Year	Population (thousands)	Labor Force (including military)	Labor Force Participation Rate (%)	Unemployed Workers (thousands)	Unemployment Rate (%)	Average Hourly Earnings* (current dollars)	(1982 dollars)
1950	152,271	63,377	41.6	3,288	5.2	1.34	5.34
1951	154,878	64,160	41.4	2,055	3.2	1.45	5.39
1952	157,553	64,524	41.0	1,883	2.9	1.52	5.51
1953	160,184	64,246	40.1	1,834	2.8	1.61	5.79
1954	163,026	65,785	40.4	3,582	5.4	1.65	5.91
1955	165,931	67,087	40.4	2,852	4.3	1.71	6.15
1956	168,903	68,517	40.6	2,750	4.0	1.80	6.38
1957	171,984	68,877	40.0	2,859	4.2	1.89	6.47
1958	174,882	69,486	39.7	4,602	6.6	1.95	6.50
1959	177,830	70,157	39.5	3,740	5.3	2.02	6.69
1960	180,671	71,489	39.6	3,852	5.4	2.09	6.79
1961	183,691	72,359	39.4	4,714	6.5	2.14	6.88
1962	186,538	72,675	39.0	3,911	5.4	2.22	7.07
1963	189,242	73,839	39.0	4,070	5.5	2.28	7.17
1964	191,889	75,109	39.1	3,786	5.0	2.36	7.33
1965	194,303	76,401	39.3	3,366	4.4	2.46	7.52
1966	196,560	77,892	39.6	2,875	3.7	2.56	7.62
1967	198,712	79,565	40.0	2,975	3.7	2.68	7.72
1968	200,706	80,990	40.4	2,817	3.5	2.85	7.89
1969	232,677	82,972	35.7	2,832	3.4	3.04	7.98
1970	205,052	84,889	41.4	4,093	4.8	3.23	8.03
1971	207,661	86,355	41.6	5,016	5.8	3.45	8.21
1972	209,896	88,847	42.3	4,882	5.5	3.70	8.53
1973	211,909	91,203	43.0	4,365	4.8	3.94	8.55
1974	213,854	93,670	43.8	5,156	5.5	4.24	8.28
1975	215,973	95,453	44.2	7,929	8.3	4.53	8.12
1976	218,035	97,826	44.9	7,406	7.6	4.86	8.24
1977	220,239	100,665	45.7	6,991	6.9	5.25	8.36
1978	222,585	103,882	46.7	6,202	6.0	5.69	8.40
1979	225,055	106,559	47.3	6,137	5.8	6.16	8.17
1980	227,757	108,544	47.7	7,637	7.0	6.66	7.78
1981	230,138	110,315	47.9	8,273	7.5	7.25	7.69
1982	232,520	111,872	48.1	10,678	9.5	7.68	7.68
1983	234,799	113,226	48.2	10,717	9.5	8.02	7.79
1984	237,001	115,241	48.6	8,539	7.4	8.32	7.80
1985	239,279	117,167	49.0	8,312	7.1	8.57	7.77
1986	241,625	119,540	49.5	8,237	6.9	8.76	7.81
1987	243,942	121,602	49.8	7,425	6.1	8.98	7.73
1988	246,307	123,378	50.1	6,701	5.4	9.28	7.69
1989	248,762	125,557	50.5	6,528	5.2	9.66	7.64
1990	251,394	126,424	50.3	6,874	5.4	10.03	7.54

*Private nonagricultural workers in nonsupervisory positions.

Principles of Economics

Fifth Edition

RYAN C. AMACHER
Professor of Economics and
Dean, College of Commerce and Industry
Clemson University

HOLLEY H. ULBRICH
Alumni Professor of Economics
Clemson University

COLLEGE DIVISION South-Western Publishing Co.

Cincinnati Ohio

Sponsoring Editor: James M. Keefe
Developmental Editor: Alice Denny
Production Editor: Sue Ellen Brown
Production House: Lifland et al., Bookmakers
Cover and Interior Designer: Craig LaGesse Ramsdell
Photo Editor: Diana Robbins Carter
Marketing Manager: Scott D. Person
Cover and Interior Illustrator: Jean Tuttle ©1992

HB67EA
Copyright ©1992
by South-Western Publishing Co.
Cincinnati, Ohio

Library of Congress Cataloging-in-Publication Data

Amacher, Ryan C.
    Principles of economics / Ryan C. Amacher, Holley H. Ulbrich. —
5th ed.
        p.   cm.
    Includes bibliographical references and index.
    ISBN 0-538-81305-9
    1. Economics.   I. Ulbrich, Holley H.   II. Title.
HB171.5.A397   1992
    330—dc20   91-18992
                                                                                 CIP

Printed in the United States of America

1 2 3 4 5 6 7 RN 6 5 4 3 2 1

Photo Credits: p. 18: (*top*) Hoover Institution, Stanford University; (*bottom*) Massachusetts Institute of Technology; p. 63: The Bettmann Archive; p. 172: Historical Pictures Service, Inc., Chicago; p. 202: The Bettmann Archive; p. 485: The University of Chicago; p. 522: Historical Pictures Service, Inc., Chicago; p. 537: Bettmann/Hulton; p. 627: The Bettmann Archive; p. 658: Photograph courtesy of The Public Relations Department of Carnegie-Mellon University; p. 667: (*top*) Peter Lofts Photography; (*bottom*) Victor Jorgensen-Scope for Fortune Magazine; p. 685: (*top*) Public Information/University of Chicago; (*bottom*) Photo by Sam Sweezy; p. 726: Brown Brothers, Sterling, Pa.; p. 778: Courtesy of Robert Schalkenback Foundation; p. 797: Courtesy of Thomas Sowell

PREFACE

Each revision of a textbook presents a major challenge. This fifth edition of *Principles of Economics* was no exception. We had to decide what to keep, what to change, and what additions or modifications were needed to make the textbook up to date and responsive to changing ideas, methods, and interests. In putting together a fifth edition, we have benefited from comments and suggestions from users of earlier editions, colleagues at Clemson University, and some careful and thoughtful reviewers.

We reiterate our goal that guided the earlier editions. We do not want to make professional economists out of students. A common complaint is that instructors and textbook authors treat the principles of economics course as the first step in work toward a Ph.D. This text is intended not to train professional economists but rather to describe the analytical tools that economic theory offers the policy analyst or adviser to governments and business firms. This book teaches enough theory to enable students to understand policy and presents enough policy situations to give them an understanding of how to apply the theory. In addition, where relevant, we present the historical context of the theory.

CHANGES IN THE FIFTH EDITION

The multi-color format allows us to be more creative with the graphs and to make the book more attractive. The figures have been prepared so that all demand-related curves are blue and all supply-related curves are red. Historical and other nonspecific information is shown in gold. Throughout the text, special features, including the International Perspectives,

Economic Profiles, Economic Insights, and summary boxes, are presented in a consistent color and format.

We have expanded the integration of the international sector in this edition. The gold-colored International Perspective pages in each chapter extend the scope of the material from the purely domestic scene to the worldwide implications and focus on related real-world international issues. Some of the perspectives show what happens to the model or theory when it is placed in the context of an open economy. Thus, we add exports and imports to supply and demand in microeconomics and to aggregate supply and demand in macroeconomics. We look at the antitrust implications of foreign competition and the link between the budget deficit and the trade deficit. Other perspectives consider how particular problems are addressed or how particular institutions work in other countries. For example, the chapter on financial markets looks at how financial markets work in Japan, and the discussion of poverty programs explores income support programs in Europe.

We recognize that students appreciate having important material summarized frequently, so we continue to include concise summaries of main points in order to make the book as user friendly as possible. Other features that are especially helpful to students have been retained, including key terms and their definitions in the margins and the numbered chapter summaries. Chapter learning objectives have been reintroduced at the request of users. The number of end-of-chapter questions has been expanded, including more problem-solving and brainstorming questions along with those that review chapter material.

On the basis of reviewer recommendations, a major effort was made in this edition to reorganize and streamline the material in the introductory chapters. The number of introductory chapters has been reduced from four to three. Each chapter emphasizes a single model and uses that model to develop basic methodological concepts. Thus, Chapter 1, "Economics, Economic Issues, and Economic Methods," now introduces the production possibilities curve. Chapter 2, "Markets, Governments, and Nations: The Organization of Economic Activity" describes the circular flow model, building on the introductory material on scarcity and choice in Chapter 1 while creating a broad overview of both microeconomics and macroeconomics. This chapter blends some materials from Chapter 2 of the previous editions with a discussion of the role of governments and the international economy, in order to set the stage for the remaining chapters. Some methodological material, which appeared in the opening chapter in earlier editions, is best understood in the context of the circular flow model. Thus, Chapter 3, "Supply and Demand," now incorporates the topics of comparative statics and equilibrium and disequilibrium. The materials that were presented in Chapter 4 in previous editions have been assigned to various micro and macro chapters as appropriate, but the basic material on the role of government has been incorporated into the new Chapter 2.

The significant changes in macroeconomics begin with Chapter 9, "Fiscal Policy." Materials on the size and composition of the federal budget are now found in Chapter 9 in connection with discussion of the budget as a policy tool. Because the broad and complex issue of the national debt and deficits dominates any discussion of fiscal policy, we have split this critical current policy debate off into a separate chapter (Chapter 10), drawing materials from several earlier chapters and incorporating new data and arguments.

In the area of money and interest rates, we felt that it was necessary to include some discussion of financial markets, as banks are increasingly becoming merely one among a host of financial intermediaries. After the discussion of money demand in Chapter 11 and banks and the Federal Reserve in Chapter 12, a new chapter has been added. Chapter 13, "Financial Markets and Interest Rates," includes materials on the interest rate, investment, and the loanable funds market, as well as a new discussion of the economic role of financial intermediaries such as the stock and bond markets. We have reorganized the final chapters of the macro part of the text so that the discussion of demand issues ends in Chapter 15 with another look at inflation and employment, as well as a brief summary of various schools of thought. Chapter 16, "Aggregate Supply and Economic Growth," includes an expanded treatment of the productivity issue and industrial policy. We have moved "Economic Development and the Third World" from the end of the textbook to Chapter 17 in the macroeconomics section, since it is logically linked to the growth chapter.

Chapter 18, "Applications of Supply and Demand," again reviews the concepts of supply and demand, with new examples and revised material brought together from several chapters of the previous edition. The presentations of elasticity in Chapter 19 and demand and consumer choice in Chapter 20 received strong support from our reviewers. Indifference curve analysis remains as an optional appendix to Chapter 20.

Chapter 21, which introduces the student to the theory of the firm, includes coverage of two new topics: households as firms and nonprofit firms. The optional appendix covering isoquant and isocost curves parallels the Chapter 20 appendix on indifference curves. Chapter 22 presents cost theory and concludes with a discussion of profit maximization. Chapters 23–25, covering perfect competition, monopoly, and monopolistic competition and oligopoly, have been updated with new examples and problems. The final chapter of this section, Chapter 26 on regulation, deregulation, and antitrust policy, includes antitrust and regulatory changes that have occurred since the last edition.

Chapter 27 discusses marginal productivity in the context of labor markets. Chapter 28 follows the labor market theory with a revised and updated discussion of U.S. labor history and the role of unions. All the material on rent, interest, and profit appears in Chapter 29, which now also includes a discussion of the functional distribution of income. Chapter 30, "Income Distribution: Poverty, Discrimination, and Welfare," concludes the section. This chapter includes two new topics: the regional distribution of poverty and transfers to the elderly, an area of great controversy.

Chapters 31 and 32 in turn discuss market failure and government failure, incorporating new material and additional examples on both sides of the argument. A new Chapter 33, "Case Studies in Market Failure and Government Failure," includes the farm problem and urban problems. Also covered in this chapter is a third area of growing interest and concern—the environment. This material is new to the fifth edition.

The international section comprises three chapters. Chapter 34, "International Trade," now includes an introduction to two additional arguments for tariffs: the optimum tariff argument and the theory of the second best. To show the role of services in the balance of payments, Chapter 35 contains an International Perspective that discusses how the United States has become a net exporter of tourism. Chapter 36, which deals with comparative systems, was revised at the last minute to incorporate the rapid changes in Eastern Europe.

IMPORTANT FEATURES OF THE FIFTH EDITION

The previous editions of *Principles of Economics* have been used by thousands of students at hundreds of institutions. The following features have made this text a useful and well-regarded teaching and learning tool.

ORGANIZATION

The length and content of the fifth edition represent a very careful weighing of thoroughness against brevity. Although we did not go quite so far as to apply "zero-based editing" by requiring each item to justify its inclusion, we did carefully rethink what to include and we did some pruning to make room for new material and ideas.

This edition of the textbook is again available in paperback splits. *Principles of Macroeconomics* contains Chapters 1–17 and 34–36. *Principles of Microeconomics* contains Chapters 1–3 and 18–36.

SPECIAL PAGES

Each chapter includes special pages. At least one special page, color-keyed gold, is an International Perspective, extending the scope of the material in the chapter to a global view. Other special pages may be Economic Profiles of important economists or Economic Insights into important institutions, relevant historical events, or pressing current issues. The special pages are placed close to the relevant chapter material and highlight the development of the theory or its application to current domestic or global problems.

PEDAGOGICAL FEATURES

Each chapter begins with learning objectives, to introduce the students to the materials that will be covered. Key terms and their definitions are highlighted in the margin of the text. A feature introduced in the fourth edition and continued in the fifth edition is the capsule summaries of the preceding section or sections, placed at strategic points in each chapter. We have again expanded the selection of end-of-chapter questions, which can be used for review, homework, or class discussion. Suggested answers are provided in the *Instructor's Manual.* The carefully annotated Suggestions for Further Reading in each chapter have been updated and expanded to include current material. All terms that appear in boldface type and in the margins of the book are defined in the Glossary.

SUPPLEMENTARY MATERIALS

In addition to the pedagogical features in the textbook—the learning objectives, key terms, questions, and summaries—there is also a *Study Guide*, an *Instructor's Manual*, and a *Test Bank*. The *Study Guide* was prepared by Patricia Pando of Houston Baptist University. The revised *Test Bank* for the fifth edition was developed by Ryan Amacher, Holley Ulbrich, and Dennis Placone of Clemson University and has again been expanded to accommodate instructors' needs. The *Instructor's Manual* was prepared by the authors of the textbook.

THE STUDY GUIDE
The *Study Guide* will be a real asset for your students. Each chapter corresponds to a chapter in the textbook. It includes a chapter overview; matching exercises based on the important terms in the chapter; a three-part self-test consisting of true/false questions, problems requiring numerical and/or graphical solutions (where appropriate), and multiple choice questions; a review of the learning objectives for the chapter; complete answers to all questions in the self-test; and chapter exercises. The chapter exercises can be used for homework or for quizzes. (Answers are provided in the *Instructor's Manual*.)

THE INSTRUCTOR'S MANUAL
The *Instructor's Manual* also contains a chapter corresponding to each chapter in the text. Each chapter of the *Manual* includes a short discussion of the purposes of the chapter; the chapter outline, learning objectives, and summary; key terms from the chapter with their definitions; suggestions for lectures, extensions, and applications; suggested answers to all end-of-chapter questions; and answers to the chapter exercises in the *Study Guide*. Transparency masters are also included in the *Instructor's Manual*.

THE TEST BANK
An extensive *Test Bank* is available to adopters. It consists of 5,000 multiple choice and true/false questions, including those in the *Study Guide* (marked with an asterisk). The *Test Bank* is also available on disk for use with MicroSWAT III test generation software. This easy-to-use, menu-driven software allows instructors to quickly and efficiently produce high-quality tests. Instructors can enter and edit questions, scramble questions and choices, and print graphs as part of a test. Included in the software is a grade book.

TRANSPARENCIES
Important illustrations from *Principles of Economics* have been reproduced on a set of color acetate transparencies available to adopters to enhance classroom presentations. The most critical illustrations appear on overlay transparencies, an innovative teaching tool.

THE MICROCOMPUTER TUTORIALS
Tutorial software, available for IBM® or IBM-compatible machines, con-

tains eight modules—four in micro, four in macro—designed for either individual or group use in reviewing basic concepts.[1] The tutorials have been thoroughly revised in response to suggestions from users and are available to adopters. Copies may be made for student use.

ACKNOWLEDGMENTS

We are grateful to the many colleagues who made specific comments concerning the fourth edition or reviewed drafts of this fifth edition:

Jack E. Adams
University of Arkansas

Andy Barnett
Auburn University

Dan Barszcz
College of DuPage

Greg Brown
Lincoln Memorial University

Heinrich H. Bruschke
St. Louis University

Gary W. Burbridge
Grand Rapids Junior College

Camille P. Castorina
Florida Institute of Technology

Rick L. Chaney
St. Louis University

Abdur Chowdhury
Marquette University

Dave Clark
Marquette University

David L. Cleeton
Oberlin College

Donald A. Coffin
Indiana University Northwest

Dean S. Dutton
Brigham Young University

Bernard Feigenbaum
California State University–
   Northridge

David W. Findley
Colby College

Vivek Ghosal
University of Florida

Patricia E. Graham
University of Northern Colorado

Ralph Gunderson
University of Wisconsin-Oshkosh

R. W. Hafer
Southern Illinois University

David L. Hames
University of Hawaii, Hilo

Raza Hamzaee
Missouri Western College

Stephen Happel
Arizona State University

Dannie E. Harrison
Murray State University

Thomas R. Ireland
University of Missouri–St. Louis

David Jobson
Keystone Junior College

Andrew Larkin
St. Cloud State University

Anton D. Lowenberg
California State University–
   Northridge

Robert McAuliffe
Babson College

Rob Roy McGregor
University of South Carolina

Patrick McMurry
Missouri Western State College

Robert Main
Butler University

John E. Marthisen
Babson College

1. IBM® is a registered trademark of International Business Machines Corporation. Any reference to IBM refers to this registered trademark.

Richard F. Measell
St. Mary's College

Hamid Milani
University of Wisconsin–Marathon
    County

Clark Nardinelli
Clemson University

Michael V. Olds
Orange Coast College

Eugene Ottle
McKendree College

John Pisciotta
Baylor University

Dennis Placone
Clemson University

Gary Quinlivin
St. Vincent College

Richard Robertson
Hinds Community College

Barbara Sherman Rolleston
Baldwin Wallace College

Malcolm Russell
Andrews University

Jody L. Sindelar
Yale University

Lawrence G. Smith
Grossmont College

Fred A. Tarpley, Jr.
Georgia Institute of Technology

Percy O. Vera
Sinclair Community College

Doug Wakeman
Meredith College

John Warner
Clemson University

Mellie Warner
Clemson University

Dale Warnke
College of Lake Country

William F. Watson, Jr.
Brunswick Junior College

Donald A. Wells
University of Arizona

Arthur L. Welsh
Pennsylvania University

Bernard J. Widera
University of Wisconsin, Madison

Jehad Yasin
Fort Valley State College

In addition, we owe a significant debt of gratitude to users and reviewers of the earlier editions of the textbook for numerous suggestions and comments. Our team at South-Western Publishing Co. has been a significant part of our textbook life. Our developmental editors—Dennis Hanseman and, for the last two editions, Alice Denny—have greatly improved our work. Sponsoring Editor Jim Keefe and Marketing Manager Scott Person have developed a classy final product. Over the years we have learned a great deal about the market from the College Division publisher's representatives, and we have enjoyed our interactions with them. We also want to thank our spouses, Susan and Carl, who continue to provide encouragement and inspiration through many editions of this textbook.

Finally, we would like to dedicate the fifth edition to the memory of Professor Jack Livingston of Ripon College and Professor Dorothy Goodwin of the University of Connecticut. Their skill and enthusiasm for teaching attracted us to economics as a profession. If they were alive to read this textbook, they would find their inspired teaching living on in its pages.

Ryan C. Amacher
Holley H. Ulbrich

BRIEF CONTENTS

CONTENTS

INTRODUCTION TO ECONOMICS

1. Define economics and distinguish between microeconomics and macroeconomics.
2. Explain why you should study economics.
3. Discuss how economics is related to other social sciences.
4. Explain the relationship between scarcity and choice.
5. Define and give examples of opportunity cost.
6. Use a production possibilities curve to show:
   a. opportunity cost,
   b. increasing opportunity cost,
   c. economic growth,
   d. unemployment of the factors of production.

CHAPTER 1

ECONOMICS, ECONOMIC ISSUES, AND ECONOMIC METHODS

7. Identify the basic elements of an economic model and explain how it can be tested.
8. Interpret the self-interest assumption and explain why it is important in economics.
9. Explain and give examples of:
   a. the association-causation fallacy,
   b. the fallacy of composition,
   c. the *ceteris paribus* fallacy.
10. List the steps followed in policy analysis.

INTRODUCTION

In this chapter, we explore what economics is, stressing the basic economic problem of scarcity and choice. In order to do that, we introduce you to your first economic model—the production possibilities curve. We then generalize from this model to some properties of models in general. Finally, we explain how economists use models to think about economic problems and develop policies to address those problems. By the end of this chapter, you will have begun to think like an economist.

WHAT IS ECONOMICS?

economics
The study of how people and institutions make decisions about production and consumption and how they face the problem of scarcity.

microeconomics
The study of individual market interactions, focusing on production and consumption by the individual consumer, firm, or industry.

Economics is the study of how people, individually and through institutions, make decisions about producing and consuming goods and services and how they face the problem of scarcity. The word *economics* comes from the Greek *oikonomos*, which means household management. The study of economics is divided into microeconomics and macroeconomics.

Micro, or *mikros*, is a Greek prefix meaning small. **Microeconomics** describes the interactions of producers and consumers in individual markets, such as the market for cars. It also examines interactions between such markets, for example, the impact of changes in the demand for steel on the price of aluminum.

The Greek prefix *macro*, or *makros*, means long or large. So, as you might expect, the study of the economy as a whole is called **macroeconomics**. Macroeconomics is concerned with **aggregates**, or quantities whose values are determined by adding across many markets. Macroeconomics studies the behavior of variables that describe the whole economy, such as the

2

value of the total output that the economy produces in a given time period. Macroeconomics also examines the behavior of such aggregates as the price level and total employment or unemployment. Values of these aggregates are derived from many individual markets taken together.

In both microeconomics and macroeconomics, the most important tools are demand and supply, which are developed in Chapter 3. Demand and supply help to explain prices and outputs in individual markets. These tools also explain the relation between prices and outputs in different markets. In microeconomics, you may look at the demand for the output of a single industry, such as bicycle manufacturing. In macroeconomics, you look at the level of prices and output for the economy as a whole, using aggregate demand and aggregate supply as the main tools. Even though microeconomics and macroeconomics are often studied separately, they are closely related.

macroeconomics
The study of the economy as a whole or of economic aggregates, such as the level of employment and the growth of total output.

aggregates
Quantities whose values are determined by adding across many markets.

ECONOMICS IN RELATION TO OTHER FIELDS

Economics is usually classed as a **social science**. This label makes economics an academic relative of political science, sociology, psychology, and anthropology. All of these fields look at the behavior of human beings, individually and in groups. They study different subsets of the actions and interactions of human beings. (For this reason, they are also sometimes termed *behavioral sciences.*)

Economics focuses on the consumption, production, and use of scarce resources by individuals and groups. Economics is also concerned with the processes by which households and firms make decisions about the use of scarce resources. This definition of the "territory" of economics leads to some overlap with the other social sciences. Psychologists and economists share an interest in what causes people to take certain actions. However, economists are primarily interested in actions that are reflected in market activity or in economic decisions made through government. Sociologists are interested in all facets of organized human activity. Economists, however, are interested mainly in organized activities that relate to the production and consumption of goods and services.

In general, economists assume that individuals pursue their own self-interest and respond to various signals or incentives in light of that self-interest. Although that assumption may seem obvious, it is a somewhat different view of human behavior from that of psychologists and sociologists. It often leads economists to draw different conclusions. As you learn more about economics, you will better understand how it overlaps with—and differs from—other social sciences.

social science
An academic field that studies the behavior of human beings, individually and in groups, and examines their interactions.

WHY STUDY ECONOMICS?

Economics is a required course for many different majors. You may be wondering why this is so. One reason is that economics interacts with almost all other academic subjects. It affects and is affected by current events. Also, it has a major effect on politics, both domestic and international.

A second reason for studying economics is the impact that economic ideas and theories have on world leaders. Much of what political decision makers do is based on economic theory. As John Maynard Keynes, an economist who has had great influence on macroeconomic policy in this century, wrote:

The ideas of economists and political philosophers, both when they are right and when they are wrong, are more powerful than is commonly understood. Indeed, the world is ruled by little else. Practical men, who believe themselves to be quite exempt from any intellectual influences, are usually the slaves of some defunct economist. Madmen in authority, who hear voices in the air, are distilling their frenzy from some academic scribbler of a few years back.[1]

Keynes was saying that if you want to understand what politicians, great or mad, are trying to do, you must understand the economic theories on which they are acting.

A third reason for studying economics is that it provides a better understanding of how society functions. Economic theory is very useful in understanding behavior because it allows the development of models with predictive power. As Alfred Marshall, another noted economist, wrote, "Economics is the study of mankind in the ordinary business of life."[2]

Finally, economics is fun, and people who are trained in economics find rewarding jobs and careers. If you like to think in a logical fashion, you will enjoy studying economics.

SCARCITY: LIMITED RESOURCES, INSATIABLE WANTS

scarcity
The central economic problem that there are not enough resources to produce everything that individuals want.

Whether you are just taking one course or planning a career in economics, the most important single problem you will address is that of **scarcity.** That is, there are not enough resources to produce all the goods and services people would like to consume. The first tool we will develop is an economic model that is used to explain how any economic system deals with the basic problem of scarcity. Human wants and desires are vast, relative to the resources available to satisfy them. Thus, in every economic system, there has to be some method for making choices among different desirable ends.

We live in a world of limited resources. Resources are whatever can be used to produce goods and services for human consumption. Some resources, such as oil and coal, are converted to energy and used up in the course of production or consumption. Others are not used up in that sense but are virtually fixed in quantity. Examples are land, diamonds, and copper. At any given time, even the quantity of resources created by people—roads, factories, machines, and skilled labor—cannot be changed quickly or cheaply.

insatiable wants
The needs and desires of human beings, which can never be completely satisfied.

Limited resources conflict with **insatiable wants**. Human wants are said to be insatiable (unable to be satisfied) because no matter how much peo-

---

1.   J. M. Keynes, *The General Theory of Employment, Interest, and Money* (London: Macmillan, 1936), 383.
2.   Alfred Marshall, *Principles of Economics*, 8th ed. (Don Mills, Ontario: Macmillan of Canada, 1920), 323.

ple have, they always want more of something. You may know people who seem perfectly content with what they have. If you questioned them carefully, however, you would probably find that they would like cleaner air, more time to play tennis or golf, or more shelters for the homeless. Since not all wants can be satisfied, individuals have to choose which ones to satisfy with limited available resources. In fact, every society is faced with the problem of scarcity and choice. Without scarcity, there would be no need to make choices about what desires or needs to satisfy—and thus no need to study economics.

OPPORTUNITY COSTS

Every decision to produce or consume something means sacrificing the production or consumption of something else. For instance, the cost of going to a football game includes the value of what is given up in order to attend. Economists use the term **opportunity cost** to denote the full value of the best alternative that is given up, or forgone. Part of the cost of attending a football game is the price of the ticket. This price represents the other goods and services you could have purchased with that money instead. However, there is another important part of the cost. This second part is the most valuable alternative use of those three hours, such as studying for a test. The opportunity cost of attending the game consists of both the price of the ticket and the difference in your test grade that three more hours of study would have produced. Even if the ticket had no monetary price, going to the game would still have an opportunity cost.

opportunity cost
The value of the other alternatives given up in order to enjoy a particular good or service.

Many people have problems grasping the concept of opportunity cost because they are used to thinking of cost as price, or the amount of money spent on an item or an activity. In economics, however, the concept of cost is much broader. It includes not only the dollar outlay (the other goods you could have purchased) but also the time cost (the earnings or satisfaction you could have produced for yourself in some other activity) and other sacrifices you might have made. Sometimes it is difficult to place a dollar value on these other costs, but they still play an important role in economic decisions.

SOME APPLICATIONS OF OPPORTUNITY COST

Your everyday life provides many illustrations of the concept of opportunity cost. For example, what is the opportunity cost of attending college? It is not simply the dollar figure given in your college's catalog. Money spent on books and tuition is certainly part of the opportunity cost. However, the expense of your room, meals, and clothing is not, because you would have incurred those costs even if you weren't in college. The catalog may list them as costs, but economists don't count them because they are not opportunity costs.

One important opportunity cost not listed in any college catalog is the income you could have been earning during the years you are spending in classes. For most students, that lost income will eventually be made up in higher future earnings. However, right now it is an opportunity cost that should be included. Even if you can earn only $5 an hour, if you have to cut your working hours by 30 hours a week during the 32 weeks a year you are in school, the lost earnings represent a cost of $4,800 a year.

For some students, the opportunity cost of going to college is even higher. Suppose you are a talented athlete who could play professionally right after high school, as many baseball and tennis players do. Your college education may cost as much as $100,000 a year in lost earnings. After several years of college, many football and basketball players face this dilemma. Even if they are straight-A students, the opportunity cost of completing a degree in terms of lost income is very high. It is not surprising that many of them choose to "turn pro" and postpone or abandon getting a degree.

Another illustration of opportunity cost is provided by the proposal of some politicians that there should be two years of national service for all young adults. This service would be in the military or some other part of the public sector and would pay very low wages. For some, the opportunity cost would be very low because they have few good employment opportunities. But for someone with an engineering or accounting degree, athletic skills, or other potential for good earnings, the opportunity cost would be very high. Universal national service is a tax on being young. Such a tax would be very different for different individuals.

OPPORTUNITY COST AND THE CHOICE CURVE

We can illustrate the concept of opportunity cost and its relationship to choice using a very simple example. Assume that you have $40 to spend and you have two choices: pizza and cola. Pizzas cost $8 each, and colas cost $2 for a six-pack. To keep things simple, we assume that you wish to spend the whole $40. Figure 1 shows the various combinations of pizza and cola that you can buy with $40. If you spend the entire $40 on pizza, you can purchase 5 pizzas (the *y*-intercept in Figure 1). On the other hand, you can

FIGURE 1
CHOICE AMONG ALTERNATIVES
If six-packs of cola cost $2 and pizzas cost $8, a person with $40 to spend has many attainable combinations of cola and pizza. The line *PR* represents the boundary between attainable and unattainable combinations. Along line *PR*, the opportunity cost of 1 pizza is 4 six-packs of cola.

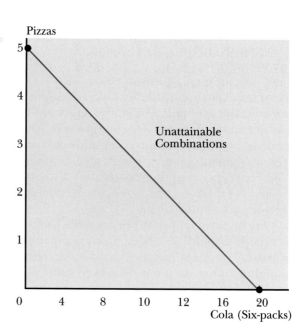

The Nobel Committee, established by the Swedish Royal Academy of Sciences, awarded the first Nobel Prize in 1901. These prizes include awards for peace, as well as physics, chemistry, literature, and medicine. They were originally funded by a bequest from the inventor of dynamite, Alfred Nobel. It wasn't until 1969, however, that the first Nobel Prize for Economics was awarded. The Bank of Sweden funded this prize to celebrate its 300th anniversary.

The addition of an economics prize puts economics in a distinguished family of academic disciplines. It is the only social science to be so honored. Receipt of a Nobel Prize is a high honor for an economist and financially rewarding.

The Nobel Prize winners in economics have made profound and very diverse contributions to this field. Many of the European winners are noted for their work in international or development economics. These include Myrdal, Meade, Ohlin, and Lewis. More than half the winners have been Americans. The following are the winners of the prize since 1969:

1969　Ragnar Frisch, Norway
　　　 Jan Tinbergen, Netherlands
1970　Paul A. Samuelson, United States
1971　Simon Kuznets, United States
1972　Kenneth J. Arrow, United States
　　　 Sir John R. Hicks, Great Britain

INTERNATIONAL
PERSPECTIVE

THE
NOBEL PRIZE
FOR
ECONOMICS

1973　Wassily Leontief, United States
1974　Gunnar Myrdal, Sweden
　　　 Friedrich A. von Hayek, Great Britain
1975　Leonid V. Kantorovich, Soviet Union
　　　 Tjalling C. Koopmans, Netherlands/United States
1976　Milton Friedman, United States
1977　James E. Meade, Great Britain
　　　 Bertil Ohlin, Sweden
1978　Herbert A. Simon, United States
1979　Sir Arthur Lewis, Great Britain
　　　 Theodore Schultz, United States
1980　Lawrence R. Klein, United States
1981　James Tobin, United States
1982　George Stigler, United States
1983　Gerard Debreu, France/United States
1984　Sir Richard Stone, Great Britain
1985　Franco Modigliani, United States
1986　James M. Buchanan, United States
1987　Robert Solow, United States
1988　Maurice Altais, France
1989　Trigve Haavelmo, Norway
1990　Harry M. Markowitz, United States
　　　 Merton H. Miller, United States
　　　 William F. Sharpe, United States

buy 20 six-packs of cola with $40 (as shown by the *x*-intercept in Figure 1). Other possibilities lie along the line that connects these two intercepts. The line represents all possible combinations of pizza and cola that total $40.[3] Of course, all combinations in the shaded area of Figure 1 are also attainable. However, these combinations wouldn't exhaust your entire $40.[4] Combinations above and to the right of the line are not attainable because they cost more than $40.

Figure 1 illustrates the array of choices and the concept of opportunity cost. The price of 1 pizza is the same as the price of 4 six-packs of cola. The decision to purchase a pizza means the sacrifice of those six-packs that could have been purchased instead. Opportunity cost is measured by the slope of the choice line.[5]

SOCIETY'S CHOICES: THE PRODUCTION POSSIBILITIES CURVE

production possibilities curve
A graph that depicts the various combinations of two goods that can be produced in an economy with the available resources.

From the perspective of the economy as a whole, the choice is not how to spend income between alternative purchases but how to allocate available productive resources between alternative goods that could be produced. This problem is illustrated by a close relative of the choice curve of Figure 1. Society's choice curve is called a **production possibilities curve**. This curve shows the various output combinations of two goods or groups of goods that can be produced in an economy with the available resources. This simple economic model is based on a few assumptions:

1. All of the economy's productive resources are fully employed. This means that everyone who wants a job has one. Also, factories, land, and other resources are being used to full capacity. (These resources will be discussed in greater detail in the next chapter.)
2. There are only two goods (or types of goods) in the economy.
3. The resources used in production are interchangeable. One worker is the same as another, one machine can be substituted for another, and all land is equally useful for producing the two goods.
4. We are looking at the economy at a specific period of time (the short run). During this time period, both the quantity and quality of resources are fixed, and the technology does not change.

Given these four assumptions, we can look at a simple example of a

---

3.   The line *PR* is a continuous line. It is easy to see that points *A* and *B* represent attainable combinations because both contain whole numbers of colas and pizzas. Connecting these points implies that you can purchase fractional units of cola and pizza, for example, half of a six-pack of cola. Since we usually purchase goods in whole units, it might seem strange to show fractional units as attainable combinations. This is merely a convenient assumption. If the numbers on the axes are large enough, for example, hundreds of pizzas and thousands of colas, then there is less problem in visualizing the array of choices as a continuous line.
4.   We have ruled out the possibility of saving part of the $40 because we are assuming only two alternative uses of funds: pizza and cola. If saving were an option, there would really be three goods: pizza, cola, and savings. Faced with only two alternatives, we can only choose how to divide the money between them.
5.   If you have forgotten how to measure the slope of a line, you should refer to the appendix on graphs to refresh your memory.

SOYBEANS (TONS)	MISSILES
20	0
16	1
12	2
8	3
4	4
0	5

TABLE 1
PRODUCTION POSSIBILITIES
SCHEDULE

production possibilities curve. Table 1 shows combinations of missiles and soybeans that an economy can produce. Figure 2 plots the numbers of Table 1 on a graph. Line *PR* in Figure 2 is a production possibilities curve. It represents all the combinations of missiles and soybeans that can be produced in this economy when the available resources are fully employed.

In Figure 2, points *A* and *B* represent two different combinations of missiles and soybeans that both lie on the production possibilities curve. Points *A* and *B* are both output combinations that can be attained in this economy with the available resources. Point *C* is also attainable. Since it lies inside of line *PR*, however, it represents unemployed resources. There are points on *PR* that have to be better than *C* because they represent more missiles, more soybeans, or more of both. The economy can do better, that is, can produce more. Therefore, *C* is inferior to points on the production possibilities curve.

The line *PR* in Figure 2 can also be used to measure opportunity cost for the economy. Line *PR* is a straight line. This fact implies that the opportunity cost of one product in terms of the other is constant. That is, the number of missiles given up to get another ton of soybeans doesn't

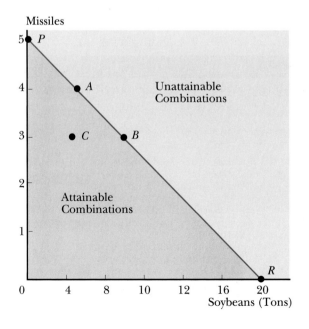

FIGURE 2
PRODUCTION
POSSIBILITIES CURVE
A production possibilities curve shows combinations of two goods that can be produced in an economy, with fixed resources and technology. Points on the curve represent the full employment of resources.

change along line *PR*. Each time the production of soybeans is increased by 1 ton, one-quarter of a missile is sacrificed. The opportunity cost of 1 more ton of soybeans is one-quarter of a missile. Conversely, the opportunity cost of 1 more missile is 4 tons of soybeans.

Opportunity cost of one good in terms of another is constant along line *PR* in Figure 2 because we assumed that all resources are alike for production purposes. That is, any unit of resources is just as good as any other unit in producing either soybeans or missiles. This assumption produces a straight-line production possibilities curve.

INCREASING OPPORTUNITY COSTS

After an economist has constructed a model, the next step is to go back and vary the assumptions to see what difference they make. Consider what happens when we drop the third assumption stated above—that productive resources are interchangeable. That is, we no longer assume that one unit of labor or land is just as productive as another for producing either good. Table 2 shows a different set of combinations of missiles and soybeans that can be produced in this economy. These combinations are plotted on the graph in Figure 3. At point *A* in Figure 3, output is 10 missiles and 200 tons of soybeans. At point *B*, output consists of more missiles, 100, but fewer soybeans, only 100 tons.

The production possibilities curve in Figure 3 is bowed, or curved, instead of being a straight line. This new shape reflects the change in the assumption that resources are alike. Here we are being more realistic and assuming that some resources are better suited to the production of missiles and others to the production of soybeans. This change in assumptions produces a model that differs from the first one in what it implies about opportunity cost.

If the economy is at point *A* in Figure 3, we can get another 10 missiles by shifting resources from soybean production to missile production. In moving from point *A* to point *C*, we must give up only a small amount of soybeans, 5 units. But to move from point *B* to point *D*, producing an-

TABLE 2
PRODUCTION POSSIBILITIES
SCHEDULE

SOYBEANS	MISSILES
205	0
(A) 200 ⎱ −5	10 ⎱ +10
(C) 195 ⎰	20 ⎰
187	30
179	40
169	50
158	60
146	70
133	80
117	90
(B) 100 ⎱ −23	100 ⎱ +10
(D) 77 ⎰	110 ⎰
50	120
0	130
0	130

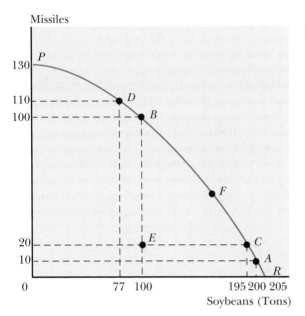

FIGURE 3
PRODUCTION POSSIBILITIES AND INCREASING OPPORTUNITY COSTS
On this production possibilities curve, the opportunity cost of additional units of soybeans increases as the economy becomes more specialized in soybeans: producing each additional unit of soybeans requires a larger sacrifice of missiles than before (increasing opportunity cost). If the economy is inside the production possibilities curve at some point such as *E*, more of both goods could be produced.

other 10 missiles requires a larger sacrifice of soybeans, 23 units instead of 5. This curved production possibilities curve illustrates the very important principle of **increasing opportunity cost**. That is, the more missiles that are already being produced, the larger the sacrifice of soybeans required to get additional missiles. Table 2 shows that between points *A* and *C*, ten more missiles cost 5 units of soybeans. Between points *B* and *D*, however, ten more missiles cost 23 units of soybeans.

increasing opportunity cost
The principle that as production of one good rises, larger and larger sacrifices of another are required.

Increasing opportunity costs are obvious in wartime. As more war goods are demanded, civilian sacrifices increase. Initially, as military production expands, additional labor and other resources are used that are relatively more productive for making missiles and relatively less productive for growing soybeans. As the switch to missiles continues, however, military production takes resources that are relatively less productive for making missiles, although they were highly productive for growing soybeans. Soybean production falls by larger and larger amounts, therefore, because more resources are stripped away from soybeans for every extra missile produced. These resources are increasingly those best suited to producing soybeans and least adaptable to missile production.

UNEMPLOYMENT

For the straight-line version of the production possibilities curve, another important assumption was that all resources are fully employed. If we drop that assumption, the production possibilities curve can also illustrate unemployment and the effect of reducing it. Suppose the economy is at point *E* in Figure 3. This point is inside the production possibilities curve because some workers, factories, land, and machines are unemployed. If the economy could move from point *E* to point *C*, it would be possible to have more soybeans (195 tons instead of 100) with no sacrifice of missiles.

Moving from point E to point B would mean producing the same amount of soybeans (100 tons) but more missiles (100 instead of 20). Finally, at point F, more of both missiles and soybeans could be produced simply by putting idle resources to work. At point E, the opportunity cost of both soybeans and missiles is zero because none of either good has to be sacrificed to increase production of the other. However, there is an opportunity cost to being at point E rather than elsewhere on the curve. This cost is equal to the output of either good that could have been produced.

From a macroeconomic perspective, unemployed resources are wasteful. They represent extra production that could be attained simply by putting idle resources to work. The opportunity cost of the goods gained is zero. Thus, economists believe that full employment is an important goal. It is important not just for the individual who needs to work in order to earn income, but also for the aggregate economy.

Both World War II and the Vietnam War made Americans aware of the importance of the full employment of resources. At the beginning of World War II, there were unemployed resources. It was therefore possible to produce more war goods (missiles) without a sacrifice of consumer goods (soybeans). Eventually, all the idle resources were employed. Then further expansion of the production of war goods required the sacrifice of consumer goods. No cars were produced for several years during World War II as auto factories switched to making military tanks and trucks. Other consumer goods were also in short supply. The Vietnam War occurred at a time of relatively low unemployment in the late 1960s. Thus, expanding production of military hardware and diverting labor from civilian activities to soldiering led immediately to reduced production of consumer goods. The economy was already on the production possibilities curve when the United States was drawn into the Vietnam War.

One of the main concerns of macroeconomics is explaining how an economy can find itself inside the production possibilities curve at a point such as E in Figure 3. How can an economic system avoid the idleness and waste of unemployed resources? If an economy finds itself at a point such as E, what can be done to get back on the production possibilities curve? These are important questions in the study of macroeconomics. The production possibilities curve is a useful technique for identifying these questions.

ECONOMIC GROWTH

Another macroeconomic issue that can be illustrated by the production possibilities model is economic growth. If technology can improve and the quantity of resources can increase, then output can grow beyond the limits of the production possibilities curve. Better technology or more resources means a change in the fourth assumption stated earlier—that both resources and technology are fixed. As labor becomes more skilled and productive, and as producers acquire new machines and plants embodying the latest technology, the production possibilities curve shifts outward.

An outward shift of a production possibilities curve is shown in Figure 4. If the economy is at point A on PR, production consists of D_1 units of soybeans and C_1 units of missiles. With the shift of the curve to P_1R_1, it is

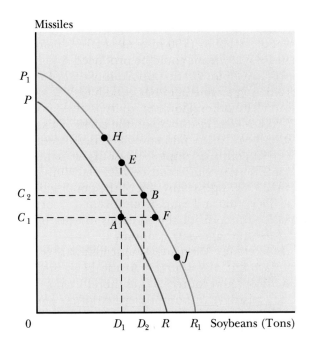

Missiles

FIGURE 4
SHIFT OF THE PRODUCTION
POSSIBILITIES CURVE
An outward shift of the
production possibilities
curve from PR to P_1R_1
means that the economy
can produce more of
both goods (economic
growth).

possible to reach some point, such as point *B*, that includes more of both soybeans (D_2 units) and missiles (C_2 units). Other possible combinations on the new production possibilities curve include the same amount of one good and more of the other (such as point *E* or *F*) or less of one good and more of the other (such as point *H* or *J*). No matter which combination is produced, the important thing about an outward shift of a production possibilities curve is that it increases the economy's capacity to respond to human wants.

Added resources, usually labor or capital, are sources of economic growth. New technology can also shift a production possibilities curve outward and account for economic growth. Invention, innovation, discovery of resources, and improvements in productivity all contribute to economic growth.

THE PRODUCTION POSSIBILITIES CURVE SHOWS:	
• Attainable combinations	Points on the curve
• Opportunity cost	The slope of the curve
• Unemployment of resources	Points below or inside the curve
• Economic growth	A shift of the curve to the right

THEORIES, HYPOTHESES, AND MODELS

The production possibilities curve is a theoretical model. Based on certain assumptions (two products, a brief time period, fixed resources, given technology), we theorized that output of one good would grow in a predictable way if output of the other good was reduced. The production possibilities curve is just one of many economic models. This book will develop and use a variety of these models. You can use them to understand the workings of markets, the behavior of producers and consumers, and the effects of various policies on a wide range of social problems.

A model represents a scientific approach to examining problems. Scientists of all kinds differ from nonscientists in that they deal with facts in a systematic way. Early scientists in all fields did little more than classify the facts they or others uncovered. This approach has limited value, however. It is very easy to get lost in a forest of facts, even when they are neatly filed and classified.

THEORIES AND HYPOTHESES

theory
A set of principles that can be used to make inferences about the world.

Theories play an important role in everything we do. A **theory** is an abstraction from reality that tries to focus on a cause-and-effect relationship between two variables. The variables can be money supply and prices in macroeconomics or labor costs and prices of cars in microeconomics. A theory is useful in that it simplifies observations by clearing away irrelevant details. In a way, a theory allows you to see the forest instead of the trees. Any interpretation of our environment is based on an implicit theory about cause-and-effect relationships. Our senses receive information, and we interpret that information on the basis of some theory about the world we have developed over time. These theories are constantly being revised and improved to better explain the facts. A good theory will develop **testable hypotheses**, which are mini-theories that can be verified or disproved by checking them against facts or experiences. Even small children, for example, quickly develop testable hypotheses based on experience: "My finger will hurt if I touch the hot stove," or "The cat will scratch me if I pull its tail."

testable hypothesis
An inference from a theory that can be subjected to real-world testing.

MODELS

model
A set of assumptions and hypotheses that is a simplified description of reality.

Economic theorists, like other scientists, develop theories that will yield testable hypotheses.[6] Then they test these hypotheses by comparing them with the facts and seeing if they are consistent.

A **model** is a formal statement of a theory, usually in the form of graphs or equations. In the simpler model of the production possibilities curve as a straight line, we assumed that all productive resources were alike. As a result, the relationship between outputs of the two goods was a constant one. In the more complex model, we introduced an alternative assumption—that all resources were not alike. The model then predicted that increased production of one good would require increasing sacrifices of the other.

An economic model will generate one or more "if-then" hypotheses about what will happen in the real world. These hypotheses are then

---

6.   Not everyone agrees that economics, or any of the other social sciences, is scientific in the same sense as the natural sciences. This debate has been going on for a century. It started with an essay by Thorstein Veblen in the *Quarterly Journal of Economics* in 1889. For a more recent discussion of this issue, see Alfred Eichner, "Can Economics Become a Science?" *Challenge* (November-December 1986): 4–12.

tested in real situations or experiments. The production possibilities model offers several such testable hypotheses. For example, according to this model, if a larger share of resources is devoted to production of military goods (missiles), then less will be available for consumer goods (soybeans). During the Vietnam War, President Lyndon Johnson was convinced that there were enough idle resources in the U.S. economy to expand both military and civilian output at the same time. As the economy quickly reached full employment, it became apparent that continuing to produce military goods and to divert some productive resources (young men) into fighting could be done only at the expense of producing less housing, education, and other goods and services for consumers.

At the beginning of the 1990s policy makers were anticipating another test of the above hypothesis—in the opposite direction. If reforms in the Soviet Union and Eastern Europe did indeed lead to reduced spending on defense in the United States, most economists expected that the resources released from military use would lead to a large increase in output of civilian goods. Politicians named those released resources the "peace dividend." They were making plans to divert them to such civilian uses as education, housing, anti-drug programs, and bailing out the savings and loan industry, when war broke out in the Persian Gulf. A peace dividend may still occur, but not as soon as many people had hoped.

ASSUMPTIONS

Unlike physical scientists, economists rarely have the chance to conduct controlled experiments to validate their models. Instead, economists most often test hypotheses by looking at actual experiences in markets. Such experiments are often referred to by economists as *ceteris paribus* experiments. *Ceteris paribus* is a Latin phrase that means "all else being equal." An economist changes one variable in a theoretical model (for example, the technology for producing missiles in the production possibilities model). The economist then predicts what would happen *ceteris paribus*, or if everything else remained constant. The **ceteris paribus assumption**, or holding everything else constant, is the most common and most important assumption in economic models. If the technology of missile production improved but there was no change in the technology of producing soybeans, the production possibilities curve would shift out as in Figure 5, from *PR* to *PR₁*. The economist would predict an increase in output of both commodities, but a relatively larger increase in the output of missiles. The economist must then untangle the effects of the change in missile technology on the mix of output (missiles and soybeans) from anything else that changed in the real world in the time period when this model is being tested.

In addition to the *ceteris paribus* assumption, one other assumption is a basic part of most economic models. This assumption is that most people behave in a self-interested way. In general, **self-interested behavior** consists of trying to get the most of something they want (to maximize some goal) out of available resources. For consumers, self-interested behavior means maximizing their satisfaction. For owners of productive resources, self-interest is expressed by seeking to maximize income or wealth. For busi-

ceteris paribus assumption
The assumption that everything else will remain constant, used for most economic models. (*Ceteris paribus* is Latin for "all else being equal.")

self-interested behavior
A basic assumption of economic theory that individual decision makers do what is best for themselves.

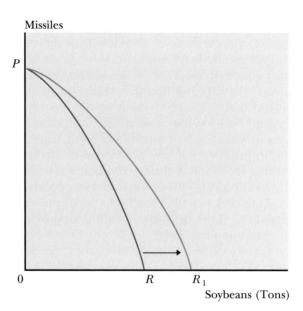

FIGURE 5
TECHNOLOGICAL CHANGE AND THE PRODUCTION POSSIBILITIES CURVE
A change in the technology of producing soybeans shifts the production possibilities curve from *PR* to *PR*₁. This shows that if all resources were devoted to soybeans, more could be produced. If all resources were devoted to missiles, however, no increase in output could occur. Increases in both are also possible.

ness firms, self-interest means maximizing profits.[7] In the production possibilities model, self-interested behavior will direct the decision as to which combination to produce out of all possible combinations. That combination is the one that maximizes the welfare or satisfaction of consumers.

The self-interest assumption has given economics, and economists, a good deal of undeserved bad press. This has occurred because self-interest is confused with selfishness. Critics of market economies argue that encouraging and rewarding self-interested behavior is a basic flaw in such systems. The ideas of social reformers such as Karl Marx and Mao Zedung have led to many experiments in socialism, such as the Fourier settlements in the United States and the Cultural Revolution in China. These experiments have been attempts to devise alternative ways of organizing economic activity. All of these experiments have tried to rebuild societies in such a way that individuals would act on nobler or higher motives than self-interest.

In fact, concern for others and for the community as a whole is not incompatible with self-interest because individuals define their own self-interest in terms of what is satisfying to them. Some individuals derive their greatest satisfaction from material possessions, others from leisure or enjoyment of the arts, and still others from helping others and building better communities. Some persons may derive satisfaction from all of these! So self-interested behavior is not inconsistent with volunteer work or charitable contributions. Such unselfish activities are not, by our definition, un-self-interested. This definition of self-interest is broad enough to cover the actions of Albert Schweitzer and Mother Teresa as well as those of the most unlovable of "greedy capitalist pigs."

When economists use the self-interest assumption in developing theory, they are simply saying that they expect individual behavior to be

---

7.   Maximization of various kinds is a central concern of microeconomics. You can refer to the appendix on graphs to review the geometry of maximization.

influenced by costs and benefits. If the cost of a course of action declines or the benefits rise, relative to alternatives, more people will choose that course of action. For example, if the price of soybeans rises relative to that of missiles, some firms will switch production from missiles to soybeans, attracted by the higher price. If salaries for public school teachers rise relative to those of accountants, more people are likely to prepare for a teaching career and fewer to study accounting. If the penalty for speeding falls, *ceteris paribus*, more people are likely to drive faster than the posted speed limit. If the cost of giving to charity rises because it is no longer tax-deductible, less will be given to charity.

Furthermore, economists do not use the concept of self-interest to predict any one person's or firm's behavior but rather to predict average or group behavior. Such predictions are similar to the use of attributes of certain groups by insurance companies to predict how often certain events will occur. Insurance companies develop norms for various groups—life expectancies, accident rates, or numbers of house fires—and use them to set prices for policies. These norms say nothing about how likely any particular member of a group is to live past the age of 80, run a car off the road, or have a house burn to the ground.

Even economists do not always agree about the best way to develop theories and construct models. Specifically, the role of assumptions has been fiercely debated by two American Nobel Prize winners in economics, Paul Samuelson and Milton Friedman. The traditional view, taken by Samuelson, is that once a theory is demonstrated to be logically correct, its usefulness depends on whether its assumptions are realistic. This view is consistent with the role of theory in the natural sciences. Friedman disagrees, arguing that the true test of the usefulness of a theory is whether it works. That is, does it accurately predict what happens in the real world? In this book, we will be looking for logically correct theories and models that pass both kinds of tests: realistic assumptions, and accurate predictions.

BASIC ELEMENTS OF THE ECONOMIC APPROACH

This discussion of theories and models suggests that economics is much like other sciences in its methods. What is unique or different about the economic approach? There are a few emphases and ideas that help set economics apart.

1. *Like the natural sciences, economic theory is positive, or nonnormative.* **Positive statements** are if-then propositions about *what is*. In contrast, **normative statements** describe *what ought to be*. In other words, economic theory strives to be scientific. However, when economists try to apply economic theory to policy questions, they often find it difficult to keep their work positive. Economic theory is value-free. However, appliers of the theory are often tempted to mix in their values in order to favor a preferred outcome or policy. It is a positive statement to say that production of more missiles will require increasing sacrifices of soybeans. It is a normative statement to say that more missiles and fewer soybeans should be produced.

positive statements
A set of propositions about what is, rather than what ought to be.

normative statements
A set of propositions about what ought to be (also called value judgements).

Milton Friedman and Paul A. Samuelson are two of the best-known contemporary American economists. Both are winners of the Nobel Prize in economics. The two men represent polar extremes with respect to economic policy. Samuelson sees an important role for government in modern industrial society. Friedman advocates a *laissez-faire* economic policy. He argues that the market economy operates very well and that the interventions Samuelson supports do more harm than good. Samuelson is a leader of the Eastern liberal school of economics. Friedman represents the conservative Chicago School.

Samuelson, a professor at the Massachusetts Institute of Technology (MIT), has an A.B. degree from the University of Chicago and A.M. and Ph.D. degrees in economics from Harvard University. His Ph.D. dissertation, *Foundations of Economic Analysis*, written when he was only 23 years old, was published as a book. It still ranks as a monumental work in the application of mathematics to economics. Graduate students still study it. Many of today's economists were introduced to economics with Samuelson's textbook, *Economics*. Samuelson is largely responsible for making MIT's economics department one of the best in the country.

Friedman is retired from the University of Chicago, where he taught for 30 years. He is presently a senior research fellow at the Hoover Institution at Stanford University. Friedman received an A.B. degree from Rutgers, an A.M. degree from the University of Chicago, and a Ph.D. degree from Columbia University. He has made notable contributions to economic theory. His policy ideas are readily available in three popular books: *Essays in Positive Economics* (1953), *Capitalism and Freedom* (1962), and *Free to Choose* (1980). Recently, Friedman has angered some of the conservatives who usually agree with him by arguing that illegal drugs should be legalized. He argues that legalizing such drugs will reduce both the profits in selling them and the crime and violence among sellers and users.

ECONOMIC
PROFILE

MILTON
FRIEDMAN

1912–

AND

PAUL A.
SAMUELSON

1915–

2. *Economic theory cannot predict the future.* It can only explain the effects of certain events. Economic theory consists of statements of the if-*A*-then-*B* type. The prediction that *B* will occur depends on whether or not *A* happens. (Note that theory does not predict the occurrence of *A*. Economists do not have a crystal ball.) In the production possibilities model, an increase in resources will result in economic growth, *ceteris paribus*. In this case, part of the *ceteris paribus* assumption is that the increased resources will be put to work and not left unemployed. There is, however, some difference between what economics *is* and what many economists actually *do*. Many economists, especially macroeconomists, spend a great deal of time forecasting future conditions. To do this, they make use of economic theory. In forecasting, an economist guesses the likelihood that *A* will occur and then uses economic theory to predict the occurrence of *B*. Sometimes, however, forecasts are wrong. This doesn't necessarily mean that the theory is incorrect. The forecaster may have been wrong in expecting *A* to occur.

3. *Most economists look first to market processes for solutions to social problems.* This market bias reflects a preference for the freedom and efficiency arising from decentralized processes. However, most economic theory is applicable to nonmarket systems as well, even though the legal and political institutions differ. Economists can apply tools developed for analyzing market economies to the workings of socialist economies and to a wide variety of nonmarket behavior.

4. *Economists pay a great deal of attention to cost.* The emphasis on opportunity cost, scarcity, and choice is fundamental to economics. Nobel Prize winner Milton Friedman underscored the importance of opportunity cost in this famous remark: "There is no such thing as a free lunch. This is the sum of my economic theory. The rest is elaboration." Harping on the subject of cost often puts economists in conflict with policy makers. Environmentalists don't like to hear economists talk about the opportunity cost of environmental purity in terms of forgone output. College admissions or recruitment officers seeking students don't like economists reminding students that the opportunity cost of a college education includes income not earned while in college.

5. *Economists are very interested in chances to substitute among alternatives.* Substitution and cost are closely related because the decision to substitute is based on the costs of the various alternatives. Sometimes substitutes are obvious, such as plastic for aluminum or electric heat for gas. Other substitutes are less apparent. A tree, for example, can substitute for gas or oil as heat or for aluminum siding on houses. Trees can also substitute for air conditioning or awnings by providing shade. An important task of economic analysis is identifying alternatives that can serve as substitutes and evaluating the costs of substituting one for another.

6. *Economists think in terms of incremental, or marginal, analysis.*[8] The marginal approach means looking at the effects on other variables of small increases or decreases in one important variable. Should we produce another (marginal) missile? If we do, what will be the (marginal) cost in terms of soybeans not produced? Most decisions in economics are

---

8. Remember that *marginal* means extra, or incremental, rather than inferior.

not all-or-nothing choices but are made at the margin. Decisions about how to spend the next hour, whether to eat another slice of pizza, and whether to hire an extra worker are all marginal decisions.

7. *Economists take the individual, rather than the group, the industry, or the community, as the basic decision-making unit.* They regard the behavior of individuals as an important influence on public policy and on decisions made in the private sector. The emphasis on individuals rather than groups reflects the importance of incentives in economics. Changes in prices, costs, profits, wages, substitutes, and opportunities are the driving forces behind individual economic decisions. It is the individual, not the group or community, that responds to incentives.

THREE COMMON FALLACIES

There are three dangerous fallacies, or errors in logical thinking, that can lead to false conclusions in economics. The following three statements could appear in the news and would seem logical to most readers. Each, however, contains a fallacy.

1. "The stock market closed up today in active trading. Analysts attributed the gain to optimism generated by the recent U.S.-Soviet summit on arms control."
2. "Layoffs in the auto industry were attributed to rising imports of cars, especially from Japan. Union leaders called for renewed emphasis on buying American goods, predicting severe unemployment in all manufacturing industries if the tide of imports continues to rise."
3. "The long expected decline in college enrollment, caused by fewer high school graduates since the mid-1980s and sharply rising tuitions, has not taken place. College enrollments appear to be stable or rising, in contradiction to forecasts."

THE ASSOCIATION-CAUSATION FALLACY

association-causation fallacy
The false notion that association implies causality.

The Latin phrase *post hoc, ergo propter hoc* translates as "after this, therefore, because of this." This kind of reasoning is called the **association-causation fallacy**. The fact that *A* changes and then *B* changes does not mean that the change in *A* caused the change in *B*. Suppose an increase in the number of students taking driver education programs is followed by an increase in accidents involving teenaged drivers. We could not conclude that driver education causes accidents. A statistical or observed association does not imply a causal relationship.

The stock market news item presented above is a familiar example. Newscasters know that the market has either risen or fallen, and they want a cause to offer as an explanation to report to their audiences. They can always find such a reason by identifying another important news event of the same day as *the* cause. The best way to avoid this fallacy is to search for a theoretical explanation for the suggested cause-and-effect relationship. Why, in terms of models and theories, should we expect a change in *A* to cause *B* to change in a certain way? There are sound theoretical reasons why an increase in profits or a decline in interest rates might lead to a

THINKING LIKE AN ECONOMIST

As you start to think about problems and policies from an economic perspective, here are some guidelines to help you.

• Positive, not normative	Try not to confuse what theory tells you will happen with what you *want* to happen
• Can the market solve it?	Economists tend to prefer market solutions because they are more efficient.
• Costs	I know there is no free lunch, but have I really counted all the costs?
• Substitutes	What are the substitutes? Where are they? What are their costs?
• Individuals and incentives	What incentives (positive and negative) does this policy create for individual buyers, sellers, and workers?
• Fallacies	Have I carefully reviewed my analysis to avoid the three common fallacies?

stock market boom. Is there any reason for an arms agreement to affect the stock market? Avoiding the association-causation fallacy is a good reason for studying and using economic theory.

THE FALLACY OF COMPOSITION

The second news item given above illustrates the **fallacy of composition**. This is the erroneous view that what holds for the parts holds for the whole as well. It is true that rising auto imports hurt auto producers and auto workers as a group. Even if most of the auto industry suffers, that is not true of all manufacturing industries. If Americans import more, some American manufacturers will manage to sell more to foreigners who earn those dollars. Thus, there will be gainers as well as losers. What is true for auto workers and auto producers is not true for the economy as a whole. In fact, the U.S. economy did quite well during some of the worst years for the auto industry in the 1980s.

fallacy of composition
The false notion that what holds for the parts holds for the whole.

THE *CETERIS PARIBUS* FALLACY

The third news item offers an example of the *ceteris paribus* fallacy. The *ceteris paribus* **fallacy** occurs when a variable does not change as predicted because the analyst has overlooked the fact that other variables have also changed. When economists make statements or predictions, they qualify them with the phrase *ceteris paribus*, meaning other things being unchanged. What happens to college enrollment when tuition rises, *ceteris paribus*? Economic theory tells us that enrollment should fall. Instead, enrollment in the 1980s held steady and even rose slightly.

The rise in tuition and decline in high school graduates, taken together, should have caused a decline in college enrollment. However, at the same time, incomes rose. Even though there were fewer students, they came from smaller families that could more easily afford to educate all their children. Also, a growing population of retired people provided a

ceteris paribus **fallacy**
The false notion that arises because an observer fails to recognize that variables other than the one in question have changed.

From the end of World War II until the mid-1970s, American students learned economics almost as though the United States were on a different planet from the rest of the world. A few textbooks had a chapter or two on international economics at the end. This material was rarely covered in class, however. This approach to economics reflected two common attitudes. The first was that the U.S. economy was so large and the share of foreign trade in U.S. economic activity was so small that the rest of the world could safely be ignored. The second was that it was important for students to learn how the U.S. economy worked, but not necessarily how institutions, policies, and solutions to common problems worked in other countries.

In the 1980s, Americans learned the economic importance of the rest of the world. The rest of the world has had a significant effect on the U.S. economy. The price of the dollar has seen some dramatic ups and downs in the last fifteen years. These fluctuations have affected imports, exports, employment, and price levels in the United States. Clearly, U.S. economists can no longer ignore the macroeconomic effects of the rest of the world.

At the microeconomic level, individual American firms, workers, and consumers have also become increasingly aware of the rest of the world. Americans who eat bananas from Central America on their cereal and drink coffee from Colombia, tea from India, or hot chocolate from Ghana for breakfast start their days in an international market. They may ride to work or school on a Japanese bicycle or in a Japanese car—although the car may have been built in the United States! When students graduate, many take jobs with multinational firms, American or foreign, in the United States or abroad. Their parents may have suffered spells of unemployment related to imports competing with domestic production of steel, autos, shoes, or textiles.

As Americans have become more aware of the impact of the rest of the world on their own

INTERNATIONAL PERSPECTIVE

THE UNITED STATES AND THE REST OF THE WORLD

economy at both the micro and macro levels, they have also become increasingly interested in learning from others. Europe has taught Americans the benefits of economic integration, which is being applied in the newly created U.S.–Canada free trade area. Americans have looked to Europe and Canada to study experiments in social policy, such as national health insurance and children's allowances. Japan has much to show U.S. firms about management and innovation. Japanese educators have been studying U.S. higher education while Americans are interested in their system of year-round education in the lower grades.

Recognizing the growing importance of the international economy as both an influence on the U.S. economy and a source of ideas, we have chosen not to relegate the rest of the world to the back of the book. Each chapter offers one or more international perspectives. Some of these extend the material in that chapter to the open, or international, economy. This allows you to see the impact of the rest of the world on economic decisions and events at home. Others look at how a model, analysis, or solution to an economic problem might be different in another environment. You will see how tax systems work in Europe, why antitrust policy in the United States is stricter than in other nations, or why unemployment is always so high in the United Kingdom. Theories and models will explore the similarities between economic systems and the impact of one nation on another. Specific institutions and solutions will highlight the variety of possible approaches to solving the common problem of scarcity and choice.

When you finish this course, you should understand not only how the U.S. economic system operates but also how it appears in perspective with many others. We hope you will use the international perspectives to broaden your horizons and your understanding of the U.S. economy as one among many.

new pool of students. Income, family size, and number of retirees were all assumed to be *ceteris paribus* conditions. However, they did not remain constant but changed. These changes offset the effects of higher tuition and fewer high school graduates. Thus, college enrollments continued to increase. The statement predicting falling enrollment is wrong because the observer failed to examine fully the *ceteris paribus* conditions. In this case, as with the other two, a careful application of economic theory will help avoid the fallacy.

MAKING POLICY CHOICES

When economic models are applied to public policy issues, it is difficult to decide when the economist's task ends and the policy maker takes over. When economic methods are used for policy analysis, there is a five-step process.

1. *State the problem.* The choice of what problem to consider and how to state it is the task of the policy maker. How a problem is stated often determines what tools the economist applies and what solutions are considered. For example, suppose the problem is illegal parking on campus, especially parking by students in faculty spaces. Let's follow that problem through the next four steps.

2. *Apply the relevant economic model.* The economist turns to the toolkit to select the most useful theoretical model. In this case, there is a fairly simple technique called cost-benefit analysis that is not a formal model. This technique simply assumes that people are self-interested, that they are aware of the opportunity costs and benefits of their actions, and that they will choose the course of action that maximizes the excess of benefits over opportunity costs. This simple model predicts that an increase in the opportunity cost of illegal student parking or a reduction in benefits will reduce the amount of such illegal parking.

3. *Identify solutions.* The most common error at this stage is to leave out some solutions. Cost-based solutions to illegal parking might include higher fines. Do you think a student would be less likely to park in a faculty space if the fine were $100 instead of $10? More police officers would raise the cost by increasing the probability of being caught. The university could reduce the benefits of illegal parking by providing more bicycle racks or free bus transportation around campus and to and from commuter parking lots. Campus officials could even sell reserved parking spaces, and let students and faculty bid for parking rights.

4. *Evaluate solutions.* This is the stage where economists are most useful, pointing to costs, substitutes, and incentives. A good economic model predicts how various solutions will affect the amount of illegal parking, who will gain and who will lose, and which solution costs least to implement. For example, more police officers would be more expensive than higher fines. On the other hand, higher fines are a burden on students, many of whom have limited incomes. Bicycle racks are cheaper than shuttle buses. However, racks are not as helpful as buses would be to commuting students, unless they live very close to campus.

5. *Choose and implement one or more solutions.* This step is *not* the task of the

economist, although it is hard to stop after carrying the process this far. The policy maker (who may have been trained as an economist) takes the economist's list of possible solutions and the evaluation and makes a policy choice.

Most arguments among economists occur when they overstep the boundaries of scientific analysis and advocate a particular solution to an economic problem. Newspapers and TV news programs often quote economists who disagree. However, economists agree far more often than they disagree. Disagreements make headlines; agreement isn't news. Throughout this book, we will point out where most economists agree and also where and why they disagree. The models we describe represent a broad range of agreement among most economists on how markets work and how individuals respond to incentives.

Economics is an exciting social science. The individual who understands the economic way of thinking will gain insight into an endless array of interesting policy questions. We wish you well. Let's get on with it!

SUMMARY

1. Economics is the study of how decisions about producing and consuming goods and services are made and how individuals and groups face the problem of scarcity.

2. Microeconomics looks at the interactions of producers and consumers in individual markets. Macroeconomics is the study of the economy as a whole and is concerned with aggregates, numbers that are determined by adding across many markets.

3. Economics is one of the social sciences, along with psychology, sociology, and political science. These fields focus on the behavior of individuals in their interactions with one another.

4. Economic theory is an abstract way of thinking that allows the development of principles, or tools, that can be used to study social issues.

5. Resources are finite, but human wants are insatiable. This conflict is the basic economic problem of scarcity. People cannot have everything they want and must make choices.

6. The production possibilities curve illustrates the problem of scarcity. In order to have more of one good, people must settle for less of another. The cost of extra units of one good is the number of units of the other sacrificed, or the opportunity cost.

7. The principle of increasing opportunity cost says that the more of one good people have, the greater the amount of other goods they must sacrifice to obtain one more unit of that good.

8. The production possibilities curve can be used to describe unemployment of resources (points inside the curve) and economic growth (a shift of the curve to the right).

9. Self-interested behavior is a basic assumption of economic theory. Although economists recognize that economic behavior is a complex process, they assume that human beings pursue their own self-interest.

10. Economic theory is positive, or nonnormative. It can't tell us what we should do, but it can make statements of an if-*A*-then-*B* type.

11. Economists tend to rely on the market to solve social problems. In analyzing problems, economists stress identifying options and looking at costs and benefits, particularly at the margin.

12. The association-causation fallacy is the false notion that association implies causality.

13. The fallacy of composition is the false idea that what holds for the parts holds for the whole.

14. The *ceteris paribus* fallacy occurs when changes in one variable fail to have the predicted effect on another variable because the observer has ignored changes in other important variables.

15. A policy decision is analyzed in five steps: state the problem, apply the relevant economic model, identify solutions, evaluate solutions, and choose and implement solutions.

16. Although economists agree on many things, their disagreements are often highlighted. Most of their disagreements are over policy choices rather than economic theory.

NEW TERMS

economics	insatiable wants	theory	normative statements
microeconomics	opportunity cost	testable hypothesis	association-causation
macroeconomics	production possibilities	model	fallacy
aggregates	curve	*ceteris paribus* assumption	fallacy of composition
social science	increasing opportunity	self-interested behavior	*ceteris paribus* fallacy
scarcity	cost	positive statements	

QUESTIONS FOR DISCUSSION

1. Do you think people exhibit behavior patterns that confirm the self-interest assumption? Does your own behavior confirm this assumption? Is a contribution to charity or volunteer work a contradiction of the self-interest assumption?

2. Why do economists theorize rather than attempt to describe reality exactly?

3. Do assumptions have to be realistic in order for a theory to work?

4. What is the difference between using theory to predict and forecasting?

5. Consider the following simple predictive model: if the speed limit is reduced, fewer highway deaths will occur. What assumptions are being made? What *ceteris paribus* conditions could change and make this prediction invalid?

6. Identify and explain the fallacy in each of the following statements.

   a. "There was a transit strike in April, and unemployment in the city rose in May. Clearly the transit strike created unemployment."

   b. "The new subway system is finally working, but downtown parking spaces are harder to find than before. The subway system hasn't relieved congestion."

   c. "Our state competed heavily to attract industry, and it worked. Unemployment is down. If all states did the same, national unemployment would fall."

7. Which of the following quantities are microeconomic, and which are macroeconomic? Which might fall between the two?

   a. price of shoes

   b. number of men aged 18 to 24 in the U.S. labor force

   c. level of interest rates

   d. unemployment in Tulsa

   e. production of agricultural products

   f. average level of prices

   g. production of butter

   h. average price of imported goods

   i. unemployment in the United States

   j. total output

   k. unemployment of carpenters

   l. number of nurses in the U.S. labor force

   m. unemployment in the northeastern states

8. What is the opportunity cost of working 10 hours a week flipping burgers while in college? If you worked more hours per week, would you experience increasing or constant opportunity cost? That is, would the extra hours require giving up alternative uses of your time that have the same value or an increasing value?

9. a. Given the following data, plot a production possibilities curve and calculate the opportunity cost of bicycles in terms of skateboards.

BICYCLES	SKATEBOARDS
10	0
8	10
6	20
4	30
2	40
0	50

   b. Assume that new technology increases the possible output of both skateboards and bicycles by 50 percent. Draw the new production possibilities curve. Calculate the new opportunity cost of bicycles in terms of skateboards.

   c. Now assume that new technology increases the amount of bicycles that can be produced by 6 units if all resources are devoted to bicycles, but does not change the amount of skateboards that can be produced. Draw a new curve, and calculate a new opportunity cost.

10. You know that the opportunity cost of books in terms of cassettes not produced is 1 book for 2 cassettes and that available resources can produce a maximum of 100 books. Can you draw the production possibilities curve for these two goods? If so, what is the maximum possible output of cassettes? If you choose to produce 40 books, how many cassettes can be produced?

11. Using the following economic data, plot a production possibilities curve for tomatoes and tomahawks:

TOMATOES	TOMAHAWKS
100	0
80	15
60	30
40	45
20	60
0	75

What is the opportunity cost of a tomato? A tomahawk? If 50 tomatoes are produced, how many tomahawks can be produced?

12. Using the data in question 11, suppose a change in technology makes it possible to increase tomato production to a maximum of 150 units. There is no change in the technology of producing tomahawks. Draw the new production possibilities curve. Now what is the opportunity cost of each good? If this economy chooses to produce 60 tomatoes, how many tomahawks can it produce?

13. Try developing a simple economic model to predict how students will respond to an increase in dormitory rents. What are your assumptions? What will happen to the number of dormitory spaces rented? What will happen to the number of off-campus apartments rented and their prices?

14. Which of the following statements are normative, and which are positive? Rewrite the normative statements to make them positive and the positive ones to make them normative.

a. "Women earn less than men."

b. "Defense spending has grown too rapidly in the last decade."

c. "Because their child-care duties interfere with their work, women with children should earn less than men."

d. "Twenty-three percent of the federal budget is spent on defense."

e. "An estimated 14 percent of the U.S. population lives in poverty, according to government standards defining poverty."

f. "The government is not doing enough to reduce poverty."

15. The economy of Southland can only produce two goods: food and clothing. Both are subject to constant costs. Draw a production possibilities curve for Southland that shows the maximum output of food as 50 cartons and the maximum output of clothing as 100 suits. Now locate each of the following on your diagram.

a. Output of 25 cartons of food and 25 suits of clothing. Label this point *U*. Does it lie on the curve? What does this point represent? What is the opportunity cost of another suit of clothing at this point?

b. Output of 50 cartons of food and 100 suits of clothing. Label this point *G*. Does this point lie on the curve? Is it attainable? If not, what must happen for *G* to be a possible output combination?

c. Output of 25 cartons of food and 50 suits of clothing. Label this point *A*. Does it lie on the curve? What is the opportunity cost of another carton of food at this point?

16. a. Suppose the two goods in question 15 are subject to increasing costs, but the end points remain the same. Draw a new production possibilities curve for food and clothing in Southland.

b. Suppose the economy of Southland has a technological change that increases the capacity to produce food but not clothing. How will the production possibilities curve shift? Is it possible to produce more of both food and clothing after this shift?

c. Suppose the economy of Southland has an increase in resources that affects both food and clothing production equally. How will the production possibilities curve shift?

SUGGESTIONS FOR FURTHER READING

Boulding, Kenneth. *Human Betterment.* Beverly Hills, CA: Sage, 1985. This recent book by one of America's best known economic philosophers makes a case for normative analysis when the values behind the analysis are clearly spelled out.

Huff, Darrell, and Irving Geis. *How to Lie with Statistics.* New York: W. W. Norton, 1954 (copyright renewed 1982). This classic guide to interpreting and misinterpreting graphs and statistics is must reading for any serious student of the social sciences.

Rhoads, Stephen E. *The Economist's View of the World: Government, Markets, and Public Policy.* New York: Cambridge University Press, 1985. Written by a political scientist, this book looks at both the useful contributions of economics to other social sciences and the limitations of economics.

Stigler, George. *Memoirs of an Unregulated Economist.* New York: Basic Books, 1988. A Nobel Prize–winning economist looks at the training of economists and the uses of economics in an account of his own experiences in the field.

APPENDIX:
ECONOMIC RELATIONSHIPS AND GRAPHS

Economic theories and models are often expressed in the form of mathematical relationships among variables. These relationships can be described by algebraic equations. Economists more often express them visually in the form of graphs. Graphs make it possible to illustrate economic theories and models in ways that make them easier to remember and to apply to the real world. Remember that everything that can be said in graphs can also be said in words. Graphs are only an aid to understanding the theory. Mastering and applying the theory is what you should be trying to achieve. If you can learn to feel comfortable with graphs as visual presentations of economic ideas, reading this textbook and understanding your professor's lectures will be much easier.

RELATIONSHIP BETWEEN TWO VARIABLES

A relationship between two variables, variable x and variable y, can be expressed in a number of ways. One is a table of values of x and y. For example, Table 1A shows the various amounts of fertilizer applied per acre and the corresponding yields of corn per acre. What does this table mean? It means that different amounts of fertilizer were applied to different plots of land and that those plots of land yielded varying amounts of corn.

This relationship could also be expressed in the form of a graph.[a] A

TABLE 1A
RELATIONSHIPS BETWEEN TWO VARIABLES

x-VARIABLE, FERTILIZER (100s OF LBS./ACRE)	y-VARIABLE, CORN (BUSHELS/ACRE)
1	1
2	10
3	40
4	80
5	100
6	110
7	115
8	110
9	100
10	70

a.   A third way to represent such a relationship is with an equation, $y = f(x)$. We will be using some equations in this book but will rely more heavily on graphs to display relationships between variables.

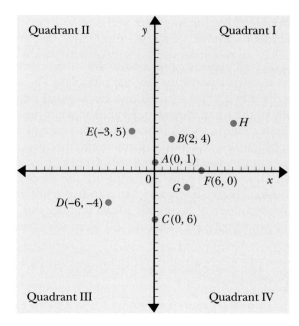

FIGURE 1A
QUADRANT SYSTEM
A four-quadrant system makes it possible to represent combinations of positive and negative values in two dimensions. Point C represents an x-value of 0 and a y-value of –6. The quadrants are labeled I to IV in the counterclockwise direction.

y-axis
The upright line in a coordinate system that shows the values of the dependent variable; the vertical axis.

x-axis
The horizontal line in a coordinate system that shows the values of the independent variable; the horizontal axis.

origin
The intersection of the vertical and horizontal axes of a coordinate system, at which the values of both the x-variable and the y-variable are zero.

coordinates
The values of x and y that define the location of a point in a coordinate system.

graph shows how the quantity of one variable changes when another variable changes. Figure 1A shows the system most commonly used for graphing. The vertical line is referred to as the **y-axis** (or vertical axis). The horizontal line is referred to as the **x-axis** (or horizontal axis). The x-axis and y-axis divide the graph into four quadrants.

The point where the axes cross (or intersect) is the **origin**. At the origin, the values of both the x-variable and the y-variable are zero. Above the x-axis, the y-variable has positive values. Below the x-axis, the y-variable has negative values. To the right of the y-axis, the x-variable has positive values. To the left of the y-axis, the x-variable has negative values. Both x and y have positive values in Quadrant I and negative values in Quadrant III. In Quadrant IV, x takes on positive values, and y takes on negative values. In Quadrant II, x has negative values, and y positive values. In this book, most of the graphs will use only Quadrant I because most economic data takes on only positive values.

Each point on a graph has a set of **coordinates**, a pair of numbers representing the x-value and the y-value. For example, point B on Figure 1A represents the value 2 for the x-variable and the value 4 for the y-variable. The x-value is always given first. For example, point E represents $x = -3$, $y = 5$. See if you can determine the coordinates of points G and H.

With this background, we can plot the relationship between fertilizer applied and corn output given in Table 1A. The first decision to make is which variable goes on which axis. If there is a cause-and-effect relationship, we usually put the "causing" variable on the horizontal axis and the variable being affected on the vertical axis. In mathematics, the causing variable is the **independent variable**, and the affected variable is the **dependent variable**. Since we think that fertilizer causes increased corn yields, we plot it on the horizontal axis (*x*-axis). Corn yield is plotted on the vertical axis (*y*-axis).

The next decision concerns establishing a scale for each axis. The scales can be whatever is convenient and do not need to be the same. In this case, the fertilizer units are hundreds of pounds per acre, and the corn units are bushels per acre. Once a scale is established and the axes are labeled, we can plot the coordinates of the points in Table 1A. Then we connect the plotted points with a smooth curve to produce a graph, shown in Figure 2A.

The value of a graph is that it gives you a visual picture of the mathematical relationship between the variables. In Figure 2A, you can easily see that as fertilizer is increased up to 700 pounds per acre, corn output increases. After that level, more fertilizer causes a decrease in output. The corn plants grow too rapidly and don't produce many ears, or the roots suffer fertilizer burn.

Not all relationships produce as tidy a graph as the one for fertilizer and corn yield. Sometimes researchers plot data to see if there is any visual pattern before trying to understand what, if any, is the relationship between the two variables. Such a plot of actual data is called a **scatter diagram**. Scatter diagrams are useful in searching for possible mathematical relationships between two variables.

Figure 3A plots actual data on the rate of inflation (vertical axis) and the rate of unemployment (horizontal axis) for the United States from 1975 to 1989. In this diagram, there doesn't seem to be a consistent rela-

independent variable
The variable, usually plotted on the horizontal axis, that affects or influences the other variable.

dependent variable
The variable, usually plotted on the vertical axis, that is affected or influenced by the other variable.

scatter diagram
A graph that plots actual pairs of values of two variables to determine whether there appears to be any consistent relationship between them.

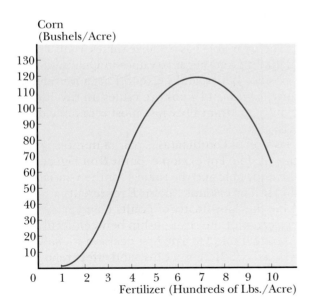

FIGURE 2A
FERTILIZER AND
CORN OUTPUT
A graph is usually plotted with the dependent variable on the *y*-axis and the independent variable on the *x*-axis. Here, as the independent variable (fertilizer) increases, the dependent variable (corn output) first increases and then decreases.

FIGURE 3A
INFLATION AND
UNEMPLOYMENT
A scatter diagram plots the coordinates for the values of two variables that may or may not have a consistent relationship. This diagram plots the unemployment rate and the inflation rate for the United States from 1976 to 1989. It shows no consistent relationship between these two variables.

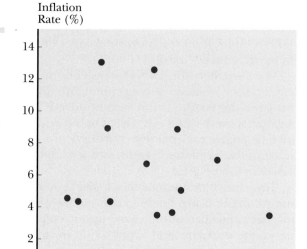

Source: Council of Economic Advisers, *Economic Report of the President* (Washington, DC: U.S. Government Printing Office, 1990).

FIGURE 4A
GNP AND MONEY SUPPLY
(BILLIONS OF DOLLARS)
This scatter diagram plots the money supply and the GNP for the United States from 1976 to 1989. Unlike the diagram in Figure 3A, this one seems to show a rather consistent relationship between the two variables.

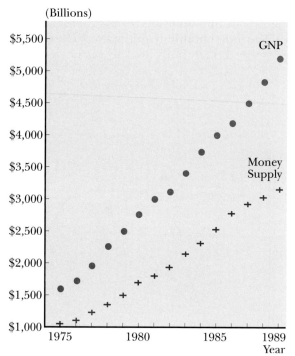

Source: Council of Economic Advisers, *Economic Report of the President* (Washington, DC: U.S. Government Printing Office, 1990).

tionship of any kind between the rate of inflation and the rate of unemployment, at least for the years plotted. Figure 4A plots the relationship between the money supply and total output, or GNP, for the United States from 1975 to 1989. As you can see, there appears to be a more consistent relationship between these two variables.

POSITIVE AND NEGATIVE RELATIONSHIPS AND SLOPES

A graph shows how two variables are related. This relationship may be positive or negative. A **positive relationship** means that an increase in the value of the *x*-variable is associated with an increase in the value of the *y*-variable, as in Figure 4A. A **negative relationship** means that an increase in the value of the *x*-variable is associated with a decrease in the value of the *y*-variable. Some relationships in economics, such as the one between fertilizer and corn output plotted in Figure 2A, are positive for some values of the *x*-variable and negative for others.

Most of the economic relationships you will encounter in this book are represented by straight lines. A straight line can have a positive slope, as in Figure 5A, or a negative slope, as in Figure 6A. The **slope** is a measure of the steepness of the line. It is the ratio of the change in the dependent variable (y) to the change in the independent variable (x). If the slope is designated by the letter m, then the equation of a straight line can be written as

$$y = mx + b,$$

where b is the value of y when $x = 0$. (The value b is also known as the y-intercept, because at this value the line crosses the y-axis.)

Even though both lines in Figure 5A are positively sloped, the rela-

positive relationship
A relationship between two variables in which an increase in one is associated with an increase in the other and a decrease in one is associated with a decrease in the other.

negative relationship
A relationship between two variables in which an increase in the value of one is associated with a decrease in the value of the other.

slope
The ratio of the change in the dependent variable (y) to the change in the independent variable (x).

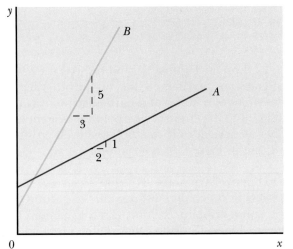

FIGURE 5A
POSITIVELY SLOPED LINES
The slope of a line is the ratio of the change in the *y*-value to the change in the *x*-value. A line sloping upward to the right has a positive slope, indicating a positive relationship between the two variables.

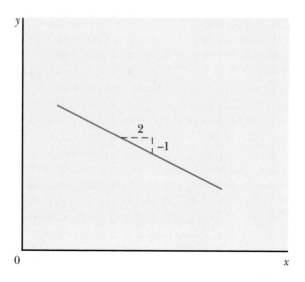

FIGURE 6A
NEGATIVELY SLOPED LINE
A negative slope represents a relationship between the variables in which an increase in the value of the independent variable is associated with a decrease in the value of the dependent variable.

tionship between the *x*-variable and the *y*-variable represented by line *A* is very different from that represented by line *B*. The same amount of change in *x* leads to a larger change in *y* along line *B* than it does along line *A*. In Figure 5A, the slope of line *A* is equal to $+\frac{1}{2}$ because the *y*-value changes by one unit for each two-unit change in the *x*-value. The slope of line *B* is $+\frac{5}{3}$, or +1.67. The steeper slope of line *B* indicates that a larger change in the value of *y* will result from a given change in the value of *x* than along line *A*. The sign of the slope is also very important. It indicates whether the relationship between the two variables is positive or negative. A slope with a positive sign designates a positive relationship. A slope with a negative sign, as in Figure 6A, indicates a negative relationship. The slope of the line in Figure 6A is $-\frac{1}{2}$.

NONLINEAR GRAPHS
AND MAXIMA AND MINIMA

tangent line
A straight line just touching a curve (nonlinear graphic relationship) at a single point. The slope of the tangent line is equal to the slope of the curve at that point.

A straight-line graph, such as those in Figures 5A and 6A, has the same slope along the entire line. The slope of a curved line, on the other hand, varies along the curve. The slope of a curve at a particular point is the slope of the straight line tangent to the curve at that point. A **tangent line** is a straight line that touches a curve at only one point without crossing it. The slope of the curved line in Figure 7A is +1 at point *A* and $-\frac{3}{2}$ at point *C*.

maximum
The point on a graph at which the *y*-variable, or dependent variable, reaches its highest value.

The slope of the curve in Figure 7A at point *B* is equal to zero. A small change in the value of *x* results in no change in the value of *y* along the straight line tangent to the curve at point *B*. Point *B* is a **maximum** because the *y*-variable reaches its highest value at that point. The highest value of *y*, y_1, is associated with an *x* value of x_1. Recall that we described

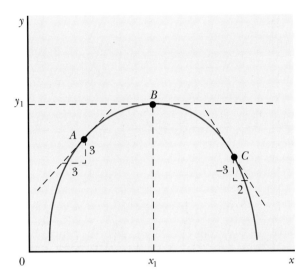

FIGURE 7A
NONLINEAR GRAPHS:
SLOPE AND MAXIMUM
On a nonlinear graph, the slope changes along the curve. The slope of the curve at any point is the slope of a straight line tangent to the curved line at that point. When the slope is zero, the value of the y-variable is either at a maximum or at a minimum. At point B, y is at its maximum value, y_1, when x has the value x_1.

self-interested behavior as consumers maximizing satisfaction, resource owners maximizing income, and firms maximizing profit. Being able to find the maximum is very important in economics.

Sometimes a slope of zero is associated with a **minimum** rather than a maximum, as in Figure 8A. The y-variable assumes its lowest value, Y_1, at point B in Figure 8A. This y-value is associated with an x-value of X_1. A firm that is trying to minimize costs, or losses, may be interested in finding a minimum point. It is also important for many kinds of economic questions to determine whether a point of zero slope is a maximum or a minimum.

minimum
The point on the graph at which the y-variable, or dependent variable, reaches its lowest value.

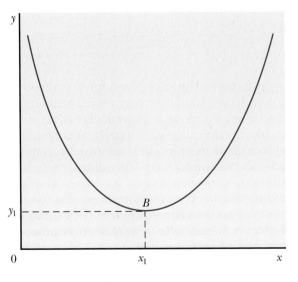

FIGURE 8A
NONLINEAR GRAPHS:
MINIMUM
This nonlinear graph also has a slope of zero at point B. In this case, point B represents the minimum value of y, y_1, which is associated with an x-value of x_1.

FIGURE 9A
THE 45° LINE
A 45° line drawn in the
first quadrant has a slope
of +1. If both axes are
measured in the same
units, the 45° line shows
all points where the
x-value and the y-value
are equal.

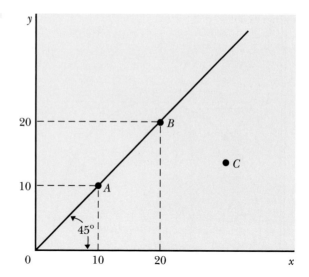

THE 45° LINE

45° line
A line in the first
quadrant, passing
through the origin,
with a slope of +1, which
divides the quadrant in
half. If the scales on the
axes are the same, the
value of the x-variable
is equal to the value of
the y-variable along the
45° line.

A geometric construction that proves very useful in economic analysis is
a **45° line**. This is a straight line through the origin that divides Quadrant
I into two equal sections. If both axes are measured in the same units, the
values of the x-variable and the y-variable will be equal at any point on the
line, and the slope will be +1. A 45° line is shown in Figure 9A. Suppose,
for example, you want to know whether the value of x is less than, equal
to, or greater than the value of y at point C. A 45° line gives you a quick
answer to that question. The value of x is greater than the value of y at
point C because point C lies below the 45° line.

GRAPHS WITHOUT NUMBERS

The graph in Figure 2A and the scatter diagrams in Figures 3A and 4A
were constructed from sets of numbers. Other graphs in this section only
give a few numerical values from which to calculate slopes. Figures 7A and
8A have no numbers on them at all. In economics, graphs of theoretical
concepts often use no numbers. For example, we might theorize that
there is a negative relationship between the price of any good that people
consume and the quantity demanded. If price is the y-variable and quantity demanded the x-variable, a negatively sloped line such as the one in
Figure 5A could represent this theoretical relationship. It doesn't matter
that we don't have specific coordinates to plot. We have instead graphed
an abstract idea. Many graphs in economics are of this abstract type.

On graphs without numbers, symbols are used for values, line segments, and areas. For example, Figure 10A is similar to graphs you will
study in Chapter 3. The y-axis shows the price per loaf of bread, and the
x-axis shows the quantity of loaves consumed per week. Particular prices
are represented by symbols such as P_1. Quantities consumed are represented by symbols such as Q_1, Q_2, and Q_3. If you have studied geometry,

Price/Loaf

P_1

0   Q_3 Q_1 Q_2 Loaves/Week

D_2

D_1

D_3

FIGURE 10A
EFFECTS OF CHANGES IN
TASTES ON THE DEMAND
FOR BREAD
Many graphs in eco-
nomics use symbols
rather than numbers on
the axes. The symbol P_1
represents a hypothetical
price, and Q_1, Q_2, and Q_3
represent hypothetical
quantities.

you will note that it would be technically correct to refer to quantity Q_1 as quantity $\overline{0Q_1}$. We will, however, use the shorthand Q_1 to minimize clutter.

In addition to using symbols to represent quantities, we will also make frequent use of the symbol delta, Δ, to represent changes in a variable. For example, the symbol ΔQ is a shorthand expression for the change from Q_1 to Q_2 in Figure 10A.

PIE CHARTS AND BAR CHARTS

All of the graphs considered so far, except for the scatter diagrams, rep-resent theoretical relationships of one kind or another. Economists also use graphs to describe the real world. Such graphs display descriptive statistics. These include the allocation of government funds between types of programs, the growth of output or the money supply over time, and the different growth rates of imports and exports.

Two common types of descriptive graphs encountered in economics are pie charts and bar charts. **Pie charts** are used to show the division of some whole into parts, usually designated by percentages. Figure 11A is a pie chart depicting the sources of household income in 1989. Pie charts have become very popular because they are easy to create on a personal computer. This visual representation often conveys a clearer sense of the relative sizes of various components than you could obtain from reading a table of numbers.

Another popular type of descriptive graph is a **bar chart**, such as Fig-ure 12A. This diagram describes the behavior of two variables, federal gov-ernment revenue and expenditures, in a series of "snapshots" from 1970 to 1989. This graph gives a much more vivid impression of how much ex-penditures have grown relative to revenues than you could derive from a set of numbers.

pie chart
A graphic represen-
tation in the shape of a
pie that expresses actual
economic data as parts
of a whole. The sizes of
the slices of the pie
correspond to the
percentage shares
of the components.

bar chart
A graphic representation
that expresses data using
columns of different
heights.

FIGURE 11A
PIE CHART OF HOUSEHOLD
INCOME FOR THE UNITED
STATES, 1989
A pie chart depicts the division of a whole into parts (percentages). This pie chart shows that the largest component of household income is wages and salaries. Transfer payments and interest are much smaller components.

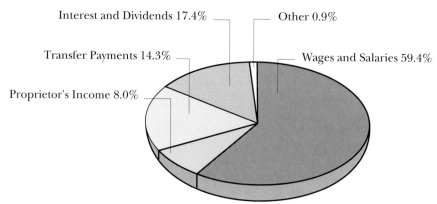

Source: Council of Economic Advisers, *Economic Report of the President* (Washington, DC: U.S. Government Printing Office, 1990).

FIGURE 12A
BAR CHART OF FEDERAL
REVENUES AND EXPENDI-
TURES, 1980–1989
A bar chart can be used in a variety of ways to present economic data in a visual fashion. This bar chart compares federal revenues and expenditures for various years.

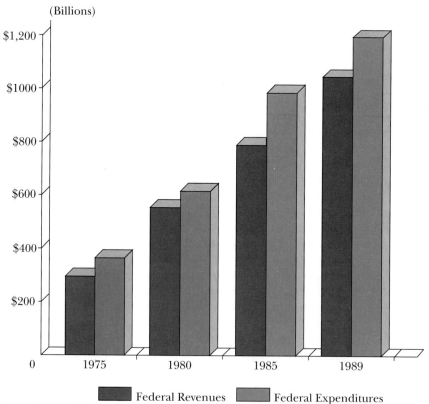

Source: Council of Economic Advisers, *Economic Report of the President* (Washington, DC: U.S. Government Printing Office, 1990).

Theoretical graphs, such as those in Figures 5A through 10A, and descriptive graphs, such as Figures 11A and 12A, are spread throughout this book. Both types are also common in textbooks in social sciences and business and in popular magazines such as *Newsweek*, *Time*, and *Business Week*. Economics is a very visual subject. Be sure that you feel secure with reading and interpreting graphs before proceeding further.

CAUTION: GRAPHS AND NUMBERS CAN MISLEAD AS WELL AS INFORM!
Graphs and statistics can be very informative. They put some concrete, real-world content into abstract models and economic relationships. However, it is very easy to present data in a misleading way. The choice of a scale along an axis can make changes look bigger than they really are. The use of averages conceals a great deal of information about variation. For example, three families with incomes of $24,000, $25,000, and $26,000 have an average income of $25,000. The same average could be the result of three incomes of $5,000, $5,000, and $65,000. The same average income describes two very different distributions of income.

A classic guide to the use and abuse of numbers and graphs is *How to Lie with Statistics*, by Darrell Huff and Irving Geis. This book has been through numerous paperback editions since it was first published in 1954. It should be required reading for anyone taking courses in the social sciences. It is a useful guide through the pitfalls of the means, medians, averages, bar charts, surveys, samples, and growth rates that are the daily news of the economic and political worlds.

Always be very cautious in accepting someone's graphs or numbers. Consider carefully what that person may be trying to persuade you to think or do and how the statistics could be manipulated to put that position in a more favorable light.

1. Identify the factors of production.
2. List the three basic economic questions that must be addressed by every economic system.
3. Use a circular flow model to show the relationships between firms and households in product markets and in factor markets in a market economy.
4. Describe how traditional, command, and market economies answer the three basic economic questions.
5. Explain and give examples of the basic economic functions of government.
6. Describe and calculate the benefits of specialization and exchange based on comparative advantage.

CHAPTER 2

MARKETS, GOVERNMENTS, AND NATIONS: THE ORGANIZATION OF ECONOMIC ACTIVITY

INTRODUCTION

Chapter 1 introduced the basic economic problem of scarcity and choice that every economy must address, regardless of its level of development or form of government. In this chapter, we explore some of the common problems and choices faced by people in all societies in using their scarce resources to satisfy their wants. We will also examine the different ways in which choices are made in different kinds of societies. Throughout this book, a series of international perspectives will remind you that the way economic problems are addressed in American society is not necessarily the way they are addressed in other countries.

In the last two decades, economists have become more aware of the importance of interactions between national economies. These interactions include trade in goods and services and movements of labor and capital. They affect the growth rate, production, employment, price level, and other important macroeconomic variables in both countries. Competition from foreign producers, foreign markets for products, and the use of foreign inputs also have important effects on prices and quantities in individual markets. Thus, another issue we introduce in this chapter is the difference between an isolated, or closed, economy and an open economy. An open economy is one that trades goods, services, and productive resources with other nations.

LIMITED RESOURCES: THE FACTORS OF PRODUCTION

To examine the process of choice, we can begin by identifying the scarce resources that exist. Scarce resources used to produce goods and services are called **factors of production**. The factors of production are divided into four broad categories: labor, land, capital, and enterprise. All resources used to produce goods and services fit into one of these four categories.

LABOR
Labor is the factor of production with which you are probably most familiar. **Labor** is the physical and mental exertion of human beings. The

factors of production
The inputs of land, labor, capital, and enterprise that a firm uses to produce outputs.

labor
The physical and mental exertion that human beings put into production activities.

41

efforts of a factory worker, a professional basketball player, a university professor, and a carpenter are all labor.

Wages are the payments labor receives for its productive services. Some labor is valued (and paid) more than other labor. Why? One reason is that some labor is more productive. Workers are born with different talents and abilities. Some are more intelligent. Others are physically stronger or better coordinated. Still others have artistic or musical ability. It is also possible to make labor more productive by devoting money and time to improving skills. Individuals invest in their labor skills by going to college, serving as apprentices, or practicing. Economists refer to this development of labor skills as an investment in human capital. **Human capital** consists of labor-enhancing abilities that increase labor's productivity. A large part of wage differences can be explained by differences in human capital.

wages
The return to labor, one of the factors of production.

human capital
The investment made to improve the quality of people's labor skills through education, training, health care, and so on.

LAND

The second factor of production is land. **Land**, to an economist, is not just rocks and soil, but all natural resources that can be used as inputs to production. By this definition, land includes minerals, water, air, forests, oil, and even rainfall, temperature, and soil quality. The income payment to this factor of production is called **rent**.

A key distinction between land and other productive resources is that land consists of natural resources or conditions, unimproved by any human activity. For example, acreage in Arizona that has been irrigated represents more than land. It also represents capital, the third factor of production. Thus, part of the payment that is called rent is a return to land, but part of it may be a return to capital.

land
Natural resources that can be used as inputs to production.

rent
The return to land, one of the factors of production.

CAPITAL

The third factor of production, **capital**, is defined as all aids to production that are human creations rather than resources found in nature. Capital includes tools, factories, warehouses, and inventories. You have also seen that capital can become attached to land or to labor (human capital) when investment is made in improvements or in skills and training. In common usage, real capital is often confused with financial capital. Financial capital is money lent to purchase real, physical capital. Economists reserve the term *capital* for real inputs to production, not for financial assets.

Capital, like land, receives a flow of income. The payments to capital are called **interest**. Interest is a reward for giving up present consumption in order to make resources available for the creation of more capital for future production. **Investment** is the act of adding to capital. Although the term *investment* is used by noneconomists for such activities as buying stocks and bonds, to an economist the term means the creation of real, tangible assets, such as machines, factories, or inventories that can be used to produce other goods and services.

capital
The durable inputs into the production process created by people. Machines, tools, and buildings are examples of capital.

interest
The return to capital, one of the factors of production.

investment
Purchases of real, tangible assets, such as machines, factories, or inventories, that are used to produce goods and services.

ENTERPRISE

The last factor of production is **enterprise**, which consists of the activities of combining the factors of production to produce goods and services, taking risks, and introducing new methods and new products (innovation). Entrepreneurs combine other factors of production by buying or

enterprise
The input to the production process that involves organizing, innovation, and risk taking.

renting them to produce a saleable product. The reward for innovation, risk taking, and organization is **profit.**

Profit is the most difficult of the four factor returns to measure in practice because it is whatever is left over after paying for land, capital, and labor. Noneconomists frequently count profit as what is left after the bills are paid. However, this measure is likely to overlook such opportunity costs as the value of the owner's labor (wages) or the return to the owner's capital (interest).

profit
The return to enterprise, one of the factors of production. Profit is whatever remains after all other factors have been paid.

THE BASIC ECONOMIC QUESTIONS

The process of choosing how to allocate scarce resources can be broken down into three broad economic questions.

- *What* goods and services will be produced and in what quantities?
- *How* will they be produced? (That is, what methods of production and combinations of inputs will be used?)
- *For whom* will they be produced? (That is, who gets what share of the goods and services produced?)

Different kinds of economic systems answer these three questions in different ways. However, people in all economic systems are faced with the problem of how to allocate scarce resources among an unlimited number of wants.

The market provides at least a partial answer to these three questions in many societies. A **market** is any setting in which buyers and sellers meet to exchange goods, services, or productive resources. A market system is an economic system that relies primarily on market transactions to answer the three basic economic questions.

market
A place where buyers and sellers meet to exchange goods, services, and productive resources.

The production possibilities curve introduced in Chapter 1 showed attainable levels and combinations of outputs, or the choices available. The production possibilities curve, however, does not explain how to choose among these combinations. What determines if an economy is at one particular point on the production possibilities curve instead of another, and who makes that choice?

WHAT, HOW, AND FOR WHOM

The *what* question asks exactly what mix of goods and services is to be produced—how many tons of wheat, thousands of textbooks, yards of fabric, pairs of jeans, and gallons of milk will make up the total national output. It is a difficult enough question in the simple two-product world of the production possibilities curve. With thousands and thousands of possible combinations of outputs, the *what* question is extremely complex. In a market system, the answer to the *what* question is determined by consumers, who "vote" in the marketplace by using their dollars to obtain particular goods and services. In other economic systems, other methods are used to determine what kinds of goods and services are produced and in what amounts.

A market economy may result in choices about the output mix that some economists or policy makers find peculiar or distasteful. Many policy makers may not share the public's taste for rock videos, gambling palaces, country music, or skateboards. However, unless people's consumption of these items can be shown to be harmful to others, a market society does not pass normative judgment on tastes. Markets produce what people want to buy.

The *how* question asks what input combination will be used to produce the chosen goods and services. Should missiles be produced by combining many workers with a few units of capital or by a more capital-intensive method? Is it better to produce soybeans using lots of tractors and machinery intensely cultivating a few acres of land or using more land and workers and relatively little capital? Should college students be taught in large classes by professors (highly skilled labor) or in small sections by teaching assistants (substituting less skilled labor)? Such questions must be answered in a systematic way. In a market system, prices guide suppliers and buyers of inputs to decisions that maximize profits or minimize costs.

The *for whom* question asks who will get the goods and services produced and how much each person will receive. This is a way of asking which of many possible distributions of income will be chosen. Should the distribution be equal or unequal? Should an individual's share be based on contributions to production, on need, or on some combination of the two? A pure market system answers this question directly: a person's rewards depend on contributions to production. Other systems, including a mixed market system, use a mixture of guidelines to determine the distribution of income.

The answers to the three questions are not independent of one another. The distribution of income will determine whether there is more demand for bread and milk or luxury yachts. The production process chosen may determine the amount of each kind of output that can be produced.

Tradition, Command, and the Market

Every society has to find a way to answer the three basic economic questions. The study of the different ways of organizing economic activity, or answering these questions, is called comparative economic systems. There are many ways of classifying economic systems, such as by who owns the productive resources or by the form of government. One useful way of classifying economic systems is by the method used to answer the three basic economic questions. This classification identifies three broad types of economies: the traditional economy, the command (planned) economy, and the market economy. Of course, no economy fits neatly into any one of these categories. All economies are mixed in that they contain elements of traditional, command, and market processes.

traditional economy
An economy in which the three basic questions are answered by custom, or how things have been done in the past.

The Traditional Economy. The **traditional economy** answers the basic economic questions by appeals to tradition, or custom. That is, the answers are determined by how the questions have been answered in the past. What is produced is whatever parents have taught their children to produce on the basis of customs developed in the past. A heavily traditional society is usually not highly sophisticated. Most of people's efforts are devoted to simple production of food, clothing, and shelter. Tradition determines what kinds of food are grown, what kinds of clothing are made, and what kinds of houses are built. It also determines what combination of these three is produced in any given period.

In a traditional economy, the techniques of production (how to produce) are also passed on, with little change, from one generation to the next. In many parts of Asia and Africa, the methods of building houses and of farming have been the same for many generations. These methods use simple materials, much labor, and very little capital equipment.

Traditional societies also have established answers to the distribution question (for whom). If you have studied cultural anthropology, you know that traditional societies often have rules on how to divide the spoils of the hunt or the fruits of the harvest. Medieval Europe was a highly traditional society, with shares of crops assigned to various claimants. There were also customary duties of military service or payments to the lord of the manor. In such a traditional society, a person's claim on society's resources is determined primarily by status in the hierarchy from peasant to king.

You may recognize elements of tradition that persist even in modern industrial societies. For example, there are still many small, rural communities almost untouched by modern farming techniques. Some ethnic groups have strong traditions of sons following their fathers' occupations. Women's roles and responsibilities continue to follow tradition in many respects. For the most part, however, tradition plays a limited role in the decision-making process in modern industrial economies.

THE COMMAND ECONOMY. The **command economy**, or planned economy, answers the basic economic questions through central command and control. A central planning authority makes all decisions regarding what and how to produce. Individual production units receive detailed plans and orders that carry the weight of law. The question concerning income distribution is answered in the process of determining what and how to produce. The central planners also set wage rates and levels of production. This planning process was the primary method of organization in the Soviet Union and other countries in Eastern Europe, before the recent rapid movement toward market economies. The major goal of perestroika was to decentralize decision making and reduce the amount of central control in the Soviet Union. The nations of Eastern Europe have made an even more rapid journey toward decentralization and the use of markets.

In any economy, people plan. That is, they think about the future and prepare for it. In a traditional society, people plan for a future that will be much like the past. In a command economy, the government plays the primary role in planning how to answer the production and consumption questions for society. This kind of planning is very different from the individual planning that goes on in a market economy. Decision making is highly decentralized in a market system.

THE MARKET ECONOMY. The third type of economic system is the market economy. The **market economy** relies on incentives and the self-interested behavior of individuals to direct production and consumption through

command economy
An economy in which the three basic questions are answered through central planning and control (also called a planned economy).

market economy
An economy in which the three basic questions are answered through the market, by relying on self-interested behavior and incentives.

market exchanges. Consumers, "voting" with their dollars, determine what is produced. The result of this market process determines what goods and services are available.

Suppliers determine how to produce. Since suppliers are self-interested and seek to maximize their profits, they tend to combine inputs so as to produce a good or service at the lowest possible cost. The answer to the *how* question depends on the prices of productive resources. Suppliers will use more of abundant resources because they are relatively cheap.

The goods and services are distributed to consumers who have the purchasing power to buy them. Households that have more purchasing power (because they own more valuable productive resources) receive more goods and services. The quantity and quality of the labor skills the individual sells are the most important determinants of individual income. About 75 percent of the income in the United States is wages and salaries. Those with high-quality, scarce skills that are in great demand receive high salaries and have more influence on the output mix. People with higher earnings have more "votes" in the form of dollars spent in the marketplace.

property rights
The legal rights to a specific piece of property, including the rights to own, buy, sell, or use in specific ways. Markets can exist and exchanges can occur only if individuals have property rights to goods, services, and productive resources.

One essential condition for undirected markets to answer the basic economic questions is the institution of **property rights**. In a command economy, most property belongs to the state. There is very limited private ownership. In fact, the process of restoring private ownership and private property rights has been slow in Eastern Europe, requiring changes in the constitutions in many cases. In a market economy, however, private property and property rights play an essential role. Markets will function only if individual buyers and sellers possess the property rights to the goods and services they want to exchange.

In a market economy, productive resources are owned by individuals. Owners of capital will not invest unless they are certain that they can claim the ownership of that capital and the products that it produces. They also need to be assured that their capital and its interest will not be taken away by the state or by force or violence. Workers will not offer their labor for hire if their rights to be paid cannot be enforced or if they know their earnings are likely to be stolen. Agreements to use productive resources and to make payments for them have to be protected from violence or breach of contract. What a market system needs, then, is a legal system that defines property rights and enforces them against any violations. Defining and enforcing property rights is an important function of government even in a pure market economy.

Beyond enforcing property rights, governments undertake some amount of central planning in all economies, including that of the United States. Federal and state governments play a substantial role in determining what is produced and how it is produced. Government policy makers make decisions about highways, schools, public parks, national defense, and other goods and services produced in the public sector. Their actions also change the distribution of income through taxes and social welfare programs. However, politicians and public policy makers are not the primary decision makers in the U.S. economy or in most other modern industrial economies, such as those of Japan, Canada, Australia, and the nations of the European Community. In these countries, most decisions are made by individuals through markets.

RESPONDING TO CHANGE. One way to compare the workings of these three types of economic systems is to consider how each responds to change. Suppose an earthquake closes some copper mines, and the supply of copper is suddenly cut in half. A traditional economy would probably have rules to ensure a fair distribution of the reduced supply. It would not, however, be very flexible in adjusting production processes or the output mix. In a command economy, government officials would determine the possible effects of the copper shortage and estimate how long it was likely to last. They would then decide which uses of copper had the highest priority and make sure that the available copper was distributed so that those uses could occur. For example, orders might be sent to firms producing electric generators to substitute some other metal for copper, in order to conserve it for uses such as house wiring.

Contrast these processes with what occurs in a market economy. When the mines close and less copper is available, copper prices rise. Consumers of copper know immediately that the price has gone up. The high price leads consumers to search for cheaper substitutes. It also attracts a sudden flow of imported copper or scrap copper to the market. The allocation of copper might not meet the traditional economy's criterion of fairness or the command economy's priorities. However, the market response is much faster. Substitution and increased supplies occur very quickly with no need for the government to process and send information. Acquiring relevant information for decisions requires the use of scarce resources. The market system economizes on the amount of costly information needed to make production and consumption decisions.

Clearly, a market system has advantages over command and traditional economies in flexibility and capacity for dealing with change. However, the market system also has some drawbacks. Many observers criticize the distribution of income that results from the workings of the market, which can create extremes of wealth and poverty. Market systems have also been criticized for encouraging self-centered behavior at the expense of community interests.

MIXED ECONOMIES

Because of the advantages of the market system, even primarily traditional or command economies incorporate some elements of markets. Conversely, the pure market system is often modified to soften some of the harshness of pure capitalism.

The blend of tradition, command, and market-decision methods varies, but most modern industrial countries such as Canada, Japan, the United States, Australia, and some of the nations of Western Europe have mixed economies. In a **mixed economy**, the basic decision method is the market, but some economic choices are made by government. These choices are designed to modify the answers to the basic economic questions reached in the course of unregulated market activity while keeping most of the benefits of markets intact. The goal is to leave economic decisions to the market when it works well, but to intervene in the economy when the market outcome is not acceptable. On a macroeconomic level, a high rate of unemployment is an example of an unacceptable market outcome. On a microeconomic level, air pollution caused by coal-fired power plants is an example of an undesirable market outcome. In both

mixed economy
An economy in which the three basic questions are answered partly by market forces and partly through government.

instances, some people argue that the government should step in to correct the performance of the market and alter its results.

All noncommunist industrial nations are properly classed as mixed economies. Increasingly, the formerly communist nations of Eastern Europe are moving in that direction as well. The mix varies significantly from country to country. Governments are much more heavily involved in the economy in Poland, Sweden, and France than in the United States and Germany. The differences in the degree of governmental involvement in economic decisions reflect variety in political systems, national values, and historical experiences. Even within economies, the division of labor between the market and the public sector changes from time to time. The movement to privatize certain activities (to shift them from the public sector to the private sector) was very strong in the 1980s in several industrial countries, including the United States and Britain. That movement has taken hold in the formerly communist nations of Eastern Europe as their governments sell off state-owned land and enterprises to private individuals.

Most of this book presents economic theory in the context of a mixed, but primarily market, economy. When we want to cite examples of how things work in reality, we will draw mostly on the experiences of the U.S. economy. The international perspectives will offer some illustrations of how things work in other countries. Despite the emphasis on the mixed economy as the model and the United States as the chief example, the economic theory we will develop is universally applicable. What differs is how often and for what purpose different governments choose to intervene in the market.

THE CIRCULAR FLOW OF ECONOMIC ACTIVITY

circular flow model
A visual representation of the relationships between the factor market (in which income is obtained) and the product market (in which income is used to purchase goods and services).

factor market
Set of markets in which owners of the factors of production sell these to producers.

product market
Set of markets in which goods and services produced by firms are sold.

Chapter 1 discussed the use of models by economists in developing simple descriptions from which wider conclusions and inferences can be made. One model that is often used to describe a mixed economy in which the market is the primary source of decisions is the **circular flow model**. This model provides an overview of the central concerns of both macroeconomics and microeconomics. The circular flow model is a visual picture of the relationships between the **factor market**, in which income is earned, and the **product market**, in which income is used to purchase goods and services.

The first economist to describe a circular flow model was François Quesnay (1694–1774), the leader of a group of French economists known as the Physiocrats. The name *Physiocrats* comes from a French word that means "rule of nature." Physiocrats believed that the economy was a part of the natural order and that there were natural laws governing the causes of wealth. Quesnay, who was also a physician, was inspired by William Harvey's discovery that blood circulated in the human body. This led him to develop the circular flow model of the macro economy. His model was based on the view that the circulation of resources and products in the economy was similar to the circulation of blood in the human body. And, like a loss of blood, any reduction in this flow was a cause for concern.

THE TWO-SECTOR CIRCULAR FLOW MODEL

In a pure market economy, there are only two kinds of actors: households and business firms.[1] Firms and households interact in two types of markets: the factor and product markets. As shown in Figure 1, households purchase goods and services produced by firms, creating a flow of dollars to firms in payment for these goods and services. The individual markets in which these exchanges take place, shown in the upper part of Figure 1, make up the product market. Firms buy factors of production (inputs or resources) from households (who own all the productive resources) in order to produce the goods and services they sell to the households. The total of the individual markets in which these transactions take place, shown

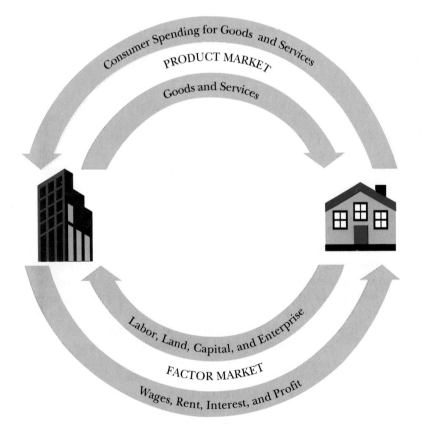

FIGURE 1
CIRCULAR FLOW OF INCOME
Households purchase goods and services in the product market and supply land, labor, capital, and enterprise in the factor market. Firms buy the services of these inputs in the factor market and supply goods and services in the product market.

---

1.   Sometimes firms and households are one and the same. A family-owned grocery store, a home-based accounting service, or a day-care facility may operate from within a household. For simplicity, we treat them as though they can be separated. That is, we assume that households own all factors of production and firms produce all goods and services.

in the lower part of Figure 1, is the factor market. The flow of productive resources to firms generates a reverse flow of dollar payments (wages, rent, interest, and profits). Quesnay saw such a system as a closed one, in which the flow would be continuous, like the flow of blood in the human body.

As you saw in Chapter 1, models are an important part of economic analysis because they permit more orderly thinking about the world. The circular flow in Figure 1 is a very simple model of the way a market economy operates. This model is a broad overview of the economy that you need to keep in mind as we proceed to look at its various specific components. We will add a few simple refinements to the model in this chapter.

Most of macroeconomics is concerned with measuring and changing the sizes of the flows of output and income, represented by the sizes of the shaded arrows. Most of microeconomics is devoted to a closer look at the operation of the individual markets that make up the circular flow and at the behavior of individual actors (households, firms, and governments).

The Circular Flow Model with Saving, Government, and International Trade

We can make the simple circular flow model more realistic in several important ways. To keep things as simple as possible, however, we will limit the model to just one flow in each market instead of two. The diagrams will show the flow of income payments through the factor market to households and the flow of purchases through the product market to the business sector.

The first adjustment to the model is to relax the assumption that the flow of income from firms to households (the lower half of Figure 1) and the flow of payments from households to firms (the upper half of Figure 1) are equal. If firms pay out all of their revenues to households and households spend every dollar they receive on purchases of goods and services, then the flows will be equal. But if households save part of their incomes, there is a leakage out of the circular flow. If firms invest (buy new capital equipment), there is an injection into the circular flow. Either an injection or a leakage can change the size of the flow. Figure 2 shows a flow of savings out of the income stream and an injection of investment spending into the income stream.

A second adjustment of the simple model is to add a government sector. You know that local, state, and federal governments produce, or cause the production of, goods ranging from schools and libraries to missiles and post offices. Governments take part of household incomes in taxes—a leakage out of the spending stream. They also purchase productive inputs from households—an injection, just like investment. Government plays an important microeconomic role because its actions affect the mix of goods and services produced and the distribution of output. At the macroeconomic level, government actions affect the amount of total production, as well as unemployment and economic growth. Figure 3 on page 52 shows a circular flow diagram with a government that collects taxes from households and purchases goods and services from business firms.

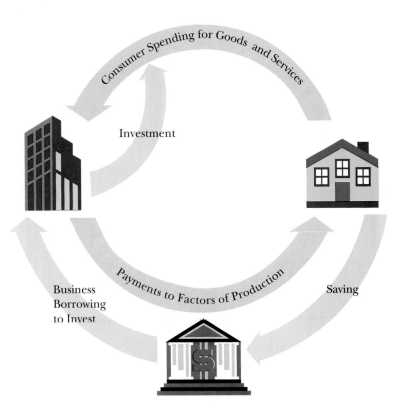

FIGURE 2
CIRCULAR FLOW WITH
SAVING AND INVESTMENT
If households do not
spend all their income,
some of it will leak out
of the circular flow in
the form of savings. If
business firms borrow
in order to invest, their
investment will be an
injection into the
circular flow.

Even this model ignores some important government transactions such
as taxes on business, transfer payments to households, purchases of labor
from households, and borrowing.

Finally, the simple circular flow model describes a closed economy
(one that has no interaction with the rest of the world). Except for Albania, which has chosen to minimize its interactions with the rest of the
world, most nations are affected by transactions with other countries. Figure 4 on page 53, therefore, adds one final change. Households purchase
imports from the foreign sector (other nations). Business firms sell exports to that sector. Imports are a leakage out of the spending stream. Income earned is not directly spent on purchases of consumer goods from
the domestic business sectors. Exports represent an injection of spending
into the flow. Exports often represent a large part of sales and income, especially in small countries. Imports may provide a large share of total consumption. In the United States, the ratio of exports to total output is only
12 percent. In some smaller countries, this ratio is much higher. Mexico,
for example, exports about 16 percent of its output, and the Netherlands
exports 49 percent of what it produces.

The government sector and the foreign sector are two very important
additions to the circular flow model. The government is what makes the
economy a mixed economy, one in which some decisions are made outside the market. The foreign sector makes the economy an open rather

FIGURE 3
CIRCULAR FLOW WITH
GOVERNMENT
Government is a third
actor in the circular flow
model. It interacts with
households and firms in
collecting taxes from
households and purchas-
ing goods and services
from firms. Here
households have two
leakages not spent on
consumption. Business
firms have three cus-
tomers for output:
households (consump-
tion), other business
firms (investment),
and government.

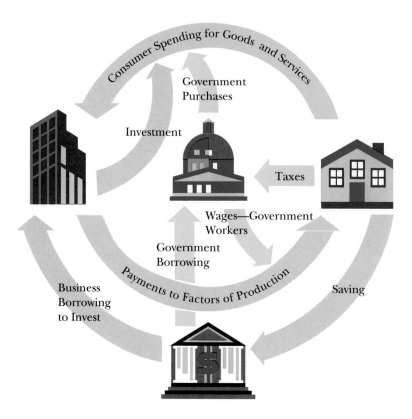

than a closed one. Actions by the three "inside" actors (households, businesses, and government) will have very different effects from what would
occur in a closed economy. We will consider each of these sectors in turn.

THE ECONOMIC ROLE OF GOVERNMENT

The next chapter will introduce you to the workings of a market. All markets work in basically the same way in any economy. Supply and demand
determine prices and quantities. In some economies or for some kinds of
exchanges, however, the market may not be allowed to perform this function. Then some other decision-making process must be used to answer
the three basic economic questions.

The most common method other than the market is to allow choices
concerning the use of resources to be made by politicians or other agents
of government. The kinds of decisions made through governments and
the kinds made through the private sector vary among nations. In the
United States, health care is private. In Canada, it is publicly financed but
privately provided. In most European countries, health care is both paid

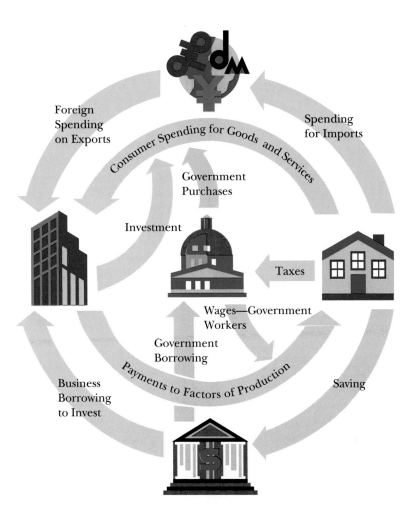

Foreign Spending on Exports

Spending for Imports

Consumer Spending for Goods and Services

Government Purchases

Investment

Taxes

Wages—Government Workers

Government Borrowing

Payments to Factors of Production

Business Borrowing to Invest

Saving

FIGURE 4
CIRCULAR FLOW WITH A FOREIGN SECTOR
Still another source of production and buyer of output is the rest of the world, or the foreign sector. Sales to foreign buyers are exports, and purchases from foreign suppliers are imports.

for and provided by government. Some governments (such as Sweden's) use taxes and social welfare programs to greatly modify the market distribution of income. Others (such as Japan's) do very little to change the distribution of income that results from market decisions.

In the United States, the preference is to make most decisions through the market. However, there are some things that the market cannot do or cannot do well. Many economists argue that the market does not do a very good job of addressing such problems as poverty, pollution, inflation, unemployment, and the market power of large firms. It is also difficult for private markets to provide enough of such collective goods and services as defense, education, and sewer systems.

Recall that a market system requires clearly defined property rights. That is, someone has to decide who owns what goods and services and to define their rights to use and trade those goods and services. The market cannot define and enforce property rights very well, so this role is usually assigned to governments. Citizens in most modern mixed economies cannot legally drive a car without a license, park in a handicapped space without a sticker,

The division of economic activity between public and private spheres in a mixed economy is not fixed. In wartime, the share of economic activity commanded by government increases. When there are changes in citizens' preferences or political philosophy, government's share of total dollars spent may rise or fall in response. For most Western economies, there has been a gradual upward trend in the share of government spending to total GNP and the share of personal income paid in taxes. In the last decade, however, several mixed economies have tried to reverse that trend and reduce the share of economic activity controlled by government. In particular, there has been a move to spin off some allocation activities of government to the private sector. This change is called privatization. In Eastern Europe, a large part of the transition away from communism has consisted of shifting activities from government to the private sector.

Privatization has been strongly advocated in a number of countries. Nowhere was it pushed as far as in Britain under Prime Minister Margaret Thatcher. There the public sector was cut 40 percent in the 1980s. This privatization effort in Britain was stronger than in the United States in part because there had been more public sector involvement in economic activity in Britain.

Privatization can mean a variety of things. It may mean that the government continues to provide a service—for example, garbage collection—but is no longer the producer of that service. Instead, the government collects taxes to pay for the service but contracts with a private firm to actually perform it. Alternatively,

INTERNATIONAL PERSPECTIVE

PRIVATIZATION IN BRITAIN

the government may get out of the business of providing a service. It will either leave provision completely to the private market or limit its role to subsidizing buyers or producers. For example, instead of owning public housing, the government could meet the housing needs of the poor by providing housing vouchers to allow them to pay for housing and letting the private market respond by producing and managing the housing units. In Britain, a large amount of housing, called council housing, was owned and managed by the local public sector. One big privatization effort in the 1980s was to sell that housing to its occupants. As owners, these people have a stronger vested interest in the maintenance and upkeep of their property.

Much of what was first privatized in Britain is traditionally in the private sector in other market economies. Companies made private included British Steel, British Airways, Rolls-Royce, and Jaguar. (Jaguar was later purchased by Ford Motor Company.) When these companies were privatized, the government issued shares of stock sold to the public, creating private ownership while raising revenue for the public treasury. It was hoped that private, profit-minded managers would be more efficient, lowering costs and prices and increasing output and exports. In the last few years, however, the British government met resistance in trying to privatize such traditionally public services as water, electricity, and roads. The privatization movement has been an important episode in the continuing search for balance between the public and private sectors.

or build a fast-food restaurant in a neighborhood zoned residential. These rules represent restrictions on property rights. An unrestricted market would allow people to do all of these things, whether or not they were considered desirable by the majority. Even in a pure market economy, government is needed to establish and protect property rights.

The activities of government are grouped into three categories: allocation, redistribution, and stabilization. Stabilization and redistribution are conducted primarily through governments in all economic systems. Allocation is a microeconomic activity that is shared by the government and the market to different extents in different systems. Much of the dispute over what government should or should not do relates to its allocation activities. Also, much of the difference between market and command economies involves how allocation is divided between the market and the agencies of government.

THE ALLOCATION FUNCTION

Allocation refers to any activity of government that affects the quantity and quality of goods and services produced (that is, anything that affects the answer to the *what* question). Allocation activities in a market-based mixed economy may include producing public education, subsidizing higher education, taxing cigarettes, regulating factory and automobile emissions, setting safety standards for cars, placing quotas on steel imports, building highways, and setting prices for electric power produced by private firms.[2] In a command economy, the array of government allocation activities is much broader. Some, maybe even most, allocation activities also affect the answer to the *for whom* question because they increase the incomes of some firms and individuals at the expense of others.

allocation
Any activities by government or its agents that affect the distribution of resources and the combination of goods and services produced.

PUBLIC GOODS AND POSITIVE EXTERNALITIES. In mixed economies, allocation activities are usually assigned to the public sector only when the good or service is considered a public good or when its production or consumption creates substantial external effects. We will explore each of these criteria in turn.

Economists define **public goods** as those goods that are nonrival in consumption and not subject to exclusion. What do these technical phrases mean? Sunsets and lighthouses are both nonrival in consumption. *Nonrival* means that a good or service is not used up in consumption. The fact that you are watching a sunset leaves no less sunset for someone else to enjoy. Sunsets and lighthouses are also hard to subject to exclusion. *Exclusion* means that nonpayers, or free riders, can be kept from consuming the good. **Free riders** are people or business firms who consume collective goods without contributing to the cost of their production. In addition to sunsets and lighthouses, national defense and mosquito spraying are examples of services for which it is very difficult, or at least expensive, to exclude nonpayers. Because nonpayers cannot easily be excluded, there is not much incentive for a self-interested private firm to produce such goods.

public goods
Goods that are nonrival in consumption and not subject to exclusion.

free riders
People or business firms who consume collective goods without contributing to the cost of their production.

---

2.   Some government allocation activities (for example, setting prices for electric power) relate to the regulation of monopoly.

positive externalities
Spillover benefits to third parties (free riders) that result from production or consumption of certain goods.

Some economists extend the term *public good* to include goods with weak rivalry or high costs of exclusion. Examples of such nearly public goods include fire fighting, education, and highways. In all these cases, benefits spill over to nonpayers. These spillover benefits to third parties are called **positive externalities**. Where there are such positive effects, the private market may not produce enough of the good or service because some who benefit can free-ride. Note that this broader group of nearly public goods can imply an expanded role for government. In fact, all of the services mentioned have at some point been produced in the private sector. Volunteer fire departments in some rural areas still will not put out fires in nonsubscribers' homes. Education through the twelfth grade is produced in both the public and the private sector. Private toll roads were the earliest form of highways in New England.

negative externalities
Harmful spillovers to third parties that result from production or consumption of certain goods.

public bads
Negative external effects of production or consumption that impact a large number of individuals—for example, acid rain.

NEGATIVE EXTERNALITIES. When people or firms consume certain goods or engage in certain activities, they pass some of the costs of production or consumption along to others. These are **negative externalities**. Those who create noise, litter, hazards, and pollution do not bear the full cost. If the negative externalities are strong enough and widespread enough, they may constitute **public bads**. These are negative effects that impact on everyone to some degree. Public bads are the polar opposite of public goods and include such broad negative effects as global warming, depleting of the ozone layer, and extinction of endangered species. Too many negative externalities and public bads are produced if all decisions are left to private markets and individuals. Many of the regulatory activities first undertaken in the 1960s and 1970s in the United States were intended to reduce such effects.

THE SCOPE OF ALLOCATION BY GOVERNMENT. Most economists agree that the government does have some responsibility to produce public goods, to encourage the production of goods with positive externalities, and to discourage the production of negative externalities and public bads. But the lines are drawn differently by different individuals within any nation. They are certainly drawn very differently in different countries. How big do spillovers have to be before government gets involved? Does the government itself have to produce public goods, or can their production be contracted out to the private sector or encouraged through subsidies? Do negative externalities have to be addressed by prohibitions or standards, or can taxes and fines do the job? An individual's, or a nation's, answers to these questions will reflect certain underlying values, ideas about the relative importance of efficiency, equity, and freedom.

Figure 5 shows a spectrum from public bads through goods with negative externalities to private goods and then to goods with positive externalities, ending with public goods. In almost all economies, it is agreed that the two ends of the spectrum call for government intervention to promote public goods and deter public bads. It is also fairly generally agreed that the market works best in the middle of the spectrum, producing and distributing private goods and nearly private goods. Nations disagree on

PUBLIC BADS	Goods with Negative Externalities	PRIVATE GOODS	Goods with Positive Externalities	PUBLIC GOODS
Acid rain Ozone depletion	Noise and litter Oil spills Cigarette smoke	Hamburgers Clothing Automobiles	Seat belts/Air bags Fire protection Education	Lighthouses National defense Mosquito spraying Prenatal care

FIGURE 5
PUBLIC GOODS, PRIVATE GOODS, AND PUBLIC BADS
Goods and services fit on a spectrum from pure public goods such as defense through weak public goods, to private goods, and then to goods that cause negative external effects to some parties. At the far end of the spectrum are activities that cause widespread harm, public bads.

where to draw the lines on either side of the middle, dividing the private from the public sphere.

In the United States, there is another division of responsibility, because the United States has a federal system of government. A federal system has another layer of government (besides the national level) with independent responsibility. In the United States, a large part of allocation by government occurs at the state and local levels. Some public goods are provided on a national scale—defense, for example. But many are provided at the community level. Different cities and towns choose different combinations of public services. One city may choose more street lights and snow removal. Another may vote for public parks and better roads. Allowing this kind of variety in local choices makes governments more responsive to the values and desires of the people who are paying the bills. This diversity is an attractive feature of fiscal federalism, a system in which the economic responsibilities of government are not concentrated at a single level but dispersed among several levels. The United States, Canada, Germany, and Australia are examples of countries in which governments at the state or province level have notable power and responsibility. Economists find a federal system attractive because the autonomous lower levels of governments are in competition for residents and business firms. This competition creates diversity and choice, and perhaps greater efficiency.

THE REDISTRIBUTION FUNCTION

The distribution of income in a market economy is based on each person's contributions to production. There is no denying that the distribution of income determined by the market is quite unequal. Some people are very wealthy, and others are very poor. One way in which economies differ greatly is the extent to which the political process is involved in redistribution. **Redistribution** means taking income from one group and giving it to another through taxes and transfer payments.

In any economy, when the government taxes individuals with high incomes, they have less incentive to work, save, and invest to increase output in future years. On the other hand, some individuals cannot earn an income through the market. They may be too old, too young, too sick, or too handicapped. Others work as hard as they can with the skills and resources at their disposal but still cannot earn enough to get by. There is some private redistribution, but private charity is subject to a free rider problem. (Many people will not participate because they know others

redistribution
Actions by government that transfer income from one group to another.

will.) Such free-riding behavior makes income redistribution more or less a public good that falls within the domain of government.

How much income should be redistributed? To whom should it go? How can redistribution be managed to minimize the negative effects on work incentives? These are difficult questions to answer. As a result, the answers are very different in different countries. In general, there is more redistribution and greater equality of income in countries at the middle of the mixed economy spectrum than in countries at either the command or the market extreme.

An obvious way to redistribute income is to use taxes and transfer payments. In the United States, transfer payments take the form of Social Security benefits, food stamps, and welfare payments. Taxes that collect relatively more from the rich than the poor, such as the U.S. federal income tax, mean that the rich pay more than the poor do for the same level of public services. This difference is a form of redistribution. In the United States, transfer payments are primarily financed by the federal government rather than state governments. The states do administer the programs and pay part of the cost. Redistributing income at the federal level makes it possible to reduce inequality between rich and poor states, as well as between rich and poor individuals within states.

Transfer payments are the most visible form of income redistribution. However, there is a redistributive side to almost everything the government does. If increased funds are spent on public education, families with school-aged children benefit more than childless households. Increased spending on health care benefits those who are sick. Quotas on steel imports benefit steelworkers but not steel users. Expanded student loan programs help college-aged people who qualify at the expense of all other taxpayers and would-be borrowers. Since it is virtually impossible for the government to spend money on anything without redistributing income, it is difficult to measure how much redistribution takes place.

Indirect kinds of income redistribution often benefit those who are not poor, that is, the middle class or the rich. Income redistribution through taxes and transfer payments is often criticized because of its effect on incentives. However, other government programs are equally vulnerable to criticism as "welfare for the rich." Examples are subsidies for large farms, tax loopholes for real estate owners and developers and oil and gas producers, bailouts for savings and loan institutions, and cost overruns by large defense contractors. This kind of redistribution is a consequence of democracy, where the rich and the middle class have more political clout than the poor. In any economy, however, how much redistribution is enough, from whom it should come, and to whom it should go are very difficult questions.

THE STABILIZATION FUNCTION

stabilization
Actions by government to reduce changes in output, employment, and prices.

The last and most recently developed task of government is stabilization. **Stabilization** refers to government actions to reduce changes in output, employment, and prices. Until recently, many people believed that stabilization problems were unique to market economies, which tended to go through severe ups and downs in output, employment, and prices. It is now clear, however, that unemployment and inflation were problems for the command economies of Eastern Europe as well.

Stabilization is mainly a macroeconomic function. However, the ways in which stabilization policies are carried out also affect the mix of goods produced (allocation) and the distribution of costs and benefits (redistribution). Government attempts to stabilize the economy consist of increasing spending or cutting taxes to increase output and employment or cutting spending and increasing taxes to control inflation. In addition, changes in the money supply are used to expand or contract economic activity.

Economists disagree about how stable a market economy would be if it were left alone. Historically, in the U.S. economy (and most market economies), there have been periods of high unemployment combined with low inflation, or occasionally even deflation (falling prices). These downturns have alternated with periods of more rapid inflation (increasing prices) and lower unemployment in a cyclical pattern. Even though such cycles have been less severe since World War II, it cannot be concluded that the U.S. economy has been more stable with government intervention than it was when the government played a much smaller role.

When spending and taxes are used to try to stabilize the economy, budget deficits or surpluses are likely to result. The rationale for deficits is that price stability and full employment should dictate whether or not the budget is balanced. However, the U.S. government has run deficits that cannot be justified on the basis of stabilization activity. The central governments of both the United States and the Soviet Union had substantial budget deficits throughout the 1980s. Since 1958, the U.S. federal budget has been in deficit in all but two years.

ECONOMIC ROLES OF GOVERNMENT

FUNCTION	EXAMPLE
• Allocation	
Public goods	Defense, courts
Goods with positive external effects	Education, seat belts
Negative external effects	Pollution controls
• Redistribution	Social Security
• Stabilization	Cutting taxes to end recession

THE ROLE OF THE FOREIGN SECTOR

The last of the four sectors is the foreign sector. All nations engage in trade with other nations to some extent, because there are goods and services they cannot produce for themselves or can produce only at a very high cost. In most nations, there is also some inflow and outflow of the factors of production—labor, capital, land, and enterprise. Some nations, including the United States, allow goods and factors to flow relatively freely. Others, especially China, Japan, and the Soviet Union, restrict the movement of one or both with tariffs, quotas, immigration restrictions, capital controls, and exchange controls.

In the circular flow diagram, the sizes of the arrows labeled "imports" and "exports" indicate the size of the foreign sector, or the importance of markets and suppliers in other countries. If the foreign sector is small, the economy is more like a closed economy. In a closed economy, activities of governments or private individuals have all or most of their impact within the economy and do not spill over to the rest of the world. Also, actions in the rest of the world have little or no impact on this kind of economy. With a large foreign sector, however, an economy is more likely to affect and be affected by the rest of the wo rld. It is more vulnerable to the effects of inflation or recession in other countries. When its export sales fall, since exports are a large share of total output, the impact is felt throughout the economy.

The larger its land area, population, and total output or income, the less dependent an economy is likely to be on trade. Trade averages 20 to 40 percent of GNP across the broad range of all countries, but there is tremendous variety within this range. The ratio of exports to total output, or GNP, in 1986 was relatively low for such large countries as India (9 percent) and China (11 percent). Countries that are geographically isolated, such as Australia (17 percent), also tend to have a lower ratio of trade to GNP because the cost of shipping is so high. At the other extreme, small countries that produce primary products (agricultural

INTERNATIONAL PERSPECTIVE

THE SIZE OF THE FOREIGN SECTOR

or mineral) often have very high ratios of trade to GNP. The small oil-producing nation of Bahrein exports 92 percent of its total output.

The tiny duchy of Luxembourg exports 72 percent of what it produces. The Caribbean nation of Jamaica, whose revenues derive from tourism, exports 62 percent of its GNP.

The importance of trade can be measured by comparing either exports or imports to GNP. For many nations, the two measures will be about the same, but some countries are very unbalanced. Japan, for example, exports 12 percent of what it produces but imports less than 8 percent of what it consumes. Imports greatly exceeded exports for the United States for most of the 1980s. By 1990, however, the two were close to equal, with exports being about 11 percent of GNP and imports about 12 percent. One of the largest gaps between exports and imports occurs in the small, developing nation of Guinea-Bissau. Its ratio of trade to GNP is only 10 percent for exports but 53 percent for imports.

By either measure, the share of trade in the GNP is a good indicator of how dependent on other nations a nation is. The higher the trade ratio, the more sensitive a country is to events in foreign markets and the more dependent it is on foreign sources of supply. The benefits of trade are substantial, but one of the prices nations pay for those benefits is less control over their own economic destiny.

BENEFITS AND COSTS OF INTERNATIONAL TRADE

In general, a nation benefits from trade in both goods and factors. Trade enables households to consume goods that are not produced at home or would be much more costly to produce there. Trade enables firms to produce for larger markets, often lowering their costs of production. Trade also forces firms to respond to competitors in other countries that are producing products that are cheaper, more appealing, or safer. A flow of labor or capital may help a country overcome its shortages in certain factors of production.

Those who work for or own firms whose products compete with imports as well as workers who compete directly with immigrant workers may not have a positive attitude toward such trade. These groups are likely to lobby for tariffs and other forms of protection in order to shield themselves from the effects of foreign competition. In addition, an economy that depends on international trade to market its products or supply needed goods and services will be affected by the actions of other countries. Interdependence with other countries reduces the amount of control that the government can exert over domestic economic activities.

For a nation as a whole, however, there are substantial gains from trade with other nations. Let's explore one of the main benefits of such trade, the gains that result from specializing on the basis of comparative advantage.

SPECIALIZATION AND COMPARATIVE ADVANTAGE

A major benefit of international trade is that it permits a nation to go beyond its production possibilities curve without acquiring more resources or improving technology. A nation can attain better combinations of output through specialization and exchange. **Specialization**, or the division of labor, means that individuals will produce more than they intend to consume of one or only a few items and will trade the excess for other things they want.

specialization
Limiting production activities to one or a few goods and services that one produces best in order to exchange for other goods.

Specialization allows individuals to take the fullest advantage of their unique talents and skills. Some people who are strong and agile can become professional athletes. Some people who are intelligent and gifted talkers can become lawyers. Specialization allows individuals to concentrate on what they do best and to produce more than they could if they tried to engage in a variety of production activities. For people with very valuable specialized skills, such as basketball stars or brain surgeons, the opportunity cost of using their time for other purposes is very high. Think about the value of the time an NBA star spends in cooking his own dinner or mowing his lawn!

Nations, states, and regions also specialize. The phrase *banana republic* used to refer to small Latin American countries that were heavily specialized in producing bananas for export. These countries used the earnings from bananas to import and consume a wide variety of products that they did not produce. Other small countries are highly specialized in oil, coffee, cocoa, sugar, and other agricultural products and raw materials. Within the United States, pineapples come from Hawaii, oranges from Florida and California, wheat from the midwest and plains states, and peaches from Georgia and South Carolina. Nations, states, and regions also specialize in certain types of goods and services. Japan is famous for small cars and electronic products, Switzerland for watches and banking, and France and Italy for wines.

By specializing, individuals, regions, and nations can produce more total output with no increase in resources or breakthroughs in technology. Thus, specialization improves a nation's standard of living and lets it move outside the production possibilities curve. Small countries especially can consume more goods and enjoy a wider range of goods and services through specialization and trade than if they were limited to what they produced. This point was strongly emphasized by the founder of modern economics, Adam Smith. In his 1776 classic *The Wealth of Nations*, he saw specialization and trade as the engine of growth.

SPECIALIZATION AND EXCHANGE. The benefits of specializing require that people or nations engage in exchange. If you choose to specialize, you will have to engage in trade because you will give up producing all the other goods and services you need. If you are concentrating on what you do well, you don't have time to spend cutting your own hair, growing your own vegetables, or repairing your own car. You certainly don't have time to build your house or manufacture your car! One thing that distinguishes modern industrial societies from less developed countries is the extent of specialization and exchange. The average American produces very little of what he or she consumes. Instead, individuals specialize in one or two products or services and purchase everything else in the market.

COMPARATIVE ADVANTAGE. How do individuals, regions, or nations decide what products to produce for exchange? How do they answer the question "In what should we specialize?" Sometimes the answer is obvious, determined by climate or other resources. In general, the answer lies in the **principle of comparative advantage**. This principle states that each person, group, or country should specialize in that product or service for which the opportunity cost of production is lowest. If that principle is followed, the total output of a group of people, an entire economy, or, for that matter, the entire world will be maximized. Higher total output will result, with no increase in resources or improvement in technology.

principle of comparative advantage
The idea that output will be maximized if people specialize in producing those goods or services for which their opportunity costs are lowest and engage in exchange to obtain other things they want.

Figure 6 illustrates comparative advantage using two straight-line production possibilities curves. Both George and Karen can produce various combinations of cookies and hamburgers with their available resources, as the curves illustrate. Before specializing, Karen is producing 30 hamburgers and 10 dozen cookies a month for her own consumption (point *A* in Figure 6). George is producing 10 hamburgers a month and 40 dozen cookies for himself (point *R* in Figure 6). Karen, who has had some experience working in a fast-food restaurant, is better at making hamburgers. Each hamburger she makes requires that she give up production of only $\frac{1}{2}$ dozen cookies. George's hamburgers cost him 2 dozen cookies per hamburger produced. Karen has a lower opportunity cost for hamburgers, which means that George must have a lower opportunity cost for cookies. Clearly, they should specialize.

If they decide to specialize, Karen will produce 50 hamburgers (point *B* in Figure 6). George will turn out 60 dozen cookies (point *S*). Total out-

Adam Smith is regarded as the founder of modern economics. He was born in Kirkcaldy, Scotland. He was educated at the University of Glasgow and at Oxford University in England and eventually became a professor at Glasgow. *The Wealth of Nations*, published in 1776, marked a break with previous economic thought. Smith stressed the role of individual self-interest in promoting overall welfare. In his view, the "invisible hand" of self-interest leads people to act in socially desirable ways. For example, you know when you arrive at a hotel in a strange city in the evening that you can count on being able to buy breakfast in the morning. People who hope to make a profit will have restaurants and coffee shops open for your business.

Before Smith, people who wrote on economic issues emphasized what government could and should do to run the economy in the national interest. Smith, however, argued that the role of government should be minimal. It should provide for national defense, produce and regulate the money supply, and support a system of laws with swift, efficient justice in the courts. Beyond these activities, private individuals pursuing their own self-interest would provide direction for economic activity. There was no need for government to intervene. For more than a century, Adam Smith's ideas led economists to view the best economic role of government as minimal.

Smith was not naive about the risks of relying on self-interest. He argued that whenever producers of the same product get together, their thoughts rapidly turn to conspiring to raise prices and increase profits. He was opposed to this type of monopoly behavior and thought that government should do nothing to encourage such practices. But as long as the government does not promote monopoly, market forces and competition will limit the ability of firms to take advantage of their customers.

Opportunity cost is another useful concept developed from the work of Adam Smith. He used the example of a village where people could hunt deer or beaver. As he pointed out, the opportunity cost of bagging one deer was the number of beaver that could have been trapped with the same time and trouble. Smith recognized that the only true cost in economics is opportunity cost.

ECONOMIC PROFILE

ADAM SMITH

1723–1790

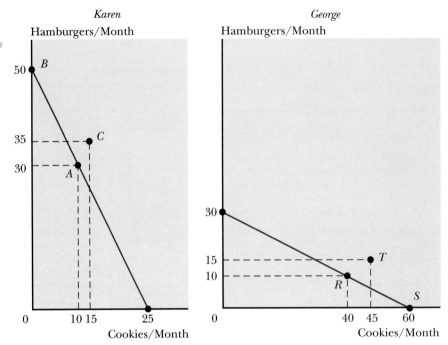

FIGURE 6
SPECIALIZATION AND
EXCHANGE
When Karen and George
specialize, total output
increases from 40
hamburgers (Karen
30, George 10) and 50
dozen cookies (Karen
10, George 40) to 50
hamburgers (Karen)
and 60 dozen cookies
(George). After ex-
change, both can
consume more than
before. Karen is at point
C instead of A and
George is at point
T instead of R.

put increases by 10 hamburgers and 10 dozen cookies. All that remains is
to divide up the gains. One combination that makes both better off is to
split the increase equally. Thus, Karen consumes at point C in Figure 6
and enjoys 35 hamburgers and 15 dozen cookies. George consumes at
point T, with 15 hamburgers and 45 dozen cookies. Both have gained because they are consuming more than before. There is more total output
with no new resources and no improvement in technology.

The principle of comparative advantage means that both trading partners gain when individuals and nations specialize in the products for
which their opportunity cost is lower and trade for what others produce
more efficiently. Comparative advantage is the basis of all trade, not just
international trade. We will return to comparative advantage in great detail in the chapter on international trade.

SUMMARY

1. The factors of production consist of labor, land, capital, and enterprise. Labor receives wages, land receives rent, capital receives interest, and enterprise receives profit.

2. Every economy must address three basic economic questions: what to produce, how to produce it, and for whom to produce. Processes for answering these questions are tradition, command, and the market.

3. In different degrees, industrial nations have tried to answer the basic economic questions by using a mixed economy, where the market is the primary method, but government officials often intervene in the marketplace in an attempt to improve economic performance.

4. The circular flow model is a useful overview of the relations among sectors in a market economy. The basic model shows the interactions of households and businesses in the factor and product markets. More realistic versions add saving and investment, government, and a foreign sector.

5. There are some necessary functions that the market cannot perform or cannot perform well. These include defining and protecting property rights, providing public goods and correcting for external effects, bringing about a "fair" distribution of income, and stabilization.

6. Allocation by government includes not only the production of public goods and the reduction of public bads, but also any activities that affect private decisions about production and consumption. These activities include taxes, subsidies, and regulation. Different societies make different choices about how much allocation is carried out by government.

7. Redistribution changes the unequal distribution of income that results from the market. Redistribution occurs mainly through taxes and transfer payments, but any action of government will have redistributive effects.

8. Stabilization refers to the activities of government aimed at creating full employment, stable prices, and a satisfactory rate of economic growth. These actions include changes in taxes, transfer payments, and spending as well as changes in the money supply.

9. International trade in goods, services, and factors of production benefits both trading partners. Some workers and firms in a nation experience losses because of foreign competition. The gains usually exceed the losses, but the losers may succeed in persuading the government to restrict trade for their protection.

10. Individuals and nations can gain a higher standard of living with the same resources and technology if they engage in specialization and exchange. Total output will be larger if individuals, regions, and nations produce those goods for which their opportunity costs are lowest and trade for other things. This is the principle of comparative advantage.

NEW TERMS

factors of production	investment	mixed economy	negative externalities
labor	enterprise	circular flow model	public bads
wages	profit	factor market	redistribution
human capital	market	product market	stabilization
land	traditional economy	allocation	specialization
rent	command economy	public goods	principle of comparative
capital	market economy	free riders	advantage
interest	property rights	positive externalities	

QUESTIONS FOR DISCUSSION

1. Is your college degree an investment in human capital? What is the opportunity cost of your degree?

2. Suppose you own a farm with buildings and machinery, all five members of your family work on the farm, and you take the risks and manage the production. Identify all the factors of production involved and classify them correctly.

3. How are macroeconomic problems handled in a mixed economy?

4. In what ways are factor markets and product markets similar? In what ways are they different?

5. List all the leakages and all the injections you have observed in circular flow diagrams.

6. Which of the following institutions or actions represent tradition, command, or market processes?

   a. the military draft

   b. the volunteer army

   c. encouraging daughters to be teachers and nurses

   d. requiring women to be teachers and nurses

   e. offering financial incentives to anyone who becomes a teacher or nurse

   f. five generations of farmers tilling the same land

   g. prohibiting the sale of marijuana

   h. taxing the sale of alcoholic beverages

7. What should be the role of government in providing education? Should it produce, subsidize, or get out of education altogether? Why do you suppose that education through the twelfth grade is "free" (actually, paid for through taxes) but only subsidized beyond that level? Does it have anything to do with who gets the benefits?

8. Can you find examples of services produced in the public sector in your area that are produced in the private sector elsewhere, or vice versa? Can you explain why the choice might not be the same in different sections of the country or in communities of different sizes?

9. Classify each of the following government actions as primarily allocation, redistribution, or stabilization.

   a. cutting taxes to end a recession

   b. making Social Security payments to the elderly

   c. paying farmers not to produce corn

   d. putting restrictions on the amount of sulphur dioxide factories are allowed to emit into the air

   e. buying paper shredders for government offices

10. Where would you put each of the following items on the spectrum in Figure 5?

   a. hospital wastes that wash up on beaches

   b. noise from a student apartment complex that bothers the neighbors

   c. highways

   d. Christmas decorations that make a house more attractive

   e. flu shots

11. Why is specialization necessary for exchange, and vice versa?

12. Angela and Arthur have been assigned the tasks of filing folders and grading papers. Angela can file 50 folders an hour and grade 20 papers. Arthur can file 25 folders per hour and grade 25 papers. The total output for these two work-study students is to grade 100 papers and file 200 folders. How long will it take if they divide the task equally? How long will it take if they specialize based on the principle of comparative advantage? How much time do they gain?

13. In Question 12, what is Angela's opportunity cost for filing in terms of grading not done? What is Arthur's? How does this information help you to determine comparative advantage?

14. Use the following information on the production of bushels of peaches and tomatoes in two countries, Upland and Downland. Plot a pair of production possibilities curves like those in Figure 6. Before trade, each country is producing 20 bushels of peaches and 30 bushels of tomatoes. Locate their initial production

UPLAND		DOWNLAND	
PEACHES	TOMATOES	PEACHES	TOMATOES
40	0	50	0
30	15	40	10
20	30	30	20
10	45	20	30
0	60	10	40
		0	50

combinations on the graphs. Determine who should specialize in what, locate the production points after specialization, and determine how much the total output will increase.

15. Individuals as well as nations have comparative advantages, which can change. How will going to college and getting a degree change your comparative advantage?

SUGGESTIONS FOR FURTHER READING

Carson, Robert B. *Economic Issues Today: Alternative Approaches,* 5th ed. New York: St. Martin's, 1991. The introduction gives an overview of alternative values and approaches underlying different economic systems.

Hoover, Kenneth, and Raymond Plant . *Conservative Capitalism in Britain and the United States: A Critical Appraisal.* London and New York: Routledge, Chapman and Hall, 1989. Offers a good discussion of the division of responsibilities between the state and the market and the ideological foundations for that choice.

Radford, R. A. "The Economic Organization of a P.O.W. Camp." *Economica* (November 1945): 189–201. This classic article demonstrates how a market economy quickly established itself in a P.O.W. camp during World War II and highlights the gains from exchange.

Wolf, Charles. *Markets or Governments: Choosing Between Imperfect Alternatives.* Cambridge, MA: MIT Press, 1988. Compares market and nonmarket alternatives for various kinds of productive activities.

1. Define supply and demand and list the factors influencing each.
2. Demonstrate the concepts of supply and demand using:
   a. words,
   b. numbers or functions,
   c. graphs.
3. Identify on a graph the differences between:
   a. changes in demand and changes in the quantity demanded, and
   b. changes in supply and changes in the quantity supplied.
4. Show how changes in the *ceteris paribus* conditions affect demand and supply.
5. Explain how equilibrium is reached, and what disequilibrium and equilibrium mean.
6. Use the supply and demand model to illustrate the concepts of
   a. marginal analysis,
   b. equilibrium,
   c. comparative statics,
   d. endogenous and exogenous variables,
   e. primary and secondary effects.
7. Discuss the functions of prices in a free market.
8. Explain how interference with the market distorts its allocative mechanism.

CHAPTER 3

SUPPLY AND DEMAND: THE BASICS OF ECONOMIC ANALYSIS

INTRODUCTION

Markets are places where buyers and sellers meet to engage in exchange. In the process of exchanging, they determine prices and quantities produced. The supply and demand model explains how buyers and sellers interact to determine prices and quantities. It is the most basic and most widely used model in economics.

Economists view **demand** as the desire and ability to consume certain quantities at various prices over a certain time period. Demand is not seen as needs or wants that can be measured in some social or biological way. The concept of need is reserved for policy makers and political decision making. For needs and wants to be demands, they must be viewed not as wishes or dreams but as what people will actually do when confronted with different sets of prices. Similarly, **supply** refers to what firms are actually willing and able to produce and offer for sale at various prices over a period of time.

demand
The desire and ability to consume certain quantities of a good at various prices over a certain period of time.

supply
The quantity of a good offered for sale at various prices during a certain time period.

DEMAND

Many things affect the demand for a good or service. There is much evidence that price is a very important determinant of demand. Thus, we focus first on what happens when the price of a good or service changes relative to the prices of other goods and services. In looking at the relationship between price and quantity, economists hold constant everything else that affects demand.

law of demand
The quantity demanded of a good or service is negatively related to its price, *ceteris paribus.*

The **law of demand** states that the *quantity demanded* of a good or service is negatively related to its price, *ceteris paribus*. In other words, if everything else is held constant, consumers will purchase more of a good or service at a lower price than at a higher price. As price rises, *ceteris paribus*, consumers will purchase less of a good or service, because its opportunity cost in terms of other goods is higher. Note that we are saying quantity demanded—not demand—is a function of price. This distinction is critical. Demand refers to a whole set of price-quantity combinations. Quantity demanded is the amount consumers want to buy at a particular price.

demand schedule
A table that shows quantities demanded at various prices during a specific time period.

A **demand schedule** shows the various quantities demanded at various prices during a specified period of time. How can we generate a demand schedule for an individual? We could develop Mary's demand schedule for potato chips since she knows all of the *ceteris paribus* conditions that apply (tastes, income, prices of substitutes, and so on). We might suggest various prices and ask her how many bags of potato chips she would buy at each price. Actual experiments with a variety of subjects support the validity of the law of demand.

The demand schedule in Table 1 shows Fred's demand for bread. As price falls, Fred chooses to consume larger quantities of bread per week as he substitutes bread for other items he might purchase. Table 1 is consistent with the law of demand because Fred demands larger quantities of bread at lower prices. Note that there is a time dimension—a week. We cannot determine how many loaves Fred will buy without specifying a time frame—per day, per week, per month, per year, or per lifetime.

demand curve
A graph representing a demand schedule and showing the quantity demanded at various prices in a certain time period.

We can represent the demand schedule of Table 1 on a graph called a demand curve, as shown in Figure 1. A **demand curve** is a graph representing a demand schedule. When we draw a demand curve, the vertical axis shows the price per unit and the horizontal axis shows the quantity per time period.[1]

MARKET DEMAND

Table 1 and Figure 1 show a demand schedule and a demand curve for a single consumer. Sellers, however, are more interested in the market demand curve for a brand of bread or even the market demand curve for all

TABLE 1
FRED'S DEMAND
FOR BREAD

PRICE PER LOAF (CENTS)	QUANTITY DEMANDED PER WEEK
50	1
40	7
30	13
20	19
10	25
5	28

1. If graphing the schedule is confusing, review the appendix to Chapter 1. We usually draw linear curves for convenience.

Price/Loaf (Cents)

FIGURE 1
FRED'S DEMAND FOR BREAD
An individual's demand curve shows the quantity that he or she will purchase during a specific period at different prices.

Loaves/Week

bread. A **market demand curve** shows what quantities will be demanded by all consumers in a certain market at various prices. The market demand curve is the sum of all of the individual demand curves. We add the demand curves for individual consumers horizontally. For example, to determine the market quantity of bread demanded at a price of 40 cents per loaf, we add the 7 loaves demanded by Fred to 2 loaves demanded by Mary, a loaf demanded by Joanna, and so on. We find a total (market) quantity demanded of 10,000 loaves at a price of 40 cents per loaf. These two numbers represent one point on the market demand curve. We then repeat the addition of quantities demanded for every other price. The result is the downward-sloping market demand curve shown in Figure 2, showing a negative relationship between price and quantity. At higher prices, buyers want fewer loaves. At lower prices, they want more.

As price changes in the market, the quantity demanded changes in the opposite direction, just as it did for Fred. Figure 2 shows that 13,000 loaves of bread are purchased at a price of 35 cents per loaf. If the price falls to 20 cents per loaf, the quantity demanded increases to 25,000 loaves. If the price rises to 45 cents per loaf, the quantity demanded decreases to 5,000 loaves.

market demand curve
The sum of all of the individual demand curves. A market demand curve shows what quantities will be demanded by all consumers in a specific time frame in a certain market at various prices.

CETERIS PARIBUS CONDITIONS AND SHIFTS IN DEMAND
Many things can affect the demand for a good or service. Economists generally focus on a few, separated into two important categories: price, and everything else. Because price is so important, economists express demand as a function of price. The price of a good affects the quantity demanded. Everything else affects demand. We held the nonprice determinants of demand constant while we focused on price. Now we want to look at the nonprice determinants and how they affect the demand curve.

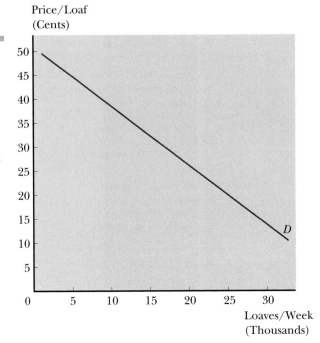

FIGURE 2
MARKET DEMAND FOR BREAD
A market demand curve is a graph depicting how much will be purchased in the market at various prices. It is the sum of all of the individual demand curves.

The nonprice determinants of demand are as follows:

1. tastes of the group demanding the good or service,
2. size of the group demanding the good or service,
3. income and wealth of the group demanding the good or service,
4. prices of other goods and services,
5. expectations about future prices or income.

Nearly everything that affects demand does so by working through one of these determinants. Weather, for example, may affect demand for bread by changing tastes. People may eat more cold sandwiches instead of hot meals in warmer weather. Economists study demand by holding all but one of these determinants constant and determining what happens when that one changes. Nonprice determinants of demand are the *ceteris paribus* conditions discussed in Chapter 1.

Changes in the *ceteris paribus* conditions change the demand for the good or service. On the graph, a change in demand is seen as a shift of the curve. Economists are careful to distinguish clearly between movements along a demand curve and changes (or shifts) of the curve itself. Movements along the curve are *changes in quantity demanded*, caused solely by a change in the *price* of the good. When the price of bread goes up, fewer loaves are demanded—a change in quantity demanded. Changes (or shifts) of the curve are *changes in demand* caused by changes in any of the *ceteris paribus* conditions. When the weather gets hot or population increases, more loaves are demanded at every possible price—a change in demand.

TASTES. How do changes in the *ceteris paribus* conditions affect the market demand for a good? Suppose people's tastes change in favor of bread because the weather is hot or a fad develops for high-fiber diets. As shown in Figure 3, this change in demand shifts the entire demand curve to the right, from D_0 to D_1. An **increase in demand** means that at every price, consumers demand a larger amount than before. The opposite would occur if tastes changed away from bread. Such a change in tastes would cause a decrease in demand, represented by a shift from D_0 to D_2. A **decrease in demand** means that at every price, consumers demand a smaller quantity than before.

increase in demand
A shift in the demand curve indicating that at every price, consumers demand a larger amount than before.

SIZE OF THE GROUP. The market demand curve, as you saw earlier, is found by adding the individual demand curves. Thus, if the number of individuals in the group of potential consumers changes, market demand will also change. Suppose demand curve D_0 in Figure 3 represents the demand for automobiles in a state with a minimum driving age of 16 years. If the law is changed to allow 15-year-olds to drive, the group of potential consumers increases. Some of them, or their families, will want an extra car for the extra driver. The demand curve will shift from D_0 to D_1. The size of the group has increased. Therefore, there has been an increase in the demand for the good, or a larger quantity demanded at every price.

decrease in demand
A shift in the demand curve indicating that at every price, consumers demand a smaller amount than before.

On the other hand, if the size of the group decreases, there will be a decrease in demand, a shift from D_0 to D_2 in Figure 3. The big drop in the birth rate in the late 1960s and early 1970s decreased demand first for baby food and diapers and then for public school teachers. In the 1990s, it is affecting demand for automobiles and college teachers.

INCOME AND WEALTH. Income changes can also shift the demand curve. You might expect that demand for all goods would increase as income increases. However, this is not always true. Whether demand increases in this case depends on whether the good is a normal good or an inferior

FIGURE 3
EFFECTS OF CHANGES IN THE *CETERIS PARIBUS* CONDITIONS ON DEMAND
If a change causes more of a good to be demanded at every price, the demand curve will shift to the right, as from D_0 to D_1. A change that causes less to be demanded at every price causes a shift to the left, as from D_0 to D_2.

normal good
A good for which demand increases as income increases.

inferior good
A good for which demand decreases as income increases.

good. A **normal good** is a good for which demand increases as income increases, *ceteris paribus*. If demand falls when income rises, the good is an **inferior good**. Most goods are normal goods. However, there are a few inferior goods.

Consider, for example, the difference between steak and hamburger. If, as an individual's income increases, the individual consumes less hamburger and more steak, then hamburger is an inferior good and steak is a normal good. However, meat or beef in general is still considered a normal good.[2] Likewise, a trailer might be considered inferior to a house, but housing in general is a normal good.

For a normal good, an increase in income would cause demand in Figure 3 to shift from D_0 to D_1. For an inferior good, an increase in income would shift demand from D_0 to D_2, as buyers could afford the more expensive substitute. For a normal good, a decrease in income would shift demand from D_0 to D_2 in Figure 3. For an inferior good, a decrease in income would increase demand from D_0 to D_1 as buyers were forced to economize with less appealing goods.

Changes in wealth have the same effect as changes in income. If the value of assets falls, leaving people less wealthy, demand for normal goods will decline. When the stock market crashed in October 1987, many analysts predicted a recession. They expected the decline in wealth to cause consumer spending to decrease. Though there was a decline in wealth, it was not large enough to spark a recession. It did, however, affect the demand for some goods and services.

complementary goods
Goods that are jointly consumed. The consumption of one enhances the consumption of the other.

substitute goods
Goods that can be interchanged. The consumption of one replaces the consumption of the other.

PRICES OF OTHER GOODS. The fourth nonprice determinant of demand is the prices of other goods and services. There are two classes of other goods: complements and substitutes. **Complementary goods** are goods that are jointly consumed. If consuming two goods together enhances the enjoyment of both, the goods are called complements. Examples are bacon and eggs, lamps and light bulbs, or hamburgers and ketchup. Substitute goods have the opposite relationship. Rather than enhancing each other's consumption, **substitute goods** replace each other. Orange juice and grapefruit juice, Coke and Pepsi, and Reebok and Adidas shoes are examples of substitute goods.

If two goods are complements, a rise in the price of one will decrease demand for the other. Referring again to Figure 3, consider D_0 as the demand curve for good x (bagels). If the price of complementary good y (lox) goes up, the demand for bagels will decrease, shifting the curve from D_0 to D_2. Buyers will consume less lox because its price is higher and will thus would demand fewer bagels at every price. If the price of lox fell, consumers would want to consume more lox and thus would demand more bagels to go with it at every price. In Figure 3, demand for bagels would shift from D_0 to D_1.

If two goods are substitutes, a rise in the price of one will increase demand for the other. Good x (Coke) and good y (Pepsi) are substitutes. Suppose curve D_0 in Figure 3 represents the demand for good x (Coke).

---

2.   A good example of an inferior good is an outhouse. As a community's income rises, the demand for outhouses decreases. In the United States, outhouses have almost become extinct.

The price of good y (Pepsi) increases relative to the price of Coke. Since this makes the opportunity cost of Coke lower, consumers will demand more Coke at every price. The demand for Coke shifts from D_0 to D_1 in Figure 3. If the price of Pepsi decreased relative to the price of Coke, the opposite would happen. The opportunity cost of Coke would be higher, and consumers would demand less of it at every price as they shifted consumption to Pepsi. The decrease in demand for Coke is shown by a shift from D_0 to D_2 in Figure 3. The shift to substitutes as price rises means that the quantity demanded of the good falls, exactly as predicted by the law of demand.

In a broad sense, all goods are substitutes for each other because they are all alternatives on which people can spend income. Some goods are closer substitutes than others, however. The more easily that good A can be substituted for good B, the more a change in the price of one will affect the demand curve for the other. A rise in the price of watches, for example, would have much less impact on the demand for hot dogs than on the demand for clocks, bracelets, or other substitutes.

People often make the error of assuming a good has no satisfactory substitutes. How often have you heard someone say, "There is no substitute for victory (or success, steak, a new car…)." In fact, there are substitutes for anything. If the price rises sharply enough, consumers will start searching harder for acceptable substitutes.[3]

REASONS FOR A CHANGE IN THE QUANTITY DEMANDED

- The quantity demanded will *increase* if the price of the good or service *decreases*.
- The quantity will *decrease* if the price of the good or service *increases*.

REASONS FOR A CHANGE IN DEMAND

- The demand for a normal good or service will *increase* if:
  buyers' tastes change to favor that good or service,
  the number of buyers in the market increases,
  the income or wealth of buyers increases,
  the prices of complementary goods fall,
  the prices of substitute goods increase, or
  buyers' expectations for the future cause them to purchase more now.

- The demand for a normal good or service will *decrease* if:
  buyers' tastes change against that good or service,
  the number of buyers in the market decreases,
  the income or wealth of buyers decreases,
  the prices of complementary goods increase,
  the prices of substitute goods decrease, or
  buyers' expectations of the future cause them to delay purchases.

---

3.   This point often makes economists seem cynical. Does honesty have a substitute? Yes. If the price becomes too high, many people (but not all) will become dishonest.

expectations
Feelings that individuals
have about future
conditions.

EXPECTATIONS. The last *ceteris paribus* condition that affects demand is **expectations**. If individuals expect anything important to change in the future, they may take action now that they would otherwise postpone. For example, if you expect that the demand for automobiles will be so high next year that their prices will rise, you may decide to buy a car now to avoid paying a higher price. If you expect your income to be higher in the future, you may demand more goods and borrow to pay for them so that you do not have to delay consumption until your income actually rises.

SUPPLY

supply schedule
A table that shows
quantities offered for sale
at various prices over a
particular time period.

A **supply schedule** shows the quantities offered for sale at various prices during a specific period of time. Price is the primary determinant of quantity supplied.

THE (NOT QUITE) LAW OF SUPPLY
Assume everything else is held constant but the price of the good or service. We can then state the **(not quite) law of supply** as follows: the *quantity supplied* of a good or service is *usually* a positive function of price, *ceteris paribus.*

(not quite) law of supply
The quantity supplied of
a good or service is
usually a positive function
of price, *ceteris paribus.*

With all else held constant, suppliers usually will supply less of a good or service at lower prices. As prices rise, the quantity supplied will increase, because it becomes more profitable to produce and sell the good. It is important to note that quantity supplied is a function of price. Note also the word *usually.* This is not quite a law because of two exceptions to this relationship. The first is when there is no time to produce more units (for example, theater seats at a sold-out performance) or when a unique supplier no longer exists (for example, paintings by Picasso). In these unusual cases, quantity supplied does not respond to price at all. The second exception occurs for certain products for which increased volume allows costs per unit to fall. For example, as a utility company increases its output of electricity, its costs per unit typically fall. These lower costs may be passed on to customers in the form of lower prices.

Table 2 shows a hypothetical supply schedule for an individual supplier—Susan's Lemonade Stand. A supply schedule shows the quantities supplied during a period of time at various prices. Like a demand schedule, a supply schedule includes a time frame—in this case, a day. Table 2 is consistent with the law of supply because Susan supplies larger quanti-

TABLE 2
SUSAN'S SUPPLY
OF LEMONADE

PRICE PER GLASS (CENTS)	QUANTITY SUPPLIED PER DAY
5	0
10	5
15	10
20	15
25	20
30	25

ties of lemonade at higher prices. The supply schedule of Table 2 can be drawn on a graph as shown in Figure 4. This **supply curve** is a diagram showing the quantity supplied in a particular time and at various prices. It shows a positive relationship—more will be offered for sale at higher prices. Price per unit is on the *y*-axis, and quantity per time period is on the *x*-axis, just as it was for the demand curve. Supply curves usually have a positive *y*-intercept, indicating that at some low price, suppliers may offer none of the good.

supply curve
A graph representing a supply schedule and showing the quantities supplied at various prices in a certain time period.

MARKET SUPPLY

The **market supply curve** is the sum of all of the individual supply schedules. Figure 5 is a market supply curve for lemonade, showing the total quantity supplied over a period of time at various prices. As price changes in the market, quantity supplied changes in the same direction. Figure 5 shows that 5,000 glasses of lemonade are supplied at a price of 10 cents per glass. If price falls to 5 cents per glass, quantity supplied decreases to zero glasses. If price rises to 20 cents per glass, quantity supplied increases to 15,000 glasses. These changes occur because most producers are willing to sell more units if the price rises enough to cover the added costs of production.

market supply curve
The sum of all of the individual supply curves. A market supply curve shows what quantities will be supplied by all firms at various prices during a specific time period.

CHANGES IN SUPPLY AND THE *CETERIS PARIBUS* CONDITIONS

A supply curve is drawn to show a relationship between price and quantity supplied, with everything else held constant. A change in one of the *ceteris paribus* conditions will cause the entire supply curve to shift. The most important of these are as follows:

1. the state of technology,
2. prices of the factors of production,
3. the number of suppliers,
4. expectations about the future,
5. prices of related goods.

FIGURE 4
SUSAN'S SUPPLY OF LEMONADE
A supply curve for an individual (or firm) shows how much of a good will be offered for sale at various prices.

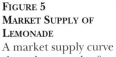

FIGURE 5
MARKET SUPPLY OF
LEMONADE
A market supply curve
shows how much of a
good will be offered for
sale at various prices. It
is the sum of all of the
individual supply curves.

Everything that affects supply works through one of these determinants.
For example, if a natural disaster destroys large amounts of capital, it will
affect supply by increasing the price of that factor of production. If the
price of corn rises relative to wheat, a farmer might decide to grow corn
instead of wheat.

TECHNOLOGY. Suppose technology improves. For instance, agricultural researchers develop a low-cost drug that causes a young steer to double in
weight rapidly. This advance in technology means that more beef will be
supplied at each price. There is an **increase in supply**, or a shift in the supply curve such that a larger quantity will be provided at every price. In Figure 6, an increase in supply is shown as a shift from S_0 to S_1. A negative
change in technology will have the opposite effect. Suppose the government discovers that the drug used to fatten steers has harmful effects on
humans who eat the beef. Farmers are forbidden to continue using the
drug. Less beef will be supplied at each price. There will be a **decrease in**
supply, represented as a shift from S_0 to S_2 in Figure 6.

increase in supply
A shift in the supply curve
indicating that at every
price, a larger quantity
will be offered for sale
than before.

decrease in supply
A shift in the supply curve
indicating that at every
price, a smaller quantity
will be offered for sale
than before.

PRICES OF THE FACTORS OF PRODUCTION. As you recall from Chapter 2, the factors of production are land, labor, capital, and enterprise. The price paid
for the use of land is rent. The price of labor's services is wages. The price
for using capital is interest. The return to enterprise is profit. If the price of
a factor—such as wages for labor—goes up, the supply of products using
that factor will be affected. Suppliers will offer less of the good at each price.
Supply will decrease because the costs of production have gone up.

Suppose S_0 in Figure 6 represents the market supply of beef. Assume
that the wage rate of meat cutters increases. This will mean less beef will

Price/Pound

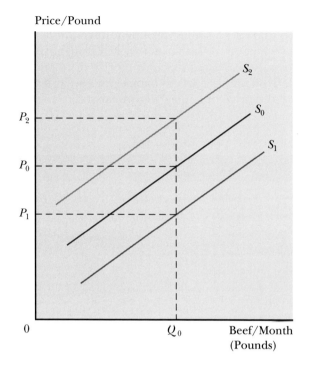

FIGURE 6
CHANGES IN THE *CETERIS*
***PARIBUS* CONDITIONS AND**
SUPPLY
Changes in a *ceteris
paribus* condition can
cause the supply curve
to shift. A change that
would cause more to be
supplied at each price is
an increase in supply and
is represented by the shift
from S_0 to S_1. A change
that causes the supply to
decrease is represented
by a shift from S_0 to S_2.

be supplied at each price. Supply will decrease from S_0 to S_2. After the increase in wages, suppliers will supply the old amount (Q_0) only at a higher price (P_2). A rise in the price of a factor of production, *ceteris paribus*, causes a decrease in supply. The cost of supplying any particular quantity has increased. Thus, less will be supplied at the old price, or the same amount will be supplied at a higher price. The opposite is also true. A decrease in the price of a factor of production will cause an increase in supply, shifting the curve from S_0 to S_1 in Figure 6.

NUMBER OF SUPPLIERS. A change in the number of suppliers will also shift the supply curve. If the number of beef ranchers declines, the supply curve will shift from S_0 to S_2 in Figure 6—a decrease in supply. In contrast, an increase in the number of beef ranchers will shift the supply curve from S_0 to S_1 in Figure 6—an increase in supply.

EXPECTATIONS. Expectations about any of the *ceteris paribus* conditions or about market price can have an effect on supply. Assume that beef ranchers expect that the price of beef will fall next year because they anticipate a poor grain harvest. (A poor grain harvest would make it more expensive to keep cattle on feedlots.) What would this expectation cause ranchers to do? They would bring more cattle to market now, before the price falls. If enough ranchers share this expectation, the supply curve for this year will increase from S_0 to S_1, as shown in Figure 6. The price of beef will fall from P_0 to P_1 because ranchers will be slaughtering more cattle. Next year, with fewer cattle available, the supply curve will shift back to the left.

PRICES OF RELATED GOODS. Changes in the prices of other goods can affect supply. If the price of a good that uses a similar production technique increases, a firm may switch production. A farmer may switch from corn to wheat when the price of corn increases relative to the price of wheat. A sewing factory might switch from men's shirts to babies' nightwear if the price of men's shirts fell and the price of babies' nightwear rose.

REASONS FOR A CHANGE IN THE QUANTITY SUPPLIED

- The quantity supplied will *increase* if the price of the good or service *increases.*
- The quantity supplied will *decrease* if the price of the good or service *decreases.*

REASONS FOR A CHANGE IN SUPPLY

- The supply of a good or service will *increase* if:
  new technology allows the good or service to be produced at lower cost,
  the prices of the factors of production decrease,
  the number of suppliers increases,
  the prices of other goods or services that can be produced with the same resources decrease, or
  suppliers' expectations for the future cause them to produce more now.
- The supply of a good or service will *decrease* if:
  the prices of the factors of production increase,
  the number of suppliers decreases,
  the prices of other goods or services that can be produced with the same resources increase, or
  suppliers' expectations for the future cause them to produce less now.

---

market equilibrium
A point at which quantity demanded by consumers is equal to quantity supplied by producers. The price at which this occurs is the equilibrium price, or market-clearing price.

market-clearing price
The equilibrium price, which clears the market because there are no frustrated consumers or suppliers.

disequilibrium
An unstable situation in which variables are moving toward equilibrium but are not yet at equilibrium.

MARKET EQUILIBRIUM

We can combine market supply and market demand schedules to determine the market equilibrium. **Market equilibrium** occurs at that price for which quantity demanded by consumers is equal to quantity supplied by producers. This equilibrium price is also called the **market-clearing price**.

EQUILIBRIUM AND DISEQUILIBRIUM

In Table 3, at a price of $2, suppliers *want* to supply 4 million pounds of coffee, and consumers *want* to purchase 8 million pounds. A price of $2 is not an equilibrium price because quantity demanded exceeds quantity supplied by 4 million pounds at that price. This situation is one of **disequilibrium**, in which variables are moving toward equilibrium but are not yet there. This is an unstable position. Some consumers will not be able to purchase the amount they desire at a price of $2. As they shop for coffee, they will offer a higher price. As the price rises, quantity supplied will rise, and quantity demanded will fall. This process will continue until the price reaches $3. At $3, the amount consumers wish to purchase is exactly equal to the amount suppliers wish to sell. This quantity is the equilibrium quan-

The number of suppliers and the number of buyers can shift the supply and demand curves, respectively. Sometimes the suppliers are offering imported goods, and sometimes the buyers live in foreign countries.

In an open economy, the market demand curve faced by producers is the sum of the domestic demand for the product and the foreign demand for the product. Consider the market demand for American corn. If there were no foreign demand, the market price would settle at P_d, and corn producers would sell Q tons of corn. (See the graph titled "Foreign Demand for Corn.") When foreign demand, D_f, is added, the price rises to P_{d+f}, and the amount sold rises to Q_{d+f}. The price of corn and the amount of corn sold have both increased. Consumers in the domestic market are paying a higher price because they now pay P_{d+f}. Since the domestic demand curve has not shifted and the price has increased, the quantity of corn demanded by domestic consumers will fall. In this example, domestic consumption falls to Q_d.

It appears that domestic corn producers have gained at the expense of domestic corn consumers. After all, consumers now pay a higher price for less corn. This conclusion is correct, but it ignores the other side of the coin. Foreign con-

sumers can only buy the corn if they sell something that earns the currency necessary to pay for the corn. The domestic supply of the product that foreigners sell to pay for the corn will have an effect in other markets.

The graph titled "Foreign Supply of Automobiles" shows the U.S. market for automobiles. Without a foreign supply, the domestic price and quantity would be P_d and Q_d. Adding foreign supply, S_f, changes the equilibrium. There is a decline in price to P_{d+f} and an increase in quantity demanded to Q_{d+f}. In this case, the domestic consumption of automobiles increased by $Q_{d+f} - Q_d$. Domestic consumers can purchase more automobiles at a lower price.

There is an important lesson in this example of supply and demand in an open economy. Relative to a no-trading situation, the opening of foreign trade will result in higher prices and less consumption of exported items and lower prices and more consumption of imported items. So there are winners and losers as a result of international trade. But, as you learned in Chapter 2, the principle of comparative advantage shows that the net effect of trade is an expansion of choices and an increase in total consumption for consumers in the domestic market.

FOREIGN DEMAND FOR CORN

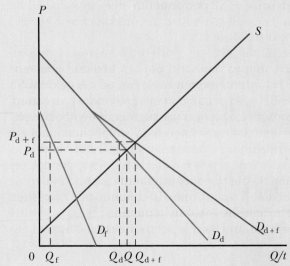

FOREIGN SUPPLY OF AUTOMOBILES

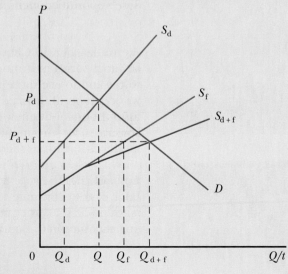

PRICE PER POUND (DOLLARS)	POUNDS SUPPLIED PER MONTH	POUNDS DEMANDED PER MONTH	DIFFERENCE
1	2 million	10 million	8 million excess quantity demanded
2	4 million	8 million	4 million excess quantity demanded
3	6 million	6 million	equilibrium
4	8 million	4 million	4 million excess quantity supplied
5	10 million	2 million	8 million excess quantity supplied

tity, and $3 is the market-clearing price, because there is no tendency for price or quantity to change.

If the price was $4 per pound, suppliers would offer 8 million pounds of coffee per month, but consumers would only wish to purchase 4 million pounds. At this price, there is an excess quantity supplied of 4 million pounds per month. Suppliers with unsold coffee will accept a lower price. As price falls, some suppliers reduce their output (a movement along the supply curve), and some consumers buy more (a movement along the demand curve) until the equilibrium price of $3 is reached. This $3 price again clears the market.

Note that the equilibrium price and quantity do not simply represent the point where the amount sold equals the amount bought. Quantities bought and sold are *always* equal, even in disequilibrium. Four million pounds per month were bought and sold at $2 and at $4. Equilibrium occurs at a price for which the quantity supplied and the quantity demanded are equal.

Figure 7 shows market supply and market demand curves for coffee, based on the supply and demand schedules in Table 3. The equilibrium price is $3, and 6 million pounds per month are sold at equilibrium. At $4, there is an excess quantity supplied, and price will fall. This causes the quantity demanded to increase and the quantity supplied to decrease. The opposite happens at a price of $2 per pound.

SUPPLY, DEMAND, AND ECONOMIC MODELS

As you learned in Chapter 1, the primary work of economists is to construct theories and models that explain and predict how the economy works and to use those theories and models to devise policies to make it work better. All theories and models share certain techniques and certain assumptions about how households and firms make decisions about using resources for production and consumption. The supply and demand model can be used to illustrate some of these techniques and assumptions.

EQUILIBRIUM. The supply and demand model represents the first use in this book of the economic concept of equilibrium. In this model, equilibrium is found at that price for which the quantity demanded is equal to the quantity supplied. Equilibrium (and its counterpart, disequilibrium) is a

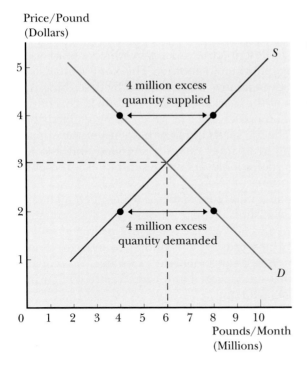

Price/Pound
(Dollars)

FIGURE 7
SUPPLY OF AND DEMAND FOR COFFEE
At equilibrium, the amount consumers wish to purchase is equal to the amount suppliers wish to sell. The price established at equilibrium is called the market-clearing price. At prices above the market-clearing price, quantity supplied exceeds quantity demanded. At prices below the market-clearing price, quantity demanded exceeds quantity supplied.

term that you will encounter often. This book will discuss equilibrium prices, equilibrium quantities, equilibrium levels of employment, equilibrium levels of gross national product (GNP), and so forth. Almost every economic model includes a definition of equilibrium. If the model has an equilibrium position, it will have a set of forces that can change that position. In the supply and demand model, these forces are called supply shifters and demand shifters. There are also forces that move an economy toward a new equilibrium position. In the supply and demand model, sellers' and buyers' responses to price changes will move the economy toward a new equilibrium.

Economists' notion of equilibrium is borrowed from the physical sciences. A system is in equilibrium when it is at rest or when it is moving at a constant rate in the same direction. That is, all the forces acting on the system are in balance, and there is no tendency to change. Equilibrium carries no sense of being good or bad, desirable or undesirable. In economics (as in physics or chemistry), if a system is left alone, equilibrium is where it will come to rest. Disequilibrium is a state in which the variables are moving away from old equilibrium values and toward new equilibrium values but have not yet arrived there. If the supply curve has shifted to the right but the demand curve is unchanged, there is a surplus at the old price. This situation is a disequilibrium. A surplus means that the quantity supplied is greater than the quantity demanded at the current price. Market forces are putting downward pressure on the price in order to move to a new equilibrium. If the price was too low for equilibrium to exist, there would be a shortage. Quantity demanded would exceed quantity supplied, and there would be upward pressure on the price.

COMPARATIVE STATICS. When a supply curve or a demand curve shifts, the diagram always identifies the original equilibrium and the new equilibrium. Economists are able to describe the process by which a market or economy moves from one equilibrium to another. This kind of analysis is called **comparative statics**. Comparative statics begins by describing the initial equilibrium position of the market (or the economy). This initial state is then compared to some later state in which some element has changed. For example, a change in technology has shifted the supply curve to the right, resulting in a larger quantity supplied and a lower price. That is, comparative statics looks at changes in equilibrium positions between two different times.

comparative statics
A technique of comparing two equilibrium positions to determine the changing relationships between variables.

Another way of looking at comparative statics is to see such an analysis as a comparison of two snapshots of the economy (or of a particular market). We take a snapshot and analyze the relationships that exist. We then change one variable, which causes the economy to move to a new equilibrium. Next, we take another snapshot of the economy. We compare the two snapshots to see what has changed and why. We are comparing static (frozen) pictures of the economy.

MARGINAL ANALYSIS. Supply and demand is just one of many economic models that involve **marginal analysis**, a technique for analyzing problems by examining the results of small changes.

marginal analysis
A technique for analyzing problems by examining the results of small changes.

Marginal refers to the extra, additional, or next unit of output, consumption, or any other measurable quantity that can be increased or decreased by incremental amounts. The concept of the margin is central to economic analysis, although it is probably new to you. Most economic decisions are made at the margin: Should I consume the extra slice of pizza or work the extra hour? Should we produce the extra unit or take on a new client at our accounting firm? These kinds of daily decisions made by households and firms determine prices, output, and other important economic quantities. In the supply and demand model, the supply curve reflects the decisions of suppliers to offer extra or additional (marginal) units for sale at higher prices. The demand curve reflects the decisions of buyers to purchase extra or additional (marginal) units at lower prices. When the price of a good falls, consumers decide at the margin whether to substitute a little more of that good for other goods whose prices have not changed.

ENDOGENOUS AND EXOGENOUS VARIABLES. All economic models contain variables. Variables that a model attempts to explain or determine are called **endogenous variables**. Variables that have an impact on the endogenous variables but are themselves determined outside the model are called **exogenous variables**. In mathematics (and sometimes in economics), these are referred to as dependent and independent variables, respectively.

endogenous variables
Variables that are explained or determined within a model.

exogenous variables
Variables that are determined outside of a model and affect endogenous variables.

In the supply and demand model, both price and quantity are endogenous variables that affect one another and are determined by the model. For example, the price of oranges is endogenous to this model. Some of the other variables in a supply and demand model are exogenous. For example, in the market for oranges, the weather in Florida is an exogenous variable. The weather affects the price of oranges, but the price of oranges does not affect the weather.

In the supply and demand model, the exogenous variables are the nonprice determinants that cause the position of the supply or demand curve to change. These determinants are technology, tastes, number of suppliers, income, prices of related goods, and so forth. Most economic models concentrate on just one or two endogenous (or dependent) variables and explain them by the behavior of a larger number of exogenous (or independent) variables.

Primary and Secondary Effects. Economists often analyze the effect of a change in one variable on other related variables. The **primary effect** is the dominant effect they seek to analyze. For instance, the demand curve shows how doubling the price of oranges would affect the quantity of oranges consumed. But there are also **secondary effects** in related markets. These effects may not be immediately apparent and may take time to work through the economy. For example, if the price of oranges doubled, the sales of cranberry juice might increase, or the consumption of bacon and eggs might decrease. These are related goods whose demand depends on the price of oranges (or orange juice). Such changes would not be as obvious or as immediately apparent as the primary effect.

primary effect
The dominant or immediate effect of a change in an economic variable.

secondary effects
Effects indirectly related to the immediate effect, often smaller and felt after some time.

A THEORY OF PRICE FORMATION

The law of demand and the (not quite) law of supply support a very powerful theory of how markets work to set and change prices. That theory is based on two propositions. The first is that quantity demanded is negatively related to price. The second is that quantity supplied is positively related to price. When these two propositions are combined, they imply several things:

1. When the quantity demanded exceeds the quantity supplied, $(Q_d > Q_s)$, price will rise.
2. When the quantity demanded is less than the quantity supplied, $(Q_d < Q_s)$, price will fall.
3. When the quantity demanded equals the quantity supplied, $(Q_d = Q_s)$, price is at equilibrium.

This theory, combined with the possible shifts in *ceteris paribus* conditions, produces all of the basic elements of a model of how prices (and quantities) are determined in a market system.

Changes in Demand and Supply
When changes occur in any of the *ceteris paribus* conditions that affect demand, the model can be used to trace the effect on market equilibrium. Assume first that there is an increase in demand, that is, an outward shift of the entire curve. This increase in demand could be a result of a change in any of the *ceteris paribus* conditions. It could result from an increase in income (for a normal good), a change in tastes in favor of the good, an increase in the price of a substitute or a decrease in the price of a complement, an increase in the size of the consuming group, or a change in expectations. The increase in demand is shown as an outward shift in the demand curve from D_0 to D_1 in Figure 8. The equilibrium price rises from

P_e to P_1, and the price increase causes quantity supplied to increase to Q_1. Consumers demand a larger quantity of the good at every price than before the shift of the curve.

Now consider a decrease in demand. A decrease in demand means that consumers will demand less of a good at every price. This decrease could result from a fall in income, a change in tastes away from the good, a decrease in the price of a substitute or an increase in the price of a complement, a decrease in group size, or a change in expectations. The decrease in demand is shown as an inward shift in the demand curve from D_0 to D_2 in Figure 8. The decrease in demand causes equilibrium price to fall from P_0 to P_2, and quantity supplied responds by falling from Q_0 to Q_2.

Changes in any condition that affects supply will shift the supply curve. An increase in supply could result from an advance in technology, a decrease in the price of a factor of production, an increase in the number of suppliers, or a change in expectations. The increase in supply appears on a graph as a rightward shift of the supply curve, from S_0 to S_1 in Figure 9. This increase in supply would cause the equilibrium price to fall from P_0 to P_1, leading to an increase in the quantity demanded from Q_0 to Q_1.

A decrease in supply could result from an increase in the price of a factor of production, a decrease in the number of suppliers, or a change in expectations. A decrease in supply is shown as a leftward shift from S_0 to S_2 in Figure 9. This decrease in supply causes the equilibrium price to rise from P_0 to P_2, causing quantity demanded to decrease from Q_0 to Q_2.

The supply and demand model is very useful in analyzing a variety of economic problems and issues. As you apply this model, keep in mind the difference between changes in demand and supply (that is, shifts in the positions of the curves) and changes in the quantity demanded and quan-

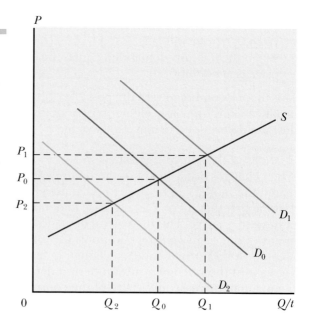

FIGURE 8
CHANGES IN DEMAND
An increase in demand from D_0 to D_1 causes the equilibrium price to rise from P_0 to P_1 and the quantity supplied to increase from Q_0 to Q_1. A decrease in demand from D_0 to D_2 causes the equilibrium price to fall from P_0 to P_2 and the quantity supplied to fall from Q_0 to Q_2.

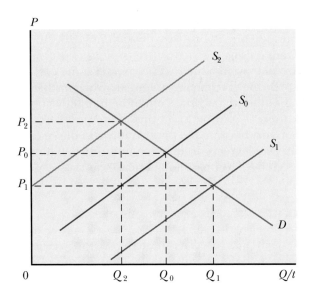

FIGURE 9
CHANGES IN SUPPLY
An increase in supply from S_0 to S_1 causes the equilibrium price to fall from P_0 to P_1 and the quantity demanded to increase from Q_0 to Q_1. A decrease in supply from S_0 to S_2 causes the equilibrium price to rise from P_0 to P_2 and the quantity demanded to fall from Q_0 to Q_2.

tity supplied (that is, movements along the curves). The importance of this difference will become very clear as you attempt to untangle situations that involve several changes in *ceteris paribus* conditions.[4]

ARE PRICES FAIR?

The analysis of supply and demand presented in this chapter has been positive rather than normative. No mention has been made of what constitutes a fair or just price. Nor has there been any comment as to whether certain minimal levels of consumption of certain goods are necessary for a fair society. Supply and demand theory predicts how an increase in demand for a good will affect price and quantity. A higher price may mean that some people can no longer afford the item, regardless of how "necessary" or "basic" it may appear to be. The supply and demand model offers no moral evaluation of what prices should be.

DIFFERENT PRICES FOR DIFFERENT BUYERS

A second adjustment to the supply and demand model is the observation that, in reality, people often pay different prices for the same good. In the supply and demand model, the equilibrium price is a single, unique price that is paid by all buyers and received by all sellers. There may be different prices for different buyers and sellers because of transactions costs. **Transactions costs** are costs associated with gathering information about markets (prices and quantities supplied) for consuming or producing. Organizing, negotiating, and searching take time and involve opportunity costs. Firms are organized to reduce transactions costs on the producing side. For consumers, the existence of transactions costs means that different people pay different prices for the same good or service.

transactions costs
Costs associated with gathering information about markets (prices and quantities supplied) for consuming or producing.

---

4.   To test yourself, work through these shifts. Determine the effect that changes in supply and demand have on price and quantity. For example, ask yourself: What is the effect on equilibrium of an increase in demand coupled with a decrease in supply?

A familiar example of such price differences is that gas stations next to expressways charge higher prices for gasoline than do stations farther away from expressways. Why? Transactions costs. Most users of an expressway are unfamiliar with the area and are in a hurry. They perceive the cost of searching for a lower price to be higher than the potential saving produced by such searching. Think about what gas prices might be in a retirement community. Do you think there would be lower and more uniform gas prices in a retirement community because the opportunity cost of the customers' time is lower? If you live near a retirement community, you might want to check on the prices charged for gasoline in nearby areas.

EVALUATING THE MARKET PROCESS

In Chapter 2, you saw that each and every economy must address three basic questions: what, how and for whom? Supply and demand—the market process—provide important signals to inform, direct, and motivate economic agents in answering these questions.

FUNCTIONS OF PRICES

Prices play a central role in a market system in allocating scarce resources and answering the basic economic questions. The primary functions of prices are to inform, direct, and motivate consumers and business firms.

INFORMING. Market prices condense a great deal of complex information into a simple form. This condensed information is useful to consumers and producers in making decisions. An increase in demand causes a market price to rise. The supplier of a product does not have to know what caused demand to change. All suppliers need to know is that the price has risen. They will respond by increasing the quantity supplied. Likewise, consumers do not need to understand anything about the production process or the associated costs. All they need to know is the market price. If the price rises, consumers decrease the quantity demanded. The market price, then, provides all participants in the market with up-to-the-minute information on the relative scarcity of goods.

DIRECTING. Market participants act on price information. If suppliers are bringing too much of a good to market, its price will fall. The decisions of consumers and producers will move the market to a new equilibrium. Market prices will signal for an increase in the production of those products of which consumers are demanding more. Firms will produce these goods by bringing resources together in a way directed by the market prices of those resources. All of this takes place without any individual or group of individuals telling consumers and entrepreneurs how or why to act. All of the necessary information is found in market prices.

MOTIVATING. The *for whom* question is also a reminder that price is a powerful motivator. Supply and demand establish a reward structure for owners and users of productive resources. Households and firms will seek to produce those goods or develop those skills that are highly desired by oth-

When the Berlin Wall was opened in the fall of 1989, writer Gloria Steinem observed that it was a very peaceful revolution. There was no violence, and everyone went shopping. In fact, the East Germans were hungry for markets, especially supermarkets and large department stores stocked with many kinds of goods. All of the nations of Eastern Europe are scrambling to relearn how markets work as they attempt to decentralize their economies, restore incentives, and obtain a greater variety of consumer goods for their citizens.

Some of the first foreign entrepreneurs attempting to become a part of the emerging markets in Eastern Europe have found the going rough. They were accustomed to working in a network of suppliers rather than interacting with government factories and collective farms to obtain their materials. McDonald's opened its first restaurant in Moscow after hurdling numerous obstacles in obtaining ingredients for its food products and materials for constructing the building. Finding workers, however, was not difficult. With meat always in short supply, prospective workers were attracted as much by the free meals as by the wages.

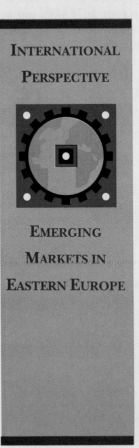

INTERNATIONAL PERSPECTIVE

EMERGING MARKETS IN EASTERN EUROPE

In spite of years of central planning, however, the market has shown a remarkable resiliency in some of the nations of Eastern Europe, where central planning has only dominated economic activity since the end of World War II. A black market—an illegal market, mostly for foreign goods and foreign currencies—has operated in these nations for the entire period. Even in the Soviet Union, some people working on collective farms were allowed to have private plots as well and to sell the output of those plots in a free market. A significant part of Soviet farm output came from those private plots, because the incentives to work hard and produce more were stronger when the workers could capture the benefits.

Private restaurants and retail shops have been quickly revived, along with farmers' markets and even one private, foreign-owned hotel in Moscow. The process of restoring the use of markets in production of manufactured goods will be slower, but the nations of Eastern Europe see markets—decentralized, efficient, with strong incentives—as their best hope for a higher standard of living in the future.

invisible hand
The idea advanced by Adam Smith that individuals pursuing their own self-interest direct the market system toward socially desirable outcomes.

ers, in order to earn rewards in the form of higher incomes. All of this happens without any government agency or central planning bureau telling people what to do. No one has to tell a gas station owner when to be open or where to build a station, or a bright young person to invest in education. People pursue certain activities because they perceive it to be in their own self-interest. This whole process of self-interested response to incentives is what Adam Smith referred to as the **invisible hand**.[5]

ALLOCATIVE EFFICIENCY

According to Adam Smith, the invisible hand informs, directs, and motivates the self-interest of market participants. Suppliers are motivated to guide resources into the production of the goods most wanted by consumers and to produce those goods with the most efficient methods and resource combinations possible. In the words of Nobel Laureate George Stigler,

… an economic actor on average knows better the environment in which he is acting and the probable consequences of his actions than an outsider, no matter how clever the outsider may be.[6]

allocative efficiency
The use of resources to produce the goods most desired by society. Free markets allow allocative efficiency.

Allocative efficiency is the use of resources to produce the goods most desired by society. It is the reason why most economists look to the market first for solutions to economic problems.

FREEDOM

Finally, an important result of a market system is that individuals enjoy a great deal of freedom to pursue their own self-interest. In a market system, the production and distribution of goods and services take place on a basis of voluntary cooperation in the pursuit of individual self-interest. Nobel Laureate Milton Friedman, like Stigler a champion of the market system, describes this advantage in these terms:

So long as effective freedom of exchange is maintained, the central feature of the market organization of economic activity is that it prevents one person from interfering with another in respect to most of his activities. The consumer is protected from coercion by the seller because of the presence of other sellers with whom he can deal. The seller is protected from coercion by the consumer because of other consumers to whom he can sell. The employee is protected from coercion by the employer because of other employers for whom he can work, and so on. And the market does this impersonally and without centralized authority.[7]

NONMARKET ALLOCATION AND THE SHORTCOMINGS OF MARKETS

Although the market is a highly efficient way to allocate resources, it does have some drawbacks, as we observed in Chapter 2. Some of those drawbacks include failure to provide public goods or to correct negative external effects, instability, and inequality in the distribution of income. Markets perform poorly when there is a lack of competition. The above

---

5. See the profile of Adam Smith in Chapter 2.
6. George J. Stigler, "Economists and Public Policy," *Regulation* (May/June 1982): 16.
7. Milton Friedman, *Capitalism and Freedom* (Chicago: University of Chicago Press, 1981): 14–15.

quotation from Friedman does not apply when monopolies interfere with freedom of choice. Often the failings of the market lead to government intervention, resulting in a mixed economy rather than a pure market economy.

Critics of the market system range from those who would replace it with central direction to those with a more middle-of-the-road approach. The latter see a variety of ways of dividing responsibilities between markets and government. If prices are not allowed to direct resources in certain situations, some other mechanism must be developed for their allocation. Government directives, waiting in line, or appeals to "good behavior" are possible allocative mechanisms. The benefits of government intervention must be weighed against the very strong advantages of markets in terms of efficiency and flexibility. The following examples suggest some areas where government intervention has reduced the efficiency of resource allocation.

TAXI FARES. One well-known example of a problem created by intervention in the market is poor taxi service in New York City. The Taxi and Limousine Commission allowed only 11,787 cabs to operate there in 1987. Because the medallions (permits) required to operate a cab were so scarce, owners paid up to $100,000 per medallion. There are a few "gypsy" cabs in New York, but the supply is limited because these drivers face severe penalties if caught operating without the required medallion. Other cities, such as Washington, D.C., allow a large number of cabs to operate and charge a relatively minimal fee for a permit. Both cities regulate the fares that cab drivers can charge, with a fixed price per mile plus a charge for standing time.

At peak traffic hours, it is difficult to get around in New York. Therefore, many cab drivers avoid working during these periods, making it even more difficult to hail a cab. Lines of well-dressed people standing forty-deep outside exclusive hotels attest to this allocation problem. In contrast, you can wave a hand at any street corner in downtown Washington, and three cabs will be immediately at your service.

What are the solutions to New York's problem? The experience in Washington suggests that visitors and residents would be better off if New York City allowed more cabs on the streets. But if you were a driver who paid $100,000 for a medallion, would you be in favor of this solution? Of course not. Another possibility would be to allow the market to set prices for taxi services. *Fortune* magazine suggested that cab drivers be allowed to change rates at peak times with "some sort of electronic display...perched atop the cab that would periodically announce new rates."[8] If cabbies could set rates and vary them by time of day, some riders would be discouraged by higher prices. Also, some cab drivers would be encouraged to put in more hours to earn higher fares. Do you think the lines outside the hotels would decrease?

ORGAN DONATIONS. Another example of markets at work occurs in the relatively new medical field of organ transplanting. Certain organs such as

---

8.   "Yellow Power," *Fortune* (15 September 1986): 144.

hearts, lungs, and eyes are donated only at death, usually from accident victims. Other organs, such as kidneys, can be donated by live donors, because humans have two kidneys and can function with just one. There have also been some successful transplants of part of a liver, since this organ can regenerate itself. As organ transplants have become more popular and more successful, a shortage of organs has developed. Newspapers and television frequently carry heartrending appeals. Some hospitals even have donor seekers who contact relatives of accident victims. One explanation for the shortage of organs is that the price is being held at too low a level. In fact, the price is zero.

One writer, Barry Jacobs, proposed establishing a market for kidneys.[9] Since individuals can get along quite well with one kidney, Jacobs's proposal was to let individuals who are cash-poor and kidney-rich sell a kidney to those who are cash-rich and kidney-poor. Also, Congressional hearings were held to consider what could be done about the shortage of kidneys for transplant. Two members of Congress proposed a federal program to fund a computer organ-marketing system and a 24-hour kidney hotline. The program would, however, establish no financial incentives for donors. What do you think might happen if there were a market for kidneys?

Some idea of the possible effect of paying for kidneys comes from an experiment by two British economists, Michael Cooper and Anthony Culver. They tried to determine the supply of blood that would be offered at various prices.[10] They found that there was a moderate supply at a price of zero. At this price, blood was given by those who were motivated by charity, altruism, or other noneconomic reasons. The supply actually fell at a nominal price of about $1.00 a pint, because the payment did not compensate some potential donors for the loss of the good feeling they obtained from giving blood for free. But as the price rose, more and more donors came forward. For many years, some people in American cities have sold their blood when they needed money. The quantity supplied is positively related to price, just as our models would predict. Do you think that kidneys would be any different?

FACULTY OFFICES. A final example of market versus nonmarket allocation comes, appropriately, from an economics department trying to allocate faculty offices in a new building. The other five departments in the school of business used various methods of allocation: seniority, first come first served, and a roll of the dice. None of these methods reflected the intensity of people's preferences for corner offices, offices with windows, large offices, and so forth. There was great dissatisfaction with the outcomes. Only in the economics department was there an attempt to use the market for allocating office space. Faculty members were invited to submit sealed bids. The highest bidders got to choose first, and the proceeds went to student scholarships. A bid indicated how important the "perks" associated with a particular office were to the bidder. Those who

---

9. "Socialized Kidneys," *Fortune* (19 March 1984): 190.
10. Institute of Economic Affairs, *The Economics of Charity: Essays on the Comparative Economics and Ethics of Giving and Selling, with Applications to Blood* (Surrey, England: Gresham Press, 1973).

worked at home more or were away from campus more would presumably bid less than those who used their offices more regularly and cared more intensely about aspects of their workplace.

The experiment was quite successful. The highest bidder paid $500 for the first choice of office, and bidders down to $75 were able to secure the more desirable offices with windows. Since those who bid too low were free to recontract with others if they changed their minds, there was general satisfaction with the outcome.[11]

Summary

1. Demand depends on the current price of the good or service as well as nonprice determinants. These other influences on supply include the size of the group demanding the good, the tastes of the consuming group, the incomes of that group, the prices of related goods and services, and the expectations concerning the future.

2. The law of demand states that the quantity demanded of a good or service is negatively related to its price, *ceteris paribus.*

3. Changes in the price of a good affect the quantity demanded of that good. That is, a price change leads to a movement along the demand curve.

4. Changes in the *ceteris paribus* conditions that affect demand cause demand to either increase or decrease. That is, there is a shift in the position of the entire demand curve.

5. When income increases, the demand for a normal good will increase, and the demand for an inferior good will decrease.

6. Two goods are complements when a price increase in one will cause a decrease in demand for the other. Two goods are substitutes if an increase in the price of one causes an increase in demand for the other.

7. Supply depends on the price of the good or service as well as on nonprice determinants. These include the prices of the factors of production, the level of technology, the number of suppliers, and expectations.

8. The law of supply states that the quantity supplied of a good or service is usually a positive function of its price, *ceteris paribus.*

9. Changes in a good's price affect the quantity supplied of that good. Changes in factors of production that affect supply cause supply to either increase or decrease. When the prices of factors of production increase, there will be a decrease in supply. An advance in technology will usually cause supply to increase.

10. The market-clearing (equilibrium) price is the price at which the amount consumers wish to purchase is equal to the amount suppliers wish to sell. When supply or demand shifts, the market is in disequilibrium until natural forces determine a new equilibrium price and quantity. The comparison of two equilibrium positions is called comparative statics.

11. The supply and demand model has two endogenous variables that are determined within the model. These variables are price and quantity. The exogenous variables are determined outside the model but influence what goes on in the model by shifting supply and demand. These variables include prices of related goods, tastes, income, expectations, and technology.

12. The supply and demand model, like most economic models, uses marginal analysis. It focuses on decisions about the next unit purchased or sold rather than on aggregate or all-or-nothing decisions.

13. Prices play an important role in informing, directing, and motivating consumers and producers.

14. Markets maximize individual freedom by allowing individuals to pursue their own self-interest.

15. Transactions costs result from the fact that organizing, negotiating, and searching take time and involve costs. The existence of transactions costs means that different people pay different prices for the same good or service.

11. William J. Boyes and Stephen K. Happel, "Auctions as an Allocation Mechanism in Academia: The Case of Faculty Offices," *Journal of Economic Perspectives* (Summer 1989): 37–40.

New Terms

demand	normal good	market supply curve	endogenous variables
supply	inferior good	increase in supply	exogenous variables
law of demand	complementary goods	decrease in supply	primary effect
demand schedule	substitute goods	market equilibrium	secondary effects
demand curve	expectations	market-clearing price	transactions costs
market demand curve	supply schedule	disequilibrium	invisible hand
increase in demand	(not quite) law of supply	comparative statics	allocative efficiency
decrease in demand	supply curve	marginal analysis	

Questions for Discussion

1. Develop a simple theory to explain (predict) student grades in this course. Identify at least two exogenous variables and one endogenous variable.

2. How can expectations about economic conditions affect supply?

3. Does the fact that some people appear to buy more of some goods, such as mink coats and diamonds, as their prices go up negate the law of demand?

4. How can belief in a future change in the availability of gasoline affect the demand for automobiles?

5. Pat, a professional student, failed an economics course and decided to sell flowers on a street corner to make ends meet. A second flower seller established a business directly across the street from Pat. Pat, unconcerned, came up with the following hypothesis: "When supply increases, demand will increase. Therefore, I will be just as well off as I was before the second flower seller arrived." Did Pat deserve to fail economics? Why or why not?

6. A market-clearing price is the price at which the amount sold equals the amount purchased. Is this correct?

7. List all of the conditions that can decrease demand or supply.

8. List all of the conditions that can increase demand or supply.

9. Why is it so important to distinguish changes in demand and changes in supply from changes in quantity demanded and changes in quantity supplied?

10. Why do some people shop at convenience stores, knowing they will pay higher prices, even when a supermarket with lower prices is open in the same block?

11. The following table lists market information you gathered about landing slots at the Atlanta airport. Suppose you are asked to make a recommendation to the airport manager about pricing the slots to reduce crowding and delays. What will you recommend?

THE MARKET FOR LANDING SLOTS FROM 8:00 A.M. TO 9:00 A.M.

PRICE($)	QUANTITY SUPPLIED	QUANTITY DEMANDED
0	12	50
250	12	40
500	12	20
1,000	12	15
1,500	12	8
2,000	12	2

12. Draw a supply curve for personal computers that slopes upward and a demand curve for personal computers that slopes downward. They intersect at an equilibrium price of $2,000 and an equilibrium quantity of 6,000 units per month. Now experiment with each of the following.

a. A breakthrough in the technology of making chips substantially lowers the cost of production. Which curve shifts, and which way? (Draw it on your diagram.) Find the new equilibrium price and quantity. Did they increase or decrease?

b. The baby boom generation has bought large numbers of personal computers, and the market is saturated. The number of potential customers in the following generation is much smaller because the birth rate fell sharply during the late 1960s and early 1970s. Does this affect supply or demand? Which curve shifts, and in which direction? What is the effect on price and quantity?

c. A foreign firm enters the market, adding a new source of supply. How does this change affect the price, quantity, and market supply curve? What is the impact on domestic firms?

13. Explain whether each of the following will shift the supply curve or the demand curve for milk and in which direction.

    a. The birth rate rises. (There are more babies.)

    b. The price of beef is very high, tempting dairy farmers to slaughter their milk cows.

    c. There is a drought, creating a shortage of feed for dairy herds.

    d. Scientists find that drinking too much milk increases the risk of heart disease.

    e. Scientists find that drinking more milk reduces the chances of developing osteoporosis.

14. If both supply and demand shift to the right, what happens to price and quantity? What happens if both supply and demand shift to the left?

15. In 1989, one of the hot gift items was the Nintendo entertainment system, which was used to play games. Only Nintendo games could be played on this system, and Nintendo games could not be played on other systems. How would a shortage of Nintendo systems affect the demand for Nintendo games?

SUGGESTIONS FOR FURTHER READING

Friedman, Milton. *Capitalism and Freedom.* Chicago: University of Chicago Press, 1981. This book presents the case for free markets by perhaps the most respected and passionate of their advocates.

Hayek, F. A. "The Use of Knowledge in Society." *American Economic Review* (September 1945): 519–528. This classic, very readable article shows the importance of markets as a source of information and coordination.

Miller, Roger LeRoy, Daniel K. Benjamin, and Douglass C. North. *The Economics of Public Issues,* 7th ed. New York: HarperCollins, 1990. An easy-to-read book that uses supply and demand to analyze issues of current interest.

INTRODUCTION TO MACROECONOMICS

1. Draw and explain the expanded circular flow model, including all leakages and injections.
2. Identify the major macroeconomic goals and tell how each is measured.
3. Discuss the costs and benefits of economic growth and the costs of unemployment and inflation.
4. Define productivity and explain its importance.
5. Draw a typical business cycle diagram, and explain how output, employment, prices, and productivity change over the course of the cycle.
6. Explain the political and economic importance of the Great Depression.

CHAPTER 4

MACROECONOMIC GOALS AND FLUCTUATIONS

INTRODUCTION

Macroeconomics is concerned with the behavior of economic aggregates, including total output and income, total employment and unemployment, and price levels and inflation. In contrast, microeconomics is focused more narrowly on the quantities and prices of specific goods, such as pizza or textbooks, and the employment of certain factors of production, such as farmland or textbook writers. If a few people are unemployed, this is probably a microeconomic problem of finding the right wage rate or the right information on job openings or of developing the right skills. If 10 million people are unemployed, this is a macroeconomic problem. If the price of eggs rises, it is a microeconomic matter. If the average price of everything rises, it is a macroeconomic problem. When one person's income rises, there is a microeconomic explanation in terms of skills or productivity. When the economy's total income rises, there is a macroeconomic explanation in terms of economic growth.

This chapter is an overview of some major macroeconomic concerns. In this chapter, we will begin to explore the issues of the rate of economic growth, price stability and inflation, and employment and unemployment.

THE CIRCULAR FLOW MODEL REVISITED

In Chapter 2, we introduced the circular flow model as a way to see the interrelationships in a market economy. The individual markets and actors that make up the circular flow constitute microeconomics. The sums of their actions constitute macroeconomics. In this chapter, we want to focus on circular flow from a macroeconomic perspective.

A simple two-sector circular flow model shows the flow of goods and services from business firms to households in the upper flow as well as a return flow of payments from households for their purchases. In the lower flow, business firms purchase the services of productive inputs from households, creating a flow of income back to households. Even in this very simple two-sector world, it is possible to identify some important macroeconomic relationships. The upper part of the diagram, the product market, represents the aggregate of the individual markets in which final goods and services are bought and sold. The lower half, the factor market, is the aggregate of the individual markets in which the services of productive inputs are bought and sold. These markets represent the total of thousands of individual markets for steelworkers, bread, rental housing, cars, machine tools, and other inputs and outputs. That is, the product market and the factor market are both macroeconomic markets.

Another important macroeconomic concept that is suggested by the circular flow diagram is the view of national income or output as a *flow*. The flow of factor income from firms to households becomes a flow back to firms to pay for purchases of goods and services. The upper flow is total output, and the lower flow is total income. The two flows are the same size in the simple circular flow model because all of the income received by households is spent to purchase the output of firms.

SAVING, INVESTMENT, AND THE CREDIT MARKET

Figure 1 adds two flows to the simple circular flow model—saving and investment.[1] These flows were introduced in Chapter 2 and are developed

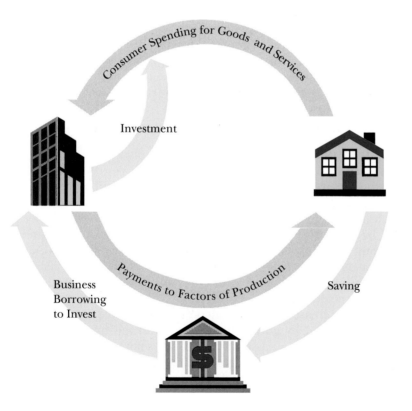

FIGURE 1
THE CIRCULAR FLOW WITH SAVING, INVESTMENT, AND A CREDIT MARKET
When there are leakages, not all household income is spent on consumption. A credit market allows saving (nonconsumption) by households to be converted into investment funds for firms. These investment funds are then spent by firms on capital goods and further production.

1. Recall from Chapter 2 that we simplified this diagram before adding other flows. We reduced the original two pairs of flows to just two flows: income payments to productive factors in the lower half and expenditure payments for goods and services in the upper half.

saving
The part of households' income flow not spent on purchases of goods and services.

investment
Purchases by firms of some real, tangible asset, such as a machine, a factory, or a stock of inventory.

credit market
The aggregate market consisting of financial institutions that channel household savings to business firms that want to invest.

leakages
Flows out of the circular pattern that occur when factor income is received but not spent directly on purchases from domestic firms. Savings, taxes, and purchases of imports are leakages.

injections
Spending added to the circular flow that is not paid for out of factor income. Business investment, government expenditures, and sales of exports are injections.

here in more detail. **Saving** is a flow from households that occurs because they refrain from spending part of their income flow on goods and services. These funds flow into the credit market instead of the product market. **Investment** is a flow from firms. Firms borrow from households through the credit market in order to purchase new plants or equipment or to add to their inventories. That is, they use the borrowed funds to purchase new capital goods from other firms or to finance the "purchase" of their own output in the form of increased inventories.[2] The **credit market** consists of financial institutions channeling household savings to business firms that want to invest. The credit market is an important macro market.

Another important pair of macroeconomic concepts is illustrated in Figure 1. These are leakages out of the income stream and injections into the income stream. **Leakages** are flows out of the circular pattern that occur when factor income is received but not spent directly on purchases from domestic firms. Examples of leakages are saving, taxes, and purchases of imports. Income leaks out of the income stream if households do not spend all of their income on consumption of goods produced by business firms. **Injections** are added flows into the circular pattern that represent spending not paid for out of factor income. Examples of injections are business investment, government expenditures, and sales of exports. There are injections in Figure 1 because the business firms spend income that is not earned but borrowed.

If leakages are greater than injections, the size of the income flow will shrink. If injections are larger than leakages, the income flow will increase. Since the level of output and income (that is, the size of the flow) is a central macroeconomic concern, leakages and injections play important roles in macroeconomic models.

GOVERNMENT IN THE CIRCULAR FLOW

When we add a third actor, government, to interact with households and firms, the picture of the macro economy becomes still more realistic. In Figure 2, governments (federal, state, and local) interact with firms and households in several ways. The government buys goods and services produced by firms. It is thus a third "customer" in addition to households, which buy goods for consumption, and business firms, which purchase goods for investment. Government purchases of goods and services are another injection into spending in the product market. The government also employs factors of production, mainly labor services. Wages paid by government increase the flow of income to households.

Taxes collected by governments are a leakage from household income. (For simplicity, we assume that all taxes fall on households.) Taxes are paid to finance the services governments provide, such as defense, police, fire protection, streets, and education. Taxes reduce households'

---

2. Some business firms may actually save and lend to others, and some households may be net borrowers. For simplicity, however, we treat all saving as coming from the household sector and all borrowing as done by the business sector.

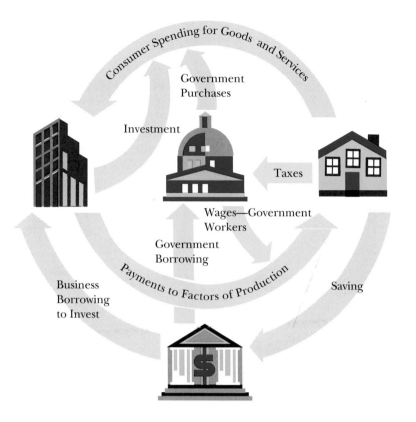

Consumer Spending for Goods and Services

Government Purchases

Investment

Taxes

Wages—Government Workers

Government Borrowing

Payments to Factors of Production

Business Borrowing to Invest

Saving

FIGURE 2
THE CIRCULAR FLOW WITH A CREDIT MARKET AND GOVERNMENT
Government subtracts from the circular flow by taxing households (leakages). It adds to the upper flow (expenditures) by buying goods and services from firms. It adds to the income flow by purchasing the services of labor from households. Governments, like businesses, also borrow in the credit market.

consumption by lowering their after-tax (disposable) incomes. Therefore, less is available to spend. Taxes may also reduce household saving.

Finally, if the government spends more than it collects in taxes, it must borrow funds in the credit market. There it will compete with business firms for the supply of household savings. A government that spends more than the revenue it takes in is running a **deficit**. A government that collects more in taxes than it spends on wages and purchases is showing a **surplus**.

The government, then, enters the circular flow model at a number of points. It takes funds out of the stream by taxing households and by borrowing in the credit market. It adds to the spending flow by purchasing goods and services from firms. It adds to the income flow by purchasing labor services from households. Taxes are leakages out of the flow. Government purchases of goods and services are injections.

deficit
A situation in which the government spends more than it collects in taxes.

surplus
A situation in which the government collects more in taxes than it spends.

THE FOREIGN SECTOR: EXPORTS AND IMPORTS

Adding the foreign sector completes the picture of the macro economy. As Figure 3 shows, it is not only another "customer" for firms' output but also another supplier of goods and services besides the domestic business sector. Buying from foreign countries and selling to other countries add a new source of leakages and a new source of injections. Purchases from foreign

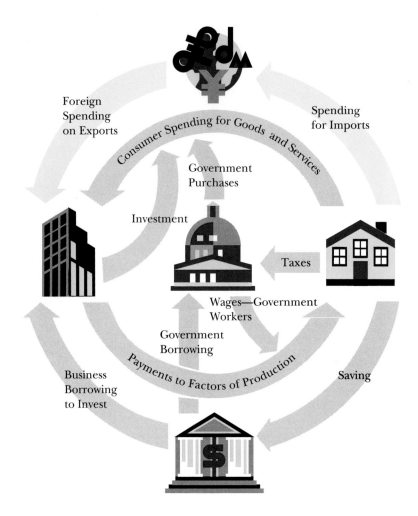

imports
Goods and services purchased from foreign sellers.

exports
Goods and services sold to foreign buyers.

balance on goods and services
The difference between the value of exports and the value of imports for a country in a given year.

firms are **imports**. Goods and services sold to foreign buyers are **exports**. Purchases of imports are flows out of the stream (leakages). Sales of exports are flows into the stream (injections). Thus, if a country increases its purchases from foreigners, *ceteris paribus*, the size of the flow will shrink. If the same country increases its sales to foreigners, *ceteris paribus*, the size of the flow will increase. The difference between exports and imports for a given country for a given year is called the **balance on goods and services**. A surplus in the balance on goods and services means that injections from the foreign market exceed leakages to it. A deficit in the balance on goods and services means that foreign market leakages are greater than injections.

For many years, exports and imports were so small relative to the total flow of income and product in the United States that they were often omitted from the circular flow diagram. In the early 1960s, the ratio of both imports and exports to total domestic output was only about 5 or 6 percent. Since then, not only has the ratio of both imports and exports to total output risen sharply in the United States, but trade has become increasingly unbalanced. By the late 1980s, exports were about 9 percent of total output, and imports accounted for 12 percent of spending. Ignoring exports and imports in the 1990s would lead to serious errors in predicting the size of the income and output flow.

THE COMPONENTS OF THE CIRCULAR FLOW DIAGRAM			
FOUR MARKETS	FOUR ACTORS	THREE LEAKAGES	THREE INJECTIONS
Product	Households	Saving	Investment
Factor	Firms	Taxes	Government purchases
Credit	Government	Imports	Exports
Foreign	Exports and imports		

MACROECONOMIC GOALS

What do people want from the economy as a whole? What are the macroeconomic goals? How can a nation measure whether it is better off or worse off? The circular flow diagram provides a picture of the macro economy. In that visual model we can implicitly identify at least one macroeconomic goal—to encourage the steady growth of the flows of income and output. The levels of income and output and the rate at which they grow are the central focus of macroeconomics. Expressed as a goal, the focus is on economic growth at a steady and sustainable rate. However, there are other important macroeconomic concerns that are not directly observed in the circular flow diagram. Two other major goals are price stability and full employment. There is almost total agreement about the centrality of these three goals, because economists and policy makers are aware of the high costs of lack of growth, price instability, and unemployment. In this chapter, we explore what these goals mean and how performance on each is measured.

ECONOMIC GROWTH

Economic growth is defined as an increase in real output per capita. The word *real* means that the number describing output has been corrected for price changes.[3] For example, if the value of the total output of soup has gone from $1 million to $2 million, you need to know what has happened to the price of a can of soup before you jump to the conclusion that there is twice as much soup. If the price of soup rose 40 percent, the real output of soup has not doubled. In fact, there is really only about 43 percent more soup.

An increase in real output per capita means that the average person has more goods and services and a higher standard of living than before. It is generally believed that a growth rate of 3 to 4 percent per year is the highest that can be sustained for any length of time. Producing more output requires more productive resources and/or improvements in technology. A rate of growth of 3 to 4 percent corresponds to an attainable combined rate of change in these two important sources of economic growth.

economic growth
An increase in the level of real output per capita.

3.   In contrast, the word *nominal* indicates that a value has *not* been corrected for price changes.

COSTS AND BENEFITS OF ECONOMIC GROWTH. For a long time, economic growth was the most widely accepted of the macroeconomic goals. Economists and others believed that if some production is good, more must be better. A higher standard of living is better than a lower one. As population grows, output has to grow just to keep per capita output and income from falling. Generally, people want economic growth to provide some improvements in the standard of living as well. Additional capacity to produce means that some more of those insatiable wants can be fulfilled. These may be private wants for better housing or collective wants for better roads.

Beginning in the 1960s, however, many people began to question the value and, especially, the costs of economic growth. More industry and a larger population created more air and water pollution, noise, and litter. Questions were raised about the effects of growth on the environment. In addition, as the birth rate dropped in the late 1960s and early 1970s, the need for growth in order to provide for additional population became much less pressing.

Critics of economic growth as a central policy goal raise a number of objections. Some point out that we live on a finite planet, with limited natural resources. Thus, growth cannot be sustained indefinitely. Growth also creates undesirable by-products, such as solid waste, hazardous wastes, and air pollution. Doubts have also been expressed about whether continued economic growth has resulted in improvements in the quality of life. Gains in productivity have seemed to go into producing more output instead of more leisure. In the 1980s, the typical European worker had a four- to six-week annual vacation in contrast to the typical two weeks for an American worker. Some Americans asked whether economic growth was worth the cost in terms of lifestyle. At the same time, younger Japanese workers questioned the benefits of their nation's rapid economic growth. Most of them had to put up with cramped housing, long commutes, and high prices for consumer goods.

infrastructure
The basic facilities and equipment, usually publicly owned, that provide community services.

Another concern that surfaced in the late 1970s was that the existing infrastructure might not be able to support continued growth. **Infrastructure** is the basic facilities and equipment that provide community services. The support system of roads, water, sewers, electric power, schools, hospitals, and parks is important to residents and businesses. Demand for infrastructure rises with economic growth. The infrastructure not only needs to grow with the population in a community but also requires regular maintenance and repair.

Many of these concerns really point to disagreements about the composition of output rather than about economic growth. If there is an increase in productive capacity, it can be directed toward more output or more leisure, more private goods or more collective goods (including infrastructure). With more resources, a society can devote more effort to improving the environment without sacrificing other goods and services. Many of these apparent objections to economic growth are really objections to how output is measured and how priorities are set for using new resources and technology.

The last two recessions, in 1981–82 and 1990–91, made Americans more aware of the costs of not growing. When economic growth is slow or stops, tax revenues decline or grow slowly. Politicians hate to raise tax rates. Rising unemployment further reduces tax revenues and creates pressures on government to spend in order to relieve unemployment. There are even political battles between generations. Retirees want a greater share of the public budget to support them, and younger people want funding for public schools. Thus, for most Americans, a steady and sustainable rate of economic growth, along with attention to the quality of life and the state of the environment, remains a central economic goal.

MEASURING GROWTH. The most widely used measure of economic growth is the rate of increase in output, which is shown in Figure 4.[4] As this figure suggests, the United States has experienced periods of rapid growth alternating with stretches of slow growth or even decline in output. The 1970s were a period of very slow growth. The rate of growth picked up again by the mid-1980s but slowed at the end of the decade. A recession developed in late 1990. The overall (compounded) rate of growth in Figure 4 has been about 3.6 percent a year, with a wide range from –9 percent a year (briefly) in 1980 to over 12 percent a year in the late 1940s.

PRICE STABILITY

Another important macroeconomic goal is price stability. Prices can either rise or fall. In recent years, however, the United States has experienced a continued rise in the general, or average, level of prices. This is **inflation**. The measure of inflation is the change in the price index. A **price index** measures the price level in any year relative to some base year. The best-known such measure is the **Consumer Price Index (CPI)**, popularly known as the cost-of-living index. The CPI measures the cost of a mar-

inflation
A sustained rise in the general, or average, level of prices.

price index
A measure of the price level in a given year relative to some base year.

consumer price index (CPI)
A well-known measure of inflation based on the cost of a selected market basket of consumer goods (also known as the cost-of-living index).

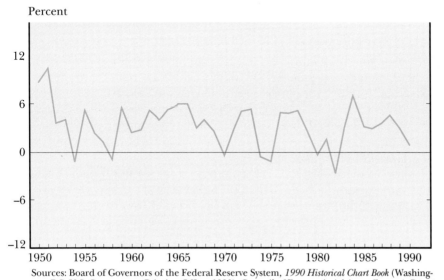

FIGURE 4
ANNUAL GROWTH RATE OF REAL GNP, 1933–1990
Growth rates of output, or real gross national product (output in constant dollars), show much variation over time. It is easy to identify recessions in this diagram as periods when real output fell (growth rates were negative).

Sources: Board of Governors of the Federal Reserve System, *1990 Historical Chart Book* (Washington, DC: U.S. Government Printing Office, 1990); Council of Economic Advisers, *Economic Report of the President* (Washington, DC: U.S. Government Printing Office, 1991).

---

4.   The output growth rates in Figure 4 have been corrected for price changes.

Both prices and productivity are measured in this chapter (Figures 5 and 7) using an index. An index is simply a weighted average, for which the absolute value has relatively little meaning. The important thing about an index is the year-to-year change in its value or the comparison of its values for different individuals, firms, cities, states, or countries.

Suppose you were asked to develop an index of academic quality of colleges. You might set up your index to reflect the number of books in the library, the average SAT scores of entering students, the average starting salary of graduates, and the faculty-to-student ratio. The table presents such data for three colleges. You assign a high weight to SAT scores (40) and equal weights (20 each) to the other three variables (weights must add to 100).

For each item, the index value is calculated by multiplying the weight (which is the same for an item for all three colleges) by the raw value of the item for each college. For example, an SAT score of 10 (1,000 raw score) multiplied by a weight of 40 percent gives a value of 4.0. The weighted index values are added to create an index for each college. The absolute values of the numbers 15.0, 17.7, and 23.8 don't mean very much. The relative values of an index are what matter. These are used to make comparisons over time (how fast prices are rising according to the price index) or space (how the productivity index in the United States compares to that of Japan).

Note that according to this index, college 3 is the "best" primarily because of high SAT scores and secondarily because of graduates' starting salaries. On the other two items, faculty-to-student ratio and number of library books, this college is weaker. If the index gave greater weight to these other items and less weight to entering SAT scores, college 3 might not rank as high. You can see from this example that it is possible to "rig" the weights to make a particular school look good. This is why you need to interpret indices with care. Note also that the indices for a school will record changes in its performance from year to year. Thus, this index can be used for one school over time as well as for comparisons among schools.

Economists use a variety of indices in their work. The price index is the most familiar. Other indices include the productivity index, the stock market index, and the quality-of-life index. Used to compare the well-being of states and nations, the quality-of-life index includes the literacy rate, the infant mortality rate, per capita income, average life span, and other measures of health and wealth.

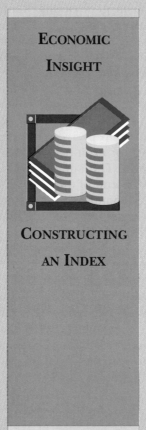

ECONOMIC INSIGHT

CONSTRUCTING AN INDEX

INDEX OF COLLEGE QUALITY

ITEM	WEIGHT	COLLEGE 1		COLLEGE 2		COLLEGE 3	
		RAW VALUE	INDEX VALUE	RAW VALUE	INDEX VALUE	RAW VALUE	INDEX VALUE
Books	20%	10	2.0	20	4.0	50	10.0
SAT scores	40%	10	4.0	9	3.6	12	4.8
Salaries	20%	25	5.0	20	4.0	30	6.0
F/S ratio	20%	20	4.0	30	6.0	15	3.0
Index			15.0		17.7		23.8

Note: Number of books is in 1,000s, SAT scores in 100s, salaries in $1,000s, and F/S ratio in faculty per 100 students.

ket basket of a selected array of consumer goods each year. The percentage change in the CPI from one year to the next is the inflation rate. The inflation rate from 1933 to 1990 is shown in Figure 5. You can see that, except for World War II, prices were relatively stable until the 1970s. High inflation in the late 1970s and early 1980s increased awareness of the many problems caused by inflation, especially when it is unexpected. Lower inflation rates in the rest of the 1980s helped to calm fears that high rates of inflation would become a permanent feature of the American economy. However, the inflation rate in 1990 was 6 percent—perhaps the start of a new round of higher inflation rates in the 1990s.

GAINERS AND LOSERS FROM INFLATION. One reason why governments try to restrain inflation is that it causes unintended and often undesirable redistribution of income and wealth. Redistribution is more likely to occur when inflation is unexpected. People make contracts and decisions on the assumption of an expected rate of inflation. Suppose, for simplicity, you are expecting zero inflation. You lend someone $100 for a year at an interest rate of 5 percent. This rate is enough to cover your risk of not being repaid and the cost of not using the money for a year, assuming no inflation. Then there is unexpected inflation of 10 percent. At the end of a year, you receive $105, but it will only purchase $95.45 in goods and services ($105/1.10). Who gained? The borrower. If you had anticipated the inflation, you would have charged a higher interest rate to cover the loss

FIGURE 5
INFLATION RATE,
1933–1990
The rate of change in the CPI is shown for each year since 1933. Note the negative inflation rates during the Depression of the 1930s, when prices were falling. There was a gradual rise from the 1940s through the 1960s, a sharp increase from 1975 to 1982, and finally a leveling off in the mid-1980s.

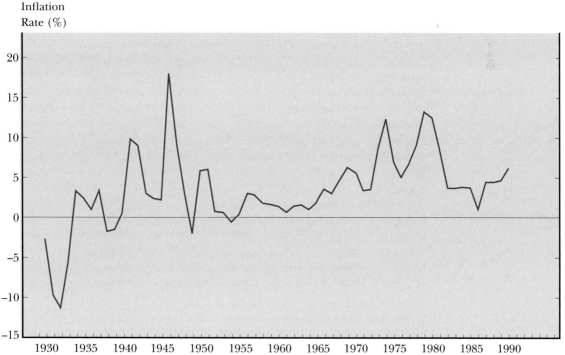

Inflation Rate (%)

Sources: Board of Governors of the Federal Reserve System, *1990 Historical Chart Book* (Washington, DC: U.S. Government Printing Office, 1990); Council of Economic Advisers, *Economic Report of the President* (Washington DC: U.S. Government Printing Office, 1991).

of purchasing power. Unexpected inflation redistributes income from lenders to borrowers.

Lenders and borrowers are not the only ones who are affected by income redistribution from unexpected inflation. People who hold any kind of fixed-dollar assets, such as life insurance policies, lose purchasing power. People who hold real, physical assets, such as land, houses, or jewelry, often find that the value of those assets rises faster than the rate of inflation. As more people shift to real assets in response to expected inflation, the increase in demand for those assets will drive their prices up even faster than the inflation rate.

Buying as much house as you could possibly afford was a popular inflation hedge in the 1970s and 1980s. Many home buyers were later able to sell their houses for much more than they paid for them as house prices increased rapidly. This pattern ended in the late 1980s. In the 1990s, the smaller number of new home buyers has led real estate experts to predict that house prices will be stable in nominal terms (falling in real terms). Thus, housing does not look like a good inflation hedge in the 1990s. Sometimes common stocks, which represent ownership claims on the real, physical assets of firms, also do better than the inflation rate. However, the future course of the price of any given stock is highly uncertain. Thus, stocks are a risky inflation hedge. Hedging against anticipated inflation is an important way to protect the value of assets, but there is no perfect instrument to use for that purpose.

Governments are often winners during times of inflation because of the progressive nature of state and federal income taxes. As prices rise, households' nominal incomes also rise, even if their real income or purchasing power is unchanged. Taxpayers find themselves in higher tax brackets, paying a higher percentage of their incomes in taxes. Changes in U.S. tax laws beginning in 1987 have made federal income taxes less progressive. In the future, the government will stand to gain less from inflation. Beginning in 1990, some aspects of the income tax code (brackets and personal exemptions) will be adjusted for inflation each year, making the federal government even less of a winner from inflation. However, even with these changes, the government will continue to reap gains in the form of increased revenues when there is inflation. This revenue gain will occur because there are still several rates and brackets in the federal income tax code and in many state income tax codes as well. Other taxes, such as sales taxes and property taxes, are less sensitive to inflation.[5]

It is important to separate the effects of inflation from the effects of changes in *relative* prices. As a worker, you may feel that you are hurt by inflation because your wages aren't rising as fast as the price level. But it's very possible that even if prices were stable your wages might fall. Your wages could fall because of declining demand in your occupation or in your area. Wages of some workers—for example, accountants, engineers,

---

5.   Generally, property taxes do not rise with inflation unless the inflation is sustained for a long period of time and reflected in property values. Property is reassessed for tax purposes relatively infrequently. In the 1970s, however, rapid inflation coincided with strong housing demand as baby boomers were forming households. As the price of houses rose even more rapidly than the general price level, property taxes also shot up rapidly, especially in California. The result was the property tax revolt from about 1978 to 1983.

and nurses—have been rising faster than the rate of inflation. Wages of other workers—such as retail clerks—have been rising more slowly. In recent years, wages for fast-food work and other entry-level jobs traditionally held by teenagers and college students have been rising sharply because of the relatively small number of people in that age group. Such relative wage changes have been caused by changes in supply and demand in those markets. As long as the average wage keeps pace with inflation, workers are not hurt by inflation, even though some workers may be suffering from a decline in demand for their particular skills.

The same is true of prices of consumer products. Even when most prices are rising, the prices of some goods are falling or rising much more slowly. If the market basket of goods you purchase is very different from that used to compute the CPI, then you will feel the effects of both inflation and changing relative prices. If your basket is full of items whose prices are rising faster than average, both inflation and changing relative prices will hit your budget. But if you are consuming less popular goods such as bicycle tires, granola, and diapers when most other consumers are driving up the prices of gasoline, oat bran, and college tuition, the cost of your basket may not be rising as fast as the CPI.

MARKET SIGNALS, INFLATION PSYCHOLOGY, AND MENU COSTS. Our discussion of relative prices versus the price level suggests another problem due to inflation. Inflation confuses the market signals on which individuals rely to make good decisions about earning, spending, saving, and investing. It is difficult to tell what is happening to relative prices when all prices are moving at once. This confusion of signals due to inflation is a major problem in market economies.

Another problem from high rates of inflation is an inflation psychology that leads people to "buy now before the price goes up." This expectation encourages consumption but discourages saving and investment. Saving and investment are important because they increase the nation's stock of capital and result in a higher rate of economic growth. Thus, high rates of inflation can have a negative effect on economic growth.

A third problem is the menu cost of inflation. Have you ever gone into a restaurant and seen prices crossed out and written over? Such price changes happen more often with inflation. Firms have to get new menus, price lists, catalogs, and other price information printed more often. All of these adjustments use real resources that could be used more productively in other ways.

Given all these drawbacks to inflation, why not try to reduce the inflation rate to zero? In fact, a target inflation rate of zero has been proposed by Alan Greenspan, the chairman of the Federal Reserve System (the central bank). One of the problems with this target, however, is that the measurement of inflation is not very precise. Therefore, what appears to be modest inflation of about 2 percent might actually be closer to zero inflation if the index were correctly computed.[6] A stronger argument

---

6.   The pros and cons of Greenspan's zero-inflation proposal are discussed by Michelle Garfinkel in "What Is an 'Acceptable' Rate of Inflation?—A Review of the Issues," *Review*, Federal Reserve Bank of St. Louis (July-August 1989): 3–15.

against the goal of zero inflation is that the costs of reducing the inflation rate to zero may be greater than the benefits. Often moderate inflation is associated with rapid economic growth, which is usually considered a desirable goal. Since most of the problems from inflation are related to high rates of inflation, rapid inflation, or unexpected inflation, a low and stable rate of inflation may be desirable.

WHAT'S WRONG WITH INFLATION?

The costs of inflation are:

- unintended redistribution of income and wealth,
- transfer of resources to government,
- confused market signals,
- lower levels of saving and investment (inflation psychology), and
- menu costs.

FULL EMPLOYMENT

full employment
The level of employment at which approximately 94 to 95 percent of those who want to work are employed.

The third macroeconomic goal is full employment. The precise amounts of employment and unemployment that constitute full employment are difficult to pinpoint. Clearly, full employment does not mean that 100 percent of the population is employed or even that 100 percent of those able are willing to take a job. One way of defining **full employment** is to identify some level of unemployment as "normal," or acceptable, and only count unemployment in excess of that amount. A level of 5 to 6 percent is currently considered normal. Thus, by this definition, an economy is at full employment when 94 to 95 percent of those who want to work are employed.[7]

frictional unemployment
Unemployment due to workers being temporarily between jobs or new entrants to the work force.

structural unemployment
Unemployment due to a mismatch between the skills or locations of unemployed workers and those of available jobs.

FRICTIONAL AND STRUCTURAL UNEMPLOYMENT. It is not possible to have a situation where everyone is always employed. Some unemployment is normal because there are new entrants into the labor force searching for jobs. Finding a job takes time. During that time, a person will be unemployed. Other workers are between jobs. They have quit one job to look for a better one, are recovering from an illness, or have moved with their families to a different part of the country. Such short-term unemployment is called **frictional unemployment**.

Another normal source of unemployment is a mismatch of workers and jobs. There may be a surplus of teachers and a need for pipefitters. There may be excess labor in Montana and a shortage of workers in Virginia. Whenever the available workers do not match the jobs in terms of skills or location, there is **structural unemployment**. This kind of unemployment tends to last longer than frictional unemployment because it takes longer for workers to retrain or relocate to match available jobs. When plants

---

7.   Still another way to define full employment is that the number of job seekers should be about equal to the number of vacancies.

close, either permanently or because the firm is moving production to another place, the result is usually some structural unemployment.[8]

Some economists argue that both frictional and structural unemployment are higher than necessary because government "subsidizes" unemployment. Workers take longer to search for a job when they can collect unemployment compensation and other benefits. That's not necessarily undesirable. They may wind up with more suitable jobs, in which they can earn more and be more productive. It does, however, raise the measured rate of unemployment, and the cost of the search falls on taxpayers.[9]

Frictional unemployment calls for better information and employment services. Structural unemployment may call for retraining and assistance in relocating. Since these policies try to make specific segments of the labor market work more efficiently, they are really closer to being microeconomic than macroeconomic.

CYCLICAL UNEMPLOYMENT. Some unemployment is related to declines in the level of aggregate output. This **cyclical unemployment** is a major policy concern in macroeconomics. Workers are laid off because of a fall in demand generally or specifically for the products they produce. Cyclical unemployment tends to be most severe in heavy industry (manufacturing equipment and some consumer goods such as cars and refrigerators). Macroeconomic policies intended to reduce cyclical employment try to create more jobs by increasing demand for total output.

cyclical unemployment
Unemployment caused by a decline in the level of total output.

Unemployment rates since 1929 are shown in Figure 6. Note the extremely low rate of unemployment during World War II and the gradual rise in unemployment during the late 1970s and early 1980s. This period was followed by a gradual decline in unemployment to the end of that decade. Unemployment rates began to rise slowly again in late 1990, as the United States entered a recession.

COSTS OF UNEMPLOYMENT. Why are macroeconomic policy makers concerned about the level of unemployment? First, unemployment is wasteful. If unemployment exists, the economy is not operating on the production possibilities curve. Unemployed labor should be producing goods and services. Although other resources can also be unemployed, policy makers and people in general are usually more concerned about unemployed labor than unemployed capital or land.

The second reason for concern about unemployment is that the system of income distribution in a market economy is very dependent on employment. If people don't have jobs, they earn no income. Employed

8. The Bureau of Labor Statistics studied the experiences of workers displaced by plant closings during the recessions in 1980 and 1981–1982. The study found that 60 percent were working again by 1984 although many were receiving lower wages.
9. These same economists would argue that some structural unemployment is caused by the minimum wage, which eliminates entry-level jobs worth less than that wage. Lack of job openings at the entry level keeps unskilled workers from acquiring the skills and experience to move up the employment ladder. In the period 1967–1981, the minimum wage more than tripled in dollar terms (from $1.00 to $3.35). However, the minimum wage was not increased from 1981 until 1990, when it was raised to $3.80, with further increases in 1991 and 1992. During this period, the value of the minimum wage in real terms (adjusted for inflation) fell by about 36 percent. Thus, the minimum wage has probably had little if any impact on employment in the 1980s.

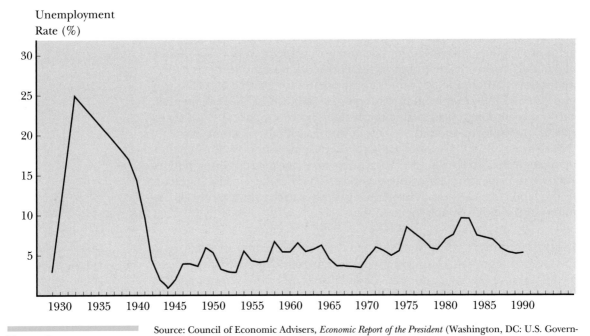

Unemployment
Rate (%)

Source: Council of Economic Advisers, *Economic Report of the President* (Washington, DC: U.S. Government Printing Office, various issues).

FIGURE 6
U.S. UNEMPLOYMENT
RATES AS A PERCENTAGE O
THE CIVILIAN LABOR
FORCE, 1929–1990
Unemployment rates
soared between 1929
and 1933. Unemploy-
ment remained high unti
World War II, when war
production required
almost complete employ-
ment of the civilian labor
force. A gradual upward
trend in unemployment
rates can be observed,
with peaks in the re-
cessions of 1959–1960,
1970, 1975, and
1980–1982.

productivity
A measure of economic
performance that shows
changes in output per
worker hour from one
year to the next.

persons wind up supporting unemployed persons through unemployment benefits, food stamps, and other social welfare programs.

Finally, unemployment is both psychologically demoralizing and
harmful to future earnings. Each period of unemployment is a lost opportunity to develop skills and experience that will make a worker more
valuable to an employer. That is, unemployment means less investment in
human capital.

PRODUCTIVITY AND MACROECONOMIC GOALS

There is one other macroeconomic variable that plays an important role in
determining changes in output, employment, and the price level. This variable is productivity. The other three variables are goals, but productivity is
a means to a goal. **Productivity** is a measure of economic performance that
shows changes in output per worker hour from one year to the next.

The productivity index for the United States is shown in Figure 7. The
growth of productivity was very high in the early postwar period. It had
slowed considerably by the 1970s and remained low into the early 1980s.
When productivity improves rapidly, there tends to be rapid economic
growth, high employment, and low inflation. When productivity grows
more slowly or not at all, there is usually slow growth, high unemployment, and higher inflation. Thus, productivity plays a key role in achieving the three major economic goals.

Much effort was devoted to trying to explain the slowdown in the
growth of productivity in recent decades and to suggest ways to improve
productivity. Inexperienced or poorly trained workers, low savings rates,

Percent

FIGURE 7
PRODUCTIVITY INDEX, 1948–1990
The index of productivity per worker hour in the private sector increased at an average rate of just under 2 percent a year, doubling in the last 40 years. The growth rates were rapid in the 1950s and 1960s, slowed down in the 1970s, and picked up slightly in the 1980s.

Source: U.S. Department of Commerce, *Business Statistics* (Washington, DC: U.S. Government Printing Office, various issues).

and not enough investment in developing new products and technology were all cited as possible causes. Some of the approaches suggested included adopting Japanese management techniques and encouraging more investment in human and physical capital. Certainly, better human capital, more physical capital, and improvements in technology are all key elements in productivity. Other economists, however, have suggested that the high rates of increase in productivity of the early postwar period were not typical and that current rates are more nearly normal.

Productivity is important because it is a major source of growth in per capita income and also a major source of wage increases not due to inflation. In order to earn more, a worker must add more to a firm's revenues. More output per hour is the key to a higher standard of living. In the last fifteen years, most increases in real household income in the United States have come from having more workers per household rather than higher real earnings per worker.

FLUCTUATIONS IN OUTPUT, EMPLOYMENT, AND PRICES

What happens when we put output, employment, and prices together? Figure 8 shows the inflation rate, the unemployment rate, and the growth rate of real output in a single diagram. As you can see, the unemployment rate and growth of output track each other quite closely, though in opposite directions. The inflation rate is less consistently related to the other two. Until the 1970s, inflation rates in the United States tended to be low when growth was slow and unemployment was high. Higher inflation rates went with rapid growth and low unemployment rates. In the 1970s, however, the U.S. economy experienced slow growth, high unemployment, and high inflation all at once. The mid-1980s saw stable growth with both unemployment and inflation rates lower than before.

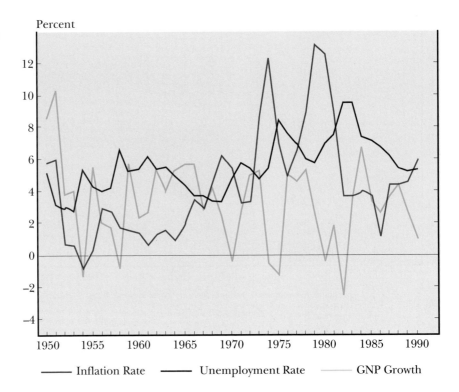

FIGURE 8
GROWTH, UNEMPLOYMENT, AND INFLATION, 1950–1990
Combining the three major macroeconomic variables in a single graph shows some pattern of their moving together. Economic growth and unemployment, in particular, move rather consistently in opposite directions. The link between these two variables and inflation is stronger in earlier periods but quite weak in the last two decades.

stabilization policy
Government actions designed to smooth out sharp changes in output, employment, and the price level.

business cycle
An observed and repeated pattern of ups and downs in real output, employment, and prices.

peak
A high point in a business cycle, where output turns downward.

recession
A state of an economy marked by a decline in real output for two or more successive quarters.

Over the course of a longer period, the major macroeconomic variables tend to move together in a rather predictable fashion, although not always in the "right" direction. When there is slow growth or even falling output, rising unemployment, and/or high inflation rates, the government often intervenes to try to "correct" the course of these variables. **Stabilization policy** consists of those actions of government designed to smooth out ups and downs in output, employment, and prices.

BUSINESS CYCLES
An observed and repeated pattern of ups and downs in output, employment, and prices was named the **business cycle** in the nineteenth century. A simplified business cycle is shown in Figure 9. In the expansionary phase of the cycle (from upturn through peak), output increases, prices rise rapidly, and unemployment falls. Productivity tends to increase as the economy emerges from the trough of a recession. Firms have kept some workers on during the recession but have not used them fully. As sales increase, firms employ these workers more fully, and productivity rises. As expansion continues, new and less experienced workers are hired. Then the increase in both productivity and output starts to slow, although employment continues to rise.

RECESSIONS, TROUGHS, EXPANSIONS, AND PEAKS. As output reaches a high point, or **peak**, and turns down, prices tend to fall also, or at least to rise at a slower rate. The downturn of output is called a **recession**. The Com-

Level of Economic Activity
(Real GNP)

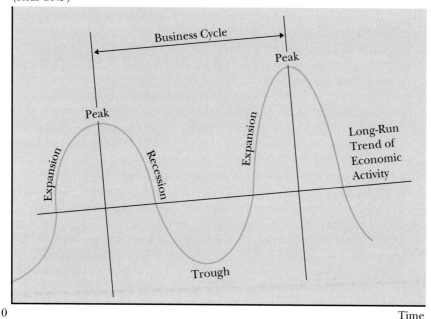

FIGURE 9
THE BUSINESS CYCLE
This typical business
cycle shows changes in
the level of economic
activity over time. In
this case, the peaks and
troughs are equal in
magnitude, and the
upturn and downturn
take the same length of
time. Actual cycles may
be less symmetric, with
upturns greater or
smaller than downturns
in size or duration. The
cycle is measured from
peak to peak. The trend
line is the underlying
growth rate of output.

merce Department's rule is that the economy is in a recession when output (adjusted for price changes) declines for two or more successive quarters. Unemployment increases and income and output fall, until the lower turning point, or **trough**, when output reaches its lowest level. Then the process starts over again. The upturn from trough to peak is an **expansion**. A complete cycle goes from peak to peak.

Each successive peak (and trough) should occur at a higher level of output because the business cycle is a fluctuation around a trend line of growing output over time. For example, a six-year business cycle with a trend growth rate of output of 2 percent a year should see a final peak of output that is 12 to 13 percent above the previous peak.

trough
A low point in a business cycle, where output turns upward.

expansion
A period of economic growth extending from a trough to the next peak in a business cycle.

EARLY BUSINESS CYCLE THEORIES. Much of the early measurement work in macroeconomics was related to the study of business cycles. Researchers identified recurring patterns of upturns and downturns at intervals of eight years (the general business cycle) and twenty years (linked to activity in building construction). In the nineteenth century, macroeconomics meant describing and attempting to explain these business cycles.

These observed ups and downs in economic activity were explained in some rather creative ways. One of these explanations was the sunspot theory, developed by English economist William Stanley Jevons. Unusually severe radioactive storms on the surface of the sun, known as sunspots, seemed to be closely linked to business cycles. This link may sound like a perfect example of the association-causation fallacy discussed in Chapter 1, but there was some plausible reasoning behind it. Sunspots do affect weather patterns on earth, and the agricultural sector (then the largest single sector of the economy) has always been highly dependent on the weather. However, even with the declining relative importance of agriculture, business cycles have continued to be observed. Sunspots may have contributed to early business cycles, but they do not appear to be the driving force in this century.

Another contributor to the mystique of business cycles was a Russian economist, Nikolai Kondratieff. Other observers noted regular cycles of eight to ten years, with shorter cycles of two to three years and longer cycles of about twenty years. Kondratieff found even longer periods of expansion and contraction of about fifty years. These cycles are called Kondratieff cycles, or long waves. Some observers argue that both the regular eight-year cycle and the long-wave cycle turned down at the end of the 1920s, contributing to the severity of the Great Depression.

It has been suggested that the fifty-year cycles are related to the development of entire new industries and complexes of industries—for example, the development of automobiles, radio and motion pictures, and household appliances in the first few decades of this century. If Kondratieff was right, another downturn in the fifty-year cycle was due in the late 1970s. However, a depression did not occur, although there was slow growth and high unemployment during that period.

Most nineteenth-century economists focused their attention on the shorter eight- to ten-year cycle and the twenty-year cycle. They looked to patterns of consumption and investment for their explanations.

U.S. ECONOMIC FLUCTUATIONS SINCE THE CIVIL WAR

Some recent business cycles in the United States can be identified in Figure 8. There was a trough in 1953–1954 and another in 1957–1958. There were particularly severe downturns in 1974–1975 and 1980–1982. The data in this figure, however, are too recent to include the most famous downturn of the twentieth century: the Great Depression, which occurred from 1929 to 1937.

depression
A very severe recession.

The U.S. economy experienced twenty-seven recessions between the end of the Civil War and 1990. On the average, a recession has occurred in the United States every 4½ years. The 1929–1933 recession was so severe it was given a special name: depression. A **depression** is a very severe recession. President Harry Truman once said that when your neighbor is out of work, that's a recession; but when you lose your job, that's a depression. In a depression, people suffer unemployment, inability to get credit, and losses of their homes, farms, savings, and businesses.

bimetallism
The use of both gold and silver as parts of the money stock.

There were upturns and downturns in real output and employment in the nineteenth century. However, the variable for which the best data is available for that period is the price level. From the end of the Civil War in 1865 until the early 1900s, wholesale prices in the United States showed a downward trend. You might think that falling prices would have been greeted with enthusiasm. This, however, was not the view of most farmers, who were in debt for equipment, seed, livestock, and land. The payments on these debts were fixed in dollars, but the prices for farm products were falling. Falling prices made it difficult for farmers to meet the payments. This problem explains why people in the western areas of the United States were enthusiastic about **bimetallism** at the end of the nineteenth

The Great Depression of the 1930s was not an American event but a worldwide event. The triggering event for the United States was the stock market crash of Black Friday, October 29, 1929. For Europeans, it was the collapse of the Kredit Anstalt Bank in Austria in 1930, a major bank. Other banks failed in its wake.

Two important conditions in the early 1930s made the Depression spread from country to country. One of these conditions was the remnants of the international gold standard, battered by World War I but still in effect. The gold standard linked the banking systems of many countries and limited the power of national banking systems to expand their money supply unless they had enough gold backing for any added currency. Nations that lost gold to foreigners were forced to contract their money supplies at a time when expansion of the money supply would have been a more suitable policy. As the Depression deepened, one country after another abandoned the gold standard, usually only after the domestic money supply had shrunk to a much smaller size.

The second condition was protectionism. Many countries, including the United States, reacted to falling output and rising unemployment by trying to "keep jobs at home." They tried to substitute domestic production for imported goods by imposing high tariffs and other restrictions—a policy known as "beggar thy neighbor." Some economists even argue that protectionism caused the Great Depression. Most economists would agree that it made the Depression even more severe. The physical volume of trade fell by one-third in the early years of the Depression. Because of falling prices, the value of trade fell by two-thirds.

INTERNATIONAL

PERSPECTIVE

THE GREAT

DEPRESSION IN

EUROPE AND

CANADA

The Depression's effects in each country can be measured by what happened to output and unemployment during the worst period, 1929–1932. Partly because of their great prosperity in the 1920s, the United States and Canada experienced the largest declines in total output, measured in current dollars. The market value of output fell 25 percent in Canada and 26 percent in the United States in that worst period. Part of the decline was in real output and part was due to falling prices. In Europe, where the 1920s had not been as prosperous, declines in the market value of output were less drastic but still striking: 12 percent in France, 16 percent in Germany, and 10 percent in Sweden. (The United Kingdom, coming off a bad decade in the 1920s, actually saw a slight rise in output of about 2 percent from 1929 to 1932.) The unemployment statistics were even grimmer. The table below shows the unemployment rates for 1929 and 1932.

The political effects of the Great Depression were far-reaching. In the United States, it spawned Social Security, unemployment compensation, welfare programs, bank regulation, and other government programs. The role of government was thus greatly expanded. In Germany and Italy, the frustrations of the Great Depression led to the rise of fascist governments under Hitler and Mussolini. Canada and many Western European nations followed the same path as the United States in building a social safety net for those who lost their source of income. Most Western European governments, however, went much further, creating welfare states that provided health care, public housing, income support programs, and similar services.

UNEMPLOYMENT RATES FOR 1929 AND 1932

YEAR	GERMANY	SWEDEN	UNITED KINGDOM	CANADA	UNITED STATES
1929	5.9%	2.4%	5.9%	2.9%	3.1%
1932	17.2%	6.8%	13.1%	17.6%	23.5%

century. This policy would have expanded the U.S. money stock by making silver serve as money along with gold.[10] Farmers hoped that this increase in the money supply would raise prices or at least help curtail falling prices. Bimetallism was not adopted, although it was an important issue in the 1896 presidential campaign. The Democratic candidate for President, William Jennings Bryan, made an electrifying speech against the gold standard and in favor of bimetallism. His theme was "You shall not crucify mankind upon a cross of gold!" and it nearly won him the election.

Price levels rose sharply during World War I, so sharply that efforts were made to measure the effects of inflation on the purchasing power of wages for shipbuilders and other war workers. The outcome of this measurement effort was the first consumer price index. After World War I, prices dropped sharply from the high levels reached in wartime. This fall was accompanied by a sharp contraction in industrial production during the postwar recession of the early 1920s. (Reliable measures of real output and changes in real output began to be available only early in the twentieth century. Growth of real output is the single best measure of the ups and downs in economic activity.)

After a relatively prosperous and mildly inflationary period for the rest of the 1920s, there was a sharp and prolonged fall in prices, output, and employment between 1929 and 1933. This downturn marked the beginning of the Great Depression. It occurred not only in the United States but in many other countries as well. Wholesale prices fell by about one-third between 1929 and 1933. As production in the United States began to recover after 1933, prices also began to rise. Then there was a sharp setback in output, employment, and prices in 1937–1938.

With the outbreak of World War II, prices began a sharp rise, both output and employment rose dramatically, and unemployment almost disappeared. The United States experienced more minor ups and downs in the late 1940s and 1950s, followed by a period of fairly steady growth from 1961 to 1968. The ups and downs resumed with the recession of 1969–1970. There was a severe downturn in 1973–1975 and another in 1980–1982.

In the years since World War II, the most significant change from the prewar period is that declining real output has been much less likely to be accompanied by a fall in prices. When prices have declined, they have not fallen nearly as much as in periods before World War II. A decline in economic activity that is not accompanied by a fall in the price level is referred to as **stagflation**. A combination of the words *stagnation* and *inflation*, this term means that the economy is stagnant (not growing), but there is also inflation at the same time. In the 1974–1975 recession, prices continued to rise sharply. Not until the relatively severe 1980–1982 recession did the rate of inflation fall sharply. Inflation rates remained low through the late 1980s.

stagflation
An economic condition of slow growth, high unemployment, and inflation.

A CASE STUDY IN BUSINESS CYCLES: THE GREAT DEPRESSION
The Great Depression brought severe economic hardships to a large portion of the U.S. population. Real output fell by more than one-third. Un-

---

10. The bimetallic standard was used in the United States from the early 1800s until 1878. Then it was abandoned and replaced by the gold standard.

employment rose to almost 25 percent of the work force in the depths of the Depression. People who had jobs were worried they would lose them. Many jobs were converted to a part-time basis in order to spread the work among more people. In addition, banks were failing. Between 1929 and 1933, the number of commercial banks in the United States fell by one-third. More than a fifth of all surviving banks had to suspend operations for some time because of financial problems. Few depositors ever recovered any of the funds they lost.

The effect on people went beyond economic hardships. America seemed to have lost its bright promise. People who had worked hard all their lives, who had saved and planned for the future, and who had believed in the work ethic found themselves wiped out. They lost homes, businesses, and jobs—through no fault of their own. Retired people found their stocks and bonds nearly worthless, and their savings vanished in bank failures. Many people's self-images and status depend on their jobs, on their success in the workday world, and on their ability to provide for their families. The Depression sowed doubt and fear among those who lost their jobs and those in danger of losing theirs. In his first inaugural address, President Franklin D. Roosevelt said, "The only thing we have to fear is fear itself." He was talking about the social, spiritual, and moral crisis in America as well as the economic problems.

The suffering during the Depression was not eased by programs available today, such as unemployment insurance, welfare, Social Security, and food stamps. These programs were in large part inspired by the experiences of the Depression. In 1933, people out of work had to rely mainly on private charity and relief from state and local governments, which were facing hard times themselves. Many city governments were unable to pay their bills because property owners had defaulted on local property taxes. Thus, local governments were in no position to help their residents. In addition, many people were reluctant to accept help either from private charities or from the government.

Economic conditions were no better abroad. The Depression affected every European country. Banks failed, and the European financial system was badly shaken. The United States and European countries raised tariffs and took other antitrade measures in an effort to create jobs by substituting domestic production for imported goods. Trade fell drastically. (The consequences of this policy will be discussed in detail in the chapter on international trade.)

The Roosevelt administration tried to deal with both the immediate emergency and the long-term issues. People had to be put back to work and, in the meantime, had to be given help. To put people back to work, Roosevelt and his advisers experimented with emergency government hiring programs. This policy was one of the early instances of the proposal that government should be the employer of last resort for people who can't find jobs elsewhere.

Beyond the emergency needs, the Roosevelt administration felt that policies had to be adopted to ensure that the Great Depression would never happen again. There should be programs to aid people in hard times as a matter of "right," so they didn't have to feel ashamed. The safety net of social welfare programs, such as Old Age and Survivors Insurance

(Social Security), Aid to Families with Dependent Children, and unemployment compensation, was created during this period. In addition, deposit insurance and other banking regulations were put in place during the Great Depression to safeguard people's savings.

Within the field of economics, the Depression and the resulting policies of the Roosevelt administration set the stage for importing the new ideas of the Keynesian revolution from England. The impact of the Great Depression on policy, programs, and economic thinking far outlasted the soup kitchens and federal relief agencies it spawned.

The misery and fear of the Depression led to political changes in many countries. In January 1933, Adolf Hitler became Chancellor of Germany, a country having severe economic problems. The Depression is also credited with helping Mussolini rise to power in Italy. In the United States, unhappy voters rejected Herbert Hoover in the 1932 election in favor of Franklin Roosevelt. The Socialist candidate, Norman Thomas, received almost 900,000 votes in that election. The Communist candidate received more than 100,000 votes.

Despite his campaign promise to balance the federal budget, Roosevelt was a pragmatic politician, willing to try various tactics to solve the pressing economic problems. One such scheme was to put people back to work by employing them on government projects such as constructing dams and public buildings, sewers and streets. Naturally, the jobless who found work on these projects were pleased. Not only were they making money, but they had also regained the dignity of having worthwhile work and providing for their families. There seemed to be no harm and much good in such projects. Jobless workers were once again providing things people could use. One of the most disturbing aspects of the Depression was the terrible paradox that many people were living in great need of goods and services while many workers couldn't get jobs to produce those things. There were, however, some abuses of these "make work" projects. A standard joke told of the government's hiring some workers to dig ditches and other workers to fill them in again. There were stories of public workers spending their days in parks, leaning on rakes or shovels. On balance, however, the majority of the American public supported such schemes to move the country out of the Depression.

By the presidential election of 1936, the country was hardly back to normal, as the unemployment rates in Figure 6 show. But in a definite sign of approval of Roosevelt's policies, the people re-elected him overwhelmingly. He carried every state except Maine and Vermont.

STABILIZATION POLICY AND THE GREAT DEPRESSION
The Depression influenced the direction of future macroeconomic policy because it was so severe that it brought many new programs and experimental policies into being as part of an effort to "do something." Roosevelt and his advisers developed their plans for government spending and government jobs to reduce unemployment during the Depression on an *ad hoc* basis, with little theory behind them. Economists had already begun to provide theoretical reasons for such approaches. Swedish economists such as Erik Lindahl and Gunnar Myrdal, members of the Stockholm School, had proposed in the late 1920s and early 1930s that

governments abandon the goal of balancing the budget annually.[11] Instead, they argued, the budget should be balanced over the course of the business cycle. According to the Stockholm School, when output is falling and unemployment is rising, government should spend more to put people back to work, even if this produces a government deficit. In boom times, the government could run a surplus by cutting back on its projects. This surplus would cool off the boom while paying off the money borrowed during the deficit years. Only over the entire course of a business cycle, then, would the government budget be balanced. This kind of government stabilization policy is called countercyclical policy. **Countercyclical policy** is any set of government actions intended to offset the cyclical ups and downs of the macro economy.

countercyclical policy
Government actions designed to offset the cyclical ups and downs of the macro economy.

Much more influential than the Stockholm School was a book that came out in 1936, the year of Roosevelt's re-election. That book was *The General Theory of Employment, Interest, and Money*, by British economist John Maynard Keynes. At that time, the Depression in the United States still had five more years to run before it would end as the country entered World War II. Recovery from the Depression was already progressing in Great Britain and in some other countries, including Germany. Keynes, his theories, and his followers did not really have much influence on either the British or the American recovery. However, the Depression convinced many people that Keynesian theory was right and that it provided sound guidelines for economic policy making. Not until the 1970s were there serious challenges to Keynesian ideas about macroeconomic policy.

The Great Depression was a painful and difficult experience for almost all Americans. It forced economists and politicians to think more carefully about macroeconomics and economic policy. The Depression set the stage for Keynes's ideas to challenge the theories and models economists had been working with. In order to test these new ideas, it was necessary to have better measures of output, employment, prices, and other variables than had been developed in the past. Beginning in the 1930s, economists devoted much more attention to measuring economic aggregates in order to have the information needed to carry out a countercyclical policy. The next chapter will address the measurement of these economic aggregates.

SUMMARY

1. The circular flow model represents the aggregate level of economic activity. Adding a credit market, the government, and a foreign sector provides a more realistic picture of the workings of the macro economy.
2. The major macroeconomic goals are economic growth, price stability, and full employment.
3. Economic growth is measured by changes in real output (or sometimes industrial production). Economic growth of about 4 percent a year is generally regarded as feasible and desirable because it raises the standard of

11. Myrdal was awarded the Nobel Prize in economics in 1974. His early work in macroeconomics was noted as well as his later work in sociology and development economics.

living and reduces unemployment. However, economic growth creates some costs in terms of environmental quality and strains on the infrastructure.

4. Price stability is measured by the inflation rate, or changes in the Consumer Price Index (CPI). Unstable prices are usually rising prices. A sustained general rise in the price level is inflation. Inflation causes a redistribution of income and wealth, confuses market signals, discourages saving and investment, and creates menu costs.

5. Full employment is usually reached when about 94 to 95 percent of the labor force is employed. That is, there is an unemployment rate of about 5 to 6 percent. Normal unemployment is partly frictional (due to new entrants in the job market or workers between jobs) and partly structural (due to a mismatch between workers and job openings). Unemployment in excess of a normal level is usually due to declines in real output. This kind of unemployment is called cyclical unemployment and is a macroeconomic policy concern.

6. Productivity is a measure of output per worker and is important for sustained economic growth.

7. Business cycles describe the ups and downs of output, employment, and prices.

8. The most significant macroeconomic event in the twentieth century was the Great Depression. It not only had important economic and political effects but also led to many changes in macroeconomic theory and policy.

NEW TERMS

saving	balance on goods and	frictional unemployment	trough
investment	services	structural unemploy-	expansion
credit market	economic growth	ment	depression
leakages	infrastructure	cyclical unemployment	bimetallism
injections	inflation	productivity	stagflation
deficit	price index	stabilization policy	countercyclical policy
surplus	Consumer Price Index	business cycle	
imports	(CPI)	peak	
exports	full employment	recession	

QUESTIONS FOR DISCUSSION

1. What are the costs and benefits of rapid economic growth?

2. Can you think of any benefits of having high rates of inflation? Of having high rates of unemployment?

3. Using the figures in this chapter, see if you can trace the relationship between changes in output and consumer prices, unemployment, and productivity for each of the following years, all of which showed signs of a recession: 1955, 1958, 1961, 1970, 1974–1975, 1980, 1982.

4. Why is productivity important? How is it likely to be affected by a large increase of new entrants into the labor force? By improvements in technology? By investment in new and better equipment? Why was there a connection among all of these in the 1970s in the United States?

5. How do you think interest rates would be affected if inflation occurred that took everyone by surprise? How would the effect be different if the inflation were expected?

6. What kinds of changes will increase the size of the circular flow? What kinds of changes will decrease the flow?

7. What is a leakage? What is an injection? Identify three kinds of leakages and three kinds of injections.

8. Which of the following are structurally unemployed, frictionally unemployed, or cyclically unemployed?

   a. a new college graduate seeking a first job

   b. a teenager who quit a fast-food job because she didn't like the hours

   c. farmers in Iowa who had to sell their farms because of inadequate demand for farm products and who are looking for a different line of work in a different area

   d. a person with a Ph.D. in classical languages, a field in which there are a hundred applicants for every available teaching position

   e. a person laid off because of a recession

9. How will each of the following affect the flow of real output in the circular flow diagram?

   a. an improvement in technology

   b. a decline in business investment

   c. an increase in taxes, with no increase in government spending as the government attempts to balance its budget

   d. an increase in exports

   e. a rise in the price level

10. Suppose there is a decline in real output. What

would you expect to happen to employment and to the inflation rate? Why?

11. Use the given data to calculate each rate of change.

a. Year 1, output index = 100; year 2, output index = 110. What is the rate of growth of output from year 1 to year 2?

b. Year 1, price index = 140; year 2, price index = 155. What is the inflation rate between year 1 and year 2?

c. Year 1, productivity index = 25; year 2, productivity index = 27. What is the rate of growth of productivity from year 1 to year 2?

12. Suggest three ways in which the Great Depression affected economic policy in the United States.

13. Why is it unlikely that a rate of economic growth in excess of 3 or 4 percent can be sustained for a long period?

14. Why were farmers in favor of expanding the U.S. money supply in the late nineteenth century?

15. How can you tell when an economy is in a recession?

16. Try constructing an index of your own, using the following data. Suppose that 40% of the cost of car repairs is labor, 50% is parts, and 10% is miscellaneous. Suppose that in the first year the cost of labor is $12 an hour, parts cost an average of $15 each, and miscellaneous costs run about $5. In the second year, labor rises to $15, parts average $20, and miscellaneous costs are unchanged. What is your "price index" for car repairs? By how much has the cost risen?

Suggestions for Further Reading

Barber, William J. *From New Era to New Deal: Herbert Hoover, the Economists, and American Social Policy.* London: Cambridge University Press, 1985. Examines attempts to stem the flood of decline in the Hoover years before Roosevelt's New Deal.

Bird, Caroline. *The Invisible Scar: The Great Depression and What It Did to American Life, From Then Until Now.* New York: Longman, 1966. A lively account of the aftereffects of the Great Depression.

Galbraith, John K. *The Great Crash of Nineteen Twenty-Nine.* Boston: Houghton Mifflin, 1979. A classic and well-written account of the events leading up to the Great Depression.

Hibbs, Douglas A., Jr. *The American Political Economy: Macroeconomics and Electoral Politics.* Cambridge, MA: Harvard University Press, 1987. Chapters 2 and 3 of this very readable blend of history, economics and politics offer a thorough discussion of the costs of unemployment and inflation.

Hughes, James J., and Richard Perlman. *The Economics of Unemployment: A Comparative Analysis of Britain and the United States.* London: Cambridge University Press, 1984. A nontechnical discussion of how unemployment is measured in both countries, why it is different, which groups are unemployed, and other unemployment issues.

James, Harold. *The German Slump: Politics and Economics 1924–1936.* Cambridge, England: Cambridge University Press, 1987. A look at the experience of the Great Depression from the perspective of the German economy.

1. Distinguish between stocks and flows and between income statements and balance sheets.
2. Explain the purposes and uses of national income accounting.
3. Describe how gross national product (GNP), net national product (NNP), national income (NI), and personal income (PI) are computed.
4. Explain the relation between the national income accounts and the circular flow model.
5. Explain why actual saving and investment must always be equal in the national income accounts.
6. Describe the drawbacks of the GNP as a measure of economic well-being.
7. Compute a simple price index.
8. Identify the major price indices and explain how each is used.
9. Describe the process by which unemployment figures are calculated.

CHAPTER 5

MEASURING ECONOMIC PERFORMANCE AND NATIONAL INCOME ACCOUNTING

INTRODUCTION

Chapter 4 introduced the basic macroeconomic goals of economic growth, full employment, and price stability. In order to determine how well an economy is doing in terms of those goals, economists have to be able to measure output, employment, and the price level. Measurement of macroeconomic variables is the subject of this chapter. All nations make some effort to track the behavior of output, employment, and prices. In the United States, measurement of output, known as national income accounting, is the responsibility of the Department of Commerce. The Department of Labor collects and reports data on employment and price level.

BASIC ACCOUNTING CONCEPTS

Two basic kinds of accounting statements are used in economics as well as in all business fields. These statements are balance sheets and income statements. In accounting, balance sheets measure stocks of assets and liabilities at a point in time. Income statements record flows of income and expenditure over time. National income accounts take the form of an income statement.

STOCKS AND FLOWS

Economists find it useful to distinguish between stock variables and flow variables. Stock variables appear on balance sheets, and flow variables appear on income statements. A **stock variable** is a variable that is defined at a point in time, such as December 31, 1991. Stocks are existing quantities of goods or assets. An example of a stock variable is the number of apartment units that exist today. Notice the date on this stock—today. A year from today, there will be more or fewer units, depending on how many new apartments are built and how many old ones are torn down.

A **flow variable** is a variable that is defined over a period of time, such as

stock variable
A variable that is defined at a point in time.

flow variable
A variable that is defined over a period of time.

125

the year 1991. Flows measure changes in quantities over time. The number of new apartments built from January 1 to December 31 of this year is a flow variable. That is, a flow is something measured over a period of time. The length of the period—hour, day, month, quarter, year, or decade—must be specified in order for the size of the flow to have any useful meaning.

What is the right interval to use in measuring a flow? It depends on the question being asked, the nature of the flow, and how expensive it is to collect information. The U.S. Census measures flows of population through births, deaths, and migration at ten-year intervals. This information is used in many kinds of economic research as well as for its original purpose, redistricting for the House of Representatives. A speculator in the wheat market, however, requires daily information on crop prospects. The operator of a nuclear reactor wants very frequent readings on the core's temperature.

In your city, new houses are built every year, and some old ones are torn down. The number of new houses built this year minus the number destroyed is the *net* flow of houses. That is, the total number of new houses built is the *gross* flow. Subtracting the number torn down gives the net flow. Even if new houses are being built, a major flood or fire could destroy more than are being created, making the net flow negative.

The flow affects the stock. Suppose there is a stock of 1,000 houses on January 1 in Townville. Also suppose that 300 new houses are built in Townville this year. That is, the gross annual flow of new houses is 300. If 100 old houses are removed from use during the year, the net flow is 200. At the end of the year, the stock of houses in Townville is 1,200. There were 1,000, but 300 new ones were built and 100 old ones were destroyed. The change in the stock of housing is equal to the net flow of new housing.

Most of the reduction in the stock of housing is not due to tearing down or destruction of houses but to a decline in value as a result of depreciation. Any physical asset tends to decline in value over time as it wears out, needs more upkeep and repairs, or becomes obsolete as better alternatives are developed. The decline in the value of an asset is called **depreciation**. In Townville, the equivalent of 100 housing units were lost. This decline in the housing stock may have consisted of 100 houses torn down. It is more likely, however, to have been the result of wearing out, lack of maintenance, and other forms of depreciation that reduced the value of the existing stock by 10 percent. If there had been no new houses built, Townville's housing stock at the end of the year would have been 900. The gross flow of new housing resulted in a year-end stock of 1,200. The net flow is the gross flow minus depreciation. Thus, the year-end stock is the January 1 stock plus the net flow, or it is the January 1 stock minus depreciation plus the gross flow.

Like most economic information, the data on housing flows just provided is rather general. It does not provide a complete picture of the state of housing in that community for the year in question. Two important missing dimensions are size and quality. If the 300 new houses are all very small and the 100 houses destroyed were the largest in town, or if the 300 new houses all have less storage space or fewer bathrooms than the destroyed houses, the figure of a 200-house increase would be misleading as an indicator of better housing conditions. If we want to consider size and quality, the stock and flow of houses are reflected somewhat more accurately in dollar values. Suppose that 500 houses worth $2.5 million are lost

depreciation
The decline in the value of an asset, such as a machine or factory, over time.

cause it is difficult to assign it a dollar value. That asset is her human capital, or her skills and education. (Recall that human capital is a part of the factor of production labor, as discussed in Chapter 2.) Most of her liabilities are related to the cost of acquiring further human capital. Thus, if Katrina's future earnings are taken into account, her financial condition is somewhat better than her balance sheet suggests.

Individuals and firms use balance sheets regularly to assess where they stand. Nations use income statements to measure total output, but we rarely see balance sheets for countries as a whole. A balance sheet will be very useful in Chapter 12, however, in understanding money and the banking system. For now, let's turn to the nation's income statement, the Gross National Product account.

BASIC ACCOUNTING CONCEPTS

INCOME STATEMENTS	BALANCE SHEETS
• measure flows,	• measure stocks,
• add income and subtract expenditures,	• compare value of assets to value of liabilities,
• have net income as the "bottom line," and	• have net worth as the "bottom line," and
• identify additions to stocks of saving or assets.	• show year-to-year changes in wealth.

MEASURING GROSS NATIONAL PRODUCT

The most widely used measure of total income and output is the **gross national product (GNP)**. GNP is the total market value of all final products produced by domestically owned factors of a given country during a given time period, most commonly a year.[1] It measures the size of the spending flow in the upper half of the circular flow diagram. GNP can be computed either by adding the production of the various sectors of the economy or by adding up sales by category of buyers.

gross national product (GNP)
The total market value of all final goods and services produced by a nation's domestically owned factors of production during a given time period, usually a year.

GROSS NATIONAL PRODUCT BY PRODUCING SECTOR
Table 3 shows GNP by producing sector for the United States in 1990. The business sector's $4,620.3 billion consists of net sales of all business firms. These figures are obtained from sales figures reported in connection with state sales taxes, corporate income taxes, and reports to stockholders. National income accountants try to determine *net* sales, eliminating double counting by subtracting sales to other firms that use the goods in further production. All goods produced should be counted, but only once. The accounts are supposed to consist of only final goods or final sales, not any

---

1.   Many other countries report a closely related measure, Gross Domestic Product (GDP). GDP is the value of final goods produced within the country. GDP would include production within the United States using foreign resources (foreign-owned factories or foreign workers) but would exclude production by U.S. corporations or workers abroad. For the United States, the difference between the two figures is about 2 percent. For other countries, the difference can be substantial.

TABLE 3
U.S. GROSS NATIONAL
PRODUCT BY PRODUCING
SECTOR, 1990 (BILLIONS
OF DOLLARS)

Business sector		$4620.3
Government sector		579.4
Federal	$178.5	
State and local	400.9	
Household and nonprofit sector	——	224.8
Foreign sector (net imports)		38.6
Gross national product		$5,463.0

Source: Council of Economic Advisers, *Economic Report of the President* (Washington, DC: U.S. Government Printing Office, 1991).

final goods
Goods that will not be further processed or resold.

intermediate goods
Goods that will be further processed before final sale.

intermediate goods. **Final goods** are those that will not be further processed or resold. **Intermediate goods** are those that will be further processed into final goods. For example, flour sold to consumers in supermarkets is counted in the GNP but flour sold to bakers is not, because they use the flour to make bread. That sale of flour will be counted in the GNP as part of the value of bread produced.[2]

The output of the business sector reflects sales of final product, measured in dollars. Most U.S. output is produced by the business sector, as you would expect in a market economy. National income accountants get a large share of their data from various financial reports of the business sector, such as sales tax returns, income tax returns, and reports by corporations to their stockholders.

Governments—federal, state, and local—also produce services such as public education, police protection, and national defense. Data for the public sector is easy to find, because all governments must report to their citizens each year how much money was received and how it was spent. Although the data is easy to come by, the market value of government output is difficult to measure because these services are not sold. Since government agencies hire employees to produce these services, national income accounts measure the value of government output by the compensation paid to employees. The services may actually be worth more or less than this amount. In the absence of a market price, however, labor cost is the only available measure of the value of government output.

A relatively small part of the GNP is produced in the household and nonprofit sector and by the foreign sector. The household and nonprofit sector accounts for the value of goods and services produced by nonprofit, nongovernmental agencies, such as private schools, museums, charitable organizations, and social clubs, as well as some small in-home businesses, such as family day care. This data is assembled primarily from income tax returns and other sources.

The foreign sector consists of producers who buy from and sell to

2.　Another way of computing GNP is the value-added approach. With this method, each product or service is counted when it is sold, regardless of whether the sale is final. However, the cost of goods and services that went into its production is subtracted. For example, if a baker buys flour, the flour is counted when it is sold to the baker. The bread that the baker sells is also counted, but the value of the baker's purchases of flour is subtracted. The difference between the value of goods and services purchased and the value of goods and services sold is the value added. This method should give the same result as adding final goods and services.

other countries. This data is easy to collect because exports and imports pass through a limited number of points of entry and exit, where they are checked by customs officials.

GROSS NATIONAL PRODUCT BY BUYING SECTOR

The upper half of the circular flow diagram accounts for GNP as spending by buying sectors. A basic assumption behind the national income accounts is that everything that is produced is also sold. If the business sector produces goods that are not sold, these goods must be added to inventories. The changes in these inventories are counted as "sales" of output to the business sector. **Business inventories** are stocks of goods held by firms from which they can make sales to meet demand.

business inventories
Stocks of goods held by firms from which they can make sales to meet demand.

Table 4 shows how U.S. GNP for 1990 was divided among the four groups of buyers to which it could be sold: households, business firms, government, and the foreign sector. These four groups correspond to the four actors in the circular flow model. This second (and more widely used) way of accounting for output also provides a cross check on the data collected for the producing sector.

consumption expenditures
Sales to the household sector.

THE HOUSEHOLD SECTOR. Sales to the household sector are called **consumption expenditures**. Since consumer purchases are final sales, they are all counted as part of GNP. Consumption expenditures in turn can be divided into various categories, which are useful because each one responds a little differently to changes in economic conditions. **Consumer durables** are such long-lasting items as refrigerators and washing machines. **Consumer nondurables** are items that have a very short useful life, such as a loaf of bread or a shirt. **Consumer services** are that part of household consumption composed of nontangible activities. Examples of services

consumer durables
Goods that last, on average, a substantial length of time.

consumer nondurables
Goods that last, on average, only a short period of time.

consumer services
That part of household consumption composed of nontangible activities.

			PERCENTAGE OF GNP
GROSS NATIONAL PRODUCT		$5,463.0	100.0
Personal consumption expenditures		$3,658.1	67.0
Consumer durables	$ 481.6		8.8
Consumer nondurables	1,194.2		21.9
Consumer services	1,982.3		36.3
Gross private domestic investment		745.0	13.6
Fixed investment (plant and equipment)	$ 524.3		9.6
Residential construction	222.9		4.1
Change in inventories	–2.2		0.4
Government purchases of goods and services		1,098.0	20.1
Federal government	$ 424.2		7.8
State/local government	673.8		12.3
Net exports of goods and services		–38.0	–0.7
Exports	$ 670.4		12.3
Imports	–708.4		–13.0

TABLE 4
U.S. GROSS NATIONAL PRODUCT BY BUYING SECTOR, 1990 (BILLIONS OF DOLLARS)

Source: Council of Economic Advisers, *Economic Report of the President* (Washington, DC: U.S. Government Printing Office, 1991).

are haircuts, concerts, being waited on at a restaurant, or having a gardener tend your yard. Services form a large part of total personal consumption, as Table 4 indicates.

THE BUSINESS SECTOR. Purchases by the business sector of final output are called **gross private domestic investment**. Gross investment is measured before subtracting capital goods that have worn out or become so obsolete they aren't worth using. Thus, if the business sector buys 10,000 tractors during one year but has to scrap 1,000 old tractors that year, the net change in the number of tractors is 9,000. Gross investment, however, is still 10,000 tractors. Net investment is 9,000.

What about the words *private* and *domestic*? The word *private* means investment by business firms, rather than by the government. The word *domestic* means that the investment was made in the United States, not in another country. In national income accounting, *investment* means the purchase of some real, tangible asset, such as a machine, a factory, or a stock of inventories. To an economist, buying bonds and making deposits in banks are actually forms of lending. When business firms use borrowed funds to purchase new plants or equipment or expand their inventories, they are investing in the sense meant by economists and national income accountants.

The components of gross private domestic investment are given in Table 4. Most investment consists of **fixed investment**, which is new plants or equipment, such as factories, tractors, drill presses, and computers. A second major component of gross private domestic investment is residential construction. If you think of investment as something that will be used to provide goods and services in the future, the idea that housing should be classed as investment rather than consumption makes a great deal of sense. Houses last a long time and produce "shelter services" to consumers in the future. (Those shelter services are counted under consumption.) Furthermore, many housing units, especially apartments, are owned by firms and rented to households. These housing units are even more like other business investments. Even when individuals purchase houses for their own use, this transaction is more like a business investment than an ordinary consumer purchase of a final good. A housing purchase, like a business investment, is a large expenditure, usually of borrowed money, that will provide a stream of services in the future.

There is no market transaction between the owner and the occupant of an owner-occupied house, because they are the same person. To determine a dollar value for those shelter services that owners "purchase" from themselves, national income accountants have to estimate the equivalent rental value. This value is what the owner-occupied housing would rent for in the market. This estimated value is then counted as a purchase of consumption services by the household sector.

The last component of gross private domestic investment is changes in business inventories. National income accountants treat inventory changes as sales by businesses to other businesses or to themselves. Since these inventories aren't used up in the current year, they are treated as final products, not intermediate goods. Inventories are counted in GNP for the year in which they are produced, not the year sold. Whatever firms

gross private domestic investment
Purchases by the business sector of final output.

fixed investment
The part of business investment that does not add to inventories; consists of new plants and equipment and residential construction.

produce that is not sold to other sectors becomes part of their investment in inventories. This method of accounting for inventories assures that the national income accounts balance. Every dollar of output produced has a buyer. If no one else wants some output, the accounts show that the firm that produced it has "bought" it to add to its own inventories. Business inventory is an important category to watch in the national income accounts. If firms experience undesired inventory changes, their efforts to restore inventories to desired levels will have a significant impact on output and employment.

THE GOVERNMENT SECTOR. A large part of a nation's income is claimed by government—federal, state and local—and a substantial share of output is produced by or for government. Total government expenditures account for about a third of U.S. national income. The federal government spent $1,273 billion in 1990. State and local governments added another $765 billion. Some of this money was spent to produce or to purchase goods and services, such as defense, health care, highways, police, education, and courts.[3] Other government expenditures were transfer payments, such as veterans' benefits, interest on the national debt, and Social Security benefits, which are not counted in GNP.

Purchase of goods and services by governments at all levels is a major component of GNP. The largest part of government expenditures is for salaries and wages for government employees. Governments produce services such as defense, education, and road repair using the labor of these employees. These services are treated as though the government "sold" them to itself.

Another component of government purchases in the national income accounts is spending for goods and services produced by other sectors, mainly the business sector. State and local governments actually purchase more goods and services than the federal government does. Some government purchases are used up almost immediately, such as food for army mess halls. Other government expenditures, such as those for dams or highways, result in goods that will last for years. These can be regarded as a form of "government investment." The national income accounts, however, do not distinguish between government consumption and government investment, but treat all government expenditures alike.

The value of government purchases in the national income accounts does not correspond to the size of the federal budget for two reasons. First, as we already indicated, national income accounts include state and local as well as federal expenditures. Second, a large part of government expenditures is not in payment for goods or productive services. About two-thirds of total government spending is for goods and services, but the rest is for transfer payments. **Transfer payments** are income payments to individuals who provide no goods or services in exchange. Veterans' benefits, welfare payments, unemployment compensation, and Social Security benefits are all examples of transfer payments. Most transfer payments

transfer payments
Income payments to individuals who provide no goods or services in exchange.

3.   As you should recall from Chapter 4, total spending by the federal government is higher than that of state and local governments, but a large part of federal spending consists of transfer payments to individuals and grants to state and local governments.

come from the federal level, although many of them are administered by state and local governments.

THE FOREIGN SECTOR. The final group of buyers is the foreign sector. Consumption, investment, and government expenditures all include some imported goods, which must be subtracted from the GNP because they are produced elsewhere. Exports are part of domestic production, so they need to be included in GNP. Thus, exports are added and imports are subtracted to arrive at gross national product, or what was produced by a country's own factors of production. For convenience, national income accounts usually group these exports and imports together and report the difference between them as net exports of goods and services.

Net exports are usually a fairly small part of GNP but receive more attention than any of the other three components. The balance on goods and services (another name for net exports) can be either positive or negative. When it is negative, there is much concern about the effects of the "flood" of imports on competing American firms and of reduced export sales on American exporting industries. The use of net exports makes the foreign sector look less significant than it really is. Exports are now approximately 12 percent of GNP, and imports account for about 13 percent of total spending. The ratios of both exports and imports to GNP have increased in the last twenty years.

TOTAL SPENDING AND GNP. The sum of spending by the four buying sectors is GNP. Adding consumption spending by households (C), investment spending by business (I), purchases of goods and services by government (G), and spending by the foreign sector, or net exports ($EX-IM$), gives this formula for GNP:

$$GNP = C + I + G + (EX - IM).$$

This formula states that everything that is produced in a year must be purchased by one of the four buying sectors.

NATIONAL INCOME

national income (NI)
Income earned by the four factors of production; consists of wages, rent, interest, profit, and proprietors' net income.

The top half of the circular flow diagram measures the flow of output, or GNP. In the process of producing GNP, income is generated. This income is paid to the factors of production and corresponds to the accounting concept of national income. **National income (NI)** is income earned by the factors of production—land, labor, capital, and enterprise. It consists of wages, rent, interest, profit, and proprietors' net income and is shown on the bottom half of the circular flow.

The key to understanding NI is that all of the income generated in producing GNP must be accounted for in some way. Most of it is paid to the four factors of production. Thus, NI consists of rent, wages and salaries, interest, and profits. In a very simple economy, all of the value of final goods and services produced (GNP) would become payments to factors of production. GNP, which measures the flow in the product market of the circular flow diagram, and NI, which measures the flow in the factor market, would be identical. Since the actual economy is not so simple, some adjustments must be made in order to convert GNP to NI.

DEPRECIATION AND NET NATIONAL PRODUCT

The first adjustment to GNP is correcting to account for the fact that part of the capital stock is used up in the production process. Depreciation (called capital consumption allowance in the GNP accounts) is a cost of production that is not received as income by any factor of production.[4] The **capital consumption allowance** is the national income accountants' estimate of the depreciation of the nation's capital stock. In Table 5, GNP minus capital consumption allowance is equal to **net national product (NNP)**. Similarly, **net private domestic investment** is defined as gross private domestic investment minus the capital consumption allowance (depreciation). Net national product is equal to

$$NNP = C + I_n + G + (EX - IM),$$

where I_n represents net, rather than gross, investment. The only difference between GNP and NNP is that GNP includes gross private domestic investment but the investment term in NNP is net private domestic investment.

NNP is a more meaningful measure of production than GNP, because it excludes all intermediate products, including capital used up in the course of the year's production. GNP is more widely used, however, for two reasons. First, GNP figures are more precise than NNP figures because depreciation is difficult to measure or even estimate accurately. Second, GNP is more closely related than NNP to the behavior of employment and prices.

The World Resources Institute, a Washington-based environmental or-

capital consumption allowance
The national income accountants' estimate of the amount of the nation's capital stock used up in production during a year.

net national product (NNP)
Equal to GNP minus the capital consumption allowance (depreciation).

net private domestic investment
Gross private domestic investment minus the capital consumption allowance (depreciation).

TABLE 5
RELATION OF GNP, NNP, AND NI FOR 1990 (BILLIONS OF DOLLARS)

GNP		$5,463.0
Less:	Capital consumption allowance	−575.7
Equals:	NNP	4,887.4
Less:	Indirect business taxes and nontax liability and business transfer payments	−475.4
Plus:	Net subsidies less surplus of government enterprises	+2.5
Plus (or minus):	Statistical discrepancy*	−3.1
Equals:	NI	$4,417.5

*The statistical discrepancy reconciles errors that arise from the two different data sources used. GNP is estimated from sales data. NI is estimated from factor income. The discrepancy is the remaining difference in estimates after the "plus" and "less" items have been added to or deducted from GNP.

Source: Council of Economic Advisers, *Economic Report of the President* (Washington, DC: U.S. Government Printing Office, 1991).

4. Firms use the capital consumption allowance more for determining their corporate income tax liability than for providing a good estimate of actual economic depreciation. If tax laws allow businesses to overstate depreciation, firms will take advantage of this opportunity to reduce their taxes. If tax laws don't allow businesses to claim all of their actual depreciation, then the official capital consumption allowance figures will understate depreciation. Federal tax laws have been very generous in allowing depreciation in the past, especially from 1981 to 1986. However, the 1986 tax reform bill greatly reduced this loophole.

ganization, has developed another version of NNP. It is arrived at by subtracting depletion of natural resources as well as depreciation of capital equipment from GNP.[5] This group argues that if capital used up is subtracted, it makes sense to also subtract nonrenewable resources that are used up. The group's first set of estimates of this new concept was made for Indonesia, because so much of that country's output is based on natural resources, mainly oil and natural gas. The correction reduced the estimate of Indonesia's output by 17% and reduced the country's estimated growth rate from 1971 to 1984 from an average of 7 percent to an average of 4 percent. No such estimates have yet been made for the United States.

FROM NET NATIONAL PRODUCT TO NATIONAL INCOME

There are a few more adjustments that must be made to NNP to obtain NI. We must subtract costs of production not paid to factors of production. These costs are indirect business taxes and business transfer payments. We need to add payments to factors of production that are not reflected in market prices. These payments consist of *net* subsidies to farmers and other businesses. Finally, the net surpluses of government enterprises, such as the U.S. Postal Service or a municipal water department, are subtracted. The resulting figure is NI, or that part of NNP that was earned by the factors of production.

Indirect business taxes, such as license fees, excise taxes, and business property taxes, are subtracted from NNP. They are reflected in the prices of final products but are not earned by any factor of production. Business transfer payments, such as private pension payments, bad debts, and prizes in promotional contests, are subtracted for the same reason. Also subtracted is the net surplus (or "profit") of any government enterprise that charges for services. Although this surplus is part of the price paid for services of the government enterprise, it is not earned by any owner of factors of production. Some such enterprises are subsidized, so their market prices reflect less than factor cost. These subsidies are *added* to NNP to determine NI. The sum of these corrections is the *net* amount added to (or subtracted from) NNP to obtain NI.

In Table 6, NI is computed as the sum of factor payments. NI consists of the total of wage and salary income, rental income, corporate profits, net interest earnings, and income of proprietors. (Proprietors are owners of small retail stores, independent farmers, and other businesses that are not corporations.) All of this income is earned by households. However, some of it is not actually paid out—such as the part of corporate profits that firms keep as undistributed profits or pay in corporate income taxes to the government.

Wages, interest, and corporate profits need no explanation, but proprietors' net income is more complicated. Net income for proprietorships consists mostly of wages and profits to the owner-worker. If the proprietor has invested funds in the business, some of this income is interest. Some of the proprietor's income is probably profit to enterprise. It is not possible to separate proprietors' net income into these components. Thus, it is listed as a single item in the national income accounts.

5. *Wasting Assets: Natural Resources in the National Income Accounts* (Washington, DC: World Resources Institute, June 1989).

NATIONAL INCOME	$4,417.5
Wages and supplements (including contributions to social insurance)	3,244.2
Proprietors' income	402.4
Rental income of persons*	6.7
Corporate profits	297.1
Net interest	467.1

*Includes the estimated rental value of owner-occupied housing.

TABLE 6
NATIONAL INCOME BY RECIPIENT, 1990 (BILLIONS OF DOLLARS)

Source: Council of Economic Advisers, *Economic Report of the President* (Washington, DC: U.S. Government Printing Office, 1991).

Note that a large part of rental income is *imputed*. National income accountants estimate how much owners would have to pay if they rented their homes instead of owning them. This imputed value of the shelter services of owner-occupied housing is included in NI. Rent paid by one business to another will be netted out, since this is an intermediate rather than a final service. One reason the rental income figure is so small is that it is net of depreciation. Gross rent was $61.4 billion in 1990, but depreciation reduced that amount by $54.8 billion.

Net interest omits all payments of interest from one member of the household sector to another. For example, the interest paid to a relative for a loan to buy a car is not included in national income. Also, interest on government bonds is treated as a transfer payment. It is included in personal income but not in national income because it is not regarded as a cost of production.

NI measures the value of factor services and provides a useful cross check on the accuracy of the GNP and NNP figures. However, from the standpoint of households, the important income flow is not what they *earn* (NI) but what they *receive*. What they receive is personal income.

PERSONAL INCOME AND DISPOSABLE INCOME

Personal income (PI) is the income *received* by households (whether earned or not). National income (NI) is the income *earned* by the household sector. The major differences between NI and PI are corporate income taxes, undistributed corporate profits, and transfer payments. The first two items are subtracted from NI to compute PI because they are earned by households but not actually paid out to them. Net transfer payments are added because they are received but not earned.

Transfer payments are not a part of NI because they represent only a movement of spending power from sector to another. These payments are not related to any current production in the top half of the circular flow model. Transfer payments include a modest amount of business transfer payments and a much larger volume of government transfer payments ($660 billion in 1990).[6] The latter include Social Security, unemployment compensation, Aid to Families with Dependent Children, and veterans'

personal income (PI)
The income received by households; computed from NI by subtracting corporate profits taxes and undistributed corporate profits and adding net transfer payments.

6.   Transfers from households to other households do not change personal income because they remain within the household sector.

TABLE 7
CONVERSION OF NATIONAL
INCOME TO PERSONAL
INCOME FOR 1990
(BILLIONS OF DOLLARS)

NATIONAL INCOME		$4,417.5
Less:	Undistributed corporate profits, corporate profits taxes (includes inventory valuation adjustments),	– 173.3
	and social insurance contributions	– 506.9
Plus:	Net interest payments	+ 213.8
	Government transfer payments	+ 659.5
	Business transfer payments	+ 35.0
Equals:	Personal Income	$4,699.6

Source: Council of Economic Advisers, *Economic Report of the President* (Washington, DC: U.S. Government Printing Office, 1991).

benefits. *Net* transfer payments are arrived at by subtracting contributions of firms and employees to social insurance from gross transfer payments. Net interest payments are also treated like transfer payments, since such payments are not related to current output. Table 7 shows how 1989 national income is converted to personal income for that year.

The household sector can use its personal income in three ways: (1) to pay personal taxes to various levels of government, (2) to spend on consumption goods, or (3) to save. The income the household sector has left after taxes is called **disposable income**. Disposable income can be spent on consumption or saved. It is very useful for forecasting household consumption, the largest component of GNP.

disposable income
Income received by households and available to spend or save; equals PI less personal taxes.

NATIONAL INCOME ACCOUNTS AND THE CIRCULAR FLOW

The concepts of NI, NNP, and GNP reflect the income and spending flows of the circular flow model discussed in Chapters 2 and 4. Let's begin with the fact that personal income can be used in three ways:

(1) PI = consumption + personal saving + personal taxes.

The relationship between NI and PI is given by

(2) NI = PI + (corporate saving + corporate profits taxes)
            – net transfer payments.

Thus, we can substitute for PI from equation (1) into equation (2) to account for all the uses of NI as follows:

(3) NI = consumption + personal saving + personal taxes
            + (corporate saving + corporate profits taxes)
            – net transfer payments.

Taxes minus transfer payments are called net tax payments, since they represent income transferred to the government less income transferred back to households. Equation (3) says that NI is spent on consumption *or* used for net tax payments (business taxes and personal taxes less transfers) *or* used for some form of saving, either by households (personal saving) or by business firms (corporate saving). By definition, whatever income is not spent or paid in taxes has to be saved.[7]

If we let T represent net taxes and S the sum of household and business saving, then

$$NI = C + S + T.$$

This equation describes how households use the income received in the lower half of the circular flow model. Ignoring depreciation, the top half of the circular flow model can be represented by

$$GNP = NNP = C + I + G + (EX - IM).$$

If we ignore some of the smaller differences between NNP and NI (indirect business taxes, business transfer payments, and net subsidies to government enterprises), then NNP = NI. That is,

(4) $\quad C + I + G + (EX - IM) = C + S + T.$

Subtracting consumption from each side of equation (4) gives

(5) $\quad I + G + (EX - IM) = S + T.$

If we move imports to the right-hand side of equation (5), we have

$$I + G + EX = S + T + IM.$$

Note that the terms on the left-hand side of the equation correspond to the three kinds of injections into the circular flow discussed in Chapter 4. The terms on the right-hand side of the equation are the leakages out of the circular flow. Thus, when the national income accounts are balanced, the sum of expenditures, $C + I + G + (EX - IM)$, is always equal to the sum of factor earnings, or NI. Also, the leakages out of the circular flow are always equal to the injections. This relationship is a very important one in macroeconomics, as you will see in later chapters.

PRICES AND PRICE INDICES

The values of GNP, NNP, and NI that we have been discussing are all nominal values. In order to use GNP either to measure economic well-being or to forecast output or employment, economists need to know what is happening to real, physical production. A price index makes it possible to correct GNP figures for changes in the price level.

A price index, like any index, is a weighted average. Index values are composites of many numerical values, which are assigned weights based on their relative importance. The absolute value of any index has little meaning. The *relative value*, especially changes in the relative value, of an index is important. The fact that the Dow Jones industrial stock index passed the 2500 mark in 1987, for example, was only meaningful if you knew what its value was in earlier years.

---

7.   Remember that consumption is defined as household expenditures on current output of final goods. If you buy an Impressionist painting (or a used bicycle or car), then you have merely passed on some of your income to someone else, who must decide whether to spend it or save it.

HOW PRICE INDICES ARE CONSTRUCTED: THE CONSUMER PRICE INDEX

A price index can be constructed in two different ways. One is to take a current-year market basket of goods and services and ask what it would have cost to buy the same collection last year or several years ago. This kind of index, a current weights index, assigns weights to the various items based on the composition of output or the consumption in the current year. The other way to construct a price index is to start with a market basket or output mix in some benchmark, or base, year. Then the behavior of the cost of that market basket is followed in succeeding years.

The most familiar price index, the Consumer Price Index (CPI), uses base-year weights. The current CPI is based on the mix of goods bought by a typical urban family of four in 1982–1983.[8] Suppose that typical family bought twenty pounds of ground beef, three pairs of jeans, five rolls of paper towels, and eight pounds of apples. Those goods and the amounts of each are used in computing the index. That basket of goods is priced at regular intervals to see what is happening to the CPI, or the "cost of living." Table 8 constructs a price index for those four items after determining their base-year and current-year prices.

Since the items in the market baskets are the same for both years, the increase from $75.00 to $88.90 must be due entirely to price changes. The index is $88.90/75.00 = 1.18$, or, as it is usually written, 118. This means that prices rose, on the average, 18 percent. Note, however, that two prices rose more than 18 percent, one price rose less, and one price actually fell.

The actual CPI is based on a market basket of hundreds of items. To find out what is happening to the prices of particular groups of goods or services—such as housing, food, energy, and health care—you can check their price indices each month in the *Monthly Labor Review*. Indices for different regions of the country are also available. Some colleges and universities compute and publish a price index for their immediate areas.

Forbes magazine constructs a price index each year called "The Forbes Four Hundred Cost of Living Extremely Well Index."[9] This index includes such items as a Russian sable coat, tuition at Harvard, season tickets at the Metropolitan Opera, a private plane, an Olympic-size swimming pool, Cuban cigars, and other luxury items. In the late 1980s, this index was rising more rapidly than the CPI. However, little sympathy was generated in political circles for the plight of the extremely well-to-do.

Another tongue-in-cheek index was constructed by James Schick for the cost of the equipment that colonists were required to provide in order to accompany Captain John Smith to the New World in 1624.[10] Schick's list of food, clothing, household equipment, tools, and transportation included such hard-to-find items as powder and shot, swords, and muskets. A careful search for equivalent items led to the conclusion

8. The items in the market basket are not changed very often because of the cost and difficulty of carrying out the survey and processing the results. Until 1987, the most recent survey available was that for 1972–1973. Beginning in 1987, the 1982–1983 survey results became available and have since been used in constructing and revising price indices.

9. "Are You Watching, Chairman Greenspan?" *Forbes* (23 October 1989): 388–390. This figure is reported in the magazine each fall.

10. James B. M. Schick, "John Smith's Bill: Then and Now," *American Heritage* (November 1989): 158–165.

ITEM	QUANTITY Q	BASE YEAR		CURRENT YEAR	
		PRICE VALUE P_1	TOTAL $(Q \times P_1)$	PRICE VALUE P_2	TOTAL $(Q \times P_2)$
Ground beef	20	$ 1.10	$22.00	$ 1.50	$30.00
Jeans	3	16.00	48.00	18.00	54.00
Paper towels	5	.60	3.00	.50	2.50
Apples	8	.25	2.00	.30	2.40
Value of market basket			$75.00		$88.90

TABLE 8
COMPUTING A PRICE INDEX

that in 1989 these items would cost $3,190 (plus transatlantic passage for the settler and possessions). John Smith's estimate for the same list of goods was 12 pounds, 6 shillings, and 3 pence, or about $55 at the old dollar/pound exchange rate. Comparing these two figures gives you a very rough estimate of inflation over the last 365 years!

USES FOR THE CONSUMER PRICE INDEX

Price indices are useful for a number of purposes. If you are comparing job offers in different parts of the country, you will want to adjust salary offers to take into account differences in the local cost of living in each area. If you want to see if your real income has improved since last year, you need to adjust this year's nominal income for price changes.[11] Suppose, for example, that between 1988 and 1989 your nominal income rose from $20,000 to $22,000, a 10 percent increase. How much did your real income increase? The value of the CPI was 118.3 at the end of 1988 and 124.0 at the end of 1989 (compared to the base value of 100 for 1982–1984). The 1989 index divided by the 1988 index is 1.048 (a 4.8 percent price increase). In 1989 dollars, your $22,000 income is worth $22,000/1.048, or $20,992. Your real income rose by $992, or 4.96 percent. Note that the 10 percent increase in nominal income is roughly equal to the sum of the real increase of about 5 percent and the price increase of 4.8 percent. This observation offers a shortcut for estimating a change in real income. You can approximate real income changes using

$$\%\Delta Y_r = \%\Delta Y_n - \%\Delta P,$$

where Y_r is the real income, Y_n is the nominal income, and P is the price level. If the change in nominal income (10 percent in this case) and the change in the price level (5 percent) are known, then their difference will be approximately equal to the percentage change in real income.

Changes in the CPI are used to adjust poverty income levels, Social Security benefits, and wages for workers who have contracts providing for cost-of-living adjustments. Even where no contract is involved, the CPI plays a role in many wage negotiations and other business and personal decisions. Housing became an attractive investment in the 1970s, for example, because of figures showing that the value of the average house was

11. Nominal income (income not adjusted for changes in the price level) is also often referred to as money income or dollar income.

Until 1973, the price of the dollar in terms of gold and other currencies was established by the U.S. government. From 1935 to 1971, $35 of U.S. currency was the equivalent of one ounce of gold. Prior to 1935, the price of an ounce of gold was $20.67. From December 1971 to February 1973, the price was $38. In 1973, the U.S. government abandoned efforts to control the price of the dollar, and the price was left for the market to determine. In the jargon of central bankers, the United States had "closed the gold window."

Since most other major currencies also had market-determined prices, the problem of measuring the ups and downs of the dollar surfaced immediately. The price of the dollar is important because it is reflected in the prices of exports and imports. Thus, it is important to have some way of measuring changes in its value. But what could be used to measure the value of the dollar? Measuring what was happening to the dollar in terms of Japanese yen would give a different picture from what was happening to it in British pounds or French francs. For example, between 1980 and 1990 the price of the dollar rose from 29.2 to 33.4 in Belgian francs. During the same period, it fell from 227 to 145 in Japanese yen. Any bilateral exchange rate reflects not only what is happening to the market for the U.S. dollar but also anything affecting the value of the second currency in terms of all other currencies.

The solution to this problem was to construct a price index for the dollar, much like the CPI or the GNP deflator. This price index is called the trade-weighted dollar. It is computed as the change in the weighted average of the values of the dollar in terms of fourteen other currencies. Weights are assigned to these values on the basis of the proportion of U.S.

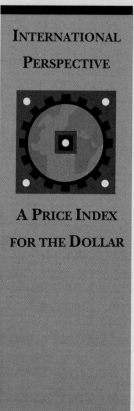

INTERNATIONAL PERSPECTIVE

A PRICE INDEX FOR THE DOLLAR

trade that each nation represents. The fourteen nations include all of the United States' major trading partners, including Canada, Japan, and the nations of Western Europe.

As you can see from the diagram, this index was set at 100 in 1973 when the U.S. dollar began to float. Between 1980 and 1990, when the dollar rose in terms of Belgian francs but fell in terms of Japanese yen, the index rose from 87.4 to 89.1, an increase of 2 percent. This increase represents the net effect of a large rise in the dollar's price in terms of Belgian francs and British pounds, a more modest increase in Canadian dollars, almost no change in terms of Dutch guilders, and a decline in terms of both Japanese yen and German marks. The index rose sharply from 1980 to 1985 (from 87.4 to 143.2) before falling back at the end of the decade to almost the same value it had in 1973.

TRADE-WEIGHTED VALUE OF THE DOLLAR, 1967–1990*

* 1972–1973 = 100.

Source: Council of Economic Advisers, *Economic Report of the President* (Washington, DC: U.S. Government Printing Office, 1991).

> ### HOW TO CONSTRUCT YOUR OWN PRICE INDEX
>
> - Step 1. By survey or some other method, come up with a typical market basket of purchases.
> - Step 2. Determine the market price for each item in the base, or beginning, period.
> - Step 3. Multiply prices by quantities and add to find the total value of the market basket in the base period.
> - Step 4. Find the prices for the same set of items in the next period.
> - Step 5. Compute the new value of the market basket as in Step 3.
> - Step 6. Divide the value of the current-year market basket in Step 5 by the value of the base-year market basket in Step 3, and multiply the result by 100.

rising faster than the CPI. (It is expected to fall behind the CPI in the 1990s, however.) Probably no other economic data is quoted as often as the CPI.

PROBLEMS WITH THE CONSUMER PRICE INDEX

Because the CPI is used so widely, it is important to recognize its drawbacks and limits. One of these is the fact that the market basket is fixed or changed very infrequently on the basis of extensive consumer surveys. The current CPI is based on a survey taken in 1982–83. Since that time, changes in the age distribution of the population, changes in tastes and technology, and development of new products have changed the mix of goods consumers buy. The longer the time that passes since the survey that was used to find the weights, the more inaccurate the CPI becomes.

A second problem has to do with changes in relative prices. The CPI measures changes in the *average* price of a representative market basket of goods and services. If your household consumes those goods and services in about that proportion, then the CPI will reflect changes in your cost of living. If, however, you spend more than average amounts on medical care and housing (whose prices have risen rapidly) and less than average amounts on clothing and furniture (whose prices have risen more slowly), then your personal price index will rise faster than the CPI. Thus, using the CPI to compare incomes over time or to adjust wages or Social Security benefits is likely to lead to overadjusting at some times and undercorrecting for inflation at others.

OTHER PRICE INDICES

There are two other widely used price indices. One is the **GNP implicit price deflator**. This index is used to correct GNP for price changes to determine what is happening to real output. It has a broader base than the CPI because it reflects all of the goods and services in the GNP, not just consumer goods. Unlike the CPI, the GNP deflator is a current-weights index. The weights for the various components are based on the proportions sold or produced in the current year, not a base year. Once the GNP deflator is computed, it is used to compute real GNP. Each of a series of

GNP implicit price deflator
A current-weights index used to correct the GNP for price changes.

nominal GNP figures is divided by its respective current-year GNP deflator in order to create a series of real, or price-adjusted, GNP figures. These figures allow economists to examine year-to-year growth without being confused by rising prices.

Nominal GNP (uncorrected for inflation) and real GNP can give very different pictures of economic performance. For example, in 1982 (a recession year), nominal GNP rose to $3,069 billion from $2,958 billion in 1981, a modest increase of $111 billion, or 3.6 percent. However, after dividing by the GNP deflator, real GNP actually fell by 2.1 percent between 1981 and 1982. The GNP deflator gives a different measure of inflation than the CPI does. The difference is partly due to the deflator's broader coverage and partly due to the fact that it uses current weights rather than base-year weights. Table 9 compares inflation measured by the CPI and by the GNP deflator for 1975 to 1990.

Producer Price Index
A group of three indices (for raw materials, semifinished goods, and finished goods) that shows what is happening to prices paid by producers and wholesalers.

Another major price index, the **Producer Price Index**, is actually a family of indices. There are three indices: one for raw materials, one for semifinished goods, and one for finished goods. These indices show what is happening to prices paid by producers and wholesalers, which will eventually affect the prices of retail goods and services. The Producer Price Index is useful in forecasting changes in the CPI and the GNP deflator.

PROBLEMS IN USING GNP FIGURES

Adjusting GNP for price changes is a very important correction. Price changes, however, are not the only problem with GNP. Omitted items, both positive and negative, limit the usefulness of GNP.

TABLE 9
COMPARISON OF INFLATION
RATES MEASURED BY THE
CPI AND THE GNP
DEFLATOR, 1975–1990

YEAR	INFLATION RATE MEASURED BY CPI (%)	INFLATION RATE MEASURED BY GNP DEFLATOR (%)
1975	7.0	9.8
1976	4.8	6.4
1977	6.8	6.7
1978	9.0	7.3
1979	13.3	8.9
1980	12.4	9.0
1981	8.9	9.7
1982	3.9	6.4
1983	3.8	3.9
1984	4.0	3.7
1985	3.8	3.0
1986	1.1	2.6
1987	4.4	3.2
1988	4.4	3.3
1989	4.6	4.1
1990	6.1	4.1

Source: Council of Economic Advisers, *Economic Report of the President* (Washington, DC: U.S. Government Printing Office, 1991).

One major use of GNP is to measure economic well-being. Are Americans better off than last year? Are Americans better off than Russians or Japanese? Another use of GNP is as a forecasting tool. Changes in GNP affect employment, prices, interest rates, government tax revenues, and exchange rates. The GNP measure that best reflects economic well-being is not necessarily the one that makes the most reliable forecasting tool. In choosing what to include or exclude, national income accountants usually base their decision on the usefulness of GNP as a forecasting tool rather than as a measure of economic welfare.

This choice leads to some interesting omissions. We have already observed that GNP does not correct for either depreciation of capital equipment or depletion of natural resources. Other omissions are nonmarket production, changes in leisure, illegal activities, and some quality improvements. To convert GNP from a forecasting tool to a welfare measure, a correction would also have to be made for any increase in negative external effects and public bads, such as noise, water pollution, and global warming.

Nonmarket production is not included in GNP. If you repair your own car, only the parts that you purchase are counted. If you take your car to a service station, all of the repairs enter into GNP. Excluding nonmarket transactions understates economic well-being and also distorts the comparative use of GNP figures. This omission of nonmarket production may not make a big difference in year-to-year comparisons within a country or comparisons of similar countries such as the United States and Canada. It does distort comparisons between 1900 and 1990 or between the United States and India. For example, as a country gets wealthier, there are more professional laundries. Less laundry is done at home. This change says nothing about how clean the clothes of the population are. In the last twenty years, as more women have entered the work force in the United States, a larger share of household services (including laundry, meals, and day care) is being purchased in the market. The change in GNP overstates the actual increase in economic well-being.

On the other hand, activities that are paid for "under the table" or by barter are difficult to track, so GNP accountants are not able to include such transactions. This omission understates economic welfare. Some transactions are excluded on purpose. Since the GNP is limited to legal markets, national income accountants exclude illegal activities such as drugs, prostitution, or gambling.[12]

An important aspect of well-being not reflected in GNP is change in leisure time. Since 1900, the average factory work week has dropped from 70 hours to less than 40 hours. That reduction clearly represents an increase in economic well-being, but it is not reflected in GNP. A partial indicator is spending for leisure-type activities (such as travel, theater tickets, and health-club memberships) or equipment (VCRs, tennis racquets, and skis), but these are poor proxies for actual consumption of leisure.

Finally, in many cases what appear to be price increases are actually quality improvements. Products may be safer, more durable, or more use-

---

12. Gambling is counted in states where it is legal (such as Nevada) but not in states where it is illegal.

ful. However, unless a specific feature can be separated out and assigned a price tag, GNP accountants have no good way of correcting for quality improvements.

There are also undesirable activities that increase measured GNP while reducing economic well-being. Suppose there is a rise in the crime rate, resulting in the hiring of more police and the building of more jails. Is the average person better off? Probably not. But the government-spending component of the GNP registers an increase in purchases of police services. In the process of producing more goods and services, the economy may be creating more air and water pollution, more noise, more litter, and more congestion. Not only are these side effects of growth not subtracted, but the costs of combating pollution, noise, and litter are added into GNP as production of additional goods and services. These costs are known as "defensive" expenditures. One estimate places such defensive expenditures (for West Germany before reunification) as high as 10 percent of measured GNP.[13]

Some economists have attempted to develop an alternative to GNP as a measure of changes in the quality of life. William Nordhaus and James Tobin estimated the value of leisure time, household work and other non-market production, and quality improvements to add to GNP.[14] They also estimated negative influences on the quality of life (pollution, crime, etc.) and subtracted those from the GNP. The result was their **Measure of Economic Welfare (MEW)**, an alternative to GNP that focuses more closely on changes in economic welfare. Nordhaus and Tobin found that, in general, MEW appears to have grown more slowly than real GNP.

Measure of Economic Welfare (MEW)
An alternative to GNP that tries to provide a better indicator of economic well-being by adding leisure and nonmarket production and subtracting public bads.

MEASURING UNEMPLOYMENT

The last important macroeconomic variable to be measured is the unemployment rate. The number of unemployed as well as the number of employed will grow with the population and with the fraction of the population that is of working age and employable. Thus, it is more helpful to measure unemployment as a percentage of the labor force than to just count the number of unemployed. The **unemployment rate** is defined as the percentage of the labor force that wants to work but does not currently have a job. That is,

unemployment rate
The percentage of the labor force that wants to work but does not currently have a job.

$$(6) \quad \frac{\text{Unemployed workers}}{\text{Labor force}} = \frac{\text{Unemployed workers}}{\text{Employed workers} + \text{Unemployed workers}}$$

The first step in measuring unemployment is to determine the size of the labor force. Until recently, only the civilian labor force was counted.

13. Leipert, Christian, "National Income and Economic Growth: The Concept of Defensive Expenditures," *Journal of Economic Issues* (September 1989): 843–855.
14. William Nordhaus and James Tobin, "Is Growth Obsolete?" *Economic Growth, Fiftieth Anniversary Colloquium V* (Cambridge, MA: National Bureau of Economic Research, 1972). A number of other extensions and qualifications to GNP are summarized in Robert Eisner, "Extended Accounts for National Income and Product," *Journal of Economic Literature* (December 1988): 1611–1684.

Once statistics are compiled, they are almost always used for comparisons. Is GNP higher than last year? Is U.S. GNP growing faster than GNP in other countries? How does the unemployment rate or inflation rate in the United States compare with that in other developed countries?

There are problems in comparing these figures between nations because GNP, unemployment, and price indices are not computed exactly the same way in all countries. The share of economic activity going through the market is much different in less developed countries. This difference affects all three indicators but especially GNP. Comparisons of the United States, Canada, Japan, Australia, and the countries of Western Europe are a

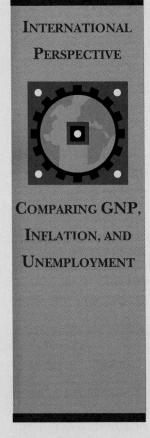

INTERNATIONAL PERSPECTIVE

COMPARING GNP, INFLATION, AND UNEMPLOYMENT

little more reliable because these countries are all at similar levels of economic development. The share of economic activity passing through the market is roughly the same, and the ways statistics are collected and presented are similar, but differences still remain.

With this warning, how does the United States compare with similar countries? As the table shows, it is *not* number one, at least not on many measures, but it doesn't fare too badly. The United States is behind Japan and about even with Canada in industrial production. It ranks in the middle of the seven countries in economic growth and inflation and is only worse than Japan in the unemployment rate.

COUNTRY	INDUSTRIAL PRODUCTION, 1988*	REAL GROWTH RATE (% CHANGE IN REAL GNP)		UNEMPLOYMENT RATE, 1989 (%)	INFLATION RATE, 1988 (%)[†]
		1976–1983 AVERAGE	1990		
Canada	136.3	2.7	2.7	7.5	5.7
France	114.0	2.5	2.5	9.6	4.6
Great Britain	118.1	1.7	1.7	7.0	3.6
Italy	126.4	3.3	3.3	7.8	5.9
Japan	159.2	4.4	4.4	2.3	9.3
United States	137.2	2.5	2.5	5.3	5.7
West Germany	117.8	2.4	2.4	5.7	3.6

*For the index of industrial production, the base year in 1977.
[†]Inflation is measured by changes in the CPI.

Source: Council of Economic Advisers, *Economic Report of the President* (Washington, DC: U.S. Government Printing Office, 1990, 1991).

Those who were employed in the military services were excluded. Newer measures include the military in the labor force, which results in lower measured unemployment rates.

labor force
Those who are working or actively seeking work.

The **labor force** consists of those who are working and those who are actively seeking work. A full-time homemaker, a child, a retiree, a full-time student, a prisoner, or anyone else not employed is not counted in either the numerator or the denominator of equation (6). People who had been seeking work but have given up and stopped looking are also excluded from the measured labor force.

The measures of both the labor force and the number of unemployed are obtained from door-to-door surveys and payroll data from business firms.[15] Respondents in door-to-door surveys are only considered unemployed if they have made some effort to find work in the last four weeks.

Like the GNP and the CPI, the unemployment rate is an imperfect indicator. Discouraged workers (those who sought work for a while, became discouraged, and gave up) are not counted as unemployed. This omission makes unemployment appear lower than it really is. Some workers may be underemployed—working below their ability or fewer hours than they would like. These workers, however, are counted as employed. On the other hand, some workers leave jobs, make a modest effort to find work in order to qualify for unemployment benefits, and avoid taking a job until their unemployment benefits run out. These people should probably not be counted as "actively seeking work." Their inclusion overstates unemployment.

The major source of short-term changes in unemployment is changes in total demand for labor that result from changes in total output. Over longer periods, total labor supply also affects the unemployment rate. An indicator that is helpful in sorting out the relative importance of these two sources of changes in unemployment is the labor force participation rate. The **labor force participation rate** measures the fraction of the adult population that is employed or actively seeking work. In 1948, the labor force participation rate was 59 percent. It remained near that level until the 1960s, when it began to rise. By 1990, 66.6 percent of the population over the age of 16 was in the labor force. This increased fraction of the population in the labor force meant that even though the U.S. unemployment rate was reaching new highs, the employment rate (the percentage of the population with jobs) was fairly stable. Part of the increase in unemployment was caused by the larger fraction of the population that was seeking employment.

labor force participation rate
The percentage of the adult population that is employed or actively seeking work.

In the 1990s, the labor force participation rate is expected to level off, primarily because there will be fewer new entrants to the labor force. (A smaller number of people will be in their late teens and early twenties.) Unemployment will remain low as the labor force grows at an average rate of only 1.2 percent a year, compared to 2.3 percent from 1976 to 1990.[16]

The increased labor force participation rate in the last two decades

15. There are discrepancies between household and establishment surveys. These differences arise partly from variations in coverage and definitions, partly because some jobs are held by illegal aliens and workers holding more than one job. See Paul O. Flain, "How Many New Jobs since 1982? Two Surveys Differ," *Monthly Labor Review* (August 1989): 10–15.
16. Howard N. Fullerton, Jr., "New Labor Force Projections Spanning 1988 to 2000," *Monthly Labor Review* (November 1989): 3–11.

reflects two factors. One is that the baby-boom generation—due to the jump in the birth rate between 1946 and 1962—grew up and entered the labor force. Thus, a larger proportion of the population was of working age. The other change was in female participation in the labor force, which rose from 38 percent at the beginning of the 1960s to 58 percent in 1990. Some of the high unemployment rates of the 1970s reflect the time required to absorb the large increase in labor force participants. The declining unemployment rates of the late 1980s, which are expected to continue into the 1990s, are as much a result of a slowdown in new entrants to the labor force as any other factor. Female participation is expected to peak, and the baby boom was followed by a "baby bust" (period of low birth rates). The number of new high school and college graduates reached a low in 1990 and is gradually increasing again. Thus, prospects are bright for a low unemployment rate in the next decade simply for demographic reasons.

SUMMARY

1. Stocks are existing quantities. Flows measure quantities over time. An income statement measures flows. A balance sheet measures stocks.

2. Gross National Product (GNP) measures final output produced in a country over a given period of time. It can be measured by producing sector or by buying sector. Its value should be the same whether it measures output produced or income created in the production process.

3. Other measures of output and income are national income (NI), net national product (NNP), personal income (PI), and disposable income. National income corresponds to the flow in the lower half of the circular flow diagram.

4. A price index, which is a weighted average of prices, is used to measure changes in price level. A price index is used to correct for price changes and measure real income or output. The most commonly used price indices are the Consumer Price Index (CPI) and the GNP deflator.

5. GNP is not perfect either as a measure of economic well-being or as a means of making comparisons in time and space. The Measure of Economic Welfare (MEW) is one alternative that tries to compute economic well-being.

6. Problems with the GNP include the omission of non-market and illegal transactions and leisure and the failure to correct for economic bads.

7. Unemployment is measured as the percentage of the labor force not working but actively seeking work. Some changes in unemployment arise from changes in the size of the labor force relative to the population rather than from changes in total output or the demand for labor.

NEW TERMS

stock variable
flow variable
depreciation
income statement
balance sheet
net worth
gross national product (GNP)
final goods
intermediate goods

business inventories
consumption expenditures
consumer durables
consumer nondurables
consumer services
gross private domestic investment
fixed investment
transfer payments

national income (NI)
capital consumption allowance
net national product (NNP)
net private domestic investment
personal income (PI)
disposable income

GNP implicit price deflator
Producer Price Index
Measure of Economic Welfare (MEW)
unemployment rate
labor force
labor force participation rate

QUESTIONS FOR DISCUSSION

1. Suppose that during a certain period GNP rises from $3,000 billion to $3,500 billion, while GNP deflator goes from 100 to 125. What has happened to real GNP?

2. Suppose another baby boom occurred and a significant number of parents dropped out of the labor force to stay home and do child care. What would happen to the unemployment rate, the labor force participation rate, and the employment rate?

3. Why is GNP not entirely satisfactory as a measure of economic well-being? Why is it better for comparisons over short time periods or between countries that are similar in economic and social conditions?

4. How would an increase in Social Security taxes affect GNP, NNP, national income, and PI?

5. Draw up a personal income statement. See if it helps you to understand why national income accountants wind up with a statistical discrepancy in matching the income side to the expenditure side.

6. Given the following information, compute the unemployment rate.

Civilian noninstitutional population	186,393,000
Civilian labor force	125,557,000
Total civilian employment	117,342,000

There were an additional 1,688,000 people in the armed forces. What would happen to the unemployment rate if these persons were counted?

7. Use the following data to compute GNP, NNP, and NI. If NI computed at factor cost is $3,387 billion, what is the statistical discrepancy? (All figures are in billions; any omitted items are zero.)

Consumption	$2,762
Government purchases	865
Gross investment	675
Depreciation	455
Indirect business taxes	349
Net exports	−106

8. Use the data in Question 7 to compute the percentage of GNP going to each buying sector. Present the results as a bar chart or pie chart.

9. Use the following data to compute NI, PI, and disposable income for the year. (All figures are in billions; any omitted items are zero.)

Wages and salaries	$2,499
Personal taxes	513
Government transfers	491
Social insurance taxes	376
Corporate profits	300
Net interest	295
Proprietors' income	279
Corporate profits taxes	103
Dividends	88
Undistributed profits	46
Business transfers	23
Rental income	16

10. Given the information in the table, compute a price index for a ten-year-old child. This child receives a weekly allowance and would like to request a raise based on the increase in the cost of the market basket of goods purchased. By how much has this consumer's cost of living risen?

ITEM	QUANTITY	LAST YEAR'S PRICE	THIS YEAR'S PRICE
Movie admission	1	$3.00	$3.25
Soft drinks	3	.50	.50
Candy bars	4	.30	.35
Pencils	2	.15	.12
Comic books	2	.75	.85

11. Explain this statement: "Everybody's CPI is nobody's CPI."

12. Suppose the government decided not to tax corporate profits, and as a result the extra funds were all paid out as dividends. How would this change affect GNP, NNP, NI, and PI?

13. Suppose a hurricane struck the coast of New England, destroying millions of dollars' worth of housing. What would be the immediate effect on GNP, NNP, NI, and PI?

14. Identify whether each of the following would be an asset or a liability on your personal balance sheet.

a. government bonds   d. a TV set
b. car loan   e. a bicycle
c. bill due for doctor's care   f. a condominium

15. Why is unemployment likely to remain low in the 1990s? If the birth rate rises in the 1990s, when and how will it affect employment and unemployment? Suppose, instead, that the birth rate does not change but immigration increases. What effect would that have on employment and unemployment?

SUGGESTIONS FOR FURTHER READING

Carlson, Keith M. "Do Price Indices Tell Us about Inflation? A Review of the Issues," *Review*, Federal Reserve Bank of St. Louis (November/December 1989): 12–30. This excellent and not very technical article discusses the historical development of the major price indices and how they are used. Provides details on some of the components for the CPI.

Council of Economic Advisers. *Economic Report of the President.* Washington, DC: U.S. Government Printing Office, annual. Gives a summary of economic developments and a variety of statistics.

Franklin, Norman. *Tracing America's Economy.* Armonk, NY:

M.E. Sharpe, 1987. A guide to locating and interpreting economic data.

Sommers, Albert T. *The U.S. Economy Demystified: What the Major Economic Statistics Mean and Their Significance for Business.* Lexington, MA: Lexington Books, 1985. A guide to macroeconomic data, its interpretation, and sources, especially the national income accounts.

U.S. Department of Labor. *Monthly Labor Review.* Washington, DC: U.S. Government Printing Office. Best source of data for the CPI; also reports regularly on changes in the CPI and interpretations of movements in consumer prices.

1. Describe the uses of the aggregate demand and aggregate supply curves.
2. Explain why the aggregate demand curve has a negative slope.
3. Discuss the different views of the slope and shape of the aggregate supply curve.
4. Identify the basic viewpoint of each of the major schools of macroeconomic thought.
5. Explain how differences in values and goals are related to differences in emphasis and interpretation in macroeconomics.

INTRODUCTION

CHAPTER 6

AGGREGATE DEMAND AND AGGREGATE SUPPLY

Chapters 4 and 5 introduced three important macroeconomic variables that measure aggregate economic performance: total output, price level, and unemployment. The level of each of these variables and how they change are explained by an economic model. For a century, economists have been in agreement on the basic microeconomic model of supply and demand, which determines individual prices and quantities, although they have disagreed about how well the market works in certain industries. There has been little agreement on what kind of model best explains how output, employment, and the price level are determined. This chapter is the first step toward developing a macroeconomic model. Recall from Chapter 1 that any model offers a simplified description of reality that can be used to understand a system and predict the effects of various changes. The aggregate supply and demand model is both simple and predictive. Thus, it is a useful way to organize the study of macroeconomics.

A GENERAL FRAMEWORK FOR MACROECONOMICS

Before looking at the details of macroeconomic theory, we need a general model, or framework. The framework we will use to explain the levels of output, employment, and prices is the aggregate supply and demand model. This framework is general enough to support a number of macroeconomic viewpoints. Once we have established this framework, we will use it to introduce some macroeconomic schools of thought, whose competing ideas will recur in later chapters.

AGGREGATE DEMAND

Think back to the microeconomic supply and demand curves for individual products developed in Chapter 3. Your first thought might be to obtain aggregate supply (*AS*) and aggregate demand (*AD*) curves by adding the supply and demand curves for all the products in the marketplace. Unfortunately, this is not the way to proceed. Why not? First, there are technical problems with adding such unlike goods as cars, toothpaste, and haircuts on the horizontal axis and the prices of each on the vertical axis. What units can you use to combine very different products, and how do you construct an aggregate price index that accurately represents all their prices?

Second, when you add across many markets, many of the effects that can shift the individual supply and demand curves drop out of the picture. For instance, the demand for toothpaste is affected by the prices of mouthwash (a substitute) and toothbrushes (a complement). On the aggregate demand curve, however, it is not possible to distinguish among individual prices. The vertical axis measures only the aggregate, or average, price level. On the horizontal axis, it doesn't matter whether consumers are buying toothpaste or mouthwash, as long as they are buying some item. More toothpaste offsets less mouthwash when both goods are combined into total real output on the horizontal axis. Thus, there is no substitution effect.

aggregate demand curve
A graph showing the amounts of total real ouput that all buyers in an economy wish to purchase at various price levels.

A microeconomic market demand curve shows how much of a given product consumers will buy at various prices, *ceteris paribus*. The **aggregate demand curve** shows the amounts of total real output that all buyers in an economy will purchase at various price levels. Figure 1 shows an aggregate demand curve (*AD*). On the vertical axis, *P* represents the price level, measured by a price index. On the horizontal axis, *Y* represents real output, or output adjusted for changes in the price level. Economists generally believe that the aggregate demand curve has a negative slope, as pictured in Figure 1. For convenience, we will usually use a straight-line aggregate demand curve.

Economists use the symbol *Y* to stand for different concepts of the flow of income or output. However, if we overlook some of the smaller differences between GNP and national income (NI), then *Y* can represent both the flow of output and the flow of income. Nominal GNP or NI is then the product of *P* and *Y* at any point. For example, at point *A* in Figure 1, a price level of $3 and total output of 1,000 units give a GNP of $3,000.

THE AGGREGATE EXPENDITURE APPROACH. One way of looking at aggregate demand is in terms of the components of GNP by purchasing sector. These components are consumption spending by households (*C*), investment spending by business (*I*), government purchases of goods and ser-

FIGURE 1
AGGREGATE DEMAND
An aggregate demand curve shows a negative relationship between the price level and real output.

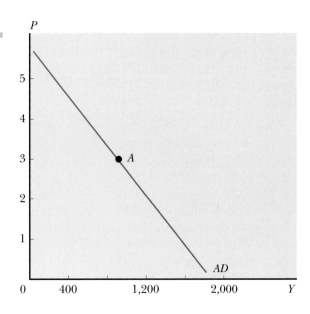

vices (G), and spending by the foreign sector, or net exports ($EX - IM$).
As you learned in Chapter 5, the national income accounts measure actual expenditures in these four categories. However, actual spending and planned spending may be different if the market is not in equilibrium. In order to plot the demand curve, you need to know, not what was actually spent, but the planned or intended level of purchases at each price level.

The only unplanned component of GNP by purchasing sector is unplanned changes in inventories, which is a component of business investment. Everything else is assumed to be planned. Thus, $C + I + G + (EX - IM)$ less unplanned changes in inventory represents a point on a demand curve —one combination of P and Y that buyers choose. However, total GNP by purchasing sector (less unplanned inventory changes) represents "demand" at only one price level, the current one. For this reason, we will refer to the sum of planned purchases, or $C + I + G + (EX - IM)$, as aggregate expenditure, or AE. In order to use information on aggregate planned expenditure in plotting an aggregate demand curve, we would have to know what real C, I, G, and $(EX - IM)$ would be at various price levels.

Although it is not possible to observe directly what $C + I + G + (EX - IM)$ would be at various price levels, there are some clues to what happens to real demand for output as the price level changes. The slope of the aggregate demand curve implies that higher prices have a negative effect on planned purchases of real output. Dollar spending ($P \times Y$) may be higher if P is sufficiently higher, but Y will be lower. People tend to be reluctant to buy as much real output at higher price levels as they do at lower ones. This is especially true if prices rise ahead of wages or more rapidly than wages or income. Several explanations based on the theory of self-interested behavior can be offered for the negative slope of the aggregate demand curve.

If the price level rises, even with no change in employment and real output, nominal income ($P \times Y$) will increase. As you saw in Chapter 4, when nominal income increases and the tax code is progressive, then tax revenues rise more than in proportion to the income increase, even if *real* income (Y) is unchanged. Households' disposable incomes fall relative to total real income and output. Higher taxes, by reducing disposable income, reduce people's ability to buy at higher prices.[1]

When the price level rises, usually exports fall and imports rise. The resulting change in net exports ($EX - IM$) will change real quantity demanded. Higher domestic prices mean that a country's exports become more expensive to foreigners. Also, imports become more attractive to residents of the country because they are relatively cheaper. Both foreigners and residents will substitute cheaper foreign products for more expensive domestic ones, reducing exports and increasing imports. A fall in net exports means that real quantity demanded is lower at a higher price level.[2] Conversely, a lower price level, *ceteris paribus*, will lead to substitution of home products for foreign products. Then real quantity demanded will be greater at lower price levels.

---

1.   The negative impact of collecting higher taxes on total spending will not be as severe if there is an increase in government spending to offset any reduction in consumption.
2.   Part, but not all, of the effect of higher prices on exports and imports is likely to be offset by changes in the price of the country's currency. We will explore this topic in more detail in the chapter on international finance.

Aggregate supply and demand are concepts developed for a closed economy (one with no foreign sector). But shifts in exports or imports can be quite large and can have a visible effect on output, employment, and prices. Between 1976 and 1990, both imports and exports grew faster in real terms than GNP for the United States. Over this period, exports rose 130 percent, imports rose 134 percent, and real GNP increased by only 47 percent. Clearly, trade is becoming a larger component of economic activity.

Aggregate supply and demand can be adapted to include goods and services that are consumed within a country but produced in foreign countries, or vice versa. To do this, it is necessary to define aggregate supply and aggregate demand a little more precisely. In an economy with a foreign sector, aggregate supply is defined as the supply of goods and services *produced* in the country, not the supply of goods and services available for consumption. Thus, aggregate supply is a production concept, not a consumption concept. In a closed economy, the two supplies would be the same.

Aggregate demand in an open economy consists of demand for goods and services produced in the country, whether the demanders are residents or foreigners. Thus, exports show up in an aggregate supply and demand diagram as an increase in aggregate demand. Imports are shown as a decrease in aggregate de-

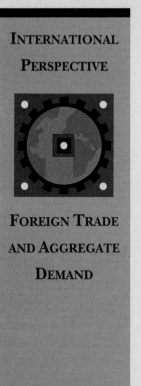
mand rather than an addition to aggregate supply. These definitions of aggregate supply and demand in an open economy are used because they reflect the impact of imports and exports (through aggregate supply and demand) on the level of output, employment, and prices.

The total spending by the foreign sector ($EX - IM$) is small relative to the rest of output. Because its two components enter into aggregate demand separately, however, each of them can have a major impact on real output and the price level. An increase in exports is an added source of demand for a nation's output, shifting aggregate demand to the right. Rising exports drive up real output and employment. Exports also tend to put upward pressure on the price level because there are fewer goods left for domestic consumers, who must compete for that limited supply.

Rising imports appear in an aggregate supply and demand diagram as a reduction in demand. Increased imports shift aggregate demand to the left, driving down domestic output and employment but also holding down the price level. From 1981 to 1985, falling exports and rising imports in the United States were blamed for slow growth of output and high unemployment. However, they also deserve some of the credit for a lower rate of inflation.

Higher prices also reduce the value of financial assets owned by households. These include savings accounts, bonds, certificates of deposit, pension funds, and insurance policies. As the value of these assets falls, households will cut back on spending in order to rebuild their assets to the desired levels. Changes in aggregate assets or wealth have the same effect on the aggregate demand curve that changes in individual wealth have on the individual demand curve. When the price level falls, the real purchasing power of financial assets rises, making households feel wealthier. Such an increase in wealth means that households are willing and able to purchase more goods and services at every level of real income (Y).

If you are thinking like an economist, it may occur to you that one household's or firm's asset may be another's debt. Your savings deposit (asset) has been loaned by the bank as someone else's mortgage (liability). Your bonds (asset) are the liability of some corporation. When the price level rises, the decreased spending by asset holders may be offset by the increased spending of debtors, who feel less burdened by their debt. This would be true if it were not for the fact that the government is a major net debtor. When the price level rises, there is a fall in the value of government debt held by households. As their wealth decreases, households spend less. However, government officials do not necessarily respond by spending more. Similarly, a fall in the price level would increase the value of government debt held by households, raising their spending. Again, there is no reason to expect that public officials would respond by spending less.

Spending by state and local governments is also sensitive to price level changes. Many of these governments are constrained by their constitutions or in other ways to limit their spending to what they receive in revenues. When the price level rises, two of the three major sources of state and local revenue—property taxes and sales taxes—tend to lag behind. These taxes are not highly sensitive to changes in the price level.[3] Therefore, state and local governments must limit their purchases to what they can buy with revenues that are rising more slowly than the price level.

Finally, higher price levels are associated with higher interest rates, for reasons we will explore in later chapters. Rising interest rates increase the opportunity cost of borrowing by business for investment, by households for purchase of consumer durables, and by state and local governments to finance construction. Lower price levels lead to lower interest rates and more of all three of these kinds of borrowing.

All of the effects described here—taxes, net exports, household wealth, government spending, and interest rates—support the notion of a downward sloping aggregate demand curve. However, none of them are very powerful—certainly not as powerful as the substitution effect in the demand for individual products. Consider, for example, the effect of a change in the value of households' financial assets. Some estimates suggest that a $1 change in a household's wealth only leads to a 6¢ change in its spending. Although all of these effects on price levels are weak, they all work in the same direction—yielding an aggregate demand curve that slopes down-

---

3. The property tax revolt in the late 1970s was a response to rising house prices that led to sharp increases in property taxes as well as income taxes. But, under more normal circumstances, there is a long time lag between rising house prices and rising property tax assessments.

ward from left to right. Because none of these effects are very powerful, the aggregate demand curve is generally believed to be quite steep.

THE MONETARY APPROACH. Another view of the aggregate demand curve is shown in Figure 2. In this figure, the curved line shows the various ways that a given national income can be divided between prices and real output. For example, a national income of $2,000 could consist of a price level of $1 and real output of 2,000 units, a price level of $5 and real output of 400 units, or any of a number of other combinations.

This aggregate demand curve is consistent with a classical explanation of how output and prices are determined. Its origins go back at least to the eighteenth-century British economist and philosopher David Hume. The classical explanation of the price level is based on the equation of exchange and the quantity theory of money. The **quantity theory of money** states that changes in the price level are proportional to changes in the money supply. This theory, like many theories in macroeconomics, developed as a way to explain certain economic events.

quantity theory of money
The theory that changes in the price level will be proportional to changes in the money supply.

Classical economists believed that there was a very simple relationship between the money supply and the price level:

$$M_s \times V = P \times Y.$$

equation of exchange
An identity based on the quantity theory of money that says that the money supply times the velocity of money equals the price level times real output.

This relationship is called the **equation of exchange**. The idea behind this relationship is that the value of spending must be equal to the value of what was bought. M_s is the money supply, and V is the velocity of money, or the number of times the average dollar is spent per year. Thus, $M_s \times V$ equals total spending. For example, if the money supply is $2,000 and $V = 3$, then total spending will be $6,000. If dollars turn over more often, then the same amount of spending could be supported by a smaller money supply. For example, with $V = 5$, the same $6,000 in spending could be sustained by a money supply of only $1,200. Classical economists generally believed

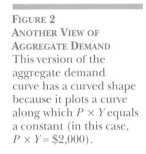

FIGURE 2
ANOTHER VIEW OF
AGGREGATE DEMAND
This version of the aggregate demand curve has a curved shape because it plots a curve along which $P \times Y$ equals a constant (in this case, $P \times Y = \$2,000$).

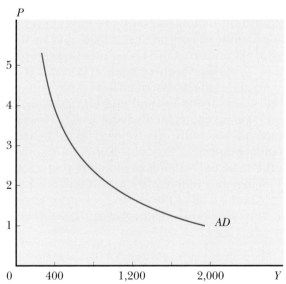

that velocity (V) was quite stable. Therefore, any change in the money supply would result in a proportional change in spending ($P \times Y$).

The variables on the right-hand side of the equation of exchange should look familiar. P is the price level, and Y is real output, so $P \times Y$ is (nominal) national income. If $M_s \times V$ is what was spent, $P \times Y$ is what was bought, and the two have to be equal. In fact, the equation of exchange is an identity. It states that what was spent has to equal the market value of what was bought.

In terms of the aggregate demand curve, the equation of exchange implies that a fixed money supply (M_s) combined with a stable velocity (V) will yield a constant value of nominal GNP, which is equal to $P \times Y$. That is, a fixed amount of money available to spend and a fairly stable frequency of spending for each unit of currency each year will determine nominal GNP. However, for any given nominal GNP, various combinations of P and Y are possible. Those combinations lie along a curve such as the one in Figure 2. You might experiment with drawing such a curve for given values of M_s and V. For example, the combinations of money supply and velocity that resulted in total spending of $6,000 could imply a price level of $1 and real output of 6,000 units or a price level of $4 and real output of 1,500 units, or various other combinations.[4]

We will explore the development of the quantity theory of money in more detail in the next chapter. For now, you can see that any given nominal money supply will determine an aggregate demand curve that slopes downward.

WHY THE AGGREGATE DEMAND CURVE HAS A NEGATIVE SLOPE

A higher price level reduces

- consumption demand,
- net exports, and
- government (state and local) spending

through

- smaller real money supply,
- higher interest rates,
- lower value of households' financial assets,
- higher (progressive) taxes,
- substitution of relatively cheaper foreign goods for domestic goods, and
- slow growth of sales and property tax revenues.

4.   Another way of looking at the quantity theory of money as an explanation of the aggregate demand curve is to rearrange the equation of exchange slightly. Dividing through by P and V gives $M_s/P = (1/V)Y$. The term on the left-hand side, M_s/P, is known as the real money supply, because it is the nominal money supply adjusted for changes in the price level. It represents the purchasing power of the money supply. Since the term $1/V$ can be regarded as roughly constant, this equation says that there is a positive relationship between the real money supply and the price level. It also says that for any given nominal money supply, there is a negative relationship between real output and the price level. An increase in the price level reduces the purchasing power of the money supply and therefore the amount of real output that people are able to demand.

aggregate supply curve
A graph showing the amounts of total real output that the producing sector will offer for sale at various price levels.

AGGREGATE SUPPLY

The **aggregate supply curve** shows the various quantities of total real output that the producing sector will offer for sale at various price levels. The equilibrium point on the aggregate supply curve corresponds roughly to NI at factor cost. However, NI at factor cost, like GNP, is computed in money terms and for only one price level, the current one. So NI is just one point on the aggregate supply curve, just as GNP less unplanned inventory investment is only one point on the aggregate demand curve. Points on the aggregate supply curve represent possible values of NI that suppliers are willing to produce and offer for sale.

THE SLOPE OF THE AGGREGATE SUPPLY CURVE. What is the shape of the aggregate supply curve? Economists would like to know the answer to that question! Probably no single graphical construction in economists' vast collection has generated as much argument as the aggregate supply curve. A large part of this dispute has to do with how firms and owners of resources respond to changes in the price level, and how quickly. Time plays an even more important role with respect to aggregate supply than with respect to aggregate demand. Thus, the dispute over the slope often centers on the difference between what the aggregate supply curve looks like in the short run and in the long run and how much time is meant in each of these cases.

Recalling the market supply curve for an individual product from Chapter 3, you are probably expecting the aggregate supply curve to slope up from left to right, like line *AS* in Figure 3(a). However, like the aggregate demand curve, the aggregate supply curve differs from the supply curves for individual products in some important ways. The problems of adding individual prices and outputs also exist for aggregate supply, so the aggregate supply curve is not simply the sum of the market supply curves for all goods and services. One of the reasons for the upward-sloping microeconomic supply curve for a single product is substitution. (Producers shift to more profitable products when prices of those goods rise relative to the prices of other goods the firm could produce.) This reason, how-

FIGURE 3
AGGREGATE SUPPLY CURVES
(a) An aggregate supply curve with an upward slope, similar to most supply curves. (b) The classical aggregate supply curve, for which the economy is producing at capacity (or full-employment level of output, Y^*). Attempts to increase output will only drive up the price level. (c) The Keynesian version of the aggregate supply curve, which assumes there are enough unemployed resources that output can be increased without driving the price level above P_0.

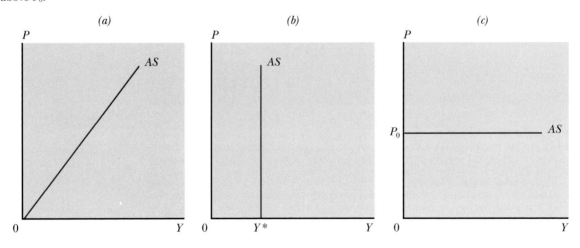

ever, has no validity at all in explaining why the aggregate supply curve slopes upward. Total real output on the horizontal axis already includes all possible substitute goods.

Nevertheless, many economists expect the aggregate supply curve to slope upward for some of the same reasons that supply curves for individual goods and services slope upward. As firms in general try to produce more output with given resources, some labor has to work overtime at higher pay, driving up costs and prices. Firms are working their capital harder, so it wears out faster and breaks down more often. Competition among producers for scarce resources drives up wages and interest rates. All of these cost increases, for individual products and for aggregate real output, will be reflected in higher prices.

Another reason for an upward-sloping supply curve, either for a single product or for goods and services in the aggregate, is that the lure of higher prices will induce producers to try to expand output. If firms and entrepreneurs can sell their products for more, and if their overall costs have not risen as much as the prices of what they sell, they can make more profit. Profit is the incentive and the reward to which producers respond. If higher prices do indeed mean higher profits, then the aggregate supply curve will slope upward.

A VERTICAL AGGREGATE SUPPLY CURVE. Before the 1930s, an even simpler view of the aggregate supply curve prevailed. It was seen as a vertical line, running straight up and down. This slope indicates that output does not respond at all to changes in the price level. Classical economists believed that the economy naturally tended toward the level of output that available resources could support. There was really only one level of real output that could occur in a properly functioning economic system, where supply and demand in labor markets assured full employment. This real output level was defined as the full-employment level of output, or capacity output. The **full-employment level of output** is the level of real output associated with full use of all factors of production, especially labor.

Figure 3(b) shows the aggregate supply curve as a vertical line (AS). The level of real output associated with full employment is labeled Y^*. In this model, the price level can vary, but it will have no effect on real output. A fixed real output level and a variable price level imply a vertical aggregate supply curve. Such a curve plays an important role in the classical macroeconomic model.

A HORIZONTAL AGGREGATE SUPPLY CURVE. The British economist John Maynard Keynes, who was introduced briefly in Chapter 4, offered a third view of the aggregate supply curve in the 1930s. He suggested that during periods when large amounts of resources were unemployed, the aggregate supply curve could be horizontal, as in Figure 3(c). It would be possible for firms to increase both individual and aggregate output without driving the price level above P_0. They could produce more simply by putting unemployed resources to work. Firms would not have to pay higher prices to compete for scarce resources. They could simply hire idle workers at the going wage and use their factories' idle capacity. A horizontal aggregate supply curve implies that the economy is inside its production possi-

full-employment level of output
The level of real output associated with full use of all of the factors of production, especially labor.

bilities curve, since there is unemployed labor (and other resources) willing to work at the present wage.

A COMPOSITE VIEW. These three views of the aggregate supply curve are sometimes combined in a composite version with three distinct regions, shown in Figure 4. The horizontal region (sometimes known as the Keynesian region) represents a situation in which there are ample idle resources. Thus, output can be increased without driving up prices. This segment corresponds to the Keynesian aggregate supply curve of Figure 3(c).

In the middle region of the composite aggregate supply curve, there are some unemployed resources. Perhaps they are not the right kind for the mix of additional output that firms are trying to produce. Attempting to expand output in this situation will drive up the price level but will also result in more output. This segment corresponds to the upward-sloping curve of Figure 3(a).

The last segment of the composite aggregate supply curve shows what happens when there are no more unemployed resources available. It is possible to produce more of good *A* only by cutting output of good *B*. As producers of *A* try to bid resources away from other uses, they drive up prices and reduce output of other goods. In this region, the economy is on the production possibilities curve. More of one kind of output can only be obtained by sacrificing output of other goods or services. Attempts to expand total real output will only drive up the price level. This segment corresponds to the classical curve of Figure 3(b).

THE SHORT RUN AND THE LONG RUN. The composite aggregate supply curve is one way to reconcile the conflicting views of how the graph should look. Another way of reconciling these conflicting views is to clarify what is meant by the short run and the long run. Part of the debate between Keynes and both his predecessors (the classical economists) and his successors (monetarists) is a matter of defining terms. Most economists

FIGURE 4
AGGREGATE SUPPLY
CURVE: COMPOSITE
VERSION
This composite aggregate supply curve is made up of a horizontal (Keynesian) region, an intermediate region in which prices and output rise or fall together, and a vertical (classical) region.

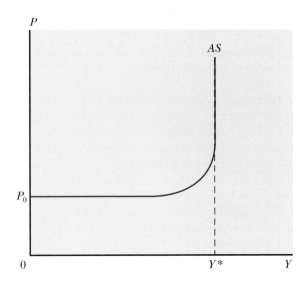

would agree that in the long run, the level of output will tend toward full employment, which corresponds to a vertical aggregate supply curve. They disagree about the curve's shape in the short run, however. Even more important, they disagree about the length of time that separates the short run from the long run. If the long run is six months, a fair amount of unemployment can be tolerated until the economy returns to "normal." If the long run is ten years, people will be less patient. Keynes and his followers pointed to the length and severity of the Great Depression as evidence of how long an economy can deviate from the long-run equilibrium level of output corresponding to full employment of resources.

AGGREGATE EQUILIBRIUM

What happens when we put aggregate supply and aggregate demand together? In Chapter 3, we combined the demand curve and supply curve for a specific good to determine an equilibrium quantity and price. In the same way, the aggregate demand and aggregate supply curves together determine the level of real output and the price level.

Consider the simplest case, a downward-sloping aggregate demand curve and an upward-sloping aggregate supply curve (Figure 5). Equilibrium occurs at Y_1 and P_1. This price and output combination is an equilibrium in the same sense that the intersection of an individual supply curve and demand curve is. If firms collectively try to produce any other level of output, forces in the marketplace will tend to push the economy toward the equilibrium level.

Consider what happens if firms try to produce a real output, Y_2, that is larger than the equilibrium level of output, Y_1. For that level of output, producers will attempt to charge prices that average out to a price level of P_2. But consumers are only willing to purchase that large quantity of output, Y_2, when the price level is much lower, P_3. At a price level of P_2, consumers are only willing to buy a total quantity of Y_3. At the higher output level, Y_2, producers will find themselves with unsold output (unplanned

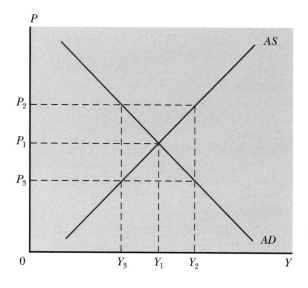

FIGURE 5
EQUILIBRIUM OUTPUT AND PRICE LEVEL
Equilibrium occurs at the intersection of *AS* and *AD*. If producers attempt to produce and sell the quantity Y_2, they will have unsold output at the desired price level. As they accumulate unwanted inventory, they will cut production. Real output and the price level will fall to Y_1 and P_1.

inventory investment) and will have to cut prices. As prices fall, the incentive to produce more output is lower. Thus, real output declines, until equilibrium is restored. You may want to go through this process for output levels below equilibrium, such as Y_3, to make sure you understand how equilibrium is restored.

In Figure 5, as in the diagrams for individual markets, the quantity sold and the quantity bought are always equal. Producers may offer quantity Y_2 at price level P_2, but they only sell quantity Y_3 at that price level. Both NI and GNP, however, are equal to $P_2 \times Y_2$. The unsold output is counted as inventory investment, and the workers and owners of capital who produced that output receive factor incomes. The national income accounts balance whether or not the economy is in equilibrium. In the circular flow model, the unplanned investment that firms make in inventory means that they will reduce their inventories in the near future. When that happens, the size of the flow will shrink back to a sustainable level of $P_1 \times Y_1$.

SHIFTS IN AGGREGATE DEMAND AND AGGREGATE SUPPLY

Changes in output and price level can result from shifts in either aggregate demand or aggregate supply. Aggregate demand can shift if any of the underlying conditions changes at every possible price level. These *ceteris paribus* conditions are the size of the money supply, household consumption, government spending, business investment, and net exports. Some of the effects that can shift individual demand curves are also still relevant. These effects are changes in consumer wealth, tastes, population, expectations, and interest rates. Two things that shift individual demand curves are not relevant here. One is the prices of substitutes and complements, which disappear when we aggregate over all goods. The other is changes in income. Since real output is also real income, income is already represented in the model and cannot be an exogenous variable.

Aggregate supply can also shift for two of the reasons that individual supply curves shift. There may be an increase or decrease in the amount of resources available or a change in technology. Other things that affect individual supply curves, such as the prices of other products the firm could produce, disappear when we look at aggregate output.

SHIFTS IN AGGREGATE DEMAND. If the aggregate supply curve slopes upward, we expect both the price level and output to increase when the aggregate demand curve shifts to the right. How much of the shift is in the price level and how much is in real output depends on the slope of the aggregate supply curve. In Figure 6, the original equilibrium is at P_1 and Y_1 on AD_1. A shift of the curve to AD_2 means that people want to purchase more real output at every possible price level. If the aggregate demand curve shifted to AD_3, this would mean that people are willing to buy less real output at every possible price level. Both the price level and total real output will fall. When the aggregate demand curve shifts, prices and real output move in the same direction.

The effect of shifts of the aggregate demand curve on real output and the price level is different if the aggregate supply curve is horizontal or vertical. Along a horizontal aggregate supply curve, increases in aggregate demand drive up real output only. Also, a decline in aggregate demand re-

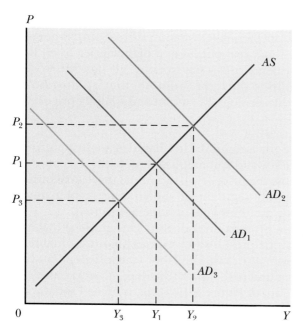

FIGURE 6
SHIFTS IN
AGGREGATE DEMAND
An increase in aggregate demand from AD_1 to AD_2 (a shift to the right) drives output and prices up. A decrease in aggregate demand from AD_1 to AD_3 (a shift to the left) drives output and prices down.

duces real output only, with no effect on the price level. With a vertical aggregate supply curve, the price level rises when the aggregate demand curve shifts to the right and falls when it shifts to the left, but real output does not change. You might experiment with the composite aggregate supply curve of Figure 4 to observe these different effects on prices and output.

SHIFTS IN AGGREGATE SUPPLY. Shifts in aggregate supply are shown in Figure 7. For simplicity, we use the upward-sloping aggregate supply curve.

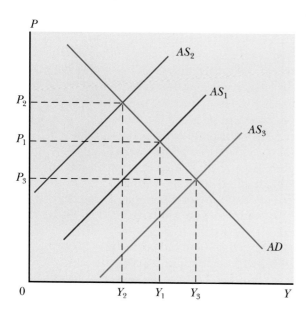

FIGURE 7
SHIFTS IN
AGGREGATE SUPPLY
A decrease in aggregate supply from AS_1 to AS_2 (a leftward shift) raises prices and lowers real output. An increase in aggregate supply from AS_1 to AS_3 (a rightward shift) lowers the price level and increases real output.

A shift in aggregate supply to the left (from AS_1 to AS_2) means that producers will be willing to supply a smaller quantity of real output at every possible price level *or* the same real output at a higher price level. Real output falls and the price level rises—the worst of all possible worlds. When aggregate supply shifts to the right (from AS_1 to AS_3), the result is the best of all possible worlds—rising real output and a falling price level.

EMPLOYMENT AND UNEMPLOYMENT

The three macroeconomic goals identified in Chapter 4 are steady growth of total output, price stability, and full employment. Since Y represents real output and P represents the price level, two of the three goals are included in the aggregate supply and demand model. This graphic model can be extended to include the third goal of full employment.

Figure 8 is an **aggregate production function**. This graph shows how much total real output can be produced by various amounts of labor. A production function is normally drawn with labor (the independent variable) on the horizontal axis and real output (the dependent variable) on the vertical axis. The diagram in Figure 8, however, is turned sideways so that the horizontal axis shows real output (Y) and the vertical axis shows the aggregate level of employment of labor (N). Assuming that the size of the labor force is stable, the higher the value of N, the lower the rate of unemployment will be.

There is a positive relationship between the number of workers employed and the level of real output. More workers will produce more output. In Figure 8, output rises as more workers are hired, but as more workers are added, total ouput grows more slowly. The best workers are hired first, and the last workers hired are usually less productive. Also, if the stock of capital is fixed, each worker added has less and less capital with which to work. So extra workers increase total output, but later ones do not add as much as previous ones.

aggregate production function
A graph showing the relationship between total real output and the number of workers employed.

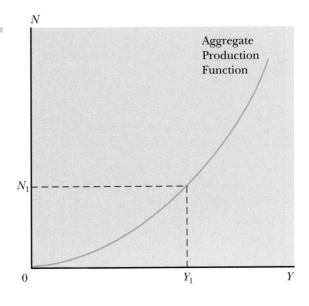

FIGURE 8
THE AGGREGATE PRODUCTION FUNCTION
The aggregate production function shows the relationship between the level of real output and the level of employment. The increase in real output gets smaller as more and more workers are hired.

Combining Figure 8 with aggregate supply and demand curves provides a view of output, employment, and prices all at once. This is done in Figure 9. Equilibrium values of the price level and real output are determined to be P_1 and Y_1, where AS crosses AD_1. Tracing real output down to the aggregate production function, we find that N_1 workers must be employed in order to produce that level of real output. Thus, aggregate supply and demand combined with a production function determine not only the price level and real output but also the level of employment and, by extension, the level of unemployment.

If N_1 is less than full employment, then the diagram in Figure 9 suggests how to get to full employment. A shift of either AD or AS to the right will cause the two curves to intersect at a higher level of real output. This shift increases employment and reduces unemployment. For example, a shift from AD_1 to AD_2 will raise output to Y_2, the price level to P_2, and employment to N_2. In this case, statistics would show an increase in both out-

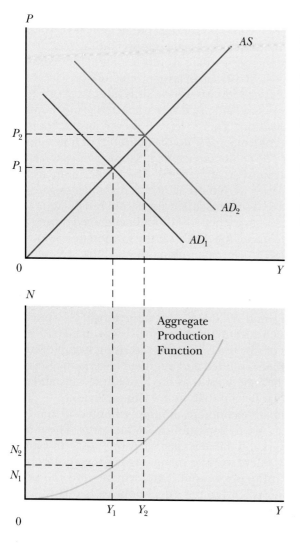

FIGURE 9
OUTPUT, EMPLOYMENT, AND PRICE LEVEL
Combining aggregate supply, demand, and production function in two interrelated graphs shows what is happening to output, employment, and the price level all at once. Shifts of AD or AS affect employment as well as the price level and real output.

put and employment but at the expense of a higher price level (inflation). You can experiment with other combinations to see how changes in aggregate supply and demand affect employment and unemployment.

AGGREGATE SUPPLY AND DEMAND AND COMPETING MACROECONOMIC IDEAS

The aggregate supply and demand model is very useful for looking at macroeconomic policy. It is also helpful in understanding some of the disputes over what policy can and cannot do. The competing ideas of the various groups of macroeconomists can be interpreted using this simple framework. Some of the differences between Keynesians and monetarists, Post-Keynesians and new classical economists, or (in the nineteenth century) the classical school and business cycle theorists can be interpreted as disagreements over how aggregate demand shifts, or whether it can be permanently shifted by government policies. Other disputes can be interpreted in terms of differences over the shape of the aggregate supply curve and whether and how it can be shifted by public policies.

Although the formal model of aggregate supply and aggregate demand is relatively new, both concepts date from the nineteenth century. Macroeconomics did not get a great deal of attention before the Great Depression. Nineteenth-century economists were mainly interested in microeconomic questions of value, cost, and price, free trade and protectionism, and monopoly and competition. There were, however, two schools of thought that disagreed over the macroeconomic questions of how output, employment, and the price level are determined. These groups were the classical school and the business cycle theorists. The former emphasized aggregate supply and the latter were more concerned with aggregate demand, although these terms were not actually used until much later.

The conflict between these two schools of thought climaxed during the Great Depression. The outcome of that clash was the Keynesian revolution, which put a new emphasis on aggregate demand and how it could be shifted. As Keynesian policies produced mixed results, new groups of economists challenged Keynes's emphasis on aggregate demand. Although these groups had a wide range of views, the dominant group that emerged during the 1960s and 1970s was the monetarists. As concern shifted from full employment to inflation, monetarists seemed to be offering better explanations of why the price level was rising so rapidly during the 1970s. Other economists refined and modified ideas in the Keynesian tradition. This group became known as the Post-Keynesians and has been much stronger in Great Britain than in the United States.

Two more schools of macroeconomic thought emerged in the late 1970s to challenge both the Keynesians and the monetarists. These new groups were the supply siders and the new classical economists (or rational expectationists). Supply siders stressed managing aggregate supply as the most effective way to influence output, employment, and the price level. New classical economists tend to regard all policies as relatively ineffective. Like supply siders, however, they emphasize aggregate supply in explaining how output and employment are determined.

Here, we provide a brief overview of the central ideas of each of these groups and how they relate to aggregate demand and supply.

THE CLASSICAL SCHOOL

Economists use the term **classical school** to refer to a diverse group of economists, from David Hume in the early eighteenth century to A. C. Pigou in the early twentieth century. What these economists had in common was a belief that the economy automatically tends toward a level of output associated with full employment. In their view, the aggregate supply curve is vertical, at least in the long run, and the long run is not very long. Because of that belief, they felt that the main goal of macroeconomic policy should be to control the price level and inflation. The core of classical macroeconomics focused on the management of the money supply to control inflation.

One of the central ideas of the classical school was the quantity theory of money introduced earlier in this chapter (and examined in more detail in Chapter 7). The quantity theory of money was originally developed as an explanation for inflation. Today, changes in the money supply are viewed as one of the major sources of shifts in the aggregate demand curve. The other central idea of the classical school was Say's law.

SAY'S LAW. Jean-Baptiste Say was a nineteenth-century French economist who was interested in business cycles. His name is associated with **Say's law**, which says that "supply creates its own demand." That is, enough income is created in the process of production to buy everything that is produced. Individual goods can be overproduced if suppliers fail to read correctly the signals from the market. These suppliers will be penalized for producing the wrong things by incurring losses. Meanwhile those who read the market signals correctly will be rewarded with profits. General overproduction for any length of time is not possible.

Say realized that this view was rather simplistic. What would happen if households let part of their income "leak" out of the circular flow in order to save, instead of spending it all on consumption? Say had an answer for that objection. Household saving would flow into banks and be lent to business firms that would inject it back into the income stream as investment. In an economy with small government and foreign sectors, saving (leakages) and investment (injections) would be equal.

What ensures that saving will be equal to investment? The incentive to save is the interest that can be earned. Interest is the reward for saving. Interest is also the price of investment. The biggest obstacle to borrowing in order to invest is the interest that must be paid. Changes in the interest rate, like changes in any price, ensure that the supply of funds (saving) will be equal to the demand for borrowing (investment). Thus, automatic forces will always push real output (Y) toward the full-employment level, or Y^* in Figure 10. Attempts to increase aggregate demand will only drive up the price level. In Figure 10, an increase in aggregate demand from AD_1 to AD_2 drives the price level up from P_1 to P_2, leaving real output unchanged at Y^*. Say's law is the reason why classical economists believed that the aggregate supply curve is vertical at the full-employment level of real output.

classical school
A group of economists in the eighteenth and nineteenth centuries who believed that the economy automatically tended toward the full-employment level of output.

Say's law
The idea that supply creates its own demand, a cornerstone of classical economics.

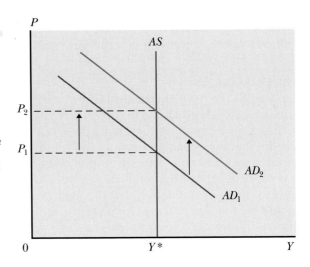

FIGURE 10
AGGREGATE SUPPLY
AND DEMAND:
A CLASSICAL VIEW
If the aggregate supply
curve (*AS*) is vertical,
shifting aggregate
demand from AD_1 to AD_2
drives the price level up,
from P_1 to P_2, leaving real
output unchanged at Y^*.
Thus, policies aimed at
increasing aggregate
demand will not be
effective.

CLASSICAL ECONOMICS AND *LAISSEZ-FAIRE*. Classical economists were the intellectual heirs of Adam Smith and his *laissez-faire* ideas about the effectiveness of free markets. Their prescription for macroeconomic policies could also be described as *laissez-faire*: Leave the macro economy alone, and it will correct itself. According to them, unemployment does occur, but it cannot last very long because the economy automatically tends toward a level of output associated with full employment. With the level of real output determined by the resources available and unemployment viewed as a short-term and self-correcting problem, the classical economists' main macroeconomic concern was the price level. Classical economists in the nineteenth century knew that increases in aggregate demand could drive up the price level. They believed that the government should try to control the money supply in order to keep aggregate demand from shifting to the right and causing inflation.

It is clear from the data presented in Chapter 4 that there were extended periods of falling output and unemployment during the time of the classical school. It is difficult to reconcile these data with an aggregate supply curve that is vertical at the full-employment level of output. However, some of the classical economists' ideas reflected their ordering of macroeconomic goals. Inflation was of greater concern to them than un-

IDEAS OF THE CLASSICAL SCHOOL

- *Output* is determined by available resources (especially labor) and will always tend toward the level associated with full employment. Thus, the aggregate supply curve will be vertical at the full-employment level of output.

- *Employment* is determined by supply and demand in the labor market. Unemployment is generally temporary and can be corrected by a reduction in real wages.

- The *price level* is determined by aggregate demand, or, more specifically, by the money supply, which determines the position of the aggregate demand curve.

employment. Also, minimal government intervention was a goal in itself. They felt that government intervention in the economy, even on behalf of the worthy goal of full employment, was likely to interfere with the more highly valued microeconomic goals of efficiency and freedom.

Finally, classical economists were primarily concerned with the long run, a time period in which the economy is normally at or near the full-employment level of output. They felt that any deviations from full employment and capacity output would be corrected if only people were willing to wait for natural market forces to operate.

THE BUSINESS CYCLE THEORISTS

Nineteenth-century economists who were concerned about large or prolonged deviations from the full-employment level of output were called **business cycle theorists**. Among them were Thomas Robert Malthus and Karl Marx. These economists challenged the classical view that market forces will return the economy automatically to full employment. They thought that view didn't seem to fit the evidence. There were long and painful periods of declining output and widespread unemployment that had to be explained and, if possible, corrected. In addition, cyclical patterns in economic activity were clearly observable, such as the business cycle illustrated in Chapter 4. None of these real-world events were consistent with an aggregate supply curve that was vertical. The business cycle theorists' picture of the economy is captured by Figure 11, which shows a fairly flat aggregate supply curve. In this model, a shift in aggregate demand from AD_1 to AD_2 drives the price level up from P_1 to P_2, but also results in an increase in real output from Y_1 to Y_2.

Business cycle theorists argued that cyclical ups and downs in output, employment, and prices occurred with such regularity and frequency that they seemed to be obeying some natural law of the marketplace. But that law was not Say's law. Unlike the classical economists, the business cycle theorists did not develop a single general theory or model to describe, explain, or predict the recurrent ups and downs in economic activity. Their

business cycle theorists
A group of economists in the nineteenth and early twentieth centuries who tried to develop explanations for cyclical patterns in economic activity.

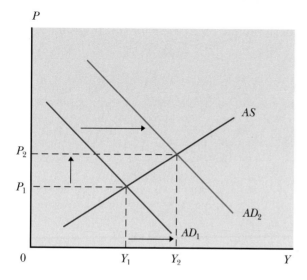

FIGURE 11
AGGREGATE SUPPLY AND DEMAND: THE VIEW OF THE BUSINESS CYCLE THEORISTS
The aggregate supply and demand model can be used to interpret the ideas of business cycle theorists. With a fairly flat aggregate supply curve, a shift of aggregate demand from AD_1 to AD_2 drives the price level up, from P_1 to P_2. It also results in an increase in real output from Y_1 to Y_2.

The Physiocrats (see Chapter 2) felt that saving could cause reductions in the circular flow that would be damaging to the economy. A later French economist, Jean-Baptiste Say, presented a theory that stated that saving (leakages) was no cause for concern. Say, a businessman turned academic, taught political economy at the *Conservatoire des Arts et Metiers*.

Say's law played a central role in classical macroeconomics. This law is based on a simple theory of self-regulating markets. Say's law contends that the aggregate supply of goods and services will always be equal to the aggregate demand for them. Say maintained that the sum of all wages, profits, rents, and interest paid in production (NI) would be equal to the value of the goods produced (GNP) and, therefore, would be sufficient to buy them. The purchasing power in a system is always enough to purchase the goods produced. The simple, popular statement of Say's law is that supply creates its own demand. Household income that does not flow directly back into the income stream in the form of consumption would be channeled as saving through the credit market. It would flow either into investment or into consumption by other households that borrow.

ECONOMIC PROFILE

JEAN-BAPTISTE SAY

1767–1832

Say never argued that overproduction of some goods and underproduction of others would not occur. He believed, however, that these imbalances would be corrected rather quickly as entrepreneurs adjusted the output mix in order to earn profits by satisfying consumer demands.

Supply side economics, which gained popularity in the 1980s, draws on Say's theory in emphasizing the role of aggregate supply. Many supply siders quoted the following passage from Say:

"The encouragement of mere consumption is no benefit to commerce; for the difficulty lies in supplying the means, not in stimulating the desire for consumption; and we have seen production alone furnishes that means. It is the aim of good government to stimulate production; of bad government to encourage consumption."[a]

a. Jean-Baptiste Say, *A Treatise on Political Economy* (Philadelphia: John Grigg, 1830).

major contribution was to point to the role of demand (or what we now call aggregate demand), specifically the behavior of consumption or investment demand, in generating changes in output, employment, and price level. When Keynes tried to explain one of the most severe downturns in economic activity in modern times, the Great Depression, he built on the work of the business cycle theorists.

What values and priorities were implicit in the work of the business cycle theorists? They were more concerned about unemployment and lost output than the classical school was. Business cycle theorists did not ignore inflation, but it was not as urgent a concern to them. Like classical economists, however, most of them (except for Marx) did not prescribe government intervention. Many of them, in fact, shared the classical school's *laissez-faire* attitude about the role of government. In addition, with no real model, it was not easy to devise an appropriate form of government intervention to stabilize the business cycle. That prescription had to await the Keynesian revolution in the 1930s.

JOHN MAYNARD KEYNES AND THE KEYNESIAN REVOLUTION

The greatest challenge to the classical school was the business cycle itself at its worst—the Great Depression. "Wait it out; the economy will correct itself" was not appealing advice in the depths of the Depression. John Maynard Keynes's often quoted answer to the classical economists was "In the long run we are all dead." He insisted that even if the problems of falling output and unemployment could not last indefinitely, they could last long enough to cause great hardship, lost output, and human suffering. Even if the aggregate supply curve was vertical in the long run, its shape could be much flatter, or even horizontal, in the short run. If aggregate supply was relatively constant, shifts in aggregate demand could have significant effects on real output and employment. Economists whose macroeconomic ideas are based on the work of this famous British economist are called **Keynesians**.

The Keynesian challenge to the classical view is one that will take several chapters to develop. Basically, Keynes started with the idea that the aggregate supply curve might be very flat, or even horizontal. In that case, the economy could be in equilibrium, with aggregate supply equal to aggregate demand, at a level of output Y_e that is substantially below the full-employment level of output, Y^*. This situation, pictured in Figure 12, could persist for a fairly long time if there was no government intervention. This view challenged the classical position that equilibrium implied full employment. To the classical economists, the situation Keynes described was a disequilibrium that would set in motion automatic corrective forces.

Keynes also challenged Say's law. He argued that just because enough income is created in the production process to buy the output, that does not necessarily mean that all of the income will be spent. Savings would not be automatically channeled into investment, and the interest rate would not be very effective in ensuring that the two were equal. (We will present a more detailed picture of this challenge in Chapters 7 and 8.) The important conclusion that Keynes drew was that private components of aggregate demand (consumption and investment) might not behave so as to restore full employment. He thought that the government should use its

Keynesian economists
Twentieth-century economists who adopted and extended John Maynard Keynes's idea that there could be persistent unemployment without government intervention.

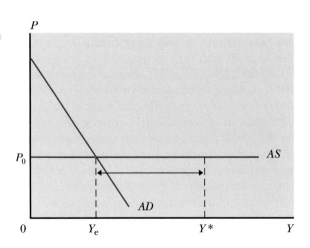

FIGURE 12
AGGREGATE SUPPLY AND
DEMAND: A KEYNESIAN
VIEW
This model shows an
equilibrium situation in
which aggregate supply
is equal to aggregate
demand. Note that the
resulting level of output,
Y_e, is substantially below
the full-employment level
of output, Y^*.

power to spend and tax in order to stabilize private economic activity. The use of government taxing and spending to influence output, employment, and prices is called **fiscal policy**. Keynes saw fiscal policy as a way to shift aggregate demand to the right, increasing output and employment.

Because fiscal policy can be inflationary (depending on the slope of the aggregate supply curve), many people believed that Keynes was more concerned about unemployment than inflation. That is not true. Some of his writings, such as *Treatise on Money* and *How to Pay for the War*, addressed the problem of inflation. In 1936, however, when the *General Theory of Employment, Interest, and Money* was published, unemployment was a very serious concern, and the price level had been falling for several years. What really set Keynes apart from the classical school was not so much his concern for unemployment as his willingness to sacrifice *laissez-faire* principles. Unlike classical economists, Keynes thought that government officials could and should intervene to speed up the process of getting back to full employment.

Again, it is not difficult to draw some inferences about Keynes's values and priorities from what he had to say. He was concerned primarily with unemployment, at least in 1936. He was not willing to let hardship, suffering, and lost output persist while the economy slowly corrected itself. Finally, Keynes was not committed to *laissez-faire* policies and a minimal role for government. He believed that the benefits of intervention in the business cycle would exceed the cost. This argument led to a political revolution with

fiscal policy
The use of government spending and taxes to try to influence the levels of output, employment, and prices.

IDEAS OF THE KEYNESIANS

In the short run, if the economy is below full employment,

- *Output* is determined by aggregate demand.
- *Employment* is determined by the level of output.
- The *price level* is unable to fall and unlikely to rise under these conditions, so it can be treated as given.

respect to the role of government. That change was as important as the intellectual revolution Keynes's ideas caused in the field of economics.

THE MONETARISTS

Keynesian ideas spread rapidly in the 1940s and 1950s. These ideas had so much influence that the impact of Keynes on macroeconomics became known as the Keynesian revolution. Inevitably, there was a counter-revolution. Keynesian economics appeared to be successful in preventing unemployment and major recessions, but neither Keynes nor his followers put much emphasis on the problem of price stability. Some critics questioned whether Keynesian economics was really in any way responsible for postwar prosperity. The most coherent and effective criticisms came from a group of economists somewhat in the classical tradition. This group was named **monetarists** by one of their best known members, Karl Brunner. Using more elaborate theories and statistical evidence than the classical school, monetarists challenged Keynes's theories and policy recommendations.

Although the monetarists are in the *laissez-faire* classical tradition, their name comes from the fact that they admit that at least one kind of government policy can have at least some short-run impact. **Monetary policy** means using changes in the money supply to try to affect levels of output, employment, and prices. Monetarists believe that monetary policy can shift aggregate demand and, in the short run, may affect real output, especially if the changes in the money supply are unexpected.

Monetarists, like classical economists, believe that the aggregate supply curve is vertical in the long run. They do concede that the curve can have a positive slope in the short run, although they expect it to be fairly steep. That is, in the short run, the economy could find itself at a level of output Y_e that is below the full-employment level of output, Y^*, as shown in Figure 13. Expanding the money supply would shift the aggregate de-

monetarists
Twentieth-century economists who criticize Keynesian economics and stress the role of the money supply.

monetary policy
The use of changes in the money supply to try to influence the levels of output, employment, and prices.

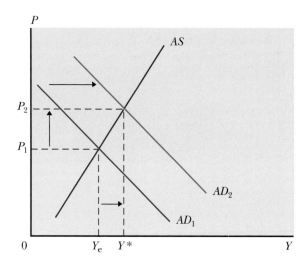

FIGURE 13
AGGREGATE SUPPLY AND DEMAND: A MONETARIST VIEW
If the economy is operating at a level of output Y_e below the full-employment level of output Y^*, expanding the money supply shifts the aggregate demand curve from AD_1 to AD_2. There is a slightly less than vertical slope on the aggregate supply curve in the short run. Thus, the price level rises from P_1 to P_2. Real output also increases slightly, from Y_e to Y^*.

mand curve from AD_1 to AD_2. With a positively sloped aggregate supply curve, the price level in the short run would rise from P_1 to P_2. Real output, however, would also increase from Y_e to Y^*. Like classical economists but unlike Keynesians, monetarists are also concerned about inflation and generally opposed to government intervention. We will look more carefully at their contributions in later chapters.

SUPPLY SIDERS
Both Keynesians and monetarists are primarily concerned with the aggregate demand curve and why it shifts. They both take the aggregate supply curve as given, even if they do disagree about its slope. In the late 1970s and early 1980s, many countries, including the United States, experienced rising prices, falling output, and rising unemployment all at the same time. If you look again at Figure 9, you will see that this combination could not have resulted from shifts in the aggregate demand curve. Something must have been happening to aggregate supply. This was the conclusion of a group of academic economists and policy makers called **supply siders**. This name reflects the fact that they were looking for solutions to problems of inflation and unemployment that would involve shifting aggregate supply to the right.

supply siders
Late-twentieth-century economists and policy makers who want to fight inflation and unemployment by trying to shift the aggregate supply curve to the right.

Figure 14 shows the supply side view. Initially, equilibrium price level P_1 and real output Y_1 are determined by the intersection of a steeply sloped aggregate supply curve (AS_1) and a stable aggregate demand curve (AD_1). Now some event happens to reduce the economy's capacity to produce real output. The most famous such event (called a supply shock) in recent history was the dramatic increase in the price of oil in the mid-1970s. Oil not only is needed for heating and transportation but also enters into the production of many other goods, such as fertilizers, plastics, and medicines. The sudden rise in the price of oil shifted the aggregate supply curve from AS_1 to AS_2, driving the price level up to P_2 and reducing real output to Y_2.

Supply siders are every bit as diverse as the business cycle theorists. They tend, as a group, to be less theoretical than some of the other schools

FIGURE 14
SUPPLY SHOCKS AND
AGGREGATE SUPPLY
AND DEMAND
A supply shock moves the economy away from its initial equilibrium price level, P_1, and real output, Y_1. The shift in the aggregate supply curve from AS_1 to AS_2 drives the price level up to P_2 and reduces real output to Y_2.

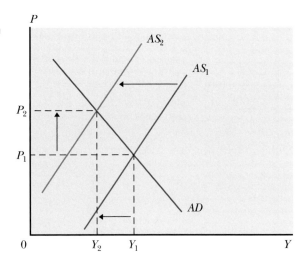

of thought. The theory on which they rely is largely a microeconomic theory of individual incentives. Supply siders are concerned about both inflation and unemployment. Supply siders generally want a strong private economy, but some of them support certain kinds of government intervention. In large part, "Reaganomics" (the economic policies of the Reagan administration from 1981 to 1989) reflected the ideas of the supply siders. We will look more closely at their ideas and experiences in the 1980s with their policy prescriptions in a later chapter.

NEW CLASSICAL ECONOMISTS

The group of economists known as the **new classical economists** (or sometimes as the rational expectations school) also emerged during the 1970s and 1980s. These economists were displeased with both the usefulness of existing theories and the performance of the economy. They take an even dimmer view of government intervention than the monetarists do. New classical economists regard both monetary and fiscal policies as ineffective because individuals find it in their own self-interest to anticipate government actions and respond in ways that offset the impact of those actions. The new classical models imply that government policies can only be effective when people are taken by surprise. Otherwise, self-interested behavior defeats the effectiveness of government efforts to shift aggregate demand.

new classical economists Late-twentieth-century economists who regard monetary and fiscal policies as ineffective because individuals will anticipate and offset government actions.

New classical economists share with classical economists (and to some extent with monetarists) a good deal of faith in the effective workings of unregulated markets and a preference for a minimal role for government. They believe that the aggregate supply curve is vertical or close to vertical even in the short run, because markets are very efficient and individuals apply new information quickly to their behavior. Their policy ideas and their view of the aggregate supply curve are quite similar to those of the classical school. However, their arguments are more sophisticated, often expressed in elaborate mathematical form. They also differ from the classical school on the issue of aggregate demand. Classical economists believe that policies can shift the aggregate demand curve. However, the shift will only cause inflation, with no effect on real output. New classical economists are skeptical about the ability of policy to shift the aggregate demand curve at all.

New classical economists believe that the aggregate supply curve is vertical in the long run and close to vertical in the short run. They argue that even if government policy makers succeed in shifting aggregate demand, the only effect will be to drive up prices. Unlike classical economists, however, new classical economists believe that monetary and fiscal policy can have some *temporary* effects on both output and price level. These effects will last until the private actors in the economy realize what the government is doing. In the long run (not a very long period of time, in the new classical view), private decisions will determine the level of output and employment. We will explore the ideas of this school in greater detail in a later chapter.

THE POST-KEYNESIANS

Every counterrevolution faces loyalists, and the attack on the Keynesian revolution was no exception. The "defenders of the faith" in this case were

Post-Keynesians
A group of late-twentieth-century economists who have refined and extended the work of Keynes. They stress market imperfections such as imperfect information, monopoly power, and inflexible wages and prices.

several groups of economists, both British and American, known as Post-Keynesians.[5] **Post-Keynesians** are economists who have refined and extended the ideas of Keynes in response to real-world experiences as well as challenges from monetarists, supply siders, and new classical economists.

In general, Post-Keynesians are skeptical about the responsiveness of markets, the flexibility of wages and prices, and the speed of the adjustment process. They point to long-term contracts, monopolies, the costs of gathering information, and other real-world considerations that can greatly slow the adjustment process. Thus, their aggregate supply curve, like that of the Keynesians, is relatively flat, and the short run is a fairly long period of time. Like Keynes, they see an important role for government in smoothing out ups and downs and, in particular, in reducing unemployment by shifting aggregate demand. We will examine Post-Keynesian ideas more closely in later chapters.

LIBERALS, CONSERVATIVES, AND POLITICAL ECONOMY

As you may have noticed, some economists support and others are opposed to government intervention to correct unemployment. In general, those who favor a larger role for government in both macroeconomic and microeconomic policy are known as liberals. Those who wish to minimize the role of government and rely on market processes are labeled conservatives.

The old name of economics was political economy, reflecting an emphasis on proposing and evaluating public policy. Although contemporary economists pride themselves on being positive rather than normative, in practice the line between positive and normative is not clearly drawn. Goals, values, and priorities tend to influence economists' thinking, development of models, and interpretation of data.

Keynesians and Post-Keynesians are generally liberal in political philosophy. They are concerned about unemployment, somewhat tolerant of inflation, and inclined to look for solutions through government. Monetarists and new classical economists, on the other hand, tend to be conservative. These two groups have much more faith in market processes and much less trust in the ability of government to improve outcomes. Both of these groups tend to worry more about inflation than unemployment. Supply siders' political philosophy falls somewhere between these two camps, closer to the conservative end. Unlike monetarists and new classical economists, supply siders are concerned about both inflation and unemployment and see some positive but limited role for government. They believe that government can create an environment in which the private sector can work effectively to shift aggregate supply to the right.

As we work through the ideas of these various groups in the next few chapters, keep in mind that even though the theories and models are positive rather than normative, their interpretation and application by particular economists or groups are inevitably tinged by political philosophy.

---

5. A number of American economists who have modified and refined some of their views in response to critics but are still within the Keynesian tradition call themselves "New Keynesians."

Summary

1. The aggregate demand curve shows the amounts of total real output that consumers will buy at various price levels. This curve slopes down from left to right.

2. A higher price level is associated with less demand for real output. This relationship is due to the effects of changes in price level on tax revenues, interest rates, exports and imports, and households' wealth.

3. Aggregate demand will shift if there is a change in consumption, investment, government spending, or net exports at every price level or if there is a change in the money supply.

4. The aggregate supply curve shows the amounts of total real output that the economy will produce at various price levels. There is much disagreement about whether this curve is horizontal, upward-sloping, or vertical. A composite aggregate supply curve has a horizontal region at low levels of output, followed by an upward-sloping range, and finally a vertical segment as output reaches capacity.

5. An upward-sloping aggregate supply curve results from higher costs of production as firms compete for increasingly scarce supplies of resources. Alternatively, an upward-sloping aggregate supply curve reflects the incentive that higher profits associated with higher prices gives to producers to increase output.

6. The aggregate supply and demand curves, taken together, determine the price level and the level of real output. Adding an aggregate production function also indicates the level of employment.

7. The two competing schools of thought in macroeconomics in the nineteenth century were the classical school and the business cycle theorists. Classical economists thought that the economy tended naturally toward full employment. Thus, the classical aggregate supply curve was vertical. The classical school advocated a *laissez-faire* approach. The business cycle theorists were concerned about the ups and downs of the market economy, which had long periods of unemployment and falling output. Business cycle theorists put more emphasis on the role of what contemporary economists call aggregate demand.

8. Keynes challenged the classical school during the Great Depression. He suggested that the aggregate supply curve could be horizontal, or at least very flat, in the short run. Thus, periods of unemployment could persist for a long time without automatic correction. He advocated government intervention in the form of fiscal policy to shift aggregate demand.

9. The principal competing schools of thought in the late twentieth century are the Keynesians and Post-Keynesians on one side and the monetarists and new classical economists on the other, with supply siders in between. They disagree about the effectiveness of policy and the steepness of the aggregate supply curve.

10. Monetarists criticized Keynesian theory and policy and recommended a return to a more *laissez-faire* approach. However, they believe that shifting aggregate demand by changing the money supply can be an effective policy tool in the short run.

11. Both Keynesians and monetarists focus on aggregate demand. Supply siders advocate shifting aggregate supply. This should result in lower prices and increased output and employment at the same time.

12. New classical economists, like classical economists, see a minimal role for government. The classical school took the position that the private economy will do well enough if left alone. The new classical economists go further. They argue that monetary policy and fiscal policy are generally ineffective because their intended impact on aggregate demand is offset by the rational expectations of households and firms. They also believe that the aggregate supply curve is close to vertical even in the short run.

New Terms

aggregate demand curve	aggregate supply curve	aggregate production function	Say's law
quantity theory of money	full-employment level of output	classical school	business cycle theorists
equation of exchange			Keynesians

fiscal policy   monetary policy   new classical economists
monetarists   supply siders   Post-Keynesians

QUESTIONS FOR DISCUSSION

1. Suppose the President proposes to increase federal spending in order to reduce unemployment. Show the effect of this change on the diagram of Figure 9. What would be the reaction of a classical economist, a Keynesian, a monetarist, and a supply sider?

2. Practice using the aggregate supply and demand curves. What kind of shift would produce a rise in both P and Y? a fall in both? a rise in P and a fall in Y? a rise in Y and a fall in P?

3. How can you shift aggregate demand and/or aggregate supply so that real output increases while prices remain stable?

4. Why does the aggregate demand curve slope down from left to right?

5. Explain how Figure 9 makes it possible to consider all three macroeconomic goals.

6. Identify whether each of these statements is most likely to be made by a classical economist, a Keynesian, a monetarist, a new classical economist, or a supply sider.

   a. "If the government doesn't do something about unemployment, it isn't going to go away any time soon."

   b. "If the government tries to increase employment, all it will wind up doing will be driving up the price level."

   c. "If the government feels it should do something in this recession, it should use monetary policy."

   d. "Whatever the government does, smart people will figure it out in advance and take actions that will wind up offsetting the effect of government policy."

   e. "If we just encourage production by making it worthwhile for business to produce, we will get out of this recession. Demand is not the problem."

7. Assume an upward-sloping aggregate supply curve. How will an increase in foreign demand for exports affect aggregate supply and demand, output, prices, and employment? Use aggregate supply and demand curves and a production function in your answer.

8. How would your answer to Question 7 be different if the aggregate supply curve were vertical? What if it were horizontal?

9. Which variables rise during the upswing of the business cycle? Do any fall? Which ones rise and which ones fall during a downturn?

10. How does Keynes's famous remark "In the long run we are all dead" relate to the debate between classical economists and Keynesians?

11. In what ways are Keynesians and Post-Keynesians liberal? In what ways are monetarists and new classical economists conservative? Why are supply siders harder to classify?

12. In the equation of exchange, suppose V is stable (constant) with a value of 4, and the money supply is $200 billion. What combinations of P and Y are possible? Identify about a dozen combinations, and plot them on a graph. Does your graph look like an aggregate demand curve? Why or why not?

13. Suppose the money supply in Question 12 increases to $300 billion. Identify some new possible combinations of P and Y. Plot the new combinations. Which way has the curve shifted?

14. What kinds of changes can shift the aggregate supply curve to the right? What kinds of changes can shift the aggregate demand curve to the right?

15. Suppose the aggregate demand curve is a straight line. One point on it is represented by a price level of $3 and a quantity of 1,500 units, and another point by a price level of $5 and a quantity of 1,000 units. What quantity of real output is associated with a price level of $4? Can you locate other points on this line?

SUGGESTIONS FOR FURTHER READING

Backhouse, Roger. *Economists and the Economy: The Evolution of Economic Ideas, 1600 to the Present Day.* Oxford and New York: Basil Blackwell, 1988. Development of economic ideas in a context of economic history; particularly strong in the development of ideas about inflation, employment, and business cycles.

Breit, William, and Roger L. Ransom. *The Academic Scribblers: Economists in Collision,* 2nd ed. Hinsdale, IL: Dryden Press, 1982. Biographical sketches and contributions of a number of famous economists of the past.

Canterbery, E. Ray. *The Making of Economics*, 2nd ed. Belmont, CA: Wadsworth, 1980. History of economic thought; emphasizes interaction of economic conditions, values, and development of economic ideas.

Maddock, Rodney, and Michael Carter. "A Child's Guide to Rational Expectations," *Journal of Economic Literature* (March 1982): 39–51. A fairly nontechnical overview of a highly technical approach to macroeconomics.

Wanniski, Jude. *The Way the World Works: How Economics Fails and Succeeds*. New York: Simon and Schuster, 1978. The best-known popularized version of supply side economics.

APPENDIX: A GLOSSARY OF SYMBOLS

Chapters 4 through 6 have introduced a number of symbols. More will appear in the next few chapters. Here, for handy reference, is a list of symbols you have already encountered.

GNP	gross national product
NNP	net national product
NI	national income
PI	personal income
Y	real output
Y^*	full-employment level of real output
N	level of employment
C	consumption
I	gross private domestic investment
G	government purchases of goods and services
T	taxes
EX	exports
IM	imports
P	price level
M_s	money supply
V	velocity of money
AD	aggregate demand curve
AS	aggregate supply curve

Here are some additional symbols you'll be encountering in the next few chapters.

C_0	that part of consumption that is independent of the level of income
b	marginal propensity to consume (also MPC)
M_d	demand for money
t	marginal tax rate
T_0	that part of taxes collected that is independent of the level of income
R	transfer payments
K	capital stock
k	the fraction of money income people want to hold in cash; equal to $1/V$
a	marginal propensity to invest
m	marginal propensity to import
RR	required bank reserves
ER	excess bank reserves
rr	reserve ratio
i_n	nominal, or market, interest rate
r_r	interest rate after correcting for inflation

DETERMINING OUTPUT AND EMPLOYMENT: KEYNESIAN MACROECONOMICS AND FISCAL POLICY

3

1. Explain how Say's law led classical economists to conclude that the economy would not go through prolonged periods of overproduction or unemployment.
2. Discuss the role of each of these self-regulating markets in ensuring that the economy will tend toward the full-employment level of output:
   a. the product market,
   b. the labor market,
   c. the credit market.
3. Use the quantity theory of money to explain how increases in the money supply lead to proportional increases in the price level.
4. Discuss the basic ideas of the business cycle theorists.
5. Identify and explain the Keynesian criticisms of the classical model.

CHAPTER 7

CLASSICAL MACROECONOMICS AND THE KEYNESIAN RESPONSE

INTRODUCTION

Modern macroeconomic theory cannot be fully understood without looking at how it developed. Before the 1930s, the dominant school of macroeconomic thought was the classical school. There are several reasons to begin the study of macroeconomic theory with the classical school. First, classical macroeconomics represents the best efforts of early economists to develop a theoretical system to explain the aggregate level of economic activity and to predict the effects of changes of various kinds on economic activity.

Second, classical macroeconomics provided the background against which John Maynard Keynes, the great British economist, developed his new ideas. The foundation of classical macroeconomics lay in three ideas: Say's law, the quantity theory of money, and self-regulating markets. Keynes began his "revolution" by attacking each of these in turn.

Finally, each of the three parts of the classical foundation has received renewed attention in the economic debates of the last two decades. New classical economists have stressed the importance of self-regulating markets, which they believe will restore full employment and frustrate attempts by policy makers to change the level of income and output. The roots of the monetarists' ideas are found in the quantity theory of money. Finally, the supply side economics so popular in the 1980s was in many ways a modern version of Say's law.

Classical macroeconomics does not describe a single approach but rather a rich and diverse group of ideas. When Keynes attacked the ideas of the classical school in the *General Theory of Employment, Interest, and Money* (1936), he was attacking the mainstream of nineteenth-century economic thought.[1] In doing so, he ignored some important recent work on the quantity theory of money by economists such as Henry Simons and Irving Fisher, who were working in the classical tradition. The ideas that Keynes criticized were those that drove the macroeconomic policies of his time. His contributions changed the policy approach to recessions and depressions for decades to follow.

---

1. From now on, we will refer to this work as simply *General Theory*.

THE CLASSICAL VIEW OF MACROECONOMICS

The aggregate supply and demand model, although not used until well into this century, is helpful in understanding the ideas of the classical school. Specifically, Figure 1 shows a vertical aggregate supply (AS) curve and a downward-sloping aggregate demand (AD) curve in the upper panel and the aggregate production function in the lower panel. Classical economists believed that the interaction of labor supply and labor demand determines the real wage and the level of employment. The level of employment (N) then determines how much total real output (Y) will be produced. In Figure 1, N_1 is determined in the labor market (not shown). N_1 is the level of employment capable of producing a real output of Y_1. Output does not vary with the price level because the level of real output is determined by the interaction of labor supply and labor demand. Thus, the AS curve is vertical at Y_1. The AD curve has no influence on real output. It only serves to determine the price level, P_1. Shifts in aggregate demand will change the price level only.

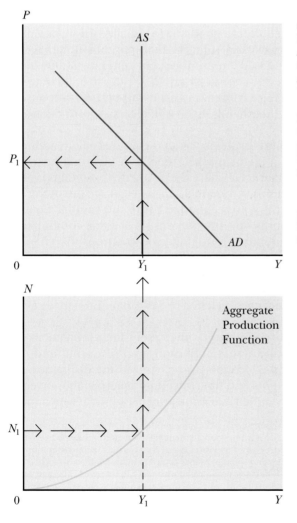

FIGURE 1
A CLASSICAL VIEW OF OUTPUT, EMPLOYMENT, AND PRICES
The level of employment (N_1), established in the labor market determines the level of real output (Y_1), and thus the location of the vertical aggregate supply curve (AS). Aggregate demand (AD) only affects the price level. It has no influence on output or employment.

SAY'S LAW

Say's law, introduced in Chapter 6, is often phrased as "supply creates its own demand." Say argued that the production of goods and services generates an amount of income equal to the value of the products produced. If firms produce output with a value of $1,000, then they also create incomes for the factors of production equal to $1,000. Since the income created is the same as the value of output, the production process creates the amount of income necessary to purchase the goods and services produced. Say further argued that the only reason people offer their labor or other productive resources in the factor market is to earn income to use for consumption spending. Production generates income, which is all spent to purchase what was produced.

This simple form of Say's law implies that a market economy will not be subject to severe or prolonged periods of overproduction. Say's law would always be true in an economy where there was no saving. However, if people save a part of their incomes, spending can be less than the value of what is produced. This level of spending results in unsold goods. As producers pile up inventories, they cut back on production and lay off workers. Output falls and unemployment rises. Thus, Say's law is not correct if there is any saving.

The circular flow model offers a good way to visualize this problem of overproduction as well as its classical solution. In the circular flow diagram in Figure 2, firms produce $1,000 in products and generate $1,000 in incomes. Households, however, choose to save $200 of their income, so there is not enough spending to purchase all the output. Left with unsold products ($200 worth) on their hands, firms will decrease production and employment.

The classical answer to this problem was to recognize that, in addition to a product market and a factor market, there is a third market—the credit market. The credit market is where the saving of households is used to provide funds for business investment. Saving is a leakage out of the circular flow, but investment is an injection back into the circular flow. In the national income accounts, investment consists of some combination of business plants and equipment, residential construction, and changes in inventories. In our example, the $200 of unsold output, or a change in inventories, is the investment that matches the saving of households. Thus, actual, or realized, saving has to be equal to realized investment. In Figure 2, $200 in realized saving is matched by $200 in realized investment in the form of added inventory.

macroeconomic equilibrium
The level of output at which there is no tendency to change. The amount that buyers wish to buy is exactly equal to what is being produced

Defining unsold output as inventory investment merely balances the accounts. It does not result in an equilibrium level of output and employment. Even in Say's time, economists recognized the distinction between a balancing of accounts and the concept of macroeconomic equilibrium.[2] **Macroeconomic equilibrium** is the level of output at which there

2.   This distinction between an accounting identity and equilibrium may be clearer if you recall the income statement in Chapter 5. Your income statement will be in accounting balance every year. What comes in is either spent or saved. However, your finances may be in disequilibrium. You may be saving less or borrowing and spending more than you planned. If so, you will adjust your flows next year accordingly. When you are satisfied with the pattern, when planned or expected income, outgo, saving, and borrowing are equal to what actually occurred, then you are in equilibrium as well as in accounting balance.

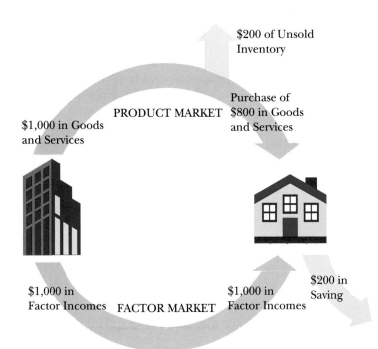

$200 of Unsold
Inventory

PRODUCT MARKET

Purchase of
$800 in Goods
and Services

$1,000 in Goods
and Services

$1,000 in
Factor Incomes   FACTOR MARKET $1,000 in
Factor Incomes

$200 in
Saving

**FIGURE 2
SAVING—A PROBLEM?**
When business firms produce $1,000 in goods and services, they generate $1,000 in incomes to the suppliers of factors of production. If $200 of this income is saved, only $800 is spent for goods and services. Thus, $200 worth of goods and services remain unsold. In response to inventory buildup, firms cut production. Incomes fall, and unemployment rises.

is no tendency to change. The amount that buyers wish to buy is exactly equal to what is being produced. If firms build up unwanted inventories, their initial response may be to cut prices. However, after cutting prices to unload excess inventories, firms are likely to cut back production in the next period. Then the size of the flow of income and output will shrink.

As long as unplanned and unwanted inventory changes are occurring, the economy is in disequilibrium. Realized saving and realized investment are always equal. In equilibrium, however, planned saving and planned investment must also be equal. The saving desired by consumers must be exactly offset by desired business investment or other planned injections so that the size of the flow is neither shrinking nor growing. Classical economists believed that equilibrium would be reached and maintained at a level consistent with full employment by the actions of three self-regulating markets. These markets are the product market, the labor market, and the credit market. If these three markets functioned properly, Say's law would hold in the sense that the sum of planned spending for consumption and for investment would be enough to purchase all that was being produced.

SELF-REGULATING MARKETS

Classical economists believed that full employment of resources was almost a sure thing in a market economy if markets were allowed to operate freely and given enough time. They did not claim that the economic system would *always* operate at a level of full employment. Occasional problems of overproduction and unemployment would occur. These problems, however, would be quickly eliminated by self-regulating markets.

self-regulating markets
Markets that quickly
resolve problems of
shortage or surplus
through price changes,
quantity adjustments, or
a combination of the two.

Self-regulating markets are markets in which automatic forces move the economy to a new equilibrium whenever there is a shift in supply or demand. Equilibrium will be restored by adjustments in either prices or output, or both, without any government intervention. Classical economists believed that the same kind of corrective forces that restore equilibrium in markets for single products are also at work in aggregate markets. Although temporary shortages or surpluses are possible in either individual or aggregate markets, a lasting general shortage or surplus of aggregate output is not possible.

THE PRODUCT AND LABOR MARKETS. The two primary markets in the circular flow diagram are the product market (upper flow) and the factor market (lower flow). The labor market is the largest part of the factor market. Classical economists believed that flexible prices and wages in the product and labor markets were the first line of defense against unemployment and recession.

The labor market played a central role in the classical model. The supply and demand for labor together determined both the wage level and the amount of labor employed. If there were unemployed workers, the quantity supplied must be more than the quantity demanded. This was a clear indication that the market price (the wage) was too high for equilibrium.

If firms find that they have unsold output, they can dispose of it by cutting prices. The idea of cutting prices when there is a surplus of wheat, autos, or plane tickets is familiar. How do price and wage adjustments work when there is an excess of output in general? Figure 3 shows the usual AD curve and a classical (vertical) AS curve. In this diagram, there is an excess of aggregate supply over aggregate demand at price level P_1, resulting in unsold output. The unsold output is equal to the difference between Y_1 and Y_2. On the diagram, this is the length of line $\overline{AB}$. This diagram seems to suggest that if all firms cut prices, the price level will fall to P_2. Output will remain at the full-employment level, Y_1.

Suppose, however, that firms respond to the piling up of unwanted inventories by cutting output to Y_2 instead of cutting prices. Then employment will fall to N_2. There will be excess labor in the labor market. Competition among workers for jobs will drive down both real and nominal wages (wages with and without adjustments for changes in the price level). With lower wages, a wheat farmer or auto producer will find it possible to produce the same output at lower cost. Firms will choose to hire more workers at the lower wages. Although sellers will have to cut prices to sell the extra output, they can afford to because of lower labor costs. The fall in output is temporary, because flexible wages and prices will always restore output to the full-employment level. In fact, some advisers to President Hoover recommended wage and price cuts in 1930 during the first stage of the Great Depression as a solution to growing unemployment.

You may have noticed a subtle flaw in this reasoning. If all firms cut prices to sell excess output, they will have to cut wages in order to avoid losses. When producers of toothpaste cut the price of their product and the wages of their workers, the wage cut has almost no impact on the market for their product. The firms' workers make up a very small part of the

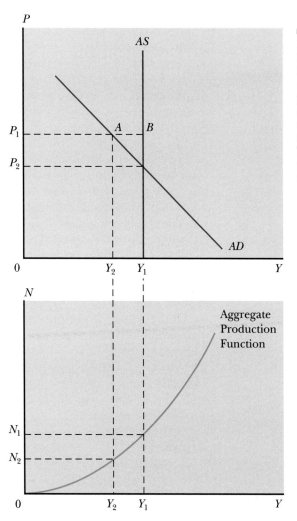

FIGURE 3
EXCESS AGGREGATE SUPPLY
Excess aggregate supply (*AB* in this diagram) will put downward pressure on the price level, either directly or through wages and the labor market. This process continues until full-employment output is restored.

total toothpaste market. What is true of a single good, however, is not necessarily true of aggregate output. If all firms cut wages, the workers (who are also the customers) will have less purchasing power with which to buy the output. Therefore, sales will fall in real terms. (Remember to beware of the fallacy of composition when you think about macroeconomics!)

THE CREDIT MARKET. Flexible wages and prices in the labor and product markets were not the only weapon in the classical armory. A self-regulating credit market was another important part of the classical explanation of why unemployment and unsold output would not persist. Through the credit market, household income that is saved flows into the hands of business firms, which in turn spend it on investment. The interest rate is the incentive to lend and the price of borrowing. Changes in the interest rate assure that planned saving and planned investment spending will be equal.

Both the classical and Keynesian models assumed that the size of the labor force is known, allowing economists to determine how many jobs are needed to reach full employment. If the population is growing at a moderate pace, then the labor force will also grow at a slow, steady pace. Thus, a labor force of a known size in the short run is a reasonable assumption for both models. The full-employment level of output (Y^*) then depends on the size of the labor force. In the real world, however, labor is free to move from country to country. High employment and rapid growth in one country may induce immigration and thus increase the size of the labor force and the full-employment level of output. Falling output will lead to unemployment, but it may also result in emigration of workers or a slow-down in immigration. Either of these will reduce the impact on domestic unemployment. Thus, unemployment may fall less during the upturn of the business cycle and rise less during a recession if some of the burden of adjustment falls on migration.

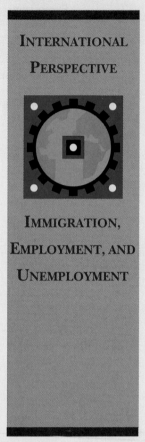

INTERNATIONAL PERSPECTIVE

IMMIGRATION, EMPLOYMENT, AND UNEMPLOYMENT

The effect of migration on unemployment can be seen using the aggregate supply and demand model. A sharp increase in the labor force due to immigration will shift aggregate supply to the right. This shift allows an increase in aggregate demand with more output as well as some price increase. A fall in the labor force due to emigration will shift aggregate supply to the right. This shift reduces the decline in prices that might otherwise occur during an economic downturn.

Two examples illustrate this point. The first is the pattern of immigration in American history, driven by conditions in both Europe and the United States. The second is the more recent experience in Germany with "Gastarbeiter" (guest workers).

Data from the nineteenth century shows that immigrants were drawn to the United States by prosperity. Peaks in immigration coincided with peaks in the business cycle in 1873, 1882, 1892, 1903, 1907, and 1910. These peaks were followed by downturns in both output and immigration. The pull of prosperity in the United States was often reinforced by pushing effects of pogroms against the Jews in Eastern Europe, bad harvests, or other adverse conditions abroad. Simon Kuznets, a historian of business cycles, has found cycles in immigration of sixteen to eighteen years in length paralleling cycles in economic growth. British economist Brinley Thomas argues, however, that immigration was less a response to growth than a cause of growth. It increased aggregate supply by providing new resources for production and also aggregate demand as immigrants purchased consumer goods with their wages. Thomas's view is in the classical tradition. In this view, the level of output is determined by the resources—especially labor—that are available.[a]

In the 1970s and 1980s, West Germany had a very slow increase in its native labor force because of low birth rates. During periods when demand was strong, West Germany issued special "guest worker" permits to encourage foreign workers to come in to supplement the domestic work force. Most of these workers came from Turkey or, more recently, from Greece. When demand was slack, priority tended to be given to native Germans. Some guest workers would return home until the next peak demand drew them back into the German labor market. With the influx of Germans from what had been East Germany after reunification, there is likely to be little future need for guest workers. Instead, the jobs will go to Germans from the east, who cannot be sent home when they are not needed. Thus, Germany's solution to ups and down in employment opportunities may have been a casualty of reunification.

a. Jonathan Hughes, *American Economic History*, 3rd ed. (Glenview, IL: Scott-Foresman, 1990).

Figure 4 shows how the credit market works to make saving available to finance investment. In the classical view, the supply of credit (loanable funds) comes from people's decisions to save. The demand for credit reflects the desire by business firms to borrow for investment purposes. The supply curve has a positive slope. This slope indicates that saving is directly related to the interest rate. People save (give up some spending) only if there is an incentive to do so. The interest rate is the incentive for saving. By saving now, individuals can earn interest and accumulate larger sums of money to spend in the future. When the interest rate rises, saving will increase because the same amount of current saving will provide more future consumption. Thus, a higher interest rate will call forth more saving, or a greater supply of loanable funds. Lower interest rates, on the other hand, will lead to less saving, or a smaller supply of loanable funds. There is less incentive to save instead of consume at lower interest rates.

The demand curve in Figure 4 shows the amount of loanable funds borrowers want at various interest rates. It has the familiar negative slope. The price of borrowing is the interest rate that firms pay to obtain credit. Investment spending increases when the interest rate declines. It decreases when the interest rate rises. Projects or purchases of investment goods that would be profitable at lower rates of interest may not look as attractive at higher interest rates. Thus, planned investment spending will be lower at higher rates of interest.

According to classical economists, the interaction of borrowers and lenders in the credit market should establish an equilibrium interest rate. At this interest rate, the quantity of planned saving will be equal to planned investment spending. This interest rate, i_1 in Figure 4, is deter-

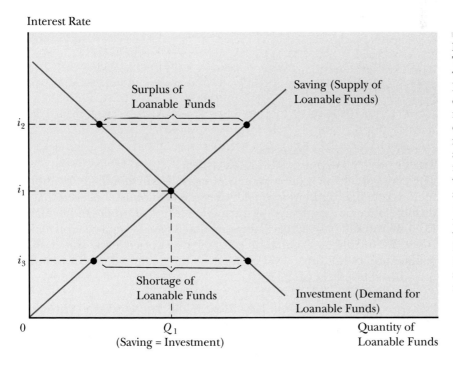

Interest Rate

Surplus of Loanable Funds

Saving (Supply of Loanable Funds)

i_2

i_1

i_3

Shortage of Loanable Funds

Investment (Demand for Loanable Funds)

0   Q_1
(Saving = Investment)

Quantity of Loanable Funds

FIGURE 4
THE CLASSICAL VIEW OF THE CREDIT MARKET
In the classical view, changes in the interest rate ensure that the quantity of loanable funds supplied (saving) and the quantity demanded (investment) would be equal. Saving and investment are equal (at Q_1) at i_1, the equilibrium interest rate. There would be a surplus at higher interest rates (such as i_2) and a shortage at lower rates (such as i_3).

mined by the intersection of the saving and investment curves. At higher interest rates, such as i_2, the quantity of loanable funds supplied exceeds the quantity demanded. The surplus of saving over planned investment spending will push the interest rate downward toward i_1. At lower interest rates, such as i_3, the quantity of loanable funds demanded exceeds the quantity supplied. This shortage causes the interest rate to be bid up to i_1 as would-be borrowers compete for the limited amount of credit.

Either the supply curve or the demand curve can shift to create a disequilibrium. Either way, natural forces will restore equilibrium in a self-regulating market. Suppose a fear of recession or a high level of consumer debt causes people to suddenly become more thrifty. The amount of saving will increase at every possible interest rate. That is, the saving curve will shift to the right. The new equilibrium interest rate will be lower than i_1. An increase in saving puts downward pressure on the price of loanable funds. The lower interest rate leads to an increase in the amount of investment spending. Thus, changes in the interest rate ensure that any income not spent on consumption will be channeled into desired investment.

ELEMENTS OF CLASSICAL MACROECONOMIC THEORY

- Employment is determined by the forces of supply and demand in the labor market.
- Output is determined by equilibrium in the labor market.
- The aggregate supply curve is vertical at the full-employment level of output.
- The price level is determined by the supply of and demand for money.
- An economy always tends toward the full-employment level of output because enough income is created during production to purchase the output (Say's law) and self-regulating markets correct temporary disequilibria.
  In the product market, falling prices ensure that all output is sold.
  In the labor market, adjustments in wages clear the labor market.
  In the credit market, changes in interest rates make saving equal to investment.

CLASSICAL AGGREGATE DEMAND:
THE QUANTITY THEORY OF MONEY REVISITED

The classical idea that the workings of markets will eliminate unemployment is one that is still widely held. Classical economists believed that individual prices are explained by the market forces of supply and demand. Even they would have agreed, however, that a more complex explanation is needed for the determination of the general price level. The classical explanation of the price level is based on the quantity theory of money, introduced briefly in Chapter 6.

INFLATION, DISCOVERY OF THE NEW WORLD, AND THE QUANTITY THEORY OF MONEY. The quantity theory of money, like many theories in macroeconomics, developed as a way to explain certain economic events. Among the early writers on this theory was the Scottish philosopher David Hume (1711–1776). Hume was interested in the very practical problem of explaining the inflation that followed the discovery of the New World. (Hume had a great influence on Adam Smith, author of *The Wealth of Nations*.)

Gold and silver were the main forms of money in Europe until the nineteenth century. The New World was discovered in the late fifteenth century and colonized by several European nations in the next two centuries. The Spaniards seized the gold and silver of the Aztecs in Mexico and the Incas in Peru and brought it to Europe. As this gold and silver flowed in, Spaniards went on a spending spree. They bid against other potential buyers and drove up the prices of goods and services all over Europe. Hume and other theorists sought to explain the link between the inflow of money and the rising price level.

Although these early theorists did not have the tools of demand and supply, their reasoning can be expressed in those terms. In the supply and demand diagram of Figure 5, an inflow of gold and silver has caused the demand for a specific good, woolen goods, to increase while the supply curve remains unchanged. In the seventeenth century, the newly wealthy Spanish demanded more woolens from both Spanish and British suppliers. Of course, the people who sold woolens then had extra money, so they too demanded more goods of all kinds. As demand for a broad range of products increased, aggregate demand shifted to the right, as shown in Figure 6.

The story didn't end there. People who supplied all kinds of goods found that the prices of their inputs were rising. Higher prices for inputs meant that their costs were rising. For example, the new, higher prices for woolens attracted more people into the business of raising sheep. Com-

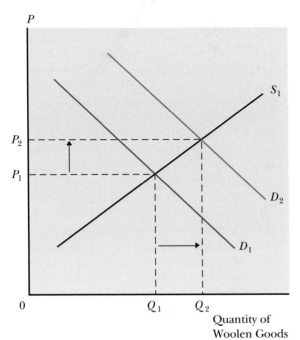

FIGURE 5
A SEVENTEENTH-CENTURY SHIFT IN THE DEMAND CURVE FOR WOOLENS
An inflow of gold and silver from the New World led Europeans to increase their demand for various goods, such as woolen goods. The rightward shift of the demand curve drove up the price of woolen goods from P_1 to P_2. Quantity increased along the supply curve from Q_1 to Q_2 in response to the higher price.

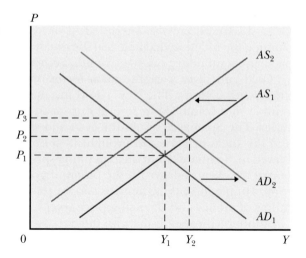

FIGURE 6
ADJUSTING TO AN INFLOW OF MONEY
The general increase in demand for goods drives up both prices and costs. The rise in costs shifts the aggregate supply curve to the left. Both P and Y increase, but equilibrium output ultimately returns to Y_1. When all prices and costs have adjusted (the supply curve has shifted as well as the demand curve), there will have been no change in output but an increase in the price level to P_3.

petition for grazing land drove up the lease payments that the sheep herders had to pay, raising the price of raw wool. Eventually these increased production costs caused the individual supply curves for wool and other goods to shift to the left. Thus, aggregate supply shifted to the left, as shown in Figure 6. A leftward shift in aggregate supply means that producers will offer the same amount for sale at a higher price than before because their costs have risen. (We are using an upward-sloping short-run aggregate supply curve here. As you will see shortly, however, the long-run aggregate supply curve will still be vertical. Classical economists tended to concentrate on the long run.)

After both aggregate demand and aggregate supply adjust to changes in the price level, the equilibrium quantity of real output will be the same as before the inflow of money. The inflow of gold and silver to Europe in the seventeenth century did not increase any of the economy's productive resources or improve its technology. Thus, there was no reason why total output would change once the economy adjusted fully to the larger money supply. As long as money was flowing into Spain and from there to the rest of Europe, prices were destined to go on rising. Aggregate demand kept shifting to the right and aggregate supply to the left. Since rising demand spilled over from Spain to other countries, the aggregate demand and supply curves in all of these countries continued to shift. Thus, the money inflow to Spain led to higher price levels throughout Europe.

When would this rise in the price level come to an end? If the inflow of money never stopped, classical economists could see no end to rising prices. However, suppose the money inflow did end. Then, they argued, the increase in the price level would be proportional to the increase in the money stock. A money stock that was twice as large would lead to a price level that was twice as high. A money stock that was four times as large would mean a price level that was four times as high. Land prices and wages would also rise in proportion to increases in the money supply.

Changes in the price level may not be exactly proportional to the rise in the money stock. While the money stock is rising, other things that affect the price level may also be changing. For example, the productivity of labor may rise. Like most economic predictions, those based on the quantity theory are subject to *ceteris paribus* conditions.

The insight that the long-run level of prices is directly related to the money stock was a notable insight of classical economics. To the question "How much will the price level change when the money stock increases?" it gives a reasonably precise answer: The price level changes in proportion to the change in the money stock. However, the quantity theory could not predict how long it would take the price level to change. Furthermore, you should have noticed in Figure 5 that output of a particular good will initially increase when demand increases. (Figure 6 shows that this also holds for goods in general.) Thus, in the short run, changes in the money supply may affect real output as well as the price level. In the long run, real output returns to the level that existed before the added money came into the system.

How much will output increase at the start? How long will it take output to settle back to its old level? The quantity theorists could not really answer these questions. The quantity theory offered a better explanation for long-run changes in the price level than for the short-run effects of changes in the money supply on real output and employment.

INFLATION AND THE NAPOLEONIC WARS. British economist David Ricardo (1772–1823) was responsible for a second important development in the quantity theory of money, this time in response to wartime inflation. Major wars are almost always accompanied by inflation. During wartime, increased production of military goods means that households receive more income as wages. However, there are no additional consumer goods for them to purchase with that added income. When purchasing power increases but output available to purchase does not, the price level will rise.

The Napoleonic Wars (1793–1813) triggered a debate about the role of banks in creating money and fueling inflation. During this period in Britain, notes (paper money) supplied by banks were an important part of the total money supply. As output of military and other goods expanded, a question arose. How much money in the form of notes should banks be allowed to issue? Policy makers were certain that too much new money would result in inflation. Bankers and public officials argued that banks should issue enough money to "meet the needs of trade." That is, banks should supply whatever firms needed to borrow in order to produce goods that had a ready market.

Ricardo pointed out that the amount of money required to meet the needs of trade depends on the price level. The price level, in turn, depends on the money supply. If the price level rises, more dollars will have to be loaned in order to expand output by a given amount. If banks meet this increased demand for loans by issuing more notes, the money stock will become even larger. This increased money stock will drive the price level even higher. At the higher price level, the needs of trade will require more loans and an even larger money supply. The result is an upward spiral, with the stock of bank notes and the price level chasing one another.

To get off this spiral, Ricardo suggested, the Bank of England (the British central bank) should place some limits on the ability of banks to create money by issuing notes. This debate over the effects of issuing bank notes on the price level reinforced Hume's conclusion that controlling the price level depends on controlling the supply of money. Thus, the lesson from wartime inflation was that there was a need for some agency, such as a central bank, to control the money supply in order to control the price level.

THE QUANTITY THEORY OF MONEY BEFORE KEYNES. Both of these historical events raised the question of how the money supply, the price level, and output were related. In the case of the inflow of gold, the money stock was clearly rising more rapidly than real output. Hume and others identified the increase in the money supply as the cause of a rising price level. In the case of wartime inflation, some output was not available for consumption. Resources were being diverted to the war effort. The money supply was at least as large as before, if not larger, but there was less real output available to purchase. Again, the consequence of different rates of growth in the money supply and (available) real output was a rise in the price level.

The government (or the central bank) exerted control over the money supply in the eighteenth and nineteenth centuries, as it does today. Classical economists wanted the government to manage the money supply in such a way as to minimize inflation. Recognizing that output (Y) would grow over time with increases in population and resources, they reasoned that the money supply (M_s) should grow only at the same rate as Y. In that way, inflation would be avoided.

The quantity theory of money underwent some changes in the late nineteenth century because of the work of British economist Alfred Marshall (1842–1924). One of Marshall's most important contributions was to reinterpret the equation of exchange ($M_s \times V = P \times Y$) as a theory of the demand for money. The **demand for money** is the amount of money that people want to hold in the form of currency or checking account balances. The demand for money is not that different from the demand for other goods and services. People demand money because it is useful in making market transactions. Holding money has a price, however. Choosing to hold money means giving up the things that it could buy or giving up the interest that could be earned if it were converted into other kinds of financial assets. Money is also unique in certain respects, especially in its almost total acceptance in transactions for all other goods and services. Thus, although the demand for money is similar to the demand for other goods and services, money plays a special role in a market economy.

Marshall argued that people normally want to hold part of their wealth in the form of money. He assumed that the amount of wealth that individuals choose to hold in the form of currency or checking account balances (as opposed to stocks, bonds, and other financial assets) is positively related to their incomes. The higher a person's income, the higher the average amount of money balances that person will want to hold to meet

demand for money
The amount of money households and businesses wish to hold for making transactions and as a financial asset.

day-to-day transaction needs. For the economy as a whole, the total demand for money should be positively related to the aggregate level of income and output.

Marshall observed that the public had to hold whatever amount of money was being supplied. That is, actual M_d had to equal actual M_s. If the money supply is \$1,000, then the public collectively has to hold (demand) \$1,000. Based on this observation, Marshall rearranged the equation of exchange, obtaining

$$M_d = k \times P \times Y = k \times \text{GNP}.$$

Money supply has been replaced by money demand because in equilibrium the two should be equal. The velocity of money, V, has been replaced by k on the other side of the equation, because $k = 1/V$ by definition. Marshall explained k as the fraction of income people desire to hold in the form of cash balances. Like V, the size of k depends on such factors as how often people get paid and have to make payments and what other forms of assets are available. Marshall expected that k, like V, would be fairly stable over long periods of time. If one accepts the classical arguments that Say's law is valid and markets are self-regulating, then Y will be stable at the full-employment level. In that case, Marshall's revised equation of exchange becomes a theory of how the price level is determined.

Suppose there is more money supplied than the amount people want to hold. The money market will be in disequilibrium. That is, $M_d < M_s$. Finding that they have larger cash balances than they wish to hold, individuals will spend more, driving up the price level (P). The rise in the price level will increase the nominal value of output ($P \times Y$), which determines the amount of money people want to hold. The public will finally be satisfied to hold exactly the amount of money being supplied at the higher price level. Similar forces are set in motion when the money supply is less than the amount people want to hold, or $M_d > M_s$. Reductions in spending as people try to rebuild their cash balances will drive down the price level until the money supply is once again equal to the money demand. Thus, a self-regulating market for money, working through the price level, should assure that the equilibrium condition, $M_d = M_s$, will be satisfied. In equilibrium, money supply and money demand must be equal, and money demand is given by

$$M_d = k \times P \times \overline{Y} = k \times \text{GNP}.$$

The bar over Y in this expression indicates that real output is constant at the full-employment level. The proportional relationship between the money supply and the price level is the same as before. This version of the equation offers an explanation of the price level in terms of money demand and the behavior of households.

A simple example will show how the behavior of households translates an increase in the money supply into an increase in the price level. Assume that the economy is at the full-employment level of output, with 500 units of output being produced ($\overline{Y} = 500$). Also, assume that the fraction of their income that people desire to hold as money is stable and equal to 25 percent of their annual income ($k = 0.25$). Finally, assume that the money supply is initially \$1,000 ($M_{s1} = \$1,000$) and that the annual value of output $(P \times \overline{Y})$ is such that the public is satisfied to hold $1,000 in money $(M_d = M_s)$. The initial price level (P_1) can be found by substituting these numbers in

(1) $M_{s1} = k \times P_1 \times \overline{Y}$.

Then we have

$$P_1 = \frac{M_{s1}}{k \times \overline{Y}} = \frac{\$1,000}{(0.25)(500)} = \frac{\$1,000}{125} = \$8.$$

The equilibrium price level is $8. That is, the average price for a unit of output is $8. The annual value of output is $4,000 ($8 × 500).

What would happen if, as a result of an influx of gold into the economy, the money supply doubled? Substituting the new value of the money supply $(M_{s2} = \$2,000)$ into equation (1) determines that equilibrium occurs at a new price level, P_2:

$$P_2 = \frac{\$2,000}{(0.25)(500)} = \frac{\$2,000}{125} = \$16.$$

According to these calculations, a doubling of the money supply (from $1,000 to $2,000) would cause a doubling of the equilibrium price level (from $8 to $16). Therefore, the annual value of nominal output would also double to $8,000 ($16 × 500), even though real output is unchanged.

How and why do prices rise in response to increases in the money supply? Given an initial equilibrium $(M_{d1} = M_{s1})$, an increase in the money supply puts people in the position of having larger money balances than they wish to hold. That is, $M_{s1} > M_{d2}$, relative to the value of total output $P_1 \times \overline{Y}$. Individuals who find themselves with more dollars than they wish to hold will increase their spending for consumer goods and services.[3] Although individuals can decrease their money holdings through spending, the economy as a whole cannot. The excess dollars are passed from person to person. The increased spending, therefore, shifts aggregate demand to the right (see Figure 6). The resulting shortages of goods and services cause price increases. Eventually, wages and other costs also rise, shifting aggregate supply to the left. The level of output returns to the original level $(Y_1$ in Figure 6) and the price level rises further (to P_3). At the higher price level, the public is willing to hold the entire money supply. The money market is again in equilibrium (quantity supplied equals quantity demanded).

Classical economists favored a strictly *laissez-faire* approach to most markets. Many of them did agree, however, that regulation of the money supply would help control ups and downs in output and employment. If a temporary decline occurred in output, falling prices and wages could be avoided by expanding the money supply. An increase in the money supply could lead to at least a short-run improvement in the level of real output as well as (or instead of) a rise in the price level.

The quantity theory of money, Say's law, and the idea of self-regulating markets provided a complete classical model of macroeconomics. This model explained the level of employment, output, and prices. According to this model, recessions would be temporary and self-correcting. Thus, the role of the government should be limited to careful management of the money supply.

THE BUSINESS CYCLE THEORISTS

In the nineteenth century, the main critics of the quantity theory of money were the business cycle theorists. They called attention to the reality of ups and downs in the economy. The classical model showed with perfect logic that prolonged unemployment was impossible. Actual unemployment seemed to defy the model by lasting for long periods of time. The classical model said that output would always be at, close to, or tending toward the full-employment level. Real-world experience showed that large and prolonged deviations from the full-employment level of output not only were possible, but occurred with alarming frequency.

Business cycle theorists, from Thomas Malthus in the nineteenth century to Wesley Mitchell and Joseph Schumpeter in the early twentieth century, observed regular cyclical patterns in economic activity. They sought to explain these patterns in terms of the nature of the market economy. Unlike the classical school, the business cycle theorists did not offer a complete model of how output, employment, and the price level are determined. Classical economists stressed natural forces that would tend to restore equilibrium. Business cycle theorists were more interested in what happened during the period when the economy was moving from one equilibrium to another. Schumpeter even described economic downturns as periods of "creative destruction." *Creative* meant that the old worn-out capital of declining industries was being replaced by new, improved capital in emerging industries.

The ideas of business cycle theorists such as Schumpeter are noteworthy because they offer a bridge from classical to Keynesian macroeconomics. Two important themes of this school of thought play an important role in Keynes's *General Theory*:

1. *The notion of underconsumption, or inadequate aggregate demand.* Malthus and other business cycle theorists argued that an unequal distribution of income affects the ability of consumers to purchase all that is produced. A small number of wealthy households consume a great deal less than their income and save a large amount. Workers earning very low wages spend most or all of their income. This amount is not enough, however, to purchase the rest of what is produced. If the saving of the wealthy few is not channeled into investment, then leakages from the circular flow will exceed injections. The size of the flow will decrease.

2. *The instability of investment.* If the government and foreign sectors are small and there is not enough consumption, then the burden of purchasing the rest of output falls on business firms. Firms must increase

their demand for funds to invest. Both Schumpeter and Keynes, writing in the 1920s and 1930s, emphasized the fact that investment demand is extremely unstable. Investment depends on changes in technology, development of new industries, interest rates, final demand, and investor psychology. All of these variables are unpredictable and highly volatile. In addition, new plants and equipment last for a long time and continue to produce consumer goods during that time. Once an increase in consumption demand has been filled by investing in new plants and equipment, very little further investment is needed in order to have enough productive capacity for current consumption. As a result, demand for investment goods tends to depend on consumer demand. If consumer demand is growing, new investment is needed to meet that demand. If consumer demand is stable, no new investment is needed. If consumer demand falls, the appropriate level of new investment may be negative as producers work off and wear out excess productive capacity.

Although business cycle theorists identified other influences, inadequate demand from both consumers and investors played the central role in explaining recessions. Business cycle theorists were concerned about aggregate demand, even though they didn't use that term. Both the government and the foreign sector played minor roles in nineteenth-century economics. Thus, the business cycle theorists focused on two major actors in the macroeconomic drama: consumers and investors. In doing so, they laid the groundwork for the Keynesian revolution.

THE KEYNESIAN REVOLUTION

The Great Depression challenged the classical model with the reality of a long depression and high unemployment. In *General Theory*, Keynes attacked the classical model in two important ways. First, he identified some flaws in the model. Second, unlike the business cycle theorists, he offered a well-developed alternative model of the macro economy. This model was the basis for the **Keynesian revolution**, the change in macroeconomic theory and policy that occurred when Keynes's ideas displaced the classical explanation of how output and employment are determined. The Keynesian model begins with aggregate demand and works from there to employment, instead of the other way around.

Keynesian revolution
The change in macroeconomic theory and policy that occurred when Keynes's ideas displaced the classical theory of how output and employment are determined.

KEYNES ON SAY'S LAW
Keynes was critical of Say's law. Classical economists argued that the existence of saving by households and investment by firms does not invalidate Say's law because changes in the interest rate will ensure that planned saving is equal to planned investment at the full-employment level of output. If planned saving is always exactly offset by planned investment, then all output will be sold to willing buyers for either consumption or investment. In that case, overproduction or lasting unemployment is not possible. Keynes argued that even though the interest rate does influence planned saving and planned investment, other important influences can keep the credit market from perfectly matching these two flows.

Keynes identified several reasons why individuals save besides earning interest: (1) to build reserves in case of unforeseen future needs, (2) to develop a nest egg for retirement, (3) to establish a financial base for an increased standard of living in the future, (4) to gain economic independence, (5) to build reserves for speculative purposes, (6) to leave an inheritance, and (7) to satisfy the urge to accumulate. These motives, he argued, generate considerable saving that is relatively independent of the interest rate.

Keynes also argued that the interest rate was only one influence on investment decisions. He argued that firms invest in new plants and equipment only if they expect to make a profit. Based on their expectations of the profit from a given investment project, businesses often borrow even when interest rates are high or refuse to borrow when they are low. According to Keynes, final demand by consumers, the size and age of existing capital stock, and new technology all play more important roles than the interest rate in determining investment.

Since both saving and investment respond more strongly to other influences than the interest rate, Keynes argued, planned saving *could* exceed planned investment at the full-employment level of output. Thus, Say's law would be invalid. According to the classical model, if planned saving exceeds planned investment, the interest rate will fall. Keynes said that a fall in interest rates may have little effect on either saving or investment, but excess saving will lead to a decline in the level of output and income. Thus, if credit markets fail to work as the classical model describes, severe depression and unemployment can persist for long periods in a market economy.

KEYNES ON SELF-REGULATING MARKETS

According to classical theory, temporary overproduction and unemployment in individual markets would be eliminated as unemployed workers competed for jobs and drove down wages. To a firm, falling wages mean lower costs. The firm could profitably cut prices and increase sales. Falling wages and prices would eliminate overproduction and restore full employment.

Keynes also argued that neither the product nor labor market would adjust quickly and automatically to eliminate unemployment and overproduction. He believed that labor unions and large corporations have enough market power to keep wages and prices from falling. Faced with rising unemployment, labor unions would fight to keep wages from declining in order to protect their members who were still working. Without declining wages, business firms would not be willing to cut their prices. Furthermore, when facing overproduction, large corporations are likely to choose to reduce production levels rather than prices. Price cutting risks cutthroat price competition. Keynes felt that in a mature, capitalistic economic system, it would be difficult to reduce either prices or wages. According to him, prices and wages are "sticky downward." Since prices and wages are not fully flexible, there will be no automatic adjustment process in product and labor markets to restore full-employment equilibrium.

Finally, Keynes pointed out that even if wages and prices could fall, the result would not necessarily be to restore output to the full-employment level. Falling prices mean that buyers can purchase more output, but falling wages mean that workers can buy less. In a macro economy, supply

John Maynard Keynes was born in Cambridge, England to a prosperous family. His father, John Neville Keynes, was a well-known economist who taught at the university there. The young Keynes grew up in an atmosphere where well-educated people were intensely interested in the public policy issues of the day. All his life, Keynes was able to dominate any group by his great intelligence, witty conversation, and forceful personality.

Keynes divided his life between teaching at Cambridge and active involvement in government and business affairs. He worked for the British Treasury, where he rose rapidly during World War I. In fact, Keynes was a British delegate to the Versailles Peace Conference, which drafted and signed the peace treaty ending World War I in 1919. He was disillusioned by the negotiations at Versailles and the harsh conditions imposed on the losers, especially Germany. In a very critical book, *The Economic Consequences of the Peace,* Keynes argued that the harsh economic conditions imposed on Germany would lead to more problems with that country in the future. This book ended Keynes's employment by the Treasury because he criticized British policy. He returned to Cambridge and turned to business, making a great deal of money with shrewd investments. He also managed the investment funds of King's College at Cambridge, to the college's great benefit.

ECONOMIC PROFILE

JOHN MAYNARD KEYNES

1883–1946

Keynes was a member of the Bloomsbury Group, which included such literary figures as Lytton Strachey and Leonard and Virginia Woolf. A man of many talents and interests, Keynes married a Russian ballerina, Lydia Lopokova, and was well known for his taste in art and literature. He wrote essays on policy topics and biographical essays on many people, including economists, as well as a treatise on the theory of probability.

Along with his other activities, Keynes did some revolutionary work in macroeconomics. During the 1920s, he wrote the two-volume *Treatise on Money,* which was published in 1930, after the beginning of the Great Depression. The *Treatise* was basically a quantity theory approach to macro problems in the spirit of Keynes's teacher, Alfred Marshall. By the time the *Treatise* was published, Keynes was unhappy with this approach and had begun what he called his "long struggle" to see macro questions from a different perspective. The new view Keynes was working toward was contained in his *General Theory of Employment, Interest, and Money,* published in 1936. This book presented an alternative macroeconomic model aimed at explaining how economies had fallen into the Great Depression and how they could get out of it.

and demand are not entirely independent because they are parts of the same circular flow.

KEYNES ON THE QUANTITY THEORY OF MONEY

Keynes admitted that the quantity theory of money was useful in describing the long-run movement of the economy from one equilibrium to another. He saw the theory as much less useful in the short run. The quantity theory was based on the assumption that, in the equation of exchange, the velocity of money was stable. That is, V was constant. Data from the early 1930s, as well as other periods, showed that this assumption did not hold in the short run.[4] The velocity of money (and therefore k) was especially unstable during the Great Depression. Between 1929 and 1933, V fell sharply, and k increased. (Remember that $k = 1/V$.) A rise in the value of k meant that the amount of money people wanted to hold, relative to GNP, had increased. The quantity theory of money offered no explanation for the sudden increase in the demand for money implied by the sharp drop in V.

Keynes pointed out that a theory that only explains what happens in the long run is not very useful. He reminded his readers that we live in the short run and "in the long run we are all dead." Keynes was more interested in developing a theoretical model to explain short-run economic activity and recommending policies to improve short-run economic conditions.

Keynes questioned the stability of money velocity, which was a basic assumption of the quantity theory. Building on the work of Alfred Marshall, Keynes reasoned that the demand for money was strongly influenced by more than the level of GNP. In addition to demanding money for making transactions, as Marshall claimed, people also want to hold money as a safeguard against changes in interest rates on bonds and other financial assets. If interest rates are low, people will avoid buying bonds and hold more of their wealth in the form of money while waiting for interest rates to rise. When interest rates are low, the opportunity cost of holding money is also low. Thus, very little is sacrificed by holding money instead of bonds or other securities. In addition, people who buy bonds when interest rates are low run a risk of locking in those rates and being stuck with low-yield assets when the rates rise.

When market interest rates are high, people will prefer to hold more of their wealth in interest-earning securities and less in money because the opportunity cost of holding money is high. Much interest is lost by holding money, which earns little or no interest, instead of interest-earning assets. In addition, if interest rates are high compared to the immediate past, people will expect them to fall rather than to rise further. Buying securities when interest rates are high enables the holder to lock in those rates for the life of the assets.

---

4. Some economists before Keynes did not share this simplistic view of velocity. Henry Simons and Irving Fisher recognized its instability, especially over the course of the business cycle. Thus, they advocated an active use of monetary policy to offset changes in velocity and keep the price level and output stable.

asset demand for money
Demand for money
to hold in order to
protect the value of one's
assets against changes in
interest rates. The asset
demand for money is
negatively related to
interest rates.

**transactions demand
for money**
Demand for money in
order to make purchases
and carry out other day-
to-day market transac-
tions. The transactions
demand for money is
positively related to
income.

Keynes called the motive for holding money as an asset the "specula-tive demand for money." Today economists prefer the term **asset demand for money**, which is the demand for money to hold in order to protect oneself against losses due to changes in interest rates. The asset demand for money is negatively related to interest rates. The motive for holding money identified by Marshall is called the **transactions demand for money**, the demand for money in order to make purchases and carry out other day-to-day market transactions. Transactions demand is positively related to income.[5]

Keynes argued that the interest rate would strongly influence the de-mand for money. If the interest rate declined, the quantity of money de-manded relative to GNP ($P \times Y$ in the equation of exchange) might in-crease, even if GNP were stable or declining. In the equation of exchange, this change in people's desire to hold money would appear as an increase in k or a decline in V. Thus, changes in V and k during the Great Depres-sion could be explained by including the interest rate as an important influence on the demand for money.

In summary, Keynes criticized the quantity theory because it neglects the role of interest rates and fails to explain short-run changes in V and k. He argued that Say's law was not valid and that long periods of over-production and unemployment *were* possible. Without Say's law and self-regulating markets, no automatic forces would bring the economy back to equilibrium during a recession. Without a stable velocity of money, even an increase in the money supply might not work. Having criticized the classical view of the way the macro economy worked, Keynes offered a different model. As you will see, in his model, only government inter-vention could bring the economy out of a downturn as severe and pro-longed as the Great Depression.

A PREVIEW OF KEYNESIAN THEORY AND POLICY

During the Great Depression, the U.S. economy experienced severe and lasting unemployment, along with falling prices and a sharp decline in real output. Classical theory could not account for such conditions. In de-veloping an alternative theory, Keynes and his followers focused on the question "What determines the level of employment in a market econ-omy?" They knew that if they could explain employment, the same model would explain unemployment.

KEYNESIAN MACROECONOMIC THEORY
In attempting to identify the cause of employment, Keynes reasoned as follows:

1. The level of employment is directly related to the level of production, or output (Y).
2. In a market economy, planned spending on the output of the business

5. Keynes identified a third motive, the precautionary demand for money. This motive drives those who hold cash for "a rainy day" (as an emergency fund). Since this demand, like transac-tions demand, is related to income, later economists combined it with transactions demand.

sector will determine the level of production. Firms adjust their levels of production to meet demand for their products. Put simply, "supply adjusts to demand." (In contrast, Say's law said "supply creates its own demand.")

3. Since employment depends on production and production responds to spending, the level of employment in a market economy depends on the level of planned spending in the economy.

Note how Keynes reversed the sequence of events from the classical model. In the classical model, the labor market determined employment, and employment determined the level of output. Therefore, the position of the aggregate supply curve is vertical. Recall from Chapter 6 that the aggregate supply curve can be very flat, even horizontal, if many resources are unemployed. The Keynesian model of the Depression economy has ample unemployed resources and a horizontal aggregate supply curve. If aggregate supply is constant (horizontal), then aggregate demand determines the level of output. In turn, the level of output determines the level of employment. Aggregate demand, which determined only the price level in the classical model, has the starring role in Keynes's model. It determines the level of real output. In Figure 7, the price level is given at P_1, and aggregate demand determines the level of output, Y_1 . Output, in turn, determines the level of employment, N_1.

Consider how this model might apply to the situation in the 1930s. Unemployment was high because planned spending was too low to generate the level of output (Y^* in Figure 7) that would result in full employment (N^*). Thus, too little spending was identified as the cause of unemployment. To reduce unemployment, planned spending had to increase. In the language of aggregate supply and aggregate demand (a model developed after Keynes), aggregate demand had to shift to the right.

How could aggregate demand be shifted to ensure a level of output that would result in higher employment and lower unemployment? Keynes's answer goes back to the circular flow model. He identified the groups of purchasers (households, firms, government, and the foreign sector) in the spending stream and considered what determines the amount of planned spending by each group. Keynes was very interested in determinants of planned consumption spending and planned investment spending.[6] He concluded that sometimes these two sources of spending will be inadequate to lead the economy to the full-employment level of output. At such times, the government, as a third major spending sector, should step in and boost planned spending (and aggregate demand) to the desired level.

What determines planned consumption and investment spending? According to Keynes, consumer spending (and saving) depends primarily on the level of income. Keynes believed that household spending habits are relatively stable and that households will spend a specific fraction of any increase in income. Investment demand, or planned investment spending, however, is much less stable. Investment depends on such

---

6.   Today, with a large and growing foreign sector, economists pay more attention to what determines exports and imports. We will consider the role of the foreign sector more carefully in the next chapter. It did not play much of a role in the original Keynesian model.

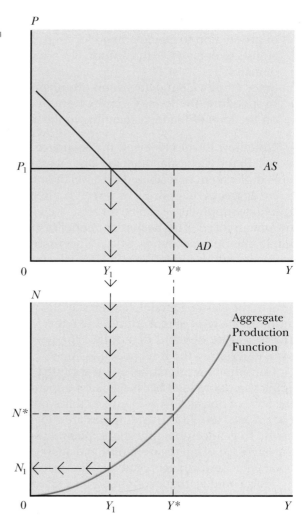

FIGURE 7
A KEYNESIAN VIEW OF AGGREGATE SUPPLY AND AGGREGATE DEMAND
When there are unemployed resources, the aggregate supply curve is horizontal. Aggregate demand determines the level of real output (Y_1). The price level (P_1) is not affected by changes in demand. The level of real output (Y_1) determines the number of workers needed to produce it (N_1) through the production function in the lower graph.

factors as expectations, interest rates, and changes in final consumer demand. Expectations are especially prone to sharp swings. Thus, Keynes believed that investment spending would shift a great deal and would be the major source of changes in output and employment. Government can offset those changes by increasing its spending when investment demand is low and by cutting it back when investment demand is high.

There is a basic difference between the Keynesian and classical models. In the classical model, investment and saving both depend on the interest rate, which balances leakages and injections in the circular flow. In the Keynesian model, however, the interest rate plays a much smaller role. The interest rate has little influence on investment. Investment is instead dominated by changing expectations about final sales and consumer demand. The interest rate also has almost no effect on saving (which responds mainly to income). Since investment and saving are determined by different forces, there is no reason to expect that planned saving will be equal to planned investment. Therefore, there is no reason to expect

> ## KEYNESIAN CRITICISMS OF THE CLASSICAL MODEL
>
> - Say's law is not necessarily valid. Just because enough income is created does not mean it will be spent.
>
> - Self-regulating markets do not necessarily guarantee full employment.
>   In the credit market, saving and investment are influenced by much more than the rate of interest.
>   In the labor market, unions and other influences can make it difficult to adjust wages downward. If wages do fall, that will also reduce demand.
>   In the product market, large corporations may cut output rather than prices.
>
> - Instead, in the Keynesian model:
>   Employment is determined by output.
>   Output is determined by the intersection of the aggregate supply and demand curves (by demand for final output).
>   The aggregate supply curve can be horizontal.

the economy to move automatically toward an equilibrium at a full-employment level of output.

THE KEYNESIAN EXPLANATION OF THE GREAT DEPRESSION

The Great Depression resulted from many complex forces and cannot be explained by a single cause or event.[7] At the time, economists trained in the classical tradition could not explain it. Keynes was able to offer a direct and plausible explanation of why planned spending by consumers and investment by firms fell so dramatically from 1929 to 1933 (see Table 1). He also explained why the economy did not recover automatically, as classical macroeconomics predicted.

Keynes observed that, after several years of rising consumption and investment spending during the 1920s, the rate of expansion began to slow. With enough plants and equipment to meet current demand, firms reduced their levels of investment spending, leading to a decline in output and employment. When employment declined, household income declined. Consumption spending also declined. Falling consumption further discouraged investment spending because of firms' expectations of poor future sales. Investment spending fell further, causing more declines in employment, income, and consumption spending. The spiral continued, and output and sales plummeted.

Consumer spending fell because there were fewer jobs and less income. Business firms reduced output because they couldn't sell their products. They weren't spending for investment because they had little confidence in the future. In fact, firms were so pessimistic about the future that they weren't even replacing machinery as it wore out. To many people, it seemed as though the whole system had broken down.

---

7. Since the 1930s, many economists have looked at the series of events and offered different views as to the key causes. These causes include the Smoot-Hawley Tariff of 1930, international monetary problems, a simultaneous downturn in eight-year, twenty-year, and fifty-year business cycles, and the Federal Reserve's inept management of the money supply. These explanations, however, evolved long after the events.

Keynesian theory suggested a way to end the Great Depression: The government should intervene in the market economy by using its power to tax and spend to increase aggregate demand. That is, the government should spend more or tax less, or both. This advice was difficult for political leaders to follow in an era of *laissez-faire* capitalism. Keynes's prescription was followed to a very limited extent until World War II. In Table 1, you can see that the process of recovery was very slow, especially in employment. Consumption, investment, and total GNP did not reach the pre-Depression levels of 1929 until twelve years later in 1941. Unemployment remained high until the war was fully under way in 1942.

Preparations for war forced the U.S. government to increase its defense spending. Congress chose to raise taxes, but by less than the amount needed to pay for the war. By 1943, the unemployment rate in the United States had fallen to 1.9 percent. Keynesian economic policy of increasing spending more than taxes had finally ended the Great Depression, but not as Keynes expected. The massive increase in government spending in the 1940s was not an exercise in Keynesian economic policy. It occurred in order to pay for World War II.

THE POLITICS OF THE KEYNESIAN REVOLUTION

Keynes's ideas were considered radical by many at the time. Keynes considered his proposals conservative. During a period when communism, fascism, and other antimarket philosophies were very popular, Keynes saw his economic policy as a way to rescue the market economy from its most serious weakness—persistent and recurring downturns in output and employment. Recessions and depressions offered fertile ground for socialist or communist proposals to shift to a more centrally planned economy. Keynes wanted to salvage the market economy by reducing its tendency to go into recessions.

After World War II, Keynesian ideas were more widely accepted. The Keynesian revolution was a huge political and economic success. The Great

TABLE 1
CONSUMPTION AND
INVESTMENT EXPENDITURES
DURING THE DEPRESSION
(BILLIONS OF DOLLARS)

YEAR	CONSUMPTION EXPENDITURES	INVESTMENT EXPENDITURES	TOTAL GNP	UNEMPLOYMENT RATE
1929	$79.0	$16.2	$103.9	3.2%
1930	71.0	10.3	90.4	8.7
1931	61.3	5.5	75.8	15.9
1932	49.3	.9	58.0	23.6
1933	46.4	1.4	55.6	24.9
1934	51.9	2.9	65.1	21.7
1935	56.3	6.3	72.2	20.1
1936	62.6	8.4	82.5	16.9
1937	67.3	11.7	90.4	14.3
1938	64.6	6.7	84.7	19.0
1939	67.6	9.3	90.5	17.2
1940	71.9	13.2	100.4	14.6
1941	81.9	18.1	125.5	9.9

Source: Council of Economic Advisers, *Economic Report of the President* (Washington, DC: U.S. Government Printing Office, various years).

Depression had brought a great deal of suffering. Classical economic theory offered no immediate relief. Classical economists advised people to wait until prices fell, markets readjusted, and equilibrium was restored. In short, their policy was to do nothing until, in the long run, the economy returned to its full-employment equilibrium. Keynes offered a policy that could make things better in the short run. This option was much more appealing to both politicians and the unemployed. At the same time, Keynes offered frustrated economists a plausible explanation of the Great Depression. Today, most government officials still adhere to at least part of the Keynesian view. They believe it is better to do something about economic conditions than to wait for the economy to correct itself—especially if the correction may not take place until after the next election!

SUMMARY

1. The view of the classical school was that the economy always tends toward the full-employment level of output. The classical aggregate supply curve is vertical. Changes in aggregate demand affect only the price level. Deviations from the full-employment level of output are temporary and self-correcting.

2. Say's law said that enough income will be created in the process of production to purchase all that is produced. Any problems are corrected through price adjustments in the self-regulating product, factor, and credit markets.

3. In the classical model, the interest rate ensures that planned saving is equal to planned investment.

4. The quantity theory of money explains how changes in the money supply are translated through household behavior into changes in the price level and/or real output. In the classical model, the velocity of money (V) and real output (Y) are constant. According to the equation of exchange, $M \times V = P \times Y$, changes in the money supply lead to proportional changes in the price level.

5. Business cycle theorists such as Malthus and Schumpeter stressed insufficient consumption and unstable investment as the main causes of ups and downs in output and employment.

6. Keynes criticized the three central elements of classical theory: Say's law, the quantity theory of money, and self-regulating markets. He argued that factors other than interest rates determine saving and investment, that prices and wages can be sticky downward, and that the demand for money is unstable.

7. Keynes stressed the role of planned spending in determining the levels of output and employment. He argued for government intervention to deal with persistent recession and unemployment.

NEW TERMS

macroeconomic equilibrium	demand for money	transactions demand for money
self-regulating markets	Keynesian revolution	
	asset demand for money	

QUESTIONS FOR DISCUSSION

1. Suppose an economy has suffered two years of falling output and rising unemployment. How would this be explained by a classical economist, a business cycle theorist, and a Keynesian? What would each recommend doing?

2. Marshall's form of the equation of exchange is $M_d = k(P \times Y)$. Let $k = \frac{1}{4}$. Suppose money national income is $3,000. What must the money supply be in order to be equal to the money demand? Suppose the money supply increases to $1,000. What must the value of total output be? What are some possible divisions of that total between P and Y?

3. Keynes argued that k was not stable, especially in the short run. Suppose when you increase the money supply to $1,000 in Question 2, k rises from $\frac{1}{4}$ to $\frac{1}{3}$. That is, people decide to hold a larger fraction of their money income in cash balances. What happens to $P \times Y$ when M_s increases in this case? What does that imply for monetary policy?

4. The variables V and k are not calculated directly but are inferred from the value of M_s and $P \times Y$ (nominal GNP). Given the following data on money supply and GNP (both in billions of dollars), compute V and k for the United States for the years shown.

YEAR	MONEY SUPPLY	GNP
1959	$141	$488
1960	143	507
1961	147	525
1962	149	565
1963	155	597
1964	162	638
1965	170	691
1966	174	756
1967	185	800
1968	199	873
1969	206	944
1970	217	993

You can repeat this exercise for other periods with data from the *Economic Report of the President*. What do you conclude about the stability of k and V?

5. Using the data in Table 1, compute the ratio of consumption to GNP and the ratio of investment to GNP for each year. Present the data as a graph. What conclusions can you draw about which form of spending is more stable?

6. Indicate whether each of the following statements about the Great Depression would be likely to be made by a business cycle theorist, a classical economist, or a Keynesian.

a. "Left alone, the economy would have corrected itself."

b. "Unequal distribution of income meant that the rich bought too little and the poor could not buy the rest, leaving a glut of unsold goods."

c. "Instability of investment means that the government has to step in to stabilize demand."

7. Why is the classical aggregate supply curve vertical? Why is the Keynesian aggregate supply curve horizontal?

8. What was revolutionary about Keynes's ideas?

9. According to classical economists, how do interest rates help to ensure that the economy will always return to the full-employment level of output?

10. Suppose that in the last six months real output has fallen by 3 percent, with a sharp rise in unemployment. What would a classical economist recommend as policy? Why? What would a Keynesian recommend?

11. What reason did Keynes give for the instability of money velocity?

12. If you expect interest rates to rise, will you hold money in cash or buy bonds? Why? What if you expect interest rates to fall?

13. Suppose there are 100 million workers in the economy, and full employment is defined as 96 percent of them being employed. Also suppose that each $10 billion in output employs 1 million workers. What is the full-employment level of output? If actual output is $850 billion, what would you expect the unemployment rate to be?

14. Sometimes the Keynesian revolution is described as a switch from "supply creates its own demand" to "demand creates its own supply." Explain this statement.

15. Why, according to Keynes, do self-regulating markets not solve the problem of falling output?

SUGGESTIONS FOR FURTHER READING

Clarke, Peter. *The Keynesian Revolution in the Making, 1924–1936.* Oxford, UK: Oxford University Press, 1988. Examines the British economic conditions in the 1920s and 1930s as a major influence on the development of Keynes's ideas.

Garraty, John A. "The Big Picture of the Great Depression," *American Heritage* (August/September 1986): 90–97. A good account of one of the most significant economic events of the twentieth century.

Heilbroner, Robert. *The Worldly Philosophers*, 6th ed. New York: Simon and Schuster, 1987. A popular and readable account of the lives and ideas of the great economists.

Hollander, Samuel. *Classical Economics.* Oxford and New York: Basil Blackwell, 1987. Traces the development of the ideas of the classical school.

Lekachman, Robert. *The Age of Keynes.* New York: McGraw-Hill, 1975. The best-known account of the life, times, and contributions of the most famous economist of the twentieth century.

Terkel, Studs. *Hard Times: An Oral History of the Great Depression.* New York: Random House, 1970. A classic retelling of personal experiences of individuals and families during the Depression.

1. Explain the importance of the consumption function in the Keynesian model of how national income and output are determined.
2. Define:
   a. consumption function,
   b. marginal propensity to consume (*MPC*),
   c. marginal propensity to save (*MPS*).
3. Discuss the role of investment spending in the Keynesian model.
4. Find the equilibrium level of national income from a table or a graph, using each of these methods:
   a. $C + I + G + (EX - IM)$ equals aggregate expenditure (*AE*);
   b. leakages equal injections.
5. Explain how unplanned changes in business inventories affect the level of income and output.
6. Calculate the value of the multiplier, given either *MPC* or *MPS*.
7. Calculate the change in the equilibrium national income, given the initial change in planned spending and the value of the multiplier.

CHAPTER 8

THE KEYNESIAN MODEL

INTRODUCTION

This chapter develops Keynes's explanation of how national income and output are determined. The Keynesian model explains how it is possible to reach an equilibrium level of income and output that is not the full-employment level.

Keynes did not agree with the classical view that the output level associated with full employment was the only possible equilibrium for the economy. He pointed out that the predictions of classical theory did not match the experience of the 1930s. In the Great Depression, the economy appeared to be at an equilibrium level of national income and output far below that required for the full employment of resources. Keynes did agree with the classical view that the economy would move automatically to an equilibrium level of national income and output. At that level, total planned spending and actual output would be equal. However, Keynes argued that it was quite possible for this equilibrium level to be a relatively low one, associated with a high level of unemployment. The Keynesian model of the economy explained how this could happen.

Keynes argued that supply adjusts to demand. That is, businesses will adjust their level of output to meet the demand as long as there are idle resources to expand production. Demand, or planned spending, plays the key role in determining how much is produced. What determines the spending plans of households and firms? Keynes believed that expenditures, especially consumption expenditures, are strongly influenced by the level of income. All income (wages, salaries, rent, interest, and profit) is received by the owners of the factors of production. There is a continuous flow from income to demand to output and back to income. Planned spending by households and firms determines the level of national income and output, but planned spending itself is influenced by national income. Thus, Keynes recognized that planned spending, output, and national income are *interdependent*. Their values are jointly determined.

In the language of aggregate supply and demand, the Keynesian model has a downward-sloping aggregate demand (*AD*) curve and a horizontal aggregate supply (*AS*) curve. A horizontal slope is one of the possible slopes for the *AS* curve presented in Chapter 6. Recall that the *AS* curve is likely to be horizontal when there are unemployed resources, which happened in the 1930s. At such a time, it is possible to expand output without driving up wages and prices. A horizontal *AS* curve allows the Keynesian model to focus on the position of the *AD* curve because that position determines the equilibrium level of national income and output. The level of real output (*Y*) that results from the intersection of the *AD* curve with Keynes's horizontal *AS* curve does not necessarily ensure full employment.

Keynes, however, did not use the terms *aggregate supply* and *aggregate demand*, at least not in the way they are used today. Instead, the central focus of his model was the relationship between consumption expenditures and disposable income. This relationship is known as the consumption function.

Investment demand also plays an important role in the Keynesian model. The sum of the two sources of planned spending—consumption and investment—is the aggregate expenditure (*AE*) function. This function determines the equilibrium level of national income and output. The multiplier concept is derived from the consumption function and shows how changes in planned expenditures affect that equilibrium level. The addition of government purchases and export and import spending provides a complete Keynesian model of the macro economy. When we have developed all these relationships, we will link the Keynesian model to the aggregate supply and demand framework of Chapter 6.

In this chapter and the next, we make a few simplifying assumptions. First, we will initially ignore the distinctions among GNP, NNP, NI, and PI. We will treat these as though they were all equivalent to *Y*, or real income and output. For the Keynesian model, the only important distinction we will need to make later on is between income before taxes and after-tax, or disposable, income (Y_d). Second, we will assume that the price level is fixed. When the price level does not change, consumption, investment, output, and income have the same values whether they are expressed in current market terms or in real (price-adjusted) terms. For analyzing periods of high unemployment when there is little upward pressure on prices, a fixed price level is a convenient and plausible assumption. (This second assumption will be relaxed toward the end of this chapter.) Third, we will initially ignore government and the foreign sector to concentrate on a simple two-sector economy. The two sectors are households that earn, consume, and save and business firms that produce and invest. Once we have built a working model of this simple economy, we can relax each assumption and bring the model closer to the real world.

THE KEYNESIAN AGGREGATE EXPENDITURE FUNCTION

aggregate expenditure (*AE*)
Total planned spending by all sectors for an economy's total output.

The Keynesian model uses a measure of planned spending that is different from aggregate demand. **Aggregate expenditure (*AE*)** is defined as total planned spending by all sectors for an economy's total output. Recall from Chapter 5 that there are four sectors in the economy: households, business firms, government, and a foreign sector. In the upper half of the circular flow, the business sector sells output to each of the four sectors, including business firms that are making investment purchases. Aggregate expenditure for a four-sector economy is the sum of the purchases of all sectors:

$$AE = C + I + G + (EX - IM).$$

Here C is planned consumption spending, I is planned investment spending, G is government purchases of goods and services, and EX and IM are exports and imports, respectively. This breakdown is not the only way of sorting planned spending into components. It is useful, however, because the forces and motives influencing planned spending are different for each of these four sectors of the economy. These four purchasers of output correspond to the four categories of purchasers used in national income accounting and to the four actors in the circular flow model.

In a simple economy with no government and no foreign trade, aggregate expenditure has just two components: consumption and investment. It is useful to start with these two to develop a model of income determination and then add the others to make the model more realistic.

THE KEYNESIAN CONSUMPTION FUNCTION

Recall that Keynes challenged Say's law by arguing that it is demand, or planned spending, that determines how much is produced. Since the largest component of spending is consumption, Keynes began building his model by examining the behavior of consumption. He argued that the amount consumers spend depends mainly on their disposable income. Keynes called this relationship the consumption function and made it a key part of his theory.

The **consumption function** is any equation, table, or graph that shows the relationship between the income of consumers (disposable income) and the amount they plan, or desire, to spend on currently produced final output. Note that this Keynesian function relates consumer spending to disposable income, not national income. The distinction between disposable income and national income is not important here, since we are considering a simple economy with no government and thus no taxes. Later it will be important to distinguish between total output and income (Y) and disposable income (Y_d). Thus, we present the consumption function here in the same form in which it will appear when we add government to the model.

The general form of the equation for the consumption function is

$$C = C_0 + bY_d$$

where C is consumption expenditures and Y_d is disposable income. This expression says that consumption is positively related to income. That is, consumption rises when income rises and falls when income falls. The expression also indicates that there is a component of consumption (C_0) that is not related to the level of income. In the simple Keynesian model, any variable that is not dependent on income is said to be autonomous, or determined by other variables not included in the model. On a graph,

consumption function Any equation, table, or graph that shows the relationship between income of consumers (disposable income) and the amount they plan to spend on currently produced final output.

the consumption function is a positively sloped straight line that crosses the vertical axis at C_0.[1] The slope of this line is b.

As an example, assume that the consumption function for a simple economy is expressed as

$$(1) \quad C = C_0 + bY_\mathrm{d} = \$200 + 0.8Y_\mathrm{d},$$

with all values in billions of dollars.

Table 1 shows some specific values for this consumption function. This table was derived by choosing various values for national income ($Y = Y_\mathrm{d}$ because there are no taxes). The values for planned consumption spending (C) were then obtained by substituting the values of Y_d into equation (1). That is, the table answers this question: "If disposable income is equal to Y_d, then how much will households spend out of that income on consumption?" For example, if

$$Y_\mathrm{d} = \$1,200 \text{ billion},$$

then

$$C = \$200 \text{ billion} + 0.8(\$1,200 \text{ billion}) = \$1,160 \text{ billion}.$$

How were the values for planned saving (S) in the fifth column of Table 1 obtained? Recall from Chapter 4 that saving is that part of income that is not spent. Therefore,

$$S = Y_\mathrm{d} - C.$$

The values for planned saving (S) were obtained by subtracting the values in the third column from those in the first. That is, consumption (C) is subtracted from income (Y_d) to see what is left. Note that saving is negative at very low levels of income. Households will draw on their accumulated savings in order to maintain some minimum level of consumption.

THE MARGINAL PROPENSITIES TO CONSUME AND TO SAVE. Note that the values in Table 1 show a consistent relationship among income, consumption,

TABLE 1
PLANNED CONSUMPTION
SPENDING (C) AND
PLANNED SAVING (S)
AT VARIOUS LEVELS OF
NATIONAL INCOME (Y)
(BILLIONS OF DOLLARS)

NATIONAL INCOME (DISPOSABLE INCOME), $Y = Y_\mathrm{d}$	CHANGE IN DISPOSABLE INCOME, ΔY_d	PLANNED CONSUMPTION SPENDING, C	CHANGE IN PLANNED CONSUMPTION SPENDING, ΔC	PLANNED SAVING, S	CHANGE IN PLANNED SAVING, ΔS
$ 600	$ —	$ 680	$ —	$–80	$—
800	200	840	160	– 40	40
1,000	200	1,000	160	0	40
1,200	200	1,160	160	40	40
1,400	200	1,320	160	80	40
1,600	200	1,480	160	120	40
1,800	200	1,640	160	160	40
2,000	200	1,800	160	200	40

1.   A linear consumption function is consistent with Keynes's ideas about the relationship between consumer spending and disposable income, discussed in Chapter 7.

and saving. In the table, every time income increases by $200, consumption increases by $160 and saving by $40. Keynes believed that consumers are creatures of habit. When disposable income changes, he expected consumer spending to change by a constant fraction of the change in income. Keynes called this fraction the **marginal propensity to consume (*MPC*)**. It corresponds to *b* in the equation for the consumption function. The marginal propensity to consume (*MPC*) is the ratio of the change in consumption spending (ΔC) to the change in disposable income (ΔY_d):

$$MPC = \frac{\Delta C}{\Delta Y_\mathrm{d}}.$$

marginal propensity to consume (*MPC*)
The fraction of any change in income that is consumed. The *MPC* is greater than 0 and less than 1.

A related concept is the **marginal propensity to save (*MPS*)**, which describes how saving responds to income changes. The marginal propensity to save (*MPS*) is the ratio of the change in saving (ΔS) to the change in disposable income (ΔY_d):

$$MPS = \frac{\Delta S}{\Delta Y_\mathrm{d}}.$$

marginal propensity to save (*MPS*)
The fraction of any change in income that is saved. The *MPS* is greater than 0 and less than 1.

Values of *MPC* and *MPS* are not shown in Table 1 but can be calculated easily from the values given there. For instance, when Y_d increases from $1,000 billion to $1,200 billion, *C* increases from $1,000 billion to $1,160 billion and *S* increases from $0 to $40 billion. Thus, for $\Delta Y_\mathrm{d} = \$200$ billion, $\Delta C = \$160$ billion and $\Delta S = \$40$ billion. The values of *MPC* and *MPS* are

$$MPC = \frac{\Delta C}{\Delta Y_\mathrm{d}} = \frac{\$160 \text{ billion}}{\$200 \text{ billion}} = \frac{4}{5}, \text{ or } 0.8,$$

and

$$MPS = \frac{\Delta S}{\Delta Y_\mathrm{d}} = \frac{\$40 \text{ billion}}{\$200 \text{ billion}} = \frac{1}{5}, \text{ or } 0.2.$$

If you calculate *MPC* and *MPS* from other values in Table 1, you will get the same values each time. Table 1 was created using Keynes's assumption that the marginal propensity to consume is constant.

In this example, *MPC* is $\frac{4}{5}$ and *MPS* is $\frac{1}{5}$ of the change in income, and their sum equals 1. In an economy with no taxes, *MPC* and *MPS* will always add up to 1 because all consumer income that is not spent on final goods and services must be saved. (If *MPC* and *MPS* are computed as fractions of changes in disposable, or after-tax, income, then they will sum to 1 even if taxes are included in the model.) When income rises by $500 billion, the additional consumption spending is the marginal propensity to consume times $500 billion. If *MPC* is 0.8, consumption spending rises by $400 billion. The amount *not* spent is (1-*MPC*) times $500 billion, or $100 billion. The amount not spent on consumption is, by definition, saving. Thus, when income rises by $500 billion, the change in saving is equal to the marginal propensity to save times $500 billion. Since all the added income must be either spent or saved, we can conclude that

$$MPS = 1 - MPC, \text{ or } MPC + MPS = 1.$$

If *MPC* is 0.9, then *MPS* must be 0.1. If *MPC* is 0.6, then *MPS* must be 0.4. If $\frac{9}{10}$ or $\frac{6}{10}$ of an increase in income is spent, only $\frac{1}{10}$ or $\frac{4}{10}$ is saved.

Figure 1 is a graphic presentation of the numbers in Table 1 and the corresponding consumption function,

$$C = \$200 + 0.8Y_d.$$

The marginal propensity to consume is equal to b, the slope of the consumption function. Recall that the slope of a line is the ratio of the change in the variable on the vertical axis to the change in the variable on the horizontal axis, moving from left to right along the horizontal axis. In Figure 1, the slope is the ratio of the change in C to the change in Y. In symbols, $b = \Delta C/\Delta Y = MPC$. Similarly, the slope of the saving function is $\Delta S/\Delta Y = MPS$. When consumers receive more income, a larger share of it normally goes to consumption than to saving. The marginal propensity to save is usually smaller than the marginal propensity to consume. Thus, the slope of the consumption function is steeper than the slope of the saving function in Figure 1. (If you have difficulty with slopes, you may want to review the appendix to Chapter 1.)

Keynes believed that the marginal propensity to consume would be relatively constant, at least over a modest range of values of income and output. That is, he expected that a rise in disposable income from $1,000 billion to $1,200 billion would lead to the same increase in consumption as a rise in disposable income from $1,200 billion to $1,400 billion. Since Keynes wrote *General Theory*, economists have devoted much attention to examining the behavior of the consumption function. When consumption functions are estimated from annual data for total consumption and

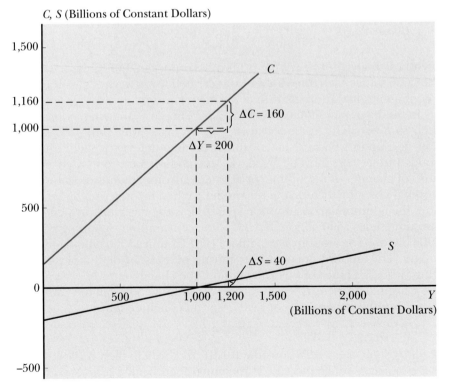

FIGURE 1
PLANNED CONSUMPTION AND PLANNED SAVING
The consumption function shows the relationship between planned consumption and national income. The saving function shows the relationship between planned saving and national income. The slope of the consumption function is equal to *MPC*. The slope of the saving function is equal to *MPS*.

KEYNES'S HYPOTHESES ABOUT *MPC* AND *MPS*

- *MPC* and *MPS* are always greater than 0 and less than 1.

- The sum of *MPC* and *MPS* must always equal 1.

- *MPC* is the slope of the consumption function, and *MPS* is the slope of the saving function.

- *MPC* and *MPS* are relatively constant. Their values do not change along the graph of the consumption function.

national income for the United States, they appear to be fairly stable, with a nearly constant marginal propensity to consume. Some of these estimates of the consumption function find a positive value for the constant term (C_0). In Table 1, for example, this constant term is $200 billion. Other estimates of the actual consumption functions appear to be closer to the form $C = bY_d$, which has no constant term. A graph of this function would cross the y-axis at the origin.

Figure 2 plots data for consumption and income in the United States

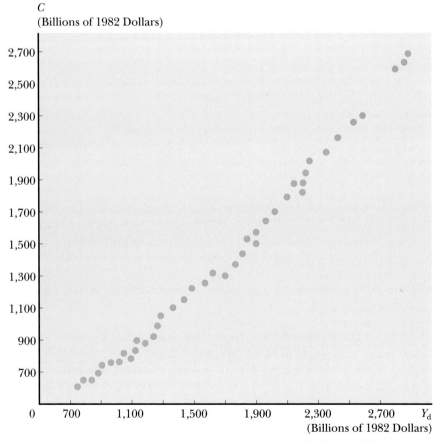

C
(Billions of 1982 Dollars)

0   700   1,100   1,500   1,900   2,300   2,700 Y_d
(Billions of 1982 Dollars)

**FIGURE 2
CONSUMPTION
EXPENDITURES VERSUS
DISPOSABLE INCOME FOR
THE UNITED STATES,
1950–1990**
The historical relationship between consumption expenditures and disposable income seems to be very stable, with an *MPC* between 0.8 and 0.9 and a C_0 term that is close to zero.

Source: Council of Economic Advisers, *Economic Report of the President* (Washington, DC: U.S. Government Printing Office, 1991).

from 1950 to 1990. This consumption-income relationship appears to be almost a straight line, with a slope (*MPC*) between 0.8 and 0.9 and no constant term. The ratio of increases in saving to increases in disposable income is relatively low, between 0.1 and 0.2. A low saving rate has concerned many economists who think Americans need to save more in order to speed up economic growth. We will explore this issue further in Chapter 16.

THE CONSTANT TERM IN THE CONSUMPTION FUNCTION. It is easy to understand why consumption might rise as income rises. But where does that constant term, C_0, in the equation for the consumption function come from? If we insert a value of zero for Y_d into the general form of the consumption function, $C = C_0 + bY_d$, this equation seems to say that there is a positive level of consumption, C_0, even when no output is currently being produced and no income is being earned. For Table 1, C_0 had a value of $200 billion. This value indicated that consumers would buy $200 billion worth of goods and services even if there were no production taking place and no income coming into households.

The constant term in the consumption function reflects two important facts. One is that it is possible to consume for a short while even with no current production. An economy could consume inventories and deplete its stock of capital for short periods of time. This process is known as **dissaving**. If an economy was in a crisis situation in which production halted, it could still continue to consume for a while. No economy ever comes to a complete standstill. However, during the revolutionary changes in Eastern Europe in late 1989 and 1990, some economies came very close—that of Romania, for example. What does happen fairly often is that economies temporarily consume more than they produce in wartime by drawing on inventories and wearing out capital without replacing it.

dissaving
Consuming by drawing on accumulated stocks (inventories) or financial assets.

The second fact embodied in the constant term C_0 is that there are many other influences on consumption besides income. The most important of these influences are

1. wealth (consumers' assets such as stocks, bonds, houses, cars, and savings deposits),
2. interest rates (which affect the cost of consumer borrowing),
3. the price level (discussed in Chapter 6 in connection with the *AD* curve), and
4. expectations (including expectations about future prices, income, and employment).

If one of these influences changes, the entire consumption function will shift up or down. Consumers will want to purchase more goods and services at every income level. This shift in the consumption function will also be reflected as a change in the value of C_0 in its consumption equation and the table of values. For example, if consumers acquired more wealth and assets over time and thus felt they did not need to save as much out of any level of income, they would increase their consumption. The value of C_0 might increase from $200 billion to $250 billion. The entire

BASIC FEATURES OF THE KEYNESIAN CONSUMPTION FUNCTION

- Consumption (C) depends on the level of disposable income (Y_d).

- Part of consumption is independent of the level of income. This constant term (C_0) changes in response to changes in such other influences as wealth, interest rates, the price level, and expectations.

- The rest of consumption (bY_d) is positively related to income. The marginal propensity to consume ($MPC = b$) is the fraction of an additional dollar of income that will be spent on consumption: $0 < b < 1$.

consumption function would shift upward as consumers spend more of every possible value of Y_d.

INVESTMENT EXPENDITURE

In a two-sector economy, there are only two kinds of planned expenditures: consumption and investment. Planned expenditures are distinguished from actual expenditures, because sometimes households or firms will find that actual spending does not equal what was planned.

We have already explored what determines consumption. How do we explain the behavior of investment demand (I)? Recall that classical economists believed that the most important determinant of planned investment spending was the interest rate. Keynes did not agree. He argued that profit expectations would be the most important determinant of investment spending. Other important influences on investment are the interest rate, the size and age of the existing stock of capital, changes in corporate taxes, and changes in technology. Some of these influences are subject to drastic and sudden changes.

In order to understand the behavior of investment, you need to recall the breakdown of gross private domestic investment into fixed investment in business plants and equipment, residential construction, and inventories. All three of these components are responsive to changes in both expectations and interest rates, but to different degrees.

Plants and equipment have a long useful lifetime. Thus, there may be a large existing stock to be used up before there will be much replacement. The same is true of residential construction. Also, housing demand is very sensitive to changes in construction costs and patterns of population growth. If a large proportion of the population is twenty to forty years old, there is high demand for new housing as new families are formed. As the population ages, housing demand does not grow as rapidly. Inventories are very dependent on actual and expected final sales. Thus, they tend to fluctuate more in the short run than other types of investment. Unplanned changes in inventories, in fact, play a very important role in moving an economy toward equilibrium. Sudden increases or decreases in inventories signal producers that they need to change their level of output.

In general, all three types of investment fluctuate much more than consumption. Because inventories are more likely than other types of investment spending to exceed or fall short of desired levels, we will assume that other plans are realized. That is, any gap between planned and actual spending will consist of unplanned changes in inventories. This is not always the case, however. In the Soviet Union, actual consumption frequently falls short of planned consumption because stores' shelves are empty and there are no inventories on which to draw.

Keynes assumed that the investment demand curve would shift so frequently that the relationship between planned investment spending and the level of income (or the rate of interest) would not be as important as the causes of its shifts. In the Keynesian model, it is the level of investment spending that matters. For this reason, we will follow Keynes for now and treat investment demand as an exogenous variable, a given value that is determined outside the model.

EQUILIBRIUM IN A TWO-SECTOR MODEL

The consumption function and some measure of investment demand are all we need to develop a two-sector model that determines the equilibrium value of national income and output (Y). Table 2 and Figure 3 add to the consumption function of equation (1) an investment demand of $200 billion, which is autonomous (independent of the level of income). In a two-sector model, consumption and investment represent all of the sources of demand. Figure 3 graphs the data in Table 2 and adds a reference line with a slope of 45°. This reference line locates those points where the value measured on the horizontal axis (total output or income) is equal to the value on the vertical axis (aggregate planned expenditure, or $C + I$).[2] Where the AE (or $C + I$) curve crosses the 45° line, aggregate expenditure is equal to total output. This value of output is, by definition, an equilibrium level. In Figure 3, equilibrium occurs at $Y = \$1,800 = C + I$.

What makes this level of output the equilibrium level? Equilibrium occurs at an output level of $1,800 because no other level can be sustained. At any other level of output, unplanned inventory changes occur. These changes direct business firms to adjust production levels in order to make output equal to aggregate planned expenditure.

Table 3 shows the important role played by unplanned inventory changes. For example, if Y were equal to $1,400 billion, aggregate planned expenditure (AE) would be $1,480 billion. Planned spending for output

TABLE 2
AN AGGREGATE
EXPENDITURE (AE)
SCHEDULE (BILLIONS
OF DOLLARS)

NATIONAL INCOME, $Y = Y_d$	PLANNED CONSUMPTION EXPENDITURE, C	PLANNED SAVING, $Y - C$	BUSINESS INVESTMENT EXPENDITURE, I	AGGREGATE EXPENDITURE, $AE = C + I$
$1,000	$1,000	$ 0	$160	$1,160
1,200	1,160	40	160	1,320
1,400	1,320	80	160	1,480
1,600	1,480	120	160	1,640
1,800	1,640	160	160	1,800
2,000	1,800	200	160	1,960
2,200	1,960	240	160	2,120
2,400	2,120	280	160	2,280
2,600	2,280	320	160	2,440

2.   This graphic tool is described in the appendix to Chapter 1. You may want to go back and review that section.

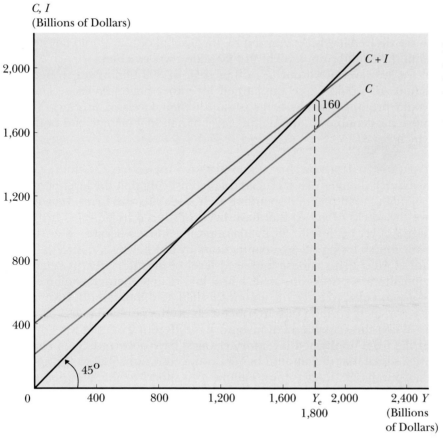

FIGURE 3
AGGREGATE EXPENDITURE AND EQUILIBRIUM OUTPUT Adding investment to the consumption function gives aggregate planned expenditure ($AE = C + I$) at every possible level of output. The 45° reference line shows the points where aggregate expenditure (measured on the vertical axis) equals total output (measured on the horizontal axis). The AE curve crosses the 45° line at the equilibrium level of output (Y_e).

would exceed current production by $80 billion. As firms tried to fill orders, their inventories would begin to decline. They would realize that production is not keeping pace with sales. Firms would respond to unplanned declines in inventories by increasing their levels of output. The expansion in output to rebuild inventories would increase the level of output to the equilibrium level of $1,800 billion.

On the other hand, if Y were equal to $2,400 billion, AE would be only $2,380 billion. In this case, current production would exceed aggregate

NATIONAL INCOME, $Y = Y_d$	AGGREGATE EXPENDITURE, AE	UNPLANNED INVENTORY CHANGES, $(Y - AE)$	BUSINESS RESPONSE	EFFECT ON NATIONAL INCOME
$1,000	$1,160	$-160	Increase output	Increase
1,400	1,480	- 80	Increase output	Increase
1,800	1,800	0	Maintain output	No change
2,000	1,960	+ 40	Decrease output	Decrease
2,200	2,120	+ 80	Decrease output	Decrease
2,600	2,440	220160	Decrease output	Decrease

TABLE 3
UNPLANNED INVENTORY CHANGES AND THE EQUILIBRIUM LEVEL OF NATIONAL INCOME (BILLIONS OF DOLLARS)

planned expenditure by $120 billion, resulting in unplanned buildup of inventories. Firms would reduce output in order to bring inventories back to the desired levels. As they did so, the level of output would fall steadily until the equilibrium level of $1,800 billion was reached.

At any level of output (Y) other than $2,000 billion, a gap between Y and AE would cause unplanned inventory changes. These changes would prompt business firms to adjust their levels of production and move the economy to the unique level of national income and output at which $Y = AE$.

THE CRUCIAL ROLE OF UNPLANNED BUSINESS INVENTORY CHANGES

Inventory changes play a crucial role in ensuring that the level of output is equal to total planned spending by households and firms. **Inventories** are the stocks of goods that have been produced by business firms but have not yet been sold. Firms maintain inventories because they do not want to risk losing sales to competitors by not having a desired item in stock.[3] Most firms choose a desired level of inventory that is related in some way to sales. For instance, a firm may plan to maintain an inventory of goods equal to twice the amount usually sold in a month. Inventories act as a safety cushion or buffer between production and sales.

When the actual level of inventory is different from the level desired by the firm, **unplanned inventory changes** have occurred. Such changes are a signal that the amount being produced is not equal to the amount that purchasers want to buy. Failure to respond to this situation could prove very costly. When sales are greater than current production, inventory declines. Eventually the firm finds that it cannot fill all of its customers' orders. When production is greater than sales, inventory rises. The firm finds itself piling up unwanted inventory. Business firms, therefore, have very strong incentives to respond to unplanned changes in inventories by expanding or contracting their output levels.[4]

LEAKAGES AND INJECTIONS IN A TWO-SECTOR MODEL

The consumption and investment approach is the most commonly used method for explaining what determines the level of output and income. This method finds the value of aggregate planned expenditure and compares it to output to find the equilibrium level. However, there is another approach that will give the same result. The second way is the method of leakages and injections, which derives from the circular flow. Equilibrium national income occurs at the level at which planned leakages from the circular flow (saving in this two-sector model) equal planned injections (or planned investment, excluding unplanned inventory changes). If

inventories
The stocks of goods that have been produced by business firms but have not yet been sold.

unplanned inventory changes
Changes that occur when the inventory level rises above or falls below that desired by a firm because the production level is too high or too low relative to current sales.

---

3.   What did you do the last time you tried to purchase an item in a store and were told that the item was sold out? You probably went elsewhere to make your purchase. The store that was out of the item not only lost the sale but created a poor image in your mind and gave a competitor the opportunity to gain a customer.

4.   The driving force of the Keynesian model is the self-interested behavior of the managers of business firms. Profit-maximizing behavior requires that output be adjusted to the level of demand for the product. This emphasis on self-interested behavior links Keynes to the classical school. In fact, it is also consistent with the recent development of "quick response" as a management strategy. Quick response means that firms are organized so as to react very quickly to unexpected inventory changes.

leakages are greater than injections, the size of the flow is shrinking. If injections are greater than leakages, the size of the flow is increasing. (Think of the level of income as the water in a bathtub, injections as the water flowing in from the faucet, and leakages as water going down the drain.) Only when planned leakages and planned injections are equal is the level of income stable, with no tendency to change. (This concept of equilibrium was introduced in Chapter 4.)

We can use the data in Table 2 to show that the level of income for which $C + I = Y$ is the same level of income at which leakages (planned saving, or S) are equal to injections (planned investment, or I). At the equilibrium level of income ($Y = \$1,800$), consumption is $1,640. Thus, the amount of planned saving (equal to income minus consumption) must be $160. Planned investment takes up the slack in demand not filled by consumption and is also equal to $160. In Table 2, leakages are equal to injections at $Y = \$1,800$. Figure 4 plots the values of investment and saving from Table 2 to locate the equilibrium level of national income (Y or Y_d). This level occurs where leakages in the form of planned saving (S) are equal to injections in the form of planned investment (I). As in Figure 3, in Figure 4 the equilibrium level of output and income is $1,800 billion.

ADDING GOVERNMENT AND THE FOREIGN SECTOR

The simple, two-sector economy with only households and business firms shows how the equilibrium level of national income is determined. A more complete Keynesian model includes all four sectors from the circu-

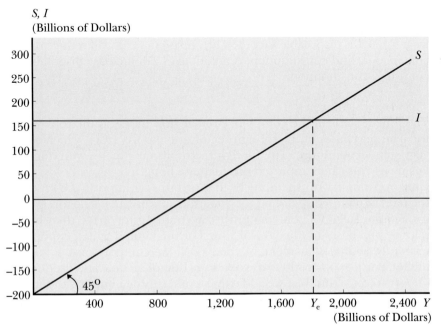

FIGURE 4
DETERMINING EQUILIBRIUM OUTPUT WITH LEAKAGES AND INJECTIONS
Another method to determine equilibrium national income is the leakages and injections approach. In a two-sector economy, the only leakage is saving (S), and the only injection is investment (I). In this case, the two are equal ($I = S$) at a value of $160 billion, which occurs at an income level of $1,800 billion.

lar flow and the national income accounts. Adding government and the foreign sector makes the model more realistic.

GOVERNMENT SPENDING AND TAXES

Adding government to the model causes leakages from the circular flow in the form of taxes (T) and injections of additional spending in the form of government expenditures (G). Government expenditures, like investment expenditures, are assumed to be determined by factors other than income. That is, they are autonomous. There may be some linkage to levels of income and output, but government spending is determined through the political process. Thus, we treat its value (G) as a given constant, like C_0 in the consumption function. When we add government expenditures, aggregate planned expenditure becomes

$$AE = C + I + G.$$

We now have another source of demand for output. Taken by itself, the addition of government expenditures to planned aggregate expenditure would increase the equilibrium level of income and output by a multiplier effect. However, there is a downside to this addition. Government purchases must be paid for, at least in part, by collecting taxes. For simplicity, we assume that taxes are independent of the level of income and that all taxes are paid by consumers.

Taxes constitute a leakage from the circular flow. A part of income received by households is not available to spend on consumption because it has been claimed by the government in taxes. Taxes do not enter the equation for aggregate expenditure directly because they do not represent planned spending for output. Instead, taxes work indirectly. The addition of taxes will reduce disposable income and therefore reduce consumption. (Consumption depends on disposable income.) Taxes (T) are incorporated into aggregate expenditure through the consumption function:

$$C = C_0 + b(Y - T),$$

where $Y - T$ is disposable income (Y_d). A rise in taxes will reduce disposable income and consumption. A fall in taxes will increase disposable income and consumption.

THE FOREIGN SECTOR

The fourth actor in the complete circular flow model is the foreign sector. The purchases of the foreign sector are exports (EX), which add to aggregate expenditure. The foreign sector also competes with domestic business firms when imported products are bought by households, firms, and government. Any spending by these groups for imports (IM) reduces the level of planned spending for domestic output (AE). The foreign sector is quite large for some countries, accounting for more than half of sales or purchases in the circular flow. For the United States, exports are currently about 10 percent of total GNP, and imports are somewhat higher. Since exports add to the domestic flow of income and product but imports reduce this flow, we add exports and subtract imports to arrive at aggregate expenditure. For now, we will assume that both export and import spending are autonomous, like investment and government spending.[5] Thus, net exports $(EX - IM)$ can be treated as a given constant. With the foreign sector in the model, the complete aggregate expenditure function looks like this:

$$AE = C + I + G + (EX - IM).$$

Changes in exports or imports as well as changes in domestic spending can shift the aggregate expenditure function and change the level of income and output. Suppose, for example, that a crop failure in another country led to a large increase in exports of wheat, soybeans, and beef from the United States. How would such a change in exports influence the equilibrium level of national income? If imports are unchanged, there will be an increase in net exports in $(EX - IM)$. This change shifts the AE curve upward and causes an increase in the equilibrium value of Y. A decrease in net exports would have the opposite effect. The AE curve would shift down, and the equilibrium value of Y would decrease.

What forces bring about changes in net exports? Changes in prices and incomes between countries, tariffs, quotas, and embargoes can all influence spending for imports and exports. The exchange rate (the price of a nation's currency) is another major influence on exports and imports. Weather, natural disasters, and wars can also have an effect. For instance, if severe winter weather in the Soviet Union ruins the wheat crop, the Soviets turn to foreign suppliers for grain. If they purchase wheat in large quantities from the United States, as they have in the past, U.S. net exports increase. In Figure 5, such an increase shifts the aggregate expenditure curve upward from AE_1 to AE_2, and equilibrium national income rises to Y_2.

The Smoot-Hawley Tariff of 1930 was designed to increase net exports by reducing imports rather than increasing exports. Fewer imports, policy makers reasoned, would create jobs in the production of import substitutes and thus increase aggregate demand. Another type of shift in net exports from the import side originates with a sudden rise in the price of an imported good. An example is the increase in the price of OPEC oil in the 1970s.[6] In the short run, expenditures for imported oil increased, and net exports fell. As shown in Figure 5, the decrease in net exports caused the aggregate expenditure curve to shift downward from AE_1 to AE_0. As a result, the equilibrium level of national income fell to Y_0. A decline in the price of oil, such as the one in the mid-1980s, has the opposite effect, shifting the AE curve upward and increasing the equilibrium level of national income.

EQUILIBRIUM IN A FOUR-SECTOR MODEL

Now we can show how the level of national income is determined in a four-sector economy. Table 4 and Figure 6 add government spending (G) and taxes (T) and a foreign sector $(EX$ and $IM)$ to the numbers of Table 2

5.   In fact, we might expect some extra spending for imports to come out of consumption, some out of business investment spending, and some out of government purchases. For simplicity, we simply add net exports to the equation without making any adjustments to domestic spending.
6.   Because oil is an important raw material, this increase also affected the aggregate supply curve, as we noted in Chapter 6.

AE
(Billions of Dollars)

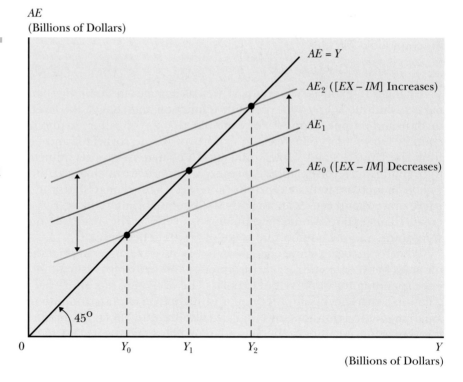

FIGURE 5
EQUILIBRIUM INCOME AND
NET EXPORTS
With aggregate expenditure and national income initially at AE_1 and Y_1, an increase in wheat sales to the Soviet Union caused the aggregate expenditure curve to shift upward to AE_2. National income increased to Y_2. When OPEC raised the price of oil, aggregate planned expenditure shifted downward to AE_0. National income decreased to Y_0.

and the diagram of Figure 3. These variables have been given values: $G = \$200$ billion, $T = \$200$ billion, $EX = \$140$ billion, and $IM = \$80$ billion. The constant term in the consumption function, C_0, is still equal to $\$200$ billion. The government has a balanced budget ($G = T$), and the nation has a positive balance of trade ($EX > IM$). As before, $I = \$160$ billion. Equilibrium occurs at an output level of $Y = AE = \$2,300$ billion, where output is exactly equal to the sum of planned purchases by the four sectors. At levels of output lower than $\$2,300$ billion, aggregate expenditure is greater than output ($AE > Y$). At levels above $\$2,300$ billion, output is greater than aggregate expenditure ($Y > AE$).

Table 4 shows that the addition of a government with a balanced budget and net exports that are positive has increased the equilibrium level of income compared to the two-sector model. In the two-sector model, equilibrium national income was $\$1,800$. Here it is $\$2,300$. The addition of more purchasers for output has more than offset the negative effects of imports on aggregate expenditure and of taxes on consumption and aggregate expenditure.

LEAKAGES AND INJECTIONS IN A FOUR-SECTOR MODEL

In the four-sector economy, when aggregate expenditure equals total output, planned leakages from the circular flow will be equal to planned injections. However, there are now three leakages (saving, taxes, and imports) and three injections (investment, government purchases, and

NATIONAL INCOME, Y	PERSONAL INCOME TAXES, T	DISPOSABLE INCOME, $Y_d = (Y - T)$	CONSUMPTION EXPENDITURE, C	INVESTMENT EXPENDITURE, I	GOVERNMENT PURCHASES, G	NET EXPORTS, $(EX - IM)$	AGGREGATE PLANNED EXPENDITURE, $AE = C + I + G + (EX - IM)$
$1,000	$200	$ 800	$ 840	$160	$200	$60	$1,260 $AE > Y$
1,400	200	1,200	1,160	160	200	60	1,580 $AE > Y$
1,800	200	1,600	1,480	160	200	60	1,900 $AE > Y$
2,200	200	2,000	1,800	160	200	60	2,220 $AE > Y$
2,300	200	2,100	1,980	160	200	60	2,300 $AE = Y$
2,400	200	2,200	2,060	160	200	60	2,480 $AE < Y$
2,500	200	2,300	2,140	160	200	60	2,560 $AE < Y$
2,600	200	2,400	2,320	160	200	60	2,640 $AE < Y$
3,000	200	2,800	2,480	160	200	60	2,900 $AE < Y$
3,400	200	3,200	2,800	160	200	60	3,220 $AE < Y$
3,800	200	3,600	3,120	160	200	60	3,540 $AE < Y$
4,200	200	4,000	3,440	160	200	60	3,860 $AE < Y$

TABLE 4
EQUILIBRIUM OUTPUT WITH GOVERNMENT AND A FOREIGN SECTOR (BILLIONS OF DOLLARS)

exports). At equilibrium income, the condition that leakages equals injections becomes

$$S + T + IM = I + G + EX.$$

Saving consists of income that is not consumed, paid in taxes, or spent

$AE = C + I + G + (EX - IM)$
(Billions of Dollars)

FIGURE 6
EQUILIBRIUM WITH THE GOVERNMENT AND THE FOREIGN SECTOR
In a four-sector economy, equilibrium occurs where aggregate expenditures, $AE = C + I + G + (EX - IM)$, is equal to current output, Y_e.

Leakages or Injections
(Billions of Dollars)

FIGURE 7
LEAKAGES AND INJECTIONS IN A FOUR-SECTOR ECONOMY
In a four-sector economy, equilibrium income occurs where the sum of the three leakages $(S + T + IM)$ from the circular flow is equal to the sum of the three injections $(I + G + EX)$ into the circular flow. The equilibrium income, $2,300 billion, is the same as in Figure 6.

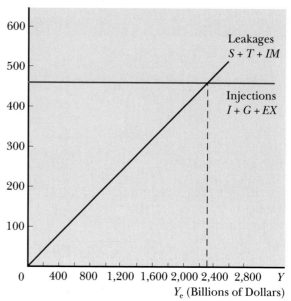

on imports. At the equilibrium level of income $(Y = \$2,300)$, consumption takes $1,980 billion of income, taxes $200 billion, and imports $40 billion, leaving $80 billion for saving. Saving plus taxes plus imports gives total leakages of $320 billion. With investment of $160 billion, government purchases of $200 billion, and exports of $60 billion, injections also total $320 billion. Be sure to note in Table 4 that leakages and injections are equal *only* at the equilibrium level of income. Below that level, injections exceed leakages, causing income to rise. Above that level, leakages exceed injections, causing income to fall. Figure 7 shows the equilibrium level of income of $2,300 billion determined by the leakages and injections method. This is the same value obtained by the aggregate expenditure method.

CHANGES IN AGGREGATE EXPENDITURE AND THE EXPENDITURE MULTIPLIER

Based on the data provided for the four-sector economy, the equilibrium level of income is $2,300 billion. Now suppose one of the components of aggregate expenditure changes. What effect will this have on the equilibrium level of income (Y)? As you may have already realized, a change in C, I, G, or $(EX - IM)$ shifts the AE curve. When aggregate expenditure changes, equilibrium income must also change. The size of the change in income depends on the magnitude and direction of the change in C, I, G, or $(EX - IM)$.

Suppose investment expenditures (I) increase by $200 billion to a new level of $360 billion at each level of national income. The aggregate expenditure curve shifts upward by $200 billion from AE_1 to AE_2, as shown

The Keynesian model was developed to describe ups and downs of income and output in developed, industrial economies. For such economies, it can be assumed that the components of aggregate expenditure—consumption, investment, government spending, and net exports—are largely independent of each other. The Keynesian model was constructed on the assumption of such independence. In a small economy with a single major export product, however, this assumption may not be valid.

Consider the economy of Ghana, an African country whose main crop is coffee. Coffee represents 60 percent of the value of Ghana's exports and 40 percent of total output. Suppose there is a large drop in Ghana's coffee sales due to changes in tastes abroad. In a developed economy, this fall in net exports would be duly entered in the aggregate expenditure function. It would have ripple effects throughout the economy through the expenditure multiplier and induced declines in consumption.

In Ghana, however, such ripples will be larger and more serious. In addition to the induced decline in consumption, the fall in coffee sales means a loss of revenue to the government. (Taxes on the export crop are often a major source of government revenues in small one-crop economies.) With little capacity to borrow, the government will be forced to reduce government purchases (G). The decline in government purchases has

INTERNATIONAL

PERSPECTIVE

THE KEYNESIAN

MODEL IN A

ONE-PRODUCT

ECONOMY

an additional downward multiplier effect on income and output. Furthermore, most of the investment occurring in Ghana is probably linked to the production of coffee. With poor sales prospects for their major crop, investors in Ghana are likely to cut back on their investment spending (I). This fall has a third downward multiplier effect on income and output.

During a boom in coffee sales, the reverse is true. Net export sales have a multiplier effect. They also create a stimulus to government spending from the additional revenue from export taxes and a stimulus to investment in the coffee industry in anticipation of future boom years. These two injections of new spending have their own multiplier effects on consumption and, through consumption, on income and output.

Thus, for such an economy, changes in economic activity are likely to be much more intense than for economies that are more diversified and less dependent on international trade. A modest dip in the level of economic activity in the country or countries to which Ghana exports its coffee could have a major impact on the level of income and output in this small, highly specialized economy. This kind of effect was responsible for a saying heard often for decades after World War II: "When the United States sneezes, the rest of the world catches pneumonia."

in Figure 8. The original equilibrium income of Y_1 ($2,300 billion) no longer holds. At this level of national income, planned spending (AE) is now $2,500 billion and exceeds Y_1 by $200 billion. Unplanned reductions in inventories occur. Business firms respond by increasing output, which increases national income. When all the effects have worked through, how much do you expect national income will have risen?

The final increase in income and output is much greater than the initial $200 billion increase in investment. The new equilibrium point in Figure 8 occurs where AE_2 intersects the 45° line. At that point, national income is at Y_2, or $3,300 billion, which is $1,000 billion higher than the original equilibrium level. Thus, the $200 billion upward shift in aggregate expenditure results in a $1,000 billion increase in equilibrium income and output because of the multiplier effect. The expenditure multiplier measures the impact of a given initial change in aggregate expenditure on equilibrium income and output. This multiplier is an important and powerful tool of Keynesian economic theory.

THE MULTIPLIER AND CHANGES IN INVESTMENT

Suppose that, as a result of changed expectations, firms increase investment expenditures (I) by $200 billion. Aggregate expenditure (AE) initially increases by the same amount. But the process of expanding output and income does not stop there. Additional investment spending creates

FIGURE 8
A SHIFT IN AGGREGATE EXPENDITURE
With equilibrium national income at Y_1, business investment spending increases by $200 billion ($\Delta I = \$200$). The aggregate expenditure schedule shifts up (from AE_1 to AE_2) by $200 billion. Equilibrium national income increases by $1,000 billion, from Y_1 to Y_2.

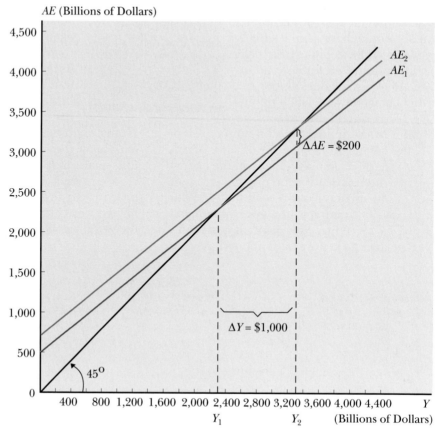

additional income for those who produce investment goods. Suppose, for example, the investment consists of building an apartment complex. The plumbers, carpenters, and electricians earn additional income, which they in turn spend to buy groceries, movie tickets, and new cars. Grocers, farmers, theater operators, actors, auto workers, and auto dealers all receive more income, which they in turn spend.

Think about what you have just learned about the relationship between income (Y) and consumption spending (C). When Y changes, C also changes, but by a smaller amount. The marginal propensity to consume describes the relationship between changes in income and the *induced* changes in consumption spending. Thus, an additional business investment of $200 billion causes incomes to increase by $200 billion. This is the round one effect. As a result of receiving this additional income ($200 billion), households will increase their spending by an amount dependent on the marginal propensity to consume. This round two spending will increase aggregate expenditure further. If *MPC* is 0.8, as in our example, the round two increase in *AE* will be $160 billion ($200 billion × 0.8). But this spending also becomes additional income to those who receive it, setting off a round three increase in spending. This round-by-round process is shown in Table 5. Each change in output and income causes a change in spending in the next round, which changes output and income. The process continues, with smaller increases in each successive round.

How long does this income-spending process go on? Table 5 traces the process through the first five rounds and then summarizes the remaining rounds. Although in theory the process goes on forever, a shortcut is available to quickly determine the total change in output and income. Note that after round one, each column entry in Table 5 is 80 percent of the entry above it. Thus, the numbers in the columns that show each round of increase in spending and income are declining at a uniform rate of 80 percent—or 0.8, the value of the marginal propensity to consume. There is clearly a relationship between income growth and the size of the marginal propensity to consume. It turns out that the overall effect of the round-by-round changes in national income is shown by

(2) $\Delta Y_f = \Delta AE_1 \times$ expenditure multiplier,

where ΔY_f is the sum of all the changes in the level of national income and

Round	Change in Aggregate Expenditure (Billions)	Change in National Income (Billions)
1	$200 (initial change)	$200
2	160	160
3	128	128
4	102.40	102.40
5	81.92	81.92
All following rounds	327.68	327.68
Total	$1,000.00	$1,000.00

TABLE 5
THE DYNAMICS OF THE MULTIPLIER PROCESS

expenditure multiplier
Measures the impact of a
given initial change in
aggregate expenditure on
equilibrium income and
output. The multiplier is
equal to $1/(1 - MPC)$.

ΔAE_1 is the initial change in planned aggregate expenditure. The **expenditure multiplier** is defined as

$$(3) \text{ Expenditure multiplier} = \frac{1}{1 - MPC} = \frac{1}{1 - b}.$$

It is possible to compute the change in the equilibrium level of national income (ΔY_f) if the initial change in aggregate expenditure (ΔAE_1) and the marginal propensity to consume (MPC) are known. First, we solve equation (3) by substituting the actual value of MPC:

$$\text{Expenditure multiplier} = \frac{1}{1 - 0.8} = \frac{1}{0.2} = 5.$$

Second, we solve equation (2) for ΔY_f by substituting the known values for ΔAE_1 and the expenditure multiplier:

$$\Delta Y_f = \$200 \text{ billion} \times 5 = \$1,000 \text{ billion}.$$

This result indicates the same change in the level of national income as in Figure 8. This change in output and income is also the value that would result from summing the effects of an infinite number of rounds in Table 5.

The expenditure multiplier applies to a change in any of the components of aggregate expenditure: C, I, G, or ($EX - IM$). For instance, a \$50 billion increase in net exports is subject to the expenditure multiplier of 5 and would, therefore, cause an increase of \$250 billion in the equilibrium level of national income. The expenditure multiplier is the same no matter where the change in spending originates. A government dollar multiplies as well as a dollar from the foreign sector. If the C_0 term in the consumption function can shift up or down with changes in consumer wealth or population or other influences, it will have the same kind of multiplier effect. The size of the multiplier, however, is usually somewhat smaller than the value we have been using here, because of a variety of leakages and other effects. The multiplier for the U.S. economy is generally believed to be about 3. That is, over a period of about two years, a given dollar change in the level of autonomous spending will raise equilibrium by about \$3.

THE MULTIPLIER AND CHANGES IN CONSUMPTION: A CASE STUDY

The consumption function is one of the most stable components of aggregate expenditure. Government spending is unpredictable, investment is volatile, and exports and imports have swings. Consumers, however, seem to buy food, cars, clothing, and other necessities and conveniences with great regularity. Once in a while, however, consumers take forecasters by surprise. They did so when forecasting output and income with the Keynesian model was in its infancy.

During World War II, output was high and unemployment was low because of massive government spending for the war effort. Since so much output consisted of military goods and so many workers were in the military, few consumer goods were being produced. Consumers worked long hours and earned big paychecks. But they were encouraged to be patriotic and purchase war bonds (save) instead of spending on the limited supply of consumer goods.

Economists had predicted a serious recession at the end of the war as government spending dropped back to normal levels. There was eventually a mild recession, but not until about four years after the war ended. What was wrong with the forecast? The consumption function shifted upward because consumers had amassed large amounts of financial assets in the form of boxes full of war bonds. After the war, they were ready to cash in these bonds to satisfy their pent-up demand for cars, houses, new clothes, and other consumer goods. Most of the decline in planned government spending for national defense was offset by an upward shift in the consumption function. In terms of the Keynesian model, the downward multiplier effect of reduced government spending was offset by the upward multiplier effect of an increase in C_0.

THE PARADOX OF THRIFT

Another application of the expenditure multiplier led to the surprising discovery that an increase in planned saving may not have a positive effect. Americans traditionally have regarded saving as a virtue. Benjamin Franklin said, "A penny saved is a penny earned." How can saving ever be bad?

Keynes questioned the value of increasing saving when an economy is operating well below the full-employment level of output. An upward shift in the saving function implies an equal and opposite downward shift of the consumption and aggregate expenditure functions. The equilibrium level of national income must fall because aggregate expenditure has fallen. As a result, actual saving may not increase at all, even though planned saving is higher. The name given to this phenomenon is the **paradox of thrift**.

paradox of thrift
The fact that attempts by consumers to increase saving cause income and output to decline. Therefore, actual saving may not increase at all.

What causes this unexpected outcome? As people become more thrifty (and thus spend less on consumption at all levels of income), their increased planned saving ultimately causes income and output to decline. Furthermore, the increase in planned saving does not necessarily result in much increase in actual saving. As income falls, households are forced to consume less and save less out of their smaller incomes. It is possible that households may wind up saving no more than before out of a lower level of income and output.

THE KEYNESIAN MODEL AND AGGREGATE DEMAND

Chapter 6 presented a model of aggregate supply and aggregate demand as the framework for the study of macroeconomics. This chapter has developed the Keynesian model in which an aggregate expenditure function determines the level of income and output. The price level receives no attention in the Keynesian model. The price level and real output receive equal billing in the aggregate supply and demand model. How are these two models connected?

The relationship between the aggregate demand (*AD*) curve of Chapter 6 and the aggregate expenditure (*AE*) curve of the Keynesian model is shown in Figure 9(*a*). The *AE* curve is drawn for a given, fixed price level. Higher price levels are associated with lower aggregate expenditure at every level of income. Chapter 6 suggested many reasons why total demand for goods and services will be lower at higher price levels. Higher price levels discourage consumption by reducing the value of household financial assets. Higher price levels are associated with higher interest rates, discouraging both investment and purchases of consumer durables. Higher price levels also discourage exports and stimulate imports, reducing the net exports (*EX – IM*) component of aggregate expenditure. The same reasons that explain why the *AD* curve slopes down from left to right also explain why there will be a different *AE* curve corresponding to

FIGURE 9
DERIVING AN *AD* CURVE FROM A FAMILY OF *AE* CURVES
(*a*) Each aggregate expenditure function determines a unique equilibrium level of real income (*Y*). There is a different *AE* curve for each possible price level. (*b*) The price level (*P*) and the unique equilibrium level of output (*Y*) corresponding to each *AE* curve are to trace out an *AD* curve.

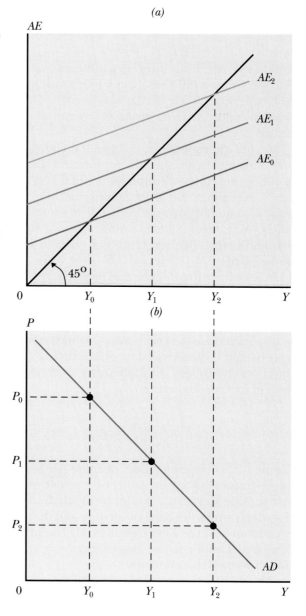

each different price level. Thus, AE_0 is associated with a high price level, P_0; AE_1 with a lower price level P_1; and so forth.

Figure 9(b) derives an AD curve by plotting the various P and Y combinations derived from the set of AE curves in Figure 9(a). For example, along AE_0, price level P_0 is associated with equilibrium real income level Y_0. Remember, the AE curve shows the amount consumers and business firms will plan to spend on consumption and investment at various *income* levels. The AD curve in Figure 9(b) shows the amounts of real output (Y) that will be demanded by households and business firms (and, in a four-sector economy, government and the foreign sector) at various *price* levels.

Both the AE curve and the AD curve represent demand for total output. The AE curve shows the relationship between demand and income. The AD curve shows the relationship between demand and the price level. When we developed individual demand curves in Chapter 3, we defined a demand curve as a price-quantity relationship. The phrase *demand curve* is therefore reserved for those graphs that plot quantity against price. A shift in aggregate expenditure for any reason *other than a change in the price level* will shift the AD curve. An increase in consumer wealth, a change in firms' expectations, a reduction in government spending, a surge in exports, or a shift away from buying imported goods can shift both the AE and AD curves. An upward shift of the AE curve due to any of these events will lead to a rightward shift of the AD curve. A downward shift of AE will shift AD to the left.

Whether you use an aggregate supply and demand model or an aggregate expenditure model, the equilibrium level of national income occurs where total output and planned aggregate expenditure are equal. In the Keynesian model, equilibrium does not mean that the economy will necessarily be at full employment with stable prices. If the economy does reach equilibrium with high unemployed resources (as during the Great Depression) or with rampant inflation (as during the late 1970s), what can be done to alter the situation? The following chapter will discuss the tools government can use to deal with undesirable equilibrium conditions.

SUMMARY

1. In contrast to classical theory, the Keynesian model shows that the macro economy can come to an equilibrium level of national income and output with a high level of unemployed resources.

2. The equilibrium level of national income occurs where output equals aggregate expenditure. In the Keynesian model, the equilibrium levels of national income and aggregate expenditure are interdependent. That is, they are jointly determined.

3. The foundation of aggregate expenditure is the Keynesian consumption function. The consumption

function shows how consumption expenditures (C) vary with disposable income (Y_d).

4. The aggregate expenditure function is the sum of four components: consumption expenditures (C), investment expenditures (I), government purchases of goods and services (G), and net exports (EX− IM).

5. The intersection of the AE curve and the 45° line defines the equilibrium level of income. This level does not assure full employment of resources.

6. At nonequilibrium levels of income, differences between aggregate expenditure and income result in unplanned changes in business inventories. These changes act both as a signal and as an incentive, causing firms to adjust their level of output to the level of spending.

7. Through the multiplier process, any initial change in planned spending will result in a larger change in the equilibrium level of national income.

8. Increases in foreign spending for U.S. exports increase aggregate expenditure and income. Increases in

Americans' spending for foreign imports reduce aggregate expenditure and income.

9. The *AE* curve shows the relationship between planned spending and income. The *AD* curve shows the relationship between planned spending and the price level. Shifts in the *AE* curve for any reason except a change in the price level will shift the *AD* curve.

NEW TERMS

aggregate expenditure (*AE*)	marginal propensity to save (*MPS*)	unplanned inventory changes
consumption function	dissaving	expenditure multiplier
marginal propensity to consume (*MPC*)	inventories	paradox of thrift

---

QUESTIONS FOR DISCUSSION

1. Suppose C_0 is $300 billion and *MPC* is 0.5. Create a table relating *C* and *S* to Y_d for all values of Y_d between 0 and $5,000 billion (by $500 billion intervals).

2. Use the following information to construct a table similar to Table 4:

  C is $200 billion when $Y_d = 0$
  $MPC = 0.75$
  $T = $300 billion
  $I = $100 billion
  $G = $400 billion
  $EX = $50 billion
  $IM = $150 billion

3. Use the information in Question 2 to construct a graph of the *AE* curve similar to Figure 8. Indicate the equilibrium level of national income on the graph. What is the dollar value of that equilibrium income?

4. Use the information from Question 2, but change *I* to $200 billion. Determine the new equilibrium income level and the value of the expenditure multiplier.

5. Use each of the following to find the value of the expenditure multiplier:

  a. $MPC = 0.40$
  b. $MPS = 0.25$
  c. $MPC = 0.67$
  d. $MPS = 0.50$
  e. $MPC = 0.90$
  f. $MPC = 0.75$

6. Assume the initial equilibrium level of national income is $4,800 billion and $MPC = 0.9$. What will be the new equilibrium level of *Y* if *I* decreases $100 billion from its initial level?

7. In what direction will each of the following shift the

AE curve? How will the *AD* curve shift? In what direction will income change?

  a. As a result of U.S. restrictions on foreign goods, there is an exogenous fall in the level of imports (*IM*).

  b. The government launches a new program to improve highways and bridges. That is, government purchases (*G*) increase.

  c. Banks are offering such attractive interest rates that consumers decide to save a larger part of their incomes and spend less.

  d. Business firms decide to change the ratio of inventories to sales from 30 percent to 25 percent. Therefore, there is a planned reduction in inventory investment.

8. Suppose the consumption function is $C = $300 + 0.85Y$.

  a. What is the value of the multiplier?

  b. What are the values of C_0, *MPC*, and *MPS*?

  c. Determine the level of consumption for $Y = $100, $300, $500, $700, $1,000, $1,200, $1,500, $2,000, and $3,000.

9. Discuss what would happen to the consumption function in Question 8 in each of the following situations.

  a. Consumers experience an increase in wealth.

  b. Taxes increase.

  c. Consumers expect prices to rise rapidly in the future.

  d. Interest rates fall.

10. Why did aggregate expenditure and aggregate demand play a more important role in the Keynesian model than in the classical model?

11. In what directions would the *AE* curve and the *AD* curve shift in each of the following cases?

a. Worried about a recession, business firms reduce their investment spending.

b. A high birth rate means that families increase their consumption at every level of income to pay for diapers, pediatricians, and day care.

c. Real income increases.

d. The government reduces taxes.

12. How is it possible to consume without any income?

13. How do unplanned inventory changes ensure that actual saving and investment are always equal in a two-sector economy, even if planned saving and investment are not?

14. If a rise in the price of the dollar reduced sales of American exports and increased Americans' purchases of imports, what would be the effect on the level of income and output? What about the price level?

15. If a point on the *AE* curve is above the 45° reference line, are unplanned inventory changes positive, negative, or zero? Why?

Suggestions for Further Reading

Breit, William, and Roger L. Ransom. *The Academic Scribblers*, 2nd ed. Hinsdale, IL: Dryden Press, 1982. A lively history of some of the great economists discussed in this and earlier chapters, including Marshall and Keynes, as well as Keynes's best-known American disciple, Alvin Hansen.

Dernburg, Thomas. *Macroeconomics: Concepts, Theories, and Policies*, 8th ed. New York: McGraw-Hill, 1989. A somewhat Keynesian intermediate macroeconomics textbook that expands on the Keynesian aggregate expenditure function in a context of aggregate demand and aggregate supply.

Dimand, Robert W. *The Origins of the Keynesian Revolution: The Development of Keynes' Theory of Employment and Output.* Stanford, CA: Stanford University Press, 1988. A recent overview of how Keynes's ideas about output and employment evolved during the 1930s and into the 1940s.

APPENDIX: THE ALGEBRA OF THE KEYNESIAN MODEL

The Keynesian model has been presented in this chapter largely in graphs and numbers. However, the model can be written in algebraic form, providing a formal derivation of the equilibrium level of income and the expenditure multiplier. In this appendix, we derive a series of versions of the Keynesian model, each more complex than the last.

MODEL 1

The simplest Keynesian model is the two-sector model in which there is no distinction between disposable and national income because there is no government. Thus,

$$Y = C + I,$$

where

$$C = C_0 + bY,$$

and

$$I = I_0.$$

So we have

$$Y = C_0 + bY + I_0$$

or

$$Y - bY = C_0 + I_0.$$

Solving for the equilibrium level of Y, we get

$$(1) \; Y_e = \left(\frac{1}{1-b}\right)(C_0 + I_0).$$

This relationship shows both the equilibrium level of income and the expression for the multiplier.

MODEL 2

The second model adds a government sector, with three activities: government purchases (G), taxes (T), and transfer payments (R). All of these activities are autonomous. With these additions, the model becomes

$$Y = C_0 + b(Y - T_0 + R_0) + I_0 + G_0,$$

or

$$Y - bY = C_0 - bT_0 + bR + I_0 + G_0.$$

Solving for the equilibrium value of Y gives the same multiplier as with the first model. There are now more variables in the expression being multiplied that can shift aggregate expenditures:

$$(2) \; Y_e = \left(\frac{1}{1-b}\right)(C_0 - bT_0 + bR_0 + I_0 + G_0).$$

The basic multiplier is unchanged, but there are more sources of shifts in the aggregate expenditure function. Note that the impact, dollar for dollar, of a given change in T or R is less than the impact of an equal change in C_0, I, or G because taxes and transfer payments work through the consumption function. This smaller impact is indicated by the fact that T_0 and R_0 are multiplied by the marginal propensity to consume, b, which always has a value of less than 1.

Model 3

The third model makes T and R dependent on the level of income, because taxes rise and transfers fall as income rises. That is,

$$T = T_0 + tY$$

and

$$R = R_0 - rY.$$

In these equations, t is called the marginal tax rate and r is called the marginal transfer rate, or the change in transfers per additional dollar of income. We have

$$(3)\ Y = C_0 + b(Y - T_0 - tY + R_0 - rY) + I_0 + G_0,$$

or

$$Y - bY + btY + brY = C_0 - bT_0 + bR_0 + I_0 + G_0.$$

The solution to the model is given by

$$Y_e = \left(\frac{1}{1 - b + bt - br}\right)(C_0 - T_0 + bR_0 + I_0 + G_0).$$

The multiplier is more complex in this model. If t is greater than r, the multiplier is smaller than in the second model. If t is less than r, the multiplier is larger. This model is applied in the next two chapters to describe the effects of fiscal policy by changing the tax rate.

Model 4

The fourth model allows investment expenditures to be at least partly responsive to the level of final demand, rather than being totally autonomous. This change makes investment expenditures, like taxes and transfer payments, a function of the level of income and output. This model uses an investment demand function of the form

$$I = I_0 + aY,$$

where a is defined as the marginal propensity to invest. Incorporating this expression in equation (3) gives

$$Y = C_0 + b(Y - T_0 - tY + R_0 - rY) + I_0 + aY + G_0,$$

or

$$Y - bY + btY + brY - aY = C_0 - bT_0 + bR_0 + I_0 + G_0.$$

Again, solving for the equilibrium value of Y gives the equilibrium condition:

$$(4)\ Y_e = \left(\frac{1}{1 - b + bt + br - a}\right)(C_0 - bT_0 + bR_0 + I_0 + G_0).$$

The multiplier in this model is larger than the one in the third model because of additional induced investment spending.

MODEL 5

The last model adds a foreign sector. Exports (EX_0) are independent of the level of income, but imports are not. The import demand function takes the form

$$IM = IM_0 + mY,$$

where m is the marginal propensity to import. This change gives the final form of the model:

$$Y = C_0 + b(Y - T_0 - tY + R_0 - rY) + I_0 + aY + G_0 + EX_0 - IM_0 - mY,$$

or

$$Y - bY + btY + brY - aY + mY = C_0 - bT_0 + bR_0 + I_0 + G_0 + EX_0 - IM_0.$$

The equilibrium condition is

$$(5)\ Y_e = \left(\frac{1}{1 - b + bt + br - a + m}\right)(C_0 - bT_0 + bR_0 + I_0 + G_0 + EX_0 - IM_0).$$

This multiplier is smaller than the one in the fourth model because of the additional leakage of funds into spending on imports in every additional round of spending.

Equation (5) is a fairly complete form of the basic Keynesian model. The multiplier reflects induced changes in consumption, taxes, transfers, investment, and imports. The aggregate expenditure function can be shifted by autonomous changes in consumption (C_0), taxes (T_0), transfer payments (R_0), investment spending (I_0), government spending (G_0), exports (EX_0), or the autonomous component of export demand (IM_0).

This model can be used as a basis for a microcomputer simulation of economic activity. There are much larger and more complex models that include interest rates, prices, the money supply, and other variables to forecast output and employment. However, you can get an idea of how these variables are interrelated by putting this model on a microcomputer with some initial values for each variable. You can then change one variable and see how the others respond.

1. Explain the Keynesian argument that active fiscal policy is the only way to assure full employment with stable prices.
2. Distinguish between automatic stabilizers and discretionary fiscal policy, and give examples of each.
3. Define:
   a. fiscal policy,
   b. recessionary gap,
   c. permanent income hypothesis.
4. Describe the use of an appropriate fiscal policy to offset the effects of changes in spending by consumers, businesses, or the foreign sector.
5. Briefly describe these experiences with discretionary fiscal policy in the United States:
   a. the Kennedy tax cut,
   b. the Ford tax rebate,
   c. the Reagan tax cut.
6. Critically analyze the arguments for and against active fiscal policy.

CHAPTER 9

FISCAL POLICY

INTRODUCTION

This chapter discusses the theory and practice of fiscal policy, based on the model in Chapter 8. **Fiscal policy** consists of changes in government expenditures (G) or taxes (T) in order to influence the level of economic activity, inflation, and economic growth. Fiscal policy is not simply any changes in government spending or taxes. Government spending and taxes existed long before the development of Keynesian economic theory. Fiscal policy is *intentional* use of taxing or government spending to affect the level of output, employment, and prices.

fiscal policy
Changes in government spending and taxes to influence the level of economic activity, inflation, and economic growth.

Some economists, especially monetarists and new classical economists, consider fiscal policy to have limited benefit and, in some cases, to even be harmful to the economy. Other economists, especially Keynesians, regard active fiscal policy as a valuable tool of the central government. In order to evaluate both sides of this argument, we must look closely at exactly how fiscal policy works in theory and practice.

WHY FISCAL POLICY?

Both classical and Keynesian economists agree that the economy automatically moves to a level of national income where total output equals aggregate expenditure (or where leakages equal injections). In the Keynesian model, however, such an equilibrium level may not be associated with full employment of resources.

Keynes believed that the equilibrium levels of output reached by major capitalistic economies such as the United States and Great Britain during the 1930s were not acceptable. Levels of unemployment were too high. He argued that governments should respond to such conditions with fiscal policy. That is, government should act so as to increase aggregate expenditure (AE) enough to ensure a socially desirable equilibrium level of income and output.

Aggregate expenditure consists of four components: consumption demand, planned investment spending, government purchases of goods and services, and net exports. An increase in any of these four components can stimulate output and employment. Keynesians, however, do not think it is realistic to expect private demand (consumption and investment) alone to solve the problem of recession combined with high unemployment.

Households and businesses are motivated more by self-interest than by social interest. Individual persons or firms cannot be expected to act in the interest of society as a whole if so acting would conflict with their perceived self-interest. In a recession, social interest calls for households to increase consumption spending and business firms to increase investment spending in the face of stagnant demand for their products. In fact, for individual households or business firms to "swim against the tide," expanding production or consumption while others are contracting, would be futile.

The self-interested behavior of the private sector (households and business firms) usually makes economic fluctuations worse instead of improving conditions. During the Great Depression, for instance, households became more frugal. Also, business firms reduced investment spending because of their uncertainty and pessimistic expectations about future income, employment, and sales. During expansionary periods, expectations of job security, pay raises, and increasing sales and profits are likely to stimulate more private spending, pushing the economy further beyond full-employment equilibrium.

Planned investment (I) is sensitive to changes in profit expectations, input costs, and interest rates. Changes in these influences will shift the investment component of aggregate expenditure. In the Keynesian model, investment is the most volatile component of total spending. It is also the one least sensitive to any direct influence by government policy.

The foreign sector also offers little hope for an automatic cure for prolonged downturns. Export demand (EX) is affected by changes in the price level in the United States relative to those in other countries, exchange rates, economic conditions in foreign countries, trade restrictions, and sometimes even the weather. Imports (IM) are affected by changes in the price level domestically and abroad, exchange rates, trade restrictions, consumer tastes, and the domestic income level. A higher level of income stimulates all kinds of private spending, including spending on imported goods.[1] Net exports ($EX - IM$) are a somewhat volatile but fairly small component of aggregate expenditure.

There are policy tools that government can use to bring about an increase in net exports. Such an increase would shift the AD curve to the right. The government can try to put downward pressure on the price of its currency. Or it can use tariffs and quotas to reduce imports of foreign goods and services. Such solutions were popular in the early years of the Great Depression. They have surfaced as proposed emergency measures in almost every downturn before or since that time. Since these actions

---

1.   In Chapter 8, to keep the model simple, imports were treated as autonomous, or independent of the level of income. In a more realistic model, imports depend on the level of income or output.

are taken at the expense of a nation's trading partners, they are referred to as beggar-thy-neighbor policies. One country may increase its level of employment by limiting imports, which will add jobs in producing substitutes. However, the problem is then passed on to the trading partner, who sees a fall in exports and thus in employment. Even if a country were to ignore the negative effects of such policies on its trading partners, their positive effect on the domestic economy would be short-lived. Other countries are likely to retaliate quickly with similar policies. Since policies that can be used directly to affect net exports are rather unappealing and the foreign sector is small, such policies are rarely considered as a potential fiscal policy tool.[2]

Self-interest leads to consumption and investment decisions that aggravate rather than dampen economic ups and downs. Since there is little prospect for help from the foreign sector, Keynesians see government spending as the only hope for stabilization. They argue that only the government can be expected to act in the social interest by using its taxing and spending powers to offset changes in private demand. Keynesian economics also provides an explanation of how income levels can be changed by government intervention. Critics have attacked Keynesians' positive view of the government and their theoretical model. We need to clarify the Keynesian view of fiscal policy before we can critique it.

HOW FISCAL POLICY WORKS

Recall how an economy reaches an equilibrium other than at full employment. Chapter 8 identified changes that could shift saving and consumption, such as changes in wealth, taxes, inflationary expectations, or interest rates. A downward shift in the consumption function due to one of these changes can lead to a fall in output, income, and employment. An upward shift in the consumption function can lead to a rise in output, income, and employment. The effect of tax changes on consumption (C) and the aggregate expenditure (AE) curve is particularly important because tax changes are one of the tools of fiscal policy. Fiscal policy in the form of tax changes can work through the consumption function to affect the level of output, employment, and prices.

Policy makers face an aggregate expenditure function that is very unstable. As consumption spending (C), investment (I), or net exports ($EX-IM$) fluctuate, aggregate expenditure changes. Through the multiplier process, the resulting changes in income, output, and employment are larger than the initial change in C, I, or ($EX-IM$). Shifts in the AE curve are translated into shifts in the AD curve, as you saw at the end of Chapter 8. Shifts in aggregate demand lead to changes in the price level as well as in real output and employment. We will work mostly with the aggregate supply and demand model in this chapter. You should keep in

2.   The role of the foreign sector in macroeconomic policy is complex. With foreign sales and purchases forming an increased share of U.S. economic activity in recent years, policy makers have become more aware of the effects of domestic policies on exports, imports, and exchange rates, and vice versa. International trade and exchange rates between currencies have a direct relationship with the level of output, prices, and interest rates in the domestic economy.

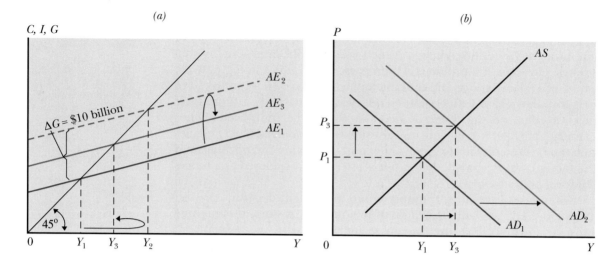

FIGURE 1
AGGREGATE EXPENDITURE,
AGGREGATE DEMAND,
AND FISCAL POLICY
(*a*) An increase in
aggregate expendi-
ture from AE_1 to AE_2
because of increased
government spending
will raise equilibrium
output from Y_1 to Y_2
if there is no change
in the price level.
(*b*) The shift in AE also
shifts the AD curve from
AD_1 to AD_2, increasing
Y by a smaller amount
(from Y_1 to Y_3) and also
increasing the price level
(from P_1 to P_3). At the
higher price level, the
economy's AE curve will
be AE_3 in part (*a*), with
an equilibrium output
level of Y_3.

mind, however, that changes in government spending and taxes shift the
AE curve and that shift in turn shifts the AD curve.

Figure 1 shows how an increase in government spending works in both
models. In part (*a*), an increase in government spending (*G*) by an
amount of $10 billion shifts the AE curve from AE_1 to AE_2, increasing the
equilibrium level of output from Y_1 to Y_2. In part (*b*) of the figure, the
same increase in government spending shifts the AD curve to the right by
a horizontal distance corresponding to $10 billion. With an upward-
sloping supply curve (AS), the impact of the added spending is divided
between a change in output (from Y_1 to Y_3) and a change in the price level
(from P_1 to P_3). Each AE curve is associated with a given price level. Thus,
when the price level rises, aggregate expenditure will be lower. As higher
prices feed back into the aggregate expenditure function, the economy
finds itself on a lower AE curve (AE_3) in part (*a*), corresponding to a
higher price level. The final level of output in both diagrams is Y_3.

Although some forms of fiscal policy may also shift the aggregate supply curve, fiscal policy is mainly directed at aggregate demand. Fiscal policy is designed to shift aggregate expenditure and aggregate demand in
the direction that will move the economy toward the desired level of output, employment, and prices. The higher demand must be sustained until conditions change. If government spending (*G*) increases only temporarily or taxes (*T*) are reduced temporarily, then when they return to
their original level, the AE and AD curves will return to their original positions. Real output and income will also fall back to the original level.

Keynesian economists do not advocate government intervention to offset every shift in aggregate expenditure. They argue that fiscal policy should
be used only to offset spending shifts that have substantial and prolonged
effects on output, employment, and prices. In reality, specific fiscal policy
actions have not been undertaken very often during the last fifty years.

THE GOAL: FULL EMPLOYMENT WITH STABLE PRICES
In order for government to use fiscal policy wisely, policy makers must
identify a target level of national income. If this target level is far from the

current equilibrium level, then the government should adjust taxes or spending in the right direction. The usual goal is an equilibrium level of national income that generates full employment with price stability. This level is represented by the symbol Y^*.[3]

In the Keynesian model developed in Chapter 8, the aggregate expenditure function was derived by summing components of planned spending—C, I, G, and ($EX - IM$)—at each level of national income. Consumption expenditures were represented by the equation $C = \$200$ billion $+ 0.8Y_d$. In this consumption function, the marginal propensity to consume (MPC) is 0.8, giving a value of 5 for the expenditure multiplier. The economy in Figure 2 is initially at full employment with stable prices when national income is \$3,500 billion ($Y^* = \$3,500$ billion). Above \$3,500 billion lie inflationary pressures. Below \$3,500 billion lies unemployment. The equilibrium level of output, which in this case is equal to Y^*, is found at the intersection of AE_2 and the 45° line.

The purpose of Keynesian fiscal policy is to assure that the level of spending in the economy is AE_2 (the level that results in Y^*) and not some other level, such as AE_1 or AE_3. If the level of aggregate expenditure is lower than AE_2, unemployment will result. If aggregate expenditure and aggregate demand are above the levels required to bring the economy to full employment, there will be a shortage of workers. Then competition for workers and other scarce resources will result in inflationary pressures.[4]

THE RECESSIONARY GAP

The difference between aggregate expenditure and the full-employment level of output is called the **recessionary gap**. A recessionary gap exists when the equilibrium level of national income is *less* than the desired level Y^*. In Figure 2, a level of planned spending along AE_1 results in a recessionary gap because the resulting equilibrium level of income is only \$3,250 billion. The recessionary gap (measured at Y^*) is equal to the vertical distance between AE_1 and AE_2. This gap, distance DE, measures how much aggregate expenditure must rise in order to bring national income up to the desired level. A recessionary gap exists when buyers are unwilling to purchase as much output as the economy would supply at the full-employment level of output (Y^*). If firms attempt to produce at the full-employment level of output, they will see unplanned increases in inventories and respond with cutbacks in production. Thus, the economy in Figure 2 is in equilibrium at Y_1.

A recessionary gap such as DE calls for expansionary fiscal policy. **Expansionary fiscal policy** consists of cutting taxes, raising transfer payments, or increasing government purchases to try to increase the level of output and employment. For the economy in Figure 2, expansionary

recessionary gap
The difference between aggregate expenditure and the full-employment level of output.

expansionary fiscal policy
Cutting taxes, raising transfer payments, or increasing government purchases to try to increase the level of income and employment.

---

3. In reality, Y^* is a range of values for Y, not a single number.
4. The Keynesian model is less useful when there is inflation because it is based on idle resources, price stability, and a horizontal AS curve. We will use this model mainly to analyze the effects of expansionary fiscal policy during recessions. Fiscal policy can also be used to reduce the level of output. It is not possible to use the Keynesian model to visualize its effects because of the absence of a variable price level. Thus, we will discuss contractionary fiscal policy only in the broader framework of an aggregate supply and demand model.

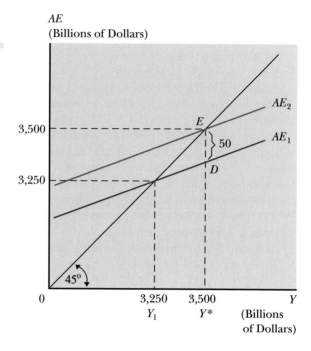

FIGURE 2
THE RECESSIONARY GAP
The full-employment
level of national income,
Y^*, is achieved when
aggregate expenditure
is AE_1. If aggregate
expenditure is AE_2, the
recessionary gap is DE.

fiscal policy needs to shift the AE curve upward by $50 billion. This shift increases equilibrium income from Y_1 to Y^*, a gain of $250 billion.

How did the economy get a $250 billion increase in equilibrium income from only a $50 billion upward shift in aggregate expenditure? The difference is a result of the multiplier effect discussed in Chapter 8. A $50 billion upward shift in the aggregate expenditure function increases output, income, and consumption through the marginal propensity to consume (MPC). With $MPC = 0.8$, the final change in real output (Y) is equal to the multiplier of 5 times the upward shift in planned spending (AE) of $50 billion. If there is any effect on prices (in the aggregate supply and demand diagram), then the change in real output will be smaller.

CHANGING NATIONAL INCOME USING FISCAL POLICY

The policy challenge is to close a recessionary gap by creating an increase in aggregate expenditure. In Figure 2, an increase in national income of $250 billion (from Y_2 to Y^*) requires an upward shift in aggregate expenditure of $50 billion. To increase spending by $50 billion at each level of national income (to shift from AE_1 to AE_2), government expenditures must increase by $50 billion. Through the multiplier process, a $50 billion change in aggregate expenditure causes national income to change by $250 billion.

Another fiscal policy tool that can be used to shift aggregate expenditure and aggregate demand is a change in taxes (T). Changes in personal taxes affect disposable income. Since consumption spending changes in the same direction as disposable income, the government can use taxes to influence consumption and, therefore, national income. A reduction in taxes will shift the AE curve upward and the AD curve to the right. An increase in taxes will lower the AE curve and shift the AD curve to the left.

An important limit to the effectiveness of fiscal policy is that much of the intended impact spills over to other nations. When Nation *A* increases its output level, its citizens demand more imports. Imports are a leakage. Every extra dollar spent on imports instead of domestic goods reduces the multiplier effects of expansionary fiscal policy. For a nation like the United States, in which imports are not a major component of GNP (about 13 percent in 1990), this weakened impact of fiscal policy is not a major problem. But in smaller countries, such as Guyana, Chad, Luxembourg, or Belgium, trade is a large fraction of total spending. In these countries, most of the impact of a fiscal policy may spill abroad, with little effect on the domestic economy.

For the same reason, there is no point in one of the states in the United States trying to pursue an expansionary fiscal policy. (The large and isolated state of Alaska did consider this option to address its local recession in the late 1980s.) If Minnesota runs a budget deficit to try to increase the state's output and employment, a large share of the impact will be felt in Wisconsin, North Dakota, and even as far away as New York and California—all places that supply a substantial amount of Minnesota's "imports."

When expansionary fiscal policy shifts aggregate demand to the right, driving up the price level as well as real output, a second problem emerges in an open economy. At higher prices, a nation's citizens want to buy more cheap foreign goods. At the same time, foreigners are less interested in the nation's high-priced exports. The value of net exports ($EX-IM$) falls. There are fewer injections (EX) and more leakages (IM). A higher price level does even more than a higher level of income to offset the initial expansionary effect of fiscal policy. Prices affect both exports and imports, but rising real income only affects imports.

The same problem plagues contractionary fiscal policy. Falling income will reduce imports, so contractionary fiscal policy is partly offset by reduced leakages. A falling price level will stimulate exports and reduce imports. Again, the effect is to offset some of the contractionary impact of fiscal policy.

Fiscal policy is a powerful tool for affecting output and employment. Some of its effects, however, may spill over to other nations, raising or lowering their incomes and outputs instead of affecting the domestic economy. It is difficult for any nation, especially a small one, to confine the impact of fiscal policy within its borders.

A cut in personal taxes works to close a recessionary gap such as *DE* by increasing consumption, which shifts the *AE* curve upward. How much must taxes be cut to shift *AE* upward by $50 billion in Figure 2? Since the marginal propensity to consume (*MPC*) is 0.8, consumption (*C*) will increase by 80 cents for every dollar increase in disposable income (*Y*$_d$) as a result of the tax cut. The change in *C* is equal to the change in *Y*$_d$ multiplied by *MPC*. In this case, we know the required change in *C* ($50 billion) and the size of the *MPC* (0.8), so we can find the required change in taxes. Taxes must be cut by $62.5 billion at each level of national income in order to change consumption by $50 billion. Once taxes have been cut and the consumption and aggregate expenditure functions have shifted upward, the multiplier process will go to work. Income (*Y*) increases by $250 billion (the multiplier of 5 times the shift in aggregate expenditure of $50 billion). It takes a $62.5 billion decrease in taxes to accomplish the same change in national income as a $50 billion increase in government spending.[5]

Fiscal Policy and the Multiplier

Why is the multiplier for a tax change smaller than the multiplier for a change in government spending? Think about how taxes and government spending enter the income stream. Every dollar of additional government spending immediately contributes another dollar to aggregate expenditure. On the other hand, every dollar not taken by personal taxes is split between saving and consumption. If, for example, the marginal propensity to consume is 0.8, then every $1 reduction in personal taxes contributes 80¢ to increased aggregate expenditure (through an increase in consumption spending) and 20¢ to increased saving. The tax change multiplier is smaller than the government spending multiplier because a portion of a tax decrease leaks immediately out of the spending stream and into saving.

Ignoring the foreign sector for the moment, recall from Chapter 8 that the equilibrium level of national income is given by

$$AE = Y_e = C_0 + b(Y - T) + I + G,$$

where *b* is the marginal propensity to consume (*MPC*) and disposable income (*Y*$_d$) is equal to *Y* − *T*. We can rearrange this expression:

$$Y_e = \frac{1}{1-b}(C_0 - bT + I + G).$$

When we arrange this expression this way, we have separated equilibrium income into two components. The first term, $1/(1-b)$, is the multiplier from Chapter 8. The second term, in parentheses, contains all the factors that can shift aggregate expenditure: C_0, *T*, *I*, and *G*.

Note that the investment, government spending, and constant consumption values are all multiplied by the multiplier, but the tax term is also multiplied by −*b*. This difference between the tax term and the oth-

---

5.   In this model, we assume that the change in taxes is not accompanied by any change in spending as a result of reduced revenue. If a fall in taxes is accompanied by a fall in government spending, the two will tend to offset each other. There will be only a very small impact on output and employment.

ers reflects two important facts. First, changes in taxes work in the opposite direction from changes in all of the other terms. An increase in taxes reduces aggregate expenditure, and a reduction in taxes increases aggregate expenditure. Changes in all of the other terms move aggregate expenditure in the same direction. Second, because b is always less than 1, the effect on output and employment of a given change in taxes will be smaller than that of a change of equal amount in any of the others. We can express this difference by writing two multipliers:

$$\text{Consumption } (C_0) \text{ Multiplier,}$$
$$\text{Government Expenditure } (G) \text{ Multiplier, } = \frac{1}{1-b}$$
$$\text{and Investment } (I) \text{ Multiplier}$$

and

$$\text{Tax Change Multiplier} = -b\left(\frac{1}{1-b}\right) = -\frac{b}{1-b}.$$

For our example, with $MPC = b = 0.8$, the government expenditure multiplier has a value of 5 and the tax change multiplier has a value of -4.

THE BALANCED BUDGET MULTIPLIER

These different multipliers bring up an interesting possibility. Suppose the government wanted to pursue an expansionary policy but did not want to unbalance the budget or increase an existing deficit. Since a given dollar amount of change in government spending has a greater impact than the same amount of change in taxes, it is possible to have equal changes in both and still have some positive effect on the equilibrium level of income. Suppose the government increases both spending and taxes by an equal dollar amount, say $20 billion, leaving the budget deficit or surplus unchanged. The increase in the level of income (Y) resulting from the change in spending (G) is the expenditure multiplier, $1/(1-b)$, times the change in G. If b is equal to 0.8, as before, then Y will increase by 5 times $20 billion, or $100 billion. Calculating the effect of the tax change is a little more complex. The $20 billion increase in taxes (T) is multiplied by the tax multiplier of -4, which is equal to $-b/(1-b)$. So the reduction in Y resulting from the tax increase is $-$80 billion.

Thus, the net change in Y from these two offsetting actions is $20 billion—exactly the same as the equal-sized changes in G and T. Is this a coincidence? No. If we add the two multipliers, $+5$ and -4, we get 1. Adding the algebraic expressions for the two multipliers also gives 1:

$$\frac{1}{1-b} + \frac{-b}{1-b} = \frac{1-b}{1-b} = 1.$$

The value of the balanced budget multiplier is always 1. An equal increase in government spending and taxes will have some modest impact on output and employment. This effect, however, will be much less than the impact of a change in only one of these two with the other held constant.[6]

---

6.   If tax collections depend on the level of income, which they normally do, the balanced budget multiplier is much more complicated to demonstrate.

THE TOOLS OF FISCAL POLICY: GOVERNMENT SPENDING AND TAXES

The tools of fiscal policy are government spending and taxes (and transfer payments, which can be treated as negative taxes). In general, conservative Keynesians prefer tax changes, leaving the size of government production and purchases constant. Liberal Keynesians are more likely to favor changes in government spending. Before we can examine fiscal policy more carefully, however, we need to examine its tools. That is, we need to consider the spending and income of governments, especially the federal government.

In the United States in the last few decades, a large share of the nation's income has been claimed by government, and a substantial share of output has been produced by or for government. Government spending has been growing faster than the economy as a whole. Between 1949 and 1990, the federal government's expenditures rose from 15 percent of national income to 23 percent. State and local governments' expenditures rose from 8 percent of national income to 14 percent. Because government plays such a major role in the economy, changes in its taxing and spending levels can be a very effective tool for influencing the level of income and output.

GOVERNMENT PURCHASES AND TRANSFER PAYMENTS

Total government expenditures—federal, state, and local—account for about one-third of national income in the United States. The federal government alone spent $1,252 billion in 1990. State and local governments added another $765 billion. Some of these funds were spent to produce or to purchase goods and services, such as defense, health care, highways, police, education, and courts.

Table 1 summarizes the major types of spending by all three levels of government. About two-thirds of government spending is for purchases of goods and services. The rest is for transfer payments to individuals who provide no goods or services in exchange. These payments include veterans' benefits, welfare payments, unemployment compensation, and Social Security benefits. Most transfer payments originate at the federal

TABLE 1
HOW GOVERNMENTS
SPEND THEIR INCOMES

FEDERAL (1990*)		STATE AND LOCAL (1989*)	
Defense	23.9%	Education	29.6%
Social Security	19.9	Public welfare	10.7
Interest payments	14.7	Highways	6.5
Transfers to state		Police	3.1
and local governments	10.4	Health, hospitals	2.3
All other	31.4	All other	47.8
Total	100.0%	Total	100.0%

*Data are for fiscal years.

Sources: Advisory Commission on Intergovernmental Relations, *Significant Features of Fiscal Federalism* (Washington, DC: U.S. Government Printing Office, 1990), and Council of Economic Advisers, *Economic Report of the President* (Washington, DC: U.S. Government Printing Office, 1991).

FEDERAL (1990)		STATE (1989)		LOCAL (1989)	
Income taxes	47.3%	Income taxes	19.2%	Property taxes	25.8%
Social insurance		Sales taxes	15.9	Income taxes	3.6
taxes	35.1	Other*	46.5	Sales taxes	2.1
Other*	4.8	Federal grants	18.4	Other*	35.6
Borrowing	12.6			State and federal	
				grants	32.9
Total	100.0%	Total	100.0%	Total	100.0%

*Includes estate taxes, excise taxes, user fees, revenues from government enterprises, and miscellaneous sources.

TABLE 2
REVENUE SOURCES FOR GOVERNMENTS, FISCAL YEARS

Source: Advisory Commission on Intergovernmental Relations, *Significant Features of Fiscal Federalism* (Washington, DC: U.S. Government Printing Office, 1990), and Council of Economic Advisers, *Economic Report of the President* (Washington, DC: U.S. Government Printing Office, 1991).

level, although some are administered by state and local governments. Defense and Social Security are the two biggest expenditures for the federal government. Education is the largest item in state and local budgets. Interest on the national debt takes a growing share of the federal budget because of continuing large budget deficits.

PAYING FOR GOVERNMENT

Table 2 lists revenue sources for all three levels of government.[7] Taxes are the major income source for governments. Major federal taxes are income taxes and social insurance taxes (Social Security taxes, workers' compensation taxes, and unemployment insurance taxes). The main revenue sources at the state and local levels are sales taxes and property taxes, respectively. Another revenue source for state and local governments is federal grants-in-aid. State and federal grants combined provide 38 percent of local government revenues. Sometimes the federal government uses these grants as fiscal policy tools to stimulate spending by state and local governments.

IMPLEMENTING FISCAL POLICY: AUTOMATIC STABILIZERS

In practice, there are two kinds of fiscal policy. One kind is put into place and left to respond automatically to changes in the level of economic activity. The second kind, used less frequently, is deliberate action to change tax laws or enact new spending programs so as to influence the level of output, employment, and prices.

7.   Table 2 suggests an implicit division of revenue sources among federal, state, and local governments. Certain revenue sources, such as income tax, may be suited to being collected by the federal government because there are some cost advantages to national collection or because a particular tax is easier to avoid at the local level than at the federal level. Since the benefits of most local government services are linked to the use of property (fire and police protection, street lights, sewer systems, and so forth), there is some logic to using the property tax at that level. Also, it is more difficult to avoid property taxes than other kinds of local taxes. Thus, it is easier for local governments to rely on that revenue source. State governments are responsible for education and highways and rely heavily on sales and income taxes for revenue. This division of revenue sources and responsibilities among the three levels of government is referred to as fiscal federalism.

Congressional legislation over the years, much of it enacted during the Great Depression, has created a system of tax collections and transfer payments that change automatically in response to changes in national income. These **automatic stabilizers** partially offset changes in private spending and tend to reduce changes in output and employment. They include changes in income tax collections, agricultural support payments, Social Security and welfare benefits, and unemployment compensation claims. Automatic stabilizers do not require further action by Congress. They are built into the economy.

automatic stabilizers
Changes in tax collections and transfer payments that are automatically triggered by changes in national income and tend to reduce changes in output and employment.

PROGRESSIVE INCOME TAXES

In the simple Keynesian model of Chapter 8, taxes (T) were independent of level of income.[8] If you have ever filled out Form 1040 to pay income taxes to the Internal Revenue Service, you know that as your income goes up, your taxes go up even faster. The federal income tax is progressive, as are some state income taxes.

An income tax, or any tax, can be regressive, proportional, or progressive. Table 3 shows examples of how each type of tax affects three income earners. A **regressive tax** is a tax that takes a smaller share (percentage) of income as income rises. In the second column of Table 3, Jones pays a higher share of his income (5 percent) than does Brown (1 percent).

regressive tax
A tax that takes a smaller share (percentage) of income as income rises.

Sales taxes on food are somewhat regressive because the proportion of an individual's budget spent on food declines as income rises. Note that a tax can be regressive even if the tax does not decline in absolute dollars as income rises. In Table 3, Brown paid $5,000, and Jones paid only $500. For Brown, however, the tax represented a smaller percentage of income. Many people object to regressive taxes because of the burden they place on low-income families.

A **proportional tax** takes the same share (percentage) of income from all taxpayers. The proportional tax of 5 percent in Table 3 takes the same share of income from each person. However, the dollar amount increases as income increases.

proportional tax
A tax that takes the same share (percentage) of income from all taxpayers.

A **progressive tax** takes a larger share (percentage) of income as income rises. In Table 3, the progressive tax takes not only more dollars from Brown than from Smith or Jones, but a higher share of Brown's income. The federal personal income tax in the United States is a moderately progressive tax, with rates ranging from 15 percent to 31 percent. The range of rates was reduced by the 1986 tax reform and again in 1990, but the tax is still progressive. That is, your federal taxes will go up more than in proportion to your income as your income rises.

progressive tax
A tax that takes a larger share (percentage) of income as income rises.

TABLE 3
COMPARISON OF AMOUNTS
PAID UNDER THREE TYPES
OF TAXES

	INCOME	REGRESSIVE TAX	PROPORTIONAL TAX	PROGRESSIVE TAX
Jones	$ 10,000	$ 500 = 5%	$ 500 = 5%	$ 500 = 5%
Smith	$ 80,000	$1,600 = 2%	$ 4,000 = 5%	$ 20,000 = 25%
Brown	$500,000	$5,000 = 1%	$25,000 = 5%	$250,000 = 50%

8. You may wish to review the discussion of endogenous and exogenous variables in the appendix to Chapter 1. In Keynesian models, taxes can be either endogenous or exogenous.

If taxes rise or fall more than in proportion to changes in national income and output, then consumption (which depends on after-tax, or disposable, income) will rise or fall *less* than in proportion to changes in national income and output. Suppose, for example, that at an income level (Y) of $3,000 billion, taxes are $300 billion, or 10 percent. Disposable income (Y_d) is then $2,700 billion. Substituting $2,700 billion for Y_d in the equation for the consumption function gives

$$C = \$200 \text{ billion} + 0.8Y_d = \$200 \text{ billion} + 0.8(\$2,700 \text{ billion})$$
$$= \$2,360 \text{ billion.}$$

The consumption component of aggregate expenditure is $2,360 billion.

What happens if Y increases by $1,000 billion, so the equilibrium level of income is $4,000 billion instead of $3,000 billion? With a marginal propensity to consume of 0.8, you might expect consumption to rise by 80 percent of the income increase of $1,000 billion, or $800 billion. However, consumption will increase by less than $800 billion even if the tax system is not progressive. If taxes take 10 percent of income, a rise in Y of $1,000 billion will raise Y_d by $900 billion. Consumption will increase by 0.8 times $900 billion, or $720 billion. If the tax system is progressive, taxes may increase from 10 percent ($300 billion) at the old level of income to 12 percent ($480 billion) of the new income. In this case, national income rises by $1,000 billion, but disposable income will rise by only $820 billion, from $2,700 billion to $3,520 billion. Substituting this value of Y_d in the consumption function, we find that consumption (C) is now $3,016 billion. This increase of $656 billion, or 28 percent, in C is less than the 33 percent increase in Y. Thus, when income rises, progressive taxes rise more than in proportion to the increase in income. The effect is to dampen consumer demand.

With progressive income taxes, a fall in national income will lead to a more-than-proportional fall in taxes. The disposable income of households will be a larger fraction of total income and output when income falls. Thus, the fall in consumption will be less than proportional to the decline in output and income. Since consumption spending is more stable than the level of output and income, progressive income taxes reduce ups and downs not only in the household standard of living but also in aggregate planned spending during good times and bad.

The mildly progressive corporate income tax is also an automatic stabilizer. Although this tax became less progressive after 1986, revenues from it still increase sharply during economic expansions and fall sharply during contractions. The corporate income subject to this tax consists of profits. Profits are highly sensitive to changes in the level of economic activity.

TRANSFER PAYMENTS

Transfer payments, many of them dating from the Great Depression, also act as automatic stabilizers. Transfer programs include unemployment compensation, Social Security, farm price supports, food stamps, and welfare benefits. All of these programs involve payments for which no production is expected in exchange.

Transfer programs such as food stamps usually set rules that determine who is eligible, rather than specifying a dollar amount to be spent. The

The term *policy maker* keeps cropping up in any macroeconomic discussion. Who are the policy makers for the U.S. economy? The Board of Governors of the Federal Reserve System, the Secretary of the Treasury, the chairman of the Council of Economic Advisers, the director of the Office of Management and Budget, and the director of the Congressional Budget Office are the macroeconomic policy makers. Most of them are highly visible, appearing on the evening news and *Meet the Press* and giving interviews to the *Wall Street Journal*.

The term *policy* in macroeconomics refers mainly to the use of fiscal policy tools (changes in taxes and government spending) and monetary policy tools (primarily changes in the money supply) to influence the level of output. Macroeconomic policy is a responsibility of the federal government. State and local governments have to stick pretty close to a balanced budget. Furthermore, if they tried to pursue an active fiscal policy, most of the benefits would probably spill over to other states.

Fiscal policy is a responsibility that is shared between the executive branch and the Congress. The President's chief policy advisers are the three economists on the Council of Economic Advisers. These economists are appointed by the President. The functions of the Council are to advise the President on the course of the economy, to participate in decision making on economic, budget, and financial policy (international as well as domestic), to oversee preparation of the annual *Economic Report of the President*, and to speak on behalf of the administration to Congress, the public, and the

ECONOMIC

INSIGHT

WHO MAKES

POLICY?

media.[a] The Secretary of the Treasury also plays an important role in recommending tax and spending policies, especially tax policies. The Office of Management and Budget prepares the annual federal budget to transmit to Congress. In the process of developing that budget, important decisions are made about the level and composition of government spending.

Since 1974, Congress has played a more active role in fiscal policy. Congress established the Congressional Budget Office then to provide an independent analysis of the executive branch's budget proposals and propose alternatives. Most fiscal policy requires congressional legislation, and Congress felt the need for a second opinion on the course of the economy and the impact of proposed legislation.

Monetary policy, which we explore in Chapters 12 and 14, is under the control of the Federal Reserve System. This central bank is a quasi-governmental agency in that its members are appointed officials. However, they are much more independent than most bureaucrats. They are not supported out of tax revenues, since the Federal Reserve System earns enough income from its normal operations to be self-supporting. The seven governors are appointed for one-time, fourteen-year terms by the President. Thus, the Board of Governors has a great deal of independence. The President may try to persuade the Fed to cooperate, but the executive branch often finds itself in conflict with the central bank. Coordination of monetary and fiscal policy is one of the most difficult challenges facing any president.

a.   Murray L. Weidenbaum, "The Role of the Council of Economic Advisers," *Journal of Economic Education* (Summer 1988): 237–244.

AUTOMATIC STABILIZERS AND HOW THEY WORK

- Progressive income taxes make disposable income (and consumption) more stable than national income. Examples are federal personal and corporate income taxes and personal and corporate income taxes in some states.

- Transfer payments rise automatically during recessions and fall in expansions. Examples are unemployment compensation, welfare, farm price supports, food stamps, and means-tested programs such as subsidized housing and heat assistance.

number of families eligible for these transfer programs rises during recessions and falls during periods of expansion. During recessions, more people qualify for unemployment benefits, apply for food stamps, go on welfare, and retire early on Social Security. As the economy recovers, some people—even some of those who retired early—go back to work. Transfer payments fall. In addition, farm prices will be higher during expansionary periods so less will be spent on farm price supports. During recessions, farm prices fall, which triggers a rise in support payments.

If you think of transfer payments as negative taxes, you can see that they work in the same way as progressive income taxes in stabilizing output and employment. Instead of changes in tax rates as the level of income in the economy rises and falls, there are changes in the number of persons who qualify for benefits.

DISCRETIONARY FISCAL POLICY

Automatic stabilizers might be considered Keynesian fiscal policy because they lead to changes in transfer payments and tax revenues that offset changes in private economic activity. For small changes in output and employment, automatic stabilizers may be sufficient to cushion the fluctuations until the economy corrects itself. For major swings in aggregate expenditure, however, automatic stabilizers are not enough. In that case, policy makers turn to discretionary fiscal policy. **Discretionary fiscal policy** consists of changes in tax rates, in levels of transfer payments, or in government purchases of goods and services in order to change the equilibrium level of national income.

At the end of World War II, political and business leaders feared that the transition from wartime to peacetime production would send the economy into another depression. In response to these concerns, Congress passed the Employment Act of 1946. The **Employment Act of 1946** was an official adoption of Keynesian ideas about the role of discretionary fiscal policy in keeping the economy on a steady path.[9] This legislation made the U.S. government responsible for achieving and maintaining full employment, steady growth, and stable prices through the use of fiscal

discretionary fiscal policy
Deliberate changes in tax rates, transfer programs, or government purchases designed to change the equilibrium level of national income.

Employment Act of 1946
A law requiring the federal government to actively promote full employment, steady growth, and stable prices through the use of fiscal and monetary policy.

9. Nobel Prize winner James Tobin argues forcefully that this act is as relevant today as it was in 1946, and that discretionary fiscal policy still has an important role to play. See "High Time to Restore the Employment Act of 1946," *Challenge* (May-June 1986): 4–12.

Economic Report of the President
An annual report to Congress describing the state of the economy and recommending policy.

(and monetary) policy. To provide policy-making advice, Congress created the three-member Council of Economic Advisers.[10] The legislation also requires the President (with the aid of the Council) to prepare an annual economic report, the ***Economic Report of the President***. This report, sent to Congress every January, describes the state of the economy and may recommend changes in policy.

Congress changes tax rates, transfer programs, and government purchases almost every year for various reasons. The end of the military threat from the Warsaw Pact was expected to result in a decline in defense spending. The Gulf War, however, made that prospect less likely. New social problems such as AIDS and homelessness put pressure on policy makers to increase spending in those areas. Congress tinkers with the income tax code regularly to change incentives to save, invest, or give to charity. These actions may affect the level of economic activity. They do not, however, constitute fiscal policy, because their primary purpose is not to influence the level of output and employment.

True acts of pure discretionary fiscal policy are relatively rare. We will examine four fiscal policy actions that took place in the last thirty years. All of them involve tax changes. They illustrate the political and economic processes at work in discretionary fiscal policy.

THE KENNEDY TAX CUT

The first major use of discretionary fiscal policy was the Kennedy tax cut of 1964. When John Kennedy ran for the presidency in 1960, he was critical of the lack of active fiscal policy during Eisenhower's terms of office. The U.S. economy had experienced two major recessions in the 1950s. Although the 5.4 percent unemployment rate and 2.2 percent economic growth rate for 1960 look attractive by current standards, they were worse than figures for earlier years. In terms of the Keynesian model of Chapter 8, the economy was in equilibrium in 1960, but national income and output were below the full-employment level. There was a recessionary gap.

Walter W. Heller, the chair of Kennedy's Council of Economic Advisers, and other Keynesian economists had high hopes for what discretionary fiscal policy could do. In his 1967 book, *New Dimensions of Political Economy*, Heller said, "Today's talk of an intellectual revolution and a 'new economics' arises not out of startling discoveries of new economic truths but out of the swift and progressive weaving of modern economics into the fabric of national thinking and policy."[11] Heller expressed confidence that active fiscal policy based on Keynesian theories offered the best hope for solving macroeconomic problems. He was the first to use "fine-tuning" to describe targeting a particular level of output, employment, and inflation and carefully managing taxes and spending so as to try to reach that goal.

A recessionary gap can be eliminated by expansionary fiscal policy, consisting of some combination of an increase in government spending and a decrease in taxes. In 1962, Kennedy proposed both a decrease in

10. For an inside look at how the Council functions today, see Martin Feldstein, "How the CEA Advises Presidents," *Challenge* (November-December 1989): 51–55.
11. Walter Heller, *New Dimensions of Political Economy* (Cambridge, MA: Harvard University Press, 1967), viii.

personal and corporate income taxes and an increase in government spending. The proposal was designed to cause an increase in all three domestic components of aggregate expenditure: consumption, investment, and government spending. The shift in aggregate expenditure and aggregate demand would increase national income and output and eliminate the recessionary gap.

Congress was hesitant to intervene in the economy on the basis of Keynesian economic theory. Many members of Congress resisted the proposed tax cut because it would increase the federal deficit. After Kennedy was assassinated, Lyndon Johnson finally succeeded in getting approval for the tax cut in 1964.

Did the Kennedy tax cut work? From Table 4, you can see that the unemployment rate declined and the economic growth rate rose for several years after 1964. These statistics do not prove that discretionary fiscal policy was responsible for the rapid economic expansion between 1964 and 1968. However, Keynesian economists felt that in this case fiscal policy had worked as theory predicted.

The Johnson Tax Surcharge

Arthur M. Okun served on the Council of Economic Advisers from late 1964 until the end of the Johnson administration. In 1968, Okun was named chair of the Council.[12] By 1966, as the unemployment rate continued to fall (Table 4), concern had shifted from slow growth and high unemployment to inflationary pressures and labor shortages. Not only was the Kennedy tax cut successful, but spending for both the Vietnam War and President Johnson's War on Poverty provided more stimulus than the economy needed. The

Year	Unemployment Rate (%)	Growth Rate of Real GNP (%)	Inflation Rate (CPI) (%)
1959	5.3	5.8	1.7
1960	5.4	2.2	1.4
1961	6.5	2.6	0.7
1962	5.4	5.3	1.3
1963	5.5	4.1	1.6
1964	5.0	5.3	1.0
1965	4.4	5.8	1.9
1966	3.7	5.8	3.5
1967	3.7	2.9	3.0
1968	3.5	4.1	4.7
1969	3.4	2.4	6.2
1970	4.8	−0.3	5.6
1971	5.8	2.8	3.3

TABLE 4
UNEMPLOYMENT, ECONOMIC GROWTH, AND INFLATION IN THE UNITED STATES, 1959–1971

Source: Council of Economic Advisers, *Economic Report of the President* (Washington, DC: U.S. Government Printing Office, 1991).

12. By 1970, Arthur Okun was less positive about the use of discretionary fiscal policy in his book *The Political Economy of Prosperity*. It was becoming apparent that an expansionary fiscal policy that succeeded in stimulating economic growth and employment was likely to also result in budget deficits and inflation. Okun was still convinced that well-designed discretionary fiscal policy could improve the performance of the economy.

contractionary fiscal policy
Raising taxes, lowering transfer payments, or reducing government purchases in an attempt to reduce the equilibrium level of output to one that is attainable with available resources.

time had come for the first (and only) experiment in using contractionary fiscal policy to "put on the brakes"—to reduce the level of aggregate expenditure and the equilibrium level of income and output. **Contractionary fiscal policy** consists of decreases in government purchases, decreases in transfer payments, or increases in taxes in order to reduce the equilibrium level of output to one that can be produced with available resources.

The contractionary policy chosen was a one-time 10 percent surcharge on income taxes (with an option for the President to extend it to a second year). Policy makers expected the surcharge to dampen demand and reduce inflationary pressures. The tax surcharge was requested by the President in 1967 but was not passed by Congress until 1968. This policy was later judged ineffective. Unemployment did rise, but the inflation rate did not fall.[13] However, there was a one-time change rather than a sustained increase in taxes, and monetary policy was expansionary at the time. Both of these facts make it difficult to assess whether or not this policy was really effective.

THE FORD TAX REBATE

By the mid-1970s, the economy was plagued with the twin evils of high unemployment and high inflation. During the administration of President Ford, income tax changes were again used as expansionary policy, in the form of a $23 billion tax rebate in 1975. As the Ford tax rebate took effect, planned spending and aggregate demand increased, and the unemployment rate fell. By 1976, unemployment had fallen slightly to below 8 percent from a high of over 9 percent in 1975. Once again, fiscal policy based on Keynesian theory appeared to produce the intended results. However, the improvement was not enough to get Ford re-elected! In fact, because of the temporary nature of the rebate, it had far less impact than the Kennedy tax cut a decade earlier.

THE REAGAN TAX CUT

In 1981, President Reagan proposed and Congress passed a major tax cut. It was not billed as fiscal policy for three reasons. First, the Reagan tax cut, like the Ford tax rebate, came at a time when both unemployment and inflation were very high. Discretionary fiscal policy is designed to address either unemployment (expansionary policy) or inflation (contractionary policy) but not both. Second, the tax cut was accompanied by (somewhat smaller) spending cuts. For maximum impact, a Keynesian would generally recommend cutting taxes without cutting spending in order to combat unemployment. Third, the tax cuts made were intended to affect aggregate supply, an issue that we will examine in Chapter 16. However, any tax cut, especially one that is larger than spending cuts, will shift both aggregate expenditure and aggregate demand. We can consider the Reagan tax cut as an act of expansionary fiscal policy and examine its effects on output and employment.

13. Note that we use the inflation rate rather than the price level in assessing economic performance, even though the aggregate supply and demand model uses the price level. This is for convenience. We also tend to use the rate of growth of real output rather than the level of output as a measure of economic growth, even though it is the level of output that is shown on an aggregate supply and demand diagram.

Personal taxes were cut by 25 percent over a three-year period. The first 12.5 percent cut took effect late in 1981, and the second took effect in July 1983. Thus, the largest effects on disposable income occurred from mid-1982 on. The most important part of the business tax cut was accelerated depreciation for new business investment. This change greatly shortened the time period over which new plant and equipment purchases could be depreciated for tax purposes. Most of the original business tax cut was later offset by increases in business taxes enacted in 1982 and 1986.

From a Keynesian standpoint, the timing of the tax cut was appropriate. It came in the midst of a major recession. Unemployment peaked in November of 1982 at 10.8 percent. At the bottom of the recession in late 1982, real GNP had fallen 3 percent from its previous peak in the third quarter of 1981. By mid-1984, unemployment had fallen to 7.2 percent, and real GNP had bounced back to 7.7 percent above the 1981 peak. From 1985 through 1989, unemployment continued to decline to 5.3 percent. Real income also grew, although at a slower rate of about 2 to 4 percent. Thus, whether or not the Reagan administration considered its actions to be discretionary fiscal policy, the tax cut was successful by Keynesian standards in increasing output and employment.

BUSINESS TAX CUTS AS FISCAL POLICY

With several of the tax cuts above, as well as at other times when there was no major change in personal or corporate income tax rates, changes in business income taxes were made in order to stimulate investment. One such change was the **Investment Tax Credit (ITC)**. This credit offers tax savings over and above depreciation for business firms investing in new plants or equipment. Firms can subtract a percentage of the investment made from their tax liability. The ITC was first introduced as part of the Kennedy tax cut in 1964. The ITC has been a political football—being modified, removed, or restored many times. Each time, Congress weighs the revenue loss against the current perceived need to stimulate investment. Business firms complain that the ITC is less effective in encouraging investment when it is uncertain. They say it should be permanent rather than on and off.

Investment Tax Credit (ITC)
Provision offering tax savings over and above depreciation for business firms investing in new plants or equipment. A percentage of the investment made can be subtracted from tax liability.

The 1981 tax cut also provided for accelerated depreciation. This change meant that for tax purposes investors in real assets of all kinds could depreciate them much more quickly than their resale value actually declined. This tax saving was supposed to provide a stimulus to investment. It is not clear how much additional investment resulted. There was, however, a definite decline in revenues from the corporate income tax. In 1986, when tax reform lowered rates across the board for both individuals and corporations, accelerated depreciation was greatly weakened.

The economic justification for both the ITC and accelerated depreciation was to focus some of the stimulus to aggregate demand on investment rather than consumption. Additional investment is an increase in both demand and the productive capacity of the economy. Thus, it shifts both aggregate demand and aggregate supply to the right, reducing the inflationary effect of fiscal policy.

FISCAL POLICY: PROS AND CONS

Advocates of fiscal policy as a way to affect output and employment claim that government spending and taxes can be used to reduce, if not eliminate, the social costs of unemployment and inflation (discussed in Chapter 4). Furthermore, increased government expenditures intended to close a recessionary gap can provide needed social goods, such as schools, parks, and highways. However, discretionary fiscal policy has been criticized since its beginnings in the 1930s. One theoretical criticism is the permanent income hypothesis, which challenges the Keynesian consumption function and the multiplier. Other criticisms of fiscal policy focus on four issues: budget deficits and the national debt, an increase in the size of government, lags, and the use of fiscal policy for political gain. Because deficits and the national debt have been a key issue for the last ten years and promise to continue to be at least until the end of the century, they are discussed separately in Chapter 10.

THE PERMANENT INCOME HYPOTHESIS

Recall that the centerpiece of the Keynesian model is the consumption function, $C = C_0 + bY_d$, from which the expenditure multiplier, $1/(1- b)$ or $1/(1 - MPC)$, is derived. In order to increase the level of income and output, the government can cut taxes (raising Y_d directly) or increase government spending. Then rounds of spending, governed by the consumption function, lead to a multiplier effect on output and income. The expenditure multiplier works in both directions. If the consumption function is very stable, the value of the expenditure multiplier derived from the consumption function will also be stable.

permanent income hypothesis
The view that consumption does not depend on current income alone but on past income and expected future income as well.

The permanent income hypothesis was a central part of Milton Friedman's attack on the Keynesian model. The **permanent income hypothesis** is the view that consumption does not depend on current income alone, but on past income and expected future income as well. Think about your own consumption. Today's spending is not based just on today's income. If you are paid every other week, you don't consume very heavily on payday and not at all for the next thirteen days! Some people may come close to that pattern, but a household's consumption usually depends on its expected income stream over time. Friedman argues that consumption depends on permanent income, which consists of past, present, and expected future income.

Casual observations of how people act seems to support this idea. Seasonal workers, such as farmers and construction workers, may only work six to eight months a year, but they consume at a fairly constant level throughout the year. Striking or laid-off workers usually maintain their consumption if the strike or layoff doesn't last too long. If these households do not have enough liquid assets (cash or other assets easily turned into cash) or access to credit, they may have to curtail consumption. But in general, Friedman argues, consumption is much more stable than actual current income because it is not based on that income alone.

Another way of understanding the permanent income hypothesis is to think about what you would do if you had less income for a short time. You would probably continue to pay those expenses that are fixed in the short run, such as house payments, car payments, and utility bills. You would still eat meals and put gas in the car but might give up seeing new movies and buying tapes or new clothes. You might cut back a little on food by eating out less and spend less on recreation and other nonessentials. In the short run, your options for cutting spending are limited, especially when the income change is temporary. If your income fell permanently, however, you might decide to sell your house and car and move to smaller quarters or make other big changes in your consumption patterns. You might drop out of school, move out of an apartment and back home or into the dorm, or make other large adjustments.

It is more difficult to argue that individuals won't increase their consumption in response to a temporary increase in income. But people will usually increase consumption less with a temporary increase in income than with a permanent increase. Thus, the permanent income hypothesis seems to make good sense in terms of how people behave.

POLICY IMPLICATIONS. The permanent income hypothesis has some important implications for fiscal policy. If consumers fail to respond to a temporary increase in disposable income by spending a large fraction of it, then fiscal policy will have less effect on output and employment. An increase or decrease in government spending or taxes will still have a first-round effect on output and employment. However, unless people are convinced that the change is permanent, subsequent rounds of changes in spending will be very small. Temporary changes in taxes or spending will have little impact on consumer spending, because a one-time tax cut or a one-year spending increase will affect permanent income much less than current income.

Consider, for example, a person who expects to live twenty-five more years. A one-time tax cut of $1,000 increases this person's current income by $1,000. But his or her permanent income increases (ignoring interest) by only $40 a year! The 1964 and 1981 income tax cuts, which were enacted as permanent changes, appear to have had more effect on income and consumption than the 1968 temporary surcharge or the 1975 one-time tax rebate.

PROBLEMS OF MEASUREMENT. The debate on the consumption function cannot be easily settled by statistical testing. In order to test whether the consumption function works better with current income than with permanent income, economists would have to be able to measure permanent income. A household's permanent income at any given time depends on both experience and expectations. As the household acquires more experience, expectations change and so does permanent income. Economists are even less able to measure permanent income for the entire economy than for one household. They can only offer examples that suggest that temporary income changes have less effect on consumption than permanent income changes do.

GOVERNMENT SPENDING

A group of economists from a relatively new branch of economics has criticized fiscal policy on the grounds that such actions tend to increase the size of the government sector relative to the private sector. **Public choice**

public choice economics
A branch of economic theory that attempts to integrate economics and politics by examining the motives and rewards facing individuals in the public sector.

For most of the period since World War II, Britain has had a large and growing public sector with poor economic performance. Unemployment was stubbornly high, growth was slow, and inflation was persistent. In 1979, Margaret Thatcher became Prime Minister and instituted a combination of economic policies very similar to those adopted later by President Reagan in the United States. Reagan cut taxes more than spending. Thatcher cut taxes only moderately, cut some forms of spending, and emphasized reducing the extent and scope of government activities. Unlike Reagan, Thatcher was successful in reducing the size of government. For a time, her policies were very popular. However, cuts in some important local services and the replacement of property taxes with very regressive poll taxes weakened her position and helped to bring about her removal as Prime Minister in 1990.

Thatcher pursued a complex policy with many goals, including privatization of industry

and redistribution of wealth. However, we can evaluate the contractionary aspect of her fiscal policies. In terms of a Keynesian model, aggregate expenditure fell in Britain because the fall in taxes was smaller than the reduction in government spending. As a result the *AD* curve shifted to the left, and unemployment rose while inflation fell. Inflation was nearly 15 percent in 1979. It fell to about 3 percent in 1987, only to finally rise again to 8 percent in 1988. This rate was still well below that when Thatcher took office. Unemployment, about 5.5 percent when she took office, rose to 13 percent in 1983 and was still at 8 percent by 1988. (These numbers are not comparable to those of the United States because of different ways of counting employed and unemployed workers.) While Reagan pursued an expansionary policy in the name of a healthier private sector and a smaller government, Thatcher pursued a contractionary policy—with the expected effects on inflation and unemployment.

economics attempts to integrate politics and economics by examining the motives and rewards for different types of behavior in the public sector. Public choice economics is the modern form of political economy. Much of public choice economics is microeconomic. However, some work in macroeconomics has been done by public choice theorists.

James Buchanan, a Nobel Prize winner, and his colleague Richard Wagner see rising deficits and resistance to collecting the taxes to pay for spending as logical consequences of the nature of the U.S. political system.[14] Buchanan and Wagner argue that policies that hurt a few citizens very intensely and benefit most others very slightly are not likely to be enacted, even if the total benefits exceed the costs. Conversely, it is politically easy to enact programs that benefit a few very greatly at a small cost to each taxpayer, even if the total costs exceed the total benefits.

Spending programs benefit specific interest groups: welfare clients, hospitals, farmers, defense firms, or industries that compete with imports. A tariff may be designed to protect the shoe industry or the textile industry. Such a policy benefits workers and owners in that industry at the expense of consumers of shoes or textiles. In addition, the costs of many spending programs, such as farm price supports or cost overruns by defense contractors, are borne by taxpayers in general. Taxpayers feel the effects as higher current taxes, more inflation, or higher future taxes to finance deficits. Recessions provide an excuse to fund such programs by borrowing rather than by raising taxes. When the recession ends, the program has acquired a constituency and cannot be axed. Over time, then, the government sector grows relative to the private sector.

Other economists, including Nobel Prize winner James Tobin, argue that the large size of the government sector relative to the private sector is a force for stability. Investment and net exports are quite unstable, as are some components of consumption—especially consumer durables. Government purchases, however, are quite stable. They change slowly from year to year. The share of total output that is bought by or produced by government is much larger now than it was in Keynes's day. With this big, stable sector providing an anchor, the economy is less likely to drift into recession. These economists argue that the growing share of economic activity passing through government is the primary reason why there has not been another Great Depression.

However, in a market system, it is inefficient to make production decisions through government when there are no compelling reasons such as public goods or strong externalities. The market does a better job of allocating resources in response to consumer demand. Thus, if greater macroeconomic stability is due to the larger share of economic activity in the public sector, there will be a difficult tradeoff between stability and efficiency.

LAGS IN FISCAL POLICY

Lags in making policy decisions provide another basis for criticism of discretionary fiscal policy. The **recognition lag** is the length of time required

recognition lag
The length of time it takes to determine that an economic problem exists.

---

14. James Buchanan and Richard E. Wagner, *Democracy in Deficit: The Political Legacy of Lord Keynes* (New York: W. W. Norton, 1977).

to become aware of, or recognize, an economic problem. Statistical measures (unemployment rate, CPI, and GNP) take from one to three months to compile. When these measures become available, they describe economic conditions for the previous month or previous quarter. These measures provide the basis for forecasting whether a recession will continue or end, whether unemployment will rise, fall or remain the same, how fast output will grow, or what the rate of inflation will be. Such forecasts are difficult to make and prone to errors. And an inaccurate forecast can result in the wrong fiscal policy.

Once a problem is recognized, more time passes as the President and Congress choose a fiscal policy solution and enact it into law. Policy makers must decide what kind of action to take—taxes, transfers, or government spending—and at what level. They must decide whose taxes to cut, what kinds of spending programs to undertake, and what section of the country should get the initial benefit. This **implementation lag** is the time it takes after a problem is recognized to choose and enact a fiscal policy in response. Some economists have recommended that Congress give limited power to change tax rates to the President in order to save valuable time.

After a fiscal policy has become law, further time passes before there is any improvement in the economy. Tax changes can be implemented fairly quickly through payroll withholding. Spending programs, on the other hand—especially those involving construction of highways or public buildings—take time to design and carry out. Once the initial round of spending takes place, then the multiplier effects are felt over a period of eighteen to twenty-four months. The **impact lag** is the time that elapses between the implementation of a fiscal policy and its full effect on economic activity.

Taken together, the recognition, implementation, and impact lags add up to a long period of time. It is quite possible that the combined lags can take up so much time that the full impact of a tax cut or an increase in spending will not be felt until after the economy has begun to move out of the recession by itself. In Figure 3, the points labeled R, I_1, and I_2 are,

implementation lag
The time it takes after a problem is recognized to choose and enact a fiscal policy in response.

impact lag
The time that elapses between implementation of a fiscal policy and its full effect on economic activity.

FIGURE 3
LAGS AND DESTABILIZING FISCAL POLICY
Along the course of this business cycle, recognition that the economy is in a recession occurs at point R. Implementation of fiscal policy takes place at point I_1, and its impact on the economy is finally felt at point I_2. Because the expansionary policy was delayed, it causes the economy to take off on the course indicated by the dashed line. The economy has been made less stable.

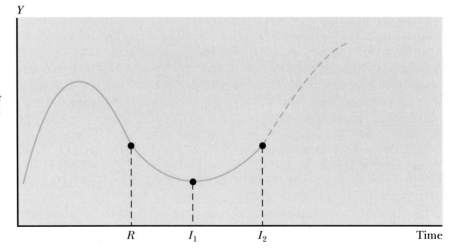

respectively, the end points of the recognition, implementation, and impact lags. As you can see, the delays mean that the policy's effect on economic activity is not actually felt until the economy is well into the recovery phase. The dashed line from point I_2 shows what the path of economic activity is likely to be as a result of poorly timed discretionary policy. The expansionary fiscal policy intended to combat recession will simply fuel inflation. Similar mistiming on contractionary policy could aggravate a recession. Discretionary fiscal policy combined with lags can actually make an economy less stable.

THE POLITICAL BUSINESS CYCLE

Public choice economists have also suggested that discretionary fiscal policy combined with the American political system can create a political business cycle. In many other countries, the political system is parliamentary. The legislative branch and executive branch are united under a prime minister. In such systems the prime minister usually has some say about when elections are called, and campaigns are relatively brief. In the U.S. political system, however, there are only two years between elections. All members of the House of Representatives and one-third of the Senate are elected every two years, and presidents are elected every four years. Consequently, the next election is never very far from the mind of anyone in Congress or the White House.

Under these conditions, the incumbent party has a strong incentive to try to reduce unemployment and inflation so that economic conditions look good at the time of the next election. Such political maneuvering gives the economy a series of short-run policies and rapid reversals to meet political needs, rather than a consistent pursuit of policies with a longer run payoff. Examples of timing spending programs and tax cuts so as to attempt to influence the outcome of an election are not hard to find. In the 1970s, Congress approved automatic changes in Social Security benefits each January based on changes in the CPI. Before that time, these benefits would typically be adjusted just before an election so as to court the elderly vote. Increases in payroll taxes to finance the added benefits would not take place until after the election. The 1981 tax cut is another example. This tax cut had its first substantial effect on withholding in 1982, a congressional election year, and the final impact was felt in the 1984 presidential election year. In fact, it is hard to find a tax cut that took effect in an odd-numbered year or a tax increase that took effect in an even-numbered year!

Some economists have suggested that there may even be a controlled business cycle designed to peak just before elections. This **political business cycle** is the result of the use of fiscal and monetary policy, especially fiscal policy, to influence the outcome of elections. A downturn can follow an election, as long as there is another peak, or at least an upturn, in time for the next election. According to this view, the level and timing of tax and spending changes (and when the Federal Reserve is willing to cooperate, changes in the money supply) tend to respond less to changes in economic activity than to the timing of elections.

American Political Economy, a recent book by Donald Hibbs, offers evidence that favorable or unfavorable economic conditions at the time of

political business cycle
A business cycle that results from the use of fiscal (or monetary) policy to influence the outcome of elections.

an election have a definite effect on the success or failure of the incumbent party.[15] President Reagan saw his party lose many congressional seats in the recession-year election of 1982. Economic conditions had improved by the 1984 presidential election, no doubt contributing to Reagan's landslide re-election. As expansion continued to the end of the decade, low unemployment and only moderate inflation undoubtedly helped Reagan's Vice President, George Bush, win the 1988 election.[16] Although economic conditions can influence political outcomes, there has been little success in using statistics to prove or disprove that politicians can actually create a political business cycle for their own benefit.

PROBLEMS WITH FISCAL POLICY

- Increase in the relative size of government
- Loss of control over budget deficits
- Difficulty in making accurate economic projections
- Lags (recognition, implementation, and impact)
- Political business cycles

FISCAL POLICY, AGGREGATE DEMAND, AND THE PRICE LEVEL

The analysis of fiscal policy in this chapter has been based on the simple Keynesian model from Chapter 8. That model focuses on aggregate expenditure with a fixed price level. It is adequate when there is severe unemployment, when aggregate supply may be horizontal. When the price level can change, this simple Keynesian model is not as useful. A better model for situations closer to full employment is the blending of the aggregate expenditure and aggregate supply and demand models. Recall that at the end of Chapter 8, we integrated the Keynesian model into the aggregate supply and demand framework.

Figure 4 shows how the slope of the *AS* curve affects the impact of expansionary fiscal policy. Expansionary fiscal policy shifts the *AE* curve upward for all price levels and thus shifts the *AD* curve to the right. Only the shifting of the *AD* curve is shown in Figure 4. If aggregate demand remains in the horizontal range of the *AS* curve (AD_1 and AD_2), all of the impact of expansionary fiscal policy falls on real output. A shift to AD_3 in the upward-sloping range of the *AS* curve means that expansionary fiscal policy will affect both real output and the price level. If the *AD* curve intersects *AS* in its vertical range, the only impact of expansionary fiscal policy will be on the price level. Because classical and new classical econ-

---

15. Donald A. Hibbs, *American Political Economy* (Cambridge, MA: Harvard University Press, 1988).
16. To the extent that Reagan's policies were truly supply side, rather than Keynesian, the impact was likely to be quite slow because such policies depend on work incentives, investment incentives, and productivity, which do not respond very rapidly. Investment in particular, since it requires a long planning horizon, may take some time to respond. We will look more closely at the effect of supply side policies in Chapter 16.

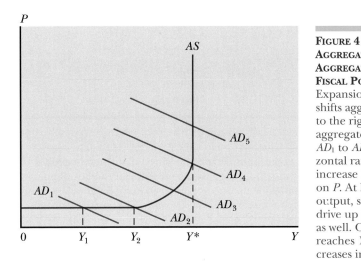

FIGURE 4
AGGREGATE DEMAND,
AGGREGATE SUPPLY, AND
FISCAL POLICY
Expansionary fiscal policy
shifts aggregate demand
to the right. A shift in
aggregate demand from
AD_1 to AD_2 in the horizontal range of AS will
increase Y with no effect
on P. At higher levels of
output, shifts in AD will
drive up the price level
as well. Once real output
reaches Y^*, further increases in AD will only
increase the price level.

omists believe the AS curve is vertical, they would not expect fiscal policy
to affect real output at all.[17]

For most of this chapter (except in discussing the Johnson surcharge),
we have concentrated on expansionary fiscal policy. Higher taxes, lower
transfers, or reduced government spending is contractionary fiscal policy.
Such policy is rarely undertaken, usually only in response to severe
inflation. Contractionary fiscal policy affects both real output and the
price level. Which of the two is affected more depends on the range of the
aggregate supply curve in which the economy is operating. Contractionary fiscal policy will have its main impact on the price level when equilibrium output exceeds Y^* on the AE diagram. This situation corresponds
to aggregate demand curves AD_4 and AD_5 in Figure 4.

Because fiscal policy shifts the aggregate demand as well as aggregate
expenditure, it is also known as demand management policy. However,
fiscal policy is not the only tool that can shift aggregate demand. Recall
from Chapter 6 that one of the factors held constant in drawing the AD
curve was the size of the money supply. Thus, changes in the money supply will also shift aggregate demand. After we have looked more closely at
debt and deficits in the next chapter, we will explore the effects of money
demand, money supply, and monetary policy on the level of output, employment, and prices.

17. Actually, classical economists considered fiscal policy ineffective, but new classical economists might expect some temporary effects if the policy was unexpected. We will explore this
view further in Chapter 15.

SUMMARY

1. Keynesian fiscal policy is based on three assumptions: (a) Equilibrium output may occur at high rates of unemployment or inflation. (b) Changes in private or foreign-sector spending may move the economy to an equilibrium that is not satisfactory. (c) Only the government can be counted on to change its spending and taxing to move the economy toward a more acceptable equilibrium.

2. A decline in aggregate expenditure that the private sector (households, firms, and foreigners) plans to make can create a recessionary gap. A recessionary gap occurs when aggregate expenditure is too low to purchase an economy's full-employment output.

3. Fiscal policy can be used to close a recessionary gap. Closing a recessionary gap requires increasing government spending, reducing taxes, or both.

4. Automatic stabilizers reduce fluctuations in economic activity without requiring legislation. Discretionary fiscal policy requires deliberate action by the executive branch or by Congress.

5. The Employment Act of 1946 makes the government responsible for achieving and maintaining full employment through the use of monetary and fiscal policy.

6. Major instances of discretionary fiscal policy were the Kennedy tax cut (1964), the Ford tax cut (1975), the Reagan tax rebate (1981–1983), and the Johnson tax surcharge (1968).

7. Advocates of active fiscal policy claim it allows the nation to reduce, if not totally avoid, the social costs of unemployment and inflation.

8. The permanent income hypothesis says that consumption is based on permanent income and income expectations, not just current income. By this hypothesis, the Keynesian expenditure multiplier is unstable and fiscal policy is less effective.

9. Public choice economists argue that active fiscal policy leads to inefficiency because it results in a larger public sector and creates an opportunity for political business cycles.

10. Discretionary fiscal policy is affected by lags in recognition, implementation, and impact.

NEW TERMS

fiscal policy	proportional tax	contractionary fiscal	public choice economics
recessionary gap	progressive tax	policy	recognition lag
expansionary fiscal	discretionary fiscal policy	Investment Tax Credit	implementation lag
policy	Employment Act of 1946	(ITC)	impact lag
automatic stabilizers	*Economic Report of the*	permanent income	political business cycle
regressive tax	*President*	hypothesis	

QUESTIONS FOR DISCUSSION

1. Do you think that economists who adhere to classical macroeconomic theory would recommend the use of fiscal policy to eliminate a recessionary gap? Why or why not?

2. Why did Keynes not expect the private sector to offer much help in stabilizing economic activity?

3. Suppose $MPC = 0.9$, $C_0 = \$300$ billion, and I, G, T, and $(EX-IM)$ are each equal to $\$100$ billion. What are the equilibrium values of Y, C, and S?

4. If G in Question 3 rises to $\$150$ billion, *ceteris paribus*, by how much will the equilibrium levels of Y, C, and S change? What would happen to the equilibrium levels of Y, C, and S if T were reduced by $\$50$ billion, *ceteris paribus*?

5. Use the information in Question 3, and suppose Y^* is $\$5,600$ billion. By how much would G have to change to bring the economy to full employment? By how much would T have to change?

6. If the United States changed its political system so that elections were held less often and called by the President at a time that he or she chose, how do you think macroeconomic policy would be affected?

7. Why are economists concerned about the lags associated with fiscal policy actions? What solutions can you suggest?

8. Using the latest issue of the *Economic Report of the President*, list the rates of unemployment, inflation, and real output growth since 1981, the year of the Reagan tax cut. What conclusions can you draw about possible effects of that tax cut as expansionary fiscal policy?

9. What are the costs and benefits of having a larger government sector and a smaller private sector?

10. According to the permanent income hypothesis, which of the following would have the greatest effect on your consumption? Why?

    a. a Christmas bonus

    b. a promotion

    c. a six-week layoff

    d. getting married to someone who is also employed

11. How does the permanent income hypothesis challenge the effectiveness of fiscal policy?

12. Why is fiscal policy less effective in an economy with a large foreign sector?

13. Why does a tax cut have less effect on the level of income and output than an equal change in government spending? What about a change in transfer payments?

14. Classify each of the following as a recognition, implementation, or impact lag.

    a. The numbers on GNP are slow in arriving from the Department of Commerce.

    b. Congress takes a recess to think things over.

    c. A new spending program has finally been put in place, and the dollars are starting to trickle through the economy.

15. How would you identify a political business cycle?

16. Under what conditions will expansionary fiscal policy be inflationary?

SUGGESTIONS FOR FURTHER READING

Blinder, Alan. *Hard Heads, Soft Hearts.* New York: Addison-Wesley, 1987. Blinder looks at fiscal policy from a perspective of efficiency (hard heads) and equity (soft hearts). Chapter 6 examines the 1986 tax reform.

Brookings Institution. *Economic Choices.* Washington, DC: Brookings Institution, annually. This annual review of public policy issues, especially fiscal policy, gives a different perspective from that of the administration, expressed in the *Economic Report of the President.*

Council of Economic Advisers. *The Economic Report of the President.* Washington, DC: U.S. Government Printing Office, annually. Gives a summary and explanation of fiscal actions on an annual basis.

Maynard, Geoffrey W. *The Economy under Mrs. Thatcher.* Oxford and New York: Basil Blackwell, 1988. Looks at fiscal policy in the 1980s in Britain.

Niskanen, William A. *Reaganomics: An Insider's Account of the Policies and the People.* London and New York: Oxford University Press, 1988. Another inside look at making policy in the 1980s written by a member of the Council of Economic Advisers.

Stein, Herbert. *Presidential Economics: The Making of Economic Policy From Roosevelt to Reagan and Beyond.* New York: Simon & Schuster, 1985. A well-written account of the ins and outs of fiscal policy in practice, with thorough coverage of its weaknesses and limitations, by an economist who was a Washington insider for several decades. More recently, Stein has also written *Governing the $5 Trillion Economy* (Oxford and New York: Oxford University Press, 1989).

Willett, Thomas D. *Political Business Cycles: The Political Economy of Money, Inflation, and Unemployment.* Durham, NC: Duke University Press, 1988. A good treatment of political business cycles and other macroeconomic issues from a public choice perspective.

1. Distinguish between a federal budget deficit and the national debt.
2. Discuss the links between fiscal policy and the national debt.
3. Explain why the national debt grew so rapidly during the 1980s.
4. Define:
    a. high-employment balanced budget,
    b. cyclically balanced budget,
    c. structural deficit,
    d. cyclical deficit.
5. Discuss the pros and cons of running deficits and a national debt.

INTRODUCTION

An economy with automatic stabilizers and some use of discretionary fiscal policy will have budget deficits at least part of the time. In the United States, federal budget deficits were one of the most pressing economic issues during the 1980s

CHAPTER 10

BUDGET DEFICITS AND THE NATIONAL DEBT

and will continue to be a concern throughout the 1990s. This chapter focuses on the deficit problem because it is central to current policy discussions.

DEBT AND DEFICITS

It is important to distinguish between national debt, which is a stock concept, and a budget deficit, which is a flow concept. A **deficit** is the amount by which the federal government's expenditures exceed its revenues in a given year (the fiscal year, which runs from October 1st to September 30th). The **national debt** is the cumulative total of all past budget deficits minus all past surpluses. It is the amount owed to lenders by the federal government.[1]

Deficits are nothing new. The United States began its history with a national debt. The Revolutionary War was financed by printing money—before there was a government with taxing power. One of the major problems facing the first Congress in 1789 was the retirement of $79 million in national debt, about two-thirds of it from the Revolutionary War. By the second term of President Andrew Jackson in the 1830s, the entire debt had been repaid.[2]

The U.S. government ran budget surpluses for much of the nineteenth century. However, both the Union and the Confederacy ran large deficits to finance the Civil War. Except for periods during the Civil War and World War I, federal budget deficits were quite small before the 1930s. In 1929, just before the Great Depression, the national debt stood at $16.9 billion, or about 16 percent of GNP. (Because economists expect debt to grow as the economy grows, they usually correct for overall growth

deficit
The amount by which the federal government's expenditures exceed its revenues in a given year (the fiscal year).

national debt
The total of all past budget deficits minus all past surpluses, or the net amount owed to lenders by the federal government.

---

1. Most of the debt is held by the public, but some of it is held by federal agencies and trust funds, including the Social Security Trust Fund.
2. For a good survey of the history of U.S. debt and deficits, see Benjamin Friedman, *Day of Reckoning* (New York: Random House, 1988), Chapter 5.

in both by comparing the debt to the size of the economy, measured by GNP.) By 1932, the federal budget had become unbalanced by a sharp drop in output, employment, and the price level. Both Herbert Hoover and Franklin Roosevelt ran for president in that year on a campaign promise to balance the budget.

By 1939, at the outbreak of World War II, the national debt had nearly tripled to $48.2 billion, or 55 percent of GNP. World War II brought a large increase in output but an even larger increase in government borrowing. At the end of the war, the national debt stood at $260.1 billion, or 122 percent of GNP. The debt was reduced slightly in the next few years. Then it began to grow very slowly, much more slowly than GNP. By 1970, the national debt had risen to $380.9 billion. Because GNP had also grown, the national debt was only 38 percent of GNP.

Rapid growth of the debt in the 1970s was matched by rapid growth of nominal GNP. However, these increases reflected inflation more than growth in real output. By 1980, the national debt stood at $908.5 billion, but had fallen in relation to GNP to 34 percent. The 1980s saw a rapid rise in both the national debt and GNP. Between 1980 and 1990, the size of the national debt tripled from less than $1 trillion to over $3 trillion. The estimated 1990 debt of $3,113 billion represents 57 percent of GNP. This figure is the highest since just after World War II. Table 1 shows the behavior of both budget deficits and the national debt over the last two decades. (A few earlier years are also included to provide a benchmark.) Figure 1 plots national debt relative to GNP for the entire post–World War II period.

The current figures for the national debt actually understate certain obligations of the government that could prove costly in the near future. The government has guaranteed not only the safety of deposits in federally insured banks but also mortgage loans, student loans, and other private sector borrowing that could represent serious future liability.

DOES KEYNESIAN FISCAL POLICY MEAN DEFICITS?

Critics of Keynesian fiscal policy claim that it is at least partly responsible for deficits in the federal budget and increases in the national debt. These economists might be less opposed to Keynesian fiscal policy if budget surpluses offset deficits over the long run. They point out that from 1950 through 1990, budget surpluses totaled less than $20 billion, and budget deficits totaled about $3,000 billion. During what might be considered the heyday of Keynesian policy, the period from 1960 to 1980, the national debt tripled from $290.5 billion to $908.5 billion. (During that period, however, debt as a share of GNP declined from 57 percent to 34 percent.)

In the 1930s, even before Keynes's *General Theory*, there was support for spending more on social projects during economic downturns and cutting back when the economy returned to full employment. However, it is politically very difficult to cut back spending or increase taxes during the expansionary phase of the business cycle. Thus, many economists fear that Keynesian policy provides a ready excuse for the long-run expansion of the relative size of the government sector.

Households and firms are limited in their ability to spend more than their income for any length of time because of the threat of bankruptcy.

YEAR	FEDERAL DEFICIT (BILLIONS OF DOLLARS)	NATIONAL DEBT (BILLIONS OF DOLLARS)	DEBT/GNP (%)
1945	− 47.6	260.1	122.5
1955	− 3.0	274.4	71.0
1965	− 1.4	322.3	47.9
1970	− 2.8	382.6	38.6
1971	− 23.0	409.5	38.8
1972	− 23.4	437.3	37.9
1973	− 14.9	468.4	36.5
1974	− 6.1	486.2	34.3
1975	− 53.2	544.1	35.7
1976	− 73.7	631.9	37.2
1977*	− 53.6	709.1	36.7
1978	− 59.2	780.4	35.9
1979	− 40.2	833.8	34.1
1980	− 73.8	914.3	34.2
1981	− 78.9	1,003.9	33.6
1982	−127.9	1,147.0	36.5
1983	−207.8	1,381.9	41.6
1984	−185.3	1,576.7	42.7
1985	−212.3	1,827.5	46.3
1986	−221.2	2,130.0	50.8
1987	−152.6	2,345.3	53.4
1988	−155.1	2,707.3	55.4
1989	−152.0	2,866.2	54.8
1990	−123.8	3,113.3	56.5

TABLE 1
NATIONAL DEBT AND
BUDGET DEFICITS FOR
THE UNITED STATES,
1945–1990

*The third quarter (July–September) of 1977 was a transition quarter, because the federal fiscal year was changed to start October 1 instead of July 1. The fiscal year for 1977 is July 1, 1976–June 30, 1977, and the fiscal year for 1978 is October 1, 1977–September 30, 1978.

Source: Council of Economic Advisers, *Economic Report of the President* (Washington, DC: U.S. Government Printing Office, 1991).

FIGURE 1
THE RATIO OF DEBT
TO GNP, 1945–1990
After falling from the
end of World War II
until 1981, the ratio of
the national debt to GNP
climbed steadily through
the 1980s.

Bankruptcy is a remote possibility for a central government. Sometimes local governments—cities, counties, school districts, and water systems—have been unable to pay their debts and filed for bankruptcy. The difference between a national government and a household, firm, or local government is the power to tax a broad range of persons in order to raise funds to pay off debts. For nations, any threat of bankruptcy comes from abroad. If a national government finances its spending through foreign loans, then it may be unable to come up with the "hard currency" (acceptable foreign currencies) to repay them. This kind of bankruptcy is not a serious concern for the United States at present, but is the heart of the Third World debt crisis (discussed in Chapter 17).

The deficits of the 1970s and 1980s are largely due to political decisions: the expansion of spending programs and several cuts in taxes. Once spending programs are created, they acquire clients and supporters. Thus, it is difficult to reduce or eliminate them. For example, it is difficult to close military bases because nearby towns will lose income and population. On the other hand, voting for higher taxes is politically unpopular. Recent budget deficits were caused not by discretionary fiscal policy but rather by problems in the budget process. The argument about how the government should spend its money—on welfare programs, national defense, or environmental and regulatory programs—often becomes confused with the debate over fiscal policy.

How Fiscal Policy Creates Budget Deficits

Fiscal policy works through changes in government spending or taxes, or both. In most cases, fiscal policy will change the balance of the federal budget, moving it toward deficit or surplus. If the government uses Keynesian fiscal policy to reduce or eliminate a recessionary gap, spending is increased or taxes are decreased. No matter which action is taken, spending will rise relative to taxes, increasing the budget deficit or reducing the surplus. Fiscal policy affects the national debt by changing the size of the budget deficit or surplus. A federal budget deficit increases the national debt, and a surplus reduces it.

Is fiscal policy responsible for the recent long series of federal budget deficits and the huge national debt? Not exactly. The deficits and the debt are mainly the result of political decisions to spend more than the government takes in. Only a small portion of the current national debt is due to deficits incurred as a result of deliberate fiscal policy actions. Furthermore, most Keynesians argue strongly that the benefits of active fiscal policy (increased employment and economic growth) more than offset the costs (budget deficits). The problem is that many politicians have used Keynesian arguments to avoid making difficult budget decisions. Keynes may have created a politically acceptable excuse for increasing spending without raising taxes.

THE GROWTH OF THE NATIONAL DEBT SINCE 1980

Between 1980 and 1990, budget deficits grew steadily in dollar terms, and the size of the national debt tripled. The most striking change, however, was in the ratio of debt to GNP, as shown in Figure 1. That ratio reached

Some journalists, as well as some economists, have used the phrase "twin deficits" to identify what they consider to be the most pressing macroeconomic problem in the United States. One of the twins is the federal budget deficit. The other is the trade deficit. The trade deficit is a deficit in the balance of trade or the current account. The balance of trade is the difference between exports and imports of goods. The current account includes the balance of trade as well as trade in services, interest and dividend payments, and a few other items. Both of these accounts are part of the balance of payments, which is discussed in detail in the chapter on international finance. By either measure, a trade deficit means that Americans bought more currently produced goods and services from foreigners than they sold to the rest of the world.

Both the balance of trade and the current account have been mostly in deficit since the early 1970s. The deficits were modest at first, and there were a few surplus years. The current account was in surplus in six of the eleven years from 1971 to 1981. The main reason for these surpluses was the fact that Americans received more interest and dividend payments from the rest of the world than U.S. firms and government paid to foreigners. The balance of trade took a big turn for the worse in the late 1970s, mostly due to higher prices for imported oil. From 1980 to 1985, the balance of trade deficit rose from $25 billion to $122 billion. The current account balance shifted from a modest $1.9 billion surplus in 1980 to a $115 billion deficit by 1985.

The deficit on the balance of trade affects output and employment, because it means that

INTERNATIONAL
PERSPECTIVE

THE OTHER
DEFICIT:
THE BALANCE
OF TRADE

net exports are negative. A negative value for net exports depresses output, employment, and the price level. Part of the reduction in inflation in the early 1980s is generally credited to falling exports and rising imports. Some of the blame for the high unemployment and slow economic growth in the same period fell on the foreign sector for the same reason—falling exports and rising imports. (You may want to check out this process with an aggregate supply and demand diagram.)

Are the two deficits related? Some economists argue that they are. If the budget deficit drives up interest rates, funds will be attracted from abroad to earn high interest. The inflow of funds will cause a demand for U.S. dollars to invest in the United States, driving up the price of the dollar. A high price for the dollar makes exports more expensive and imports cheaper. (We will explore this process in more detail in the international finance chapter.) Thus, interest rates provide a link between the budget deficit and the trade deficit.

As the budget deficit peaked and began to fall in the mid-1980s, real interest rates also began to decline. The price of the dollar fell, and the balance of trade began to improve, although slowly and erratically. By 1990, the balance of trade deficit was $94 billion, still high but smaller than the record $155 billion for 1987. If the budget deficit continues to fall during the 1990s and real interest rates decline as well, foreign investment in the United States should decline. The result will be a further decline in the value of the dollar, an expansion of exports, and a gradual reduction in the trade deficit.

a ten-year low in 1981 at 33.6 percent, only to shoot up to over 56 percent in 1990. The current intense concern about the deficits and debt is not based only on the fact that both are large and growing. More serious is the unpleasant reality that both have risen much more rapidly than total output over the last ten years.

Most of the growth in deficits in the 1980s was not based on Keynesian theory or justified as expansionary fiscal policy. There are various ideas as to exactly what Reagan's advisers had in mind in 1981 when they proposed a 30 percent reduction in personal income taxes and an even bigger cut in corporate profits taxes. (The actual cut was 25 percent.) Some supply siders argued that the increased incentives to work, save, and invest would actually result in increased revenues.[3] That did not occur. A second group (including David Stockman, Reagan's first director of the Office of Management and Budget) argued that the purpose of the tax cut was to cut off the revenue source that was feeding government spending. Lower revenues would force a reduction in spending and in the size of government. A third group claimed that the growth of the deficits was due not to the tax cut but to excessive spending, which they blamed on Congress.

Most observers attribute the deficits of the early 1980s to attempting the impossible—cutting taxes while increasing defense spending. (The latter grew from 5 to 6.5 percent of GNP between 1980 and 1983.) Even attempts to reduce nondefense spending could not bridge the gap. In addition, there were two other contributing factors. One was the recession of 1980–1982, and the other was high interest rates.

THE 1980–1982 RECESSION

The United States entered a recession in 1980, with a sharp drop in GNP during the second quarter. The economy then rebounded, only to see a second sharp decline in output and a rise in unemployment in 1982. Real output fell by 2.5 percent in 1982, and unemployment rose to 9.5 percent in 1982, remaining at that level during 1983. During the recession, the automatic stabilizers did their job. Tax revenues fell even further than they would have with the tax cut alone, and payments for food stamps and unemployment compensation rose. Temporarily, the deficit increased more than it would have under more normal conditions. However, cyclical increases in the deficit are normally corrected by an ensuing expansion. Thus, the recession can only absorb a small part of the blame for the high deficits.

HIGH INTEREST RATES

A second factor contributing to the deficit problem was the fact that both nominal interest rates and real interest rates (nominal rates corrected for inflation) remained high throughout the early 1980s.[4] From 1979 to 1983, the interest rate on a three-month Treasury bill (a very short-term, riskless investment) was over 10 percent. Although interest rates fell in the

---

3.   In *Day of Reckoning* (Chapter 10), Benjamin Friedman argues persuasively that the increases in work effort, saving, and so on would have to be much more massive than had ever been observed in order for this supply side idea to work.

4.   The relationship between nominal and real interest rates is discussed in Chapter 13.

latter part of the 1980s, the T-bill rate was still higher than it had been for most of the preceding three decades. Interest rates were slow to fall even in nominal terms. In real terms, they have remained high into the 1990s.

When the government borrows money, it must pay interest. Interest must be paid not only on new debt (the deficit) but on all outstanding debt as well (the national debt). In 1980, net interest payments amounted to 8.9 percent of total federal spending. By 1990, interest payments had risen to 14.7 percent of spending. A combination of a larger debt and high interest rates accounted for the increase in the interest payments from $53 billion in 1980 to $171 billion in 1990. This large annual commitment of funds makes it much harder for the President and Congress to cut spending.

GRAMM-RUDMAN-HOLLINGS AND A BALANCED BUDGET

The rapid growth of the national debt alarmed some politicians and created pressure for restricting Congress's unlimited ability to spend. After many years of proposing a balanced budget amendment to the Constitution, which would require a balanced budget on an annual basis, Congress took action by passing the Gramm-Rudman-Hollings Act in 1985. This act set a timetable for reducing the deficit from over $200 billion in 1986 to zero in 1990. Targets were set for each year. However, the President and Congress were required to meet the targets only in the projected budget (based on assumptions about economic conditions), not the actual budget. Failure to meet the targets (not to mention failure to enact a budget at all by October 1st, which often occurs) would automatically trigger painful across-the-board cuts in most federal spending programs.

Clearly, the zero-deficit goal for 1990 was not attained. The size of the deficits did decrease for several years but rose again in fiscal 1990. The deficit reduction plan was revised and extended first to 1993, then to 1996. Each fall still seems to bring a serious crisis as the threat of Gramm-Rudman-Hollings looms over the budget process. Some of the decline in the deficits from 1986 to 1989 was the result of spending cuts and gradual increases in tax revenues from economic growth. Part of the deficit reduction consisted of accounting tricks, sales of assets, and increased revenues in the Social Security Trust Fund. At the end of the 1980s, it seemed that there might be reduced defense spending, the so-called peace dividend, a result of changes in Eastern Europe. This reduced spending combined with rising tax revenues and holding the line on nondefense spending would gradually reduce the deficit. However, the 1990–1991 recession, the war in the Persian Gulf, and the huge cost of the savings and loan bailout sharply increased the 1990 and 1991 deficits and dimmed hopes for reducing deficits in the next few years. (The savings and loan crisis is discussed in a later chapter.)

Both the Gramm-Rudman-Hollings Act and a frequently proposed constitutional amendment requiring a balanced budget involve limits on the freedom of the President and Congress to spend. They also make it more difficult to pursue expansionary fiscal policy or to respond to other needs. Neither policy solves the basic dilemma of how to link the level of public spending to tax revenues while allowing for year-to-year changes based on the state of the economy and the needs of public policy.

SHOULD THE BUDGET BE BALANCED?

The debate over balancing the budget arises from the conflicting needs for appropriate fiscal policy and some degree of budgetary control. This debate is far from new. Before Keynes, the conventional wisdom called for an **annually balanced budget**. In this view, revenues should be equal to expenditures on an annual basis. An annually balanced budget would force Congress to collect taxes to pay for spending programs and thus restrict the growth of government. It would not allow the use of any kind of fiscal policy.

Keynesian economists suggested, instead, a **cyclically balanced budget**. In this case, surpluses during the expansion phase of the business cycle would offset deficits incurred in the recession phase. Over the course of the cycle, the budget would balance. The cyclically balanced budget was a nice idea in theory but hard to apply in practice. For example, a prolonged recession followed by a weak and brief expansion would generate a large deficit and then a small surplus.

Economists who raised such practical objections searched for other approaches to the problem of deficits. Some wanted to throw out the whole idea of balancing the budget and simply let a surplus or deficit emerge from the need to stabilize the economy. This idea was called **functional finance**. The problem with functional finance was that it ignored the issue of putting some limits on government spending.

THE HIGH-EMPLOYMENT BALANCED BUDGET

In the 1960s, a new idea about balancing the budget arose. The **high-employment balanced budget** incorporated the concern about balancing taxes and spending, the need for fiscal policy, and the newly recognized automatic stabilizers. In this view, the actual budget need not be balanced, but tax rates and transfer programs should be set so that the budget would be balanced at the full-employment level of output (Y^*). Those who developed this idea said that the actual deficit or surplus is not important. What is meaningful is what the surplus or deficit would be at the full-employment level of output. The adoption of a high-employment balanced budget as a policy goal was a major victory for Keynesian ideas.

The actual deficit is a poor measure for fiscal policy because it reflects not only decisions about taxing and spending but also the state of the economy. If output (Y) falls far below the full-employment level (Y^*), progressive income taxes and transfer programs will create a deficit as tax revenues fall and transfer payments rise. This deficit is acceptable from a Keynesian standpoint because it helps to stabilize the level of income and output. But if the economy were producing at Y^*, even with no action by Congress, there might not be a deficit. What policy makers need to look at is not the actual deficit but what the deficit would be at Y^*. Figure 2 shows the various levels of taxes (T) and spending (G) that a particular set of tax rates, transfer programs, and spending programs will generate at various national income (Y) levels. At an equilibrium level of income ($Y_e = \$2,500$), the deficit is $70 billion. If the economy were at full employment ($Y^* = \$3,500$), there would be a surplus of $25 billion.

The notion of a high-employment surplus gives policy makers both a

annually balanced budget
The view that government revenues should be equal to expenditures on an annual basis.

cyclically balanced budget
The idea that surpluses during expansionary periods should offset deficits during recessionary periods so that the budget balances over the course of the business cycle.

functional finance
The idea that a balanced budget is less important than a stable economy.

high-employment balanced budget
The view that tax rates and transfer payments should be set so as to balance the budget at the full-employment level of output Y^*. (The actual budget need not be balanced.)

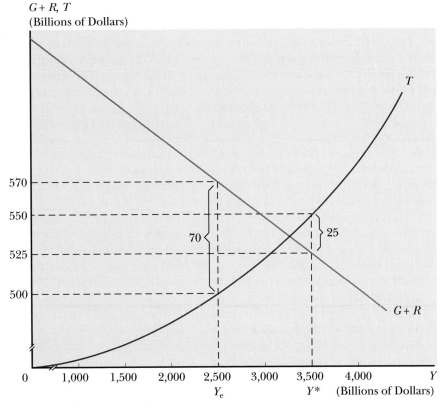

$G + R, T$
(Billions of Dollars)

Figure 2
**Balancing the Budget
at the Full-employment
Level**
The budget surplus or
deficit is equal to
government purchases
of goods and services (G)
plus transfer payments
(R) minus taxes (T).
When income rises,
transfers fall and taxes
rise. There is a surplus
of $25 billion at the full-
employment level of
income ($Y^* = \$3,500$
billion) but a deficit of
$70 billion at the current
equilibrium income
($Y_e = \$2,500$ billion).

goal to work toward and a measure of the direction of fiscal policy (whether it is contractionary or expansionary). Just because a deficit exists
doesn't necessarily mean that the government is pursuing an expansionary fiscal policy. The President and Congress may even be pursuing a contractionary policy. The deficit may simply be the result of automatic stabilizers and recessionary conditions. When economists want to measure
the direction of fiscal policy, they look at changes in the high-employment
budget surplus or deficit rather than the actual deficit.

The Structural Deficit and the Cyclical Deficit

Two new terms were created in the 1980s to distinguish between the part
of a deficit related to a downturn of the economy and the part of a deficit
that would persist at full employment. The **structural deficit** is the part
of a deficit that would persist even if the economy were at the full-
employment level. This term is closely related to the concept of a high-
employment balanced budget. However, the high-employment balanced
budget is regarded as a policy target, but the structural deficit has no such
normative meaning. The **cyclical deficit** is that part of a deficit that is due
to a downturn in economic activity.

Both these concepts take their meaning from the comparison of potential output to actual output. **Potential output** is another name for the
output the economy could produce if all its resources were fully employed. Potential output is thus a number or range of numbers that cor-

structural deficit
The part of a deficit that
would persist even if the
economy were at the full-
employment level of
output.

cyclical deficit
The part of a deficit
that is due to a downturn
in economic activity.

potential output
The output an economy
could produce if all of its
resources were fully
employed.

responds to the full-employment level of output (Y^*) from the aggregate supply and demand and Keynesian models. If the structural deficit is zero, then all of the budget deficit is due to the economy falling short of its potential. That is, there are many idle resources. With unemployment hovering around 5 percent at the beginning of the 1990s, however, the U.S. economy is quite close to full employment. Thus, most of the current deficit is structural rather than cyclical.

THE PROJECTED DEFICIT AND THE ACTUAL DEFICIT

One of the problems with taming the deficit is that its size is difficult to predict and control. The automatic stabilizers that appear to be so helpful in directing the economy toward a more stable path create problems in forecasting the deficit. When Congress enacts a budget, it does not legislate a level of revenue but rather a tax structure that will yield varying amounts of revenue under varying economic conditions. Similarly, entitlement programs such as Aid to Families with Dependent Children, food stamps, veterans' benefits, and Social Security are budgeted not as precise dollar sums but as estimates based on how many people will be eligible. If more people are eligible than estimated, the deficit will be larger than expected.

To make budget proposals look rosier, Congress or the President can make optimistic assumptions about the levels of output, employment, and prices. Both have been more inclined to make such assumptions under the pressures of the Gramm-Rudman-Hollings Act. If output grows rapidly and unemployment is low, then tax revenues will be higher and transfer programs will cost less. If inflation remains low, there will be less pressure to increase transfer payments or salaries for public employees. Inflation also affects the revenue side. With low inflation rates, taxpayers do not find themselves in higher tax brackets because of increased nominal income. For all these reasons, the budget surplus or deficit projected by both the Office of Management and Budget and the Congressional Budget Office is likely to be very different from the actual budget. Output, employment, and inflation rates often differ from what the budget makers assumed.

Another source of error in estimating the deficit is changes in interest rates. With interest payments on the national debt accounting for about 14 percent of federal spending, market interest rates have an important influence on the spending side of the budget. When the Treasury has to sell newly issued bonds, interest rates that are higher than expected will add to the deficit, and lower than expected rates will reduce it.

Long-range projections of the deficit are even more prone to error. They must anticipate changes in output, exchange rates, labor force participation, investment, productivity, and other determinants of government revenues and expenditures. Forecasts of declining deficits in the late 1980s did not anticipate how expensive it would be to bail out failed savings and loans, a major drain on the federal budget in recent years. By 1989, some economists were projecting that in the absence of a recession, the budget deficit would gradually decline if the President and Congress held firm on new spending programs while tax revenues continued to rise with economic growth. The combination of a recession and the unexpectedly large cost of the savings and loan bailout made their predictions far off the mark.

Political factors play a role in forecasts as well. For most of the 1980s, the executive branch (home of the Council of Economic Advisers) was under the control of one political party, while Congress (home of the Congressional Budget Office) had a majority from the other. The forecasts by the CEA were often more optimistic than those of the CBO. The CEA projected higher real growth and lower unemployment. However, a careful comparison to private forecasts shows that, while both the CEA's and the CBO's forecasts are prone to error, neither shows any permanent bias toward erring on the side of optimism or pessimism.[5]

Balancing fiscal policy with controlling the size of the public sector and limiting the size of the deficit is a tough political task. It is made much more difficult by the fact that the actual deficit is not known until after the fiscal year is over.

Obviously, there is a political incentive for the administration to use clever accounting to conceal or reduce the apparent size of the deficit. Presenting the actual deficit as well as the budget in such a way as to make the deficit look smaller is an old practice. Beginning in 1967, the Johnson administration changed the way the budget was presented to a unified format that included Social Security revenues and expenditures. This change was made at least partly to gloss over the deficit by making it appear smaller. When the President and Congress came up with the savings and loan bailout plan in 1989, they put large parts of it "off budget." That is, the bailout is being financed outside the regular budget and is thus not counted in the deficit. When the government sells assets, as it did often in the late 1980s in an effort to at least approach the Gramm-Rudman-Hollings targets for deficit reduction, the proceeds help to reduce the deficit, but only in the current year.

SOCIAL SECURITY AND THE DEFICIT

The federal budget deficits peaked in 1986, then declined steadily in nominal terms before rising again in 1990 and 1991. A large part of the improvement in 1986–1989 was due not to direct Congressional action or better economic conditions, but rather to reforms in the Social Security system, enacted in 1983. Noting that there would have to be increased outlays in the period after the year 2000, as the baby boomers began to reach retirement age, a special presidential commission proposed increasing Social Security taxes to build up a surplus in the Social Security Trust Fund. Since Social Security taxes are collected and benefits are paid out by the federal government, the taxes appear as revenue and the benefits as expenditures in the combined federal budget. Technically, Social Security funds are separate, but the number reported as the overall budget deficit or surplus has included them since 1967.

When the Social Security Trust Fund runs a surplus, those funds are invested in federal government bonds until they are needed to pay benefits. What will happen when the baby boomers start to retire? In theory, other taxes will be increased or other spending decreased in order to provide the revenue to retire those bonds and pay the benefits. In other

5.   Michael T. Belongia, "Are Economic Forecasts by Government Agencies Biased? Accurate?" *Review of the Federal Reserve Bank of St. Louis* (November/December 1988): 15–23.

TABLE 2
FEDERAL REVENUES,
EXPENDITURES, AND
DEFICITS WITH AND
WITHOUT SOCIAL
SECURITY FOR FISCAL
YEARS 1980–1990
(BILLIONS OF DOLLARS)

YEAR	FEDERAL REVENUES		FEDERAL EXPENDITURES		FEDERAL DEFICIT	
	WITH SS	WITHOUT SS	WITH SS	WITHOUT SS	WITH SS	WITHOUT SS
1980	$ 517.1	359.3	$ 590.9	$240.8	$ 73.8	$118.5
1981	599.3	416.6	678.2	538.6	78.9	112.0
1982	617.8	416.3	745.7	589.7	127.9	173.4
1983	600.6	391.6	808.3	637.6	207.8	246.0
1984	666.5	427.1	851.8	673.6	185.3	246.5
1985	734.1	547.9	946.3	757.7	212.3	209.8
1986	769.1	485.2	990.3	791.5	221.2	306.3
1987	854.1	550.8	1,003.8	796.4	149.7	246.4
1988	909.0	574.7	1,064.1	844.7	155.1	270.0
1989	990.7	727.0	1,144.1	915.1	151.9	188.1
1990	1,031.3	749.7	1,251.7	969.7	123.7*	181.6*

*Estimated.

Source: Council of Economic Advisers, *Economic Report of the President* (Washington, DC: U.S. Government Printing Office, 1991), pp. 398–399.

words, Social Security revenues are being used to finance a part of the regular budget deficit. There will have to be future budget surpluses to repay the "loan" from the Social Security Trust Fund.

There are other special funds and off-budget categories, but Social Security is by far the largest. Table 2 shows federal revenues, expenditures, and deficits with and without Social Security, from 1980 to 1990. As you can see, much of the recent apparent reduction in the deficit is due to increased net revenues in the Social Security system. Social Security revenues have been increasing more rapidly than other federal revenues, while Social Security expenditures have risen more slowly.[6]

The Social Security Trust Fund represents a real policy challenge. It is projected to rise by a large amount in the next thirty years, then drop sharply until about 2050. One option for public policy is to ignore these changes and balance the rest of the budget (which would make the budget deflationary for the next thirty years). Another option, more or less the one that has been pursued for the last twenty-five years, is to treat the federal budget as a single entity. Thus, current Social Security revenues offset deficits in the rest of the budget. In terms of the current impact of federal spending and taxing on the economy, this approach makes a great deal of sense. But unlike other revenues, Social Security revenues carry a deferred commitment to pay benefits. Paying those benefits (by repaying the Trust Fund) will require higher taxes or less spending for other purposes in the future.

In the 1990 *Economic Report of the President*, the Bush administration put forth a proposal addressing the relation of Social Security to budget deficits. This proposal called for continued reduction in the deficit for the

6.   The use of Social Security revenues to reduce the deficit has received a lot of attention in the last few years. For example, in 1990 Senator Daniel Moynihan proposed reducing the Social Security payroll tax and addressing the deficit in other ways. For two views on this issue, see Lee Smith, "Trim That Social Security Surplus," *Fortune* (August 29, 1988): 84–89; and Alan S. Blinder, "Congress Should Keep Its Hands off This Nest Egg," *Business Week* (July 4, 1988): 20.

combined budget, with a goal of zero deficit by 1994. After that, further deficit reductions would be pursued until the regular budget was in balance. Then there would be a net surplus for the combined budget, reflecting the surplus in the Social Security Trust Fund.

DO DEFICITS MATTER?

The major advantage of being able to run deficits is that they make it possible to use fiscal policy in order to stabilize the level of output and unemployment. However, there are costs associated with running deficits. A number of problems have been attributed to deficits and the growing national debt. Are deficits a problem? Economists differ on this question.

YES: THE GROWTH OF THE PUBLIC SECTOR

When deficits are not controlled, there is no constraint on the size of the public sector. If the government had to finance all its spending out of tax revenues, it would have to weigh the pleasure citizens derive from spending programs against their pain in paying taxes. The necessity to tax would be a constraint on spending. With deficits, legislators can adopt a "spend now, pay later" approach. And "later" is likely to be after they have left office. When the cost of spending programs is not immediately apparent as higher taxes, both legislators and citizens may underestimate the cost of government programs. The expansion of government programs may then take too large a share of total resources. Being able to spend without taxing, at least in the short run, means that added spending has zero opportunity cost for politicians.

YES: HIGHER INTEREST RATES AND INTEREST PAYMENTS

When the government runs a deficit, it borrows by issuing bonds, just as corporations do. In selling bonds, the government competes for funds in the credit market, driving up interest rates for all borrowers. The real interest rate measures the actual cost of repaying a loan in dollars at the time the loan is repaid. The real interest rate is the market interest rate minus the expected rate of inflation. Through the 1980s, this rate remained high relative to the past.

The large deficits of recent years have made many economists concerned that competition from the federal government in the credit market and the resulting high interest rates have discouraged borrowing for private investment. This effect is known as **crowding out**. In fact, the high interest rates have attracted foreign funds to the United States, which have limited the crowding out of private investment.

crowding out
The negative effect on borrowing for private investment due to competition from the federal government in the credit market.

The high interest rates, especially in the early 1980s, also increased the fraction of federal spending going to interest payments on the national debt from 8.9 percent in 1980 to 14.7 percent in 1990. With more and more funds diverted to interest payments, Congress has less choice about the use of funds or about budget cutting. Cutting the size of the deficit in any given year has almost no impact on the interest liability. Only surpluses that actually reduce the debt and/or lower interest rates would reduce this large piece of the budget.

A group of U.S. economists told a Joint Economic Committee hearing in 1989 that the budget deficit was causing a reduction in public investment in two areas critical to the nation's future. Those two areas are physical infrastructure and children. They named this failure to invest the "third deficit."

During the 1980s, budget makers had to hold the line on nondefense spending because of a political commitment to higher defense spending without any increase in taxes. As a result, funding for existing nondefense programs was scarce, and that for new programs almost nonexistent. This failure to spend in certain key areas may have a long-term impact on productivity and economic growth, according to these economists. One group of neglected expenditures, in their view, includes spending for highways, bridges, mass transit, airports, water supply, and waste disposal. All of these things are highly important to industry as well as to households. The other area of concern of these economists is investment in education for low-income children and youth. Not enough is being done in teaching basic skills, dropout prevention, and job training.[a]

Total government spending grew by 79 per-

ECONOMIC
INSIGHT

THE THIRD
DEFICIT?

cent (not adjusted for inflation) between 1981 and 1990. The areas identified by the concerned economists grew much more slowly. Their first area of concern fits into the budget category of transportation and community and regional development. Their second concern matches with the budget heading of education, training, employment, and social services. Spending in these categories grew by only 11 percent between 1981 and 1990. Such a small nominal increase translates into a large decrease after correcting for inflation. These two categories now constitute a much smaller share of the budget.

The debate on the "third deficit" highlights the fact that the budget is an expression of priorities and values as well as a fiscal policy tool. In the 1980s, there appeared to be a strong consensus for lower taxes and more defense spending. These choices were combined with increasing interest payments on the national debt, growth in a few transfer programs, and a growing determination to contain the size of the deficit. Cuts had to come somewhere. Some of the tradeoff has clearly come out of the kinds of nondefense spending that this group of economists has identified.

a. This argument, put forth by a group of economists at the Economic Policy Institute, was summarized in "Pay Now or Pay Later," *Washington Post National Weekly Edition* (July 31–August 6, 1989): 5.

Maybe: A Burden on Our Grandchildren?

The burden of the debt usually means the problems that will arise when it is repaid. President Eisenhower was the first to worry publicly about passing a burden of debt to our grandchildren. Often the size of the national debt is given per person. People who worry about the burden of the debt on the next generation point out that every child born today assumes a national debt burden of more than $11,000.[7]

How valid is this concern? Does a free-spending generation pass on a heavy burden to the next? Not necessarily. Basically, the burden of the national debt falls on the generation in which the debt is incurred. These people are the ones who give up consumption in order to make resources available for government spending. Deficit financing of government spending, just like taxation, takes resources away from the private sector and transfers them to the government. The loss of current consumption is borne by the generation that lent to the government, not their grandchildren. During World War II, the government ran large deficits to finance the war effort. The cost was borne by those who were working, paying taxes, and buying war bonds between 1941 and 1945. They paid by consuming fewer goods and services, because the output mix was skewed toward military production.

Sometimes the national debt is incurred in ways that benefit the next generation. Fighting World War II created benefits for the next generation in terms of the kind of world they inherited. If the government had not borrowed money to fight the war, you might have been born into a totalitarian society. Future generations may benefit from debt incurred through expansionary fiscal policy. If the government borrows to expand the productive capacity of the economy and put idle resources to work, then future generations will inherit a larger capital stock and enjoy a higher output. They will benefit from the borrowing and spending activity that created the debt. When the time comes to repay the debt, it can be repaid more easily out of the higher national income that will result from the productive use of borrowed funds in an earlier time.

Running deficits can create some future problems, however. If funds are borrowed by the government during a period when the economy is close to full employment, such as the last half of the 1980s, then resources may have been diverted away from productive investment. As the government drove up interest rates in the credit market, some private borrowers who wanted funds to build housing, factories, and shopping centers were priced out of the credit market. (We will look more closely at the relationship between deficits, interest rates, and private investment in Chapter 13.) Thus, future generations may be worse off as a result of current borrowing, because of the productive capital that was not created during this period.

When and if the government repays part of the debt, some citizens will be taxed to repay the maturing bonds owned by others. If most bond holders are rich, repaying the debt will mean some redistribution of income from the poor to the rich. In addition, if the government must cut spending programs in order to use tax revenues to repay the debt, the people

---

7.   To be accurate, that burden should be adjusted for inflation, so that it is expressed in terms of constant purchasing power.

THE COSTS OF THE NATIONAL DEBT

- The private sector output given up at the time the debt was incurred
- Lack of constraint on the growth of the public sector
- Higher interest rates that discourage private investment and reduce the future capital stock
- Future repayment of debt held by foreigners
- Income redistribution when the debt is repaid

who would benefit from those spending programs will essentially be "taxed" to pay back the debt.

Finally, Americans no longer simply owe the debt to themselves. High interest rates in the United States during most of the 1980s attracted foreign lenders. Many of them bought U.S. government bonds. About 20 percent of the national debt owed to individuals is owed to foreigners, mostly Japanese. Currently, about $30 billion in interest payments on the national debt is sent abroad. When those bonds are redeemed, the United States will have to transfer real goods and services away from domestic uses in order to pay back the bond holders.[8] Repaying the debt to foreigners is a burden that will fall on future generations.

No: Ricardian Equivalence

Economist Robert Barro has argued that the choice of deficit spending versus tax financing doesn't matter.[9] According to Barro, rational consumers will recognize that debt financing simply means higher future taxes to pay off the debt. Thus, any increase in their current spending because of higher disposable income would be offset by a reduction in current spending because of anticipated lower future disposable income. That is, they will consume less and save more because of anticipated higher future taxes. This concept is called Ricardian equivalence.

Few economists accept Barro's argument that the impact of tax and debt financing is exactly the same, and there has been little real-world evidence to support the theory. However, Barro does offer a useful insight: The difference in impact between different methods of government financing may be smaller than expected.

No: The Real Deficit Argument

Another argument that minimizes the importance of deficits is the real deficit argument. Some economists, most notably Robert Eisner, claim that the deficit that matters is not the nominal deficit but the real deficit.[10]

---

8. In addition, if a lot of foreign-held debt is redeemed at once, the loss of foreign funds could create a shortage of loanable funds in credit markets and drive up interest rates for domestic borrowers of all kinds, including the government.

9. Robert Barro, "Are Government Bonds Net Wealth?" *Journal of Political Economy* (December 1974): 1094–1118; "The Ricardian Approach to Budget Deficits," *Journal of Economic Perspectives* (Spring 1989): 37–54.

10. Robert Eisner, "Budget Deficits: Rhetoric and Reality," *Journal of Economic Perspectives* (Spring 1989): 73–93. Eisner also suggests a number of other adjustments to the deficit, such as separating out investment-type expenditures and not counting sales of government assets.

The **real deficit** measures the federal budget deficit as the change in the real (inflation-adjusted) value of the national debt from one year to the next. During a period of inflation, the real value of the debt falls. Thus, a budget deficit during an inflationary period could occur at the same time as a fall in the real value of the national debt. If the deficit is measured as the change in that real value, what was a deficit by usual measures might turn out to be a surplus!

This may sound like lying with statistics. We can make the argument more concrete with some numbers. Suppose the national debt at the beginning of a year is $200 billion, and the current-year deficit is $10 billion. Prices rise by 10 percent. At the end of the year, the $210 billion in debt (including $10 billion in new debt from the current deficit) is worth, in real terms, only $210 billion/1.10 = $190.9 billion. The deficit of $10 billion disappears when it is measured in real terms. By such a measure, the deficit should be equal to the change in the value of the outstanding debt. That adjustment turns a $10 billion deficit into a surplus of $9.1 billion!

The deficits of the 1980s do look a little less frightening when measured either in real terms or as a fraction of GNP. The sleight-of-hand trick in the preceding paragraph cannot convert the deficits of the 1980s into surpluses, but it does bring them down to less alarming levels. Table 3 shows what happens to the nominal deficit and the change in national debt when they are measured as the real deficit and as a fraction of GNP.

The data in Table 3 don't change the fact that the deficit grew in the 1980s—in nominal terms, in real terms, and as a percentage of GNP. Furthermore, however the debt and deficits are measured, the basic problem remains. The ability to run unlimited deficits frees politicians from the need to raise the money in taxes for programs they want to fund. That political reality has contributed to the growth of government beyond what

real deficit
A measure of the federal budget deficit as the change in the real (inflation-adjusted) value of the national debt from one year to the next.

TABLE 3
NOMINAL DEFICIT AND REAL DEFICIT FOR THE FISCAL YEARS 1980–1990

YEAR	NOMINAL DEFICIT (BILLIONS OF DOLLARS)	CHANGE IN NATIONAL DEBT* (BILLIONS OF DOLLARS)	REAL DEFICIT† (BILLIONS OF DOLLARS)	NOMINAL DEFICIT/GNP (%)
1980	73.8	69.5	81.6	2.7
1981	78.9	75.5	84.4	2.6
1982	127.9	134.4	135.0	4.0
1983	207.8	211.8	204.4	6.1
1984	185.3	169.0	158.3	4.9
1985	212.3	199.4	177.0	5.3
1986	221.2	236.8	206.3	5.2
1987	150.4	151.9	128.1	3.4
1988	155.1	161.9	133.5	3.0
1989	152.0	139.1	110.1	2.9
1990	220.4	220.1	162.6	2.3

*Increase in the debt from the end of the previous year to the end of the current year, held by the public. Social Security revenues are subtracted from the revenue side, and that part of the debt held by the Social Security Trust Fund is not counted as part of the total national debt.

†Change in the national debt divided by the GNP deflator (equal to 100 in 1982).

Source: Council of Economic Advisers, *Economic Report of the President* (Washington, DC: U.S. Government Printing Office, 1991).

taxpayers might choose if they were paying the bill directly. In that sense, deficits are still a matter for concern.

No: The State and Local Surplus

The total impact of government taxes and spending on output involves the combined actions of all governments—federal, state, and local. Local governments usually come quite close to balancing their budgets. State governments rather consistently ran surpluses throughout the 1980s. From 1980 to 1990, these surpluses totaled $511.0 billion, or about 52 percent of the federal deficits during that period.

To some extent this argument mixes apples and oranges. State governments are quite different from the federal government. For one thing, states are much more limited in their ability to run long-term deficits. Many of them are constrained by their constitutions. Even those that do not have balanced budget requirements find their bonds harder to sell if they keep running deficits. Even if states could run deficits for long periods, there is no way to integrate those deficits into fiscal policy. Congress can influence state and local spending through changes in federal grants but cannot exercise any direct control over state and local budgets. As a tool of fiscal policy, only the federal budget is under the control of the policy makers.

Furthermore, the states' surpluses appear to have been temporary. A large part of them was due to retirement contributions. As state employees begin to retire in larger numbers in future years, those surpluses will shrink. Declining federal defense spending has hit certain states hard. Falling incomes and declining property values in some states have turned budget surpluses into deficits and forced tax increases. In most states, there are increased pressures to build prisons, combat homelessness, take care of Medicaid patients, and replace parts of the infrastructure (especially roads and schools). These demands on the states, which have been receiving smaller and smaller amounts of federal aid, mean that their surpluses are projected to be smaller in the 1990s. State and local budget surpluses may help to mitigate federal deficits, but they seem likely to be of less help in the near future than they were in the last decade.

Summary

1. The United States has run large budget deficits for the last decade. As a result, there has been a large increase in the national debt, both in nominal terms and relative to GNP.

2. Fiscal policy can lead to a larger national debt if deficits exceed surpluses. Most deficits are at least partly due to politicians' reluctance to raise taxes or cut spending.

3. The growth of the national debt in the early 1980s was the result of the 1981 tax cut, increased defense spending, the 1981–1982 recession, and high interest rates.

4. The Gramm-Rudman-Hollings Act of 1985 represented an attempt to force Congress and the President to reduce the deficit by targeted amounts over a period of several years.

5. Differing ideas about when or whether to balance the federal budget include the annually balanced budget, functional finance, the cyclically balanced budget, and the high-employment balanced budget. A surplus or deficit for the high-employment balanced budget is used as a measure of the direction of fiscal policy.

6. The cyclical deficit is that part of the deficit resulting from a gap between actual and potential output. The structural deficit is the deficit that would still persist even if the economy were at the full-employment level of output.

7. The actual deficit is difficult to control because it depends on economic conditions. In forecasting the expected deficit, politicians may use optimistic assumptions to make it look smaller.

8. Increased Social Security revenues with only modest increases in benefit payments offset part of the federal budget deficits in the 1980s. Such revenues bring with them the obligation to pay benefits in the future.

9. Deficits are a matter of concern because they may increase the size of government, drive up interest rates, and impose a burden on future generations because of lost productive investment and higher debt to foreigners.

10. One argument that deficits do not matter is based on the idea of Ricardian equivalence—that people will save more in anticipation of higher future taxes. Another argument stresses the real deficit, or changes in the inflation-adjusted value of the debt. State and local surpluses also partly offset the federal deficit.

NEW TERMS

deficit
national debt
annually balanced
   budget
cyclically balanced
   budget
functional finance

high-employment
   balanced budget
structural deficit
cyclical deficit
potential output
crowding out
real deficit

QUESTIONS FOR DISCUSSION

1. What is the real deficit? What are the risks of using this measure instead of the nominal deficit?

2. Suppose the consumption function is $C = \$300$ billion $+ 0.9Y_d$ and the values of I, G, and $(EX - IM)$ are each $\$100$ billion. Taxes (T) and transfer payments (R) are dependent on the level of income according to $T = -\$40$ billion $+ 0.15Y$ and $R = \$500$ billion $- 0.1Y$. Since you know that $Y_d = Y - T + R$, the new consumption function is $C = \$300 + 0.9(Y + \$40 - 0.15Y + \$500 - 0.1Y)$, where all figures are in billions. Use this relationship to determine the equilibrium value of Y. What is the actual surplus or deficit in the government budget? If $Y^* = \$4,000$ billion, what is the high-employment surplus or deficit? Does this indicate that fiscal policy is expansionary or contractionary?

3. Given the following relationships, develop a table that shows the surplus or deficit in the government budget at Y values (in billions) of $\$500$, $\$1,000$, and $\$1,500$. At what level of Y will the government's budget balance?

$G = \$150$
$T = -\$25 + 0.2Y$
$R = \$125 - 0.1Y$

4. Does Keynesian fiscal policy necessarily mean deficits?

5. Will the federal borrowing in the 1980s impose a burden on future generations? Why or why not? How is it different from federal borrowing during the 1930s?

6. What would happen to the real deficit if there was high inflation but no change in the nominal deficit?

7. Suppose businesses in the United States adopt early retirement plans on a large scale. As a result, a much higher proportion of workers decide to retire at sixty-two (when they are first eligible for Social Security benefits) rather than at sixty-five. What would happen to the federal budget deficit?

8. Why does the actual deficit almost always turn out to be very different from the projected deficit?

9. What is a structural deficit? A cyclical deficit? Which is of greater concern?

10. Why is the high-employment surplus or deficit rather than the actual surplus or deficit used to determine the direction of fiscal policy?

11. Why do some politicians advocate an annually balanced budget? What problems would this policy create?

12. Why do some economists say the budget deficit should be measured as the combined federal, state, and local deficit? What problems would this create?

13. Which measure of the deficit would you use for each of the following purposes?
   a.   determining the direction of fiscal policy
   b.   measuring the inflation-adjusted deficit
   c.   estimating the deficit that would persist even at full employment
   d.   determining the part of the deficit due to unfavorable economic conditions

SUGGESTIONS FOR FURTHER READING

Aaron, Henry J., Barry P. Bosworth, and Gary Burtless. *Can America Afford to Grow Old?* Washington, DC: Brookings Institution, 1989. A close look at the demographics, economics, and politics of the Social Security system.

Blinder, Alan. *Soft Heads, Hard Hearts.* New York: Addison-Wesley, 1987. This readable book by a well-known contemporary economist takes a critical look at budget deficits and other current issues, such as trade policy and welfare, from a moderately liberal perspective.

Friedman, Benjamin. *Day of Reckoning.* New York: Random House, 1988. A critical look at U.S. policies in the 1980s that led to the increase in federal budget deficits and an outline of policies to address those concerns in the 1990s.

Savage, James D. *Balanced Budget and American Politics.* Ithaca, NY: Cornell University Press, 1988. A historical and political look at the controversy over balancing the federal budget.

MONEY, FINANCIAL MARKETS, AND MONETARY POLICY

4

1. Explain why money replaces barter as a society becomes more complex and specialized.
2. List the four functions of money and briefly discuss the meaning of each one.
3. Identify the desirable properties of money.
4. List and explain the motives for holding money.
5. Define each of the following kinds of monetary assets:
   a. bank notes,
   b. greenbacks,
   c. commodity money,
   d. full-bodied money,
   e. fiat money,
   f. certificates of deposit,
   g. checkable deposits,
   h. time deposits,
   i. near money.
6. Explain the differences between M1, M2, and M3.
7. Describe the relationship between changes in the money supply and aggregate demand.

CHAPTER 11

MONEY: WHAT IT IS AND WHY PEOPLE HOLD IT

INTRODUCTION

Consumption, investment, government spending, and net exports—the key variables in the last three chapters—are the real flows of goods and services in the circular flow diagram. However, the circular flow diagram also shows flows of money payments and even a credit market. Starting in this chapter, we will expand this model to include money, financial instruments, banks, and financial markets.

The word *money* means different things to different people. The variety of meanings often leads to misunderstandings between economists and noneconomists. Here are some ways in which economists *don't* use the word money:

1. How much money (income) did you earn last year?
2. Most of his money (wealth) is tied up in bonds.
3. It's almost impossible to get mortgage money (credit) in today's market.
4. This country does not have enough money (resources) to increase both military and social spending.

When economists use the word *money*, they usually mean items (cash and checking account balances) that are generally accepted as a means of payment. For example, "if I didn't keep some money on hand, I'd have to use my credit card every time I wanted to buy a candy bar."[1]

Money is not income, wealth, credit, or productive resources, although it is sometimes confused with each of those. This chapter discusses what money is, how it has evolved, and what the U.S. money supply consists of

1. Adapted from Ira Kaminow, "The Myth of Fiscal Policy: The Monetarist View," *Business Review,* Federal Reserve Bank of Philadelphia (December 1969).

in the 1990s. We will also look at what money does and how people decide how much money to hold.

Recall from Chapter 6 that we assumed a given money supply in drawing the aggregate demand curve and identified changes in the money supply as one of the factors that can shift that curve. Changes in the money supply were used to explain changes in the price level in the classical model in Chapter 7. The last three chapters, however, have put money on hold while developing the Keynesian explanation of how the levels of output and employment are determined. The simple Keynesian model assumes a fixed price level and a large quantity of idle resources. We will develop a more general model that applies when the economy is at or near full employment and the price level can rise. In such a model, changes in the supply and demand for money, as well as changes in consumption or investment demand or fiscal policy, can shift the aggregate expenditure and aggregate demand curves.

WHAT IS MONEY?

It is difficult to define money without knowing what it does. Let's start with a working definition: Money is something that people accept as payment for a good or service. (Later, after looking at the properties of money, the functions of money, and the reasons for holding money, we will be able to give a more precise definition.) This working definition draws attention to a basic requirement for anything that serves as money. It must be generally acceptable to those who are exchanging goods and services in markets.

If you go into a store and buy some socks or rent a video, chances are you pay with dollar bills, or Federal Reserve notes. Paper money has been used in the United States for nearly 300 years, since colonial times. The paper by itself is worth only a few cents, but you know you can exchange the bills for goods and services in stores, restaurants, and theaters. Other people are willing to accept these pieces of paper in trade for goods and services because they know they can, in turn, spend the money and pass it on to someone else. If you believed that no one would take the money, you wouldn't be interested in having it. If everyone thought the money was worthless, no one would take it. Then it really would be worthless because it couldn't be used to buy anything. Money has value because it is accepted as the means of exchange.

BARTER AND THE INVENTION OF MONEY

Your professors make a living by providing you with high-quality teaching services. They teach, not out of altruism, but because they want to get things in return, such as housing, food, books, and vacations. Professors, like other workers, sell their services in the resource market in order to make purchases in the goods market. And professors, like most people in modern industrial economies, specialize in producing just one or a few goods or services but want to purchase many different ones.

In societies that have only a few goods, trade can be carried out fairly easily. Certain tribes of pygmy hunters in Zaire trade ivory from their elephant hunts for the metal they need to make arrows and spears. They also trade for a few agricultural goods. Because most of their trade is in metal and tusks, prices are measured not in money but in terms such as arrow tips per tusk. Money is not needed here because few goods are traded. People can easily arrange to trade what they have for what they want. This type of direct trade of goods and services is called **barter**.

barter
Direct exchange of one good or service for another without the use of money.

Consider a barter economy in which a potter wants to buy a pizza. Such trades require a **double coincidence of wants**. That is, each trader must find a trading partner who wants what he or she offers and offers what he or she wants. If the potter goes to the market and the pizza maker wishes to exchange a pizza for a ceramic bowl, all is well. But what if the pizza maker isn't interested in pottery and wants a shirt instead? The potter then has to find someone who wants to trade a shirt for a bowl before going to trade with the pizza maker. In addition, a pizza or a shirt may not be equal in value to a bowl, raising the problem of making change. Barter is costly in terms of the time and effort required to find a trading partner.

double coincidence of wants
The necessary requirement for barter that each trader has what the other wants and wants what the other has.

A large or highly specialized economy cannot function by barter. A better system eliminates the need for the double coincidence of wants by finding one commodity that everyone will accept in trade. The most common solution to the problems of barter is to use money. This solution is extremely efficient because using money saves on the search and transactions costs that are involved in bartering. Although money has other uses, carrying out transactions is its most important role.

Even in modern industrial economies, people still engage in barter. Newspapers sometimes report creative barter transactions made to avoid taxes. Barter is common among friends and neighbors. Lawn mowing is traded for babysitting or the use of tools for some help with a fix-up project. Doctors have been known to perform operations in exchange for a two-week vacation at a beachfront condominium. Most transactions in the United States and other developed countries, however, are made with money rather than by barter.

THE FUNCTIONS OF MONEY

medium of exchange
A function of money in simplifying transactions by allowing people to exchange the goods and services they produce for money and then exchange money for other goods and services they want.

Because barter can be inconvenient, money developed as a means for trading in goods and services. That is, money serves as a **medium of exchange**. As a medium of exchange, money simplifies transactions by allowing people to exchange the goods and services they produce for money and then exchange money for other goods and services they want. People receive their wages in the form of money and use it to buy clothes, food, housing and other items. In the jargon of economics, money reduces transactions costs. This function is so important that it is the first part of our definition of money: In order for something to be money, it must be used to carry out transactions.

unit of account
A function of money in providing a measuring unit in terms of which goods can be valued and thus readily compared with each other.

A second function of money is to serve as a **unit of account**, a way to compare the costs, values, or prices of various goods.[2] In this sense, money is the equivalent of such measures as lengths or weights. If people did not

2.   Because money does so many things, it's difficult to separate its function as the medium of exchange from that as a unit of account. It might help to think in terms of the bit, which is a rare example of a unit of account that is not also a medium of exchange (a coin or bill in circulation). Two bits equal 25 cents. The Spanish dollar used in the New World for some time consisted of pieces of eight. Each eighth of such a dollar was a bit.

have prices and money as a way of making comparisons, they would have to keep track of the value of each good in terms of all other goods. The price of an apple might be $\frac{2}{3}$ of an orange, or $\frac{1}{500}$ of a pair of shoes. In fact, in a barter economy that had only 100 goods, there would be 4,950 prices without money. (Imagine being an accountant in a barter economy!) Having money to serve as a unit of account reduces those 4,950 prices to 100 prices.[3]

The third function of money is to serve as a **standard of deferred payment**, allowing people to make contracts that extend into the future. As a standard of deferred payment, money gives borrowers and lenders a medium in which to express the repayment of debt in the future. If you work for someone today, you may be paid two weeks later. If you charge something on your credit card, you are agreeing to make a future payment. (If you don't know that, read the fine print on the back of the card!) In this way, money allows an economic link to the past and the future. It is easier to specify a repayment in terms of money than as a list of a number of goods and services.

The fourth and final function of money is to serve as a **store of value**, or financial asset. As a store of value, money provides a general form of purchasing power that can be held in order to buy goods and services in the future. A decision to store your wealth as automobiles works well only if you happen to need a car in the future or can easily and quickly find a car buyer when you need cash. Not knowing what their future needs will be, people usually want to store some wealth in a form that can serve as a medium of exchange. Then they will be able to easily convert their wealth into goods and services. The ease with which an asset can be converted into the medium of exchange is called **liquidity**. Money is the ultimate liquid asset because it already is the medium of exchange. In its function as a store of value, money competes with other (substitute) financial assets such as savings bonds or certificates of deposit. These assets offer interest but do not serve as a medium of exchange.

This list of functions makes it possible to replace the working definition of money with a more precise definition. Money is what money does. That is, anything that performs all four of the functions just listed is money. **Money** is any financial asset that serves as a medium of exchange, a unit of account, a standard of deferred payment, and a store of value.

DESIRABLE PROPERTIES OF MONEY
Money can take all kinds of forms. What should be used for money? Fishhooks? Stones? Shells? Beads? Tobacco? All of these have served as money at some time. Some of the desirable properties of money can be inferred by considering the forms of money that have been used for long periods and those that haven't made the grade. Experience suggests that money should have a stable value, be somewhat scarce (but not too scarce), and be portable, durable, uniform, divisible, acceptable, and transferable. Let's explore each of these properties.

---

standard of deferred payment
A function of money in providing borrowers and lenders a medium for the repayment of debt in the future.

store of value
A function of money in providing purchasing power in a general form that can be held in order to buy goods and services in the future.

liquidity
The measure of how quickly a financial asset can be converted into the medium of exchange.

money
Any financial asset that serves as a medium of exchange, a unit of account, a standard of deferred payment, and a store of value.

---

3. For 100 items, each having 99 prices in terms of the others, you might think there are 9,900 prices. But half of these can be eliminated. The price of apples in terms of oranges is just the reciprocal of the price of oranges in apples. That leaves 4,950 prices—still a lot to keep track of!

STABILITY OF VALUE. Stability of value means that purchasing power doesn't change very rapidly. If the value of a currency is stable, one currency unit (such as a dollar) buys about the same amount of goods and services, even though the prices of some items may rise or fall in response to changes in supply and demand in individual markets. A stable value is of key importance in making people want to use money and accept it. Inflation means that money is losing purchasing power. If further inflation is expected, money is a poor store of value.

Stability of value is especially important if money is to function as both a store of value and a standard of deferred payment. Money whose value is being eroded by inflation is not a satisfactory standard for determining loan repayment. The money repaid will have less value than the money borrowed. If you fear that the value of your money is in danger of being rapidly eroded by price increases, you may be tempted to switch some of your store of value into land, buildings, fine art, rare coins, diamonds, or gold. These other assets are real goods whose value rises when prices increase. Owning them thus partly protects you against inflation. The amount of money you hold as a store of value will depend on what you expect to happen to its future value. Stability of value depends on controlling the money supply (as you learned when we discussed the quantity theory of money in Chapter 7).

If several forms of money are available, the one whose value is most stable will be hoarded and disappear from circulation. People will choose to hold the more stable form of money as a store of value and attempt to use the money whose value is unstable as a medium of exchange. Sellers, however, will be reluctant to accept such money. If they do, they will try to pass it on quickly. This behavior has been observed so often that it has the status of a law. Gresham's law says, "Bad money drives out good [out of circulation]."[4]

Confederate money in the closing days of the Civil War offered a good example of Gresham's law at work. A more recent example occurred in Poland and Yugoslavia. In those two countries, U.S. dollars were hoarded and highly valued by those who could get them. Thus, dollars largely disappeared from circulation. The local currencies—the zloty and the dinar—circulated rapidly because, unlike dollars, both were a poor store of value. Zlotys and dinars were more acceptable as a unit of account and a medium of exchange. Reforms in 1990 stabilized the purchasing power of the zloty and the dinar and made them more acceptable as a store of value.

SCARCITY. Scarcity of money is a key property. The general level of prices tends to increase directly with the quantity of money in circulation. Sand, for example, meets many of the other criteria for money but is too easy to scoop up in large quantities. Scarcity was one reason for the popularity of precious metals as money in the past. Today, governments try to maintain the scarcity of the money supply by limiting the quantity of money they produce.

---

4.   Gresham's law dates back to the fifteenth century but is commonly attributed to Sir Thomas Gresham, the founder of the Royal Exchange in Great Britain in the nineteenth century.

Yap, one of the Caroline Islands, lies in the western Pacific Ocean, north of the equator and the island of New Guinea and east of the Philippines. The fame of Yap lies in its stone money, called *fei*, first described in anthropological literature early in this century. The *fei* are large wheel-shaped stones, with holes in the center to allow them to be carried on poles. The stones range in size from one foot to eight feet in diameter. They aren't portable or divisible, but they are not easily counterfeited. A new stone had to be brought from Palau or Guam by raft or canoe, costing a certain amount of human time and effort. These costs ensure the scarcity of Yap's stone money.

Each stone is quite valuable. Together they represent most of the island's financial wealth. As you can imagine, the stones aren't used in everyday transactions. The usual currencies are tridacna shells, used for large transactions, and mother-of-pearl, used for smaller transactions. The stones are mainly used as a store of value, a unit of account, and a standard of deferred payment rather than as the common medium of exchange. They are still

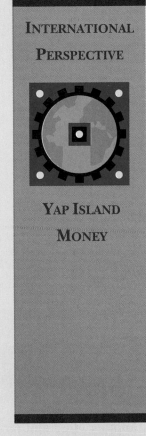

INTERNATIONAL PERSPECTIVE

YAP ISLAND MONEY

thought of as money, however. The larger stones are well known, and possession can change hands without the location being changed. Indeed, even stones that are now under the sea (lost in shipment between islands) maintain their value, and their ownership (though not their locations) can be changed. The stone in the Smithsonian Institution is probably still a part of the Yap money supply!

Yap's experiences with modern currencies explains why the stones have retained their monetary role. The Spanish first claimed Yap, but after defeat in the Spanish-American War, they sold the island to Germany in 1899. After Germany's defeat in World War I, Yap was transferred as a League of Nations trust territory to Japan. The Japanese controlled it until the end of World War II, when it came under the jurisdiction of the United States. All these nations introduced their currencies to Yap. Upon the introduction of U.S. currency, a Yap chief said, "First Spanish money no good, then German money no good, now Japanese money no good. Yap money always good!"[a]

a. "The Trust Territory: Its 2,130 Islands Form a New U.S. Domain in the Pacific," *Life* (25 April 1949): 100.

PORTABILITY. Medieval Swedish copper coins and the stone money of the Island of Yap were both very heavy. In general, however, portability is an important attribute of money. Portable forms of money—usually gold—have been very useful in crises. Some people, such as refugees fleeing political upheaval or persecution, discovered how critical portability is when they had to convert their assets to a form that could be carried and concealed.

DURABILITY. Durability is another important quality of money. Perishable commodities such as apples or fragile commodities such as glass would not serve well as money. Paper money is not extremely durable, but it is easy to replace. You can turn in a tattered U.S. dollar bill for a new one at a bank, which then turns in the old bill to the Federal Reserve. The tattered bill is destroyed, typically after a useful lifetime of about sixteen months. Coins, in contrast, have a useful lifetime of about twenty years.

UNIFORMITY. Uniformity is an essential quality of money that rules out many commodities. Variations in quality complicated the use of tobacco as money in the South during colonial times. Cows can be fat or thin, healthy or sick, and their value as money would vary accordingly. The advantage of paper money or precious metals is that it is easy to verify uniformity. The purity of gold and silver can be tested by weight or vouched for by a stamp of approval, as on coins.

DIVISIBILITY. Divisibility of money is essential in making transactions. It has to be possible to make change. Small denominations and coins are needed for this purpose. Divisibility as well as portability makes cows, houses, and other large, heavy assets very unsatisfactory forms of money. Divisibility helps to account for the popularity of both gold and silver as money.

ACCEPTABILITY. Another important property of money in its function as a medium of exchange is acceptability. To be useful, money must be acceptable; people must be willing to take it in payment for goods and services. A person will accept money only because of the belief that others will also accept it.

representative money
Money that is redeemable in a commodity (or commodities), such as gold.

If the substance used as money is also a commodity with nonmonetary uses (such as gold), its value as a commodity sets its minimum value, which gives it some general acceptability. If the money is not itself a commodity but is always redeemable in a commodity, the acceptability and value of the commodity transfer to the money. Such money is known as **representative money**. The gold certificates and silver certificates used as currencies in the United States until 1933 and 1963, respectively, were representative monies. Bank deposits were representative money if the bank promised to redeem them in gold. The acceptability of representative money depends on whether people believe it will be redeemed as promised.

fiat money
Money that is not a commodity and is not redeemable in any commodity.

legal tender
Money that, by law, must be accepted by private parties and governments in payment of debts and obligations.

Modern money, however, is normally neither a commodity nor redeemable as a commodity. It is usually **fiat money**, which is whatever the government declares to be money. What gives such money its value and acceptability? Part of the answer lies in the term **legal tender**. By law, certain forms of money (currency in the United States) are "legal tender for all debts, public and private." That phrase is printed on all U.S. bills. If something is legal tender, all persons are required to accept it in payment of debts. Governments must also accept paper money for the payment of taxes if it is designated as legal tender. Since most households have a fairly large tax obligation, this guarantee is one good reason to accept legal tender in exchange for goods or services of real value. Even people who don't have to pay taxes can feel confident that this money will be of value and acceptable to others.

FORMS OF MONEY

An incredible variety of items have served as money throughout history. All monies have had at least some of the desirable properties of money but in different degrees. Milk—a very nondurable item (but liquid!)—has been used as money. Cattle and slaves have also served as money, though they are neither very homogeneous nor divisible. Even cannons have been used as money, despite the fact that they are not very portable.

Various precious metals, such as gold and silver (and copper, though it is not as rare), have frequently served as money. The value of coins made from precious metals can be reduced by clipping, chipping, or shaving, either by private citizens or by the issuing governments. Precious metals can also be combined with less expensive (base) metals. In the Middle Ages, it was not uncommon for a monarch to call in all the coins, melt them, add base metals, recast them, and redistribute twice as many coins. The increased number of coins drove up the prices of goods and reduced the value of each coin. This **debasement of money** made the value of coins suspect. How much gold (or silver) was really in a coin?

During World War II, prisoners of war in German detention camps used cigarettes as money. They received cigarettes as part of their rations from the Red Cross and elsewhere. There were more cigarettes than people wanted to smoke, so they were traded for other goods. The supply was well known, so cigarettes gradually became recognized as a form of money with a fairly stable value. Toward the end of the month, before new cigarette rations arrived, many of the cigarettes had been smoked. The value of a cigarette in terms of most other goods, such as chocolate bars, tended to rise until a new shipment came in.

Money in the form of coins has been around for a long time. Originally, coins were made out of precious metal, and the stamp of the royal authority (often complete with a flattering profile) certified to their value. Such coins were **full-bodied money**, with a value in other uses equal to their monetary value. Modern coins are **token money**. Their value as money is greater than the value of the metal they contain. Currency and checks, mostly issued by banks, are somewhat more recent than coins but still have a long history.

In the United States, money consists of coins, currency, and checkable deposits. **Currency** is paper money with a specified value. In the United States, official currency is now issued solely by the central bank (the Federal Reserve System). In the past, paper money has been issued by the Treasury (gold and silver certificates), private banks, and even state governments. In some countries, private banks continue to issue currency.

debasement of money
The practice of reminting coins of gold or silver with base metals added, thus increasing the number of coins, driving up the prices of goods, and reducing the value of each coin.

full-bodied money
Money that has a value in other uses equal to its monetary value. Coins made of precious metals are the best examples.

token money
Money whose monetary value is greater than its commodity value. Modern coins, for example, are worth more as money than the metal they contain.

currency
Paper money with a specified value, issued by the government or central bank.

checkable deposits
Balances in accounts at depository institutions on which checks can be drawn.

Traveler's checks, a form of money issued by U.S. banks, are a safe and acceptable medium of exchange that is very close to currency. **Checkable deposits**, the principal component of the money supply, consist of balances in checking accounts at banks and other depository institutions. All of these forms of U.S. money have the desired properties of money.

BANKS AND MONEY

Banks play an important role in the creation of money. Modern banking evolved from the services provided in the Middle Ages by goldsmiths. Goldsmiths made jewelry and decorative objects and kept a stock of gold for their own use. Because they maintained safe storage facilities, goldsmiths began storing other people's gold. They issued receipts for the gold left with them. Depositors often found it more convenient to use those receipts as money than to retrieve the gold. The receipts began to circulate as currency, fully redeemable in gold. Goldsmiths were thus the earliest bankers.

The emergence of banks resolved several problems with existing forms of money. Coins were bulky, inconvenient to carry in large amounts, and easy to steal. Paper money, on the other hand, needed some guarantee of its value. One form of guarantee was its convertibility into coins. Thus, banks could provide safe storage for and convenient access to coins and could issue currency that had some guarantee of value. Another need fulfilled by banks was the need for a credit market—a way of transferring money balances from those individuals who did not wish to use them at the moment to those who did. Your local bank or savings and loan still offers these basic banking services today.

BANK NOTES, CHECKING ACCOUNTS, AND OTHER FORMS OF MONEY

By the late eighteenth century, bank notes like the receipts issued by goldsmiths had become a substantial part of the money supply in England and many other countries. Such bank notes carried a promise to give the bearer the specific sum of gold stated on the face. Sometimes banks failed because they could not meet their obligations to redeem these notes in gold as promised.

Governments also issued notes redeemable in gold or silver on demand. Like banks, governments were sometimes unable to keep their promise to redeem this paper money for gold or silver. During the Civil War, the U.S. government issued notes called **greenbacks** that were not redeemable in gold. The Confederate States of America also issued nonredeemable notes. When the war was going well for the Union forces, greenbacks traded at close to their face value in gold. Greenbacks fell in value during periods when the war was going badly for the North. Confederate notes became virtually worthless toward the end of the war. It became clear that the Confederacy would lose, and the notes would not be redeemed. Confederate notes are now popular collectors' items, but you would have a hard time getting anyone to accept them in payment!

Until 1862, most U.S. banks were chartered by individual states. The National Banking Act (1863) imposed a federal tax on bank notes issued by

greenbacks
Paper money issued by the U.S. government during the Civil War that was not redeemable in gold.

Most countries have coins in various denominations as well as currency. In many countries, as in the United States, a decimal system is used. The currency is divided into 100 units, as the U.S. dollar is divided into 100 cents. The British currency was one of the last major currencies to change to a decimal system. Before the 1970s, there were 12 pence to a shilling and 20 shillings to a pound. The pound is now divided into 100 pence as a result of currency reform, and the shilling has ceased to be coined.

Many currencies have only one unit. There is the peso in Mexico, the yen in Japan, the franc in France and Switzerland, the mark in Germany, and the lira in Italy. Often the unit has a historic name. The franc is a name going back to the Dark Ages, when the tribe inhabiting the area that is now France was the Franks. The bolivar in Venezuela is named for a Latin American hero, Simon Bolivar. The krone of several Scandinavian countries simply means "crown," indicating that it is issued by the king or queen. The pound sterling originally was worth one pound of sterling silver. Sometimes the name is changed in a currency reform. In 1986, Brazil called in its cruzeiros and replaced them with a new currency, the cruzado, at a ratio of 1 cruzado for 1,000 cruzeiros.

INTERNATIONAL PERSPECTIVE

MONEY AROUND THE WORLD

The basic currency unit may be very large or very small. That is, it may take a large number or a small number of currency units to buy a newspaper or a loaf of bread. In most cases, the size of the currency unit says nothing about the currency's value or stability. The yen is a small currency unit but has a stable and rising value. The pound sterling is a large currency unit but has much smaller purchasing power relative to other currencies than it had ten, twenty, or forty years ago. Sometimes a currency unit changes from large to small as a result of severe inflation. For example, in early 1989, it took 78,000 australs to buy a car in Argentina. A year later, 78,000 australs bought dinner for four at a nice restaurant in Buenos Aires.[a]

The value of the currencies of the major industrial countries is determined by supply and demand in the international marketplace. Here are the values of a few of the major currencies in terms of U.S. dollars in early 1991.

CURRENCY	PRICE IN U.S. DOLLARS
Japanese yen	0.0076
German mark	0.6782
French franc	0.1994
Canadian dollar	0.8604
British pound	1.9675

You can check on currency prices in most major daily newspapers.

a. *Washington Post National Weekly Edition* (4–10 March 1990): 20.

state-chartered banks. This act was an attempt to force banks to obtain federal charters and come under federal regulation. Instead, it virtually drove bank notes out of existence and encouraged the development of checking accounts as a substitute for gold and bank notes in the United States.

demand deposits
Bank deposits on which checks can be written (also known as checking accounts).

Checking accounts, or **demand deposits**, first appeared in fifteenth-century Italy. They have some advantages over bank notes. There is no problem of making change, because a check can be written for the exact amount. Checking accounts are easier to protect from theft than cash because you can stop payment on checks if your checkbook is stolen. Checking accounts have one important drawback, however. The person who accepts a check has no easy way to verify that the check will be accepted by the bank on which it is written. If the check writer doesn't have enough funds on deposit, the check will "bounce"—right back to the person who accepted it in payment. Thus, especially if you are young, move around a great deal, or don't have satisfactory identification, your check is not always as widely accepted as currency or coins.

In the last twenty years, the variety of accounts offered by banks has increased. The federal government eliminated many of the regulations on the kinds of accounts banks could offer and the interest rates they could pay. The revolution in banking began when interest rate ceilings were suspended in the 1970s. Banks had to compete more aggressively for deposits in order to have funds to lend. Instead of offering toasters and other premiums, they offered new kinds of accounts with higher interest rates. The first new type of account to develop was the **certificate of deposit** (**CD**). CDs are deposits with financial institutions for specific periods, with higher interest rates than savings accounts and a penalty (often substantial) for early withdrawal. They function well as a store of value, but they are not very liquid.

certificate of deposit (CD)
A deposit made with a financial institution at a specified interest rate for a given (fixed) period of time.

In the early 1980s, for the first time since the 1930s, bank depositors could have an account that offered both interest on deposits and check-writing privileges. These accounts were introduced under various names, such as negotiated order of withdrawal (NOW) accounts and money market accounts. Many of these new accounts allow unlimited check writing and electronic transfers of funds. Even ordinary checking accounts began to pay interest once deregulation made it possible.

MEASURING THE MONEY SUPPLY

Because of these changes, economists had to rethink exactly what to count in measuring the money supply. Until the late 1970s, there were two widely used definitions of the money supply. One definition included currency plus demand deposits at commercial banks. The second definition added savings accounts. Which measure would an analyst use? The answer depended on which one seemed to do the best job of explaining people's behavior. Usually the two measures would move together. Sometimes, when there was switching between checking and savings accounts, one measure might rise while the other fell.

Before the development of such options as CDs and money market accounts, there was a wide gap between demand deposits, which are considered money by even the strictest definition, and savings accounts, which cannot be used directly for transactions. Changes in the banking system have filled this gap with NOW accounts, credit union share draft accounts, automated funds transfers between accounts, and money market deposit accounts. There is a much wider variety of checkable deposits offered by all types of depository institutions.

Before 1980, there was a clear line that separated money from near money. A financial asset—coin, currency, CD, or bond—was either a medium of exchange (money) or an interest-earning asset (near money). With a whole new array of interest-bearing checking accounts, the dividing line became blurred. Economists have had to decide where these new kinds of deposits fit into the various definitions of the money supply.

Liquidity is the most important criterion for deciding what financial assets are a part of the money supply. Since money is highly liquid, the amount of liquidity that a financial asset has is useful for deciding whether it should be considered money or near money. **Near money** is a financial asset that is a close but not perfect substitute for money as a medium of exchange.

Today, the **M1 money stock** is defined as the total of those kinds of financial assets that function as a medium of exchange. It includes currency in circulation (outside banks), traveler's checks, demand deposits at commercial banks, and other checkable deposits (NOW accounts, credit union share draft accounts, and demand deposits at thrift institutions).

The **M2 money stock** is equal to M1 plus small time and savings deposits, money market accounts at banks and other financial institutions, and a few other specialized monetary assets. Time and savings deposits are those on which you can earn interest and on which you cannot write a check. Money market accounts with banks or mutual fund companies are deposits invested in short-term liquid assets (such as Treasury bills), on which the owner can write a limited number of checks. A still broader measure, the **M3 money stock**, is equal to M2 plus large time deposits, repurchase agreements, and a few other items. Table 1 gives exact definitions and current magnitudes of these three widely used measures.[5]

THE MONEY SUPPLY AND THE EQUATION OF EXCHANGE

The equation of exchange, $M_s \times V = P \times Y$, was introduced in Chapter 7. Of the three measures of the money supply, how do economists decide which to use for M_s in this equation? This decision is important because the equation is used to predict changes in the price level and real output (and as we will see later, changes in interest rates as well). The choice is not easy. Suppose you decide to use M1 for the money supply in the equation of exchange. Everything not a part of M1 is then near money. However, savings and time deposits at banks, which are a part of M2 but not M1, are very good substitutes for checking accounts. With an automatic teller card, it is possible to withdraw cash from a money market account just as easily as from a checkable deposit.

Clearly, there will always be some near money that is close to the money

near money
Assets that are very similar to the kinds of assets included in the money stock. Near money is usually highly liquid.

M1 money stock
The total of all financial assets in the United States that function as a medium of exchange: currency, traveler's checks, demand deposits, and other checkable deposits.

M2 money stock
The total of M1 and small-denomination time and savings deposits at all financial institutions, money market accounts, and a few other items.

M3 money stock
The total of M2 and large-denomination time deposits, repurchase agreements, and a few other items.

---

5. There are other measures of the money supply that become more inclusive, all the way up to a measure called L (for liquidity) that includes a broad array of assets. The definitions for these other measures are given in the *Federal Reserve Bulletin*.

TABLE 1
MONEY STOCK MEASURES
AND COMPONENTS,
OCTOBER 1990
(BILLIONS OF DOLLARS)

MEASURES

M1	$ 820.1
M2	3,320.1
M3	4,088.2

MAJOR COMPONENTS

Currency	$ 244.0
Demand deposits	276.8
Other checkable deposits	291.0
Savings/time deposits	1,172.3
Money market accounts	376.3

M1 money stock: currency held by the public plus commercial bank demand deposits, traveler's checks of nonbank issuers, and other checkable deposits (which include NOW and ATS accounts, credit union share draft accounts, and demand deposits at thrifts).

M2 money stock: M1 plus small-denomination savings and time deposits at all depository institutions, money market deposit accounts and money market mutual funds (except those owned by institutions), overnight repurchase agreements at commercial banks, and overnight Eurodollars.

M3 money stock: M2 plus large-denomination savings and time deposits at all depository institutions, term repurchase agreements at commercial banks and savings and loans, term Eurodollars, and money market mutual funds (institutions only). (There is another correction for interbank deposits.)

Source: *Economic Indicators* (Washington, DC: U.S. Government Printing Office, January 1991).

concept you choose. If you use M2 in the equation of exchange, you will find that deposits at savings and loan associations, which are not included in M2, are not very different from similar accounts at commercial banks. If you choose M3, which includes negotiable CDs, you will find that short-term U.S. government obligations, such as Treasury bills, are fairly good substitutes for those CDs because there are active resale markets for Treasury bills.

In order to use the money supply as a policy tool or a forecasting tool for prices, employment, and real output, it is important to agree on the best measure. Some economists use the one that is the most accurate in predicting the money value of GNP. That measure is usually M2. M2 is also more stable than M1. When individuals look for higher-yielding assets, they often switch to some of the interest-bearing accounts included in M2. Such changes make M1 fluctuate a great deal more than M2.

Other economists argue for M1 because it corresponds to money's function as the medium of exchange. M2 incorporates more of money's function as a store of value, which is important both in the Keynesian model and in modern monetarist explanations of what determines interest rates, the price level, and real output. By the late 1980s, the preference among model builders and policy makers had shifted from M1 to M2, but not all economists agreed with the change.

DEMAND FOR MONEY

Now that you have a working definition of what money is, what it does, and what the money supply consists of, we can use the equation of exchange to see the effects of changes in money supply and demand on output, employment, and the price level. The demand for money developed here is based on the quantity theory of money introduced in Chapter 7. The supply of money is closely linked to the banking system, which we will describe in the next chapter. Changes in the supply and demand for money can shift the aggregate demand curve introduced in Chapter 6. By shifting that curve, they affect the levels of output, employment, and prices.

Motives for Holding Money

Two of the four functions of money—as the medium of exchange and a store of value—relate directly to its uses by individuals and business firms. People hold money because it is convenient for market transactions. They also may hold money as one of many forms in which to store wealth.

Economists believe that individuals decide how much money to hold in the same way they decide which goods and services to buy. That is, they compare the satisfaction obtained from holding money with the satisfaction obtained from holding alternative assets. Money is useful for two important purposes: making transactions and storing purchasing power for future use.[6] Whenever money is used to carry out transactions or held in anticipation of transactions in the near future, those funds are satisfying the transactions demand for money, or the desire for cash balances to meet day-to-day spending needs. Recall from Chapter 7 that the transactions demand for money is positively related to income.

The classical quantity theory of money was based on the role of money as a medium of exchange, or the transactions demand for money. If people hold money mostly for making transactions, the amount they wish to hold is related to the volume of transactions they expect to make. For an individual, the amount of money held for transactions is proportional to income. For the economy as a whole, the amount of money demanded for transactions is proportional to the aggregate volume of transactions, which is roughly equal to GNP (or $P \times Y$).[7] Recall that the equation of exchange can be written as either

$$M_{\mathrm{d}} = k \times P \times Y = k \times \text{nominal income}$$

or

$$M_{\mathrm{s}} \times V = P \times Y,$$

where $k = 1/V$. Classical economists expected that k and V would be con-

---

6.   Money also provides some degree of security against unexpected events that might require an outlay of cash. Money held for such purposes is said to satisfy the precautionary demand for money. Since both the transactions demand and the precautionary demand for money depend on the level of nominal income $(P \times Y)$, they are often lumped together under transactions demand.
7.   It is not exactly the same because there will be transactions in used goods, illegal goods, and financial assets that are not reflected in GNP. But if the relationship between the volume of these transactions and GNP is a fairly constant ratio, GNP is a good approximation for the dollar value of transactions.

The underground economy in the United States consists of a mix of barter and cash transactions, some legal and some not. Many people who transact business in the underground economy are trying to avoid payment of income taxes and Social Security taxes. Some want to avoid losing welfare benefits. Others, such as drug dealers, are more worried about the police than the Internal Revenue Service. Transactions are more difficult for the government to uncover if they are made by barter or in cash instead of by check.

The underground economy is a major source of demand for currency instead of checkable deposits. Cash transactions can be used to avoid taxes. Wages are often paid in cash to retired persons on Social Security who would lose some benefits if their earnings were reported. Some workers who get tips in cash don't want to pay income tax or Social Security taxes on those earnings. Cash wages to illegal aliens can help them avoid deportation.

One measure of the size of the underground economy is the growth of currency (Federal Reserve notes) relative to other forms of money. Currency rose from 23 percent of the money supply in 1970 to 30 percent in 1983. High Social Security taxes, a progressive income tax, and high inflation made the underground economy attractive during that period. Several factors combined to reduce the demand for cash by the end of the 1980s: lower marginal tax rates, lower inflation rates, and more intensive monitoring of large cash transactions by tax officials. By 1990, these factors had dropped the currency ratio slightly to 28 percent of the money supply, suggesting a modest decline in underground activity.

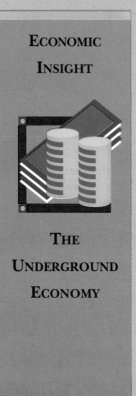

ECONOMIC INSIGHT

THE UNDERGROUND ECONOMY

stant, or at least stable, because transactions demand reflects patterns of earning and spending that do not change very rapidly.[8] Think about your own spending and earning. The money you receive—from a part-time job, from scholarships, or from your parents—comes in at regular intervals and you spend it at a rather steady and predictable pace.

During the Great Depression, however, there was a large decline in the velocity of money that took many economists by surprise. In the 1930s, people wanted to hold more money at every level of GNP. In the equation of exchange, this change in preferences meant that k increased and V fell. When people attempted to increase their money holdings, they engaged in fewer transactions and, on average, held each dollar longer. As they spent less, both GNP ($P \times Y$ in the equation of exchange) and V declined. Keynes attempted to explain changes in people's desired cash balances in terms of other reasons for holding money besides transactions demand.

INTEREST RATES, RISK, AND THE ASSET DEMAND FOR MONEY

Despite the advantages of money for transactions and precautionary purposes, individuals don't choose to keep all of their wealth in cash or checking accounts. There are costs associated with holding money. A major cost is the opportunity cost of the interest that could be earned by holding other assets instead of money.[9] Keynes explored the manner in which yields on other assets can affect the demand for money. Specifically, he identified a third kind of demand for money. He labeled it the speculative demand for money, but it is now more often called the asset demand for money (as we discussed in Chapter 7). The asset demand for money is the amount of money people wish to hold as a store of value in preference to other kinds of financial assets. This demand for money depends on the interest rates on other kinds of financial assets. The asset demand is negatively related to the interest rate.

Keynes further clarified the relationship between the interest rate and the demand for money. He pointed out that it is not only the current interest rate that affects the decision to hold money, but also how that rate compares to past and expected future rates. Suppose that for the past decade the yield on bonds had averaged 6 percent, but this year it dropped to 4 percent. You would tend to prefer cash balances to bonds because the opportunity cost is lower. But there is another reason to stay away from bonds. If you think that 6 percent interest is "normal" and the 4 percent yield is temporary, then you expect the yield on bonds to go back up to 6 percent in the near future. If you buy bonds now, not only will you get a low yield, but you will be risking a capital loss. A bond that you purchase for $1,000 at 4 percent with a very long maturity period (twenty years or more) will be worth only $667 when the interest rate rises to 6 percent.[10]

---

8. Late nineteenth-century economists and early twentieth-century economists in the classical tradition, such as Irving Fisher and Henry Simons, did not share this view. They were concerned about the instability of velocity, especially in the short run, and although they would agree with this equation, they would not regard either k or V as constant.

9. Another cost comes from the fact that money's value, or purchasing power, rises and falls with changes in the price level. Holding money is costly during periods of rising prices. We will explore this concern in more detail in Chapter 13.

10. If the maturity period were shorter, the individual could hold the bond to maturity to collect the face value. We will explore bond prices and interest rates in Chapter 13.

WHY PEOPLE HOLD MONEY	
MOTIVE	**CHARACTERISTICS**
Transactions demand for money	• To meet day-to-day expenses
	• Reflects money's function as the medium of exchange
	• Positively related to level of income
Asset demand for money	• As a store of wealth or as one asset among many
	• Reflects money's function as a store of value
	• Negatively related to interest rate

Suppose the Federal Reserve System (described in Chapter 12) tries to increase aggregate demand by increasing the money supply. The increased money supply will reduce interest rates and should result in more investment spending. However, if interest rates are already low relative to past experience, a larger money supply may have little effect. Banks, firms, and individuals will just increase their holdings of cash. Thus, the larger money supply will have little effect on lending, interest rates, and investment. Velocity will fall, as it did during the Great Depression. We will explore this issue further in Chapter 14.

EXPECTED PRICE LEVEL CHANGES AND THE DEMAND FOR MONEY. A more general theory of money demand can build on both the classical quantity theory and Keynes's asset demand. Such a theory includes three important influences on money demand: real output/income (classical transactions demand), interest rates (Keynes's asset demand), and the price level (including changes in both actual and expected prices).

Changes in price expectations influence the demand for money. Consider how changes in the price level affect the purchasing power of money. When prices rise, a dollar buys less. When prices fall, it buys more. People will be concerned that a rising price level will cause money holdings to decline in value. If the price level was expected to rise, this would provide an incentive for people to shift part of their assets out of money and into other kinds of financial assets that are less vulnerable to losing value through inflation. They might try to purchase real assets (such as land, coins, or houses) whose value rises with the price level. Or they may purchase financial assets with yields high enough to offset the expected loss of purchasing power. As people try to exchange their money for other kinds of assets, such as bonds, desired money balances fall relative to GNP ($P \times Y$ in the equation of exchange). Velocity (V) increases, or k declines.

An expected drop in the price level would have just the opposite effect. As money increases in purchasing power and is expected to increase further in the future, people will expect the value of their money holdings to rise. As they cut spending, GNP falls. Since the money supply is unchanged, the equation of exchange must be balanced by a decline in V or a rise in k.

THE STABILITY OF VELOCITY. The combined influence of interest rates and price expectations on the demand for money explains why k and V vary in the short run. It is easy to verify that this was the case in the 1930s when V fell and k rose. After the stock market crash of 1929 and the many bankruptcies of the early 1930s, many people wanted to hold a larger fraction of their assets in the form of money. The interest rates on bonds and other financial assets were very low. In 1933, the yield on a three-month Treasury bill was only 0.5 percent, compared to about 6–7 percent in recent years. Furthermore, the price level was falling in the early 1930s and was expected to fall further.

Velocity, measured by comparing GNP to M1, declined sharply again in the late 1980s. However, this time the decline in velocity was not tied to a recession. A gradual decline in interest rates played some role. The decline in velocity was also related to changes in financial markets and the emergence of new forms of near money. These changes made M1 a less satisfactory measure of the money supply as more close substitutes appeared for its components. An imperfect measure of the money supply would give an imperfect measure of velocity, since $V = \text{GNP}/M_s$.

How often and how much does the velocity of money change? Figure 1 on page 310 plots two values of V ($V_1 = \text{GNP}/\text{M1}$ and $V_2 = \text{GNP}/\text{M2}$) as well as the interest rate on a Treasury bill for the period from 1970 to 1990. You can see from this diagram that V_1 is less stable than V_2, but that both seem to be related to the interest rate. We will consider the stability of velocity and its implications in Chapter 14.

DETERMINANTS OF VELOCITY

The velocity of money (V) is determined by

• Interest rates	Higher interest rates increase velocity. Lower interest rates reduce velocity.
• Price expectations	Inflationary expectations increase velocity. Deflationary expectations reduce velocity.
• Institutional changes	Different forms of money or payment periods will change spending habits and affect velocity.

MONEY DEMAND, MONEY SUPPLY, AND AGGREGATE DEMAND

The money supply is largely under the control of the central bank, which uses tools that are described in Chapter 12. Until now, we have treated the amount of money in the economy as an exogenous variable or a given number. Money demand, however, is subject to many influences, including (1) the interest rate, which determines the demand for money as a store of value, (2) the level of income, which determines transactions demand, and (3) the price level and price expectations. Money demand is positively related to the level of money income ($P \times Y$).[11]

---

11. In the equation $M_d = k \times P \times Y$, nominal money demand ($M_d$) is a function of nominal income ($P \times Y$). If the equation is written as $M_d/P = k \times Y$, real money demand (M_d/P) is a function of real income (Y).

FIGURE 1
VELOCITY OF MONEY,
1960–1990
Velocity is equal to GNP divided by the money supply (M1 or M2). In the last thirty years, V_1 has increased, but with ups and downs around the upward trend. Presently the value of V_1 (GNP/M1) is in the range of 5.5–7. The value of V_2 (GNP/M2) is around 1.5–2.0.

Source: Calculated from data in the *Economic Report of the President,* 1991.

EQUILIBRIUM IN THE MONEY MARKET

Figure 2 shows the relationship of money demand and money supply to nominal income. An increase in $P \times Y$ will increase the amount of money demanded along the curve M_{d1} in Figure 2. Equilibrium occurs at that

FIGURE 2
MONEY SUPPLY, MONEY
DEMAND, AND INCOME
Here the money supply is considered as given, or independent of the level of money income. Money demand is positively related to the level of money income, *ceteris paribus.* A change in some other factor, such as interest rates, will shift the money demand curve from M_{d1} to M_{d2}.

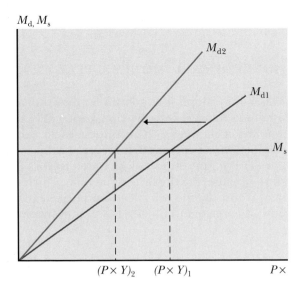

level of $P \times Y$ at which the quantity of money demanded is equal to the quantity supplied, which occurs at $(P \times Y)_1$ in Figure 2.

Suppose interest rates fall. With a lower opportunity cost of holding money, people will choose to hold larger cash balances at every level of income. The demand curve for money shifts to M_{d2} in Figure 2. Since V and k measure the relationship between money demand and money income, another way of saying the same thing is that velocity has fallen. At income level $(P \times Y)_1$, there is a shortage of money balances. Money demand exceeds money supply.

How does this economy return to equilibrium? As people try to build up their cash balances, the decline in spending reduces the level of income and output to $(P \times Y)_2$. At that lower income level, individuals will demand smaller cash balances. Note that the money market is back in balance, but money income has fallen.

Not all of the burden of adjustment falls on output and the price level. As individuals try to build up their money balances, less is available to lend. Interest rates begin to rise as borrowers compete for a limited supply of funds. As interest rates rise, some individuals will settle for smaller holdings of money as an asset. They will choose to use money to purchase financial assets offering attractive interest rates. These higher interest rates will shift the money demand curve back toward M_{d1} in Figure 2. Changes in interest rates will cushion some of the impact of increasing demand for money on output and the price level.

Suppose, instead, the money supply increases. In Figure 3, this development is shown as a shift in the horizontal money supply curve from M_{s1} to M_{s2}. Note that there is now too much money in the system. Quantity supplied exceeds quantity demanded. When the money supply increases, how do individuals respond? If money demand is unchanged, people have larger money balances than they want. When people have excess money balances, they have only two choices about what to do with the money:

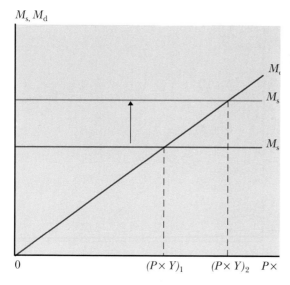

FIGURE 3
AN INCREASE IN THE MONEY SUPPLY
An increase in the money supply shifts the money supply curve from M_{s1} to M_{s2}. The result is an increase in the level of money income from $(P \times Y)_1$ to $(P \times Y)_2$ as households spend their excess cash balances and drive up income and the price level.

spend it or lend it. (If they choose to leave the money in their bank accounts, the bank will lend it to someone.) Spending it drives up output and prices. The economy moves along the money demand curve to a larger quantity of money demanded at a higher level of $P \times Y$. Lending the money drives down interest rates. At lower interest rates, people will be willing to hold larger cash balances (lower velocity of money). A combination of a lower velocity and a higher level of $P \times Y$ will ensure that the larger money supply brings the equation of exchange back into balance.

THE MONEY MARKET AND AGGREGATE DEMAND

Recall from Chapter 6 that the aggregate demand curve reflects the idea that a given money supply will buy various combinations of P (price level) and Y (real output). If we add aggregate demand to the analysis above, we can determine how much of the impact of a change in money demand or supply will be on real output and how much on prices. There are other factors that affect the slope and position of the aggregate demand curve, but money supply and demand are both important. If M_s increases and that increase is not entirely offset by a decline in V, there will be an increase in aggregate demand for goods and services. The AD curve shifts to the right, as shown in Figure 4. The result is an increase in P or Y or both. The exact combination depends on the slope of the AS curve. In Figure 4, the price level rises from P_1 to P_2, and real output rises from Y_1 to Y_2. The supply and demand for money are reflected in aggregate demand and therefore affect output, employment, and prices.

The addition of money to the aggregate supply and demand model identifies another source of shifts in aggregate demand besides fiscal policy or changes in consumption or investment habits. The fiscal policy tools used to shift aggregate demand are under the control of Congress and the executive branch. The money supply is under the control of the banking system, mainly the Federal Reserve System. In order to understand how this tool for shifting aggregate demand can be used, you need to know more about the banking system and how it works. The Federal Reserve System and the creation of money are described in the next chapter.

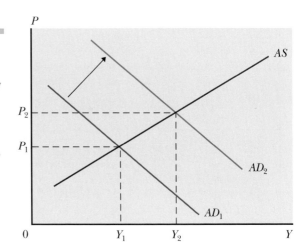

FIGURE 4
MONEY AND
AGGREGATE DEMAND
An increase in the money supply (or a decrease in the demand for money) creates a surplus of money. As it is spent on consumption or invested, aggregate demand shifts to the right (from AD_1 to AD_2) and drives up the price level (from P_1 to P_2) and real output (from Y_1 to Y_2).

SUMMARY

1. People accept money because it can be exchanged for other things they want. Money is desirable and useful only to the extent that it is accepted.

2. Barter is extremely costly and inefficient. The use of money allows people to carry out market transactions more economically.

3. The functions of money include its use as a medium of exchange, unit of account, standard of deferred payment, and store of value (asset). A variety of items have been used as money.

4. Desirable properties of money include stability of value, transferability, portability, durability, acceptability, recognizability, divisibility, and scarcity.

5. Several different measures of the money stock are used today in the United States. Whatever measure is used, money will have close substitutes, called near money. To draw the line between money and near money, economists usually try to determine which measure of the money stock works best for the problem they are working on.

6. Banking developed from goldsmiths' acceptance of deposits for safekeeping. Over time, the goldsmiths began to issue written promises to return a certain amount of gold. These promises were an early form of paper money.

7. Bank notes gradually replaced gold and were in turn replaced by checking accounts. It is not necessary for paper money or checking accounts to be redeemable in gold. For money to work well, it simply has to be generally acceptable.

8. The demand for money is expressed by the equation $M_d = k \times P \times Y$, another form of the equation of exchange, $M \times V = P \times Y$. Transactions demand for money is related to the level of income. Money is also demanded as an asset. Asset demand for money is higher when the interest on other financial assets is low.

9. Changes in the money supply affect output and prices through money demand. Excess money balances will be spent or lent, increasing aggregate demand and driving up prices and/or output.

NEW TERMS

barter	store of value	full-bodied money	certificate of deposit
double coincidence of	liquidity	token money	(CD)
wants	money	currency	near money
medium of exchange	representative money	checkable deposits	M1 money stock
unit of account	fiat money	greenbacks	M2 money stock
standard of deferred	legal tender	demand deposits	M3 money stock
payment	debasement of money		

QUESTIONS FOR DISCUSSION

1. In terms of the desirable properties of money, why have precious metals (gold and silver) been such popular choices for money? Why would each of the following be a poor choice: peanuts, seashells, glass, diamonds, teeth, cows, and trees?

2. Do you sort out your money on hand into transactions money, precautionary money, and asset money? Why do you think economists make these distinctions?

3. Part of the U.S. money supply (M1) is currency, and part of it is checkable deposits. Why might the ratio of currency to checkable deposits change? That is, why might people prefer to keep more of their money in currency or more of it in checkable deposits?

4. Draw a line labeled "Liquid" at one end and "Not very liquid" at the other end. Place the following financial assets along the line from most liquid to least liquid:

currency, twenty-year bonds, money market accounts, NOW accounts, savings accounts, checkable deposits, certificates of deposit, real estate, and Treasury bills (short-term obligations that mature in less than a year). Explain how this continuum relates to the problem of defining the money supply.

5. In each case, solve for the missing term in the equation of exchange.

    a. $M_s = \$500$, $V = 3$, $Y = \$750$, $P = $ _____

    b. $M_s = \$600$, $P = 3$, $Y = \$500$, $V = $ _____

    c. $M_s = \$800$, $V = 2$, $P = 0.75$, $Y = $ _____

    d. $V = 4$, $Y = \$1,400$, $P = 1.5$, $M_s = $ _____

6. Using the equation of exchange and the quantity theory of money, explain how each of the following would affect the money value of GNP.

    a. Workers get paid more often. (*Hint*: What happens to the average balance in their checking accounts?)

    b. A big promotional campaign persuades individuals to buy more government bonds. Thus they hold smaller cash balances.

    c. An evening TV program convinces people that rampant inflation is coming back soon.

7. Classify each of the following as transactions demand, precautionary demand, or asset demand for money.

    a. lunch money in your wallet (cash)

    b. money set aside in your checking account to pay next week's bills

    c. a coin bank in the kitchen for emergencies

    d. the proverbial stock of money kept in the mattress because of fear of banks

    e. funds in a NOW account that will be put into bonds when interest rates rise

8. In the *Federal Reserve Bulletin*, find the most recent figures for the sizes of M1, M2, and M3. List the components (for example, currency and checkable deposits) of each. What is the largest component of the money supply?

9. What are the benefits of holding cash? What are the costs or risks?

10. Take a bill from your wallet and answer the following questions:

    a. How do you know it is legal tender?

    b. Whose signatures are on it?

    c. By whom and in what city was it issued?

11. How would each of the following affect people's demand for money?

    a. lower interest rates

    b. higher price level

    c. higher expected inflation rate

    d. lower real income

12. Why did the velocity of money fall so sharply during the Great Depression?

13. Why, according to Keynes, is the relationship between current interest rates and "normal" interest rates important in determining how much money to hold as an asset?

14. "If you have excess money balances, your only choices are to spend the money or lend it." What does this statement mean? Can people collectively get rid of excess money balances?

15. If it is not possible for people as a group to get rid of excess money balances (Question 14), how is equilibrium restored in the money market when people have more money than they currently wish to hold?

Suggestions for Further Reading

Galbraith, John K. *Money: Whence It Came, Where It Went.* New York: Bantam Books, 1976. A delightfully readable account of money by one of the most talented writers in economics.

Mayer, Thomas, James S. Duesenberry, and Robert Z. Aliber. *Money, Banking and the Economy,* 4th ed. New York: W. W. Norton, 1990. A very up-to-date look at money and the monetary system.

Polanyi, K., M. Arenseberg, and H. W. Pearson, eds. *Trade and Markets in the Early Empires.* Chicago: Regnery Gateway, 1971. Looks at the history of money.

Radford, R. A. "The Economic Organization of a P.O.W. Camp." *Economica* (November 1945): 189–201. Many times reprinted, a classic article that looks at the use of cigarettes as money in an actual situation.

1. Explain how banks create money.
2. Explain why a central bank is necessary.
3. Describe the structure and functions of the Federal Reserve System.
4. Define each of the following terms related to the money creation process:
   a. reserves,
   b. required reserve ratio,
   c. excess reserves,
   d. discount rate,
   e. open market operations,
   f. currency drain,
   g. money multiplier.
5. Explain how the Fed uses each of following tools to influence the money supply and interest rates:
   a. open market operations,
   b. the reserve ratio,
   c. the discount rate.
6. Calculate the maximum possible change in checkable deposits that would result from each of the following:
   a. an open market operation,
   b. a change in the reserve ratio.
7. Describe the federal funds market and explain how the Fed influences the federal funds rate.

CHAPTER 12

MONEY CREATION AND THE FEDERAL RESERVE SYSTEM

INTRODUCTION

You know that changes in the money supply shift the aggregate demand curve. In Chapter 11, we explored the mechanism by which this shift takes place. Increases in the money supply mean that people's money balances are larger than they wish to hold. As they attempt to get rid of the excess money by spending or lending, they drive up consumption and investment demand, shifting the aggregate demand curve to the right. The opposite happens when the money supply shrinks.

Left unanswered in Chapter 11 were the questions of exactly where money comes from and how the supply can be changed. This chapter provides the answers to these questions by explaining the source of the money supply. The key players in the creation of money are the central bank and all depository institutions, including commercial banks and thrift institutions (savings banks, savings and loan associations, and credit unions). We will refer to all depository institutions as banks to simplify the discussion.

Recall from Chapter 11 that the M1 money supply consists of coins, currency (Federal Reserve notes), and checkable deposits. Coins, issued by the U.S. Treasury, are a very small part of the money supply. Federal Reserve notes are issued by the Federal Reserve System, and checkable deposits are held by depository institutions. Thus, money creation (except for the small amount of money in coins) is under the control of the depository institutions and the central bank.

The United States was one of the last modern industrial countries to

315

Federal Reserve System (Fed)
The central bank of the United States.

establish a central bank. The **Federal Reserve System (Fed)**, established in 1914, is the central bank of the United States. In addition to regulating banks, the Fed exerts control over the size of the money supply. This chapter will discuss the events leading up to the creation of the Fed and the tools it uses to influence the money supply.

WHAT BANKS DO

As you learned in Chapter 11, goldsmiths were responsible for the development of the first paper currency and were also the first modern bankers. Goldsmiths issued notes as receipts for gold deposits, and the notes began to circulate as currency. It didn't take the goldsmiths very long to discover that they had few day-to-day requests from depositors to redeem these notes for gold. They could safely lend out some of the depositors' gold (as well as their own), earning interest and eventually paying interest on deposits.

Suppose a prosperous medieval baron deposited 100 florins in gold with a goldsmith, accepting a paper receipt, or note, in exchange. This paper note, redeemable in gold, could serve as money. In fact, in some ways the note served better as money than the 100 gold florins because it was just as acceptable but much easier to carry. The goldsmith could lend someone else 50 florins of the baron's gold, which would also be money.

The deposit of 100 florins expanded the money supply by 50 florins. The original deposit of 100 florins was still money but so was the 50 florins lent by the goldsmith. This kind of transaction by goldsmiths is the origin of fractional reserve banking, a fundamental principle of all modern banking systems. **Fractional reserve banking** is the practice of holding a fraction of money deposited as reserves and lending the rest. This practice is the basis for money creation in most market economies.

fractional reserve banking
The practice of holding a fraction of money deposited as reserves and lending the rest.

The development of banking was as great an innovation as the development of money. By replacing barter, money solved the problem of meeting the double coincidence of wants in order to make trades. When banking came into being, it was no longer necessary to hunt for an individual who was willing to lend as much as the borrower wanted to borrow for the desired time and on acceptable terms. Just as money simplified the problem of matching traders, banks simplified the problem of matching lenders with borrowers. The most important function of a bank is to be a wholesaler in the lending business, gathering up small sums from depositors and lending larger amounts to borrowers. Banks pay some interest to depositors, charge more interest to borrowers, and make their profit and pay their expenses out of the difference.

It is risky for individual lenders to deal with individual borrowers because a lender loses the entire amount of the loan if the borrower fails to repay. If individuals lend through a bank rather than directly, they are "buying" a piece of the whole range of loans made by the bank. Although one or two borrowers may default, most of the loans will be repaid.

THE BANK'S BALANCE SHEET

A bank is a business firm, just like a grocery store or a shirt factory. It is in business to earn a profit for its owners, who are stockholders. The balance sheet of any firm provides a picture of its financial situation. The balance sheet of a bank lists its assets in order of liquidity (from most liquid to least liquid), its liabilities, and its net worth. Table 1 is a balance sheet for Amacher National Bank. The first thing you should notice is that the balance sheet balances. That is, assets equal liabilities plus net worth. A balance sheet must always balance. The fact that it balances says nothing about how well the bank is doing. To determine the bank's condition, we must look at some individual assets and liabilities.

For Amacher National, reserves are the most liquid asset. **Reserves** are bank assets that can be used to pay depositors when checks are presented for payment. Reserves consist of currency on hand (vault cash) and deposits at the central bank. It is important for a bank to keep enough reserves to meet the day-to-day withdrawals of customers. However, a bank does not want to keep any more reserves than necessary because reserves do not earn interest, and loans do.

The interest-earning assets of Amacher National are government bonds and loans to the public. Note that the bank's assets are others' liabilities. Government bonds are liabilities of the U.S. Treasury, and loans are liabilities of the households and businesses who borrowed the money. The fixed assets of Amacher National consist of the bank's building, furnishings, and other equipment. This kind of asset is the least liquid on the list because it is the most difficult to convert to cash.

The largest liability for Amacher National is its checkable deposits of $50,000. A small volume of savings or other deposits and some loans that the Fed has made to this bank (which will be explained later in the chapter) make up the rest of the bank's liabilities. The net worth of $8,000 represents the value of the bank to its stockholders.

The balance sheets of banks and savings and loans (thrifts) have received a great deal of public scrutiny in the last few years. During the late 1980s, there were many depository institutions whose assets came to have much less value than their liabilities, leaving these institutions with negative net worth. We will examine this banking crisis in more detail in the next chapter. For now, we are mainly interested in the balance sheet as a tool to describe the process of money creation.

reserves
Bank assets that can be used to pay depositors when checks are presented for payment, consisting of currency on hand and reserve deposits at the central bank.

T-Accounts and Money Creation
The items on a bank's balance sheet play an important role in the money creation process. Rather than relisting all assets and liabilities, it is simpler

Assets		Liabilities	
Vault cash	$ 1,000	Checkable deposits	$50,000
Reserves at the Fed	19,000	Other deposits	5,000
Government bonds	15,000	Loans from the Fed	2,000
Loans to the public	20,000		
Fixed assets	10,000	TOTAL LIABILITIES	$57,000
TOTAL ASSETS	$65,000	NET WORTH	$ 8,000
		TOTAL LIABILITIES AND NET WORTH	$65,000

Table 1
Balance Sheet for Amacher National Bank

T-accounts
Partial balance sheets
showing changes in assets
and/or liabilities
resulting from a trans-
action or group of
transactions.

to look at only those that change. We will use a partial balance sheet, called a **T-account**, that shows changes in assets and/or liabilities resulting from a transaction or group of transactions. The only items listed on a T-account are those that have changed. If the balance sheet balances at the start, then as long as the changes on the T-account offset each other, the balance sheet will still be in balance after the transaction is completed.

Table 2 shows how T-accounts are used to record changes in Amacher National's balance sheet for two sample transactions. Suppose Susan Smith came in with $100 in cash to deposit in her checking account, and the bank took the deposit and put it in the vault. There would be a $100 increase in assets (vault cash, or reserves) and a $100 increase in liabilities (checkable deposits). The balance sheet would still be in balance. In the second transaction, Amacher National sells a $1,000 bond and uses the proceeds to make a loan. The balance sheet would still be in balance after this transaction because the increase in one kind of asset (the loan) would be exactly offset by the decrease in another (the bond).[1] T-accounts are useful for following the process of money creation in banks.

Note that the plus and minus signs in the T-accounts refer to increases and decreases, not to assets or liabilities. The +$100 represents an increase in reserves in transaction 1, and the –$1,000 refers to a reduction in bonds in transaction 2.

The way today's banks create money is not very different from the way medieval goldsmiths increased the money supply—by making loans with the gold others had deposited for safekeeping. The goldsmiths discovered that on any given day, most depositors did not withdraw much of their gold. A fractional amount was all goldsmiths had to hold to meet daily demand. Although gold has ceased to play much of a role in the money supply, banks still lend part of the reserves created by deposits. Banks' checkable deposits serve as money, just as the notes issued by the goldsmiths served as money.

How much can Amacher National lend? The balance sheet in Table 1 shows that this bank already has $20,000 in loans outstanding. The balance sheet also shows that the bank has reserves of $20,000 (including vault cash) and checkable deposits of $50,000. To keep things simple, we

TABLE 2
SAMPLE TRANSACTIONS AND T-ACCOUNTS

TRANSACTION 1:
Susan Smith puts $100 in cash in her checking account; Amacher National Bank adds the $100 to its reserves.

ASSETS		LIABILITIES	
Reserves	+$100	Checkable deposits	+$100

TRANSACTION 2:
Amacher National Bank sells a bond and makes a loan.

ASSETS		LIABILITIES	
Loans	+$1,000		
Bonds	–$1,000		

1.   There would really be two sets of changes on the asset side. When the bond was sold, bond holdings fell and reserves rose. When the reserves were lent, reserves fell and loans rose.

will assume that banks keep reserves only to back up checkable deposits. Amacher National's reserves are 40 percent of its checkable deposits. This is a fairly high level of reserves. This bank can probably lend more without worrying about meeting the demands of depositors.

Assume that Amacher National has decided to reduce reserves to only 20 percent of deposits. Twenty percent of the $50,000 in checkable deposits is only $10,000. Thus, Amacher National can expand its loans by $10,000. Remember, reserves do not earn interest, but loans do. When the next promising borrower comes in, the bank will make a $10,000 loan. The bank will probably not give the borrower cash but will simply credit the borrower's checking account, increasing the bank's checkable deposits (liabilities) by $10,000. The T-account for this transaction is shown in Table 3.

The balance sheet of Amacher National is still in balance, and the bank has increased the money supply by $10,000 in new checkable deposits. It looks as if Amacher National could lend still more because the note at the bottom of the T-account points out that reserves are still $20,000 and checkable deposits are $60,000. The bank only needs to keep $12,000, or 20 percent, in reserves to back up $60,000 in checkable deposits.

Amacher National did not lend more than $10,000 because the loan officer knew that Joe's Barber Shop intended to spend the money. Those funds will not stay in the firm's checking account very long. Joe will spend them on equipment for his shop, and Joe's supplier will probably deposit Joe's check in another bank. When a check drawn on one bank is deposited in another, the first bank loses reserves and checkable deposits. The bank that receives a check drawn on another bank finds its reserves and checkable deposits increasing. The receiving bank's ability to make loans and expand the money supply will increase. If Joe's supplier deposits the check in Ulbrich Savings Bank, the T-accounts for the two banks will be as shown in Table 4 on page 320.

After this transfer of reserves, Amacher National is "all loaned up." It cannot make any more loans until it somehow acquires more reserves. However, Ulbrich Savings can make new loans. If this bank also keeps a 20 percent reserve behind checkable deposits, then it needs only $2,000 in reserves behind the $10,000 in new checkable deposits. Ulbrich Savings can safely lend the other $8,000 of newly acquired reserves.

MAXIMUM EXPANSION OF THE MONEY SUPPLY

Amacher National lent $10,000 in **excess reserves**, which are reserves above the level required by law. Then Ulbrich Savings Bank expanded its lending by $8,000. It's not hard to see that Ulbrich's lending will create new reserves for a third bank, which will in turn lend and create new reserves

excess reserves
Reserves above the level required by law.

AMACHER NATIONAL BANK MAKES A LOAN TO JOE'S BARBER SHOP.		
ASSETS	**LIABILITIES**	
Loans +$10,000	Checkable deposits +$10,000	

Note: Total reserves = $20,000; total checkable deposits = $60,000.

TABLE 3
T-ACCOUNT FOR A LOAN TRANSACTION

TABLE 4
T-ACCOUNTS FOR A TRANSFER OF RESERVES FROM ONE BANK TO ANOTHER

AMACHER NATIONAL BANK

ASSETS		LIABILITIES	
Reserves	−$10,000	Checkable deposits	−$10,000

Note: Total reserves = $10,000; total checkable deposits = $50,000.

ULBRICH SAVINGS BANK

ASSETS		LIABILITIES	
Reserves	+$10,000	Checkable deposits	+$10,000

for a fourth bank, and so on. How long will this process continue? If we know what ratio of reserves to deposits banks wish to maintain, we can identify the upper limits of the money expansion process.[2]

Any bank can expand its loans as long as it has excess reserves. The banking system as a whole can expand loans as long as there are excess reserves in the system. Thus, expansion of the money supply must stop only when there are no more excess reserves in the banking system. The only way to get rid of excess reserves is for banks to lend them.

Suppose all banks in the system hold reserves of 20 percent of checkable deposits, either voluntarily or because they are required to do so by law. Each bank wants to lend out any excess reserves (ER) in order to earn interest. The money creation process will stop only when there are no more excess reserves. That is, no more money will be created when all bank reserves (BR) in the entire banking system have been converted to required reserves (RR). The **reserve ratio** (rr) is the fraction of deposits that banks are required to hold in reserves. Banks' required reserves are thus $rr \times D$, where D = checkable deposits. The banking system (as well as any individual bank) is fully loaned up when RR equals BR, or

$$(1)\ RR = BR = rr \times D.$$

Dividing equation (1) by rr gives

$$(2)\ D = \frac{1}{rr} \times BR.$$

reserve ratio
Fraction of deposits that banks are required to hold in reserves.

The steps in the money expansion process are shown in Table 5. This table shows the change in deposits, reserves, and loans for the first five banks as well as the totals for the process. Note that the bottom line satisfies equation (2). That is, newly created checkable deposits are equal to the initial excess reserves multiplied by the deposit multiplier, $1/rr$. The **deposit multiplier** is the ratio between the maximum increase in the money supply and a given increase in excess reserves. It equals the reciprocal of the reserve ratio.[3] The deposit multiplier depends only on the ratio of required reserves to checkable deposits.

deposit multiplier
Ratio between the maximum increase in the money supply and a given increase in excess reserves. It equals the reciprocal of the reserve ratio.

2. The maximum money supply may not be reached because no one can force a bank to make loans from its pool of excess reserves. If there are no loan customers that look worthwhile, a bank can simply hold some excess reserves. We will consider this effect a little later.
3. This term should not be confused with the Keynesian expenditure multiplier discussed in Chapter 8.

BANK	CHANGE IN CHECKABLE DEPOSITS	CHANGE IN BANK RESERVES	AMOUNT THE BANK LENDS
Amacher National	$ —	$ —	$10,000
Ulbrich Savings	+10,000	+2,000	8,000
C	+8,000	+1,600	6,400
D	+6,400	+1,280	5,120
E	+5,120	+1,024	4,096
All others	+20,480	+4,096	16,384
Total	$+50,000	$+10,000	$40,000

TABLE 5
INCREASE IN MONEY SUPPLY WITH INITIAL EXCESS RESERVES OF $10,000 AND A RESERVE RATIO OF 20 PERCENT

According to equation (2), checkable deposits (*D*) can change only if the reserve ratio (*rr*) changes or if all bank reserves (*BR*) change. Using the symbol Δ to represent "change in," we have:

$$\Delta D = \frac{1}{rr} \Delta BR = \Delta M_s.$$

Thus, the change in checkable deposits will be equal to the reciprocal of the reserve ratio (*rr*) multiplied by the change in bank reserves (ΔBR). In our example, *rr* = 0.20, so the value of $1/rr$ is 5. If the ΔBR equals $10,000, then $\Delta D = 5 \times \$10,000 = \$50,000$.

Expansion of checkable deposits can occur only when there are excess reserves. If all reserves are being held to meet the desired ratio of reserves to deposits, then there are no excess reserves available. In that case, the money supply cannot increase.

WHY EXPANSION MAY BE LESS THAN THE MAXIMUM

The actual expansion of the money supply may be less than the maximum that existing bank reserves can support. One reason why this may occur is that the public may decide to hold more of its financial assets in currency and less in checkable deposits. Individuals may make this choice because of concerns about bank safety or because they are using cash transactions to avoid income taxes or to hide illegal activities (such as drug dealing).

A **currency drain** is an increase in cash held by the public that causes a dollar-for-dollar decline in bank reserves. Since currency is part of reserves when it is in the banking system, a currency drain means a reduction in bank reserves. If reserves decline, the banking system cannot support as many checkable deposits. For every dollar of currency flowing out of the banks and into circulation, bank reserves (*BR*) fall by $1. With a 20 percent reserve ratio (*rr*), $5 of potential new deposits are eliminated.

A second reason why expansion of the money supply may fall short of the maximum lies with banks. Banks may choose to hold more reserves than are legally required. Usually banks like to keep reserves down to the required minimum because reserves earn no interest. But if economic conditions are depressed, loan prospects are risky, or interest rates on loans are so low that the only direction they can go is up, banks may choose to hold some excess reserves until conditions improve. In addition, during recessionary times, banks may choose to hold some reserves in case there are large withdrawals during a run, or bank panic. Even if

currency drain
An increase in cash held by the public that causes a dollar-for-dollar decline in bank reserves.

banks are willing to lend, households and firms may not be anxious to borrow. If households and firms are already heavily in debt or have gloomy expectations, they may be reluctant to borrow from banks.

CONTRACTING THE MONEY SUPPLY

The process of contracting the money supply is the expansion process in reverse. Suppose that, for some reason, Amacher National Bank lost reserves. Perhaps a customer withdrew currency from her account in the amount of $2,000. If Amacher National Bank was all loaned up before this withdrawal, this loss of reserves will put the bank below the required reserve level. Amacher has lost $2,000 in reserves and $2,000 in deposits. With a 20 percent reserve ratio, the bank was holding only $400 in reserves behind that deposit. The shortfall of $1,600 must be made up by not making loans or by selling bonds. As Amacher works to rebuild its reserves, however, it gains reserves at the expense of the other banks in the system. Table 6 shows the first few stages of this process. The deposit multiplier is the same here as for the expansion process. Thus, the initial loss of $2,000 in reserves will lead to a maximum contraction of the money supply of $10,000 if no banks had any excess reserves before the first transaction.

BANKS AND THE CENTRAL BANK

This description of the money expansion and contraction process raises two important questions. Where do reserves come from, and who sets the reserve ratio? Deposits and withdrawals of currency by the public are one source of changes in bank reserves, but these flows are relatively small in the U.S. banking system. The major source of bank reserves, including cash in the form of Federal Reserve notes, is the central bank, the Federal Reserve System. The Fed not only creates reserves but also sets and changes the reserve ratio.

CENTRAL BANKING IN THE UNITED STATES

The Federal Reserve System was created by Congress in 1914 in response to two perceived needs. The public wanted Congress to regulate banks in order to prevent them from making risky loans that threatened the safety of deposits. There was also a demand for a lender of last resort to rescue basically sound banks that were threatened with failure and bankruptcy because of temporary economic conditions. Later, a third goal was established: managing the size of the money supply so as to promote economic growth, high employment, and a stable price level. This goal is now the Fed's most important function, but it was not part of the original design of the system. It has only become significant since the Great Depression.

TABLE 6
DECREASE IN MONEY
SUPPLY FOLLOWING
A LOSS OF RESERVES
OF $2,000

BANK	CHANGE IN CHECKABLE DEPOSITS	CHANGE IN BANK RESERVES	REDUCTION IN BANK LENDING
Amacher National	$ —	$–2,000	$–1,600
Ulbrich Savings	–1,600	–1,600	–1,280
Bank C	–1,280	–1,280	–1,024

The U.S. Constitution gave the federal government the power to "coin money and regulate the value thereof." It said nothing, however, about establishing banks. Two early attempts to establish a central bank failed. Alexander Hamilton, the first Secretary of the Treasury, was the mastermind behind the creation of the Bank of the United States in 1791. Located in Philadelphia, the bank was privately owned but chartered by the federal government. Its role was to supervise other banks, promote bank safety, and serve as a lender of last resort. Its charter expired in 1811. In 1816, the Second Bank of the United States was created. When its charter was not renewed in 1836 for political reasons, the United States no longer had a central bank.

BANKING PROBLEMS IN THE NINETEENTH CENTURY

The nineteenth century was marked by frequent bank panics in the United States. **Bank panics** are sudden waves of fear that banks will not be able to pay off their depositors. In the nineteenth century, banks made loans by issuing their own bank notes rather than creating checkable deposits. These notes were supposed to be redeemable in gold. Banks did not maintain enough reserves to redeem all their notes at the same time. As long as the note holders believed they could redeem their notes, very few would actually do so on any given day. The day-to-day demand for redemption in gold could easily be met.

During bank panics, some banks only had problems of liquidity. That is, they did not have enough reserves to meet current demand. Most of the loans they had made would eventually have been repaid, but not quickly enough to meet depositors' current withdrawals. Other banks had more serious problems of solvency. These banks had so many bad loans that the value of their assets was less than the value of their deposits.

For banks that followed unsound lending practices, there usually came a day when too many notes were presented for redemption. The bank's reserves would be too low to redeem all of them. When this happened at one bank, people sometimes panicked and tried to redeem notes at other banks as well. At the height of the bank panics, many sound and well-managed banks were unable to redeem the large numbers of notes presented in a single day. These banks failed, or closed, even though they were basically sound. People who had deposited money in failed banks lost it, and people who needed loans could not get them. Even the banks that didn't fail had to greatly reduce their lending to build reserves against a run of withdrawals.

A run could occur at a perfectly sound bank. All that was needed was a rumor of possible failure that was believed by enough people. To prevent sound banks from going under in a panic, a lender of last resort was needed. A **lender of last resort** is a source of funds for rescuing sound banks by lending them as much as they need to meet temporary high demand from depositors. If sound banks could obtain funds from a lender of last resort, depositors would be less likely to panic. Thus, panics would be less likely to occur in the first place and would be less severe when they did occur.

Does this description of bank panics sound like the banking crisis of the late 1980s? There are some similarities between the two crises and some important differences. Because of federal deposit insurance (discussed later

bank panics
Sudden waves of fear that banks will not be able to pay off their depositors.

lender of last resort
A source of funds for rescuing sound banks by lending them as much as they need to meet temporary high demand from depositors.

in this chapter), few depositors in the 1980s crisis suffered losses. The numerous bank failures of the 1980s represented problems of solvency, not liquidity. These banks had made ill-advised loans and investments. When the value of those investments fell, many banks became insolvent. We will examine the banking crisis in more detail in the next chapter.

EARLY ATTEMPTS AT CONTROL

Without a central bank to regulate unsound banking practices in the nineteenth century, some larger private banks tried to fill the void. A major bank, or group of banks, that was concerned about overissuing of notes and unsound loan practices at Bank A could exert pressure by presenting Bank A's notes to be redeemed in gold. This action drained gold from Bank A and slowed down its issuing of notes. (Such a process was carried out with some success by the Suffolk Bank and its affiliated banks in New England.) Such actions by private banks did not work very well or last very long. Private banks did not have the power to examine another bank's books and lending practices or to force it to stop making bad loans. They lacked the legal authority to regulate other banks and weren't financially strong enough themselves to withstand a major panic. Also, state governments' oversight of banks was generally ineffective and varied widely from state to state.

The logical conclusion seemed to be that only the federal government had the effective power to regulate banks, as well as the financial resources to act as the lender of last resort. However, political battles over whether to give central banking powers to the federal government went on for nearly a century. One reason for the resistance to a central bank was the fear that the centralized power would be used to benefit rich and powerful bankers. The Bank of the United States, originally chartered by the federal government, had tried to restrain the excesses of other banks. Many people felt that the Bank of the United States had used governmental power to benefit the bank's owners, their friends, and business associates. These feelings led to the failure of the first two attempts to establish a central bank.

Another source of resistance to a central bank was disagreement about the importance of sound money and the dangers of inflation. Conservative bankers wanted to limit the expansion of loans for fear it would lead to inflation. If that happened, the value of the loan repayments they received would fall. Rapid money growth and inflation did not seem like problems to some other groups, however. The people who wanted loans—for example, farmers on the Western frontier or small businesses in the East—looked on the expansion of loans as a good thing. People who were in debt had their interest payments fixed in dollar terms. In times of rising prices, they had increasing incomes with which to make their payments. In times of falling prices, they had to make these fixed payments out of a falling income. Borrowers and debtors were afraid that a central bank would pursue a conservative policy that would make life more difficult for them.

National Banking System
Agency that chartered and regulated national banks during the latter half of the nineteenth century, before the Federal Reserve System.

THE NATIONAL BANKING SYSTEM

During the Civil War, Congress tried again to make banks safer. The **National Banking System**, established in 1863, allowed banks to apply for federal instead of state charters (formal permission to incorporate and operate). Banks that receive their charters from the federal government are called **national banks**. A **state bank** is chartered and regulated by one of the states.

The agency that is charged with chartering and regulating national banks is the Comptroller of the Currency in the Department of the Treasury. State banks are regulated by various agencies and commissions in the different states. After 1863, state banks continued to exist alongside national banks. Since state regulation was rather weak and ineffective, the National Banking Act did not substantially improve the stability of banks. Furthermore, there was still no lender of last resort.

THE FEDERAL RESERVE ACT

The panic of 1907 and the recession that followed convinced Congress to hold hearings on banking problems. After a series of compromises designed to quiet some of opponents' fears, the Federal Reserve Act was passed in 1913. The Federal Reserve System, modeled after the British central bank (the Bank of England), began operating in November 1914. The Federal Reserve System was intended to be an agency that regulated banks and served as a lender of last resort.

STRUCTURE AND FUNCTIONS OF THE FEDERAL RESERVE SYSTEM

The Federal Reserve System was structured to allay fears people had about concentrating financial power at the federal level. The United States is divided into twelve Federal Reserve districts, each with its own Reserve Bank (see Figure 1).[4] The purpose of having districts was to keep the management of the Federal Reserve Banks in closer touch with the people, instead of concentrating power in Washington, DC or New York City.[5] In addition, the board of directors of each district bank was to contain specific numbers of representatives of the banking industry, agriculture, and the general public in order to prevent domination by bankers.

The district banks play an important role in clearing checks from bank to bank. Suppose you write a check for $100 on your account at Student Union Bank in Boston and send it to a firm in Georgia. The firm deposits your check in its account in Citizens and Southern Bank. Citizens and Southern records an entry of $100 in the firm's account and sends the check to the Atlanta Federal Reserve Bank, which credits the Citizens and Southern reserve account with $100 and forwards the check to the Boston Federal Reserve Bank. The Boston Fed takes $100 out of the reserve account of Student Union and transfers it to the account of the Atlanta Fed.

national banks
Banks chartered by the federal government and subject to its rules and regulations.

state banks
Banks chartered and regulated by individual states, as opposed to the federal government.

---

4. You can easily determine which district bank issued a Federal Reserve note. To the left of the portrait on the face of each bill is a seal that gives the name of the district bank. The letter in the middle of the seal corresponds to the number that appears four times near the corners. For example, a bill from the Federal Reserve Bank of Dallas, Texas will have the letter K in the seal and four 11's near the corners. Dallas is the 11th Federal Reserve district, and K is the 11th letter of the alphabet.

5. It was also thought that each district could experiment with different policies, which would allow everyone to learn which strategies worked best. This idea never really worked out, as it became apparent that monetary policy had to be coordinated at a national level.

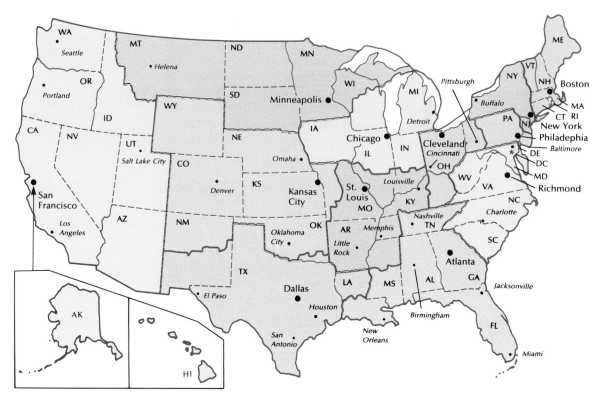

* Board of Governors of the Federal Reserve System
• Federal Reserve Bank Cities
· Federal Reserve Branch Cities

Source: Board of Governors of the Federal Reserve System, *Federal Reserve Bulletin,* June 1990.

FIGURE 1
THE FEDERAL RESERVE SYSTEM
There are twelve Federal Reserve districts, each with its own bank. Most of these banks have branches. The Board of Governors of the Federal Reserve System is located in Washington, DC.

Finally, the check is returned to Student Union, which loses $100 in reserves (an asset) and deposits (a liability). Complex as this process sounds, it is more efficient than what happened before the Fed existed. Checks were passed from bank to bank to bank until they returned to the point of origin, often months later.

When the Federal Reserve System was created, national banks were required to be members. State-chartered banks were allowed but not required to join. The incentives for state banks to join voluntarily were the privileges of borrowing from the Fed and of having direct access to its interbank check-clearing services. Both of these privileges were limited to member banks. In 1980, the law was changed to place all depository institutions under the control of the Fed.

Board of Governors
Central governing body of the Federal Reserve System.

To provide for some central control, a **Board of Governors** was established as the governing body of the Federal Reserve System. The seven governors are appointed by the President for fourteen-year, staggered terms. There can be no more than one governor from any of the twelve districts. Most governors have a background in law, banking, or economics.

Most countries have central banks. In fact, the United States was one of the last developed, industrial countries to establish a central bank. All central banks attempt to control the money supply, provide services to banks, manage monetary policy, issue currency, and perform other central banking functions. However, most other central banks have an easier job than the Fed.

The setup of the Fed reflects the fact that the United States is a federal country. The nation is made up of states with some degree of independence. (There are not very many other federal countries. Among the few are Canada, Australia, Brazil, and West Germany.) In countries with unitary (nonfederal) systems, there is less need to provide representation for states and regions in policy making and no need for regional banks of the central bank. In the United States, the transition from state to federal regulation of banking required some compromises that were not made in most other countries.

A typical name of a foreign central bank is the Bank of England or the Bank of Italy. The first central bank of the United States was called the Bank of the United States. When this country took another stab at central banking, a new name was needed. The central bank was named the Federal Reserve System to reflect its federal nature and what was originally re-garded as its primary function, storing and supplying reserves.

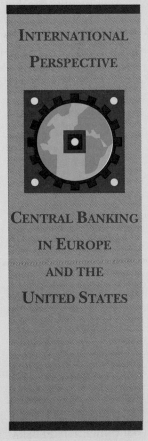

INTERNATIONAL

PERSPECTIVE

CENTRAL BANKING

IN EUROPE

AND THE

UNITED STATES

In European countries, the central bank's task of supervising banks and carrying out monetary policy is easier because there are only a few large banks with many branches. The United States has a large number of individual banks, many of them not members of the Federal Reserve System. Branch banking and inter-state banking are recent developments in this country, partly because of the suspicions of Westerners about the power of large Eastern banks. In Europe, large banks with branches have a long history. Some extend back into the Middle Ages. Many less developed countries that were formerly colonies of European nations (especially of France or Britain) have banking systems and central banks that were copied from those of the colonial power.

Finally, European governments do not face one major political problem that confronts the President and Congress in the United States. Control of monetary policy is assigned to an agency that operates independently of both the executive and legislative branches of the U.S. government. Central banks in most other countries are a part of the government and are under its control. This arrangement makes it much easier to coordinate monetary and fiscal policy.

Because the governors serve such long terms, it is rare for even a two-term President to appoint more than a bare majority of the board. These long terms give the Fed a degree of political independence from the executive branch. Technically, the Fed is outside both executive and legislative control, operated by the Board of Governors. The Fed is accountable to its regional boards, its stockholders, and the banks, but there is no effective way for the President or Congress to exercise any control except by the appointments to the Board. Political insiders in Washington have labeled the chairperson of the Fed's Board of Governors, currently Alan Greenspan, as the second most powerful person in Washington.

In the late 1970s, the Federal Reserve System was losing members because member banks were subject to higher reserve ratios than most non-member banks, whose reserve ratios were set by state regulators. Although the Fed offered member banks access to borrowing and check-clearing services, smaller banks could obtain these services indirectly through correspondent relationships with member banks. With high market interest rates, the opportunity cost of holding reserves was very high. Legislation in 1980 eliminated this disadvantage of belonging to the Federal Reserve System by phasing in uniform reserve ratios for the same type of deposits for all banks, whether or not they were member banks.[6] This action stemmed the loss of membership and helped the Fed to retain more control over the banking system and the money supply.

Federal Open Market Committee (FOMC)
Committee that supervises the conduct of the Fed's monetary policy.

Within the Fed, the most powerful group is the **Federal Open Market Committee (FOMC)**, which supervises the conduct of monetary policy. This committee consists of the Board of Governors plus the presidents of five district banks, always including the president of the New York Federal Reserve Bank. The FOMC meets regularly to make decisions about changes in bank reserves and the money supply. All district bank presidents, not just those currently on the FOMC, attend these meetings.

ARE BANKS SAFER UNDER THE FEDERAL RESERVE SYSTEM?

Bank safety was one of the primary reasons for establishing the Federal Reserve System. The first test of the Fed was the Great Depression. Based on the number of bank failures, the Fed flunked. Two deposit insurance agencies, the Federal Deposit Insurance Corporation (FDIC) and the Federal Savings and Loan Insurance Corporation (FSLIC), were created in the 1930s. These two insurance corporations were designed to protect bank depositors, not banks or bank stockholders, from insolvency. Originally deposits were insured up to $2,500, but the ceiling was raised several times and is currently $100,000. The insurance is required for all members of the Federal Reserve System and is financed by premiums paid by the member banks. Both the FDIC and the FSLIC (which were merged in 1990) supervise member banks for safety and compliance with federal banking regulations. The bank insurance system seemed to work well until the late 1980s when a number of bank failures shifted the burden of protecting depositors to the federal government. We will consider this issue in more detail in Chapter 13.

---

6. Although all depository institutions and all types of accounts are treated alike, there is a distinction based on size. The reserve ratio is higher for banks with deposits of over $40 million.

Thus, national banks are subject to a great deal of oversight because they must belong to the Federal Reserve System and carry deposit insurance. The Fed supervises its member banks, the Comptroller of the Currency supervises national banks, and the FDIC supervises its member banks. Some state-chartered banks, however, are supervised only by their state's banking commission and any state or private deposit insurance group to which they belong.

Recall that there are two sources of bank failure. One is a liquidity problem—a lack of ready cash to meet excessive withdrawals by the public. The insurance of deposits by the FDIC and FSLIC and the existence of the Fed as a lender of last resort have largely resolved that problem. The other problem is one of solvency—the value of a bank's assets is not enough to cover outstanding liabilities, such as deposits. A bank becomes insolvent if it has too many assets in loans that may never be repaid. When a bank becomes insolvent, it will go out of business or be taken over by another bank in a merger. Such a merger is often forced by the insuring agency.

The FDIC and the Comptroller of the Currency also regulate kinds of investments that banks can make. This regulation provides stockholders and depositors some protection against insolvency. Even in a regulated industry such as banking, it is important to allow unsuccessful firms to fail and leave the industry if the market system is to function effectively. However, a very high failure rate, such as occurred in the late 1980s, overstrains the capacity of the regulatory authorities and the resources of the insurance corporations.

There were some spectacular failures of major banks in the late 1970s and early 1980s. For example, Franklin National Bank in New York City, Continental Illinois in Chicago, and Penn Square in Oklahoma failed. Failures of state-chartered banks in Ohio, Nebraska, Mississippi, and Maryland in 1984 and 1985 led to demands for reform to provide greater protection for depositors. After a two-year wave of failures (79 banks in 1984 and 120 in 1985) and a number of shotgun mergers, many of the surviving state-chartered banks became members of the FDIC or FSLIC.

In the late 1980s, bank failures were far less spectacular but much more numerous, threatening the soundness of the two deposit insurance corporations. A number of banks—especially savings and loans—developed some serious solvency problems. On their balance sheets, the value of assets had fallen below the value of liabilities, leaving them with negative net worth. Some of these banks were suffering from mismanagement by own-

FUNCTIONS OF THE FED

- Preventing bank crises and panics by serving as the lender of last resort
- Supervising banks
- Providing currency and check-clearing services
- Providing banking services to the Treasury
- Conducting monetary policy

ers who made loans to themselves and their friends on the basis of property with inflated values. Others ran into regional economic problems. Banks that served rural, agricultural communities saw the value of loan collateral drop sharply with falling prices for farmland and high bankruptcy rates among farmers. Similar problems affected banks in Texas and Oklahoma that had made many loans to oil companies. A number of big urban banks had to write off bad loans to less developed countries or extend them with a risk of never being repaid. In 1990 and 1991, several major New England banks failed as the recession and falling real estate prices hit that region harder than the rest of the country. We will explore the origins of this banking crisis and its consequences in the next chapter.

THE BALANCE SHEET OF THE FEDERAL RESERVE SYSTEM

Like all banks, the Federal Reserve System has a balance sheet that lists its assets, liabilities, and net worth. Table 7 shows a simplified balance sheet for the Fed for 1990. Note that member banks' reserves are assets to those institutions but liabilities of the Fed. Federal Reserve notes, now the only legal form of U.S. currency, are another major liability of the Fed. Treasury deposits are a relatively small entry on the liability side. One of the original but now less important functions of the Fed is to be a bank to the U.S. Treasury. The Treasury also keeps funds in commercial banks. The main assets of the Fed are government bonds of various maturities, which are used in open market operations. The Fed also holds gold certificates, issued by the Treasury when it acquires gold. A small amount of the Fed's assets consists of loans outstanding to banks.

On a balance sheet, the best measure of financial health is net worth, or assets minus liabilities. For a corporation, net worth represents the value of ownership rights of stockholders. Who owns the Fed? Member banks do, and they earn a guaranteed return on their shares. Any earnings in excess of that guaranteed return go to the U.S. Treasury, since the Fed is both a privately owned firm and an agency of the government.

In Chapter 11, we used T-accounts to show the effect of single transactions for Amacher National Bank. A T-account can also be used to describe the transactions of the Fed. The main transactions of interest are those that relate changes in member bank reserves, because bank reserves determine bank lending and the size of the money supply. Thus, the most

TABLE 7
FEDERAL RESERVE BALANCE
SHEET, OCTOBER 1990
(MILLIONS OF DOLLARS)

ASSETS		LIABILITIES	
Government securities	$237,763	Reserves of banks	$ 34,546
Loans to banks	591	Federal Reserve notes	255,866
		Treasury deposits	7,607
Gold certificates	11,060	Other liabilities	10,628
Other assets	65,653	TOTAL LIABILITIES	308,641
		NET WORTH	6,426
		TOTAL LIABILITIES	
TOTAL ASSETS	$315,067	AND NET WORTH	$315,067

Source: Board of Governors of the Federal Reserve System, *Federal Reserve Bulletin* (Washington, DC: U.S. Government Printing Office, January 1991).

important items on the balance sheet are government securities, loans to banks, and reserves of banks.

Table 8 shows two sample transactions and T-accounts for the Fed. In transaction 1, the Fed buys a $10,000 government bond from Amacher National Bank. In transaction 2, the Fed makes a $20,000 loan to Ulbrich Savings Bank. When the Fed buys the bond, we assume that Amacher National is paid by a credit to its reserve account at the Fed. When the Fed makes the loan to Ulbrich Savings, we assume that Ulbrich requests that the funds be paid in Federal Reserve notes.

THE FED AND THE MONEY SUPPLY

Actions concerning bonds, reserves, loans to banks, and Federal Reserve notes are the tools of monetary policy. The Fed uses the money supply and interest rates to affect output, employment, and the price level. The Fed has three methods of influencing the money supply: open market operations, changes in the reserve ratio, and changes in the discount rate. Open market operations involve buying and selling bonds to affect banks' reserves. Changes in the reserve ratio affect their excess reserves. The discount rate affects the borrowing done by the banks.

OPEN MARKET OPERATIONS

The Fed's most frequently used tool is open market operations, although it is the most recent of the three to develop. **Open market operations** are purchases and sales of government securities (bonds) by the Federal Reserve on the open market in order to affect bank reserves.[7]

open market operations
Purchases and sales of government bonds on the open market by the Fed in order to affect bank reserves.

Open market operations are a very flexible tool. The impact on reserves can be precisely determined to be as large or small as desired. Open market operations can be reversed if necessary and can be done without any fanfare. As a result, the Fed relies most heavily on open market operations for monetary policy.

Open market operations are carried out at the open market desk at the Federal Reserve Bank of New York. Bonds are bought and sold through brokers in New York City. The New York district bank has this responsibility because New York is the financial center of the country. The

TABLE 8
SAMPLE TRANSACTIONS AND T-ACCOUNTS FOR THE FED

TRANSACTION 1:
The Fed buys a bond from Amacher National.

ASSETS		LIABILITIES	
Government bonds	+$10,000	Reserves of banks	+$10,000

TRANSACTION 2:
The Fed makes a loan to Ulbrich Savings.

ASSETS		LIABILITIES	
Loans to banks	+$20,000	Federal Reserve notes	+$20,000

7.   The term *bond* is used here to refer to all U.S. Treasury securities. In reality, a large part of open market operations is carried out in short-term Treasury obligations, or T-bills.

open market desk, however, does not buy and sell on the basis of its own decisions. It carries out the overall directives of the FOMC.

How do the Fed's open market operations affect bank reserves? Suppose Bank A has reserves of $1,000,000 that it holds in the form of deposits with the Fed. The Fed buys $100,000 worth of government bonds from Bank A. The Fed now owns the government bonds and pays for them by writing on its books that Bank A has $100,000 more in deposits (reserves) with the Fed. Thus, Bank A's reserves are now $1,100,000. These changes are shown on the T-accounts of Bank A and the Fed in Table 9. Suppose the Fed buys a bond from an individual or a business firm. The seller is a customer of some bank, so the check received from the Fed will be deposited in a bank. The bank will then clear the check through the Fed, and the bank's reserves with the Fed will increase by the amount of the sale. No matter where the Fed buys bonds, bank reserves increase by the amount of the Fed purchase. Conversely, open market sales of securities by the Fed decrease the reserves of banks by the amount of the sale. Through open market operations, the Fed can directly affect the reserves of banks.

FIRST-ROUND EFFECTS OF OPEN MARKET OPERATIONS. Assume that the level of required reserves is 20 percent of checkable deposits and that all of Bank A's reserves were required reserves prior to the purchase of $100,000 in government bonds by the Fed. As shown in Bank A's T-account in Table 9, this transaction affects its reserves. The bank's interest-earning assets in the form of government bonds have fallen by $100,000. Its reserves have risen by $100,000. Now its excess reserves, total reserves *minus* required reserves, are $100,000.

This change in the makeup of Bank A's assets is only the first-round effect of the open market operation. What will Bank A do with these excess reserves? It now has fewer interest-earning assets because it sold the $100,000 bond to the Fed. When the next customer asks for a $100,000 loan, it will be granted if that customer is a good risk. Further, the bank may be a little more eager to make loans on easier terms. The bank may even be willing to lend at a lower interest rate. The new loan of $100,000 is shown in Table 10 as an increase in both checkable deposits (liabilities) and loans (assets) of Bank A.[8]

Bank A had new deposits of $100,000 and new reserves of $100,000. Of these new reserves, 20 percent of new deposits, or $20,000, were required reserves. Why didn't Bank A lend more money? Because, as mentioned earlier in this chapter, the loaned money is likely to be withdrawn from the bank very soon. Borrowers usually do not take out loans just to

TABLE 9
EFFECTS OF AN OPEN MARKET OPERATION ON BANK A AND THE FED

BANK A				THE FED			
ASSETS		LIABILITIES		ASSETS		LIABILITIES	
Reserves	+$100,000			Government bonds	+$100,000	Reserves of banks	+$100,000
Government bonds	−$100,000						

8.   If you were drawing up a T-account for the borrower, that person's T-account would show an increase in checkable deposits as an asset and a loan to be repaid as a liability.

ASSETS		LIABILITIES	
Loans	+$100,000	Checkable deposits	+$100,000

TABLE 10
T-ACCOUNT FOR BANK A'S
LOAN EXPANSION OF
$100,000

let the money sit idle in a checking account. For instance, a builder will take out a loan to finance the construction of a new office building and will use the funds to pay for materials and hire construction workers. When the borrower's checks are deposited in other banks, they will be presented for payment to Bank A. When checkable deposits are withdrawn, reserves will decline by the same amount.

The lesson for a single bank is clear. It can safely lend only its excess reserves because it can afford to lose these reserves and still meet the reserve ratio. As long as a bank lends only reserves that are in excess of its required reserves, it will be able to meet its reserve requirement, even if all the loaned funds leave the bank.

OPEN MARKET OPERATIONS AND THE DEPOSIT MULTIPLIER. What happens to the funds that the borrower pays out? Bank A will lose reserves and deposits, but another bank will gain both, just as before. The new reserves the Fed has created will remain in the banking system until the Fed withdraws them (perhaps by an open market operation in the opposite direction).[9] These reserves can be passed around from bank to bank, but banks cannot create new reserves. As long as they are in the banking system, they can support additional checkable deposits and thus a larger money supply. The amount of additional deposits they can support depends on the reserve ratio, according to the relationship developed earlier in this chapter:

$$\Delta D = \frac{1}{rr} \Delta BR = \Delta M_s.$$

The change in checkable deposits (ΔD) from the $100,000 open market operation ($\Delta BR = \$100,000$) with a reserve ratio ($rr$) equal to 0.20 is $100,000/0.20, or $500,000. How did this happen? Initially, member bank reserves increased by $100,000. Since the reserve ratio was unchanged, all of these additional reserves were excess reserves, available for lending. As loans and deposits expand, however, the excess reserves gradually become required reserves behind newly created checkable deposits. This process continues until all of the new reserves are serving as required reserves.

CONTRACTING THE MONEY SUPPLY. Open market purchases of bonds by the Fed are expansionary. When the Fed purchases bonds, it pays for them by increasing member banks' reserves. If the Fed wishes to contract the money supply or prevent banks from expanding the money supply, it will offer to sell bonds to the banks. Very small changes in their yield[10] will

---

9. Certain actions by the U.S. Treasury, foreigners, and the public can reduce member bank reserves. We will neglect these for the moment.
10. A slight fall in the price will raise the yield, which is equal to interest income divided by price paid. We will explore this relationship further in the next chapter.

make it extremely profitable for banks to purchase these bonds. The Fed thus has no trouble finding buyers. (If banks do not wish to buy, their customers will, and the effect on reserves is the same.) When the Fed sells bonds, it accepts payment by decreasing the bank's reserve account.

As a result of the sale of government bonds by the Fed, bank reserves fall. The deposit multiplier works on this reduction in reserves in the same way it works on an expansion of reserves. The money supply that can be supported by existing reserves is smaller than before. If banks were fully loaned up before this transaction, there would be a decrease in the money supply.

CHANGING THE RESERVE RATIO

The second tool used by the Fed is its power to set and change the reserve ratio. Items that a bank can count toward meeting the required reserve consist of two assets. One is the currency and coins the bank has on its premises, called vault cash. The second, and larger, consists of funds the bank has on deposit with its district Reserve Bank. The Fed requires depository institutions to hold reserves equal to certain fractions of the different kinds of deposits they have.[11] One reason why banks collapsed during panics before the Fed was created was that their reserves were too small or not readily available. In practice, reserves now have little to do with the safety of checking and savings account deposits. Their safety is ensured by the federal deposit insurance. However, reserves do ensure that banks will have some ready funds to meet withdrawals.

THE RESERVE RATIO AND BANK LENDING. The reserve ratio is less important as a way to ensure a cushion of liquidity and solvency than as a means for the Fed to control the ability of banks to lend and create money. To see how this works, assume that banks have to hold reserves equal to 20 percent of their checkable deposits. Suppose Bank A has exactly the required reserve level: deposits of $1,000,000 and reserves of $200,000. If people withdraw $100,000 from their checking accounts (checkable deposits), Bank A will have only $100,000 left in reserves supporting checkable deposits of $900,000. Required reserves behind that level of deposits are $180,000. Thus, Bank A's reserves are now $80,000 below the level required by the Fed. The bank must make up these reserves or face fines by the Fed. When Bank A, and other banks, are forced to contract lending to make up reserves, the money supply will shrink.

A change in the reserve ratio increases or decreases banks' ability to lend money. With a given level of reserves, an increase in the reserve ratio from 20 percent to 25 percent would create a reserve shortage and make bankers less willing to lend. A reduction in the reserve ratio from 20 percent to 15 percent would convert some required reserves to excess reserves and make bankers more willing to make loans. (Normally changes in the reserve ratio are much smaller than that, no more than 0.5 percent at a time.)

---

11. Historically, the Fed had different reserve ratios for different types of deposits and different sizes of banks. Nonmember banks and other depository institutions had still different reserve ratios set by their regulatory agencies. All this was changed in 1980. Now reserves vary only with the kind of account and not with the type or size of the depository institution. All checkable deposits, whether at commercial banks, savings banks, or credit unions, have the same reserve ratio. The Fed can adjust the requirements within a range of 8–14 percent. Reserve ratios are graduated by total volume of deposit.

There are two international financial institutions that perform certain banking functions for nations. One is mostly concerned with the international market for national currencies. The other is primarily a lending institution that makes long-term loans in order to promote economic growth in less developed countries.

Representatives of the major nations met in Bretton Woods, New Hampshire in 1944 to make plans for international monetary coordination in the postwar period. The result of that meeting was the creation of the International Monetary Fund (IMF) and the International Bank for Reconstruction and Development (World Bank). The first problem that the delegates were concerned about was the international monetary system. The gold standard had died, and nations wanted to maintain stable currency prices. Most delegates thought that stable currency prices would require a "manager." There would also be a need for a place where nations could go to borrow foreign currency when they had temporary shortages and needed to pay for imports. That is, the "manager" would also be a lender of last resort for countries.

The IMF was intended to be that manager, supplying liquidity to nations to meet temporary crises. The IMF supplies liquidity by lending currencies of other countries that can be used to meet international obligations. Since 1973, when the major industrial nations shifted

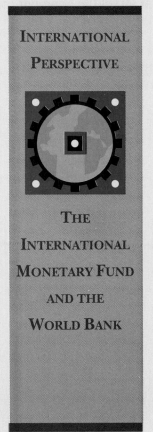

INTERNATIONAL
PERSPECTIVE

THE
INTERNATIONAL
MONETARY FUND
AND THE
WORLD BANK

from fixed currency prices to floating exchange rates, the role of the IMF in international finance has been much less important.

The World Bank's primary role is as a long-term lender and technical adviser to developing nations. It was created to assist in the reconstruction of Europe after World War II and to help former colonies to get on their feet. Today, the World Bank receives contributions from the developed nations and borrows money in financial markets in order to make long-term, low-interest loans to less developed nations. The loans are used for such developmental projects as roads, dams, electric power plants, and water systems. As these loans are repaid, the World Bank recycles the funds to other nations and other projects.

Neither the IMF nor the World Bank is a bank in the sense of creating money. Since gold ceased to play a monetary role, there has been no true international money, although the U.S. dollar has functioned as such to some degree for most of the last forty years. The IMF does operate as a bank in lending to nations in need of foreign currencies, and the World Bank plays a banker's role as a wholesaler of loanable funds. Without a single world government to create and direct a worldwide central bank, the IMF and the World Bank represent as much international central banking as we are likely to have.

Both open market operations and changes in the reserve ratio affect the amount of checkable deposits by changing excess reserves. The difference between the two tools is that changes in the reserve ratio leave the amount of reserves the same but convert some required reserves to excess reserves, or vice versa. A reduction in the reserve ratio increases the size of the money supply that can be supported by any given amount of bank reserves. An increase in the reserve ratio reduces the size of the potential money supply.

The impact of a change in the reserve ratio is shown on a T-account for Bank A in Table 11. Suppose the Fed reduces the reserve ratio from 20 to 10 percent. Bank A's reserves are still $200,000, but required reserves have fallen to $100,000, and excess reserves have risen to $100,000. With $100,000 in excess reserves, Bank A can be expected to expand its lending, just as it did when an open market sale of a bond to the Fed increased its reserves. Table 11 traces the response by Bank A, which is similar to its response to the open market operation. Whether excess reserves result from an open market operation or a change in the reserve ratio, they are still something of a "hot potato." They move from bank to bank and can be eliminated only by being turned into required reserves.

What happens when the reserve ratio is raised? If excess reserves are initially zero, an increase in the reserve ratio will result in a reserve deficit. Checkable deposits will fall as banks are forced to contract loans. The maximum money supply that any given volume of reserves can support will be smaller because the deposit multiplier will be smaller.

THE RESERVE RATIO AND THE DEPOSIT MULTIPLIER. A change in the reserve ratio changes the maximum size of the money supply, not by changing bank reserves (BR), but by changing the deposit multiplier ($1/rr$). The deposit multiplier is the reciprocal of the reserve ratio. When the reserve ratio changes from 20 percent to 10 percent, the deposit multiplier increases from 5 to 10. Thus, a reduction in the reserve ratio has a double impact on the money supply. First, it converts some required reserves into excess reserves. Second, it increases the size of the deposit multiplier. An increase in the reserve ratio works in the opposite way. The higher reserve

TABLE 11
BANK A RESPONDS TO A
CHANGE IN THE RESERVE
RATIO FROM 20 PERCENT
TO 10 PERCENT

BANK A BEFORE THE CHANGE IN THE RESERVE RATIO:

ASSETS		LIABILITIES	
Reserves	$200,000	Checkable deposits	$1,000,000
Loans and government bonds	800,000		

After the change in the reserve ratio, Bank A makes a loan of $100,000. When the borrower spends the funds, Bank A loses reserves and deposits to another bank.

ASSETS		LIABILITIES	
Reserves	$100,000	Checkable deposits	$1,000,000
Loans and government bonds	900,000		

ratio creates a shortfall of excess reserves and also reduces the size of the deposit multiplier.

A change in the reserve ratio is more complex than open market operations because of this double impact. Because it is such a powerful tool, changes in the reserve ratio are made rarely and in small amounts. Even a change of a fraction of 1 percent can have a very large (and somewhat uncertain) impact on the economy and can be very unsettling to banks. In the last two decades, the Fed made adjustments to the reserve ratio an average of three times a year, most of them affecting only one or two types of deposits.[12]

DISCOUNTING AND THE DISCOUNT RATE

One additional way for banks to make up a shortage of required reserves is to borrow from the Fed. This lending power is the Fed's third tool of monetary control. It derives from the role of the central bank as a lender of last resort. A bank borrows from the Fed by putting up some of its assets as backing, or collateral, for the loan. Only certain kinds of assets held by banks are eligible to serve as collateral. A loan is made when the bank discounts such an asset with its district Reserve Bank.

The term *discounting* refers to the method by which the Fed charges interest on a loan to a bank. Discounted loans can be made by banks to their customers as well as by the Fed to a bank. This type of loan simply deducts the interest in advance. Normally, if you borrowed $10,000 for a year, you would receive $10,000 and expect to repay $11,000 or more. The difference between the principal (the amount borrowed) and the total repaid is the interest. With a discounted loan, the principal would still be $10,000, but the borrower might receive only $9,000. The interest is subtracted at the beginning instead of added during or at the end of the term of the loan.

Borrowing from the Fed by banks is called "using the discount window." The interest rate the Fed charges banks is called the **discount rate**. Changing the discount rate is one of the tools of monetary policy. The higher the rate charged, the less eager banks are to borrow. The lower the rate, the more willing banks are to increase reserves by borrowing. The Fed may deny use of the discount window to banks that have made unwise loans. The discount rate is almost always below other interest rates at which banks could borrow.

discount rate
The interest rate the Fed charges on loans to banks.

THE DISCOUNT WINDOW AND CHANGES IN THE RESERVE RATIO. Recall what happens when an increase in the reserve ratio leaves banks with too little reserves. Banks are forced to contract their deposits by selling some interest-earning assets or eliminating loans. Such a forced contraction is a very difficult situation for both banks and their loan customers. It takes time to make the transition to the new conditions. For this reason, the Fed may choose to cushion the impact of a decline in bank reserves by keeping the discount window open—by standing ready to make loans to banks as needed.

---

12. A list of these changes is given by Michelle R. Garfinkel and Daniel L. Thornton in "The Link Between M1 and the Monetary Base in the 1980s," *Review*, Federal Reserve Bank of St. Louis (September-October 1989): 35–52.

With an open discount window, instead of immediately calling in loans and selling bonds, banks can borrow reserves from their district Bank. What they borrow is deposits with that Federal Reserve Bank. An increase in the Fed's lending activity means an increase in member bank reserves. However, banks have taken out loans with the Fed that they will eventually have to repay. They will still have to make the adjustment by reducing their assets, but they have bought some time in which to adjust more gradually.

Each Federal Reserve Bank sets a discount rate at which the depository institutions of its district can borrow. Since the Board of Governors must approve the rate, the rates are usually the same in all twelve districts. Normally the discount rate is slightly below the market interest rate. To keep banks from borrowing from the Fed at low rates and lending to customers at high rates, the district banks ration the borrowing privilege, and banks are warned by Fed officials about abusing the discounted loans. Many people are under the impression that the Fed sets market interest rates, but the discount rate is the only rate the Fed sets directly. We will discuss how the Fed has an indirect effect on the general level of market interest rates in Chapter 14.

The discount rate functions as a signal more than as a direct tool of monetary control. An increase in the discount rate indicates to banks that the Fed wants to cool down the economy by reducing bank lending. A decrease signifies the Fed's desire to stimulate the economy. Changes in the discount rate also alter the profitability of borrowing from the Fed in order to relend. Raising the rate makes it more expensive to borrow. In that case, banks are expected to borrow less and hold larger excess reserves in order to avoid borrowing. A lower rate makes borrowing from the Fed more attractive and encourages banks to hold fewer excess reserves. They know they can easily borrow from the Fed if necessary.

Raising and lowering the discount rate is not as powerful a tool as changes in the reserve ratio or open market operations. Its impact is harder to measure than the others, since the magnitude of the effect depends on bankers' reaction to the change. If this tool were used too often, it would lose its effectiveness as a signal of the Fed's policy direction.

federal funds market
The market in which banks borrow reserves from each other.

federal funds rate
The interest rate charged in the federal funds market.

THE FEDERAL FUNDS MARKET. Banks can borrow reserves from each other as well as from the Fed. These loans between banks are made in the **federal funds market**. If Bank A has excess reserves, it can lend some of these (for one day at a time) to Bank B. The rate charged is the **federal funds rate**. If the annual rate is 12 percent, it costs the borrowing bank approximately $1/30$ of 1 percent for a one-day loan. Such loans can be renewed, but a bank can get its loaned funds back after one day if it so desires.

The Fed does not directly set the federal funds rate, but it does set a target range for that rate, such as plus or minus $1/8$ of 1 percent around 12 percent. Then, if the federal funds rate drops to $11\frac{7}{8}$ percent, the Fed will sell bonds to drain reserves from the banking system. As excess reserves of member banks fall relative to the demand for them, the federal funds rate will be driven up. Similarly, if the rate rises to $12\frac{1}{8}$ percent, the Fed will buy bonds to inject reserves into banks. The supply of reserves increases relative to demand, driving the federal funds rate back down toward 12 percent. Many economists think that this indirect control of the federal funds rate plays a very important role in monetary policy and in how well the policy works. The federal funds rate is usually slightly above the discount rate because banks prefer to borrow from other banks rather than from the Fed.

OTHER TOOLS OF THE FEDERAL RESERVE SYSTEM

The Fed has a few more specialized tools. From time to time, the Fed has been authorized to set maximum repayment periods and minimum down payments for consumer credit. It can also set the fraction of stock purchases that a buyer can finance with credit (the margin requirement). These tools, called selective credit controls, are not used very frequently. They have become less useful in the last few decades with the growth of alternative sources of funds (nonbank financial institutions) to which borrowers can turn.

The Fed can also use **moral suasion**. That is, it can try to convince banks to do what it favors. For example, the Fed may think that the money supply is growing too quickly. The Board of Governors will urge banks not to make as many new loans in order to hold down the rate of growth. Since the Fed regulates banks and controls their access to the discount window, banks have to pay some attention to such requests. Although the Fed has some success in persuasion, this approach is generally less effective than open market operations as a way of controlling the money supply.

The way in which the Fed has used its monetary policy tools has cre-

moral suasion
Attempts by the Fed to convince depository institutions to do what the Fed favors.

FEDERAL RESERVE TOOLS

TOOL	WORKS THROUGH	PLUSES AND MINUSES	FREQUENCY OF USE
• Open market operations	Changing bank reserves	Flexible Broad impact	Used frequently
• Changes in the reserve ratios	Changing excess reserves	Broad impact Extremely powerful	Used rarely
• Changes in the discount rate	Changing the amount of borrowing banks will do	Useful as signal Affects interest rates	Used relatively infrequently
• Selective credit controls	Changing terms of consumer loans and borrowing to buy stock		Used infrequently
• Moral suasion	Persuading banks to change amount of lending	Limited in effectiveness	Used occasionally

ated disagreements among economists as well as politicians. The debates of the nineteenth century over how freely banks should lend are still alive. There is still support for easy money, unlimited credit, and inflation among those who are in debt and want to be able to borrow more and pay it back with cheaper dollars. There are also several groups of hard-money backers, ranging from those who simply want monetary growth carefully controlled to those who would like to return to full-bodied money, usually a gold standard. Developments in banking and financial markets in the last fifteen years have changed the nature of banking in the United States in ways that have yet to be fully seen. The next chapter will take a closer look at some of these changes as part of a broader examination of financial markets and interest rates.

SUMMARY

1. The banking system in the United States is based on the principle of fractional reserve banking, first applied in the Middle Ages by goldsmiths.

2. Depository institutions make loans, which expands the money supply. The upper limit on such expansion is determined by the amount of reserves banks must keep to back up deposits.

3. The Federal Reserve System was created in 1913 to limit the damage to the economy from bank panics in the nineteenth and early twentieth centuries. It was designed to serve as a regulator and lender of last resort to member banks.

4. There are twelve Federal Reserve districts in the United States, each with a Federal Reserve District Bank. The central authority is the Board of Governors in Washington, DC. A main concern of the Fed is monetary policy, which is carried out by actions that influence interest rates, credit conditions, and the money supply.

5. The Fed has three main tools it can use in implementing monetary policy: open market operations, changes

in the reserve ratio, and lending at the discount rate.

6. Open market operations are purchases and sales of government bonds by the Fed on the open market. Open market operations go on daily.

7. The reserve ratio determines the amount of reserves banks must hold as a fraction of checkable deposits. Required reserves must be held in the form of vault cash and deposits in a Federal Reserve Bank.

8. Both changes in the reserve ratio and open market operations work by changing banks' excess reserves. Excess reserves are total reserves minus required reserves. As excess reserves expand, banks can increase their loans and, thus, the money supply. Reductions in excess reserves tend to force contractions of loans and the money supply.

9. Banks can borrow from the Fed at the discount rate to cushion reductions in reserves.

10. Both the reserve ratio and the discount rate are changed infrequently. Open market operations are the main tool of monetary policy.

NEW TERMS

Federal Reserve System (Fed)	excess reserves	National Banking System	open market operations
fractional reserve banking	reserve ratio	national banks	discount rate
	deposit multiplier	state banks	federal funds market
reserves	currency drain	Board of Governors	federal funds rate
T-account	bank panics	Federal Open Market Committee (FOMC)	moral suasion
	lender of last resort		

QUESTIONS FOR DISCUSSION

1. Why are there twelve Federal Reserve districts? In which district are you? What is the Board of Governors?

2. Which of the following items appear on the Fed's balance sheet? For each item that appears on the balance sheet, indicate whether it is an asset or a liability.
   a. government bonds
   b. reserves of banks
   c. deposits by the Treasury
   d. deposits by the public
   e. loans to banks
   f. currency

3. Which of the following items appear on a bank's balance sheet? For each item that appears on the balance sheet, indicate whether it is an asset or a liability.
   a. government bonds
   b. reserves
   c. deposits by the Treasury
   d. deposits by the public
   e. loans to the public
   f. currency

4. What are the three main tools of the Fed? Which one is used most often? Why?

5. Suppose the reserve ratio is 20 percent. If an extra $2 billion in excess reserves are injected into the banking system through an open market purchase of T-bills by the Fed, by how much can checkable deposits rise? What would your answer be if the reserve ratio were 10 percent? Does the total of checkable deposits have to rise?

6. Would it make a difference in your answers to Question 5 if the increase in excess reserves came about because the Fed lowered the discount rate and thus induced banks to borrow $2 billion?

7. Suppose bank reserves are $100 billion, the reserve ratio is 20 percent, and banks are fully loaned up (that is, excess reserves are zero). Now suppose the reserve ratio is lowered to 10 percent and banks once again become fully loaned up. What is the new level of checkable deposits? Do this problem again, but assume the reserve ratio rises to 25 percent.

8. List the steps by which a sale of government bonds by the Fed affects output and the price level through aggregate supply and demand.

9. If the Fed sells bonds, what is likely to happen to each of the following?
   a. bank reserves
   b. interest rates
   c. the money supply
   d. output and/or prices (money GNP)

10. How did the inflation of the 1970s add to the pressure for bank deregulation in the early 1980s?

11. Why do banks borrow from one another instead of from the Fed?

12. How are the effects of changes in the reserve ratio on bank lending and the money supply different from the effects of open market operations?

13. How does the Fed's role differ from what was originally envisioned?

14. Why did it take the United States so long to establish a permanent central bank?

15. List all of the actions the Fed can undertake to try to increase lending, the money supply, and the level of economic activity.

SUGGESTIONS FOR FURTHER READING

Goodhart, Charles. *The Evolution of Central Banking.* Cambridge, MA: MIT Press, 1988. Explains why and how central banks evolved, drawing on the experiences of several countries.

Greider, William. *Secrets of the Temple.* New York: Simon and Schuster, 1987. A critical look at the working of the Federal Reserve System.

Mayer, Thomas, James S. Duesenberry, and Robert Z. Aliber. *Money, Banking and the Economy,* 4th ed. New York: W. W. Norton, 1990. An excellent intermediate book with thorough coverage of theory, institutions, and history.

1. Discuss the effects of deregulation on banks.
2. Explain the relationship between:
   a. bond prices and bond yields,
   b. real and nominal interest rates,
   c. risk and interest rates.
3. Describe each of these nonbank financial markets or institutions:
   a. the stock market,
   b. the bond market,
   c. mutual funds,
   d. pension funds,
   e. insurance companies.
4. Discuss the effect of interest rates on investment spending, output, and income.

CHAPTER 13

FINANCIAL MARKETS AND INTEREST RATES

INTRODUCTION

Financial markets are shown as the outer flow in the bottom half of the circular flow diagram in Figure 1. The role of financial markets, or the credit market, is to gather funds from households and other savers and channel them to borrowers (households, government, or business firms) or to firms that sell ownership rights (stock). The prices at which funds are borrowed in the credit market are interest rates. Ownership claims convey a right to a share in the profits of the firm.

The last two decades have seen dramatic changes in financial markets. There are more kinds of institutions offering more kinds of deposits, financial instruments, and services. The 1980s saw bank deregulation, the invention of junk bonds, and a stock market crash. There was also a banking crisis that continues into the 1990s.

The Fed is interested in lending, borrowing, and interest rates mainly as a channel of monetary policy. But it cannot ignore the close links between the market for stocks and the market for loanable funds. This chapter describes the workings of financial markets in the wake of all the changes that have occurred since the 1970s.

BANK DEREGULATION IN THE 1980s

The functions of banks and the rules under which they operate have changed dramatically in the last two decades. The typical commercial bank of the early 1970s offered checking accounts (which paid no interest), passbook savings accounts, and a few other financial services, such as safe deposit boxes, traveler's checks, and loans. In 1970, there were no money market accounts, no NOW accounts, and no certificates of deposit (CDs). Handy automatic teller machines (ATMs) dispensing cash and accepting deposits were yet to be developed. Interest rates on passbooks were regulated, and interest on checking accounts had been forbidden since the 1930s. Banks that wanted to compete for deposits offered trading stamps, free gifts, and other rewards instead of higher yields. Interstate banking was forbidden. In many states, even branch banking (multiple offices for

343

FIGURE 1

THE CIRCULAR FLOW WITH A CREDIT MARKET
The credit market gathers savings from households and channels them into business and government investment. The major participants in this market include banks, savings and loan institutions, credit unions, the stock market, the bond market, mutual funds, insurance companies, and pension funds.

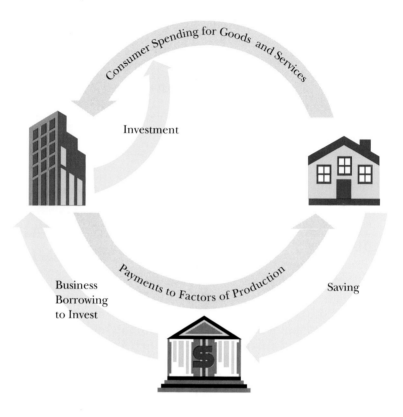

a single bank) was forbidden. Thus, unlike many foreign countries, the United States had no large nationwide or even regional banks. Around 1975, all of these rules and practices began to change.

DEVELOPMENTS IN THE BANKING INDUSTRY

High inflation rates and high market interest rates in the 1970s were the stimulus for some major changes in the banking system. One such change occurred in New England. State-chartered and state-insured savings banks, not subject to federal regulations on interest on deposits, pioneered a new type of savings account that allowed depositors to write negotiated orders of withdrawal. These NOW accounts were the first interest-bearing checking accounts in forty-five years. Funds started flowing out of national banks in New England into these accounts. Finally, those banks were allowed to compete by offering this type of account, but with an interest rate no higher than the regulated passbook rate. NOW accounts later spread nationwide.

Competition from money market mutual funds, offered by nonbank financial institutions, became a serious threat to the banking system in the 1970s. Money market mutual funds are financial instruments with high yields, fairly low minimum balances (ranging from $500 to $5,000), and high liquidity. For the first time, someone with only a few thousand dollars, or even less, could earn the kind of high rates that had required a

$10,000 minimum. Although money market mutual fund accounts, un-like bank deposits, were not insured, the funds were invested quite safely in commercial paper (short-term business borrowing) and T-bills. Some of these accounts also allowed check writing. Banks offered no compara-ble type of deposit to compete with money market mutual funds. The re-sult was a massive loss of deposits from banks and savings and loans.

A third important development during the 1970s was the loss of mem-ber banks by the Federal Reserve System. Although the Fed offered its member banks check-clearing services and borrowing privileges, the banks also had to meet higher reserve ratios than most state banks. Since reserves earn no interest, higher required reserves meant that member banks were losing interest earnings. Thus, banks began exchanging their federal char-ters for state charters. Fewer banks were under the direct control of the Fed, making it more difficult for the Fed to carry out monetary policy.

LEGISLATIVE CHANGES

The result of these developments was the passage of two major pieces of legislation that were intended to bring about bank deregulation. **Bank deregulation** is a policy enabling banks to compete more aggressively with nonbank financial institutions by reducing the regulations affecting them. The first deregulatory act was the Depository Institutions Deregulation and Monetary Control Act (DIDMCA) of 1980. This act put all depository in-stitutions—commercial banks (with either state or national charters), sav-ings banks, savings and loan associations, and credit unions—under the control of the Fed. All gained access to Fed services and became subject to the same reserve ratios for the same types of deposits. This act also provided for gradual phasing out of interest ceilings on deposits and authorized all banks to offer interest-bearing checking accounts. The role of savings banks and savings and loan associations was expanded. These banks for-merly offered mostly passbook savings accounts and invested almost exclu-sively in home mortgage loans. Under DIDMCA, they were allowed to of-fer a full range of accounts and invest in a greater variety of loans and assets.

In 1982, Congress passed the Garn–St. Germain Act to expand the range of accounts that could be offered by banks. This act allowed banks, including thrift institutions, to issue checkable, interest-bearing deposit ac-counts similar to the money market mutual funds available from nonbank institutions. These accounts are known as money market accounts, super NOW accounts, or other names. They generally pay slightly lower interest rates than money market mutual funds, but they offer the advantages of deposit insurance and convenient access at local branches and ATMs.

Another provision of the Garn–St. Germain Act opened the door to in-terstate banking. National banks had been forbidden by the 1927 McFad-den Act to engage in interstate banking unless so authorized by state law. Failures of thrift institutions in the early 1980s were so numerous that the Federal Savings and Loan Insurance Corporation (FSLIC) had to find many merger partners to take over the assets of failed banks. Often the most attrac-tive candidates were from out of state. The Garn–St. Germain Act allowed an out-of-state bank to take over a failed bank if it was the only candidate.

bank deregulation
A policy enabling banks to compete more aggressively with nonbank financial institutions by reducing the regulations affecting them.

Bank deregulation was intended to benefit depositors, banks, and the Fed. The two federal laws made it possible for banks to offer a wider range of services and more attractive interest rates to small depositors and middle-income households. Although interest rates on all assets had fallen by the end of the 1980s, depositors still had a choice among a much wider variety of accounts than before. Armed with these new types of accounts, banks could compete more effectively with nonbank institutions in attracting deposits. The Fed gained better control over the money creation process.

Partly as a result of the Garn–St. Germain Act and partly as a result of new technology, both branch banking and interstate banking increased during the 1980s. A number of states had severe restrictions on both of these practices. The use of ATMs made it increasingly difficult for these states to determine exactly what constituted branch banking. Bank holding companies were created to get around prohibitions on interstate banking, leading to further demands by banks that state legislatures relax these prohibitions. Finally, the wave of bank failures in the 1980s put pressure on legislatures to allow the development of larger (and presumably safer) banks. The combined impact of these developments was that many states did relax restrictions on both branch banking and interstate banking. This move allowed the development of larger banks with more diversified assets and greater economies of scale. In many small towns, the bank is now a local unit of a statewide or even interstate bank.

Why did Congress suddenly decide to deregulate the banking industry after decades of regulation? Most of the federal bank regulations originated in the 1930s to prevent bank failures. Banks did not object to regulation as long as they had no serious competition from other firms offering deposit accounts. Regulation kept banks from competing with each other to attract deposits by offering interest on checking accounts. They could lend the funds deposited in checking accounts without having to pay depositors any interest.[1] Consumers, whether they liked it or not, were being protected from bank failure at the sacrifice of higher yields and a greater array of accounts and services. It was really the inflation of the 1970s that brought an end to regulation of interest rates. Inflation drove up market interest rates and widened the gap between what banks were allowed to pay and what other depository institutions were willing to pay. Banks lost deposits to these other institutions, where depositors could earn higher rates, a process known as disintermediation. Deregulation enabled banks to fight back and regain some of the lost deposits.

THE BANKING CRISIS

Although the benefits of deregulation were soon apparent, the costs were slower to appear. Freed from interest rate ceilings, banks began to compete aggressively for deposits. With fewer restrictions on the kinds of assets they could hold, some thrifts—especially savings and loans—began to make riskier investments. When the 1981–1982 recession hit, banks took a double hit. Interest rates fell on the loans they were making, while funds

---

1.   Some payments were made to depositors, in the form of free checks, free access to other bank services, or sometimes premiums or gifts for new deposits. These payments were an indirect form of interest.

Each country's system of banks and financial markets is unique, but most have some features in common. Japan's financial system provides an interesting comparison to that of the United States.[a]

Japan has had a central bank, the Bank of Japan, since 1882. Like the Fed, the Bank of Japan issues currency, serves as a bankers' bank and a depository bank for the government, and conducts monetary policy. The banking system consists of city and regional banks, *sogo* banks, *shinkin* banks, and postal savings. There are only twelve city banks, which hold 20 percent of all deposits of financial institutions and lend to large corporations. (The Japanese government also invests directly in business ventures.) The sixty-four regional banks, located in medium-sized cities, hold individual deposits (mostly time deposits for one year or more). Thus, one major difference is the smaller number of what are called commercial banks in the United States.

Sogo banks are roughly equivalent to U.S. savings banks or savings and loans. *Shinkin* banks are the Japanese equivalent of credit unions. These banks are much more numerous than the city and regional banks and serve the needs of individuals. However, Japanese

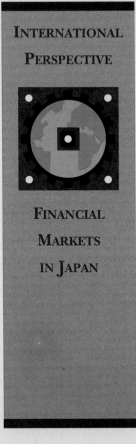

INTERNATIONAL
PERSPECTIVE

FINANCIAL
MARKETS
IN JAPAN

households also maintain large deposits in postal savings (deposits at the post office). Such deposits were important in the United States at one time but no longer exist. Like the United States, Japan has deposit insurance. However, the government protects the Japanese deposit insurance system from large demands by imposing strict collateral requirements on most loans in order to ensure bank solvency.

Bank deregulation hit Japan at about the same time as the United States and for a similar reason. The development of medium-term government bond funds with higher yields than bank deposits led to an outflow of households' and small firms' funds from the banking system. Interest rates were then allowed to rise. More generous funding of the deposit insurance system and stricter collateral requirements have helped Japan to avoid bank failures.

Partly for cultural reasons and partly because there is no Social Security system, Japanese households save a much larger share of their incomes than American households do. Thus, the banking system plays an even larger role in overall financial markets in Japan than it does in the United States.

a.   This description is based on Yoshio Suzuki (ed.), *The Japanese Financial System* (Oxford: Clarendon Press, 1987).

in CDs were locked in for periods from one to seven years at the old high interest rates. In addition, many of the banks' loans were in default.[2]

spread
The difference between the average interest rate earned on loans and the average interest rate paid on deposits.

Banks earn an income by charging more interest on loans than they pay on deposits. Banks' earnings fall when there is a decline in the **spread**, the difference between the average interest rate earned on loans and the average interest rate paid on deposits. Banks will then be tempted to make riskier loans in order to earn higher interest rates and restore earnings. In the early 1980s, market interest rates dropped sharply. The average interest rate on banks' loan portfolios responded very quickly, because banks hold a large amount of short-term assets, such as T-bills and commercial paper (very short-term business loans). As these assets matured, banks tried to replace them with higher-earning ones, even though most of those involved greater risk. In spite of such efforts, average bank earnings on investments fell. It took somewhat longer, however, for banks to bring about a change in the average interest paid on deposits, because many deposits were long-term CDs. For some banks, the spread was not enough to cover operating expenses, so they suffered losses (negative net earnings). Since the net worth of banks grows or shrinks depending on their earnings, negative net earnings reduced many banks' net worth.

At the same time, there was a decline in the market value of banks' assets. Banks in Texas, Oklahoma, and Louisiana had made many loans to oil companies. These assets became worthless when the price of oil dropped sharply. Because oil is such an important part of economic activity in these three states, the drop in its price had widespread effects. The prices of houses in Houston and other oil centers dropped sharply, threatening mortgage holders (usually savings and loans) with losses. As owners defaulted, the houses they abandoned to the bank usually had a resale value less than the balance due on the mortgage. Office buildings in large cities in these three states, especially in Houston, had few tenants. When rental income was not enough to meet mortgage payments, developers abandoned buildings to the bank, again with a poor resale market. In addition to these problems, defaults on loans to Third World countries hit some of the larger banks.

Savings and loans had also taken advantage of the freedom created by deregulation combined with the safety net of deposit insurance to make some very risky loans. Banks that were close to insolvency were tempted to make such loans. If the loans paid off, at high interest rates, the bank could become solvent again. If the gamble failed, depositors were protected by deposit insurance.

To understand the nature of the insolvency problem, consider the simple balance sheet of Petroleum Savings and Loan in Table 1. As you can see, this bank has $100 million in assets, consisting of reserves, mortgages, and commercial loans. It has $94 million in deposits as liabilities and a net worth of $6 million. This bank exceeds the current capital requirements imposed on banks by regulatory agencies. Its capital is 7 percent of its loans ($6 million divided by $85 million).[3] Capital requirements are being raised but will rise to only 3 percent of loans by 1995.

2. A loan is in default when the lender fails to make regularly scheduled payments of principal and interest.
3. Bankers and investors, unlike economists, use the word "capital" when talking about money. Therefore, the word is used in that sense in this chapter.

ASSETS		LIABILITIES	
Reserves	$ 15	Deposits	$ 94
Mortgages	40		
Commercial loans	45		
TOTAL ASSETS	$100	TOTAL LIABILITIES	$ 94
		NET WORTH	$ 6
		TOTAL LIABILITIES	
		AND NET WORTH	$100

TABLE 1
BALANCE SHEET OF PETROLEUM SAVINGS AND LOAN (MILLIONS OF DOLLARS)

Suppose a soft housing market results in foreclosures on a number of Petroleum Savings and Loan's mortgages. The bank takes over some of the houses and sells them to pay off the mortgages. Assume that the bank forecloses on $10 million in mortgages, but distress sales of those properties bring in only $5 million. The value of the mortgage part of the bank's portfolio of assets drops to $30 million. The bank adds the $5 million received from property sales to its reserves. At the same time, suppose some of the bank's commercial loans do not pay off. A few borrowers go bankrupt and are able to pay only a small fraction of what they owe. The value of commercial loans drops to $38 million. Now the bank's balance sheet looks like Table 2.

This bank is still liquid—in fact, its reserves have increased. However, it is no longer solvent—the value of its liabilities is greater than the value of its assets. Unless matters improve quickly, this bank will have to file for bankruptcy. Its assets will be sold to pay the claims of depositors. After the bank pays off $88 million worth of deposits, the remaining $6 million (of deposits up to $100,000) will be paid by the Federal Deposit Insurance Corporation (FDIC) if this bank is a member.

The experience of Petroleum Savings and Loan is typical of what happened to many depository institutions in the 1980s. From 1980 to 1988, 879 commercial banks and 517 savings and loan associations were closed because of solvency problems. In comparison, 80 commercial banks and 43 savings and loans closed during the 1970s, and 58 commercial banks and 43 savings and loans closed during the 1960s. Clearly something had happened to the banking system. Commercial banks that failed from 1980 to 1988 represented 6 percent of those existing at the beginning of the decade. The failure rate for savings and loans during the same period was

ASSETS		LIABILITIES	
Reserves	$ 20	Deposits	$94
Mortgages	30		
Commercial loans	38		
TOTAL ASSETS	$ 88	TOTAL LIABILITIES	$94
		NET WORTH	–$ 6
		TOTAL LIABILITIES	
		AND NET WORTH	$88

TABLE 2
REVISED BALANCE SHEET OF PETROLEUM SAVINGS AND LOAN (MILLIONS OF DOLLARS)

13 percent.[4] Although the vast majority of both commercial banks and savings and loans remained healthy, those that failed rolled up huge losses. The payoffs to depositors far exceeded the financial resources of the deposit insurance agencies, the FDIC and the FSLIC.

BAILOUT LEGISLATION

Response to the crisis in the banking industry was slow to emerge. Legislation was finally passed in 1989. The Financial Institutions Reform, Recovery and Enforcement Act (FIRREA) merged the FDIC with its savings and loan counterpart, the FSLIC. It also set up a new agency, the Resolution Trust Corporation (RTC), to deal with the problems of insolvent banks, including the sale of their assets. The insurance premiums banks pay for deposit insurance were increased, and banks were made subject to higher capital-to-loan ratios to provide a larger cushion for solvency.[5] These higher ratios mean that the bank's stockholders have more to lose from risky loans, and the concerns of stockholders should force banks to be more cautious and thus less likely to be insolvent in the future. However, these changes still leave the taxpayers facing a bill for the bailout that is currently estimated at $130–176 billion, including some $40 billion spent prior to passage of the law.

The process of restoring health to the banking industry will take many years. Housing demand and prices are expected to be stable or declining in the 1990s, as the smaller generation following the baby boom reaches the stage of family formation. Since savings and loans are still heavily committed to mortgages, a weak housing market may endanger some institutions that are currently healthy. In 1990, the Bank of New England, the flagship of a bank holding company that controlled several large New England banks, declared bankruptcy as a result of declining real estate prices in Massachusetts and Connecticut. By the end of the century, however, the United States should have a leaner, safer banking industry, with fewer small banks and more conservative portfolios of assets than in the go-go years of the 1980s.

THE LOANABLE FUNDS MARKET AND INTEREST RATES

market for loanable funds
The market in which transactions between borrowers and lenders determine the interest rate and equate quantities of loanable funds offered to quantity demanded.

Banks are only one group of players, although a very important group, on the lending side of financial markets. The other major lenders in the loanable funds market are stockbrokers, bond dealers, insurance companies, pension funds, credit unions, and mutual funds. The borrowers are business firms, households, and government. The **market for loanable funds** is the market in which transactions between borrowers and lenders determine the interest rate, which ensures that the quantity of loanable funds offered is equal to the quantity demanded. The price in this market is the interest rate.

4. Data from Dwight M. Jaffee, "Symposium on Federal Deposit Insurance for S&L Institutions," *Journal of Economic Perspectives* (Fall 1989): 3–10.
5. For a description of this legislation and the events leading up to it, see Dwight M. Jaffee, "Symposium of Federal Deposit Insurance for S&L Institutions," *Journal of Economic Perspectives* (Fall 1989): 3–10.

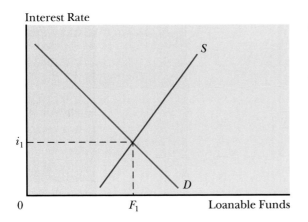

Interest Rate

i_1

0   F_1 Loanable Funds

FIGURE 2
THE MARKET FOR
LOANABLE FUNDS
The demand curve for loanable funds slopes downward because at lower nominal interest rates, borrowers want to borrow more. The upward-sloping supply curve shows that at higher nominal interest rates, lenders are willing to lend more. At the equilibrium interest rate i_1, the amount borrowers want to borrow equals the amount lenders want to lend (F_1).

The demand for loanable funds (to invest) is negatively related to the interest rate, as shown in Figure 2. More will be borrowed at lower rates, *ceteris paribus*, and less at higher rates. The supply of loanable funds, which consists of savings plus newly created money, rises with the interest rate. The interest rate is the price of loanable funds. Like any price, this rate rises and falls to clear the market and make quantity demanded equal to quantity supplied. The interest rate is a very important macroeconomic variable because it affects business investment decisions, household purchases of consumer durables, demand for the U.S. dollar, and the cost of servicing the public debt.

THE RANGE OF INTEREST RATES

We have been using the term *interest rate* as if there were a single interest rate paid by all borrowers in the market. In fact, there is a whole complex of interest rates. A few of these are

- interest rates on home mortgages and car loans,
- interest rates on bonds (ranging from the lowest on T-bills to the highest on junk bonds),
- interest rates that banks pay the Fed (the discount rate) and each other on borrowed reserves (the federal funds rate), and
- interest rates banks pay on checking and savings accounts and CDs.

The interest rate for a loan depends on who the borrower is and how much risk the borrower poses, as well as on how long the repayment period is. Short-term loans usually carry lower rates than long-term loans. Risky borrowers pay more than safe, dependable borrowers. Table 3 lists interest rates from 1981 to 1990 on a variety of loans, including bonds. The lowest rate is usually the discount rate, followed by the T-bill rate and the rate on municipal bonds. Interest rates on municipal bonds are low because the interest is exempt from federal income taxes. In general, the interest rates included in the table rise and fall together. In the late 1970s

YEAR	GOVERNMENT BONDS			CORPORATE BONDS		MORTGAGES (NEW HOMES)	DISCOUNT RATE (NEW YORK FED)
	T-BILLS	THREE-YEAR	MUNICIPALS	AAA	BAA		
1981	14.0%	14.4%	11.2%	14.2%	16.0%	14.7%	13.4%
1982	10.7	12.9	11.6	13.8	16.1	15.1	11.0
1983	8.6	10.5	9.5	12.0	13.6	12.6	8.5
1984	9.6	11.9	10.2	12.7	14.2	12.4	8.8
1985	7.5	9.6	9.2	11.4	12.7	11.6	7.7
1986	6.0	7.1	7.4	9.0	10.4	10.2	6.3
1987	5.8	7.7	7.7	9.4	10.6	9.3	5.7
1988	6.7	8.3	7.8	9.7	10.8	9.2	6.2
1989	8.1	8.6	7.2	9.3	10.2	10.1	6.9
1990	7.5	8.3	7.3	9.3	10.4	10.1	7.0

*For bonds, the figure is current yield rather than the interest rate, which is equivalent. Corporate and municipal bonds are graded by bond-rating services according to the degree of risk from Aaa downward. The lowest investment grade recommended for purchase by individuals is Baa. The highest-rated bonds pay the lowest rates of interest because there is little risk of default on either interest payments or principal.

Source: Council of Economic Advisers, *Economic Report of the President* (Washington, DC: U.S. Government Printing Office, 1991).

TABLE 3
INTEREST RATES,
1981–1990*

and the beginning of the 1980s, they all rose to levels that were very high compared to past experience. Home mortgage rates, which had been in the 6–8 percent range, rose to 14 percent and higher. T-bills, which had been paying interest at a rate ranging from 4 to 6 percent in previous decades, peaked at 14 percent in 1981.

RISK AND INTEREST RATES

Although all the interest rates rise and fall, the differences among them will vary over the course of the business cycle. During downturns, some private borrowers may have a higher risk of default as their businesses teeter on the edge of bankruptcy. As private borrowers begin to look riskier relative to the government, lenders will be more reluctant to lend to them and be more inclined to buy safer assets such as T-bills. The rate that lenders charge private borrowers rises relative to the T-bill rate. The difference between interest rates charged to the safest borrowers and those charged to less safe borrowers for the same length of time is called the **risk premium**. Risk premiums vary from borrower to borrower, but they generally rise during recessions and fall during expansions.

With so many interest rates, it is difficult to choose one to serve as an indicator of how the market is doing. Generally the interest rate on T-bills is used as the market indicator. The T-bill rate is the interest rate the U.S. government, the safest borrower of all, pays on its short-term borrowing.

REAL AND NOMINAL INTEREST RATES

Why did interest rates rise so sharply in the late 1970s and early 1980s? To answer this question, we need to distinguish between the real rate of interest and the nominal rate of interest. The rate that people observe, or the market rate, is nominal. The **nominal rate of interest** is the rate of interest actually charged, without any correction for inflation. The real rate of interest is not observed. The **real rate of interest** is the nominal rate of

risk premium
The difference between interest rates charged to the safest borrowers and those charged to less safe borrowers for the same length of time.

nominal rate of interest
The rate of interest actually charged, without correction for inflation (also known as the market rate of interest).

real rate of interest
The nominal rate of interest minus the expected rate of inflation.

COMPONENTS OF THE INTEREST RATE

THE MARKET INTEREST RATE CONSISTS OF:	WHICH IS:
• the real rate of interest	the amount people are willing to pay for the right to spend now instead of later *or*
	the rate of return on investment
• plus the risk premium	a measure of the probability that the borrower will fail to repay the loan
• plus the inflation adjustment	the expected rate of inflation over the life of the loan

---

interest minus the expected rate of inflation or the actual rate of inflation.[6] If the price level is rising, the dollars repaid on a loan will be worth less and less with each successive payment. Lenders aren't interested in just getting their dollars back. They want to be repaid the purchasing power they lent plus some interest. Similarly, borrowers make calculations as to what a loan really costs them, considering that they can repay with depreciating dollars. Thus, an inflation premium is included in the interest rate.

Consider what happens when Joan lends Peter $100 for a year, charging him 5 percent interest. At the end of the year, Peter repays Joan $105. Suppose, however, that the price level rose by 10 percent during the year. The $105 that Joan gets back at the end of the year will only purchase $105/1.10 = $95.45 worth of goods and services. Instead of earning a positive real return, Joan has less purchasing power. If she had added an inflation premium of 10 percent, Peter would have paid back $115, which would have purchased $104.54 worth of goods. Joan wouldn't have made quite 5 percent in real terms, but she would have come close.[7]

Some estimated values of real interest rates from 1965 to 1990 are shown in Table 4.[8] Expected inflation rates were assumed to be equal to the actual inflation rates for each period. Under that assumption, real rates are computed by subtracting the percent change in the GNP deflator from the interest rate on T-bills. Note that the real rate of interest is quite small but is also much more stable than the nominal rate. There were seven years in the 1970s when the real rate was negative. Negative real interest rates occur when lenders do not correctly anticipate inflation and charge too small an inflation premium. When negative real interest rates occur, there is a surge in loan demand. Negative interest rates are a good reason to borrow! In the 1970s, borrowers were offered loans at 8 percent

---

6.   This is an approximation. Technically, $i_n = i_r + \dot{p} + (i_r \times \dot{p})$, where i_n is the nominal interest rate, i_r is the real interest rate, and $\dot{p}$ is the rate of inflation. The last term, however, is usually small enough to ignore.

7.   If you use the equation in footnote 6, you can compute exactly how much Joan would have had to increase the interest rate to get a real return of 5 percent.

8.   These values are estimates because the *actual* rate of inflation was used rather than the *expected* rate of inflation. If expected and actual inflation rates are the same, then these estimated real interest rates would be the same as the actual ones.

TABLE 4
NOMINAL INTEREST,
INFLATION, AND REAL
INTEREST

YEAR	T-BILL RATE	PERCENT CHANGE IN GNP DEFLATOR	REAL INTEREST RATE
1965	3.95%	2.2%	1.75%
1966	4.88	3.2	1.68
1967	4.32	3.0	1.32
1968	5.34	4.4	0.94
1969	6.68	5.1	1.58
1970	6.46	5.4	1.06
1971	4.35	5.0	−0.65
1972	4.07	4.2	−0.13
1973	7.04	5.8	1.24
1974	7.89	8.8	−0.91
1975	5.84	9.3	−3.46
1976	4.99	5.2	−0.21
1977	5.27	5.8	−0.53
1978	7.22	7.4	−0.18
1979	10.04	8.6	1.44
1980	11.51	9.2	2.31
1981	14.03	9.6	4.43
1982	10.69	6.0	6.69
1983	8.63	3.8	4.83
1984	9.58	3.7	5.88
1985	7.48	3.3	4.38
1986	5.98	2.7	3.28
1987	5.82	3.0	2.82
1988	6.69	3.3	3.39
1989	8.12%	4.1	4.02
1990	7.51	4.1	3.41

Source: Council of Economic Advisers, *Economic Report of the President* (Washington, DC: U.S. Government Printing Office, 1991).

interest when the inflation rate was over 10 percent. The opposite problem occurred in the early 1980s when lenders overestimated inflation and added too much of an inflation premium to interest rates. As a result, real interest rates rose sharply.

EXPECTED INFLATION AND THE MARKET FOR LOANABLE FUNDS

Changes in expected inflation rates will shift both the demand and supply of loanable funds and thus lead to a new equilibrium value of i, the nominal interest rate. Suppose people come to expect a higher rate of inflation. The demand curve for loanable funds shifts to the right, from D_1 to D_2 in Figure 3. Individuals want to borrow more at any given interest rate because they think the inflation rate is going to be higher. The higher the inflation rate, the less valuable are the dollars the borrower must repay. Exactly the same sort of reasoning applies to business demand for borrowing. Business firms will be much more willing to borrow at any given interest rate if they expect to be able to charge higher prices for the goods they produce.

The supply curve for loanable funds will shift to the left if there is an increase in the expected inflation rate. Lenders look at the purchasing

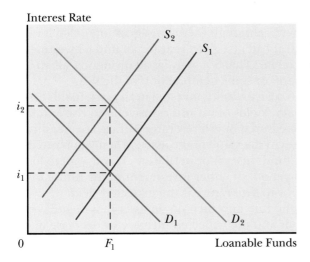

Interest Rate

Loanable Funds

FIGURE 3
EXPECTED INFLATION AND THE LOANABLE FUNDS MARKET
An increase in the expected rate of inflation increases demand for loans at every market interest rate (the demand curve shifts from D_1 to D_2), because loans are cheaper to repay. The supply of loanable funds falls (the supply curve shifts from S_1 to S_2), because each market rate on the vertical axis represents a lower real rate of interest. The demand and supply curves shift the same distance, intersecting at a market (nominal) interest rate that reflects the higher expected inflation rate. The volume of loanable funds (F_1) is the same as before.

power they will have when they get their funds *plus interest* back from the borrower. For example, if you lend $100 at 10 percent interest for one year, you will get back $110 at the end of the year. If the price level is the same as it was at the start of the year, you will be able to buy 10 percent more real goods. But if the price level also rises by 10 percent, then the $110 you get back will buy only the same amount of goods that $100 would have bought at the start of the year. If lenders demand 10 percent more in real goods in order to give up the current use of their funds, they won't lend at 10 percent interest if they expect 10 percent inflation. In fact, to get a 10 percent return in terms of real goods, lenders will demand an interest rate of 20 percent. The supply curve shifts to the left because lenders are willing to lend the same amount only at a higher nominal interest rate.

Thus, when the expected rate of inflation rises, both the demand and supply curves shift, driving up the equilibrium nominal interest rate. In fact, the nominal interest rate should rise by about the same amount as the increase in the expected rate of inflation. Lenders and borrowers will adjust the market rate they are willing to accept or pay to correct for the rising price level.

INTEREST, DIVIDENDS, AND YIELD ON AN ASSET
Interest is not the only form in which lenders receive a return on their funds. Suppose you purchase one share of stock in IBM. You probably will

receive some dividends, although you can't be sure how much. Also, the value of your share may go up, although there is no guarantee that it will. Suppose you come out $10 ahead in a given year for an initial investment of $100, a return of 10 percent.[9] That $10 may be all dividends, all an increase in the price of a share, or some combination of the two.

yield
The return on funds invested in an asset measured as a percentage of the price paid for the asset.

The **yield** is the rate of return on funds invested in an asset. In this case, 10 percent is the actual yield. Yields of various assets tend to rise and fall together. Many yields are measured by interest rates. Others are measured by dividends or by increases in the value of the asset. When you try to decide whether to hold your funds in cash or in IBM stock, you want to look at what you can expect to get out of either investment in the future over and above what you paid for it. This figure is the expected yield.

expected yield
The rate of return on an asset that includes expected interest or dividends and the expected increase or decrease in its price.

The **expected yield** is the rate of return on an asset that includes expected interest or dividends and the expected increase or decrease in its price. Expected yield is heavily influenced by the degree of perceived risk of the investment. **Risk** is a measure of how much the actual yield on an asset may vary from the expected yield. A high-risk asset may have a large yield in some years and a low or even negative yield in others. A low-risk asset will have a much more stable yield. The risk for a given asset can change depending on market conditions. An increase in the actual yield or a decrease in risk will increase the expected yield. A decrease in the actual yield or an increase in risk will reduce the expected yield.

risk
A measure of how much the actual yield on an asset may vary from the expected yield.

Because other financial assets are substitutes for money, anything that increases demand for those other assets will lead to a decrease in demand for money. An increase in yield will cause people to increase their holdings of stocks or bonds and reduce their holdings of money. Why? Think of the yield on stocks or bonds as the opportunity cost of holding money. When people hold money, they are giving up the earnings they could gain from other assets. When the yield on other assets increases, the opportunity cost of holding money also rises. Individuals respond by holding more stocks and bonds and less money. The opposite is true when yields on other assets decline. Thus, interest rates and yields on competing financial assets are important to the Fed in trying to influence the demand for money.

INTEREST RATES AND NONBANK FINANCIAL INSTITUTIONS

Changes in interest rates played an important role in bank deregulation and the rise of new types of financial assets in the 1970s. By the late 1970s, banks had become increasingly conscious of the fact that they were competing with a number of other institutions that also gathered up funds from various sources and made them available to borrowers. Because of inflation, market interest rates had risen. Banks were regulated as to the interest rates they could pay on deposits, but their nonbank competitors were not. Banks began losing funds to these competitors. As a result, economists and policy makers began to take greater interest in these other participants in financial markets.

---

9.   Suppose you buy one share of stock for $100. A year later, you receive a dividend of $4, and the price of the share has risen to $106. You could sell the share and be $10 ahead ($4 from the dividend and $6 from the increase in the share price). You made $10 on your investment of $100. That is, the higher price ensures that the investment yielded a 10 percent annual rate of return. The yield is a combination of dividend and capital gain (an increase in value).

Taken together, banks and nonbank financial institutions make up the credit market at the bottom of the circular flow diagram (see Figure 1). The principal nonbank financial institutions are stockbrokers and the stock market, bond dealers and the bond market, mutual funds, insurance companies, and pension funds. There are other players in financial markets, but these major ones should be enough to give you a sense of how financial markets work. Stockbrokers and bond dealers purchase and sell one type of financial asset. Mutual funds, insurance companies, and pension funds are more like banks in that they collect funds at "retail" and invest in diversified assets.

STOCKS, STOCKHOLDERS, AND THE STOCK MARKET

The **stock market** is a financial market in which ownership claims on corporations are bought and sold.[10] Most daily trades involve just one stockholder selling shares to another. However, new stock is also issued. Individuals make investment funds available to corporations by purchasing the newly issued shares of stock. The performance of the market is measured daily in terms of several indexes of stock prices as well as the daily volume of shares traded. We are primarily interested in the stock market as an economic device for attracting loanable funds to corporations and allowing individuals to share the risks of losses in the hope of gain.

stock market
A financial market in which ownership claims on corporations are bought and sold.

STOCKS AND STOCKHOLDERS

Only corporations can issue stock. A share of **stock** is an ownership claim in a corporation. Stockholders, who own shares of stock, have a claim on the profits of the corporation after all expenses are paid. Stockholders are therefore risk takers. They are taking the chance that there will be no profits and thus no earnings. If the corporation goes bankrupt, the value of their stock will fall sharply, perhaps to zero. Then they will lose their capital as well as their earnings. If the corporation succeeds, however, stockholders gain both by an increase in the value of their shares and by higher earnings. Some of a corporation's net earnings are paid as dividends to stockholders. Other parts of net earnings are reinvested to increase future earnings. Such reinvestment normally increases the net worth of the corporation and therefore increases the value of a share of stock.

Stockholders also enjoy voting rights in the corporation. They can attend the annual meeting to vote on the board of directors and comment on company policy. Few stockholders take advantage of this privilege. Some, however, have chosen to vote their shares to change a corporation's leadership, to redirect its market strategy, and sometimes even to involve it in social policy. In the 1980s, the focus of many corporate annual meetings was shifted by a minority of stockholders to issues such as environmental awareness, disinvesting in South Africa, and increasing opportu-

stock
An ownership claim in a corporation.

10. The stock market is too complex to describe fully in just a few pages. If you are interested in this fascinating subject, there are many books that can provide you with more detailed information and many newspapers and magazines that can help you watch the market.

In October 1987, the major indexes that measure the average price of a stock on the New York Stock Exchange all dropped sharply, the largest decline since the 1929 stock market crash that marked the beginning of the Great Depression. The Dow-Jones Industrials average dropped 30 percent in about three weeks. Standard and Poor's 500 index fell about 22 percent. The most widely used indicator, the Dow-Jones Industrials, had broken 2,000 points earlier in the year only to fall from its September level of 2,571 to a December low of 1,910. It took almost two years, until August 1989, for the market to recover to pre-crash levels. The 1929 stock market crash was even more severe. The market fell by 34.8 percent from its peak in September 1929 to the end of that year. It continued to fall until it hit its low point in 1932, with the average price of a share down 89 percent from its peak value.

How does a stock market crash affect the rest of the economy? The links between the stock market and overall economic activity run through four channels. First, when stock prices fall, it is more difficult for firms to raise equity capital in order to invest. Thus, a weak stock market discourages investment. Second, stocks are part of the assets of households. When the value of household assets falls, households experience a decline in wealth and respond by cutting back consumption. Both these actions will shift the *AD* curve to the left, reducing output and the price level. Third, investors often borrow in order to finance their stock purchases. When the value of the stocks that serve as collateral for their loans falls, they have to come up with some cash to reduce the size of the loan in line with the lower value of their stocks. The reduction in loans also tends to reduce output and prices.

Finally, the market both reflects and creates expectations about the current and future condition of the economy. A stock market crash may reflect generally negative expectations, or it may create them. Negative expectations tend to reduce lending, borrowing, and spending, thus

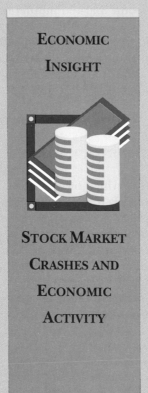

ECONOMIC INSIGHT

STOCK MARKET CRASHES AND ECONOMIC ACTIVITY

having the effect of lowering economic activity.

Because the stock market is one of the dozen leading indicators used to predict downturns and upturns in economic activity, the crash in 1987 was widely heralded as a forecast of an impending recession. As you may have noticed, there was no recession during the following year. Both nominal and real GNP continued to rise and unemployment continued a slow decline for almost three years. A major reason for this positive outcome was that the Fed rushed to pump loanable funds into financial markets. In fact, stock market declines are not very reliable as a forecaster. During the period from the end of World War II until 1990, there have been eight major stock market declines, of which only three were associated with a recession.

In 1929, stocks were one of the few financial assets available to small investors. Today, individuals have access to many types of assets, and stocks make up a smaller part of their portfolios. Thus, the impact of the 1987 crash on consumption was much weaker. In addition, requirements about borrowing to buy stocks are much stricter now than they were in the 1920s. Fewer stock buyers were caught in 1987 with large loans on stocks that had fallen in value. Finally, the consensus of observers after the 1987 crash was that the market decline did not reflect general pessimism about the economy.

When the average price of a stock, or prices of stocks in general, rise more rapidly than is justified by the underlying value of the companies issuing the stock, a correction eventually takes place. Stock prices will fall to more realistic levels. Many large institutional investors (such as mutual funds and pension funds) have programmed trading plans that respond automatically to price changes. These investors may thus tend to overreact and buy or sell too much. The stock market showed large swings in the 1980s, largely because these large buyers and sellers dominated the market and had a great influence on prices.

nities for minorities and women. Other stockholders are more interested in such bread-and-butter issues as new product development, marketing strategy, and profitability.

THE STOCK MARKET

The organized stock market in the United States has its primary center in the New York Stock Exchange, where ownership shares of large corporations are traded. Other exchanges are the American Stock Exchange and the Pacific Stock Exchange. Stocks that are not traded as frequently or that are issued by smaller corporations are traded through brokers in the over-the-counter market. Buyers may also invest through foreign exchanges, such as the London or Tokyo stock exchange.

The average price of a share on the New York Stock Exchange is considered a leading indicator, forecasting downturns and upturns in the business cycle. There are several indexes that provide a handy guide to the performance of the market on any particular day. The Dow-Jones Industrials and Standard and Poor's 500, for example, follow the prices of a fixed group of stocks and measure the change in the average price.

Although individuals see the stock market as an opportunity for gain through sharing corporate risk, the most important economic function of the stock market is to provide equity funds for corporations. Equity refers to ownership. In contrast, debt, or borrowed funds, has a fixed interest rate and must be repaid at some future date. Stock ownership provides a way to share the risks of new ventures, new technology, new products, or expanding in an uncertain market among a large number of individuals holding shares in the corporation.

BONDS AND THE BOND MARKET

The second major financial market is the **bond market**, in which the debt instruments of governments and corporations are traded. Sometimes governments and corporations borrow by taking out a loan from a bank or other financial institution at a specified interest rate. Such loans involve formal agreements about regular payments of capital and interest until the sum is repaid. More often, however, governments and corporations issue bonds. A **bond** is a debt instrument issued by a corporation or a government agency and having a fixed face value, annual interest payment, and maturity date. The face value is the dollar amount for which the bond can be redeemed at maturity. The maturity date tells how long a time period will elapse between when the bond is issued and when it is redeemed.

bond market
A market in which the debt instruments of governments and corporations are traded.

bond
A debt instrument issued by a corporation or a government agency and having a fixed face value, annual interest payment, and maturity date.

WHO ISSUES BONDS?

Corporations issue bonds in order to raise money to invest. The federal government issues bonds in order to finance the deficit in the federal budget. As you learned in Chapter 12, such bonds are a major asset of the Federal Reserve System and its member banks. These bonds are attractive because they are safe, offer reasonably good yields, can be readily marketed if necessary, and have a wide range of maturities. In addition, federal agencies such as the Federal National Mortgage Association issue bonds (called agency bonds) in order to help finance mortgage loans and for other purposes. State and local governments also issue bonds in order to finance capital projects, such as school buildings and sewer systems. These bonds are called **municipal bonds** regardless of whether they are issued by a state, city, county, or school district. They are attractive to investors because the interest on them is not subject to federal (and sometimes state) income tax.

municipal bond
Any bond issued by a state or local government to finance a capital project.

Governments are major borrowers. In 1989, about 25 percent of all the funds raised in the U.S. credit market went to finance the borrowing of federal, state, and local governments. Some critics of government borrowing argue that competition from the government makes it harder for private firms to sell their bonds or to borrow. If funds are limited, the federal government will have its demand satisfied first because it is a safer borrower. Private borrowers may have to settle for borrowing less at higher interest rates. When government borrowing drives up interest rates and chokes off some private borrowing, crowding out has occurred.

The 1980s saw the emergence of a popular but very risky type of bond, called **junk bonds**. Junk bonds are high-yield, high-risk securities that are usually issued to finance a takeover of one corporation by another. During the wave of corporate mergers and takeovers in the 1980s, a large number of these bonds were issued to raise the cash to buy the stock of the corporation being acquired. When the dust settled, the newly merged firm was saddled with a very large burden of debt at a very high interest rate. A number of the merged corporations wound up in bankruptcy. Holders of junk bonds suffered severe losses as scheduled interest and principal payments were not made and the market value of their bonds fell sharply.

junk bonds
High-yield, high-risk securities that are usually issued to finance a takeover of one corporation by another.

BONDS VERSUS STOCKS

Bonds other than junk bonds are usually considered a safer investment than stock because bonds have a prior claim on a corporation's assets. Bond prices do fluctuate with changes in interest rates but are generally more stable than stock prices. Interest payments on bonds are safer and more certain than dividends from stock shares.

The annual interest rate is fixed when the bond is sold, but the yield is not. The yield on a bond is the annual income from it (the annual interest payment plus any change in its market price) divided by the current selling price of the bond. Since the selling price of the bond can go up or down, the yield varies with that price. When interest rates are high, buying bonds is a way to lock in high yields. Even if you have to sell the bonds before they mature, you will get some of the high yield in the form of a **capital gain**, an increase in the market price of the asset (bond). If your bond is yielding 12 percent when newly issued bonds are paying only 9 percent, buyers will bid up the price of your higher yielding bond.

capital gain
An increase in the market price of an asset.

The advantage of bonds when interest rates are high becomes a disadvantage when interest rates are low. If you buy bonds when interest rates are low, not only are you getting a low yield, you may also suffer a capital loss if interest rates rise. When interest rates are low, two other assets are more attractive than bonds: stocks and money. Stocks are more attractive because the dividend and the potential for capital gains look better when bonds are offering low yields. Money is more attractive because its opportunity cost (the bond interest forgone) is lower and the risk of capital loss on bonds is higher if interest rates go back up.

BOND YIELDS, INTEREST RATES, AND BOND PRICES

There is a fairly simple relationship between the price of a bond and its yield. Higher bond prices mean lower yields, and vice versa. An example will illustrate this relationship. Assume that the federal government issues bonds maturing in ten years with a face value of $10,000 and an annual interest payment of $900. At this price, their yield is 9 percent. Now suppose the Fed engages in open market operations, buying so many of these bonds that their price rises by $100. (In the bond market, like any other market, an increase in demand with no change in supply will drive up the price.) This price increase will reduce the current yield on these government bonds to 8.91 percent ($900/$10,100).[11]

Because financial markets are interrelated, lower interest rates on government bonds will spread to other assets. Imagine that both government and low-risk corporate bonds are priced at $10,000 with yields of 9 percent. Most buyers would not prefer one to the other. But if the price of a government bond rises to $10,100, its yield will fall, as in the example just given. Corporate bonds, whose yield remains at 9 percent, then become more attractive than government bonds, and buyers will shift from government to corporate bonds. As buyers demand more corporate bonds, their prices will also be driven up, and yields will fall.

NONBANK FINANCIAL INTERMEDIARIES

There are some nonbank financial institutions that also collect funds from households and pass them on to borrowers and to firms raising equity capital (issuing stock). Recall that one of the major reasons for bank deregulation was the competition for both loan customers and depositors from nonbank financial institutions. Although these nonbank competitors cannot provide a substitute for money as a medium of exchange, they can provide good substitutes for money as a store of value. Individuals who hold deposits in banks can shift those deposits to other specialized financial assets, such as shares of mutual funds. Individuals may also own financial assets that are serving several purposes, such as deposits in pension funds and life insurance policies. These financial assets are a store of value, but also provide funds for retirement income or to take care of dependents in case of death.

Pension funds, insurance companies, and mutual funds are known as **institutional investors**. Because these investors deal in much larger volumes than the individual investor, their purchases and sales can affect the market price of a stock or bond. If institutional investors become more cautious and switch from stocks to bonds, the stock market suffers a decline. If institutional investors become bullish (optimistic about stocks), stock

institutional investors
Large investors, including insurance companies, pension funds, and mutual funds, whose purchases and sales have an impact on the prices of investment assets.

11. The Fed usually sells T-bills, which are bonds with a very short maturity. Then prices will not fall nearly that far because the owner always has the option of holding the T-bill until it matures, which is very soon. On a bond with a long time to maturity, however, large price swings such as this one are observed when interest rates change.

market indicators will rise. Institutional investors have become much more important players in the stock market in the last few decades. Some market watchers attribute the wider swings in average stock prices to the increased role of institutional investors.

MUTUAL FUNDS

Mutual funds compete directly with banks for the deposits of households and small businesses. Like banks, mutual funds invest in a variety of assets. The most common assets held by mutual funds are stocks and bonds. A **mutual fund** is a financial institution that pools money from many individuals in order to invest in a diversified portfolio of assets. Through a mutual fund, a small investor could own a small share of a wide array of assets instead of taking the risk of owning stock or a bond of one corporation. Mutual funds charge a small fee for their management services, but often offer an excellent return with minimal risk. Although deposits at mutual funds are not insured, most of them are not risky.

mutual fund
A financial institution that pools money from many individuals in order to invest in a diversified portfolio of assets.

As mutual funds became more popular, a whole array of options developed. You can buy shares in a fund that specializes in municipal bonds, or small corporations, or socially responsible companies. You can invest in a fund that stresses safety, or income, or risky growth. International portfolios, diversified by both industry and country, are available through mutual funds. An especially popular type of fund during the late 1970s was the money market mutual fund, which was invested in short-term government bonds (T-bills) and commercial paper (short-term business loans) and offered check-writing privileges. It was mainly competition from these funds that led to deregulation of bank interest rates in the early 1980s.

INSURANCE COMPANIES

There are many insurance companies and types of insurance policies covering homes, automobiles, health care, disability, and death. These companies accumulate investment funds in reserves against expected future losses. The insurance companies with the largest sums to invest are the life insurance companies. Life insurance companies sell two types of policies that accumulate a cash value while they are in effect. (Thus, the cash value is an asset on a household's balance sheet.) The first type is whole, or universal, life insurance, which pays off when the policyholder dies or can be cashed in for some sum during the policyholder's lifetime. The other type of policy is an annuity, which involves making current payments in return for an income later on, usually after retirement. Both types of policies provide life insurance companies with large cash reserves, which are invested in a variety of assets. Earnings on these assets, along with premiums paid by policyholders, provide enough funds to pay off present and estimated future claims as well as the costs of operation and profit for stockholders.

commercial paper
Short-term loans by financial institutions to business firms.

Insurance companies often invest in major construction projects such as office buildings and shopping centers. They also invest in stocks and bonds and make short-term loans, called **commercial paper**, to business firms. (Banks also hold a large amount of commercial paper.) Insurance companies are often a source of venture capital, which is funding for starting new businesses or developing new and unproven products or technologies.

PENSION FUNDS

Pension funds are very similar to insurance companies in that they take in large amounts of cash that they hold and invest. The cash reserves are used for payments to pensioners. Pension funds do not have stockholders. Usually pension funds are connected to an employer or a union, although some large ones cover a broad industry. For example, the Teachers' Insurance and Annuity Association (TIAA) is a large pension fund that covers many school and college teachers across the country. Because workers normally pay into the fund for many years before collecting benefits, pension funds have very large sums available to invest. They are generally quite cautious in their investments, preferring a safe low yield to a riskier higher one.

THE BORROWER'S SIDE: INVESTMENT AND INTEREST RATES

We have examined the motives of lenders and the structure of financial markets. Now we need to complete the picture by looking at why firms and individuals borrow. (We looked at government borrowing in an earlier chapter.) We know that many households borrow in order to finance the purchase of houses, cars, and consumer durables. This section concentrates on borrowing by businesses for investment purposes. Bear in mind, however, that much of what we say about business borrowing also applies to borrowing by households and state and local governments. Like business firms, these actors borrow to buy durable assets that will yield a stream of services in the future.

THE INVESTMENT DEMAND SCHEDULE

A business firm makes a decision to invest by comparing the expected rate of return on the investment to the market interest rate. Assume that a manufacturing firm is considering three investment projects for the coming year: (1) an automated welding machine that costs $20,000, (2) a computerized accounting system that costs $60,000, and (3) a forklift that costs $30,000. The firm has calculated the expected revenues and costs of operation for each piece of equipment over its useful life to the firm. These calculations also took into account the initial cost and salvage value. With this information, the firm's accountants have calculated that the expected rate of return on investment is 14 percent for the welding machine, 22 percent for the accounting system, and 8 percent for the forklift.

Based on this information, we can construct an investment demand schedule for the manufacturing firm. An **investment demand schedule** ranks all possible investment projects for a firm in order of decreasing expected rate of return. The investment demand schedule for this firm is shown in Figure 4. The schedule looks like a set of steps rather than a smooth line because the firm is considering three separate projects, each of which requires a lump sum expenditure.

For the economy as a whole, aggregate business investment spending will also depend on how the interest rate compares to the expected rate of return on investments. An investment demand schedule that sums the schedules of every firm in an economy is a smooth line, as shown in Fig-

investment demand schedule
A graph that ranks possible investment projects for a firm in order of decreasing expected rate of return.

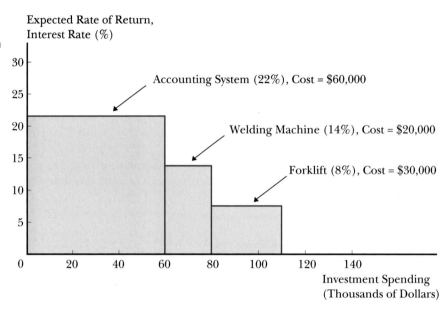

FIGURE 4
AN INVESTMENT DEMAND
SCHEDULE FOR A FIRM
Three possible invest-
ment projects for a
manufacturing firm are
ranked according to their
expected rates of return.
The firm decides which
investment to undertake
by comparing their
expected rates of return
to the market interest
rate.

marginal efficiency of investment (*MEI*) curve
A graph that sums the investment demand schedules for all firms in an economy. It ranks all investment possibilities for all firms according to their expected rates of return.

ure 5. The economy's investment demand schedule in Figure 5 is also known as the **marginal efficiency of investment (*MEI*) curve**. This diagram ranks all investment possibilities for all firms according to their expected rates of return.

Given the *MEI* curve for an economy, the market interest rate will determine the amount of investment spending. Every investment with an expected rate of return equal to or exceeding the market interest rate will be undertaken. For instance, at an interest rate of 20 percent, the level of

FIGURE 5
AN INVESTMENT DEMAND
SCHEDULE FOR AN
ECONOMY
Aggregate investment
spending depends on the
interest rate, *i*. If *i* is 20
percent, then total
investment will be $50
billion. If *i* declines to 12
percent, investment will
increase to $100 billion.
Investment demand is
negatively related to the
interest rate.

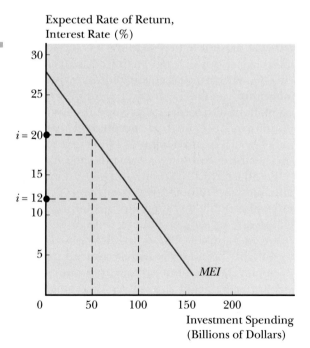

investment spending for the entire economy will be $50 billion in Figure 5. There are $50 billion worth of investment projects with an expected rate of return exceeding 20 percent. At an interest rate of 20 percent, the firm in Figure 4 would invest in the accounting system because its expected rate of return (22 percent) exceeds that interest rate. Neither the welding machine nor the forklift would be purchased. At an interest rate of 12 percent, the firm would invest in the welding machine as well as the accounting system. For the entire economy, a 12 percent interest rate would result in $100 billion of investment spending.

Investment demand and interest rates are negatively related. When interest rates rise, investment spending declines. When interest rates decline, investment spending rises. Higher interest rates raise the cost of investing so that only the most desirable investments will be undertaken. Less promising projects may become cost-effective at lower interest rates.

Note that the interest rate is relevant whether the firm is borrowing or not. When a firm borrows funds to invest, it wants to be sure that it will earn enough to pay all costs and interest, with some profit left over. If the firm is using its own funds to finance a project, there is still an opportunity cost. The firm must consider whether investing those funds in financial assets (bonds or other corporations' stock, for example) instead would offer a higher return than investing in new physical capital.

INVESTMENT SPENDING AND NATIONAL INCOME

This discussion of the borrower's side completes the picture of the loanable funds market. Investment demand, household demand for auto and mortgage loans, and borrowing demands of all levels of government combine to create a downward-sloping demand curve for loanable funds, as shown in Figures 2 and 3. The supply of loanable funds is positively related to the interest rate. Higher yields will induce lenders to make more funds available through financial markets. Lower yields will make them more likely to hold cash and wait for more attractive yields.

Financial markets are linked to aggregate supply and aggregate demand through changes in planned investment, which is a highly volatile component of aggregate demand. Other borrowing decisions (by households and governments) are also translated into changes in aggregate demand. Recall from the Keynesian model in Chapter 8 that a change in consumption, investment, government spending, or net exports causes a shift of the aggregate demand (*AD*) curve and a change in the equilibrium level of national income. Thus, if interest rates fall in financial markets, more firms will borrow or issue bonds in order to invest. The resulting increase in investment spending will shift the *AD* curve to the right. The increase in aggregate demand increases the equilibrium level of national income, employment, and prices. An increase in the interest rate has the opposite effect. Investment declines, the *AD* curve shifts to the left, and national income and output, employment, and the price level all decline.

Monetary policy has an important influence on interest rates, lending and borrowing, and investment, both directly through banks and indirectly through other players in financial markets. The next chapter will explore some of the problems in making monetary policy have the intended impact on output, employment, and the price level.

SUMMARY

1. The Depository Institutions Deregulation and Monetary Control Act (DIDMCA) of 1980 made all depository institutions members of the Federal Reserve System. It also greatly reduced the differences among types of depository institutions.

2. Bank deregulation combined with conditions in the oil industry and the real estate market, among other things, resulted in the failure of a number of savings and loans and banks in the 1980s.

3. The real rate of interest is the nominal, or market, rate of interest adjusted for the expected rate of inflation. When lenders guess wrong about inflation, the real rate of interest they earn can be negative. The real rate, not the nominal rate, governs money demand and investment decisions.

4. The rates of interest on various assets are all related, but they differ because of differences in risk and maturity.

5. A higher inflation rate will shift the demand curve for loanable funds to the right and the supply curve to the left, driving up the market interest rate.

6. The two major financial markets are the stock market and the bond market. Buyers and sellers exchange ownership shares in corporations in the stock market

and debt instruments of governments and corporations in the bond market.

7. Bonds are generally less risky than stocks. The yield on a bond is inversely related to its current market price. When a bond's price rises, its yield falls.

8. The major nonbank financial institutions, or institutional investors, are mutual funds, insurance companies, and pension funds. These institutions gather funds from households and other sources and invest them in stocks, bonds, or major construction projects. They also invest in commercial paper and provide capital for new business firms.

9. Business firms compare the expected rate of return on an investment to the market rate of interest in deciding whether to undertake that investment. The ranking of investments by their expected rates of return is a firm's investment demand schedule. For the economy as a whole, the investment demand schedule is the sum of the demand schedules of all firms and is called the marginal efficiency of investment (*MEI*) curve.

10. Changes in the interest rate affect the level of investment by shifting aggregate expenditure and aggregate demand so as to influence output, employment, and the price level.

NEW TERMS

bank deregulation	yield	bond	commercial paper
spread	expected yield	municipal bond	investment demand
market for loanable	risk	junk bonds	schedule
funds	stock market	capital gain	marginal efficiency of
risk premium	stock	institutional investors	investment (*MEI*)
nominal rate of interest	bond market	mutual fund	curve
real rate of interest			

QUESTIONS FOR DISCUSSION

1. How do banks and financial institutions today differ from what they were in 1979?

2. Suppose you were the manager of Petroleum Savings and Loan, and you knew that federal regulators were aware of your problems and would soon be check-

ing your books and deciding whether to close your bank down. What might you do? How is your self-interested behavior likely to make the problem worse?

3. In terms of a balance sheet, what does it mean to say that a bank has become insolvent?

4. A one-year bond issued today will pay $1,000 at maturity. Calculate the yield on this bond for prices of $999, $975, $950, $925, $900, $850, and $800.

5. Suppose the equilibrium real rate of interest is 3 percent and that people always try to earn this rate. If they believe inflation will be 5 percent, what should the nominal rate of interest be? What if they believe inflation will be 12 percent? Suppose they believe inflation will be 12 percent, but it turns out to be 15 percent. What is the actual real rate of interest that people will receive? (*Hint:* When people try to earn the equilibrium real rate in every period, the difference between the expected real rate of interest and the actual real rate is the expected inflation rate minus the actual inflation rate.)

6. Is it possible for the real rate of interest to rise while the market rate is falling? How would this happen?

7. In Table 3, why is the interest rate on Baa corporate bonds always higher than the rate on T-bills?

8. You own a bond with a face value of $1,000 and a yield of 6 percent. That is, it pays interest of $60 a year. Now the nominal rate of interest rises to 8 percent. In order for your bond to yield 8 percent, to what level must its price rise or fall?

9. What would happen to the price of the bond in Question 8 if the market interest rate fell to 5 percent?

10. What are the two major financial markets? What does each deal in? How are they related?

11. What is the difference between a stock and a bond? Which would you prefer to own if you were willing to take risks in hope of profits? Which would you prefer if you wanted safety and interest income?

12. What are institutional investors? Why are they so important in financial markets?

13. Using the investment demand schedule in Figure 5, assume that *i* declines from 20 percent to 15 percent. How would the amount of investment spending change?

14. Why is the level of investment for a firm or an economy negatively related to the interest rate? Does it make any difference whether the firm borrows or uses its own funds?

15. How would a decline in the interest rate affect aggregate demand?

SUGGESTIONS FOR FURTHER READING

Cargill, Thomas F., and Gillian G. Garcia. *Financial Reform in the 1980s.* Stanford, CA: Hoover Institution Press, 1986. Reviews the history of financial changes and their impact on monetary policy from a monetarist perspective.

Kane, Edward J. *The S&L Insurance Mess: How Did It Happen?* Washington, DC: Urban Institute Press, 1989. A good history of how the savings and loan problem evolved and evaluation of the bailout policy.

Lewis, Michael. *Liars' Poker: Rising through the Wreckage on Wall Street.* New York: W. W. Norton, 1989. A novel that describes the action in the New York bond market and how the major firms created new markets in the 1980s.

Mishkin, Frederick S. *The Economics of Money, Banking, and Financial Markets*, 2nd ed. Glenview, IL: Scott, Foresman, 1989. A textbook with a thorough treatment of financial markets.

1. Explain the Keynesian view of the monetary transmission mechanism.
2. Discuss the effect of interest rates on investment and money demand.
3. Evaluate interest rates and monetary aggregates as alternative targets for monetary policy.
4. Recount the main monetary policy actions of the Federal Reserve System.
5. Explain how each of the following raises questions about the effectiveness of fiscal policy:
   a. the stability of the multiplier versus the stability of the velocity of money,
   b. crowding out.
6. Discuss the advantages and disadvantages of the three ways of financing government spending:
   a. by taxes,
   b. by borrowing,
   c. by printing money.
7. Identify the major areas of agreement between economists.

CHAPTER 14

MONETARY POLICY IN THEORY AND PRACTICE

INTRODUCTION

In the last three chapters, we have discussed money, the banking and financial systems, the Federal Reserve System, and the role of interest rates. Now we can take a closer look at how monetary policy works in the aggregate supply and demand model. Although monetary and fiscal policy focus attention on different aspects of demand management, both work by shifting aggregate demand (*AD*). Monetarists and Keynesians, or economists in the broad classical and Keynesian traditions, disagree about the effectiveness of monetary policy and about how it works to influence the levels of output, employment, and prices. This chapter looks at how monetary policy works in theory and practice and then summarizes the arguments from both sides about its effectiveness.

HOW MONETARY POLICY AFFECTS AGGREGATE DEMAND

There are two approaches to explaining how monetary policy affects aggregate demand. Monetarists stress demand for cash balances (transactions demand) and the equilibrium between money supply and money demand. Keynesians emphasize the role of interest rates (asset demand for money). These explanations do not necessarily contradict one another. Both mechanisms can work at the same time to translate changes in the money supply into shifts in aggregate demand. Those shifts lead to changes in output, employment, and the price level.

When the money supply and monetary policy are added to the simple Keynesian model, it becomes more realistic in two important ways. Interest rates become another exogenous variable, and the expanded model allows for changes in the price level. Interest rates play a modest but important role in the Keynesian model, because they influence consumption

369

and investment decisions. The price level was ignored in the simple version of the Keynesian model, in which output was so far below the full-employment level that the *AS* curve could be treated as horizontal. Since changes in the price level are closely linked to changes in the money supply, it was difficult to use that model to explore the impact of contractionary as well as expansionary fiscal policies. The more complete model, including money and interest rates, enables us to consider the use of both monetary and fiscal policies in both expansionary and contractionary directions.

MONETARY THEORY BEFORE KEYNES

To discuss the role of money in the Keynesian model, we need to review some of the ideas of the classical economists on the subject of money. Recall that the classical economists made the quantity theory of money the center of their macroeconomics. According to the quantity theory, when the money supply (M_s) expands, both individuals and private banks find that they are holding larger money balances than they want. Demand for money to hold for transactions depends mainly on money income, as shown by the money demand equation,

$$M_d = k \times P \times Y.$$

Figure 1 shows the demand for money as a function of money income. The graph is a straight line with a positive slope of k and an intercept of zero.[1] Since the money supply is given (determined by the Fed), it can be represented as a horizontal line, such as M_{s1}. Now suppose the money supply increases to M_{s2} in Figure 1. At the current level of money income, $(P \times Y)_1$, money supply exceeds money demand. People attempt to spend

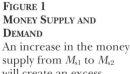

FIGURE 1
MONEY SUPPLY AND
DEMAND
An increase in the money supply from M_{s1} to M_{s2} will create an excess supply of money. As people try to spend the money, they drive up nominal income from $(P \times Y)_1$ to $(P \times Y)_2$. At the higher level of income, people are satisfied to hold larger money balances.

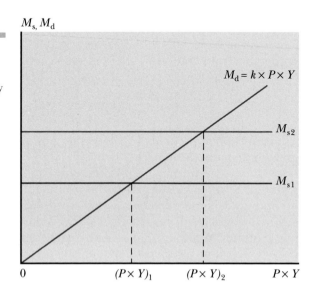

1.   It is also possible to plot money demand as a function of real income, *Y*, rather than money income, *P* × *Y*. If money demand is plotted versus real income, then changes in *P* can also shift the demand curve.

their excess cash balances. As they do, the level of money income will tend to rise. This process will continue until people are satisfied with their larger cash balances as a fraction of a larger money income, $(P \times Y)_2$. Thus, classical economists saw changes in the money supply as affecting spending directly, rather than working indirectly through interest rates.

A KEYNESIAN VIEW OF MONETARY POLICY

The classical view of how changes in the money supply lead to increases in demand was generally accepted before the 1930s. Keynes, however, stressed the effects of monetary policy working through changes in interest rates. An increase in the money supply will reduce interest rates, at least initially, because more funds will be available for banks to lend, if people do not immediately anticipate an offsetting rise in the price level.[2] (Inflationary expectations will be slower to change during a recession or depression.) The lower interest rates will stimulate investment demand. Changes in investment demand shift the *AD* curve, causing changes in output and income. Thus, according to Keynes, monetary policy works by influencing interest rates, which influence investment, which then affects output and income. The process of translating money supply changes into changes in demand, output, and the price level is called the **transmission mechanism**. Figure 2 shows this process. Let's consider each step in more detail.

transmission mechanism
The process of translating money supply changes into changes in demand, output, and the price level.

FROM MONEY TO INTEREST RATES. Recall that there are only two things that individuals can do when they have more money than they wish to hold: spend it or lend it. (If you leave money in a checking or savings account, the bank will lend it for you.) Classical theory puts a strong emphasis on spending as the way to get rid of the extra money. The Keynesian model puts an equally strong emphasis on lending.

When the Fed creates money by buying bonds, most of it enters the marketplace in the form of additional excess bank reserves. Banks will want to lend these reserves in order to earn interest.[3] To entice borrowers, banks may have to offer lower interest rates. In fact, the process of monetary expansion itself will tend to lower interest rates, at least in the

FIGURE 2
THE MONETARY TRANSMISSION MECHANISM: A KEYNESIAN VIEW
Keynesians think that monetary policy affects output and income mainly through interest rates. If the Fed buys bonds, the money supply increases, and interest rates fall. Lower interest rates stimulate investment, driving up aggregate expenditure. Higher aggregate expenditure causes output and income to rise through the multiplier effect.

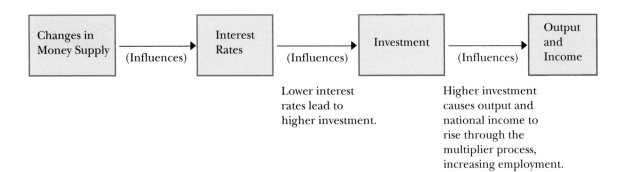

Lower interest rates lead to higher investment.

Higher investment causes output and national income to rise through the multiplier process, increasing employment.

2. If the increase in the money supply means that people expect more inflation, the inflationary expectations component of the market interest rate will rise. Thus, any effect of monetary expansion on interest rates is likely to be temporary.
3. If the Fed buys a bond from an individual, it's also very possible that that person will want to reinvest (lend) the money received.

short run. Recall the relationship between bond prices and bond yields. When the Fed uses open market operations to expand the money supply, it buys bonds. The increased demand for bonds drives their prices up and their yields down. As the lower yields on bonds spread to other assets and other financial markets, interest rates in general tend to fall.

Modern macroeconomists have tried to build their theories and models on a solid foundation of microeconomics. That is, they have sought to develop models that are firmly anchored in the self-interested behavior of individuals. In the Keynesian model, the response of banks and individuals to money creation is based on how they respond to changes in interest rates as the opportunity cost of holding money. If open market operations by the Fed result in banks holding more excess reserves than they would like to, bankers will be eager to lend those excess reserves even at lower interest rates. If individuals find themselves with larger cash balances than they need, they will make some of them available for lending in order to earn interest. Both of these actions will increase the supply of loanable funds and tend to put downward pressure on the market interest rate.

FROM INTEREST RATES TO INVESTMENT DEMAND. The next step in the transmission mechanism is from interest rates to investment demand. Recall from Chapter 13 that the relationship between investment demand and the interest rate is shown by the *MEI* curve. In Figure 3(a), the *MEI* curve, representing private investment demand, is the only source of demand for borrowing.[4] When the supply of loanable funds increases due to expansion of the money supply, the interest rate falls from 15 percent to 12 percent and the quantity of loanable funds demanded for investment purposes increases from $100 billion to $125 billion.

FIGURE 3
THE MONETARY TRANSMISSION MECHANISM AND AGGREGATE DEMAND
(*a*) The process of transmitting changes in the money supply into changes in output and the price level begins in the market for loanable funds. Increased loanable funds depress the interest rate and increase investment demand from $100 billion to $125 billion.
(*b*) The increased investment demand shifts aggregate expenditure upward, from AE_1 to AE_2.
(*c*) The increase in aggregate expenditure shifts aggregate demand to the right, from AD_1 to AD_2.

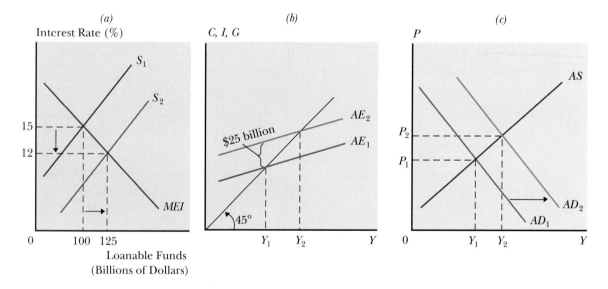

4.   Investors are not the only possible borrowers. Two other components of aggregate demand may also respond to lower interest rates. Consumers borrow to finance the purchase of houses, cars, and appliances. (Recall from Chapter 8 that one of the things that can shift consumption is a change in the interest rate.) Also, state and local governments borrow to finance capital projects, such as schools and roads. They also may borrow more at lower interest rates.

Since investment is an important component of aggregate expenditure, the *AE* curve will shift from AE_1 to AE_2 as shown in Figure 3(*b*). The vertical shift will equal the $25 billion increase in investment demand. (Actually, the whole family of *AE* curves shifts upward. We have shown only one pair.) The upward shift in the *AE* curve will shift the *AD* curve to the right as shown in Figure 3(*c*), increasing output and the price level.

PROBLEMS WITH THE TRANSMISSION MECHANISM
Thus, monetary policy works through interest rates and investment demand to influence the levels of output and prices. In the Keynesian view, however, there are several things that could go wrong in the process of translating changes in the money supply into changes in output.

BANK LENDING AND EXCESS RESERVES. The first thing that could go wrong is that banks might choose to hold excess reserves. Banks are more likely to make that choice during a recession, when interest rates are already low and the potential borrowers look risky. If the Fed buys bonds from the public rather than banks, the individuals who sell the bonds might choose to hold cash. If interest rates are low, individuals find that the opportunity cost of holding money instead of interest-bearing assets is also low. Thus, currency drains and excess bank reserves can reduce the expansionary effect of open market operations on the money supply.

Keynes believed that both excess reserves of banks and increased money holdings by households were very likely in response to an increase in the money supply under recessionary conditions of low interest rates and pessimistic expectations. He thought that the demand for excess reserves by banks and for cash balances by households would be very sensitive to interest rates, at least during recessions.

HOW SENSITIVE IS MONEY DEMAND TO INTEREST RATES? Even if banks or individuals lend some of the newly created money in the form of bank loans or purchases of other financial assets, it is possible that the interest rate might not fall very much, or at all. Figure 4 shows two views of the negative relationship between money demand and interest rates. The demand curve in both cases slopes down from left to right because interest

FIGURE 4
MONEY DEMAND, MONEY SUPPLY, AND INTEREST RATES
(*a*) If money demand is very sensitive to interest rates, expanding the money supply lowers interest rates only from i_0 to i_1. (*b*) If money demand is less sensitive to interest rates, changes in the money supply have more effect on interest rates, dropping then from i_0 to i_2.

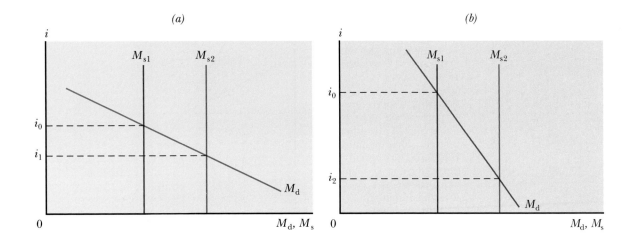

is the opportunity cost of holding money, and when that cost is lower, more money will be demanded. The real issue between Keynesians and monetarists is not the negative slope but the steepness of the money demand curve.

Part (*a*) of Figure 4 shows a Keynesian money demand curve. Here the quantity of money demanded is very sensitive to interest rates (interest-elastic). Part (*b*) shows a monetarist money demand curve. In this case, the quantity of money demanded does not respond very much to interest rates (interest-inelastic). In both parts of the figure, the money supply expands by the same amount, shifting from M_{s1} to M_{s2}. Interest rates fall much more in part (*b*) than in part (*a*).

Why does a given expansion of the money supply bring about a smaller decline in interest rates, when money demand is highly sensitive to interest rates? A very small drop in interest rates is enough to induce banks and households to hold much more cash and fewer other financial assets, such as loans and bonds. The responsiveness of money demand to interest rates is a major point of disagreement between Keynesians and monetarists.

INVESTMENT DEMAND AND INTEREST RATES. Even if interest rates did fall, investment demand might not be very responsive to the lower rates. In Figure 5, the investment demand curve labeled I_1 is relatively flat. A small decline in interest rates leads to a big change in investment demand along this curve, from I_A to I_C. The investment demand curve labeled I_2 is relatively steep. Here the same fall in interest rates increases investment demand only from I_A to I_B. Keynesians argue that the investment demand curve is more like I_2, which shows interest rates having little influence on investment demand. According to this view, investment demand is more dependent on changing expectations and other influences than on interest rates. Shifts in investment demand are so frequent that the steepness of the investment demand curve isn't really very important.

It is very difficult to measure the responsiveness of investment demand to changes in the interest rate. Both investment demand and interest rates are highly sensitive to changes in demand, expectations, and other eco-

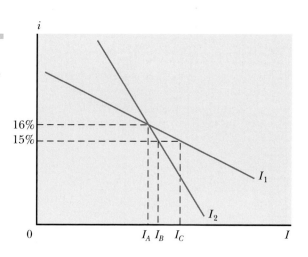

FIGURE 5
INTEREST RATES AND THE SLOPE OF THE INVESTMENT DEMAND CURVE
When the interest rate falls from 16 percent to 15 percent, the change in quantity of investment is larger along the more responsive investment demand curve, I_1, than along the steeper investment demand curve, I_2.

nomic conditions that vary over the course of the business cycle. Thus, investment demand and interest rates may move in the same direction because of other influences that offset or hide any negative relationship between the two. There has been no conclusive proof one way or the other.

EMPIRICAL EVIDENCE ON MONEY DEMAND

The relative importance of money income and interest rates in determining money demand is an issue that may be resolved using empirical tests. In a famous article from 1973, Stephen Goldfeld estimated the money demand function.[5] He found that a 1.0 percent change in money income leads to a 0.19 percent change in money demand (transactions demand) in the short run (three months) and a 0.68 percent change in the long run (two years). Thus, money demand is positively related to money income, but the response is rather small in the short run. According to Goldfeld, the demand for money is negatively related to both short-term and long-term interest rates. However, the effect of interest rates on money demand is less powerful than the effect of money income. For example, Goldfeld found that a 1.0 percent increase in the interest rate on time deposits led to a reduction in money demand (asset demand) of 0.045 percent in the short run and 0.16 percent in the long run. In general, his evidence clearly shows that interest rates do influence money demand, but not as much as Keynesians would expect.

Recent tests using data from the 1980s show a greater impact of interest rates on money demand. In tests done for the National Bureau of Economic Research by Dennis Hoffman of Arizona State University and Robert Rasche of Michigan State University, a 1.0 pecent increase in interest rates generated a reduction in long-run money demand of 0.5–0.6 percent, much higher than what Goldfeld found.[6] Thus, the modern version of money demand as a function of both income and interest rates appears to hold up well under empirical testing.[7]

IS MONETARY POLICY EFFECTIVE?

Suppose banks do not lend, or the public holds cash, or interest rates do not fall very much, or investment demand does not respond to lower interest rates. If any one of these occurs, it might require a very large increase in the money supply to bring about much of a change in aggregate expenditure, output, and employment. Thus, the possibility that money demand is very sensitive to interest rates while investment demand is not is, in the Keynesian view, a serious drawback to monetary policy. In this view, monetary policy should play a supporting role for fiscal policy, keeping credit available and interest rates low when fiscal policy is expansionary and keeping credit tight when fiscal policy is contractionary. Keynesians argue that you can lead investors to money, but you can't make them

5.   Stephen M. Goldfeld, "The Demand for Money Revisited," *Brookings Papers on Economic Activity* (Washington, DC: Brookings Institution, 1973).

6.   Dennis Hoffman and Robert H. Rasche, "Long-Run Income and Interest Elasticities of Money Demand in the United States," National Bureau of Economic Research Working Paper No. 2949, April 1989.

7.   The appendix to Chapter 15 describes how economists conduct empirical tests, using real-world data and statistical tests to support or disprove economic theories.

Both the Keynesian and monetarist models of monetary policy are based on a closed economy. That is, they ignore the rest of the world. However, the fraction of U.S. output entering international trade has grown in recent decades. Flows of money and financial assets between countries have also expanded. It has become increasingly clear that neither monetary policy nor fiscal policy can ignore the rest of the world.

Suppose the Fed is pursuing an expansionary policy. According to the monetarist model, there will be an excess supply of money. As people try to spend it, their purchases will drive up both real output and the price level, in some combination. In an open economy, however, some of their purchases will be imported goods rather than domestic products. As the price level starts to rise, sales of exports will fall, and imports of relatively cheaper foreign goods will rise. A fall in exports and a rise in imports mean that the aggregate demand curve shifts to the left. This shift reduces the impact of expansionary monetary policy on output and the price level. Some of the extra money is, in effect, exported, increasing demand in the rest of the world as well as at home.

In the Keynesian model, monetary policy works mainly through interest rates. As interest rates start to fall in an open economy, domestic firms will want to borrow more in response to the lower rates. Lenders, however, are more

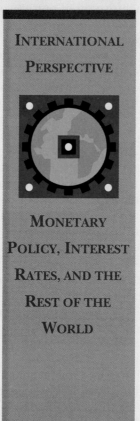

INTERNATIONAL

PERSPECTIVE

MONETARY

POLICY, INTEREST

RATES, AND THE

REST OF THE

WORLD

likely to want to make loans in other countries where higher interest rates are offered. Some of the newly created money goes abroad in search of higher interest rates. In addition, the inflow of funds from abroad shrinks as domestic interest rates fall. The net increase in loanable funds is fairly small, and there is little effect on investment.

The same problems occur with contractionary monetary policy in a Keynesian model. Spending falls, but some of the decline is in spending for imports, rather than domestic goods and services. Thus, there is less impact on aggregate demand, output, and the price level. Higher interest rates will attract an inflow of foreign funds, frustrating any attempts to reduce investment demand.

Thus, although Keynesians and monetarists disagree about the process, they concur that monetary policy is less effective in an open economy. Regardless of whether monetary policy works directly through spending or indirectly through interest rates, it will be less effective in an economy that is very open (has a lot of economic interactions with other countries). Small countries, such as Guyana, Taiwan, the Netherlands, and Costa Rica, find it virtually impossible to pursue an independent monetary policy because most of the effects leak out of the economy instead of staying at home.

spend. If fiscal policy is successful in inducing investors and other spenders to borrow, however, then it is important that funds be available to them. Keynesians do not deny that monetary policy is important, but they think it clearly takes a back seat to fiscal policy, especially during recessions. To Keynesians, money matters, but not very much.

Monetarists share the view of classical economists about the importance of the interest rate to investment decisions. Keynesians are firmly grounded in microeconomic behavior with respect to money demand and interest rates. But monetarists have the solid microeconomic foundation in their view of what determines investment demand. Recall that, in the classical model, the interest rate ensured that investment demand and the supply of savings would always be equal. Interest is the price that firms must pay for the use of funds now rather than later. Firms compare that interest rate to the rate of return on the investment, whether they are borrowing funds or using their own funds that could be earning interest.

The debate over the role of interest rates in affecting lending and borrowing is not just theoretical. It has important policy implications. If the Keynesian view is correct, then monetary policy is relatively ineffective, especially during recessions. If the monetarist view is correct, monetary policy is much more important and powerful as a tool to influence the price level and real output.

There is no simple test of whether Keynesians or monetarists are more nearly correct about the impact of monetary policy. One interesting comparison, however, is shown in Figure 6, which plots the percent change in

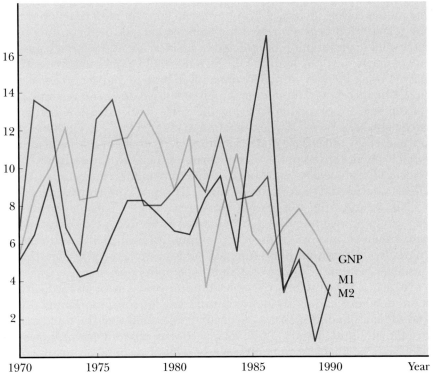

Rate of Growth of M1, M2, GNP (%)

FIGURE 6
CHANGES IN M1, M2, AND GNP, 1970–1990
This figure plots changes in the M1 and M2 measures of the money supply versus changes in nominal GNP for a twenty-year period. Note that the relationship between M1 and GNP has become weaker in recent years.

money supply (both M1 and M2) versus the percent change in nominal GNP for the period 1965–1989. Note that the relationship of M1 and GNP was much closer in the earlier part of the period than in more recent years. M2 tracks GNP a little better than M1 does for the entire period. This graph does not prove anything, but it does at least suggest that monetary policy has some influence on GNP. Since the relationship is not extremely close, the graph suggests that other factors besides monetary policy are also influencing GNP.

VELOCITY OR THE EXPENDITURE MULTIPLIER: WHICH IS STABLE?

Monetarists argue that monetary policy is more effective than fiscal policy because of the way households respond to changes in the money supply and changes in real income. They argue that households respond in predictable ways to changes in the money supply. That is, the velocity of money (V in the equation of exchange) is stable. Monetarists also claim that the marginal propensity to consume (MPC) is not stable. Therefore, the Keynesian consumption function and expenditure multiplier are not stable. Since fiscal policy depends on multiplier effects, this attack on the consumption function raises questions about the effectiveness of fiscal policy.

Velocity and the marginal propensity to consume cannot both be stable. If V is stable, MPC is unstable, and so is the expenditure multiplier. Keynesians and monetarists agree that both cannot be stable. They disagree about which is unstable.

Why can't both V and MPC be stable? Consider what happens when the money supply increases. The Keynesian consumption function shows the relationship between real disposable income and real consumption. How would consumption be affected by an increase in the money supply? According to Keynesians, unless the increase in the money supply is accompanied by an increase in real income, it will have no impact on consumption. The increase in the money supply will drive down interest rates, reducing velocity or perhaps raising the price level. In the equation of exchange, $M_s \times V = P \times Y$, a combination of lower velocity (V) and a higher price level (P) will ensure that real output (Y) is unchanged. If real output is unchanged, consumption will not change either. Keynesians believe that velocity is unstable. Monetary policy is therefore ineffective, because it only affects velocity and the price level, not real output (and employment).

Not so, argue the monetarists. An increase in cash balances creates an excess supply of money. People will spend more to get rid of the excess cash balances, increasing their consumption out of their given real income. It is the consumption function, not the velocity of money, that is unstable. Monetary policy works, and fiscal policy does not.

Which is more stable, the consumption function or the velocity of money? When economists look at annual data for consumption spending and the marginal propensity to consume, they find that the fluctuations in MPC are quite large. Despite its year-to-year ups and downs, however, MPC stays pretty close to an average of 0.89 of disposable income over the long run.

Velocity averages about 6 (relative to M1). It rose steadily in the 1970s, then fluctuated. Velocity is positively related to real income, prices, and interest rates. Like the marginal propensity to consume, velocity is highly unstable over the short run. The measurement of velocity for recent years has been complicated by changes in the measurement of the money supply and the introduction of new kinds of financial assets (such as money market accounts). Until recently, velocity appeared to show a steady upward trend in the long run. However, it tends to rise during expansions and fall during recessions and appears to be fairly sensitive to interest rates.

What can we conclude from this debate about the stability of velocity, the stability of the expenditure multiplier, and the relative effectiveness of monetary and fiscal policy? No definite conclusions emerge. Both the Keynesian expenditure multiplier and the velocity of money are fairly unstable in the short run, especially over the course of the business cycle. An unstable Keynesian expenditure multiplier makes the effects of fiscal policy less certain. An unstable velocity of money that is sensitive to interest rates seems to support the Keynesian view and to make monetary policy less effective.

MONETARY POLICY IN PRACTICE

Keynesians argue that monetary policy works mainly through interest rates. As a result, some economists argue that the target of monetary policy should be controlling interest rates. Monetarists place less emphasis on interest rates and more on the direct effects of changes in the money supply on spending. They believe that the Fed should emphasize controlling the size of the money supply. Interest rates and the money supply are alternative targets for monetary policy, and there has been an ongoing dispute about which works better.

This dispute is important for two reasons. First, the Fed's impact on market interest rates is limited and temporary. If the Fed tries to reduce interest rates by expanding the money supply, there will eventually be upward pressure on the price level. Inflationary expectations will spread. Since these expectations are an important influence on interest rates, market interest rates will rise.

The second reason why the dispute is important is that the Fed cannot pursue both targets at once. If the Fed tries to control interest rates, it must adjust the money supply to whatever level is needed to maintain the desired rates. If interest rates rise above the desired level, the Fed must buy bonds and increase bank reserves to stimulate lending and bring interest rates back down. If interest rates fall below the desired level, the Fed must cut back on the money supply to try to bring them back up. If the Fed tries to control the money supply, then it cannot control interest rates. When the Fed chooses one target, it loses control of the other.

MONEY SUPPLY OR INTEREST RATES?
The Fed can direct its attention to controlling the growth of the money supply or to controlling the level of interest rates. Monetarists usually favor controlling the size of the money supply and its rate of growth.

KEYNESIANS VERSUS MONETARISTS ON MONETARY POLICY

Keynesians believe:

• Money demand is sensitive to interest rates.
• The velocity of money is unstable.
• Investment is insensitive to interest rates.
• Monetary policy is not very effective in changing aggregate demand, output, and employment.

Monetarists believe the opposite:

• Money demand is insensitive to interest rates.
• The velocity of money is stable.
• Investment responds to changes in interest rates.
• Monetary policy is effective in influencing aggregate demand, output, and employment in most cases.

Keynesians usually prefer an interest rate target. This choice reflects the Keynesian belief that interest rates exert an important influence on business activity.

In addition, some Keynesians argue that it is difficult, if not impossible, for the Fed to control the growth of the money supply within narrow limits. This argument is based on the fact that the Fed does not exercise direct control over the money supply. The Fed affects the money supply indirectly through its control of bank reserves and currency (Federal Reserve notes). Banks' decisions about excess reserves and individuals' decisions about cash balances will affect how large a money supply a given monetary base supports.

money multiplier
The ratio of the actual money supply to the monetary base.

monetary base
The currency in the hands of the public plus reserves held by banks.

THE MONEY SUPPLY AS TARGET. The Fed can influence bank lending by influencing bank reserves, but it cannot directly control lending and the money supply. Recall the deposit multiplier ($1/rr$) from Chapter 12. This multiplier determines the maximum money supply and the maximum expansion or contraction that could result from a given change in bank reserves. A slightly different concept is the **money multiplier**, a ratio which gives the relationship of the actual money supply to the monetary base. The **monetary base** consists of the currency in the hands of the public plus reserves held by banks. (Currency in people's hands is part of the monetary base because it becomes bank reserves if it is deposited in banks.) Thus, the monetary base is used either as cash holdings for the public or as reserves to support bank deposits.

The money supply can be defined by the relationship

$$M_s = m \times B,$$

where M_s is the money supply, B is the monetary base, and m is the money multiplier. The money multiplier is then

$$m = \frac{M_s}{B}.$$

Thus, the money multiplier (m) is closely related to the deposit multiplier ($1/rr$) in the equation $D = (1/rr) \times BR$, developed in Chapter 12. However, B includes currency as well as bank reserves (BR). Thus, instead of being determined by the Fed, as the deposit multiplier is, the money multiplier is influenced by the decisions of banks and individuals whether to hold cash or reserves or to lend.

Different money multipliers correspond to the different measures of the money supply. For example, suppose M1 = $400 billion, M2 = $1,000 billion, and B = $200 billion. Then the M1 money multiplier is

$$m_1 = \frac{\text{M1}}{B} = \frac{\$400 \text{ billion}}{\$200 \text{ billion}} = 2,$$

and the M2 money multiplier is

$$m_2 = \frac{\text{M2}}{B} = \frac{\$1,000 \text{ billion}}{\$200 \text{ billion}} = 5.$$

Both the size and the stability of the money multiplier are important because the Fed can control the monetary base, but it cannot control the money supply directly. Changes in the money supply are caused by changes in the monetary base, the money multiplier, or both.

If the Fed wants to increase the monetary base, it can use open market operations to buy government bonds. If the Fed buys the bonds from a bank, their market value is automatically added to the bank's reserves. If the Fed buys the bonds from a private citizen, the citizen will ultimately deposit the Fed's check in a bank. In either case, the monetary base (B) will rise by the amount of the purchase. If m is constant, M_s will increase by m times the change in B. For example, a $1 billion increase in B would cause M_s to rise by $2 billion if m were 2, by $3 billion if m were 3, and so on.

If the money multiplier is not constant, however, changes in its value can affect the money supply even with no change in the monetary base. Suppose B is $200 billion and m is initially 2.5. Then M_s equals $500 billion (2.5 × $200 billion). A fall in m of only 0.1, to 2.4, means that M_s becomes $480 billion (2.4 × $200 billion), a fall of $20 billion. Thus, a very small change in m has a large effect on M_s.

The Fed controls B, which is one source of change in M_s. The other source of change, variations in m, is only partly under the Fed's control. A portion of an increase in B could go to extra holdings of currency, so there would be less of an increase in bank reserves. In this case, the public's decision to hold more currency and coins instead of checkable deposits would keep M_s from rising as much as it otherwise would. If an increase in B goes entirely to reserves, banks could decide not to lend all these reserves. In either case, an attempt to make M_s rise by a certain amount by increasing B could be frustrated in part by an offsetting fall in m.

Monetarists argue that the money multiplier is fairly stable over periods of a few quarters and that most changes in the money supply are therefore caused by changes in the monetary base. Thus, to monetarists, controlling the money supply is very important. Controlling the monetary base can allow the Fed to control the money supply fairly well.

Table 1 gives the values of m for two measures of the money supply, M1 and M2, for the period 1970–1990. In each case, m was calculated by dividing the money supply by the monetary base. The numbers in each column seem quite close. But note that the spread from the lowest value of the M1 multiplier (in 1980) to the highest (in 1972) is 0.32/2.70, or about 12 percent. For the M2 multiplier, the maximum spread is 32 percent. During the 1980s, however, the M2 multiplier was more stable than the M1 multiplier. Because the money multiplier is less than perfectly stable, the Fed usually sets its targets in terms of the growth of the money supply and adjusts the monetary base rather than the other way around.[8]

Another problem in targeting the money supply is choosing among the different measures of that supply. The Humphrey-Hawkins Act of 1978 requires the Fed to report its monetary growth targets for the year to Congress, and Congress interprets that target as M1. With more kinds of financial institutions and deposits, the Fed has shifted its monetary target from M1 to M2. This change was made partly because the link between the monetary base and M2 (see Table 1) seems to be slightly more stable and partly because M2 seems to be more closely linked to the level of economic activity (money income, or $P \times Y$). In any case, the target is not a

TABLE 1
MONEY MULTIPLIERS,
1970–1990

YEAR	M1 MONEY MULTIPLIER	M2 MONEY MULTIPLIER
1970	3.02	8.84
1971	3.01	9.40
1972	3.02	9.76
1973	2.96	9.66
1974	2.85	9.42
1975	2.80	9.97
1976	2.78	10.51
1977	2.78	10.78
1978	2.76	10.69
1979	2.74	10.64
1980	2.70	10.71
1981	2.73	11.15
1982	2.74	11.30
1983	2.77	11.61
1984	2.73	11.72
1985	2.83	11.70
1986	3.00	11.65
1987	2.92	11.28
1988	2.87	11.14
1989	2.80	11.28
1990	2.66	10.90

8. The link between the monetary base and M1 in the 1980s was affected to some degree by reforms that brought all depository institutions under the Fed's control and provided for uniform reserves. For a discussion of this relationship, see Michelle R. Garfinkel and Daniel L. Thornton, "The Link between M1 and the Monetary Base in the 1980s," *Review*, Federal Reserve Bank of St. Louis (September-October 1989): 35–52.

precise number or a specific rate of growth but a range of growth rates for the various monetary aggregates: the monetary base, M1, M2, and related measures.

INTEREST RATES AS TARGET. Until the late 1970s, the Fed paid more attention to interest rates than to the money supply. Letting interest rates rise too high could discourage investment and cause a recession. The decision to target interest rates instead of the money supply was reinforced by the fact that the Treasury has to borrow by selling U.S. government securities to the public. The government budget deficit is financed through these bond sales, and the Treasury prefers low, stable interest rates to high, unstable ones.

The Fed attempts to control interest rates by keeping the federal funds rate (the interest rate banks charge each other when lending and borrowing reserves) within a certain range. If, for example, Bank A needs $1 million in reserves to meet the reserve requirement, it can borrow them from Bank B and pay that bank interest at the federal funds rate. Bank B notifies the Fed to transfer $1 million from its reserve account to Bank A's account.

The Fed targets a range for the federal funds rate, such as 7–7.5 percent. If the demand for reserves rises, driving up the federal funds rate, the Fed will buy government bonds. The prices of bonds will rise, and their yields fall. As lower interest rates spread from bonds to other assets, the federal funds rate is kept from rising above 7.5 percent. If demand for reserves falls, and the federal funds rate seems likely to fall below 7 percent, the Fed will sell government bonds. Open market sales of bonds will depress bond prices and put upward pressure on interest rates.

An interest rate target requires the Fed to keep adjusting the monetary base to whatever is demanded in the market for loanable funds. Thus, the Fed cannot control both the money supply and interest rates at the same time. The Fed was widely criticized by monetarists in the 1970s for giving interest rate targets priority over money supply targets. In an abrupt shift, the Fed changed its priorities from interest rates to the money supply in the fall of 1979. This change, under the leadership of chairman Paul Volcker, was regarded as a milestone in monetary policy and a victory for monetarist ideas. The policy of focusing on the money supply remained in place until 1982, but pressure on the Fed during the recession then forced it to moderate that policy. In addition, changes in the banking system made it more difficult to forecast and control relationships between the size of the monetary base and the money supply in the 1980s. Since 1982, the Fed has been using a mix of targets: a range of growth rates for the several measures of the money supply and a range of market interest rates.

GNP TARGETING

In recent years, there has been an attempt by the Fed to shift from targeting interest rates or the money supply to **GNP targeting**. This policy calls for the Fed to aim at some level of nominal GNP by influencing a number of variables that affect it. These variables include the measures of the money supply as well as total credit and interest rates. However, even

GNP targeting
A monetary policy that calls for the Fed to aim at some level of nominal GNP by influencing a number of variables that affect GNP.

if changing GNP is the ultimate goal, the Fed must choose intermediate targets that are within its control to try to attain that goal. Those targets are still some combination of money supply and interest rates.[9]

LAGS IN MONETARY POLICY

Lags present another problem in implementing monetary policy. Monetary policy is affected by the same kinds of lags that affect fiscal policy: recognition, implementation, and impact lags. The recognition lag is probably about the same length for both monetary and fiscal policy. Unlike fiscal policy, however, monetary policy has a very short implementation lag. The Federal Open Market Committee (FOMC) meets regularly and makes decisions about changes in the money supply. Because of the Fed's independence from Congress and the executive branch, it can move quickly without asking anyone's permission.

In discussions of monetary policy, the recognition and implementation lags are combined and known as the inside lag. The impact lag—known as the outside lag in monetary policy—can be quite long. In the 1960s, it was estimated that it took one to two years for money supply changes to be fully reflected in prices and output. By the 1980s, the lag appeared to be getting shorter. The inflation of the late 1970s had made lenders and borrowers more sensitive to the need to acquire and use current information to form correct expectations about inflation. Shorter lags also reflect increased competition in financial markets as a result of bank deregulation.

The length of the outside lag depends on how quickly people recognize and respond to a change in the money supply. It takes time for banks to increase or decrease their lending or for individuals to adjust their spending. In general, it is estimated that, because of the outside lag, it takes at least two quarters for monetary policy to have half its ultimate impact and eighteen to twenty-four months for the full effect to be felt.

Lags are an important concern because they can cause monetary policy to have the wrong effect, just as they can for fiscal policy. From 1945 to 1982, cycles of economic activity have been brief, with the average recession lasting only eleven months. A policy that cannot be implemented quickly and have a rapid impact may be worse than no policy at all.

SECTORAL EFFECTS

Monetary policy does not affect all sectors of the economy equally. When monetary policy is tight, those economic activities that depend on borrowing are affected more heavily. Business investment in plants and equipment, housing, consumer durables (especially automobiles), and state and local government capital projects are very dependent on borrowing and sensitive to changes in monetary policy. Consumers, the auto industry, and the construction industry resent being singled out to bear more than their share of the battle against inflation when monetary policy is tightened. Adjustable-rate mortgages (ARMs) and other innovations in home financing have somewhat lessened the impact of monetary pol-

9.   For a more detailed discussion of GNP targeting, see Michael D. Bradley and Dennis W. Jansen, "Understanding Nominal GNP Targeting," *Review*, Federal Reserve Bank of St. Louis (November-December 1989): 30–40.

icy on housing. However, this and other parts of the private sector are still sensitive to changes in interest rates and the availability of funds.

In the 1980s, the foreign sector became more sensitive to monetary policy. A tight monetary policy that drives up interest rates will attract funds from abroad and drive up the price of the dollar (see the International Perspective). When the price of the dollar rises, exporters find it harder to sell their goods abroad. Also, some firms in this country find that foreign competitors can more easily undersell them. Thus, the international sector of the economy has become increasingly sensitive to monetary policy.

POLITICAL PROBLEMS

Even though the Fed is technically independent, it is not immune to political pressures. The best-known instance of political pressure on the Fed was when it helped to finance the government deficit immediately after World War II. In recent years, Congress has put pressure on the Fed to keep interest rates low, often in response to the construction and auto industries and others who want low interest rates. The Fed was often pressured by Congress or the President to ease monetary conditions in election years. The Fed is also under pressure from banks, which would like to be able to lend freely (and borrow freely from the Fed) during times of high loan demand.

All of these forces tend to push the Fed in the direction of monetary expansion. It was only after some painful experience with the resulting inflation that the Fed was able to fight back and tighten monetary conditions in the late 1970s and early 1980s. The Fed now resists pressure to expand the money supply for political reasons, especially to make incumbents look good at election time.

RULES VERSUS DISCRETION

Many economists, especially monetarists, have not been happy with the Fed's performance. They blame the Fed for both recessions and inflation, as the course of monetary policy zigzags between expansion and contraction. The Fed has come under criticism in recent years for monetary tightness during the Great Depression. The same criticism was levied at the Fed during the 1980–1982 recession. A proposed regulation requiring the Fed to chart a course of growth in the money supply at some predetermined, steady rate is called a **monetary rule**. Such a regulation would replace discretionary monetary policy.

monetary rule
A proposed regulation requiring the Fed to make the money supply grow at some predetermined, steady rate.

The most commonly suggested form of monetary rule is to allow the money supply to grow at about the same rate as, or just a little faster than, real output over the long run, keeping inflation at a tolerable rate of 1–2 percent a year. This rule would call for a growth rate of 4–5 percent a year for the money supply. When output growth slows down because of a recession, monetary policy would be mildly inflationary. (If M_s is growing at 4–5 percent a year and velocity is stable, then $P \times Y$ must grow at the same rate. If Y is growing more slowly, P must take up the slack.) If the economy is overheated and demand is fueling growth of, say, 7 percent a year, monetary policy would be contractionary. Proponents of such a rule argue that attempting to respond to imperfect information from the marketplace, with the added hindrance of lags, is worse than having no monetary policy at all. Nobel Prize winner Milton Friedman is probably the best-known advocate of having a monetary rule.

The Fed is not likely to adopt such a binding rule voluntarily. It has, however, tried to stabilize the monetary growth rate and give more emphasis to the money supply as target rather than interest rates in recent years. Although monetarists are still unhappy with the Fed's performance in the last decade, especially with rapid monetary growth in the early 1980s, this change in targets represented a victory for monetarist ideas.

Another proposed "rule" is to return to a gold standard. Being on a gold standard requires a nation to have enough gold to redeem its currency in gold on demand. The stock of gold would place limits on the size of the money supply, and the Fed's discretionary policy role would be greatly reduced. The United States went off the gold standard in 1934 and is not likely to return, but some conservatives find the idea of an automatic limit on monetary expansion very attractive.

MONETARY POLICY UNDER THE FED, 1914–1990

When the Federal Reserve System was established in 1913, one of its primary functions was to keep the United States in compliance with the international gold standard. Complying meant that the Fed had to allow the size of the U.S. gold stock held by the Treasury to set an upper limit on the size of the money supply, in some fixed ratio. Such a requirement severely limited the Fed's freedom to expand the money supply.

The first problem confronted by the Fed was helping the federal government finance its deficit during and after World War I. The Fed cooperated in keeping interest rates low and buying any government bonds that could not find a buyer. These actions were inflationary. When the Fed recognized that the ratio of money to gold was getting too high, it began to contract the money supply. That action played a role in bringing about the 1920–1921 recession.

THE FED AND THE DEPRESSION

The biggest controversy over the Fed's policy centers on its actions from 1929 to 1937. The money supply fell by 25 percent from August 1929 to March 1933, in part because of widespread bank failures. Such a wave of failures was exactly what the Fed was intended to prevent. The Fed, aided by large inflows of gold, did keep the discount rate low during the early years of the Depression. It was the money supply, not the monetary base, that fell sharply. The monetary base remained stable while the ratio of currency to deposits rose (as people withdrew cash from the banking system) and the ratio of deposits to reserves fell (as banks held more excess reserves). Widespread bank failures led to large cash withdrawals from banks. Thus, the same monetary base supported fewer deposits. Banks saw few good loan prospects, and interest rates were low. Therefore, they chose to hold large excess reserves. Cash withdrawals combined with excess reserves meant that the money multiplier was smaller.

The most vocal critics of the Fed's actions in this period have been Milton Friedman and Anna Schwartz, who did a thorough study of these actions.[10] They argued that the Fed was too passive, failing to pump up reserves to offset what was happening in the private sector. The Fed did not shrink the monetary base but did not allow it to expand either. However, the Fed was constrained with respect to the size of the money supply by the gold standard until 1934. The most controversial policy decision by the Fed during the Depression took place after the United States went off the gold standard. The Fed chose to raise reserve requirements in 1936, trying to "mop up" excess bank reserves. This action was widely blamed for sparking an economic downturn in 1937.

Peter Temin argued that Friedman and Schwartz came down too hard on the Fed.[11] The money supply can change from either the supply side or the demand side. The return on investment was low during the early years of the Depression. If there is low return on investment and weak consumption demand, interest rates will fall. That fall will lead both individuals and banks to hold onto more cash and make less available to borrowers. The opportunity cost of holding currency and excess reserves will be low because of demand factors, which are largely outside the control of the Fed.

The Fed did not cause the Depression, but perhaps a more aggressive expansionary monetary policy would have made it shorter and milder. Bear in mind, however, that the Fed had had only seventeen years of experience when the Depression occurred. Also, some of its actions prior to 1935 were restricted by its need to comply with the gold standard.

THE ACCORD

During and after World War II, the Fed's main task was helping the Treasury finance the enormous debt incurred during the war at acceptably low interest rates. The Fed abandoned monetary targets in order to hold down interest rates. The result was inflation, because every time the Fed bought Treasury obligations to keep interest rates down, it expanded bank reserves. In 1951, the Fed and the Treasury reached an agreement. This agreement, called **The Accord**, stated that the Fed was no longer obliged to hold interest rates low to assist with the Treasury's debt financing. In 1952, the Fed was finally free to turn its monetary policy in the direction of stabilizing economic activity.

For most of the rest of the 1950s, the Fed used free reserves as its target. **Free reserves** consist of bank excess reserves less bank loans from the Fed. If free reserves were large, the Fed took that as a signal of too much slack in the credit market. The Fed defined its role during this time as "leaning against the wind." That is, the Fed was determining the direction of economic activity and trying to steer the economy back toward a middle ground of steady growth, stable prices, and high employment.

MONETARY POLICY IN THE 1960S AND 1970S

The inflation rate began to creep up in the late 1960s and rose faster in the 1970s. From 1965 to 1979, the CPI rose 130 percent. For most of this

The Accord
The 1951 agreement between the Fed and the Treasury that the Fed was no longer obliged to hold interest rates low to assist with the Treasury's debt financing.

free reserves
A bank's excess reserves less its loans from the Fed.

---

10. Milton Friedman and Anna J. Schwartz, *A Monetary History of the United States* (Princeton, NJ: Princeton University Press, 1963).
11. Peter Temin, *Did Monetary Forces Cause the Great Depression?* (New York: W. W. Norton, 1976).

credit crunch
The 1966 shortage of loanable funds caused by the sudden slowing of monetary growth rates by the Fed.

period, monetary policy was expansionary. The one major exception was the 1966 credit crunch. The **credit crunch** was a shortage of loanable funds caused by the sudden slowing of monetary growth rates by the Fed. The Fed abruptly reduced the rate of growth of M1 from 4.6 percent in 1964 and 1965 to 0 percent in mid-1966. This reduction was a response to what it perceived as a threat of inflation. The housing industry ground to a halt. Savings and loan associations lost deposits to higher interest assets elsewhere as interest rates rose sharply in response. The Fed reversed its course and continued monetary expansion through the end of the 1960s. Inflation rates (predictably) began to rise.

The 1970s began with a financial crisis, a sharp drop in the stock market combined with the failure of Penn Central. That railroad was a major borrower from commercial banks. The Fed earned some of its highest marks ever for monetary policy during this crisis. It announced that the discount window was open and lowered reserve requirements. As the 1970s wore on, inflation took hold, pushed by the OPEC oil price hike. The Fed responded with a more restrictive monetary policy, which probably contributed to the 1974–1975 recession.

By the late 1970s, after flip-flopping between targeting the money supply and targeting interest rates, the Fed began to move more in a monetary direction, while keeping an eye on interest rates. An abrupt change of direction in October 1979 was later named the "Saturday night special." Instead of interest rates, the Fed decided to make the growth of the various measures of the money supply, especially M1, the focus of its policy actions. The Fed cut the monetary growth rate sharply at the end of 1979, which drove interest rates to all-time highs. This action contributed to the recession (and drop in the inflation rate) of the early 1980s. The 1979 shift marked a firm choice of money supply targets over interest rate targets.

RECENT MONETARY POLICY

Through most of the 1980s, the Fed was chaired by Paul Volcker. Volcker and the Fed emerged as heroes with a fairly restrictive monetary policy. This policy was credited with helping to reduce both the inflation rate and nominal (but not real) interest rates. Part of the decrease in inflation and interest rates, however, was the result of a decline in velocity rather than a slowing of the growth of the money supply. Monetary policy in the 1980s was complicated by rapid growth in the federal debt, an influx of foreign lending, changes in bank regulations, and more numerous bank failures. In 1982, the Fed backed off from its 1979 decision to focus solely on money supply targets and began to pursue interest rate targets as well. In addition, M1 competed with other measures of money and credit for the role of primary money supply target.

In 1987, Volcker was succeeded by Alan Greenspan as chairman of the Fed. A combination of changing leadership and experience has changed the Fed's operating style and priorities. The experience of the 1970s and early 1980s made the Fed much more concerned about inflation and much more aware of the effects of high interest rates on the economy. Bank deregulation, increasing involvement of foreigners in U.S. money and credit markets, and the gradual weakening of the close link between

M1 and GNP have made the Fed much more uncertain about the effects of its actions on the economy.[12]

GOVERNMENT BORROWING, CROWDING OUT, AND MONETARY POLICY

As you have seen at several points in this brief history of monetary policy, monetary and fiscal policy are closely related. Financing government borrowing is one area in which the two policies must be coordinated. In the 1980s, the most important links between fiscal and monetary policy had to do with the effects of government deficit financing on interest rates and private investment and the Fed's response to crowding out.

Monetarists argue that increased government spending (G) may not have much effect on aggregate expenditure (AE) or aggregate demand (AD) because it is likely to be offset by a decline in private investment. How does this happen? If government spending is financed by borrowing, this drives up interest rates. Higher interest rates discourage private investment. Thus, the increase in G is offset by a fall in gross private domestic investment (I).

As you learned in Chapters 10 and 13, reductions in private borrowing and investing because of increased government borrowing, which drives up interest rates, is called crowding out. In extreme cases, total spending may not increase at all. The simple Keynesian model has no crowding out. In that model, the interest rate does not rise when G increases. Instead, AE rises by the full amount of G, with the usual effect on output and employment due to the expenditure multiplier.

Figure 7 shows how crowding out occurs, using supply and demand curves for loanable funds at various rates of interest. Assume that the initial demand curve, D_0, reflects only demand for private investment. Ini-

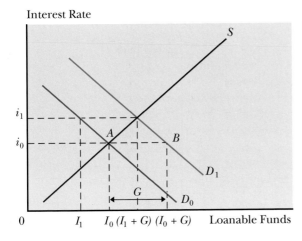

Interest Rate

i_1

i_0

A B

S

D_1

G D_0

0 I_1 I_0 $(I_1 + G)$ $(I_0 + G)$ Loanable Funds

FIGURE 7
SUPPLY AND DEMAND FOR LOANABLE FUNDS AND CROWDING OUT
Increased demand for loanable funds to finance government spending shifts demand from D_0 to D_1. Increased demand drives up interest rates and reduces private borrowing. Total borrowing rises to $I_1 + G$, but private investment falls from I_0 to I_1.

12. Council of Economic Advisers, *Economic Report of the President* (Washington, DC: U.S. Government Printing Office, 1990), 83–84.

tially the government is not borrowing at all. The interest rate is i_0, and the volume of lending and borrowing is I_0. Suppose the government adds its demand (to finance an increase in G with no additional taxes). The combined demand curve shifts to D_1. The horizontal distance between the two demand curves at the initial interest rate is AB, the amount of increased G financed by borrowing. The interest rate rises to i_1. At that interest rate, private borrowers (still represented by D_0) only want to borrow I_1. Total demand for loanable funds (as well as the total expenditure function AE) has risen, but actual lending increases only by the difference between I_0 and $(I_1 + G)$. That amount is much smaller than the increase in G.

THE KEYNESIAN CASE

How much crowding out actually occurs? Figure 8 diagrams two extreme cases: one with a horizontal supply curve of loanable funds in part (a) and one with a vertical supply curve in part (b). The horizontal version represents the extreme Keynesian view, perhaps appropriate to conditions like those of the Great Depression. In this case, banks have excess reserves but are reluctant to lend to risky private borrowers. However, they will lend freely to the government because they are certain of being repaid. Thus, government borrowing has no effect on interest rates because there are funds available at the existing rate. No crowding out occurs. Aggregate expenditure will rise by the full amount of G, the distance between I_0 and $(I_0 + G)$, and the interest rate will not change. There will be a large shift of aggregate demand to the right, driving up output and prices—the normal result of fiscal policy in the Keynesian model.

THE MONETARIST CASE

Part (b) of Figure 8 represents an extreme monetarist view. In this case, banks are already all loaned up when the government issues new bonds. Government borrowing can occur only at the expense of private borrowers. These borrowers include not only business investors but also state and

FIGURE 8
THE SUPPLY CURVE FOR
LOANABLE FUNDS
(a) In the Keynesian view, there are ample loanable funds available at the current interest rate. When G increases, no crowding out occurs, interest rates do not rise, and aggregate expenditure increases by the full amount of G. Aggregate demand shifts to the right (from D_0 to D_1). Real output and/or the price level rises. (b) In the monetarist view, the rise in G is fully offset by a decline in I as interest rates rise sharply. Aggregate expenditure is unchanged, and there is no effect on aggregate demand, real output, or the price level.

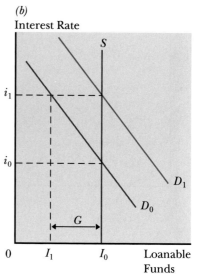

local governments (borrowing to build schools and sewer plants) and consumers (borrowing for houses, autos, and stereo systems). The rise in G is offset by an equal fall in I from I_0 to I_1 as interest rates rise from i_0 to i_1. Thus, part (b) shows total crowding out. Expansionary fiscal policy has no effect on the level of real output. There is no shift in aggregate expenditure because the upward shift caused by rising G is offset by an equal and opposite fall in I. Aggregate demand is unchanged.

THE INTEREST RATE AND THE SUPPLY OF LOANABLE FUNDS

The slope of the supply curve for loanable funds depends on how sensitive the demand for money is to changes in interest rates. Money that households do not wish to hold becomes available to lend in the loanable funds market. If money demand is very responsive to interest rates, the supply curve for loanable funds will be relatively flat. Only a small rise in interest rates will be needed to induce individuals to switch from holding money to lending it. A supply curve for loanable funds drawn by a Keynesian would be very flat, although not as flat as the curve in Figure 8(a). Interest rates hardly change at all when the government enters the market as a borrower.

The monetarist supply curve for loanable funds is vertical, or nearly so. Monetarists do not expect money demand to be very responsive to the interest rate. When interest rates rise, the funds lent to government are exactly offset by a reduction in business borrowing, with no increase in aggregate expenditure or aggregate demand.

Who is right? Both sides are partly correct. According to the empirical tests cited earlier, money demand is moderately responsive to changes in interest rates. If money demand is responsive to interest rates, higher interest rates will call forth more loanable funds as banks lend excess reserves and individuals cut down on their cash balances. Thus, under normal circumstances, there should be partial but not total crowding out.

The experience of the 1980s did not provide a good test of the crowding out hypothesis, because of the effect of foreign lending. A part of both government and private borrowing was financed by foreign funds flowing into the United States. This flow of funds reduced direct competition between government borrowing and business borrowing for the same pool of funds. Instead, the inflow of foreign funds drove up the price of the dollar and made U.S. exports more expensive and U.S. imports cheaper. Thus, instead of the crowding out of investment, there appears to have been some crowding out of net exports.

THE INTEREST RATE AND INVESTMENT DEMAND

It is not only the slope of the supply curve for loanable funds but also the slope of the marginal efficiency of investment (*MEI*) curve that determines how much crowding out takes place. The slope of this demand curve represents the responsiveness of investment demand to interest rates. Recall that Keynesians think investment is influenced more by aggregate demand, expectations, and other factors than by interest rates. Monetarists expect investment to be affected more by interest rates.

These two views are pictured in Figure 9. An upward-sloping supply curve for loanable funds is paired with a very steep or unresponsive

The huge U.S. government budget deficits in the 1980s appear to have resulted in very little crowding out of investment. Between 1981 and 1985, foreign investment in the United States rose sharply, attracted by high interest rates, an appealing business climate, and other factors. As a result, international capital flows provided funds for investment.

When foreigners purchase U.S. bonds, stocks, or whole firms or make bank deposits, they must first convert their currency (yen, pounds, francs, Canadian dollars, or whatever) into U.S. dollars. As foreigners demand more dollars, the price of the dollar, or the exchange rate, rises. Between 1981 and 1985, the price of the U.S. dollar rose 60 percent.

Was this development good or bad? Both. A higher price for the dollar is great if you want to visit Europe or buy a foreign car. American dollars will buy more foreign currency and thus more foreign goods. A more expensive dollar is also good news on the inflation front. Relatively cheap imports will keep the CPI from rising as rapidly. If, however, you are an exporter or compete with imported products, a higher dollar price presents problems. When dollars are expensive, American goods are expensive, and foreign goods are rel-

INTERNATIONAL PERSPECTIVE

THE BUDGET DEFICIT AND THE EXCHANGE RATE

atively cheap. It is hard to sell goods abroad or to compete at home. Exports fell steadily as the dollar rose during the early 1980s. Slow growth of real output and employment was blamed on the high price of the dollar, the flood of imported goods, and the decline in U.S. exports. Thus, some of the pressures for protection against competition from imports in the first half of the 1980s reflected the high price of the dollar.

The rising tide of foreign investment in the United States and the rising price of the dollar both halted in 1985. These changes occurred partly because there were better investment opportunities elsewhere and partly because federal deficits stablized and began to fall, reducing interest rates. Between 1985 and 1990, the price of the dollar fell 38 percent. If the lower price for the dollar holds in the 1990s, the United States can expect more exports, fewer imports, more jobs—and higher prices. In economics, there is no free lunch and no unmixed blessing. The inflow of foreign investment in U.S. stocks, bonds, and bank accounts bring both costs and benefits and so does a slowdown in such investment.

(a)
Interest Rate

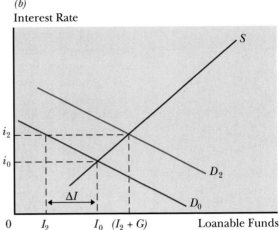

(b)
Interest Rate

(Keynesian) investment demand curve in part (*a*) and a very flat or responsive (monetarist) investment demand curve in part (*b*). In both cases, crowding out is measured by the decline in private investment. When demand shifts from D_0 to D_1 in part (*a*), very little crowding out occurs. Interest rates rise, but investment demand is not affected much. More crowding out occurs in the monetarist model in part (*b*) when demand shifts from D_0 to D_2. If an increase in government spending is partly offset by a decline in investment, then the resulting shift in aggregate expenditure and aggregate demand will be smaller. There will be less impact on output, employment, and the price level.

The debate over crowding out is not yet resolved. Empirical tests have not proved whether increased government borrowing has much effect on interest rates and, as a result, on the amount of private borrowing. In the early 1980s, real interest rates did remain high when the government borrowed heavily to finance record deficits. However, very little crowding out of investment was observed because the high interest rates attracted an inflow of foreign funds. This inflow of foreign funds not only increased the supply of loanable funds but also drove up the price of the dollar from 1980 to 1985. In effect, it crowded out net exports to some degree. As the level of government borrowing stabilized and began to fall during the late 1980s, the price of the dollar fell. There was some increase in net exports, due to a reduction in imports at first and later some increase in exports as well.

HOW SPENDING IS FINANCED

Borrowing is not the only way to finance an increase in government spending (*G*). There are three ways: raising taxes, borrowing, and printing money. Each of these methods affects aggregate demand differently. Only raising taxes is pure fiscal policy. The other two methods involve a blend of monetary and fiscal policy.

Tax financing of *G* may be slightly expansionary, according to the Keynesian model. As you learned in Chapter 9, the government expen-

FIGURE 9
CROWDING OUT AND THE INVESTMENT DEMAND CURVE
(*a*) When government borrows, interest rates rise from i_0 to i_1, but private investment falls only from I_0 to I_1.
(*b*) Investment is very sensitive to interest rates. Government borrowing drives interest rates from i_0 to i_2. There is a large fall in private investment from I_0 to I_2.

ditures multiplier $[1/(1 - b)]$ is a little larger than the tax multiplier $[-b/(1 - b)]$. However, the effect of expansionary fiscal policy on output and employment is much larger when the increase in G is not accompanied by higher taxes (T). Fiscal policy that consists of equal changes in G and T requires a very large change in both to have any effect.

Financing an increase in G by borrowing is a standard Keynesian policy prescription. On the other hand, G can be held constant while taxes are increased or decreased, which also changes the level of borrowing. In either case, expansionary policy runs the risk of crowding out investment. To the extent that crowding out occurs, the impact of the change in government spending on output and employment is smaller.

ACCOMMODATING MONETARY POLICY. One way to avoid crowding out when the government spends more than it collects in taxes is to expand the money supply. In order to keep interest rates from rising when the government borrows, the Fed buys the excess government bonds. When the Fed buys bonds, bank reserves increase, and the money supply expands. Monetary expansion that is undertaken to help the Treasury finance deficits without driving up interest rates very much is called **accommodating monetary policy**. Monetarists argue that expansionary fiscal policy supported by accommodating monetary policy is not fiscal policy at all, but monetary policy. If an increased deficit leads to increases in output and employment, they believe, the higher output is caused by monetary expansion, not fiscal policy. It is clear that when an increased deficit is financed with a larger money supply, it is difficult to tell whether changes in output, employment, and the price level are the effects of monetary or fiscal policy.

accommodating monetary policy
Monetary expansion that is undertaken to help the Treasury finance deficits without driving up interest rates very much.

DO FINANCING METHODS MATTER? Economist Robert Barro of the University of Rochester argues that the method of financing government spending has no impact on private spending.[13] People will perceive that increased government spending now, financed by borrowing, will mean increased taxes in the future to pay off the debt. If they are consuming on the basis of permanent income, as Friedman argues, then they will reduce their consumption because of the expected future increased taxes. Thus, the effect of higher government spending will be to increase current income, decrease future income, and leave permanent income unchanged.

Barro's argument is based not only on the permanent income hypothesis but also on the macroeconomic idea that people have rational expectations. That is, they make economic decisions using all available information and they avoid repeating previous errors. That people have rational expectations is a central idea of the new classical school. According to this view, people may not be misled into changing their behavior in response to temporary policy changes. The policy implications of rational expectations, an approach to macroeconomics that has been strongly advocated by Robert Lucas and Thomas Sargent, will be explored further in the next two chapters. Barro's view that financing methods do not have

13. Robert Barro, "Are Government Bonds Net Worth?" *Journal of Political Economy* (November/December 1974): 1095–1117.

any effect on output and employment has produced a great deal of debate, but so far has not won wide acceptance among either Keynesians or monetarists.

DOES POLICY DO ANY GOOD?

The question of whether policy can help reflects a final basic difference between Keynesians and monetarists. Keynesians believe that policy makers should be concerned about the short run. The long run, or the period in which the economy may adjust to some full-employment equilibrium, is very long. In the interim, there may be an unacceptable amount of suffering from unemployment, inflation, or both. Most monetarists share the classical view that the economy should be left to correct itself, but they go one step further. Monetarists believe that activist policy, especially fiscal policy, may do more harm than good. How is a policy maker to know what to do if economists can't agree among themselves?

DO ECONOMISTS EVER AGREE?

Although monetarists and Keynesians disagree about macroeconomic theory and policy, they agree about a number of things. More than two decades ago, Milton Friedman said, "We are all Keynesians now." That is, most economists use a modified Keynesian framework to discuss macroeconomic issues. Since that time, mainstream economists would tend to add, "We are also all monetarists now." The model of the loanable funds market that was used in Chapter 13, for example, incorporates both monetarist and Keynesian views. The aggregate supply and demand model is broad enough to encompass not only Keynesian and monetarist views but others as well.

Here is a list of some points of agreement between Keynesians and monetarists:

1. The money supply can affect output as well as prices, although the effects on output may be only short-run.
2. Velocity is more stable in the long run than in the short run.
3. The demand for money depends on both income and interest rates, although income has a stronger effect.
4. Expectations about income, prices, and interest rates are an important influence on consumption and investment.
5. Fiscal policy can have some effects on real output in the short run. The long-run effects are much less certain.
6. Both inflation and unemployment beyond a certain minimum are undesirable.
7. Lags may distort the intended effects of monetary and fiscal policy.
8. Some crowding out is a likely result of a deficit-financed increase in government spending.

Note all the qualifiers in this list: "may," "to some degree," "some," and "in the short run." Monetarists and Keynesians disagree about the slope of the aggregate supply curve, the importance of crowding out, and the relative length of the long run and the short run. But even when they disagree, Keynesians and monetarists are using the same ideas: the aggregate expenditure function, the quantity theory of money, and the aggregate supply and demand model.

SUMMARY

1. The Keynesian view of monetary policy is that it works by lowering interest rates. In turn, lower interest rates stimulate investment and increase aggregate expenditure and aggregate demand. However, Keynesians do not think that monetary policy is always very effective at lowering interest rates or that lower interest rates are very effective in stimulating investment.

2. Monetarists believe that monetary policy works directly by creating a money supply that exceeds money demand. The excess money is spent, driving up prices and/or output.

3. The effectiveness of monetary policy depends on how sensitive money demand is to interest rates and how responsive investment demand is to changes in interest rates.

4. The Fed can attempt to control either the money supply or interest rates, but not both. In recent years, more emphasis has been placed on targeting the money supply.

5. Monetary policy suffers from lags, regional effects, and political pressures. Because of these problems with

monetary policy, some economists support a monetary rule that would set a fixed rate of growth for the money stock.

6. Monetarists believe that the velocity of money is stable (at least in the long run) and the expenditure multiplier is not. Keynesians argue the opposite. Stable velocity means monetary policy is more effective. A stable expenditure multiplier means fiscal policy is more effective.

7. Velocity rises during business expansions and falls during recessions. It has had a long-term upward trend in the last twenty years.

8. Fiscal policy will not be effective if government borrowing drives up interest rates and crowds out private borrowers.

9. If an increase in government spending is financed by higher taxes, the taxes reduce the impact of fiscal policy. Financing government spending by printing money makes it hard to separate the effects of fiscal and monetary policy.

NEW TERMS

transmission mechanism
money multiplier
monetary base
GNP targeting

monetary rule
The Accord
free reserves
credit crunch

accommodating
    monetary policy

QUESTIONS FOR DISCUSSION

1. The monetarist transmission mechanism accepts "spend it" as the explanation of what happens to an increase in the money supply. The Keynesian transmission mechanism follows the "lend it" route. Explain the difference.

2. If $MPC = 0.75$, what change in Y would occur if i decreased from 20 percent to 15 percent? Use Figure 3 to determine your answer.

3. Let $i = 15$ percent and $MPC = 0.9$. Further, suppose

the economy is in equilibrium and $Y = \$2,000$ billion. If $Y^* = \$2,200$ billion, what change in i would be necessary to bring the economy to the full-employment level of national income? Use Figure 3 to determine your answer.

4. Let B be \$200 billion. If m is 3 and then rises to 3.2, what is the change in M_s? What is the dollar change in M_s if B rises from \$200 billion to \$225 billion, and m is constant at 3?

5. Why do Keynesians think that monetary policy is

likely to be less effective than fiscal policy?

6. If money demand is sensitive to changes in interest rates and investment demand is not, how would that affect the relative effectiveness of monetary and fiscal policy? What if money demand is not sensitive to interest rate changes but investment demand is?

7. Why can't the Fed control both the money supply and interest rates at the same time? Discuss the advantages and disadvantages of each target.

8. Which sectors are most affected by changes in monetary policy? Why?

9. How might each of the following have differed if the Fed had been following a 4 percent monetary growth rule?

a. the 1936–1937 recession (during the Depression)

b. the postwar interest rate agreement with the Treasury

c. the 1966 credit crunch

10. If you were in charge of the Fed and concerned about inflation, would you pursue an interest rate target or a money supply target? Why?

11. Why can't both velocity and the expenditure multiplier be stable at the same time? If the demand for money is sensitive to interest rates, how is velocity affected?

12. If the government is pursuing an expansionary fiscal policy, which of the following conditions will make that policy more effective and which will make it less effective? Why?

a. Money demand is very sensitive to interest rates.

b. Investment demand is very sensitive to interest rates.

c. Monetary policy is accommodating.

13. If the Fed is pursuing an expansionary monetary policy, which of the following conditions will make that policy more effective and which will make it less effective? Why?

a. Money demand is very sensitive to interest rates.

b. Investment demand is very sensitive to interest rates.

c. Fiscal policy is also expansionary.

14. If the government tries to increase the level of output by increasing G, what difference does it make how that increase is financed?

15. According to Barro, why should the financing method in Question 14 make no difference?

Suggestions for Further Reading

Burns, Arthur. *The Anguish of Central Banking.* Washington, DC: American Enterprise Institute for Public Policy Research, 1980. Monograph on monetary policy by a former chair of the Board of Governors.

Federal Reserve Bank of St. Louis. *Review.* Published six times yearly. Follows the Keynesian-monetarist debate closely, from a strongly monetarist perspective.

Friedman, Milton, and Walter Heller. *Monetary versus Fiscal Policy.* New York: W. W. Norton, 1969. A classic debate by two influential economists.

Greider, William. *Secrets of the Temple: How the Federal Reserve Runs the Country.* New York: Simon and Schuster, 1987. A critical and highly controversial look at how the Fed has conducted monetary policy in recent years.

Mayer, Thomas, James S. Duesenberry, and Robert Z. Aliber. *Money, Banking and the Economy,* 4th ed. New York: W. W. Norton, 1990. Chapters 20 through 25 offer a thorough evaluation of recent monetary policy.

1. Discuss how decisions made by individuals may lead to undesirable aggregate outcomes.
2. Describe the shape of the Phillips curve and explain what makes it shift.
3. Describe the stagflation of the 1970s and the challenge it posed to both Keynesian and monetarist models.
4. Define:
   a. the natural rate of unemployment,
   b. demand-pull inflation,
   c. cost-push inflation.
5. Evaluate the Post-Keynesian policy of wage and price controls as a method for dealing with stagflation.
6. Identify the major differences among the six schools of macroeconomic thought.

CHAPTER 15

INFLATION AND UNEMPLOYMENT: CHALLENGES TO DEMAND MANAGEMENT

INTRODUCTION

Thomas Schelling, a Harvard economist, has developed some very creative approaches to analyzing the aggregate results of individual choices. In one of his many books on this subject, *Micromotives and Macrobehavior*, he offers a wide range of examples of the unfortunate effects when individuals make choices without considering the choices of others.[1] His examples include choosing seats at a concert, picking a route when commuting to work, and buying or selling a house in a racially mixed neighborhood. The outcomes are likely to be an empty front section at a concert, overcrowding on some roads and little use of others, or panic selling and housing segregation. Schelling shows that outcomes are usually less satisfactory for everyone than would be the case if individuals were somehow able to devise strategies to cope with the effects of interdependence.

Consider, for example, what might happen in an economy where everyone had pessimistic expectations and decided to save more as a hedge against recession. With such expectations, it is likely that some of the added savings would not be reinvested. As a result of increased saving (and lower consumption), demand and income would both fall. Increased planned saving would be offset by less actual, or realized, saving out of lower income. (This effect is the paradox of thrift discussed in an earlier chapter.) Fear of recession and a self-interested response to that fear would help to cause a recession.

If a group is small enough—such as a family, a club, a small town, or a class—its members are aware of their interdependence. Their individual contributions to an outcome are each large enough to make a difference. As a group gets larger, however, it matters less what any one person does because each has such a small effect on the aggregate outcome. Thus, individuals make self-interested decisions without considering the effects of interdependence. The outcome may be unsatisfactory for everyone.

This problem of an aggregate outcome that is unsatisfactory to every-

---

1. Thomas Schelling, *Micromotives and Macrobehavior* (New York: W. W. Norton, 1978).

one, or at least to a majority, is the central concern of macroeconomics. The sum of individual and collective decisions can lead to a rate of inflation and a level of unemployment that few people find satisfactory. Citizens call on government to offset the effects of these choices and to provide a better outcome. The demand management (fiscal and monetary) policies discussed in the last eight chapters suggested some ways to act collectively through government in order to offset some of the undesirable effects of self-interested private decisions.

We began our discussion of macroeconomics by identifying three important macroeconomic goals: economic growth, price stability, and full employment. We can complete our discussion of price stability and full employment (and their mirror images, inflation and unemployment) at this point, because both of these goals are closely linked to demand management. (Economic growth is closely linked to aggregate supply, so we will discuss that goal in the next two chapters.)

Until this point, we have looked at demand management policies under the assumption that policy makers had a clear sense of direction, either to reduce unemployment or to contain inflation. In this chapter, we consider some of the problems of using either monetary or fiscal policy during a period of stagflation, when inflation rates and unemployment rates are both high. We will also look at wage and price controls as an alternative policy tool to contain inflation without creating unemployment. Finally, we will conclude our discussion of demand management policies by looking again at the various schools of macroeconomic thought. Although each group has a slightly different approach, they basically fall into two camps. One group, consisting of Keynesians and Post-Keynesians, believes that the actions of the private sector (households and business firms) lead to unsatisfactory outcomes that must be corrected by government. The other group, which consists of the descendants of the classical school (the monetarists, new classical economists, and supply siders), believes that correction can be left to market forces. Both groups may agree that outcomes are unsatisfactory at any given moment. However, the first group calls for corrective action, and the second group relies on existing corrective forces.

STAGFLATION AND THE PHILLIPS CURVE

According to the simple Keynesian model, too low a level of aggregate planned expenditure results in unemployment. When aggregate planned expenditure is too high, relative to full-employment output (Y^*), the result is inflation. In this model, it is not possible to experience both inflation and unemployment at the same time. The stagflation of the 1970s presented a major challenge to Keynesian thinking.

The monetarist model is somewhat better suited to describing stagflation. In this model, inflation results when the money supply grows faster than real output. During the 1960s, monetarists developed an explanation of the relationship between inflation and unemployment called the natural rate hypothesis. The stimulus for this work came from a diagram describing the historical relationship between changes in wages (or price level changes) and changes in unemployment. That diagram was

developed by British economist A. W. Phillips. Later work by Edmund
Phelps, who explained Phillips's results using the natural rate hypothesis,
contradicted the prevailing Keynesian view of the inflation-unemployment
relationship. These new approaches were used by economists to explain
the stagflation of the 1970s.

Is There an Unemployment-Inflation Tradeoff?

The simple Keynesian model is based on a horizontal aggregate supply
curve. The more general version of the Keynesian model uses a composite aggregate supply curve with a horizontal region at low levels of output
and an upward-curving region where the economy approaches full employment. At that point, the aggregate supply curve becomes vertical.
With such a composite aggregate supply curve, as shown in Figure 1, a
movement of the aggregate demand curve from AD_1 to AD_2 increases output (and employment) with no change in the price level. A shift from AD_3
to AD_4 drives up prices with no change in output. A shift from AD_2 to AD_3
increases output (and employment) and the price level.

When economists look for an explanation of the relationship between
unemployment and inflation, they usually begin with the aggregate supply and demand curves, which determine output and the price level.
Changes in employment and unemployment are very closely linked to
changes in production, or real output. The inflation rate is a measure of
the rate of change in the price level.

It is important to distinguish between a one-time change in the price
level and inflation. A sustained and continuous rise in the price level is
inflation. The aggregate supply and demand model explains the price
level, not the inflation rate. It takes a single shift in aggregate supply or
aggregate demand to change the price level. There must be continuous
shifts to produce sustained inflation.

In the 1950s and 1960s, economists generally believed that there was a
consistent negative relationship between the inflation rate and the unem-

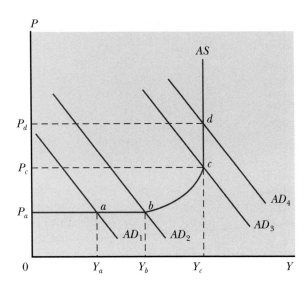

Figure 1
Aggregate Demand and
Aggregate Supply:
A Composite View
When aggregate demand
shifts in the range from
Y_a to Y_b (from AD_1 to
AD_2), only output and
employment rise. Prices
are unchanged. From Y_b
to Y_c, further rightward
shifts in aggregate
demand (to AD_3)
increase both prices and
output (and employ-
ment). Beyond Y_c,
rightward shifts in
aggregate demand (to
AD_4) only drive up the
price level.

ployment rate. That kind of relationship between inflation and unemployment is shown in Figure 2. The vertical axis measures the inflation rate, and the horizontal axis measures the unemployment rate. The curve in Figure 2 corresponds closely to the composite aggregate supply curve in Figure 1. The zero inflation rate and the levels of unemployment at points a' and b' correspond to output levels Y_a and Y_b in Figure 1. These points lie on the horizontal section of the inflation-unemployment tradeoff curve in Figure 2. When aggregate demand shifts from AD_1 to AD_2 in Figure 1, unemployment falls from a' to b' in Figure 2, with no inflation (no change in the price level). A shift to point c in Figure 1 and point c' in Figure 2 means a decline in unemployment but a rise in the price level (or inflation). Output level Y_c in Figure 1 is defined as the full-employment level of real output, corresponding to an unemployment rate of 4 percent. This amount of unemployment was generally accepted as the definition of full employment during the 1950s and 1960s.

Note that, according to Figures 1 and 2, increases in the price level and the unemployment rate cannot occur together as a result of shifts in aggregate demand. A rightward shift of the aggregate demand curve will reduce unemployment or raise the price level, or some combination of the two. A leftward shift of the aggregate demand curve will increase unemployment or lower the price level (or the inflation rate), or both.

The actual unemployment and inflation rates for 1961 to 1970 are shown in Figure 3. With one exception, these points seem to lie on or fairly close to a smooth curve, like the one in Figure 2. Until the late 1960s, a relatively stable composite aggregate supply curve, combined with changes in aggregate demand, seemed to offer an accurate description of the relationship between unemployment and inflation. This curve was consistent with the general Keynesian model.

FIGURE 2
INFLATION AND UNEMPLOYMENT WHEN AGGREGATE DEMAND SHIFTS AND AGGREGATE SUPPLY IS STABLE
The inflation and unemployment rates at a', b', c', and d' correspond to the points of intersection of AD_1, AD_2, AD_3, and AD_4 with AS in Figure 1.

Inflation Rate (%)

FIGURE 3
INFLATION AND
UNEMPLOYMENT
IN THE U.S. ECONOMY,
1961–1970
The data for this period
seem to show a consistent
negative inflation-
unemployment relation-
ship, except for 1970.
Later evidence suggested
a shift to the right of the
Phillips curve beginning
in 1970 (the dashed line).

Source: Council of Economic Advisers, *Economic Report of the President* (Washington, DC: U.S. Government Printing Office, 1982).

Figure 4 plots the unemployment and inflation rates for 1970 to 1989.
Note that a negative relationship between the two rates is not apparent
here. In fact, during the late 1970s, inflation and unemployment seemed
to have a positive relationship. Most observers attribute the change in the
relationship between inflation and unemployment to shifts in the aggregate supply curve. By the 1980s, aggregate supply seemed to have stabilized
somewhat, restoring the inflation-unemployment link. However, the relationship was still not as close and consistent as it was two decades earlier.

Inflation Rate (%)

FIGURE 4
INFLATION AND
UNEMPLOYMENT IN
THE U.S. ECONOMY,
1970–1990
The data for this period
seem to suggest a much
less consistent relation-
ship between unemploy-
ment and inflation than
in earlier periods. Most
observers attribute the
lack of a relationship to
shifts in aggregate supply.
It is possible to trace two
patterns, one for the
1970s and one for the
period 1982–1990.

Source: Council of Economic Advisers, *Economic Report of the President* (Washington, DC: U.S. Government Printing Office, 1991).

THE DEVELOPMENT OF THE PHILLIPS CURVE

The unemployment-inflation relationships plotted in Figures 2 through 4 had their origin in the work of British economist A. W. Phillips. In 1958, Phillips published a paper in which he reported an observed negative relationship between the rate of wage increases and the level of unemployment in Great Britain for the period 1861–1913. Figure 5 reproduces one of the graphs from Phillips's article.

In the early 1960s, Paul Samuelson and Robert Solow, two Nobel Prize winners in economics, reinterpreted the Phillips curve as offering society a choice, or tradeoff, between various combinations of inflation and unemployment. Since both wages and production costs are closely related to prices, Phillips's original diagram was transformed into an inflation versus unemployment curve. A graph that shows the relationship between the rates of inflation and unemployment for a country over a specified period of years is called a **Phillips curve**. Phillips curves have also been interpreted as offering a menu of tradeoffs between inflation and unemployment. For example, along the Phillips curve in Figure 5, a society could opt for low unemployment such as that at point *A* and pay the price of rapid increases in prices. On the other hand, it could keep price increases low, as at point *B*, at the cost of higher unemployment.

Phillips presented evidence suggesting that a tradeoff existed between inflation and unemployment, but he offered no theoretical explanation. Early explanations for the Phillips curve focused on how changing conditions in the labor market influenced prices. When aggregate demand is increasing, business firms expand output and increase employment. As

Phillips curve
A graph showing the relationship between the rates of inflation and unemployment for a country over a specified period of years.

FIGURE 5
A PHILLIPS CURVE
This Phillips curve was created by A. W. Phillips with data for Great Britain from 1861 to 1957. Note the negative relationship between the rate of change of nominal wages and the unemployment rate. The curve is not very steep at high rates of unemployment (say, 10 percent) but is quite steep at low rates of unemployment (say, 1 percent). Thus, reducing employment from 10 percent to 9 percent would not cost much in extra wage inflation, but reducing unemployment from 2 percent to 1 percent would result in a lot of extra wage inflation.

Source: A. W. Phillips, "The Relation between Unemployment and the Rate of Change of Money Wage Rates in the United Kingdom, 1861–1957," *Economica* 25 (1958): 283–300.

the unemployment rate falls, the labor market becomes tighter. It becomes increasingly difficult to hire qualified workers at the prevailing wage rates. Business firms must, therefore, offer higher wages to attract new workers. Because aggregate demand is increasing, those higher wages can be passed along to consumers in the form of higher prices. Thus, falling unemployment rates are associated with continuous increases in the wage rate and the price level, or inflation.

THE PHILLIPS CURVE IN THE 1960s. In the 1960s, the idea that the Phillips curve represented a menu of choices for economic policy makers was reinforced by the behavior of inflation and unemployment rates. Take another look at Figure 3, which is a Phillips curve for the U.S. economy using unemployment and inflation data for 1961–1970. Recall that the 1964 Kennedy tax cut was intended to reduce the unemployment rate. As Figure 3 shows, from 1965 through 1969, lower unemployment rates were traded for higher inflation rates. This choice of a specific unemployment-inflation target at which fiscal policy could be directed was called "fine tuning" the economy during the Kennedy-Johnson years.

SHIFTS IN THE PHILLIPS CURVE. In 1970, the U.S. economy moved to a higher level of unemployment and a higher rate of inflation, as you can see in Figure 3. One explanation for this unexpected change was that something had caused the tradeoff between unemployment and inflation to worsen. That is, the Phillips curve had shifted to the right (the dashed line in Figure 3). Early explanations for this shift of the Phillips curve focused on random supply shocks and changes in the makeup of the labor force. Several supply shocks affected the U.S. economy in the early 1970s, increasing the price level without lowering the unemployment rate. These shocks included the devaluation of the dollar with respect to other currencies in 1971 and again in 1973 and the series of dramatic increases in the price of OPEC oil beginning in 1973. Although these shocks affected both aggregate demand and aggregate supply, we will focus on the effects on aggregate supply.

Devaluation meant that the dollar bought fewer units of foreign currency. As a result, the dollar price of imports increased.[2] Higher import prices contributed to general price increases in the economy. Because the physical volume of imports declined very little, however, there was no reduction in the unemployment rate. The rise in oil prices had an even wider effect on the U.S. economy. Gasoline prices quadrupled between 1973 and 1980. In addition, because petroleum and its derivatives are used for many other purposes, including heating and as raw materials, rapidly rising prices for imported oil set off price increases throughout the economy.[3]

2. For example, suppose that a German exporter sold Volkswagen vans for 32,000 DM (Deutsche Marks). At an exchange rate of $1 for 4 DM, a U.S. importer could have purchased a van for resale in the United States for $8,000. If $1 bought only 3 DM after devaluation, the U.S. importer would have to pay $10,666 for the same van.
3. The opposite effect occurred in the 1980s. A sharp drop in the price of crude oil from about $35 to under $15 a barrel appeared to shift the aggregate supply curve to the right and contributed to the drop in the inflation rate.

With the move away from command economies in Eastern Europe, one of the most striking developments has been the emergence of
both inflation and unemployment
as serious macroeconomic problems. In Poland, for example, the
early months of 1990 saw a 70 percent rise in the price level, along
with a sharp decline in wages and
rising unemployment. What has
happened? Did the restructuring
of these economies toward greater
decentralization and use of markets shift the aggregate supply
curve back to the right, resulting in
severe stagflation?

No. The stagflation in Eastern
Europe can be interpreted in an aggregate supply and demand framework, but not as a sudden decrease
in aggregate supply at the time of
the change. For many years, the
economies of Eastern Europe suffered from repressed inflation and
disguised unemployment. An inefficient system of production failed
to produce enough output to keep
pace with the normal growth of aggregate demand. When aggregate
demand exceeds aggregate supply
at a given price level, the price level
is normally expected to rise. However, price
controls in Eastern European countries kept
the price level from rising. Instead, there was a
chronic gap between aggregate supply and aggregate demand at the artificially low price
level maintained by the state. That gap showed
up as empty shelves, chronic shortages of con-

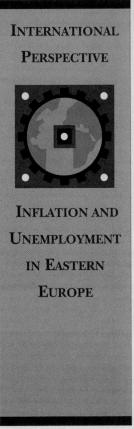

INTERNATIONAL
PERSPECTIVE

INFLATION AND
UNEMPLOYMENT
IN EASTERN
EUROPE

sumer goods, long lines, and long waiting lists
for telephones, apartments, and other goods
and services. When prices were allowed to adjust, they rose quickly. As output
begins to expand under a more
efficient system, prices should stabilize. In the meantime, shelves are
full again at the higher, more realistic prices.

The rising unemployment in
Eastern Europe also represents a
surfacing of what used to be disguised. The Communist governments guaranteed a job and a pay-
check for everyone who was able
and willing to work. Those workers
were not necessarily productive,
however. (A standing joke in Eastern Europe went like this: "The
government pretends to pay us,
and we pretend to work.") Incentives to work and to manage and
use workers effectively were missing because of the lack of market
signals. Now that some production
is being privatized, most of the new
owners and managers get to choose
how many workers to employ and
what to pay them. They may even
be allowed to fire those who do not
earn their keep.

Many Eastern Europeans are fearful about
the transition to a market-based economy
where there is no job security. The tradeoff between a higher standard of living and job security is one that workers in market-based
economies have always faced. It is one of the
costs of a productive market system.

Total spending on imports increased, resulting in a fall in net exports ($EX - IM$) and a leftward shift of the aggregate demand curve. According to the Keynesian model, this reduction in total spending should have resulted in a decrease in national income and output and an increase in unemployment. The increase in oil prices clearly had price effects as well as output effects. Those price changes could not be accounted for in a simple Keynesian framework.

Price increases resulting from random economic shocks cause the inflation rate associated with any given unemployment rate to be higher than before the shocks. That is, the Phillips curve shifts to the right, and the aggregate supply curve shifts to the left. Such shifts are depicted in Figure 6. Point A represents the inflation-unemployment combination on the Phillips curve in part (b), corresponding to point A' on the aggregate supply curve in part (a) prior to the random shocks. Point B is the inflation-unemployment combination after the shocks. The movement from A to B implies a shift in the Phillips curve from PC_1 to PC_2. Thus, random economic shocks provide one plausible explanation for why the Phillips curve shifted in the 1970s.

Another explanation for the higher unemployment rates and inflation rates in the 1970s focuses on the changing makeup of the U.S. labor force. From 1960 to 1980, the proportion of women and young people in the labor force rose significantly. These new and less experienced workers had higher unemployment rates and also increased the size of the labor force as a fraction of the total population. Thus, the unemployment rate rose relative to the level of output, because of the changing makeup of the labor force. In this case, higher rates of unemployment will be observed at each inflation rate. In contrast, the explanation based on random shocks suggested a higher inflation rate at each unemployment rate. In both cases, however, the Phillips curve shifts up and to the right.

THE INSIDER-OUTSIDER MODEL AND THE PHILLIPS CURVE. Another explanation of the worsening inflation-unemployment tradeoff received considerable

FIGURE 6
SHIFTS IN AGGREGATE SUPPLY AND THE PHILLIPS CURVE
When aggregate supply shifts to the left, as in part (a), it is possible to have rising prices and rising unemployment at the same time. This outcome is depicted as a shift in the Phillips curve in part (b) from PC_1 to PC_2. Points A' and B' correspond to points A and B.

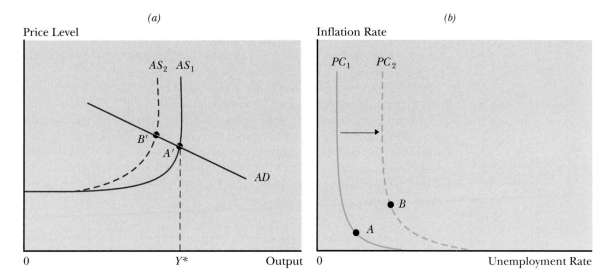

insider-outsider model
An explanation of labor market behavior that assumes that insiders (employed union members) will negotiate for higher real wages for themselves at the expense of jobs for outsiders, thus worsening the inflation-unemployment tradeoff.

attention in the 1980s. This model is based on the power of insiders (employed union members) relative to outsiders (nonunion members).[4] The **insider-outsider model** rests on the assumption that, with a union, those already employed (insiders) will bargain for a higher wage even at the expense of employment for those on the outside. During economic downturns, some workers are laid off and become outsiders. When economic activity increases, insiders will bargain for a higher real wage in preference to more jobs. If this kind of bargaining is widespread, the upturn in economic activity will be accompanied by more inflation and less reduction in unemployment than would otherwise be the case. The insider-outsider model is in the Keynesian and Post-Keynesian tradition of market power and market imperfections. It offers an explanation for stagflation that was missing in the simpler Keynesian model.

CRITICISMS OF THE PHILLIPS CURVE

Some economists were dissatisfied with all of these explanations for the worsening tradeoff between unemployment and inflation. Monetarists, in particular, were skeptical about whether there really was a stable tradeoff between unemployment and inflation and a resulting menu of policy choices. They countered with another view of the Phillips curve, developed by Milton Friedman in his presidential address to the American Economic Association in 1967. Friedman argued that any tradeoff was purely short run, that no real tradeoff between inflation and unemployment existed in the long run. The basis of Friedman's argument lay in expectations. To understand his criticism, we need to look closely at the role of expectations in determining the response to a change in aggregate demand.

CORRECT VERSUS MISTAKEN EXPECTATIONS

Suppose the government attempts to reduce unemployment by increasing the money supply. The increase in the money supply shifts the demand for output to the right, as shown by the shift from AD_1 to AD_2 in Figure 7. Initially, business firms keep prices at P_1 and produce total output of Y_1. However, at P_1, people will demand the larger quantity of output Y_2, even though firms would like to supply only Y_1. Firms will sell a total of Y_2 by using up part of their inventories. Output has not yet changed, but sales have risen. Thus, inventories fall.

If firms were satisfied with their initial inventories, they will try to rebuild them to that desired level. Inventory is important in building a clientele. In order to attract and retain customers, firms implicitly promise to sell as many units as buyers demand at the price set in the short run. For example, if you go to a hardware store for a doorknob, you expect to find doorknobs in stock at the usual price. If the store doesn't have them, you will probably go to another store. The first store runs a good chance of losing a customer, perhaps permanently.

4.   Assar Lindbeck and Dennis Snower, "Wage Setting, Unemployment and Insider-Outsider Relations," *American Economic Review Papers and Proceedings* (May 1986): 235–239.

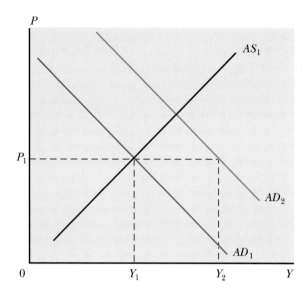

FIGURE 7
EXPANSIONARY FISCAL POLICY SHIFTS THE AGGREGATE DEMAND CURVE
When government spending increases, there is a shift in aggregate demand. At the old price level, firms sell Y_2 units, but only Y_1 units are produced. The unplanned reduction in inventories induces producers to expand output. Increased demand for inputs puts upward pressure on prices.

When demand shifts to the right, as in Figure 7, many firms will experience falling inventories. They will order new inventories from their suppliers or begin to produce more themselves. Output will start to rise. Prices will also start to rise. Any business firm that holds its prices at P_1 will find inventory falling steadily. As firms replenish their inventories by buying more inputs or semi-finished goods, they find themselves competing for limited supplies. Market forces drive up the prices of inputs. Suppliers will be charging higher prices. The aggregate supply curve will start to shift to the left, from AS_1 to AS_2 in Figure 8.

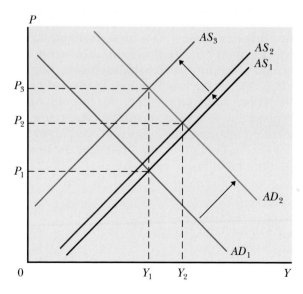

FIGURE 8
AGGREGATE SUPPLY SHIFTS WITH INFLATION
As sellers respond to higher demand with more output and higher prices, the price level rises to P_2. Y_2 is beyond the long-run productive capacity of the economy. Competition for resources continues to drive up prices until the short-run aggregate supply curve reaches AS_3. There it intersects the aggregate demand curve at the full-employment level of output, Y_1, and the new higher price level, P_3.

In Figure 8, the quantity of real output demanded at a higher equilibrium price level, P_2, exceeds the economy's full-employment level, Y_1. The aggregate supply curve has not shifted left as much as it eventually will because expectations have not yet completely adjusted. Suppliers have not yet made their full price adjustments. Workers have not yet made the full wage demands that they will make when they completely anticipate the new, higher price level. Curve AS_3 in Figure 8 reflects the ultimate equilibrium of the economy. The aggregate supply curve has fully adjusted to the new, higher money supply. The market has settled back to the initial output (Y_1), but the new, higher price level (P_3) reflects the higher money supply.

It might well be that output first expands, as in Figure 7, without a rise in the price level because expectations of inflation have not yet changed. For some time, aggregate output may still be larger than expected. However, the price level will start to rise as experience with inflation and inflationary expectations cause aggregate supply to shift to the left. The final equilibrium in Figure 8 occurs when everyone has come to expect the new, higher price level.

THE NATURAL RATE OF UNEMPLOYMENT

natural rate of unemployment
The rate of unemployment that is determined by frictional and structural factors and toward which the economy tends to return.

Another attack on the Phillips curve was based on the idea of a natural rate of unemployment. The **natural rate of unemployment** is the rate of unemployment determined by frictional and structural factors. It is the rate toward which the economy tends to return. The natural rate of unemployment corresponds (approximately) to the structural and frictional unemployment discussed in Chapter 4. These kinds of unemployment are due to changes in the number, location, and job skills of people in the labor force and to changes in the demand for labor. For example, if the demand for aluminum workers increases and the demand for steelworkers falls, there will be temporary unemployment while workers shift from one industry to another. The full-employment level of output, Y^*, is the level corresponding to the natural rate of unemployment.

THE NATURAL RATE AND OKUN'S LAW. Economist Arthur Okun, who served on the Council of Economic Advisers in the 1960s, used the natural rate of unemployment as a basis for policy in the short run. The economy might indeed return to the level of output associated with the natural rate of unemployment in the long run, but the loss of output in the short run represented a serious policy concern. Okun focused on the output forgone in spells of unemployment that exceeded the natural rate. He concluded that there was a consistent relationship (known as Okun's law) between the excess of unemployment over the natural rate and the loss of potential GNP. He estimated the relationship as 2.5 percent of GNP forgone for every 1 percent that unemployment exceeded the natural rate.

FRIEDMAN AND THE NATURAL RATE HYPOTHESIS. Nobel Prize winner Milton Friedman used the idea of the natural rate of unemployment to challenge the Keynesian view that the Phillips curve represents a stable menu of attainable combinations of inflation and unemployment. In his words, "There is always a temporary tradeoff between inflation and unemployment; there is no permanent tradeoff."[5] Friedman stated that there may be a short-run tradeoff between inflation and unemployment because of mistaken expectations, but in the long run the Phillips curve is vertical at the natural rate of unemployment.

Friedman argued that workers' expectations about inflation influence their decisions in the labor market. Those decisions in turn collectively determine the level of employment and wage rates. The short-run trade-off between inflation and unemployment will exist only if the actual inflation rate turns out to be different from what workers expected it to be. If inflation is fully anticipated (as it is more likely to be in the long run), no tradeoff will occur. The current rate of unemployment might change in the short run in response to monetary and fiscal policies, but the natural rate of unemployment would not be affected.

Workers' expectations are not the only reason why policy actions may be more effective in the short run than in the long run. Consider a discretionary fiscal policy action, such as an increase in government spending to reduce the unemployment rate. The resulting rightward shift of the aggregate demand curve causes temporary shortages at the current price level. Excess aggregate demand begins to pull the price level upward. Rising prices result in rising profits for business firms, which respond by increasing output. In order to produce more output, more workers must be hired. The newly employed workers take jobs at the prevailing wage rate. Even though prices have begun to rise, wage rates do not respond at once to the changed conditions. The price increases are initially perceived as changes in particular prices, not in the general price level. Even after people recognize that there is an increase in the general price level, wages are slow to adjust because many wage rates are determined by contracts that are renegotiated only once every two or three years. There is some lag between rising prices and the upward adjustment of wage rates. This lag allows firms to earn more profits.

Thus, in the short run, unemployment declines and the inflation rate rises, as the Phillips curve suggests. By increasing spending, the government buys a reduction in the unemployment rate at the cost of an increase in the inflation rate. But, Friedman argues, the new inflation-unemployment combination is not stable. The decline in the unemployment rate is achieved only because workers expect no inflation. Workers will eventually realize that prices in general have risen and are continuing to rise, reducing the purchasing power of their wages. They will adjust their expectations about inflation and demand higher wages to restore the purchasing power of their earnings. Higher wages will cut business profits back to their original levels. Business firms will reduce output to the old level at the new higher price level, and the unemployment rate will rise to its original level. If aggregate demand is maintained at the new, higher level by expansionary fiscal policy and continued growth in the money supply, the economy will remain at the new, higher inflation rate. Unemployment will remain at the natural rate. These rates represent a stable combination of inflation and unemployment because they are based on expected and actual inflation being the same.

---

5.   Milton Friedman, "The Role of Monetary Policy," *American Economic Review* (May 1968): 1–15.

Friedman concluded that after all adjustments to inflation are complete and the labor market is in equilibrium, unemployment will return to the natural rate. The inflation rate can be at any level, depending on whether aggregate demand continues to shift to the right. Thus, in the long run, the Phillips curve will be vertical at the natural rate of unemployment.

THE NATURAL RATE, AGGREGATE DEMAND, AND AGGREGATE SUPPLY. The natural rate hypothesis can also be described using aggregate supply and aggregate demand curves. In Figure 9, the economy is initially in equilibrium at point A, at output level Y_1 and price level P_1. Again, no inflation is expected. Assume the government wishes to increase output to Y_2 in order to reduce unemployment from, say, 6 percent to 4 percent. Expansionary fiscal policy shifts the aggregate demand curve from AD_1 to AD_2. Both real output (Y) and the price level (P) rise as the economy moves to point B.

However, the upward slope of the short-run aggregate supply curve, AS_1, is based on incorrect expectations about inflation. Workers are willing to supply more labor and firms more output only because they do not realize that the higher wages and prices are general, rather than specific to their labor or their product. Once workers realize that the price level as a whole is rising and the purchasing power of their wages is falling, they will demand higher nominal wages. Costs will rise, eroding the temporary profits of business firms. As the cost-profit relationship returns to its original level, firms will want to produce the same real output at the new higher prices, represented as a shift in the short-run aggregate supply curve from AS_1 to AS_2.

At the new equilibrium, at point C in Figure 9, output has returned to the old level, Y_1, corresponding to the natural rate of unemployment, but the price level is higher, at P_3. The economy is once again operating on the long-run vertical aggregate supply curve, AS^{lr}, corresponding to the natural rate of unemployment.

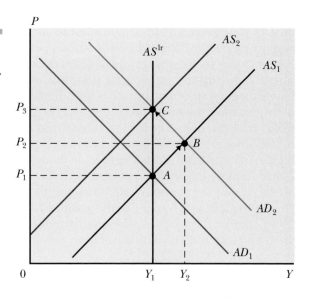

FIGURE 9
AGGREGATE SUPPLY AND DEMAND AND THE NATURAL RATE OF UNEMPLOYMENT
A rightward shift of the aggregate demand curve can temporarily increase employment and output with some rise in prices. Eventually, however, the aggregate supply curve will shift to the left. There will be no long-term increase in output or employment, just higher prices.

If government uses expansionary monetary or fiscal policy again, the same thing will happen. Real output will always return to the full-employment level, Y^*, corresponding to the natural rate of unemployment but at a higher price level. This "Christmas tree" pattern of changes in Y and P is illustrated in Figure 10. The heavy arrows trace the path of output and prices in response to successive doses of expansionary fiscal (or monetary) policy shifting the aggregate demand curve up and to the right. Thus, attempts to reduce unemployment below its natural rate using demand management policies may have temporary success but will ultimately only drive up the price level.

This emphasis on expectations and aggregate supply was developed largely from the ideas of the new classical school about rational expectations. We have discussed those contributions briefly in earlier chapters and will encounter them again in the next chapter when we explore aggregate supply more fully. Both new classical economists and monetarists expect policy actions to affect the price level but not to have much impact on real output in the long run. New classical economists believe that expectations adjust very rapidly and thus the short run is a very brief period of time. In their view, the economy returns very quickly to the long-run aggregate supply curve, on which policy actions will have no effect on real output and employment.

DEMAND-PULL AND COST-PUSH INFLATION

The inflationary process described in the preceding section is the result of shifts in aggregate demand. **Demand-pull inflation** is inflation that

demand-pull inflation
Inflation that starts as a result of a rise in aggregate demand, usually due to expansionary monetary or fiscal policy.

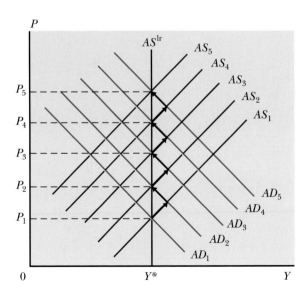

FIGURE 10
THE NATURAL RATE OF UNEMPLOYMENT AND REPEATED SHIFTS IN AGGREGATE DEMAND AND AGGREGATE SUPPLY
The arrows trace a path of shifts of the short-run aggregate demand curve to the right followed by shifts in the aggregate supply curve to the left as workers and other owners of inputs react to higher prices and wages. Output always returns to the level associated with the natural rate of unemployment (Y^*). There is, however, a series of temporary increases in output (and decreases in unemployment) and continued increases in the price level.

starts as a result of a rise in aggregate demand, usually due to expansionary monetary or fiscal policy. Increases in the money supply, which shift the *AD* curve rightward, are one possible source of demand-pull inflation. Expansionary fiscal policy is another, and that's why inflation is often blamed on government deficits. An increase in the federal budget deficit can shift the *AD* curve rightward and set off inflation, although there is no precise link between deficits and inflation. (The record-breaking budget deficits of the 1980s were associated with very low inflation rates.) However, the private sector can also initiate demand-pull inflation if consumers or businesses increase demand. Regardless of how inflation begins, it cannot be sustained for very long without monetary expansion. The velocity of money can't rise indefinitely. There is a limit to how fast money can change hands. So if there is no monetary expansion, demand-pull inflation will eventually grind to a halt.

Another type of inflation is initiated by a rise in costs, which decreases aggregate supply. **Cost-push inflation** is inflation that starts as a result of a leftward shift of the *AS* curve because of wage or price increases. We have already considered some shocks to the economy that had this effect, such as devaluations of the dollar in 1971 and 1973 and the OPEC oil price hikes. Shocks can come from within the economy, too. Unions blame business firms, and business firms blame unions for inflation. Is there any truth to these claims?

Figure 11 illustrates cost-push inflation. Assume that nationwide union contracts have, on the average, resulted in wage increases that are higher than can be justified by increases in productivity. The wage increases raise costs to businesses, and they try to pass these higher costs on to the consumer as higher prices. The resulting shift from AS_1 to AS_2 leads not only to a higher price level (P_2) but to lower output (Y_2), which means higher unemployment.

What happens next depends on the government's response. If policy makers are more upset about the rise in unemployment than the rise in

cost-push inflation
Inflation that starts as a result of a decrease in aggregate supply due to wage or price increases.

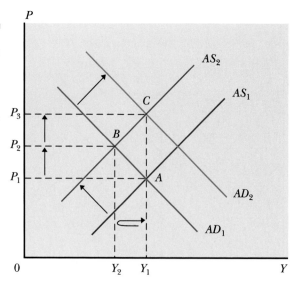

FIGURE 11
COST-PUSH INFLATION AND EXPANSIONARY POLICIES
When a decline in aggregate supply increases unemployment, the government responds with expansionary monetary or fiscal policy, shifting aggregate demand from AD_1 to AD_2. Employment and output return to the original level, but prices rise further.

inflation, they will try to "cure" the unemployment by shifting aggregate demand from AD_1 to AD_2 through expansionary fiscal or monetary policy. This shift will drive up prices further. The unemployment rate will return to where it started as output returns to Y_1. The process may end there, or it may repeat itself. If the process is repeated, with continual expansion of the money supply, stagflation is likely to result.

Sometimes business firms are portrayed as the villains in this drama. They seem to start the process by charging higher prices to their customers. It really doesn't matter how the process gets started. The important thing is that inflation cannot be sustained without expansionary monetary or fiscal policy.

How can you tell if inflation is demand-pull or cost-push? Once it gets started, it's hard to trace its roots. But if you look at Figures 9 through 11, you can see that demand-pull inflation starts with increases in both output (Y) and prices (P), followed by a fall in Y and a further rise in P. On the other hand, cost-push inflation starts with a fall in Y and a rise in P. Only when policy makers respond by shifting aggregate demand does Y go back up and P rise further.

THE POST-KEYNESIANS

The discussion of theoretical and policy approaches to dealing with stagflation has been cast in terms of just two rival views, those of the Keynesians and those of the monetarists. In the 1970s, another school of thought, called Post-Keynesianism, began to attract attention. Post-Keynesians are economists in the Keynesian tradition who believe that market power and institutional rigidity keep macroeconomic markets from arriving at full-employment equilibrium. The primary source of Post-Keynesian ideas was Cambridge University in England. The leading figure in the group was the British economist Joan Robinson (1903–1983), who was a colleague of Keynes.

EFFECTS OF MARKET POWER

When market power is concentrated, Post-Keynesians argue, firms often cut output instead of prices when demand is weak. Cutting output when aggregate demand declines leads to more unemployment rather than a falling price level. When aggregate demand increases, firms with market power are likely to raise prices instead of output. Thus, since prices are flexible upward but not downward, it is possible to experience chronic unemployment along with inflation during periods of expanding demand. This behavior of prices should make demand management policies effective—a very Keynesian conclusion. However, policies to expand demand will reward the powerful firms with higher prices and profits. Post-Keynesians are concerned with the distributional effects of such policies. Expansionary policies appear to benefit monopolistic firms. Contractionary policies put the burden on workers in the form of higher unemployment.

Lester Thurow of the Massachusetts Institute of Technology shares some of the views of the Post-Keynesians on issues such as the role of income distribution, market imperfections, and the importance of economic power in determining the effects of monetary and fiscal policy. He argues that differences in distributional preferences will guarantee disagreement among economists in the near future.[6] He and others believe that the existence of different schools of macroeconomic thought, each holding to different theoretical models and empirical conclusions, is really the result of differences in distributional preferences.

Groups hurt by inflation are different from those hurt by unemployment, although there is some overlap. Those who benefit from active fiscal policy are different from those who benefit from a *laissez faire* approach. Those who gain from supply side policies may or may not overlap with those who benefit from easy or tight monetary policies. Recall that tight monetary policy falls heavily on housing, investment, and industries that export and compete with imports. Supply side policies benefit high-income groups, those making certain favored investments, and entrepreneurs. Benefits to the poor or to average workers may trickle down as the result of increased output, investment, and productivity.

Wage and Price Controls

Post-Keynesians have made useful contributions to the recent debates on macroeconomic theory and policy. Here we are interested in their approach to stagflation. The focus on market power and income distribution makes the Post-Keynesians the only major school of economic thought to advocate the use of wage and price controls to contain inflation during periods of expanding demand.

wage and price controls
Government-imposed restrictions on increases in prices or wages in order to contain inflation.

Wage and price controls are government-imposed restrictions on increases in prices or wages in order to contain inflation. They were used during World War II, when aggregate demand increased and the United States was hitting the limits of its productive capacity. Most market-oriented economists—monetarists, supply siders, classical and new classical economists, and many Keynesians—are critical of such controls because of the problems they create.

Figure 12 illustrates the problem of controls in the market for a single product. The controlled price, (P_c), is set below equilibrium. The controlled price reduces the quantity supplied from Q_e to Q_s and increases the quantity demanded to Q_d. The result is an excess demand at that price. Market signals are prevented from calling forth an increase in quantity supplied to eliminate the shortage. Instead, the limited supply, Q_s, must be rationed among consumers using lines, coupons, or other means. These methods are less efficient than using prices to determine what mix of goods to produce and to ensure that goods go to those who want them most, measured by the prices they are willing to pay.

During periods of excess demand for goods and services in general, changes still occur in relative demand and supply of particular goods and services. Demand for shoes may increase relative to demand for toothpaste, or the cost of building houses may rise faster than the cost of pro-

---

6.   Lester Thurow, *The Zero-Sum Society* (New York: Penguin Books, 1981) and *Dangerous Currents: The State of Economics* (New York: Random House, 1984). Thurow and other U.S. economists in the Keynesian tradition (especially at Harvard and MIT) who do not subscribe to all of the Post-Keynesian views often call themselves New Keynesians.

Price/Unit

FIGURE 12
EFFECTS OF WAGE-PRICE
CONTROLS
In the market for an individual product, a price ceiling of P_c reduces quantity supplied from Q_e to Q_s and increases quantity demanded to Q_d. A shortage results.

ducing haircuts. Under controls, the same limits on raising prices (and wages) apply across the board, making relative price adjustments very difficult. This lack of flexibility is a major defect in the use of controls.

Given the drawbacks, why do Post-Keynesians advocate controls? One reason has already been suggested. When government uses demand-expanding policies, the resulting distribution of income may favor the most powerful elements—the largest firms and the strongest unions. Such changes in income distribution can be minimized when wage and price controls are used in conjunction with demand-expansion policies. Post-Keynesians also favor controls when deflationary policies are in effect. Again, distributional effects are part of the reason. However, Post-Keynesians also see controls as having a psychological effect on inflationary expectations. If people observe a lower rate of inflation—which controls will provide, at least for a time—they may revise their expectations more rapidly and speed up the adjustment process.

Probably the most effective criticism of wage and price controls is that they are not a substitute for demand management policies. If demand management policies are expansionary, then controls will merely suppress inflation for a time. If demand management policies are anti-inflationary, they will eventually work with or without controls and without the distortions in market signals that controls create.

In spite of their drawbacks, controls have a great deal of political appeal. They were last used in the United States during the early 1970s by the Nixon administration. Inflation did slow briefly, but monetary and fiscal policy remained expansionary. As soon as the controls were lifted, prices skyrocketed, just as they did after World War II. Controls can be a complement to demand management policies but not a substitute for them.

During the 1970s, some sophisticated approaches to controls were developed that tied allowable increases in prices and wages to tax breaks and penalties and used market incentives to attempt to control price in-

tax-based inflation policy (TIP)
A sophisticated approach to wage and price controls that ties allowable increases in prices and wages to tax breaks and penalties and uses market incentives to attempt to control price increases.

creases. The best known of these plans was called **tax-based inflation policy** (**TIP**). This modified market approach generated a great deal of interest in 1970s. Declining inflation rates in the 1980s put most innovative anti-inflationary ideas on the shelf. They may be revived if and when the inflation rate becomes unacceptably high.

THE CLASH OF MACROECONOMIC IDEAS

The United States has had a number of macroeconomic problems in the last twenty years. The period has seen slow economic growth and poor productivity. In addition, there have been several recessions and very large federal budget deficits. In the late 1970s and early 1980s, both unemployment and inflation were higher than normal. Interest rates were at record highs. The international value of the U.S. dollar skidded through the late 1970s. It rose sharply from 1981 to 1985 and then took an abrupt fall from 1985 to 1989. By the end of the 1980s, the value of the dollar had stabilized and even risen slightly.

The macroeconomic models used in the 1960s and early 1970s were not adequate to deal with these problems because both the Keynesian model (as well as the Post-Keynesian alternative) and the monetarist model were focused on demand management. Problems of productivity, slow growth, and stagflation have to be explained in terms of the behavior of the aggregate supply curve. We will explore those relationships in more detail in the next chapter.

The issue of whether or not to call for government to improve on market outcomes is the touchstone that most strongly differentiates the various schools of economic thought. The six schools that we have identified—classical, monetarist, supply side, new classical, Keynesian, and Post-Keynesian—can be divided into two broad groups. Here is a rundown of where each group stands:

1. *The classical group.* This group includes four schools of thought that in various ways call for a minimal role of government: classical economists, monetarists, new classical economists, and supply siders.

    Classical economists argued that unsatisfactory outcomes are only temporary. Market forces would correct such mistakes, just as market forces lead commuters to less congested freeways to save valuable time or make it attractive for a couple to move into a racially mixed neighborhood because the price of housing is relatively cheaper there. Although there are no classical economists today, their ideas persist in three schools of thought.

    Monetarists agree with the classical view that market forces do move the economy in the right direction but recognize that these forces operate at uncertain speeds. However, monetarists also believe that the corrections proposed by Keynesians are likely to prove less satisfactory than waiting for the problem to resolve itself.

    Supply siders argue that government intervention has been misdirected. The proper role of government is to provide adequate incentives to work, earn, save, and invest through appropriately targeted tax-

The question of whether the business cycle is dead recurs during every period of extended prosperity. The long recovery of the U.S. economy from 1982 to 1990 was no exception. An article in the *Washington Post* was just one of many that asked whether the business cycle had gone out of business.[a] Drawing on the work of several economists, *Post* writer Jodie Allen cited such changes as more responsive financial markets, a leaner and stronger manufacturing sector, more rapid assimilation of information, and better policy (mainly monetary). Unfortunately, the 1990–1991 recession began before the end of the year in which Allen wrote this upbeat assessment.

In fact, the fluctuations in economic activity during the entire period since World War II have been mild by his-torical standards. A number of reasons have been offered for this experience. First, some economists credit the greater stability to automatic stabilizers and stabilization policy, both monetary and fiscal. Second, others point to the fact that the United States is a more open economy (a higher ratio of trade to GNP), and shocks are now dampened by spillovers to the rest of the world. Still others claim that a larger government sector has been a source of stability. Fluctuations may be milder, but there have been two recessions in the last decade: the rather severe (but brief) recession of 1981–1982, and the 1990–1991 recession. The business cycle has been declared dead before, usually—like this time—just on the eve of the next recession.

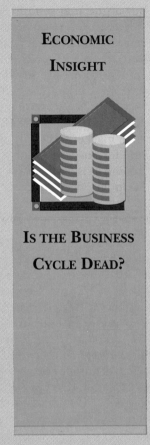

ECONOMIC INSIGHT

IS THE BUSINESS CYCLE DEAD?

---

a.   Jodie Allen, "Has the Business Cycle Gone the Way of the Dodo?" *Washington Post National Weekly Edition* (15–21 January 1990): 25.

ing and spending policies. In addition, supply siders argue that government should not tamper with market incentives.

New classical economists put little faith in any kind of government action. They argue that self-interested individuals quickly anticipate and often offset the effects of any demand-expanding policies. Unsatisfactory macro outcomes will be quickly changed because rational individuals will act in their own self-interest. These economists argue that government intervention often makes things worse and that the role of government should be reduced.

2. *The Keynesian group.* Both Keynesians and Post-Keynesians believe that unsatisfactory outcomes can persist for long periods of time and that the corrective market forces are weak and ineffective. Thus, they see an active role for government in moving the economy to a more satisfactory outcome. Post-Keynesians put more emphasis than Keynesians do on monopoly power and distributional effects of inflation and unemployment.

This list brings us back to a basic macroeconomic question raised in Chapter 4. Should the government be asked to try to stabilize economic activity? Should—or can—the government do anything to control unemployment and inflation? If so, what actions should it undertake, and how effective will they be? These are questions to which the two groups of economists give very different answers. The four schools that are part of the classical group share a faith in the effectiveness of market processes, the importance of incentives, and the self-correcting nature of the economy, at least in the long run. Both Keynesians and Post-Keynesians see a larger role for government and more evidence of market failure of various kinds. They also share a concern about the short run as well as the long run.

The differences among the various schools of thought can be grouped into four major areas, as shown in Table 1:

1. what determines the level of output and employment,
2. the role of interest rates,
3. the goals and values that can be inferred from the theories, and
4. the general thrust of policy recommendations.

THE AGGREGATE SUPPLY CURVE

Chapters 7–15 concentrated on the aggregate demand curve. This emphasis on demand reflects the dominance of Keynesian and monetarist ideas in economics. Both of those schools focus attention on the pros and cons of demand management strategies. The only attention we have paid to the aggregate supply curve has been to see how its shape affects the outcome of changes in aggregate demand.

Shifts in the position of the aggregate supply curve received little attention until the late 1970s. At that point, some economists started looking more closely at the determinants of the aggregate supply curve, both its position and its slope, as a possible explanation for stagflation. As we

SCHOOL OF THOUGHT	DETERMINATION OF OUTPUT AND EMPLOYMENT	ROLE OF INTEREST RATES	GOALS AND VALUES	POLICY
THE CLASSICAL GROUP				
Classical	Output tends toward the full-employment level. Supply creates its own demand.	Interest rates fluctuate to make saving and investment equal.	Minimum government, price stability, and steady growth.	None (*laissez-faire*).
Monetarist	Output is determined by planned spending in the short run but tends toward the level associated with the natural rate of unemployment in the long run.	Interest rates influence investment spending, may frustrate fiscal policy through crowding out, and have a modest influence on money demand and velocity of money.	Minimum government, price stability.	Monetary policy with stress on stable monetary growth, minimal fiscal policy.
Supply Side	Output is determined mainly by the location of the aggregate supply curve.	Interest rates are not central. High interest rates can discourage capital formation.	Growth, productivity, full employment, low inflation, reliance on private sector.	Deregulation, tax policy stressing work and investment incentives.
New Classical	Output tends to move rapidly toward the level associated with the natural rate of unemployment.	Interest rates affect demand for financial assets (including money) fairly quickly and have some effect on investment.	Use and respect market processes, minimum government.	Only fiscal and monetary surprises affect output and then only temporarily.
THE KEYNESIAN GROUP				
Keynesian	Output is determined by planned spending. Output level is not necessarily at or near full employment.	Interest rates have little influence on investment. Interest-elastic demand for money makes monetary policy ineffective.	Full-employment, role of government as a stabilizing force.	Fiscal policy primarily, with monetary policy in a supporting role.
Post-Keynesian	Output can deviate from the full-employment level for long periods. Demand plays a central role.	Interest rates (and other prices and wages) tend to adjust slowly.	Pessimistic about market processes, perceive a lot of institutional barriers to quick adjustments, see government as a stabilizer.	Wage-price controls, activist fiscal policy, control the concentration of economic power to reduce wage and price rigidities.

TABLE 1
DIFFERENCES AMONG SIX
SCHOOLS OF THOUGHT IN
MACROECONOMICS

have seen, supply siders emphasize policy tools to shift the aggregate supply curve. New classical economists have looked more closely at the curve's slope and concluded that it is vertical, or nearly so, in the short run as well as the long run. Economists in general have begun to pay more attention to the behavior of aggregate supply. Aggregate supply, productivity, and economic growth are the subject of Chapter 16.

SUMMARY

1. The aggregate outcome of individual decisions may not be satisfactory to everyone or even to a majority. The purpose of macroeconomic policy is to avoid or change that kind of outcome.

2. The Phillips curve shows the various combinations of inflation and employment that an economy has experienced in a specific period of time. Early Phillips curves showed a negative relationship, leading economists to view the Phillips curve as a menu of policy choices between inflation and unemployment.

3. Experience in the last two decades has led economists to doubt that the Phillips curve offers a stable menu of policy choices.

4. Friedman developed the natural rate hypothesis to explain why there is no long-run tradeoff between inflation and unemployment.

5. When expectations about inflation are correct, expansionary policy will have only a temporary effect on output, driving up the price level only and restoring the natural rate of unemployment.

6. Post-Keynesians are concerned about market power

and the distributional effects of inflation and unemployment. They advocate some temporary use of wage and price controls as a complement to contractionary monetary and fiscal policies.

7. There are six schools of macroeconomic thought. The classical group includes the classical, monetarist, new classical, and supply side schools. The Keynesian group consists of Keynesians and Post-Keynesians. The two groups differ primarily in their views of the shape of the *AS* curve and their goals, values, and policy recommendations.

8. The Phillips curve appears to show a tradeoff between inflation and unemployment, but the relationship shifted in the 1970s. Friedman argues that the long-run Phillips curve is vertical at a level of output corresponding to the natural rate of unemployment.

9. Demand-pull inflation is started by a rightward shift of the *AD* curve, with the *AS* curve shifting in response. Cost-push inflation is begun by a shift of the *AS* curve to the left, with policy makers responding by shifting the *AD* curve to the right.

NEW TERMS

Phillips curve	natural rate of	demand-pull inflation	wage and price controls
insider-outsider model	unemployment	cost-push inflation	tax-based inflation policy (TIP)

QUESTIONS FOR DISCUSSION

1. Why, according to Schelling, are aggregate outcomes more likely to be unsatisfactory as the group size increases?

2. According to the simple Keynesian model, the economy can't experience both inflation and unemployment at the same time. Why not?

3. What difference does it make for a Phillips curve whether aggregate supply is stable or not?

4. What difference does it make to monetary and fiscal policy if the long-run Phillips curve is vertical?

5. If the Phillips curve has shifted to the right, what does that suggest about the direction and relative size of shifts in aggregate supply and aggregate demand?

6. What is the natural rate hypothesis? Why does it imply that policy is ineffective in the long run?

7. How can you tell cost-push inflation from demand-pull inflation by looking at shifts in the *AD* and *AS* curves, ?

8. In what way are Post-Keynesians similar to Keynesians? How do the two schools differ?

9. How would a Keynesian deal with stagflation? A monetarist? A Post-Keynesian?

10. What are the costs and benefits of using wage and price controls?

11. Identify some of the distributional effects of expansionary and contractionary policies.

12. Why do economists disagree over macroeconomic policy recommendations?

13. If there were high unemployment and low inflation, what would each of the six schools of thought recommend? How would the policy recommendations differ if both unemployment and inflation were high?

14. What is the role of interest rates according to each of the schools of thought?

15. Trace the adjustment process in Figure 7, beginning with a decrease in the money supply.

SUGGESTIONS FOR FURTHER READING

Blinder, Alan. *Hard Heads, Soft Hearts.* New York: Addison-Wesley, 1987. A very readable, fairly Keynesian look at policy options with a concern for distributional effects. Chapters 2 and 3 look at unemployment, inflation, and demand management.

Eichner, Alfred (ed.). *A Guide to Post-Keynesian Economics.* New York: M. E. Sharpe, 1979. A collection of essays by major Post-Keynesians outlining the central ideas of that school.

Klamer, Arjo. *Conversations with Economists: New Classical Economists and Opponents Speak Out on the Current Controversy in Macroeconomics.* Totowa, NJ: Rowman and Allanheld, 1984. Informal dialogues between new classical economists and their critics on the current state of macroeconomics.

Schelling, Thomas. *Choice and Consequence.* Cambridge, MA: Harvard University Press, 1984. One of several unusual works by an economist with a unique perspective on the collective effects of individual choice.

Sheffrin, Steven M. *The Making of Economic Policy.* Cambridge, MA: Basil Blackwell, 1989. Discusses the current state of stabilization policy and the areas of consensus that have emerged in the last two decades.

Thurow, Lester. *Dangerous Currents: The State of Economics.* New York: Random House, 1984. Looks at the state of macroeconomic theory and why policy has not been successful, from a liberal Keynesian viewpoint.

APPENDIX: ECONOMETRICS, MODEL BUILDING, AND EMPIRICAL EVIDENCE

What does it mean to say, for example, that the empirical evidence supports the interest-sensitivity of the demand for money? How do economists prove or disprove theories? Econometrics is the branch of economics that deals with testing economic hypotheses by applying statistical methods to economic models, using available data.

One of the problems that faces economists is that they rarely get to conduct experiments. They usually have to rely on data gathered for other purposes to help frame answers to their questions. This problem is shared not only by other social sciences, including political science and sociology, but even by such natural sciences as astronomy and meteorology.

Sometimes the government "gives" economists an experiment. What happens to exports and imports when the value of the dollar changes? The rise and fall of the U.S. dollar from 1980 to the present have helped economists to answer that question. Does a permanent tax cut have more effect on consumption than a temporary cut? The tax cuts of 1982 and 1986 (permanent) and the tax increase of 1969 (temporary) gave some indications. Even in these cases, economists cannot control all of the other relevant variables.

TESTING SIMPLE MODELS

Resolving many of the issues dividing monetarists and Keynesians calls for empirical evidence. Suppose, for example, you wanted to test the crowding-out hypothesis. Does government borrowing drive up interest rates and reduce private borrowing? You could test the statistical relationship between government borrowing and private borrowing. For example, you might use the relationship

$$PB_t = A_1 + A_2 GB_t + u,$$

where PB_t is private borrowing during a certain time period, GB_t is government borrowing during the same period, and u is an error term. PB_t and GB_t are knowns. You can find values for both of these kinds of borrowing from a number of published sources, such as the *Survey of Current Business*. You can pick as long a time period as you like. The values of A_1 and A_2 will be estimated by a statistical procedure called *regression analysis*, which fits a straight line to the data and estimates the intercept (A_1) and the slope (A_2).

The regression procedure also provides another piece of information, R^2, which tells what percentage of the variation in PB_t is explained by the variation in GB_t. If R^2 is high, you have a "good fit." If it is low, there are probably other factors that have more effect on private borrowing.

Even if GB_t has a large coefficient A_2, the effect of GB_t on PB_t might not be very significant. There are tests (called *significance tests*) that measure how much effect variable x actually has on variable y. If the equation above related several variables to PB_t, significance tests would help to determine which of them had an important influence and which had little effect. For example, drawing on the crowding-out hypothesis, the theoretical model might say that the existing capital stock would significantly affect private borrowing. Thus, you might add that variable to the equation. But, in looking at the results, the capital stock may turn out not to be a significant determinant of private borrowing.

PROBLEMS WITH SIMPLE MODELS

There are some problems with simple models that have just one explanatory variable (such as GB_t) and one dependent variable (such as PB_t). For example, there are really two steps to the process of crowding out. Government borrowing affects interest rates, and then interest rates affect private borrowing. Thus, a more accurate model would split the process into two components, with an equation for each part:

$$i_t = A_1 + A_2 GB_t + u \quad \text{and} \quad PB_t = B_1 + B_2 i_t + u,$$

where i_t is the rate of interest for the period in question. The first equation is used to predict a value of that interest rate. That value is then used in the second equation to predict a value for PB_t.

There are other influences on private borrowing in addition to government borrowing and interest rates. Income, monetary policy, and expectations are important influences. They are *ceteris paribus* assumptions that are held constant in drawing graphs. But when economists test econometric models, these variables must be included. Otherwise, the model will suffer from what econometricians call a *specification error*. The estimates for the values of the coefficients (the A's and B's in the equation above) will be incorrect. A famous instance of a specification error was mentioned in Chapter 8. Economists incorrectly forecast a recession after World War II because they ignored the effects of liquid assets on consumption.

MODELS, FORECASTING, AND SIMULATION

Economists build and test models in order to forecast the effects of various actions, including monetary and fiscal policy. There are some elaborate models, such as the MIT model and the Chase econometric model, which contain many equations and many variables. These models attempt to forecast income, output, employment, prices, interest rates, and other economic aggregates from quarter to quarter. Forecasting is the activity the general public most often expects from economists.

Models are also used for simulation purposes. A simulation uses a model in which the coefficients have already been estimated from past data. Changes are then made in some of the assumptions. For example, a simulation might incorporate a change in export demand or an increase in the money supply and see how all the other variables are affected. On the basis of models, economists can estimate the effect of various policy changes and give advice about what to do and how much to do.

Econometrics has developed over the last forty years into a highly sophisticated technique used by virtually all economists. If you read an article in a professional journal or a thesis or dissertation in economics, you will find that most professional economic writing today follows a standard format. The writer discusses the development of the idea under consideration, builds a mathematical model, and tests the model with data using accepted econometric methods. Econometrics is a basic part of an economist's toolkit.

AGGREGATE SUPPLY, GROWTH, AND DEVELOPMENT

AFTER STUDYING THIS CHAPTER, YOU SHOULD BE ABLE TO:

1. Discuss the role of expectations and market conditions in determining the slope of the the aggregate supply curve.
2. Identify the sources of economic growth, which are the factors that can shift the aggregate supply curve.
3. List some policy tools for improving productivity and for shifting the aggregate demand curve to the right.
4. Explain what industrial policy is and how it is implemented.

INTRODUCTION

CHAPTER 16

AGGREGATE SUPPLY AND ECONOMIC GROWTH

Classical macroeconomics was displaced in the 1930s and 1940s by the Keynesian revolution. The Keynesians replaced the classical emphasis on aggregate supply with a new emphasis on aggregate demand. During the 1960s and 1970s, the Keynesians were in turn challenged by the monetarists. Starting in the mid-1970s and increasingly in the 1980s, both new classical economists and supply siders entered the debate. These two groups' different approaches to macroeconomic policy drew heavily on the work of classical economists. They built on the microeconomic foundations of effective markets and self-interested behavior.

Even though many of the ideas of the new classical and supply side economists have been challenged, their work did focus attention on the aggregate supply (*AS*) curve, its slope and what makes it shift. The slope of the *AS* curve determines how much output will increase when the aggregate demand (*AD*) curve shifts to the right in the short run. Shifts in the *AS* curve are the sources of economic growth. Thus, a closer look at the slope of this curve and what makes it shift will complete our macroeconomic model. It will also provide some insight into the all-important macroeconomic goal of growth of real output.

For the United States and most other industrial nations, economic growth during the 1980s was not very good. The average real growth rate for the decade was about 2.5 percent for both the United States and Western Europe. Even Japan experienced a decline in its rate of growth compared to the preceding periods. When growth slows down, real incomes rise very slowly. If population grows faster than output, per capita income can actually fall. In fact, in real terms (1982 dollars), the average weekly earnings for workers in the private sector in the United States fell from its 1972 high of $315.44 to $259.98 in 1990. Real per capita GNP did rise from $14,183 to $16,580 between 1979 and 1990 (less than 2 percent per year). However, this gain was largely due to putting a larger proportion of the population to work.

A steady rate of economic growth is the most central of macroeconomic goals. Like any goal, the goal of economic growth involves some tradeoffs. Growth is often accompanied by inflation, which redistributes income. Growth may benefit the rich but fail to trickle down to the poor. Growth may come at a cost in terms of leisure, environmental quality, or security. Against these costs a society must weigh the very considerable benefits of growth. Growth allows a society to absorb a growing labor force without rising unemployment. Growth increases the standard of living. Out of the "growth dividend," a society can (if it chooses) provide for the elderly, the homeless, the poor—needs that can be addressed less painfully out of new resources and new income. In this chapter, we will assume that there is a societal consensus in favor of growth. The discussion will concentrate on how to make it happen and how it relates to the aggregate supply and demand model.

EXPECTATIONS, MARKETS, AND THE SLOPE OF THE AGGREGATE SUPPLY CURVE

Chapter 6 presented different shapes for the aggregate supply curve. The four versions are shown in Figure 1: (*a*) horizontal, (*b*) vertical, (*c*) upward sloping, and (*d*) composite. Each shape has different implications for the effects of changes in aggregate demand on real output and the price level.

With the horizontal curve in Figure 1(*a*), increases in aggregate demand increase real output only—the extreme Keynesian case. With the vertical curve in part (*b*) of the figure, when real output is fixed at the full-employment level (corresponding to the natural rate of unemployment), increases in aggregate demand will raise the price level only. The upward-sloping curve in part (*c*) suggests that increases in aggregate demand will always raise both prices and output. The composite curve in part (*d*) has a horizontal segment (the Keynesian range), an upward-sloping segment (the intermediate range), and a vertical segment (the classical or monetarist range). With this curve, the relative impact of a change in aggregate demand on real output and the price level will depend on how close the economy is to full employment. Thus, the slope of the aggregate supply curve is important because it determines the impact of demand management policies.

THE SHORT RUN AND THE LONG RUN
The extreme Keynesian case of a horizontal aggregate supply curve reflects ample idle resources and involuntary unemployment in the short run. Although such conditions have not recurred since the Great Depression, this case forms a part of the composite view in Figure 1(*d*). The

FIGURE 1
FOUR SHAPES FOR THE AGGREGATE SUPPLY CURVE
(*a*) In the extreme Keynesian (depression) case, the *AS* curve is horizontal. Output can expand indefinitely without a rise in prices when aggregate demand increases. (*b*) The classical long-run *AS* curve is vertical at the full-employment level of output. Increasing aggregate demand only raises prices. (*c*) When the *AS* curve has an upward slope, both prices and output will rise when aggregate demand increases. (*d*) This curve is a composite of all three views.

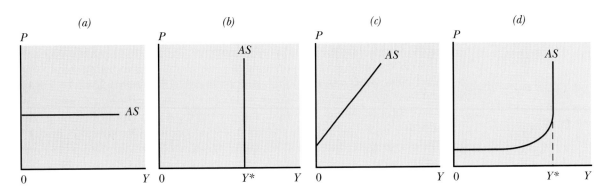

horizontal part of the composite aggregate supply curve implies that, if the level of output is well below full employment, it is possible to increase output without any increase in the price level.

In recent years, the debate over aggregate supply has concentrated on the alternatives of vertical versus upward sloping—parts (b) and (c) of Figure 1. It is generally agreed that the short-run aggregate supply curve is upward sloping rather than vertical. The upward slope results from imperfections in the marketplace, such as immobile resources, imperfect information, incorrect expectations, or delayed responses to information. The real issue is how strong those imperfections are and how long it takes the market to overcome them. Keynesians, especially Post-Keynesians, argue that the imperfections are large and the market works slowly to overcome them. Economists of the classical group—monetarists, new classical economists, and supply siders—support Milton Friedman's natural rate hypothesis, discussed in Chapter 15. This hypothesis predicts that a higher price level will not call forth more real resources or real output in the long run. Only in the short run will people confuse higher money wages or profits with higher real wages and profits. In the long run, they will have accurate information and the opportunity to incorporate correct expectations into their decisions.

The rationale for an upward-sloping (rather than vertical) aggregate supply curve does not rest totally on confusion, imperfect information, or incorrect expectations. A case can be made for the existence of opportunities for real (short-run) profit from a rising price level. Some workers, entrepreneurs, investors, and consumers are able to respond more quickly than others. These individuals can gain from rising prices. Suppose, for example, you are a shoe manufacturer. Prices in general are rising, and you can sell your shoes for more. However, your contracts with workers and suppliers include prices that are fixed for six months. If, during those six months, you can obtain resources at those fixed prices and sell the shoes for higher prices, you can increase your profits. At the end of six months, your contracts will be up for renewal. You know that wages and prices of materials will rise and your temporary profit surge will end in the long run. In the meantime, however, you have an incentive to expand output.

The longer the contract period, the longer the original short-run upward-sloping aggregate supply curve will be valid. When contracts expire, the short-run aggregate supply curve will shift upward. A new short run will begin on a new curve. Once again, economists are faced with this question: How long is the short run? Economists of the Keynesian group argue that the short run is very long indeed. Economists of the classical group claim that the short run is really not a very long period of time.

The long-run and short-run aggregate supply curves are shown in Figure 2. The long-run aggregate supply curve, AS^{lr}, is vertical at Y^*, which is the real output level corresponding to the natural rate of unemployment. The short-run aggregate supply curve, AS_1, is upward sloping. Initially the economy is in short-run and long-run equilibrium at P_1 and Y^*. Then aggregate demand shifts from AD_1 to AD_2. Moving along AS_1, output increases to Y_2, and the price level begins to rise to P_2. Producers raise prices and expand output in response to increased demand.

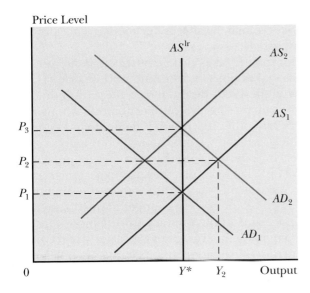

Price Level

FIGURE 2
SHORT-RUN AND LONG-
RUN AGGREGATE SUPPLY
When the *AS* curve slopes
upward in the short run
but is vertical in the long
run, an increase in
aggregate demand (shift
from AD_1 to AD_2) raises
both real output and the
price level. Eventually
rising prices drive up
input costs, shifting the
short-run *AS* curve
upward (from AS_1 to
AS_2). Real output returns
to Y^*, and only the price
level increases.

Eventually, however, the rising price level affects the prices of productive inputs: workers, capital, and raw materials. The real value of workers' earnings falls. As soon as factor owners have an opportunity to renegotiate wages and prices, those wages and prices rise. Rising costs produce an upward shift in the short-run aggregate supply curve to AS_2. Once again the economy is in short-run and long-run equilibrium at a higher price level, P_3. However, there has been no permanent increase in the level of output and employment.

This view of the world implies that demand management policies—fiscal or monetary—cannot permanently alter output and employment unless the long-run aggregate supply curve shifts to the right. Monetarists, new classical economists, and supply siders thus offer policy prescriptions based on the factors that shift aggregate supply, not aggregate demand.

RATIONAL VERSUS ADAPTIVE EXPECTATIONS

The most important market imperfections that make the aggregate supply curve slope upward are (1) lack of accurate information or incorrect expectations and (2) inability to respond quickly and correctly to accurate information. New classical economists (rational expectationists) argue that this view of how market participants behave is too pessimistic. They argue that it is in people's self-interest to acquire, interpret, and respond to information that affects their economic well-being.

If producers, workers, consumers, and investors have accurate information about present and future price levels and other relevant data, and if they know how to act on that information, they will adjust their wage demands, money holdings, and purchases very quickly when conditions change. That is, not only policy makers but also participants in labor, product, and financial markets quickly acquire, process, and act on correct information. If these conditions exist, the short run will be quite short. A vertical or nearly vertical aggregate supply curve will be the appropriate model for policy making. If, on the other hand, the process of acquiring and responding to information works more slowly, the upward-sloping aggregate supply curve may be the better model. That process could be slow for two reasons.

First, information is not free. It takes real resources to generate and acquire information. It also takes time to distribute information. These lags became much shorter in the 1980s (aptly labeled the start of the "Information Age") because of increasing use of telecommunications networks, personal computers, and other information technology. However, information is still not widely available on an instantaneous basis.

Second, people may learn from their mistakes, but they do not always learn immediately or adapt fully. For example, they may expect next year's rate of inflation to be the same as this year's, rather than adjusting their forecasts upward or downward on the basis of changes in the money supply, the unemployment rate, and other relevant information. On the other hand, they may keep in mind an average of the last few years' data, to which they add some current information about changes in policy and market conditions in order to form expectations about next year. People will adjust their behavior in the right direction but not completely. They may not correctly anticipate the actual rate of inflation. Individuals acquire, process, and act on relevant economic information in their own self-interest, but they never have information that is entirely accurate or complete. This view of how expectations are formed is summarized by the concept of **adaptive expectations**.[1]

adaptive expectations
Expectations about the future that are formed by economic actors on the basis of current and past experience and that adjust slowly to changing conditions.

The experience of the late 1970s and early 1980s was consistent with the view that individuals' expectations are adaptive. That experience also suggested that people adapt more quickly as the payoff from acquiring and using accurate information gets higher. Throughout the 1950s and 1960s, inflation rates were low and steady, so past experience was a good guide to the future. Conditions changed in the mid-1970s. Many people—mortgage lenders, investors, workers, and producers—were surprised by the high rates of inflation. They saw their real wages and the value of their assets fall because they had not correctly anticipated the inflation. By the end of the 1970s, cost-of-living adjustment clauses in contracts, variable-rate mortgages, and other developments allowed markets to react more quickly to changes in the inflation rate. In terms of Figure 2, the short-run aggregate supply curve shifted upward more quickly and also became steeper as many price adjustments became automatic.

In the 1980s, as the rate of inflation began to fall, the opposite problem surfaced. With many contracts fixed, the real rate of interest rose sharply because the market rate included too high an inflation premium. Wage contracts had to be quickly renegotiated because they were based on higher inflation rates.[2] Within a year or two, however, people were incorporating lower expected rates of inflation in their economic decisions.

The rational expectations (new classical) view of how market partici-

1.   An even simpler model is called extrapolative expectations. This model suggests that people expect the current period to be just like the preceding one.
2.   An example of a delayed response to inflation was the introduction of indexing into the federal income tax with the 1981 law, to take effect in 1985. By the time indexing took effect, inflation rates had dropped sharply. With the reduction in the number of rates from fourteen to three in the 1986 tax reform, indexing was eliminated.

pants behave is an extreme one. It requires individuals to obtain large quantities of information quickly, sort out the relevant information, and process it through a sophisticated economic model about how changes in some variables will impact on others. However, even though this model represents an extreme, it is helpful in understanding the long run. When the payoff for obtaining and using correct information is high enough, people will make the effort to seek it out and act on it to the greatest extent possible. When the costs of ignorance and the benefits of possessing accurate information rise, the speed of reaction will also rise. Furthermore, it is not necessary that each and every market participant acquire and respond to information. It is only necessary that the search for and use of information take place at the margin.

While economists have been arguing over adaptive versus rational expectations, psychologists have been studying how people actually form expectations. Their work suggests that expectations typically consist of a mixture of recent past experience, current experience, and some projections of future events. That is, they are closer to adaptive than to rational expectations. Work with psychologists may help economists clarify how expectations are formed and how rapidly they adjust.

AUCTION MARKETS AND CONTRACT MARKETS

Even if expectations are rational, the aggregate supply curve will not be vertical if the process of changing wages, prices, and interest rates is slow. When aggregate demand increases, a slow response of wages, prices, and interest rates means that output may expand for a fairly long period of time before the short-run aggregate supply curve shifts up. A decline in aggregate demand may lead to long periods of low output and high unemployment until prices finally respond. This possibility is stressed by Post-Keynesians.

Although people may have accurate information, some time may pass before they are in a position to act on it. In some cases, it may not be desirable to act at all because the cost of responding is too high. Acting on accurate information may require changing jobs, selling assets, or other drastic actions. Thus, some people may choose to wait until the rate of inflation falls back to what they had expected. Often the costs of responding depend on the kinds of product markets and resource markets in which individuals are buying and selling. People will be more likely to relocate, for example, if their houses can be sold quickly at acceptable prices and if new jobs at satisfactory wages are easy to find.

auction markets
Markets characterized by good information, many buyers and sellers, and rapid adjustments of price to changing conditions.

Markets characterized by good information, many buyers and sellers, and rapid adjustments of price to changing conditions are known as **auction markets**. Typically, auction markets have many buyers and sellers making frequent transactions. You may have been to an estate auction, an antique auction, or a livestock auction. At these auctions, a fixed stock of goods is offered for sale, one item at a time. The price moves up the demand curve until one buyer pays the final price bid. Price bears all the burden of adjustment, and price changes rapidly.

contract markets
Markets characterized by few buyers and sellers, imperfect information, long-term contracts, and sluggish price adjustments.

Other markets are **contract markets**. In these markets, buyers and sellers enter into long-term agreements at fixed prices. The contract protects both buyer and seller from risks of price changes or other uncertainties.

Typical transactions in contract markets are long-term fixed-rate mortgages, tenure appointments for college faculty members, apartment leases, labor union contracts, and business or government contracts for major construction projects. Contracts of pro athletes or college football coaches reflect past performance. Such contracts may run for several years and be very expensive to change if the player or coach fails to live up to expectations. Prices move slowly in contract markets because it takes time for old contracts to expire. During that time, the cost of violating a contract can be very high.

If auction markets are typical, then prices will adjust quickly to changes in demand at both the micro and macro level. That is, a relatively small increase in aggregate demand will drive the price level up quickly with little effect on real output. The aggregate supply curve will be vertical, or nearly so. If contract markets are more typical, then price adjustments will be slow and the aggregate supply curve flatter. In the long run, even contract markets become auction markets because no contract lasts forever.[3] Rent controls expire. The 99-year leases in Hong Kong end in 1997 and will not be renewed. The typical contract is much shorter and more flexible.

Thus, rational expectations and auction markets suggest that the long-run aggregate supply curve is vertical or at least very steep. Adaptive expectations and contract markets suggest that the short-run aggregate supply curve could be fairly flat and that the short run itself may be a fairly long period of time.

EXPECTATIONS, MARKETS, AND AGGREGATE SUPPLY

• IF expectations are rational	People are correctly informed about current conditions and form appropriate expectations about the future.
and markets are efficient (auction),	Prices adjust quickly to changing conditions.
THEN the aggregate supply curve is vertical in the long run and very steep in the short run.	Demand management policies have little if any effect on real output.
• IF expectations are adaptive	Information is acquired gradually, and expectations adjust slowly.
and markets are contractual (contract),	Prices cannot change rapidly because it is too difficult to change them.
THEN the aggregate supply curve is upward sloping, at least in the short run (which can be fairly long).	Demand management can have a significant impact on short-run output.

3. In long-term contracts, the benefits to one side will be capitalized, that is, reflected in the value of the property the contract concerns. For instance, houses with guaranteed low utility costs will sell for a higher price than comparable houses not offering that benefit. However, this doesn't help the utility company!

ECONOMIC GROWTH: SHIFTING THE AGGREGATE SUPPLY CURVE

Although economists disagree about the slope of the aggregate supply curve, they agree about what makes it shift. Economists know that the long-run aggregate supply curve will shift to the right in response to increases in the capital stock, improvement in the size and/or quality of the labor force, additional natural resources, improvements in productivity, or technological advances. Increases in resources or productivity will shift the aggregate supply curve to the right. Encouragement of production through reduced taxes or regulations that lower costs to firms will also shift the curve to the right. Anything that shifts the aggregate supply curve to the right is a source of economic growth. That is, the shift will produce a rise in real per capita income, the measure of a nation's standard of living. Thus, what causes economic growth can be visualized in graphic terms as the factors that increase aggregate supply.

The aggregate supply curve can also shift to the left, indicating negative growth, or a decline in a nation's standard of living. Factors that can shift the curve to the left include resource depletion, a decline in the size and/or quality of the labor force, and public policies (taxes or regulations) that discourage productive activity.

Long-term economic growth requires steady rightward shifts of the aggregate supply curve. Economic growth has been a major concern in the United States for at least thirty years. Economists are constantly examining the growth rate of the U.S. economy to make sure that the standard of living is rising, or that Americans are economically more successful than the Soviets or as successful as the Japanese. Economists are also concerned that output expand fast enough to create enough jobs for a growing labor force. The antigrowth voices of the early 1970s became muted when Americans started realizing the costs of not growing in terms of inflation, unemployment, and a lower standard of living, if population grew faster than real output. During the 1980s and into the 1990s, the continuing debate has not been over *whether* to grow but rather *how* to grow. Economists try to determine what strategies are most successful for shifting the aggregate supply curve to the right.

GROWTH IN INVESTMENT AND SAVING

Between 1960 and 1990, real output increased 150 percent in the United States. Some of that growth was a result of increased resources, specifically labor and capital. Gross investment in constant dollars was 173 percent higher in 1990 than it was in 1960. However, recall from Chapter 5 that a large (and increasing) part of gross private domestic investment goes to replacement of worn-out capital. After correcting for depreciation, real net investment was only 64 percent higher in 1990 than it was in 1960. Thus, the real growth rate of investment was much lower than the rate of economic growth.

Because investment is so volatile, year-to-year comparisons must be treated carefully. Figure 3 plots both gross and net investment expenditures as percentages of GNP for 1950 to 1990. The growth of gross in-

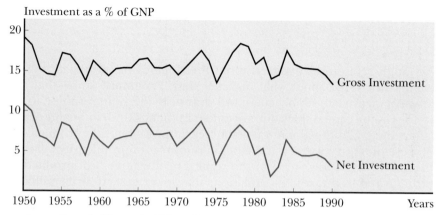

Source: Council of Economic Advisers, *Economic Report of the President* (Washington, DC: U.S. Government Printing Office, 1991).

vestment over that whole period was greater than the growth of total GNP
but was very erratic. Net investment is investment in new plants, equipment, and housing as opposed to replacement of worn-out facilities and
equipment. It actually fell relative to GNP. Note that in recession years,
such as 1975 and 1982, investment declines even more than GNP, reducing the stock of capital available for future economic growth.

PRIVATE SAVING. Private saving is the major source of funding for investment to expand future output. Saving by households and business firms,
which provides the funds for investment, has not kept pace with the
growth of GNP in recent years. From 1980 to 1990, business and household saving rose 64 percent in current dollars, while GNP increased by
100 percent. In addition, much of the saving in the 1980s was absorbed in
financing the large federal budget deficits. The combination of low private saving and negative saving in the public sector resulted in a substantial inflow of funds from abroad to cover the shortfall.

savings rate
The ratio of combined
business, household, and
government saving to
GNP.

The most commonly used indicator of what is happening to saving is
the **savings rate**, or saving by households, business, and government combined as a percentage of GNP. The current U.S. rate is low compared to
past experience and to savings rates in many other industrial countries.
However, saving has fallen in other industrial countries as well in the last
two decades. From 1960 to 1980, the United States saved 19.6 percent of
GNP, somewhat below the average for seventeen industrial countries,
which was 23.4 percent. (Japan, at 35 percent, had the highest ratio.) Demographic factors such as the maturing of the baby boomers contributed
to the low savings rate in the United States. As individuals grow older, they
enjoy higher incomes and finish paying for houses and educating their
children. Their savings rates will rise. Such a rise should occur in the
United States in the next two decades.

The savings rate fell throughout the 1980s in both the United States
and other industrial countries. By 1988, the U.S. savings rate was 15.1 percent, compared to an average of 20.3 percent for other industrial countries. This decline was fueled less by demographic changes than by a fall

in government saving. Federal deficits combined with state and local government surpluses reduced the overall savings rate by about 2 percent of GNP.[4] The national savings rate was the focus of much attention in the 1980s as economists tried to explain why it was so low and policy makers tried to invent creative ways to induce households to save more.

Gross private domestic investment and saving each accounted for about 12 percent of GNP in 1990. Inflows of funds from abroad were an important source of investment financing in the 1980s because domestic saving was not sufficient to both meet private investment demand and fund federal budget deficits. In 1988, more than $200 billion in foreign investment flowed into the United States, including $58 billion in direct investment. (Direct investment consists of developing or acquiring ownership of office buildings, factories, and other tangible assets.) Even after allowing for an outflow of $82 billion for investment abroad, the net foreign funding of private and public sector borrowers in the United States in 1988 came to $112 billion.

One of the major sources of foreign funds was Japan, which invested more than $40 billion in the United States in 1988–1989. A large part of Japanese investment was in the auto industry. Some of these investments were joint ventures, and others were entirely Japanese-owned. Between 1982 and 1988, investments by Toyota, Suzuki, Honda, Mazda, Mitsubishi, Fuji, and Nissan created 32,000 jobs and the capacity to produce 2.4 million cars a year in seven plants in the United States and three in Canada. Although some Americans resented the invasion of the Japanese and other foreign investors, others were happy to have new plants and job opportunities in their communities.

PRIVATE AND PUBLIC INVESTMENT. Business investment in new equipment is a key source of economic growth. Additional equipment gives each worker more capital with which to work and thus increases productivity. New equipment embodies new technology, which also increases productivity. Thus, the slowdown in investment in the 1970s and 1980s led to a search for policies that would stimulate investment. Tax incentives of various kinds were proposed and implemented. In the 1981 tax law, accelerated writeoffs of new investment greatly reduced corporate income taxes. Those revenues were partly restored by reforms in the 1986 tax law. Since 1986 there has been a great deal of interest in restoring to the tax code the special treatment of capital gains, which are currently taxed as ordinary income. Capital gains are "profits" that result from the sale of assets at a higher price than they cost. Many policy makers argue that favorable tax treatment of capital gains would stimulate more sales of business firms and corporate stock.

A higher level of investment was seen as the cure for stagflation because it would shift the aggregate supply curve to the right. Such a shift would increase employment without more inflation. Although stagflation is no longer the main problem, investment is still very important. The pattern of the last few years has been one of slow growth, steady inflation of

4. Data from Andrew Dean et al., "Savings Trends and Behavior in OECD Countries," *OECD Economic Studies* (Spring 1990): 7–58.

4–5 percent, and unemployment that is perhaps just a little above the natural rate. Higher investment would address all of these concerns, so the focus on increasing investment can be expected to continue in the 1990s.

The policy emphasis in the last decade has been on private capital as a way to increase economic growth. However, the role of infrastructure as capital should not be overlooked. Most of this capital is in the state and local public sector, where the growth of the capital stock has slowed considerably from earlier decades. The transportation network of highways and airports on which private business depends is provided in the public sector. Investment in human capital also requires local public sector investments in schools and health care facilities.

GROWTH IN THE LABOR FORCE

Another source of economic growth is a larger and/or more skilled labor force. Increases in both the size and the quality of the labor force can contribute to economic growth. If only the size increases, as occurred during the 1970s, real GNP may increase but there will be little if any increase in real per capita GNP, which measures improvements in the standard of living. A more skilled and productive labor force, which has more capital and better technology to work with, is the essential ingredient for an increase in real per capita GNP.

THE SIZE OF THE LABOR FORCE. During the 1970s, the labor force grew by 29 percent. A large part of that increase reflected the entry of the baby boom generation into the labor force. Another large part of the increase was due to the increased participation of women, many of whom were entering the labor force for the first time. Thus, labor force growth was much more rapid than before, but the average level of workers' skill and experience fell. This fall slowed the growth of GNP and the rightward movement of the aggregate supply curve.[5]

In the 1980s, the labor force grew much more slowly. From 1980 to 1990, it grew by only 16 percent, much less than the 22 percent growth of the preceding decade. In 1970, 16 percent of the population was between sixteen and twenty-four years old, the age group that makes up most of the new entrants to the labor force. By 1990, those in that age group made up only 13.4 percent of the population. Thus, if labor is to make a contribution to economic growth in the 1990s, the emphasis must shift to the quality of the labor force, or the labor force must be expanded by immigration or by a higher labor force participation rate.[6]

INVESTMENT IN HUMAN CAPITAL. Investment is traditionally defined as the creation of new capital in the form of tangible productive assets, such as buildings, machines, and roads. The notion of capital is, however, broader

5.   As the labor force ages in the next century, there is a risk that productivity will decline because there will be more older workers with obsolete skills.
6.   The 1990 *Economic Report of the President* considered the labor force an important enough issue to devote an entire chapter (Chapter 5) to the subject. Immigration in the 1980s averaged 580,000 persons per year, a large proportion of them of working age. Many of them are unskilled. These immigrants generally filled slots in the lower end of the labor market and did very little to address the increasing need for skilled workers (although immigrants to the United States in 1990 included 48,000 Chinese graduate students, hardly unskilled!).

than just physical tools. Capital is anything used to increase the flow of output. Human capital thus includes "investment" in health, vigor, education, or training—anything that will increase the productivity of the individual worker.

Both individuals and firms can invest in human capital. An individual's decision to seek additional education is very similar to an entrepreneur's decision to purchase a new piece of equipment. In both cases, the investment is productive if the return (discounted) exceeds the cost (also discounted).

The largest investment in human capital in the United States is in the public schools, which offer "free" education through grade 12. This education is supplemented by post-secondary education in colleges, universities, technical schools, and vocational training programs, adult literacy and retraining programs, and on-the-job training. Estimates by Jacob Mincer in the 1970s indicated that as much as half of human capital in the United States was derived from on-the-job training.[7]

The United States invests heavily in education at all levels but most heavily in elementary and secondary schools. In 1959, expenditures per pupil were $1,635 (measured at 1982–1983 prices). By 1988, this figure had risen to $2,239, a real increase of about 36 percent. This amount compares favorably with educational expenditures in other developed nations. Of other major industrial nations, only Switzerland spends more per pupil. Canada, Japan, Australia, and the other nations of Western Europe all spend less.[8] The median amount of education (years of schooling completed) of persons twenty-five years old and over has also risen steadily in the United States, from 10.5 years in 1960 to 12.7 years in 1987. In 1987, 76 percent of the adult population had at least a high school diploma. The United States spends about 6.3 percent of GNP on education at all levels, compared to about 10 percent of GNP on business investment in plant and equipment.

The U.S. educational system has come under much criticism for failing to produce a well-educated labor force. Public schools were among the scapegoats for the slow economic growth in the 1970s and early 1980s. Parents, taxpayers, and educators pointed to falling SAT scores and high dropout rates. Employers complained about lack of basic skills in writing and computation. The result has been a careful examination of how effectively resources invested in education are being used. At the elementary and secondary levels, a number of states have enacted reforms in order to use those resources more effectively. Those reforms include tougher attendance laws, stricter teacher certification, basic skills testing for students, and other measures designed to improve the quality of public education. A few business leaders have even offered to provide college funds for those who make it through twelfth grade in certain inner city schools. That guarantee has lowered the dropout rate in those schools. All of these steps are attempts to improve the quality of human capital. The result would be an increase in aggregate supply and in the U.S. standard of living.

---

7. Jacob Mincer, *Schooling, Experience, and Earnings* (New York: National Bureau of Economic Research, 1974).
8. Comparative international data is taken from John Hood, "Education: Money Isn't Everything," *Wall Street Journal* (2 February 1990): A-10.

The Gulf War has raised once again the question of whether military spending is responsible for the slower growth rate of the United States compared to those of other industrial countries. For example. Lloyd Dumas argues that "owing to the disproportionate allocation of scientific and engineering talent to military research, the rate of commercial innovation has declined appreciably since the late 1960s. Rising prices and deteriorating relative quality have made U.S.-produced goods increasingly noncompetitive in both world and domestic markets, forcing production cutbacks and plant closures in the United States and creating additional inflationary pressures."[a]

This statement is stronger than many observers would make. It does, however, highlight a concern about the role of military spending in the economy. Does defense spending displace infrastructure investment or funding for human capital? Does more for military research and development mean less for private industry?

The first question is a difficult one to answer. In the United States, 5.5 percent of GNP went to defense spending in 1990, a slightly higher share than the average for all industrialized countries as reported by the World Bank.[b] It is not clear how those funds would have been spent if defense outlays were reduced. The result might have been lower deficits or lower taxes rather than more spending on infrastructure and human services.

The second question is a little easier to address. Research and development (R&D) spending, public and private, accounts for about 2.8 percent of GNP. This figure is comparable to levels in West Germany (prior to reunification) and Japan (both at 2.8 percent). It exceeds the share of GNP that goes to R&D in France and the United Kingdom (both at 2.4 percent). However, a large share of that R&D spending in the United States was devoted to

ECONOMIC INSIGHT

DEFENSE SPENDING AND THE CIVILIAN ECONOMY

military research and technology, with very limited spinoffs in terms of civilian production. Nondefense R&D spending in the United States amounts to about 2 percent of GNP compared to 2.8 percent for Japan and 2.6 percent in West Germany (before reunification). With defense R&D eliminated, the gap in R&D spending between the United States and France or the United Kingdom was also much narrower—2 percent of GNP in the United States compared to 1.8 percent in both those countries.

The distinction between military and civilian R&D spending would be less important if there were substantial spillover benefits between the two. The one great success of military R&D that was translated into profitable civilian applications is the transistor. However, other examples are hard to find. In fact, Hewlett-Packard argues that defense is now a net user of civilian-created technology in electronics, rather than the other way around.[c] The military is generally more interested in performance than in price. The civilian market is sensitive to both concerns. Thus, for example, machine tool manufacturing in the United States has been stimulated by military demand, but the result has been an industry that has been more attentive to high performance than to cost. The more price-sensitive civilian sector of the market has gone to the Germans and the Japanese.

Some of the greatest military innovations with spinoffs to the private sector have not been in technology but in management. Cost-benefit analysis, operations research, and planning-programming-budget systems originated in the military and spread quickly to private industries. Overall, however, it is difficult to evaluate whether high levels of defense spending, with or without the Gulf War, have increased, reduced, or had no impact on U.S. economic growth.

a. *The Political Economy of Arms Reduction*, Selected Symposium 80, American Association for the Advancement of Science, 1982.
b. World Bank, *World Development Report 1990* (New York: Oxford University Press, 1990)
c. Jacques S. Gansler, *Affording Defense* (Cambridge, MA: MIT Press, 1989).

GROWTH IN NATURAL RESOURCES

The last category of inputs that can shift the aggregate supply curve is natural resources. In the late 1960s, a group of doomsayers called "The Club of Rome" used a computer simulation model to predict massive shortages of natural resources by the end of this century. Many economists are not very concerned about resource shortages because they have observed how market forces have dealt with such problems in the past. The market has several mechanisms to address problems of declining resource availability. When high-grade sources are exhausted, lower-grade sources are substituted. When a given resource becomes scarce, its price rises. Users then turn to natural or synthetic substitutes. Higher prices also stimulate searches for new sources of supply. Finally, technological change has helped to lower extraction costs and make lower-grade deposits worth exploiting.

Economists V. Kerry Smith and John V. Krutilla have examined experience with natural resources over the last hundred years. They do not lightly dismiss concerns over increased resource scarcity, but they found the record of the past to be encouraging.[9] Higher prices typically called forth the kinds of responses just described.

With one exception, increased resource prices did not have much to do with the slowdown of the last two decades. That exception was oil, whose price rose tenfold in just seven years, leading to a temporary leftward shift of the aggregate supply curve. Even in that case, with a dramatic price increase of a widely used natural resource, producers and consumers adapted. More fuel-efficient cars, alternative energy sources, insulation, modified production methods, and other responses minimized the long-run effect on the economy. The higher price also ultimately called forth additional oil supplies, shifting the aggregate supply curve back to the right to some extent.

RESEARCH AND DEVELOPMENT

Increased productive resources are not the only source of increases in aggregate supply. If new ways of using resources can create more output, then those technological changes can also shift the aggregate supply curve to the right. New technology may be embodied in new capital or in a change in methods of production. Research and development, or R&D, consists of efforts to develop new products and new production methods and put them to use.

Technological change is a two-step process. The first step requires investment in research into new products and new methods. This step results in inventions. The second step is to translate those inventions into something that is commercially feasible and cost-effective. This second step is **innovation**, or the translation of new methods and products into actual production and marketing. A special issue of *Business Week* devoted to innovation suggested that Americans excel at the invention phase, but the Japanese are much more successful in making the transition from invention to innovation and exploiting the profit potential of new ideas.[10]

innovation
The translation of inventions into products and processes that are commercially feasible and cost-effective.

9. V. Kerry Smith and John V. Krutilla, "Economic Growth, Resource Availability, and Environmental Quality," *American Economic Review Papers and Proceedings* (May 1984): 226-230.
10. "Innovation in America," *Business Week* (special issue), 1989.

Technological change is difficult to measure in the aggregate. It is possible to measure changes in spending on research and development and new equipment, which embodies the latest technology. There is no easy way, however, to measure the extra output due to the new technology. The United States does spend heavily on research and development. About 2.8 percent of GNP goes to research and development, much of it funded by the federal government and carried out by industry and universities. In the 1970s and 1980s, however, about 25 percent of U.S. spending on research and development was directed to defense-related research, which has limited applications to other markets. Other countries (especially Japan) have put much more effort directly into industrial research.

Research and development spending usually requires investment in new capital that embodies the newly developed technology. Thus, research and development spending and new capital spending go hand in hand to shift the aggregate supply curve to the right and promote economic growth.

REAL BUSINESS CYCLES

A growing economy typically exhibits some instability, because innovations resulting from research and development and investment spending do not occur at a steady pace. Thus, such an economy would be expected to exhibit business cycles, as described in Chapter 4. The Keynesian model explains such cyclical fluctuations in output, employment, and the price level in terms of shifts in aggregate demand in both directions, combined with a relatively stable aggregate supply curve that gradually moves rightward over time.

Another explanation of cyclical fluctuations, in the classical tradition, was developed in the 1980s. Its roots go back to such early twentieth-century economists as Wesley Clair Mitchell (who first measured business cycles) and Joseph Schumpeter. This explanation holds that cyclical economic fluctuations result from changes in aggregate supply rather than in aggregate demand. The cyclical pattern is called the **real business cycle**. If changes in aggregate supply as a result of technology shocks and other disturbances occur irregularly in large bursts, they can generate cyclical fluctuations in output.[11]

real business cycle
A cyclical pattern of economic activity resulting from changes in aggregate supply (rather than aggregate demand).

The supply-induced explanation of fluctuations was a response to the experience of the 1970s and early 1980s. At that time, supply influences, such as a less experienced labor force and higher oil prices, appeared to shift the aggregate supply curve to the left. Such a shift would result in the usual decline in output and employment that indicates a recession. Unlike most recessions, however, there would be no fall in the price level (or the inflation rate), as would normally be the case. In a supply-induced recession, in contrast to a demand-induced recession, real output can fall while the price level rises. A subsequent shift of the aggregate supply curve

11. A temporary shock, such as a drought, earthquake, crop failure, or short-term oil price hike, will produce a temporary backward shift in the *AS* curve. In contrast, long-term resource depletion, technological change, or capital accumulation or depreciation produces longer-term shifts.

to the right would expand both employment and real output. What happened to the price level during such an expansion would depend on whether aggregate demand also shifted to the right during that period.

In general, a real business cycle—one based on shifts in aggregate supply—would tend to imply rising price levels or higher inflation rates during recessions and lower price levels or lower inflation rates during expansions. This pattern is somewhat consistent with the experience of the 1970s but does not generally describe cyclical fluctuations for longer periods. Evidence to support a real business cycle on a regular and recurring basis has been weak.[12] The major cyclical fluctuations of the last century can be explained in terms of aggregate demand, as has been done by both Keynesians and monetarists.

THE PRODUCTIVITY DILEMMA

New and better capital and methods of production are one of the most important sources of increased labor productivity. **Productivity** is the measure of real output per worker hour. Like the price level, productivity changes are measured by an index. Table 1 shows the increase in productivity by decade for the United States.

According to studies by economist Edward Denison, increases in labor productivity accounted for about two-thirds of U.S. economic growth from 1929 to 1982.[13] (The remainder was due to an increase in the size of the labor force.) Increases in the productivity of labor resulted from having more capital with which to work as well as such important factors as education and technological change.

The slow growth of productivity in the last two decades is a dramatic change from earlier periods. The problem is not unique to the United States. A similar slowdown in productivity growth has plagued all of the developed industrial countries. The concern over productivity, slow growth, and the combination of rising prices and rising unemployment

productivity
A measure of real output per worker hour.

PERIOD	PRODUCTIVITY INDEX*	AVERAGE ANNUAL INCREASE (%)
	1950 = 50.2	
1950–1960	1960 = 65.9	+2.8%
1960–1970	1970 = 87.3	+2.9%
1970–1980	1980 = 99.2	+1.3%
1980–1990	1990 = 111.9	+1.2%
*1977 = 100.		

TABLE 1
U.S. PRODUCTIVITY
GROWTH, 1950–1990

Source: Council of Economic Advisers, *Economic Report of the President* (Washington, DC: U.S. Government Printing Office, 1991).

12. The pros and cons of this highly technical subject are discussed in Charles I. Plosser, "Understanding Real Business Cycles," *Journal of Economic Perspectives* (Summer 1989): 51–78, and N. Gregory Mankiw, "Real Business Cycles: A New Keynesian Perspective," *Journal of Economic Perspectives* (Summer 1989): 79–89.
13. Edward F. Denison, *Trends in American Economic Growth 1929–1982* (Washington, DC: Brookings Institution, 1985).

led to many efforts to explain what was occurring and to devise suitable policies to get the economy moving again.[14] Former Prime Minister Margaret Thatcher's program of "Thatcherism," a uniquely British set of supply side policies, was perhaps the most dramatic political response to concerns about productivity.

One type of policy to increase productivity consists of various types of incentive, bonus, or profit-sharing schemes to encourage labor to work harder and become more skilled. Under such plans, workers are paid for output rather than input. Their pay is based on what they produce, rather than being an hourly wage or annual salary. Economist Alan Blinder has reviewed a number of studies on productivity incentives and concluded that at least some evidence suggests that such incentives do increase productivity.[15]

The explanations for the productivity slowdown are not hard to find. Although the labor force has grown, there has been some (short-term) decline in its quality as a result of a fall in the average age, training, and experience of workers, a situation that will gradually improve during the 1990s. The rates of saving and investment have remained stubbornly low. The pace of technological change has been slow. A great deal of research and development spending has been directed toward defense rather than commercial innovations. Finally, there have been problems with the cost and availability of some natural resources. All of these factors either failed to shift the aggregate supply curve to the right fast enough or, in some cases, pushed it to the left. The search was on for supply side policies.

POLICIES TO SHIFT AGGREGATE SUPPLY

It is virtually impossible to devise a policy to shift aggregate supply that does not also shift aggregate demand. Unlike the supply and demand curves for individual products, the aggregate supply and demand curves are not entirely unrelated. A tax cut, for example, may encourage work and investment, which shifts the aggregate supply curve to the right. However, it also stimulates spending on consumption and investment, which shifts the aggregate demand curve to the right. In the late 1970s and early 1980s, a group of economists, policy makers, and business journalists proposed that the United States adopt policies that would be aimed at shifting aggregate supply to the right more than aggregate demand. The result was supposed to be larger output and employment at the same or lower prices.

Supply side economics, unlike Keynesian theory or monetarism, does not consist of a clearly defined theoretical model. In the narrow sense, supply siders are a group of economists advocating a specific group of policies relating to deregulation, tax incentives, and work incentives. In designing those policies, supply siders emphasize certain microeconomic foundations of aggregate supply. In a broader sense, all economists are supply siders in that they believe that factors that can shift the aggregate supply

---

14. Issues of productivity growth are discussed in detail in a symposium edited by Stanley Fischer in the *Journal of Economic Issues* (Fall 1988): 3–98.

15. Alan S. Blinder (ed.), *Paying for Productivity: A Look at the Evidence* (Washington, DC: Brookings Institution, 1990).

In the 1980s, U.S. economic policy seemed to be out of step with much of the rest of the world. European countries were committed to demand management policies, and the United States was pursuing supply side policies. In recent years, however, just as supply side policies fell out of favor in the United States, they became more popular in European countries. As more conservative politicians came into power in France, Denmark, and the United Kingdom, a less progressive tax system aimed more at incentives and less at redistribution of income became a U.S. "export." Similar tax reforms were also undertaken in New Zealand and Canada.

The reasons that led these countries to re-examine the incentive effects of their tax systems are twofold. First, most of the countries of Western Europe, as well as Canada and New Zealand, were dissatisfied with their economic performance in the 1980s. Growth rates in the twelve member countries of the European Community, as well as in New Zealand, have been lower than growth rates in the United States and Japan for the last ten years. Unemployment is high in most European countries. Most of them have had higher rates of inflation than the United States. Canada's growth has kept pace with that of the United States, but Canada has suffered from slightly higher unemployment and inflation.

Second, the changes in the U.S. tax system legislated in 1981 and 1986 have had important implications for the major trading partners of the United States. As a result of lower marginal tax rates, the United States has become a more attractive place to work, earn, live, and invest. Some other industrial countries have seen an outflow of highly skilled workers to the United States, such as college professors, medical doctors, entertainers, and artists. There has also been a flow of investment from Europe into the United States. Other industrial countries have

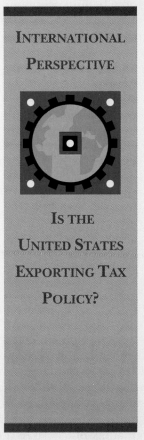

INTERNATIONAL PERSPECTIVE

IS THE UNITED STATES EXPORTING TAX POLICY?

felt pressured to lower their marginal income tax rates in order to compete with the United States for investment and skilled workers and to increase rates of growth of output and employment. Canada reformed its income tax in 1988, reducing the number of brackets from ten to three. However, marginal rates dropped very little for most families.[a] In New Zealand, tax reform enacted in 1987 lowered the top rate from 66 percent to 33 percent and reduced the number of brackets to only two.[b]

Prime Minister Margaret Thatcher in Great Britain went even further than reformers in the United States, Canada, and New Zealand. As her government reduced dependence on the income tax, some responsibilities were shifted from the central government to the local government, just as was done in the United States. In the United States, however, some of the responsibilities fell on state rather than local governments. State governments rely on income and sales taxes, but local governments in both the United States and Britain rely mainly on property taxes. Since there is no state government in Britain, the burden shifted to the property tax. The Thatcher government attempted to take some of the pressure off the property tax by reinstituting an old and very regressive tax called the poll tax. The poll tax generated a tax revolt in Britain far more widespread than the property tax revolt in the United States a decade earlier. Other countries have confined their tax reforms to reducing the progressivity of the income tax, and most are watching the reforms in Britain with interest.

American economists have generally found little evidence that supply side policies had a significant impact on saving, investment, or productivity. However, some of the countries of Western Europe have jumped on the tax incentive bandwagon for fear they will be left behind.

a. "Will Canada's Tax Reform Have a Supply Side Effect?" *Wall Street Journal* (3 September 1988): 15.
b. "New Zealand's Painful Economic Cure," *Wall Street Journal* (11 October 1988): 17.

curve are important for long-term economic growth. In fact, a Keynesian or a monetarist is often an advocate of some supply side policies.

Supply siders insist that economic incentives are important and that the driving force behind economic decisions is the self-interested behavior of individuals. Recall the importance of incentives and response to the role of interest rates in money demand, bank lending, and business investment decisions on the aggregate demand side of the market. The responses of individuals in their roles as workers, managers, investors, and savers to changes in the reward structure of their environment is also important for aggregate supply. Supply siders point out that the government has a great deal of influence on this reward structure.

THE TAX WEDGE AND WORK INCENTIVES

tax wedge
The gap between prices paid by consumers and the prices (incomes) received by sellers (factor owners).

Supply siders are concerned about the effects of taxes, especially income taxes, on incentives and economic activity. Higher taxes taxes drive up costs of production and consumer prices.[16] Taxes to support government activity create a **tax wedge**, which is the gap between prices paid by consumers and the prices (incomes) received by sellers (factor owners). Thus, the tax wedge discourages both consumption and production. If the government borrows instead of raising taxes to finance additional spending, this action raises the cost of borrowing to private firms. The rise in the cost of borrowing drives up their costs and discourages private-sector investment. Either way, supply siders argue, the growth of government contributes to rising costs.

Supply side economists argue that the growth of the tax-transfer system reduces incentives to work, save, invest, and innovate, all of which contribute to productivity. High marginal tax rates discourage individuals from putting forth extra effort and encourage tax avoidance. Under a progressive income tax system (and the U.S. federal income tax was fairly progressive until 1986), increases in nominal income push workers into higher marginal tax brackets. As a result, a significant portion of the return to increased effort and productivity is taxed away. Consequently, workers are likely to opt for more leisure (longer vacations, increased absenteeism, less moonlighting, and earlier retirement).

Consider Ms. A, a skilled accountant earning $35 an hour. She is considering either putting in an extra four hours for a client on Saturday morning or spending that time cleaning her carpets. If she works, her gross income will be $140. A commercial carpet cleaner charges $100. Without considering taxes, it makes sense for her to work four hours, pay the carpet cleaner, and come out $40 ahead. Resources would be efficiently allocated. The value of her time as an accountant is higher than the value of her time as a carpet cleaner. However, taxes may change her decision. If her marginal income tax rate (federal plus state) is 40 percent, then after taxes she will earn only $84. It would be cheaper to clean her own carpets. A lower tax rate would induce her to use her time where it is most productive—as an accountant, not as a carpet cleaner. These con-

16. The extent to which taxes fall on consumers, rather than on producers or factors of production, depends on the kind of tax and the amount of market power possessed by the producers. However, most economists would agree that the tax wedge has some impact on both producers and consumers.

cerns about the incentive effects of high marginal tax rates were reflected in the 1981 tax cut and the 1986 tax reforms. Both of these policy actions sharply reduced marginal income tax rates for individuals.

Supply siders also argue that transfer payments discourage productive work. Unemployment compensation programs encourage workers to stay unemployed until their benefits are exhausted. Welfare programs, including not only cash transfers but also food stamps, subsidized housing, and Medicaid, discourage people from taking low-wage jobs. The wages they could earn may barely offset the loss of welfare payments plus other benefits. Consider Mr. B, who currently receives $120 a week in welfare benefits. A job becomes available, which would require Mr. A to work forty hours a week at the minimum wage of $4.25 an hour. If he takes the job, he loses his welfare benefits. He will earn $170 a week instead of $120. The "tax" on his earnings will be $120/$170, or about 71 percent. Is it worth working forty hours a week to earn $50 more? (After Social Security and other taxes, Mr. B's net earnings increase may actually be negative.) This argument was popularized by Charles Murray in his book *Losing Ground* in the early 1980s. He argued that welfare actually discourages people from investing in human capital.[17] Workfare programs in some of the states and finally on the national level in the late 1980s were designed to overcome this problem by allowing people who go off welfare to accept jobs to keep more of their earnings.

Clear evidence is hard to find, but there is some support for the argument that marginal tax rates affect those at the bottom of the ladder. There is also some weak support for a similar effect on those in high tax brackets. Economists Gary Burtless and Robert Haveman, summarizing a variety of studies of the effects of taxes and transfers, conclude that the loss of welfare benefits was a deterrent to work effort in some experimental programs to test work incentives. They also found that possible loss of Social Security benefits had a negative effect on work effort among the elderly.[18]

TAXES, SAVING, AND INVESTMENT

Supply siders also raise the tax issue with respect to saving and investment. An individual's reward for saving depends on both the interest rate and the marginal tax rate on the next dollar of income. For any given interest rate, there is less incentive to save additional dollars at a higher marginal tax rate. Less credit will be available to borrowers. Thus, a progressive income tax discourages saving and indirectly, through the higher cost of borrowed funds, discourages investment.

Supply siders also apply this argument to entrepreneurial or management risk taking. In deciding whether to expand productive facilities or to implement new technologies, owners or managers must weigh the risks that are involved against the expected profits *after taxes*. The higher the marginal tax rate, the smaller the expected profit will be, and the less eager investors will be to assume risks. As a result, less new technology is adopted, and both output and productivity growth are retarded.

17. Charles Murray, *Losing Ground: American Social Policy, 1950–1980* (New York: Basic Books, 1984).
18. Gary T. Burtless and Robert H. Haveman, "Taxes and Transfers: How Much Economic Loss?" *Challenge* (March–April 1987): 45–51.

There is not much evidence from the 1980s to support this view of supply siders. Despite two major reductions in the marginal income tax rate, neither saving nor investment responded very strongly during the 1980s.[19] The 1981 tax law even contained some tax breaks for special savings accounts, such as All Savers Certificates and Individual Retirement Accounts (IRAs). Despite these incentives, the share of after-tax income that people saved continued to fall. Investment did not show much response either.

In the late 1980s, a modified supply side argument became popular. Some economists and policy makers argued that the special tax treatment of capital gains, eliminated in the 1986 tax reform, should be restored. (Recall that capital gains are earnings that result from an increase in the market value of an asset over its purchase price.) Under a highly progressive tax system, capital gains are likely to push their recipient into a higher tax bracket and generate more tax liability than they would have if they were received over several years instead of all at once. Special tax treatment (a lower rate) for capital gains is believed to be an incentive to invest in riskier ventures and thus provide capital for innovation and growth. However, there is no conclusive evidence about the effect of this tax break on investment.

OTHER EFFECTS OF TAXES ON OUTPUT

Supply siders also argue that progressive taxes cause resources to be allocated inefficiently. Resources flow to certain sectors of the economy, such as real estate, that enjoy tax advantages. All depreciation, taxes, and interest expenses are deductible on real estate investments. Individuals in high marginal tax brackets find that their after-tax yields are higher from investing in real estate than in other assets. Thus, supply siders argue that too many financial resources flow into the real estate market, instead of more productive uses. The 1986 tax reform eliminated some but not all of the special tax provisions for certain types of investments.

Finally, supply siders stress that high marginal tax rates cause too many scarce resources to be devoted to avoiding taxes. Time spent looking for tax loopholes (by individuals and their hired attorneys and accountants) could be used more productively.

REGULATION AND DEREGULATION

Supply siders are also very critical of government regulations in environmental and health and safety areas that increase costs of production and drive up prices without increasing output. In addition to the direct costs of compliance, these regulations place a heavy burden of paperwork on industry. Although the purposes of the regulations might indeed be desirable, they divert real resources from producing goods and services to complying with regulations and filing forms. These higher costs shift the aggregate supply curve to the left. Deregulation should shift it back to the right.

Deregulation was a central feature of the policies of the Reagan administration. Some regulations were repealed. Others were simply not enforced. Experiments with deregulation in the 1980s in the airline indus-

---

19. Supply siders point out that a large part of the tax cut was offset by increased Social Security taxes and higher state and local taxes in many cases. Thus, some of the expected benefits did not occur.

try, telephone service, and banking, however, generated mixed results. The enthusiasm for deregulation appears to have peaked in the mid-1980s. The policy is currently being reassessed.

PUBLIC POLICY TOWARD RESEARCH AND DEVELOPMENT

Since the federal government plays a major role in the allocation of research and development funds, it has an important direct influence on the activities of invention and innovation. In addition to direct expenditures, the federal government also finances the education of many scientists and engineers, protects property rights to inventions through the patent system, and offers special tax breaks for research and development spending in the private sector.

Profits are the incentive to engage in research and development. The outcome of a research and development effort will be more profitable if the resulting product reaches the broadest possible market. One effort to increase the return to research and development, therefore, has concentrated on opening foreign markets to new U.S. products and better protecting patents and copyrights on a worldwide basis (protecting rights in "intellectual capital").

SUPPLY SIDE ECONOMICS IN THE 1980s

For the most part, what President Reagan did in his first term was a textbook application of supply side economics. Congress and the President reduced some social welfare programs and enacted a three-stage, 25 percent cut in personal income taxes in 1981. Accompanying the tax cuts were some incentives to save and invest. Also, efforts were made to reduce the burden on business of complying with government regulations. The goal was to shift aggregate supply to the right, increasing saving, investment, productivity, output, and employment while reducing inflation.

It is difficult to evaluate supply side policies because it is impossible to conduct *ceteris paribus* experiments. Tight monetary policy combined with lower inflation rates drove real interest rates to record highs. The worldwide recession from 1980 to 1982 led to falling output and employment and probably deserves some of the credit for lower inflation rates. Since recovery from a recession is generally associated with rising productivity, it is hard to know how much productivity was affected by the Reagan program. The most noteworthy changes were the drop in the inflation rate and the steady recovery and expansion since the 1981–1982 recession. The massive budget deficits that followed the tax cut are also at least partly the result of these supply side policies.

In addition, the supply side program was often criticized on distributional grounds. Critics argued that the package of tax cuts and incentives was "welfare for the rich," who received the biggest tax cuts and benefited the most from saving and investment incentives. Defenders of these policies countered that the rich were paying the most to begin with. In addition, as a group they tend to include the most productive workers (measured by their high salaries) and the individuals most willing and able to save and invest. Thus, any program aimed at encouraging work effort, saving, and investment has to focus on incentives for individuals with higher incomes. But, the defenders argued, the resulting economic growth, lower inflation rates, and higher productivity will eventually benefit everyone.[20]

Supply side ideas have declined in popularity in the last few years. There has been a lack of hard evidence of their effectiveness. There has also been concern about the distributional effects of higher taxes on the poor (especially Social Security) combined with tax breaks for the rich.

IS INDUSTRIAL POLICY THE ANSWER?

industrial policy
A growth strategy consisting of government programs to identify and encourage promising industries and to ease the decline of old industries.

Supply side economics is a politically conservative growth strategy, relying on private market forces. In the last few years, a competing growth strategy has been proposed. This politically liberal strategy, known as **industrial policy**, consists of government programs to identify and encourage promising industries and to ease the decline of old industries. Japan has often been cited as an example of the successful use of industrial policy. European countries also pursue similar strategies.

The tools of industrial policy usually include subsidies, tax incentives, government-sponsored research and development, low-interest loans, and other devices designed to promote an industry or group of industries. Often restrictions on imports or promotion of exports is part of the policy. The basic goal is to identify promising industries and help them to develop to the point where they can continue to grow and prosper on their own. In some cases, industrial policy is proposed as a way to avoid the pain of structural change in declining industries by propping them up and helping them to survive. In other cases, industrial policy attempts to ease the transition for labor and capital out of declining industries and into other areas with more promising futures.

The primary goal of industrial policy is competitiveness. Much of the interest in industrial policy was spurred by the decline in exports and the rise in imports in the United States in the 1980s. To a large extent, the change in the balance of trade (exports minus imports of goods and services) was a result of the rise in the price of the U.S. dollar from 1981 to 1985. As the price of the dollar declines, some of the problem of competitiveness may be resolved.

The United States already has an industrial policy of sorts, although it is not deliberate and coordinated. Existing tax, subsidy, and regulatory policies, as well as government spending for research and training programs, favor certain industries at the expense of others. Concentration of research in agriculture, defense, and space programs favors industries in those areas and suppliers to those industries. The minimum wage, by *not* favoring industries that use large amounts of unskilled labor, has tipped the balance in favor of industries using more capital and/or skilled labor. The Investment Tax Credit and accelerated depreciation, until modified in 1986, favored capital-intensive industries. The list is endless. The point

---

20. The notion that benefits to the rich will eventually spill over to lower income groups is known among development economists as the trickle-down theory. Those who suggest direct aid to the poor to help them earn and be more productive, with benefits spilling over to higher-income groups, call their approach the bubble-up theory.

Japan and the European Community (EC) offer good examples of positive and negative industrial policy. Japan pursues a more positive policy of identifying and promoting industries that seem to have growth potential. Since Japan has the best record of economic growth of any industrial country since World War II, other countries have shown much interest in its policies. As a general rule, the nations of the EC have pursued a more negative approach. This approach consists of protecting and supporting declining industries, trying to get them back to a competitive level.

The key to Japan's program is the Ministry of Trade and Industry (MITI), which selects the industries to assist. Methods used in the 1950s and 1960s included organizing cartels, providing loans at low interest rates to targeted industries, and controlling imports. In the 1970s and 1980s, the government did offer aid to declining industries in the form of tax breaks and loan guarantees. Overall industrial policy in Japan has been directed much more at supporting promising industries through accelerated depreciation allowances, tax benefits, research support, and loans. The U.S. government usually makes such benefits available to all firms, but Japan is more selective in deciding which industries to favor. Critics have argued, however, that the MITI is not always successful in identifying which industries to promote. It has backed some losers and missed some potential winners, such as the auto industry. Although the Japanese strategy is mostly positive, selected industries, such as agriculture, are heavily protected.

The EC's primary strategy has been to slow

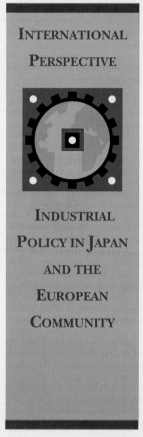

INTERNATIONAL PERSPECTIVE

INDUSTRIAL POLICY IN JAPAN AND THE EUROPEAN COMMUNITY

structural changes that cause losses and unemployment in declining industries. Low-interest loans and import restrictions play a key role. Agriculture has benefited from subsidies and import controls, despite its comparative disadvantage. Other declining industries that have been singled out for special treatment are shipbuilding, steel, textiles, and footwear. One exception to the EC pattern has been Italy, which has relied heavily on antitrust policy, deregulation, and reducing the size of the public sector in order to make its industries more competitive within as well as outside the EC. At the same time, Italy is promoting small and medium-sized industries with technical assistance and low-cost loans in order to enable them to compete with larger firms in both Italy and the EC.[a] Italy's strategy, intended to position Italian industry to compete when the EC becomes a single integrated market after 1992, is more forward-looking than those of some of its neighbors. It will be difficult to support, subsidize, and protect specific industries against competition within a unified twelve-nation market with uniform product standards, no trade barriers, and free flow of goods and productive resources.

American policy makers interested in industrial policy have been attracted to the Japanese positive model because of Japan's high growth rate. However, policy proposals and practice in the United States seem to more closely resemble the EC model. They have emphasized protection from foreign competition and focused on rebuilding declining industries rather than developing promising new ones.

a.   "Italy's Industrial Policy Challenged by 1992," *Wall Street Journal* (27 June 1988): 15.

is that every nation has an industrial policy. The real question is whether it is pursued as a deliberate strategy and the results are evaluated to see if the industries the nation wishes to help are indeed the ones benefiting.

The foremost advocate of industrial policy in the United States has been economist Robert Reich, who laid out such a strategy for the United States in his 1983 book, *The Next American Frontier.* Among his recommendations were replacing the income tax with an expenditure tax (to encourage saving), increased federal spending for research and science training, tax incentives for human capital investments, and aid to declining industries to encourage conversion to other areas.

Critics of industrial policy point out that it involves second-guessing the market. The government, rather than the market, is selecting the industries to develop, using its judgment instead of the judgment of consumers, entrepreneurs, and owners of productive resources. In addition, industrial policy creates a field day for lobbyists and special interest groups trying to make a case that their industry is most deserving of any special benefits.

The debate over industrial policy began in the 1980s when it was put forth as a liberal answer to conservative strategies of tax cuts, deregulation, and reduced government spending. This debate will continue well into the 1990s.

SUMMARY

1. There are four shapes for the aggregate supply curve: horizontal, vertical, upward sloping, and composite. Each shape has different implications for the effects of a change in aggregate demand on prices, output, and employment.

2. If the long-run aggregate supply curve is vertical, shifts of the aggregate demand curve can affect output in the short run but only the price level in the long run.

3. An upward-sloping aggregate supply curve may be the result of imperfect information or a limited ability to adapt to changing conditions. If expectations are rational and markets work well, the aggregate supply curve is vertical, at least in the long run.

4. The aggregate supply curve can be shifted by changes in the quantity and quality of resources avail-

able or by changes in technology.

5. Increases in capital, including human capital and improvements in technology, increase worker productivity. Productivity growth in industrial countries has been slower in recent decades than in earlier periods.

6. Supply side economics is a group of policies intended to shift the aggregate supply curve to the right. These policies include work incentives, saving and investment incentives, and deregulation. The Reagan administration implemented a supply side program in the 1980s.

7. Industrial policy is an alternative to supply side economics. It also emphasizes tax and production incentives but aims to promote and encourage a specific industry or a group of industries.

NEW TERMS

adaptive expectations	savings rate	productivity
auction markets	innovation	tax wedge
contract markets	real business cycle	industrial policy

QUESTIONS FOR DISCUSSION

1. How can a tax cut be both a demand side (Keynesian) and a supply side policy? Does it make any difference what kinds of taxes are cut?

2. Why is the shape of the *AS* curve important?

3. What determines the slope of the *AS* curve?

4. Economists who believe in rational expectations assume that individuals will acquire and process all relevant information to make economic decisions in their own self-interest. If you watch key variables and expect the inflation rate to rise, how will that affect your consumption, saving, and work behavior?

5. Sketch the four versions of the aggregate supply curve shown in Figure 1 and show how a leftward shift of *AD* (a reduction in aggregate demand) affects prices and output in each case.

6. Which of the following can be classed as auction markets and which as contract markets?

    a. the stock market

    b. the mortgage market

    c. the labor market

    d. the market for new houses

    e. the market for tickets to a baseball game

7. Why are both rational expectations and auction markets necessary in order to have a vertical *AS* curve in the short run?

8. What is industrial policy? How is industrial policy different from supply side economics?

9. How would each of the following affect measured productivity?

    a. new and better capital equipment for many workers

    b. a sharp rise in the labor force participation rate

    c. higher prices for natural resources in general

10. What are some of the factors that can increase labor productivity?

11. Ms. Karcher is retired and receiving Social Security benefits, but she is considering working part-time. If she works part-time, she will pay about 15 percent of her earnings in federal income tax, 4 percent in state income tax, and 7.3 percent in Social Security tax. What is her marginal tax rate on earnings? If she works twenty hours a week, she will earn a gross income of $100. What is her net income and her net hourly wage? Should she take the job?

12. Mr. Stewart is trying to decide whether to work on Saturday for three hours at an hourly rate of $20 or to spend the three hours cleaning his garage. He can hire two neighborhood boys to clean the garage, but they charge $35. What should he do if his combined tax rate (federal income tax, state income tax, and Social Security tax) on the additional income totals 30 percent? What if the combined tax rate totals 50 percent?

13. Does business investment shift aggregate supply or aggregate demand? How do you think increased business investment will affect prices and real output?

14. Were supply side policies successful in the 1980s? Why or why not?

15. According to Smith and Krutilla, why have natural resources not been a serious limit to growth?

SUGGESTIONS FOR FURTHER READING

Aschauer, David A. "Does Public Capital Crowd Out Private Capital?" *Journal of Monetary Economics* (September 1989): 171–188. Explores the relationship between public and private capital as both complements and substitutes in promoting economic growth. Aschauer concludes that public sector capital does make a significant contribution to growth.

Blinder, Alan S. (ed.). *Paying for Productivity: A Look at the Evidence.* Washington, DC: Brookings Institution, 1990. Examines the potential for increasing workers' productivity through various types of pay incentives.

Council of Economic Advisers. *The Economic Report of the President.* Washington, DC: U.S. Government Printing Office, annual. Policies to promote growth are always emphasized. The 1990 edition has a thorough discussion of growth policy.

Dertouzos, Michael L., et al. *Made in America: Regaining the Productive Edge.* Cambridge, MA: MIT Press, 1989. Examines the productivity decline and offers proposals for improvement.

Hicks, Donald A. *Is New Technology Enough? Making and Remaking the Basic Industries.* Washington, DC: American Enterprise Institute, 1988. Looks at whether technology will help basic manufacturing industries survive. Includes case studies of machine tools, steel, automobiles, textiles, ceramics, and fiber optics.

Perry, George. "Reflections on Macroeconomics." *American Economic Review Papers and Proceedings* (May 1984): 401–407. Discusses the shapes of the *AS* curve and some reasons why it has an upward slope.

Sheffrin, Steven M. *The Making of Economic Policy.* Cambridge, MA: Basil Blackwell, 1989. Chapter 3 discusses real business cycles.

Stein, Herbert, "Should Growth Be a Priority of National Policy?" and Heller, Walter, "Activist Government: Key to Growth?" *Challenge* (March/April 1986). Two former chairs of the Council of Economic Advisers, one from the Nixon administration in the 1970s and one from the Kennedy and Johnson administrations in the 1960s, debate the growth policy issue.

1. List and discuss the characteristics of less developed countries.
2. Define:
   a. per capita income,
   b. dependency ratio,
   c. the crude birth rate,
   d. the crude death rate.
3. Explain what development economists call the vicious circle of poverty.
4. Compare and critically evaluate the economic development theories of Karl Marx and W. W. Rostow.
5. Contrast the following strategies for economic development:
   a. big push versus leading sectors,
   b. *laissez-faire* versus government-directed development.
6. Describe the problems that population growth and international debt create for development and discuss possible remedies.
7. List the proposals of the New International Economic Order (NIEO).

CHAPTER 17

ECONOMIC DEVELOPMENT AND THE THIRD WORLD

INTRODUCTION

Growth is a matter of concern for developed, industrial countries like the United States. However, it is closer to a life-or-death matter for many less developed countries (sometimes referred to as LDCs).[1] The problems facing these countries encompass the whole operation of the economy. The term *economic growth* used in Chapter 16 is too narrow to describe the goal of most of the poorer nations of the world. Economic development is a total process of transformation. It means not only raising current standards of living but also building a solid foundation of human and physical capital, technology, infrastructure, and economic institutions that will support continued improvement in the future. This chapter takes a closer look at conditions in less developed countries, using some of the economic concepts developed in earlier chapters to explain some of the reasons for differences in the levels of development.

It is easy to blame the poor countries themselves for their failure to attain a high standard of living, or to blame the rich for the problems of the poor. One development economist, writing from the perspective of analysts in the industrial world, identifies two explanations:

One says that we are so rich and they so poor because we are so good and they so bad; that is, we are hardworking, knowledgeable, educated, well-governed, efficacious,

---

1. In the jargon of development economists, the name for less developed countries has changed frequently. The changes have in part reflected the increasing political power of these countries. In the 1950s and 1960s, the term "underdeveloped countries" was most commonly used. (Before that, they were often called "backward countries.") In the late 1960s and early 1970s, the term "less developed countries" emerged. In the late 1970s, the term "Third World" was in vogue. In the early 1980s, U.N. publications used the terms "low-income countries," "middle-income countries," and "industrialized countries" to designate the levels of development. In most recent U.N. publications, the term "developing countries" is used. These countries often refer to themselves as the Group of 77.

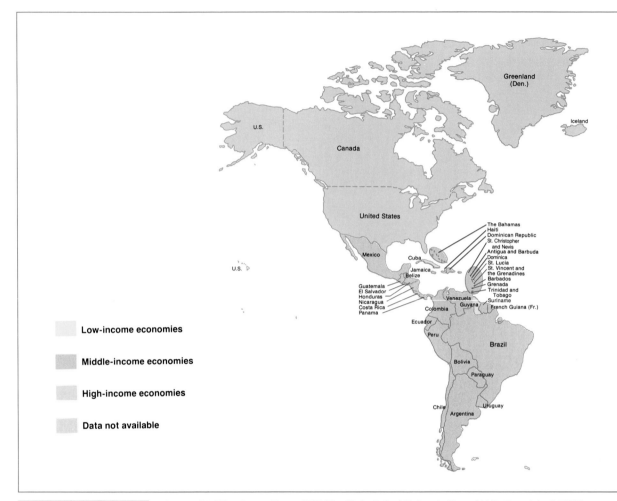

Source: *World Development Report, 1990* (New York: Oxford University Press, 1990). Copyright © 1990 by the International Bank for Reconstruction and Development/The World Bank.

FIGURE 1
WORLD BANK ECONOMIC CLASSIFICATIONS
Although it is common to divide the world's nations into three eonomic groups, there is no agreement as to name and which countries belong in each group. The World Bank has developed its own classification system and terminology suitable to its needs.

and productive, and they are the reverse. The other says that we are so rich and they so poor because we are so bad and they so good; we are greedy, ruthless, exploitative, aggressive, while they are weak, innocent, virtuous, abused, and vulnerable.[2]

Neither of these "good guys, bad guys" versions fully captures the extent to which relations between rich and poor countries affect the growth and development of both partners. This quotation does suggest, however, that the industrial world has a role to play. We will explore the role the developed, industrial countries can play in assisting the development process.

CHARACTERISTICS OF LESS DEVELOPED COUNTRIES

Although less developed countries are diverse, they share a number of important characteristics. The most obvious characteristic of a less devel-

2.   David S. Landes, "Why Are We So Rich and They So Poor?" *American Economic Review Papers and Proceedings* (May 1990): 1.

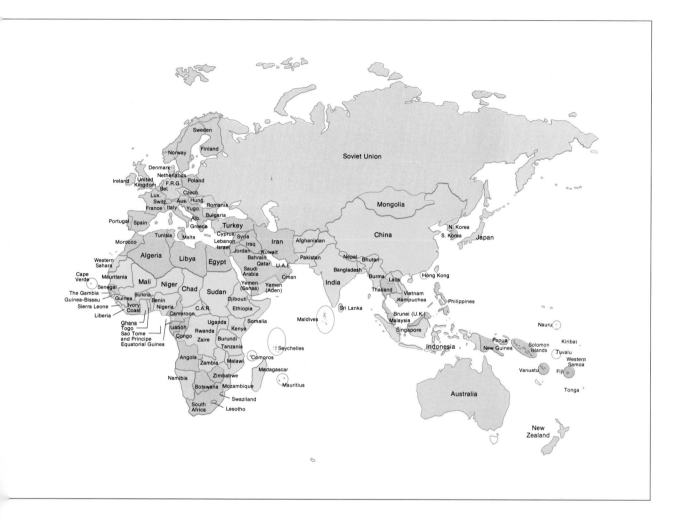

oped country is low per capita income. This criterion is used to sort nations out into various stages of economic development. Accompanying
low per capita income, however, are several other important characteristics that contribute to the persistence of poverty.

LEVEL OF PER CAPITA INCOME

The World Bank considers any country with a GDP of less than $500 per
capita (in 1988 U.S. dollars) as a low-income country. GDP differs very little from GNP for most countries. GNP measures all the output produced
by a country's citizens, at home or elsewhere. GDP measures all production that takes place within the country, whether by citizens or foreigners.
Forty-two countries were categorized as low-income countries in 1989. Another thirty-seven countries were classed as lower middle-income, with per
capita GDP ranging from $570 (Bolivia) to $2,160 (Brazil). Seventeen
countries were classed as upper middle-income, with a range from $2,290
(South Africa) to $5,420 (Libya). Only twenty-five countries made the list

of high-income countries, including both industrial market economies and high-income oil exporters. Among this prosperous group, per capita incomes ranged from $6,200 (Saudi Arabia) to $27,500 (Switzerland). Figure 1 identifies the World Bank's low-, middle-, and high-income economies.

Table 1 presents the World Bank's most recent figures for per capita gross domestic product (GDP) and growth rates of GDP for selected countries at various income levels. (Because of recent changes in Eastern European countries and because data from those countries tends to be unreliable and incomplete, we have left them out of the table. We will discuss

TABLE 1
BASIC INDICATORS OF
ECONOMIC DEVELOPMENT
FOR SELECTED COUNTRIES

	PER CAPITA GDP, 1988	YEARLY GROWTH RATE OF PER CAPITA GDP, 1965–88
LOW-INCOME COUNTRIES	$280	3.1%
Bangladesh	170	0.4
Uganda	280	−3.1
India	340	1.8
Lesotho	420	5.2
Indonesia	440	4.3
LOWER MIDDLE-INCOME COUNTRIES	$1,380	2.6%
Philippines	630	1.6
Egypt	660	3.6
Paraguay	1,180	3.1
Chile	1,510	0.1
Mexico	1,760	2.3
UPPER MIDDLE-INCOME COUNTRIES	$3,240	2.3%
South Africa	2,290	0.8
Hungary	2,460	5.1
Argentina	2,520	0.0
Portugal	3,650	3.1
HIGH-INCOME COUNTRIES*	$17,080	2.3%
Saudi Arabia	6,200	3.8
United Kingdom	12,810	1.8
Kuwait	13,400	−4.3
France	16,090	2.5
Federal Republic of Germany	18,590	3.2
United States	19,840	1.6
Japan	21,020	4.3

*Note that Kuwait's per capita income will fall in the next few years because of the Gulf War, but it had been falling before 1990. Also, the unification of the two Germanys will reduce per capita income.

Source: Adapted from *World Development Report, 1990* (New York: Oxford University Press, 1990). Copyright © 1990 by the International Bank for Reconstruction and Development/The World Bank.

developments in the centrally planned economies of Eastern Europe in a later chapter.)

Table 1 both exhibits and conceals a great deal of diversity. The oil-exporting countries in the high-income category are subject to the fluctuations of the world oil market and must eventually find other economic activities to replace their dwindling oil reserves. Although Bangladesh is very poor and its growth in per capita GDP has been slow because of a high birth rate, it has made progress in agricultural production. Thus, it probably has more hope of development than some of the poor and largely desert nations of sub-Saharan Africa. Some of the middle-income countries, notably Mexico, although better off than the poorer countries, are saddled with heavy debt burdens. Measures to resolve that problem, as well as to contain inflation, have brought the growth process to a virtual standstill not only in Mexico but in several other Latin American nations as well.

The figures in Table 1 must be used with caution. Per capita GDP is not very reliable for comparison purposes. The problems of accurately measuring income and production are even greater in less developed countries than in developed ones. Less developed countries cannot use sophisticated methods of gathering and processing data. In addition, a much larger share of output in these countries does not pass through the market. In rural areas especially, a family is likely to grow its own food, build its own house, and make its own clothes. This output is difficult to estimate and value at market prices. Finally, a major problem is the use of exchange rates to convert figures into a common currency, the U.S. dollar. Fluctuations in the value of the dollar can create impressions of faster or slower growth than actually took place.[3]

Growth rates are very important over time. The spread in growth rates among the four groups in the table is quite narrow. Compare the 2.3 percent per year for the lower middle-income group to the 3.1 percent for the low-income group. However, this narrow spread in rates of growth does not imply that income gaps are closing. First, the averages conceal the fairly wide country-to-country variation within each group, including some rates that are negative. Second, starting from a lower base of per capita income, it is possible for one country to grow at a faster rate than another and still fall further behind in absolute dollars. If country A starts at $100 per capita and grows at 5 percent a year while country B starts at $1,000 and grows at 3 percent a year, at the end of ten years, country A will have a per capita income of $163, and country B will have a per capita income of $1,344. The gap between the two will have widened from $900 to $1,181.

Even very small differences in growth rates can matter a great deal. Consider the growth rate of 2.3 percent for the lower middle-income group versus 3.1 percent for the low-income group. A country starting out at a per capita income of $1,000 will see its income rise to $1,243 in ten years at a 2.3 percent growth rate. The same per capita income will rise to $1,450 in ten years at the higher growth rate of 3.1 percent.

3.   An effort to develop more meaningful estimates was undertaken in the 1970s. A composite market basket of goods was chosen and priced in each country, with a comparison to the United States as a standard. This process was quite complex and has not been repeated. The estimates were published by Irving B. Kravis in *World Product and Income: International Comparisons of Real GDP* (Baltimore, MD: Johns Hopkins Press, 1982).

The issue of whether income differences among countries are growing or shrinking has long fascinated economists. The prediction that these gaps will narrow over time through the transfer of technology and innovation is called the **convergence hypothesis**. Economist William Baumol looked at the historical evidence on convergence from 1870 to 1979. He found the strongest convergence among the industrialized countries, with much less convergence between rich and poor countries. Other economists, however, have criticized his findings for not covering enough countries or for being biased by the strong convergence of the last thirty years.[4]

convergence hypothesis
The prediction that income differences among countries will shrink over time because of the transfer of technology and innovation.

POPULATION, BIRTH RATE, AND THE DEPENDENCY RATIO

One of the most striking differences between less developed and more developed countries is in the area of population. The population is characterized by the birth rate, the population growth rate, and the age distribution of the population. The study of population characteristics is called demography. Table 2 shows some important differences in population characteristics between less developed and more developed countries.

The **crude birth rate** is the number of births per thousand of population. As Table 2 shows, there is a large difference in the crude birth rates of poor and industrialized countries. An important consequence of a high birth rate is a high **dependency ratio**, or the percentage of the population not of working age (under fifteen or over sixty-four). Low-income countries have much higher dependency ratios. Almost half of the population of low-income countries is not of working age, compared to less than 33 percent in the industrial economies. A high dependency ratio means that a smaller proportion of the population is available to engage in productive labor. More resources must be used to meet the needs of dependent persons (a few of them elderly, but mostly children) for food, clothing, shelter, medical care, and basic education. Those resources will not be available to promote economic development through building factories

crude birth rate
Number of births per thousand of population.

dependency ratio
The percentage of the population not of working age (under fifteen or over sixty-five).

TABLE 2
POPULATION CHARACTERISTICS AT VARIOUS LEVELS OF DEVELOPMENT

	CRUDE BIRTH RATE, 1988*	CRUDE DEATH RATE, 1988*	POPULATION GROWTH RATE, 1980–88	PERCENTAGE OF POPULATION AGED 0–14, 1988
Low income	3.1	1.0	2.8	35.7
Lower middle-income	3.0	0.8	2.3	38.0
Upper middle-income	2.6	0.8	1.8	33.4
High-income countries	1.4	0.9	0.7	20.5
*Births per 100 people and deaths per 100 people per year.				

Source: Adapted from *World Development Report, 1990* (New York: Oxford University Press, 1990). Copyright © 1990 by the International Bank for Reconstruction and Development/The World Bank.

4. William J. Baumol, "Productivity Growth, Convergence, and Welfare: What the Long Run Data Show," *American Economic Review* (December 1986): 1072–1085. A later article by J. Bradford DeLong questioned whether Baumol has really proved convergence. See "Productivity Growth, Convergence, and Welfare: Comment," *American Economic Review* (December 1988): 1138–1154.

and power plants, providing worker training, and developing transportation systems.[5]

There are many reasons for high birth rates. Women marry soon after puberty in many poor countries, because they have few economic alternatives except marriage. They produce children early because children, especially sons, are useful as labor and for old-age insurance. These economic motives are reinforced by cultural patterns that frown on failure to marry and have children.

Population growth due to high birth rates may have positive consequences. A larger population can result in more specialization and economies of scale. Julian Simon has been one of the few voices in favor of population growth as a development strategy. In his book *The Ultimate Resource*, Simon argues that the negative aspects of growth and development—pressure on limited food supplies, land, and energy, slow growth of per capita income, and increasing pollution—are vastly overstated. An additional person is a productive resource who will ultimately add more to production than society had to invest in his or her care, feeding, and education up to maturity.[6] Most economists, however, consider a large number of dependent children as a drag on economic development. We will explore the population problem in more detail later in this chapter.

Table 2 also shows that people in poorer countries have a shorter life expectancy. Life expectancy reflects health, nutrition, and infant mortality factors. A shorter life expectancy means that the productive work life of the average adult is not as long. The consequence of the short life expectancy and the high birth rate in less developed countries is a large number of children with relatively few adults to support them. This age distribution is a major barrier to achieving the goal of increasing output and raising the standard of living.

THE DEATH RATE AND THE POPULATION EXPLOSION. Recent health care advances have greatly lowered the death rate in most poorer countries. It has remained almost constant in industrialized countries. The crude death rate fell from 1965 to 1987 in the low-income and lower middle-income countries: from 1.6 per 100 to 1 per 100 in low-income countries and from 1.4 to 0.8 in lower middle-income countries. The **crude death rate** is the number of deaths per hundred of population. The consequence of the declining death rate and the high and stable birth rate has been a population explosion in many less developed countries. This population growth means that these countries must grow rapidly in productive capacity just to stay *even* in per capita income.

crude death rate
Number of deaths per thousand of population.

The effect of the population explosion on per capita income is easily seen by referring to Figure 2. The figure shows the average annual growth rate of GDP in low-income, lower middle-income, upper middle-income, and high-income countries. But the picture is very different for growth in per capita GDP, also shown in Figure 2. The poorest countries have managed to stay ahead of population growth, largely because of a slowdown in birth rates in China and India. (Outside of those two countries, the pop-

5. For a thorough discussion of this issue, see Allen C. Kelley, "Economic Consequences of Population Change in the Third World," *Journal of Economic Literature* (December 1988): 1685–1728.
6. Julian L. Simon, *The Ultimate Resource* (Princeton, NJ: Princeton University Press, 1981).

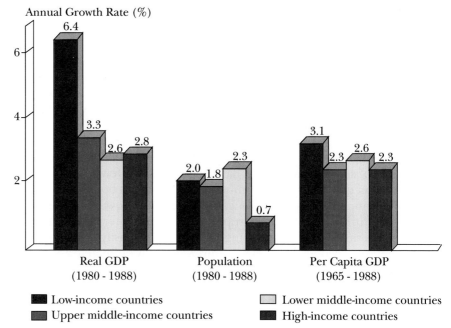

Source: *World Development Report, 1990* (New York: Oxford University Press, 1990). Copyright © 1990 by the International Bank for Reconstruction and Development/The World Bank.

ulation growth rate for the low-income countries has been 2.8 percent.) High rates of population growth have meant that both groups of middle-income countries have slower than average growth rates of per capita GDP.

INVESTMENT IN HUMAN CAPITAL. Most low-income countries invest very little in human capital, or the health, education, and skills of their citizens. Labor that is healthy and well-educated is more productive. Investment in humans can do as much to increase productivity as investing in machines, bridges, and power plants. Of course, one reason why low-income countries invest little in human capital is that they have little to invest. One of the reasons they have little to invest is that they have had such low levels of investment in human and other kinds of capital in the past. This trap is called the **vicious circle of poverty**. There is little investment because there is a low level of income, and there is a low level of income because there has been little investment.

Table 3 gives some indications of the levels of investment in human capital at different levels of development. Investment in health care is reflected in the number of people per physician. There are many more persons per physician in less developed countries than in high-income countries. Another important area of investment is in education, which is measured in Table 3 by school enrollment data. Low school enrollments in the low-income countries reflect the need for everyone to work to support the family in a subsistence economy. Education is a luxury that the family can rarely afford, especially for more than one child. Girls are less likely than boys to be enrolled in school. The effect of low school attendance is an uneducated and therefore less productive work force.

vicious circle of poverty
A trap in which many low-income countries are caught—there is little investment because of a low level of income, and a low level of income because of little investment.

	NUMBER OF PEOPLE PER PHYSICIAN, 1984	SCHOOL ENROLLMENT RATE, 1986 (%)*		
		PRIMARY	SECONDARY	HIGHER EDUCATION
Low-income countries	5,580	104	37	3
Lower middle-income countries	3,030	104	54	16
Upper middle-income countries	1,220	104	67	20
High-income countries	940	102	93	39

*Figures exceed 100 percent because older children and adults are enrolled in primary school.

TABLE 3
INVESTMENT IN HUMAN CAPITAL AT VARIOUS LEVELS OF DEVELOPMENT

Source: Adapted from *World Development Report, 1990* (New York: Oxford University Press, 1990). Copyright © 1990 by the International Bank for Reconstruction and Development/The World Bank.

AGRICULTURE

One characteristic of most less developed countries is the large share of resources devoted to agriculture. Some of this agriculture is large-scale and relatively modern, producing export crops such as cocoa, coffee, and bananas. Most of it, however, is basically subsistence agriculture. Simple, labor-intensive technology is used to produce food for individual families rather than crops to be sold for cash. Rural overcrowding, small land holdings that preclude modern economical cultivation, and low agricultural yields per acre are typical. A dominant role for the agricultural sector is strongly linked to low levels of per capita income. In order to escape poverty, a country must have some resources left over after feeding itself, either directly (by producing enough food for home use and export) or indirectly (by exporting enough nonfood items to import needed foodstuffs).

Table 4 shows some important differences in the agricultural sector at various levels of development. In the low-income group, about one-

	SHARE (%) OF GDP FROM AGRICULTURE, 1988	SHARE (%) OF MERCHANDISE EXPORTS FROM AGRICULTURE, 1988
Low-income countries	33	23
Lower middle-income countries	14	30
Upper middle-income countries	10	13
High-income countries	3	12

TABLE 4
ROLE OF AGRICULTURE AT VARIOUS LEVELS OF DEVELOPMENT

Source: Adapted from *World Development Report, 1990* (New York: Oxford University Press, 1990). Copyright © 1990 by the International Bank for Reconstruction and Development/The World Bank.

Just because a country becomes highly developed doesn't mean it stays that way. At different times in history, Egypt, Rome (Italy), Greece, and Babylonia (now Iraq) were highly developed by the standards of their time. All are relatively poor today.

Argentina, which was once one of the richest countries in the world, offers a twentieth-century example of negative development. In 1900, New Zealand and Argentina, with growth fueled in part by agricultural exports to Europe, had the two highest GNPs in the world. Wage rates in Argentina in 1910 were 25 percent higher than in Paris and 80 percent higher than in Marseilles. Europeans were migrating to Argentina in large numbers. Over the fifty-year period before 1914, Argentina's economy grew by an average rate of 5 percent per year, an achievement that still ranks as one of the highest and longest episodes of long-term economic growth. At the turn of the century, the Argentinean rancher played much the same role in French plays as the vulgar Texas oil tycoon did in *Dallas.*

In 1987, Argentina had a per capita GNP of $2,767, and that of New Zealand was $10,000. New Zealand was labeled (by the World Bank) as a high-income country, and Argentina was labeled an upper middle-income country. Between 1965 and 1988, Argentina's real per capita GNP did not grow at all. New Zealand's average growth rate was 0.8% per year.

What happened? Argentina taxed its exports heavily. Very little was invested. Argentines spent—Buenos Aires became the center of high living. Elvio Baldinelli, an Argentine trade expert, explained it well: "Argentina despised its export industries and taxed them very heavily, yet lived off them very well until markets closed and prices fell." Norman Gall wrote in *Forbes* magazine that Baldinelli's lament and the explanation for the decline of Argentina can be summed up in one sentence: "To succeed in the modern world, a country needs economic policies that encourage, not hamper, economic initiative."[a]

Economic development is not something that is achieved and then enjoyed forever. The decline of the Roman Empire, the decline of Britain in the 1960s and 1970s, and the rapid rise and fall of some of the oil-rich countries suggest that attention to the causes of economic growth are important for even the most developed countries.

a. Norman Gall, "The Four Horsemen Ride Again," *Forbes* (28 July 1986): 96.

third of GDP is derived from agriculture. In both low-income and lower middle-income countries, the agricultural sector is a major source of exports. In low-income countries, an average of 70 percent of the population is in agriculture, compared to 44 percent in middle-income countries and 7 percent in high-income countries. In the United States, only 2 percent of the labor force produces enough to feed the entire nation, with a surplus for export. In general, agriculture tends to be much more productive in upper middle-income and high-income countries. In those countries, agriculture is highly mechanized and a small part of the population produces an abundant harvest, including some for export. The table shows a consistent pattern of declining reliance on agriculture as a nation becomes wealthier.

As a producing sector, agriculture faces certain problems in both developed and less developed countries. Supply is unpredictable, depending on the weather. Demand is not very responsive to price changes. Thus, a bumper crop will lead to a big price drop. A poor harvest will command high prices, but high prices are little comfort to farmers with little or nothing to sell. These problems are more serious when agriculture is a large share of GDP. For this reason, reducing dependence on agriculture is a goal of every development program.

A major contributor to improved agricultural output in a number of less developed countries in the last two decades was the development of high-yield dwarf varieties of rice and wheat. This agricultural innovation, known as the **Green Revolution**, was undertaken by the Rockefeller Foundation, initially in Mexico and then in other countries. This project had to overcome obstacles such as lower resistance to pests in the new varieties. The new strains also required changes in techniques toward farming methods requiring more fertilizer, irrigation, and use of machinery. Nevertheless, the Green Revolution led to a rapid increase in production of these two basic foodstuffs in some less developed countries.

Green Revolution
An agricultural innovation consisting of the development of dwarf, high-yield varieties of wheat and rice that have enabled some less developed countries to improve food production.

CLIMATE

Almost all the poorest countries are in tropical climates. Conversely, all the industrialized countries are in temperate climates. This relationship between climate and development is so strong that it seems unlikely to be a coincidence. In fact, the gap between levels of development between the regions is sometimes referred to by development economists as the "North-South problem." Some development economists have suggested that warmer climates produce lower human effort, more diseases, and unfavorable agricultural conditions. There is no winter to wipe out large numbers of disease-bearing pests and parasites. In addition, many tropical countries are largely jungle or desert, neither of which is hospitable to agriculture.

DUALISM

A final characteristic of almost all less developed countries is the coexistence of two societies in the same country—one modern, urban, and market-oriented and the other made up of rural peasants who are illiterate, largely employed in agriculture and with very little of their economic activity passing through the market. This coexistence is called **dualism**.

dualism
The coexistence of a modern, urban, market-oriented society and a rural, agriculture-based, traditional peasant society, characteristic of most less developed countries.

The cities in less developed countries contain many poor people, but also have modern transportation and plumbing, manufacturing and service jobs, culture, a concentration of educated people, and a modern market economy. Birth rates are lower and in most cases women have access to education and market opportunities. Rural areas, in contrast, tend to maintain simple, traditional lifestyles with centuries-old farming methods, early marriage with many children, and much home production with few market transactions. The majority of the population in the rural areas lives in poverty or near poverty, generating little saving and investment, little improvement in human capital, and little interest in innovation.

Dualism can be a major handicap to development. The urban population in a dual economy is too small to provide a market for manufacturing and services or to generate enough saving and investment in human and physical capital.

MODELS OF ECONOMIC DEVELOPMENT

The study of economic development has resulted in few elegant theoretical models. The field has tended to attract practitioners and field economists rather than theorists. There are, however, a few models or theories that attempt to describe and predict various aspects of the development process. These models have, at times, been the basis of policies aimed at encouraging development.

The basic elements of the development process are the same as those outlined in Chapter 16 for economic growth in developed countries. The production possibilities curve and the aggregate supply curve must both be shifted to the right. To do that, either existing resources must be used more effectively or additional resources must be created or acquired. Technology and cultural change are the keys to better resource use. Additional resources can come from within, through sacrificing consumption today to invest in physical and human capital for tomorrow, or from other countries.

CLASSICAL ECONOMICS AND ECONOMIC DEVELOPMENT

The original theorist of economic development was also the person who is regarded as the founder of market economics. The complete title of Adam Smith's *Wealth of Nations* (1776) was *An Inquiry into the Nature and Causes of the Wealth of Nations*. In that book, Smith set forth the classical principles of economic development. These principles rested on a *laissez-faire* governmental policy (nonintervention) toward private industry and commerce. The division of labor and the resulting increase in productivity were limited only by the size of the market. Smith advocated free trade as a way to promote this division of labor by exploiting each nation's comparative advantage in production.

Some of Smith's successors in the classical tradition were less optimistic about the development process. David Ricardo developed the theory of diminishing marginal productivity. This theory suggested that as an economy grew, additional resources would add less and less to total output. Thomas Robert Malthus is best known for his dismal predictions about the race between population and the food supply. He saw population growth as the surest way to slow down or even reverse the growth of per capita output and the rise in the standard of living.

Karl Marx as a Development Economist

Karl Marx is best known as the intellectual founder of communism, but he also described a sequence for economic development. Marx saw all society passing through a series of historical stages: (1) primitive society (tribal communism), (2) slavery, (3) feudalism, (4) capitalism, (5) socialism, and, finally, (6) communism. At this final stage, Marx argued, scarcity would no longer exist, and workers would produce without material incentives. His contributions to economic development were in three areas. First, he discussed problems of income distribution as economies developed. Second, he described a pattern of relationship between capitalistic economies and the peripheral nations that is still cited today by Third World critics of the industrial nations. Third, the Soviet model of Marxism has been copied by a number of less developed countries as a development strategy.

Marx and his early followers predicted that a class struggle would emerge between the workers (the proletariat) and the capitalists. According to the labor theory of value, widely held among economists in the early nineteenth century, capitalists would pay workers only the minimum amount necessary to subsist. Wages would always tend toward the subsistence level because capitalists, seeking to maximize profits, would pay the minimum amount necessary. Marx labeled the difference between the value of the goods produced by labor and the subsistence wage the workers received **surplus value**. This surplus value, which accrued to capitalists, represented their exploitation of workers. It was this exploitation, Marx believed, that would eventually lead to the overthrow of capitalism by the workers.

surplus value
The difference between the value of the goods produced by labor and the subsistence wages the workers received.

This prediction did not hold up well in subsequent years. Industrialization did spread throughout the Western world in the aftermath of the Industrial Revolution. However, the pattern of capitalist exploitation of the working masses did not emerge. In fact, the material well-being of workers increased rapidly with spreading industrialization.

Marx's second contribution, a view of the relationship between the capitalistic countries and the Third World, was closely related to his view of income distribution. With workers living at the subsistence level, markets for the products of capitalism would have to be found in other countries. The capitalist machine would also need the foodstuffs and raw materials from the Third World. By keeping Third World countries dependent on the capitalist nations for manufactured goods and exploiting their agriculture, capitalists could siphon off income and wealth from them.

Although this view of the relationship between developed and less developed countries is simplistic, many citizens in less developed countries continue to believe it. However, keep in mind that, according to the theory of comparative advantage, both parties are better off as a result of specialization and trade. Contacts with the developed world have brought new methods, ideas, products, capital, and opportunities to the Third

World. The relationship is much less one-sided than Marx would have us believe.

The third, more indirect, contribution of Marx was to encourage a socialist, state-directed approach to development to avoid the supposed evils of capitalism. Marxist ideas continue to hold sway in a decreasing number of nations today, including Cuba, Albania, Angola, and China. These countries have nationalized the means of production in order to ensure that economic growth is for the benefit of the workers rather than capitalists. To date, these nations have had little success in accelerating growth. Some countries have engaged in land reform under the umbrella of Marxism. Large land holdings have been broken up in order to create co-operative farms or give small holdings to the peasants. These co-operative farms have generally shown low productivity because workers have little incentive to produce. The distribution of land to peasants (private ownership) has generally been more successful in increasing output.

W. W. Rostow: The Stages of Economic Growth

W. W. Rostow, in a book entitled *Stages of Economic Growth*, responded to Marx's theory with a different development theory in the same historical tradition.[7] Based on the experience of the modern industrial countries, Rostow argues that all countries go through five stages of economic growth. He believes that it is possible to classify countries according to their current stage. This classification enables researchers to look for the barriers that have kept some countries from advancing into the next stage in their development process.

The first stage is the traditional society, in which economic decisions are made on the basis of custom and obligation. The second stage develops the preconditions for takeoff. In this stage, cultural barriers to development are overcome, advances in agriculture take place, and an entrepreneurial class of risk takers begins to emerge. Takeoff is the third stage, during which there is a large increase in the rate of saving. Increased saving finances capital investment in the leading sectors (the industries that are developing most quickly). The leading sectors grow rapidly, and their growth pulls other sectors along. The takeoff is, of course, the key to emerging as an industrialized country. The Industrial Revolution in Western Europe and the United States marks the takeoff in these countries.

The final two stages are the drive to maturity and high mass consumption. During the drive to maturity, lagging sectors of the economy catch up to the leading sectors. The takeoff is consolidated into sustained growth. The fifth stage, high mass consumption, describes the present level of development in the United States and Western Europe. In this stage, the economy settles into a steady pace of growth that provides a high level of consumption for most members of the society.

Rostow's theory of stages implies that all countries follow a (roughly) similar path to development. Critics of the theory have pointed out that although the stages might describe the development process of the pres-

---

7. W. W. Rostow, *Stages of Economic Growth*, 2nd ed. (New York: Cambridge University Press, 1971).

ent industrialized nations, the present less developed countries will not necessarily follow the same sequence. The dualism in the typical less developed country, for example, makes it very different from seventeenth-century England, where the level of technological development was similar in all sectors of the economy.

Economist Simon Kuznets, a Nobel Prize winner, has pointed out that there are many differences between conditions in today's less developed countries and the preindustrial phase of today's developed countries.[8] Among the most important of these differences is agricultural production. Per capita agricultural output in today's less developed countries is about one-fourth the level it was in preindustrial stages of the present developed countries. Another significant difference is that population is still growing much more rapidly in less developed countries than it was in today's developed countries at a similar stage in their development. Social and political obstacles are also more formidable in many less developed countries. Thus, some of the preconditions are not yet met in the majority of less developed countries, and little progress is being made in getting ready for takeoff.

THE BIG PUSH STRATEGY

Broad theories are less helpful in prescribing policies than specific strategies are. One specific approach is the **big push strategy**. It calls for a major thrust on all fronts in the economy by government or by private enterprise with the government's support. This strategy is based on the classical notion that growth in the output of an industry is limited by the extent of the market. At low levels of economic development, it is futile for any one industry to expand its output to a larger scale. It would be unable to sell its added product. But if all industries expand in a big push, the inputs needed for the production of one commodity become the demands for other industries' output. Also, the incomes generated will create a large demand for the final products. The big push must be orchestrated by the government, its proponents argue, because no single entrepreneur or group of entrepreneurs has the incentive to expand production unless there is expansion in other industries at the same time.

big push strategy
The development strategy calling for a major thrust on all fronts in the economy by government or by private enterprise with government inducement.

THE LEADING SECTORS STRATEGY

Albert O. Hirschman, a development economist with a great deal of field experience, takes a different tack from the big push strategy.[9] Hirschman supports a **leading sectors strategy** for economic growth. He argues that a country should concentrate on developing successful sectors that will then influence other sectors in the chain of production through backward and forward linkages.

For example, if there is a successful sardine fishing industry, it could be linked forward to a canning operation, which in turn could be linked forward to a packing and shipping industry. Backward linkages could develop effective demand for cans and shipping cartons, stimulating a min-

leading sectors strategy
The development strategy calling for concentration on a few successful sectors, which will then pull along other sectors in the development process.

---

8.   Simon Kuznets, *Economic Growth and Structure* (New York: W. W. Norton, 1965).
9.   Albert O. Hirschman, *The Strategy of Economic Development* (New Haven, CT: Yale University Press, 1958).

ing industry and a paper industry. In this view, if the government is to be involved in the development process, it should concentrate its efforts on encouraging those sectors or industries that maximize the number of potential linkages. Private entrepreneurs would then take over in response to the demand created through the linkages. The role of the government would be limited. The market would play the primary role in allocating productive resources.

GOVERNMENT AND THE DEVELOPMENT PROCESS

The theories and strategies just discussed prescribe a variety of roles for government. The Marxist extreme calls for state ownership of resources and direction of production. Adam Smith would recommend a *laissez-faire* approach. The big push strategy calls for a strong government role. The leading sectors approach relies more on the private sector.

Development policies of some less developed countries and policies advocated by some development economists call for governments to direct the development process. Many of these views grew out of the experience of the 1930s and 1940s, when the Soviet Union was able to grow very rapidly by applying severe authoritarian techniques.[10] As a result of the apparent Soviet success, some economists began to argue like this:

No policy of economic development can be carried out unless the government has the capacity to adhere to it. . . . Quite often, however, democratic governments lose equanimity and determination in the face of opposition. . . . This is the dilemma of most democratic governments. It is here that socialist countries . . . have an immense advantage: their totalitarian structure shields the government from the rigorous and reactionary judgments of the electorate. . . . Another advantage of the socialist countries is their passionate conviction and dedication to the objective of economic growth—which contrasts visibly with the halting and hesitant beliefs and actions of most democracies. The firm and purposive sense of direction . . . is in pointed contrast to the extensive revisions and changes in policies and methods which are prompted by minor setbacks in most democratic governments and which produce a sense of drift and helplessness. The political economy of development appears to pose a cruel choice between rapid (self-sustained) expansion and democratic processes.[11]

The idea that development requires authoritarian leadership has been dealt a severe blow by recent events in Eastern Europe and by troubles in the Soviet economy. However, this notion was challenged earlier in an empirical study by U.S. government economist G. William Dick.[12] He divided the independent less developed countries into three classifications: authoritarian, semicompetitive, and competitive. An authoritarian country is headed by one political party. A competitive country has two or more political parties competing for power, with free elections at regular intervals. A semicompetitive country has one majority party and several mi-

10. This drastic approach to development is sometimes called the Stalinist model.
11. Jagdish Bhagwati, *The Economies of Underdeveloped Countries* (New York: McGraw-Hill, 1966), pp. 203–204.
12. G. William Dick, "Authoritarian versus Nonauthoritarian Approaches to Economic Development," *Journal of Political Economy* (July/August 1974).

nority parties or one political party that conducts legitimizing elections. In any case, there is much less extensive control of individual choices in a semicompetitive country than in an authoritarian country. Dick examined the growth rates of real per capita GDP in each of the less developed countries. He found that the authoritarian countries generally had lower growth rates than the competitive countries. Growth is a complex process that cannot be reduced to a single factor, but the main lesson of Dick's empirical study is that rapid growth and democracy may be linked.

Most approaches to development are at neither the totalitarian nor the *laissez-faire* extreme. Government is usually expected to play some role. One important role it can play is to create a set of taxes and regulations that is favorable to development of private enterprise. Another important role for government is the development of human capital through health and education. Government also needs to provide infrastructure, such as roads, water systems, and airports. Finally, it is important for government not to become an obstacle to development by dissipating scarce and valuable resources on political goals or as favors to special interest groups.

PROPERTY RIGHTS AND DEVELOPMENT

Although there are no definitive theories of development, there is ample evidence that private ownership of property and competition can play important roles. Private property, the ability to buy and sell and exchange the products of one's labor, is an essential condition for individual incentives to work, save, invest, and take risks. When governments restrict property rights, they can reduce these work and investment incentives, slowing the economic growth process. (We discussed the role of private property and property rights in Chapter 2 when the stage was being set for the study of economics.)

Governments influence the amount of competition that exists. Government monopolies, or government-sponsored monopolies, can prevent competition from developing. Monopolies have less incentive to expand output, innovate, or take risks because there are no competitors nipping at their heels. Many African countries that were formerly under British rule inherited colonial policies that created government monopolies in many export industries, licensing of private sector producers, and state enterprises that spawned huge bureaucracies. With established public monopolies, or government-created private monopolies, it is difficult to create the kind of competitive environment in which economic growth is more likely to take place.

A 1988 study by Gerald Scully explored the role of the economic and political environment in development. Scully classified 115 economies on the basis of political rights, individual rights, and use of a free market. He found that those that most strongly emphasized political and individual rights and the use of markets had been growing at a rate 2.7 times as fast as those that did not.[13] Thus, the institutions of democratic capitalism appear to make a significant contribution to the development process.

---

13. Gerald W. Scully, "The Institutional Framework and Economic Development," *Journal of Political Economy*, 1988, 96(3): 652–662.

MILITARY SPENDING AND DEVELOPMENT

The war in the Persian Gulf in early 1991 was a dramatic reminder of another obstacle to development. In many less developed countries, a large share of public expenditure is diverted into military uses. Several African countries have been fighting guerrilla wars for a long time. Other ongoing battles are in Sri Lanka, the Philippines, and Central America. Iraq and Iran ended a long and bloody conflict not long before Iraq invaded Kuwait. The result of the Gulf War has been a sharp drop in both population and income for Iraq and Kuwait. It will take a long time to rebuild infrastructure and restore levels of output in both those countries.

According to the World Bank, world military expenditures in the 1980s accounted for about 5 percent of total world income. Developing countries spent $173 billion on defense in 1987, which accounted for 5.1 percent of GNP and 19.2 percent of central government budgets in those countries.[14] Defense takes a much larger share of GNP in some countries. Pakistan, with a per capita GNP of only $350, spends 6.4 percent of GNP on defense. Yemen spends almost 10 percent.

In addition to the absolute amount of resources used, another problem created by defense spending in less developed countries is that much of that spending is for imported arms. These imports use scarce foreign exchange needed in industrial and agricultural development. Even if these countries do not actually go to war, their military spending is taking resources badly needed in other sectors. If military spending increases the likelihood of war, there is an additional potential loss of lives and infrastructure.

THE ROLE OF DEVELOPMENT ASSISTANCE

Still another role for government in development is a flow of economic aid from governments of already developed countries. The United States and Canada received substantial aid, both public and private, in their earliest days. Israel is often cited as a modern-day developmental miracle. It has received massive infusions of foreign capital of all kinds—physical, financial, and human. Japan and the Soviet Union, on the other hand, developed almost in isolation. Thus, although aid can be helpful, it apparently is not essential to development.[15]

Agency for International Development (AID)
An agency that is part of the U.S. State Department and is in charge of U.S. aid to foreign countries.

The United States concentrates its official development assistance through the **Agency for International Development (AID)**, which is part of the State Department and is in charge of U.S. aid to foreign countries. A publication of AID states:

Programs to assist these people reflect an American tradition of sharing and helping the needy as well as enlightened national self-interest. In part, foreign aid is an expression of the American people's sense of justice and compassion. It also plays an important role in the continuing effort to achieve an enduring structure of world peace. This role is essential to the quest for global tranquility, freedom and progress. There are many things, however, that foreign aid cannot do. Experience has shown that it cannot right all social wrongs or solve every economic problem in

14. World Bank, *World Development Report 1990* (New York: Oxford University Press, 1990), p. 17.
15. Agency for International Development, *AID's Challenge in an Interdependent World* (Washington, DC: Office of Public Affairs, 1978), p. 3.

A report published in 1987 by The Overseas Development Council describes the attitudes of U.S. citizens toward economic development and U.S. development assistance.[a] This very comprehensive survey was carried out by the Strategic Information Research Corporation and turned up some surprising conclusions. Here are the pollsters' findings:

- Americans are aware of the problems of poverty and underdevelopment that face the Third World and do not believe that much progress has been made in improving Third World living conditions over the last decade.
- Americans have strong negative perceptions of Third World *governments*, but not of the *people* of those countries.
- A majority of Americans favor U.S. efforts to assist Third World countries with development.
- Policy makers perceive public support for U.S. economic assistance to be weak and fluctuating.
- Most Americans are poorly informed about U.S. foreign policy, the Third World, development issues, and U.S. relations with developing countries.
- Most Americans are aware in very general terms of the existence of economic relationships between the United States and the Third World and believe such relationships to hold potential mutual benefits.
- The perceived tradeoff between promoting *domestic* well-being and helping those *overseas* limits public support for specific U.S. trade, aid, and financial policies to promote Third World growth or alleviate poverty.

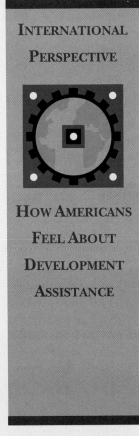

INTERNATIONAL PERSPECTIVE

HOW AMERICANS FEEL ABOUT DEVELOPMENT ASSISTANCE

- Most Americans recognize that the United States has political or strategic interests in the Third World, but many are concerned about U.S. overinvolvement in the affairs of developing countries.
- The major reason for public support for economic assistance is a humanitarian concern or a sense of responsibility. Economic or political self-interest rationales are generally less compelling.
- Americans consider economic assistance a legitimate tool to use in pursuing U.S. political or strategic objectives, but they are concerned that this result is not always achieved.
- In some cases, public preferences about the U.S. aid program appear to be at odds with official policy.
- Americans express a strong preference for those types of U.S. economic aid aimed at delivering help directly to poor people.
- Economic aid is widely perceived to be ineffective or wasted. However, this opinion does not dissuade many Americans from supporting assistance efforts.
- The American public makes little distinction between private and official aid.
- A small—but not insignificant—proportion of Americans have been personally involved in efforts to eliminate poverty and stimulate development in the Third World. A larger active constituency may, however, exist.
- Personal experience or personal approaches are most likely to motivate Americans to become actively involved in efforts to promote development or to alleviate poverty in Third World countries.

a. Christine Contee, *What Americans Think: Views on Development and U.S.–Third World Relations* (New York: InterAction and The Overseas Development Council, 1987).

a developing country. It cannot bring about instant progress. Some economists even claim that it has not been very effective in promoting economic development. Economic aid must be considered as a complement to other elements of foreign policy.[16]

The United States is a major contributor to the development programs of low-income countries. In 1988, the United States contributed 24 percent of all the aid given by Western industrialized countries and gave far more than any one of the other countries. However, as a percentage of GNP, thirteen countries gave a much larger share to low-income countries than the 0.25 percent contributed by the United States. France, for example, gave more than 1 percent of GNP to development aid.

At the end of the 1980s, pressures for renewed and expanded foreign aid came mainly from the fledgling democracies of Eastern Europe. They looked to the West for aid in rebuilding their economies. East Germany received aid mainly from West Germany before and after reunification. Poland, Hungary, Romania, and Czechoslovakia looked to Japan, the United States, Canada, and Western Europe for equipment, technical assistance, and other forms of aid.

The New International Economic Order

New International Economic Order (NIEO) A proposal by the Group of 77 calling for changes in international economic institutions to redistribute income from richer nations to poorer nations through trade preferences, increased aid, and other measures.

Economic aid and trade are two of the major issues underlying a call by many Third World countries for a **New International Economic Order (NIEO)**. This proposal calls for a change in international economic institutions in order to redistribute income from richer nations to poorer nations. In particular, it calls for developed nations to assume more responsibility for speeding up the development process.

The NIEO was proposed by a group of less developed countries in the United Nations called the Group of 77. Among its proposals were increased foreign aid and preferential tariff treatment and reduced regulations to allow less developed countries to export more to the developed nations. It also proposes that developed nations support price stabilization programs for tropical agricultural products, much like the farm price support programs in the United States and Europe. To this point, the success of the NIEO has been small. One outcome has been increased attention to the problems of less developed countries in trade negotiations in the 1970s and the 1980s.

Help from the Private Sector: Multinationals

In addition to aid from government to government, many countries' development efforts benefit from direct foreign investment by private firms and individuals, which supply scarce capital. Both private loans and multinational corporations (MNCs) transfer capital to these countries. Private loans have contributed to the debt problem, discussed later in this chapter.

A multinational corporation is a firm with headquarters in one country and one or more branch plants in other countries. Multinational corporations are headquartered in every developed, industrial country and a few less developed ones. Most of them have their branch plants in in-

---

16. The debate over the effectiveness of economic aid is summarized in Robert Cassin et al., *Does Aid Work? Report to an Intergovernmental Task Force* (New York: Oxford University Press, 1986). This report, written for the World Bank, provides some good data and a review of the arguments.

dustrial countries. There has been a foreign corporate presence in most less developed countries at least since World War II, and in many cases going back to the beginning of the century.

The impact of multinational corporations on development is hotly disputed. Multinational corporations often choose locations in less developed countries for access to raw materials or to local and regional markets for products they cannot easily export from home, because of either distance, perishability, or trade barriers. They do bring in capital, provide job opportunities, and increase foreign exchange. However, the good jobs are often filled by foreign nationals, not local workers. A multinational corporation may have no meaningful linkages to the rest of the host economy. It will then fail to act as a leading sector that spreads development to other sectors. A multinational corporation may be the largest taxpayer, largest export earner, and major employer in a small country. Thus, it may wield more real power than the host government. Multinational corporations can play a useful role in economic development. Any benefit they bring, however, may not be enough to overcome the many obstacles that developing nations face.

One of the major concerns about multinational corporations is that they tend to transplant technology developed in their home country, usually a nation with abundant capital and skilled labor, but scarce unskilled labor. Critics point out that these firms rarely adapt their methods of production to make the best use of local resources. This process is called technology adaptation, and its result is **appropriate technology**. In addition, they do not usually make their technology available to other companies in related fields in the less developed countries. Thus, there are none of the linkage effects necessary to promote development.

appropriate technology Methods of production that have been adapted to take advantage of the mix of resources available in less developed countries.

TIME BOMBS IN THE DEVELOPMENT PATH

There are two major problems that developing countries must address. The first is control of population growth. The second is the huge debt that many of them have compiled in recent years.

THE POPULATION BOMB

As you saw earlier in this chapter, even countries experiencing economic growth can see their per capita income decline if their population is growing at a faster rate than income. Yet discussions of managing population growth are very sensitive. Many countries regard foreign advice concerning birth rates as inappropriate.

In 1800, the world's population is estimated to have been about 1 billion. In 1988, it was 5.1 billion. By the year 2000, it will have swelled to 6 billion. The world's population is growing by 250,000 people per day, or 90 million people per year. The problem for development is that more than 90 percent of that projected growth will occur in the less developed countries.

Table 5 shows estimates of expected populations and population growth rates for the world's most populous countries. It is important to note that no developed industrial country can be found in the list of countries with rapid population growth.

FASTEST-GROWING NATIONS	POPULATION IN 2000 (MILLIONS)	AVERAGE ANNUAL GROWTH RATE, 1987–2000 (%)	SLOWEST-GROWING NATIONS	POPULATION IN 2000 (MILLIONS)	AVERAGE ANNUAL GROWTH RATE, 1988–2000 (%)
Oman	2	3.9	Hungary	10	–0.2
Rwanda	10	3.8	West Germany	61	0.0
Ivory Coast	18	3.8	Denmark	5	0.0
Yemen Arab Republic	13	3.6	Belgium	10	0.0
Jordan	6	3.6	Austria	8	0.1
Libya	6	3.6	Italy	58	0.1
Syria	18	3.6	Greece	10	0.2
Malawi	12	3.5	Finland	5	0.2
Zambia	11	3.5	Ireland	4	0.3
Uganda	24	3.5	Britain	59	0.3
Kenya	34	3.4	Switzerland	7	0.4
Tanzania	37	3.4	Sweden	9	0.4
Iraq	26	3.4	Portugal	11	0.4
Togo	5	3.3	Spain	41	0.4
Congo People's Republic	3	3.3	France	59	0.4
			Japan	129	0.4
Niger	11	3.3	Norway	4	0.4

Source: Adapted from *World Development Report, 1990* (New York: Oxford University Press, 1990). Copyright © 1990 by the International Bank for Reconstruction and Development/The World Bank.

TABLE 5
PROJECTED POPULATIONS AND GROWTH RATES OF FASTEST- AND SLOWEST-GROWING NATIONS

DEFUSING THE POPULATION BOMB. Understanding why populations grow provides a clue to a solution. During the Industrial Revolution in Western Europe and the United States, populations grew rapidly but not at the explosive rates of today's less developed countries. There were somewhat different reasons for those increases. As the standard of living began to rise during the Industrial Revolution, the birth rate increased, and death rates slowly began to decline. After incomes increased to higher levels, the birth rate also declined. Today, medical advances, inoculations, and many life-lengthening techniques have spread throughout the world, reducing death rates even in less developed countries. As a result, those countries have high birth rates and declining death rates and, therefore, an exploding population.

Birth rates didn't decline in the developed world until most countries had attained relatively high levels of per capita income. In most nations, death rates fell first as better health care, better nutrition, and higher standards of living lengthened lifespans. After a time, birth rates fell. A nation that has bridged the developmental gap from falling death rates to falling birth rates, thus slowing population growth and reducing the dependency ratio, has made the **demographic transition**.

demographic transition
The bridging of the developmental gap from falling death rates to falling birth rates, resulting in slower population growth.

Less developed countries are feeling pressure from both within and abroad to try to influence their birth rates even though income levels are still low. In the present developed countries, the demographic transition occurred naturally. Most efforts to deliberately encourage or even enforce population control have occurred in Communist countries, although India has made some strong efforts toward voluntary sterilization and birth control. In China, the Communist authorities have instituted a get-tough campaign that denies many state-supplied benefits to couples with more than one child. This "planned" approach has slowed China's population growth rate to 1.3 percent. It has had many unintended side effects, however, including claims of female infanticide and a very high number of late-term abortions.

POPULATION AND POVERTY. Economists must be careful in their analysis of the problems of overpopulation. After all, the existence of large numbers of people by itself has little to do with poverty. Many stories of famine and the problems of the population explosion are reported from areas of the world such as Africa, by a reporter standing in the middle of the most densely populated city in one of the poorest countries in the world. The implication is clearly that there is a link between population density and poverty. Yet the report will probably be produced in and certainly broadcast from New York City or Washington, D.C., two of the richest *and* most densely populated places on earth. Clearly, people aren't starving because of dense population. They are starving because they are poor. As we saw above, population growth and slow economic growth may be interrelated, but the relationship is not causal. If the less developed countries could speed up economic growth, fast food franchisers would be bidding for prime spots in their large cities.

THE DEBT BOMB

One of the elements of the vicious circle of poverty is a low level of investment. It seems logical, then, that one way to break this circle would be for both the public and private sectors in less developed countries to borrow from the developed world. For many years, the World Bank operated with this goal in mind. The World Bank made low-interest loans to less developed countries to build roads, dams, and power plants. The modest amount of borrowing from private-sector financial institutions was mainly short-term commercial credit and was not viewed as a serious developmental problem.

This pattern began to change in the 1970s, as more and more private banks lent to both governments and private firms to undertake projects in less developed countries. These projects were expected to boost GNP enough to allow the borrowing country to make the interest and principal payments and still be better off.

By 1982, problems had begun to surface. Not all of the loans were being used for capital investment that would generate income to make repayment. Many of the loans went to finance current consumption (especially oil imports) or ill-conceived investment projects. Loans to Mexico were singled out as being used unwisely, because funds often lined the pockets of corrupt politicians. The crisis became apparent in the U.S. banking community. Some banks had made so many risky loans to developing countries that default could lead to bank failure. Some nations were unable to service their debts (to meet scheduled payments of interest and/or principal). As a result, banks were increasingly reluctant to extend or renew existing loans to those countries (to say nothing about making new loans).

By 1987, the total external public debt of Third World countries exceeded $911 billion. Brazil topped the list in debt size, with a total debt of almost $90 billion. Seven countries had annual payments of principal and interest amounting to more than 10 percent of GNP, with Jamaica heading the list at 17 percent. Private debt was large (over $1 billion) in eighteen of the ninety-seven less developed countries. Most of the debt, however, is public sector debt, usually foreign aid loans, for which terms are generally favorable and renegotiable.

There really is only one long-term solution to the Third World debt problem, although it may have several aspects. The solution is that of any debtor: consumption must be cut, and income must be generated to repay the debt. The debtor nations must improve their trade balances to earn income to repay or refinance the loans. This can be done by decreasing imports, allowing more foreign investment, and setting realistic exchange rates. Another solution that has been proposed is a debt-equity swap, whereby debt is exchanged for ownership of local assets. First proposed by American bankers and public officials, the idea was not well received in debtor countries.

Growth in both the debtor nations and the industrial market economies that buy their exports will aid the process of bringing debt under control. As developed nations grow, they demand more imports from the less developed countries. These imports allow the less developed countries to earn foreign currency needed to repay their debt.

In the past few years, negotiations between governments and banks have worked out interim solutions for some of the nations most deeply in debt. Some have worked out agreements for partial or deferred payments. No actual major default has occurred, but banks are increasingly cautious about lending without firmer guarantees of repayment.

A DEVELOPMENT SUCCESS STORY: THE NEW ASIAN TIGERS

The most remarkable story in economic development in recent decades is a group of Asian countries that have been reclassified from less developed countries to newly industrializing countries (NICs). These four countries—Hong Kong, Taiwan, South Korea, and Singapore—have been nicknamed "The Asian Tigers." They have grown rapidly in the last twenty years in a climate of private enterprise, hard work, minimal regulation, and open trade.[17] Two more Asian countries, Thailand and Indonesia, may be repeating the success of the other four.

All four of these nations have seen rapid growth of both GNP and exports with low inflation rates and high employment. There is a consistent pattern of high levels of saving and investment relative to GNP and a strong emphasis on development of exports and export markets. In some ways, all four have followed the Japanese model. In other ways, each of them is unique. What they have in common is average growth rates from 1981 to 1988 ranging from 5.4 to 9.9 percent, per capita GNPs ranging from $3,600 (South Korea) to $9,070 (Singapore), and bright prospects for the future. All of them have deliberately embarked on a strategy involving a strong private sector and a government that plays a supporting rather than directing role in the growth process. These development success stories make a powerful case for a market-oriented approach to development.

17. Lawrence A. Veit, "Time of the New Asian Tigers," *Challenge* (July-August 1987): 49–55.

SUMMARY

1. Less developed countries are characterized by low per capita income, high population growth, dualism, and a large part of productive activity in the agricultural sector. A tropical climate and a culture that is not favorable to economic activity are common in these countries.

2. Low-income countries invest little in human capital, that is, in the health, vigor, and education of the population. An unhealthy and uneducated labor force is relatively unproductive.

3. Marx offered a historical model of economic development in which countries advance through stages from primitive society to communism. He emphasized the role of income distribution and the relationship between capitalistic countries and peripheral countries. He felt that state ownership and control would promote economic development.

4. Rostow's theory of economic development sees each country passing through stages of growth. It is based on how development occurred in the present developed countries.

5. The big push strategy suggests that government can speed the process of economic development through a major coordinated thrust on all fronts of the economy. The leading sectors strategy strongly suggests that if effort is concentrated in some key sectors and linkages are developed, those sectors will pull along the other sectors.

6. The United States has traditionally aided less developed countries. Much U.S. aid is channeled through the Agency for International Development (AID). U.S. aid is large in an absolute sense, but other Western nations contribute a larger share of GNP than does the United States.

7. The New International Economic Order (NIEO) is a call for a new international economic system that gives preference to less developed countries in international trade and involves greater aid from the industrial countries.

8. Multinational corporations also channel capital to less developed countries, but the effects on development are mixed.

9. Population growth creates problems for economic development because of the diversion of resources into caring for those too young or too old to be productive workers.

10. The debt of developing countries is an increasingly serious problem for those countries and for the U.S. banks that have been granting development loans.

11. Evidence from the newly industrializing countries (NICs) of Southeast Asia suggests that market forces are positively linked with economic growth. Government can play an important role in providing infrastructure and investment in human capital.

NEW TERMS

convergence hypothesis
crude birth rate
dependency ratio
crude death rate

vicious circle of poverty
Green Revolution
dualism
surplus value

big push strategy
leading sectors strategy
Agency for International
    Development (AID)

New International
    Economic Order
appropriate technology
demographic transition

QUESTIONS FOR DISCUSSION

1. Does development change the cultural environment or does the cultural environment cause economic development?

2. What role do you think the United States should play in world development?

3. If you were to advise the government of a less developed country on steps to take toward development, what would be your top four priorities? Why?

4. Suppose you visited a less developed country and the local officials told you that they were pursuing a big push strategy instead of a leading sectors strategy. How could you tell if this was true?

5. In recent years, there has been a great deal of television coverage concerning drought and famine in Africa. Is this an agricultural problem or an economic development problem?

6. Why is the study of demographic trends so important in the study of economic development?

7. What is the New International Economic Order (NIEO)? How would it help less developed countries?

8. What do development economists have in mind when they speak of linkages?

9. What is the vicious circle of poverty?

10. What are Rostow's preconditions for takeoff?

11. Suppose you were in charge of development for a less developed country and were approached by a multinational corporation interested in locating in your country. What kinds of concerns might you have?

12. Suppose the multinational corporation in Question 11 was in the business of printing books to ship abroad. What kinds of linkages might be involved?

13. What role should government play in the development process? How does this differ from what governments actually do?

14. Which of the following pieces of data are useful in determining whether countries are less developed countries? Why?

GNP (or GDP)

per capita GNP

population growth rate

death rate

literacy rate

share of GNP derived from agriculture

15. Who are the Asian Tigers and what are they doing right?

SUGGESTIONS FOR FURTHER READING

Bianchi, Andres, Robert Devlin, and Joseph Ramos. *External Debt in Latin America: Adjustment Policies and Renegotiation.* Boulder, CO: The United Nations Economic Commission for Latin America and the Caribbean, 1985. A description of the magnitude of the debt problem with some calm and reasoned solutions.

Hagen, Everett W. *The Economics of Development,* 4th ed. Homewood, IL: Irwin, 1986. A thoughtful and thorough textbook that emphasizes differences in the problems facing the various developing countries.

Kang, T. W. *Is Korea the Next Japan? Understanding the Structure, Strategy, and Tactics of America's Next Competitor.* New York: Free Press, 1989. A book that examines the reasons for Korea's rapid economic development in the 1980s.

McCord, William, and Arline McCord. *Paths to Progress.* New York: W. W. Norton, 1986. Two field sociologists argue that Third World countries must make profound cultural, political, and social changes if they are to experience economic development.

Meier, Gerald (ed.). *Pioneers in Development.* Oxford and New York: Oxford University Press, 1988. Examines major contributions to understanding the process of economic development.

Reynolds, Lloyd G. *Economic Growth in the Third World.* New Haven, CT: Yale University Press, 1985. A book that contains good statistical surveys on forty countries.

Rostow, Walt Whitman. *Rich Countries and Poor Countries: Reflections on the Past, Lessons for the Future.* Boulder, CO: Westview Press, 1987. This collection of essays on the world economy includes some comments on the development process from one of the best-known twentieth-century development economists.

Schumacher, Ernest Friedrich. *Small Is Beautiful: Economics as If People Mattered.* New York: Harper & Row, 1976. A somewhat dated, but still popular book that questions the value of economic growth and stresses the importance of developing appropriate technologies.

DEMAND AND CONSUMER CHOICE

6

1. Calculate the expected cost of a crime given the probability of arrest and conviction and the penalty.
2. Define:
   a. price ceiling,
   b. price floor,
   c. shortage,
   d. surplus,
   e. black market.
3. Diagram the economic effects of:
   a. rent control,
   b. the minimum wage,

CHAPTER 18

APPLICATIONS OF SUPPLY AND DEMAND: THE BASIC MICROECONOMIC TOOLS

   c. price supports in agriculture,
   d. regulation of the price of natural gas.
4. Discuss how markets allocate scarce resources.
5. Describe the effects of natural gas regulation and deregulation.
6. Discuss the economic aspects of the health care crisis.
7. Identify market adjustments that have occurred in the numbers and incomes of physicians.
8. Explain how disasters can be caused by humans or governments instead of being natural.

INTRODUCTION

This chapter makes use of some of the basic microeconomic models and theories developed in the first three chapters. These economic tools can yield profound insights into a variety of social issues. Equipped with these tools of analysis, you can understand such diverse issues as crime, rent control, the minimum wage, the energy crisis, and the effects and causes of natural disasters.

THE ECONOMICS OF CRIME:
USE OF THE SELF-INTEREST ASSUMPTION

We can use one of the assumptions from Chapter 1, the self-interest assumption, to analyze crime and prevention. Assume that criminals are rational people who commit crimes when it is in their self-interest to do so. This type of simplifying assumption bothers some people who argue that some criminals are not rational. Addicts who commit crimes while on drugs are a case in point. Are they rational? Probably not in a psychological sense. Yet, as you will see, this assumption allows us to develop a model with testable implications.

   The critical point for the economic model of crime is whether criminals make decisions to commit more crimes if the cost of committing crimes goes down or is perceived to be lower. The model says that a criminal calculates the costs and benefits of each crime and commits those crimes for which the benefits exceed the costs. The hypothesis is that a criminal calculates costs (C) and benefits (B) of criminal activities and commits those for which B is greater than C. According to this hypothesis, crime is an economic activity, and the criminal behaves like any entrepreneur.

The benefits are what the criminal hopes to realize by the activity. For crimes involving the theft of property, it is relatively easy to place a value on this. The anticipated benefit is the market value of the take. For other crimes such as vandalism, illegal parking, or littering, we have to impute some value to the activity. This value may not be monetary. For example, it may consist of time saved due to parking illegally rather than searching for a legal parking spot.

The cost is the penalty (P) adjusted for the probability (π) that the criminal will be caught and the penalty will be imposed. The penalty for illegal activity is not imposed every time a crime is committed. Thus, adjusting the penalty by the probability of incurring it produces an expected cost of committing the crime. The prospective criminal compares B to $P \times \pi$. For example, suppose the fine for littering is $500, but on the average one will be caught and fined only once every 500 times. The expected cost of littering is then $1 ($500 × $\frac{1}{500}$). The economic model of crime thus suggests that if some people get more than $1 worth of benefit from littering, they will litter.

There are three elements to the simple model just developed. First, the model says that crime depends on the benefits from the activity so, *ceteris paribus*, as the value of those benefits goes up, so will the amount of criminal activity. Second, it says that as the penalty goes down (with no change in the probability of being caught), the criminal activity will increase. Third, it says that if the probability of being caught goes down, *ceteris paribus*, the amount of criminal activity will go up. This simple model can now be applied to crimes more serious than littering, such as armed robbery.

THE ECONOMICS OF ROBBERY

The economic model of crime can be used to advise policy makers on how to decrease the amount of armed robbery. Policy makers have three options. One possibility is to decrease the potential take, or profit. This is difficult to do, but you have probably noticed that most convenience stores and gas stations open late at night advertise that they don't keep much cash on hand. That's one way of reducing the take. Private citizens in New York City have also exercised this option by placing signs reading "no radio" in their parked cars.

The second possibility for reducing robbery is to increase the penalty. In one suburb of Washington, D.C., the local police chief recently announced that squad cars would be equipped with rifles with exploding shells (outlawed by the United Nations as being too inhumane for warfare). In addition, officers had been instructed to shoot first and ask questions later when investigating robberies. Almost immediately, the robbery rate fell in this town and increased in adjacent areas. This result is predicted by the model, which says as the potential penalty rises, criminal activity will fall. Of course, some people object to such a policy even if it does reduce crime. Remember that economic models are positive, not normative. They only indicate what the consequences of a policy will be. They don't say if it's good or bad in a moral sense.

The third option for reducing the robbery rate would be to increase the probability that robbers will be arrested and convicted. This might be accomplished by adding more police, improving the court system, putting television cameras in banks, or other similar measures.

In an economic study of crime, William Trumbull shows that the probability of punishment and the severity of the punishment both have an effect on the crime rate.[1] He shows that the certainty of punishment has a greater deterrent effect than the severity of punishment, but both have significant effects. His research also shows that when the returns to legal activity increase (the outlook for jobs improves), illegal activity declines. Illegal activity is a substitute for regular employment when jobs are scarce.

The Economics of the Death Penalty

The preceding analysis may have led you to conclude that economists would argue that the death penalty deters crime by increasing the expected cost. At least one economist, Isaac Ehrlich, has argued that the death penalty does act to reduce the amount of murder.[2] If you are a doubter, answer this question: Would you ever litter if the probability of getting caught was 1 in 500, and the penalty was death? To answer yes, you would have to place a high value on being able to litter or a low value on your own life. However, some people argue that murderers have such a distorted view of reality that they underestimate the probability of being caught, convicted, and sentenced to death. These people argue that the death penalty provides little deterrence. More importantly, just because positive economic theory says that the death penalty deters crime, that does not mean that you, or anyone else, has to support the death penalty if you object on moral (normative) grounds. You can still be opposed to the death penalty on humanitarian grounds even if you accept the implications of the model.

The Economics of Illegal Parking

Some of you may still be skeptical about this simple economic model of crime. Let's apply it to an action that you have probably committed or at least thought about committing—illegal parking on campus. On almost all college campuses, the quantity of parking spaces supplied is less than the quantity demanded at a zero price. As a result, there are benefits to parking in an illegal space. Suppose the fine for illegal parking is $10, and you find from experience that you get a ticket one out of every four times you park illegally. The expected cost of the crime is thus $2.50 ($10 × ¼). It is difficult to estimate the benefits that accrue to those who park illegally. Since there are many violators, however, it's clear that those benefits are substantial. Assume that you are appointed to a committee formed by the college president to solve the parking problem. Using the simple economic model, your committee identifies three options: (1) The college

---

1.   William N. Trumbull, "Estimations of the Economic Model of Crime Using Aggregate and Individual Level Data," *Southern Economic Journal* (October 1989): 423–439.
2.   Isaac Ehrlich, "The Deterrent Effect of Capital Punishment: A Question of Life and Death," *American Economic Review* (June 1975).

Gary Becker has extended the application of microeconomic theory into many areas that had been considered noneconomic. He has examined criminal behavior as the result of rational economic calculation and the selection of a spouse as an exercise in the demand for characteristics that have an economic dimension. He has also examined racial discrimination, the decision to have children, time allocation, and the pursuit of education as an investment decision.[a] His ideas about crime prevention came to him when he was rushing to a student presentation at Columbia University and couldn't find a parking place. His thoughts went to the costs, the benefits, and the probability of being caught if he parked illegally. This "intellectual flash" formed the basis for his work on crime prevention.

Becker presently teaches at the University of Chicago. He has also been on the faculty at Columbia University. He received his undergraduate education at Princeton University and his Ph.D. degree from the University of Chicago. In 1967, Becker received the John Bates Clark Award, which is awarded by the American Economic Association to an outstanding economist under forty years old. Gary Becker is a good bet to eventually win a Nobel Prize in economics.

ECONOMIC PROFILE

GARY BECKER

1930–

a.   See Gary Becker, *The Economic Approach to Human Behavior* (Chicago: University of Chicago Press, 1976), *The Economics of Discrimination* (Chicago: University of Chicago Press, 1957), *Human Capital*, 2nd ed. (New York: Columbia University Press, 1975), *Essays in the Economics of Crime and Punishment*, with W. M. Landes (New York: Columbia University Press, 1974), and *A Treatise on the Family* (Cambridge, MA: Harvard University Press, 1981).

could lower the benefits of illegal parking by buying shuttle buses to transport students from parking areas to the classroom buildings. (2) The college could increase the likelihood of being caught by hiring more police and increasing the number of times they check the parking areas. (3) The college could raise the cost of the crime by having illegally parked cars towed away. This last solution raises the cost of the crime in two ways. Violators would have to pay towing fees in addition to the parking fine. Also, getting towed involves a great deal of time and trouble.

If you still don't think the model works, there is an empirical test you can carry out. Observe the amount of illegal parking on your campus on a nice sunny day. Then the next time it rains, observe that activity again. What does the model predict? On rainy days, the benefits of the crime go up, *ceteris paribus*; they include being closer to class plus arriving in class dry. The probability of being caught also goes down, *ceteris paribus*, because campus police don't like to get wet either. The model thus predicts that there will be more illegal parking on rainy days. Check it out—test the model!

THE ECONOMICS OF BASKETBALL "CRIME"

Economists Robert E. McCormick and Robert D. Tollison applied a similiar economic model for criminal activity to the game of basketball.[3] They picked college basketball as a subject of analysis because there is a great deal of data available and the number of referees (police) increased from two to three in 1978. Their empirical test showed that increasing the number of officials from two to three caused the number of fouls (crimes) to decline.

PRICE CEILINGS AND PRICE FLOORS

price ceilings
Upper limits on prices imposed by a governmental unit. The ceiling is a price that cannot be exceeded.

Chapter 3 described how free markets reach equilibrium. It is possible for this market process to be interfered with. Such interference is usually the result of governmental action. **Price ceilings** are upper limits on prices imposed by a governmental unit. The ceiling is a price that cannot be exceeded. **Price floors** are minimum limits on prices established by a governmental unit. The floor is a minimum price that cannot be undercut. Price ceilings and price floors disrupt the market-clearing process. Microeconomic tools make it possible to see the effects of these disruptions.

price floors
Minimum limits on prices established by a governmental unit. The floor is a price that cannot be undercut.

PRICE CEILINGS

A price ceiling that is set below the equilibrium price prevents the market from clearing. The amount that consumers wish to purchase at the imposed price is greater than the amount suppliers are willing to supply at that price. Figure 1 demonstrates this problem. In Figure 1, the equilibrium price is P_e and equilibrium quantity is Q_e. The government imposes a price ceiling at P_c. The amount that consumers wish to consume at price P_c is Q_d. The amount suppliers are willing to supply at that price is Q_s. The result is a shortage.

shortage
The amount by which the quantity consumers wish to purchase at some price exceeds the quantity suppliers wish to supply at that price. A shortage can occur on a lasting basis only when a price ceiling is in effect.

A **shortage** exists when the amount that consumers wish to purchase at

3.   Robert E. McCormick and Robert D. Tollison, "Crime on the Court," *Journal of Political Economy* (April 1984): 223–235.

some price exceeds the amount suppliers wish to supply. A shortage can occur on a lasting basis only when a price ceiling is in effect. It is important to realize that the shortage is caused by the ceiling. Without the ceiling, the price would rise. The quantity demanded would decrease and the quantity supplied would increase until the price reached P_e and the market cleared.

If a price ceiling is to be maintained, government officials must replace the market with some other way of allocating the good or service. Consumers will be frustrated as they try to obtain the good or service at the lower price. Some means other than price must be used to determine who will get the available supply of the good or service. The means might be ration coupons, a first-come, first-served rule, or other nonmarket allocating mechanism. Nonmarket methods of allocation waste resources in unproductive activities as consumers attempt to obtain goods in roundabout ways. People might spend hours waiting in line for goods that are priced below market-clearing prices, or they might invest resources in political activity aimed at gaining an advantage in the allocation scheme.

This allocation problem was common in the planned economies of the Soviet Union and Eastern Europe before the recent reforms. Price ceilings were maintained on many consumer goods. There were shortages of these goods and long lines of consumers waiting for a chance to purchase. Consumers would often get into any line when they saw it developing, knowing that a line meant there was some scarce product available.

In almost all cases where price ceilings are imposed, black markets spring up. **Black markets** are markets in which people illegally buy and sell goods or services at prices above government-imposed price ceilings.[4] We'll have more to say about black markets later.

black markets
Markets in which people illegally buy and sell goods and services at prices above government-imposed price ceilings.

---

4. You should be able to show why a price ceiling that is imposed *above* the equilibrium price has no noticeable effect on the market.

rent control
A price ceiling imposed
by a governmental unit
on housing rents.

RENT CONTROL. Price ceilings are used by various levels of government. Let's look at the effect of price ceilings on apartment rentals.

The governments of many cities, including New York City and Washington, D.C., have imposed price ceilings on apartment rents. This kind of ceiling, imposed by governmental units, is referred to as **rent control**. At first glance, the goal of rent control seems admirable. This goal is to keep rents low so that everyone, including those who are poor, can find a place to live at a reasonable price. To see the effect of rent control, refer again to Figure 1. At a price less than the market-clearing price, there will be a shortage of rental units. More people will be looking for rental units than the number of units available. Something other than market forces will determine who gets the rental units. Landlords may impose criteria for prospective tenants because, for any vacancy, there will be a number of people eager to rent the apartment. Without rent control, a landlord is more likely to rent to any prospective tenant rather than leave the apartment vacant, because the market is clearing. With rent control, the landlord can choose from the backlog of prospective tenants. The landlord can exclude those who are young (or old) or those who have pets or children. Since landlords cannot raise rents, they will instead choose tenants who seem likely to cost the least in terms of damage, noise, complaints, or hassles. Interference in the market has replaced impartial market forces with a system that encourages discrimination.

Rent control, like many other governmental intrusions into the market, has outcomes other than those intended by the well-meaning politicians who advocate them. This is certainly true of rent-controlled housing in New York. Some of the richest members of society gain from rent control, and some of the poorest are left with no housing. Donald Trump reports in his book that the actress Mia Farrow had a rent-controlled apartment for $2,000 per month that would have had a market rent of about $10,000 per month.[5] Trump thought that the most notorious example of the inequity of rent control is that Ed Koch, former mayor of New York City, has a very nice three-bedroom apartment with a terrace in a beautiful part of Greenwich Village, for $350 per month. The market rent would be close to $1,800 per month.

Rent control laws live on even though their effects are apparent. A case study of the experience in Santa Monica, California shows the political appeal of rent control. Santa Monica enacted rent control in 1979. The city rolled back rents and limited increases to about two-thirds of the increase in the Consumer Price Index. The original law was promoted by politician Tom Hayden (former husband of Jane Fonda) as a way to preserve the existing population mix, which included large numbers of blacks, Hispanics, the elderly, and low-income families. Since 1979, many apartment complexes have been abandoned by their owners, who would rather have them vacant than rent them at the controlled rents. Abandoned rent-controlled apartments sit adjacent to homes selling for more than $500,000. The problem is made worse by the fact that the owners of the abandoned apartment buildings find it very difficult to sell. Many want to

5.   Donald J. Trump (with Tony Schwartz), *Trump: The Art of the Deal* (New York: Warner Books, 1987), pp. 255–256.

tear down the buildings and build new office or residential space. But the city passed a law to prevent such reconstruction. In order to tear down any rental unit, the owner must pay to build replacement units in the city. One apartment owner had his building spray-painted with the words "We want perestroika now."

The irony of the situation in Santa Monica is that the rent-controlled units have become a haven for rich young professionals. The parking lots outside these $350-per-month, two-bedroom apartments are filled with BMWs and Audis. The population mix that Tom Hayden wanted to preserve has not been preserved. So why isn't the law being changed? Perhaps the fact that 75 percent of the voters of Santa Monica are tenants offers a hint.[6]

These examples show the impacts of rent control on the distribution of income and the production of new housing. The short-run effects of rent control are mainly distributional. Landlords in rent-controlled areas choose to rent to richer tenants because they may cause fewer problems and "know the right people" to get in. In the long run, fewer housing units are built and the existing stock of housing units deteriorates.

BLACK MARKETS. As mentioned earlier, black markets tend to develop when price ceilings are imposed. In Santa Monica, it has been reported that "key money," up-front payments of up to $5,000, was required of some prospective tenants. This practice was one form of black market.

Assume that Figure 2 represents the market for tickets to one of the biggest college football games of the year, the Orange Bowl. The stock of tickets is completely fixed in the short run because the stadium has a seating capacity of 70,000. The athletic departments of the two colleges are selling the tickets at a price ceiling of $20 per ticket. For this game, the market-clearing price would be $30. The price ceiling creates a shortage of 30,000 tickets. At that price, there is going to be a larger quantity of tickets demanded than exist. The athletic departments have to allocate

Price/Ticket

FIGURE 2
THE ORANGE BOWL
A price ceiling is often imposed by universities in selling tickets to popular events. If such a price ceiling is below the market-clearing price, it creates a black market for the underpriced tickets.

6. See Marc Beauchamp, "Bankrupt Landlords in Wonderland," *Forbes* (20 March 1989): 105–107.

During World War II, the U.S. government tried to control the prices of some basic commodities, such as gasoline and sugar. Ration tickets were distributed to determine who got the limited supplies. These ration tickets were sold on black markets. Since governments at all levels in the United States usually refrain from trying to set price ceilings, there has been little black market activity in the United States except for that episode. About the only direct experience you might have with a black market is the scalping of tickets to athletic events and concerts.

However, you may be aware of black markets that exist in other countries. One important black market is in currencies. Many countries attempt to control the price of their currency in terms of other currencies. Economists refer to this price as the exchange rate. Attempts to control the exchange rate always produce black markets for foreign currencies. If you went before 1990 to Eastern Europe, the Soviet Union, or some parts of Asia, you were probably approached on the street by furtive individuals who wanted to exchange their currency for dollars at a much better exchange rate than any bank provides.

Currency exchange is not the only kind of black market exchange abroad. You have probably heard stories about the black market for jeans in the Soviet Union. If you travel to the Soviet Union, pack a couple pair of extra jeans so you can finance part of your trip out of all the rubles you can get for them on the black market. But don't get caught!

INTERNATIONAL

PERSPECTIVE

BLACK MARKETS

Governments usually attempt to control a broad range of prices during and after wars. This effort is made more difficult by the fact that consumer goods are usually more scarce at those times. Equilibrium prices would therefore be rising rapidly while the government was trying to control them. Perhaps the extreme examples of such controls happened in Germany and Japan after World War II.

In both Germany and Japan following World War II, there were enormous national debts that were financed by monetary expansion. These large increases in the money supply led to severe inflation. At the same time, the governments of these countries imposed strict controls on food prices, even rationing the caloric intake of individuals. These strict controls led to black markets and the phenomenon of "trekking." Urban residents would leave town to go to the countryside to make black market deals with farmers. The stricter the controls, the more the trekking grew. It was reported that on one day more than 900,000 residents of Tokyo left town for the countryside. In Germany, the controls came to an end with the Erhard reforms of 1948. With the end of controls, the incentive to trek evaporated. As with most economic forces, there was a secondary effect. Railroad passenger traffic in Germany fell immediately to less than 40 percent of the prereform level. This drop in rail traffic was evidence of the volume of the trekking that had been taking place.

Sources: Jerome B. Cohen, *Japan's Economy in War and Reconstruction* (Minneapolis: University of Minnesota Press, 1949); and Lucius C. Clay, *Decision in Germany* (New York: Doubleday, Inc., 1950).

the tickets by some other means than the market. Tickets will be sold to those fans who are willing to wait in line or those who donate to the booster club. The shortage of tickets will produce a black market. Some of those who are able to get the tickets for $20 will be willing to sell them. These people will engage in black market activity by selling their tickets to those who are willing to pay more.

Black marketers dealing in tickets to sports or entertainment events are referred to as scalpers. Scalping generally has a bad connotation. But consider that a scalper is performing the service of transferring tickets from people who value other goods more highly than they value the tickets to people who value the tickets more highly than other goods. Thus, the scalper is being paid for performing a service. In most states, scalping has been outlawed. In Texas, it is legal and organized reselling of tickets takes place. In Washington, D.C., it is illegal to resell tickets—even at prices below the original price!

Why Ceilings? If price ceilings are so disruptive, why do they exist? One answer is that not all people are hurt by ceilings. Those who are able to purchase the good or service at the artificially low price are better off. As a result, they approve of the ceiling. For example, people who already have an apartment and don't want to move would be better off with rent control. These people would probably vote for rent control because it would make them better off. Also, those who don't mind waiting in line or those who get tickets because they are team boosters like low ticket prices.

It is important to realize that price ceilings do not generally help the poor. If there is one $20 ticket left for the big game, who do you think will get it? A poor fan who likes football more than anything else $20 would buy, or the governor who thinks it would be good politics to be seen at the game? Whenever the market is replaced, another mechanism must be substituted to allocate goods. This mechanism usually depends heavily on power and influence. Thus, the poor are not generally helped by price ceilings.

Price Floors

A price floor that is set above the equilibrium price keeps the market from clearing. The amount that suppliers offer for sale at the imposed price is greater than the amount consumers wish to purchase at that price. Figure 3 demonstrates this case. In Figure 3, the equilibrium price is P_e, and the equilibrium quantity is Q_e. The government imposes a price floor at P_f. The result is that the quantity supplied at price P_f is Q_s, and the quantity consumers demand at that price is Q_d. The higher price has attracted more suppliers into the market. At the same time, it has discouraged buyers or caused them to shift to substitutes. The result is a surplus equal to $Q_s - Q_d$.

A **surplus** exists when the amount that suppliers wish to supply at some price exceeds the amount that consumers wish to purchase. A surplus can only occur on a lasting basis when a price floor is in effect. The surplus is created by the price floor. If the floor didn't exist, the price would fall. The quantity demanded would increase and the quantity supplied would decrease until the market cleared.

surplus
The amount by which the quantity suppliers wish to supply at some price exceeds the quantity consumers wish to purchase at that price. A surplus can occur on a lasting basis only when a price floor is in effect.

FIGURE 3
PRICE FLOOR
If the government imposes a price floor above the market-clearing price, a surplus will be created. At the price imposed by the government, suppliers will desire to sell more units than consumers will be willing to purchase. Demand would have to increase to $D + D_G$ to clear the market after the price floor was imposed.

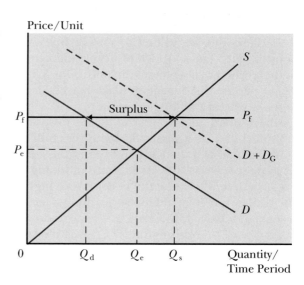

It can be difficult for the governmental agency that imposes a price floor to keep prices from falling below the floor. Some suppliers will attempt to cut prices in order to sell the quantity they want to supply. The most effective way for the government to prevent this price cutting is to purchase the excess quantity supplied. By purchasing the surplus, the government in effect is shifting the demand curve outward to create a new equilibrium at the desired price. In Figure 3, the dashed demand curve represents the demand at the price floor (D) plus the added governmental demand (D_G). A shift to demand curve $D + D_G$ would allow the price to remain at P_f.

The best example of price floors that work in this way are the price supports operated by the Commodity Credit Corporation (CCC) for some agricultural products in the United States. The **Commodity Credit Corporation (CCC)** is a U.S. government agency that makes loans to farmers as part of federal price support programs. Suppose the federal government wants to maintain a price for grain that is above the market-clearing price. To maintain this price floor, it is necessary for the CCC to purchase some grain. The effect of this is to shift the demand curve to the right (as with $D + D_G$ in Figure 3) so that the higher price can be maintained.

Commodity Credit Corporation (CCC)
A U.S. government agency that makes loans to farmers as part of federal price support programs.

THE MINIMUM WAGE

The **minimum wage** is a price floor imposed by the federal government in the labor market. Looking again at Figure 3, a minimum wage (P_f) set above the market wage (P_e) causes a surplus of labor ($Q_s - Q_d$). If the minimum wage is set above the market-clearing wage rate, the amount of labor that workers will supply at the minimum wage will be greater than the amount of labor that firms will wish to employ, resulting in unemployment.

minimum wage
A price floor imposed by the federal government in the labor market.

In 1978, Congress raised the wage floor to $2.65 an hour, up from the $2.30 an hour that was set in 1974. In addition, a formula was adopted that ensured automatic increases up to $3.35 an hour in 1981. In 1989, Congress passed legislation to raise the minimum wage to $3.80 in 1990 and $4.25 in 1991.

Economists generally agree that minimum wage laws cause unemployment to be higher than it would be otherwise. Unemployment will especially affect young people, for whom the market-clearing wage might be much lower than the minimum wage. There is strong statistical evidence from a large number of economists that increases in the minimum wage result in higher youth unemployment. Robert Goldfarb and Edward Gramlich independently reviewed eight empirical studies by economists.[7] The studies agreed that increases in the minimum wage cause increases in unemployment among teenagers. The studies predicted that a 15 percent increase in the minimum wage would increase teenage unemployment by 3.4 to 5.3 percent.[8]

If there is agreement among economists about the harmful effects of minimum wage laws, why are they enacted? The reason is very similar to the rationale for price ceilings. Not all people are hurt by the wage floor. Some workers receive pay increases when the legislation is enacted. Those who are laid off or who seek work but are unable to find it at the new minimum wage usually don't understand the role of the higher minimum wage in causing their problems. The result is that it is politically popular with some groups—organized labor, for example—to support minimum wage increases. Remember that the economic model only predicts that such laws cause decreased employment. It does not say that minimum wage legislation is a good or bad thing in other respects. A society may decide that it is better to have fewer people employed at a higher wage rate than to have a larger number employed at a lower, market-clearing wage rate.

During the Reagan administration, the minimum wage was not increased. Thus, its impact declined as market wages rose relative to the stable minimum wage. For most workers, the equilibrium wage was already above the floor, so it did not cause much, if any, unemployment. In fact, there is some evidence that the increase to $4.25 in 1991 will have little impact, for two reasons. First, the legislation allows a subminimum wage of $3.35 per hour for training purposes. This training wage can be paid for six months. Second, it appears that for most employers in most markets the equilibrium wage is already at or above $4.25. McDonald's, for example, pays an average of $4.65 per hour. Wendy's International pays $4.25. The only region where the higher minimum wage may cause some unemployment is in the South, where both wages and skill levels of employees tend to be lower.

MARKETS AS ALLOCATION MECHANISMS

Auctions are markets in which there are seldom any barriers to letting the price allocate scarce goods. If there are enough people bidding on the items offered, the price that results should be an equilibrium price. Auc-

7.   Robert Goldfarb, "The Policy Content of Quantitative Minimum Wage Research," *Industrial Relations Research Association Proceedings* (December 1974): 261–268; Edward M. Gramlich, "Impact of Minimum Wages on Other Wages, Employment and Family Incomes," *Brookings Papers on Economic Activity*, No. 2 (1976): 409–451.
8.   These estimates were based on calculating the elasticity of supply and demand for teenaged workers.

tions are, therefore, a good way to allocate scarce resources. Yet people often object to using auctions because they think that they will do better if some mechanism other than the market is used for allocation.

A case study from Arizona State University is a good example of this phenomenon.[9] When the university built a six-story addition to its business college, whole departments had to relocate to the new facility. As in most buildings, some offices were better than others (some had windows, some didn't, some were large, some were small). The departments faced the problem of allocating a scarce resource without a market.

The chair of the management department adopted the allocation mechanism used most frequently in traditional societies—seniority (defined as the length of time spent on the faculty at Arizona State). The marketing and accounting departments followed the example of management and used a seniority system. Some of the younger assistant professors thought this to be very unfair, because they spent time in their offices doing research and preparing for classes while the full professors spent more time consulting and less in their offices. The chair of the finance department agreed that seniority allocation seemed unfair. A sign-up sheet was placed by the chair's office, and offices were allocated on a first-come, first-served basis. The result was that those professors who spent a lot of time roving the halls got the best offices. Those doing research, on sabbatical, or on a trip ended up with small offices and no windows. The chair of the statistics department decided to use a random drawing of names to allocate offices. This met with faculty approval because everyone would be treated equally. After the draw, those with seniority forced the chair to cancel the outcome and use seniority instead.

The chair of the economics department wanted to use the market to allocate the scarce resources. Being a good bureaucrat, he asked the faculty for suggestions. Surprisingly, in a department of economists, no one suggested using prices to allocate a scarce resource. Instead, the chair was advised by the most senior faculty member to use seniority as is done at "all great institutions." Other suggestions were to allocate the offices based on research productivity, teaching effectiveness, height, race, sex, and religion. One member suggested office "wrestlemania"—a brawl. The chair decided on a sealed bid auction with the proceeds going to a scholarship fund. After three weeks, the twenty-four bids were opened. The highest bid was $500 and the second highest was $250. All twenty-four bids totaled $3,200. Offices were allocated in order of the sizes of the bids. The only complaint was from the person who bid $500, who overestimated the equilibrium price, bidding twice as much as the next highest bidder and almost four times the average bid.

Trouble was brewing. A professor used the experiment as an example in a principles of economics course. The students thought it was a good idea. They even understood that it was only important that the price had to be paid. It didn't matter where the money went. One student, who happened to be a reporter for the campus newspaper, thought that the

9.   This case is drawn from William J. Boyes and Stephen K. Happel, "Auctions as an Allocation Mechanism in Academia: The Case of Faculty Offices," *Journal of Economic Perspectives* (Summer 1989): 37–40.

office auction was such a good idea that it was reported on the front page. The story was then picked up by the Phoenix media and went out on the AP wire. The chair faced an onslaught of criticism from university administrators and local politicians who accused the chair of selling state property. Eventually, the publicity calmed down, largely because the money had gone to fund a scholarship. But the lesson was loud and clear: Many good opportunities to use the market as an allocation device are overlooked.

A LESSON FROM THE ENERGY CRISIS

You may have been a preschooler when your parents had to wait in line for gasoline at the height of the energy crisis in the mid-1970s. Times change, and some gas stations have even returned to the old practice of giving away road maps to their customers. Policy makers in the United States should not forget that crisis, however. There is an old saying: "What goes around, comes around." Policy makers should prepare for future rounds of energy policy by asking what can be learned from past mistakes. Indeed, some policy makers are predicting a second energy crisis. Secretary of the Interior Donald Hodel warned in 1987 that people would be sitting in gas lines by 1992.

In 1978, President Jimmy Carter gave a speech to the U.S. public about the energy crisis wearing a sweater and sitting next to a fire. He declared that the energy crisis was the moral equivalent of war. President Carter ultimately ordered the deregulation of natural gas prices and a windfall profits tax on large oil companies. President Reagan continued the phased deregulation but eliminated the windfall profits tax in his 1981 tax reform. Problems continue to confront the natural gas market. The tools developed in other chapters can be used to analyze many aspects of the energy "crisis." The natural gas shortage provides a good case study for that purpose.

THE CREATION OF A CRISIS: REGULATION OF NATURAL GAS

In 1938 Congress passed the Natural Gas Act, and in 1954 the Supreme Court placed all firms selling natural gas in more than one state under the regulation of the Federal Power Commission (FPC).[10] The law was intended to keep prices "just and reasonable" for consumers by allowing suppliers only a "fair" rate of return. After the Supreme Court ruling, the FPC attempted to regulate the price received by each individual producer engaged in the interstate sale of natural gas. The system broke down in 1960 because a giant backlog of cases had developed as a result of attempting to regulate more than 4,000 firms.[11] Thus, the FPC ruled in 1965 (affirmed by the Supreme Court in 1968) that it would set prices sepa-

---

10. The brief discussion that follows does not do justice to the complexity of natural gas regulation. For more information and other references, see Edward J. Mitchell, *U.S. Energy Policy: A Primer* (Washington, DC: American Enterprise Institute for Public Policy Research, June 1974).
11. Edward J. Mitchell called this "the outstanding example of the federal government in the breakdown of the administrative process" (*U.S. Energy Policy: A Primer*, p. 7).

rately for each geographical area and each individual petroleum commodity. This decision took eight years to be implemented, and during this entire period, prices were kept at 1960 levels. This individual commodity approach to pricing was next to impossible to implement because natural gas is jointly produced with crude oil. The method requires that certain costs be allocated to the production of natural gas, even though it is produced in a joint process. What were the effects of this regulation?

Paul W. MacAvoy, a member of President Ford's Council of Economic Advisers, has extensively examined the economics of the natural gas industry. In a series of books and articles in professional journals, he has studied the market for natural gas to determine the effects of regulation. MacAvoy concluded that regulation has held prices below the equilibrium level. Between 1964 and 1967, prices would have been about twice as high without regulation. The result of the artificially low prices was that 40 percent fewer new reserves were added to production than would have been added in the free-market context. The effect of the lower new reserves was painfully obvious. In the absence of the price-rationing function of the market system, there was a shortage. Existing supplies then had to be rationed, and consumers (including industry) had to substitute more expensive fuels for the cheaper natural gas that was not available. The government, in order to keep the price of natural gas low, produced a shortage that required consumers to buy more expensive gasified coal, imported liquid natural gas, or some other substitute.

This shortage of natural gas is shown graphically in Figure 4. Assume that the price originally set by the FPC was near or at equilibrium. That

FIGURE 4
THE MARKET
FOR NATURAL GAS
In 1960, P_{1960} was an equilibrium price. The amount consumers *wished* to purchase was exactly the amount suppliers *wished* to sell. A shortage was created because the price was frozen at P_{1960} and demand increased to D_{1968} or D_{1981}. Allowing the price to rise to P_{1981} reduced the shortage. Some shortage remained as long as the price was controlled at a level below equilibrium.

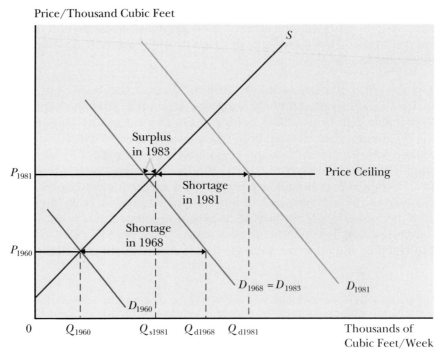

Price/Thousand Cubic Feet

The Japanese motorist pays double the world market price for gasoline and three times what the U.S. motorist pays. Yet the Japanese oil industry is sick. There is excess capacity, a strange pricing structure, gas stations in the wrong places, and very low profit margins. The responsibility for this situation can be placed on Japan's powerful Ministry of International Trade and Industry (MITI).

For years, MITI has tightly regulated and controlled the Japanese oil industry. Japan is almost totally dependent on imported oil. An attempt to gain control of a source of oil was one of Japan's motivations for invading Southeast Asia during World War II. After the war, foreign oil producers quickly set up business in Japan. In 1962, the Japanese government passed a law strengthening MITI's power to control the market and to protect domestic refiners against foreign competition.

MITI intervened with a vengeance. It allocated crude oil to refiners, set production quotas, limited imports of refined products, and regulated gas station openings. In order to keep oil prices low for industry and farmers, the government forced gasoline users to pay more than their proportionate share of refining costs. In

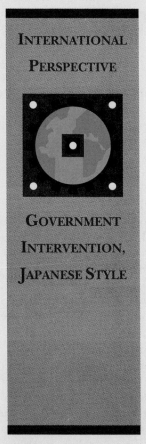

INTERNATIONAL PERSPECTIVE

GOVERNMENT INTERVENTION, JAPANESE STYLE

many years, the refiners lose money on all products except gasoline, and gasoline accounts for only about 20 percent of the refining volume.

MITI also controls the distribution of oil and gas. Many Japanese gas stations are owned by local businessmen with political clout. Under the MITI licensing scheme, a new gas station can be opened only if an old one is closed. Old inefficient stations are maintained in rural areas. The average station in Japan pumps less than one-third as much gas as the average station in the United States.

In 1987, MITI admitted that it had a problem. MITI announced a five-year plan to deregulate the Japanese oil refining industry. In April 1989, MITI phased out the quota system for gasoline production. In 1990, the restrictions on opening new gas stations were lifted. In 1992, MITI will stop allocating crude oil to refineries. However, there is no plan to reform the pricing of refined products. Unfortunately for Japanese motorists, they will continue to subsidize industrial and agricultural users of oil. This anti-consumer policy is typical of Japan's business-government partnership.

Source: Andrew Tanzer, "World's Worst Oil Policy?" *Forbes* (24 July 1989): 245–248.

price is represented by P_{1960} and the equilibrium quantity by Q_{1960}. The price ceiling was not changed for eight years. During this period, there were tremendous changes in the *ceteris paribus* conditions affecting demand. For example, household income increased greatly during this period. Thus, by 1968, the demand curve had shifted from D_{1960} to D_{1968}, resulting in a shortage. At P_{1960}, the quantity supplied was still Q_{1960}, but the quantity demanded had become Q_{d1968}. There was 40 percent less production than there would have been with a free market. In 1981, the problem was still present. Demand had increased to D_{1981}. Although the FPC allowed the price to rise to P_{1981}, that rise lagged behind the demand increase. There was still a government-induced shortage because at P_{1981}, the quantity supplied is Q_{s1981} and the quantity demanded is Q_{d1981}.

It is important to realize that the shortage was caused by the price ceiling. Natural gas is scarce, but scarcity and shortage are different concepts. Scarcity simply means that an item is not as plentiful as people would like it to be. With scarcity, rising prices ensure equilibrium. A shortage means that at the prevailing price, the quantity demanded exceeds the quantity supplied. This distinction is important because much of the debate about the energy crisis confuses these two concepts.

The energy crisis and the oil industry are subjects of hot debate between politicians and analysts. These debates often center on predictions of dire consequences because the price of oil is too high (as in 1975) or too low (as in 1988). Such predictions are nothing new. As early as the beginning of the nineteenth century, some commentators were predicting the first energy crisis. At the time, houses were lit by oil-burning lamps. Demand for these lamps was increasing rapidly because of income and population growth. The lamps were fueled by oil from sperm whales. Many people predicted that the whale population would soon be depleted and, therefore, houses would be dark. In other words, they were predicting greater scarcity of whale oil. What happened? Prices rose rapidly, from about 40 cents per gallon to about $2.50 per gallon in thirty years. The higher prices caused the quantity demanded to decrease, as users found substitutes for whale oil. A shortage did not occur because prices rose in the face of greater scarcity. Shortages can only occur with artificially imposed low prices. It is disturbing that the shortage of natural gas occurred in a market where there was a potentially large quantity supplied.

THE POLITICAL DILEMMA OF DEREGULATION

Another disturbing fact is that, even after economists recognized that government regulation was creating havoc in the natural gas market, it was politically very difficult to remove the controls. Why? Those individuals who were lucky enough, or had enough political power, could purchase natural gas at below-market prices. In 1977, the regulated price of natural gas was $1.34 per thousand cubic feet. At that time, it was estimated that markets would have cleared at $3.00 per thousand cubic feet. People bought gas furnaces, and firms installed gas-driven equipment because of the low cost. The dilemma for politicians who advocate deregulation is clear. It appears to consumers as if the deregulator, not the market forces, produces the sharp rise in price. Voters might turn against a member of Congress who votes to deregulate. It is important to realize that if Congress had not interfered with the market mechanism in the first place, voters probably would not hold Congress responsible for the higher gas prices after deregulation!

THE SHORTAGE TURNS INTO SURPLUS—AND PRICES RISE?

It was a major goal of the Carter administration to lift the price ceiling. The necessary legislation was approved by Congress as the Natural Gas Policy Act of 1978. The Carter deregulation came after a hard-fought legislative battle. It immediately raised prices 25 percent and allowed for a 10 percent increase per year until 1985, when all ceilings on newly found natural gas were scheduled to be removed. The story of the legislated deregulation didn't end with the planned removal of all ceilings. Different problems began to surface in late 1982.

The recession of 1981–1982 (and warm weather) decreased the demand for natural gas, shifting the demand curve to D_{1983} in Figure 4 (shown as the same curve as D_{1968} to keep the diagram simple). In fact, in 1983, only about 85 percent of the natural gas produced was consumed, creating a surplus in 1983, as shown in Figure 4. In a deregulated market, a surplus should cause prices to decrease. Unfortunately, the Natural Gas Policy Act of 1978 didn't deregulate all natural gas. Instead, it freed prices on new gas and kept old gas prices at low levels. The immediate effect was that the price of the new gas rose dramatically and a (sort of) equilibrium was reached.

As demand for natural gas fell, supply and demand analysis predicted that the surplus would push prices downward. However, some consumers (utilities) were locked into long-term "take or pay" contracts. These contracts stemmed from the days of regulation. Utilities would enter into twenty-year contracts with gas suppliers to share the risk of price fluctuations. The gas suppliers, faced with a surplus, expanded output of the more expensive gas (the new gas) and reduced production of the cheap gas (the old gas). As a result, the price of natural gas rose.

The regulatory distinction of old gas and new gas thus had the effect of raising natural gas prices to consumers. Its intent had been to keep prices from rising as much by controlling the price of already discovered gas.

THE MARKET FINALLY CLEARS

The natural gas story didn't even end with the complete decontrol of prices in 1985. By 1987, natural gas prices were at very low levels, in part because of deregulation, but largely due to the collapse of the oil cartel and the large decline in the worldwide price of oil and related products. In August 1989, President George Bush signed legislation ending all wellhead price controls on natural gas. This end came thirty-five years after the Supreme Court placed natural gas under the regulation of the FPC. As one industry analyst put it, "Supply and demand will come into balance in 1990."[12] After thirty-five years, the market will finally be allowed to clear.

This brief review of natural gas regulation is only one example of the effect that price regulation can have on market forces. Similar kinds of ef-

12. Kenneth R. Sheets, "The Wonder Fuel for the 1990s," *U.S. News & World Report* (31 July 1989): 38.

fects can be found throughout the U.S. economy. One need only scan the headlines for this month's crisis—the meat shortage, the cement shortage, or the capital shortage. The problem is likely to have been caused by well-intentioned interference with market forces.

THE HEALTH CARE INDUSTRY

The rapidly rising price of health care has been receiving much attention from journalists and politicians in recent years. This increased interest is also due to the fact that health care has become one of the fastest growing industries in the United States. Between 1950 and 1980, total spending on health care increased from $11 billion annually to more than $200 billion annually. Then this figure tripled again between 1985 and 1990 (adjusted for inflation). In 1950, health care expenditures represented 4.5 percent of total national income. In 1990, they represented more than 13 percent of national income. It is possible to analyze the potential problems of the health care industry using the basic economic tools of supply and demand.

Figure 5 illustrates what has happened in the health care industry. The market in 1950 is represented by supply curve S_{1950} and demand curve D_{1950}. Equilibrium is at P_1 and Q_1. Between 1950 and 1990, there were some changes in the *ceteris paribus* conditions in the health care market. On the supply side, the sophistication of the care supplied by hospitals and doctors greatly increased. There has been a virtual explosion of technological advances in the industries that make diagnostic, surgical, and therapeutic equipment. This equipment is expensive and increases the cost of supplying health care (even as it improves that care). The effect of this more expensive care has been to shift the supply curve from S_{1950} to S_{1990} in Figure 5.

FIGURE 5
THE MARKET
FOR HEALTH CARE
The health care market is characterized by decreasing supply due to increasing costs and increasing demand due to rising incomes and the aging of the population. As a result, the equilibrium price of health care has been rising rapidly.

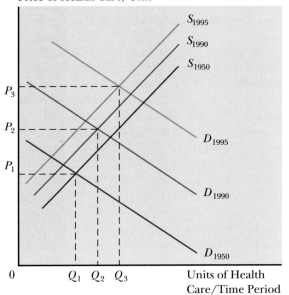

Price of Health Care/Unit

S_{1995}
S_{1990}
S_{1950}

D_{1995}

D_{1990}

D_{1950}

P_3
P_2
P_1

0 Q_1 Q_2 Q_3 Units of Health Care/Time Period

On the demand side, the changes have been equally significant. First and foremost, the income of U.S. citizens rose over this period. The demand for health care increased rapidly as incomes increased. Second, there has been an increase in Medicare, Medicaid, and employer-provided health insurance. Since payment would be made by a third party, many individuals demanded more health care. Third, the age distribution of the U.S. population has shifted. This will become an even greater problem for health care as baby boomers age. Fourth, the very success of health care delivery creates more demand for health care in the future. As health care improves, the population lives longer. More health care is then demanded because the population is now older, and older people have more health problems. Fifty years ago, many of these people would have died of measles, polio, or tuberculosis before they would have been old enough to develop the maladies now associated with older age. The increased demand for health care is represented by the shift from D_{1950} to D_{1990} in Figure 5.

The result of these changes in supply and demand has been for the price of health care to rise to P_2 and a new level of consumption to be established at Q_2. The magnitude of the shift from P_1 to P_2 can be understood by comparing the price index for medical services to the consumer price index. Between 1950 and 1990, the price index for medical services rose 978 percent. This increase was 2.2 times the change in the consumer price index (CPI).

THE COMING CRISIS IN HEALTH CARE

What about the future? It is likely that the supply curve for health care will continue to shift leftward, representing an increase in the price of the factors of production used to produce that service. It is also likely that demand will continue to increase as incomes rise and the population ages. Thus, in response to a shift in demand from D_{1990} to D_{1995} and a shift in supply from S_{1990} to S_{1995} in Figure 5, there should be an increase in price to P_3 and an increase in the equilibrium quantity to Q_3. But this prediction supposes that the government does not intervene in this market. A quick review of Congressional interest in the health care industry would be enough to convince you that this is not a realistic assumption. The most likely governmental solution to the rapidly rising prices of health care is twofold: some form of national health insurance and/or price controls.

Senator Edward Kennedy and others have made national health insurance a major political issue. His bill, "Minimum Health Benefits for All Workers Act," would require all employers to provide health care insurance for workers and their dependents. President Reagan supported catastrophic health insurance for older Americans. The economic effects of such programs are easy to predict. Since national health insurance would make health care affordable to more citizens by shifting a large part of the cost to taxpayers in general, it would increase the demand curve even beyond D_{1995} in Figure 5. National health insurance would put even greater upward pressure on prices.

There is also increasing pressure to intervene in the health care market with price controls. Congress is talking about the "immorality" of the high price of health care. Price controls have been suggested as a solution. The effect can be predicted by examining Figure 5. At a ceiling price of P_2, the effect would be a shortage. The severity of the shortage would depend on the magnitudes of the increase in demand and the decrease in supply. There would be the same type of crisis as affected the natural gas market. Even though Congress demonstrated in the 1980s that it understood how controls implemented in the 1950s helped create the energy crisis, it is flirting with similar controls for the health care industry in the 1990s.

Does this conclusion mean that politicians can't justify supporting a national health program that would ensure health care to all citizens? Not at all! All that economics says is that such a program would increase demand and put upward pressure on prices of health care. You may decide that this upward pressure on prices is an acceptable cost and that you would support such a program. The contribution of economics is to point out that these pressures are there and they can't be ignored when deciding on policy.

PHYSICIANS AND THE MARKETPLACE

Before the mid-1950s, doctors in the United States often made house calls, drove Buicks, and were viewed as upper middle-class pillars of the community.[13] In 1955, doctors' incomes averaged $16,017. All that has changed: doctors have moved to clinics and hospitals, drive Porsches and Mercedes, and are viewed by most of us as the privileged rich. Their average pretax income jumped to $28,960 in 1965, to $58,440 in 1975, and to $108,400 in 1985. That represents an increase of 677 percent over a thirty-year period, or an average annual increase of 22.5 percent, far more than the increase in the general price level.

Until 1965, the ranks of physicians were increasing at about 2 percent per year, and spending on medical care was increasing at 10 percent per year. That goes a long way toward explaining the 22.5 percent annual increases in pretax income. But, as you have learned, supply curves slope upward. The increases in income created incentives for the number of physicians to increase. In 1965, there were 277,600 doctors in the United States, 1 for every 697 Americans. In 1986, there were 506,000, or 1 for every 471 Americans.

What has happened? First, the rate of increase in physicians' income has slowed dramatically. From 1983 to 1985, their real pretax mean income rose 2 percent per year.[14] That's drastically below the thirty-year average but a result the supply and demand model would predict. Medical school applications have declined. In 1975, there were 42,624 applications for 14,579 slots. In 1985, there were 32,893 applications for 16,268 slots. In 1990, there were 26,915 applications for 16,983 slots. As *Forbes* magazine put it, "Hippocrates Meets Adam Smith." These adjustments in price and quantity suggest that the health care "crisis" may have market

13. Facts and quotes in this section are from "Hippocrates Meets Adam Smith," *Forbes* (10 February 1986): 63–66.
14. The fact that physicians' incomes are slowing in growth may seem in conflict with the fact that the costs of health care are rising. Because doctors' charges are only a small part of health costs, it is possible for their income to be falling at the same time that total health care costs are rising.

solutions. Government intervention through national health insurance or setting prices may not be needed.

A few other adjustments are worth noting. Many doctors have begun to advertise. In 1965, medical advertising was considered unprofessional and illegal. Other doctors now have television sets in their waiting rooms instead of year-old magazines. One doctor in a Beverly Hills mall gives her patients beepers that summon them from shopping when she is ready to see them so they don't have to languish in her waiting room. More of these adjustments can be expected as doctors face the facts of the market.

MICROECONOMICS AND SOCIAL POLICY: THE ECONOMICS OF NATURAL DISASTERS

One more aspect of the use of microeconomics as a policy tool can be demonstrated by looking at an area of social policy that hasn't received much attention from economists. This example will highlight the **unintended effects of policy**, those results that are unanticipated by policy makers but become evident through careful economic analysis. Policy makers might avoid the pitfall of creating institutionalized incentives by making use of microeconomic analysis.

unintended effects of policy
Results that are unanticipated by policy makers but become evident through careful economic analysis.

Economists have devoted little effort to studying the economics of natural disasters. There are some important areas in which microeconomics can be brought to bear on the analysis of how people respond to floods, earthquakes, hurricanes, and other natural disasters.

GOVERNMENT POLICY TOWARD DISASTERS

The U.S. government has provided a great deal of disaster relief in recent years. Before the mid-1960s, disaster victims received little economic aid from the federal government, although private relief for emergency needs was provided by the Red Cross. Before the 1960s, the federal government did give aid to state and local governments to rebuild schools, hospitals, and roads. However, it offered little in the way of disaster relief for individuals and businesses. In 1989, in the aftermath of Hurricane Hugo in South Carolina and the earthquake in northern California during the World Series, there was a massive outpouring of private, state, and federal assistance. The amount of federal aid was huge, even though these disasters paled in comparison to earlier ones such as the 1900 hurricane that took 6,000 lives in Galveston, Texas.

Why the large increase in aid? The increased information brought by television coverage and congressional involvement offer possible explanations. Disasters were brought to the attention of the nation, and local political leaders found they could expect relief since the cost could be spread to all taxpayers. This political cost-sharing game was easy to play. To mount opposition was to appear unsympathetic with victims. The result has been the present policy of massive federal aid to disaster victims.

Microeconomics can shed light on several other aspects of that policy. One lesson is that if you want to get other people to help you, they have to be reminded of your need. Television news is a good vehicle for such a campaign to "generate a demand for assistance."

THE CONSEQUENCES OF DISASTER RELIEF

The normative question "Should relief be given?" is moot politically because assistance can and will be given. Instead, microeconomists can ask the positive question "What are the consequences of disaster relief?"

The most obvious one is the uneconomic use of the nation's resources. Economic efficiency requires that economic decision makers bear the costs and benefits of their decisions. This implies risk taking. If policy shifts the risks from the individual to the government, different decisions will be made. Along with creating sympathy for disaster victims, television also shows the results of such social policy. Homes are rebuilt following mud slides in California with little thought given to the possibility of a recurrence of the disaster. The same holds for building in floodplains and coastal areas frequently hit by hurricanes. The risk of destruction is shifted from the owner to the public, and the taxpayer swallows the consequences.

Some economists have argued that, in the case of floods, the government should not give disaster relief but instead should mandate the purchase of private flood insurance. They argue that such insurance would ensure the efficient use of floodplains by creating the proper set of incentives. The insurance costs would reflect the risk. In the highest-risk areas, insurance would be so expensive that little building would occur. The use of the floodplains would then be determined by markets. The floodplains would probably be used for agriculture rather than for housing. What happens instead is that disaster relief distorts incentives. Housing development occurs in floodplains. In a sense, the destruction and loss of life from the inevitable floods are artificial (or government-induced) disasters.

One might argue that it would be unnecessary to mandate flood insurance if the government would simply cease to provide flood relief. The availability of disaster relief is viewed by many as a form of "free" disaster insurance. On the other hand, private individuals may choose not to purchase disaster insurance, even if they have no expectation of government relief, because of the huge cost of insurance in disaster-prone areas.

The conclusion from such analysis and from the generous disaster relief approved by Congress in recent years is clear. Public policy is encouraging uneconomic use of land and, in fact, is contributing to larger disaster losses by subsidizing economic activity in potential disaster areas.

BEHAVIOR AFTER DISASTERS

Yet another interesting issue in "disaster economics" is the behavior of disaster victims. The self-interest assumption (discussed in Chapter 1) would seem to predict selfish behavior by disaster victims and their neighbors—such actions as hoarding, price gouging by suppliers, and looting of disaster sites. In fact, after Hurricane Hugo, the city of Charleston passed a law to prevent price gouging, because prices of some critical items such as ice and chain saws were far above normal. Yet many observers have reported helpful, cooperative, and generous behavior immediately after disasters. This behavior can be explained in terms of self-interest as informal insurance and alliance activity. In other words, in a crisis situation, people do unto others as they would have others do unto them.

An alternative explanation of the behavior of disaster victims is the cost of not cooperating. Individuals may choose not to loot or hoard, especially in small communities, because their behavior will be observed and they will be subject to future sanctions. Similarly, business firms may choose not to "gouge" consumers because the disaster will be short-lived, and they dare not incur the bad feelings that would result. Both the positive informal insurance theory and the negative social sanctions theory explain behavior in terms of a calculation of costs and benefits.

RECOVERY FROM DISASTERS

The long-term economic effects of disaster on communities have been carefully analyzed by economists. The results of such studies are consistent. The long-term economic effects of a disaster are not profound, and there are few lingering economic effects on the local community. Indeed, the speed of recovery is often astonishing. The devastation from Hurricane Hugo in South Carolina was followed by recovery to normal economic activity in a short time.

Such rapid recovery is not surprising because modern history has shown that nations quickly repair from the destruction caused by wars. The economy of the Soviet Union recovered very rapidly from the great devastation caused by the Bolshevik Revolution of 1917. The New Economic Policy restored the economy to its prerevolution level of output in just two years. The post–World War II experience in Western Europe and in Japan was similar. In fact, new, modern capital was put into place, and economic growth resumed at faster rates than before. It will be interesting to observe the speed of recovery in Iraq and Kuwait now that the hostilities in the Gulf have ended.

THE ROAD AHEAD

Microeconomics is concerned with how incentives influence decision making and the ways in which institutions and changes in institutions influence incentives and, in turn, the behavior of individuals. This method of looking at markets gives economists powerful insights into the impact that policies have. That impact is often very different from what was intended. In order to address more complex microeconomic issues, you will need tools beyond the supply and demand model. The next few chapters develop some of these tools.

SUMMARY

1. The basic tools of microeconomics are useful in analyzing a wide range of social policy issues.
2. Crime can be modeled and analyzed as an economic activity resulting from a rational decision by the criminal. To decrease criminal activity, it is necessary to decrease the benefits the criminal receives or increase the costs the criminal must pay, or both. This holds for the entire range of crime, from illegal parking to armed robbery or murder.
3. Price ceilings are attempts to keep prices from

rising to their equilibrium level. Price ceilings cause shortages, and black markets often develop in response to the shortages. Rent control is an example of a price ceiling.

4. Price floors are attempts to keep prices from falling to their equilibrium level. Price floors cause surpluses that must be absorbed to prevent the price from falling. Agricultural price supports and minimum wages are examples of price floors.

5. Prices and markets allocate goods and services efficiently. Other methods of allocation may be viewed by participants as "fairer," but often result in problems.

6. The regulation of natural gas is a good example of how price ceilings disrupt markets. The lesson is that price ceilings are very difficult to remove even after the damage they cause is well understood. Even after partial deregulation is achieved politically, the effect of past disruptions to the market persist.

7. The health care industry in the United States is one of the fastest-growing industries. Prices have risen because of increasing demand and increasing costs. There have been political calls for regulation, but the lesson of natural gas regulation is relevant.

8. Many governmental policies have unintended effects that can be determined by applying microeconomic tools of analysis. For example, analysis of disaster relief shows that present public policy may in a sense "create" new disasters.

New Terms

price ceilings	rent control	minimum wage
price floors	surplus	unintended effects of
shortage	Commodity Credit	policy
black markets	Corporation (CCC)	

Questions for Discussion

1. Why does a price ceiling that is set above the equilibrium price have no immediate effect on the market?

2. Can you formulate models like the simple economic model of crime for other decisions, such as having children, getting married, or getting a divorce?

3. How is the minimum wage maintained at higher than market-clearing rates? Why don't the unemployed workers agree to work for lower wages and thereby circumvent the imposed price floor?

4. Many price controls were used in the United States during World War II. Using the models developed in this chapter, how well do you think they worked?

5. Suppose you have an 8:00 a.m. economics class that is far away from the student parking lot. You learn over time that if you park in a faculty spot but move your car by 9:15 a.m., you are ticketed every fourth time. The ticket cost is $15. What value are you implicitly placing on that illegal parking space? If the university raised the ticket price to $30, would you still park illegally? What effect would a towing policy have on your behavior?

6. The price, total demand, and total supply of winter wheat on the Chicago grain market in March 1989 are as follows:

Price per Bushel (Dollars)	Bushels Demanded (Thousands)	Bushels Supplied (Thousands)
4.65	90	77
4.85	85	78
5.05	80	80
5.25	75	82
5.45	65	86

What is the equilibrium price? What is the equilibrium quantity? Why is this the equilibrium? Explain the forces that bring the market to this equilibrium, starting at a price of $5.25.

7. Draw the demand and supply curve for winter wheat using the data in Question 6.

8. What would happen if the federal government set a price floor (a support) for winter wheat of $5.45 per bushel? Draw this price floor on the diagram you produced in Question 7.

9. What would happen if the federal government set a price ceiling for winter wheat of $5.45 per bushel? Draw this price ceiling on the diagram from Question 7.

10. Usury laws are laws that set maximum interest rates.

These laws are price ceilings in the market for loanable funds. What will happen in states that have usury laws when the equilibrium interest rate exceeds the established ceiling? Why then are usury laws politically popular?

11. Even when many people know the negative impacts of rent control, rent control laws are hard to repeal. Why?

12. How might the Federal Savings and Loan Insurance Corporation (FSLIC) have contributed to the savings and loan crisis?

13. What is causing the demand for health care to increase? What is causing the supply of health care to decrease? If supply decreases and demand increases, what will happen to the equilibrium price of health care?

14. In 1991, the minimum wage in the United States increased to $4.25. This increase was not met with predictions by economists of dire consequences, as previous increases in the minimum wage were. Why?

15. Why do bureaucracies seldom make use of markets to allocate scarce resources?

SUGGESTIONS FOR FURTHER READING

Benjamin, Daniel, Douglass C. North, and Roger LeRoy Miller. *The Economics of Public Issues*, 8th ed. New York: Harper & Row, 1990. A highly readable description of some innovative applications of the basic tools of microeconomics.

Butler, Stuart M., and Edmund F. Haislmair (eds.). *Critical Issues: A National Health System for America.* Washington: Heritage Foundation, 1989. Chapter 1 presents a detailed history of the health care system in the United States.

Maccaro, James A. "The Folly of Rent Control," *The Freeman* (January 1990): 18–21. A very readable essay that lays out the simple economics of rent control.

Scully, Gerald. *The Business of Major League Baseball.* Chicago: University of Chicago Press, 1989. A book that uses basic economic analysis to explain the economics of baseball.

1. Define elasticity.
2. Calculate the coefficient of elasticity for each of the following measures:
   a. price elasticity of demand,
   b. income elasticity of demand,
   c. cross elasticity of demand,
   d. price elasticity of supply.
3. Identify the range of values for the coefficient of price elasticity of demand when demand is:
   a. elastic,
   b. inelastic,
   c. unit elastic.
4. Identify the range of values for the coefficient of the income elasticity of demand when a good is:
   a. inferior,
   b. normal.
5. Identify the range of values for the coefficient of cross elasticity of demand when two goods are:
   a. substitutes,
   b. complements,
   c. independent.
6. Use the concept of elasticity to determine the incidence of an excise tax.

CHAPTER 19

ELASTICITY: THE MEASURE OF RESPONSIVENESS

INTRODUCTION

This chapter extends the concepts of supply and demand by developing another tool of the microeconomist—the elasticity measurement. **Elasticity** is the measure of the sensitivity, or responsiveness, of quantity demanded or quantity supplied to changes in price (or other conditions). We will develop several elasticity measures and then demonstrate their usefulness in the analysis of public policy.

elasticity
The measure of the sensitivity or responsiveness of quantity demanded or quantity supplied to changes in price (or other factors).

SUPPLY AND DEMAND REVISITED

Supply and demand are basic to economic analysis. It is worth reviewing them before beginning to expand your kit of economic tools.

When developing the concept of demand, we stressed the distinction between shifts in demand curves and movement along demand curves. Any movement along a demand curve occurs in response to a change in price and is referred to as a *change in quantity demanded*. Any shift of the demand curve is called a *change in demand*. Changes in demand occur in response to changes in one or more of the *ceteris paribus* conditions that underlie the demand curve: the tastes of the group demanding the good or service, the size of that group, the income and wealth of that group, the prices of other goods and services, or expectations about any of these conditions.

Similarly, there is an important difference between changes in supply and changes in quantity supplied. The phrase *change in quantity supplied* indicates to the economist that the change that occurred was in response

509

to a change in price. The phrase *change in supply* means that the change occurred in response to a change in one or more of the *ceteris paribus* conditions affecting supply: the prices of the factors of production, the number of sellers, the technology used to produce the good, or expectations about any of these conditions.

These principles and terms are useful in explaining economic events. Figure 1 is a diagram of supply and demand in the market for automobiles. Stable *ceteris paribus* conditions have been assumed, and differences in autos' quality, size, and gas mileage have been ignored (so that a demand curve for like units can be drawn). The market determines an equilibrium price of P_1 and quantity of Q_1. Now suppose the price of gasoline increases. Since gasoline and automobiles are complements, you know that the increase in the price of gasoline is going to cause the demand for automobiles to shift from D_1 to D_2 in Figure 1. That is, with gasoline being more expensive, people drive less, reducing the demand for automobiles. This decrease in demand for autos causes the price to fall to P_2 and the quantity supplied to decrease to Q_2. Remember that quality and other factors are held constant. Thus, the decrease in the demand for automobiles could represent a switch to smaller cars or less frequent trade-ins for newer models.

ELASTICITY AS A GENERAL CONCEPT

Elasticity measures the way one variable responds to changes in other variables. The dependent variable is the variable that changes in response to some other variable, called the independent variable. The de-

FIGURE 1
THE MARKET
FOR AUTOMOBILES
Gasoline is a complementary good to automobiles. If the price of gasoline rises, there will be a decrease in the demand for automobiles. The price of autos will fall from P_1 to P_2, and the equilibrium quantity will decrease from Q_1 to Q_2. There has been a decrease in the quantity supplied.

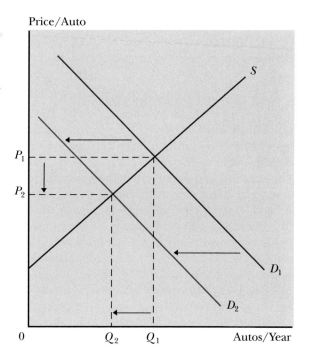

pendent variable (y) is written as a function of one or more independent variables (x_i):

(1) $y = f(x_1, x_2, x_3, \ldots, x_n)$.

Elasticity measures how the dependent variable responds to changes in any of the different independent variables. The formula to determine this responsiveness can be expressed as follows:

$$(2)\ E_1 = \frac{\%\Delta y}{\%\Delta x_1},\ E_2 = \frac{\%\Delta y}{\%\Delta x_2},\ \ldots,\ E_n = \frac{\%\Delta y}{\%\Delta x_n}.$$

This formula says that elasticity (E) is the percent change (the symbol Δ represents change) in the dependent variable (y) divided by the percent change in the particular independent variable (x) being examined.

In examining demand, economists are interested in how the quantity demanded responds to changes in price and to changes in certain other *ceteris paribus* conditions that affect demand. The quantity demanded of good A (Q_A^d) is thus the dependent variable, and the independent variables are the price of good A (P_A), income (I), tastes (T), the price of complements (P_c), and the price of substitutes (P_s). We can thus rewrite equation (1) as

$$Q_A^d = f(P_A, I, T, P_c, P_s).$$

It is now possible to determine how Q_A^d responds to change in any of the independent variables by holding all but one of them constant and calculating the elasticity coefficient using equation (2). For example, to see how quantity demanded responds to price, we use

$$E_d = \frac{\%\Delta Q_A^d}{\%\Delta P_A},$$

where E_d is the coefficient of price elasticity of demand. This formula gives us the price elasticity of demand. **Price elasticity of demand** is the measure of the relative responsiveness of the quantity demanded to changes in price.

price elasticity of demand
The measure of the responsiveness of the quantity demanded to changes in price.

PRICE ELASTICITY OF DEMAND

In the late nineteenth century, the famous English economist Alfred Marshall developed the concept of elasticity to compare the demands for various products. When comparisons are made, it is necessary to concentrate on the *relative* responsiveness of the quantity demanded to price changes rather than the absolute responsiveness. Relative comparisons make it possible to measure and then describe the sensitivity of the demand relationship. For example, in Figure 2, two demand curves are drawn. One is the demand curve for coffee, the other is the demand curve for orange juice. Although the price increases by the same amount for each curve, there are different changes in the quantity demanded. The two goods have different sensitivities to the price change. That is, they have different relative elasticities.

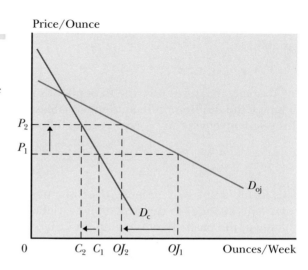

FIGURE 2
DEMAND CURVES WITH
DIFFERENT ELASTICITIES
Demand curves may have different relative elastici-ties. For example, these demand curves are for orange juice (D_{oj}) and coffee (D_c) The same price change has a much greater impact on the quantity of orange juice demanded. Therefore, the demand for orange juice is more elastic than the demand for coffee between every pair of prices.

coefficient of price elasticity of demand (E_d)
The numerical measure of price elasticity of demand, equal to the percent change in quantity demanded of a good divided by the percent change in its price.

The **coefficient of price elasticity of demand (E_d)** is the numerical measure of price elasticity of demand. It is the percent change in quantity demanded of a good divided by the percent change in price. That is, as you have seen, for good A,

$$E_d = \frac{\% \Delta Q_A^d}{\% \Delta P_A}.$$

Since percent change is the change in the variable divided by the base amount of the variable, this can be rewritten as

$$(3) \; E_d = \frac{\dfrac{\Delta Q_A^d}{Q_A^d}}{\dfrac{\Delta P_A}{P_A}}.$$

With most demand curves, the elasticity coefficient varies along the curve. However, some demand curves have a *constant* price elasticity of demand. We will examine three special cases before looking at more typ-ical demand curves.

Figure 3 shows a vertical demand curve. With this curve, quantity de-manded is totally unresponsive to changes in price. As price changes from P_1 to P_2, there is no change in the quantity demanded. The elasticity coefficient is

perfectly inelastic demand
Demand represented by a vertical demand curve with a coefficient of price elasticity of demand that is equal to zero. There is no response in quantity demanded to changes in price.

$$E_d = \frac{\dfrac{\Delta Q^d}{Q_1}}{\dfrac{\Delta P}{P_1}} = 0.$$

This vertical demand curve is a limiting case that violates the law of de-mand and is not known to exist in the real world. This curve is called a perfectly inelastic demand curve. **Perfectly inelastic demand** occurs when

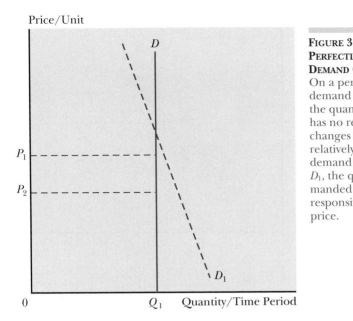

Price/Unit

P_1

P_2

0   Q_1 Quantity/Time Period

FIGURE 3
PERFECTLY INELASTIC
DEMAND CURVE
On a perfectly inelastic
demand curve, such as D,
the quantity demanded
has no responsiveness to
changes in price. With a
relatively inelastic
demand curve, such as
D_1, the quantity de-
manded is not very
responsive to changes in
price.

the coefficient of price elasticity of demand is zero. There is no response
of quantity demanded to changes in price.

Although the vertical demand curve doesn't exist in the real world, there
may be curves that are close to it, such as D_1, the dashed line in Figure 3.
This curve is a *relatively* inelastic demand curve. A highly inelastic demand
exists for goods such as medicine for a heart condition. Individuals who purchase such medicine probably do not respond very much to changes in
price, especially if they are wealthy or have ample health insurance.

Figure 4 shows a horizontal demand curve, another limiting case. At
P_1 or at any price below P_1, an infinite quantity of the good is demanded.
If the price rises above P_1, the quantity demanded drops to zero. Calculating the elasticity coefficient for a price change from P_1 to P_2 yields

$$E_d = \frac{\dfrac{\Delta Q}{Q_1}}{\dfrac{\Delta P}{P_1}} = \infty.$$

A horizontal demand curve is called a perfectly elastic demand curve because the response to changes in price is infinite. **Perfectly elastic demand**
occurs when the coefficient of price elasticity of demand is infinite.

A demand curve such as D_1, the dashed line in Figure 4, is a *relatively*
elastic demand curve. A highly elastic demand exists for the wheat production of an individual farmer in the United States. The price of a bushel
of wheat is determined by the market. At that price (or any lower price),
buyers will demand all of the farmer's wheat that is available. But if a
farmer raises the price even slightly, the quantity demanded from that
farmer will go to zero.

A third kind of demand curve is shown in Figure 5. The mathematical
term for this curve is a rectangular hyperbola. Any percent decrease or

perfectly elastic demand
Demand represented by a
horizontal demand curve
with a coefficient of price
elasticity of demand that
is equal to infinity. The
quantity demanded
responds in an infinite
way to a change in price.

FIGURE 4
PERFECTLY ELASTIC
DEMAND CURVE
On a perfectly elastic
demand curve, such as
D, the quantity demand-
ed has an infinite re-
sponse to changes in
price. If price rises above
P_1, no amount of the
good will be purchased.
If price falls to P_2, all that
is available will be pur-
chased. With a relatively
elastic demand curve,
such as D_1, quantity
demanded is very
responsive to changes
in price.

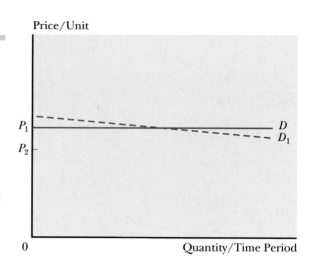

increase in price causes the same percent increase or decrease in the
quantity demanded. This means that the elasticity coefficient at any point
along this demand curve is equal to 1. For example, if you calculated the
elasticity coefficient for a price change from P_1 to P_2, you would find that

unit elastic demand
Demand represented
by a demand curve that is
a rectangular hyperbola
with a coefficient of price
elasticity of demand
equal to one. The quanti-
ty demanded responds at
the same rate as any
change in price.

$$E_d = \frac{\dfrac{\Delta Q}{Q_1}}{\dfrac{\Delta P}{P_1}} = 1.$$

Such a demand curve is referred to as a unit elastic demand curve. **Unit
elastic demand** occurs when the coefficient of price elasticity of demand
is unitary (equal to 1).

FIGURE 5
UNITARY ELASTIC DEMAND
CURVE
With a unitary elastic
demand curve, a change
in price brings about the
same percentage change
in quantity demanded.

A GUIDE TO ELASTICITY COEFFICIENTS		
NUMERICAL VALUE OF COEFFICIENTS	**RESPONSIVENESS OF QUANTITY DEMANDED TO A CHANGE IN PRICE**	**TERMINOLOGY**
• $E_d = 0$	No response	Perfectly inelastic
• $0 < E_d < 1$	Quantity demanded changes by a smaller percentage than the price changes	Inelastic
• $E_d = 1$	Quantity demanded changes by the same percentage as the price changes	Unit elastic
• $1 < E_d < \infty$	Quantity demanded changes by a larger percentage than the price changes	Elastic
• $E_d = \infty$	Quantity demanded becomes infinite, or all that is available is demanded	Perfectly elastic

Most demand curves are not shaped like those in Figures 3, 4, and 5. Most straight line demand curves look like the one in Figure 6. Demand curve *D* has a *range* of elasticity coefficients from infinity (at the intersection with the vertical axis) to zero (at the intersection with the horizontal axis). When the coefficient is *less* than 1, demand is *inelastic* because the percent change in quantity demanded is less than the percent change in

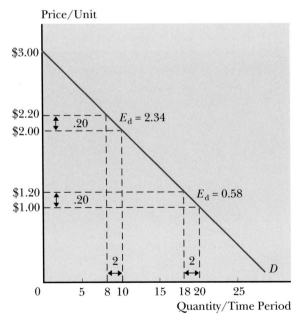

FIGURE 6
STRAIGHT-LINE DEMAND CURVE WITH VARYING ELASTICITY COEFFICIENTS
A straight-line demand curve has elasticity co-efficients that vary from zero at the horizontal-axis intercept to infinity at the vertical-axis intercept.

price. When the coefficient is *greater* than 1, demand is *elastic* because the quantity demanded changes relatively more than the price. Of course, there are degrees of responsiveness. The larger the coefficient, the greater the responsiveness.

The best way to understand elasticity is to calculate and interpret some elasticity coefficients. Before we do this, we need to clarify two points.

Before an elasticity coefficient can be calculated, it is necessary to decide whether elasticity is to be calculated at a single point or between two points. The elasticity between two points is the value of the coefficient at the midpoint between the points. This value is called **arc elasticity**. Many economists use a different, but related, measure called **point elasticity**, which uses calculus to evaluate the responsiveness of quantity demanded to price at a particular point on a demand curve.[1] Basically, the elasticity is measured at a point by assuming tiny changes in price and quantity demanded. However, we will use arithmetic to calculate particular coefficients and will be working with sizable changes. The numbers we will compute will be values of arc elasticity.

The second important point is that the formula for an elasticity coefficient will always produce a negative number because demand curves are negatively sloped. In practice, economists ignore the minus signs on coefficients of price elasticity of demand. An E_d value of -5 is considered to be larger than an E_d value of -4, for example. That is, these coefficients are treated as absolute values. It will be important later when considering other measures of elasticity to keep track of their signs, but the sign is not important for price elasticity of demand.

The demand schedule of Table 1 can be used to calculate some coefficients of price elasticity of demand. Again, the formula is

$$E_d = \frac{\text{percent change in quantity demanded}}{\text{percent change in price}}.$$

arc elasticity
The elasticity at the midpoint between two points on a demand curve.

point elasticity
The elasticity at a particular point on a demand curve.

TABLE 1
DEMAND SCHEDULE FOR STRAIGHT-LINE DEMAND CURVE IN FIGURE 6

PRICE	QUANTITY DEMANDED
$0.50	25
1.00	20
1.20	18
1.40	16
1.60	14
1.80	12
2.00	10
2.20	8
2.40	6
2.60	4
2.80	2
3.00	0

1.   This concept relies on differential calculus. For those who have had calculus, elasticity at a particular point can be measured using the formula $E_d = dQ/dP \times P/Q$, where dQ/dP is the first derivative of the demand function $Q = f(P)$.

For our purposes, this reduces to

$$E_{\mathrm{d}} = \frac{\dfrac{\Delta Q}{\dfrac{Q_1 + Q_2}{2}}}{\dfrac{\Delta P}{\dfrac{P_1 + P_2}{2}}}.$$

Since we are calculating arc elasticity, we use averages. That is, we divide both the sum of the beginning price and the ending price and the sum of the beginning quantity and the ending quantity by two. If, instead of average values, we used the beginning or ending price and quantity as the bases, the formula would produce different elasticity measures between the same two points.

We can now compute the elasticity coefficients for two different price changes on the demand curve in Figure 6. First, the elasticity coefficient for the increase in price from \$1.00 to \$1.20:

$$E_{\mathrm{d}} = \frac{\dfrac{20 - 18}{\dfrac{20 + 18}{2}}}{\dfrac{\$1.00 - \$1.20}{\dfrac{\$1.00 + \$1.20}{2}}} = \frac{\dfrac{2}{19}}{\dfrac{-\$0.20}{\$1.10}} = \frac{0.105}{-0.182} = 0.58$$

Recall that economists ignore the minus sign and just look at the absolute value of price elasticities of demand.

Now for the elasticity coefficient for the increase in price from \$2.00 to \$2.20:

$$E_{\mathrm{d}} = \frac{\dfrac{10 - 8}{\dfrac{10 + 8}{2}}}{\dfrac{\$2.00 - \$2.20}{\dfrac{\$2.00 + \$2.20}{2}}} = \frac{\dfrac{2}{9}}{\dfrac{-\$0.20}{\$2.10}} = \frac{0.222}{-0.095} = 2.34$$

Note that the elasticity is different at different points along this demand curve, which has a constant slope. In fact, all linear demand curves except those that are vertical or horizontal have elasticity coefficients that range from zero through infinity. On a demand curve such as the one shown in Figure 7, all points above price P_1 (which corresponds to the midpoint on a straight-line demand curve) have an elasticity coefficient greater than 1. At those points, demand is elastic. At price P_1, the elasticity coefficient is equal to 1. At that point, demand is unit elastic. All points below P_1 have an elasticity coefficient less than 1. In this region, demand is inelastic.

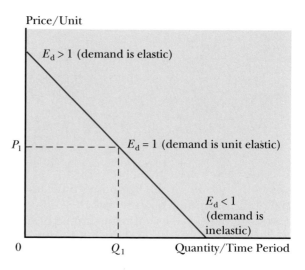

FIGURE 7
THE UNIT ELASTIC PRICE AND THE DEMAND CURVE
The point on the demand curve where $E_d = 1$ represents the unit elastic price (P_1) and divides the curve into two regions. At all prices above the unit elastic price, demand is elastic. At all prices below the unit elastic price, demand is inelastic.

    To see how important it is to average the quantity demanded and the price for the bases, you can calculate the effect of an increase in price from $1.00 to $1.20 and then of a decrease in price from $1.20 to $1.00 using equation (3), which does not use averaging. If you do this, you will get two different elasticity coefficients, depending on whether the price is decreasing or increasing. The average, or arc, elasticity between two points is found by employing averaging and gives the same measure in either direction.

    This example clearly demonstrates that elasticity is an entirely different concept from the geometric concept of slope. Because the demand is a straight line, the demand curve in Figure 6 has a constant slope. However, the elasticity coefficients vary along this straight-line demand curve.

ELASTICITY AND SUBSTITUTABILITY

Price elasticity of demand depends, in large part, on the number of substitutes a good or service has. If a product, such as table salt, has relatively few substitutes, it will tend to have a relatively inelastic demand. This is just another way of saying that the quantity demanded of a good like table salt isn't very responsive to changes in price over a wide range of prices. The elasticity of demand for a broad category of goods will be lower than that for a specific good. For example, the elasticity of demand for salt in general will be lower than the elasticity of demand for Morton's salt.

    Another determinant of the elasticity of demand is time. The longer the period of time consumers have to adjust, the more elastic the demand becomes. The reason for this is that a longer time period allows more opportunities to modify behavior and substitute different products. A good example is the elasticity of demand for natural gas. In the short run, the demand is likely to be very inelastic. Over time, however, as industry and homes convert to other sources of energy, the elasticity will increase. Table 2 lists estimated elasticities for some commonly purchased items in the range of their typical prices.

ITEM	E_d
Fresh tomatoes	4.60
Medical care	3.60
Canned tomatoes	2.50
Airline travel	2.40
Radios and televisions	1.25
Automobiles	0.80

TABLE 2
SOME ESTIMATED
ELASTICITIES

Source: Adapted from Dean A. Worcester, Jr., "On Monopoly Losses: Comment," *American Economic Review* (December 1975): 1016.

PRICE ELASTICITY OF DEMAND AND TOTAL REVENUE

Demand curves illustrate price and quantity relationships. Quantity, or the number of items sold, multiplied by price equals the **total revenue** generated. The relationship between total revenue and price elasticity of demand explains how firms set and change prices. This relationship was first considered by French mathematician and economist Antoine Augustin Cournot (1801–1877). He wondered what the owner of a hypothetical mineral spring should charge for the spring's water, which was desired for its healing powers. Cournot made three assumptions: that the spring cost nothing to operate, that it produced an unlimited quantity of output, and that the owner wanted as much income as possible.

To determine the correct price, Cournot first recognized that a price change has two (opposite) effects on total revenue. The first effect is that a price decrease, by itself, will decrease total revenue. The other effect is that a price decrease causes quantity demanded to increase, thus increasing total revenue. The net effect of these two changes on total revenue depends on whether the relative price decrease exceeds the relative increase in quantity demanded, or vice versa. This is exactly the information that the price elasticity of demand provides.

For a concrete application of this principle, look again at Figure 6 and Table 1. At a price of $2.00, the total revenue (*TR*) is $20.00. An increase in price from $2.00 to $2.20 causes *TR* to fall from $20.00 to $17.60. *TR* drops because the 10 percent increase in price caused an even greater percent decrease in quantity demanded. The elasticity coefficient at that point was greater than 1. Conversely, if the price rises from $1.00 to $1.20, *TR* increases from $20.00 to $21.60 because the percent increase in price is greater than the percent decrease in quantity demanded. The elasticity coefficient at that point is less than 1.

Figure 8 illustrates the same principle. On both demand curves, the price falls from P_1 to P_2, and quantity demanded increases from Q_1 to Q_2. This price change causes the total revenue to change. Some revenue is lost and some revenue is gained. In Figure 8, the red area represents revenue that has been lost and the gold area represents revenue that has been gained. With the relatively inelastic demand curve in part (*a*), the decrease in price brings about a decrease in total revenue. With the relatively elastic demand curve in part (*b*), the decrease in price brings about an increase in total revenue.

total revenue
The amount of money a firm takes in, equal to the quantity of the good or service sold multiplied by its price.

When a country runs a surplus or deficit in its balance of trade, adjustment in the value of its currency is one way to restore equilibrium in trade. In the early 1980s, the value of the U.S. dollar had risen a great deal in terms of other currencies, especially those of U.S. trading partners in Europe. As Americans began importing more foreign goods, however, the supply of dollars rose. Since the value of the dollar is determined in money markets, the large supply of dollars caused the value of the dollar to decline relative to the European currencies. Between 1985 and 1988, the value of the dollar fell by about 50 percent.

The decline in the value of the dollar should have reduced the trade deficit, which is the difference between the value of exports and the value of imports. The decline in the trade deficit should have come about because imports became more expensive to Americans, causing the quantity of imports demanded to decrease. Imports were more expensive because it took more dollars to buy a given amount of foreign currency. At the same time, U.S. exports to foreigners became cheaper, causing the quantity of exports demanded to increase. The experience, however, at least in the short run, was that the deficit remained high. The explanation is to be found

INTERNATIONAL PERSPECTIVE

THE PRICE ELASTICITY OF DEMAND FOR IMPORTS AND EXPORTS

in the differences between short-run and long-run elasticities.

In the short run, the demand for imports is very price-inelastic. So, when the value of the dollar falls, making imports more expensive, the quantity demanded falls, but not very much. Similarly, foreign demand for exports is inelastic. When price falls, the quantity demanded increases, but not very much. As time passes, importers in the United States have more time to adjust to the increased prices of foreign goods, and foreigners have more time to adjust to the lower prices of U.S. exports. Gradually the trade balance will come back into equilibrium.

In the short run, a cheaper dollar may actually make the trade deficit worse before it gets better. This curious result is due to the fact that short-run elasticities are much lower than long-run elasticities. Economists have come to call this worsening of the balance of trade in the face of a cheaper currency the "J-curve effect." The curve is shaped like a J because the trade deficit initially gets worse before it turns around and improves. Although this is a technical economic concept, the term has been widely adopted into the jargon of newswriters. You are quite likely to see the term "J-curve" if you read the *Wall Street Journal* or other business publications.

(a) Relatively Inelastic Demand

(b) Relatively Elastic Demand

FIGURE 8
CHANGES IN TOTAL
REVENUE
Equal price changes
bring about different
changes in total revenue,
depending on the
elasticity of the demand
curve. (a) If the demand
curve is relatively
inelastic, a decrease in
price will bring about a
decrease in total revenue.
(b) If the demand curve is
relatively elastic, the same
decrease in price will
bring about an increase
in total revenue.

In other words, you can determine what will happen to total revenue when price changes if you know the elasticity of demand. A reduction in price will always cause an increase in quantity demanded, but total revenue will decrease with inelastic demand and increase with elastic demand. Similarly, a rise in price will cause total revenue to fall when demand is elastic and to rise when demand is inelastic.

The answer to Cournot's question is that the owner of the mineral spring should not try to charge the highest possible price or sell the largest possible amount. The owner should set the price where the elasticity coefficient is 1. To see why, imagine that the price is where the elasticity coefficient is 0.5. (Demand is inelastic.) If the owner raises the price, quantity demanded will decrease, but by only half the rate of the price increase. Therefore, total revenue will rise. On the other hand, if the elasticity coefficient is 2 (or demand is elastic), the owner should decrease the price. If the price is lowered, the quantity demanded increases at twice the rate of the price. The owner will maximize total revenue when the demand coefficient is 1, or demand is unit elastic. So the mineral spring owner should set the price at P_1 in Figure 7. At price P_1, the area $P_1 \times Q_1$ represents maximum possible total revenue.

A good example of the importance of the elasticity of demand to setting prices occurred in the U.S. airline industry. The airline industry, believing that the demand for air travel was inelastic, had historically been against deregulation. The reason was that increased competition would result in lower fares. When deregulation occurred, the revenues of the airline companies increased dramatically despite the lower fares. The experience indicated that the demand for air travel was relatively elastic, or at least much more elastic than the airlines had thought. The airlines had set their prices based on incorrect estimates of the elasticity of demand.

Perhaps the best example of the effect of price elasticity on total revenue is that of Henry Ford's Model T. When Ford entered the scene, automobiles were a curiosity for the rich. Ford's strategy was to make autos for the average person through mass production—but he had to sell

Antoine Augustin Cournot was one of the first economists to view economic theory as a set of tools that could be used to analyze economic and social problems. Cournot showed that both supply and demand determine price and that, in time, price influences both supply and demand. Cournot used two-dimensional diagrams to demonstrate these relationships.

Cournot is now recognized as a great economist, but this was not the case when he was alive. He did some of the most original thinking in economic theory, but his life was a tragic one. Cournot studied mathematics at the Ecole Normale in Paris. He read constantly, despite very poor eyesight that eventually developed into blindness. While a student, Cournot worked as a secretary to one of Napoleon's generals. In 1834, with the support of the famous statistician Poisson, Cournot became a professor of mathematics at Lyons. In 1838, Cournot published his great

work in mathematical microeconomics, *Researches into the Mathematical Principles of the Theory of Wealth.* This book did not have much impact and was hardly noticed. Some sources indicate that not a single copy was sold! In later years, as his sight was failing, Cournot published less mathematical versions of this work, which were more widely read. When Cournot died in 1877, his highly innovative work in economic theory was largely unnoticed.

The irony of Cournot's life is that, although he was not well known during his own lifetime, his vision of economics as a set of highly mathematical tools that could be used to examine a large number of social problems is very close to the thinking of most present-day economists. If Cournot were around today, he would be surprised to see how his radical vision has come to reflect the accepted role of the economist.

them. He found that by reducing prices, he sold more autos and increased profits. In the process, Ford Motor Company revolutionized production. In the early years of the Model T, Henry Ford said: "Every time I reduce the charge for our car by one dollar, I get a thousand new buyers."[2]

ELASTICITY AND TOTAL REVENUE

PRICE CHANGE	CHANGE IN QUANTITY DEMANDED	COEFFICIENT OF ELASTICITY	CHANGE IN TOTAL REVENUE
• Rise	Decrease	$E_d > 1$	Decrease
• Rise	Decrease	$E_d = 1$	Unchanged
• Rise	Decrease	$E_d < 1$	Increase
• Fall	Increase	$E_d > 1$	Increase
• Fall	Increase	$E_d = 1$	Unchanged
• Fall	Increase	$E_d < 1$	Decrease

PRICE ELASTICITY OF DEMAND AND POLICY CHOICES: SMOKING

For many years, the U.S. government, primarily through the office of the Surgeon General, has pursued a policy of trying to discourage cigarette smoking.[3] It may not be appropriate for government to try to intervene in personal decisions such as smoking, but various levels of government are doing so. Many state and some local governments have required public places, such as restaurants, to set up no-smoking sections and have prohibited smoking in hospitals, doctors' offices, and public buildings.

In the 1980s Surgeon General C. Everett Koop made it his goal to create a "smoke-free society" by the year 2000. But in a report issued before he left office, he painted a picture that indicated that this goal would have to be much longer-term. In his report, he noted that in recent years the decline in cigarette smoking has been about 1.5 percent per year. At that rate, U.S. consumers will still be consuming 470 billion cigarettes annually in the year 2000. That's a pack a day for 64 million people.

Koop's report showed that cigarette smoking is less prevalent at higher socioeconomic and income levels. The ethnic group with the heaviest smoking rate is Alaska natives at 56 percent. That group is followed by Mexican-American men at 43 percent, Puerto Rican men at 40 percent, all blacks at 34 percent, all whites at 29 percent, and college graduates at 16 percent. Cigar and pipe smokers follow a different pattern. Among men with a family income over $40,000, there is a 5 percent rate of cigar smoking.

In commenting on Koop's report in *Fortune* magazine, Daniel Seligman was critical of the Surgeon General's suggestions for reducing cigarette smoking.[4] Koop's report called for more education, more regulation

---

2. *Forbes* (12 January 1987): p26.

3. Evidently the Surgeon General feels that smoking is only a problem for U.S. citizens. The warning about smoking being hazardous to health is printed only on cigarettes manufactured for domestic consumption. Cigarettes manufactured for export do not contain the warning unless it is required by the government of the importing country.

4. *Fortune* (13 February 1989): 123. Additional data on smoking and elasticity studies can be found in *Business Week* (18 June 1990): 20–21.

of smokers' behavior, and more restrictions on advertising. Seligman suggested that raising excise taxes on cigarettes was a solution brushed off too quickly in the report.

Koop's report reviewed studies of the price elasticity of demand for cigarettes. One study showed that the elasticity coefficient for smokers aged twelve to seventeen was 1.4. The elasticity coefficient for smokers as a whole was 0.7. This figure and the concept of price elasticity of demand can be used to make a policy recommendation.

Suppose the President decides to declare an all-out "war" on cigarette smoking. Assume that the President calls in the Secretary of Health and Human Services and tells the Secretary that cigarette smoking should be cut by 25 percent in the next year. The Secretary asks you, a recently hired economist at the Department of Health and Human Services, to write a memo outlining a plan to accomplish this goal.

You return to your office to begin work. Based on your study of microeconomics, you do not think that prohibitions and warnings will work. You have studied enough economics to be convinced that the only way to proceed is to unleash market forces to create the incentives that will accomplish the desired policy goal. (Remember, as an economist, you apply positive theory, without any normative considerations of whether or not the policy should be carried out.) You decide that the best way to bring about the desired reduction in smoking is to let the market do it. The best way to accomplish this is to raise price by putting an additional federal excise tax on cigarettes. Your job is now relatively simple: determine the appropriate tax.

You need data on cigarette consumption and how it responds to changes in cigarette prices. The data are not that difficult to find. You decide to use $E_d = 0.7$ from the study cited in the Koop report. It is now a simple matter to compute the tax necessary to have the desired impact on consumption. You know that the President wants to cut consumption by 25 percent and that the present average price of a pack of cigarettes is $1.42. You simply substitute into the formula to determine the tax:

$$E_d = \frac{\%\Delta Q}{\%\Delta P}$$

$$0.70 = \frac{0.25}{\%\Delta P}$$

$$\%\Delta P = \frac{0.25}{0.70} = 0.36 = 36 \text{ percent.}$$

You can now write your memo. In order to attain a 25 percent decrease in quantity demanded, it is necessary to have a 36 percent increase in price. The required additional excise tax would, therefore, be 51 cents per pack ($1.42 × 0.36), making the price of a pack of cigarettes $1.93. This price increase will reduce smoking even more among those aged twelve to seventeen, because the elasticity of demand is higher among that group.

You have used a simple economic tool in the same way that economists giving policy advice would use it. Although the example was made up, the data were real and the estimates were based on sound theory.

POLICY APPLICATION: RECRUITING STUDENTS

For many years, colleges didn't pay too much attention to the problem of recruiting students because the post–World War II baby boom produced a seemingly endless supply of new students. Many schools greatly expanded their facilities during this boom period, especially state-supported institutions. This "bubble" in the population is now past college age, and demographic data show that the college-aged population will continue to decline until 1997. This smaller pool of prospective students presents serious problems to both private and state-supported institutions of higher learning. Private institutions must attract students because tuition is often their main source of revenue. Public institutions also need students because their state funding is tied to the number of students they have enrolled.

It is a little easier to view this problem from the standpoint of the student as a demander of college services. (Since the number of students who "buy" becomes the supply of students to colleges, it is also possible to view the problem as a problem of supply.) The demand curve is like most other demand curves. It has a negative slope. If colleges raise the price, students will decrease the quantity of educational services they demand, and the number of students will be lower than before the price increase.

The situation is a supply and demand problem with elasticity considerations. To attract enough students in a competitive world, colleges have to lower their prices. But if they lower their prices to everyone, they "give back" revenue to some students who aren't the best and the brightest while significantly lowering their operating revenues. Can you think of a solution? Colleges lower the price to some selected students—those whose demand is more elastic because they have good alternatives—by giving them scholarships and other types of financial aid.

OTHER DEMAND ELASTICITIES

Price elasticity of demand is not the only microeconomic measure of responsiveness. It is possible to calculate the elasticity of almost anything because what an elasticity coefficient measures is the responsiveness of one measurable quantity to another. Two other demand elasticities are quite common in economics.

The first of these other concepts is the **income elasticity of demand**. This measures the way in which quantity demanded responds to changes in income, assuming all other things, including price, are held constant. The formula is expressed as

$$E_i = \frac{\text{percent change in quantity demanded}}{\text{percent change in income}}.$$

income elasticity of demand
The measure of the responsiveness of quantity demanded to changes in income.

The sign of the coefficient of the income elasticity of demand is important. If the sign is negative, indicating an inverse relationship between income and quality demanded, the good is said to be an inferior good. If the sign is positive, the good is a normal good.

For normal goods, if $E_i > 1$, demand for the good is income elastic. If $E_i < 1$, demand for the good is income inelastic. Goods that have high and positive income elasticities are classed as luxury goods. In fact, the concept of income elasticity of demand is used as a definition of what a luxury good is. Necessities, such as food, have a low but positive income elasticity. Luxuries, such as sports cars and foreign travel, have a high positive income elasticity.

Income elasticity is useful to producers in forecasting sales. If producers can forecast changes in consumer income and know the income elasticity of demand for their product, they can estimate how much more to produce. This is one of the reasons why firms are interested in economic forecasts.

cross elasticity of demand
The measure of the responsiveness of changes in the quantity demanded of one good to changes in the price of another.

The other common demand elasticity concept is the **cross elasticity of demand**. Cross elasticity measures the responsiveness of changes in the quantity demanded of one good to changes in the price of another. The formula for the coefficient of the cross elasticity of demand is

$$E_{AB} = \frac{\text{percent change in quantity demanded of good } A}{\text{percent change in price of good } B}$$

If the cross elasticity is equal to anything but zero, the two goods are related. They are either complements or substitutes. Two goods that are completely unrelated (independent of one another) have a zero cross elasticity of demand. If the sign of the coefficient is negative, the relationship is an inverse one. An increase in the price of good B will bring about a decrease in the quantity demanded of good A. A negative cross elasticity coefficient thus indicates that good A and good B are complements. Complements are goods that are used together, such as coffee and cream or pens and paper. A positive cross elasticity coefficient indicates a substitute relationship between good A and good B. An increase in the price of good B will lead to an increase in the quantity demanded of good A. Substitute goods can be used in place of each other. Examples are coffee and tea, and beef and chicken. The size of the coefficient tells how strong the complementary or substitute relationship is between the two goods. As we will see in later chapters, cross elasticity is useful in defining markets and industries because it is a measure of how closely goods are related.

PRICE ELASTICITY OF SUPPLY

price elasticity of supply
The measure of the responsiveness of the quantity supplied to changes in the price.

coefficient of price elasticity of supply (E_s)
The numerical measure of price elasticity of supply, equal to the percent change in the quantity supplied of a good divided by the percent change in its price.

The concept of elasticity of demand is also applicable to supply schedules and supply curves. **Price elasticity of supply** is the measure of the responsiveness of the quantity supplied to changes in the price. The **coefficient of price elasticity of supply (E_s)** is the numerical measure of price elasticity of supply. The equation for the coefficient of price elasticity of supply is

$$E_s = \frac{\text{percent change in quantity supplied}}{\text{percent change in price}},$$

or, in a more workable form,

$$E_s = \frac{\dfrac{\Delta Q^s}{Q^s}}{\dfrac{\Delta P}{P}}.$$

As with the price elasticity of demand, when $E_s = 1$, supply is unit elastic. If $E_s > 1$, supply is elastic. If $E_s < 1$, supply is inelastic. The analogy to price elasticity of demand stops there. The coefficient of price elasticity of supply is usually positive because supply curves normally have positive slopes. Since supply curves are positively sloped, the relationship between elasticity and total revenue established for price elasticity of demand doesn't hold. Higher prices result in higher total revenue, regardless of whether supply is elastic or inelastic.

Special cases of supply curves are classified as perfectly inelastic, unit elastic, or perfectly elastic. With the vertical supply curve in Figure 9, the quantity supplied is totally unresponsive to changes in price. It is perfectly inelastic. Examples of perfectly inelastic supply curves are rare. In the short run, however, it is often impossible to produce more of a good regardless of what happens to price. This inability to produce more will affect the supply curve, which shows the amount people are willing to supply at various prices. Consider the supply of Rembrandt paintings, for example, or of Rose Bowl tickets. A rise in the price of Rembrandt paintings (even in the long run) or Rose Bowl tickets (in the short run) does not cause the quantity supplied to increase.[5] These supply curves are perfectly inelastic.

Figure 10 shows both a perfectly elastic supply curve and a unit elastic supply curve. S_1, a horizontal line, is a perfectly elastic supply curve. Any straight-line supply curve that is drawn through the origin, as is S_2 in Figure 10, is unit elastic over its entire range. Along such a curve, the percent changes of the two variables will always be equal to each other. Other linear supply curves are elastic at every price if they intersect the price (vertical) axis above the origin and inelastic at every price if they intersect the quantity (horizontal) axis to the right of the origin. This is true even though elasticity changes along both curves. Two such curves are shown in Figure 11.

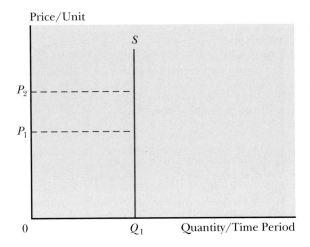

FIGURE 9
PERFECTLY INELASTIC
SUPPLY CURVE
A perfectly inelastic supply curve is a vertical line. It would exist if suppliers offered a fixed amount of a good, regardless of any changes in its price.

5.   This isn't quite correct because some individuals who own Rembrandt paintings will become suppliers if the price gets high enough.

Price/Unit

FIGURE 10
UNIT ELASTIC SUPPLY CURVE AND PERFECTLY ELASTIC SUPPLY CURVE
A perfectly elastic supply (S_1) curve is a horizontal line. With such a curve, a change in price produces an infinite response in the quantity supplied. A straight-line supply curve drawn through the origin has a unitary coefficient of elasticity along the entire curve.

PRODUCTION COSTS

Price elasticity of supply depends on the costs of production and how these costs change as the output of a good or service is increased. If costs rise rapidly as output is expanded, the quantity supplied will not be very responsive to changes in price. The supply curve is inelastic. On the other hand, if costs don't increase very much as output is increased, a rise in price will increase the profits of supplying firms and the output response could be substantial. The supply curve is elastic. Price elasticity of supply and the costs of production are so intertwined that we will discuss them in more depth in later chapters.

RESOURCE AVAILABILITY AND TIME

Elasticity of supply is the measure of responsiveness of quantity supplied to changes in price. The major factor affecting this responsiveness is the

Price/Unit

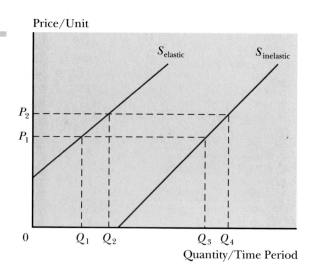

FIGURE 11
INELASTIC AND ELASTIC SUPPLY CURVES
A straight-line supply curve that intersects the price (vertical) axis will be elastic over its entire length. A straight-line supply curve that intersects the quantity (horizontal) axis will be inelastic over its entire length.

availability of resources that can be attracted away from other uses. Another factor is the time period under consideration. As the time period increases, the possibility of obtaining new and different inputs to increase the supply increases. For the two earlier examples of fixed supply, you will recognize that in the long run the stadium could be expanded and the quantity of Rose Bowl tickets increased. Rembrandts, however, have a perfectly inelastic supply because additional inputs don't exist.

These two factors—availability of inputs and time—affect elasticity of supply. Normally the elasticity of supply coefficient becomes larger with time and is larger for products that use relatively unspecialized or abundant inputs.

WHO PAYS THE EXCISE TAX: AN EXERCISE IN THE ELASTICITY OF SUPPLY AND DEMAND

Debates over tax policy can be quite confusing. Consumers are often convinced that they ultimately pay all taxes, yet business firms often fight hard to prevent tax increases on their products. If consumers pay all taxes, why should a business firm care if its product is taxed or not? The answer is not simple. The correct answer to the question of who ultimately pays such a tax is "It depends on supply and demand in the relevant market." This problem is an exercise that involves elasticity of both supply and demand.

An **excise tax** is a tax on the purchase of a particular good, such as liquor, cigarettes, or electricity, or a broad class of goods, such as food.

Let's look at an example with normally sloped supply and demand curves. Figure 12 illustrates the market for beer. Beer is a good example because excise taxes are often placed on items such as alcohol and cigarettes. These taxes are sometimes called "sin taxes." Assume that the market settles on a price of $3.00 per six-pack, with X_e representing the equilibrium quantity of six-packs per week. Now suppose the government

excise tax
A tax on the purchase of a particular good, such as liquor, cigarettes, or electricity, or a broad class of goods, such as food.

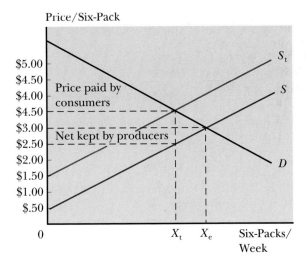

FIGURE 12
AN EXCISE TAX ON BEER
An excise tax on beer causes its supply curve to shift upward by the amount of the tax (from S to S_t). Less of the commodity is purchased at the higher price. Part of the tax is borne by consumers, and part of the tax is borne by producers.

places an excise tax of $1.00 per six-pack on beer and collects this tax from producers. The costs of production have been increased by $1.00 per six-pack. This means that the supply curve will shift up by the amount of the tax. One way to view the tax is that the producer must pay $1.00 per six-pack for the permission to produce beer. In terms of Figure 12, the supply curve shifts up at all points by $1.00. The post-tax supply curve is S_t. The equilibrium price will rise to $3.50 per six-pack, and the new equilibrium quantity is X_t.

Note that the new price is less than the sum of the old price and the tax. If the entire tax had been shifted onto consumers, the consumer would end up paying the old price of $3.00 plus the tax of $1.00, or $4.00 per six-pack. It is also clear that the amount of money the producer actually receives has fallen. Before the tax, the producer received $3.00 per six-pack, but now the producer receives $2.50 per six-pack ($3.50 price minus the $1.00 tax). The tax caused prices to rise, which caused the quantity demanded to fall. Because supply is relatively inelastic in this case, beer producers did not pass along the full amount of the tax in order to try to maintain sales. As a result, the producers sell a smaller quantity at a lower price than before. In this example, then, part of the tax was paid by consumers and part was paid by producers. Each paid half of the excise tax.

The amount of a tax paid by consumers or producers depends on the supply and demand elasticities for the goods being taxed. Figure 13 shows clearly how the elasticity of supply and the elasticity of demand affect the tax incidence. Tax incidence is the economist's term for who really pays the tax. **Tax incidence** is the place where the burden of a tax actually falls. It identifies those who pay the tax after all shifting has occurred.

tax incidence
The place where the burden of a tax actually falls after all shifting has occurred.

Part (*a*) of Figure 13 shows a normally sloped supply curve and a perfectly inelastic demand curve. When the excise tax is placed on the good, the supply curve facing consumers shifts from S to S_t. The result is that price rises from P_e to P_t. Price has risen by the full amount of the tax, and the equilibrium quantity is unchanged. In this case, the incidence of the excise tax falls fully on the consumers of this good. The tax has been shifted forward to consumers by the full amount of the tax.

Part (*b*) of Figure 13 shows a normally sloped supply curve and a perfectly elastic demand curve. The post-tax supply curve is again S_t. After the tax is imposed, price is unchanged at P_e, but the equilibrium quantity has fallen from Q_e to Q_t. Since the price to consumers is unchanged, the producer is paying the entire tax. The incidence of the tax falls fully on the suppliers of this good.

The principle demonstrated by the first two parts of Figure 13 is clear: The more inelastic the demand for a good, the more any excise tax placed on the good will fall on consumers of that good. Conversely, the more elastic the demand, the more any excise tax placed on the good will fall on the producers.

In order to see the effects of different supply elasticities, it is necessary to refer to another graph. The usual way to represent a tax increase on a graph is by an upward shift in the supply curve. However, we can also represent a tax increase by a downward shift of the demand curve. In the case of perfectly inelastic supply, it is necessary to shift the demand curve because it is impossible to shift the supply curve.

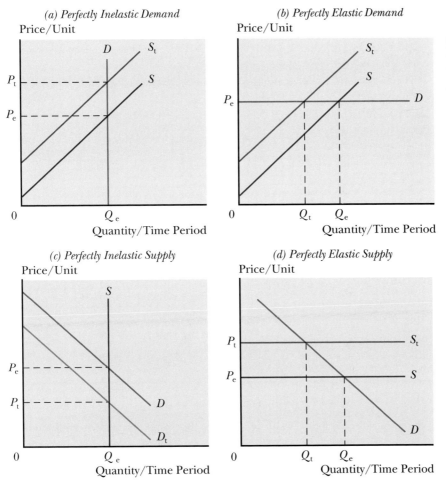

(a) Perfectly Inelastic Demand

(b) Perfectly Elastic Demand

(c) Perfectly Inelastic Supply

(d) Perfectly Elastic Supply

FIGURE 13
ELASTICITY AND TAX
INCIDENCE
Tax incidence, or where
the tax burden falls,
depends on the elasticity
of demand or supply.
(*a*) With perfectly in-
elastic demand, the con-
sumer pays the entire tax.
(*b*) With perfectly elastic
demand, the producer
pays the entire tax. (*c*) With perfectly
inelastic supply, the pro-
ducer pays the entire tax.
(*d*) With perfectly elastic
supply, the consumer
pays the entire tax.

In part (*c*) of Figure 13, *D* still shows what consumers are willing to pay
for various quantities, including the tax. However, D_t is the demand curve
as the producer sees it, after the tax has been subtracted. The tax does not
affect the quantity, which is determined by the perfectly inelastic supply
curve. The industry views the demand curve as the curve with the amount
of the tax subtracted from the price. The equilibrium quantity is unchanged
by the shift. The price the firm receives falls from P_e to P_t. In other words,
the entire amount of the tax has been paid by the suppliers of the good.

Part (*d*) of Figure 13 shows a perfectly elastic supply curve. An excise
tax shifts the supply curve from *S* to S_t to account for the higher price at
each output. After the shift, the price of the item has increased from P_e
to P_t, by the exact amount of the tax. In this case, consumers are paying
the entire tax. Less is being sold, so some producers may be worse off in
that sense. However, consumers are paying more for Q_t, and this increased amount is exactly equal to the amount of the tax.

The complete answer to the question of who pays the excise tax should
now be clear. The answer is "It depends on the relative elasticities of sup-

INCIDENCE OF AN EXCISE TAX

- The more inelastic the demand, the more price rises. The tax falls more heavily on consumers.
- The more elastic the demand, the less price rises. The tax falls more heavily on producers.
- The more inelastic the supply, the more the tax is paid by producers.
- The more elastic the supply, the more price rises. The tax is paid mostly by consumers.

ply and demand for the good on which the tax is placed." These elasticities depend on whether substitutes are available and are how consumers choose among competing goods when prices change. The next chapter will develop a theory of consumer choice that explains this process of adjustment.

SUMMARY

1. Elasticity is the measure of the sensitivity or responsiveness of quantity demanded or quantity supplied to changes in price (and to changes in other *ceteris paribus* conditions).

2. Straight-line demand curves, except for those that are perfectly vertical or horizontal, have points on them that range from elastic to inelastic and one point that is unit elastic.

3. Price elasticity of demand is a measure of how many substitutes a good or service has. The more substitutes an item has, the more elastic demand for it will be. Consumers will have more options and respond more readily to changes in price.

4. Elasticity of demand is greater when the time period is longer because consumers have more opportunity to substitute between goods.

5. Total revenue is closely related to elasticity because a demand curve is a price-quantity relationship, and total revenue is price times quantity. When price changes, the quantity demanded changes. This change affects total revenue. The amount of the change in total revenue

will depend on the responsiveness of consumers to changes in price, or elasticity.

6. Income elasticity of demand measures the responsiveness of changes in quantity demanded to changes in income.

7. Cross elasticity of demand measures the responsiveness of changes in the quantity demanded of one good to changes in the price of another good.

8. Price elasticity of supply is the measure of the responsiveness of changes in quantity supplied to changes in price.

9. As time passes, the elasticity of supply increases. The longer the time period, the more chance there is for adjustments to take place.

10. The concepts of supply, demand, and elasticity can be used to determine tax incidence. The more inelastic the demand for a good or service and the more elastic the supply, the greater is the amount of an excise tax on the good or service paid by consumers. The more elastic the demand and the more inelastic the supply, the greater is the amount of the tax paid by producers.

NEW TERMS

elasticity	perfectly inelastic	total revenue	coefficient of price
price elasticity of	demand	income elasticity of	elasticity of supply (E_s)
demand	perfectly elastic demand	demand	excise tax
coefficient of price	unit elastic demand	cross elasticity of	tax incidence
elasticity of	arc elasticity	demand	
demand (E_d)	point elasticity	price elasticity of supply	

QUESTIONS FOR DISCUSSION

1. Several years ago the *Wall Street Journal* ran an article entitled "Chicago's Troubled Transit System Takes Unorthodox Steps to Attract Commuters." The main "unorthodox" step was to reduce fares. What does this decision indicate about what the head of the Illinois State Department of Transportation thinks about the price elasticity of demand for the services of the transit system?

2. To demonstrate the importance of using average price and quantity changes when determining elasticity, use the correct formula for calculating the coefficient of price elasticity of demand for a change in price from $2.20 to $2.40 in Table 1. Then calculate the coefficient again for a price increase from $2.20 and a price decrease from $2.40, without using averaging. Explain the difference in your answers.

3. Would the elasticity of demand for Pepsi be higher or lower than that for soft drinks in general? Why?

4. Why is public policy aimed at decreasing oil imports frustrated by the fact that demand for gasoline is income elastic and price inelastic?

5. During the energy crisis, the *Wall Street Journal* ran a headline, "Europe's Drivers Don't Reduce Gasoline Use Despite Soaring Prices." Data from the article showed that gas prices were up 120 percent in Europe, and the general price level rose 140 percent during the same period. What was wrong with the headline?

6. If the government wants to place a tax on some good for the purpose of generating revenue, should it look for a good that has a relatively inelastic demand curve or a relatively elastic one?

7. For the demand schedule below, calculate the values for the total revenue column by multiplying price times quantity demanded. Then use the formula to calculate the coefficients of price elasticity of demand based on the changes in price and total revenue.

PRICE	QUANTITY DEMANDED	TOTAL REVENUE (*TR*)	COEFFICIENT OF PRICE ELASTICITY OF DEMAND (E_d)
$0.50	25	_____	_____
1.00	20	_____	_____
1.20	18	_____	_____
1.40	16	_____	_____
1.60	14	_____	_____
1.80	12	_____	_____
2.00	10	_____	_____
2.20	8	_____	_____
2.40	6	_____	_____
2.60	4	_____	_____
2.80	2	_____	_____
3.00	0	_____	_____

8. Suppose one firm is the only seller of the product represented by the demand schedule in Question 7. What would you do if the price were $2.00 when you took over that firm's marketing department?

9. The price of good *X* increases from $1.10 to $1.15, and the quantity of good *Y* consumed increases from 1,100 units to 1,750 units. What is the cross elasticity of demand? What does this imply about goods *X* and *Y*?

10. If the coefficient of the cross elasticity of demand for good *A* and good *B* is infinite, what kind of goods are *A* and *B*?

11. In the discussion concerning an excise tax on cigarettes, we calculated that a 36 percent increase in price was needed to cut cigarette consumption for all consumers by 25 percent. If the 36 percent increase in price occurred, how much would the consumption of cigarettes by those aged twelve to seventeen change?

12. Why is the coefficient of the price elasticity of demand higher for those aged twelve to seventeen than for all smokers?

13. Which of the following pairs of products are complements and which are substitutes?

    a.   men's suits and ties

    b.   butter and margarine

    c.   Pepsi and Coke

    d.   gasoline and Cadillacs

    e.   women's swimsuits and jackhammers

14. For each of the pairs in Question 13, is the coefficient of the cross elasticity of demand negative or positive? Do you expect the coefficient to be a large or small number? Why?

15. Why is the value of the price elasticity of demand negative? Why do we ignore the negative sign?

SUGGESTIONS FOR FURTHER READING

Browning, Edgar K., and Jacquelene M. Browning. *Microeconomic Theory and Applications*, 3rd ed. Boston: Little, Brown, 1989. This book contains a good treatment of elasticity, with problems to solve.

Lindsay, Cotton Mather. *Applied Price Theory*. New York: Dryden Press, 1984. A well-written, intermediate textbook on price theory with many elasticity applications.

1. Define:
   a. utility,
   b. income effects,
   c. substitution effects,
   d. consumer surplus.
2. Use marginal utility to calculate total utility, and derive a marginal utility curve from a total utility curve.
3. Use the equation for maximizing total utility to determine an individual's consumption pattern.
4. Derive an individual demand curve for a good based on:
   a. the equation for maximizing total utility,
   b. the principle of diminishing marginal utility.
5. Explain the solution to the diamond-water paradox based on:
   a. marginal utility and total utility,
   b. value in exchange and value in use.
6. Discuss the argument over a progressive income tax in terms of:
   a. the marginal utility of income,
   b. interpersonal utility comparisons.

CHAPTER 20

DEMAND AND CONSUMER CHOICE

INTRODUCTION

We have used demand and supply curves to develop a variety of predictions about the outcome of different market processes. Most of our analysis made use of market demand curves, which we derived by aggregating individual demand curves. Since individual demand curves form the bedrock of microeconomic analysis, we need to consider the factors that underlie them.

The first approach economists took in examining consumer demand—the classical approach—involved the concept of measurable utility. We will use this approach to examine some problems and suggest some applications for demand analysis. The second approach to consumer demand—indifference curve analysis—is discussed in an appendix to this chapter.

CHOICE, VALUE, AND UTILITY THEORY

The idea that households and firms must make choices because of scarcity is the fundamental notion of economic analysis. We now want to expand on that analysis to determine why consumers react in the way they do. Why does a person demand a certain good or service? An obvious answer is that the good or service is expected to satisfy some need or desire of the consumer. Economists, unlike other social scientists, are content with this simple answer.

There may be moral or ethical dimensions to the desires people have. Why do people want to buy guns, pornography, narcotics, sports cars, liquor, or cigarettes? These are questions to which psychologists, moral-

535

ists, and many others devote a great deal of attention. But economists generally are not interested in why desires exist or why people should buy some goods and not others. It is not because they think such questions are unimportant. In fact, such questions may be more important than the questions economists try to answer: What would happen to the sales of Porsches if their price increased by $1,000? What would happen to the sales of potatoes if the price of wheat went up $1 per bushel? Economists accept the fact that people have a certain psychological or ethical makeup. Without approving or disapproving of it or asking where it came from, economists start their analysis from there.

Economists' view of consumer choice is based on five assumptions about the psychology of consumer behavior:

1. Individuals (or households) must make choices because they have limited income and are forced to choose which of their many wants to satisfy.
2. Individuals make rational choices when they make these consumption decisions. That is, they weigh costs and benefits and make the decision that gives them the most satisfaction.
3. Individuals make these choices with imperfect information. In other words, they don't know (with certainty) all the attributes of the goods they are choosing to consume.
4. As increasing amounts of a good are consumed, the additional satisfaction gained from an additional unit becomes smaller.
5. Many goods have qualities that make them satisfactory substitutes for other goods.

All of these statements may seem simple and obvious, but they will enable us to make some powerful conclusions about the nature of demand.

The History of Utility Theory: The Diamond-Water Paradox

In the early development of economic theory, economists often posed questions that they then debated. One of the popular debate topics was what determined value. Adam Smith wrote that value could mean either "value in use" or "value in exchange." He posed (in 1776) what became known as the diamond-water paradox:

The things that have the greatest value in use have frequently little or no value in exchange; and on the contrary, those which have the greatest value in exchange have frequently little value in use. Nothing is more valuable than water: but it will purchase scarce anything; scarce anything can be had in exchange for it. A diamond, on the contrary, has scarce any value in use; but a very great quantity of other goods may frequently be had in exchange for it.[1]

diamond-water paradox
The fact that diamonds, although less useful than water, are more expensive than water. That is, things with the greatest value in exchange (price) often have little value in use.

The **diamond-water paradox** was the problem that classical economists used when they argued that value in use could not determine price (value in exchange). Diamonds, although less useful than water, are more expensive than water. The discussion about the diamond-water paradox

---

1.   Mark Blaug, *Economic Theory in Retrospect* (Homewood, IL: Richard D. Irwin, 1968), writes that Smith, in what may be the greatest understatement in the history of economic thought, conceded that his explanation of value was obscure.

William Stanley Jevons had one of the greatest minds in the history of economic thought. Jevons combined utility theory with marginal analysis and applied it to consumer choice. He thus constructed the theory that underlies the theory of demand.

Jevons was both a theoretical and a practical economist. He was born in Liverpool and studied chemistry and mathematics at University College, London. Financial problems caused him to move to Australia to accept a job with the Sydney Mint. He spent five years in Australia. During that time, he became interested in political economy. In 1859, he returned to the University of London and studied political economy until 1865. In 1865, he published a book, *The Coal Question*, which thrust him into prominence in economic circles. His most famous book, *Theory of Political Economy*, was published in 1871.

Jevons accepted a professorship at Owens College, Manchester, in 1866. There he worked on a wide range of intellectual pursuits, from statistical analysis of commodity prices to very abstract economic theory. He even developed a

sunspot theory to explain business cycles. His work generated a great deal of interest in political circles, but Jevons himself had little contact with those who made economic policy. This was largely because of his personal habits. He was, perhaps, the original "strange professor." He once wrote to his sister that he had never attended a party "without impressing upon all friends the fact that it is no use inviting me." He didn't regret his solitude. In fact, he argued that reserve and loneliness are necessary to develop ideas. He felt that social intercourse ensured that thoughts would "never rise above the ordinary level of the others." A colleague of Jevons wrote: "There never was a worse lecturer, the men would not go to his classes, he worked in flashes and could not finish anything thoroughly, the only point about Jevons was that he was a genius."

Unfortunately for economics, Jevons died at the age of forty-seven. At the time of his death, he was working on a massive book entitled *Principles of Economics*, which of course was never completed.

went on for a long time. Many famous mathematicians, economists, and philosophers took part in the debate. The confusion over the diamond-water paradox arose because of a lack of distinction between total units and marginal units and arguments over what the term *useful* meant.

In the 1870s, William Stanley Jevons, Carl Menger, and Leon Walras, all writing separately, solved the paradox by developing a theory of value in which demand and utility came to the forefront. Their solution played a major role in developing the theory of consumer demand.

Part of the debate underlying the diamond-water paradox was an argument over whether value (or price) was determined by supply or demand. In a famous analogy, Alfred Marshall, the great British economist, said that you could no more say whether supply or demand determined value than you could say which blade of a pair of scissors did the cutting. That is, value (or price) is determined by the interaction of supply and demand.

We'll consider the influence of demand on value first and leave supply for later chapters. Demand theorists used the notion of utility. In economics, if an individual wants a good or service, then that good or service has utility for that person. **Utility** is the satisfaction an individual expects to receive from consuming a good or service. The same good may have a great deal of utility for one person and none or very little for some other person. Like beauty, utility is in the eye (or mind) of the beholder.

Utility is strictly a before-the-fact concept. That is, utility measures the way an individual feels about a good *before* buying or consuming it. You may see a cake in a bakery window and have great desire for it—that's utility. If you buy and eat the cake, you may get sick and receive no satisfaction from its consumption—that's irrelevant economically. Utility is the satisfaction you *expect* to get, not what you actually get. The reason for this distinction is that utility is used in the development of the demand curve, and the demand curve shows the amounts that people will buy based on anticipated satisfaction. It does not consider the amounts of satisfaction actually received after having made the purchase.

TOTAL UTILITY AND MARGINAL UTILITY

A good unit for the measurement of utility, like the pound or gallon or mile, does not exist. Since utility is unique to the individual, however, an arbitrary (and imaginary) unit called the **util** can be employed. As long as no attempt is made to compare the number of utils of different people, this is a satisfactory measuring device. Such comparisons between people are inappropriate because the number of utils is a subjective measure of a certain individual's satisfaction and as such is not subject to meaningful comparisons. Imagine—some people prefer the beach to the mountains!

A relationship expressing a consumer's desire to consume differing amounts of a good is called a **utility function**. For example, suppose you try to construct your utility function for a certain brand of soft drink. First, choose a convenient time period, such as a day. Then, for 1 unit (1 can) of Coke per day, assign a number of utils, say 20. (You can choose any number at all: 1, or 1,000, or 47½.) Ask yourself, if I get 20 utils from 1 can, how many would I get if I consumed 2 cans per day? Suppose, after much

utility
The satisfaction that an individual expects to receive from consuming a good or service.

util
An arbitrary unit used to measure individual utility.

utility function
A relationship expressing a consumer's desire to consume differing amounts of a good.

reflection, you say 38. Ask yourself the same question about 3 cans per day, 4, 5, 6, and so on. You use these figures to construct a utility schedule, as shown in Table 1.

Marginal utility (*MU*) is the amount of utility that one more or less unit consumed adds to or subtracts from total utility. It is the change in satisfaction provided by one more or one less unit of consumption. The formula for marginal utility is

$$MU = \frac{\text{change in total utility}}{\text{change in quantity consumed}}.$$

In Table 1, the marginal utility is determined by calculating how much each additional can of Coke adds to total utility. For example, the first can of Coke adds 20 utils to total utility. The fourth can of Coke adds 13 utils to total utility (67−54 = 13). Marginal utility is found by subtracting the total utility of consuming three Cokes from the total utility of consuming that number plus one.

PRINCIPLE OF DIMINISHING MARGINAL UTILITY

The important feature of the schedule shown in Table 1 is that, although the total utility becomes larger the more you consume per day (up to a point), the additions to total utility from each additional unit consumed become smaller. The fact that additional, or marginal, utility declines as consumption increases is called diminishing marginal utility.

The **principle of diminishing marginal utility** states that the greater the level of consumption of a particular good in a given time period, the lower the marginal utility of an additional unit. For some goods there may be increasing marginal utility in a short range. The advertisement for potato chips that says "Bet you can't eat just one" implies that the satisfaction from the second is greater than that from the first. Such examples of increasing marginal utility are exceptions that exist for only the first few units. In most cases, as you consume more units of a good, the later units yield less of an addition to total utility than the preceding units did. For instance, the seventh Coke is expected to provide less additional pleasure than the sixth

marginal utility (*MU*)
The amount of utility that one more or one less unit of consumption adds to or subtracts from total utility.

principle of diminishing marginal utility
The fact that the additional utility declines as quantity consumed increases. Less satisfaction is obtained per additional unit as more units are consumed.

CANS OF COKE PER DAY	TOTAL UTILITY (UTILS)	MARGINAL UTILITY (UTILS)
0	0	0
1	20	20
2	38	18
3	54	16
4	67	13
5	77	10
6	84	7
7	88	4
8	89	1
9	87	−2
10	82	−5

TABLE 1
UTILITY SCHEDULE FOR COKE

Coke. This principle is reflected in Table 1. Marginal utility falls from 7 utils for the sixth Coke to 4 utils for the seventh.

Figure 1 (*a*) shows the total utility curve plotted from Table 1. Figure 1 (*b*) shows the marginal utility curve that corresponds to the table. Note that when the total utility curve reaches its maximum, marginal utility is zero. This makes sense because marginal utility must become negative for total utility to decline. In Table 1, total utility reaches a maximum at 8 Cokes per day because the ninth Coke has a negative marginal utility. The only way a total of anything can decline is for changes in that total to be negative.

Utility and Consumer Behavior

The concepts of utility and price can be combined to show how consumers make choices in the marketplace. Consumers are confronted with a range of items and also a range of prices. A consumer may not neces-

Figure 1
Total and Marginal Utility
Total utility increases as consumption increases to a certain level, in this case 8 Cokes per day, and then it declines. When total utility is increasing, marginal utility is declining, illustrating the principle of diminishing marginal utility. At the point where total utility begins to decline, marginal utility becomes negative.

sarily choose the item that has the greatest utility because its price and the consumer's income are also important factors. In other words, consumers don't always buy their first choice. You may prefer a Porsche to a Chevrolet, but you may purchase the Chevrolet. The explanation for this behavior lies in the relationship between price and utility.

Suppose, for example, you are considering purchasing a six-pack of soft drinks. You are presented with the three possibilities shown in Table 2. Coke is your first choice because it yields the most utility. But the relevant question is not which soft drink has the most utility, but which has the most utility *per dollar*. Therefore, you choose to buy a six-pack of Pepsi. This choice implies that the extra satisfaction of Coke over Pepsi is not worth $.75, but the extra satisfaction of Pepsi over 7-Up is worth $.25. There are other things you can do with the extra $.75. You are saying that $.75 spent on something other than Coke will yield more additional utils than the difference between the utility of Coke and the utility of Pepsi, but that $.25 spent on other goods will not yield more utils than spending it on Pepsi instead of 7-Up.

Thus, in deciding how to spend your money, you look at marginal utility per dollar rather than marginal utility alone. You do this because money is the common measure of what you have to give up. Dollars can be used to buy any available good. So for each dollar you spend, you want to choose the item with the highest utility per dollar. In doing so, you economize by getting the most satisfaction per dollar.

Maximizing Total Utility

The self-interest assumption implies that individuals will act to maximize their total utility. To see how marginal utility and price influence how a consumer maximizes total utility, consider an example with only two goods, Coke and pizza. A unit of Coke costs $.50 and a unit of pizza costs $1. The consumer's utility schedules for the two goods are presented in Table 3. The consumer has a given amount of income, called a budget constraint. A **budget constraint** is a given level of income that determines the maximum amount of goods that may be purchased by an individual. Let's allow this consumer a budget constraint of $13, and see how that amount will be allocated between the two goods to achieve maximum utility.

The first dollar will be allocated to pizza because a dollar's worth of pizza (1 piece) yields 32 utils of satisfaction compared with 29 utils for a dollar's worth of Coke (2 cans). The next dollar will also be spent on pizza because it yields 31 utils, which is still greater than the first dollar's worth of Coke, the alternative purchase. In other words, the consumer buys 2

budget constraint
A given level of income that determines the maximum amount of goods that may be purchased by an individual.

Choice	Marginal Utility (utils)	Price (dollars)	Marginal Utility per Dollar (utils)
Coke	30.0	3.00	10
Pepsi	27.0	2.25	12
7-Up	20.0	2.00	10

Table 2
Hypothetical Utility-per-Dollar Comparisons

COKE				PIZZA			
QUANTITY PER WEEK (CANS)	MARGINAL UTILITY, MU (UTILS)	MU/P (P = $.50)	TOTAL UTILITY, TU (UTILS)	QUANTITY PER WEEK (PIECES)	MARGINAL UTILITY, MU (UTILS)	MU/P (P = $1.00)	TOTAL UTILITY, TU (UTILS)
1	15	30	15	1	32	32	32
2	14	28	29	2	31	31	63
3	13	26	42	3	28	28	91
4	12	24	54	4	$24\,^3/_4$	$24\,^3/_4$	$115\,^3/_4$
5	11	22	65	5	$20\,^3/_4$	$20\,^1/_4$	136
6	$10\,^3/_4$	$21\,^1/_2$	$75\,^3/_4$	6	18	18	154
7	$10\,^1/_4$	$20\,^1/_2$	86	7	17	17	171
8	10	20	96	8	16	16	187
9	9	18	105	9	14	14	201
10	8	16	113	10	12	12	213
11	7	14	120	11	11	11	224
12	$6\,^1/_2$	13	$126\,^1/_2$	12	9	9	233

TABLE 3
UTILITY SCHEDULES
FOR A CONSUMER
OF TWO GOODS

pieces of pizza before buying any Coke. The third dollar is spent on Coke because the 29 utils of satisfaction gained from purchasing 2 cans are greater than the 28 utils that are yielded by a third piece of pizza. The process continues until the entire income of $13 is spent. In maximizing total utility, the consumer will spend $5 on 10 cans of Coke and $8 on 8 pieces of pizza. This allocation produces 300 utils of satisfaction—the maximum total utility that can be purchased with $13 of income. You cannot find a consumption pattern that will produce more satisfaction (try reducing Coke consumption by 2 cans and increasing pizza consumption by 1 piece, or vice versa).

The consumer's choices are based on a maximization rule that says that total utility is maximized when the last dollar spent on good A yields the same utility as the last dollar spent on good B. In algebraic form, total utility is maximized when

$$\frac{MU_A}{P_A} = \frac{MU_B}{P_B}.$$

The marginal utility of a can of Coke, when 10 cans per week are consumed, is 8 utils, and the price of a can is $.50. Thus,

$$\frac{MU_{cola}}{P_{cola}} = \frac{8}{\$.50} = 16 \text{ utils per dollar.}$$

For pizza, at the optimum consumption rate, the marginal utility is 16, and the price is $1. Thus,

$$\frac{MU_{pizza}}{P_{pizza}} = \frac{16}{\$1.00} = 16 \text{ utils per dollar.}$$

This can be generalized to include all goods by saying an individual maximizes utility when

$$\frac{MU_x}{P_x} = \frac{MU_y}{P_y} = \cdots = \frac{MU_n}{P_n}.$$

Of course, individuals don't spend all their income on goods. Sometimes individuals hold money as they do any other commodity. Including money (symbolized by $) , the equation for maximization of utility is

$$\frac{MU_A}{P_A} = \frac{MU_B}{P_B} = \frac{MU_\$}{P_\$}.$$

Since the price of a dollar is \$1, $MU_\$/P_\$$ can be written simply as $MU_\$$. Thus, total utility is maximized when

(1) $$\frac{MU_x}{P_x} = \frac{MU_y}{P_y} = \cdots = \frac{MU_n}{P_n} = MU_\$.$$

Utility maximization is the process by which a consumer adjusts consumption, given a budget constraint and a set of prices, in order to attain the highest total amount of satisfaction. Equation (1) is a very complete expression for utility maximization. It includes all commodities, even money. This equation says that in order to maximize total utility, the marginal utilities per dollar of all goods consumed have to be equal and also have to equal the marginal utility of money. If this is not the case, a change in the consumption pattern can produce more satisfaction for a given budget constraint. This equation is just a formal way of saying that people allocate their income so as to yield the most satisfaction possible. When utility is being maximized, the additional satisfaction from any use of a dollar will equal the additional satisfaction from any other use of that dollar. When this is not the case, the individual can reallocate personal income from one good to another and gain more satisfaction.

To see how a given consumption pattern can be adjusted to achieve maximum utility, look again at Table 3. Let's give Susan an income of \$9 and say that she uses it to buy \$3 worth of cola and \$6 worth of pizza. The expression $MU_{cola}/P_{cola} = MU_{pizza}/P_{pizza}$ doesn't hold because

$$\frac{10\,{}^{3}\!/\!_{4}}{.50} > \frac{18}{1}.$$

Susan isn't maximizing her utility because the last dollar she spent on cola yielded more utils than the last dollar she spent on pizza. Susan should reallocate her consumption outlays. By giving up a dollar's worth of pizza, she will lose 18 utils. But she will gain 20 utils by spending that dollar on more cola. Her total utility will thus rise by 2 (rounded off), and

$$\frac{10}{.50} \approx \frac{20\frac{1}{4}}{1}.$$

By purchasing 8 cans of cola and 5 pieces of pizza, Susan is maximizing utility with a \$9 budget constraint.

MARGINAL UTILITY AND THE LAW OF DEMAND

Utility theory makes it possible to derive an individual's demand curve for a good (good x). Suppose there are only two goods, x and y. Remember, demand curves are drawn using the *ceteris paribus* assumption. That is, income, tastes, and the prices of all other goods (good y) are held constant. The consumer is initially in equilibrium, maximizing utility when

$$\frac{MU_x}{P_x} = \frac{MU_y}{P_y}.$$

utility maximization
The process by which a consumer adjusts consumption, given a budget constraint and a set of prices, in order to attain the highest total amount of satisfaction.

At this equilibrium, MU_{x_1} corresponds to the consumption of x_1 units of good x in Figure 2. The price of x_1 units is represented by P_1 in Figure 2. The equation should now be written

$$\frac{MU_{x_1}}{P_1} = \frac{MU_y}{P_y}.$$

Now suppose the price of good x falls to P_2. This change throws the expression out of equilibrium because the denominator on the left side is now smaller, making the left side of the expression larger:

$$\frac{MU_{x_1}}{P_2} > \frac{MU_y}{P_y}.$$

To get back into equilibrium, the individual has to lower the value of the left side of the expression and/or raise the value of the right side. How can this be done? If the individual consumes more of x, MU_x will decline because of the principle of diminishing marginal utility. As consumption moves to x_2 on Figure 2, the marginal utility of good x falls. Furthermore, consuming more of x will mean some reduction in the consumption of y. As consumption of y falls, MU_y rises. When this happens, the expression will move toward

$$\frac{MU_x}{P_x} = \frac{MU_y}{P_y}.$$

Utility-maximizing behavior requires that when the price of good x falls (as from P_1 to P_2 in Figure 2), the consumer will increase consumption of x. Since this is necessary for utility maximization, it demonstrates that the demand curves of individuals must have a negative slope. That is, the lower the price of a good, the greater the quantity demanded.

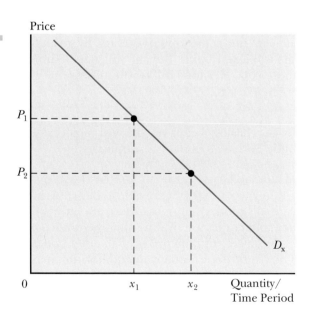

FIGURE 2
DEMAND CURVE
FOR GOOD X
When price falls from P_1 to P_2, the consumer's utility maximization is thrown out of equilibrium. Equilibrium will be restored if the consumer increases consumption to x_2.

PROBLEMS WITH UTILITY THEORY

There are two major problems with a demand theory based on utility. The first problem is that some goods are not divisible. The second, more serious problem is that utility cannot be measured.

The theory works well enough to describe the consumption of certain kinds of goods, such as soft drinks or pizzas. When the good being consumed is an automobile or a home, however, it is difficult to talk about additional units because the purchase is what economists call "lumpy." It is very difficult to consume a part of a house or a part of a car, but it is common to consume part of a six-pack of cola. The theory is somewhat weakened, then, by the fact that the consumer can't always make continuous decisions about successive amounts of consumption.[2]

A greater problem with utility theory is that it is impossible to measure utility. We have proceeded as if there were a way we could strap a meter to a consumer and exactly measure the utility expected from consuming one more unit, somewhat like measuring temperature or blood pressure. This is, of course, not possible. Psychology has not developed such sophisticated technology. But before you reject utility theory as useless, remember that it is a theoretical tool. It really isn't that important for the theory of demand to be able to measure utility. The purpose of utility theory is to develop a better understanding of why and how quantity demanded will change when prices change.

SOME APPLICATIONS OF UTILITY THEORY

You have practiced and observed utility maximization even though you may not have thought of it in the formal language of economics. Suppose, for example, you are organizing the beer concession for a fund-raising event. There are two ways to run the concession. You can charge an admission fee to the event and then allow unlimited consumption, or you can charge a set price for each beer, say $.50 per glass. Utility theory predicts different levels of consumption for these two alternatives and thus different requirements for planning the supply. In the first case, beer drinkers will consume beer until the marginal utility per glass is zero because the price per additional glass is zero. In the second case, beer drinkers will consume beer until the marginal utility per glass equals the marginal utility of $.50. You can predict, then, that there will be more drunken, rowdy behavior if the party is financed by an admission charge.

If you don't agree with this analysis, reflect back on parties you have observed. Were the most rowdy ones the pay-as-you-go type or the admission type? With the growing awareness of alcohol abuse on campus, student organizations on some campuses have outlawed keg beer parties

---

2.   This problem with utility theory is really not a major flaw. Consumers can still make adjustments with most lumpy purchases. Consider a house as an example. Suppose the individual decides after the purchase that the house is too large and that other purchases would yield more marginal utility. Over time, expenditures on the house can be lowered by a lessening of routine maintenance so that more can be spent on the other goods that yield a higher marginal utility. Buying a smaller house, buying one at a less desirable location, and renting are also available alternatives.

("all you can drink") and required that they be replaced with can-only beer parties (pay by the can). These campus rule-setters understand diminishing marginal utility whether they know it or not.

This example may seem insignificant because the consumption of beer isn't a very earth-shaking issue. Let's change the good from beer to medical services. If the government decides to provide free national health care, what do you predict will happen to the consumption of these services?[3] Of course, people will consume them until the marginal utility of the last unit is zero. This is exactly what tends to happen with a prepaid or tax-financed health care system. If you have ever participated in such a program in the military, at a university, or under a health maintenance plan, you probably have consumed more medical services than before. Since there is no charge per visit, more services are consumed. You may also have noticed that with the free system, the waiting time is usually longer, the waiting rooms are less comfortable, and the workers are less congenial than with a fee-for-service system.

THE DIAMOND-WATER PARADOX EXPLAINED

Adam Smith (and others) argued that utility (and thus demand) could not be a determinant of price because diamonds, while less useful than water, are more expensive than water. The paradox disappears if we distinguish between total utility and marginal utility. The total utility of water is high. However, since there is a great deal in existence and large quantities are consumed, its marginal utility is low. The total utility of diamonds, on the other hand, is relatively low. However, since diamonds are rare, their marginal utility is high. Price, then, is determined by marginal utility, not total utility. Economists say that marginal utility determines value in exchange (price) and that total utility determines value in use. Price, then, is related to scarcity through utility. If something has a low marginal utility at all quantities consumed, it will have a low price, regardless of how scarce it is. If something is relatively scarce and has a high marginal utility, it will be valuable and thus expensive.

INCOME AND SUBSTITUTION EFFECTS

substitution effect
An increase in the quantity demanded of a good (or service) because its price has fallen and it becomes a better substitute for all other goods.

income effect
An increase in demand for a good (or service) when its price falls, *ceteris paribus*, because the household's real income rises, and the consumer buys more of all normal goods.

The law of demand, which you studied in Chapter 3, states that as the price of a good or service declines, the quantity demanded increases, *ceteris paribus*. This law is true because of two effects that result from the price decline.

The first effect is called the **substitution effect**. When the price of a good (or service) falls, the good becomes less expensive relative to all other goods. As a result, consumers purchase more of it because it has become a better substitute for other goods as it has become cheaper. Steaks and ground beef provide a good example. As the price of steak falls, more people will switch from ground beef to steaks.

The second effect of a price decline is called the **income effect**. When the price of a good or service falls, *ceteris paribus*, the individual consumer's real income, or purchasing power, rises. That is, after buying the same amount as before (of the good for which price has fallen), the consumer has more income left over. With this higher real income, more of

---

3.   By "free" we mean there is no monetary cost to the patient. That is, price is zero.

all normal goods will be consumed. Thus, the consumption of the good that experienced the price decline also will increase (if it is a normal good). These income and substitution effects are important forces, which will become clearer in this chapter.

UTILITY THEORY AND THE PROGRESSIVE INCOME TAX

Many noneconomists believe that money and income are subject to diminishing marginal utility. This idea is one of the main arguments (but not the only one) for a progressive income tax.[4] A progressive tax takes a larger percentage of dollars from the rich because for them the dollars' marginal utility is thought to be low. A smaller percentage of dollars is taken from poorer taxpayers because for them a dollar's marginal utility is thought to be much higher. This argument assumes that it is possible to measure utility *and* to make **interpersonal utility comparisons**. Such comparisons are attempts to compare the utility of one individual with that of another. One way to avoid directly comparing utilities for different people is to assume that individuals all have the same utility schedule for given levels of income. With these two assumptions, proponents of the progressive income tax argue that society can maximize total utility by taking income away from high-income individuals who have lower marginal utilities of income and transferring it to low-income individuals who have higher marginal utilities of income.

> **interpersonal utility comparisons**
> Attempts to compare the utility of one individual with that of another (or others).

Those who apply principles of individual utility maximization to a society as a whole are on very shaky ground, however. First, economists generally believe that interpersonal utility comparisons are not feasible. People are different. There is no way you can prove that an additional $100 of income gives less satisfaction to actress Linda Evans than to an unemployed auto worker. In fact, Ms. Evans may get more satisfaction because she is such an expert consumer. It is impossible to prove that one individual gets more or less satisfaction from an increment to income than any other individual does.

A second and more fundamental problem with this analysis is that it assumes a diminishing marginal utility for income, or goods and services in general. This proposition cannot be verified. The principle of diminishing marginal utility, you will remember, states that the marginal utility of a *particular good* declines as consumption is increased. Increased income, however, represents an increase in the consumption of all goods. If wants are insatiable, there is no reason to believe that the principle of diminishing marginal utility holds for money or income. Even so, it is probably the case that most people think that income has diminishing marginal utility. What about you? Do you think a $100 bill would give your "rich" economics instructor more or less satisfaction than it would give you?

SHOPPING FOR BARGAINS

Economists have used the concept of utility-maximizing behavior to analyze shopping behavior. The idea is that a buyer will search for bargains until the expected savings in value or utility equals the cost of continued searching.

---

4.   For a comprehensive treatment of this subject, see Walter J. Blum and Harry Kalven, Jr., *The Uneasy Case for Progressive Taxation* (Chicago: University of Chicago Press, 1970).

Several predictions can be made from this theory. The first is that the larger the amount individuals expect to save, the longer they will continue to search. In other words, the bigger the item in terms of your budget, the more you will shop around. You will search longer for a good price on a car than for a good price on a loaf of bread. You might even buy bread at a convenience store, where you know the price is higher, to save some shopping time. The second prediction is that, in percentage terms, the variation in prices for bigger budget items should be smaller than the variation in prices for smaller budget items. The search process will drive high-price sellers of large items out of business or force them to reduce their prices. The third prediction is that where search costs are higher, price differences between sellers could be higher without driving the high-priced sellers out of business. Have you ever noticed that prices of gasoline are higher near freeways than in towns? Utility-maximizing theory can explain this phenomenon. Users of freeways are going somewhere, often in a hurry. Their search costs are high. They therefore do less shopping around and as a result pay higher prices.

CONSUMER SURPLUS AND UTILITY

consumer surplus
The extra utility derived from a purchase that has a value to the consumer greater than the market price.

Consumers often benefit in a market economy because they are able to purchase a good or service by sacrificing something that is worth less to them than the value of what they receive. **Consumer surplus** is the extra utility derived from a purchase that has a value to the consumer greater than the market price. Utility theory provides a measure of consumer surplus.

Consider the demand curve for a single consumer (or group of homogeneous consumers) in Figure 3. At price P_1, the individual will consume Q_1 units of the good. According to the theory of utility-maximizing

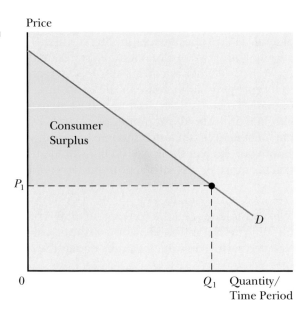

FIGURE 3
CONSUMER SURPLUS
The consumer surplus is the shaded area above the price P_1 and below the demand curve.

Tariffs have many effects. They reduce the efficiency of resource allocation. They redistribute income between countries and between producers and consumers within countries. They raise revenue for the countries that impose them. All of the economic effects of tariffs are important and will be discussed in the chapter on international trade. It is possible, however, to use the concept of consumer surplus developed in this chapter to see how tariffs affect consumer well-being.

In the graph below, S_d is the domestic supply curve and S_w is the world supply curve. World supply is perfectly elastic at the world price P_f. Consumers are demanding quantity Q, of which quantity A is sold by domestic producers and quantity $Q - A$ is imported. The triangle formed

by S_w, D, and the vertical axis represents consumer surplus. What happens if the government imposes a tariff equal to t? The price rises by the amount of the tariff to P_t, creating a new supply curve, S'_w. Consumers now purchase quantity B from domestic producers and $C - B$ from foreign producers. Consumer surplus is now represented by the triangle formed by S'_w, D, and the vertical axis. There has been a reduction in consumer surplus equal to the difference between the two triangles, or the shaded area. What this example demonstrates is that a tariff permits domestic producers to sell more of a product at a higher price and that government revenues rise by the amount of the tariff times the imported quantity. However, consumers experience a decline in consumer surplus.

TARIFFS AND CONSUMER SURPLUS

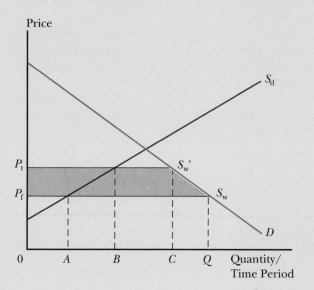

behavior, the marginal utility of the last unit purchased is equal to the price of the unit. This means that the marginal utility of each previous unit purchased was greater than price P_1. The consumer would have been willing to pay higher prices for those previous units, so at the market price of P_1, the consumer receives a bonus in terms of utility on all units but the last one. The total purchase is worth more to the consumer than the total amount (price times quantity) that is paid. This extra utility gained is called consumer surplus and is represented by the shaded area in Figure 3. Consumer surplus will be an important concept when we study monopoly. The International Perspective describes an application of consumer surplus in international trade.

ADVERTISING, MARKETING, AND DEMAND

The theory developed in this chapter explains a great deal about demand and consumer equilibrium. It does not say anything about the role of advertising and marketing. Advertising and marketing are difficult topics for economists to deal with because economic analysis usually assumes that consumers are informed, rational utility maximizers who know their own tastes and preferences. Advertising and marketing are not, however, inconsistent with those basic assumptions.

Advertisers spend a great deal of time trying to alter consumers' tastes and perceptions. If enough tastes and perceptions can be changed that the average consumer's utility from the firm's product can be increased, more will be demanded. Changes in tastes do not mean that the consumer is not rational. Even without advertising, tastes would change over time with changes in age, education, and other factors. Some tastes even change regularly with the change of season.

Advertisers also spend a great deal of time generating information for consumers about prices. This behavior of advertisers fits with the description of consumers' search behavior. If the cost of getting information falls, the cost of the search falls and consumers will do more searching. As a consequence, they may alter their purchasing patterns and buy from sellers offering lower prices.

Much advertising is directed toward making consumer demand more inelastic by convincing buyers that similar products are not satisfactory substitutes for the one being advertised. In other words, the advertiser attempts to widen the spread between the utility of its product and the utility of potential substitutes. From what you have learned in this chapter, you can see that if this strategy succeeds, an advertiser can charge a higher price for its product without losing many sales.

EXPERIMENTAL ECONOMICS: ECONOMICS ACCORDING TO RATS

Economics is beginning to borrow from experimental psychology. Some economists are carrying out work in lab settings to test some fundamental propositions in economics. At the University of Arizona, Vernon Smith has conducted research on market behavior using human subjects, usually students. At Texas A&M, economists Ray Battalio and John Kagel have experimented with human and animal subjects. These economists did experiments in mental hospitals with token economies. Patients were paid tokens for tasks and were free to spend these tokens on personal items. Some of the results of these investigations were fascinating. They found that the distribution of income earned was closely parallel to that in the U.S. economy. Perhaps even more startling was the fact that earning differences between male and female patients were similar to those between men and women in the U.S. economy.

This result led the two economists to experiment with rats. They found that rats trained to do "work for pay" (hit a bar for food) reduced their work effort after some point, choosing more leisure over additional income. They also found that among low-income rats (those that had to work hard for a little food), such work reduction patterns were more common. These experimental results are consistent with behavior patterns of individuals in real-life situations based on diminishing marginal utility.

SUMMARY

1. Total utility is the total amount of satisfaction expected from consuming an item.

2. Marginal utility is the change in total utility from consuming one more or one less unit of a good.

3. Consumers, in deciding among items, choose those items with the highest marginal utility per dollar.

4. An individual maximizes total utility by consuming all items so that their marginal utilities per dollar spent are equal.

5. When the price of a good or service falls, the quantity demanded increases because of income effects and substitution effects.

6. Utility theory is useful in explaining how much effort people will make to search for bargains.

7. Utility theory has been criticized on the grounds that utility is not measurable. Another criticism is that some items consumed are not perfectly divisible, as the theory of utility maximization requires. Despite these criticisms, utility theory is a useful tool for analyzing consumer behavior.

8. Consumer surplus is a measure of the extra benefit derived from a purchase in excess of the price that is paid.

9. Marketing and advertising can be viewed as attempts to reduce search costs and change tastes. Attempts to alter tastes are not in conflict with utility theory.

10. Experimental results have supported some of the basic propositions of marginal utility theory.

NEW TERMS

diamond-water paradox	marginal utility (*MU*)	utility maximization	interpersonal utility
utility	principle of diminishing	substitution effect	comparisons
util	marginal utility	income effect	consumer surplus
utility function	budget constraint		

QUESTIONS FOR DISCUSSION

1. Does something have to be useful to have utility? What does it mean for a good or service to be useful?

2. What is happening when the price of a good such as petroleum is increasing without a decrease in consumption?

3. Does the fact that water is inexpensive and diamonds are expensive conflict with the theory developed in this chapter? Explain.

4. If the marginal utility of one good is 4 and its price is $2 and the marginal utility of another good is 5 and its price is $1, is the individual consumer maximizing total utility? If not, how could more utility be obtained?

5. Does advertising increase or decrease the utility you get from consuming certain goods? Is this good or bad?

6. What would you expect to happen to a normal consumer's total utility for bacon if the Surgeon General established a link between bacon and cancer? How would this announcement affect the individual's demand curve for bacon?

7. The following table shows the marginal utility that Roger gets from buying various amounts of cola, pretzels, nuts, and pizza and from holding dollars. Assume that Roger has an income of $106.

What quantities of cola, nuts, pretzels, and pizza will Roger purchase? How many dollars will he hold?

8. The material in this chapter discusses rational consumer behavior. Is it ever rational to be irrational?

9. Observers of the wealthy often comment on the fact that they waste a lot of things, such as food, but are very careful in their use of time. Is this irrational behavior?

10. Use a graph to explain how a demand curve can be derived from indifference analysis.

11. Given an indifference map, a set of indifference curves, and a budget line, where does the consumer maximize satisfaction?

12. Suppose Kim Hagen's demand for escargot is represented by the following schedule. Assume that the market price of escargot is $6 per ounce.

PRICE OF ESCARGOT/OUNCE	OUNCES OF ESCARGOT/MONTH
$10	1
8	2
7	4
6	6
5	9
4	11
3	13

What is the maximum amount that Kim would pay for the first ounce of escargot per month? By how much

UNITS OF COLA (P = $18)	*MU*	UNITS OF PRETZELS (P = $4)	*MU*	UNITS OF NUTS (P = $6)	*MU*	UNITS OF PIZZA (P = $24)	*MU*	DOLLARS HELD	*MU*
1	72	1	15	1	24	1	36	1	5
2	54	2	12	2	15	2	30	2	4
3	45	3	8	3	12	3	24	3	3
4	36	4	7	4	9	4	18	4	2
5	27	5	5	5	7	5	13	5	1
6	18	6	4	6	5	6	7	6	$\frac{1}{2}$
7	15	7	$3\frac{1}{2}$	7	2	7	4	7	$\frac{1}{4}$
8	12	8	3	8	1	8	2	8	$\frac{1}{8}$

does this exceed the actual price? How much would Kim pay for the second ounce of escargot per month? By how much does this exceed the actual price? How much would Kim be willing to pay for the third and fourth ounces of escargot per month? By how much does this exceed the actual price? How much would Kim be willing to pay for the fifth and sixth ounces of escargot per month? By how much does this exceed the actual price?

13. According to the schedule in Question 12, how many ounces of escargot will Kim Hagen purchase per month? How large is Kim's consumer surplus?

14. Geno Hagen, Kim's husband, learns that the price of caviar has fallen significantly. If Kim's demand curve is their family demand curve, what will happen to their demand for escargot? What is the substitution effect? Do you think that it will be positive or negative? What is the income effect? Will it be significant in this example?

15. Some restaurants in Maryland advertise "all you can eat" crab feasts. How is this offer related to the theory in this chapter? Can you think of any restrictions a restaurant might make on the behavior of customers who buy this meal?

SUGGESTIONS FOR FURTHER READING

Browning, Edgar K., and Jacquelene M. Browning. *Microeconomic Theory and Applications*, 2nd ed. Boston: Little, Brown, 1986. A very well-written intermediate textbook on microeconomic theory.

Easterlin, Richard A. "Does Money Buy Happiness?" *Public Interest* (Winter 1973): 3–10. A short essay that challenges the notion that more goods mean more utility (happiness).

APPENDIX: INDIFFERENCE ANALYSIS, AN ALTERNATIVE APPROACH TO CONSUMER CHOICE

The marginal utility theory discussed in this chapter has the drawback that it requires precise numerical values to be assigned to alternatives (cardinal utility). A later innovation in the economic theory of choice was based on ordinal utility. Ordinal utility requires only that the utility of the choices can be ranked. Instead of saying "The next slice of pizza has 30 units of utility" or "The next Coke has 25 units of utility," the consumer needs only to be able to say "I prefer another slice of pizza to another Coke."

indifference analysis
An approach to analyzing consumer behavior based on ranking the utility of choices relative to one another.

In the late 1800s, Italian economist Vilfredo Pareto and British economist F. Y. Edgeworth, working separately, developed an approach to analyzing consumer behavior based on ordinal utility—**indifference analysis**. It wasn't until 1939, when Nobel Prize winning British economist Sir John Hicks published his classic book *Value and Capital*, that this technique became popular with economic theorists and teachers. The theory swept the economics profession, and for a while, marginal utility analysis fell into disrepute.

Pareto, Edgeworth, Hicks, and others were not trying to discredit utility theory but rather were proposing an alternative way of viewing consumer behavior. The major improvement of their theory is that it does not require the measurement of units of utility. All that is necessary is that consumers be able to rank bundles of goods in the order, from low to high, in which they prefer them.

INDIFFERENCE OR PREFERENCE

Indifference and preference seem better than marginal utility for describing the way consumers actually make decisions. Individuals make choices between bundles, or collections, of goods. For example, you might choose between four tickets to a football game and two tickets to a concert. In indifference analysis, the consumer is viewed as making choices between collections of goods and services. The only assumption is that the individual is able to state preferences for different collections or to profess indifference between some of them. In other words, confronted with a choice between going to a movie and going to a football game, the individual might rank the football game as the preferred choice. Or the individual might say, "I don't have a preference. I'm indifferent between the two choices."

indifference set
Any number of combinations of goods among which the individual consumer is indifferent (has no preference).

Suppose Mary is considering different combinations of cans of Coke and slices of pizza, as indicated in Table 1A. Combination *A* consists of 16 cans of Coke and 3 slices of pizza, and combination *B* consists of 12 cans and 4 slices. When these two combinations are offered to Mary, she states that neither combination *A* nor combination *B* is preferred over the other. They are equal in the amount of satisfaction she expects to derive. Therefore, she is indifferent between the two. Offering Mary the choice among combinations *C*, *D*, and *E* yields the same response—indifference. Mary has indicated that all five combinations of pizza and Coke yield the same amount of satisfaction. These five combinations comprise an **indifference set** for her.

COMBINATION	GOOD X (CANS OF COKE)	GOOD Y (SLICES OF PIZZA)
A	16	3
B	12	4
C	0	5
D	8	7
E	6	9

TABLE 1A
MARY'S INDIFFERENCE SET

An indifference set can be represented graphically by an indifference curve. An indifference curve corresponding to the indifference set in Table 1A is shown in Figure 1A. An **indifference curve** shows all combinations of two goods (or services) among which a consumer is indifferent.

Indifference curves are negatively sloped because for a consumer to be indifferent, all points on the curve must represent equal amounts of utility. If more of one good is added to the combination, some of the other must be removed. Each combination represents a trade-off. In Mary's case, if combination B has more pizza than combination A, it must have less Coke, since the combinations yield the same level of satisfaction. If one combination had more pizza and more Coke than any other, or if it had more of one without having less of the other, it would be preferred. The consumer would no longer be indifferent. This is yet another way of saying that more is preferred to less.

The indifference set represented by a higher indifference curve is preferred to that represented by a lower indifference curve. As Mary moves from I_1 to I_2 to I_3 to I_4 in Figure 2A, she receives more satisfaction. Such a series of indifference curves is called an **indifference map**. Every individual consumer has such a map, and movement to a higher curve on the map represents a gain in utility.

indifference curve
A plot of all combinations of goods that the consumer is indifferent among.

indifference map
A set of indifference curves. Higher curves represent higher levels of utility.

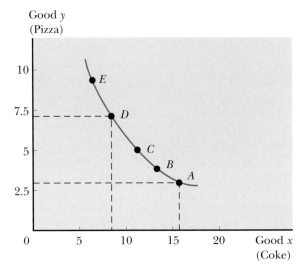

FIGURE 1A
INDIFFERENCE CURVE
An indifference curve represents combinations of two goods among which the consumer is indifferent. All combinations on the same indifference curve give the same level of satisfaction.

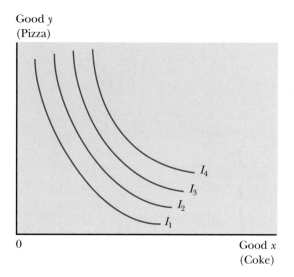

FIGURE 2A
INDIFFERENCE MAP
An indifference map is a
set of indifference curves,
each corresponding to a
different level of satisfaction. Higher curves on
the map represent higher
levels of satisfaction.

The shape of the typical indifference curve for two goods will be somewhat convex with respect to the origin. The convexity means that as a consumer gets more units of one good and fewer units of the other, it takes
more and more units of the more abundant good to compensate for the
loss of one unit of the good that is becoming more scarce. For example,
at point *A* in Figure 3A, the individual is consuming relatively large
amounts of good *y* and small amounts of good *x*. In order to compensate
for a reduction in consumption of 1 unit of *y*, the person would only require 2 units of *x* in order to be satisfied with such a trade. At point *B*, however, since less of *y* and more of *x* are being consumed compared to point
A, it will take a larger quantity of *x* (5 units) to compensate for the loss of

FIGURE 3A
CONVEXITY FEATURE OF
INDIFFERENCE CURVES
A typical indifference
curve is convex to the
origin. This convexity
means that it takes
increasingly larger
amounts of the abundant
good to compensate for
losses of the good that is
becoming more scarce.

1 unit of *y*. At point *C*, the person is consuming a large amount of *x* and very little *y*. To give up 1 unit of *y*, 20 more units of *x* would be needed to have the same utility as before.

Why do economists expect such preference relations to hold? First, most of us would agree that this is the way we would behave in such a trade-off situation. Second, the opposite conclusion seems highly unlikely. It would say that the less you had of a good, the less you would want of it relative to other goods, and the more you had of a good, the more valuable additional units of it would become. Indifference curves reflect the concept of diminishing marginal utility for two goods without assigning numerical values to utility.

DIMINISHING MARGINAL RATES OF SUBSTITUTION

The trade-off ratio along an indifference curve is called the **marginal rate of substitution (*MRS*)**. The marginal rate of substitution of *x* for *y*, MRS_{xy}, shows the willingness of the consumer to substitute between goods *x* and *y*:

$$MRS_{xy} = \frac{\text{number of units of } y \text{ given up}}{\text{number of units of } x \text{ gained}}.$$

In Figure 3A, the MRS_{xy} at point *A* is $\frac{1}{2}$. That is, 1 unit of *y* must be sacrificed to gain 2 units of *x*. At point *B*, the MRS_{xy} is $\frac{1}{5}$, and at point *C*, it is $\frac{1}{20}$. The declining value of MRS_{xy} is a reflection of the **principle of diminishing marginal rates of substitution**. That is, as more of one good (*x*) is substituted for the other good (*y*), the value of good *x* in terms of good *y* declines.

BUDGET CONSTRAINTS

An indifference map makes it possible to compare points representing combinations of two goods to determine whether the individual prefers one such combination or feels indifferent among several. All points on any single indifference curve are equivalent to each other in utility, even if utility cannot be measured numerically. Points on indifference curves located to the right and above other indifference curves are preferred combinations.

Which combinations are actually attainable for the individual? The answer depends on the income available and on the prices of the goods. Keep in mind that the consumer faces prices that are determined in markets and cannot influence them. Income constrains the consumer from buying all that might be desired. The income is the budget constraint and, when drawn on the indifference map, is called the budget line.

We limit the analysis to two goods (you could think of one of them as "all other goods"). Again assume that Mary can consume either slices of pizza or cans of Coke. Suppose she has a disposable income (*DI*) of $10.00 and pizza (good *y*) and Coke (good *x*) sell for $1.00 and $.50, respectively, per unit. The construction of the budget line is illustrated in Figure 4A. If she spends her entire income (*DI*) on pizza, she can buy 10 slices. This number is determined by dividing income by the price of the good:

$$\frac{DI}{P_y} = \frac{\$10.00}{\$1.00} = 10 \text{ slices of pizza.}$$

marginal rate of substitution (*MRS*)
The trade-off ratio along an indifference curve.

principle of diminishing marginal rates of substitution
The fact that as more of one good is consumed, more and more of the other must be given up to maintain indifference between the two.

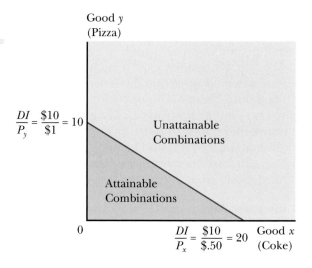

Thus, 10 is the *y*-intercept. The *x*-intercept is calculated in the same manner:

$$\frac{DI}{P_x} = \frac{\$10.00}{\$.50} = 20 \text{ cans of Coke.}$$

A straight line connecting the two points that represent buying all good *y* (pizza) or all good *x* (Coke) shows all possible combinations that Mary can purchase with a given income level of $10. For example, $10 will buy 5 slices of pizza and 10 Cokes or 6 slices of pizza and 8 Cokes. Any combination outside (above) the line is unattainable at that income level. It is outside her budget constraint. In other words, the budget line is the dividing line between those combinations that are attainable and those that are unattainable at a given level of prices and a given level of income.

CHANGES IN INCOME AND CHANGES IN PRICES

The budget line is developed holding prices and income constant. How do changes in income and prices affect the budget line? An increase in income means that more of both goods can be purchased, if prices stay the same. A doubling of income means that twice as much of both goods can be purchased, if prices remain constant. An increase in income is represented by a parallel outward shift of the budget line. A decrease in income is represented by a parallel inward shift of the budget line. Such shifts are shown in Figure 5A.

A change in the price of one good affects the maximum amount of that good that can be purchased, but does not affect the maximum amount of the other good that can be purchased. If the price of cola rises and Mary spends all her income on pizza, the price rise has no effect on the amount of pizza purchased. A price rise, then, will only affect the intercept of the budget line with the axis for the good that has experienced the price rise. Such a change is shown in Figure 6A. A price rise for good *x* from P_{x_1} to P_{x_2} causes the *x*-intercept of the budget line to move closer to the origin, reflecting the fact that less of good *x* can now be purchased with constant in-

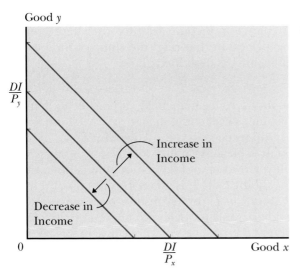

FIGURE 5A
THE EFFECT OF INCOME CHANGES ON BUDGET LINES
An increase in income is represented by an outward parallel shift of the budget line. A decrease in income is represented by an inward parallel shift of the budget line.

come. A decrease in the price of good x from P_{x_1} to P_{x_3} means more of good x can be purchased. The x-intercept of the budget line moves away from the origin, reflecting increases in the potential consumption of good x.

Price changes cause the slope of the budget line to change. The slope of the budget line is $\Delta y / \Delta x$. Note that the slope is the negative of the ratio of the y-intercept to the x-intercept, or

$$-\frac{\dfrac{DI}{P_y}}{\dfrac{DI}{P_x}}$$

which is equal to

$$\frac{P_x}{P_y}.$$

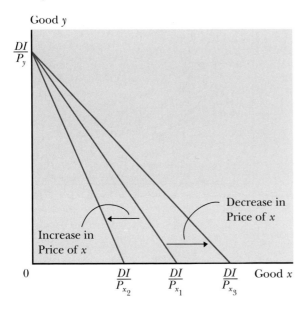

FIGURE 6A
THE EFFECT OF PRICE CHANGES ON BUDGET LINES
An increase in the price of one good changes the slope of the budget line because if all disposable income is spent on that good, less of it can be purchased. As a result, the intercept of the budget line will shift closer to the origin. The opposite holds for a decrease in price.

The slope of the budget line changes when the ratio of the prices of the two goods changes. A change in income, on the other hand, represents no change in relative prices. In that case, the slope of the budget line remains the same, but it shifts as described above.

MAXIMIZATION OF CONSUMER SATISFACTION

Adding a budget line to an indifference map makes it possible to demonstrate maximization of consumer satisfaction. In Figure 7A, at point A, the budget line is tangent to indifference curve I_2. Any point on I_3, such as point B, is preferred to point A because higher indifference curves represent higher levels of utility. However, point B is not attainable because it is outside the budget line. Point C on I_1 is attainable, but a point on I_2 is also attainable, and any point on I_2 represents more satisfaction than any point on I_1. The individual wants to reach the highest attainable indifference curve. The highest attainable curve will be one that is tangent to the budget line because no higher curve can be reached with the given income and prices. In this example, the consumer is maximizing utility, or is in equilibrium, at point A on indifference curve I_2.

You should remember from geometry that two curves that are tangent have equal slopes at the point of tangency. At the point of tangency between the indifference curve and the budget line, the marginal rate of substitution is equal to the ratio of the price of x to the price of y.[a] That is,

$$MRS_{xy} = \frac{P_x}{P_y}.$$

This expression means that the marginal rate of substitution expresses the willingness of the consumer to trade a certain amount of x for a certain amount of y, and the slope of the budget line reflects the market's will-

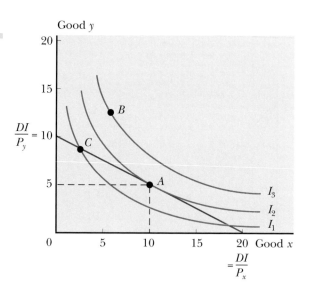

FIGURE 7A
MAXIMIZATION OF CONSUMER SATISFACTION
An individual maximizes consumer satisfaction at the point where the budget line is tangent to the highest attainable indifference curve.

a.   Technically, MRS_{xy} is equal to the negative of the slope of the indifference curve. The price ratio, as we have seen, is the negative of the slope of the budget line. Therefore, at the (equilibrium) point of tangency between the indifference curve and the budget line, $MRS_{xy} = P_x/P_y$.

ingness to trade a certain amount of *x* for a certain amount of *y*. The impersonal forces of the market impose the relative prices on the consumer, so the consumer adjusts consumption amounts in such a way that his or her trade-off is the same as the trade-off in the market.

Suppose you are consuming 15 units of *y* and 5 units of *x* (you are at point *A* in Figure 8A). According to your indifference curve (I_1), you would be willing to give up 5 units of *y* if you received 2 additional units of *x*. The market, however, is willing to give you 5 units of *x* in exchange for 5 units of *y* (note point *B*). You would probably consume less *y* and more *x*. In fact, you would be able to increase your utility by moving in the direction of the tangency of some higher indifference curve with the budget line.

CONSUMER REACTION TO INCOME CHANGES. The best feature of indifference curve analysis is that it allows us to analyze the reaction of consumers to price and income changes. Using the indifference map and the budget line, we can trace the adjustment process that takes place when a household experiences a change in income. In Figure 9A, for example, if the household's income is represented by the budget line DI_1, and *x* and *y* sell for P_x and P_y, respectively, the optimum utility is at point *A*. A decrease in income is represented by budget line DI_0, and two increases in income are represented by budget lines DI_2 and DI_3. The respective optimum positions representing tangencies of these budget lines with an indifference curve are points *B*, *C*, and *D*. Connecting points *A*, *B*, *C*, and *D* generates an **income-consumption curve**. This curve shows how consumption of the two goods changes as income changes. Recall the discussion of the income elasticity of demand in the preceding chapter. The income elasticities of both good *x* and good *y* in Figure 9A are positive because consumption of both goods increases as income increases. (Remember that a positive income elasticity indicates that a good is a normal good. An inferior good has a negative income elasticity since, in that case, as income increases, consumption of the good decreases.)

income-consumption curve
A curve that uses parallel budget lines to show changes in consumer equilibrium when income changes.

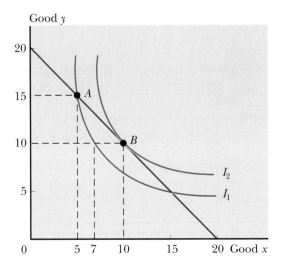

FIGURE 8A
TANGENCY ONCE AGAIN
Lower indifference curves that are within the budget constraint represent lower levels of utility than the highest, but still attainable, indifference curve.

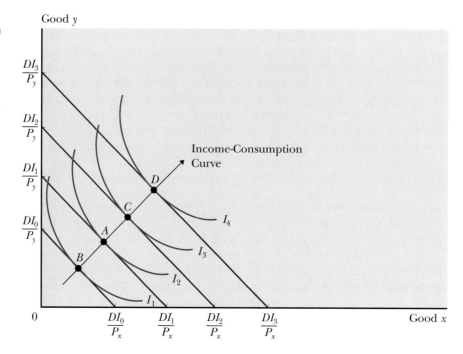

FIGURE 9A
INCOME CHANGES AND THE
INCOME-CONSUMPTION
CURVE
An income-consumption
curve traces the response
of consumption combina-
tions to changes in
income.

Figure 10A shows a case where one commodity, good x, is a normal good for a household until its income reaches DI_3. When income increases above DI_3, the household buys less of x. So x is a normal good up to point A and then becomes an inferior good as the income-consumption curve bends backward. There is nothing derogatory about the term *inferior*. A daily newspaper might be considered an inferior good for some buyers. As income falls, a person may buy the paper more often because it is a less expensive form of entertainment and also because it offers job listings. Remember, also, that a normal good to some people may be an inferior good to others.

CONSUMER REACTION TO PRICE CHANGES. Let's look at how the optimum consumption combination will be affected by price changes. Initially the consumer is at the point of maximum utility (point A in Figure 11A). As the price of x falls from P_{x_1} to P_{x_2}, the budget line rotates out to intersect the x-axis at DI/P_{x_2}, and the consumer now has a new optimum at point B on indifference curve I_2. Another decrease in price to P_{x_3} allows the consumer to reach a still higher indifference curve, I_3, and a new optimum at point C. Connecting the points A, B, and C produces a **price-consumption curve**. This curve shows how consumption changes when relative prices change.

The theory behind this change in consumption patterns relies on the income and substitution effects again. When the price of a good falls, there are two forces at work to cause the consumer to increase purchases of that good. First, when the price of a good falls, the market trade-off between this good and other goods (or the substitution rate) changes. This part of the response to a price change is the substitution effect. Second,

price-consumption curve
A curve that shows changes in consumer equilibrium when the price of one good on an indifference curve changes.

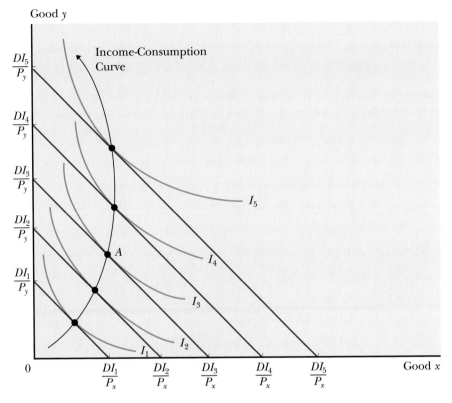

FIGURE 10A
INCOME-CONSUMPTION CURVE FOR AN INFERIOR GOOD
The income-consumption curve for an inferior good bends backward, indicating that less of the good is consumed as income increases beyond a certain level.

the individual has a larger real income, meaning that with the same nominal income, more of both (or all) goods can be purchased (and will be purchased as long as the good is not an inferior good). This part of the response to a price change is the income effect.

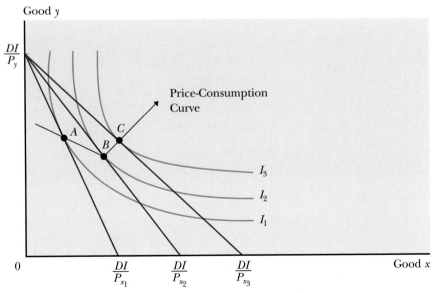

FIGURE 11A
PRICE-CONSUMPTION CURVE
A price-consumption curve depicts how consumption changes when relative prices change.

INDIFFERENCE ANALYSIS AND THE LAW OF DEMAND

Indifference analysis can be used to derive an individual's demand curve and demonstrate the law of demand. This demonstration is a *ceteris paribus* experiment in which the price of one good is changed. Part (*a*) of Figure 12A shows an indifference map and a budget line for goods x and y. The consumer is at an optimum at point A. At point A, the individual consumes x_1 units of good x at a price of P_{x_1}. Price and quantity demanded of good x are plotted in part (*b*). Now suppose the price of x falls to P_{x_2}. As

FIGURE 12A
DERIVING A DEMAND CURVE
When the price of good x decreases, the consumer can reach a higher indifference curve. This increased consumption of good x at a lower price means that the demand curve must have a negative slope.

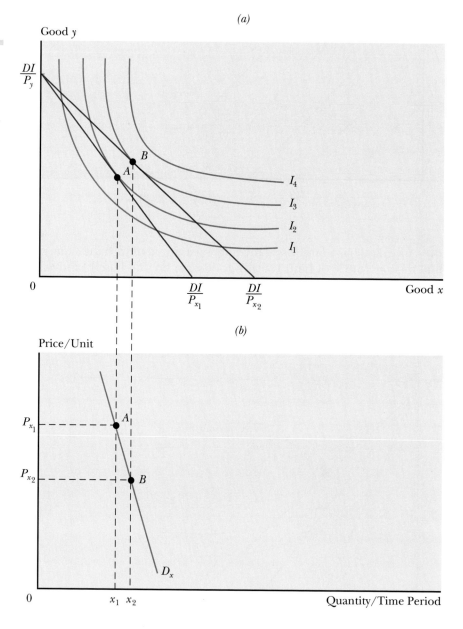

before, this decline in price causes the budget line to rotate outward. A new optimum is reached at point B, where the new budget line is tangent to indifference curve I_3. The change in price has caused the quantity demanded to increase from x_1 to x_2, as shown in part (b). The line connecting two price-quantity points in part (b) is a demand curve for good x, and it has the usual negative slope.

PRODUCT MARKETS

7

1. Define the various types of firms, including profit-seeking firms, nonprofit private sector firms, and nonprofit governmental firms.
2. List the advantages and disadvantages of the various forms of business organization.
3. Calculate the least-cost method of production to determine economic efficiency.
4. Use a production function to explain increasing and diminishing returns.
5. Diagram total, average, and marginal product.
6. Show how a firm chooses its mix of inputs to maximize output.

CHAPTER 21

FIRMS AND PRODUCTION

production
The process of transforming inputs into marketable outputs.

INTRODUCTION

The next two chapters set the stage for examining the behavior of firms. Before we can analyze firms as sellers of products in different types of markets, we must look at how firms organize the process of production. The firm buys factors of production (also known as inputs) and attempts to transform them into marketable outputs. Remember that the factors of production are land, labor, capital, and enterprise. This chapter examines the process of transforming inputs into marketable outputs, which economists call **production**.

THE FIRM IN THEORY

It is easy to take the existence of firms for granted because we have all had dealings with many types of firms. We need to stop, however, to ask why firms exist. Economic theory recognizes that firms exist to accomplish certain economic objectives and are organized in different ways to meet those objectives.

HOUSEHOLDS AS FIRMS
In many ways, households compete with firms. Firms exist to organize production, and households also organize some production. Thus, there are aspects of household activities that are similar to the activities of firms. Firms put "things" together to make other "things" that have economic value. Households clearly do, too. Households cook meals, and so do restaurants. Households make clothes, and so do tailors. Households organize entertainment, and so do movie theaters.

An interesting economic question is why households don't do everything for themselves. Why don't they make their own cars, for example? That's an easy one. They don't make their own cars because it is more efficient for them to buy cars from firms that produce cars. It gets more difficult when we ask why households don't make their own granola or build their own homes. The answer is that some do. As the price of granola and homes produced by firms increases, more households may compete with organized business firms to produce their own products for consumption.

In fact, as relative market prices change, the kinds of production carried out by households change. In recent years, many households have

568

started to grow their own vegetables in response to rising food prices and the lifestyle changes that emphasize gourmet cooking with high-quality, organically grown vegetables. This home production, in turn, affected the demand for products of firms that produced canning equipment and related products.

WHAT BUSINESS FIRMS DO

Firms are organizations that plan production. They assign tasks, monitor those tasks, and generate incentives that reward individuals for completing assigned tasks. An important point is that there are many different sizes of firms. At one extreme, households behave like very small firms. At the other, governments can be seen as extremely large, multipurpose firms. In the Soviet Union, the government has historically acted as a single firm in that it plans, organizes, and provides incentives. As market reforms proceed in the Soviet Union, it will be interesting to watch how the relationship between firms and the government evolves. The Soviet Union has had central planning for so long that there are very few experienced entrepreneurs to take on the organizing function of business firms. This problem of reform in previously centrally planned economies will be discussed in detail in a later chapter.

Within the category of business firms, there is great diversity. Many firms in the U.S. economy are **vertically integrated firms**, which means they perform many steps in a production process. For example, a firm may grow cotton, weave cloth, dye the cloth, and finally sew it into garments. Firms that are not vertically integrated may simply weave cloth or make garments. Still others are **horizontally integrated firms**, which means that they perform many similar production operations in the same industry. For example, a firm may produce men's, women's and children's shoes. Some firms are **conglomerates**, which means that they engage in many, often quite unrelated, activities.

Economic theory should help to explain why these different organizations can all coexist in a market economy. Part of the answer to this question can be found in the incentives that bring about such organizations. Ronald Coase, in a now famous article, showed that transaction costs create firms.[1] He argued that buying and selling imposes costs. **Transaction costs** are costs associated with the conduct of a business. For example, organizing and negotiating involve costs. These transaction costs are minimized by the formation of firms. What Coase was talking about was the effort that a buyer and seller in a market economy must make in continually exploring options. Buyers must search for quality and price. Sellers must monitor the changing demands of buyers.

The transaction costs of these activities can often be reduced by carrying out more research and exploration within a firm. Workers agree to join a firm that provides a workplace, incentives, and guidelines. The firm exists because it economizes on the transaction costs. But the firm also faces constraints. Costs may rise as the size and complexity of the firm increase. Thus, smaller firms (maybe even households) will become potential competitors. In other words, firms exist in many organizational forms

vertically integrated firms
Firms that perform many sequential steps in a production process.

horizontally integrated firms
Firms that perform many similar production operations in the same industry.

conglomerates
Firms that perform many unrelated operations or produce many unrelated products or services.

transaction costs
Costs associated with the conduct of a business.

---

1.   Ronald Coase, "The Nature of the Firm," *Economica* (November 1937): 286–405.

and sizes because various forms and sizes make the most efficient use of information and reduce transaction costs for different kinds of production activities.

Further developments in this theory of organization added other elements to the reasons why firms exist. Armen Alchian and Harold Demsetz added two important elements to this analysis.[2] First, firms exist because the production of many types of products is more efficiently carried out by teams than by individuals. **Teams** are groups of employees that work together to produce something. Firms exist to organize teams to produce goods or services efficiently. Second, when team production is not organized in a firm (as with volunteer activities), it is difficult to measure the contribution of the individual. There are incentives to **shirk**, to put forth less than the agreed-on effort.

The firm exists, then, to reward individuals for team effort and to monitor shirking behavior. Management is primarily responsible for developing organizational forms that use both negative and positive incentives in order to limit shirking.

teams
Groups of employees that work together to produce something.

shirk
To put forth less effort than agreed on.

THE BUSINESS FIRM IN PRACTICE

business firm
An organization formed by an entrepreneur to combine inputs in order to produce marketable outputs.

industry
A group of firms producing similar or related products.

A **business firm** is organized by an entrepreneur (or group of entrepreneurs) to combine inputs of raw materials, capital, labor services, and technology in order to produce marketable outputs of goods and services. Firms are parts of industries. There are many ways to define an industry. In general, what economists mean by an **industry** is a group of firms producing similar or related products. For example, the automobile industry might include just the big three—General Motors, Ford, and Chrysler. Or the industry might also include all foreign auto makers selling in the U.S. market and all small domestic producers. It might also include firms that supply parts, materials, and services to automobile producers or automobile consumers. There are no absolute rules on how to define a specific industry. The definition usually depends on the purpose or the particular problem or issue being studied.

FORMS OF ORGANIZATION
In the United States, firms are organized primarily in three ways. These categories are legal, not economic, and they differ mainly in the legal liability of the owners. Some interesting economic questions arise because of the different types of ownership and the different treatment under the law. These issues will become clearer as we proceed through the next six chapters.

sole proprietorship
A form of enterprise in which no legal distinction is made between the firm and its owner.

SOLE PROPRIETORSHIPS. A **sole proprietorship** is a form of enterprise in which no legal distinction is made between the owner and the firm. The financial resources of the firm are limited to those of the individual owner and what can be borrowed from friends or financial institutions. Thus, the

---

2.   Armen A. Alchian and Harold Demsetz, "Production, Information Costs and Economic Organization," *American Economic Review* (December 1972): 777–795.

profits and losses accrue solely to that individual. The owner also bears unlimited liability for any and all debts of the firm. Success of the firm is success of the owner; bankruptcy of the firm is bankruptcy of the owner. This close relationship usually means a constant involvement of the owner with the affairs of the firm. There are obviously great incentives for hard work and diligence in a sole proprietorship.

Compared to other forms of business enterprise, a sole proprietorship can be established or go out of business very easily. In certain lines of business, government approval is required, because licenses or permits are needed. Typically, however, the sole proprietor starts or ends a business by simply doing so. The IRS reported that, in 1990, 69 percent of the business firms in the United States were sole proprietorships. Most farmers and many small firms, especially in retailing and services, are sole proprietorships. Although dominant in numbers, sole proprietorships account for only 10 percent of annual business sales.

PARTNERSHIPS. Partnerships are similar to sole proprietorships except they have more than one owner. The firm does not have a legal existence separate from the owners (the partners). Like sole proprietorships, firms organized as partnerships tend to be quite small. They are typically found in professional services: medicine, law, consulting, and financial services.

There are more personal and financial resources available to a partnership than if only one person formed the firm. Besides funds, each partner may also bring special skills, knowledge, energy, or decision-making powers. Offsetting these advantages are the frictions that usually arise in operating the firm. Partners have to agree on the proportions of ownership owned by each partner, which may be dictated by the amounts of funds contributed, the amounts of work, or the amounts of other kinds of value contributed (such as ideas or patents). Partners also have to agree on joint rights and responsibilities. The partners share in any profits, but each partner bears unlimited liability for any debts incurred by the firm.

The disadvantages of a partnership arrangement apparently outweigh the advantages. The IRS reports that, in 1990, only 10 percent of the business firms and only 5 percent of annual business sales in the United States were accounted for by partnerships.

CORPORATIONS. The dominant form of business organization in the United States, measured in any way except absolute numbers, is the corporate form. A corporation is more formal and complex than the other types of business organization. A **corporation** is a form of enterprise in which persons who own shares of stock are the owners of the firm. Owners of a corporation are called **stockholders**. The legal liability of stockholders is limited. The IRS reports that, in 1990, corporations accounted for 21 percent of business firms and about 85 percent of annual business sales.

The number of stockholders may run into the hundreds of thousands, although some corporations have only a few stockholders. The stockholders vote, according to the number of shares they hold, for a board of directors. The board, in turn, appoints officers of the corporation to manage it along the guidelines set by the charter of incorporation and the di-

partnership
A form of enterprise in which there is more than one owner, and the firm does not have a legal existence separate from the owners.

corporation
A form of enterprise in which stockholders are the owners of the firm but have limited liability.

stockholders
The owners of a corporation.

In the United States, there have been few experiments with labor-managed firms. In contrast, almost all firms in Yugoslavia are owned and managed by the workers. This type of firm might become more popular as the nations of Eastern Europe struggle with reform in the 1990s. This hybrid form of organization may appeal to reformers in countries such as Poland and Romania because it has a somewhat Marxist flavor to it.

In the United States, worker management exists in a few craft industries and has been attempted in a few instances when manufacturing plants were about to close, mostly in the steel industry. The closest parallel to a labor-managed firm in the United States is profit sharing by labor in some industries. In Yugoslavia, however, the workers actually own the plant and decide how it wili be managed through councils. The ownership rights end when a worker leaves the firm, so these ownership rights are different from stockholder rights in U.S. corporations. The labor-

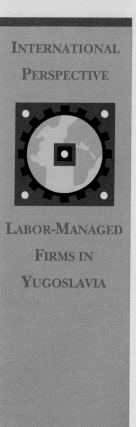

managed firm is an interesting concept for a socialist country because such worker democracy is closer to Marxist philosophy than the state-owned and -managed firms that exist in most communist countries. The question for economists is how such organization and control by workers affects incentives and ultimately the economic development of the country.

Entrepreneurs maximize profits. If the firm is owned by workers, will something other than profit be maximized? Worker self-management means that workers may seek to maximize wages and other benefits that they can capture while they are with the firm. Since workers have no ownership rights that they can sell, they may opt for a management policy that increases the short-term income of the firm over policies that would increase the firm's value over time. This bias would tend to reduce the firm's investments, which in turn (in the aggregate) would reduce the long-term economic growth of the country.

rectors. A **board of directors** consists of individuals elected by the stockholders of a corporation to select the managers and oversee the management of the corporation.

One of the strengths of the corporate form of business organization is the relative ease of acquiring capital. Capital is often acquired by issuing shares of **stock**, which are certificates of ownership in a corporation. A corporation can borrow funds by issuing **bonds**, which are interest-bearing certificates issued by governments or corporations. A corporation can also borrow directly by taking out loans from banks or other financial agencies. (Only the third option for obtaining outside funding is available to partnerships and sole proprietorships.)

The attractiveness of the corporation as a form of organization stems from the fact that the stockholders are the legal owners and have rights to the profits, but their legal liability is very limited. **Limited liability** means that the stockholders of a corporation cannot be sued for failure of the corporation to pay its debts. Only the corporation itself can be sued. This limited liability is the critical advantage of the corporate form of business. In many countries, corporations are referred to as limited liability companies, and the letters Ltd. appear after the name of the firm. The letters Inc. (Incorporated) after the name of a firm in the United States mean the same thing. Thus, a corporation, defined in law as a legal person in its own right, can go bankrupt without the owners going bankrupt. Of course, individuals who have most of their wealth in the stock of one corporation might go bankrupt because the stock would no longer have any value.

A second important advantage of corporate organization is the ease of transferring ownership. Ownership rights can be transferred through the sale of stocks, and markets (stock exchanges) have evolved to handle such transfers. The costs of transfer of ownership are for this reason significantly lower for corporations than for partnerships or sole proprietorships. The major drawback of corporate organization is double taxation. Corporate income is subject to corporate income taxes, and then part of that income is taxed again when it is distributed to stockholders as dividends.

In the late 1980s, a hybrid type of corporation evolved very rapidly in the United States. The **S corporation** enjoys some of the advantages of a corporation, most notably limited liability, but is not subject to double taxation. The income of an S corporation is simply passed to the owners and only taxed once as personal income. Most S corporations tend to be relatively small. The S corporation is replacing sole proprietorships and partnerships as a form of business organization in many industries.

Different types of ownership cause managers of firms to behave in different ways. For instance, an owner-manager of a sole proprietorship may make decisions that are different from those of the hired manager of a large corporation, because the owner-manager benefits more directly from higher profits. For now, we will ignore such differences. We'll assume that business firms, however they are organized, exist for only one purpose—to increase the wealth of their owners. To do this, firms try to maximize profits. This assumption of profit maximization makes it possible to develop a powerful theory to predict the economic effects of different market structures.

board of directors
The individuals elected by the stockholders of a corporation to select the managers and oversee the management of the corporation.

stocks
Certificates of ownership in a corporation.

bonds
Interest-earning certificates issued by governments or corporations in exchange for borrowed funds.

limited liability
The fact that the stockholders of a corporation cannot be sued for failure of the corporation to meet its obligations.

S corporation
A hybrid type of corporation that passes income directly to the owners, avoiding the double taxation of corporate profits.

FORMS OF ORGANIZATION	
• Sole proprietorship	No legal distinction between owner and firm
	Financial resources limited to those of owner
	Profits accrue solely to owner
	Owner is liable for debts
• Partnership	More than one owner
	Partners bring different skills and greater financial resources
	Partners share profits and legal liability
• Corporation	The legal liability of stockholders is limited
	Board of directors oversees management
	Ownership is transferred with ease
	Face double taxation, except S corporations

ENTERPRISE, ENTREPRENEURS, AND THE FIRM

Enterprise is the factor of production provided by an entrepreneur. The entrepreneur is the founder and often the guiding spirit of a business firm. Many business schools now offer courses in entrepreneurship. But what is it that entrepreneurs do? They identify consumer demands, organize production, allocate resources, and acquire assets. In the process, they take risks. Entrepreneurs are rewarded with profits if they have good hunches or go bankrupt if they are wrong. Many more go bankrupt than succeed, yet we read in the newspapers about the most successful. A *Fortune* survey about getting rich in America concluded that "most successful entrepreneurs didn't start out as fortune seekers; they were pursuing visions, not the almighty buck."[3]

More than 4 million men and women operate small businesses in the United States, employing about 10 percent of all workers. Two economists who have looked at the characteristics of entrepreneurs found that age and labor market experience have no bearing on the likelihood of becoming an entrepreneur.[4] They also found that men who have been unemployed and changed jobs frequently have a higher probability of becoming self-employed. This finding is consistent with the view of sociologists that entrepreneurs are "misfits." Also, individuals who score high on a psychological test known as the Rotter Scale have a higher propensity to start a new business. This test measures the belief that personal success depends largely on one's internal locus of control.

THE NONPROFIT FIRM

Although economic models assume that business firms exist to maximize profits or wealth, an increasingly large number of firms are organized as nonprofit organizations. These firms differ from for-profit firms mainly

3.   Monci Jo Williams, "How the Wealthy Get That Way," *Fortune* (13 April 1987): 38.
4.   David S. Evans and Linda Leighton, "Some Empirical Aspects of Entrepreneurship," *American Economic Review* (June 1989): 519–535.

in that they do not have a residual claimant. A **residual claimant** is an individual, or group of individuals, who shares in the profits (if any) of an enterprise. Thus, it is difficult to determine who owns a nonprofit organization. We can separate nonprofits into two categories: those in the private sector and those in the government sector.

residual claimant
Individual, or group of individuals, who shares in the profits of an enterprise.

NONPROFITS IN THE PRIVATE SECTOR

Nonprofit firms in the private sector are not part of, or sponsored directly by, a governmental unit. They exist for many reasons. Many of them (for example, health clinics and soup kitchens) are engaged in private transfers. Some provide collective goods that cannot conveniently be provided through government.

The manager (organizer) of a private nonprofit firm usually receives a salary for managing the firm. Economists expect more shirking behavior to occur in these firms because the manager cannot convert increased efficiencies into profits that affect his or her salary. Such shirking behavior has been documented by economist Kenneth Clarkson.[5] He found that nonprofit hospitals had higher budgeted expenses for supervisory positions than for-profit hospitals did. The chief manager of a nonprofit hospital was also much less concerned with the price and productivity of equipment. Automatic, across-the-board pay increases were more frequent in nonprofit hospitals. This method of giving raises is a type of shirking behavior. It would require more effort to separate good employees from bad employees.

Most economists would argue that nonprofit firms have significant organizational disadvantages that introduce inefficiencies. Yet nonprofits have increased rapidly in recent years. Why have they become such a popular form of organization? Earl Thompson has suggested an answer.[6] He points out that most nonprofit firms are associated with charitable organizations. Contributors to these charitable organizations are usually remote from the production or use of the product or service they are supporting. These contributors would have a difficult time monitoring the managers of these firms. They wouldn't be able to determine easily whether a manager was using their gift to produce the charitable product or was simply "taking it home" in the form of higher wages. However, tolerating the inefficiencies caused by managers who are not profit seekers is less costly to contributors than is monitoring manager behavior. As a result, charitable donors accept some inefficiency in preference to supporting the provision of the products or services through the for-profit or governmental sector. Thompson argues that one way to lessen the problem is to specify certain salaries for the managers.

It is also true that tax laws play a role in encouraging the formation of nonprofit organizations. In some cases, individuals can create nonprofit firms that produce output for their own consumption. They can then support this production through tax-deductible "charitable" contributions. You might, for example, create a nonprofit organization to support the

---

5.   Kenneth W. Clarkson, "Some Implications of Property Rights in Hospital Management," *Journal of Law and Economics* (October 1972): 363–384.

6.   Earl Thompson, "Charity and Nonprofit Organizations," in *The Economics of Nonproprietary Organizations*, eds. K. W. Clarkson and D. C. Martin (Greenwich, CT: JAI Press, 1980): 125–128.

local theatre in which you act and make tax-deductible gifts to this non-profit organization.

NONPROFITS IN THE GOVERNMENT SECTOR

Everyone does business with some nonprofit governmental firms. Often these firms compete directly with private, business firms. The U.S. Postal Service competes with United Parcel Service and Federal Express. City and county hospitals compete with private hospitals. Municipal golf and tennis clubs compete with private country clubs. City bus lines compete with private cab companies. Public and private colleges and universities compete for students. The list goes on and on.

What characterizes these governmental firms? To begin, like a private nonprofit firm, a governmental nonprofit has no profit and no residual claimant to that profit. Second, the manager of a governmental nonprofit usually has little control over price. If a price is charged, it is usually set by a board or some political entity. The price is often below the operating costs of the firm. In addition, the customers often cannot influence the behavior of the organization. Customers can express frustration with a private firm by switching to a competing firm. This is not always possible when dealing with a governmental firm.

The tendency to shirk is prevalent in governmental firms for the same reasons as in private nonprofits. In addition, a bureaucratic manager can get promoted by being "better" than other bureaucratic managers. In many instances, causing the agency to grow is taken as a sign of success and a cause for advancement. We will discuss this bureaucratic incentive in the chapter on market and government failure.

Some economists argue that the quality of products produced by governmental nonprofit firms is likely to be poorer than that of similar private, for-profit firms. This poorer quality results from the fact that prices charged by the governmental organization are usually lower. Customers will often choose the low-priced product or service, even though it is of lower quality. Research on Veterans Administration hospitals in comparison to private, for-profit hospitals supports this observation.[7]

WHAT ABOUT THE PROFITS OF NONPROFIT FIRMS?

In recent years, many private and governmental nonprofit organizations have entered into profit-making activities. The profits from these activities are often referred to instead as "excess of revenues over expenses." Hospitals are selling health-related equipment, universities are selling in-company training programs, university presses are producing best sellers, alumni groups are selling tours, and religious organizations are selling condos at theme parks. Profits from such activities are not taxed because they are intertwined with the nonprofit firms' noncommercial activities.

In addition, nonprofit firms may have the advantages of access to referrals and free space for doing business. They can also use bulk mail instead of paying first-class rates, as the private sector must. These factors give a cost advantage to these firms over private-sector firms in the same business.

---

7.   See C. M. Lindsay, "A Theory of Government Enterprise," *Journal of Political Economy* (October 1976): 1061–1077.

Delegates to the 1990 White House Conference on Small Business voted that the second biggest problem facing small businesses was nonprofit organizations using their tax-exempt status to compete with the private sector. (This problem ranked after government-mandated employee benefits and before liability insurance.) This subsidized competition from nonprofit organizations has led private-sector firms to pressure the U.S. Congress to change the law as it relates to profit-making activities of tax-exempt nonprofit organizations. In the late 1980s, the House Ways and Means Committee held hearings on the tax status of nonprofit organizations. As one witness from New Jersey put it, "I'm not opposed to the Girl Scouts having an annual cookie sale, but if the Girl Scouts want to open a cookie store next door to a Mrs. Fields cookie store, they should have to pay the same taxes."[8]

ECONOMIC EFFICIENCY

The firms that produce most of the U.S. output are private, profit-maximizing firms. An entrepreneur must combine resources efficiently if the firm is to maximize profits.[9] To do this, entrepreneurs must decide among competing ways of producing a given product. Suppose, for example, that the printer producing this textbook was faced with the alternatives listed in Table 1. The production engineer told the production manager that 100,000 copies could be produced in any of these four ways. The production manager informs the president and CEO of the firm, the entrepreneur, who must decide how to actually produce the textbooks. The entrepreneur must have a decision rule in order to select a production alternative. This is where profit maximization comes into play. Without profit maximization as a goal, the entrepreneur might choose on some other basis, such as a consideration of physical units of input or output.

TABLE 1
ALTERNATIVE WAYS TO
PRODUCE 100,000 COPIES
OF THIS TEXTBOOK

METHOD	CAPITAL (MACHINES)	PRICE OF CAPITAL SERVICES (PER MACHINE)	LABOR (WORKER-YEARS)	PRICE OF LABOR SERVICES (PER WORKER-YEAR)	LAND (ACRES)	PRICE OF LAND SERVICES (PER ACRE)	TOTAL COST
A	5	$30,000	5	$4,000	1	$10,000	$150,000 + $ 20,000 + $10,000 = $180,000
B	4	30,000	10	4,000	1	10,000	$120,000 + $ 40,000 + $10,000 = $170,000
C	3	30,000	15	4,000	1	10,000	$ 90,000 + $ 60,000 + $10,000 = $160,000
D	2	30,000	25	4,000	1	10,000	$ 60,000 + $100,000 + $10,000 = $170,000

8. "Profits? Who, Me?" *Forbes* (23 March 1987): 108.
9. Entrepreneurs combine factors of production, inputs, or resources. Economists use all three of these terms synonymously. Historically, factors of production was most commonly used. In this book, we use all three, but when we want to be precise, we usually fall back on factors of production.

technical efficiency
The basis for minimizing the physical inputs to a production method according to some specific rule (an engineering concept).

The method that would minimize the inputs in a physical sense would be method *A*, which uses the fewest inputs. The basis for choosing this method is technical efficiency. **Technical efficiency** refers to the minimizing of the physical inputs to a production method according to some specific rule. It is an engineering concept with little economic relevance. The drawback of this decision rule is that it requires the decision maker to compare physical units of such diverse inputs as machines, acres of land, and worker-years of labor.

Technical efficiency has been widely used in command economies, such as that of the Soviet Union. The reforms in the Soviet Union and Eastern Europe have put this type of decision rule in question. In the 1990s, these countries will be struggling to replace such calculations with more appropriate decision rules.

economic efficiency
The least-cost method of production.

A market system puts the inputs into dollar terms and lets the entrepreneur choose the least-cost method of producing. The least-cost method, or the economically efficient method, is chosen by the entrepreneur because of the assumption of attempted profit maximization. **Economic efficiency** is therefore defined as the least-cost method of production. In Table 1, the entrepreneur would choose method *C* to produce the textbooks. Regardless of the price of the textbooks, method *C* maximizes profits (or minimizes losses) because costs are minimized. However, the entrepreneur must know the prices of the various inputs in order to make this choice. This price information is not usually available in a command economy. Lack of market price information is one of the major problems facing the command economies of Eastern Europe as they try to implement reforms.

PRODUCTION FUNCTIONS IN THE SHORT AND LONG RUN

production function
A description of the amounts of output expected from various combinations of inputs.

A **production function** is a description of the amounts of output expected from various combinations of inputs. It is usually expressed in the form of a table or graph, but it also can be shown by a mathematical formula. The production function describes a technical or technological relationship. The input combinations and the corresponding output quantities are determined by engineers, agronomists, chemists, or other technical experts.

Only the technically efficient input combinations are included. For example, it might be that an output of 100 units could be produced by 5 units of capital, 20 units of labor, and 2 units of land or by 6 units of capital, 30 units of labor, and 3 units of land. The second combination is inferior to the first because it takes more of all inputs to produce the same output. That method of production would be ignored. The production function reflects the most efficient technology available to produce a given level of output.

fixed factors
The factors of production that cannot be varied in the short run.

Usually entrepreneurs are interested in only a portion of the production function. For instance, it is often convenient to ask what would happen to total production if all but one of the inputs were at a given level. When considering a production function, it is possible to distinguish between fixed factors and variable factors. **Fixed factors** are the factors of

Economists view a firm, whether a sole proprietorship or a corporation, as existing to make profits for the owners. Some economists argue that it is improper for a corporation to be involved in philanthropy (charity) because it is giving away the profits of its stockholders. They argue that the profits should be distributed to the stockholders, who can give it to charity themselves if they wish. However, corporations have been giving money to various causes for decades. For many years, this corporate giving was at the whim of the CEO, or whoever had the ear of the CEO. In recent years, the pattern has changed dramatically. Corporate giving is more likely to be based on self-interest, accountability, and cause-related marketing.

Corporate philanthropy is big business. More than $5 billion was given away in 1990. American Express started cause-related marketing with its promise to earmark a portion of its revenue to the Statue of Liberty restoration program. That identified American Express with patriotism. Ben Cohen (of Ben & Jerry's Ice Cream) has set up

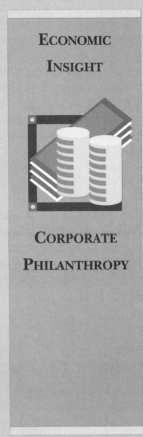

ECONOMIC INSIGHT

CORPORATE PHILANTHROPY

a company that will give 40 percent of the revenue from the flavor Rainforest Crunch to protect the Amazon rainforest. Such gifts serve worthy causes while creating a good image and potential future customers. An investment in philanthropy may make a corporation even more profitable in the long run.

The biggest givers in corporate America are some of the biggest corporations. The table lists seven of these and the main beneficiaries of their corporate largesse. You will notice from the table that corporations tend to support universities. Often these gifts are to universities in the corporation's geographic area or universities that do research of immediate benefit to the corporation. Other corporate gifts are made to promote affirmative action goals or community development in the region in which the corporation is located. In some cases, the tie between the company and the recipient is clearly business-related. Time Warner, Inc. combats illiteracy by selling its Time to Read Program to other corporate sponsors.

CORPORATION	RECIPIENTS
IBM	Recipients not made public!
General Motors	University of Michigan, GM Cancer Research Foundation
Exxon	New Jersey Science-Technology Center, Community Summer Jobs Program
Hewlett-Packard	MIT, Stanford University Hospital
RJR/Nabisco	University of Delaware, West End Neighborhood House
AT&T	Stanford University, National Urban League

Source: "What's in It for Me?" *Business Month* (November 1989).

variable factors
The factors of production that can be increased or decreased in the short run.

short run
The period of time that is too short to vary all the factors of production.

long run
The period of time in which all inputs, including plant and equipment, can be varied.

principle of diminishing returns
The fact that as more and more units of a variable factor are added to a set of fixed factors, the resulting additions to output eventually become smaller.

production that cannot be varied in the short run, such as the size of the plant. **Variable factors** are the factors of production that can be increased or decreased in the short run. Which factors are fixed and which are variable usually depends on the problem under consideration. In many cases, however, the land and the buildings of a firm (the physical plant) are considered fixed factors and labor the variable factor.

When economists distinguish between fixed and variable factors, they are referring to a time period called the short run. In this context, the **short run** is the period of time that is too short to vary all the factors of production. The **long run** is the period of time in which all inputs, including plant and equipment, can be varied. Short-run decisions are those concerning the profit-maximizing use of the existing (fixed) plant and equipment. The plant is used more intensively by increasing the amount of variable factors, such as labor or new machines. Long-run decisions are those concerning the selection of a plant size that will maximize profits.

These time horizons cannot be defined in the calendar sense, because they are different in different industries. In some industries, firms may be able to increase in size very rapidly. In some cases, contractions can occur more quickly, depending on whether the plant and equipment are adaptable for other uses. It is primarily for convenience of analysis that decisions are classed as being either short-run or long-run. Keep in mind that such decisions are inherently interrelated. Once a long-run decision to build a plant of a certain size is made, a whole series of short-run decisions are affected because they must deal with that size of plant.

INCREASING AND DECREASING RETURNS

As more and more units of a variable factor are added to a set of fixed factors, the resulting additions to output will eventually become smaller. This economic conclusion is referred to as the **principle of diminishing returns**. It is easy to see that returns must eventually diminish. Otherwise, all the wheat needed to feed the world could be produced on one acre of land by simply adding more seed, more fertilizer, more water, and more labor.

The principle of diminishing returns is a fascinating and pervasive phenomenon. The principle is almost never contradicted by real-world observations. A tree grows more slowly as it grows larger. Little pigs put on more weight from a given amount of corn than big ones do. It is more costly to add a floor to a twenty-story building than to a ten-story building. Adding water to parched soil yields remarkable crop improvement, but adding the same amount of water to already moist soil has very little effect. If a firm adds a worker when its labor force is already large, the increase in output is less than if a worker is added at a time when the labor force is small. These are only a few examples of the principle of diminishing returns.

Note that the principle of diminishing returns applies to the short run and says nothing about the long-run production function. It only says that if more and more variable input is added to a fixed factor, after a while the return will decline. Think of your own experience in studying for exams. The output is your test score, and the variable factor is the time you spend studying. Assume that you could get a score of 55 percent without studying. One hour of studying would boost your score to 66 percent, two hours to 75 percent, three hours to 80 percent, four hours to 84 percent, five hours to 86 percent, and so on. Each additional unit of variable input (hour spent studying) produces a smaller increment in output (improvement in test score). The first hour of studying produces an improvement of 11 percentage points, the second hour yields 9 points, the third hour 5 points, and so on. There is a diminishing return to studying. It is up to you to decide when the return for an additional hour of studying is not worth the opportunity cost of that hour in terms of the other things you could be doing. So you see, even deciding how much to study is an exercise in rational economic choice.

AVERAGE AND MARGINAL RELATIONSHIPS

There is a very important relationship between average values and marginal values. Think of your grade point average. If your grade in this course (the marginal grade) is below your grade point average for all courses you have taken, your average will fall. If your grade in this course is above your grade point average, your average will rise. If a basketball player's lifetime shooting percentage (average) is higher this week than last week, you know that in the intervening games, the player has shot higher-than-average (marginal) percentages. If a marginal value is above average, it will pull the average up. If the average value is falling, the marginal value must be below the average.

In production, the important relationship of marginal and average values is between marginal physical product and average physical product. In order to describe more precisely the relationship between inputs and outputs, economists use the concept of the marginal physical product. **Marginal physical product (*MPP*)** is the change in total output that is produced by a unit change in a factor of production. The marginal physical product of labor, for example, is the change in total output per unit change in the use of labor service. That is,

$$MPP_L = \frac{\Delta TPP}{\Delta L},$$

where MPP_L is the marginal physical product of labor, ΔTPP is the change in the total physical product, and ΔL is the change in the number of units of labor employed. The **total physical product (*TPP*)** is the amount of output that a firm produces in physical units. The **average physical product (*APP*)** of a factor of production is simply the total physical product divided by the number of units of the factor employed. For example, the average physical product of capital (APP_K) is

$$APP_K = \frac{TPP}{K},$$

where K is the number of units of capital used.

Table 2 illustrates these relationships for a short-run production function. All the factors of production are fixed except labor. Labor, the variable input, can vary between 1 and 10 units. In Table 2, as more variable input is added to the fixed inputs, output goes through three distinct

marginal physical product (*MPP*)
The change in total output that is produced by a unit change in a factor of production.

total physical product (*TPP*)
The amount of output that a firm produces in physical units.

average physical product (*APP*)
The total physical product (output) divided by the number of units of a factor used.

TABLE 2
A SHORT-RUN PRODUC-
TION FUNCTION

VARIABLE INPUT (UNITS OF LABOR)	TOTAL PHYSICAL PRODUCT (UNITS OF OUTPUT)	MARGINAL PHYSICAL PRODUCT OF LABOR	AVERAGE PHYSCIAL PRODUCT OF LABOR
1	6	6	6.0
2	14	8	7.0
3	24	10	8.0
4	32	8	8.0
5	38	6	7.6
6	42	4	7.0
7	44	2	6.3
8	44	0	5.5
9	42	–2	4.7
10	36	–6	3.6

stages. When the first three units of labor are added, output increases at an increasing rate. That is, the marginal physical product of labor is increasing. Adding the fourth unit of labor causes output to increase but by a smaller amount than for the third unit of labor. The marginal physical product of labor is now declining. The eighth unit of labor produces no increase in output, and the ninth and tenth units of labor actually cause total output to fall.

Figure 1 shows the relationships of Table 2 in graphical form. From zero to L_1 units of labor, the total physical product is increasing at an increasing rate. This means that marginal physical product and average physical product of labor are also increasing. At L_1, the marginal physical product of labor reaches its maximum. From L_1 to L_3, total physical product is increasing at a decreasing rate. This is the region of diminishing returns. The marginal physical product of labor is declining throughout this range. At L_2, the average physical product of labor is at its maximum. At L_3, the total physical product reaches its maximum. Adding further units of labor produces no more output. The marginal physical product of labor is equal to zero at L_3.

THE CHOICE OF INPUTS

We can use the concepts of production function and diminishing returns to consider the choice of a production method. Earlier in this chapter, we demonstrated the concept of economic efficiency by showing how a printer might choose to produce this textbook. We can now add complexity and realism to this example.

Assume that we are again looking at the production of textbooks by a firm that is of a given size. This means that the firm is in the short run and, as a result, its size cannot be altered. Let's also assume that there are only two variable inputs: labor and printing presses. Table 3 shows the possible quantities of labor and printing presses and their corresponding marginal physical products. You can see from those values that this firm is in the range of diminishing returns. This corresponds to the range between L_1 and L_3 in Figure 1.

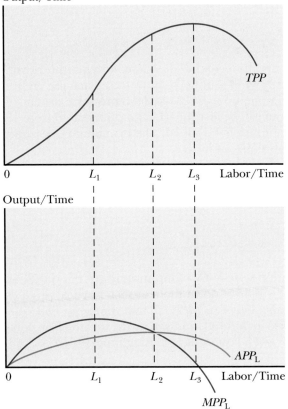

FIGURE 1
PRODUCT CURVES
When *TPP* is increasing at
an increasing rate, *MPP* is
increasing. When *TPP* is
increasing at a decreasing
rate, *MPP* is diminishing.
When *TPP* is at a maxi-
mum, *MPP* is equal to
zero.

The question facing the firm is to determine which combination of labor and presses will produce the largest amount of textbooks for a given
expenditure of dollars. Let's say that presses cost $2 per unit per day, la-
bor costs $1 per unit per day, and the firm has a budget of $26 per day.

The firm will maximize output by using labor and presses to the extent that will make their marginal physical products per dollar spent
equal. This is written as follows:

$$\frac{MPP_L}{P_L} = \frac{MPP_P}{P_P}.$$

VARIABLE INPUT— LABOR (UNITS)	MARGINAL PHYSICAL PRODUCT OF LABOR (MPP_L)	VARIABLE INPUT— PRESSES (UNITS)	MARGINAL PHYSICAL PRODUCT OF PRESSES (MPP_P)
7	6	5	10
8	5	6	9
9	4	7	8
10	3	8	6
11	1	9	3
12	0	10	0

TABLE 3
FACTOR INPUTS FOR
PRINTING THIS TEXTBOOK
AND THEIR MARGINAL
PHYSICAL PRODUCTS

The firm would use 10 units of labor and 8 presses per day because

$$\frac{3}{\$1} = \frac{6}{\$2}.$$

You can easily see why this input combination maximizes output, given a spending constraint of $26. Add 2 units of labor to replace the eighth press, for example. This combination also costs $26. If presses are reduced from 8 to 7, 2 units of output will be lost, and if labor is increased from 10 to 12 units, only 1 unit of output will be added. The firm would lose a unit of output with this alternative mix of inputs.

We now can see that a firm maximizes output by choosing its mix of inputs so that the marginal physical product of a dollar's worth of each input is equal to the marginal physical product of a dollar's worth of every other input. If

$$\frac{MPP_a}{P_a} > \frac{MPP_b}{P_b},$$

the firm reallocates its inputs to use more of input a and less of input b. As the firm uses more of a, it will drive down the marginal physical product of a and bring about equality between MPP_a/P_a and MPP_b/P_b. This conclusion can be generalized to include all inputs by saying that the firm maximizes its production for a given cost outlay by using inputs $(a, b, \ldots, n)$ so that

$$\frac{MPP_a}{P_a} = \frac{MPP_b}{P_b} = \cdots = \frac{MPP_n}{P_n}.$$

You will note that the principles developed here are very similar to those developed for utility analysis. According to utility theory, the consumer maximizes utility for a given income, or budget constraint. Here the firm maximizes output given a cost constraint. The principles of maximization are the same.

ON TO COSTS

The principles of production are a foundation for analyzing costs. In the next chapter, we will see how production functions and the principle of diminishing returns relate to the cost functions firms face.

PRODUCTION FUNCTIONS AND INPUTS

- At least one input is fixed in the short run.
- All inputs are variable in the long run.
- The marginal physical product of an input is the change in output produced by a one-unit change in that input.
- Diminishing returns is a short-run phenomenon.
- If the marginal physical product is negative, total physical product is declining.

SUMMARY

1. Firms are organized by entrepreneurs to produce outputs by combining inputs. The entrepreneur does this in such a way as to maximize profits.

2. Nonprofit firms, both private and governmental, face different incentives than for-profit firms do because nonprofit firms have no residual claimants.

3. Sole proprietorships are the dominant form of business organization by number. Corporations account for about 85 percent of annual business sales in the United States. S corporations have become popular because they are not subject to double taxation of corporate profits.

4. Economic efficiency is the basis for selecting that combination of resources that minimizes the cost of producing a certain level of output.

5. A production function is the technical relationship between factors of production and outputs.

6. In the short run, some factors are fixed. In the long run, all factors are variable.

7. In the short run, as variable factors are added to fixed factors, the firm may experience increasing returns at low levels of output but eventually will incur diminishing returns at some higher levels of output.

8. Firms choose their input mix from the production function to maximize output subject to cost constraints.

NEW TERMS

production
vertically integrated firms
horizontally integrated firms
conglomerates
transaction costs
teams
shirk

business firm
industry
sole proprietorship
partnership
corporation
stockholders
board of directors
stocks
bonds

limited liability
S corporation
residual claimant
technical efficiency
economic efficiency
production function
fixed factors
variable factors
short run

long run
principle of diminishing returns
marginal physical product (*MPP*)
total physical product (*TPP*)
average physical product (*APP*)

QUESTIONS FOR DISCUSSION

1. How does the short run differ from the long run? What would the short run be for farming, for a lemonade stand, and for electricity generation?

2. Is there a parallel between diminishing marginal utility in consumption and diminishing returns in production? Describe any similarities you see.

3. List some of the differences you have observed between private for-profit firms and nonprofit firms that produce the same good.

4. In professional sports, there are very few player-coaches. Yet many players become coaches immediately after their playing days end. Can you think of any reasons why this may be the case, based on economic theo-

ries of why firms are formed and what managers do in these firms?

5. Suppose the following production function describes three ways to produce 1,000 shirts in a sewing factory.

METHOD	UNITS OF CAPITAL (SEWING MACHINES)	UNITS OF LABOR (SEWER WEEKS)	UNITS OF LAND (ACRES)	UNITS OUTPUT (SHIRTS)
A	4	60	⅕	1,000
B	10	10	⅕	1,000
C	30	5	⅕	1,000

If you were the plant manager of this sewing factory, which method of production would you choose?

6. If the cost basis of the capital services of sewing machines in Question 5 is $3,000 per 1,000 shirts and the wage rate is $6.25 per hour (forty-hour week), which method of production would you choose?

7. What would happen to your choice of inputs if the sewing factory in Question 5 were successfully unionized and the union contract specified a wage rate of $10.65 per hour?

8. The price of land was irrelevant to your decision in Questions 5–7 because the plant uses ⅕ of an acre of land for all three methods of production. What would your reaction be (as plant manager) if the governor in a neighboring state offered you free land in an industrial park and forgave all property taxes on that land for 10 years?

9. Classify the firm resulting from each of the following mergers as vertically integrated, horizontally integrated, or a conglomerate.

    a.   An oil company buys a chain of gas stations.

    b.   A cosmetics company buys a financial institution.

    c.   An airline buys a travel agency.

    d.   An airline buys an interstate bus line.

    e.   A movie company buys a television studio.

    f.   A supermarket chain buys a rental car company.

10. Deming management, quality circles, and similar techniques that increase worker involvement in the manufacturing process have become popular. These techniques are sometimes referred to as the Japanese style of management. How does such a style of management address the problem of shirking behavior?

11. Should corporate philanthropy be applauded or condemned from the standpoint of economic efficiency?

12. What is the advantage of an S corporation?

13. Why must the marginal physical product of labor be equal to zero at the point where the total physical product is at its peak?

14. Your grades on weekly quizzes are 90, 85, 75, 65, 90, and 95. What was your average grade after three weeks, four weeks, and five weeks? When your average fell, was the marginal grade below or above the average? What about when your average rose?

15. The typical isoquant curve is curved and convex to the origin. What does this shape imply?

Suggestions for Further Reading

Eckert, Ross D. *The Price System and Resource Allocation*, 10th ed. Hinsdale, IL: Dryden Press, 1988. An intermediate text that goes into greater detail on some of the topics discussed in this chapter.

Lindsay, Cotton M. *Applied Price Theory*. Hinsdale, IL: Dryden Press, 1984. An intermediate price theory text that develops the material found in this chapter in much greater detail.

Moore, John H. *Growth With Self-Management*. Stanford, CA: Hoover Institution Press, 1980. A very readable account of the economics of labor-managed firms.

White, Michelle J., ed. *Nonprofit Firms in a Three Sector Economy*. Washington, DC: Urban Institute Press, 1981. A collection of articles looking at the behavior of private nonprofit firms.

APPENDIX: PRODUCER CHOICE

If you have not already done so, you should study the preceding chapter's appendix, which describes indifference analysis and consumer choice. A similar approach can be used to analyze producer choice.

ISOQUANT CURVES

An **isoquant** (called a producer indifference curve by some economists) is a curve that shows all combinations of quantities of two inputs that can be used to produce a given quantity of output. ("Isoquant" means equal quantity.) Along an isoquant, the amount of output produced remains the same, but the combinations of inputs vary. There is a separate isoquant for each level of output.

isoquant
A curve that shows all combinations of two inputs that can be used to produce a given output.

Suppose Eric, an entrepreneur, is considering the use of the different combinations of capital and labor shown in Table 1A. Combination *A* consists of 16 units of labor (measured in person-years) and 3 units of capital (measured in number of machines used per year). Combination *B* is 12 units of labor and 4 units of capital. Eric states that neither combination *A* nor combination *B* is preferred. They are equal with respect to the amount of output he expects to produce, and therefore, in the absence of prices, he is indifferent between these input combinations. When Eric considers input combinations *C*, *D*, and *E*, he has the same response because they all produce the same output, 1,000 dozen shirts. Such production choices can be plotted as an isoquant curve. An isoquant curve corresponding to the production choices in Table 1A is shown in Figure 1A. The isoquant curve shows all combinations of two inputs that produce a given output.

Input combinations lying on a higher isoquant curve are associated with larger quantities of output. As Eric moves from I_1 to I_2 to I_3 to I_4 in Figure 2A, he is producing more output. Figure 2A is an isoquant map. An isoquant map makes it possible to compare points representing combinations of inputs *x* and *y* so as to determine whether the producer prefers one such combination. All points on any single isoquant curve represent the same level of output. Points on isoquant curves located to the right of and above a particular curve are combinations that produce greater levels of output.

The typical isoquant curve has a negative slope, which means that in order to produce the constant output, some extra amount of one input is necessary to compensate for the loss of some amount of the other. In other words, each combination of two inputs on the same isoquant curve

COMBINATION	INPUT X (LABOR)	INPUT Y (CAPITAL)
A	16	3
B	12	4
C	10	5
D	8	7
E	6	9

TABLE 1A
INPUT COMBINATIONS FOR PRODUCING 1,000 DOZEN SHIRTS

FIGURE 1A
ISOQUANT CURVE
Isoquants are curves
representing combina-
tions of two inputs that
produce the same output.
All combinations on the
same isoquant represent
the same level of output.

has more of one of the inputs but less of the other compared to other combinations on that same isoquant curve.

DIMINISHING MARGINAL RATES OF SUBSTITUTION

The curvature of the isoquant is convex to the origin. The convexity
means that as a producer uses more units of one input and fewer units of
the other input, it takes more and more units of the more abundant input to compensate for the loss of one unit of the input that is becoming
more scarce. Just as with indifference curves, the convexity of the isoquant
reflects the principle of diminishing marginal rates of substitution.

The trade-off ratio along the isoquant curve is called (as before with
indifference curves) the marginal rate of substitution. The marginal rate

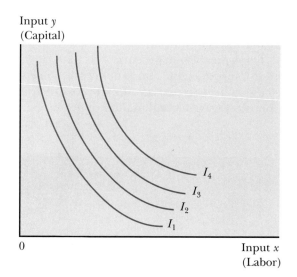

FIGURE 2A
ISOQUANT MAP
An isoquant map is
a set of isoquant curves,
each corresponding to a
different level of output.
Higher curves on the
map represent higher
levels of output.

of substitution of input x for input y, MRS_{xy}, shows the willingness of the producer to substitute between the inputs:

$$MRS_{xy} = \frac{\text{number of units of } y \text{ released}}{\text{number of units of } x \text{ substituted}} .$$

As more of one input (x) is substituted for the other input (y), the value of input x in terms of input y declines.

COST CONSTRAINTS

Which combination of inputs should a producer choose? The answer depends on the budget of that producer and on the prices of the inputs. Keep in mind that the producer faces input prices that are determined in markets. The typical producer cannot influence these prices. Total costs constrain the producer from buying all the inputs that might be desired. For every possible value of total costs, there is an **isocost line**. ("Isocost" means equal cost.) This line identifies all combinations of inputs the firm can purchase for a given total cost. This concept is analogous to the budget line in indifference analysis.

A straight line connecting the two points that represent buying only input y or only input x will show all possible combinations that can be attained with a given cost outlay. Any combination outside (above) the line is unattainable at that cost outlay. It is outside the budget constraint. In other words, the isocost line is the dividing line between those input combinations that are attainable and those that are unattainable at a given level of prices and a given cost outlay. An isocost line is shown in Figure 3A. The intercept on the axis representing each input is determined by dividing the total cost outlay (TC) by the price of that input (P_x or P_y). The slope of the isocost curve is therefore the ratio of the per-unit costs of the two inputs.

isocost line
A line that shows the amounts of two inputs that can be purchased with a fixed sum of money (a firm's budget line).

CHANGES IN COST OUTLAY OR PRICES OF INPUTS

The isocost line is developed by holding prices of inputs and total cost out-

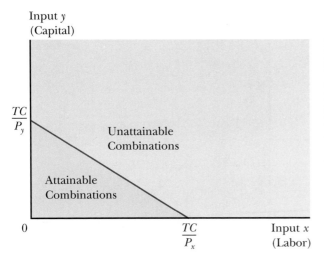

FIGURE 3A
ISOCOST LINE
An isocost line shows the input combinations that are possible at a given level of total cost outlay. Any combination outside (above) the line is unattainable.

lay constant. How do changes in total cost outlay or prices affect the iso-cost line?

An increase in total cost outlay (or the firm's budget) means that more of both inputs can be purchased, if input prices stay the same. A doubling of cost outlay means that twice as much of both inputs can be purchased. Increases in cost outlay are represented by a parallel outward shift of the isocost line. Decreases in cost outlay are represented by a parallel inward shift of the isocost line. Such shifts are shown in Figure 4A.

A change in the price of one input only affects the amount of that input that can be employed, not the amount of the other input. A price rise, then, will affect only the intercept of the isocost line with the axis for the input that has experienced the price rise. The effect of such a change is shown in Figure 5A. A price rise for input x from P_{x_1} to P_{x_2} causes the x-axis intercept of the isocost line to move closer to the origin. This shift reflects the fact that less x can now be purchased with the same cost out-lay. A decrease in the price of input x from P_{x_1} to P_{x_3} would mean that more of x could be purchased. The x-intercept moves away from the origin, reflecting increases in the potential employment of input x.

Price changes cause the slope of the isocost line to change. Note that the slope is the negative of the ratio of the prices of the two inputs, or $-(P_x/P_y)$. The slope of the isocost line changes when the ratio of the input prices changes. A change in total cost outlay, on the other hand, represents no change in relative prices. The slope of the isocost line remains the same in that case, shifting in a parallel fashion as described above.

CHOOSING THE OPTIMUM COMBINATION OF INPUTS

Drawing the isocost line on an isoquant map makes it possible to demonstrate the choice of input combination. In Figure 6A, at point A on isoquant I_2, the isocost line and isoquant I_2 are tangent. Any point on I_3, such as point B, is preferred to point A because higher isoquant curves

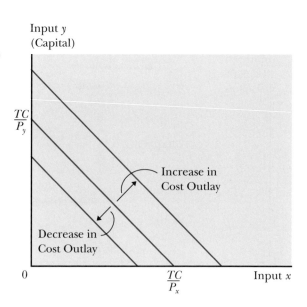

FIGURE 4A
THE EFFECT OF CHANGES IN TOTAL COST OUTLAY ON THE ISOCOST LINE
An increase in total cost outlay is represented by a parallel outward shift of the isocost line. A decrease in total cost outlay is represented by an inward parallel shift of the isocost line.

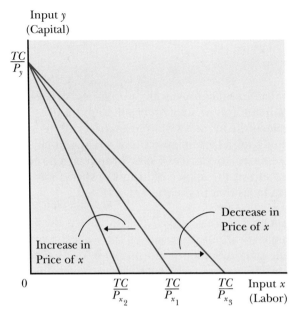

FIGURE 5A
THE EFFECT OF INPUT
PRICE CHANGES ON THE
ISOCOST LINE
An increase in the price
of one input changes the
slope of the isocost line.
An increase in the price
of an input means that if
all of the firm's cost
outlay is spent on that
input, less of it can be
purchased. As a result,
the intercept of the
isocost line with the axis
for that input will shift
closer to the origin.
The opposite holds for
a decrease in the price
of an input.

represent higher levels of output. However, point B is not attainable because it is outside the isocost line. Point C on I_1 is attainable. Point A on
I_2 is also attainable, however, and any point on I_2 represents more output
than any point on I_1. The producer wants to reach the highest attainable
isoquant. The highest attainable curve will be one that is tangent to the
isocost line because no higher isoquant can be reached with the given cost
outlay and prices.

You should remember from geometry that two curves that are tangent
have equal slopes at the point of tangency. At the point of tangency be-

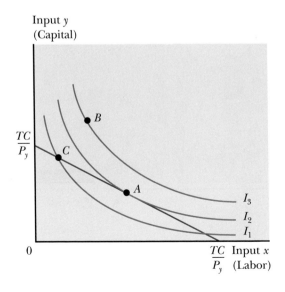

FIGURE 6A
THE CHOICE OF INPUT
COMBINATIONS
A producer maximizes
output for a given cost
outlay at the input
combination where
the isocost line is tangent
to the highest attainable
isoquant curve.

tween the isoquant curve and the isocost line, the marginal rate of substitution is equal to the ratio of the price of x to the price of y:[a]

$$MRS_{xy} = \frac{P_x}{P_y}.$$

The marginal rate of substitution expresses the willingness of the producer to substitute a certain amount of x for a certain amount of y. The slope of the isocost line reflects the market's willingness in terms of prices to trade a certain amount of x for a certain amount of y. The impersonal forces of the market impose the relative prices on the producer. The equation says that the producer adjusts the choice of inputs in such a way that his or her trade-off is the same as that of the market.

THE FIRM'S REACTION TO PRICE CHANGES

Figure 5A shows how changes in input prices affect the isocost line. We can now see how the optimum combination of inputs will be affected by price changes. Suppose a producer is initially at a point of maximum output at point A on isoquant I_1 in Figure 7A. As the price of output x falls from P_{x_1} to P_{x_2}, the isocost line rotates out to intersect the x-axis at TC/P_{x_2}, and the producer now has a new optimum at point B on isoquant I_2. Another decrease in price to P_{x_3} allows the producer to reach a still higher isoquant, I_3, and a new optimum at point C. Connecting points A, B, and C produces an expansion path, which shows how the input combination changes when relative input prices change.

FIGURE 7A
THE FIRM'S EXPANSION PATH
An expansion path depicts how the firm's choice of inputs changes when relative prices change.

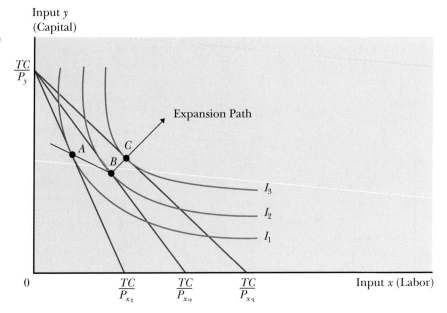

a.   Technically, MRS_{xy} is equal to the negative of the slope of the isoquant curve. The price ratio, as we have seen, is the negative of the slope of the isocost line. Therefore, at the (equilibrium) point of tangency between the isoquant curve and the isocost line, $MRS_{xy} = P_x/P_y$.

1. Define:
   a. explicit cost,
   b. implicit cost,
   c. accounting cost,
   d. accounting profit,
   e. economic profit,
   f. normal profit.
2. Use a total cost schedule to calculate:
   a. average total cost (AC),
   b. average fixed cost (AFC),
   c. average variable cost (AVC),
   d. marginal cost (MC).
3. Graph total cost (TC), total variable costs (TVC), total fixed costs (TFC), average cost (AC), average variable cost (AVC), average fixed cost (AFC), long-run average cost ($LRAC$), and marginal cost (MC).
4. List the reasons for economies and diseconomies of scale.
5. Determine the profit-maximizing level of production using:
   a. total revenue and total cost,
   b. marginal revenue and marginal cost.
6. Calculate the present value of a future stream of income using a table.

CHAPTER 22

COSTS AND PROFITS

INTRODUCTION

In the preceding chapter, we examined firms and how they carry out production. We developed the concept of a production function and the idea that a firm chooses its mix of inputs using a production function. Such choices translate into costs and cost functions. This chapter focuses on the cost relationships that result from production decisions.

We also explained in the preceding chapter how an entrepreneur attempts to minimize costs to achieve economic efficiency. But we need to be careful how we define cost. Costs of inputs should be expressed in terms of their opportunity cost. You were introduced to opportunity cost earlier, and now you need to apply it with a vengeance. Measuring costs of inputs in this way can be a problem if you are not used to thinking in terms of opportunity cost and are more used to thinking in terms of explicit cost. **Explicit costs** are accounting costs or money outlays. **Implicit costs** are those additional costs implied by the alternatives given up. When economists talk of costs, they include opportunity costs—explicit and implicit.

Some examples can make this clearer. Suppose you have the option of working two hours of overtime at $10 an hour or going to a concert that costs $5. The cost of attending the concert is the $5 ticket charge *plus* the $20 you could have earned working overtime. Attending the concert will cost you $25. The explicit cost is $5. The implicit cost is $20. Or suppose your rich aunt in Great Britain sends you her "old" Rolls Royce that is worth $100,000. She doesn't care what you do with it. You are excited because now you can drive a classic car at very low cost. You need only pay for gas, oil, insurance, and repairs. Right? No! You have forgotten to in-

explicit costs
Accounting costs or money outlays.

implicit costs
Costs measured by the value of alternatives given up.

clude a calculation of the implicit cost. If you sold the car, you could invest the $100,000. You could put the money in a high-yield account that earns 10 percent per year. In other words, you are giving up $10,000 per year if you choose to drive the Rolls. The total cost is the implicit cost of that $10,000 plus the explicit costs of gas, oil, insurance, and repairs. Do you still want to drive the Rolls?

ACCOUNTING PROFIT AND ECONOMIC PROFIT

accounting profit
The difference between total sales and explicit costs.

In Chapter 3, Susan's lemonade stand was used as an example of a firm as a supplier. Now suppose we can obtain Susan's account books in order to calculate her profits. Let's say she had total sales of $15,000 for the summer. Her books say that she has accounting (explicit) costs of $11,500. Her **accounting profit** is $3,500, determined by subtracting her explicit costs from her total sales. These are the profits reported for tax purposes. But economists think that profits figured in this way give a misleading view of a firm's health because implicit costs are ignored. If Susan's skills and talents are worth $2,000, then her opportunity cost, which is her implicit costs plus her explicit costs, is $13,500. She will be earning an economic profit of $1,500. **Economic profit** is the difference between total revenue and the total of explicit and implicit costs of production. An entrepreneur who does not earn a profit that is at least equal to his or her opportunity cost will quit the endeavor.

economic profit
The difference between total sales and the total of explicit and implicit costs of production.

OPPORTUNITY COST AND NORMAL PROFIT

normal profit
The opportunity cost of capital and enterprise, or the rate of return that is necessary for a firm to remain in a competitive industry.

The opportunity cost of capital and enterprise is referred to as **normal profit**. A normal profit represents the rate of return that is necessary to keep capital and enterprise in an industry. Say, for example, the normal profit is 8 percent. Then a firm earning an 8 percent rate of return is earning zero economic profit because its capital and enterprise could earn 8 percent elsewhere. The concept of normal profit is used by regulators in setting prices for public utilities (such as electric and telephone companies). If an electric utility is not granted a price increase and the rate of return on its capital falls below the normal profit, capital will leave that industry to try to earn its opportunity cost elsewhere.

In other words, normal profit is part of the implicit cost structure of firms. Just like the "free" Rolls Royce, a firm's capital, even if it is paid for, represents wealth that could be sold and invested elsewhere. The calculation is, in principle, exactly the same as in the Rolls Royce example.

Figure 1 shows the relationships of the concepts of accounting profit, economic profit, and normal profit. Total revenue is the same in both bars, but the difference between economic profit and accounting profit is the implicit costs, including normal profit.

A correct definition of costs is important because economists use costs and profits to predict behavior. When economic profits are positive, economists predict that new firms will enter an industry. When economic profits are negative, firms will leave the industry. When economic profits are zero, existing firms will remain and earn normal profits, but no new ones will enter. Economic profit serves as a signal, calling forth entry into

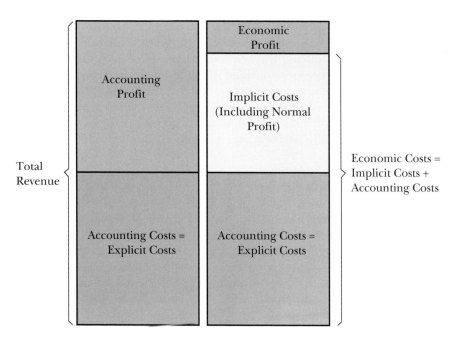

Total Revenue

Accounting Profit	Economic Profit
Accounting Profit	Implicit Costs (Including Normal Profit)
Accounting Costs = Explicit Costs	Accounting Costs = Explicit Costs

Economic Costs = Implicit Costs + Accounting Costs

FIGURE 1
ECONOMIC PROFIT AND
ACCOUNTING PROFIT
Economic profit differs
from accounting profit
by the amount of implicit
costs.

or exit out of an industry. If a firm isn't earning a normal profit in its present industry, its resources will flow to an industry where a higher rate of return can be earned. If more than a normal profit is being earned in an industry, resources will be attracted to it.

THE USE OF ACCOUNTING PROFITS IN ECONOMIC ANALYSIS

Economic theory is based on the concepts of economic costs and economic profit, but these data aren't usually available for real-world analyses. Economists are suspicious of accounting costs and accounting profits for at least two reasons. The first has to do with the way in which accounting costs are gathered. The second has to do with the discrepancy between accounting costs and economic costs.

Since federal income tax is paid on accounting profits, firms have incentives to make profits look as small as possible for the IRS and as large as possible for potential investors. There are many things that can be done to manipulate accounting profits. Some flexibility in measuring profits comes from the very different ways in which firms can account for items whose value is estimated subjectively. Several years ago, *Fortune* magazine asked experts at several "Big Eight" accounting firms how they could "pump up" the profits of a mythical $10-billion-a-year company. These experts reported a number of accounting techniques that could boost reported profits as much as 15 percent.[1] These techniques fall into three categories: altering approved accounting methods, manipulating managers' estimates of costs, and changing the time periods in which costs are paid and revenues are received.

1.   Ford S. Worthy, "Manipulating Profits: How It's Done," *Fortune* (25 June 1984): 49–54. For an interesting article that shows how Hollywood movie makers manipulate accounting profits, see Danna Wechsler, "Profits? What Profits?" *Forbes* (19 February 1990): 38–40.

Even though economists argue that accounting data do not reflect economic reality and can be manipulated, that data is all that is available for them to use in studying the economy. The use of accounting data is subject to much debate by economic researchers. Some argue that studies that use accounting data are meaningless. Others hold that accounting data are all that is available, and as long as economists are careful, using such data is worthwhile.[2] This debate will go on as long as economists attempt to measure the performance of firms and industries.

COSTS IN THE SHORT RUN

The production function relates inputs to outputs. The inputs in the production function have prices and represent costs to the firm. These input prices, which are determined in factor markets, may or may not be affected by the actions of the firm itself. Given the prices of inputs and the production function, it is possible to derive cost data for the firm. Although the derivation can be done formally, we will show the relationship on a graph and then derive the costs in a simpler fashion.

DEFINING COSTS

An example of a cost profile for a firm is given in Table 1. **Total cost (TC)** is simply the sum of all the costs of production for a given level of output. Total cost is made up of two components: total fixed costs (TFC) and total variable costs (TVC). That is, $TFC + TVC = TC$. **Total fixed costs (TFC)** are the costs of the fixed factors of production. Therefore, they can't be avoided or changed in the short run. These costs will be the same re-

total cost (TC)
The sum of all the costs of production for a given level of output.

total fixed costs (TFC)
The costs of the fixed factors of production, which can't be avoided in the short run.

TABLE 1
COST PROFILE FOR A FIRM

OUTPUT PER WEEK (Q)	TOTAL FIXED COSTS (TFC)	TOTAL VARIABLE COSTS (TVC)	TOTAL COST (TC)	AVERAGE FIXED COST (AFC)	AVERAGE VARIABLE COST (AVC)	AVERAGE TOTAL COST (AC)	MARGINAL COST (MC)
0	$60	$ 0	$ 60	$—	$ 0	$—	$ 0
1	60	40	100	60	40	100	40
2	60	76	136	30	38	68	36
3	60	108	168	20	36	56	32
4	60	140	200	15	35	50	32
5	60	175	235	12	35	47	35
6	60	216	276	10	36	46	41
7	60	262	322	$8^4/_7$	$37^3/_7$	46	46
8	60	312	372	$7^1/_2$	39	$46^1/_2$	50
9	60	369	429	$6^2/_3$	41	$47^2/_3$	57
10	60	430	490	6	43	49	61

2.   The most recent exchange in this debate was kicked off by George J. Benston, "The Validity of Profits-Structure Studies With Particular Reference to the FTC's Line of Business Data," *American Economic Review* (March 1985): 36–67. Thirteen economists responded to Benston's article in the March 1987 issue of the *American Economic Review*. See also Franklin M. Fisher and John J. McGowan, "On the Misuse of Accounting Rates of Return to Infer Monopoly Profits," *American Economic Review* (March 1983): 82–97. A series of comments in opposition to their position can be found in the June 1984 issue of the *American Economic Review*.

gardless of how many units of output the firm produces. **Total variable costs (*TVC*)** vary directly with output. Variable costs increase as more output is produced because more of the variable factors of production have to be purchased if more output is to be produced. Total fixed costs and total variable costs are shown in the second and third columns in Table 1. In this cost schedule, we assume that the firm has already identified that combination of inputs that minimizes the total variable costs for every level of output. These figures represent the cost of the economically efficient input combinations. Why should the firm pay a higher total variable cost than it has to?

Given the information in the first four columns of Table 1, the rest of the columns are computed as follows: **Average fixed cost (*AFC*)** is total fixed costs of production divided by the number of units of output. **Average variable cost (*AVC*)** is total variable costs divided by the number of units of output. That is,

$$AFC = \frac{TFC}{Q}, \quad \text{and} \quad AVC = \frac{TVC}{Q}.$$

Average total cost (*AC*) is equal to the total costs of producing a level of output divided by that level of output. That is,

$$AC = \frac{TC}{Q}.$$

Marginal cost (*MC*) is the change in total cost as a result of producing one more (or one less) unit of output. That is,

$$MC = \frac{\Delta TC}{\Delta Q} = \frac{\Delta TVC}{\Delta Q}.$$

Marginal costs are really marginal *variable* costs because there are no marginal fixed costs. When output changes, the change in fixed costs is zero.

Cost Curves

We can draw a series of cost curves from the data given in Table 1. The curves are drawn smoothly to better emphasize their relationships.[3]

The total fixed costs, total variable costs, and total cost curves are shown in Figure 2. The shape of the production function determines the shapes of the total cost curve and the total variable costs curve. As the amount of the variable factor of production increases, both output and total costs increase. If output increases more rapidly than factor cost, total cost (as well as total variable costs) increases at a decreasing rate, and returns increase. In Figure 2, the production function shows decreasing costs, or increasing returns to the variable factor, as output increases from zero to Q_1. From Q_1 to higher levels of output, output increases less rapidly than the factor cost increases. Then total cost (along with total variable costs) increases at an increasing rate. The principle of diminishing returns operates beyond output level Q_1.

total variable costs (*TVC*) The costs of the factors of production that vary directly with output, increasing as more output is produced.

average fixed cost (*AFC*) Total fixed costs of production divided by number of units of the output.

average variable cost (*AVC*) Total variable costs of production divided by the number of units of output.

average total cost (*AC*) Total costs of producing a level of output divided by the number of units of output.

marginal cost The change in total cost from producing one more (or one less) unit of output.

---

3.   Drawing the curves smoothly assumes that the gaps between the discrete points in Table 1 can be filled in with a continuous curve.

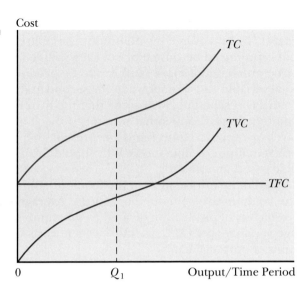

FIGURE 2
TOTAL COST CURVES
The shapes of the total cost (*TC*) curve and total variable costs (*TVC*) curve are a reflection of the production function. From zero output to an output level of Q_1, total cost and total variable cost increase at a decreasing rate. Beyond output level Q_1, diminishing returns set in. Then costs increase at an increasing rate.

Consider this simple example. Suppose a firm hires 1 additional worker and output increases by 10 units. The variable cost increases by the wage of that worker (for a given time period). Now, if it takes 2 more workers to increase output by 10 more units, total variable costs would increase by the wage rate times 2. Clearly the cost would be increasing at an increasing rate.

Now let's look at average and marginal costs. Figure 3 shows the average fixed costs (*AFC*), average variable costs (*AVC*), average cost (*AC*), and marginal cost (*MC*) curves for a firm. The *AFC* curve declines continuously, getting closer and closer to the horizontal axis of the graph.

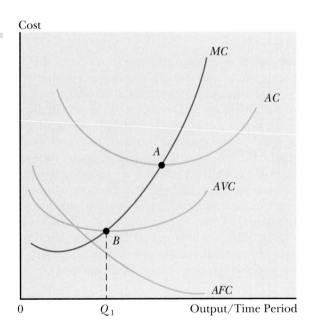

FIGURE 3
MARGINAL AND AVERAGE COST CURVES
The average fixed costs (*AFC*) curve declines continuously. The average variable costs (*AVC*) and average cost (*AC*) curves decline, reach a minimum, and then increase, resulting in a U shape. The marginal cost (*MC*) curve intersects the *AVC* and *AC* curves at their minimum points.

This decline occurs because fixed costs are constant, since average fixed costs are calculated by dividing that constant amount by an ever increasing quantity (levels of output). Thus, the average fixed costs become smaller and smaller as output increases.

Average variable costs first decline and then increase, as does average cost. The U-shaped AVC curve represents returns to the variable inputs that at first increase and then diminish. The variable inputs are being added to a given quantity of fixed factor, such as a fixed-size plant. Increasing returns occur for output levels up to Q_1 in Figure 3.

At output levels above Q_1, returns to the variable factors decline. That is, returns are diminishing. Increasing returns mean decreasing average costs, and diminishing returns mean increasing average costs. The AVC and AC curves are U-shaped because of decreasing costs (increasing returns) for small levels of output and then increasing costs (diminishing returns) for higher levels of output. Average cost declines sharply at first because average fixed costs drop rapidly and then more slowly.

Note that the MC curve intersects the AC and AVC curves at their lowest points—points A and B in Figure 3. These points illustrate the relationship between average and marginal values, discussed in the preceding chapter. For the AC and AVC curves to be declining, the marginal cost must be below the average cost. For the AC and AVC curves to be rising, the marginal cost must be above the average cost. Thus, marginal cost and average cost must be equal where the AC curve is at its minimum point. Think about how your grade point average goes up or down depending on your grade in an added (marginal) course. Also, note that when the MC curve starts to rise as output is increased, it is still below the AVC curve. Thus, average variable costs are still falling. An average value falls as long as the marginal value is below it, regardless of whether the marginal value is falling or rising.

THE RELATIONSHIP BETWEEN PRODUCT CURVES AND COST CURVES

We have said that cost curves could be derived from production functions. This derivation is an advanced topic in economics, but you can see the relationship between a production function (represented by product curves) and cost curves in Figure 4.

Part (a) of Figure 4 shows the marginal physical product (MPP) and average physical product (APP) curves discussed in the preceding chapter. In this case, the variable factor is labor. Part (b) represents the cost curves that are derived from the production function that produced the product curves. The marginal cost (MC) curve is a mirror image of the MPP_L curve. At those output levels where marginal physical product is increasing, reflecting increasing returns, marginal cost is decreasing. When the MPP_L curve is at its maximum, the MC curve is at its minimum point. When marginal physical product is declining, reflecting diminishing returns, marginal cost is rising.

Similar relationships hold for the APP and AVC curves. When average physical product is increasing, average variable costs are decreasing, and when average physical product is decreasing, average variable costs are increasing. The maximum and minimum points of the two curves also coincide.

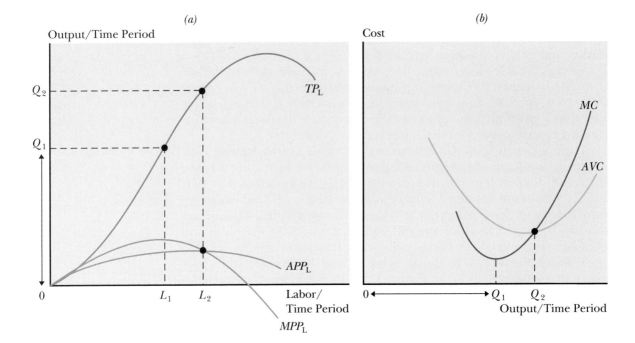

FIGURE 4
THE RELATIONSHIP
BETWEEN PRODUCT CURVES
AND COST CURVES
The cost curves are
mirror images of the
respective product curves.
When the product curve
is increasing, the cost
curve is decreasing, and
vice versa. Q_1 on the
vertical axis of part (a)
is the same as Q_1 on the
horizontal axis of part
(b). L_1 in part (a)
represents the units of
labor required to
produce Q_1 units
of output.

This relationship is based on simple logic. The cost curves are simply monetary measures of inputs needed to produce a given output, and the production function measures outputs for a given amount of inputs. Given prices of resources, increasing returns have to mean decreasing costs and diminishing returns have to mean increasing costs.

COSTS IN THE LONG RUN

In the long run, all factors of production are variable. Therefore, there are no fixed factors of production. As a result, there are no fixed costs in the long run. All costs are variable in the long run. In fact, the long run is defined as the period long enough to vary all inputs.

The most important long-run decision is what size plant to build. Each possible size is represented by a short-run average cost (AC) curve. The long-run decision is based on the selection of the desired short-run average cost curve. That choice will be based on the output the firm expects to produce. Figure 5 illustrates this decision. Suppose the technological factors (given by the production function) are such that only three plant sizes are feasible. These plants are represented by curves AC_1, AC_2, and AC_3 in Figure 5. The long-run decision of which short-run curve to operate on will depend on the planned output of the firm. If output is to be less than Q_1, then the plant represented by AC_1 should be built because its size will produce any output level between zero and Q_1 at a per-unit cost that is lower than it would be for any other size. If an output level between Q_1 and Q_2 is planned, the plant represented by AC_2 should be built. If output is to be greater than Q_2, the plant represented by AC_3 should be built.

Cost

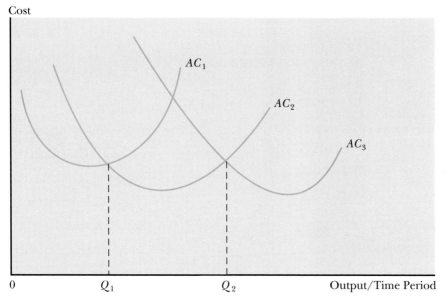

FIGURE 5
ALTERNATIVE PLANT SIZES
The determination of
which size plant to build
is a long-run decision of
a firm. This decision is
based on selection of
the short-run cost curve
that is optimal for the
expected output level.

It is likely that more than three alternative plant sizes would be feasible. They would all be examined in the planning stage. Assume the firm faces all the short-run average cost curves depicted in Figure 6. All these possible short-run curves are tangent to a curve that is sometimes referred to as a planning curve. A **planning curve** is the long-run average cost curve. It is called a planning curve because any point on the curve could be chosen in the planning stage by deciding to build a certain size of plant. Such a planning curve, more commonly called the long-run average cost curve, is shown in Figure 6. The **long-run average cost (*LRAC*) curve** rep-

planning curve
The long-run average cost
curve used in the
planning stage.

**long-run average cost
(*LRAC*) curve**
A curve tangent to all
the possible short-run
cost curves and representing the lowest attainable
average cost of producing
any given output.

Cost

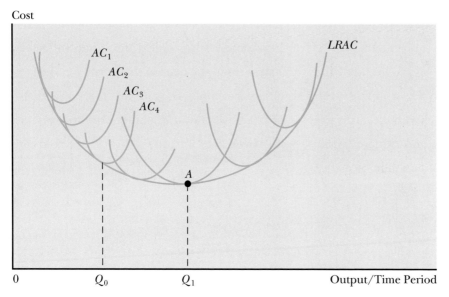

FIGURE 6
LONG-RUN AVERAGE
COST CURVE
All the possible short-run
cost curves are tangent to
the planning curve. This
planning curve is the
long-run average cost
(*LRAC*) curve and
represents the lowest
attainable average cost
of producing any level
of output. The optimal
plant size is represented
by point *A*, where the
minimum point on a
short-run average cost
curve is tangent to the
long-run average cost
curve at its minimum
point.

Manufacturing is quite often subject to economies of scale over a relatively large output range. As a result of these large-scale economies, policy makers have argued that manufacturing in less developed countries needs to be protected from foreign competition in order to get a toehold in domestic markets and someday be able to compete with industry in developed countries. This position, called the infant industry argument by economists, was strongly advocated by Alexander Hamilton (1755–1804), who served as the first Secretary of the U.S. Treasury in George Washington's cabinet. Hamilton was a promoter of economic growth and a strong federal government.

Hamilton argued that it would be very difficult for the U.S. economy to develop in a system of free trade because Great Britain had entrenched manufacturers with established trade networks. He argued that the only way U.S. firms could compete with developed foreign firms was with the "interference and aid" of the federal government. These infant industries could stand on their own after

INTERNATIONAL
PERSPECTIVE

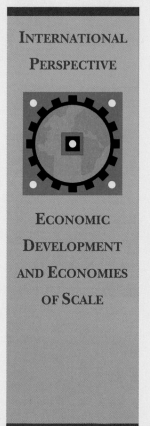

ECONOMIC
DEVELOPMENT
AND ECONOMIES
OF SCALE

a "nursing period." An important element of this argument is that the new firm needs to grow to a size at which it enjoys economies of scale before it faces foreign competition.

The infant industry argument is used by many countries today. In fact, many observers point to the sort of policy advocated by Hamilton when they examine the Japanese experience with industrialization in the postwar period. The Japanese government and business leaders defined a few key industrial sectors. They nurtured these key industries with subsidies and high-tariff barriers until the industries attained economies of scale and low enough long-run average costs to be competitive in world markets.

The problems with the infant industry argument should be obvious. How can policy makers recognize promising industries in advance? Also, unless the infant industries have a domestic market that is large enough to attain economies of scale that make them cost-competitive on world markets, the government may have to protect the industries into old age.

resents the lowest attainable average cost of producing any given output. It is a curve tangent to all the possible short-run average cost curves. For example, if you knew you were going to produce exactly Q_0 units of output, the plant size represented by AC_4 would have the lowest average cost.

Only at point A in Figure 6, which corresponds to an output of Q_1 units, is there tangency between the minimum point on a short-run AC curve and the minimum point on the $LRAC$ curve. This point indicates the optimal-size plant. The **optimal-size plant** is represented by the short-run average cost curve with the lowest attainable per-unit costs.

ECONOMIES AND DISECONOMIES OF SCALE

The $LRAC$ curve in Figure 6 is U-shaped. This shape means that, at first, as plant size and firm output increase, long-run average costs fall. After a certain point (point A on Figure 6), however, bigness becomes costly. As the plant continues to increase in size, average cost begins to rise. Economists refer to these changes in long-run average cost due to increased plant size as economies and diseconomies of scale. **Economies of scale** are declines in long-run average cost that are due to increased plant size. **Diseconomies of scale** are increases in long-run average cost that are due to increased plant size. As scale (plant size) increases, economies (cost savings) result. After a while, further growth results in diseconomies (higher costs).

Economies and diseconomies of scale are distinct from increasing and decreasing returns. Increasing and decreasing returns are the result of using a given size plant more or less intensively in the short run. Economies and diseconomies of scale result from changes in the size of a plant in the long run.

It is easy to see how economies of scale result from an increase in plant size. As a firm increases its scale of operations, it usually can employ more specialized machinery. Also, jobs can be more specialized. Equipment can be used more efficiently. By-products of the operation that might be uneconomical to recover or exploit in a small-scale plant may become economical for a large operation. A large firm is often able to obtain quantity discounts on intermediate products from other firms. Political influence that has economic value is also more likely to accrue to a large, rather than a small, firm. These are just a few of the reasons for the negative slope of the $LRAC$ curve as the scale of operations increases.

Diseconomies of scale are slightly harder to grasp. However, anyone who has dealt with giant bureaucracies, public or private, will have seen evidence of them. Diseconomies result from the fact that as an organization becomes very large, communication and coordination become more difficult and time consuming, and control from the top diminishes. After a firm has taken advantage of the gains to be achieved by growing larger, managerial inefficiencies set in. With further growth, the $LRAC$ curve turns upward.

OPTIMAL-SIZE PLANTS IN THE REAL WORLD

If you look at real-world industries, you see many different sized firms operating side by side in the same industry. Steel, for example, is produced by both very large and very small firms. If there is a single, optimal size plant

optimal-size plant
The plant represented by the short-run average cost curve with the lowest attainable per-unit costs.

economies of scale
Declines in long-run average cost that are due to increased plant size.

diseconomies of scale
Increases in long-run average cost that are due to increased plant size.

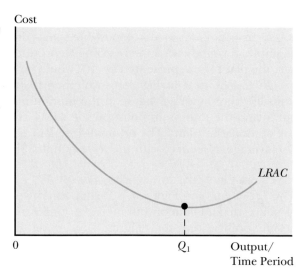

FIGURE 7
**ECONOMIES OF SCALE AND
A FEW VERY LARGE PLANTS**
When economies of scale
exist over large ranges of
output, one large plant or
a few large plants are
most efficient.

for each industry, why do firms of so many different sizes exist? Economists have spent much time investigating real economies of scale. Several different types of *LRAC* curves are represented in Figures 7, 8, and 9.

Figure 7 shows economies of scale over a large range of output. This situation occurs in the auto industry, where there are a few very large firms. The optimal-size plant in Figure 7 is that producing output level Q_1, which conceivably might represent the normal sales of the entire industry. In such industries, a natural monopoly can occur. A **natural monopoly** is a monopoly that emerges because of economies of scale. The size of the market is such that there is room for only one optimal-size firm. Many public utilities (gas and electric), for example, need to have all the sales in a market in order to become large enough to be of optimal size.

In Figure 8, a large number of plants of different sizes can be of optimal size. Firms in a range of sizes can all produce efficiently in the same

natural monopoly
A monopoly that emerges
because economies of
scale mean that there is
room for only one firm in
the market.

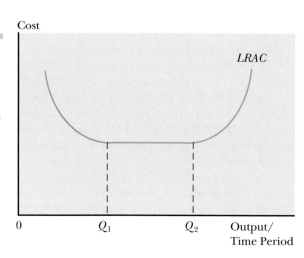

FIGURE 8
**MANY OPTIMAL-SIZE
PLANTS OF DIFFERENT
SIZES**
A range of outputs for
the optimal-size plant can
exist. When this situation
exists, plants of distinctly
different sizes can all
produce efficiently in the
same industry.

Cost

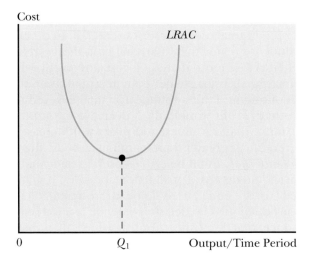

0   Q_1 Output/Time Period

FIGURE 9
MANY OPTIMAL-SIZE
PLANTS OF SIMILAR SIZES
If there is a unique
minimum point on the
long-run average cost
curve, all the plants in
an industry will be similar
in size.

industry at the same per-unit (or average) cost. In Figure 8, any firm producing an output between Q_1 and Q_2 would be efficient. If the demand for the product is large enough to support many firms in this size range, a very competitive situation exists. This situation prevails in many industries, such as textiles, publishing, and packaged food products.

Figure 9 illustrates an industry in which there are rapidly achievable economies of scale and diseconomies of scale. This kind of *LRAC* curve occurs when all the firms in an industry are of a similar size. The optimal-size plant in Figure 9 is the one whose short-run average cost curve hits a minimum point at Q_1.

The benefit of economies of scale may not be passed along to consumers. Economies of scale mean that it is efficient to have production carried out by large firms. However, these large-scale firms may exert monopoly pricing power so that lower costs are not passed on to consumers. We will return to this problem in the chapter on monopoly.

PROFIT MAXIMIZATION

The choice of plant size is one of several decisions that determine a firm's profits. The firms examined here and in the next three chapters are all profit-maximizing firms. What does profit maximization mean in terms of production decisions? It means that, in the short run, the firm will attempt to choose the output that maximizes the difference between total revenue and total cost. **Total revenue (*TR*)** is the price an item sells for multiplied by the number of units sold. **Marginal revenue (*MR*)** is the change in total revenue from selling one more (or one less) unit.

Profit will be maximized at the level of output at which marginal revenue equals marginal cost, or $MR = MC$. For any output level where marginal revenue is greater than marginal cost ($MR > MC$), total revenue is increasing faster than total cost when output and sales increase. This means that profit is increasing (or losses are decreasing). If output were

total revenue (*TR*)
The price an item sells for multiplied by the number of units sold.

marginal revenue (*MR*)
The change in total revenue from selling one more (or one less) unit.

reduced when marginal revenue was greater than marginal cost, total revenue would decline by more than total cost, so profit would fall. In other words, when marginal revenue is greater than marginal cost, if output is increased, total revenue will increase more than total cost, and profit will rise. On the other hand, if marginal cost is greater than marginal revenue ($MC > MR$), an increase in output and sales would cause total cost to increase more than total revenue. Profit would fall. A decrease in output and sales will reduce costs more than revenues, and profit will increase.

Therefore, if marginal revenue is greater than marginal cost, the firm should expand production and sales, and if marginal cost is greater than marginal revenue, the firm should decrease production and sales. If marginal revenue and marginal cost are equal, it would be unprofitable to either increase or decrease production. The decision rule for profit maximization, then, is to produce that level of output at which marginal revenue equals marginal cost ($MR = MC$). This rule is just another way of saying "Produce where total profit is at its maximum" or "Produce where total revenue exceeds total cost by the largest amount." Generally, the $MR = MC$ rule is the most convenient to work with.

It's easy to see this relationship on a graph. In Figure 10, the firm is a price taker, which means that the price is given as far as this firm is concerned. Thus, the total revenue (TR) curve in Figure 10(a) is a straight line from the origin. The marginal revenue (MR) curve in part (b) is a horizontal line at the level of the price of the product. The total cost (TC) curve is consistent with the law of diminishing returns beyond output level Q_2. (From zero output to Q_2, the TC curve represents increasing returns and decreasing average costs.) The vertical distance between TR and TC is greatest at output level Q_2. At that point the slopes of TR and TC are equal. The slope of TR is MR, and the slope of TC is MC. Thus, it is clear that $MR = MC$ at output level Q_2. This can be seen in part (b). Note that if output were decreased below Q_2, MC would fall below MR, and TR would fall by more than TC. Thus, profit would fall. If output were increased above Q_2, TC would increase more than TR, and MC would be above MR. Again, profit would fall. Profit is at a maximum at Q_2.

The decision to produce that output where marginal revenue equals marginal cost will come up again and again, so it is important to make sure you understand it. It will always be true that maximum profit will be obtained by operating at the point where $MR = MC$.

RULES FOR PROFIT MAXIMIZATION

- $MR > MC$ Expand output
- $MR = MC$ Profits maximized, output unchanged
- $MR < MC$ Reduce output

PRESENT VALUE

The discussion of costs and the movement from the short run to the long run has ignored both uncertainty and differences between present and

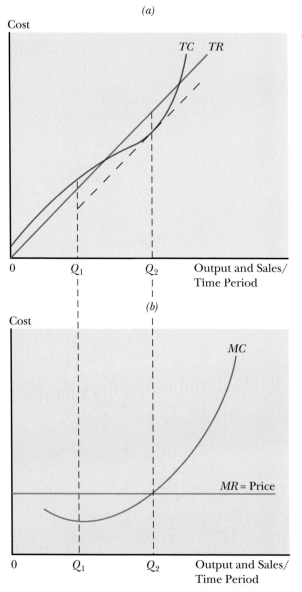

(a)

Cost

TC   TR

0   Q_1 Q_2 Output and Sales/
                                   Time Period

(b)

Cost

MC

MR = Price

0   Q_1 Q_2 Output and Sales/
                                   Time Period

FIGURE 10
PROFIT MAXIMIZATION
Profit is maximized where marginal cost is equal to marginal revenue. The vertical distance between total revenue (*TR*) and total cost (*TC*) is greatest in part (*a*) at Q_2, the same level of output where marginal cost (*MC*) equals marginal revenue (*MR*) in part (*b*).

future income. It is important to keep in mind that when an entrepreneur makes the decision of which plant to build, based on forecasted production, much uncertainty surrounds that decision. To make production forecasts, a great deal of information must be gathered and many factors must be considered. Production decisions (in fact, most economic decisions) affect costs and revenues over a number of periods of time. The decision maker needs a way of comparing revenues and costs in different time periods because a dollar cost or a dollar revenue today is not the same as a dollar cost or a dollar revenue next year or ten years from now.

To compare future dollars (costs or revenues) for different periods with present dollars, firms calculate the present value of the future dol-

Many state governments use legalized gambling to generate revenue for public projects. The most common form of this sanctioned gambling is a state-run lottery. It has even been suggested that the federal government run a lottery and use the profits to retire the federal deficit. State governments usually earmark the proceeds from a lottery for some special purpose. The most common use is to support education.

Some people feel that lotteries are a very regressive form of tax because the poor spend a higher percentage of their income in buying lottery tickets. Others who support the lottery concept argue that a lottery ticket is a voluntary purchase. Thus, a lottery cannot be viewed as a tax because people purchase the tickets of their own free will. These advocates point out that people are going to gamble and the state might as well get involved and make some profit to do "good things," such as spending more on education.

In many states, the newspapers on Sunday morning now carry a headline about the latest millionaire created by the lucky drawing on Saturday night. These drawings are usually done on television to add to the drama. In early January 1990, it was reported in the *Rocky Mountain News* that a Denver carpenter, Don Wittman, Jr., was the co-winner of $4 mil-

ECONOMIC INSIGHT

PRESENT VALUE AND LOTTERY JACKPOTS

lion.[a] "It hasn't hit me yet," he said, smiling broadly under the brim of a new Colorado Lottery baseball cap. "But I wouldn't know what to do if I quit my job. I like to work."

Let's look at the present value of Wittman's jackpot using a 10 percent interest rate and assuming that he will be paid in one lump sum on December 31 of each year. The *Rocky Mountain News* reported the amount to be received each year, after deductions for state and federal taxes: $1.583 million of the $2 million will actually be paid out, after $417,000 or about 21 percent is withheld in taxes. We have rounded off these payments to simplify the arithmetic. The table below shows what the reported $2 million is really worth. The present value of the $1.583 million at 10 percent is only $526,516. This low present value results from the fact that the payout is made over a long period of time and larger payouts are made in the most distant years.

In all, Wittman's payout adjusted for taxes and present value was only 26.3 percent of what the headlines reported. This is still a very nice prize. Most of us would be happy to be in his shoes. But perhaps it is a good thing that Wittman "likes to work." A critic of lotteries referred to state-run lotteries as a "weekly tax on stupidity." This critic understood present value.

	YEAR	PAYOUT IN DOLLARS	PRESENT VALUE IN DOLLARS		YEAR	PAYOUT IN DOLLARS	PRESENT VALUE IN DOLLARS
		$ 38,000	$ 38,000				
1.	1990	40,000	36,306	14.	2003	66,000	17,358
2.	1991	41,000	35,137	15.	2004	68,000	16,252
3.	1992	43,000	32,293	16.	2005	72,000	15,624
4.	1993	45,000	30,735	17.	2006	74,000	14,578
5.	1994	46,000	28,520	18.	2007	77,000	13,783
6.	1995	48,000	27,072	19.	2008	80,000	13,040
7.	1996	50,000	25,650	20.	2009	83,000	12,284
8.	1997	52,000	24,232	21.	2010	87,000	11,745
9.	1998	54,000	22,896	22.	2011	90,000	11,070
10.	1999	56,000	21,560	23.	2012	94,000	10,528
11.	2000	58,000	20,300	24.	2013	97,000	9,894
12.	2001	61,000	19,398	Total:		$1,583,000	$526,000
13.	2002	63,000	18,207				

a. "Carpenter Claims Half of Lotto Jackpot," *Rocky Mountain News* (3 January 1990): 7.

lars. **Present value (*PV*)** is the capitalized value of an item to be paid for or sold in the future. It is a future value discounted to the present. **Discounting** is the technique of calculating present values by adjusting for interest that would be earned between now and some specified future time. It works simply and has many important uses in daily life.

Present value is based on the fact that you can choose to save (refrain from consumption) and receive interest as a reward for your saving. As a result, you are always better off delaying a payment of a fixed sum that you must make and speeding up a payment of a fixed sum you are to receive. For example, suppose you owe a friend $100, and your friend doesn't care when you pay off the debt within the next year. If the interest rate is 10 percent, you could take $90.90, put it in the bank now, and in one year receive from the bank $100 to pay your friend—the $90.90 you deposited *plus* interest of $9.10. In other words, the present value of $100 to be paid in one year at 10 percent interest is only $90.90. Another way of saying this is that the $90.90 you put in the bank today will be equivalent to the $100 you pay to your friend a year from now. On the other hand, if you were owed $100, you would want the money now so you could put $100 in the bank and have $110 at the end of a year. Two principles emerge from this example of discounting:

1. The higher the interest rate, the lower the present value.
2. The longer the time period, the lower the present value.

The formula for calculating present value is

$$\frac{V_t}{(1+r)^t},$$

where V_t is the value in year t, r is the interest rate, and t is the number of years. Table 2 shows the present value of $1 received in various future years (up to fifty years) at different interest rates. You can use the table to see that the present value of $100 for one year at a 10 percent interest rate is $90.90 ($0.909 \times $100).

Applications of present value surround you in your day-to-day life. Let's look at an example. Suppose that on your job as project manager, you are given the task of planning a new phase of operations. The engineer tells you the necessary equipment can be built in any of three ways over a period of three years. In each case, the firm's cash outlay will be spread out differently over the years. The alternatives are listed in Table 3. All alternatives are equal in the sense that each costs $600, all have the same date of completion, and all payments are made at the end of the year. Which should you choose? The only way to determine which alternative will maximize profit is to use present value analysis and discount the future dollar amounts. Using Table 2, we calculated the present value of each amount in Table 3, at a 10 percent interest rate. We totaled the present value amounts to find the least-cost method of production, which turns out to be alternative *C*. The present value of the outlay for alternative *C* is 5 percent less than that of alternative *A* and 9 percent less than that of alternative *B*. Choosing *C* means a substantial savings for the firm.

A profit-making firm that expects to be in business for a while will try to maximize profits. However, it will maximize the present value of profits

present value (*PV*)
The value of a future payment or series of future payments discounted to the present.

discounting
The technique of calculating present values by adjusting for interest that would be earned between now and some specified future time.

YEAR	3%	4%	5%	6%	7%	8%	10%	12%	15%	20%	YEAR
1	0.971	0.962	0.952	0.943	0.935	0.926	0.909	0.893	0.870	0.833	1
2	0.943	0.925	0.907	0.890	0.873	0.857	0.826	0.797	0.756	0.694	2
3	0.915	0.890	0.864	0.839	0.816	0.794	0.751	0.711	0.658	0.578	3
4	0.889	0.855	0.823	0.792	0.763	0.735	0.683	0.636	0.572	0.472	4
5	0.863	0.823	0.784	0.747	0.713	0.681	0.620	0.567	0.497	0.402	5
6	0.838	0.790	0.746	0.705	0.666	0.630	0.564	0.507	0.432	0.335	6
7	0.813	0.760	0.711	0.665	0.623	0.583	0.513	0.452	0.376	0.279	7
8	0.789	0.731	0.677	0.627	0.582	0.540	0.466	0.404	0.326	0.233	8
9	0.766	0.703	0.645	0.591	0.544	0.500	0.424	0.360	0.284	0.194	9
10	0.744	0.676	0.614	0.558	0.508	0.463	0.385	0.322	0.247	0.162	10
11	0.722	0.650	0.585	0.526	0.475	0.429	0.350	0.287	0.215	0.134	11
12	0.701	0.625	0.557	0.497	0.444	0.397	0.318	0.257	0.187	0.112	12
13	0.681	0.601	0.530	0.468	0.415	0.368	0.289	0.229	0.162	0.093	13
14	0.661	0.577	0.505	0.442	0.388	0.340	0.263	0.204	0.141	0.078	14
15	0.642	0.555	0.481	0.417	0.362	0.315	0.239	0.183	0.122	0.065	15
16	0.623	0.534	0.458	0.393	0.339	0.292	0.217	0.163	0.107	0.054	16
17	0.605	0.513	0.436	0.371	0.317	0.270	0.197	0.146	0.093	0.045	17
18	0.587	0.494	0.416	0.350	0.296	0.250	0.179	0.130	0.081	0.037	18
19	0.570	0.475	0.396	0.330	0.277	0.232	0.163	0.116	0.070	0.031	19
20	0.554	0.456	0.377	0.311	0.258	0.215	0.148	0.104	0.061	0.026	20
25	0.478	0.375	0.295	0.232	0.184	0.146	0.092	0.059	0.030	0.0105	25
30	0.412	0.308	0.231	0.174	0.131	0.0994	0.057	0.033	0.015	0.0042	30
40	0.307	0.208	0.142	0.0972	0.067	0.0460	0.022	0.011	0.0037	0.0006	40
50	0.228	0.141	0.087	0.0543	0.034	0.0213	0.008	0.003	0.0009	0.0001	50

TABLE 2
PRESENT VALUE OF $1.00

over a period of several years, not just the current period. The concept of present value is very important in business decisions but is *not* understood by many decision makers. It is often joked that the first year of an MBA program should be devoted solely to getting students to understand and make use of present value.

TABLE 3
PRESENT VALUE OF THREE
ALTERNATIVES AT A 10
PERCENT INTEREST RATE

ALTERNATIVE	COST IN YEAR 1	COST IN YEAR 2	COST IN YEAR 3	TOTAL COST
A	$200.00 ($PV$ = 181.80)	$200.00 ($PV$ = 165.20)	$200.00 ($PV$ = 150.20)	$600.00 ($PV$ = 497.20)
B	$400.00 ($PV$ = 363.60)	$100.00 ($PV$ = 82.60)	$100.00 ($PV$ = 75.10)	$600.00 ($PV$ = 521.30)
C	$100.00 ($PV$ = 90.90)	$100.00 ($PV$ = 82.60)	$400.00 ($PV$ = 300.40)	$600.00 ($PV$ = 473.90)

Summary

1. Economists calculate both implicit and explicit costs of production. Implicit costs are those costs implied by alternatives given up. Explicit costs are money expenditures, or accounting costs.

2. When total cost (both implicit and explicit costs) is equal to total revenue, economists say there is zero economic profit. This means the firm is covering all economic costs, including a normal profit. When costs exceed revenues, firms and resources will leave an industry in order to earn the opportunity cost associated with those resources.

3. In the short run, as variable factors of production are added to the fixed factors, the firm may experience increasing returns at low levels of output. Eventually the firm will incur diminishing returns at some higher levels of output.

4. Increasing and diminishing returns account for the U shape of the short-run average cost curve.

5. The U shape of the long-run average cost (*LRAC*) curve is due to economies and diseconomies of large-scale production.

6. Profit maximization means that an entrepreneur will produce that level of output that equates marginal cost and marginal revenue. This choice ensures that total revenue exceeds total cost by the largest possible amount.

7. Present value calculations are used to make dollar amounts to be received or paid in the future comparable with dollar amounts in the present.

New Terms

explicit cost	total fixed costs (*TFC*)	marginal cost (*MC*)	diseconomies of scale
implicit cost	total variable costs (*TVC*)	planning curve	natural monopoly
accounting profit	average fixed cost (*AFC*)	long-run average cost	total revenue (*TR*)
economic profit	average variable cost	(*LRAC*) curve	marginal revenue (*MR*)
normal profit	(*AVC*)	optimal-size plant	present value (*PV*)
total cost (*TC*)	average total cost (*AC*)	economies of scale	discounting

Questions for Discussion

1. Why are cost curves normally U-shaped both in the long run and in the short run?

2. What is a normal profit? Why is it necessary for a firm to earn at least a normal profit?

3. The famous epigram of the Chicago School of Economics is "There is no such thing as a free lunch." What does this mean?

4. At what size do universities start experiencing diseconomies of scale? What does the existence of many different sizes of universities indicate about the optimal-size university?

5. Does a university have to reach a certain size to have an efficient (winning) sports program? How would you gather empirical evidence on this?

6. What is the difference between diminishing returns and diseconomies of scale?

7. Would you rather win $6 million in a lump sum or $1 million a year for 10 years? Use a present value table to find an answer. What interest rate did you use? Why?

8. Give an example of an explicit cost and an implicit cost of your college education. Why does enrollment in colleges and graduate schools increase when economic times are bad and unemployment rates are high?

9. Complete the table on the following page. (You will

Total Output Per Day (Q)	Total Fixed Costs (TFC)	Total Variable Costs (TVC)	Total Cost (TC)	Average Fixed Cost (AFC)	Average Variable Cost (AVC)	Average Total Cost (AC)	Marginal Cost (MC)
0	$10.00	$ 0	$10.00	$—	$—	$—	$—
1	___	___	15.00	___	___	___	___
2	___	___	___	___	___	9.00	___
3	___	___	___	___	3.33	___	___
4	___	___	21.00	___	___	___	___
5	___	___	___	___	___	___	2.00
6	___	16.00	___	___	___	___	___
7	___	___	___	___	___	___	4.00
8	___	___	___	___	3.13	___	___
9	___	___	41.00	___	___	___	___
10	___	___	___	___	___	___	7.00
11	___	___	56.00	___	___	___	___

be referring back to this table when you answer questions at the end of the next two chapters.)

10. Graph the values of AFC, AVC, AC, and MC from the table in Question 9. Why does MC cut AVC and AC at their low points?

11. In 1990, major league baseball salaries exploded. The large increases were the result of the end of salary collusion by the owners and greatly enhanced revenues. Each day a record salary was reported in the newspapers. Mark Langston, a pitcher with the California Angels, signed for a reported $16 million over five years. With the table below, calculate the present value of

Year	Salary (Millions of Dollars)	Present Value (Millions of Dollars)
1. 1990	3.2	___
2. 1991	3.2	___
3. 1992	3.2	___
4. 1993	3.2	___
5. 1994	3.2	___
Total	16.0	

Langston's salary at the time of the contract (1989), using an 8 percent interest rate. (For ease of calculation assume the salary is paid in one lump sum on December 31 of each year.)

12. You are running a lottery and the current interest rate is 7 percent. Assume that you sell $10 million worth of tickets and that it costs you $40,000 for printing and other related expenses. If you make one payment of $10 million to the winner at the end of ten years, how much profit will you make?

13. In this chapter a distinction was drawn between short-run and long-run costs. What is the length of time that distinguishes between short-run and long-run costs? Can it be different in different industries?

14. What is the infant industry argument? How is it related to economies of scale?

15. Why are profits maximized when MC = MR?

Suggestions for Further Reading

Davis, John S., and J. J. Kanet. "Net Present Value Made User-Friendly," *Bobbin* (September 1989): 23–26. A business article that shows how present value can be used by decision makers in the garment industry.

Dung, Tran Hu, and Robert Premus. "Do Socioeconomic Regulations Discriminate against Small Firms?" *Southern Economic Journal* (January 1990): 686–697. This article shows how federal regulations to hire the handicapped impact more significantly on smaller firms. The cost of complying with regulations is another element that impacts on the long-run average cost curves in an industry.

Eckert, Ross D. *The Price System and Resource Allocation*, 10th ed. Hinsdale, IL: Dryden Press, 1988. An intermediate price theory text that develops the material found in this chapter in much greater detail.

1. List the assumptions of perfect competition.
2. Diagram the relationship between a representative firm and the total market.
3. Identify the profit-maximizing level of output.
4. Calculate profits, given information on quantity, marginal revenue, marginal cost, average cost, and price.
5. Define the shutdown point in terms of:
   a. price and average variable costs,
   b. total fixed costs and losses.
6. List the characteristics of each of three kinds of industries:
   a. constant cost industry,
   b. increasing cost industry,
   c. decreasing cost industry.
7. Describe the short-run and long-run equilibrium for the firm and the industry under perfect competition.
8. Explain how economic rent can exist in perfect competition, even in long-run equilibrium.

CHAPTER 23

PERFECT COMPETITION

INTRODUCTION

The last two chapters developed the principles of production and the general cost relationships derived from the production process. Any firm that makes production decisions will relate potential, or forecasted, revenues to costs in order to determine output levels. However, the forecasted revenues will depend on the market conditions faced by the firm.

This and the next two chapters look at four different models, referred to as market structures. The model discussed in this chapter is perfect competition. **Perfect competition** is the market structure in which there are many sellers and buyers, firms produce a homogeneous product, and there is free entry into and exit out of the industry. It is important to keep in mind that this is a theoretical model and does not precisely describe reality. The model is useful, however, because it allows the development of tools that indicate what determines price and quantity when conditions are close to those of perfect competition. The perfectly competitive market is the abstract ideal to which we will compare other market structures. This model underlies the basic supply and demand model developed earlier.

perfect competition
The market structure in which there are many sellers and buyers, firms produce a homogeneous product, and there is free entry into and exit out of the industry.

CHARACTERISTICS OF PERFECT COMPETITION

There are six basic assumptions for the model of perfect competition. In developing the theory, we assume that six characteristics exist in the market in which a firm is selling its product.

The first assumption is that there is a large number of sellers (producers) in the market. No specific number is indicated. A large number means there are so many sellers of the product that no single seller's decisions can affect price. For example, no single wheat farmer can influence the price of wheat. A farmer could sell the entire crop or none of the crop. The farmer's decision wouldn't affect the price of wheat one bit because the market for wheat is so large relative to any single producer.

The second assumption is that there is a large number of buyers (consumers) in the market. Again, a large number means that no one buyer can affect the price in any perceptible way. In other words, no single purchaser has any **market power**.

market power
The ability of buyers or sellers to affect price.

The third assumption is that perfectly competitive firms produce a homogeneous product. The product of one firm is no different from that of other firms in the industry. Since this is the case, purchasers have no preference for one producer over another. If you are a miller and want to purchase wheat, you don't care if it was produced by Farmer Jones or Farmer Smith—a bushel of number 1 winter wheat is a bushel of number 1 winter wheat!

The fourth, and very important, assumption is that there is free entry into and free exit out of the market. This means that if one firm wishes to go into business or if another firm wishes to cease production, it can do so without any kind of constraint. This assumption is crucial in distinguishing perfect competition from monopoly, which we will examine in the next chapter.

The last two assumptions are that there is perfect knowledge and perfect mobility of resources. These assumptions are even more unrealistic than the others because information is costly to acquire and resources are usually costly to move. The effect of these two assumptions is that when economic profits exist, firms will find out about these profits and enter the industry. Even though these assumptions are unrealistic, the resulting model is valuable because it shows what adjustments would take place in an ideal setting.

If these six assumptions are met, a market will be perfectly competitive. These assumptions create a model market in which no firm or individual has the power to exert control over the market. This means that neither buyer nor seller has any influence over price.

The six assumptions were first stated more than two centuries ago by Adam Smith in a general outline of the perfectly competitive model in his book *The Wealth of Nations*. In the nineteenth century, the model of perfect competition was the main way of looking at how firms and markets determine price and output levels. The study of other market structures arose later.

COMPETITIVE ADJUSTMENT IN THE SHORT RUN

Since the perfectly competitive firm is small relative to the market and its product is the same as that of other firms, this firm views itself as having no influence on market price. If the perfectly competitive firm wants to sell any of its output, it must sell at the market price. A firm in perfect competition is referred to as a **price taker** because it has no influence on price. It can sell any amount at the market-clearing price. The firm takes that price as its selling price. If it sets a higher price, none of its output will be sold because buyers will be able to purchase an identical product at the lower market price elsewhere. On the other hand, it makes no sense

price taker
A seller (or buyer) in perfect competition that has no influence on price and can sell any amount at the market-clearing price.

to sell below the market price because the firm can sell all it produces at that market price.

The market demand and supply curves and the firm's resultant demand curve are shown in Figure 1. (The graphs in this chapter are based on models first developed by Alfred Marshall.) Market demand (D) and supply (S) curves are such that the market equilibrium price is P_1. If the market is in equilibrium, the perfectly competitive firm can sell as much of its product as it wishes at price P_1. From the firm's viewpoint, the demand curve is perfectly elastic at price P_1.

The demand schedule a firm faces is also its average revenue schedule. If, for example, the price consumers pay in the market is $15, the average revenue a seller receives per unit sold is also $15. As price changes along a market demand curve, the average revenue that sellers receive will also change. Total revenue of a firm is the price times the quantity sold ($TR = P \times Q$). **Average revenue (AR)** is total revenue divided by the quantity sold. It is the revenue per unit sold, or the price of the product. A demand curve is an average revenue curve. With perfect competition, price does not vary with output. Thus, $AR = (P \times Q)/Q = P$ is a constant. The firm's perfectly elastic demand curve in Figure 1 is also a perfectly elastic average revenue curve.

Recall that a profit-maximizing firm always produces that quantity for which marginal revenue is equal to marginal cost. Thus, we need to determine what the competitive firm's marginal revenue curve looks like. Marginal revenue is the change in total revenue from selling one more (or one fewer) unit:

$$MR_n = TR_n - TR_{n-1}.$$

In Figure 1, the change in total revenue if sales increase from x_1 to x_2 (where x_2 is one unit more than x_1) is $P_1(x_2 - x_1)$. If sales increase from x_2 to x_3, the change in total revenue is $P_1(x_3 - x_2)$. In other words, in the case of a perfectly elastic demand curve, such as the firm's demand curve in Figure 1, $D = P = AR = MR$. The marginal revenue curve associated with

average revenue (AR)
Total revenue divided by the quantity sold, or the revenue per unit sold (the price).

FIGURE 1
ELASTIC DEMAND AT MARKET EQUILIBRIUM
In perfect competition, a firm's demand curve is perfectly elastic at the market equilibrium price.

a perfectly elastic demand curve is the same as the demand curve. The demand curve is always the average revenue curve for any market structure. The demand curve is equal to the marginal revenue curve only in perfect competition. Remember the relationship between average and marginal values—if the average value doesn't change, the marginal value must be the same as the average.

Using marginal cost and marginal revenue, we now can determine how a perfectly competitive firm will adjust its output to changed prices in the short run. The demand curves for the market and a representative firm are depicted in Figure 2. A **representative firm** is a typical firm in perfect competition, one of the many similar firms in this market. In Figure 2, the representative firm's marginal cost curve is also shown. This firm maximizes profit by producing quantity x_1 when the price per unit is P_1 because at that output level, $MR = MC$. Now assume the market demand increases to D_1. The market price rises to P_2. The firm's demand curve, average revenue curve, and marginal revenue curve change to $D_1 = AR_1 = MR_1$. The firm responds by increasing its output level to x_2, where $MR_1 = MC$.

In Figure 2, the firm's short-run marginal cost curve is the same as its short-run supply curve. A **short-run supply curve** is a supply curve for the period in which the size of the plant cannot be varied (the short run). In perfect competition, the short-run marginal cost curve is the short-run supply curve. As market price rose, the firm in Figure 2 increased its output along its marginal cost curve. Further increases or decreases in price would cause further movements along the marginal cost curve, or the short-run supply curve. We will soon see how these short-run supply curves relate to the market (or industry) supply curve.

PROFITS, LOSSES, AND SHUTTING DOWN

We have just seen how a representative firm adjusts in the short run to changes in market demand. We don't yet know whether the firm has a profit or a loss, or how large this profit or loss is. To find out, we need to add the average cost curve to the graph. Also, in order to decide if the

representative firm
A typical firm in perfect competition, one of the many identical firms in the market.

short-run supply curve
The supply curve for the period in which the size of the plant cannot be varied (in perfect competition, the same as the short-run marginal cost curve).

FIGURE 2
PROFIT MAXIMIZATION
An increase in market demand causes the equilibrium price to rise. The demand curve the firm faces adjusts by the amount of the increase in price, and the firm increases its output to equate MC and MR. The adjustment process is such that the firm's marginal cost curve is its short-run supply curve.

firm should continue to produce if losses are encountered, we need to add the average variable cost curve.

In Figure 3, the firm is maximizing profit by producing output x_1 at price P_1, where $P = MR = MC$. The average cost of producing x_1 is measured by distance x_1C in Figure 3. The total cost of producing x_1 is represented by the area of the rectangle $0P_1Cx_1$. Total revenue in Figure 3 is also the area of $0P_1Cx_1$, so $TR = TC$. This firm is therefore making zero economic profit, although it is meeting its opportunity costs. Remember that total cost includes normal profit, which is the return on capital and enterprise necessary to keep firms in an industry.

If the firm's average cost (AC) curve is the one drawn in Figure 4, the average cost of producing x_1 is the distance x_1A. Total revenue (TR) is still $P_1 \times x_1$, or the area of $0P_1Bx_1$. Total cost is now the area of $0CAx_1$. Since $TR > TC$, there is an economic profit equal to the area of CP_1BA in Figure 4. On the other hand, if the firm's average cost curve is the one drawn in Figure 5, the average cost of producing x_1 is the distance x_1A. Total revenue is the area of $0P_1Bx_1$, and total cost is the area of $0CAx_1$. In this case, $TC > TR$, so losses are being incurred. The loss is equal to the area of P_1CAB in Figure 5.

Should the firm of Figure 5 continue to produce and, if so, for how long? It is suffering a loss, which means the factors of production employed by this firm could earn more in some other use. Revenues are less than opportunity costs. But keep in mind that this diagram shows the short run, which means that some factor is fixed. This fixed factor means that there are fixed costs that cannot be eliminated. Fixed costs must be paid in the short run even if production ceases. We need to include the average variable cost (AVC) curve to determine the conditions under which the firm should cease production, because variable costs are the only ones under the firm's control in the short run.

The short-run cost curves of a firm are depicted with several equilibrium points in Figure 6. At a price of P_1, which represents a marginal revenue of MR_1, the firm maximizes profits by producing x_1. At P_1, the firm is making an economic profit because total revenue (area of $0P_1Ax_1$) is greater than total cost (area of $0C_1Dx_1$). At price $P_2 = MR_2$, the firm would

Price, Cost

P_1

MC AC

C

$D = AR = MR$

0 x_1 Quantity/Time Period

FIGURE 3
A FIRM EARNING ZERO ECONOMIC PROFIT
The average cost (AC) curve is used to determine if a firm is making an economic profit. If average revenue (price) is equal to average cost, the firm is making zero economic profit.

FIGURE 4
A FIRM EARNING AN ECONOMIC PROFIT
If the firm's average revenue is greater than its average cost at the level of output being produced, the firm is making an economic profit.

produce x_2 and make zero economic profit because total revenue (area of $0P_2Bx_2$) is equal to total cost (area of $0C_2Bx_2$).

Examine carefully what happens when price falls to P_3 and marginal revenue falls to MR_3. The profit-maximizing or loss-minimizing output is now x_3. At output level x_3, losses are incurred because total revenue is the area of $0P_3Sx_3$, and total cost is the area of $0C_3Ex_3$. Losses are thus represented by the rectangle P_3CES. The firm needs to answer this question: Should it produce and incur this loss or should it cease production? Remember, if production is halted, fixed costs must still be paid. In Figure 6, if the market price is P_3, the firm is earning a total revenue equal to the area of $0P_3Sx_3$, and its total variable costs ($TVC = AVC \times Q$) are $0P_3Sx_3$. In other words, the firm is covering (exactly) its total variable costs and losing an amount equal to its total fixed costs. It must pay the fixed costs even if it shuts down, so at price P_3 the firm is indifferent about shutting down or continuing to produce. If the price falls below P_3, the firm will shut down in order to minimize losses. By shutting down, it will lose only total fixed costs, instead of total fixed costs plus some portion of variable costs if it continues to produce. The minimum or low point on the AVC curve (S in Figure 6) is called the **shutdown point** because if price (P or MR) falls below that point, the firm loses less by ceasing production.

shutdown point
The minimum point on the average variable cost (AVC) curve, or the level of output at which a perfectly competitive firm minimizes its losses by ceasing operation.

FIGURE 5
A FIRM SUFFERING A LOSS
If the firm's average cost is greater than its average revenue at the level of output being produced, the firm is incurring a loss.

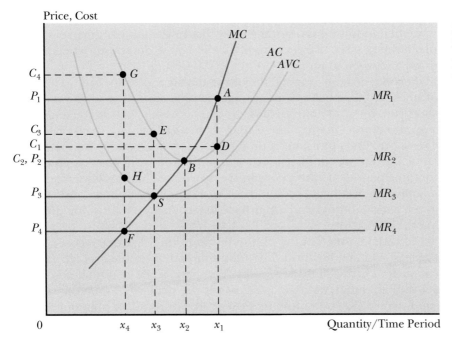

Price, Cost

FIGURE 6
THE SHUTDOWN POINT
If a firm's average revenue is greater than its average variable cost, the firm will be able to cover total variable costs and make a payment toward total fixed costs. If price falls below average variable costs, the firm will lose less money if it shuts down than if it continues to produce. The shutdown point in this case is point S at a price of P_3.

Consider price P_4 (or MR_4) in Figure 6. The $MR = MC$ rule tells the firm that at P_4 it should produce output level x_4. However, at x_4 the firm is losing P_4C_4GF ($0P_4Fx_4 - 0C_4Gx_4$). Total revenue of $0P_4Fx_0$ does not cover the total variable costs of producing x_4, which are x_4H times x_4. In other words, the firm is losing more than its total fixed costs. It is making variable cost outlays that it wouldn't have to make if it stopped production entirely. The firm would be better off to shut down and only incur its fixed costs.

Because the firm shuts down, we need to modify the earlier statement that the firm's marginal cost curve represents its short-run supply curve. That statement is not completely correct. A firm's short-run supply curve is represented by its marginal cost curve only *above* the shutdown point (point S in Figure 6). Below the shutdown point, the firm will produce no output, so only the part of the marginal cost curve above the minimum point on the average variable costs curve is the firm's supply curve.

The model has just told us that in the short run, the firm will shut down when price falls below average variable cost. It says nothing about the real-world timing of such a shutdown. The decision to shut down is more difficult in reality than in theory. It depends on many factors, including time and anticipated changes. A few examples may illustrate such problems.

First, imagine yourself the owner of a sporting goods store in a ski area or a beach resort. Shutdown may be a seasonal decision. If revenues fall below average variable costs (clerks' wages, electricity, and so on) in the off-season, you may close up, bearing only your fixed costs (such as rent on the store) until crowds return and your revenues increase. In this case, shutdown does not mean you are moving your investments in plant and equipment into other businesses. It simply means that you lose money in certain seasons and you lose less money if you shut down. You fully intend to reopen for business when the snow flies or the temperature sends people to the beaches. Past experience helps you to determine when to shut down and when to reopen.

Second, imagine yourself the owner-manager of a steel mill. The price of steel has fallen below your average variable costs of production. In the short run, you shut down (if laws and union contracts allow you to do so—a union contract might change labor from a variable to a fixed resource). The short run is too short a time period for you to vary your plant size (which is one way of saying that you can't move your fixed resources in this time period). However, if you are convinced that this low price is permanent, you will begin to liquidate. You will sell equipment and attempt to sell your buildings and other fixed assets. As you do this, you are moving to the long run.

To review, note that the minimum point on the average cost curve is the least-cost combination. The minimum point on the average variable costs curve is the shutdown point. The part of the marginal cost curve above the average variable cost curve is the perfectly competitive firm's supply curve. Keep in mind that these are all short-run phenomena. We will trace the long-run adjustment later.

AN EXAMPLE OF PRODUCTION DECISIONS

The short-run output decisions and profit determination for a perfectly competitive firm can be illustrated with a simple example. Table 1 presents some production cost data for a firm. Assuming that different market prices are the result of different market equilibrium situations, it is possible to determine the firm's response to different prices. In Table 2, six different market prices corresponding to different market conditions are assumed. When the market price is $61, the demand and marginal revenue curves the firm faces are perfectly elastic at $61. The firm produces 10 units (where $MR = MC = \$61$) and earns an economic profit of $120. This situation corresponds to the graph in Figure 4. At a market price of $46, the firm maximizes profit where $MR = MC = \$46$, which is at an output of 7 units. Since $TR = TC$ at 7 units, there is zero economic profit. This situa-

TABLE 1
PRODUCTION
COSTS FOR A FIRM

OUTPUT	AVERAGE VARIABLE COSTS (AVC)	AVERAGE COST (AC)	MARGINAL COST (MC)	TOTAL COST (TC)
1	$40	$100	$40	$100
2	38	68	36	136
3	36	56	32	168
4	35	50	32	200
5	35	47	35	235
6	36	46	41	276
7	$37\frac{3}{7}$	46	46	322
8	39	$46\frac{1}{2}$	50	372
9	41	$47\frac{2}{3}$	57	429
10	43	49	61	490

MARKET PRICE (MR)	FIRM'S OUTPUT	TOTAL REVENUE (TR)	TOTAL COST (TC)	FIRM'S PROFITS
$61	10	$610	$490	$120
50	8	400	372	28
46	7	322	322	0
41	6	246	276	−30
35	5	175	235	−60
32	4	128	200	−72

TABLE 2
PRODUCTION DECISIONS
AT VARIOUS MARKET
PRICES

tion corresponds to Figure 3. When market price falls to $41, the firm reacts by decreasing its output to 6 units (where $MR = MC = \$41$). At 6 units of output, it incurs a loss of $30. This economic loss corresponds to that shown in Figure 5.

The firm will continue to produce in the short run unless price falls below $35 because the minimum value of average variable costs (minimum point on the AVC curve) is at $35. To see why, look at how the firm responds when market price falls to $32. At $32, the firm produces 4 units. However, it loses $72 ($TR = 4 \times \$32 = \$128$, $TC = 4 \times \$50 = \$200$, and $\$128 - \$200 = -\$72$). If it shuts down, the firm loses only $60 in total fixed costs. The total variable cost (TVC) would have been $140 if production had taken place ($TVC = 4 \times \$35 = \$140$ and $TFC = \$200 - \$140 = \$60$). So the firm loses less if it ceases production. At any price less than $35, the firm will shut down.

A MARKET SUPPLY CURVE

We can now look at the relationship between the firm's supply (marginal cost) curve and the market supply curve. The firm's supply curve represents its output response to increased market prices. If we were to add (horizontally) the short-run supply curves for all firms, we would construct the short-run market (or industry) supply curve. The market supply curve is simply the aggregate of all the firms' supply curves. The short-run market supply curve, then, is the aggregate of the portions of all firms' marginal cost curves that lie above their average variable cost curves. In the long run, more firms can enter an industry as a response to economic profits. The market supply curve will shift to the right because it is made up of more individual supply curves. On the other hand, as firms leave an industry due to losses, the market supply curve will shift to the left, representing a decrease in supply. This decrease is due to the fact that there are fewer individual supply curves to be summed.

THE LONG RUN: CONSTANT, INCREASING, OR DECREASING COSTS

The process of determining price and output when firms have time to alter their fixed inputs and when new firms can enter the industry is illustrated in Figure 7. The D_1 and S_1 curves are the equilibrium demand and supply curves for the industry. The industry is in long-run equilibrium

In many countries, markets are not as well developed as they are in the United States. In these countries, many nonmarket institutions have strong holds on culture in ways that affect production, distribution, and consumption. The laws of supply and demand still hold, but customs, systems of land tenure, village and family organization, religious practices, and corruption all have an impact on the functioning of markets.

Cultural differences affect the emergence of entrepreneurs and the profit motive. In poor countries, entrepreneurs may lack the help of markets to bring together materials, labor, and capital. If individuals are not inherently risk takers, their reaction may be to say "no" to new business opportunities. In fact, in some cultures, risk taking is viewed as unacceptable behavior, and minorities become the entrepreneurs. Jews played this role in medieval Europe, the Chinese in some countries in South America, and Indians in Africa. This kind of cultural bias is a serious obstacle to economic development in many less developed countries, because development requires a strong entrepreneurial class. Also, if the ruling structure of a society does not en-

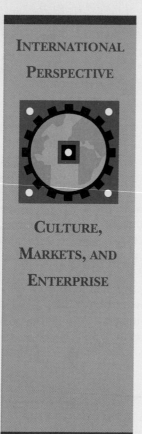

INTERNATIONAL PERSPECTIVE

CULTURE, MARKETS, AND ENTERPRISE

courage entrepreneurial development but supports the stability of a traditional society, the effect is to slow economic growth. In such traditional societies, a trauma often produces a spurt of economic growth. The trauma of World War II and its shakeup of the power structure in Japan is a case in point.

Another difference between the markets of less developed and industrialized countries is that retail markets are often less organized and products are less standardized. As a consequence, neither buyers nor sellers are price takers. Much time and effort is expended in negotiating prices. This time does not go into producing goods and services. Also, the market information widely available in industrialized countries is absent. The absence of this information adds to the cost of doing business in a traditional society and offers another cultural barrier to exchange, enterprise, and economic growth. It is easy for people in developed, industrialized countries to take markets and entrepreneurs for granted and overlook the role they play in creating and sustaining a high standard of living.

when no economic forces are working to cause it to expand or contract (or to cause the price to change). In part (*a*) of the figure, the firm is making zero economic profit at price P_1 and output x_1. Let's assume this firm is representative of 1,000 identical firms. Thus, the market supply curve (S_1) in part (*b*) is the summation of 1,000 *MC* curves (above the *AVC* curves). Since these firms are making zero economic profits at P_1, the industry is in equilibrium with an industry output of Q_1. Since each firm is producing x_1, $1,000 \times x_1 = Q_1$. Now suppose there is an increase in market demand to D_2, brought about by an increase in consumers' real income, and assume that the good under consideration is a normal good. When market demand shifts to D_2, market price rises to P_2. The demand curve for the firm rises to D_2 and is perfectly elastic at price P_2.

The firm's initial (short-run) response is to increase its output to x_2 because $MR_2 = MC$ at output level x_2. Thus, the increase in market demand from Q_1 to Q_2 is met by an increase in output by each of the 1,000 firms, from x_1 to x_2. Note, however, that each firm will then make an economic profit equal to the shaded area in Figure 7(*a*). Economic profit, you recall, means that factors of production are earning more than their opportunity cost. This profit means that the industry is out of equilibrium. Other firms are going to attempt to get some of this profit. The existence of profit is the signal for new firms to enter this industry.

Since free entry and perfect knowledge are assumed to be characteristics of perfect competition, entrepreneurs will be aware of this profit and will enter the industry. As firms enter the industry, the market supply curve will shift because it now is the summation of the 1,000 original *MC* curves plus the *MC* curves of the new entrant firms. In fact, firms will keep entering the industry until equilibrium (zero economic profit) is restored. This is illustrated in Figure 7. If all firms have the same costs (that is, all firms are exactly like the representative firm) and if nothing happens to change these costs, equilibrium will be restored when the price has been reduced to P_1, the original equilibrium price. If the new equilibrium price is P_1 and industry output is Q_3, each firm is producing x_1 units.

FIGURE 7
LONG-RUN ADJUSTMENT TO AN INCREASE IN MARKET DEMAND
An increase in market demand will cause the price to rise. The demand curve the representative firm faces will shift upward. Economic profit will result, and new firms will enter the industry in response to this profit. As new firms enter, the market supply curve shifts to the right, causing price to fall to the point at which the representative firm is again earning zero economic profit.

(a) Firm

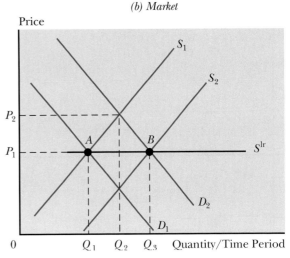

(b) Market

The summation of the firms' output (1,000 plus the number of new firms times x_1) is equal to the industry output (Q_3). Connecting the market equilibrium points, points A and B in Figure 7(b), gives the industry's long-run supply curve, S^{lr}. This curve represents what firms will supply after all adjustments have taken place.

You can check your understanding of this process by tracing the response to a decrease in demand. In Figure 8, the industry is initially in equilibrium at price P_1 and output Q_1. Firms are making zero economic profits and producing x_1 units of output each. Now suppose medical researchers discover that the product is dangerous to people's health. This news causes market demand to decrease to D_2. Market price falls to P_2, and industry output falls to Q_2. In the short run, each firm adjusts its output to x_2 (where $MC = MR_2$). At x_2, however, each firm is incurring losses represented by the shaded area in part (a). The industry is now out of equilibrium.

Just as profits are the signal for firms to enter an industry, losses are the signal for firms to exit an industry. Entrepreneurs move their factors of production to other uses, seeking to earn their opportunity cost elsewhere. Perfect knowledge is assumed, so entrepreneurs will know where they can earn at least normal profit. As firms leave the industry, the short-run market supply curve will shift to the left because it is now derived by adding up the short-run supply curves of fewer firms. Firms will leave the industry until the remaining firms have zero economic profits. Equilibrium is restored when the market supply curve shifts to S_2 in Figure 8(b) and restores a price of P_1. Industry output is now at Q_3, with each of the remaining firms producing x_1 units of output. As before, the long-run supply curve (S^{lr}) can be found by connecting the industry's equilibrium points, which are represented by points A and B in Figure 8(b).

CONSTANT-COST INDUSTRIES

The adjustments traced in Figures 7 and 8 assumed that factor prices, and thus costs, were unaffected by the quantity of output the industry pro-

FIGURE 8
LONG-RUN ADJUSTMENT TO A DECREASE IN MARKET DEMAND
A decrease in market demand will cause the price to fall. The demand curve the representative firm faces will shift downward. Losses will be incurred, and some firms will leave the industry. As firms leave, the market supply curve shifts to the left, causing price to rise until a remaining representative firm is earning zero economic profit.

(a) Firm

(b) Market

duced. As firms entered the industry (Figure 7) or exited the industry (Figure 8), the price of the factors of production did not change. As a result, the average and marginal cost curves didn't change. When cost curves don't change as an industry expands or contracts, the industry is referred to as a constant cost industry. A **constant cost industry** is an industry in which expansion of output does not cause average costs to rise in the long run. In a constant cost industry, as more steel, labor, electricity, and other inputs are purchased, the cost of those inputs does not increase. Constant costs are most likely to occur when the industry's purchase of inputs is small relative to the market supply of those inputs. If the industry's use of inputs is small relative to the market supply, increased demand for those inputs would not increase their prices. For example, consider the home computer industry. If profits exist and firms enter, these firms will demand more inputs. They will demand more plastic, more labor, and more microchips. If all the computer-producing firms use a small fraction of the total supply of these inputs, the increase in demand will not cause the price of plastic, labor, and microchips to rise.

constant cost industry
An industry in which expansion of output does not cause average cost to rise in the long run.

Figures 7 and 8, then, represent long-run contractions and expansions in constant cost industries. The short-run response to a contraction in demand is a decrease in price. An expansion in demand produces a short-run increase in price. The market adjustment, however, will return price to its original level, with fewer firms in the case of the contraction or more firms in the case of the expansion. The long-run supply curve in a constant cost industry is perfectly elastic, even though the short-run supply curve has a positive slope.

INCREASING COST INDUSTRIES

Sometimes an expansion in industry output will cause costs to increase in the long run. In this case, as an industry expands output and demands more inputs, the increased demand causes prices of inputs to rise. For example, an increase in demand for chicken causes new firms to enter the packing industry and to demand more chicken coops, chicken pluckers, land, and plastic bags. If the increased demand causes the price of chicken coops, chicken pluckers, land, or plastic bags to rise, the average production costs of the representative firm will increase as a result of the increased demand for chicken. Also, less efficient factors and firms may be drawn into the industry. These conditions describe an increasing cost industry. An **increasing cost industry** is an industry in which expansion of output causes average costs to rise in the long run.

increasing cost industry
An industry in which expansion of output causes average cost to rise in the long run.

Figure 9 illustrates the long-run adjustment process in an increasing cost industry. The industry is originally in equilibrium at price P_1 and output level Q_1. Each firm is producing x_1 units of output. Market demand increases to D_2. As a result, market price rises to P_2. The firm's demand is now represented by $D_2 = AR_2 = MR_2$. The firm's short-run response is to increase output to x_2, where $MC_1 = MR_2$. The industry's output is now at Q_2. At this increased output, two things will happen. First, new firms will enter the industry because of the economic profits that now exist. Second, costs will rise as a result of the increased demand for inputs. This rise in cost is represented by the upward shift in the marginal and average cost curves to MC_2 and AC_2 in Figure 9(a).

FIGURE 9
LONG-RUN ADJUSTMENT
TO INCREASING DEMAND
IN AN INCREASING COST
INDUSTRY
When demand increases
in an increasing cost
industry, the firms that
enter the industry bid up
the prices of the factors
of production for all
firms in the industry.
As a result, price does
not return to the old
equilibrium. Instead, a
new equilibrium with the
representative firm
earning zero economic
profit is established at
a price above the old
equilibrium price.

The upward shift of the marginal and average cost curves is based on the assumption that all costs increase at the same rate. In most cases, this would not be true, since the prices of some inputs (the scarcer ones) would rise faster. However, the example is clearer if we assume that all factor prices rise proportionally, and this assumption does not seriously affect the analysis. Firms, as purchasers of inputs, are likely to have much influence in some input markets and little influence in others. In the chicken-packaging example, as the demand for chicken increases and firms enter the industry, there may be no effect on the price of land but a large effect on the price of machines used to pluck chickens. This kind of cost increase is most likely when specific, rather than general, factors are used in the production process. It is also possible that the new firms attracted to an industry will be less efficient at producing the good in question. In this case, the representative firm will have higher costs, indicating less efficient production.

The net result of an increased number of firms and increased costs is a rightward shift in the short-run market supply curve. The supply curve shifts to the right because it is the sum of the supply curves of more firms. However, it will not shift as far to the right as it did in the constant cost industry because costs have risen for every firm. The new short-run market supply curve will be S_2 in Figure 9(b). Equilibrium is reached at price P_3, where firms are no longer making profits. Industry output is now Q_3, and each firm is producing x_1 units, where $MR_3 = MC_2$.

As before, the long-run market supply curve connects the industry's equilibrium points on all of the short-run supply curves. Connecting points A and B in Figure 9(b) produces a long-run supply curve (S^{lr}) with a positive slope, indicating an increasing cost industry.

Diagraming the adjustment process to a decrease in demand for an increasing cost industry is left as an exercise for the reader.

DECREASING COST INDUSTRIES

decreasing cost industry
An industry in which
expansion of output
causes average cost
to fall in the long run

To complete the analysis, we must consider a decreasing cost industry. A **decreasing cost industry** is an industry in which an expansion of output

David Ricardo may have been the most influential of all the classical economists. Ricardo was born into a wealthy family and was sent from London to Amsterdam for an education. He returned to enter his father's business at age fourteen. The group of businessmen he joined was the prosperous community of Jewish merchants and stockbrokers in London. To his family's horror, he fell in love with a Quaker. He was disowned and expelled from the family business. He had no alternative but to go into business for himself. Ricardo quickly became very successful and then grew bored. In 1814, Ricardo retired from business to devote his time to political economy. He became a leading intellectual. His experience contrasts with that of almost all the other classical economists, who pursued rigorous programs of formal education in philosophy. In 1819, Ricardo became a member of Parliament and, with the help of James Mill (father of the great economist John Stuart Mill), founded the Political Economy Club of London. This club became the forum in which the classical economists discussed their ideas.

Ricardo was a prolific writer of letters and pamphlets intended to influence policy discussions on economic matters. His chief formal work, *On the Principles of Political Economy and Taxation*, was published in 1817. He is best remembered for his statements on the principles of comparative advantage and his support of free trade. These ideas are only a part of his comprehensive work. In fact, much of his early interest in economics was generated by his interest in international trade and in showing the benefits of such trade. Ricardo also developed a labor theory of value that greatly impressed Karl Marx, who extended and radicalized it.

ECONOMIC PROFILE

DAVID RICARDO

1772–1823

causes average costs to fall in the long run. In a decreasing cost industry, as more firms enter the industry, causing the demand for inputs to increase, input prices fall. Falling input prices imply that there are economies of scale in an industry that is supplying an input to the decreasing cost industry. For example, as more electricity is demanded, more efficient generators are built and the price of this input falls.

Figure 10 derives a long-run supply curve for a decreasing cost industry. The initial market equilibrium price, P_1, is determined by the intersection of the market demand and supply curves, D_1 and S_1. The representative firm is in equilibrium producing x_1 units at price P_1. Now suppose there is an increase in the price of a substitute good, so that demand for the product of this industry increases to D_2. The short-run response is that price rises to P_2, shifting the firm's demand curve to $D_2 = AR_2 = MR_2$. The representative firm responds by increasing its output to x_2, where $MR_2 = MC_1$. Profits now exist and new firms will enter this industry. As new firms enter, two things happen. First, the market supply curve will shift to the right because it is now composed of individual supply curves. Second, as industry output increases, costs fall. In Figure $10(a)$, the decrease in costs is assumed to be a proportional decrease in the cost of all inputs.[1] The decrease in costs for the representative firm is shown in Figure $10(a)$ as a shift from AC_1 to AC_2 and from MC_1 to MC_2.

The industry's decrease in costs and increase in supply cause the market price to fall. A new equilibrium at a price such as P_3 will be reached. At P_3, the representative firm faces demand curve D_3. Equilibrium is reached at output x_1, where $MR_3 = MC_2$. No economic profits exist.

As before, the long-run supply curve connects the equilibrium points in the market. These points are represented by points A and B in Figure

FIGURE 10
LONG-RUN ADJUSTMENT TO DECREASING DEMAND IN A DECREASING COST INDUSTRY
When demand increases in a decreasing cost industry, the firms that enter the industry cause the prices of the factors of production to fall for all firms in the industry. As a result, a new equilibrium price is established that is below the old equilibrium price.

1.   Again, this assumption is not essential, but it is convenient because it simplifies the graph. If costs decrease with industry expansion, it is more likely that the decrease results from a decline in the price of a major input rather than a proportional decline in the price of all inputs.

$10(b)$. The long-run market supply curve is represented by S^{lr}. This curve has a negative slope, meaning that an increase in market demand would eventually lead to a new equilibrium at a lower price for the industry's product. Decreasing cost industries thus have negatively sloped long-run supply curves. (The short-run market supply curves are still positively sloped, since they are the aggregate of individual firms' short-run marginal cost curves.)

Diagraming the effects of a decrease in demand in a decreasing cost industry is left as an exercise for the reader.

COMPETITIVE EQUILIBRIUM: WHAT'S SO GREAT ABOUT PERFECT COMPETITION?

The nature of perfect competition is such that the firm and industry are driven to equilibrium at zero economic profit. This equilibrium is the appeal of perfect competition as a standard against which to judge other market structures. Economists view this equilibrium as an ideal, or a social optimum. In equilibrium, resources are optimally allocated among competing uses. Figure 11 shows a perfectly competitive firm in equilibrium. At equilibrium, price (P) is equal to average cost (AC) and also is equal to marginal cost (MC).

First, consider $P = MC$. This means that allocative efficiency is being achieved and that the resources of the firm are being allocated exactly as consumers wish. It means that firms are expanding production exactly to the level desired by consumers. If P were greater than MC, it would mean that not enough resources were going into the production of the good in question. Consumers would be willing to pay a higher price (P) than it costs to produce another unit of the good (MC). If P were less than MC, too many resources would be devoted to the production of the good. Con-

FIGURE 11
THE EQUILIBRIUM CONDITION FOR A PERFECTLY COMPETITIVE FIRM
In short-run equilibrium with perfect competition, allocative efficiency is met. This means that the resources of the firm are being allocated as consumers wish.

sumers would not be willing to pay as much as it costs to produce another unit of the good. In other words, where $P = MC$, the correct amount of resources is being devoted to producing the good.

Second, consider $P = AC$. This means that firms are earning only normal profits. There is no incentive for firms to enter or leave the industry. It is important to note the role of profits in the perfectly competitive model. Economic profits serve as the signal for firms to move in or out of an industry. When profits exist, entrepreneurs rush in to attempt to capture them. The industry is forced to a new equilibrium. When losses are present, entrepreneurs leave to seek higher returns elsewhere. Equilibrium is attained because of the profit-seeking nature of firms. In equilibrium, there is efficiency. It is not because of some altruistic behavior on the part of entrepreneurs that firms are efficient. Entrepreneurs are assumed to be profit maximizers motivated by individual self-interest, and their response to changing profits brings about efficiency. In the competitive model, self-interest and the quest for profits produce the efficiency that benefits consumers. The firm is striving not for efficiency but for profits. When economic profits have served their signaling function, they disappear.

Third, consider $MC = AC$. This means that average cost AC is at a minimum. Therefore, the representative firm in this industry is using the least-cost combination of inputs. The variable resources are being combined as efficiently as possible.

In long-run equilibrium, the short-run average cost (AC) curve also will be tangent to the long-run average cost ($LRAC$) curve at its minimum point, where $AC = LRAC$, as in Figure 12. This means that all firms are at the most efficient size and are also combining the variable resources efficiently. The firms are using the least-cost combination of inputs and the optimal plant size. All firms must be efficient, or they will be driven from the market by losses. If any one firm is more efficient than normal (more efficient than the representative firm), it will be able to make an economic profit even though the other firms don't. At long-run equilib-

FIGURE 12
LONG-RUN
EQUILIBRIUM WITH
PERFECT COMPETITION
In long-run equilibrium
with perfect competition,
average cost is equal to
long-run average cost.
This means that all firms
are at the optimal size
and are also combining
variable resources
efficiently. This is the
ideal of efficiency to
which other market
structures are compared.

WHAT EQUILIBRIUM IN PERFECT COMPETITION MEANS	
• $P = MC$	Production is at the level consumers indicate (through the market) they want.
• $P = AC$	Firms are earning normal profits. There is no movement into or out of the industry.
• $AC = MC$	Firms are using the least-cost method of production.

rium, then, $P = AC = MC = LRAC = LRMC$, since the long-run marginal cost curve ($LRMC$) crosses $LRAC$ at its minimum point.

The model of perfect competition is not meant to be a precise description of reality. Nor is it, in every case, the ideal state that society should be striving to reach. In certain industries, it may be too costly to bring about the necessary conditions for perfect competition. In that case, society can accept less than the ideal. The model of perfect competition is a tool for the economist. The economist can compare the real-world situation to the hypothetical world of perfect competition to determine what would be the case if perfect competition existed. In this sense, perfect competition is a benchmark, or yardstick, by which economists can measure the performance of other market structures.

AN EXAMPLE OF PERFECT COMPETITION

In recent years, the financial services industry has become close to the model of a perfectly competitive industry. The services that this industry offers are very homogeneous. A checking account at a financial institution in a given city is pretty much the same as a checking account anywhere else. In addition, the Depository Institutions Deregulation and Monetary Control Act (DIDMCA) of 1980 opened up entry into this industry. As a result, insurance companies, stockbrokers, and savings and loan institutions all began to compete with commercial banks for checking account business. One of the results is that consumers now earn interest on their checking accounts. This interest is equivalent to a lower price for bank services. This market entry was beneficial to consumers and drove bank profits down to normal levels.

LARGE NUMBERS OF BUYERS: COMPETITION ON THE BUYER'S SIDE

We have concentrated on developing a theory of firms in perfect competition, or competition on the sellers' side of the market. The assumption of many sellers means that all sellers perceive the demand curve they face to be perfectly elastic at the market price. Keep in mind, however, that we also assumed large numbers of buyers, so many that none possessed market power.

Concentrating on the firm should not obscure the importance of competition on the buyers' side of the market. In order for markets to be competitive, there must be enough buyers that none can affect the price by withholding purchases or increasing purchases. A competitive market cannot be "cornered" by buyers with market power or wealth. A competitive market is too big and too impersonal to be influenced by single buyers. In most of your transactions as a buyer, you will find that you are a perfect competitor—too small to influence the price.

ECONOMIC RENT IN PERFECT COMPETITION

According to the model of perfect competition, in industries in which free entry exists, profits will be driven to normal rates of return. Yet we all know of individuals who have become rich in industries that are very competitive and that have relatively free entry. How can this happen without totally invalidating this model? To explain how returns in excess of normal profits can exist in the long run, even under perfect competition, we must introduce some new concepts.

ECONOMIC RENT

economic rent
A payment to a factor of production in excess of its opportunity cost.

Rent is a familiar term. You pay rent on your apartment. But economists have a special (and very different) meaning for this term. **Economic rent** is a payment to a factor of production in excess of the opportunity cost of that factor of production. Let's say, for example, you are trained as a teacher and could earn $20,000 per year in that profession. However, you also have beautiful teeth and can do toothpaste commercials, for which you earn $50,000 per year. Economists would say that $30,000 of your income is economic rent because it is the amount by which your earnings exceed your opportunity cost. They would predict that you would do the commercials for $20,001 per year since you would then be earning more than your opportunity cost.

Economic rent, then, is more general than economic profit. Since economic profit is defined as revenue in excess of all the implicit costs (including normal profit) and explicit costs of production, economic profit is rent to entrepreneurs. Entrepreneurs will earn only normal profits in perfect competition because new entry will drive out higher rates of return. But it is possible that economic rents to other factors of production will exist. Thus, we need to relate the concept of economic rent to the model of perfect competition.

REPRESENTATIVE FIRMS AND ECONOMIC RENTS

The theory of perfect competition uses a representative firm that is one of many firms with cost structures that are identical. This assumption is not always realistic. Consider agriculture as an example. Some farmland is far superior to other farmland. It is more fertile, gets more rainfall, or is located where the weather is warmer. The quality of the land will affect the farmer's costs of production. Economic rent will always be earned on the better land, and entry of new firms will not eliminate such rent. In other competitive industries, location, family connections, or talent will make firms' cost structures different, creating economic rents.

DIFFERENTIAL RENT THEORY

Economic rent does not weaken the theory of perfect competition. In 1817, classical economist David Ricardo reconciled the existence of economic rents with perfect competition by developing differential rent theory. He was interested in explaining the fact that fertile farmland earned a higher rent than poor farmland.

Consider, for example, the cost and revenue functions of two farms, shown in parts (*a*) and (*b*) of Figure 13. The market is represented in part (*c*). Supply and demand are such that market price for the farms' product is *P*. Farm *A* is earning zero economic profit ($P = AC_A$). Farm *B* is earning an economic profit equal to the shaded area. This economic profit comes from the fact that the land used to produce the farm product is much more fertile for farm *B*. As a result, the costs of production are lower.

Farmers would be willing to pay the owner of the land owned by farm *B* a higher price for being able to farm that land. This higher price becomes a cost of production to farm *B* because economic rent for the more fertile land will rise as farmers seek to either purchase or lease this land. Even if the owner of the land is also the farmer, economic rent is still an opportunity cost of production because the owner could lease the land to other farmers.

The result of differential rent to factors of production is that rents rise on more productive factors. This rise equalizes the average cost of production among firms. In other words, the economic profit for farm *B* is a result of a superior factor of production, more fertile land. The user of the factor (it could be the owner of the farm or someone else) will receive this rent. When the rent is paid, AC_B will, in fact, rise until the shaded area for farm *B* disappears.

The point is that competitive firms may appear to earn economic profits (more than a normal rate of return), but these returns are economic rents to unique factors of production, not economic profits. In many cases, the firm's entrepreneur is the owner of the factors. As a result, the rent looks like an economic profit. In fact, many times the en-

FIGURE 13
DIFFERENTIAL RENTS IN PERFECT COMPETITION
Farms *A* and *B* both face perfectly elastic demand curves at price *P*, determined in the market for their product, part (*c*). Because its land is more fertile, farm *B* has lower average costs and earns a profit shown by the shaded area in part (*b*). That profit will be converted to economic rent as competition for the fertile land bids up its price.

(a) Farm A

(b) Farm B

(c) Market

trepreneur has special skills that form the basis for the firm. The return to these skills is an economic rent to the factor of production enterprise. It is not an economic profit. The concept of economic rent is an important one and will be discussed in more detail in several upcoming chapters.

SUMMARY

1. Perfect competition is characterized by large numbers of buyers and sellers, homogeneous products, ease of entry into and exit out of the industry, perfect knowledge, and mobility of resources.

2. A firm in a perfectly competitive market faces a perfectly elastic demand curve at the price determined by equilibrium in the market.

3. The firm's short-run supply curve is the same as its short-run marginal cost (MC) curve above the minimum point on the average variable cost (AVC) curve, known as the shutdown point.

4. Long-run adjustments to changes in market demand are dependent on the cost characteristics for the industry. Since entry is easy, additional firms will enter an industry as long as economic profits are present. Thus, economic profits, brought about by an increase in demand, will lead to new entry.

5. An industry can be characterized by constant, increasing, or decreasing costs. The slope of the long-run market supply curve will depend on which of these cost situations prevails.

6. At perfectly competitive equilibrium, $P = AC = MC = LRAC = LRMC$. This condition describes the ideal efficiency of perfect competition, to which other market structures are compared.

7. Profits are the force that drives the perfectly competitive model to efficiency. The firm is seeking not efficiency but profits. This search for profits produces the efficiency that characterizes the model of perfect competition.

8. Large numbers of buyers in a perfectly competitive market ensure that no single buyer can influence price.

9. Economic rent is a payment (return) to a factor of production over the opportunity cost of that factor.

10. Competitive firms may appear to be earning long-run economic profits, but these returns are actually economic rents to specific factors of production in the firms.

NEW TERMS

perfect competition	average revenue (AR)	shutdown point	decreasing cost industry
market power	representative firm	constant cost industry	economic rent
price taker	short-run supply curve	increasing cost industry	

QUESTIONS FOR DISCUSSION

1. Show how the long-run market supply curve will be determined by short-run supply adjustments in an increasing cost industry.

2. Draw the graphs for a decreasing cost industry in perfect competition, showing a market equilibrium and a representative firm. Then for a decrease in market demand, trace through the short-run and long-run adjustments.

3. "If the price of wheat doesn't rise, farmers will lose money and the long-run price will be even higher." Analyze this statement.

4. Why does profit maximization bring about efficiency?

5. What situations cause long-run supply curves to be positively sloped?

6. Explain in your own words why a firm might keep producing in the short run even if it were incurring a loss.

7. What does it mean to say that perfectly competitive equilibrium means that $P = AC = MC = LRAC = LRMC$?

8. Explain how the return to a good location for a firm (for instance, a gas station) in perfect competition does not violate the conclusion that economic profits are driven to zero by new entry.

9. Assume that the data from the table in Question 9 in the last chapter represent the unit-cost data for a perfectly competitive firm in a constant cost industry. What will the firm produce in the short run if the market price is $7.00? Why? What is the economic profit or loss? If this is a representative firm, where is the market price going to settle?

10. What would happen to the firm in Question 9 if the market price fell to $2.50? Why?

11. What would happen to the price, output level, and profit for a firm in a perfectly competitive industry if the price of capital increased? Distinguish between short-run and long-run changes.

12. The assumptions of perfect competition include both large numbers of sellers and large numbers of buyers. Why is it important that there be large numbers of buyers?

13. Why do economists use the term *price taker* when discussing a firm in perfect competition?

14. Why do some restaurants stay open all year and others are open only during certain times and/or certain seasons?

15. Why is it that entrepreneurs in perfectly competitive firms can't earn economic rent in the long run, but other factors can?

SUGGESTIONS FOR FURTHER READING

Eckert, Ross D. *The Price System and Resource Allocation*, 10th ed. Hinsdale, IL: Dryden Press, 1988. Develops the graphical analysis in this chapter in great detail.

Stigler, George J. "Perfect Competition, Historically Contemplated," *Journal of Political Economy* (1957). Reprinted in Edwin Mansfield. *Microeconomics: Selected Readings*. New York: W. W. Norton, 1975, 167–187. A classic article that reviews the historical development of the theory of perfect competition.

Stigler, George J. *The Theory of Price*, 4th ed. New York: Macmillan, 1987, Chapter 10. A classic introductory price theory text by a Nobel Prize-winning economist.

1. Define monopoly.
2. Calculate and diagram average revenue and marginal revenue, given data on price and output.
3. Label sections of a downward-sloping demand curve with the price elasticity, given information on marginal revenue.
4. Diagram average revenue, marginal revenue, marginal cost, and average cost curves for a monopolistic firm making:
   a. an economic profit,
   b. a loss,
   c. a normal profit.
5. List natural and artificial barriers to entry into an industry.
6. Discuss how a monopolist misallocates resources in terms of price and costs.
7. Explain why a monopolist does not have a supply curve.
8. Describe two types of price discrimination.
9. Discuss the alternatives to profit maximization.
10. Define:
    a. dumping,
    b. local monopoly,
    c. natural monopoly.

CHAPTER 24

MONOPOLY

INTRODUCTION

Monopoly is at the other end of the market continuum from perfect competition in the sense that perfect competition involves many firms and monopoly involves just one. The word *monopoly* is derived from the Greek words *mono* for "one" and *polein* for "seller." **Monopoly** is the market structure in which there is a single seller of a product that has no close substitutes.

Monopoly is a theoretical model. As with perfect competition, real-world examples of monopoly are almost nonexistent. The theory is still useful, however, as a tool to examine real-world situations. Although there are no pure monopolies, there are many firms that have some degree of monopoly power. **Monopoly power** is the ability to exercise power over market price and output. As you learned in the last chapter, firms in perfect competition are price takers. In this chapter, you will see that, because it has some control over price, a monopoly is a price searcher. A **price searcher** is a firm that sets price in order to maximize profits. A price-searching firm has monopoly power. It searches for the price-quantity combination that will maximize its profit.

One of the best examples of monopoly in U.S. history is the Aluminum Company of America (Alcoa). Before World War II, Alcoa was the only aluminum producer in the United States. But even this example falls short of absolute monopoly because aluminum does have some close substitutes. For example, soft drinks can be put into glass bottles, steel cans, or plastic containers instead of aluminum cans. Because everything has substitutes in some uses, it is difficult to find a real monopoly. Let's analyze market adjustments under monopoly and then compare the allocation of resources under monopoly to that under perfect competition.

monopoly
The market structure in which there is a single seller of a product that has no close substitutes.

monopoly power
The ability to exercise some of the conomic effects predicted in the model of monopoly by restricting output.

price searcher
A firm that sets price in order to maximize profits and thus has monopoly power.

DEMAND AND MARGINAL REVENUE

A perfectly competitive firm faces a perfectly elastic demand curve. As a result, price (or average revenue) and marginal revenue are equal. However, a monopolistic firm faces the *market* demand curve because the firm is the single seller and is, therefore, the industry. This distinction is very important because market demand curves have negative slopes. Since the monopolist's demand curve has a negative slope, its marginal revenue curve will lie below that curve, which is also the average revenue curve. The common sense reason why the marginal revenue curve lies below the average revenue curve is that the monopolist must lower price in order to sell more units of output. The price reduction applies to *all* units of output that the monopolist sells, not just the last, or marginal, unit. Each additional unit sold adds to total revenue by the amount it sells for (its price) but takes away from total revenue by the reduction in price on each unit sold. Thus, the change in revenue (the marginal revenue) must be less than the change in price.

Some data illustrating the relationship among average, total, and marginal revenue for a monopoly firm are presented in Table 1. When 3 units are sold, the total revenue is $186 ($3 \times \$62$). In order to sell 4 units, the monopolist must reduce the price from $62 to $60. Total revenue will then increase by $60 because an additional unit is being sold for $60. At the same time, it will decrease by $6 because the other 3 units now sell for $2 less each (for $60 each rather than for $62). The net result is that the monopolist has added $54 ($60 − $6) to total revenue by reducing the price from $62 to $60. Note that marginal revenue is $54 and price (average revenue) is $60 for 4 units. Marginal revenue has to be smaller than average revenue whenever units other than the marginal one suffer a price reduction.

This relationship is graphed in Figure 1. When demand is inelastic, decreases in price will cause total revenue to decline. If total revenue is declining, additions to total revenue must be negative. That is, marginal revenue is negative. In Figure 1, a reduction in price below P_1 will decrease total revenue because marginal revenue will be negative. This corre-

TABLE 1
AVERAGE, TOTAL, AND
MARGINAL REVENUE FOR
A MONOPOLIST

UNITS SOLD	PRICE (AVERAGE REVENUE)	TOTAL REVENUE	MARGINAL REVENUE
1	$64	$ 64	$ 64
2	63	126	62
3	62	186	60
4	60	240	54
5	58	290	50
6	56½	339	49
7	55	385	46
8	52	416	31
9	47	423	7
10	40	400	−23

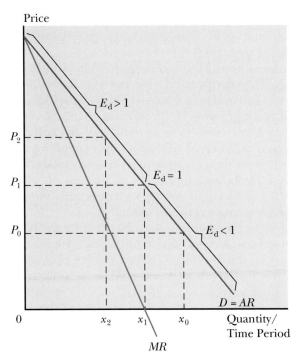

Price

P_2

$E_d > 1$

P_1

$E_d = 1$

P_0

$E_d < 1$

$D = AR$

0   x_2 x_1 x_0 Quantity/
Time Period

MR

FIGURE 1
DEMAND AND
MARGINAL REVENUE
The marginal revenue curve lies below the average revenue curve when there is a negatively sloped demand curve. In showing the relationship between average and marginal revenue, the marginal revenue curve will intersect the *x*-axis exactly halfway between the origin and the point where the average revenue curve intersects the *x*-axis. Demand is elastic above P_1 and inelastic below P_1.

sponds to the inelastic portion of the demand curve. However, a reduction in price from P_2 to P_1 would increase total revenue because the demand curve is elastic in this range.

Think back to the discussion of demand elasticity and Cournot's analysis of the mineral spring owner's situation. In that problem, the monopoly owner of a mineral spring with no production costs maximized profits by setting price where the price elasticity of demand was unitary. We can now apply the profit maximization rule $MR = MC$ to this case. If costs were zero, the MC curve would lie along the horizontal axis. In Figure 1, the monopolist would maximize profits by producing x_1 units (where $MR = MC = 0$) and selling them at price P_1. Since monopolists are profit maximizers, they produce the quantity where $MR = MC$ and sell the product for whatever the market will pay. The demand curve shows what price buyers will pay for any quantity of output. The mineral spring monopolist will increase sales of water as long as marginal revenue is positive, since it costs nothing more to produce another unit. You should note that this does *not* mean the mineral spring monopolist sells as much as possible. The monopolist sells the quantity that maximizes profit. In this case, it happens that the quantity at which profit is maximized is at a marginal revenue of zero, since costs are zero.

PRICE AND OUTPUT DECISIONS UNDER MONOPOLY

In the more general case, where costs are positive, the monopolist finds the profit-maximizing level of output by equating marginal cost and marginal revenue. The perfectly competitive firm is a price taker. The monopoly firm is a price searcher. A monopolist searches for the profit-maximizing price, not the highest price. This process can be seen by looking at the cost relationships graphically.

In Figure 2, a monopolist is producing a certain good for which the market demand curve is D. The marginal revenue curve (MR), derived from D, and the average cost (AC) and marginal cost (MC) curves are also given. The monopolist will maximize profit by producing x_1 units because at that level of output, $MR = MC$. If MR is greater than MC (that is, if output is less than x_1), the monopolist can increase profits by expanding output. Additions to output will cause total revenue to increase by more than the increase in total cost. On the other hand, if MR is less than MC (that is, if output is greater than x_1), the monopolist will reduce output because additions to output add more to total cost than to total revenue.

After choosing output level x_1, the monopolist will search for the highest price it can charge and still sell that amount of output. In Figure 2, this price is P_1. The monopolist can sell x_1 units of output at price P_1 because the demand curve in Figure 2 shows that P_1 is the maximum that consumers will pay for that level of output.

At P_1 and x_1, the monopolist is making an economic profit. The average revenue (price) is P_1, and average cost is C_1. Since P_1 is larger than C_1, the monopolist is making a profit of $P_1 - C_1$ on each unit for a total profit of $(P_1 - C_1) \times x_1$. In Figure 2, total cost is represented by rectangle $0C_1Bx_1$, and total revenue is represented by rectangle $0P_1Ax_1$. Total revenue minus total cost equals economic profit, or rectangle C_1P_1AB. Since the cost curves include both explicit and implicit costs, the monopoly firm is making more than its opportunity cost. That is, the firm is earning more than is necessary to keep its resources employed in this industry—it is making an economic profit.

FIGURE 2
THE PROFIT-MAXIMIZING POSITION OF A MONOPOLIST
The profit-maximizing monopolist will produce x_1 units of output, where $MC = MR$. Since average cost (C_1) is less than average revenue (P_1) for output level x_1, this monopolist is making an economic profit.

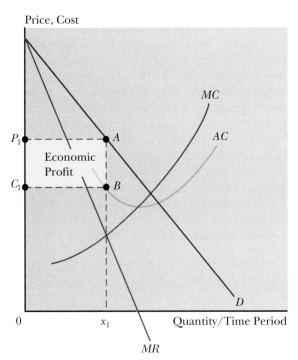

Output and Sales	Total Cost (TC)	Average Cost (AC)	Marginal Cost (MC)	Average Revenue (AR)	Total Revenue (TR)	Marginal Revenue (MR)
0	$ 60	$ —	$ —	$ —	$ 0	$ —
1	100	100	40	58	58	58
2	136	68	36	57	114	56
3	168	56	32	56	168	54
4	200	50	32	55	220	52
5	235	47	35	54	270	50
6	276	46	41	53	318	48
7	322	46	46	52	364	46
8	372	$46\frac{1}{2}$	50	51	408	44
9	429	$47\frac{2}{3}$	57	50	450	42
10	490	49	61	49	490	40

TABLE 2
COST AND REVENUE DATA FOR A MONOPOLIST

Table 2 combines the revenue data of Table 1 with cost data for the same monopolist. The monopolist would maximize profits at an output level of 7 units, where $MC = MR = \$46$. Price should be set at $52 because the demand curve (AR) indicates that 7 units will sell for $52 each. At a price of $52, total revenue is $364 (7 × $52) and total cost is $322 ($46 × 7), which means that the monopolist is making a profit of $42 ($364 − $322). If you don't believe this is maximum profit, calculate the profit at each level of output from 1 to 10 units. You will see profit is maximized at 7 units because at that level, $MR = MC$.[1]

THE MONOPOLIST'S SUPPLY CURVE

A supply curve shows how much output will be offered for sale at various prices. In order to determine a supply curve, it is necessary to show that a firm will supply a unique quantity of output at any given price. This supply is by definition independent of demand. A monopoly firm does not have a supply curve in this sense. A monopolist sets the price at the profit-maximizing level of output, so it doesn't make sense to ask how much will be supplied at various prices. For a monopoly, the profit-maximizing output, where $MC = MR$, will depend on the location and shape of the demand curve. A monopoly firm therefore doesn't have a supply curve that is independent of demand.

To convince yourself that the monopolist does not have a supply curve, examine Figure 3. In part (a), two different prices, P_1 and P_2, are consistent with output x_1, depending on where the market demand curve is located (D_1 or D_2). The marginal revenue curves that are derived from the demand curves D_1 and D_2 both intersect the monopolist's marginal cost curve at the same level of output. In part (b), two different output levels,

---

1. If you do the calculation, you will find that profit is $42 at an output of 6 units and at an output of 7 units. This result is due to the fact that this numerical example uses whole-number data. The principle of profit maximization implies producing where $MR = MC$, but a unique point exists only when dealing with functions and using calculus. In this example, the actual profit-maximizing output would be somewhere between 6 and 7 units of output.

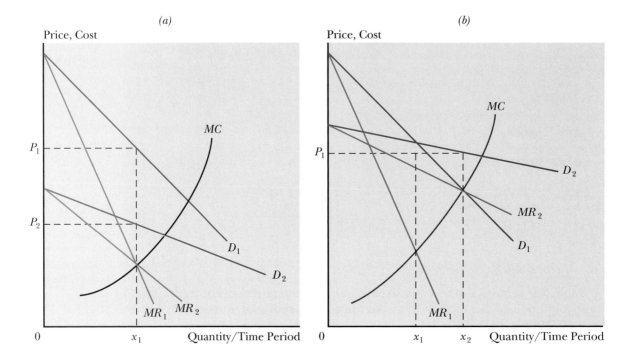

(a)   (b)

FIGURE 3
ONE OUTPUT WITH
TWO PRICES OR ONE
PRICE FOR TWO OUTPUTS
It is possible to trace out
a supply curve only if a
unique price is associated
with a certain output.
(*a*) Here there are at least
two prices, P_1 and P_2,
consistent with output x_1.
(*b*) Here there are at least
two outputs, x_1 and x_2,
consistent with price P_1.

barriers to entry
Natural or artificial
obstacles that keep new
firms from entering an
industry.

x_1 and x_2, can be produced at price P_1, depending on whether market demand is represented by D_1 or D_2.

Figure 3 shows that it is impossible to identify a supply curve for a monopolist. There is no way to predict what the monopolist will do without knowing the demand curve. In this sense, then, the monopolist has no supply curve. The predictive powers of economists are, therefore, more limited in an analysis of monopoly. In this case, economists cannot say that an increase in demand will cause price to rise, *ceteris paribus*.

PROFITS AND BARRIERS TO ENTRY

If a monopolist is earning profits, other entrepreneurs will want some of those profits. As a result, there will be pressure from new firms entering the industry. But wait! A monopoly is a *single* seller producing a product for which there are no close substitutes. If there is new entry, there is no longer a monopoly. If a monopoly is to persist, there must be some forces at work to keep new firms from entering. **Barriers to entry** are natural or artificial obstacles that keep new firms from entering an industry. Without such barriers, monopoly cannot continue.

Economies of scale provide a natural barrier to entry. If the long-run cost curves are such that the optimal-size plant is very large relative to the size of the market, there may be room for only one cost-efficient firm in the industry. If there are great economies of scale, one firm that is bigger than any of the others will be able to undersell the rest. In such a case, the bigger firm will cut its price below that of its rivals and capture their customers. Eventually the large firm will become the only firm in the industry. When just one firm emerges in this way, the firm is called a natural monopoly. This happens in very few industries.

Public utilities such as telephone companies, electric companies, and cable television companies fit this category. The government recognizes that these are natural monopolies and therefore regulates their prices and output levels. Problems associated with such regulation will be discussed in a later chapter. Some economists argue that even public utilities are not really natural monopolies. Since the occurrence of a natural monopoly is rare, most of the monopoly power that exists in our economy is due to artificial barriers.

An artificial barrier to entry is one that is contrived by the firm (or someone else) to keep others out. It doesn't take much imagination to come up with a list of such barriers. The least sophisticated, but perhaps the most effective, would be the use of violence. Suppose you have a monopoly on the illegal numbers racket in South Chicago. If new entrepreneurs move in to reap some of these profits, you simply "do away" with them—very effective! This sort of tactic may sound barbaric, but business history contains many examples of the use of violence to keep out competitors. The early history of oil exploration and drilling is one example—private armies were often a must.

On a more civilized level, it may be possible to erect artificial barriers that are legal, or at least quasi-legal. If exclusive ownership of all the raw materials in an industry could be captured, entry could be controlled by refusing to sell to potential new entrants. Alcoa enjoyed a monopoly before World War II because it controlled almost all the known sources of bauxite, the essential ore for the production of aluminum.

A current example of the use of artificial barriers occurs in the sale of diamonds. The de Beers Company of South Africa controls most of the world's diamond supply. This firm effectively controls the mining and marketing of new diamonds and has a great influence on price. In this case, there is still competition because all diamonds produced in the past are potential competitors. If de Beers manipulated production to drive price "too high," individuals might enter the market as suppliers, selling diamonds they presently own.

Another way to create artificial barriers is to own the patent on a process or machine that is vital in production. Patent rights give sole authority to use the process or machine to the holder of the patent. The problem with a patent, however, is twofold. First, it expires after seventeen years in the United States, and then everyone is entitled to use the idea. Second, to get a patent, detailed plans on how the item is produced must be provided, and these plans are available to potential competitors at the Library of Congress. So it appears a patent is not a very effective entry barrier to anyone who is willing to risk a lawsuit brought by the patent holder (and patent holders don't always win their cases). A good alternative to patents is secrecy. If a firm can keep its vital process or machine secret, it can keep new firms out of its industry. Now you know why there is barbed wire around some research and development offices, why you aren't told the formula for Pepsi Cola, and why corporate spying is big business.

GOVERNMENT AND BARRIERS TO ENTRY
It is very difficult to be a monopolist because it is very hard to keep new entrants out of an industry—unless you can get the government to help

you. Let's look briefly at two industries where firms have significant market power: the steel industry and the taxicab industry.

Suppose firms in the U.S. steel industry are earning economic profits. Firms that are producing steel in other countries see profits being earned and gear up to export steel to the United States to earn some of these profits. In effect, the foreign steel firms are entering the U.S. industry. The domestic firms then appeal to Congress and/or the President to keep the foreign firms out (to block their entry). Tariffs or quotas may be put into effect. These tariffs or quotas serve as artificial barriers to entry for foreign firms by raising the price of foreign goods or prohibiting their sale in the United States.

Next, consider the taxicab industry. You probably consider this to be a competitive industry since in any large city there are cabs from many companies on the street every day. But, if you decide to start a cab business, you might be in for some trouble. Suppose you already own a car, so the entry costs are relatively small. All you need to do is to mark your car so that it can be recognized as a cab, and perhaps install a meter. However, you will need a permit, which in some cities will be very difficult and expensive to obtain. If you operate as a "gypsy," an underground cab that avoids city regulations, you will make the existing cab owners very unhappy. In many cities, cabs are a monopoly enterprise, and it is government that protects the monopoly.

In these examples, government supplied the artificial barriers to entry. Federal, state, and local governments all restrict entry and thereby ensure protected market positions. It should not be too surprising that many instances of corruption in government have centered on the granting of monopoly privileges. A government official or agency protects a monopoly by keeping competitors out. The monopolist is often willing to pay for this with campaign contributions, favors, or outright bribes, such as direct cash payments, free vacations, or jobs for relatives.

If monopoly power persists for a long period of time, there is very likely to be some explicit or implicit government role in creating barriers to entry. Monopoly profits are a very powerful and attractive force, and new entry is very difficult for the monopolist alone to block. As a result, monopolies usually try to enlist governmental support of one kind or another.

IS MONOPOLY BAD?

Any entrepreneur would prefer to sell in a monopoly rather than a perfectly competitive industry, because economic profit always tends to zero. A firm that can create a successful monopoly will be rewarded with continuing profits. (This ability to use power in markets is stressed in marketing and management courses—thus, there are no marketing courses for wheat farmers!) Monopoly is obviously good for the monopolist, but monopoly can be bad for society.

How Monopoly Compares to Perfect Competition

To see what's so bad about monopoly, look at Figure 4. First, assume that Figure 4 represents a perfectly competitive industry. The market demand

Many multinational corporations are very large relative to the countries in which they operate. It is conceivable that some companies may have worldwide net sales that are larger than the GNP of the country in which they are operating. Thus, multinationals have a large amount of monopoly power in small host countries.

The political and economic dilemmas faced by multinational corporations and host governments have even come to the United States. For decades, U.S. policy makers were confronted with only one side of the problem, that of U.S. corporations in foreign countries. Recently, however, the United States has become a host country for foreign, primarily Japanese and European, investment.

Small less developed countries face a political dilemma in bargaining with large multinational companies. At the onset, such a country may have very little bargaining power with the multinational because the company can "shop around" for hospitable governments. If the country's policy makers want to pursue economic growth, they may have to agree initially to the multinational's terms. As time passes and the company invests more fixed capital assets in the country, the host government can increase taxes and capture more of the monopoly profits. However, a delicate balance must be maintained. Taxes and government controls di-minish the profitability of investment and future investment for the multinational. Other multinationals may be driven away by changes in a host country's business climate.

Host country controls on multinationals can take several forms. Some countries impose foreign exchange regulations that require the foreign firm to convert earnings at exchange rates that are different from market exchange rates. Another control is a rule requiring the foreign firms to use their earnings to buy local products and export them to countries with freely exchangeable currencies. Some countries (such as India) require foreign companies to divest their assets over time by selling them to native investors. This policy is a form of expropriation with compensation. Still other countries force foreign firms to purchase a certain percent of the components in a manufacturing process from domestic sources. Finally, although it may be illegal (or if not illegal, at least hushed), politicians in some countries may require bribes as a condition for doing business. This is not uncommon in countries with dictators.

In a small country, multinational companies not only exert monopoly power but also must confront monopoly power exerted by the host government. In this situation, with one monopoly confronting another, it is not always clear who wins.

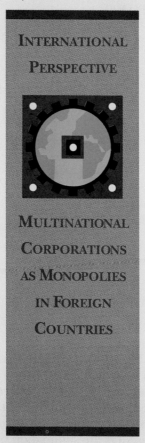

INTERNATIONAL
PERSPECTIVE

MULTINATIONAL
CORPORATIONS
AS MONOPOLIES
IN FOREIGN
COUNTRIES

Price, Cost

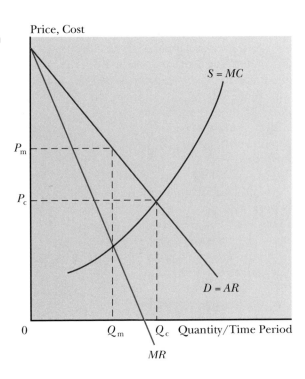

FIGURE 4
PRICE AND OUTPUT
DETERMINATION UNDER
MONOPOLY AND PERFECT
COMPETITION
The monopolist, equating marginal cost and marginal revenue, produces output Q_m and sells it at price P_m. If this same firm were perfectly competitive, the price would be P_c and output would be Q_c.

curve ($D = AR$) is that faced by the numerous sellers, and the marginal cost (MC) curve is the summation of all the individual firms' marginal cost curves. The competitive price and output are P_c and Q_c. Now suppose the industry is monopolized by one firm that has bought up all the competitive firms but still has the same cost curves. The monopoly firm, then, will face the same cost conditions that the aggregate of competitive firms faced. The *market* supply curve becomes the monopolist's marginal cost curve because it is the summation of the purchased firms' marginal cost curves. The monopoly firm also faces the *market* demand curve and its corresponding marginal revenue curve. The monopoly firm will produce at Q_m and P_m. In this case, it is a very simple matter to contrast monopoly with perfect competition. The monopolist produces a smaller output ($Q_m < Q_c$) and charges a higher price ($P_m > P_c$) than the perfectly competitive firms did. This is possible because entry into the industry is blocked. Since new firms cannot enter, consumers are not getting the optimal amount of the good produced by the monopolist. Monopolies restrict output. This is the principal economic argument against monopoly.

The monopolistic output and price, then, represent misallocation of resources if the monopoly has the same cost conditions as the aggregate of the competitive firms. Note that the misallocation under monopoly could be even worse if, in buying up the individual firms, the monopoly introduced some inefficiencies of large-scale management. Such inefficiencies would cause an upward shift of the cost curves in Figure 4.

The misallocation of resources in a monopoly is illustrated in Figure 5. The monopoly is in equilibrium producing x_1 units at a price of P_1. The monopolist's profits, which are total revenue minus total cost, are represented by rectangle CP_1AB. Let's examine closely what is going on at this

FIGURE 5
MISALLOCATION OF
RESOURCES IN A
MONOPOLY
A monopoly misallocates
resources because price is
greater than marginal
cost. This means the
value consumers place on
the item exceeds the
opportunity cost of
producing it.

equilibrium. First, price P_1 is greater than average cost (which is x_1B per unit). That is, $P_1 > AC$, and economic profits are being earned. Second, price is greater than marginal cost ($P_1 > MC$), which means the value consumers place on the last unit (P_1) exceeds the opportunity cost of producing it (MC). From the consumer's point of view, more should be produced. The monopolist prevents that from happening by restricting entry. Third, average cost at output x_1 is greater than marginal cost at x_1. That is, $AC > MC$. This means that x_1 units are not being produced using the least-cost combination of factors. The monopolist is not forced to be fully efficient. You can easily see, therefore, what economists mean when they say that monopoly misallocates resources.

MONOPOLY PROFITS AND LOSSES

There is a common misconception that a monopoly situation guarantees profits. A monopoly is not a license to make profits. If the U.S. government granted you an absolute monopoly in the sale and manufacture of Conestoga wagons, you might lose money. High costs or insufficient demand may cause a monopolist to lose money.

Figure 6 shows a monopoly suffering a loss. The monopoly is producing x_1 units and charging the profit-maximizing price, P_1. Average costs of producing are x_1A per unit. As a result, the monopolist is incurring losses equal to rectangle P_1CAB. Since the demand curve is below the average cost curve, there is no way to avoid losses. Will the monopolist continue to produce? If price is above average variable costs, as is the case in Figure 6, the monopolist will be better off in the short run if it continues producing. In the long run, if demand does not increase, the monopoly

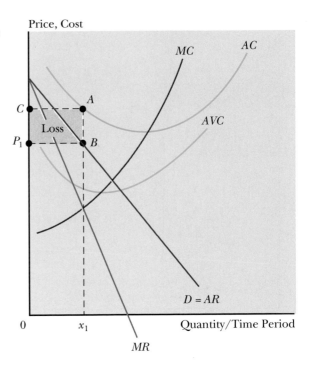

FIGURE 6
A MONOPOLY
SUFFERING LOSSES
The monopolist might suffer losses in the short run. If average cost is greater than average revenue, the monopolist is suffering a loss.

will go out of business. The presence of losses indicates that the factors of production are not earning their opportunity cost. Those factors will move to more productive uses.

A monopolist can also earn only normal profits. Figure 7 illustrates this case. The monopoly is producing x_1 units and charges price P_1. Total revenue is equal to rectangle $0P_1Ax_1$. In this instance, the monopoly is earning its opportunity cost. There will be no incentive for other firms to try to enter this industry or for this firm to leave the industry. Price is equal to average cost, which means that producers are not earning economic profits. However, price is still greater than marginal cost, indicating that more units should be produced.

You can see, then, that monopolies don't always make profits. In fact, they often incur losses and go out of business. Also, monopolists do not charge the highest price possible. Remember the mineral spring example? Monopolists charge the profit-maximizing price, and this price will depend on the demand conditions and costs in the industry.

MONOPOLY IN THE LONG RUN

The monopolist, unlike the perfectly competitive firm, can continue to earn economic profits in the long run. As long as the barriers to entry remain, economic profits can be maintained. Sustaining these barriers in the long run is very difficult, however, because the economic profits will attract new firms, substitute products, and new processes. In principle, then, even with government help, the power of any single monopoly is likely to decline in the very long run.

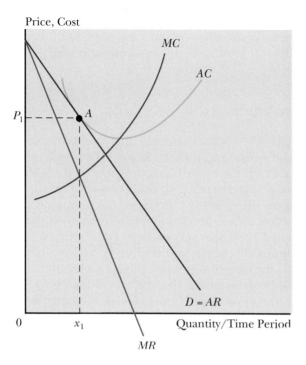

Price, Cost

P_1

A

MC

AC

$D = AR$

MR

0 x_1 Quantity/Time Period

FIGURE 7
A MONOPOLY
EARNING NORMAL PROFITS
It is possible that a monopoly might earn only normal profits. In this case, there is no incentive for other firms to enter the industry and no need for barriers to entry.

REAL-WORLD MONOPOLIES

We have pointed out that there are no examples of true monopoly in the real world. A complete monopoly cannot exist, because all products or services have some substitutes with which they compete. There are, however, firms with some monopoly power. The model of monopoly is useful in explaining the behavior of these firms. Public utilities, for example, are considered natural monopolies and are regulated as a result. Monopolies that are set up by some nations to engage in international trade are also monopolistic.

Local monopolies are another form of real-world monopoly. A **local monopoly** is a firm that has monopoly power in a geographic region. Even though close substitutes for the firm's product exist, the distance to other sources of supply creates a virtual monopoly. If you grew up in a small, remote town, there may have been only one movie theater or perhaps only

local monopoly
A firm that has monopoly power in a geographic region because of the large distance from other suppliers of its product (or substitutes).

COMPARISON OF MONOPOLY AND PERFECT COMPETITION	
MONOPOLY	**PERFECT COMPETITION**
• One firm	• Many firms
• Barriers to entry	• Free entry
• $P \neq AC$, so economic profits exist	• $P \neq AC$, only normal profit earned
• $MC \neq AC$, not producing at least-cost combination	• $MC = AC$, producing at least-cost combination

one grocery store. A firm in such a situation is a local monopoly because the substitutes are costly in the sense that you must travel to reach them. Economists use the model of monopoly to examine the effects of monopoly power in such real-world situations.

MONOPOLY POWER AND PRICE DISCRIMINATION

In analyzing monopoly behavior, we have assumed that the monopolist charges the same price to all consumers and the same price for all units sold to a specific consumer. If, on the other hand, the monopolist is able to charge different consumers different prices or charge a given consumer different prices depending on the quantity purchased, the monopolist is practicing **price discrimination**. Price discrimination is a way to expand monopoly profits by extracting consumer surplus from consumers.

To see how price discrimination works, you need to recall the discussion of consumer surplus in the chapter on utility theory. Consumer surplus is the extra utility gained by consumers who end up paying less for an item than they would be willing to pay for it. Consumers purchase an item until the marginal utility of the last dollar spent on the item is equal to the marginal utility of spending the dollar on any other good or of holding the dollar. The marginal utility of previously purchased units was greater than the price paid for those units because they were all purchased at the price of the last unit. The consumer would have been willing to pay higher prices for those units. Figure 8 illustrates this concept. At price P_1 in Figure 8, the consumer was receiving a "bonus" in terms of utility. This extra utility is called consumer surplus, represented by the shaded area in Figure 9.

A monopoly producer might be able to deal separately with consumers depending on the number of units purchased. In terms of Figure 9, the

price discrimination
The practice of charging different prices to different consumers or to a single consumer for different quantities purchased.

FIGURE 8
CONSUMER SURPLUS
Consumer surplus is the difference between the total utility received from the purchase of a product and the total revenue generated by the product. It exists because the marginal utility of each previous unit purchased was greater than price P_1.

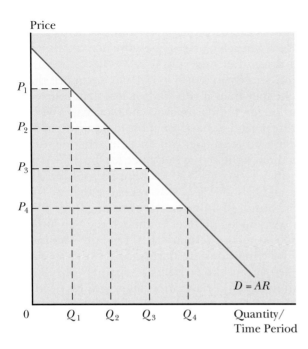

Price

P_1

P_2

P_3

P_4

0   Q_1 Q_2 Q_3 Q_4 Quantity/
Time Period

$D = AR$

FIGURE 9
A PRICE-DISCRIMINATING MONOPOLIST
A price-discriminating monopolist can capture most of the consumer surplus by charging different prices for different amounts of consumption.

monopolist could say, "You may buy up to Q_1 units for P_1, from Q_1 to Q_2 units for P_2, from Q_2 to Q_3 units for P_3, and from Q_3 to Q_4 units for P_4." By doing this, the monopolist extracts most of the consumer surplus and converts it into revenue for the firm. Compare the shaded areas in Figure 9 to the shaded area in Figure 8. Both represent consumer surplus. In Figure 9, by charging different prices for different amounts of consumption, the monopolist has expropriated much of the consumer surplus. It is theoretically possible for the monopolist to capture all of the consumer surplus by charging different prices for each number of units.

The second type of price discrimination occurs when a monopolist can separate markets and charge different prices to different groups of consumers. If the monopolist can separate the markets and prevent resale, it can price discriminate by adjusting output for the different demand elasticities in the two markets.

PRICE DISCRIMINATION IN PRACTICE
In practice, the first type of price discrimination is common. It requires that the seller have the power to separate sales on a unit-by-unit basis. This form of price discrimination is what is being practiced when multiples of a product can be purchased for a total that is less than the per-unit price times the number purchased. "Artichokes 40¢, two for 65¢" and "Coffee 50¢ a cup, refills a quarter" are examples of this type of price discrimination.

The second type of price discrimination requires that the seller be able to separate markets according to different elasticities of demand. Bookstores offer lower prices to professors than to students. Airlines charge lower fares to students and vacationers than to businesspeople. University athletic departments offer lower-priced tickets to sports events to students and faculty. Medical doctors charge different patients different fees for the same service. Senior citizens get discounts on all kinds of items, from prescriptions to theater tickets. In each of these cases, the market with the greater elasticity gets lower prices. Let's see why.

Consider plane tickets. If you fly to Europe and stay for more than fourteen days, the fare is cheaper than if you stay for less than fourteen days. If you stay a month or longer, flights are even cheaper. Why? Which class of consumers of air transportation have the most inelastic demand? Business travelers, of course, who tend to travel on tight schedules and have bosses who don't want them sight-seeing in France for fourteen days! With airline deregulation, major carriers have developed sophisticated techniques to set and change fares. *Business Week* reported that in 1985 American Airlines had over a hundred traffic analysts working three shifts seven days a week. Their job was to juggle fares to "match the bargain offerings of low-cost rivals while protecting [American's] full-fare business."[2]

It should be clear that two conditions are necessary in order to practice price discrimination. First, it must be possible to separate consumers into groups that have different demand elasticities. These groups need to be economically identifiable. If it costs too much to identify the groups, discrimination might not pay. When economists talk about price discrimination, they're not talking about discriminating on the basis of race, sex, or national origin, unless different races, sexes, or nationalities have different demand elasticities for certain products. Many times, age is used to identify groups with different demand elasticities. Senior citizens and students have more elastic demand curves because they typically have a tighter budget and more time to shop around than middle-aged people do. In the case of airfares, the classes of consumers are separated by length of stay. Businesspeople seldom want to stay at a destination for more than a few days.

Time-of-day price discrimination includes matinee performances of cultural events and movies, bowling alley use, and lunch and dinner menus. In these cases, demand is more inelastic at night because some consumers are limited to night consumption. Magazine publishers charge higher prices for magazines purchased at newsstands than for subscriptions. Sometimes subscription prices are only a fraction of the newsstand prices. Newsstand demand is more inelastic because it is a spur-of-the-moment, unplanned purchase. Book publishers charge much higher prices for hardcover novels than for softcover versions of the same novel. They separate the markets by publishing the softcover version after the hardcover demand has been satiated. Some colleges charge in-state and out-of-state tuition because it is very easy to separate these two markets. Has your car ever broken down when you were out of town? Your demand is very inelastic in such a situation. You have little information about services available, and you are easy to identify as a one-time customer (you may have an out-of-state license plate). What do you think happens? You're right! You pay much more than a local person with car trouble would pay.

The second major requirement for price discrimination is that the monopolist *must* be able to prevent the resale of goods or the movement of

2.   *Business Week* (2 December 1985): 34.

customers between markets. Consider charging different prices to different classes of customers for tickets for a college football game. It only works if the customers paying the lower price are prohibited from reselling their tickets. If not, the college is no longer a monopolist in the sale of the higher-priced tickets. Is it any wonder that the athletic department requires you to show your picture I.D. card *and* your ticket at the gate? The higher-priced ticket holders are only required to present their tickets. Price discrimination works well where resale is very difficult. Services are good candidates for price discrimination because it is very difficult to resell a service. Medical doctors are very successful in practicing price discrimination because they have easily recognizable submarkets with different elasticities (by income and insurance category) *and* because resale is almost always ruled out.

The seller often justifies price discrimination as helping a group. For example, doctors might claim they practice price discrimination (charging less to some groups) in order to "help" the poor. Students or senior citizens might be charged less "to help them out." In reality, price discrimination is almost always practiced because it increases profit.

GAINERS AND LOSERS FROM PRICE DISCRIMINATION

Price discrimination does have a positive side effect. It will usually cause output under monopoly to increase. Earlier in this chapter, you learned that one of the disadvantages of monopoly is that it restricts output. If a monopoly can, however, sell output one unit at a time, output will be pushed to the point where price equals marginal cost. This is common sense because the monopolist only restricts output in order to keep price from falling on all units. If price falls only on the additions to output (not other units), then price equals marginal revenue, and output will be increased to the point where price equals marginal cost. This is the same conclusion as for perfect competition. The difference, of course, is that more of the benefit accrues to the monopolist. Price discrimination converts consumer surplus into monopoly profits, making monopolists wealthier and consumers worse off.

Many people believe price discrimination is unfair because people pay different prices for the very same product. Why should an airplane ticket be cheaper because someone is a tourist rather than a business traveler? Why should professors get their books and pens for lower prices than students? Why should students pay less for a football ticket than nonstudents?

Interestingly, it is sometimes the group that benefits from price discrimination that complains. Price discrimination is common in international trade because the separation of national markets is often easy to maintain. Tariffs and transportation costs can help prevent resale. When firms in a country sell in a foreign market at a lower price than they do at home, they are engaging in price discrimination. Demand in the foreign country may be more elastic than domestic demand because there is more competition, and, therefore, more good substitutes are available. The foreign monopolist sells to foreigners at a lower price than at home. The U.S. Treasury calls this form of price discrimination **dumping**. Dumping occurs, for example, when the Japanese sell televisions in the United States at a lower price than they sell the same sets at home.

dumping
The practice of selling in foreign markets at lower prices than in domestic markets (a form of price discrimination).

State trading occurs when a government acts as a monopoly buyer or seller of a product in international markets. Although most nations engage in some state trading, especially in military goods, it has been more common in centrally planned economies. The communist countries of Eastern Europe and the Soviet Union have historically carried out all their international trade through state trading monopolies. These monopolies determined how much was to be imported or exported and the prices at which this trade would take place. In many instances, trade was carried out in a manner that economists call countertrade. If a firm wanted to do business with the Soviet Union, it would have to accept payment in Soviet goods rather than in hard currency.

Countertrade resulted in complicated arrangements that discouraged some Western firms from exporting to the Soviet Union. Some examples can show how complicated countertrade could be. If a U.S. firm wanted to sell computers to the Soviet Union, it might, for example, have to take payment in vodka. The U.S. firm would then have to find a firm that wanted to buy the vodka or set up a firm to distribute the vodka to liquor stores. A firm that wanted to sell textile equipment to East Germany might have to take payment in the cloth that this equipment produced. The firm would then have to somehow market the cloth.

Another difficulty that Western firms faced in dealing with state trading companies is that the state monopoly could have an unfair advantage in the market. It was one firm dealing with competitive firms from all other countries. The power of the monopoly was even greater because it was the government. There is evidence that these state monopolies were able to get better than market deals because of their monopoly power.

All these relationships are likely to change in the next few years. The political reforms that swept Eastern Europe and the Soviet Union in the early 1990s are bound to have important economic effects. There is great potential for increased trade between firms in the West and those in the formerly communist countries. It is still too early to tell how the institutions of this trade will develop. If democratic market economies emerge, however, most state trading could be a thing of the past.

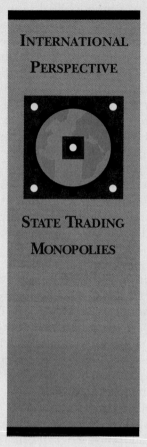

INTERNATIONAL PERSPECTIVE

STATE TRADING MONOPOLIES

The odd thing is that dumping has a bad reputation. When the Japanese dump televisions in the United States, the U.S. government takes action against Japan. This is curious because Japanese firms are giving U.S. consumers a better deal than Japanese consumers.[3] Complaining about being offered a lower price doesn't seem to make sense. Seen from the producer's angle, however, dumping is worth complaining about. You can understand why domestic manufacturers don't particularly approve of foreign competitors selling in this country more cheaply than in their own home market.[4]

PRICE DISCRIMINATION AND MONOPOLY

We developed the concept of price discrimination in connection with the study of monopoly. Price discrimination is not limited to monopolies, however. It will never occur in perfect competition but could occur in monopolistic competition and oligopoly, which we will study in the next chapter. However, since the opportunity to use price discrimination is greater if consumers have few good substitutes, it is easiest to price discriminate under monopolistic conditions.

THE COSTS OF MONOPOLY

We have made the point that a monopoly misallocates resources by contriving shortages—producing less than the competitive output to create monopoly profits. There are, however, other costs associated with monopoly. Figure 10 depicts a monopoly firm with constant marginal costs and, thus, constant average costs. Constant marginal costs and average costs are assumed for simplicity.

The monopolist will produce output level Q_m and set price at P_m. A perfectly competitive structure would have produced an output of Q_c at price P_c. As a result of restricting output, the monopolist earns a monopoly profit equal to the shaded area in Figure 10. This shaded area represents a transfer from consumers (in terms of lost consumer surplus) to the monopolist (in terms of monopoly profit). This transfer, however, is not the only cost the monopoly creates.

DEADWEIGHT LOSS

The crosshatched triangle in Figure 10 represents lost consumer surplus that was not converted into monopoly profits. This lost consumer surplus is received by no one. Consumers have lost it because the monopoly has restricted output, but it has not been received by anyone in the economy. The lost consumer surplus is referred to as the deadweight loss of monopoly. The **deadweight loss** is the lost consumer surplus due to monopolistic restriction of output. It is a deadweight loss because nothing is received in exchange for the loss. It is equivalent to throwing a valuable resource away.

deadweight loss
The lost consumer surplus due to monopolistic restriction of output.

---

3.   In fact, the dumping case concerning Japanese television sets was a rarity in that the initial complaint came from Japanese consumers.
4.   There may be some other objections to dumping. The U.S. government may fear that the Japanese are selling below cost to drive U.S. firms out of business in an attempt to corner the market on televisions. Or the government may fear that Japan is transmitting macroeconomic disturbances to the United States by weakening the U.S. television industry.

FIGURE 10
THE DEADWEIGHT
LOSS OF MONOPOLY
A monopoly converts
some consumer surplus
to monopoly profit. The
crosshatched area,
however, represents
consumer surplus that is
lost. It is the deadweight
loss associated with
monopoly.

Many years ago, Arnold C. Harberger attempted to measure this deadweight loss of monopoly.[5] He estimated that deadweight loss (he referred
to it as the welfare loss from monopoly) was quite small. In 1954, for example, only about $\frac{1}{10}$ of 1 percent of GNP was lost due to the deadweight
loss effect. This small fraction of GNP amounted to about $1.50 for each
U.S. citizen in 1954. Since Harberger's study, other economists have attempted to measure deadweight loss. Most of their estimates are also small
and tend to congregate in the range of 1 percent of GNP.[6] This is still a
surprisingly low figure, although it is ten times larger than Harberger's
original estimate. Harberger's work implies that, if the transfer from consumers to monopolists (the captured consumer surplus) is ignored,
monopoly has little effect on welfare.

MONOPOLY RENT SEEKING
Gordon Tullock believes that deadweight loss estimates are likely to underestimate the costs of monopoly. Tullock argues that since the
monopoly profits (the captured consumer surplus) are potentially huge,
monopolists spend a great deal of time, effort, and resources in establishing a monopoly.[7] He developed his argument by drawing an analogy
to theft. If thieves steal $100 million, they transfer that $100 million from
victims to themselves. This transfer is just like the transfer of consumer
surplus. But thieves invest time, effort, and resources in guns and getaway
cars. In addition, victims invest money in protecting themselves from

5. See A. C. Harberger, "The Welfare Loss from Monopoly," *American Economic Review* (May
1954): 77–87. For a recent study confirming Harberger's result and summarizing many other
studies, see Micha Gisser, "Price Leadership and Welfare Losses in U.S. Manufacturing," *American Economic Review* (September 1986): 756–767.
6. For a review of these other studies, see F. M. Scherer, *Industrial Market Structure and Economic
Performance*, 2nd ed. (Chicago: Rand McNally, 1980), Chapter 17.
7. G. Tullock, "The Welfare Costs of Tariffs, Monopolies and Theft," *Western Economic Journal*
(June 1967): 224–232.

theft. Both of these costs are wasted from the viewpoint of society as a whole. Tullock argues that the same holds true for monopoly. Monopolists "waste" resources (from a societal viewpoint) in seeking to establish a monopoly. Society also expends resources trying to break up and prevent monopolies. The efforts and resources expended by those attempting to establish monopolies to earn monopoly profits have become known as **monopoly rent seeking**. This is a cost of monopoly because these resources are no longer available to produce goods and services. We will discuss monopoly rent seeking in greater detail in a later chapter.

monopoly rent seeking
The efforts and resources expended by those attempting to establish monopolies to earn monopoly profits.

MANAGERIAL INEFFICIENCY

Still another cost of monopoly has been identified by Harvey Leibenstein.[8] Leibenstein argues that competitive firms are forced to be efficient by the market, but this does not hold true for monopolies. Since the monopolist is not punished by the market for slack management, it will tend to have more managerial "looseness" than a competitive firm. This looseness will manifest itself in corporate jets, limousines, expense accounts, and golden parachutes. Leibenstein coined the term *x*-**inefficiency** to describe the inefficiency associated with the "slack" management of monopoly firms. The monopolist escapes the market discipline and is therefore less conscious of management efficiencies. Leibenstein estimated this cost to be as high as 2 percent of GNP.

x-**inefficiency**
The inefficiency associated with the "slack" management of monopoly firms because of the lack of market discipline.

WHO RUNS THE FIRM? ALTERNATIVES TO PROFIT MAXIMIZATION

We have consistently assumed that firms are profit maximizers. This assumption makes it possible to predict how a firm will adjust to changes in demand in the market structure of perfect competition. What happens in the realm of giant firms run by professional managers? Corporations account for about 85 percent of the annual business sales in the United States. Corporations are run by hired managers, not owners. Managers might operate by some principle other than profit maximization. This idea is sometimes referred to as the **separation of ownership and control**, which simply means that managers who control corporations may behave differently than owner-managers would. Different behavior will occur only if the managers have different goals *and* if owners can't control managers. It has been argued that separation is part of the reason behind some of the takeovers in the 1980s. Leveraged buyouts occurred, according to this argument, because hired managers were not running their firms as profitably as owner-managers would have.

separation of ownership and control
The idea that large firms are run (controlled) by hired managers, not the owners, and the managers might have different goals from those of the owners.

The hypothesis that managers' behavior deviates from profit maximization is based on organizational theory. (You may have studied that theory in a course on social psychology or management.) The hypothesis assumes that managers will follow standard procedures even if these procedures result in lower profits. Managers of big business firms are seen as bureaucrats who make conservative decisions to avoid mistakes and to minimize liability, like managers in the military, the federal bureaucracy,

8.   H. Leibenstein, "Allocative Efficiency vs. x-Inefficiency," *American Economic Review* (June 1966): 392–415.

Nobel Prize winner Herbert Simon was born in Milwaukee, Wisconsin, and educated at the University of Chicago. Simon has held teaching positions at the University of California, the Illinois Institute of Technology, and the University of Pittsburgh. He is presently at Carnegie-Mellon University. Simon has never held a teaching post as an economist. Instead, he has held professorships in political science, administration, psychology, and information sciences. He is an economist in the broadest sense of the word, like the early classical economists.

In awarding the 1978 Nobel Prize in Economics to Simon, the Royal Swedish Academy noted his work concerning the development of alternatives to profit maximization. The committee made the following statement in its official announcement: "In his epoch-making book, *Administrative Behavior*

ECONOMIC PROFILE

HERBERT SIMON

1916–

(1947), and in a number of subsequent works, he (Simon) described the company as an adaptive system of physical, personal, and social components that are held together by a network of intercommunications and by the willingness of its members to cooperate and to strive towards a common goal. What is new in Simon's ideas is, most of all, that he rejects the assumption made in classic theory of the firm as an omnisciently rational, profit-maximizing entrepreneur."[a]

Simon has had an impact on more academic disciplines than any other Nobel Prize winner in economics. His work in management science and public administration is credited with bringing scientific approaches to the study of management. Herbert Simon is perhaps the best example of an economic theorist who has made a major impact on business and public administration.

a. "The Nobel Memorial Prize in Economics," *The Scandinavian Journal of Economics*, 81, no. 1 (1979): 72–73.

or any large organization. Those who argue that managers do not maximize profits offer several alternatives to that standard assumption. Let's look briefly at some of these.

The **satisficing** hypothesis argues that the management of a firm does not seek maximum profits but rather looks for certain target levels of output and profits that are satisfactory to the ownership interests. Owners' goals might include size or market share, altruism or philanthropy. Unfortunately, in order to test this hypothesis and determine its validity, it would be necessary to specify a firm's target. Otherwise, any result that is found would be consistent with satisficing behavior. The proponents of the satisficing hypothesis have not as yet found a way to specify targets. As a result, the hypothesis cannot be proved or disproved.

satisficing hypothesis
The argument that managers do not seek to maximize profits but rather seek target levels of output and profits that are satisfactory to the ownership interests.

Another goal that might be substituted in place of profit maximization is religious or racial discrimination. Firms with monopoly power and little threat of competition may sacrifice some of their profits in order to sell to, or hire, a particular group of people. A very interesting test of this hypothesis was conducted several years ago by Armen Alchian and Reuben Kessel.[9] They classified Jewish and non-Jewish graduates of the Harvard Business School according to the market structures of the industries in which they were employed. In the years examined, 36 percent of the school's graduates were Jewish. Alchian and Kessel discovered that employment of Harvard MBAs in monopolized industries was 18 percent Jewish compared with 41 percent Jewish in competitive industries. This evidence is consistent with the hypothesis that monopoly power makes discrimination against minorities easier (less costly) and points to yet another cost of monopoly power.

Thomas DiLorenzo disagrees with the satisficing hypothesis and argues that rational profit-maximizing behavior of managers of private monopolies will not be more lax than that of their counterparts in competitive firms.[10] He maintains that monopoly managers will try just as hard because they get to share in monopoly profits in the form of salary increases and added benefits.

Another hypothesis has been suggested by William Baumol. Baumol argues that given some level of profits, managers' primary goal is to increase the sales of the firm. In essence, Baumol is saying that managers are rewarded by stockholders, according to the relative size of the firm in the market, for increasing the firm's relative share of the market, say, from 15 to 20 percent. This hypothesis is called **constrained sales maximization**. The implication of this hypothesis is that monopoly might not be as bad as we concluded earlier. If sales, rather than profits, are the primary goal of a monopoly, the firm will charge lower prices and produce more output than a profit-maximizing monopolist. With lower prices and increased output, there will be less misallocation of resources than predicted with profit maximization.

constrained sales maximization
The hypothesis that managers' primary goal is to increase the sales of the firm because they will be rewarded by stockholders for increasing the firm's relative share of the market.

A rejoinder to these competing hypotheses is the long-run profit maximization hypothesis. **Long-run profit maximization** says that even if man-

long-run profit maximization
The argument that even if managers seem to behave in accord with satisficing or constrained sales maximization, they only do so because it leads to higher profits in the long run.

9. A. Alchian and R. A. Kessel, "Competition, Monopoly, and the Pursuit of Money," in H. G. Lewis et al., *Aspects of Labor Economics* (Princeton, NJ: Princeton University Press, 1962).
10. Thomas J. DiLorenzo, "Corporate Management, Property Rights, and the x-istence of x-Inefficiency," *Southern Economic Journal* (July 1981): 116–124.

agers seem to behave in accord with satisficing or constrained sales maximization, they do so only because it leads to higher profits in the long
run. According to this hypothesis, if the firm maximizes sales, it is doing
so because this will lead to higher profits in the long run. Also, if a firm
demonstrates a concern for social responsibility or philanthropy, it may
be doing so in the interest of long-run profits. The problem with the hypothesis of long-run profit maximization is that unless a distinct time period is specified, almost any behavior could be consistent with the
hypothesis. There is no way to prove or refute this hypothesis.

Competing theories of monopoly behavior highlight our earlier discussion of what theory is and what it does. Theory abstracts from the real
world by concentrating on the important aspects or effects of a phenomenon. If profit maximization is a valid assumption, it will yield reasonably accurate predictions about firms' behavior. Profit maximization
is a cornerstone of many hypotheses that have been empirically tested and
found to be valid. Alternative assumptions have yet to be rigorously tested.

FALLACIES AND FACTS ABOUT MONOPOLY

In this chapter, we have developed a model of monopoly. Although there
is no such thing as a true monopoly in the real world, there are firms that
have monopoly power. The model is useful in describing their behavior.
Since there are so many misconceptions about monopoly, it is worthwhile
to summarize a few fallacies and facts about monopolies.

FALLACY—MONOPOLIES CHARGE THE HIGHEST POSSIBLE PRICE
The public often believes that monopolies charge the highest possible
price and "rip off" consumers. This view is often supported by the press
and by consumer lobby groups. As you have seen in this chapter, however,
monopolies produce the profit-maximizing output and then sell that output on the market at a price that is constrained by the market demand
curve.

FALLACY—MONOPOLIES ALWAYS EARN (HIGH) PROFITS
A similar, but slightly different, fallacy is that monopolies always earn
profits. You have seen in this chapter that some monopolies earn profits,
some earn normal profits, and others suffer losses. To be sure, monopolists try to earn profits, but if demand changes, they might lose money.
The key difference between monopoly and competition is that profits of
a monopoly can persist because they don't lead to new entry. In cases
where monopolies suffer losses, however, the resources will flow to other
industries. In some cases, the government has tried to keep unprofitable
monopolies from going out of business.

FALLACY—MONOPOLISTS DON'T HAVE TO WORRY ABOUT DEMAND
It is a commonly held belief that monopolists don't have to worry about
demand. Some social critics have even suggested that monopolists can
manipulate demand. You have seen, however, that monopolists are constrained by the market demand for the good or service they produce.

Their search for the price that maximizes their revenue is strictly tied to that demand curve.

FACT—MONOPOLIES CHARGE A PRICE HIGHER THAN MARGINAL COST

You have seen in this chapter that a monopoly restricts output in order to earn economic profits. This restriction of output means that the price charged is greater than marginal cost. Compared to perfect competition, monopolies are less efficient in allocating resources to match consumer preferences.

FACT—MONOPOLISTS PRODUCE WHERE DEMAND IS ELASTIC

It is often mistakenly believed that a monopoly will produce where demand is inelastic. You have seen, though, that monopolies will always raise the price if demand is inelastic. Every monopoly will always be producing in an elastic portion of its demand curve.

FACT—MONOPOLIES DO NOT HAVE SUPPLY CURVES

As you have seen in this chapter, a monopoly is a price searcher. The monopoly establishes the profit-maximizing output and then sets the price equal to average revenue. As a result, the concept of a supply curve is meaningless. This lack of a supply curve makes the model of monopoly less useful than the model of perfect competition because it is difficult to analyze supply responses to demand shifts.

FACT—THE MONOPOLIST ULTIMATELY FACES COMPETITION

The model of monopoly assumes that the firm faces little or no competition because it defines a market structure consisting of a single firm producing a good with no close substitutes. In reality, however, the monopolist that earns a profit will be pursued by potential competitors, and the natural or artificial barriers to entry will be difficult to maintain. In a global economy, even if there are no domestic competitors, there is almost always a threat of competition from abroad.

As a closing note, it is appropriate to quote Alfred Marshall, the great neoclassical economist, on this subject:

It will in fact presently be seen that, though monopoly and free competition are really wide apart, yet in practice they shade into one another by imperceptible degrees: that there is an element of monopoly in nearly all competitive business: and that nearly all the monopolies, that are of any practical importance in the present age, hold much of their power by an uncertain tenure; so that they would lose it ere long, if they ignored the possibilities of competition, direct and indirect.[11]

CONTESTABLE MARKETS

contestable markets
Markets composed of large firms that are nevertheless efficient because easily reversible entry into the market is possible.

A number of economists have developed a new theory of industry structure called contestability theory.[12] **Contestable markets** are markets com-

11. Alfred Marshall, *Industry and Trade*, 4th ed. (London: Macmillan, 1923): 397.
12. William J. Baumol, John C. Panzar, and Robert D. Willig, *Contestable Markets and the Theory of Industry Structure* (New York: Harcourt, Brace, Jovanovich, 1982).

posed of large firms that are nevertheless efficient because easily reversible entry into the market is possible. This theory attempts to bring more reality to microeconomics by analyzing large multiproduct firms. The theory is very complex because it relies heavily on mathematical models, but the insights produced are essentially quite simple.

The basic idea is that the ease of entry into their market constrains the behavior of large firms and makes them efficient. Using contestability theory, economists argue that it is no longer necessary to assume that there are large numbers of firms, each a price taker, acting as if their production had no impact on the market in order to obtain efficiency. If easily reversible entry is possible, efficiency can be shown to coexist with large-scale production. In the past, this large-scale production might have been labeled monopoly.

Elizabeth Bailey, a proponent of contestability theory, was a commissioner at the Civil Aeronautics Board during the Carter administration. She suggested that contestability in the airline industry was enough to ensure efficiency because capital there consists mostly of aircraft, and capital costs can be recovered with little loss. In other words, entry into a particular air travel market is easy. She argued that even if a route were flown by only one airline, it is unlikely that monopoly prices would be charged because those prices would elicit entry by contesting airlines. According to this theory, it is the recovery of capital costs rather than economies of scale that is important.

Critics of this theory argue that it says nothing new. They argue that the model is not much different from models that show that the possibility of entry limits the pricing behavior of monopolists. Regardless of who wins the debate, it is important to note that entry conditions are important in both theories. Monopoly cannot persist in open markets, and whether one refers to this threat as competition or contestability makes little difference for public policy.

SUMMARY

1. Monopoly is a market structure in which there is a single seller of a product with no close substitutes.

2. The monopoly firm faces a negatively sloped demand curve and a marginal revenue curve that lies below that demand curve.

3. The monopolist maximizes profits by producing the output level at which marginal revenue equals marginal cost. The price is the one on the demand curve at which exactly that amount of output can be sold. Since price is often greater than average cost for a monopoly, economic profits may exist.

4. A monopolist is sometimes able to erect barriers to entry that allow profits to persist in the long run. Such barriers are very difficult to maintain. As a result, mo-

nopolists often appeal to the government for help in maintaining entry barriers.

5. Monopolies produce a lower output at a higher price than do competitive firms. At equilibrium, the monopoly firm is producing at a level of output where price is not equal to average cost or marginal cost.

6. Monopoly power is not a guarantee of profits. Some monopolies go out of business because of persistent losses. Others make only normal profits.

7. A monopoly can increase its revenues if it practices price discrimination. For price discrimination to be successful, customers must have different demand elasticities, and they must be separated and prohibited from reselling the product or service.

8. The costs of monopoly include misallocation of resources, deadweight loss, monopoly rent seeking, and x-inefficiency.

9. The satisficing hypothesis and the constrained sales maximization hypothesis are both derived from the idea of the separation of ownership and control. These hypotheses suggest that hired managers, as opposed to owner-managers, may attempt to meet satisfactory profit targets or to maximize sales rather than to maximize profits.

10. Although no examples of pure monopoly exist, the model of monopoly is useful in analyzing monopoly power.

11. Contestability theory says that large firms are forced to efficient outcomes if there is free entry into their markets.

New Terms

monopoly
monopoly power
price searcher
barriers to entry
local monopoly

price discrimination
dumping
deadweight loss
monopoly rent seeking
x-inefficiency

separation of ownership
  and control
satisficing hypothesis
constrained sales
  maximization

long-run profit
  maximization
contestable markets

Questions for Discussion

1. Explain in your own words why marginal revenue is less than average revenue under conditions of monopoly.

2. Should business firms be socially responsible? Respond to the argument that they should maximize profits and leave social responsibility to elected and appointed officials.

3. List as many barriers to entry as you can. Which are the most effective?

4. Why will a monopolist never attempt to produce in the inelastic portion of its demand curve?

5. Should government subsidize monopolies that are losing money to keep them in business?

6. Is some supermarkets' practice of giving trading stamps a form of price discrimination? If so, how does it work?

7. The following table describes the demand curve faced by a monopoly firm. Complete the marginal revenue column.

Price	Quantity Demanded	Marginal Revenue (MR)
$10	0	_____
9	1	_____
8	3	_____
7	4	_____
6	5	_____
5	6	_____
4	7	_____
3	8	_____

8. Assume that the cost data you calculated in Question 9 in the chapter on costs and profits represent the cost data of the monopoly firm of Question 7. How much would the monopolist produce in the short run? Why? What price would the monopolist charge?

9. What is the monopolist's profit, using the data from Question 9 in the chapter on costs and profits?

10. What will happen in the long run, based on the data used in the preceding two questions?

11. Years ago the U.S. government banned advertising of cigarettes on television. Can you speculate on how this ban might have affected the cigarette companies?

12. If you buy a round-trip airline ticket that includes a Saturday night stay at your destination city, the ticket price is often less than half that for the same round trip without a Saturday night stay. Is this price discrimination? Why is Saturday night the important night in this pricing scheme?

13. How does a monopolist maximize profits?

14. In what ways is monopoly thought to be inefficient?

15. What is x-inefficiency?

SUGGESTIONS FOR FURTHER READING

Asch, Peter. *Industrial Organization and Antitrust Policy*, rev. ed. New York: John Wiley and Sons, 1983. The first chapter of this book contrasts monopoly and competition.

Browning, Edgar K., and Jacquelene M. Browning. *Microeconomic Theory and Applications*, 2nd ed. Boston: Little, Brown, 1986. Chapters 11 and 12 present in-depth treatment of monopoly theory.

Bulow, Jeremy, and John Roberts. "The Simple Economics of Optimal Auctions," *Journal of Political Economy* (October 1989): 1060–1090. Shows how the seller's problem in auctions is identical to the monopolist's problem of price discrimination.

CHAPTER 25

MONOPOLISTIC COMPETITION AND OLIGOPOLY

INTRODUCTION

The last two chapters have examined the two theoretical extremes of market structures. At one extreme is monopoly, and at the other is perfect competition. There are no perfect real-world examples of either extreme. For many years, however, all real-world industries were analyzed in terms of these two models. In the 1930s, theories were developed that filled out the spectrum. Market structures between the two extremes show imperfect competition. Economists divide the middle of the spectrum into monopolistic competition and oligopoly. We will study these two market structures in this chapter.

The theory of monopolistic competition is usually associated with Edward Chamberlin and Joan Robinson. Chamberlin was a Harvard professor who published a book in 1933 entitled *The Theory of Monopolistic Competition.* Joan Robinson taught at Cambridge University in England and published *The Economics of Imperfect Competition,* also in 1933. (Robinson, who died in 1983, was only thirty years old when this classic was published!)

In 1934, German economist Heinrich von Stackelberg published a book entitled *Market Structure and Equilibrium.* It discussed the idea of firms' interdependence and formed the basis of the model of oligopoly. Oligopoly is the market structure in which a few firms compete imperfectly. The scarcity of sellers is the key to firms' behavior in oligopoly. In oligopoly, firms realize that their small number produces mutual interdependence. As a result, each firm will forecast or expect a certain response from its rivals to any price or output decision that it might make. We will examine the model of oligopoly after we study monopolistic competition.

MONOPOLISTIC COMPETITION

monopolistic competition
The market structure in which a large number of firms sell differentiated products.

differentiated product
A good or service that has real or imagined characteristics that are different from those of other goods or services.

product group
A market for a set of goods that are differentiated but have a large number of close substitutes.

The model of **monopolistic competition** describes an industry composed of a large number of sellers. Each of these sellers offers a **differentiated product**, which is a good or service that has real or imagined characteristics that are different from those of other goods or services. This differentiation can take many forms. The salespeople may be nicer, the packaging prettier, the credit terms better, or the service faster. It could even be that a famous person is associated with the product, as Bill Cosby is with Jell-O gelatin and puddings. It is important to note that a product is differentiated if consumers perceive it as different. For example, chemists tell us that aspirin is aspirin, that there is no real difference among the various brands. Yet many consumers view the brands as different, so there is product differentiation.

In monopolistic competition, the industry consists of a large number of firms, each producing a differentiated product. A very important assumption is that entry into this industry is relatively easy. New firms can enter the industry and start selling products that are similar to those already being produced. In Chamberlin's original description of monopolistic competition, a market for a set of goods that were differentiated but had a large number of close substitutes was called a **product group**. Chamberlin characterized monopolistic competition as the large-group case where there was rivalry between many firms in a product group.

You may have recognized monopolistic competition as a familiar market structure, since retail firms often fit this model. Monopolistic competition is generally what most people think of when they think of competition. Perfect competition, with its homogeneous products, simply does not fit the popular idea of competition in which firms are scrambling to make their products different.

Short-Run Equilibrium

Analysis of the short-run equilibrium of the monopolistically competitive firm is very similar to that for the monopolistic firm. Figure 1 shows the demand curve for a representative firm in monopolistic competition. When we depicted perfect competition, we started with the market and derived the representative firm's demand curve. In analyzing monopolistic competition, we begin with a representative firm, rather than with the market. With product differentiation, each firm faces a unique demand curve. The firm's demand curve in Figure 1 is negatively sloped, unlike the perfectly elastic demand curve faced by the perfectly competitive firm. The negative slope is a result of the differentiated nature of the firm's product. If the product's price is raised, the firm will not lose all its customers because some will continue to prefer this product to substitutes that are close but not perfect. Likewise, if the price is lowered, the firm will gain customers, but some customers will remain loyal to the products produced by other firms.

The elasticity of the demand curve is a measure of the degree of differentiation within the industry. If the products are only slightly differentiated, then they are close substitutes and each firm's demand curve will be very elastic. If the products are highly differentiated, the demand curve

Joan Robinson and Edward Chamberlin are given joint credit for developing the theory of monopolistic competition. Chamberlin published his *Theory of Monopolistic Competition* (1933) six months before Robinson published *The Economics of Imperfect Competition* (1933). Chamberlin, in later years, was preoccupied with trying to differentiate his ideas from Robinson's. Robinson is reported to have commented on Chamberlin's anguish over having to share the credit by saying at one point, "I'm sorry I ruined his life."

Chamberlin was born in the state of Washington but attended high school in Iowa, where he was a successful student and athlete. He later attended the University of Iowa and the University of Michigan, and ultimately received his Ph.D. from Harvard. He taught there until his death.

Joan Robinson developed her ideas quite independently of Chamberlin (they did not know each other) while a junior faculty member at Cambridge University in England. After the appearance of her path-breaking book, Robinson expanded her interests and research over a wide range of economic policy issues. She was an outspoken critic of the market system. Her antimarket publications include

ECONOMIC PROFILE

JOAN ROBINSON

1903–1983

AND

EDWARD CHAMBERLIN

1899–1967

An Essay on Marxian Economics (1956), *Economic Philosophy* (1962), and *Freedom and Necessity* (1970).

Robinson thought that economic analysis should begin with monopoly and that perfect competition should be studied only as a special case. She was one of the first economists to draw marginal cost curves the way we do now. Her account of monopolistic competition differs from Chamberlin's and from the model in this chapter. Robinson thought it natural for profits to exist in the long run.

Both Robinson and Chamberlin have had a significant impact on economics, but their careers were strikingly different. Chamberlin's career was characterized by a single pursuit—the development of the theory of monopolistic competition. Few economists have applied themselves to so narrow a purpose and yet achieved fame. Perhaps this in part explains Chamberlin's pain at having to share his fame with Robinson. Unlike Chamberlin, Robinson had wide-ranging interests. After contributing to micro theory, she worked with Keynes and helped to develop macroeconomics. Subsequently, she became a fiery social critic.

FIGURE 1
SHORT-RUN PROFITS
IN MONOPOLISTIC
COMPETITION
In the short run, an
economic profit can exist
for firms in monopolistic
competition. Such profits
will cause new firms to
enter the industry.

will be relatively inelastic, indicating that the firm can more easily raise the
price without losing many customers. Its customers are more loyal. Think
of aspirin, for example. Some people are willing to pay more for Bayer than
for Brand X because they think it is different. The makers of Bayer are able
to charge a higher price without losing a large number of customers. Bayer
will be limited in price flexibility by the amount of differentiation it is able
to create. As price goes higher and higher, fewer people will be willing to
pay for the differentiation. Some people may be willing to pay 10¢ more
for Bayer than for a different brand, but if the price of Bayer is increased
further, more and more people will shift to the other brands.

The demand curve in Figure 1 has a negative slope, indicating product differentiation. However, demand is very elastic, indicating that there
are many good substitutes. Since the demand (average revenue) curve is
negatively sloped, the marginal revenue curve will lie below it, for the
same reasons it does in the case of monopoly. The firm will, of course,
maximize profits at price P_1 and output x_1, where marginal revenue is
equal to marginal cost. The firm in Figure 1 is earning an economic profit
because average revenue, P_1, exceeds average cost, C. Total revenue is represented by rectangle $0P_1Ax_1$, and total cost is represented by rectangle
$0CBx_1$. Economic profit is thus the area of the shaded rectangle CP_1AB.

This analysis is very similar to the one developed in the preceding
chapter for monopoly in the short run. The most important difference is
that the demand curve here is very elastic. The monopolistically competitive firm is, in one sense, a minimonopolist for a product with close substitutes. The key to whether it is more like a perfectly competitive firm or
more like a monopoly depends on what happens in the long run in response to the economic profit.

LONG-RUN EQUILIBRIUM

What about long-run equilibrium in a monopolistically competitive industry? Figure 1 shows that a short-run equilibrium results in an economic

profit. Robinson thought the analysis ended here, with the firms able to earn economic profits in the long run. We assume instead that new firms can respond to these economic profits.

Entry into monopolistically competitive industries is assumed to be relatively easy. Thus, new firms will enter the industry in response to the economic profits. As firms enter the industry, the demand curve that is faced by any representative firm will shift to the left because the new firms will be attracting customers away from firms already in the industry. This is what happens, for example, when a new grocery store opens in an area. It draws customers away from the existing stores. The existing firms' demand curves will continue to shift down and to the left as new firms enter, and new firms will enter as long as economic profits are to be made. Long-run equilibrium will occur when all firms are earning zero economic profit (or normal profit). Such an equilibrium is depicted in Figure 2. Price is P_1 and output is x_1. Total revenue and total cost are represented by rectangle $0P_1Ax_1$. There are no economic profits being earned, and no additional firms will attempt to enter this industry.

Of course, too many firms might enter an industry due to a mistaken anticipation of economic profits. If this happens, losses will be realized, and some firms will leave the industry as the long-run adjustment proceeds. Figure 3 shows a monopolistically competitive firm suffering a loss equal to rectangle P_1CBA. Firms would respond to such losses by leaving the industry. The demand curves faced by the remaining firms would shift up and to the right until the equilibrium shown in Figure 2 was restored. The long-run adjustment process under monopolistic competition produces an equilibrium with zero economic profits.

MONOPOLY AND COMPETITION

As you can see, the model of monopolistic competition borrows from the model of monopoly and the model of perfect competition. In the short run, the monopolistically competitive firm is a mini-monopolist produc-

FIGURE 2
LONG-RUN EQUILIBRIUM IN MONOPOLISTIC COMPETITION
Since entry into a monopolistically competitive industry is relatively easy, there can be no long-run economic profits. Firms will enter until all firms are earning only a normal profit.

FIGURE 3
SHORT-RUN LOSSES
IN MONOPOLISTIC
COMPETITION
Short-run losses, indi-
cated by the shaded area,
will cause some firms to
exit the industry. Firms
will exit until the
remaining firms are
earning a normal profit,
as in Figure 2.

ing the profit-maximizing output and searching for the best price that can
be charged for this output. In the long run, the economic profits disappear as new firms enter the industry. The demand curve of each firm then
shifts to the left because market demand is shared by more firms. This result is similar to the long-run outcome in perfect competition. The market structure of monopolistic competition is at once both monopolistic
and competitive, which explains its name.

EXCESS CAPACITY

excess capacity
The unutilized part of
existing production
facilities by a monopolistically competitive firm.

In long-run equilibrium, the monopolistically competitive firm chooses
an output that does not fully utilize existing plant size. The unutilized part
of the production facilities, called **excess capacity**, is depicted in Figure 4.
The profit-maximizing output is x_1, where $MR = MC$. This is not, however,
the output that would have resulted under perfect competition. Under
perfect competition, the firm would use the least-cost combination of inputs, where average cost is at a minimum. This is the socially optimal output because it represents maximum attainable efficiency. This efficient
level of output is represented by x_2 in Figure 4. In other words, in long-
run equilibrium, the monopolistically competitive firm produces less
than the quantity that would efficiently use its full productive capacity.

Is excess capacity a bad thing? To answer this, it is necessary to consider what causes it. The firm is producing less than the socially ideal output because it maximizes profits by producing a lower output. This lower
output results from the fact that the demand curve for the monopolistically competitive firm slopes downward. You can see this by examining
Figure 4. Begin with demand curve D_1. The monopolistically competitive
firm is producing quantity x_1 at price P_1. Now make the demand curve
more elastic by rotating it counterclockwise. As the demand curve becomes more and more elastic and finally perfectly elastic, at D_2 in Figure
4, the output will increase toward the socially efficient output x_2. Excess
capacity is a result of the negative slope in the demand curve. This nega-

Price, Cost

FIGURE 4
EXCESS CAPACITY
Excess capacity results
from the negative slope
of the demand curve. As
the demand curve
becomes more elastic, the
excess capacity dimin-
ishes. It disappears when
the curve becomes
perfectly elastic.

tive slope, you recall, is a result of the product differentiation. The excess
capacity, therefore, results from product differentiation.

It can be argued that this excess capacity is not necessarily a bad thing.
Consumers may be willing to incur the extra cost in return for the perceived benefits of product differentiation. It would indeed be a very bor-
ing world without product differentiation. We might all be wearing khaki-
colored shirts, for example.

The major problem with this argument lies in separating desired from
undesired product differentiation. A consumer who is faced with a wide
range of product choices but little price competition is not able to choose
whether or not to pay extra to get the differentiated product. This problem isn't likely to be too important, however, when there are many firms,
as in monopolistic competition. Consider aspirin. If the only products in
the industry were Anacin, Bayer, Bufferin, and Excedrin, the consumer
would not have a low-price choice, since these brands compete almost ex-
clusively by advertising rather than by cutting prices. But the consumer
actually does have a choice of lower-priced generic brands of aspirin. So
in choosing Anacin over Brand X, the consumer voluntarily chooses product differentiation. In this case, product differentiation seems to be a
good thing because the consumer making the choice is maximizing individual utility. If, on the other hand, there are no lower-priced products
and the consumer must choose among products that compete only
through advertising, then the consumer does not really have a choice
about bearing the cost of the differentiation (unless, of course, he or she
simply does without the product altogether).

PRODUCT DIFFERENTIATION AND ADVERTISING

The firm in monopolistic competition will try to differentiate its product
in order to shift its demand curve to the right and to make demand more
inelastic by developing consumer loyalty. The firm will advertise as well as

make changes in color, style, quality, and so on. Advertising can inform consumers about higher quality or develop brand loyalty. Either of these results creates product differentiation. Competing with rival firms through advertising, style changes, color changes, and techniques other than lowering price is referred to as **nonprice competition**.

Advertising does not necessarily cause an increase in price. Even though costs rise because of advertising expenditures, it is possible that the increased output that the advertising generates will result in lower prices because of economies of scale. You can see this by examining Figure 5. In Figure 5, AC_1 represents a firm's long-run average cost before advertising. With sales of x_1 units, the price consumers pay is P_1. Advertising raises costs, shifting the firm's average cost curve to AC_2. If output increases because the firm gains sales because of the advertising, price can fall to P_2 because of economies of scale. On the other hand, if sales and output stay at x_1, average cost will rise to P_3.

If effective use of nonprice competition differentiates a firm's product enough that other firms' products do not seem to be good substitutes, the firm can earn an economic profit in the long run. Nonprice competition will often be gradual, so the firm can avoid a price war in which all firms will lose. A firm that is successful in such nonprice competition has in essence turned its share of the monopolistically competitive market into a long-run minimonopoly. The profit of such a firm could exist in the long run and not be driven to zero by new entrants.

Fast-food preparation is a monopolistically competitive industry. There are large numbers of firms, and entry is relatively easy. If a firm is able to successfully differentiate its product so that consumers don't consider the products of other firms close substitutes, the firm will be able to earn a long-run economic profit because it can keep would-be competitors out of its segment of the market. For example, McDonald's can't keep

nonprice competition
Competing with rival firms through advertising, style changes, color changes, and techniques other than lowering price.

FIGURE 5
A DECLINE IN PRICE DUE TO ADVERTISING
AC_1 represents long-run average costs without advertising. AC_2 represents costs made higher by advertising. If the firm increases output from x_1 to x_2 because of advertising, it is possible for the price charged to fall from P_1 to P_2. If sales do not increase, price will rise to P_3.

firms out of the hamburger market, but it can keep firms out of the Big Mac market. If enough people believe there's nothing like a Big Mac, this persistent brand loyalty might allow McDonald's to maintain an economic profit in the long run. Remember—Robinson thought this would be the equilibrium state.

It is easy to determine how successful a firm is at product differentiation by examining the difference between its prices and its competitors' prices. The consumer may go to McDonald's if a Big Mac costs 15¢ more than the competition, but what if it cost 55¢ more or $1.15 more? There is some price at which the other products will become good substitutes. That price is a measure of the success of product differentiation. It may be that a Big Mac is worth more to the consumer because of higher quality or because McDonald's has a very successful advertising and public relations program. The point is that it doesn't matter what causes the differentiation. The economic impact is that McDonald's may be able to earn an economic profit in the long run.

CHARACTERISTICS OF MONOPOLISTIC COMPETITION

- There are many sellers of similar but differentiated products.
- Economic profits can exist in the short run..
- Price is equal to average cost in the long run.
- Excess capacity exists in the long run (price is greater than marginal cost).
- Nonprice competition increases product differentiation.

RESOURCE ALLOCATION IN MONOPOLISTIC COMPETITION

The model of monopolistic competition has several implications for the allocation of resources. The resulting allocation will be different from the societal ideal achieved with perfect competition. First, even at the long-run equilibrium with zero economic profit, there will be excess capacity with monopolistic competition. This means that price will be greater than minimum average cost. Consumers are paying only the average cost of production, but this cost is higher than it would be with the most efficient level of production.

Second, if costs are the same under perfect competition and monopolistic competition, prices will be higher with monopolistic competition because price is greater than marginal cost (or marginal revenue). Third, firms in monopolistic competition will provide a wider variety of styles, colors, qualities, and brands. These choices are, unfortunately, related to the product differentiation and excess capacity that cause average cost to be higher.

Fourth, in monopolistic competition, there will be advertising and other forms of nonprice competition. This outcome is not necessarily bad. To the extent that advertising adds to customer satisfaction and the product is voluntarily purchased, it can be a good thing. Some social critics consider any advertising that does more than convey information to be a bad thing. Economists would argue that advertising is undesirable only if people don't have the option to consume alternative goods.[1]

OLIGOPOLY

oligopoly
The market structure in which a few firms compete imperfectly and recognize their interdependence.

The last of the four market structures is oligopoly. Oligopoly is important because there are so many real-world examples of it. **Oligopoly** is the market structure in which there are only a few firms. Since there are few firms, the actions of the firms are interdependent.

In some people's minds, oligopoly and monopoly are essentially the same. Among economists, this view is expressed by John Kenneth Galbraith. Galbraith argues, "So long as there are only a few massive firms in an industry, each must act with a view of the welfare of all."[2] This view, which is not widely shared among economists, regards oligopoly as shared monopoly. **Shared monopoly** is the model of oligopoly that says that oligopolists coordinate decisions and share markets to act as a monopoly.

shared monopoly
The model of oligopoly that says that oligopolists coordinate and share markets to act as a monopoly.

Most economists view oligopoly as more complex and difficult to analyze than monopoly. There is no single model of oligopoly, as there is for the other three market structures. The difficulty stems from the interdependence that characterizes oligopoly. Because of the complexity of oligopoly, economic analysis of it often includes heavy doses of descriptive economics rather than formal models with graphs. We will follow this tradition and describe several types of oligopoly and forms of oligopolistic behavior.

pure oligopoly
An oligopolistic industry that produces a homogeneous product.

differentiated oligopoly
An oligopoly that produces heterogeneous products that are very close substitutes.

price clusters
Groupings of prices for similar, but not homogeneous, products.

Oligopolies are sometimes categorized by the type of product they produce: homogeneous or differentiated. An oligopolistic industry that produces a homogeneous product is referred to as a **pure oligopoly**. The distinction is important because in pure oligopolies a single price is charged for the output of all the firms. An example of a pure oligopoly is the cement industry. As a consumer, you would be indifferent about which firm produced the sack of cement you purchased.

In contrast, a **differentiated oligopoly** produces products that are different. The auto industry is a good example. In differentiated oligopolies, there are **price clusters**, which are groupings of prices for similar, but not homogeneous, products. The range of prices within a cluster will depend on the amount of product differentiation. The more differentiated the products, the greater the price divergence. Tight price clusters indicate very little product differentiation.

COLLUSIVENESS AND OLIGOPOLIES

Perhaps the most useful classification tool for analyzing oligopolies is the system of definitions proposed by Fritz Machlup.[3] Machlup divided

---

1. The theory of monopolistic competition has been criticized by George Stigler as not offering any additional insights into or predictions of firms' behavior. Stigler admits that monopolistic competition is more descriptive of the real world, but he argues that the theory of perfect competition offers the same insights and predictions. See G. Chris Archibald, "Chamberlin versus Chicago," *Review of Economic Studies* (October 1961): 1–28.
2. John K. Galbraith, *American Capitalism*, 2nd ed. (Cambridge: Riverside Press, 1956), 83.
3. Fritz Machlup, *The Economics of Sellers' Competition* (Baltimore: Johns Hopkins Press, 1952).

oligopolistic behavior into three classes based on the degree of communication, coordination, and collusion among the firms in the industry. **Communication** refers to the firms' ability to signal their intentions to one another. **Coordination** refers to the firms' ability to relate their production decisions to those of the other firms in the industry. **Collusion** refers to agreements between the firms in an industry to set a certain price or to share a market in certain ways. It should be obvious that the abilities to communicate, coordinate, and collude will depend on the number of firms in an industry. As the number of firms increases, the cost of these activities will increase.

Machlup's system identifies three categories of oligopolies. The first category is characterized by formalized market coordination. The second is characterized by informal market coordination. The third category displays no market coordination.

FORMALIZED MARKET COORDINATION: CARTELS

Organized, collusive oligopolies are cartels. **Cartels** are groups of independent firms that agree not to compete but rather to determine prices and output jointly. A perfect cartel, which is able to behave as a monopoly, corresponds to Galbraith's concept of a shared monopoly.

In striving for joint profit maximization, a cartel must set prices, outputs, and marketing areas. However, the cartel can't always set these variables so that each individual firm in the cartel is maximizing its own profit. Figure 6 shows this problem clearly. In Figure 6, there are two firms, A and B, in a cartel that produces a homogeneous product. The marginal cost curves of these firms are MC_A and MC_B. MC_t is the horizontal summation (total) of MC_A and MC_B. The cartel will maximize profits, behaving exactly as a monopoly, by producing x_C where $MR = MC_t$. This output level results in a price of P_C.

Now the cartel must enforce this decision by requiring firms A and B to produce x_A and x_B, respectively. The difficulty is that neither firm would be at its individual profit-maximizing output. If each firm views onehalf of the market as its own, its demand curve is represented by MR in Figure 6.[4] The firms' profit-maximizing outputs are where $MC_A = MR_A$ and where $MC_B = MR_B$. Firm A would like to produce x_a, and Firm B would like to produce x_b.

In short, profit maximization for the cartel as a whole is not necessarily consistent with profit maximization for each individual member. In the example of Figure 6, firm A would prefer to produce *more* and sell it at a *higher* price, and firm B would prefer to produce *less* at a *lower* price. This example points out the most important problem faced by cartels. Joint profit maximization and individual profit maximization are often in conflict. As a result, a cartel is very unstable.

Perhaps the greatest threat to a cartel's existence is that members find it in their own self-interest to cheat on the cartel. **Chiseling** refers to cheating on a cartel agreement by lowering prices in an attempt to capture more of the market. If, for example, a cartel agrees on a set price, such as P_C in Figure 6, individual members may attempt to give secret price cuts

communication
Firms' ability to signal their intentions to each other.

coordination
Firms' ability to relate their production decisions to those made by other firms in an industry.

collusion
Agreements between firms in an industry to set a certain price or to share a market in certain ways.

cartel
A group of independent firms that agree not to compete but rather to determine prices and output jointly.

chiseling
Cheating on a cartel agreement by lowering prices in an attempt to capture more of the market.

---

4.   Remember that $MR = \frac{1}{2}D$. So if each firm views half the market as its own, the demand curve that each firm faces would be identical to the marginal revenue curve for the market.

FIGURE 6

PROFIT MAXIMIZATION BY A CARTEL

Joint profit maximization by two firms occurs where $MC_t = MR$. This quantity establishes a price of P_C and output of x_C. The cartel must then force firms A and B to produce output x_A and x_B, respectively. Assuming that each firm could view one-half of the market represented by the demand curve (D) as its own, individual profit maximization would establish a price of P_a and output of x_a for firm A and a price of P_b and output of x_b for firm B. To succeed, the cartel must compel firm A to produce less and firm B to produce more than its individual profit-maximizing output.

and capture more of the market. The total demand for a cartel is inelastic, so price cuts would reduce total revenue. However, the demand facing one member is elastic if it cuts price and the others do not.

If any firm in a cartel believes the others to be untrustworthy, it will have more of an incentive to chisel. As the number of firms in a cartel increases, it becomes increasingly likely that individual firms will become suspicious of the other members. The amount of chiseling is thus closely related to the number of firms in a cartel. The fewer the firms, the more closely the cartel will be able to monitor their behavior to determine if any firm is chiseling. Other factors can help a cartel control chiseling. For example, if the number of buyers is small and if the price is widely publicized, the cartel will not worry so much about one of its members chiseling.

Another threat faced by cartels is new entry. If a cartel is successful in acting as a monopoly and earning higher than normal profits, it must create barriers to entry. Otherwise, new firms might enter the market and compete with the cartel.

Let's briefly examine a few cartel-type organizations to see what elements affected their success or failure.

CARTELS IN THE REAL WORLD. The history of cartels is not impressive. Most have held together for only short periods of time, mainly because of chis-

Commodity cartels have a long history of failure. In the 1950s, commodity agreements, which are essentially cartels of commodity-producing countries, existed for tin, coffee, sugar, and wheat. The success of OPEC in 1973 reenergized some of these cartels as many commodity-exporting countries tried to emulate OPEC. The result was a flurry of activity that produced the following official organizations:

International Bauxite Association (IBA)

International Coffee Organization (ICO)

Intergovernmental Council of Copper-Exporting Countries (CIPEC)

International Sugar Association (ISA)

International Tin Council (ITC)

Organization of Banana Exporting Countries (OBEC)

In addition, there were attempts in the late 1970s and early 1980s to organize cartels in iron ore, nickel, rubber, tungsten, molybdenum, cobalt, columbium, and tantalum. Very few of these cartels, however, enjoyed the success that OPEC had in the 1970s.

Several lessons can be learned from the ex-

INTERNATIONAL
PERSPECTIVE

COMMODITY
CARTELS

perience of these commodity cartels and the success of OPEC. To be successful, a commodity cartel must:

1. have few members,
2. produce a product with few substitutes (have inelastic demand),
3. have buoyant world demand (have high income elasticity),
4. pursue a moderate pricing policy,
5. have at least tacit approval of consuming nations, and
6. have effective sanctions against chiselers.

Most cartels have great difficulty with the last three requirements and, as a result, break down rather quickly.

The effects of commodity cartels are often mixed up with economic development and world politics. Members tend to be less developed countries, and the consuming nations tend to be developed countries. The reasons for the formation of the cartel are often put in terms of a "fair" price that will redistribute wealth from rich to poor countries. Cartels are anti-consumer. Although some of those consumers live in high-income countries, many are poor people in poor countries. The OPEC oil price hike caused more hardship in poor countries than it did in rich countries.

eling. In the few cases where cartels have had long-term success, there has usually been direct government support. Once a government is involved, it becomes more difficult to chisel because the government can police and penalize this behavior.

Organized, collusive activity in private industry in the United States has usually been invalidated by the courts. However, General Electric and Westinghouse engaged in a conspiracy in the late 1950s to act as a cartel. They decided on a scheme that allowed them to submit low bids alternately on government contracts. The scheme depended on the phases of the moon. At either full or new moon (every two weeks), the firm designated to be the low bidder would gain the contract because the other firm would submit an uncompetitively high bid. This plan worked well because there were only two firms dealing with one buyer, the federal government. Each firm would know if the other was cheating because the bids were made public. In this case, the government was inadvertently helping the cartel overcome the chiseling problem.

Another example, involving a large number of firms, was an attempt to form a cartel known as the National Farm Organization (NFO). The industry for milk and beef production is composed of large numbers of firms (farms), and the NFO cartel only included about 10 percent of them. In 1967 and 1968, the NFO attempted two separate actions: one to raise milk prices and the other to raise beef prices. The cartel tried to organize farmers to keep production from the market. In order to raise prices, cartel members were to destroy milk and keep cattle away from the market. If the NFO members had been successful in raising prices, the nonmembers who continued to produce and sell would have benefited. They would have reacted to the higher prices by expanding output. Also, as prices began to rise, there would have been tremendous pressure on cartel members to chisel on the withholding action. In fact, the chiselers would have benefited much more than the members who refused to chisel. The attempt to organize the cartel resulted in violence. Cattle scales were blown up. NFO farmers sat in the roads to keep others from taking their products to market. Some farmers even resorted to taking cattle to market in house trailers to avoid detection. The lesson is clear: A cartel with many members will find it very difficult to succeed.

Cartels are much more common in Europe than they are in the United States. In Europe, cartels are permitted and often encouraged by governments. In Nazi Germany, all the major industries operated as cartels. Currently in Western Europe, the Common Market Commission is actively promoting cartels in steel, textiles, and shipbuilding.

Cartels are—with one exception—illegal in the United States. The one exception, based on the Webb-Pomerene Act of 1921, allows the formation of cartels when they are necessary to participate in foreign trade. These Webb-Pomerene cartels have not been successful in raising prices, primarily because of the large number of firms participating.

OPEC—A DECADE OF SUCCESS. The best-known cartel of recent years is the Organization of Petroleum Exporting Countries, known as OPEC. In the 1950s, international oil companies controlled a major portion of the world's oil supply. These companies frequently engaged in price competition. In an attempt to stop price cutting, some Arab governments and a few non-Arab governments formed OPEC in 1960. At first, OPEC enjoyed little success. But this changed in 1973, as the Arab-Israeli war heated up and the Arab countries banded together. On January 1, 1973, the price of oil was $2.12 per barrel. Of this $2.12, $1.52 went to the OPEC governments. By January 1, 1974, the price was $7.61 with $7.01 going to the governments. By January 1975, the price was about $10.50. By 1982, the price had risen to $35.00.

How did this cartel, which had been in existence since 1960, come to flex its muscles in 1973? At that time, importing governments helped by posting prices and dealing with OPEC in open forums, so individual members were less likely to chisel. More important, however, Saudi Arabia was willing to cut back its production of oil to allow other members to sell all they wanted to produce at the high prices set by the cartel.[5] In 1984, after production had to be cut back by 5 million barrels a day to prevent the cartel from collapsing, Saudi Arabia's willingness to bear this cost began to weaken.

The price of oil began to fall. The January 1984, price was $29 per barrel, down from the 1982 high of $35. The slide continued. In January 1987, the price was $13 per barrel. In January 1990, it was under $12 per barrel. As prices fell, chiseling became more common. The predictions made by economists in the 1970s that the cartel would eventually weaken started to come true. Some of the Persian Gulf countries, notably Kuwait, the United Arab Emirates, and Qatar, were experiencing cash flow problems. These countries started grandiose development schemes when their oil revenues were in excess of $300 billion per year. Their revenues fell significantly because of the decreased price, but the development projects still had to be paid for. Kuwait began shipping more oil than allowed by OPEC agreements—one of the factors underlying the Gulf War. In 1986, Nobel Prize winner Milton Friedman wrote an editorial entitled "Right at Last, an Expert's Dream" reminding readers that he had predicted in 1974 that OPEC would not last very long.[6]

As we pointed out earlier, all cartels face two problems. The first is chiseling, or secret price cutting. OPEC faced this problem in the presence of oil surpluses. The second problem a cartel faces is new entry. Large amounts of oil have been coming into the market from non-OPEC sources, such as the North Sea and Alaska. In addition, other sources of energy, such as solar and nuclear energy, which were uneconomical when oil was $2 per barrel, became profitable at the much higher prices. The new entry has been slow to develop, but the future should prove even more difficult for OPEC as new firms producing oil and other competing products enter the market and challenge the cartel's cohesiveness.

The impact of new oil supplies is evident in the statistics. In 1973, OPEC's share of world oil production was 56 percent. In 1975, its share was 51 percent. In 1980, it was 45 percent, and in 1984, it was 35 percent. In 1990, OPEC's share had fallen to 28 percent. This declining share of

5.   An interesting side issue is that much public criticism was leveled on the oil refining companies rather than the OPEC members. This is odd because the cartel profits are not going to the oil companies but to the governments of the OPEC member countries.
6.   Milton Friedman, "Right at Last, an Expert's Dream," *Newsweek* (10 March 1986): 8.

production signaled the weakening of the cartel better than any other piece of data. If a cartel is going to set prices, it must control a large share of total production.

In addition to the new oil supplies, the high oil prices have also had an effect on quantity demanded. The decade of OPEC's dominance resulted in adjustments in consumer demand. Perhaps the most evident of these adjustments is the increased fuel efficiency of automobiles.

INFORMAL MARKET COORDINATION

tacit collusion
Unorganized and unstated attempts by informally coordinated oligopolies to practice joint actions.

Informally coordinated oligopolies engage in unorganized and unstated attempts to practice joint actions. Such **tacit collusion** is much weaker than the collusion among members of a cartel. It is weaker because all the incentives to chisel are still present, but organized vigilance against chiseling is not. Tacit collusion is found in U.S. industries because cartels are illegal under federal antitrust laws. Informal cooperation among oligopolistic firms can be viewed as an attempt to form cartels while avoiding antitrust laws. Such collusion usually takes the form of informal agreements to behave in certain ways. Often these agreements arise naturally, without any need for formal organization. The most common form of tacit, informal agreement is based on price leadership.

price leadership
The form of tacit collusion in an oligopolistic industry in which one firm, the price leader, sets the price or initiates price changes and the other firms follow that lead.

dominant firm
The most influential firm in an industry, usually the largest firm.

PRICE LEADERSHIP. Price leadership is a form of tacit collusion in an oligopolistic industry in which one firm, the price leader, sets the price or initiates price changes and the other firms follow that lead. The firm that is the most influential in an industry is called the **dominant firm**. It may be either the largest firm or the lowest-cost firm. Price leadership is most effective where firms are few and have clearly similar products (for example, in the auto, cigarette, and steel industries). It helps if the demand for the product is price-inelastic since this will further discourage price cutting. When the demand curve for the product is perfectly inelastic, a firm that chisels on price will gain sales only at the expense of other firms. The lower price will not bring about additional sales for the industry. Thus, the conflict between firms will be sharper when demand is not very responsive to price cuts.

competitive fringe
The smaller competitors in informally coordinated markets with one large, dominant firm.

THE DOMINANT FIRM. In price leadership, the dominant firm sets a profit-maximizing price, and the other firms divide up the market at that price. The other firms, known as the **competitive fringe**, act much like firms in perfect competition. This result can be seen in Figure 7. The market demand curve for the product is D. The marginal cost curve of the dominant firm is MC_d, and the summation of all the other firms' marginal cost curves is MC_f. Those firms (the fringe) will make production decisions as price takers and will always produce where price is equal to their marginal cost. MC_f can thus be viewed as their supply curve. The demand curve that the dominant firm faces can be derived by subtracting the amount supplied by the fringe firms (MC_f) from the market demand curve (D). This subtraction gives the dominant firm's demand curve, D_d, and thus its marginal revenue curve, MR_d. The dominant firm will set a profit-maximizing price and output of P_1 and x_d. Once price P_1 is determined, the fringe firms view this price much as competitive firms view the market

Price, Cost

FIGURE 7
A DOMINANT FIRM WITH
A COMPETITIVE FRINGE
The dominant firm
views a part of the
market, D_d, as its own.
D_d is determined by
subtracting the supply
curve of the competitive
fringe, MC_f, from the
market demand, D. The
dominant firm produces
where $MC_d = MR_d$,
setting price P_1 and
producing x_d units. The
fringe firms face a
perfectly elastic demand
curve at P_1, and produce
x_f units (where
$P_1 = MR = MC_f$).

price. The fringe firms will produce x_f units at the market price P_1 because for them $P_1 = MR$ and they want to produce where $MR = MC_f$. The sum of the production of the dominant firm (x_d) and the production of the fringe firms (x_f) satisfies the market demand of x_m at price P_1.

This model of price leadership is applicable to the oil refining industry in the United States. There is a small group of dominant firms and a large number of small fringe firms. Price leadership by a dominant firm also appears to have prevailed at one time or another in the aluminum, automobile, and cigarette industries in the United States.

HISTORICAL PRICE LEADERSHIP. In a few cases, especially in mature industries, it is possible for a firm to emerge as the price leader because it is convenient for the other firms in the industry to follow the leader and thus coordinate their pricing. This type of price leadership, called historical price leadership, is very similar to cartel behavior. Its intent is collusion—to achieve industrywide profit maximization. Historical price lead-

---

CHARACTERISTICS OF OLIGOPOLY

- There are only a few sellers of homogeneous or differentiated products.
- Interdependence leads to attempts at communication, coordination, and collusion.
- Cartels may be formed to determine industry pricing and output.
- Price leadership may be used to coordinate industry pricing.
- The price leader may be a dominant firm.
- Nonprice competition increases product differentiation.

ership, however, is unorganized and thus not illegal in the United States. It was rampant within U.S. oligopolies. General Motors was the recognized price leader in autos, U.S. Steel in steel, and DuPont in chemicals. In the last ten years, the price leadership of these domestic oligopolies has been severely limited by foreign competition.

SUCCESSFUL PRICE LEADERSHIP. In order to be successful—that is, in order to raise industry profit levels—price leadership must produce a kind of cartel but still avoid legal sanctions. This means walking a tightrope. As the tacit collusion embodied in price leadership becomes successful, the incentive to chisel increases. As a result, most successful price leadership not involving a dominant firm occurs in industries in which there are only a few firms. The record of such tacit collusion shows that such industries are characterized by rigid prices. Price changes, when they occur, are generally small. Such industries are usually those that can blame price increases on rising costs and can punish firms that do not follow the price increase. The steel and auto industries are two examples. In these industries, potential chiselers know they cannot easily get away with not following the price leader.

THE GARY DINNERS. The way in which oligopolies can coordinate markets informally is clearly demonstrated by what have come to be known as the Gary Dinners. In 1901, U.S. Steel put together mergers that made it the dominant firm, supplying 65 percent of the domestic steel market. From 1907 to 1911, Judge Elbert H. Gary, chairman of the board of U.S. Steel, held a series of dinners for executives of competing companies. Gary explained that the close communication *and contact* developed at these dinners "generated such mutual *respect and affectionate regard* among steel industry leaders that all considered the obligation to cooperate and avoid destructive competition *more binding . . . than any written or verbal contract.*"[7] Efforts to prosecute U.S. Steel's behavior as an antitrust violation were unsuccessful.

In recent years, there haven't been any reported "informal" gatherings as effective as the Gary Dinners. However, trade associations, country clubs, and other such business and social gathering places can serve as forums for developing cooperative behavior among potential competitors.[8]

NO MARKET COORDINATION

Unorganized, uncollusive oligopolies are characterized by independent action. Firms in these oligopolies practice profit maximization independently but are affected by the actions and responses of their rivals. Each firm tries to anticipate the response of its rivals and then takes that prediction into account when making decisions. Economists tried to develop a model for this behavior in the early nineteenth century. In 1838, A. Augustin Cournot (1801–1877) published a theory of duopoly (a market

---

7.   F. M. Scherer, *Industrial Market Structure and Economic Performance* (Chicago: Rand McNally, 1980), 170. Italics indicate Judge Gary's actual words, taken from a government antitrust brief.
8.   Adam Smith recognized the potential for such collusion. Here is his famous statement on this subject from *The Wealth of Nations*: "People of the same trade seldom meet together, even for merriment and diversion, but the conversation ends in a conspiracy against the public, or in some contrivance to raise prices."

with only two firms). His theory and those that followed (up to the post–World War II period) were unsatisfactory because they assumed that the rival firm would not react to the action of the firm being analyzed. The post–World War II developments in oligopoly theory rest heavily on game theory. Game theory is a relatively new field of mathematics that can provide insights into oligopolistic behavior.

GAME THEORY. Game theory, a theory of rational decision making under conditions of uncertainty, was first developed by John von Neumann (1903–1957) and Oskar Morgenstern (1902-1977) in a book entitled *The Theory of Games and Economic Behavior*.[9] Game theory says that players try to reach an optimal position through strategic behavior that takes into account the anticipated moves of other players. This model describes very accurately how oligopolists behave.

Standard microeconomic decision-making theory is based on the assumption that the outcomes of various decisions are known with certainty. Game theory suggests rational solutions when the outcomes are uncertain. Games are usually described as being either zero-sum or non-zero-sum. Zero-sum games are those in which one player's gain is another player's loss. Non-zero-sum games open the door to collusion or cooperative action because all players may gain (or all may lose) from a certain course of action. This aspect of game theory has proved very useful in the study of oligopolies in which each firm must take into account the reactions of its competitors.

One of the most famous of non-zero-sum games is called the Prisoner's Dilemma. Two prisoners are interrogated separately. Each one knows that if neither confesses, both will go free. However, if one confesses and implicates the other, the one who confesses can go free and the other will be convicted. The interrogator separately offers each prisoner the opportunity to confess and go free. The rational course of action for the self-interested prisoner is to confess and implicate the other. Since both face the same incentive and the same uncertainty about the other's action, both will confess. The outcome of the two rational decisions will make both of the prisoners worse off. They would both be better off if they could engage in collusion. This lesson holds for oligopolistic firms.

THE KINKED DEMAND CURVE. One explanation of why prices in oligopolistic industries tend to be less flexible than prices in other market structures was presented by Paul Sweezy. Sweezy hypothesized that price rigidity exists because the firms in an oligopoly face a **kinked demand curve**. The demand curve has two sections because the firms come to believe that if they cut prices, their rivals will also do so. The price cut will not produce much of an increase in sales. A price increase, on the other hand, will not be imitated and will, therefore, result in a loss of sales for the firm making the increase. As a result, once a price is reached in an oligopoly, it tends to remain in effect for long periods.

game theory
A mathematical theory about rational decision making under conditions of uncertainty that can provide insight into oligopolistic behavior.

kinked demand curve
A demand curve with a bend in it at the price settled on in an oligopolistic industry because other firms' price cuts, but not price increases, are matched.

9.   For a detailed and highly mathematical treatment of game theory, see John von Neumann and Oskar Morgenstern, *The Theory of Games and Economic Behavior* (Princeton, NJ: Princeton University Press, 1949). For a short survey on game theory, see F. M. Scherer, *Industrial Market Structure and Economic Performance* (Chicago: Rand McNally, 1980), 160–166.

You can see the effect of a kinked demand curve by examining Figure 8. There is a kink in the demand curve D at point A (or at price P). Below point A, the other firms in the market will match any price decrease, making the demand curve relatively inelastic. A firm won't increase sales very much by decreasing price below P. Any increase in price above P will have the opposite effect. Competing firms will not match the increase. As a result, the demand curve above point A is relatively elastic. At the kink in the firm's demand curve, the corresponding marginal revenue curve, MR, is discontinuous. As you can see, MR has a break in it between B and C in Figure 8. This break allows a large variation in marginal cost with no effect on the profit-maximizing price, P, or output, x. For example, marginal cost could change from MC to MC_1 with no effect on price and output. Sweezy used this model to explain why prices were so rigid in oligopoly.

NONPRICE COMPETITION. All oligopolists, whether organized or unorganized, compete in dimensions other than just the price dimension. In formulating models, economists tend to treat goods as homogeneous and view competition as occurring mostly through price adjustments. In the real world, however, competition can take other forms. Firms can change the quality, color, texture, design, size, advertising, and a host of other attributes of a product.[10] Even an apparently homogeneous product can be differentiated by the quality of customer service.

OLIGOPOLY ADVERTISING. Casual observation leads to the conclusion that a great deal of the advertising on television is done by firms in oligopolistic

FIGURE 8
A KINKED DEMAND CURVE
In this model, the firm faces a kinked demand curve, D, because prices above P will not be matched and prices below P will be matched. The kink creates a discontinuity in the marginal revenue curve, which causes the price to be very rigid at the kink (P).

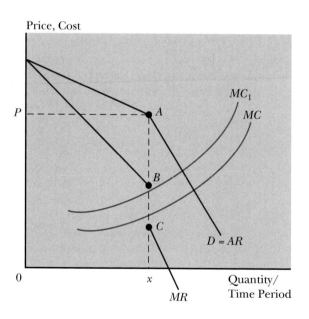

10. Sometimes quality changes substitute for price changes. For example, if the price of a candy bar remains at 45¢ but the amount of chocolate or nuts decreases, this change is equivalent to an increase in price. Oligopolists often engage in this kind of disguised price changing because it seems to provoke less response from rivals.

George Stigler and Paul Sweezy represent polar extremes in economic analysis. Both have written extensively in the field of industrial organization, but the similarities end there.

George Stigler is the personification of the Chicago School of free-enterprise capitalism. He received a bachelor's degree from the University of Washington, an MBA from Northwestern University, and a Ph.D. from the University of Chicago. In 1982, Stigler was awarded the Nobel Prize in economics. Paul Sweezy is an American Marxist. He has a B.A. degree and a Ph.D. in economics from Harvard University.

Both economists are coeditors of prestigious journals that are at opposite ends of the ideological spectrum. Stigler is coeditor of the *Journal of Political Economy*, and

Sweezy is coeditor of the *Monthly Review*. Stigler's views are best delineated in *The Theory of Price* (1966) and *Organization of Industry* (1968). Sweezy's views can be found in *The Dynamics of U.S. Capitalism* (1972), *Introduction to Socialism* (1968), and *Modern Capitalism and Other Essays* (1972).

Stigler and Sweezy have clashed over Sweezy's use of the kinked demand curve to explain why prices in oligopolies are more stable than prices in other market structures. This model has been severely criticized by Stigler, who argues that Sweezy's theory is wrong. Stigler says that Sweezy's claim that prices in an oligopoly are more stable than in other market structures does not stand up to real-world evidence.

markets. Most informational advertising is done on radio or in the print media. Most of the major ads on television appear to be aimed at a goal other than informing consumers.

There may be several economic goals of this advertising. George Stigler points out that institutional advertising, saying, for example, "our firm is the oldest or largest in the industry," is meant to convey to the consumer the comfort of reliability.[11] The idea is that the firm must treat consumers well or it wouldn't be large or old. **Name brand capital** is the value that consumers place on a product because of experience, reputation, or image. This name brand capital can be very important in terms of maintaining market share in the face of price (or quality) competition from new rivals that don't have it. In the extreme, name brand capital is a barrier to entry that may allow the firm to behave in a monopolistic fashion.

name brand capital
The value that consumers place on a product because of experience, reputation, or image.

Robert Wills and Willard Mueller have examined the effect of brand advertising on pricing in oligopolistic markets.[12] They were motivated in part by the fact that in some markets consumers show a preference for high-priced brands even though competing brands are physically identical. Brands of lemon juice concentrate, evaporated milk, and household bleach, for example, are exactly the same in every respect except packaging. In addition, blind taste tests of some products, such as beer and cookies, show that consumers often cannot distinguish their preferred brand from competing brands. The research by Wills and Mueller showed that monopoly power in such markets produces price premiums and higher profits. This monopoly power was created by advertising. They conclude that large firms will tend to advertise more heavily, have higher prices, *and* have higher profits than their smaller competitors.

An oligopolistic firm may resort to nonprice competition in an attempt to increase its market share. We can apply the model of oligopoly to these other types of competition. For example, a firm contemplating a new advertising program has to consider whether the program will increase its market share or prompt a rival to undertake a similar program. In the first case, the program may be worthwhile. In the second, it would probably only increase costs without creating a larger market share. Thus, even with respect to advertising, firms in an oligopoly are interdependent and need to consider the reactions of rivals.

FACTORS DETERMINING MARKET COORDINATION BY OLIGOPOLIES

As you have seen, there are benefits to be gained by oligopolists who can coordinate output and pricing, whether such coordination is formal or informal. There are strong forces pulling in opposite directions. It is worthwhile to review some variables that facilitate or limit such market coordination.

THE NUMBER OF FIRMS. The number of firms in an oligopoly has the most obvious impact on the likelihood of formal or informal market coordination. As the number of firms increases, the incentive and ability to coordinate diminish. In addition, as the number of firms increases, the cost of

---

11. George Stigler, *Memoirs of an Unregulated Economist* (New York: Basic Books, 1988), 81.
12. Robert L. Wills and Willard F. Mueller, "Brand Pricing and Advertising," *Southern Economic Journal* (October 1989): 383–395.

coordinating and policing the agreement increases. It is obvious that as the size of the group increases, the probability that it will include a maverick also increases. As the number of firms increases, the likelihood of effective coordination diminishes rapidly. Some economists have suggested that after the number of firms in a market reaches ten, it is likely that they will ignore each other's actions, making coordination impossible.[13]

BARRIERS TO ENTRY. Barriers to entry play a key role in determining market coordination because they are related to the number of firms. An oligopoly will not be able to practice effective coordination if it can't limit entry. New firms will destroy market coordination and erode any economic profit created by it. The lesson is a simple one. If strong barriers to entry (including barriers created by government) exist, the possibility of coordination exists. If barriers to entry are weak, coordination is highly unlikely.

THE SIZE OF FIRMS. If the oligopolistic industry is dominated by one firm, or if several of the firms are large relative to the others, the possibility of market coordination is enhanced. In such a case, coordination would only require agreement by the dominant firm or firms.

SECRECY. Coordination requires the elimination of secrecy so that uncooperative behavior can be punished. Monitoring chiseling is easier in an environment in which secret deals don't stay secret long. Government has often aided in market coordination by requiring the full disclosure of contract details.

UNSTABLE OR FLUCTUATING DEMAND. If demand fluctuates or is otherwise unstable, a firm in an oligopoly will have difficulty determining if changes in its demand are the result of market forces or, alternatively, the competitive behavior of a rival. As a result, unstable or fluctuating demand will make market coordination more difficult.

PRODUCT DIFFERENTIATION. The more homogeneous a product is, the easier it will be to coordinate the sale of that product. As product differences increase, firms will be unable to determine whether the price concessions of rivals are attempts to chisel or are due to actual differences in product characteristics.

INDUSTRY SOCIAL STRUCTURE. As you have already seen, the maturity of an industry can affect market coordination. The social structure of an industry is also important. Do the leaders know and trust each other? Do they get together at meetings? Do they play golf or engage in other recreational pursuits? If they do, coordination might be easier. Note, however, that socializing does not mean that entrepreneurs are not competitive. What appears to be cooperation may be a subterfuge for future chiseling on a coordinated effort. Remember, if an oligopolist can get all the oth-

13. See F. M. Scherer, *Industrial Market Structure and Economic Performance*, 3rd ed. (Boston: Houghton Mifflin, 1990).

ers in the market to agree and then can chisel on the agreement, it can be very profitable.

ANTITRUST ACTIVITY . The U.S. antitrust laws make collusion illegal. If these laws are vigorously enforced, it will make coordination more costly. The antitrust laws will serve to limit attempts at coordination.

MARKET STRUCTURES IN REVIEW

This chapter concludes the discussion of the four theoretical market structures. Table 1 summarizes some of the important characteristics that differentiate these market structures. The key to understanding the theory of the firm is a solid understanding of monopoly and perfect competition. Oligopoly and monopolistic competition expand the models of monopoly and perfect competition and, in effect, generalize from those models to real-world situations.

TABLE 1
SUMMARY OF MARKET STRUCTURES

TYPE	NUMBER OF FIRMS	PRODUCT DIFFERENTIATION	CONTROL OVER PRICE	TYPE OF NONPRICE COMPETITION	EXAMPLES
Perfect competition	Many	Homogeneous product	None	None	Financial markets
Monopolistic competition	Many	Slightly differentiated products	Some	Advertising and product differentiation	Retail trade and service industry
Oligopoly	Few	Homogeneous *or* differentiated products	Some to considerable (it depends)	Advertising and product differentiation	Auto and steel industries
Monopoly	One	Unique product (no close substitutes)	Considerable	Public relations	Some utilities and aluminum industry before 1945

SUMMARY

1. Monopolistic competition is a market structure characterized by many firms selling differentiated products.

2. Key assumptions in the model of monopolistic competition are a large number of producers, product differentiation, and relative ease of entry.

3. Economic profits can exist in the short run in this market structure, but entry of new firms will ensure a long-run equilibrium with zero economic profit.

4. Because of product differentiation, a monopolistically competitive firm at equilibrium produces less than the socially optimal output. The production facilities that are not used are referred to as excess capacity.

5. Monopolistically competitive firms produce a smaller output at a higher price than firms (with the same costs) engaged in perfect competition.

6. In long-run equilibrium in monopolistic competition, marginal cost is not equal to average cost.

7. Oligopoly is the market structure in which there are only a few firms competing imperfectly. Because there are so few firms in an oligopoly, they are interdependent. They take this interdependence into account in their economic decision making.

8. Oligopolies can be divided into three classes: those characterized by formalized market coordination (cartels), those characterized by informal market coordination, and those characterized by no market coordination.

9. Cartels are threatened by chiseling behavior on the part of individual members and by new entry. The larger the number of firms in a cartel, the more difficult it is for the cartel to hold together. Barriers to entry are thus important in oligopoly, just as they are in monopoly.

10. Successful cartels have often been supported by governments, which police chiseling behavior.

11. Price leadership is common in oligopolies where formalized market coordination is not possible. The price leader can be a dominant firm or, in mature industries, a historical leader.

12. Oligopolies are characterized by extensive use of nonprice competition.

13. Economic forces that work to limit coordination in oligopoly or to facilitate it pull in opposite directions.

NEW TERMS

monopolistic competition	oligopoly	coordination	dominant firm
differentiated product	shared monopoly	collusion	competitive fringe
product group	pure oligopoly	cartel	game theory
excess capacity	differentiated oligopoly	chiseling	kinked demand curve
nonprice competition	price clusters	tacit collusion	name brand capital
	communication	price leadership	

QUESTIONS FOR DISCUSSION

1. Firms in monopolistic competition earn only normal profit in the long run, unless they can successfully convince consumers that their product is different. List four examples of product differentiation. Do you think the differences are real, imagined, or created? Does product differentiation make any economic difference?

2. What are the differences between the model of perfect competition and the model of monopolistic competition? What assumption is different?

3. What is excess capacity? Is it a good or a bad thing?

4. Would you consider the National Collegiate Athletic Association (NCAA) a cartel? How do some universities (firms) chisel on the agreement? Why do they do this?

5. Explain how the expectation of new entry would limit cartel formation.

6. How would you expect the number of firms in a cartel to affect the probability of its success? Why?

7. In what sense is monopolistic competition like monopoly and in what sense is it like competition?

8. What does the kinked demand curve imply about the oligopolists' response to the pricing of rivals? What does the kinked demand curve say about prices in oligopolistic industries? On what grounds has this model been criticized?

9. How would you characterize the market in which the major television networks compete with each other? Are NBC, CBS, and ABC monopolists, oligopolists, or monopolistically competitive firms? How do they compete with one another?

10. Suppose advertising in an oligopolistic market does not increase the total volume of sales but only the distribution of sales among the oligopolistic firms. How does this fit with the Prisoner's Dilemma game?

11. How can changes in technology affect oligopoly? Reconsider your answer to Question 9 in light of this answer.

12. Some experts have predicted that the energy crisis will be back to haunt the United States by 1992 and that OPEC will again be an effective cartel. How would each of the following events affect the probability of OPEC becoming as powerful as it was from 1974 to 1982?

　a. Reforms in the Soviet Union permit the entry of Western oil companies to develop the vast Soviet oil reserves as joint ventures.

　b. Research on the accident at Chernobyl causes most Western governments to shut down all nuclear power plants.

　c. Environmental concerns over acid rain cause the United States to prohibit the burning of soft coal.

　d. The President authorizes an increase in California off-shore drilling.

　e. The international debts of some members of OPEC grow significantly.

13. Twenty years ago, the U.S. steel industry was a coordinated oligopoly. New technology now allows smaller steel producers to compete with the larger firms. What effect do you think this has had on labor unions in the steel industry?

14. How do oligopolies compete?

15. Figure 2 depicts the long-run equilibrium for monopolistic competition.

　a. What is the equilibrium rate of output?

　b. What is the equilibrium price?

　c. What is the average cost?

　d. What is average revenue?

　e. What is the level of profit?

　f. What output level is necessary to reach the least-cost combination?

　g. What is the level of excess capacity?

SUGGESTIONS FOR FURTHER READING

Breit, William, and Roger L. Ransom. *The Academic Scribblers: Economists in Collision*, 2nd ed. New York: Dryden Press, 1982. Covers the ideas of several of the economists discussed in this chapter.

Friedman, James W. *Oligopoly Theory.* New York: Cambridge University Press, 1984. A thorough study of oligopoly theory using numerical examples.

Scherer, F. M. *Industrial Market Structure and Economic Performance*, 3rd ed. Boston: Houghton Mifflin, 1990. A reference work on industrial organization, market structure, and antitrust that contains a good review of monopolistic competition and oligopoly theory.

1. Explain what a code number in the Standard Industrial Classification system means.
2. Identify the characteristics of the structure of an industry.
3. Discuss the merger movements of the 1980s and 1990s.
4. Calculate a concentration ratio and a Herfindahl Index for an industry.
5. Interpret a concentration ratio as an indication of monopoly power.
6. Describe the results of studies of the relationship between concentration and prices and between concentration and profits.
7. Diagram the regulation of monopoly power through price regulation and through taxation.
8. Calculate a Lerner Index and discuss its limitations as a tool of antitrust policy.
9. Identify and discuss the major events in the history of antitrust legislation.
10. Discuss the economic consequences of antitrust activity.
11. Discuss the nature of recent antitrust actions and conglomerate mergers.
12. Describe the public policy debate concerning competitiveness.

CHAPTER 26

THEORY IN THE REAL WORLD: REGULATION, DEREGULATION, AND ANTITRUST POLICY

INTRODUCTION

The preceding chapters examined four theoretical market structures. In this chapter, we will apply these models to the real world and examine the extent of monopoly power in U.S. industry. We will look at empirical industry studies to illustrate the real-world monopoly problem. **Industry studies** are investigations of specific industries to determine the degree of competitive behavior. This subfield of economics is sometimes referred to as industrial organization.

If an industry possesses some degree of monopoly power, it may be desirable to control or mitigate the worst effects of that power. Monopoly power could be reduced through antitrust action, monopoly profits could be taxed away, or the monopoly could be regulated and thus forced to behave in some prescribed fashion. In some cases, however, the answer might be to do nothing. This chapter will examine the theory and practice of regulation and the development of antitrust laws in the United States. It concludes with an assessment of the success of regulation and antitrust policy and an examination of recent trends in merger activity in U.S. industry.

industry studies
Investigations of specific industries to determine the degree of competitive behavior.

WHAT IS AN INDUSTRY?

We have, up to this point, been using the term *industry* without carefully defining it. In general, an **industry** is a group of firms producing the same, or at least similar, products. The difficulty with this definition is that it does not specify how dissimilar products must be before they are thought

industry
A group of firms that produce the same or similar products.

691

of as being produced in different industries. Consider containers. Are firms producing glass bottles and aluminum cans similar enough to be included in the container industry? How about firms making paper cups or even pewter mugs? Most consumers regard pewter mugs and paper cups as quite different. If you are willing to pay substantially more for a pewter mug than for a paper cup, you regard them as being distinct products. What about a plastic Ronald McDonald glass? Is it closer to a paper cup or a pewter mug? These questions demonstrate that whatever scope is assigned to an industry will be arbitrary to some extent. Some people, even some economists, may disagree with a classification of two products as belonging to the same industry or to different industries.

Cross elasticity of demand, a concept we discussed earlier, can be useful in determining whether products belong to the same industry. If the cross elasticity of demand between two products is positive, the goods are substitutes.[1] Goods that are close substitutes have a positive and very high cross elasticity of demand. If economists could agree on a value of this cross elasticity that would define goods as belonging to the same industry—again an arbitrary decision—they could use that number to draw the boundaries between industries.

The problem of assigning firms to industries is made even more difficult by the fact that some multiproduct firms produce a variety of goods that might be included in different industries. In which industry is a firm that produces coffee in addition to soap and cake mixes? General Electric produces goods as unrelated as jet engines and toasters. Informed judgments and somewhat arbitrary definitions are necessary in order to move from the world of theory into the real world of industry studies.

There is a standard set of data available from the U.S. government in which these judgments have already been made. The Commerce Department classifies firms according to the **Standard Industrial Classification (SIC) system**.[2] The SIC system divides the economy into about 400 industries and assigns them different four-digit code numbers. These four-digit industries can be combined into three-digit or two-digit industry groups or further differentiated into five-digit (or even seven-digit) product classes. Table 1 presents an example of how a code becomes more specific as more digits are added. The purpose of the SIC system is to provide a

Standard Industrial Classification (SIC) system
A code devised by the U.S. Census Bureau for classifying industries using about 400 four-digit numbers.

TABLE 1
SAMPLE CODES FROM THE
SIC SYSTEM

CODE	EXAMPLE	DESIGNATION	NAME
Two-digit	20	Major Industry Group	Food and kindred products
Three-digit	201	Industry Group	Meat products
Four-digit	2011	Industry	Meat-packing plants
Five-digit	20111	Product Class	Fresh beef

Source: U.S. Bureau of the Budget, *Standard Industrial Classification Manual* (Washington, DC: U.S. Government Printing Office, 1988).

1. E_{xy} = (percent change in quantity demanded of good x) / (percent change in price of good y).
2.   See U.S. Bureau of the Census, *Standard Industrial Classification Manual* (Washington, DC: U.S. Government Printing Office, 1988).

workable, consistent classification of U.S. industries. This system is used in studies cited in the remainder of this chapter.

INDUSTRY STRUCTURE

Once an industry has been defined, it is possible to determine its market structure, or where it lies on the spectrum from perfect competition to monopoly. The structure will depend on several characteristics of the industry. The degree of concentration and conditions of entry are especially important characteristics. Entry affects concentration because high barriers to entry result in a more concentrated industry.

CONCENTRATION RATIOS

Concentration refers to the extent to which a certain number of firms dominate sales in a given market. Measures of concentration have, for many years, been a major tool of industry studies. A **concentration ratio** is used by economists to provide a measure of the distribution of economic power among firms in an oligopolistic market. To calculate a concentration ratio, the economist lists all the firms having a particular four-digit SIC code in order of decreasing size. The next step is to calculate the percentage of that industry's total sales accounted for by a certain number of the largest firms.[3] For example, a four-firm concentration ratio measures the percentage of sales accounted for by the four largest firms in an industry. Other commonly used concentration ratios are for the largest firm, the three largest firms, the eight largest firms, and so on. Most industry studies employ four-firm ratios. Table 2 gives four-firm concentration ratios for a few industries.

It could be argued that the percentage of sales accounted for by the largest firms is not the best measure of concentration in an industry. Concentration ratios might instead be calculated using percentage of assets, percentage of employees, or value of shipments. The various measures of concentration are all closely related, however, so the choice of a ratio isn't crucial.

concentration ratio
A measure of the distribution of economic power among firms in an oligopolistic market.

PRODUCT	CONCENTRATION RATIO
Automobiles	94%
Chewing gum	93
Window glass	89
Sewing machines	82
Detergent (household)	80
Tires	71
Canned beer	66

TABLE 2
FOUR-FIRM
CONCENTRATION RATIOS
FOR SELECTED INDUSTRIES

Source: Federal Trade Commission, *Selected Statistical Series* (Washington, DC: U.S. Government Printing Office, 1990).

3. Prelaw students might anticipate a strategy for defense in antitrust cases—have the concentration ratios calculated on the basis of the most general category possible to ensure that any one firm has a small share of the sales in the industry.

The more concentrated an industry, the more likely it is that there will be a recognized interdependence and joint action of either a collusive or noncollusive nature. When the four-firm concentration ratio exceeds 50 percent, the degree of interdependence in the industry is likely to be very high.

BARRIERS TO ENTRY

Entry conditions are the second characteristic affecting market structure. If barriers to entry are high and the industry is highly concentrated, it is more likely that joint action can be undertaken to create monopoly profits. You saw earlier that cartels are very unstable and that economic profits will strongly attract new firms into the industry. If concentration is high and entry is blocked, the existing firms will be in a better position to restrict output, raise price, and maintain persistent profits.

THE HERFINDAHL INDEX

Herfindahl Index
A summed index of concentration that takes into account all the firms in an industry.

The U.S. Justice Department has been using the **Herfindahl Index,** a summed index of concentration, to replace the more traditional concentration ratios.[4] The Herfindahl Index takes into account the market shares of all of the firms in an industry, not just the market share of the few largest firms. Later in this chapter, we will look at how the Herfindahl Index was used by the Justice Department in the 1980s.

The Herfindahl Index is the sum of the squares of market shares in an industry. The formula for this sum is

$$H = (S_1)^2 + (S_2)^2 + \cdots + (S_n)^2,$$

where H is the Herfindahl Index and S_1 through S_n are the market shares of individual firms 1 through n. These market shares total 100 percent. An industry that had ten equal-sized firms each having 10 percent of the market would have a Herfindahl Index of 1000.

Table 3 shows how the Herfindahl Index is calculated for two industries and compares each index to a four-firm concentration ratio. Note

TABLE 3
SAMPLE CALCULATIONS OF THE HERFINDAHL INDEX

	INDUSTRY A			INDUSTRY B	
FIRM	MARKET SHARE (%)	SQUARE MARKET SHARE	FIRM	MARKET SHARE (%)	SQUARE MARKET SHARE
1	90	8100	1	24	576
2	2	4	2	24	576
3	2	4	3	24	576
4	2	4	4	24	576
5	1	1	5	1	1
6	1	1	6	1	1
7	1	1	7	1	1
8	1	1	8	1	1

Four-Firm Concentration Ratio = 96%. Herfindahl Index = 8116.

Four-Firm Concentration Ratio = 96%. Herfindahl Index = 2308.

4.   The Herfindahl Index was developed in 1950 by Orris Clemens Herfindahl in his Ph.D. dissertation at Columbia University.

that both industries have four-firm concentration ratios of 96 percent, but industry *A* has a much higher Herfindahl Index (8116) than industry *B* (2308). These Herfindahl Index values show that industry *A* is 3.5 times more concentrated than is industry *B*. The table demonstrates that the Herfindahl Index has a much higher value for industries that have a firm or group of firms that are relatively large. This higher value is the result of squaring the individual market shares to construct the index.

THE NUMBER EQUIVALENT

M. A. Adelman has developed another way to interpret the Herfindahl Index. The **number equivalent** is the reciprocal of the Herfindahl Index (1 divided by the value of the Herfindahl Index). It shows the theoretical number of equal-sized firms that should be found in an industry. Industry *A* in Table 3 should have 1.2 equal-sized firms, and industry *B* should have 4.3. Adelman would conclude that, *ceteris paribus,* industry *B* would be more competitive than industry *A* because *A* has a higher likelihood of collusion.

number equivalent
A measure of the theoretical number of equal-sized firms that should be found in an industry (the reciprocal of the Herfindahl Index).

CONCENTRATION AND PERFORMANCE

It might seem that the number of concentrated, oligopolistic industries in the U.S. economy is high. But just how concentrated is U.S. industry? And does the concentration make any difference? In other words, would you as a consumer be better off if U.S. industry were generally less concentrated and, thus, perhaps more competitive?

STUDIES OF CONCENTRATION TRENDS

Given the difficulty of defining industries and the fact that any classification scheme requires arbitrary judgments, it is not surprising that studies have reached widely differing conclusions on the degree and trend of concentration in U.S. industry. The studies can be divided roughly into three groups.

One group of studies, which investigated trends in concentration in the first half of the twentieth century, concluded that there had been a pronounced increase in industrial concentration in the United States. This group of studies is associated with and represented by the work of Gardiner Means. Means found that the percentage of total assets controlled by the 200 largest nonfinancial corporations in the United States increased from 33.3 percent to 54.8 percent between 1909 and 1933. In contrast, a second group of studies done more recently by the Federal Trade Commission (FTC) using the same method that Means used showed that the percentage of assets controlled by the 200 largest nonfinancial corporations has not changed since 1950.[5]

5.   Gardiner Means, National Resources Committee, *The Structure of the American Economy* (Washington, DC: U.S. Government Printing Office, 1939); Norman R. Collins and Lee E. Preston, "The Size Structure of the Largest Industrial Firms," *American Economic Review* (December 1961); Adolf A. Berle and Gardiner C. Means, *The Modern Corporation and Private Property* (New York: Macmillan, 1933); Richard Duke, "Trends in Aggregate Concentration," FTC Working Paper No. 61 (June 1982).

The studies that found increased concentration in the early part of the century were challenged in a third group of studies begun by G. Warren Nutter. Nutter argued that industrial concentration declined in the United States between 1901 and 1937. His studies were attacked on the grounds that they relied heavily on data from 1899, which he took as a starting point. Critics argued that these early numbers were suspect because of the poor quality of data for that period. Later, Nutter's study was updated and extended by Henry A. Einhorn.[6] Einhorn used Nutter's data for 1939 as a benchmark and sought to determine if concentration had changed between 1939 and 1958. Einhorn concluded that between 1939 and 1958, roughly 60 percent of national income was generated by firms producing in a competitive structure. The monopolistic sector declined slightly, and the governmental sector increased slightly. The conclusion of Nutter and Einhorn's research is that market concentration in the twentieth century has been surprisingly stable.

William Shepherd looked at a later period using a method similar to Nutter and Einhorn's.[7] Shepherd divided firms in the economy into pure monopoly, dominant firm, tight oligopoly, and effective competition. He then categorized firms according to these in 1939, 1958, and 1980. Shepherd concluded that there was a slight increase in effectively competitive firms between 1939 and 1958. He found a significant increase in competitiveness between 1958 and 1980. The share of effectively competitive firms increased from 56.3 percent in 1958 to 76.7 percent in 1980. Shepherd attributed this growth in effectively competitive firms to increased competition from imports, deregulation of U.S. industries (airlines, banking, and trucking), and government antitrust activity.

Can we draw any conclusions from these seemingly conflicting studies? At one extreme in the debate is the position that the level of monopoly power has been stable. At the other extreme is the position that concentration in U.S. industry increased dramatically in the early part of this century and then increased at a much slower pace since World War II.

Keep in mind that these measures of concentration are all aggregate measures. That is, they measure concentration at the national level. These measures may understate the degree of monopoly power in U.S. industries because they ignore or understate the power of local and regional monopolies. The food distribution industry is a good example. At the national level, there is a good deal of competition among supermarket chains. However, in some regions, the concentration ratios are much higher. In some smaller markets, there is a virtual monopoly. Thus, the national figures might lead to the conclusion that the industry is competitive, but the regional or local figures might suggest that the industry consists of a series of local monopolies.

THE MERGER WAVE OF THE LATE 1980s

Beginning in 1983, U.S. industry experienced what many observers think is the greatest reshuffling of corporate assets in its history. Between Jan-

6.   G. Warren Nutter and Henry A. Einhorn, *Enterprise Monopoly in the United States: 1899–1958* (New York: Columbia University Press, 1969).
7.   William G. Shepherd, "Causes of Increased Competition in the U.S. Economy 1939–1980," *Review of Economics and Statistics* (November 1982): 601–631.

uary 1983 and January 1987, 12,200 companies worth at least $490 billion changed hands. And this was just the beginning. In 1989, the fifty largest acquisitions, mergers, and recapitalizations set a record of $144 billion in combined value. In the 1980s, $1.3 trillion in assets of U.S. corporations were acquired, merged, or purchased.[8]

For the most part, the public and political leaders thought the merger wave was bad for the economy. In 1987, a Louis Harris poll indicated that "the American people are fed up with takeover raiders. Such types are viewed as little better than predators."[9] Most of the corporate raiders and many economists see the situation differently. They see takeovers as a catalyst that is necessary to shake up complacent managers. Often a company is completely restructured in the wake of a takeover or attempted takeover. Companies have eliminated whole levels of management after they are victims of a takeover or in order to prevent a takeover.

Business journalist Leonard Silk points out that the boards of directors of most public companies are not looking out for the stockholders because inside directors owe their careers to the CEO and the outside directors are usually close friends of the CEO.[10] Indeed, Michael Jensen has argued: "The publicly held corporation, the main engine of economic progress in the United States for a century, has outlived its usefulness."[11] Jensen believes that the merger movement of the 1980s was not a merger movement in the usual sense but, instead, an organizational revolution. He believes it is a positive step, because it will resolve the conflict inherent in a public corporation. This conflict is due to the separation of ownership and control that we discussed in the chapter on monopoly. It is the conflict over the control of corporate resources and the use of those resources.

A study by Randall Morck, Andrei Shleifer, and Robert Vishny showed that corporate boards of directors have not been the main force behind removing unresponsive managers in industries that have been performing poorly.[12] Instead, these corporate managers have been removed through hostile takeovers. This academic study confirms the anecdotal stories offered by corporate raiders.

THE MERGER WAVE OF THE EARLY 1990s?

As the decade of the 1980s ended, the activity in leveraged buyouts (LBOs) came to an end. The end was due to problems in the junk bond market, which meant that the raiders couldn't find financing for their deals. A second difficulty was the recession that began in 1990. Stephen Schwarzman, President of the Blackstone Group, commented: "When we look back on 1989, it will be the year the LBO party ended."[13] The wave

---

8. A detailed report of the fifty largest mergers and acquisitions in 1989 is found in *Fortune* (29 January 1990): 136–145. *Fortune* publishes an annual report (in January) of the preceding year's fifty largest mergers or acquisitions. *Business Week* reports on the two largest deals in each year of the decade, (15 January 1990): 52–57. It also profiles the ten best and the ten worst deals of the 1980s.

9. *Fortune* (27 April 1987): 10.

10. Leonard Silk, "On Outside Directors," *Business Month* (November 1989): 11–13.

11. Michael C. Jensen, *Harvard Business Review* (September/October 1989); 43.

12. Randall Morck, Andrei Shleifer, and Robert W. Vishny, "Alternative Mechanisms for Corporate Control," *American Economic Review* (September 1989): 842–852.

13. Christopher Knowlton, "Deals of the Year," *Fortune* (29 January 1990): 136.

of LBOs required the confluence of a strong economy, lower interest rates, and a lower stock market.

The LBO mania of the 1980s is expected to be replaced in the 1990s by friendly mergers of big firms in related industries. The criteria for these friendly mergers are reported to be bigness and synergy. There are signs that U.S. companies are becoming more interested in foreign acquisitions. Many of these friendly mergers have been transatlantic deals between U.S. firms and European firms in the same industry. Some of these mergers may be motivated by the fears of U.S. firms about being excluded from the European market after the European Community becomes fully integrated in 1992.

THE MARKET CONCENTRATION DOCTRINE

Since the merger movement of the 1980s probably increased concentration in U.S. industry to some degree, we should examine the assumption that concentration, *per se*, is undesirable. Industrial organization economists typically see a sequence relating (1) the structure of the industry to (2) the behavior of firms in that industry (conduct) and then to (3) the performance of the industry itself. According to this line of thought, a highly concentrated structure will produce the antisocial behavior and unsatisfactory performance of a monopoly. The industrial organization economist, therefore, examines the structure of an industry to predict price and output behavior. This structure-conduct-performance chain has been termed the market concentration doctrine.

market concentration doctrine
The hypothesis that the degree of concentration in an industry is a reliable index of monopoly power and that a high concentration ratio is likely to be associated with undesirable monopoly behavior.

The **market concentration doctrine** holds that the degree of concentration in an industry is a reliable index of monopoly power and that a high concentration ratio is likely to be associated with undesirable monopoly behavior. Strict application of this doctrine might lead policy makers to suggest antitrust action or some other form of control when concentration ratios reach a certain level. Before examining policy action against monopoly, let's first look at the observations underlying this doctrine.

Those who support the market concentration doctrine base their arguments primarily on two empirical observations. The first is that prices are more rigid (less flexible) in concentrated industries. The second is that profit rates and concentration are positively correlated. Supporters of this doctrine believe that both rigid prices and higher profit rates reflect the effects of the monopoly power that is associated with high degrees of concentration.

administered prices
Prices that are relatively rigid, or changed only infrequently.

ADMINISTERED PRICES. The lack of price flexibility in concentrated industries was first noted by Gardiner Means, whose findings were published in a famous monograph.[14] Looking at data from 1926 to 1933, he argued that price movements in different industries varied in frequency. In some industries, prices changed very often. In others, prices tended to be constant for relatively long periods of time. He labeled prices that were relatively rigid, or changed only infrequently, **administered prices**. Later he

---

14. Gardiner Means, *Industrial Prices and Their Relative Inflexibility*, Senate Document 13, 74th Congress, 1st Session (17 January 1935).

In 1992, the European market becomes unified. Most observers believe that this unification will produce an economic boom for the countries in the European Community (EC). There seems to be a move on the part of U.S. firms to merge with European firms to "protect" their ability to participate in this boom. U.S. firms want to merge with European firms in case the EC becomes more protectionist toward the United States and Japan.

According to business writer Joel Kotkin, however, not all business firms in the EC have been looking forward to 1992. Some firms are worried about the increased regulation and bureaucratization the unification is likely to bring. Regulation will shift from the individual national governments to the powerful 12,000-member EC bureaucracy in Brussels. These regulators are often referred to by their critics as "Eurocrats."

Small businesses are especially concerned about their future in a unified Europe. The Eurocrats appear to be insensitive to the concerns of small and medium-sized companies. Alexander Flach is a case in point. Mr. Flach does not fear competition. His German firm, Afri-Cola Bluch Corp., produces cola and has competed with Coca-Cola and PepsiCo in Europe for generations. Looking to 1992, Mr. Flach says, "I have no fears of open markets." What he is afraid of is the political power of the Eurocrats. He has already had problems from Brussels. Recent regulations of the Eurocrats established strict standards for listing the contents of soft-drink bottles. This regulation weighed more heavily on the small regional bottlers. Yet, when Mr. Flach tried to lobby in Brussels, he couldn't even get an appointment.

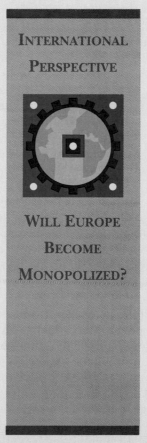

INTERNATIONAL
PERSPECTIVE

WILL EUROPE
BECOME
MONOPOLIZED?

Kotkin argues that what is the most disturbing to entrepreneurs in Europe is the mindset of the Eurocrat, a conviction that what Europe needs is larger, more centralized firms. This attitude worries European entrepreneurs, who believe that, in order to be competitive in a world market, they need to foster a competitive entrepreneurial economy. These entrepreneurs worry that if bigness prevails, it might promote a political move for protectionism within Europe. "Fortress Europe" would be the result, and the experiment with unification would lead to economic stagnation rather than economic growth.

Perhaps the concern is best summed up by Manfred Kotter, who owns a speciality metals shop in Mainz, Germany: "They say we are building a great market and economy. But so far it looks like we're doing it on the maps, not in our minds. We seem to be forgetting the role of competition in making this happen. A common market cannot be competitive if industries are dominated by two or three companies and by the bureaucrats. I wonder if we are capable of learning from the history of the past forty years."

Source: Adapted from Joel Kotkin, "Will Europe Blow It?" *INC.* (December 1989): 41–42.

demonstrated that administered prices were related to the degree of concentration in the industry.[15]

This early work by Means had a significant influence on discussions of public policy toward industry. As is usually the case, the data and methods used by both sides in the debate have been criticized. Competing researchers criticized Means's study because his data were gathered from reports submitted by firms to the Bureau of Labor Statistics. Since firms reported at different intervals, his reported price flexibility (or inflexibility) might simply have reflected a different frequency of reporting.[16] Other researchers claimed that the Bureau's data were composed of prices *asked* by firms and that the relevant data are prices *paid* by consumers.[17] In order to hide their price cuts from their competitors, firms in oligopolies often grant buyers secret cuts on posted prices. For this reason, there could be significant discrepancies between prices asked and prices paid.

Even though this issue of administered prices has been scrutinized by economists for some time, there hasn't been a scientific conclusion. The conventional wisdom that has become part of public policy debates is that there is a loose association between concentration and price inflexibility. The economist, however, in the capacity of scientist, would be hard put to prove this relationship.

CONCENTRATION AND PROFIT LEVELS. The second observation underlying the market concentration doctrine is that profits and concentration ratios are positively correlated. The theoretical explanation for this relationship is that a small number of firms finds it easier to behave collusively. The empirical link between concentration and profits began with the work of Joe Bain.[18] Bain found that profit rates and concentration ratios were positively correlated for a sample of forty-two manufacturing industries. Bain also found that when the concentration ratio exceeded 70 percent, there was a significant increase in average profit rates. George Stigler, on the other hand, conducted similar research and found there was no clear-cut relationship between concentration ratios and profit rates.[19] In his study, Stigler defined an industry as concentrated if the four-firm concentration ratio for the value of output exceeded 60 percent. Other studies examining this link concluded that there is a weak, but positive, relationship between concentration and profit rates.[20]

There has been debate about the tendency for profits to be higher in

15. National Resources Committee, *The Structure of the American Economy* (Washington, DC: U.S. Government Printing Office, 1939).
16. U.S. Congress, Joint Economic Committee, *Government Price Statistics*. Hearings before the Subcommittee on Economic Statistics of the Joint Economic Committee, 87th Congress, 1st Session (1961).
17. George J. Stigler and James K. Kindahl, *The Behavior of Industrial Prices* (New York: National Bureau of Economic Research, 1970).
18. Joe S. Bain, "Relation of Profit-Rate to Industry Concentration: American Manufacturing, 1936–1940," *Quarterly Journal of Economics* (August 1951).
19. George J. Stigler, *Capital and Rates of Return in Manufacturing* (Princeton, NJ: Princeton University Press, 1963).
20. For a review of these studies, see Harold Demsetz, *The Market Concentration Doctrine* (Washington, DC: American Enterprise Institute for Public Policy Research, 1975).

concentrated industries over the years. In 1967, President Johnson's Task Force on Antitrust Policy concluded that such a correlation exists:

The adverse effects of concentration on output and price find some confirmation in various studies that have been made of return on capital in major industries. These studies have found a close association between high levels of concentration and persistently high rates of return on capital. It is the persistence of high profits over extended time periods and over whole industries rather than in individual firms that suggests artificial restraints on output and the absence of fully effective competition. The correlation of evidence of this kind with very high levels of concentration appears to be significant.[21]

Bain's conclusion has also been challenged by Yale Brozen.[22] Brozen calculated more recent profit rates for the same industries considered in earlier studies. He found that, with the passage of time, there was a tendency for rates of profit in concentrated industries to converge with those of less concentrated industries. Rates of profit increased in the industries that previously had below-average profit levels and decreased in the industries with above-average profit levels.

DOES CONCENTRATION PREDICT PERFORMANCE? Thus, the relationship between concentration and profit levels, like the relationship betwen concentration and price rigidity, has been challenged. There appears to be some evidence to dispute the conventional wisdom that concentration ratios are a good predictor of monopoly performance, especially over time.

Why is this issue important? It is important because present policy proposals to reformulate antitrust law use market concentration as a guide. If concentration is made illegal because it is taken as an indicator of monopoly behavior and performance, many industries may be restructured by the courts simply because they are concentrated. If, instead, these industries are concentrated because there are economies of scale or because they have better, more aggressive managers or more innovation, why break them up? In such cases, antitrust activity would only serve to introduce inefficiencies into the market. In addition, many economists view the increase in concentration in the 1980s as a restructuring of corporate form rather than an increase in monopoly power.

In short, the challenges to the market concentration doctrine are significant enough to deserve closer examination. It is important that economists reach a scientific consensus on this important issue before policy makers take public action to restructure U.S. industry on the basis of a model that has not been empirically validated.

POLICIES AIMED AT REDUCING MONOPOLY POWER

In the remainder of this chapter, we will discuss policy aimed at correcting the problems associated with monopoly power. Even though there is

21. White House Task Force on Antitrust Policy, *Role of the Giant Corporation* (Washington, DC: U.S. Government Printing Office, 1967), 883.
22. Yale Brozen, "The Antitrust Task Force Deconcentration Recommendation," *Journal of Law and Economics* (October 1970): 279–292.

disagreement over the connection between concentration and monopoly behavior, for most policy decisions, a high level of concentration is taken as implying monopoly behavior.

THE CASE FOR MONOPOLY

In the chapter on monopoly, we examined in detail the costs associated with monopoly. The arguments in favor of policy against monopoly are based on a perceived need to reduce those costs. You should review the chapter on monopoly if you are unclear as to what those costs are. At least two arguments have been made in support of monopoly power. These arguments concern countervailing power and the promotion of technological progress.

countervailing power
The offsetting power possessed by both sides of the market in a monopoly.

COUNTERVAILING POWER. John Kenneth Galbraith has developed the notion of **countervailing power**. He argues that monopoly produces power on both sides of the market, and these two kinds of power countervail, or offset, each other. According to Galbraith, the U.S. economy is made up of big unions, big government, and big firms. In bargaining with each other, these big units are equally powerful. Although Galbraith did not develop the concept of countervailing power as a defense of monopoly, other economists have used it for that purpose.

This argument seems to make some sense. Concentrated tire manufacturers deal with concentrated automobile producers. Large retail chains purchase from concentrated industries that manufacture the products they sell, and labor unions are most successful in concentrated industries, such as steel, autos, and mining. Consumers are, however, left out of this process, as Galbraith points out. The costs associated with monopoly still hold for them. In essence, countervailing power redistributes the monopoly profit only among monopoly sellers, monopoly buyers, and monopoly unions.

INNOVATION. Some economists, most notably Austrian-born economist Joseph Schumpeter and John Kenneth Galbraith, have argued that monopoly, or at least oligopoly, is more conducive to technological innovation than competition is. They argue that the costs of monopoly power are offset by the dynamic innovation that monopolistic firms introduce into the economy. Schumpeter called his conclusion that monopoly power leads to innovation "shocking," since traditional analysis showed that monopoly would not be innovative because it did not face the pressure of competition.[23]

Years later Galbraith sounded the same theme, that monopoly power and bigness promote innovation:

In the modern industry shared by a few large firms, size and the rewards accruing to market power combine to insure that resources for research and technical development will be available. The power that enables the firm to have some influence on prices insures that the resulting gains will not be passed on to the public by imitators (who have stood none of the costs of development) before the outlay for de-

23. Joseph Schumpeter, *Capitalism, Socialism, and Democracy*, 2nd ed. (New York: Harper and Row, 1942), 81–82.

velopment can be recouped. In this way, market power protects the incentive to technical development.[24]

The argument that bigness allows a financial commitment to research and development seems logical. For years, General Electric advertised that progress was its most important product. But what are the facts? The facts, or more correctly the case histories, of invention and innovation are not so convincing. Researchers have found that the majority (as high as two-thirds) of important inventions are the products of individuals working independently and had no support from large research labs funded by giant corporations.[25]

MONOPOLY REGULATION

You have seen that monopoly power is present in the U.S. economy. For an optimal allocation of resources, monopoly is a bad thing. Society may decide that it is best to regulate rather than restructure a monopoly. Two common ways to do this are through price regulation and taxation.

MARGINAL COST PRICING

Consider the monopoly represented in Figure 1. The monopoly is maximizing its profits by producing output level Q_1 at price P_1. Assume that the government wants to force the firm to produce the amount that would

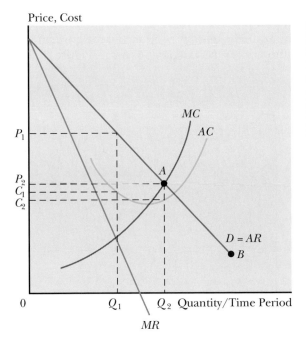

FIGURE 1
MARGINAL COST PRICING
If the regulator imposes a price of P_2, the monopoly would produce output level Q_2. Per-unit profits would decrease from $P_1 - C_1$ to $P_2 - C_2$.

24. John Kenneth Galbraith, *American Capitalism*, 2nd ed. (Boston: Houghton Mifflin, 1956), 86–87.
25. John Jewkes, David Sawers, and Richard Stillerman, *The Sources of Invention* (New York: St. Martin's Press, 1959).

be produced if this were a purely competitive market, that is, to produce where the marginal cost curve intersects the demand curve. If the government set a price ceiling of P_2, the monopoly would react by producing Q_2 units of output because the demand curve the monopoly would face would be represented by line P_2AD. The firm, as always, produces where $MR = MC$, and MR would be equal to line P_2A because demand is perfectly elastic for that line segment. The setting of such a price ceiling is sometimes called marginal cost pricing. **Marginal cost pricing** is a policy tool for forcing a monopoly to behave more like a competitive firm by regulating the monopoly price so that it is equal to marginal cost. Note that regulating monopoly in this way reduces per-unit profits from $P_1 - C_1$ to $P_2 - C_2$. Why not lower the price below P_2, since every decrease in price from P_1 to P_2 increases output even more? The problem is that for output levels greater than Q_2, every unit produced costs society more than it is willing to pay $(MC > P)$. This larger output is just as inefficient as monopoly behavior when $MC < P$, because the cost of an extra unit is less than society is willing to pay.

Now let's look at a more realistic example, a natural monopoly. Remember, a natural monopoly is one that results from a constantly declining average cost curve. In Figure 2, the profit-maximizing monopolist produces output level Q_1 at price P_1 and receives profit of $P_1 - C_1$ per unit. Now suppose a regulated price of P_2 is imposed on the monopolist. At P_2, it appears that the monopolist would increase output to Q_2. But note that at price P_2 and output level Q_2, the monopolist would lose $P_2 - C_2$ per unit sold. Price would be below average cost, so the monopolist would leave the industry. In other words, the optimal output from society's viewpoint would be where $MR = MC$, but this output would force losses on the monopolist.

The output Q_2 could, however, be feasibly produced if the government would make up the loss, the area of rectangle P_2C_2AB in Figure 2. The

marginal cost pricing
A policy tool for forcing a monopoly to behave more like a competitive firm by regulating the monopoly price so that it is equal to marginal cost.

FIGURE 2
MARGINAL COST PRICING AND LOSSES
If the regulator sets a price of P_2, the monopolist would lose $P_2 - C_2$ per unit of output sold. The monopolist would thus only produce if the regulator subsidizes it.

monopolist would then produce output level Q_2 at price P_2. The problem with this solution is that if the government subsidizes an industry out of general tax revenues, it is transferring income from taxpayers in general to the consumers of the good produced by the monopoly. Most people (except consumers of the good) would view such a transfer as an unfair redistribution of income. The trick, then, for the would-be price regulator is to set price equal to marginal cost at the point where the *MC* curve intersects the demand curve, but only if price is equal to or greater than average cost for that level of output. This might not be possible in the case of a natural monopoly.

TAXATION OF MONOPOLISTS

Another approach is to use a tax to regulate monopoly power. Suppose government officials impose a license fee (tax) on the monopolist. In Figure 3, before the tax, the monopolist is producing output level Q_1 at price P_1. The average cost curve is AC_1. The monopolist is earning profits of $P_1 - C_1$ per unit. If the monopolist is charged a fee for the right to do business, the fee represents an increase in its fixed cost, but no change in variable or marginal cost. The *AC* curve shifts up by the amount of the fee, to AC_2 in Figure 3. The monopolist still maximizes profits by producing output level Q_1 at price P_1, but profits have been reduced to $P_1 - C_2$ per unit. Note that it is possible to set the fee so as to capture all the monopoly profit and shift average cost to AC_3 in Figure 3. However, no increase in output would occur.

There are practical difficulties with both methods of regulating monopoly, and they have quite different effects. Price regulation can cause the monopolist to produce the competitive output at a lower price.

FIGURE 3
TAXING A MONOPOLIST
A license fee will be viewed by a monopolist as a fixed cost and will increase average cost but not marginal cost. The monopoly profit can be taxed away with no effect on output.

Taxation, on the other hand, leaves price and output unchanged. A tax simply captures the monopoly profit for the public coffers. It should be clear, then, that for optimal allocation of resources, price regulation is preferred because it increases output and lowers price. Taxation only corrects for the effect of monopoly on the distribution of income. The monopoly profit goes to the government instead of the monopolist and is spent on governmental projects. In this case, there is still an impact on the distribution of income because consumers will be paying "too much" for the product.

THE LERNER INDEX OF MONOPOLY POWER

Lerner Index of Monopoly Power (LMP)
An index that evaluates the gap between price and marginal cost as a measure of monopoly power.

The theory of regulation just discussed suggested a policy of marginal cost pricing as one way to correct for the misallocation of resources by a monopoly. That suggestion is based on the theoretical notion presented in the last two chapters that the degree of monopoly power is measured by the gap between marginal cost and price. Using this concept, Abba P. Lerner developed an index to measure monopoly power. The **Lerner Index of Monopoly Power (LMP)** evaluates the gap between price and marginal cost as a measure of monopoly power. The index is calculated as follows:

$$\text{LMP} = \frac{\text{price } - \text{ marginal cost}}{\text{price}}.$$

In a purely competitive industry, LMP would be zero because price would equal marginal cost. If monopoly power is present, LMP takes on positive values because price will exceed marginal cost. As the gap between price and marginal cost increases, the value of the index rises. Using LMP values permits a researcher to compare the monopoly power of firms.

The LMP is a valuable theoretical tool, but the difficulty of determining marginal cost limits its value in empirical work. If average cost data are used to approximate marginal cost data, the results will be misleading. Purely competitive firms might even appear to have monopoly power in the short run because price could be greater than average cost and at the same time equal to marginal cost.

REGULATION IN PRACTICE

cost-plus pricing
The form of price regulation that allows firms a markup that is a percentage of average costs of production.

Attempts at regulation often increase the power of oligopolies as the regulatory bodies are "captured" by the industry. The firms use the regulation to create barriers to entry, thus increasing their monopoly power. Even if regulators are pursuing the public interest in setting prices to regulate monopoly power, they may not be able to determine marginal costs. They must, in that case, turn to the alternative of regulating price on the basis of average cost information. Although it may not be the most efficient solution, such average cost pricing solves "the problem" of natural monopoly illustrated in Figure 2.

The usual practice is to allow the firm a markup that is a percentage of average costs of production. This most common form of price regulation is referred to as **cost-plus pricing**. This type of regulation creates some distortions. If the monopolist is allowed to charge a price, say, 10 percent above its average cost, it has less incentive to minimize costs. However, consumer demand gives the firm some incentive not to let price get too high.

Perhaps the best example of this form of regulation is in the present regulatory environment for utilities—electricity, gas, water, and so forth. Since utilities are considered natural monopolies, they are regulated for the public interest. Such regulation is based on cost-plus pricing. The markup is often called a fair rate of return. A **fair rate of return** is the normal profit that a regulated industry must earn in order to stay in business. Under such a regulatory policy, utilities have less incentive to cut costs than profit-oriented firms do. For those firms, profits increase whenever costs decrease.

fair rate of return
The normal profit that a regulated industry must earn in order to stay in business.

Some communities have debated whether utilities should be allowed to advertise their products. The argument against such advertising is that it simply raises average costs and results in higher prices to consumers. The argument in favor of such advertising is that it usually increases demand, which leads to more output at lower average cost and thus lower prices. The analysis here tends to support the first argument. Interestingly, the assumption of self-interested behavior would predict that a certain group in the community would support utility advertising. Any guesses? Of course, it would be the news media. The news media have strongly supported utility advertising, often on the grounds of free speech.

Regulation not only makes a firm less cost-conscious, but can also raise the actual cost of doing business. The costs of compliance (and noncompliance) with regulation could mean that less is produced at higher prices because costs are higher. In this case, regulation does not promote the goal of making monopolies produce a larger output. Regulation is also rarely limited to price regulation. Most often, regulatory bodies interfere in a wide range of the firm's decisions. Regulation often changes the firm into a quasi-governmental firm, rather than a firm that is responsive to market forces.

ANTITRUST LAWS IN THE UNITED STATES

Toward the end of the nineteenth century, there was a substantial increase in the number of large business organizations in the United States. This period saw the establishment of legal arrangements such as **trusts**, which were organizations set up to control the stock of other companies through boards of trustees, and **holding companies**, which were firms set up for the sole purpose of owning and thus controlling other firms. Trusts and holding companies enabled robber barons, as they have been called by economic historians, to control and coordinate the activities of many previously independent firms. At first, these new types of companies were viewed as a natural outgrowth of the Industrial Revolution in the United States.

trusts
Organizations set up to control the stock of other companies through boards of trustees.

holding companies
Firms set up for the sole purpose of owning and thus controlling other firms.

Eventually the public began to view some of these arrangements with suspicion. One of the earliest groups organized to oppose the trust movement was the National Grange. The Grange was a farm-based group or-

Sherman Antitrust Act
The first federal antitrust law in the United States, passed in 1890. Section 1 of the act declared every contract, combination, or conspiracy in restraint of trade to be illegal. Section 2 made it illegal to monopolize or attempt to monopolize.

Clayton Act
Federal law, passed in 1914, prohibiting the acquisition of the stock of a competing company if such an acquisition would "substantially lessen competition."

tying contracts
Agreements between producers and retailers that call for the retailer to stock certain items in return for being allowed to stock other items.

Robinson-Patman Act
A federal law that amended the Clayton Act in 1936, making predatory pricing illegal.

predatory pricing
The act of selling below cost to destroy competitors.

Celler-Kefauver Antimerger Act
A federal law that strengthened the Clayton Act in 1950 by making it illegal in certain circumstances for a firm to merge with another by purchasing its assets.

ganized in 1867 to oppose trusts. The efforts were mainly directed at the railroad trust, because of the high monopoly prices it set and also because it was able to practice price discrimination in the hauling of agricultural products.

In response to the Grange and other political movements against trusts, several states enacted antitrust statutes that regulated businesses chartered in those states. These state laws failed because corporations were able to obtain charters in less restrictive states. Two of the more lenient states were New Jersey and Delaware. By 1888, the antitrust sentiment had become so widespread and intense that both national political parties had an antitrust plank in their platforms.

In 1890, Congress passed the **Sherman Antitrust Act**, the first federal antitrust law. This act had two major provisions. Section 1 declared every contract, combination, or conspiracy in restraint of trade to be illegal. Section 2 made it illegal to monopolize or attempt to monopolize.[26] The language of the act is strong, but it is also vague, and the courts took years to determine its scope. We will trace some of the important decisions, after identifying the other major antitrust laws.

The **Clayton Act**, passed in 1914, made illegal certain business practices that could lead to monopoly. It prohibited a company from acquiring the stock of a competing company if such an acquisition would "substantially lessen competition." The act also prohibited tying contracts and price discrimination. **Tying contracts** are agreements between producers and retailers that call for the retailer to stock certain items in return for being allowed to stock other items. In 1936, the **Robinson-Patman Act** amended the Clayton Act to make predatory pricing illegal. **Predatory pricing** is selling below cost to destroy competitors. Although the Clayton Act prohibited the acquisition of competing firms through stock purchase, firms could get around this obstacle because the law did not prohibit acquisition of physical assets. The **Celler-Kefauver Antimerger Act**, passed in 1950, made it illegal in certain circumstances for a firm to merge with another by purchasing its assets. This act strengthened the Clayton Act.

In 1914, Congress passed the **Federal Trade Commission Act**. This act set up the Federal Trade Commission (FTC) to police unfair and deceptive business practices. Initially, the FTC had many powers, but in 1919 the Supreme Court denied it the power to issue cease and desist orders without judicial review. In 1938, the FTC Act was amended by the **Wheeler-Lea Act**, which added "unfair or deceptive acts or practices in commerce" to the list of transgressions. The **Hart-Scott-Rodino Antitrust Improvement Act** further amended the FTC Act in 1970. It required firms contemplating a merger or acquisition to notify the FTC and the Department of Justice before carrying it out.[27]

---

26. "Section 1: Every contract, combination in the form of trust or otherwise, or conspiracy, in restraint of trade or commerce among the several States, or with foreign nations, is declared to be illegal.... Section 2: Every person who shall monopolize, or attempt to monopolize, or combine or conspire with any other person or persons, to monopolize any part of the trade or commerce among the several States, or with foreign nations, shall be deemed guilty of a misdemeanor." (Sherman Antitrust Act, Sec. 1, 26 Stat. 209, 1890).
27. For more detail on all these laws, see J. G. Van Cise, *Understanding the Antitrust Laws* (New York: Practicing Law Institute, 1973).

Antitrust activity like that in the United States is not found in most other countries. Interestingly, after World War II, the U.S. government imposed antitrust policies on the defeated powers, Japan and Germany. Occupation forces set up new governments in Germany and Japan and imposed stringent antitrust measures aimed at deconcentrating industry. There were two stated goals. The first was to punish leading industrial groups for their wartime efforts, and the second was to weaken the German and Japanese industrial base so that those countries would be less able to pursue future wars.

This second objective was inconsistent with domestic antitrust policy in the United States at the time. Domestic policy was to pursue antitrust actions to limit monopoly power and make the U.S. economy *more* efficient. At the same time, foreign policy was to break up German and Japanese trusts to make them *less* efficient. After the United States decided that Japan and Germany should be allowed to grow economically, to counter Soviet expansion in the Cold War period, the first policy changed was the antitrust policy. One might legitimately ask what caused policy makers to view concentration as good for Germany and Japan and bad for the United States.

International Perspective

Antitrust Abroad

Except for the vigorous antitrust policy imposed temporarily on Germany and Japan, there have been no antitrust laws in other countries that are concentration-based and result in divestiture. In the mid-1970s, there was vigorous debate about proposed legislation for divestiture in Japan, but it was not enacted. Japan's trading conglomerates, called *sogo shosha*, are informal associations of industrial, financial, and commercial companies. They could not exist under U.S. antitrust laws.

Much of the relevant law in Europe is based on the Treaty of Rome, which established the European Economic Community. Individual countries tend to monitor the activities of "market-dominating" firms and regulate their price-setting ability. The emphasis is not on breaking up monopolies or potential monopolies but rather on preventing the abuse of any market power. A typical remedy is a price rollback and a requirement of government approval of future price increases. European governments often monitor the prices, costs, and profit rates of large firms.

Federal Trade Commission Act
A federal law passed in 1914 that set up the Federal Trade Commission (FTC) to police unfair and deceptive business practices.

Wheeler-Lea Act
A 1938 federal law amending the FTC Act to make unfair or deceptive acts or practices in commerce illegal.

Hart-Scott-Rodino Antitrust Improvement Act
A 1970 federal law amending the FTC Act to require firms to report mergers or acquisitions to the FTC and Department of Justice before the fact.

UNITED STATES ANTITRUST LAWS

ACT AND YEAR PASSED	MAJOR PROVISION(S)
• Sherman Antitrust Act (1890)	Makes it illegal to monopolize or attempt to monopolize. Makes contracts, combinations, or conspiracies in restraint of trade illegal.
• Clayton Act (1914)	Prohibits the acquisition of the stock of another company if that action will substantially lessen competition. Prohibits tying contracts and price discrimination.
• Robinson-Patman Act (1936)	Amendment to the Clayton Act that makes predatory pricing illegal.
• Celler-Kefauver Antimerger Act (1950)	Amendment to the Clayton Act that makes it illegal to purchase the assets of another company if that action will substantially lessen competition.
• Federal Trade Commission Act (1914)	Established the FTC to police unfair and deceptive business practices.
• Wheeler-Lea Act (1938)	Amendment to the FTC Act that makes unfair or deceptive trade practices illegal.
• Hart-Scott-Rodino Antitrust Improvement Act (1970)	Requires that the FTC and Justice Department be notified prior to mergers or acquisitions.

THE HISTORY OF ANTITRUST ENFORCEMENT

It took some time for the courts to determine the scope of the Sherman Act, in particular, to form a legal definition of the phrase "in restraint of trade." Under a strict economic definition, a firm with any monopoly power (that is, power to restrict output or to increase price) would be guilty of restraint of trade. In two famous cases against Standard Oil and American Tobacco in 1911, the Supreme Court interpreted the law using the rule of reason, which said that monopolies that behaved well were not illegal. In effect, the Court defined—some might say rewrote—the Sherman Antitrust Act to make only "unreasonable" restraints of trade illegal. The test of reasonableness was itself difficult to define. The Court held that the existence of competitors was sufficient to demonstrate reasonable behavior. In 1920, U.S. Steel, despite its dominance of the steel industry, was found not to be an unreasonable monopoly. The Court stated that the law did not make mere size an offense.

In 1945, after thirteen years of litigation, the rule of reason was dropped. Judge Learned Hand ruled in a case against Alcoa that size itself *was* enough to prove the exercise of monopoly power. The change was so fundamental that the ruling became known as the "new Sherman Act." The Alcoa case was based on estimates of market power and structural aspects of the industry. In such cases, the way in which an industry is defined is extremely important. In fact, to a large degree it determines defense and prosecution strategies. As you might guess, the defense would prefer the industry to be broadly defined, both geographically and by the number of products included, since that definition tends to reduce the importance of any one firm in any particular industry.[28]

The DuPont Cellophane case in 1956 gave further indication of what the courts thought about markets. The Justice Department filed suit against DuPont for monopolizing the cellophane market because the company controlled 75 percent of U.S. sales. DuPont's lawyers successfully argued that the relevant market was not that for cellophane only, but rather that for flexible wrapping materials. These included waxed paper, aluminum foil, and vegetable parchment. The court said that products that are "reasonably interchangeable" must be included in the definition of a market. DuPont controlled only 20 percent of the market for a "reasonably interchangeable" set of wrapping products.

In 1982, the Justice Department's case against IBM, initiated in 1969, was dismissed. The case began when the Justice Department accused IBM of monopolizing the "general-purpose computer and peripheral-equipment industry." In 1969, IBM controlled 70 percent of the large mainframe computer market and 40 percent of the office equipment market. When the case was dismissed, IBM still controlled 70 percent of the mainframe computer market but was experiencing strong competition in office equipment and microcomputers. This case, like the others, centered on market share and the definition of the industry or market. The trend seems to be toward defining markets in a much broader way.

Another significant change in antitrust activity took place much more recently. The Sherman Antitrust Act provides that private parties who are victims of monopoly under Sections 1 and 2 are entitled to sue for treble damages. In other words, if a firm is convicted under the Sherman Antitrust Act, individuals can recover three times the damages they have sustained. Historically, it was seldom invoked. Recently, however, consumer groups have brought many class action lawsuits under the provisions of the antitrust laws. Consumer groups bring action on behalf of the entire class of consumers, and treble damages in these cases can be very large.

Although the courts have made some significant changes in enforcement, they can only rule on cases brought before them. In general, very few antitrust cases have been brought by damaged firms or individuals. This raises an important question: Who initiates most antitrust cases? The decision on whether to bring charges or not rests largely with the Antitrust Division of the Department of Justice. This decision is made by a presidential appointee, the assistant attorney general for antitrust. Antitrust policy therefore reflects the wishes of the President. Theodore Roosevelt campaigned as the great "trust-buster." When he became President, he set up the Antitrust Division, and his administration brought the first cases.

Franklin Roosevelt's first term saw virtually no activity on the antitrust scene. On the contrary, in the early years of the Depression, the federal

---

28. For some examples of the ridiculous lengths to which defense lawyers will go in defining the relevant market, see Franklin M. Fisher, "Diagnosing Monopoly," *Quarterly Review of Economics and Business* (Summer 1979): 7–33.

government actually fostered anticompetitive practices through the National Recovery Administration (NRA). The **National Recovery Administration (NRA)** was a major New Deal program aimed at business recovery. It allowed and encouraged agreements between firms. It set up cartels in virtually every industry, but they eventually were declared unconstitutional. In 1937, the Roosevelt administration changed its position and vigorously pursued antitrust cases, including the Alcoa case, which ultimately reversed the rule of reason.

Both the Eisenhower and Kennedy administrations pursued active antitrust programs. Johnson's administration retreated from vigorous antitrust policy, although the IBM case was filed at the end of his term in office. Nixon's first assistant attorney general, Richard McLaren, worked at restricting conglomerate mergers (in which a company buys a firm unrelated to its existing business). The Ford administration pursued an active antitrust policy. A major case was launched against AT&T, and many price-fixing cases were filed.

Carter appointees promised to use the antitrust laws to change the concentration of power. They also promised to attack shared monopolies (in which very few firms control an industry) and to speed up the litigation process so cases would not drag on for years. Very little was accomplished along these lines during Carter's tenure.

In 1980, Reagan's appointees made it clear that they did not equate big business with bad business practices. William Baxter, Reagan's first assistant attorney general for antitrust, believed that the purpose of antitrust activity should be to promote efficiency. To this end, Baxter argued that government should not interfere with most vertical mergers (mergers in which a company acquires other firms involved in different stages of production in the same production process). He also felt that conglomerate mergers should be allowed. Baxter argued that vertical mergers and conglomerate mergers seldom foster price fixing and do not reduce competition. On the other hand, Baxter approved of tough action against horizontal mergers (in which a firm acquires a competitor).

Baxter changed many of the practices of the Antitrust Division, dropping the Nixon administration's attack on conglomerates and the Carter administration's attack on shared monopoly. Reagan's first chair of the FTC, James C. Miller III, engineered a similar policy change there. These policy changes encouraged the merger movement of the 1980s. Most observers feel that many of those mergers would never have been permitted by previous administrations.

In 1986, the policies of the Reagan administration were supported by the Supreme Court, which ruled that antitrust laws were not meant to prevent mergers just because they create larger, more formidable competitors. The Supreme Court overturned two lower court decisions in allowing Cargill to buy Spencer Beef, combining the second and third largest beef packing companies.

When George Bush was elected President in 1988, it was believed that his administration would follow the laissez-faire policies of the Reagan administration. However, by 1990, it became clear that the policies of the Bush administration were decidedly different from those of the Reagan administration. The business news was full of reports with headlines such as "Return of the Big Stick" and "Psst! The Trustbusters Are Back in Town."[29] President Bush's chief antitrust appointees, Janet D. Steiger, chair of the FTC, and James F. Rill, assistant attorney general for antitrust, have expressed skepticism about the Reagan view that bigness means efficiency and will benefit consumers. They have been stepping up antitrust and regulatory activity.

In the Reagan era, the FTC stayed out of most merger proposals. In late 1988, executives at Winn-Dixie tried to increase their market share in Florida by buying U-Save Supermarkets. Under Reagan, this purchase would not have been challenged by the FTC, but Steiger demanded so much data from Winn-Dixie that the merger was abandoned in early 1990. Increased FTC scrutiny will surely discourage mergers in the 1990s. The FTC is also investigating U.S. subsidiaries of foreign corporations. For example, Steiger announced in early 1990 that the FTC would investigate Toyota, Nissan, and Honda to determine if they are violating antitrust laws by favoring Japanese suppliers of parts for their American-produced cars.

At the Justice Department, antitrust activity is being extended to deal with countries that exclude U.S. imports. Rill has participated in trade talks between the United States and Japan and is examining ways in which U.S. law can be used to strike at bid rigging in Japan. It is argued that this bid rigging hurts U.S. exports of semiconductors, wood products, and other goods to Japan.

THE ROLE OF ECONOMIC VARIABLES IN FILING CASES

Economists and lawyers have used statistical analysis to study case-bringing activity of the Justice Department. The first such study, by Richard Posner, found that in the first eight decades of the Sherman Act, 1,551 cases were brought by the Justice Department.[30] Antitrust activity can also be initiated by the FTC and even by private citizens. Posner found that, contrary to popular belief, the antimonopoly activity of the FTC has not increased over time. However, the number of cases brought by private citizens has increased continuously since 1949.

Antitrust enforcement by the states has also been stepped up. This change, in part, resulted from a 1976 law that allows state attorneys general to sue suspected price fixers for treble damages on behalf of citizens. Politics often influence the use of this power. State attorneys general are often campaigning for re-election or for higher office. They will bring lawsuits for publicity value but will be careful to avoid suits against powerful groups that may help them in future elections. Cases are often brought against out-of-state firms. This approach creates good publicity but doesn't damage the attorney general's support from in-state businesses.

Although many antitrust cases last as long as five and six years, the success rate of the Justice Department is very high. The success rate is much lower for FTC and private cases. However, the remedies the court imposes have been far from successful in terms of restoring competition. In civil cases, the remedy has often taken the form of regulation. The goal of anti-

29. "Return of the Big Stick," *U.S. News & World Report* (4 June 1990): 54; "Psst! The Trustbusters Are Back in Town," *Business Week* (25 June 1990): 64.
30. Richard A. Posner, "A Statistical Study of Antitrust Enforcement," *Journal of Law and Economics* (October 1970).

trust activity is restoring competition, but regulation is in fact an admission that competition cannot be restored. The problems that regulation introduces make it a very unsatisfactory remedy. Criminal cases have resulted in very weak penalties for those found guilty. Not until the late 1950s was an individual sentenced to jail for price fixing. In 1960, seven more executives were sentenced to jail. In the few cases in which sentences have been imposed, the terms have been very short. In addition, the fines levied have been too small to have much of a deterrent effect.

Posner's study spawned some attempts to examine the determinants of antitrust activity. Posner pointed out that the level of antitrust activity and the kinds of cases did not seem to be related to economic conditions in the country. He also found that the political party of the President does not seem to affect the number of cases initiated. This, of course, does not mean that politics does not affect the Justice Department's antitrust activity. It only means that the amount of political interference has not, on the average, been too much affected by which party holds the presidency.

William Long, Richard Schramm, and Robert Tollison analyzed case-bringing patterns of the Justice Department and found that cases were more likely to be brought in larger industries, measured by sales.[31] Other variables that may more meaningfully indicate monopoly power, such as profit rates on sales and concentration, were found to be less important in explaining Justice Department cases. John Siegfried has found that economic variables have little influence on the kinds of cases filed by the Justice Department.[32] The work of Siegfried and Peter Asch suggests that the case-bringing criteria of the Justice Department are complex and difficult to forecast using economic variables.[33] The limited role of economic considerations is probably not surprising, since the Justice Department is staffed by lawyers rather than economists.

THE ECONOMIC CONSEQUENCES OF ANTITRUST ACTIVITY

In addition to looking for an economic explanation of antitrust activity, economists have begun to examine its economic consequences. Several of these empirical studies are informative. Peter Asch and J. J. Seneca found that firms that were known to be engaged in collusion were, surprisingly, less profitable than firms that were not known to be in collusion.[34] Robert Feinberg argued that these results were actually due to the deterrent effect of antitrust cases.[35] Dosoung Choi and George Philippatos found that the filing of antitrust cases caused restraint in pricing but that this restraint decreased with the number of times the firm had been indicted.[36] This finding implies a diminishing return to bringing cases

---

31. William F. Long, Richard Schramm, and Robert Tollison, "Economic Determinants of Antitrust Activity," *Journal of Law and Economics* (October 1973).
32. John J. Siegfried, "The Determinants of Antitrust Activity," *Journal of Law and Economics* (October 1975).
33. Peter Asch, "The Determinants and Effects of Antitrust Activity," *Journal of Law and Economics* (October 1975).
34. Peter Asch and J. J. Seneca, "Is Collusion Profitable?" *The Review of Economics and Statistics* (February 1976).
35. Robert Feinberg, "Antitrust Enforcement and Subsequent Price Behavior," *The Review of Economics and Statistics* (November 1980).
36. Dosoung Choi and George Philippatos, "The Financial Consequences of Antitrust Enforcement," *The Review of Economics and Statistics* (August 1983).

against a single firm, an implication that any beginning student of economics should be able to explain. Finally, and not too surprisingly, Kenneth Garbade, William Silber, and Lawrence White have found that the announcement of an antitrust suit against a firm has a negative impact on the stock price of that firm.[37]

ANTITRUST, GOVERNMENT-SPONSORED MONOPOLY, AND DEREGULATION

In recent years, the policy discussion about monopoly has shifted to looking at the role of government in fostering monopoly. Harold Demsetz has argued that there are two systems of belief about monopoly.[38] One system views private sector monopoly as a major threat to the economy. This view is held by supporters of the market concentration doctrine, who think such monopolies should be aggressively regulated and pursued by strictly defined antitrust policy. The other system, which Demsetz calls "the new learning," views the more serious economic threat as coming from monopolies that are sponsored and protected by government. Reducing the threat from this type of monopoly calls for deregulation and less governmental control. The new learning approach is helpful in understanding antitrust activity in the 1980s because it represents the Reagan administration's view of monopoly.

THE ALPHABET SOUP OF REGULATORY AGENCIES

Regulation at the federal level has resulted in a host of regulatory agencies aimed at protecting consumer welfare. The acronyms for these agencies read like a can of alphabet soup: CAB, EEOC, EPA, FCC, FDA, FTC, ICC, NHTSA, OSHA, ITC, and SEC. The number of such agencies grew very rapidly in the 1960s and 1970s. The Reagan administration cut back their budgets and staffing. Presumably, lower budgets and fewer people meant less regulation. The Bush administration seems less intent on starving regulatory agencies, so some of them may gain increased power in the 1990s. This is especially likely for the Environmental Protection Agency (EPA).

In many cases, regulatory agencies that were formed for consumer protection actually inhibited competition and innovation. Before airline deregulation, the Civil Aeronautics Board (CAB) set fares and prohibited entry. The Food and Drug Administration (FDA) still tightly controls innovation and entry in drug markets, forcing U.S. citizens to travel to foreign countries for access to certain medical procedures and drugs. On a local level, most cities regulate taxicabs by setting minimum prices, controlling entry, or both. Ironically, in many instances, regulatory agencies set up for consumer protection are responsible for the monopoly power that exists in the regulated market. Many companies defend the regulatory status quo because they have already met the regulations, and these regulations serve as an effective barrier to new entry and new competition. These firms are the government-supported monopolies that Demsetz identified.

37. Kenneth Garbade, William Silber, and Lawrence White, "Market Reaction to the Filing of Antitrust Suits: An Aggregate and Cross Sectional Analysis," *The Review of Economics and Statistics* (November 1982).
38. Harold Demsetz, "Two Systems of Belief about Monopoly," in H. Goldschmid, H. M. Mann, and J. F. Weston (eds.), *Industrial Concentration: The New Learning* (Boston: Little, Brown, 1974).

A Case Study of Deregulation

In 1978, the Airline Deregulation Act took many operational decisions about running an airline away from the CAB and gave them back to the private managers.[39] In the twelve years between 1978 and 1990, the airline industry and air travel were revolutionized. But there have been calls for reregulation of the airline industry. An article in *Fortune* magazine painted the following picture of air travel:

A plane rips open like a sardine tin in mid-flight, spilling an unfortunate stewardess to her death. Just about every aircraft you board seems packed. Just about every flight seems late. The attendants are too often unsmiling, the food unspeakable. Once-mighty airlines like Eastern and Pam Am struggle to stay aloft as enraged workers and creditors pick over bare corporate bones. Something is very, very wrong here, and someone had better do something about it—fast. Is that scenario accurate? Many Americans emphatically think it is. They consider each flight a grim possibly perilous ordeal. We could add to that the complaints of business travelers. In the regulated days, they could count on a plane when they wanted it, where they wanted it, and it was on time. Best of all it wasn't crowded so they could work if they wanted to. Who cares if the prices were higher, they had expense accounts to cover the cost. Right?"[40]

We have all heard these complaints about airline deregulation. Perhaps you have made them yourself. Should the airlines be reregulated? To answer this question, we need to look at what has actually happened since deregulation in 1978. David Swierenga, who analyzes data for the Air Transport Association, says, "When you look at the really important issues, the big picture if you will, deregulation has to be considered a public policy triumph."[41]

Contrary to the popular perception, air safety has improved with deregulation. The major air carriers recorded an average of 33 fatal and nonfatal accidents per year and 1,459 fatalities in the nine years before deregulation. In the nine years following deregulation, the number of accidents fell to 20 per year and the number of fatalities declined to 1,036. Given the huge increase in passenger miles, this record is very impressive. Fatal accidents per million miles traveled fell 57 percent.

Airlines flew 85 percent more miles in 1989 than they did in 1978, before deregulation. Before deregulation, half of all Americans had never flown on a commercial aircraft. Since deregulation, three out of four Americans have done so. Passenger boardings per year have increased from 275 million in 1978 to 455 million in 1989. It's no wonder that aircraft seem more crowded. This increase in consumption has been generated by the decreased price of air travel.

The most compelling argument in favor of deregulation is that air fares, adjusted for inflation, decreased 21 percent between 1978 and 1988. The FTC estimates that this decline in prices saved passengers about $100 million. A portion of this $100 million was saved by business firms

39. This case study is based on Kenneth Labich, "Should the Airlines Be Reregulated?" *Fortune* (19 June 1989): 82–90.
40. Labich, "Should the Airlines Be Reregulated?" 82.
41. Labich, "Should the Airlines Be Reregulated?" 82.

that use air travel as an input and lowered their cost of producing goods and services.

However, deregulation has not done away with problems in air travel. Crowding *is* a problem in planes and terminals. Those harried business travelers are correct—it isn't as "nice" as it was before deregulation, it's just cheaper. Furthermore, it isn't cheaper in all markets. Before deregulation, higher fares on well-traveled routes were used to subsidize travel to remote cities. After deregulation, fares to remote spots were increased or service was terminated. Congestion at airports is a big problem. Landing fees and times at major airports are regulated, and at present they do not respond to market forces. Landing fees are based on a plane's weight. A corporate jet may pay $25, and an airliner carrying 400 passengers may pay $800. Yet both require the same time and the same attention from air traffic controllers. In addition, some airlines control available landing slots based on a historical basis. The ownership of the slots represents a barrier to entry for new airlines. A discussion in Congress centers on whether there should be more regulation of these slots or whether they should be auctioned to create more efficiency. The private aviation lobby makes such reform very difficult.

COMPETITIVENESS

Those who propose a national economic policy to improve competitiveness seem to draw their ideas from the success of the Japanese economy. There is a belief that that success stems from the government's working closely with private industry to ensure that private industry is successful. The idea, in part, is that government should take steps to back industrial "winners" to make them even more successful. Such proposals rest on the premise that the U.S. economy is in serious decline and that other countries (notably Japan) have had a positive experience that is a result of industrial-governmental "partnerships."

Regardless of the form that a policy fostering competitiveness may take at the federal level, it would represent an increased governmental role in making economic decisions. Proponents of such a policy are quick to point out that the United States already has a kind of industrial policy because every action of government in taxing and spending rewards some participants in the economy and penalizes others. Those individuals argue that a coordinated and intentional policy would be preferable to what exists at present. A competitiveness policy, however, would result in a more active role for government in the economy than most market-oriented economists would find acceptable.[42]

The latest argument for an industrial policy has come out of Silicon Valley in California. The high-tech manufacturers there want the United States to form a cohesive industrial policy to help them compete with what they refer to as "Japan, Inc." At the beginning of the Bush administration,

---

42. For a thorough review of the industrial policy debate, see R. D. Norton, "Industrial Policy and American Renewal," *Journal of Economic Literature* (March 1986).

TABLE 4
INDUSTRIAL POLICY
PROPOSAL BY THE
ELECTRONICS INDUSTRY

GOAL	SHORT-TERM ACTIONS	LONG-TERM ACTIONS
Lower-cost capital	Create a "patient" venture capital corporation with funding from government Provide federal aid for critical but very risky technologies Make R&D tax credits permanent Shorten depreciation schedules for high-tech equipment	Stimulate more savings Trim the federal deficit Reduce consumer and business debt Curtail leveraged buyouts Index the capital gains tax to zero on long-term investments End the double taxation on corporate dividends
Fair trade	Enforce existing antidumping laws	Require reciprocity with foreign nations
Antitrust reform	Exempt collaborative manufacturing under some conditions Eliminate treble damages in private suits against consortiums	Adjust rules to take account of offshore competition

Source: *Business Week* (5 February 1990): 57.

their lobbyists in Washington were hopeful that the new administration would develop a plan to help them. They soon learned that Bush's advisers were opposed to industrial policy. As his chief of staff, John H. Sununu, put it, "I assure you, our commitment is to try and create a competitive climate without falling into the trap of a competitiveness vehicle, which may itself be a vehicle for mischievous legislation."[43]

The trade associations of the electronics industry have banded together to continue to try to persuade the administration to come to their aid. However, many of their proposals are general ones aimed at encouraging investment and economic growth. A few are aimed specifically at foreign competition. Table 4 highlights what the electronics industry wants as industrial policy.

The competitiveness debate has a different focus at the state level. Policy makers at that level have become very involved in economic development activities. Almost every state has a state development board that aids the governor in recruiting new firms to the state from other states and foreign countries. Government officials use all types of tax breaks and other incentives to lure new firms to their states. In this context, fostering competitiveness can mean writing state tax laws, changing state regulatory activity, and examining state services, to make a state competitive with other states. Such competition puts constraints on state governments because if state officials create an environment that is hostile to business, firms will migrate to more friendly states.

43. "The Future of Silicon Valley," *Business Week* (5 February 1990): 59.

ALTERNATIVES FOR CONTROLLING INDUSTRY

There is a great deal of monopoly power, or at least concentration, in U.S. industry, and monopoly power is undesirable from society's point of view. Unfortunately, attempts to control monopoly or to restore competition through antitrust actions have not always produced the desired results. Antitrust cases drag on for many years. The economic analysis in these cases is very complex and often conflicting. The arguments are difficult to present, and juries, judges, and even lawyers do not always understand them. Generally, the result is government intervention in the market that can introduce new inefficiencies.

There does, however, seem to be at least one policy action that could increase competition without endangering the efficiency resulting from economies of scale. This policy is based on the benefits from the threat of new entry. If public policy could support new entry by dismantling artificial barriers to entry, competitive pressure would increase. These artificial barriers are both privately and publicly imposed. In many cases, the threat of new entry alone would be enough to alter the behavior of oligopolies.

Internationalization of the economy destroys many domestic barriers. As world markets become more integrated, the relevant market for antitrust activity becomes larger. If international trade is expanded, there may be less need to worry about domestic monopolies, from an antitrust perspective.

SUMMARY

1. Industries can be defined by SIC codes established by the Commerce Department. These groupings can be used to calculate concentration ratios, which are measures of the degree to which markets are concentrated.

2. The Herfindahl Index may be a better measure of monopoly power than a concentration ratio because it accounts for all of the firms in the industry.

3. There is no conclusive evidence on the trend of concentration in U.S. industry. Some researchers have found the concentration level to be quite stable. Others have found an increase in competitive firms.

4. The merger movement of the 1980s may have increased the concentration of some U.S. industries. This movement involved $1.3 trillion in assets. Some economists believe that the business trend of the 1980s was more a restructuring of corporate management than a traditional merger movement.

5. Mergers in the 1990s seem to be motivated by a desire to become internationalized, especially with respect to the European market.

6. The market concentration doctrine states that the structure of an industry determines its ultimate performance in terms of prices and profits. This model implies that concentrated industries should be restructured.

7. There is a good deal of debate concerning the degree to which concentration leads to higher profit rates and more rigid prices.

8. Countervailing power and innovation are sometimes considered to be positive aspects of monopoly power.

9. Regulation of monopoly leads to cost-plus pricing, which destroys the incentive to minimize costs.

10. Taxation of monopoly is an alternative to regulation. It simply captures monopoly profits without affecting price or output.

11. A Lerner Index of Monopoly Power (LMP) measures the percentage difference between price and marginal cost. It is perhaps the best measure of monopoly power, but unavailability of marginal cost data limits its use.

12. U.S. antitrust law began with the Sherman Antitrust Act in 1890. The Sherman Act and later laws have been applied with varying vigor and success.

13. The record of antitrust enforcement is not too impressive. Lawsuits take a long time and rarely restore competition. Politics plays an important role in antitrust activity.

14. Deregulation of the airline industry has increased competitiveness, lowered prices, increased the numbers of people flying, and (contrary to popular opinion) increased safety.

15. Competitiveness became a major public concern in the late 1980s. At the federal level, it is an aspect of industrial policy. At the state level, it relates to economic development.

NEW TERMS

industry
industry studies
Standard Industrial
   Classification (SIC)
   system
concentration ratio
Herfindahl Index
number equivalent
market concentration
   doctrine

administered prices
countervailing power
marginal cost pricing
Lerner Index of
   Monopoly Power
   (LMP)
cost-plus pricing
fair rate of return
trusts
holding companies

Sherman Antitrust Act
Clayton Act
tying contracts
Robinson-Patman Act
predatory pricing
Celler-Kefauver
   Antimerger Act
Federal Trade
   Commission Act
Wheeler-Lea Act

Hart-Scott-Rodino
   Antitrust Improvement
   Act
National Recovery
   Administration (NRA)

QUESTIONS FOR DISCUSSION

1. Are profits a good measure of monopoly power? Is concentration a good measure of monopoly power? Discuss the advantages of using either or both.

2. What would happen in a regulated industry if the price were set such that a representative firm could not earn a normal profit?

3. If prices charged by all firms in an industry are identical, is this evidence of an antitrust violation?

4. Do concentration ratios provide any useful information about changes in conglomerate merger activity?

5. The following data are for the soft drink industry in a certain country.

FIRMS	ANNUAL SALES (IN DOLLARS)
1	$400,000,000
2	300,000,000
3	200,000,000
4	150,000,000
5–35	300,000,000

What is the four-firm concentration ratio for this industry?

6. Now assume that the entire soft drink industry is made up of the first four firms listed in Question 5. What is the four-firm concentration ratio? What is the Herfindahl Index? What is the number equivalent? What does the number equivalent tell you?

7. What would happen to the concentration ratio in Question 5 if the industry were defined as the beverage industry? As the name-brand, nationally advertised soft drink industry?

8. Why is it so difficult to regulate a natural monopoly?

9. Why do some economists favor deregulation as a way of dealing with monopoly rather than "better" or "tougher" regulation?

10. Imagine that the President has just appointed you the major national adviser on antitrust. Convince the Cabinet that the government should pursue an active antitrust policy. After you have done that, take the opposite side and argue that monopoly is not so bad and the government shouldn't worry too much about it.

11. A comprehensive study of the U.S. economy argued that it became more effectively competitive between 1958 and 1980. What are the three reasons for this increase in the number of competitive firms? How did each of these three reasons work to increase competitiveness?

12. Some economists argue that the merger movement of the 1980s was different from earlier movements because of the inherent problem of the separation of ownership and control in U.S. corporations. What do these economists have in mind?

13. Why would U.S. firms want to merge with foreign firms, especially European firms?

14. What has been the outcome of the Airline Deregulation Act of 1978?

15. The term *competitiveness* is used increasingly in political campaigns. How does the meaning of the term differ when it is used by a candidate for federal office as opposed to a candidate for state office?

SUGGESTIONS FOR FURTHER READING

Adams, Walter, and James Brock. *Dangerous Pursuits: Mergers and Acquisitions in the Age of Wall Street.* New York: Pantheon, 1989. A critique of the merger wave of the 1980s by two economists who argue that the long-run effects will be greater concentration and reduced innovation.

Asch, Peter. *Industrial Organization and Antitrust Policy.* New York: John Wiley and Sons, 1986. A textbook that gives detailed accounts of important antitrust cases.

Bauer, Paul W. "Airline Deregulation: Boon or Bust?" *Economic Commentary,* Federal Reserve Bank of Cleveland (1 May 1989). A commentary on the issues surrounding airline deregulation.

Hermaann, Werner, and G. J. Santoni. "The Cost of Restricting Corporate Takeovers: A Lesson from Switzerland." *Review, Federal Reserve Bank of St. Louis* (November/December 1989): 3–11.

According to this article, the Swiss experience shows that restricting corporate takeovers has serious consequences on the wealth of stockholders.

Newcomb, Peter. "No One Is Safe." *Forbes* (13 July 1987): 121–160. An account of how the largest firms ebb and flow, keeping concentration in flux.

Reich, Robert B. *Tales of a New America.* New York: Times Books, 1986. A book on competitiveness by one of the advocates of industrial policy.

Scherer, F. M. *Industrial Market Structure and Economic Performance.* Chicago: Rand McNally, 1980. A source book with detailed references to the literature on regulation and antitrust matters.

FACTOR MARKETS

8

1. Distinguish between product markets and factor markets and describe their relationship to each other in terms of the circular flow model.
2. Explain what makes the demand for labor different from the demand for final goods in terms of:
   a. derived demand,
   b. interdependent demand,
   c. technologically determined demand.
3. Explain how to calculate each of the following:
   a. marginal physical product of labor (MPP_L),
   b. value of the marginal physical product of labor (VMP_L),
   c. marginal revenue product of labor (MRP_L),
   d. marginal resource cost of labor (MRC_L).
4. Describe how a profit-maximizing firm decides how much labor to employ in terms of its marginal revenue product and marginal resource cost.
5. Use a factor market diagram to illustrate:
   a. pure competition versus monopoly in the product market,
   b. pure competition versus monopsony in the factor market.
6. Explain why a monopsonist has fewer workers at a lower wage.
7. Discuss the effects of investment in human capital on wages.
8. Explain how the difference between white and nonwhite income levels relates to human capital.
9. List arguments for and against comparable worth legislation.

CHAPTER 27

MARGINAL PRODUCTIVITY THEORY AND LABOR MARKETS

INTRODUCTION

Income is earned through ownership of any (or perhaps all) of the factors of production. Most individuals receive income from their labor. Many others own land or capital, or are entrepreneurs. Personal income flows to all these factors. In most discussions, much more attention is given to the equity aspects of the distribution of personal income than to the reasons for this distribution. This chapter explains how labor income is determined in a market system and why the distribution of income is what it is. In a later chapter, we will discuss actions that can be taken if society doesn't like the distribution of income that is produced by the market process.

Earlier in this book, we examined the circular flow as a starting point. It is worthwhile to return briefly to that discussion. Figure 1 reproduces the circular flow diagram from Chapter 2. It shows the firm involved in two markets: the product market and the factor market. We have studied the theory of the firm in the product market, the upper half of the circular flow diagram. We now turn our attention to the theory of the firm in the largest part of the factor market, the labor market.

The demand for labor is similiar to other types of demand we have studied. In earlier chapters, we described product markets, in which firms or individuals sell the goods and services they produce to consumers. Now we want to examine the labor market, the market in which firms buy—or

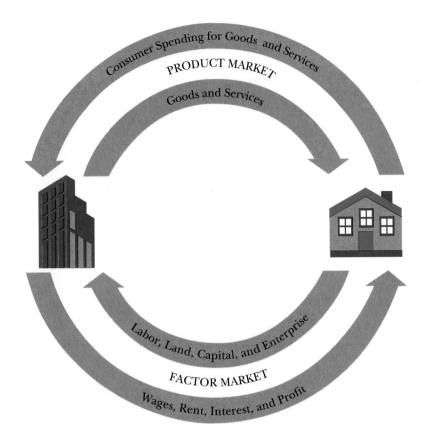

FIGURE 1
THE CIRCULAR FLOW OF
INCOME
Households purchase
goods and services and
supply land, labor,
capital, and enterprise.
Firms buy these factors of
production and supply
goods and services. In the
product market, buyers
and sellers exchange
goods and services. In the
factor market, buyers and
sellers exchange the
services of factors of
production (resources).

rent—the services of labor from individuals. We can adopt many of the
same analytical tools we used to study product markets. There are, however, some differences between labor and product markets, and we will
concentrate on these differences.

SPECIAL FEATURES OF THE DEMAND FOR LABOR

The demand for labor has three features that make it somewhat different
from the demand for a product. The first is that the demand for labor is
derived demand. A firm demands labor because the labor can be used to
produce goods that consumers are demanding. The demand for labor is
thus derived from the demand for the product it produces. If there were
no consumer demand for wood, there would be no demand for loggers.
This principle holds for all factors of production. They are only valuable
to a firm if they help to produce products that consumers value.

The second feature of the demand for labor is that it is **interdependent
demand**. It depends on the demand for other factors. In other words, the
amount of labor demanded will depend on the amounts of other factors
a firm plans to use. The amount of labor a firm demands depends on the
amounts of land, capital, and enterprise that will be used in combination
with the labor. It is also true that the demand for most products is interdependent with the demand for other products. As you know, almost all

derived demand
Demand for a productive
resource that results from
demand for a final good
or service. For example,
the demand for labor is
derived from the demand
for the product that the
labor produces.

interdependent demand
Demand that depends on
another type of demand.
For example, a firm's
demand for labor
depends on the amount
of other factors that the
firm plans to use.

John Bates Clark was the first person born in the United States to achieve an international reputation as an economic theorist. He was a reformer and an activist who helped form the American Economic Association and later became its third president.

Clark was born and raised in Providence, Rhode Island. He graduated from Amherst College in 1872. He studied economics at the University of Heidelberg and the University of Zurich. After returning to the United States, Clark taught political economy at Carleton College and then moved to Smith College, Amherst, Johns Hopkins, and finally to Columbia, where he taught political science from 1895 to 1923. After 1911, he became very active in pacifist causes and was the first director of the Carnegie Endowment for International Peace.

The nature of Clark's theoretical interests reflected the times in which he lived. The American Industrial Revolution caused Clark to examine problems of production and distribution. In his book *The Distribution of Wealth* (1899), he developed a positive theory based on the competition of rational, self-interested people. This approach was a radical change from that in his earlier work, *The Philosophy of Wealth* (1887), in which he attacked the "hedonistic" assumptions of the classical economists. His influence on later economists stems from the analytical tools he developed.

Clark's status in the U.S. economics profession is recognized by the John Bates Clark Prize of the American Economics Association. Every two years, this prize is awarded to an economist under the age of forty who has made a significant contribution to economic theory. The list of winners reads like a *Who's Who* of American economists.

ECONOMIC PROFILE

JOHN BATES CLARK

1847–1938

goods have substitutes and many goods have complements. However, the interdependence of the demand for labor with the demand for other factors of production is unusual in that the other factors can be both complements and substitutes at the same time.

The third feature is that the demand for labor is in part **technologically determined demand**. That is, the demand for labor will depend on techniques of production and on technological progress, or the production function. Recall that the production function tells how much labor is needed to produce a certain level of output, given a certain production process and amounts of the other factors of production. This technological relationship can change with new inventions and new innovations. Any change resulting in a new technology or a new innovation will have an impact on the demand for factors of production, including labor.

These basic elements are combined in marginal productivity theory, which was originally developed by John Bates Clark. **Marginal productivity theory** explains how the distribution of income is determined in a market system. Each factor is paid according to its contribution, or its marginal productivity. The more productive factors will be paid more. We will follow Clark's lead by developing marginal productivity theory in terms of labor supply and demand. The theory holds for all factors of production, but most interest centers on labor and the returns to labor.

technologically determined demand
Demand that depends on techniques of production and technological progress. For example, the demand for labor will be affected by the introduction of new technology in a firm or industry.

marginal productivity theory
An explanation of how the distribution of income is determined in a market system. Each factor is paid according to its contribution, or its marginal productivity.

SPECIAL CHARACTERISTICS OF FACTOR MARKETS

- Demand is derived from the demand for the final product.
- Demand is interdependent with demand for other inputs.
- Demand is technologically determined.

THE MARKET FOR LABOR WITH PERFECT COMPETITION

Remember that a demand curve shows the relationship between price and quantity demanded. A demand curve for labor shows how much labor will be demanded at various wage rates. In order to develop a theory about the market demand for labor, we start by asking how much labor an individual firm will employ at various wage rates. Then we sum the results for all firms in the same way we added individual demand curves to find the market demand for a product.

Consider a firm that is selling its product in a perfectly competitive product market and buying its labor in a perfectly competitive labor market. This means that the firm will take both the price of its product *and* the price of labor as given. The firm is too small to have any effect on either product prices or wage rates.

THE DEMAND FOR LABOR
What determines the firm's demand for labor? Suppose the production function is such that, as the firm increases the amount of labor employed,

ceteris paribus, the resulting increases in the amount of total product become smaller. This production function reflects the principle of diminishing marginal productivity, which we discussed in an earlier chapter. Holding constant the quantities of land and capital, it is possible to determine how the firm's output varies with the quantity of labor it uses. As the firm employs more labor in combination with fixed amounts of the other factors, the additional amounts of output per additional unit of labor eventually decline. If this were not the case, it would be theoretically possible to grow the entire world's supply of wheat on one acre of land just by employing more workers.

The amount of total physical product associated with various amounts of labor inputs for the firm is given in the second column of Table 1. This output depends on the technical relationship defined by the production function. Once we know the total product, we can determine how much extra product is produced when labor inputs are added. That value is the marginal physical product of that unit of labor (MPP_L). It is the marginal physical product because the output is in physical units, such as number of autos or tons of coal.

To put a market value on the additional output, we simply multiply the number of added units of the product by the price at which the firm can sell it. This value is called the **value of the marginal product of labor (VMP_L)**. It is listed in the sixth column of Table 1. The VMP_L, which is $P \times MPP_L$, is a measure of the value of the additional output that each additional unit of labor adds to the firm's total. The **marginal revenue product of labor (MRP_L)** is the amount that an additional unit of labor adds to the firm's total revenue. It is found in the seventh column of Table 1. It is found by multiplying MR by MPP_L. With perfect competition in the product market, $VMP_L = MRP_L$. These values are equal because the product price remains constant ($P = MR$). The firm can produce and sell as much as it wants at the market-determined price, which is \$2 in this example. When the firm faces a given price, marginal revenue is exactly equal to that price in the model of perfect competition. Later in this chapter, we will

---

value of the marginal product of labor (VMP$_L$) A measure of the value of the additional output that each unit of additional labor adds to a firm's total, found by multiplying the marginal physical product by the price at which the firm can sell the product.

marginal revenue product of labor (MRP$_L$) The amount that an additional unit of labor adds to a firm's total revenue.

TABLE 1
THE DEMAND FOR LABOR IN A PERFECTLY COMPETITIVE PRODUCT MARKET

Units of Labor	Total Physical Product	Marginal Physical Product of Labor (MPP_L)	Product Price	Total Revenue	Value of Marginal Product of Labor (VMP_L)	Marginal Revenue Product of Labor (MRP_L)
0	0		\$2	\$ 0		
		10			\$20	\$20
1	10		2	20		
		8			16	16
2	18		2	36		
		6			12	12
3	24		2	48		
		4			8	8
4	28		2	56		
		2			4	4
5	30		2	60		

look at how the value of the marginal product and the marginal revenue product differ when there is monopoly power in the product market.

The values of VMP_L and MRP_L from Table 1 are plotted on a graph in Figure 2. The MRP_L curve is the firm's demand curve for labor. It shows the value of each additional unit of labor to the firm. Thus, it shows how much labor the firm will purchase at various prices (wage rates). If you know the price of labor, you will be able to determine how much labor this firm will demand.

THE SUPPLY OF LABOR

An individual's supply curve of labor looks like the other supply curves we have considered. As wage rates rise, the quantity of labor supplied increases. This supply curve of labor, like most supply curves, is upward sloping. As wage rates rise, an individual will want to work more hours. In general, as wages rise, more people will choose to give up leisure in favor of more income. This trade-off of income for leisure is the substitution effect of a wage increase. Individuals will substitute the increased consumption of goods and services that higher wages represent for leisure. This substitution effect occurs along the upward-sloping portion of Figure 3.

There is also an income effect associated with the increased income brought about by a wage increase. Individuals want to consume more leisure at higher incomes because leisure is a normal good. The income effect of a higher wage is that individuals want to supply a lower quantity of labor. At some point, the income effect of a wage increase could dominate the substitution effect. In that case, an increase in the wage rate would bring about a decrease in the quantity of labor supplied. This is represented by the crook in the individual's supply curve in Figure 3. For this individual, an increase in the wage rate above $15 per hour causes the quantity of labor supplied to decrease. Economists refer to a supply curve with this shape as a **backward-bending supply curve**. It is important to keep in mind that this is an individual supply curve. Where the bend oc-

backward-bending supply curve
A labor supply curve that slopes back to the left at the point where the income effect dominates the substitution effect.

Price, Cost

$VMP_L = MRP_L = D_L$

Quantity/
Time Period

FIGURE 2
THE FIRM'S DEMAND FOR LABOR IN A PERFECTLY COMPETITIVE PRODUCT MARKET
The marginal revenue product of labor (MRP_L) curve is the firm's demand curve for labor. When the firm's product market is perfectly competitive, MRP_L and the VMP_L are identical.

Wage Rate (Dollars/Hour)

FIGURE 3
AN INDIVIDUAL'S LABOR
SUPPLY CURVE
When the substitution effect of a wage increase for an individual exceeds the income effect, the quantity of labor supplied increases. Up to some wage ($15 per hour here), the income effect dominates. Above that wage, further increases in the wage rate cause the quantity of labor supplied to decrease.

Quantity of Labor Supplied (Hours/Week)

curs is an individual decision. Some entertainers perform less as they get more famous. Others appear to keep increasing the quantity of labor supplied as their wage rate increases.

The market supply curve of labor (S_L) is the aggregate of all the individual supply curves. It shows how much labor is available at different wage rates, as in Figure 4. This market supply curve is not backward-bending because more workers will enter the market at higher wage rates and different individuals have different opportunity costs and will make choices resulting in different substitution effects and income effects. In other words, higher wages are needed to attract additional workers who have higher opportunity costs.

FIGURE 4
PERFECTLY COMPETITIVE
LABOR MARKET
In a perfectly competitive labor market, the firm faces a perfectly elastic supply curve (S_f). If the supply curve is perfectly elastic, the marginal resource cost (MRC_L) curve is also perfectly elastic. The firm can purchase as much labor as it wants at the market-determined wage rate.

We assumed that the firm is in perfectly competitive factor markets. Perfect competition in the labor market means the firm can purchase labor at the market wage without affecting that wage. The equilibrium wage rate is W in Figure 4. The firm can purchase as much labor as it wants at the wage rate W. The supply curve the firm faces, represented by S_f in Figure 4, is thus perfectly elastic at W. If the supply curve a firm faces is perfectly elastic, the cost of each additional unit of labor is the same, or constant. The cost of each additional unit of labor is the **marginal resource cost of labor** (MRC_L). For a firm in a perfectly competitive labor market, the marginal resource cost curve of labor, MRC_L, is the same as the labor supply curve.

marginal resource cost (MRC)
The cost of each additional unit of a productive resource.

EQUILIBRIUM IN THE PERFECTLY COMPETITIVE LABOR MARKET
The MRC_L curve is the supply curve the firm faces because it shows the relationship between price and additional units of labor supplied. A profit-maximizing firm will employ or purchase labor until $MRP_L = MRC_L$. If a unit of labor adds more to revenue than to cost (if $MRP_L > MRC_L$), it will be profitable for the firm to purchase more units of labor. However, if a unit of labor adds more to cost than to revenue (if $MRP_L < MRC_L$), the firm should purchase fewer units. The firm will hire laborers until the amount they add to total cost (MRC_L) is exactly equal to the amount they add to revenue (MRP_L). In Figure 4, the firm would employ x_1 units of labor at wage rate W. In terms of the numbers in Table 1, the firm would employ 4 units of labor if the market wage was $8 per unit. If the market wage was $4 per unit, 5 units of labor would be employed.

A COMPETITIVE LABOR MARKET WITH A MONOPOLISTIC PRODUCT MARKET

We now consider a firm that sells its product under monopoly conditions. The monopolist's demand for labor is shown in Table 2. The difference be-

UNITS OF LABOR	TOTAL PHYSICAL PRODUCT	MARGINAL PHYSICAL PRODUCT OF LABOR (MPP_L)	PRODUCT PRICE	TOTAL REVENUE	VALUE OF THE MARGINAL PRODUCT OF LABOR (VMP_L)	MARGINAL REVENUE PRODUCT OF LABOR (MRP_L)
0	0	0	$ 0	$ 0		
					$100	$100
1	10	10	10	100		
					72	62
2	18	8	9	162		
					48	30
3	24	6	8	192		
					28	4
4	28	4	7	196		
					12	−6
5	30	2	6	180		

TABLE 2
THE DEMAND FOR LABOR IN A MONOPOLISTIC PRODUCT MARKET

Give me your tired, your poor,
Your huddled masses yearning to breath free,
The wretched refuse of your teeming shore,
Send these, the homeless, tempest-tossed to me:
I lift my lamp beside the golden
    door.

—Inscription on the Statue
of Liberty

The United States is a country of immigrants and descendants of immigrants—a "melting pot," as you learned in elementary school. In the early nineteenth century, Europeans, mostly from Western Europe, flooded into the United States. In the late nineteenth century, a wave of Chinese immigrated to California. In the early twentieth century, a huge flood of immigrants arrived from Southern and Eastern Europe. The most recent large waves of immigrants have been from Southeast Asia after the end of the Vietnam War, and from Central America. Many of those coming from Central America are illegal immigrants, making them distinct from most of the other waves of immigrants.

Each influx of immigrants caused a great debate among Americans who were already citizens. The issue was always the same—whether or not to shut the door to new immigrants. Often the answer was yes, and new restrictions were passed. There was the Chinese exclusion law in 1882, the "Gentlemen's Agreement" with Japan in 1907 (halting the immigration of Japanese), and the national-origin quotas in 1921 and 1924. These quotas were designed to freeze the ethnic composition of the United States by limiting the entrance of any one nationality to a small percentage of the number of people of that nationality who were already here. The Quota Law of 1921 limited immigration from any Eastern Hemisphere country to 3 percent of the foreign-born persons from that country living in the United States in 1910. In 1924, the Immigration Origins Act set an annual quota of 2 percent of each country's U.S. residents in 1920. In 1965, Congress did away with

**INTERNATIONAL
PERSPECTIVE**

**U.S.
IMMIGRATION
POLICY AND
WAGE RATES**

the national-origin quotas and placed a yearly limit of 290,000 on all immigrants.

Many legal restrictions on immigration are racist in origin. Many groups support immigration of those who are like themselves but are opposed to altering the racial mix of the country. This motivation was clear in the 1924 act.

There is at least one economic motive for restricting immigration. Immigration makes the supply of labor much more elastic for each skill level, putting downward pressure on wage rates. It isn't surprising that organized labor groups are often opposed to liberalizing immigration policy. In fact, some states even prohibit the transfer of certain occupational skills within the United States. For example, a CPA in Wisconsin who plans to migrate to Arizona will not be licensed until he or she passes an Arizona exam. This requirement clearly reduces the supply of accounting services in Arizona. As a result, accountants in Arizona have higher incomes than they would otherwise.

In October 1986, the U.S. Congress passed an immigration reform bill that offered citizenship to illegal aliens who could prove they entered the United States before January 1, 1982. However, the law imposed strict penalties on employers who hire illegal aliens. If effectively enforced, this law will put upward pressure on wage rates in the unskilled labor markets in the South and Southwest, where illegal aliens are a large fraction of the work force. In 1986, there was evidence that the law was deterring illegal immigration. Illegal border crossings declined, and there were numerous reports of employers firing undocumented workers. By 1988, this trend seemed to have reversed. Field observations at the busiest illegal crossing point reported an increase in illegal crossing to the level recorded before the law went into effect. Data on the apprehension of illegal aliens confirms that this law has not substantially deterred entry as long as enforcement was weak and the wage pull was strong.

tween this case and the firm of the preceding section is that product price (fourth column) declines as the firm produces and sells more of its product. VMP_L and MRP_L are calculated in the same way as before. VMP_L is the value of the labor's marginal physical product, so $VMP_L = MPP_L \times P$. MRP_L is found by calculating the change in total revenue due to additional units of labor. For example, when the third worker is added, total revenue rises from \$162 to \$192. Thus, MRP_L for the third worker is \$192 − \$162 = \$30. Note that VMP_L is greater than MRP_L for all but the first unit of labor, because in a monopoly, product price is greater than marginal revenue.

Both the VMP_L curve and the MRP_L curve are graphed in Figure 5 using the data from Table 2. The MRP_L curve is the monopolist's demand curve for labor. This firm, like the perfectly competitive firm, will employ labor until $MRP_L = MRC_L$. Although this firm is selling its product in a monopolistic product market, it is purchasing labor in a competitive labor market.

The supply and demand curves for the monopolist in the competitive labor market are diagrammed in Figure 6. The market demand curve for labor is, as usual, found by summing the MRP_L curves for all firms purchasing this type of labor. The market supply curve (S_L) is the sum of individual supply curves of workers. The market-determined wage is W. This firm can purchase as much labor as it desires at W, since the supply curve it faces, S_f, is perfectly elastic at W. Since S_f is perfectly elastic, MRC_L for this firm is constant. The firm maximizes profits where $MRC_L = MRP_L$, so it hires x_1 units of labor. Note from Figure 6 that the monopolist pays W, the market wage. The fact that MRP_L is less than VMP_L does not mean that the monopolist exploits labor by paying too little. The monopolist has to pay the market wage just like any other employer in this market. Because MRP_L is less than VMP_L, the monopolist *does* employ fewer workers than similar competitive firms would employ. Recall from the chapter on

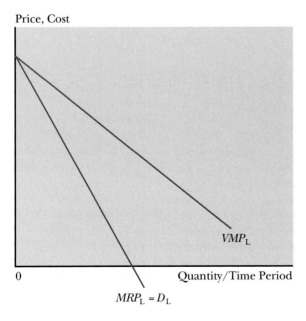

Price, Cost

0   Quantity/Time Period

VMP_L

$MRP_L = D_L$

FIGURE 5
THE MONOPOLIST'S
DEMAND FOR LABOR
When a firm has monopoly power in the product market, the MRP_L will lie below VMP_L. This is because product price is greater than marginal revenue under monopoly. Thus, $P \times MP_L$ is greater than $MR \times MP_L$.

FIGURE 6
A MONOPOLISTIC FIRM
FACING A PERFECTLY
COMPETITIVE LABOR
MARKET
A firm with monopoly
power in the product
market and in a perfectly
competitive labor market
will face a perfectly elastic
supply curve. The firm
will hire units of labor
until the marginal
revenue product of labor
is equal to the marginal
resource cost of labor
($MRP_L = MRC_L$).

monopoly that the monopolist restricts output to keep price high. The result of this restriction of output in the factor market is that the monopolist uses fewer inputs, including labor. If this were a competitive firm rather than a monopolist, it would want to be on the VMP_L curve (which would then also be the MRP_L curve) and hire x_2 workers.

MONOPSONY

We have looked at competitive and monopolistic firms demanding labor in competitive labor markets. Now we want to consider a firm that has an influence on price in the labor market. We have assumed to this point that the purchasing firm has no effect on wage rates. But what if the firm does affect wage rates? What if the wage rate rises as the firm hires more labor? We refer to such a firm as having monopsony power. The word *monopsony* comes from a Greek word meaning "one purchaser." A monopoly is the market structure in which there is a single seller of a product. A **monopsony** is a market structure in which there is a single purchaser of a factor of production.

monopsony
A market structure in
which there is a single
purchaser of a factor of
production.

We begin by assuming that we know what the monopsonist's MRP_L curve is, shown in Figure 7. It doesn't matter if this firm is selling its product in a competitive market or a monopolistic market. We also know the market supply curve of labor to this firm, S_L. Table 3 provides values that correspond to Figure 7. The market supply curve, S_L, is the labor supply curve the firm faces because the firm is the market for this labor by the definition of monopsony. In a competitive market, this situation of supply and demand would have resulted in a wage rate of W_c and employment level of Q_c. However, since the firm in this case faces the upward-sloping supply curve, S_L, the MRC_L curve lies above that supply curve, as shown in Figure 7. To see why this is the case, refer to Table 3. The supply curve is, of course, the graph of the values in the first and second columns of

Price, Cost

MRC_L

S_L

A

W_c

W_m

$MRP_L = D_L$

0 Q_m Q_c

Quantity/Time Period

FIGURE 7
MONOPSONY
The monopsonist faces the market supply curve for labor (S_L). Since this curve has a positive slope, the marginal resource cost (MRC_L) curve lies above it. The monopsonist thus hires Q_m units of labor at a wage rate of W_m.

the table. Since the curve is upward sloping, the firm must pay a higher wage rate as it hires more labor. This result is different from that for a firm hiring in a competitive labor market. The total wage costs go up with additional workers in monopsony for two reasons. First, the wage must rise to attract more labor. Second, wage costs rise because all the other workers receive a higher wage as the firm hires more workers.

UNITS OF LABOR	WAGE RATE	WAGE COST	MARGINAL RESOURCE COST OF LABOR (MRC_L)
0		$ 0	
			$ 5
1	$ 5	5	
			7
2	6	12	
			9
3	7	21	
			11
4	8	32	
			13
5	9	45	
			15
6	10	60	
			17
7	11	77	
			19
8	12	96	
			21
9	13	117	
			23
10	14	140	

TABLE 3
THE DEMAND FOR LABOR IN A MONOPSONY

The amount that each additional worker adds to total wage cost is the marginal resource cost of labor (MRC_L). You can see by comparing the second and fourth columns that the MRC_L curve will lie above the S_L curve, as shown in Figure 7. The firm, as before, maximizes profits where $MRP_L = MRC_L$. Profit maximization occurs at point A in Figure 7, where the firm employs Q_m units of labor. But MRC_L is not equal to the wage rate. Remember, the supply curve indicates what has to be paid to hire Q_m units of labor. The firm will pay wage rate W_m.

monopsonistic exploitation
The difference in wages paid by a firm that has monopsony power, compared to what would be paid in a competitive market.

Note that W_m is less than W_c, so the monopsonist is paying a lower wage than would have been paid in a competitive labor market. Economists refer to this situation as monopsonistic exploitation. **Monopsonistic exploitation** is the underpayment of wages by a firm that has monopsony power. Labor receives less than it would receive in a competitive market. This does not mean that workers are forced to work at wage rates below what they are willing to accept. The monopsonist simply restricts input, just as the monopolist restricts output.

Monopsony in the Real World

Are there any real-world examples of pure monopsony in a labor market? No, because all labor has some other possible employment. Pure monopsony, like pure monopoly, is a theoretical extreme. There are, however, real-world examples of some degree of monopsony power. You may have heard the song about the miner who "owes his soul to the company store." This song was written about mining companies when they dominated the labor market as the major employer in certain areas. Company towns—small towns with only one major employer—were common in the early twentieth century. An example was Pullman, Illinois, where railroad sleeping cars were manufactured. A large college or university in a small town provides a more current example of monopsony power in a labor market. If you compared secretarial salaries at similar-sized schools in cities of varying size, you would find that where the college or university dominates the labor market, the salaries are lower. This lower pay may in part be due to monopsony power.

Perhaps the best example of monopsony in a labor market in the U.S. economy comes from professional sports. Congress has made sports leagues exempt from the federal antitrust laws. This exemption allows the leagues to hire as monopsonists by drafting players and maintaining control through reserve clauses.[1] Players are not free to quit one team and go to work for another unless they become a free agent. As a result, wage rates for professional athletes are lower than they would be if the teams competed for players on an open market. An early study of the economics of baseball by Gerald Scully found empirical evidence of monopsonistic exploitation in that sport.[2] Scully found that the typical MRP_L for star pitch-

1.   Reserve clauses have been and are being challenged. Players can now lay out their options, thus reducing the monopsony power of the owners.
2.   Gerald W. Scully, "Pay and Performance in Major League Baseball," *American Economic Review* (December 1974): 915–930. Thomas H. Bruggink and David R. Rose, Jr. calculated the MRP_L of 103 major league baseball players and compared them to their salaries: "Financial Restraint in the Free Agent Labor Market for Major League Baseball: Players Look at Strike Three," *Southern Economic Journal* (April 1990): 1029–1043.

ers in 1969 was $405,300, but the typical salary was only $66,800. Think about basketball player Michael Jordan. He receives a very high salary, but consider what he adds to his team's (and the league's) marginal revenue. He fills up the arena for practically every game he plays. His salary is surely less than his MRP_L.[3]

The formation of the United States Football League (USFL) in the early 1980s had a profound effect on salaries in professional football. The new league introduced competition for players and the effect was startling. Rookie salaries in 1983 jumped an average of 52 percent over 1982 salaries. Many of football's general managers called this trend an "economic disaster" and blamed it on players, agents, and other teams. If they had studied economics, they would have realized it was due to the breakdown of monopsony power. When the USFL folded, the upward pressure on football salaries declined.

Except for such special cases, where buyers are purchasing very specialized labor skills, there are few instances of real monopsony power. In general, improved transportation and communication in the United States have increased labor's mobility. With increased labor mobility, there is less monopsony power. If miners are aware of job possibilities in other areas and in other occupations, the mine will be forced to pay a competitive wage. Indeed, if even a small percentage of miners are willing to pull up stakes, the mine will be forced to pay competitive wages. Complete mobility of labor isn't necessary to reduce monopsony power. It's enough to have mobility at the margin.

MONOPSONY POWER AND MINIMUM WAGES

The minimum wage is a price floor set above the market-clearing price and, thus, generally causes a surplus of labor, or unemployment. However, if there is no monopsony power, a minimum wage can cause employment to increase. In Figure 8, the monopsonist would employ Q_m units of labor at wage rate W_m. Now suppose a minimum wage of W_1 is imposed. Part of the market supply curve is replaced by a horizontal line at W_1, the imposed minimum wage. In effect, the monopsonist is forced to accept the minimum wage. The market supply curve is now represented by the line W_1AC. The marginal resource cost labor curve is now W_1A, because the supply curve is perfectly elastic in the range W_1A. At a wage rate of W_1, Q_1 units of labor would be employed. If the minimum wage imposed is W_2 instead of W_1, the supply curve the firm faces is W_2BC. The firm will face perfectly elastic supply and MRC_L curves in the range W_2B. In this case, the firm will employ Q_m units of labor at wage rate W_2. You can see that if the minimum wage that is imposed lies between W_m and W_2, more employment at a higher wage rate will result.

What we have just considered is an exception to the usual case where minimum wages result in unemployment. Be careful, though. This result

---

3. *Sports Illustrated* reported that the Milwaukee Bucks realized an additional $700,000 profit during Kareem Abdul-Jabbar's first season. His salary was $250,000. So, for Abdul-Jabbar's team, $MRP_L > MRC_L$. Although salary figures are not available for Michael Jordan's 1986–1987 year with the Chicago Bulls, *Sports Illustrated* reported in December 1987 that Jordan brought in 276,996 more fans than had attended the previous season. At the average ticket price of $13.14, that represented $3.71 million in marginal revenue.

FIGURE 8
MONOPSONY POWER AND MINIMUM WAGES
A minimum wage of W_2 in a monopsonistic labor market changes the market supply curve from S_L to W_2B and the part of S_L above B. The marginal resource cost curve is the same as W_2B, the perfectly elastic portion of the supply curve.

only occurs when there is monopsony power in the labor market. A monopsony is relatively uncommon except in certain labor markets for specialized skills, such as the market for professional basketball players. Most empirical studies of the effects of minimum wages show that the monopsony exception to the negative effects of a minimum wage on employment is not very common.[4]

DETERMINANTS OF THE ELASTICITY OF THE DEMAND FOR LABOR

At the beginning of this chapter, you learned that the demand for labor has three features making it somewhat different from the demand for a product. These features also influence the elasticity of the demand for labor, because they determine how the quantity of labor demanded will respond to changes in the wage rate. In other words, the demand for labor has a price elasticity just as the demand for products does. This elasticity is influenced by the distinguishing features of the demand for labor.

ELASTICITY OF THE DEMAND FOR THE PRODUCT
If the wage rate falls for all of the firms in the product market, the cost of producing the product will also fall. There will, as a result, be a decline in the selling price of the product. As the price of the product declines, consumers will increase their consumption of the product. The price elasticity of the demand for a product determines how much more of the product consumers will purchase in response to a decline in its price. Thus, the price elasticity of the demand for the product affects the price elasticity of the demand for labor. If the product demand is elastic, the firm

4.   For a review of these empirical studies, see Jack Hirshleifer, *Price Theory and Applications*, 4th ed. (Englewood Cliffs, NJ: Prentice-Hall, 1988), 336–340.

will hire more labor in order to increase production to respond to the increased quantity demanded by consumers. The larger the increase in quantity demanded of the product, the larger the increase in quantity demanded of labor will be. As a result, labor demand is more elastic when the demand for the final product is more elastic.

SHARE OF LABOR IN FACTOR COSTS

The second element that affects the elasticity of demand for labor is a bit more complex. First, assume that only labor is used to produce the product. Labor costs are 100 percent of product cost. If the price of labor falls 10 percent, the cost of production falls 10 percent, and price (in perfect competition) falls 10 percent. Now, more realistically, let labor costs constitute only 50 percent of product cost. Then if the price of labor falls 10 percent, the cost of production would fall only 5 percent. In other words, the larger the share of labor cost in total production cost of a product, the more a change in the wage rate will affect the cost of production and the price of the product. As a result, the larger the share of the total cost of production that wages represent, the greater the elasticity of demand for labor will be.

OPPORTUNITIES FOR FACTOR SUBSTITUTION

In actual production, a great deal of substitution among the factors of production is possible. We discussed this factor substitution in detail in the chapter on production. The choice of which combination of factors of production to use depends, as you learned earlier, on the prices of those factors. As the price of labor increases, entrepreneurs will substitute capital and land for labor to the extent that such substitution is feasible in the production function. Substitution can occur for all the factors of production. Perhaps it is most visible in the substitution that takes place among land, labor, and capital in urban versus rural areas. In urban areas, where land is expensive, labor and capital are substituted for land. High-rise structures, which use much more labor and capital, are built. In rural areas, low-rise office buildings and housing units are constructed. They use far less labor and capital than the high-rise structures of the central city.

Consider what happens when the wage rate falls. To the extent that labor can be substituted for other factors of production, more labor will be hired. The greater the degree of substitutability in production, the greater will be the price elasticity of the demand for labor.

SHIFTS IN THE DEMAND FOR LABOR

The demand curve for labor, like the demand curve for products, can shift in response to changes in underlying conditions. Two of the most important causes of such shifts are changes in demand for the product and changes in the employment of the other factors of production.

CHANGES IN THE DEMAND FOR THE PRODUCT

The demand for labor is derived from the demand for the product it is used to produce. To see this more clearly, look again at Table 1 and Table

2, which show the situations for a competitive and a monopolistic firm, respectively. Suppose there is an increase in demand in the product market. The market demand curve will shift to the right. This shift will cause the product price to increase for the competitive firm, because the value of the marginal product of labor will be larger at all levels of production. That is, the values of MRP_L in Table 1 will increase in proportion to the increase in product price. In most cases, an increase in product demand will also increase the monopolist's values of MRP_L compared to those given in Table 2.[5] The MRP_L curve shifts outward for either kind of firm, representing an increase in the demand for labor.

In a competitive labor market, each kind of firm will want to hire more labor at the existing wage rate. The market demand for labor could increase, raising both the level of employment and the wage rate. The amount by which the market wage increases will depend on how large the industry is relative to the labor market. If the industry is small, there may be only a very slight increase in wages. If it is large, however, the wage rate could rise significantly. Even in a monopsonistic labor market, the result will be an increase in wages and employment.[6]

EFFECT OF CHANGES IN OTHER INPUTS

A second important cause of shifts in the demand for labor results from the fact that the demands for different factors of production are mutually interdependent. Refer again to Table 1 and Table 2. Suppose the capital stock of the firm is doubled. If labor and capital used together are complementary in the sense that an increase in capital makes labor more productive, each unit of labor will have a larger physical product. This is a fairly general phenomenon. Consider an example. Suppose there is a great blizzard of 1993 and you and your friends have a few days off because your school has been closed. Four of you decide to make some extra cash by pulling stranded vehicles out of snowdrifts. It turns out that the effort is profitable enough that instead of relying on your jeep and a chain, your group invests the profits in a tow truck. When it snows the next time, how do you think your physical product will compare to the first experience?

If the capital stock is increased, the total physical product in Table 1 and Table 2 will increase. As a result, the values of MPP_L will increase and the values of MRP_L will also increase. The MRP_L curve will shift outward, signifying that the demand for labor has increased. This is what is meant by complementarity: an increase in usage of one factor raises the marginal revenue product of the other.

Increased productivity resulting from an increased capital stock can have several effects. Consider what happens if the capital stock expands in one firm but not the whole industry. The firm's demand curve (MRP_L) would shift to the right in Figures 4 and 6 without any (noticeable) effect on the market demand curve, because the firm is very small relative to the industry. The result would be that the firm would employ more units of labor at the market-determined price.

---

5.   It is possible to think of cases in which the demand facing the monopolist increases at every price, but marginal revenue, and thus marginal product, actually falls so the demand for labor falls.

6.   You should work through the geometry of such increases.

On the other hand, consider the effect of an industrywide increase in the capital stock. All firms in the industry have an increase in capital, causing their individual MRP_L curves and the industry MRP_L curve to shift outward. More labor is employed at a higher wage rate. Such a situation is depicted in Figure 9. The initial equilibrium occurs where the firm employs x_1 units of labor at the market wage of W_1. The industry is employing Q_1 units of labor. Now there is an industrywide increase in capital. The firm's MRP_L curve shifts to MRP'_L. Since all the firms in the industry experience this increase in MRP_L, the industry demand curve for labor will also shift, from D_L to D'_L in Figure 9. The market wage rises to W_2. As a result, the horizontal supply curve that the individual firm faces shifts from S_f to S'_f. The firm will now employ x_2 units of labor at wage rate W_2. Industry employment has risen from Q_1 to Q_2. The response of the firm to an increase in its capital stock was to hire more workers at higher wages because the increase in capital increased the marginal productivity of the workers. The demand for the two factors labor and capital can thus be seen to be interdependent.

Some U.S. manufacturing industries have hired more workers because of increases in the capital stock in recent years. The textile industry is a good example. The technology of weaving cloth has changed dramatically from shuttle looms to air jet and water jet shuttleless looms. Investment in this new technology has greatly increased the physical productivity of workers in the weaving sector of the textile industry.

PRODUCTIVITY AND HUMAN CAPITAL

In this chapter, we have applied marginal productivity theory to labor markets. We have shown that labor becomes more productive and wages rise when the labor is used with more capital. The notion of capital is, however,

FIGURE 9
AN INDUSTRYWIDE INCREASE IN CAPITAL
An increase in the capital stock will increase the productivity of labor if capital and labor are complementary factors. This increase in productivity will shift the marginal revenue product curve from MRP_L to MRP'_L and the market demand curve for labor from D_L to D'_L.

(a) Firm

(b) Industry

broader than simply physical tools. Capital is anything used to increase the flow of output. For example, economists define human capital as anything such as health, vigor, education, or training that (1) can be enhanced by "investment" and (2) increases the productivity of the individual.

Just as a firm can increase its investment in physical capital, an individual can invest in human capital. An individual's decision to seek additional education is similar to an entrepreneur's decision to purchase a new piece of equipment. In both cases, the investment is productive if the return (properly discounted) exceeds the cost (properly discounted).

HIGHER EDUCATION AS AN INVESTMENT

Your decision to pursue higher education is a form of investment. The costs are the direct costs (tuition, fees, books, and so on) plus the opportunity costs, primarily lost income (which you could earn instead of going to college). The return is the present value of the increased future earnings caused by the investment in education.

The anticipated future wage rate will have a profound impact on the type and amount of education that is pursued. For example, if wages of accountants rise relative to those of engineers, economists would expect more students to study accounting. Wages in professions that require long periods of study will have to be higher to attract new entrants, for three reasons. First, those in school for long periods of time (like medical doctors) incur greater current costs. Second, they sacrifice a great deal of present income. Third, their future income is a longer way off. As you know, income a long way into the future is worth a great deal less than income now. As we discussed in an earlier chapter, incomes of medical doctors have stopped rising as rapidly as they did decades ago. As a result of these declining (relative) incomes, applications to medical schools declined sharply in the 1980s.

This analysis does not deny that people attend universities and colleges for other reasons besides the return to investment in human capital. Some engage in education for its consumption value. For example, retired people returning to school are not investing in human capital, because their productive years have ended. Instead, they are acquiring education for its consumption value. There are many consumption-related benefits to education, ranging from enjoyment of literature and fine arts to the thrill of solving a tricky problem in logic. There are also many consumption benefits related to being a student. If you are a member of a fraternity or a sorority or enjoy the "big game" or homecoming weekend, you are familiar with some of these consumption benefits.

Not everyone makes career decisions on a strictly economic basis, and we don't want to imply that you should. You are going to spend the rest of your life working. Why not pick out an occupation or profession that you find enjoyable? This discussion of human capital and education is similar to many policy debates in economics. An economic model of human capital formation may seem dehumanizing, but you shouldn't view it that way. It is just another way of analyzing a complex process, and it will give you important insights. These insights can help explain why workers enjoy different income levels or why two workers in the same occupation working for the same firm may receive different salaries. Let's explore some of these insights.

HUMAN CAPITAL AND RACE

The idea that differences in human capital result in differences in wage rates is related to the issue of racial (or sexual) discrimination. The important economic question is how much of the income difference between whites and blacks in the United States is the result of discrimination and how much is a market phenomenon—the result of differences in human capital.

Many economists have examined income differences between blacks and whites from a human capital perspective. In 1955, Morton Zeman's doctoral dissertation at the University of Chicago began the debate over the cause of such differences.[7] Zeman examined the effects of schooling and on-the-job training, two elements of human capital formation, on income differences. He reported that increases in schooling and training increased the incomes of both whites and blacks, but increased the earnings of whites more. In other words, the rate of return to this investment in human capital appeared to be higher for whites. Zeman's work implied that the income differences were the result of different pay for the same skill (that is, discrimination) and that increasing the schooling of blacks would do little to change these differences.

As more data became available in the 1960s, Zeman's result appeared to be confirmed. Blacks gained access to more schooling, yet income differences seemed to become more pronounced. In 1974, Finis Welch found support for a human capital explanation of the income differences.[8] Welch showed, using newly available and more extensive data, that rates of return to education were in fact as high for blacks as for whites.

James P. Smith of the Rand Corporation studied the effects of race on human capital formation using historical records.[9] Smith found that the increase in black education after the Civil War had important implications for income differences. This human capital approach also helped to explain the differences between the findings of Welch and those of other researchers. Before the Civil War, every Southern state had laws prohibiting the schooling of slaves. As a result, 95 percent of all black Southerners were illiterate in 1860. At the end of the Civil War, the difference in average schooling of blacks and whites was enormous. Smith reported that whites of either sex (on the average) finished four to five more years of schooling than blacks did. In the first two decades after the war, blacks began to close this gap. In the next two decades (1886 to 1906), however, black schooling made little progress, and human capital formation of whites outstripped that of blacks. This difference was the result of two factors: the disenfranchisement of blacks in the South and the increase in the number of whites in the North who finished high school. Finally,

7. Morton Zeman, "A Comparative Analysis of White and Non-White Income Differentials" (unpublished dissertation, University of Chicago, September, 1955).
8. Finis Welch, "Education and Racial Discrimination," in Orley Ashenfelter and Albert Rees (eds.), *Discrimination in Labor Markets* (Princeton: Princeton University Press, 1974).
9. James P. Smith, "Race and Human Capital," *American Economic Review* (September 1984): 865–898.

Smith found that the differences in education between blacks and whites continually narrowed from 1906 to 1950.

Smith concluded that education, or human capital formation, profoundly affects race-related income differences, but with a great lag. Smith shows that interruptions in the progress of black schooling in the early 1900s are still influencing the income difference. The lesson of this research is that the key to further narrowing the income gap between the races (or sexes) will depend in large part on the availability of education and on-the-job training. It further shows that such changes are slow and evolutionary.

COMPARABLE WORTH

comparable worth
A standard for determining wages that calls for equal pay for jobs that require similar levels of training, responsibility, and skills.

A public policy area in which issues of perceived labor market inequities and human capital are important is the debate concerning comparable worth. **Comparable worth** is a standard for determining wages on the basis of equal pay for jobs that require similar levels of training, responsibility, skills, and so on. Support for such a standard is a response to the fact that women earn an average of about 67 percent of what men earn and are heavily concentrated in nursing, teaching, retail sales, and secretarial and clerical jobs. The comparable worth standard is criticized heavily by many economists and is also politically controversial.

THE PROS AND CONS OF COMPARABLE WORTH

Advocates of using comparable worth to adjust wages argue that the Equal Pay Act of 1963 and the Civil Rights Act of 1964, which require equal pay for equal work, do not go far enough. They claim that these laws are inadequate because average female pay is only about 67 percent of average male pay. Comparable worth advocates argue that there should be equal pay for jobs requiring similar levels of training, responsibility, and abilities.

The argument for comparable worth is based on two observations: the existence of sex discrimination and monopsony power in labor markets. If employers practice discrimination on the basis of race or sex and federal laws prohibit discrimination in pay in the same job category, then an indirect way to perpetuate discrimination is to separate jobs into categories. These categories would be predominately black or white, or male or female, and different wages would be offered for jobs with similar skills and responsibilities. Since competition would undermine such subtle discrimination, it could only persist if there is monopsony power in the labor market.

The chief difficulty with comparable worth as a way of determining wages is that it substitutes bureaucratic judgments about job classifications for the forces of the marketplace. Shifts in supply and demand for products and services, subtle differences in skills, varying attractiveness of occupations, and other market determinants of wages are difficult to identify and can change more rapidly than a bureaucratic system could handle.

Peter F. Orazem and J. Peter Mattila highlight some problems of setting wages according to any comparable worth scheme. The fundamental problem is that the valuation of different jobs is subjective. Equally in-

In the United States, comparable worth legislation has been limited to public sector employment. In Canada, a recent law extends comparable worth adjustments into the private sector. This legislation could have an indirect impact on firms in the United States since many Canadian firms affected by the law are subsidiaries of U.S. firms.

The law was passed in the Province of Ontario in 1987 and went into effect January 1, 1990. In the first phase, every firm that employs more than 500 people must publish the results of a comparable worth study for the firm and solicit comments from employees. The pay-equity plan must reflect employees' comments and criticisms.

The law did not specify how the pay-equity plans were to be developed, but it did offer suggestions. It suggested that each job be allocated points on a scale of 1 to 100. The points should be based on the job's requirements, such as education, experience, physical exertion, mental exertion, money handling, personnel supervision, type of equipment operated, physical environment, stress, and working conditions. Employers should then identify any job classification in which more than 60 percent of the workers are female. The wages in these job classifications must then be compared to wages in male-dominated classifications with the same score. For example, if the secretarial job classification has a score of 50, the employer must compare wages in that classification with the wages for a male-dominated classification with a score of 50. If the male-dominated classification has a higher average wage than that of the female-dominated classification with the same score, the firm must raise the pay of the female-dominated group.

An interesting twist is that if the male-dominated classification is paid less than the female-dominated classification with the same score, the law says that the wages of the female-dominated group cannot be cut, *and* employers are not required to raise the pay of the male-dominated group. In essence, this plan is not comparable worth, but pay adjustment for females.

The preliminary results of this law are starting to unfold. The Canadian headquarters of Campbell Soup Co. may have to raise the average salaries of secretaries by $3 per hour to make them comparable to earnings of janitors. This adjustment may, however, take some time. The law does not require firms to increase their payroll cost by more than 1 percent per year to meet these goals.

Some U.S. advocates of comparable worth think that the Canadian law may give women leverage in U.S. lawsuits. They believe that if discrimination is identified by the subsidiary of a U.S. corporation in Canada, that fact could be used as evidence in a sex discrimination case against the parent company in the United States.

INTERNATIONAL PERSPECTIVE

COMPARABLE WORTH, CANADIAN STYLE

Source: Frank Swoboda, "How Many Secretaries Are Worth One Janitor?" *The Washington Post National Weekly Edition* (26 November 1989): 21.

formed, unbiased, and qualified analysts can come up with very different results. Orazem and Mattila found that the potential gains for female state employees in Iowa under a proposed scheme were greatly modified by interest groups in the bureaucratic setting. Gains were shifted away from women and toward special interest groups. "Through a series of modifications to the plan and through collective bargaining compromises, other interest groups such as unions, supervisors, and professionals were able to avoid potential losses in pay that would have accrued under the original plan. Indeed, these groups ended up with pay raises."[10]

HUMAN CAPITAL AGAIN

Discrimination is not the only explanation of male-female wage differences. Some observers claim that women bring less human capital to the market. Less human capital could be the result of less education and on-the-job training or the result of lower strength, vigor, dependability, and health of women in general. Historically, females have invested less in education and training than have males. As a result, the average market value of their skills is lower. However, like the educational gap between whites and blacks, the gap between male and female education levels is closing. Over the past thirty years, women have been enrolling in colleges and completing degrees at rates approaching those of men. The economics of this trend is simple. As human capital equalizes, wage differences between men and women should decline. We will explore this issue further in the chapter on income distribution.

MARGINAL PRODUCTIVITY AND INCOME

The analysis in this chapter leads to an important conclusion of marginal productivity theory. In a competitive labor market, the interaction of the value of the marginal product of labor and the supply of labor determines the wage rate. In turn, the productivity of labor depends on the inherent qualities of the labor, the quantity of labor employed, and the amounts of the other factors that are used. This is another way of saying that the distribution of income is determined by the relative marginal revenue products of the different factors of production. Since wages make up the incomes of laborers, more productive workers will have higher incomes. Laborers that are less productive will have lower incomes.

John Bates Clark, the creator of this theory, claimed that it presented a "morally correct" outcome of economic activity. Morality is not the province of economic theory, however. Economic theory is positive. The marginal productivity theory says nothing about whether the income distribution that results is a good one. Rather, the theory indicates that if labor markets are competitive, each worker will receive returns based on individual productivity. If people don't like the outcome, they can work to change it through political action (a topic that will be discussed in a later chapter). The theory also indicates that output will be maximized in societies in which labor is paid according to its marginal productivity.

10. Peter F. Orazem and J. Peter Mattila, "The Implementation Process of Comparable Worth: Winners and Losers," *Journal of Political Economy* (February 1990): 43.

Summary

1. A firm is a supplier in the product market and a demander in the factor market.

2. The demand for labor differs from the demand for a product in that it is derived, interdependent, and technologically determined.

3. A firm demands labor because labor is productive. The marginal revenue product of labor (MRP_L) curve is the firm's demand curve for labor.

4. In a competitive labor market, the firm faces a perfectly elastic labor supply curve (S_L). When the labor supply curve is perfectly elastic, the marginal resource cost of labor (MRC_L) curve is the same as the labor supply curve.

5. A firm that is a monopolist in a product market uses less labor than a competitive firm would use, because the firm restricts inputs in the process of restricting output.

6. A monopsony is a market structure in which there is a single purchaser of a factor of production. Monopsony results in fewer units of labor being purchased at less than the perfectly competitive wage, because the marginal resource cost curve lies above the supply curve. The difference between the monopsonistic wage and the competitive wage is monopsonistic exploitation. Improved market information and mobility of workers greatly reduce monopsony power.

7. The elasticity of demand for labor is greater when the price elasticity of demand of the product it is used to produce is greater, when labor is an important share of the cost structure of the product, and when the opportunity for factor substitution is present.

8. The decision to pursue more education can be viewed as an investment decision that adds to one's stock of human capital. As education rates of blacks and whites converge, the human capital argument predicts that income levels will also converge.

9. The comparable worth movement calls for equal pay for jobs of equal worth.

10. Marginal productivity theory explains how the distribution of labor income in a market economy is determined. It says nothing normative about the morality of this distribution.

New Terms

derived demand
interdependent demand
technologically
  determined demand
marginal productivity
  theory

value of the marginal
  product of labor
  (VMP_L)
backward-bending
  supply curve

marginal revenue
  product of labor
  (MRP_L)
marginal resource cost
  of labor (MRC_L)

monopsony
monopsonistic
  exploitation
comparable worth

Questions for Discussion

1. Can you describe a situation that might involve monopsonistic exploitation? What would you recommend as a correction?

2. The demand for accountants has skyrocketed in recent years and the salaries of accountants have increased significantly. Is the demand for accountants a derived demand? If so, from what?

3. Why are professional athletes opposed to reserve clauses?

4. Discuss your decision to attend college in human capital terms. Include your opportunity costs and projected income. Will continued investment be required to keep your human capital from depreciating?

5. How could the potential of career interruptions have an impact on starting salaries and create a difference between women's and men's earnings?

6. Firms operate in both the factor market and the product market. How does the market structure in the product market affect the market structure in the factor market? In other words, is a monopolist always a monopsonist, or vice versa?

7. Describe how an entrepreneur decides how much labor to employ.

8. How is a change in the quantity of labor demanded different from a change in the demand for labor?

9. Does the fact that undergraduate students with high grade-point averages are recruited by "Big Eight" accounting firms have any impact on the supply of accounting professors?

10. How can the elasticity of demand for the product that labor is producing affect the elasticity of demand for that labor?

11. Do you think minimum wage legislation is a good idea? Why or why not?

12. Why might janitors earn higher wages than secretaries, even though the secretaries could do the janitors' job, but the janitors could not do the secretaries'?

13. How is equilibrium in the factor market different for a competitive firm and a monopsonistic firm? How are they the same?

14. Name three factors that could cause a firm's demand for labor to increase. How would such a shift affect the relative wages of the firm's employees?

15. What if the factors that caused the increase in demand in Question 14 affected the whole industry and not just the specific firm?

SUGGESTIONS FOR FURTHER READING

Bergmann, Barbara R. *The Economic Emergence of Women.* New York: Basic Books, 1986. An argument for comparable worth made by an economist who chaired the Committee on the Status of Women in the Economics Profession of the American Economics Association for a number of years.

Hill, John K., and James E. Pearce. "The Incidence of Sanctions against Employers of Illegal Aliens," *Journal of Political Economy* (February 1990): 28-44. A well-written analysis of the effects of U.S. Immigration Bill of 1986, restricting illegal immigration.

Leftwich, Richard H., and Ross Eckert. *The Price System and Resource Allocation*, 10th ed. Homewood, IL: Dryden Press, 1988. Chapters 15 and 16 provide a standard treatment of factor markets at the intermediate level.

1. List the economic goals of unions and the ways they can be achieved.
2. Define:
   a. exclusive union,
   b. inclusive union,
   c. featherbedding,
   d. bilateral monopoly,
   e. yellow-dog contract,
   f. secondary boycott,
   g. closed shop,
   h. union shop,
   i. right-to-work laws,
   j. mediation,
   k. arbitration.
3. Discuss the effects of unions on wages and productivity.
4. Diagram and analyze the economic effects of:
   a. an exclusive union,
   b. an inclusive union,
   c. a bilateral monopoly.
5. Trace the history of the labor movement.
6. List the economic factors that strengthen and weaken unions.

CHAPTER 28

THE LABOR MOVEMENT IN THE UNITED STATES

INTRODUCTION

Having looked at labor markets in theory, we can now examine the effect that unions have on those markets. Unions in many countries have goals that are social and political as well as economic. However, for the most part, unions in the United States have concentrated on economic goals such as higher salaries, job security, and good pensions. The most important goal has been to raise wages, so we will concentrate on the effects unions have had on the wage rate. We will begin with a theoretical look at determining how unions attempt to raise wages. We will then consider empirical evidence of the success of unions in raising wages and discuss at whose expense these increased wages have come. Finally, we will take a look at the history of the labor movement in the United States and examine some recent trends.

THE ECONOMICS OF UNION GOALS

Labor unions have been formed for all sorts of reasons, many of which are social and political. However, the most successful labor unions in the United States have concentrated on economic goals. When we speak of economic goals, the bottom line is the real income of union members. It is largely correct, though oversimplified, to think of unions as existing to increase the wages of their members. Unions do pursue goals other than increasing wages, such as shorter hours and better working conditions. These goals also have the effect, *ceteris paribus*, of increasing the well-being of union workers. If wages are unchanged and working conditions have improved, the worker has received an increase in real income. In order to increase wage rates in a competitive labor market, such as those shown in Figures 1 and 2, the union must do one of two things. It must either increase the demand for labor (from D_L to D'_L in Figure 1) or decrease the supply of labor (from S_L to S_u in Figure 2).

Increasing the demand for labor is very difficult for a union. In Figure 1, the demand curve for labor depends on both the demand for the product the labor produces and the productivity of the labor. One way for the union to increase the demand for labor is by increasing the demand for the product the firm produces. Unions have advertised in an attempt to influence people to "buy union-made." They have also lobbied to decrease imports through tariffs and quotas, in an attempt to increase the demand for domestically produced (union) products. Unions have encouraged educational training programs aimed at increasing productivity and thus increasing the demand for labor. Unions have also tried to persuade the government to help by buying union-made goods and by using macroeconomic policy to increase the demand for such goods. In some instances, unions could keep demand from falling by preventing jobs from being eliminated in declining or dying industries. All things considered, however, it is very difficult for unions to significantly increase the demand for labor.

featherbedding
The maintenance of jobs that management claims are unnecessary or redundant.

One way to maintain jobs is the practice of **featherbedding**, or keeping jobs that management claims are unnecessary or redundant. The classic example of featherbedding concerns railroad firemen. The advent of diesel and electric power made firemen obsolete, but railroad unions were successful in maintaining the job. Featherbedding is also common in the newspaper industry, where typesetters' unions have forced the hand setting of some layouts that could be prepared by computer. In the

FIGURE 1
EFFECT OF INCREASED DEMAND FOR LABOR
One way in which a union can raise its members' wages above competitive levels is to increase the demand for union labor. An increase in demand from D_L to D'_L would increase wages from P_c to P_u. This increase in demand would cause employment to increase.

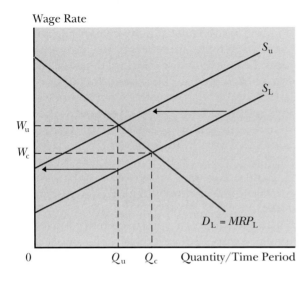

Wage Rate

FIGURE 2
EFFECT OF DECREASED
SUPPLY OF LABOR
Another way in which a
union can raise its
members' wages above
competitive levels is to
decrease the supply of
labor. A decrease in the
labor supply from S_L to
S_u will cause wages to
rise from W_c to W_u. This
decrease in supply causes
employment to decrease.

theater industry, Broadway producers are required to use a certain number of union members regardless of need. For example, a backstage crew of four union members is required no matter what kind of show is being staged. This kind of union success may be only temporary, however, because the added costs may speed the decline of an already dying industry, and the decline of the industry ultimately weakens the union.

Because of the difficulties of increasing demand, unions often focus on the supply side of the market, attempting to shift the supply curve leftward, as illustrated in Figure 2. Historically, many of the "social" goals of unions have had the effect of restricting the supply of labor. Unions have sought to reduce immigration, limit child labor, encourage compulsory and early retirement, enforce a shorter work week, and enact minimum wage legislation. Whatever else you may think of these goals, they all make economic sense for unions if the goal is to increase the wage rate of union members.

Regardless of whether unions focus on demand (Figure 1) or supply (Figure 2), their efforts have the same effect on wages. In both cases, successful union activity will cause the wage rate to rise. The effect on employment, however, is quite different. An attempt to increase demand, as shown in Figure 1, will cause employment in the industry to rise. If, however, the union tries to decrease supply, as in Figure 2, employment in the industry will decline. Since unions are much more effective at reducing supply than at increasing demand, a key economic implication of unions is that they probably reduce employment in those industries in which they are most successful at organizing.

TYPES OF UNIONS

From a theoretical point of view, we can class unions into two basic types: exclusive and inclusive.

EXCLUSIVE UNIONS

exclusive union
A union that restricts the supply of labor and maintains a higher-than-competitive wage for its members by excluding workers from a trade or occupation. Craft unions are exclusive unions.

An **exclusive union** is a union that restricts the supply of labor and maintains a higher-than-competitive wage for its members by excluding workers from a trade or occupation. Because of this exclusion, the wage rate is higher in that part of the work force than it would be in the absence of the union. Figure 3 represents the labor market with such a union. Curve S_L represents the competitive supply of labor, and D_L represents the demand for labor. In the absence of any union organization, the wage rate would be W_c, and Q_c units of labor would be employed. The exclusive union attempts to exclude additional workers from the industry and thus shift the supply curve to S_u. If the union were to succeed in keeping new entrants out, the wage rate for union workers would be W_u, and the number of those workers hired would be Q_u.

The key, then, to an exclusive union is that it restricts entry into a job or occupation. The most familiar example of an exclusive union is a **craft union**, which is composed of specific kinds of skilled laborers, such as plumbers or carpenters. These unions very often require workers to serve apprenticeships and internships in order to become members.

craft union
A union composed of specific kinds of skilled workers, such as plumbers or carpenters.

It should be obvious that a successful exclusive union is very powerful because increases in the wage rate result directly from the exclusionary tactics. The union doesn't need to bargain, coerce, or threaten to strike. Its power to exclude competing workers is sufficient to cause the market wage to increase. The power of the exclusive union is difficult to challenge once the union has been established.

It is also difficult to exclude workers from a union. When wages rise, there will be pressure from outside workers seeking employment in these trades. This natural economic force makes it necessary for the union to be able to control licensing. Many exclusive unions owe their success to getting the government to help them by requiring a worker to earn a license or permit to be a member of the trade. If the union can gain control of this licensing function, it has an automatic way of excluding labor.

FIGURE 3
EFFECT OF AN
EXCLUSIVE UNION
With an exclusive union, union membership is a precondition for employment. As a result, the union can exclude workers and decrease the supply of labor from S_L to S_u.

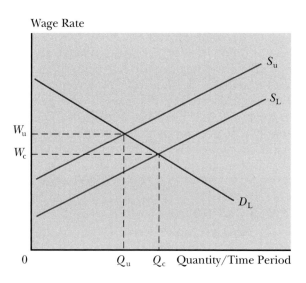

This is one way in which plumbers and electricians have maintained their union power. Professional associations, such as the American Medical Association or the American Bar Association, are similar to craft unions in their effects on the labor market for their members. Also, entry is restricted through licensing and control over professional schools.

INCLUSIVE UNIONS

The **inclusive union** attempts to organize all the workers in an industry and to maintain a strong bargaining position with respect to the management of firms in that industry. Inclusive unions, also referred to as **industrial unions**, include the United Steelworkers, the United Auto Workers, and the Teamsters. The goal of an inclusive union is to bring all workers in an industry into the union, resulting in a strong bargaining position. It is also important that an industrial union organize most of the firms in an industry. Otherwise, non-unionized firms will enjoy a cost advantage and be able to undersell union-organized firms. This competitive disadvantage will create an incentive for non-unionized firms to try to break the union. Inclusive union organization has been most successful in oligopolistic markets, where there are fewer firms in which the labor needs to be organized.

The labor market with an inclusive union is represented by Figure 4. The competitive wage and employment are W_c and Q_c, respectively. The union organizes the industry and bargains the wage rate, W_u. The bargained rate W_u has the same effect as a minimum wage in this industry, so employment will be Q_u. At W_u, however, the quantity of labor supplied will be Q_s. There will be a surplus of labor. Some extra workers would like to work at the bargained wage, and they may offer their services if a strike occurs. This surplus of labor is the so-called scabs you often see on television when management is trying to break a strike by hiring non-union workers.

inclusive union
A union that attempts to organize all the workers in an industry and to maintain a strong bargaining position with respect to management.

industrial union
An inclusive union that gains power by organizing all (or a large share) of the workers in an industry.

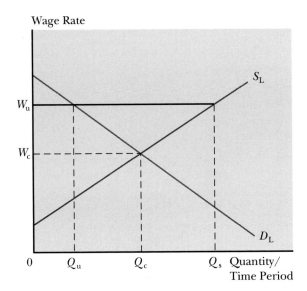

FIGURE 4
EFFECT OF AN INCLUSIVE UNION
An inclusive union attempts to organize all labor in an industry and then to bargain a wage. This bargained wage works like a price floor (or minimum wage) in this labor market.

It should be clear that the ability of an inclusive union to raise wages depends on the strength of its bargaining position, which will, of course, depend on how large a share of the employment in the particular industry is held by its members. It is important that an inclusive union have a significant membership in the industry in which it operates because its success depends on its ability to threaten the firms in that industry.

bilateral monopoly
Market structure in which monopolies deal with each other as buyers and sellers, such as when an inclusive union sells labor to a monopsonistic firm.

Inclusive unions have been most successful in industries that are very concentrated. The firms in these industries may possess monopsony power in labor markets, and an inclusive union can offset some of that power. **Bilateral monopolies** are market structures in which monopolies deal with each other as buyers and sellers, such as an inclusive union selling labor to a monopsonistic firm. Such bilateral monopolies may exist in the steel, auto, and farm machinery industries, where there are both big unions and big oligopolies. This situation is depicted in Figure 5. In the absence of the union, the monopsonistic firm would employ Q_f units of labor at a wage rate of W_f. The competitive wage rate and employment level would have been W_c and Q_c.

In the absence of monopsony power on the part of the purchaser, the union would want a wage of W_u because it faces a downward-sloping demand curve (D_L) for its product (labor). Since the demand curve is downward sloping, the marginal revenue curve lies below it. The union is a monopolist in the selling of its labor. The marginal revenue of the union is thus represented by MR in Figure 5. The union maximizes its gains where MR is equal to MC, at an employment level of Q_u. The result in terms of the wage rate is logically indeterminate. That is, the theoretical model will not say exactly where the resulting wage will fall. All it will say is that the wage will be between W_f and W_u. Whether it is closer to W_f or to W_u will depend on the relative bargaining strengths of the union and the monopsony firm. Note that if the wage is anywhere between W_m and W_f, unionization in a monopsonistic industry increases employment over

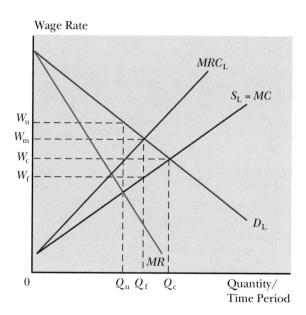

Wage Rate

FIGURE 5
WAGES IN A BILATERAL MONOPOLY
In a bilateral monopoly, a monopolistic seller (the union) sells labor to a monopsony firm. The wage rate will depend on the relative bargaining strengths of the two participants.

the non-union level, Q_f. The monopsonist hired fewer workers than would have been the case with competition. If the union is successful in bargaining a wage rate of W_c (the competitive rate), employment will rise to Q_c. Note that this result is very similar to the effect of a minimum wage in a monopsonistic labor market, which was discussed in the last chapter.

ECONOMIC EFFECTS OF UNIONS

Much of the controversy over unions centers on their effects on wages, income distribution, productivity, stock prices, and inflation. We will examine each of these issues.

DO UNIONS RAISE WAGES?

Regardless of the power of a union, there are constraints on the degree to which it can influence wages. Competitive pressure from non-union labor and the possibility of substituting other inputs will always put limits on union demands. For example, consider a union attempting to organize migrant workers. In response to higher wages resulting from the union, the farmer may substitute machinery for labor. A second powerful restraint on unions' demands exists in the product market. If unions raise wages, costs and prices rise. Consumers will react to an increased price by shifting consumption to non-union products. The demand for union-made products, and thus for union labor, will then fall. These constraints are always present, and the union can do very little to offset them.

Given these limitations, how successful have unions been in increasing the wages of their members? The difficulty in answering this question lies in separating wage differences due to varying productivity from those based solely on union power. The path-breaking empirical study in this area was done by H. Gregg Lewis.[1] Lewis based his study on data from the 1940s and 1950s. He found that union workers received on average from 10 to 15 percent higher wages than non-union workers with similar productivity characteristics. Later studies using Lewis's techniques and more recent data indicate that union salaries are 15 to 25 percent higher for workers with similar productivity characteristics.[2] These same studies also indicate that craft unions are more successful in raising wages than industrial unions are.

In 1980, C. J. Parsley published an extensive review of empirical studies on the effects of unions on wages.[3] His survey of U.S. studies is summarized in Table 1. Parsley's review showed that wages are consistently higher in unionized sectors. The evidence seems to indicate that unions increase wages. Parsley, however, gave an important warning. He pointed out that the previous studies only showed that high wages and unioniza-

1.   H. Gregg Lewis, *Union Relative Wage Effects: A Survey,* (Chicago: University of Chicago Press, 1986), p. 56.
2.   See M. J. Boskin, "Unions and Relative Real Wages," *American Economic Review* (June 1972); and P. M. Ryscavage, "Measuring Union-Nonunion Earnings Differences," *Monthly Labor Review* (December 1974).
3.   C. J. Parsley, "Labor Union Effects on Wage Gains: A Survey of Recent Literature," *Journal of Economic Literature* (October 1980).

TABLE 1
EFFECT OF UNIONS
ON WAGES

AUTHOR	TIME PERIOD OF DATA	INDUSTRY OR OCCUPATION	UNION/NON-UNION WAGE DIFFERENTIAL
Lewis (five studies)	1923–1958	Industrial workers	0–25%
Throop (two studies)	1950–1960	Selected industries	25–29.7%
Personick	1972	Construction	35–70%
Personick and Schwenk	1971	Shirt manufacturing	7–16%
Ashenfelter	1961–1966	Firefighters	6–16%
Schmenner	1962–1970	Public employees	12–15%
Weiss	1959	Craftsmen—operators	6–8%
Stafford	1966	Various occupations	–8–52%
Boskin	1967	Various occupations	–5.3–24.7%

Source: C. J. Parsley, "Labor Union Effects on Wage Gains: A Survey of Recent Literature," *Journal of Economic Literature* (October 1980); and H. Gregg Lewis, *Union Relative Wage Effects: A Survey, 1986* (Chicago: University of Chicago Press, 1986).

tion were correlated. A correct statistical approach would also have to show that the unionization affected wages rather than wages affecting unionization. In other words, workers may unionize after the wages are already higher. Parsley notes, however, that this argument is paradoxical if laborers join unions because they believe that unionization raises wages!

Where do union members' higher wages come from? Your first reaction may be that they come out of business profits, but can this be so? Recall the theory developed in earlier chapters. Wages are a cost of production. If markets are competitive, the increased cost of higher wages will result in higher prices because in the long run, with or without unions, the average firm will only be earning a normal profit. If the firm possesses some monopoly power, the higher labor costs might reduce monopoly profits, but part of the increased costs will be passed forward in higher prices.

In addition, in any product market structure faced by the firm, the increased costs of union-made products will cause the quantity demanded to be lower than it would have been without a union. The reduction in sales in unionized industries means a loss of jobs in those industries. As unemployed workers from unionized industries seek jobs elsewhere, wage rates will fall in the non-union sector.

This analysis implies that the higher wages of union workers are paid partly by consumers in the form of higher prices for union-made goods and partly by non-union workers in the form of lower wages. H. Gregg Lewis has also done empirical research in this area. He concluded that non-union wages are 3 to 4 percent lower because of union-increased wages in the organized labor sector.[4] There also appears to be some evidence that non-union wages are higher in some sectors because non-unionized firms raise wages as a defensive tactic to keep unions out.[5]

UNIONS, WAGES, AND PRODUCTIVITY

As you saw earlier in this chapter, if unions could raise the marginal revenue product of labor, the demand for labor would increase and wage rates would rise. Increasing the demand for labor is difficult to do. In fact,

4. Lewis, *Union Relative Wage Effects.*, p. 78.
5. See Barry Hirsch and John Addison, *The Economic Analysis of Unions* (Boston: Allen and Unwin, 1986).

some critics argue that unions are not only unsuccessful at raising worker productivity but, in fact, may introduce inefficiencies that decrease the marginal revenue product of labor.

Examples of these inefficiencies are well known. There are work rules requiring that certain jobs be performed by certain workers. A light bulb can't be changed by a custodian because the work rules require that the job be performed by an electrician, or a display for a convention must be unloaded by a teamster. Featherbedding, which we mentioned earlier, is another form of inefficiency. Unions can also introduce inefficiency into the production process through disruptive strikes. Strikes cause production to fall, and strikes in major industries can even cause production to be disrupted in related industries. The third way unions can introduce inefficiency is through the effects of wage increases. If unions raise wages in an industry above competitive levels, they must restrict entry into the jobs in that industry, and output is reduced.

Labor in a unionized industry might be more productive because of success in raising wages. If unions raise wages, there will be an incentive for firms to substitute capital for labor. As you learned in the last chapter, if more capital is employed in an industry, the labor in that industry will be more productive.

In a recently published book, economists Richard Freeman and James Medoff argue that unions can increase productivity because of their effect on worker turnover. They argue that unions give workers a "voice/response mechanism" that enables management and workers to iron out problems. This mechanism, they argue, "changes the employment relationship from a casual dating game, in which people look elsewhere at the first serious problem, to a more permanent 'marriage,' in which they seek to resolve disputes through discussion and negotiation."[6] Freeman and Medoff go on to argue that unionization produces loyal employees who are more skilled and have higher levels of productivity. In fact, they argue, productivity is between 20 and 25 percent higher in the unionized sector of U.S. manufacturing.

STOCK PRICES OF UNIONIZED FIRMS

Another area where unions may have an economic impact is the stock prices of firms. Economists have increasingly looked to the stock market to analyze the effect that economic events have on the value of a firm. The price of a firm's stock gives a measure of what an economic event has done to the value of the company.

A study by John M. Abowd examined the effect of union contracts on the value of the stock of the company that signs the contract. Abowd shows that shareholders' wealth moves in the opposite direction from union members' wealth.[7] There was a dollar-for-dollar trade-off between the two variables. This finding suggests that the union can negotiate a contract that extracts economic profit from a firm that has market power. This union contract then takes wealth away from the stockholders. This suggests that if unions are successful in raising wages, the increased wages

---

6.   Richard B. Freeman and James L. Medoff, *What Do Unions Do?* (New York: Basic Books, 1984), p. 38.
7.   John M. Abowd, "The Effects of Wage Bargains on the Stock Market Value of the Firm," *American Economic Review* (September 1989): 774–800.

A great deal of personnel managers' attention is focused on dealing with problem employees. If you are a business major, you will spend time studying psychology in your personnel course in order to better understand such problems. If you go to work in business and end up managing workers, your firm is likely to enroll you in a special course to help you better handle employees who seem to be constantly complaining and causing trouble.

Management has paid considerable attention to this problem in recent years. Entire jobs have been overhauled to make them more "interesting" and "meaningful." Pay and benefits packages have been improved to help keep employees happy. However, a study at the University of Minnesota suggests that the problem is much more basic. It may be in the genes. The study suggests that job satisfaction is related to stable personality characteristics. Or as *U.S. News & World Report* puts it, "some people may be born to whistle while they work."

The study grew out of the famous twin research at the University of Minnesota. A team at the Minnesota Center for Twin and Adop-

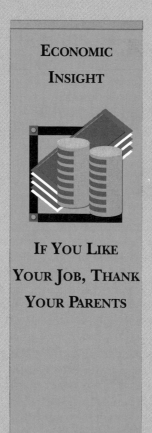

ECONOMIC
INSIGHT

IF YOU LIKE
YOUR JOB, THANK
YOUR PARENTS

tion Research studied thirty-four pairs of identical twins who were separated at birth and raised apart. Since identical twins are genetic equals, any behavioral similarities may be based on characteristics that are inherited rather than learned.

The twins were asked questions that related to pay, the chance to work independently, the amount of praise received, and general job satisfaction. The results surprised the researchers. Some twins' questionnaires were so similar that the same person might have filled them out. Twins tended to choose jobs with the same level of complexity, motor skills, and physical requirements. A research chemist's twin was a systems analyst. A coal miner's twin was a machinist. One set of twins even chose the same occupation—firefighting. Clearly, although human capital is acquired, the decisions about where to employ it and how much to invest in it are heavily influenced by heredity. From a management perspective, choosing the right worker for the job may be more important than supervising the worker or dealing with problems later.

Source: *U.S. News & World Report* (24 October 1988): 61.

come at the expense of owners of capital. The study also suggests that unions will only be successful in raising wages in industries where the firms have some degree of monopoly power. Interestingly, Abowd's results are inconsistent with Freeman and Medoff's conclusion that unions enhance productivity. A dollar-for-dollar loss of stockholders' wealth would mean that the stockholders could not expect to recoup any of the additional wage cost through productivity increases.

Do Unions Cause Inflation?

You have just seen that unions cause wages and prices to be higher in unionized industries than in non-unionized ones. But do unions cause inflation? The answer is no! Unions are only affecting relative prices across industries—not the absolute level of prices. Of course, unions bargain for higher wages and businesses raise prices in inflationary times, but these are responses to inflation, not causes of it. In fact, the empirical evidence indicates that union wages rise less rapidly during the early stage of an inflationary period than do non-union wages.[8] This is partly because unions are unaware in the beginning how high the inflation will be. Even if unions anticipate that inflation will occur, they may already have committed their members to long-term contracts with wage increases less than the inflation rate. When these contracts expire, the unions try to make up for the inflation in their wage demands. It sometimes appears as if unions are responsible for the inflation, rather than victims who are trying to catch up.

There are some indirect ways in which union activity can be inflationary. If unions are successful in raising wages above competitive levels in one sector of the economy, employment in that sector will fall. If the unemployed workers from that sector of the economy are unable to find employment in other sectors, unemployment rates will rise. Then, if policy makers pursue expansionary monetary and fiscal policy to reduce the unemployment rate in response to union pressures, inflation might result. In this sense, then, unions may encourage an inflationary bias in macro policy.

A second way that unions might have an inflationary effect is through a successful effort to raise wages faster than productivity increases. Again, unemployment could result, putting pressure on policy makers to pursue expansionary policies. Keep in mind, though, that unions and businesses do not cause inflation. Government policy makers cause inflation through expansionary monetary and fiscal policy.

A SHORT HISTORY OF THE LABOR MOVEMENT

Around the turn of the century, the U.S. economy shifted from a largely agrarian base to an industrial one. By 1910, employment in industry exceeded employment in agriculture. The industrial labor force grew rapidly, and labor organizers became more successful. In 1914, about 7 percent of the work force was unionized. Growth in the labor force and

---

8.   See Albert Rees, "Do Unions Cause Inflation?" *The Journal of Law and Economics* (October 1959).

growth in unionization were accompanied by a rapidly rising real wage rate. That rise in wages was largely due to rapid advances in technology and in the human capital of wage earners. Both union and non-union labor received substantial wage increases during this period.

THE EARLY UNSUCCESSFUL YEARS

The best way to understand the labor movement in the United States is to view it in historical perspective. In the early nineteenth century, the labor movement was unsuccessful in organizing large numbers of workers, and its operations were mostly limited to cities in the eastern United States. During this period, the workday changed from sunup to sundown to ten hours. Workers still spent twelve hours on the job but received two one-hour (mid-morning and mid-afternoon) breaks.

It became apparent by the middle of the century that a coordinated national effort to organize labor was necessary if unions were to be effective. Even if labor did successfully raise wages above the free market equilibrium wage in a certain area, the gains were short-lived. Labor from other regions of the country produced cheaper goods that could be shipped via the rapidly growing, low-cost transportation network. The U.S. Constitution forbids any interference with interstate commerce, so regions or states could not place tariffs on goods from other regions or states. Thus, all or most of the labor in the firms of an industry had to be organized if unionization was to be successful.

National Labor Union
The first successful national union in the United States, founded in 1867 by William Sylvis.

The first successful national union was organized by William H. Sylvis. Sylvis had been treasurer of the short-lived Iron Molders International Union. In 1867, he founded the National Labor Union. The **National Labor Union** was involved in political action and favored the eight-hour day, arbitration, and cooperatives (firms owned by the union members who worked there). The union published a journal, *The Workingman's Advocate*, to voice its political aims. The union grew rapidly to a membership of 600,000 but quickly fell apart after Sylvis's death in 1869.

Knights of Labor
Organized as a secret organization by Uriah Stevens in 1869, it won the first major strike in the United States against the railroad industry but had political reformist goals that led to its demise.

In 1869, the **Knights of Labor** was organized by Uriah Stevens as a secret society. The secrecy was to protect members from reprisals by management, but it also led to suspicion of the union and bad public relations. As a result, the policy of secrecy was dropped in 1879. The Knights' greatest accomplishment was to win the first major strike in U.S. history. This strike was one against the Wabash, Missouri-Kansas-Texas, and Missouri Pacific railroads, which were owned by Jay Gould, one of the most famous of the robber barons. By the turn of the century, however, the Knights of Labor had become unimportant as a force for labor reform. The reasons for its decline were important for future labor organizations. The Knights' philosophical goal for labor reform was to abolish the wage system and replace it with worker cooperatives. It thus had a reformist political agenda rather than "bread and butter" economic goals. The focus on reformist political goals, coupled with some unsuccessful large strikes and some violent acts of sabotage, contributed to the union's failure.[9]

9.   The Knights of Labor was linked to the infamous Haymarket bomb-throwing incident in Chicago in which seven policemen were killed. Eight anarchists were arrested. One was a Knight and the local union refused to expel him because of his involvement. This incident caused many people to identify the Knights with the most radical elements of the labor movement, which was politically costly to the labor movement in general.

The **American Federation of Labor (AFL)** was founded in 1886 by Samuel Gompers.[10] The AFL was an association of exclusive unions primarily made up of skilled workers. It was the first business union, which allowed it to overcome many of the problems earlier national unions had faced. A **business union** was defined by Samuel Gompers as a union that worked for economic goals without wanting to change or destroy the business organization or the political environment in which it worked. Gompers was, above all, pragmatic. He set a single goal of economic gains for the union's members, with no political reformist goals. Gompers thought that national labor leaders had to have the sole authority to call strikes and control membership dues. This principle has remained important in the U.S. labor movement to the present.

Gompers was elected the first president of the AFL. By 1904, membership had grown to nearly 2 million. Much of the union's success was due to Gompers's abilities. Although Gompers had been a radical in his younger days, he realized that the labor movement had to shed its radical-socialist image in order to succeed in the United States. He worked hard to overcome organized labor's negative image, which was generated by the management of large corporations and fed by the activities and tactics of radical unions. Gompers joined the National Civic Federation, an association of wealthy Eastern capitalists, editors, professional people, and corporation officers. This organization emphasized that labor unions' strength did not undermine U.S. business and that strong business was good for labor.

Perhaps the best evidence of Gompers's success was his acceptance by the political establishment. During World War I, President Wilson appointed Gompers to the advisory commission to the Council of National Defense. In 1919, at the Versailles Peace Conference, Gompers served as chairperson of the Commission of International Labor Legislation. He proved that labor leaders were respectable citizens, not communist radicals seeking to overthrow U.S. capitalism.

The early struggles of organized labor were understandable, since it was easy to break strikes and weaken labor organizations because there was a steady supply of eager workers pouring in from Europe. World War I brought prosperity and high labor demand and marked the beginning of success for American unions. Membership increased steadily during this period, and the image of unions started to improve. Much credit for this is due to Gompers. Unions flexed their muscles during the war period, and there were many strikes in 1917. These strikes were caused by the war-generated inflation and booming labor demand and the effect this inflation had on long-term union contracts. In 1918, labor was successful in negotiating an eight-hour day and collective bargaining rights in exchange for a no-strike agreement. As a result, labor emerged from World War I stronger than it had ever been.

The postwar period brought increased inflation and more strikes aimed at increasing wages. The **Industrial Workers of the World (IWW)** was an international union that organized steelworkers after World War I.

American Federation of Labor (AFL)
An exclusive union for skilled workers founded by Samuel Gompers in 1886 as the first business union.

business union
According to Samuel Gompers, a union that works for economic goals without wanting to change or destroy the business organization or the political environment in which it functions.

Industrial Workers of the World (IWW)
An international union that organized U.S. steelworkers after World War I and was viewed as a socialist organization, which contributed to its demise.

10. In 1881, Gompers founded the Federation of Organized Trades and Labor Unions, which is regarded as the precursor of the AFL.

Marxism was to be the workers' revolution. "Workers of the world unite!" Yet workers and independent labor unions have not fared too well in the Soviet Union.

As in the United States, some of the most aggressive union actions in the Soviet Union have been in the mining industry. In 1989, Gorbachev faced a wave of strikes by Soviet coal miners. These miners' strikes have been truly a mass movement. Unlike other movements in the Soviet Union, the miners' unrest crosses ethnic, religious, and geographic boundaries. The miners' grievances are longstanding, and their activism is representative of the real challenge that Gorbachev's reform faces.

In the 1970s, a small group of coal miners (Russians and Ukrainians) began to organize a free trade union outside the control of the state and the KGB. The organizer was Vladimir Klebanov, and the union was called the Association of Free Trade Unions of Workers in the Soviet Union. The primary aim was to protest violations of labor rights guaranteed under the Soviet constitution. The union had reformist political goals like some of the early U.S. unions.

INTERNATIONAL PERSPECTIVE

LABOR STRIKES, SOVIET STYLE

In the early 1980s, Alexei Nikitin, a mine-safety engineer, was arrested for his activity with these union groups and was confined to a psychiatric hospital for the criminally insane. When a psychiatrist, Anatoli Koryagin, diagnosed Nikitin and several other union activists as sane, he was arrested and convicted of crimes against the state. In 1983, the Soviet Union withdrew from the World Psychiatric Association rather than face censure for this episode.

Soviet governments have used two different tactics for dealing with labor unrest in the mining industry. The first is the type of repression just discussed. The second is temporary appeasement. Brezhnev would buy time by filling empty stores with food and promising changes in the mining communities. For the latest protest by the miners, Gorbachev used the same tactic, but the Ukrainian miners held out for more. They got what they wanted—a series of political and economic concessions. Ultimate success of Gorbachev's reforms will put goods in the stores where the miners shop. Getting to that point is the challenge facing perestroika.

Source: Kevin Klose, "Behind the Strikes: An Oppressed and Neglected Proletariat," *The Washington Post National Weekly Edition* (6 August 1989): 7–8.

These workers were unskilled laborers and thus not members of the AFL. The IWW had been associated with several prominent socialists and was regarded as a radical movement. At this time, after the Russian Revolution, the fear of a worldwide Bolshevik revolution gripped the United States. The IWW went on strike against U.S. Steel in 1920 and lost. The breaking of the strike was a major victory for steel companies, who successfully branded the union leaders as socialists who were attempting to overthrow capitalism. The IWW's failure, coupled with the recession of 1920 to 1922, halted what had been a steady rise in union prestige and membership.

The 1920s proved to be a difficult time for the labor movement. The Republican Presidents Harding, Coolidge, and Hoover were pro-business, and business at that time was aggressively opposed to organized labor. The federal government sanctioned **yellow-dog contracts**, which required the employee to agree to refrain from union activity as a precondition of employment and which allowed the firm to discharge a worker for violation of that agreement. In addition, the courts were hostile to union activity. This hostility was apparent in the ease with which management was able to get court injunctions. An **injunction** is a court order to cease some action. In labor-management disputes, it was often used to order labor back to work. A section of the Clayton Act (1914), which had been hailed by Samuel Gompers as the Magna Carta of labor because it limited the use of injunctions against labor, was declared unconstitutional in 1926.

SUCCESS AND POWER

Bad times for unions ended with the election of Franklin D. Roosevelt in 1932. Roosevelt campaigned as the friend of the worker. The legislation that was proposed and passed during Roosevelt's terms established a bond between organized labor and the Democratic party that still exists today. The two key pieces of legislation were the Norris-La Guardia Act (1932) and the Wagner Act (1935). These acts vastly strengthened the power of labor unions and set the stage for their rapid development. They gave workers the right to organize and made it illegal to interfere with this right.

Under the **Norris-La Guardia Act**, yellow-dog contracts were outlawed. Injunctions against unions and their activities were limited to unlawful acts, and businesses were required to engage in collective bargaining and to bargain in good faith. Thus, the most common union-bashing tactic of employers was thwarted by the Norris-La Guardia Act. Court-issued injunctions had been used to stop strikes, boycotts, and other union activities. The intent of this act was to make the federal government neutral with respect to labor policy. Compared to past practices, this was a strong stimulus to union activity.

The **Wagner Act** made it federal policy that every worker should "have full freedom of association, self-organization, and designation of representatives of his own choosing, to negotiate terms and conditions of his employment." The act also established the **National Labor Relations Board (NLRB)**. The NLRB was empowered to investigate unfair labor practices by employers and to determine the legitimate bargaining agent for labor when there are competing unions. The Wagner Act was challenged in the courts and declared to be constitutional by the Supreme Court in 1937. Under this act, private sector workers were given the right

yellow-dog contracts
Contracts that require employees to agree to refrain from union activity as a precondition for employment and that allow firms to discharge workers who violate that agreement.

injunctions
Court orders to cease some activity, such as ordering labor to stop a strike or walkout.

Norris-La Guardia Act
A law passed in 1932 that vastly strengthened the power of labor unions by limiting the court's use of injunctions in labor-management disputes.

Wagner Act
A law passed in 1935 that gave employees the right to organize and bargain collectively and outlawed certain unfair labor practices by employers.

National Labor Relations Board (NLRB)
A board established by the Wagner Act in 1935 and empowered to investigate employer unfair labor practices and to determine the legitimate bargaining agent for labor when there are competing unions.

Congress of Industrial Organizations (CIO)
An affiliation of industrial unions that was organized when the AFL decided not to move into mass-production industries.

Taft-Hartley Act
Act passed in 1947 to reverse some of the Wagner Act's favoring of labor by shifting some legal rights back to employers.

closed shops
Firms where workers must be union members before being employed.

union shops
Firms where union membership is necessary for a worker to remain employed.

right-to-work laws
State laws that allow people to hold jobs without belonging to unions.

secondary boycotts
Union actions to stop an employer from doing business with other firms.

mediation
Third-party intervention in a dispute consisting of attempts to keep the parties together and talking by offering suggestions and clarifying issues.

arbitration
Third party intervention in a dispute consisting of hearing the arguments of both sides, studying their positions, and rendering a decision. In binding arbitration, both sides must abide by the decision.

to organize without interference from management. In practice, if organizers can get 30 percent of the work force in a place of employment to sign authorization cards, the NLRB steps in and conducts a vote. If the majority of the workers support the union in the vote, the management of the company must recognize the union and bargain with it.

During the early 1930s, a debate was going on within the AFL concerning whether it should organize unions in mass-production industries such as steelworking, automobile manufacturing, and mining. The AFL, primarily an organization of craft unions, decided not to organize in these industries. As a result, a number of its affiliated unions broke away from the AFL in 1935 and formed the Committee for Industrial Organization. The name was soon changed to the **Congress of Industrial Organizations (CIO)**. John L. Lewis, the colorful, forceful head of the United Mine Workers, became its first president.

WORLD WAR II AND THE 1950S

The boom economy of the World War II years brought a number of serious strikes. The Wagner Act had given unions more legal power, and the coffers of union treasuries were full. Unions flexed their muscles through a wave of work stoppages. Although the unions were successful in achieving sizable settlements, public sympathy began to shift away from organized labor. As a result, Congress passed the **Taft-Hartley Act** in 1947, which was designed to offset some of the labor gains created by the Wagner Act. President Truman vetoed the act, but Congress overrode the veto, an indication of the anti-union political atmosphere.

The Taft-Hartley Act shifted some legal rights back to employers. **Closed shops,** in which workers were required to become union members before employment, were made illegal. **Union shops,** in which union membership was necessary for a worker to remain employed, remained legal under the act. However, states were given the right to pass **right-to-work laws**, which allowed people to hold jobs without belonging to unions. These laws obviously undermined union power. As you saw earlier in this chapter, an inclusive union must present a united front if it is to be successful in bargaining with management. Right-to-work laws greatly undermined the ability of inclusive unions to present this united front.

The Taft-Hartley Act also required unions to bargain in good faith and outlawed featherbedding and secondary boycotts. **Secondary boycotts** are union actions to stop an employer from doing business with other firms. In other words, a union not only boycotts the firm it has a grievance against, which would be a primary boycott, but it also boycotts firms (and their products) who do business with that firm. A secondary boycott is more powerful than a picket line because it involves actions against and pressures on third parties. In certain instances, the Taft-Hartley Act empowers the President to call an eighty-day cooling-off period before a strike. During this period, mediation is attempted by a government-appointed fact-finding board.

Mediation is third-party intervention into a dispute. The mediator attempts to keep the parties together and talking by offering suggestions and clarifying issues. This process is different from arbitration. In **arbitration**, a third party hears the arguments of both sides in a dispute, studies their positions, and renders a decision. If the dispute has been submitted to binding arbitration, both parties must abide by that decision.

Union leaders fought the Taft-Hartley Act as a "slave labor law" every step of the way. They continue to campaign to reverse some of its provisions. Despite the Taft-Hartley Act, however, unions have continued to show great strength, which has been enhanced by careful and well-organized political activity.

Business and labor are not always at odds. Unions and management have often worked together to lobby for reduced pollution controls, to curb imports, and even to urge tax cuts for business. In some cases, union organization brings stability to an industry. An oligopolistic industry may even use labor power to help monopolize the industry. Before the days of the United Mine Workers, mine operators had a very difficult time with labor because miners were (and are) a very independent lot. The **United Mine Workers (UMW)** is the industrial union for mine workers founded in 1890. Under the leadership of John L. Lewis, it brought organization *and* discipline to mine labor. When Lewis ordered the miners back to work, they went back to work! In later years, however, the leadership of the UMW has not been able to exercise such strong control, and **wildcat strikes**, which are local strikes unauthorized by the national union, have been frequent.

In 1955, the American Federation of Labor and the Congress of Industrial Organizations merged to form the **AFL-CIO**. This merger unified the labor movement under the leadership of Walter Reuther and George Meany. The **Landrum-Griffin Act**, passed in 1959, was a response to public concern over union power and certain questionable practices. The act made unions more democratic, prohibited Communist Party members and convicted felons from union leadership, and strengthened the Taft-Hartley Act by making picketing illegal under certain circumstances.

RECENT LABOR HISTORY

The real world of labor-management relations does not always run the way a review of the law would indicate. The NLRB is often slow to act and sometimes slow to rule in cases of unfair labor practices. The battleground of labor-management relations has shifted to the South, where much of recent industrial growth in the United States has taken place. It is also mainly in the South that right-to-work laws are found. Some economists attribute at least part of the growth of industry in the South to those laws.

The 1960s and 1970s saw a decline in the share of the labor force that was unionized. This trend was partly a result of the fact that the economy was becoming more service-oriented and less manufacturing-oriented. Thirty-five years ago, almost 40 percent of the U.S. labor force was unionized. Today, less than 20 percent is unionized. Some observers predict that by 1995 relative union membership will be at the same level as before the wave of unionization in the mid-1930s.

One exception to this trend was a dramatic increase in the membership of public employee unions. The **American Federation of State, County, and Municipal Employees (AFSCME)** was one of the few unions

United Mine Workers (UMW)
The industrial union for mine workers.

wildcat strikes
Local strikes that are unauthorized by the national union.

AFL-CIO
Organization formed by the merger of the American Federation of Labor and the Congress of Industrial Organizations in 1955, which gave labor a more unified political front.

Landrum-Griffin Act
An act passed in 1959 and aimed at curbing union power by making unions more democratic, restricting Communist Party members and convicted felons from union leadership, and making picketing illegal under certain circumstances.

American Federation of State, County, and Municipal Employees (AFSCME)
A union of public employees that was one of the few unions that grew in the 1970s.

that grew in the 1970s. In the early l970s, under the leadership of Jerry Wurf, AFSCME was politically active. However, in 1977 the union lost its first major battle in a confrontation with Mayor Maynard Jackson of Atlanta. Garbage workers affiliated with the union struck the city of Atlanta. Mayor Jackson refused to bargain with the local AFSCME chapter and hired strike breakers. A high level of unemployment in the city aided the strike breaking, and the jobs were quickly filled. In August 1981, President Reagan dealt the public sector union movement another blow when, in response to an unauthorized strike, he disbanded the Professional Air Traffic Controllers Organization (PATCO).[11]

Humphrey-Hawkins Act
A 1978 amendment to the Employment Act of 1946 that set specific targets for output, employment, and prices.

In late 1978, President Carter signed the Humphrey-Hawkins Act. The **Humphrey-Hawkins Act** was an amendment to the Employment Act of 1946 that set specific targets for output, employment, and prices. The original bill included increases in public sector jobs and was strongly supported by organized labor. The version that finally passed Congress was viewed by many labor leaders as meaningless. The act set national goals to reduce unemployment to 4 percent in 1983, and to cut inflation to 3 percent in 1983 and to zero by 1988. Full employment was defined as the right to full opportunity for useful employment at fair rates of compensation for all individuals able and willing to work. The bill was regarded by labor as merely symbolic. It did not include any means to reach the goals specified, such as more public sector jobs, but left that to future legislation.

There has been little labor legislation since the Landrum-Griffin Act, except for an increase in the minimum wage approved in 1989, the first since 1981. Labor has campaigned vigorously to repeal some aspects of the Taft-Hartley Act. The two most important pieces of legislation that organized labor currently favors are the repeal of right-to-work laws and the common situs picketing bill. The latter bill grants any union the right to picket an entire construction job even when the union represents only a small part of the labor used on the project.

In the 1980s, the situation of organized labor was affected by President Reagan's policies toward the union movement. In his first term, the administration was antagonistic toward unions, an attitude perhaps best exemplified by the dismantling of PATCO in 1981. Reagan's appointees to the NLRB reversed earlier NLRB decisions that were favorable to organized labor. These reversals began in December 1983, when Reagan appointees gained a majority on the board. The effect of these reversals was to make it more difficult for labor to receive favorable rulings. For example, the board ruled that all grievance procedures must be exhausted before an appeal to the NLRB is allowed and that the NLRB cannot force a company to bargain with a union unless the union proves it represents a majority of the workers.

The 1980s was a decade of decreased influence for labor unions. NLRB data show that unions won 60 percent of the certification elections they held in 1965. In 1989, they won less than 20 percent. This decline is the result of active policy on the part of many business firms to fight unionization. Also, firms have increasingly used sophisticated labor con-

11. For a review of the public sector union movement, see Richard B. Freeman, "Unionism Comes to the Public Sector," *Journal of Economic Literature* (March 1986).

SUMMARY OF MAJOR LABOR LAWS	
STATUTE (YEAR)	**MAJOR PROVISIONS**
• Norris-La Guardia Act (1932)	Outlawed yellow-dog contracts and made picket lines and secondary boycotts legal. Limited injunctions against labor to illegal acts and required management to bargain in good faith with unions.
• Wagner Act (1935)	Established right to form unions and set up NLRB.
• Taft-Hartley Act (1947)	Made closed shops illegal. Permitted union shops but also allowed states to pass right-to-work laws.
• Landrum-Griffin Act (1959)	Strengthened Taft-Hartley Act and made unions more democratic.
• Humphrey-Hawkins Act (1978)	Set employment targets, but did not provide any implementation.

sultants who advise them on how to prevent union-forming activity. In 1990, the Bureau of Labor Statistics reported that union membership had declined by more than 3 million members between 1980 and 1990. This figure represented a drop in the unionized part of the labor force from 23 percent to 17.7 percent. During Reagan's terms, total union membership declined by 16 percent. This period also saw a decline in union strike activity. Strike activity put 454,000 workers on the picket line in 1990, compared to 432,000 workers in 1982.

Nowhere is the weakness of the labor movement more obvious than in wage settlements in the 1980s. Because of increased pressure from imports and because of deregulation in some sectors, companies have sought lower wage contracts with unions in attempts to be more competitive. What evolved was a system of two-tier labor contracts. In these contracts, which were very popular in the mid-1980s, the union agreed to accept lower wages for future employees as a way of maintaining the higher wages of existing members. These contracts created significant pay differences. A new pilot for TWA was paid $22,000, while a pilot with seniority on foreign routes was paid $110,000. The Giant Foods contract called for $6.96 per hour for "old hires" and $5.00 per hour for "new hires." The same type contract at Briggs & Stratton produced a wage of $5.50 per hour for new workers and $8.00 per hour for old workers. The strategy started to backfire on union leaders in 1987. New union members eventually become old union members. They form powerful voting blocs. They pay the same union dues and resent being treated differently.

Finally, the structure of the U.S. economy has been changing in such a way that there are fewer jobs in the industries that have traditionally been unionized. Union leaders were slow to grasp the implications of the changing structure and internationalization of the economy. At the beginning of the 1980s, many labor leaders argued that recruits from the expanding service sector of the economy would offset losses in the manufacturing industries. This has failed to happen, partly because firms in the service sector are usually smaller than firms in manufacturing and therefore harder to organize. Service workers accounted for 70 percent of the U.S. work force in 1990, but only 10 percent of them were unionized. In

During the Reagan administration, it seemed that the AFL-CIO and the President should be the bitterest of enemies. After all, Reagan cut the budget of the U.S. Department of Labor and destroyed the union of the air traffic controllers by firing more than 11,000 controllers when they went out on strike. In foreign policy, however, the AFL-CIO and the President were strange bedfellows. In fact, in 1985 alone, the AFL-CIO spent $43 million in eighty-three foreign countries, much of it on anti-communist projects. Many of these sound as though they come from a spy novel. A union in El Salvador complained that it was undermined by the AFL-CIO because it criticized José Napoleòn Duarte, who was supported by Reagan. In another instance, Prodemca, a private group supported by AFL-CIO officials, sponsored tours of the United States by Contra leaders.

Spending by the AFL-CIO in foreign countries is done through four operating groups: The American Institute for Free Labor Department, The African-American Labor Center, The Asian-American Free Labor Institute, and The Free Trade Union. These four make up the AFL-CIO's International Affairs Department. Their 1985 expenditure of $43 million was almost equivalent to the AFL-CIO's domestic U.S. budget of $45 million for that year. The $43 million was fi-

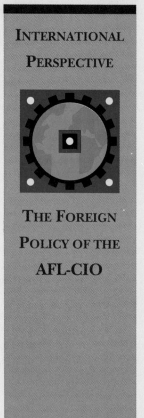

INTERNATIONAL PERSPECTIVE

THE FOREIGN POLICY OF THE AFL-CIO

nanced partly from union dues ($5 million) but mainly from U.S. government funds ($38 million). Most of the government funds were transfers from the U.S. Agency for International Development.

In 1984, $20,000 of government funds channeled through the AFL-CIO went to fund a union in Panama. The Panamanian union used the money to hold an election rally that featured the candidates supported by the military. The U.S. Ambassador to Panama, Everett Briggs, sent a cable to the U.S. State Department accusing the AFL-CIO of meddling in Panama's election. He wired that "the embassy requests that this harebrained project be abandoned before it hits the fan."[a]

Although you might expect pro-business *Forbes* magazine to argue that foreign policy should be left to the U.S. government, in 1990 *Forbes* congratulated the AFL-CIO on its foreign policy success in Poland. When Solidarity was persecuted by the Polish government, the AFL-CIO gave money to the underground and smuggled printing presses and electronic equipment to them. As M. S. Forbes, Jr. put it, "by acting upon their principles, Kirkland (President of the AFL-CIO) and American labor played a vital part in the most dramatic expansion of human freedom this century has seen."[b]

a. *Business Week* (4 November 1985): 92–96.
b. "Fact and Comment II," *Forbes* (22 January 1990): 27.

1990, only 26 percent of manufacturing workers were unionized, compared to 38.7 percent of transportation, communication, and public utility workers and 35.7 percent of government employees. In the private sector, only 15.3 percent of the work force was unionized.

THE FUTURE OF UNIONS

Despite recent trends, many union leaders still think in terms of "old-style" unions. This attitude is revealed in an article by labor economist Audrey Freedman reporting on an AFL-CIO gathering she attended. The chairperson broke the attendees into two groups by saying: "The real unions—steelworkers, boilermakers, etc.—go into the room next door. Pantywaist unions—communications workers, teachers—stay here."[12] However, the "pantywaist" unions have been growing, and the "real" unions have shrunk. This trend is exemplified by the autoworkers. In 1978, the UAW won a hard-fought battle with General Motors and Ford. The settlement called for more than $3 billion in wage increases. Despite this success at the bargaining table, UAW membership shrank by 270,000 members by 1990. Many labor leaders are unaware of or unwilling to accept the fact that any growth in union membership will have to come in the white collar and service trades.

The late 1980s witnessed a battle over labor legislation related to plant closings. In 1987, labor supporters in Congress proposed a bill that would require all U.S. firms with more than 100 employees to give sixty-days' notice before shutting down or making large-scale layoffs. The bill was called the **Worker Adjustment and Retraining Notification Act** (**WARN**). The political lines were clearly drawn over WARN. Republicans in Congress warned that if the bill were passed it would choke off economic growth. Democrats countered that WARN was only fair to workers and would have little negative impact. Michael Dukakis, who was the Democratic candidate for President, campaigned with a banner that read: "60 days is only fair." Organized labor launched a major radio campaign supporting the bill and Dukakis. In late 1988, Congress passed WARN for the second time. This time President Reagan, who had vetoed the first bill, signed it into law—even though he had earlier called it a "ticking time bomb." Dukakis was robbed of an issue, and candidate Bush did not have to explain away a Reagan veto.

What is the impact of this hotly debated labor legislation? In theory, it gives workers more search time to find a new job. It is in effect a type of severance pay. There is some evidence that workers receiving advance notification are able to find new jobs more quickly than workers who receive no notice.[13] However, the out-of-work employees covered by the law hardly regard it as a major victory for the working class. As the mayor of Sanford, N.C., Rex McLeod, put it, when a company citing WARN notified its employees in that town that it would shut down: "The only notification WARN gave me was that I was notified I had a bigger problem."[14]

Worker Adjustment and Retraining Notification Act (WARN)
An act passed in 1988 that required all firms with more than 100 employees to give sixty-days' notice before shutting down or laying off workers.

12. Audrey Freedman, "What Has Happened to Unions?," *Bell Atlantic Quarterly* (Autumn 1985): 11.
13. See Paul Swaim and Michael Podgursky, "Advance Notice and Job Search," *Journal of Human Resources* (Spring 1990): 147–178.
14. Matthew Cooper and Allen Homes, "The Disaster That Never Happened," *U.S. News & World Report* (26 February 1990): 47.

THE BROAD PICTURE

As the union movement developed in the United States, several motives for unionization were evident. These different motives are reflected in union goals. Some unions were welfare unions (the Knights of Labor, for example), which had lofty ideals of social welfare and sought these goals by advocating an end to the wage system and the establishment of worker cooperatives. Other unions were revolutionary unions (the International Workers of the World), which sought changes in the social order. Still others were business unions (the American Federation of Labor), which ignored social and political goals and sought only to better the economic status of their members. History indicates that only this third type has been successful and able to survive in the U.S. economic system.

The development of unions in the United States can be divided into several periods. The early period from the late eighteenth century until 1930 might be called the repression phase because of the hostility of the government and the courts. This was a difficult time for union organization and one in which the successes of unions were few and far between. The period from 1930 to 1947 might be termed the encouragement phase. Government support and key labor legislation greatly increased the power and prestige of unions. Unions reached their peak of influence during this period. The period from the passage of the Taft-Hartley Act in 1947 to 1980 could be labeled the intervention phase. Government intervened in labor disputes, took away some of labor's earlier gains, and attempted to put big business and big labor on a more equal footing. The current period, since 1980, should perhaps be labeled the decline phase. The basic underpinnings of the labor movement are in a state of flux, the membership mix is changing, and unions are being challenged by government and business firms at all levels.

FORCES THAT STRENGTHEN UNIONS

After more than a century of organized labor, the future of unions depends on the economic forces that work to make unions stronger, as well as those that weaken unions. Monopoly power and inelastic demand strengthen unions.

MONOPOLY POWER

Market power in the product market means that the firm has some degree of control over the price of its product. As a result, the firm has less incentive to fight attempts at unionization. Therefore, unions should be more successful in monopolistic or oligopolistic industries.

ELASTICITY OF FACTOR DEMAND

The preceding chapter discussed the determinants of the elasticity of factor demand. The elasticity of demand for labor directly affects the strength of unions. The more inelastic the product demand, the more inelastic the demand for labor will be and the stronger the union can be.

The share of total cost that is labor cost is the second determinant of the elasticity of the demand for labor. The smaller the share of labor cost, the more inelastic the demand for labor will be and, as a result, the stronger the union will be.

The substitutability of factors also affects elasticity of factor demand. The fewer opportunities the firm has to substitute other factors of production for labor, the more inelastic the demand for labor will be and, again, as a result, the stronger the union will be.

FORCES THAT WEAKEN UNIONS

Any factor that increases the competitiveness in the economy (decreases monopoly power) or increases the elasticity of demand for labor will work to weaken union power. Such factors are simply the opposites of the factors that strengthen unions. However, there are a few additional forces that have weakened unions in recent years and deserve special mention.

CHANGING STRUCTURE OF U.S. INDUSTRY

The changing structure of U.S. industry has weakened the labor movement. More than 70 percent of the work force is now employed in service sector jobs. Fewer than 10 percent of these workers are unionized. As the economy becomes more service-oriented and less industrial, organized labor will suffer erosion of its membership.

RIGHT-TO-WORK LAWS

Twenty states, mostly Southern and Southwestern, have right-to-work laws. Table 2 lists these states. Right-to-work laws, coupled with favorable tax laws, abundant labor supply, and nice weather, attracted industry from the "Rust Belt" to the "Sun Belt" during the 1970s and 1980s. This movement presents a challenge to unions and undermines their strength. The products that these largely non-unionized workers produce compete with union-made products and weaken unionized firms. The unions have responded by attempting to unionize workers in right-to-work states but firms there have successfully resisted these attempts. A study of organizing activity in right-to-work states concluded that union organizing is reduced by 50 percent in the first five years after passage of right-to-work legislation and that union membership is reduced by 5 to 10 percent.[15]

DEREGULATION

The increased deregulation of certain industries undermines the strength of unions in those industries. This trend is most obvious in the transportation industry, which underwent widespread deregulation in the early 1980s. Deregulation makes a previously regulated monopoly subject to competition, and firms may find it hard to compete if labor has previously bargained for higher-than-competitive wage rates. For example, before deregulation of the airline industry, salaries over $100,000 were common for airline captains. Post-deregulation airlines were offering much lower salaries. Continental Airlines, for example, declared bankruptcy,

15. David Ellwood and Glenn Fine, "The Impact of Right-to-Work Laws on Union Organizing," *Journal of Political Economy* (April 1987): 250–273.

TABLE 2
RIGHT-TO-WORK STATES

STATE	YEAR OF LEGISLATION
Alabama	1953
Arizona	1946
Arkansas	1944
Florida	1944
Georgia	1947
Iowa	1947
Kansas	1958
Louisiana	1976
Mississippi	1954
Nebraska	1946
Nevada	1951
North Carolina	1947
North Dakota	1947
South Carolina	1954
South Dakota	1946
Tennessee	1947
Texas	1947
Utah	1955
Virginia	1947
Wyoming	1963

reorganized, tore up pilots' contracts, and offered starting salaries of $43,000. In addition, airlines increased work weeks for pilots to forty-hour, five-day weeks, and required them to do administrative work when not flying. American West Airlines, one of the new carriers that entered the industry in the competitive environment, offered pilots $32,500 and received 4,000 applicants for twenty-nine positions.

The lesson is an important one. Regulation protects not only businesses in regulated industries, but also unions. Don't be surprised to see unions fighting deregulation.

IMPORTS

Imports, like deregulation, undermine monopoly power and union power in some industries. The steel and auto industries are examples. The United Auto Workers (UAW) was successful over the years in negotiating wage contracts significantly above competitive wage rates. These high wages made the U.S. auto industry less competitive on world markets. Foreign autos have been a threat to union strength because they represent competition. As auto imports increased and auto profits fell in the early 1980s, the UAW found wage negotiations increasingly difficult. The unions and the automakers joined ranks and went to Washington to plead, successfully, for import restraints.

SUMMARY

1. Exclusive unions are more likely to be successful at raising wages than inclusive unions.

2. Evidence indicates that unions have been successful in raising wages and that these increases have been partly at the expense of consumers and non-union labor and partly at the expense of business profits.

3. Unions may add to productivity if they reduce employee turnover.

4. Union wage increases tend to reduce the stock value of unionized firms.

5. Early unions in the United States had reformist political goals and were largely unsuccessful. When Samuel Gompers turned the American Federation of Labor toward strictly economic goals, he was successful.

6. Beginning in 1932, with the election of Franklin Roosevelt, unions received active encouragement from government. The Norris-La Guardia Act (1932) and the Wagner Act (1935) greatly enhanced the power of unions.

7. The Taft-Hartley Act (1947) and the Landrum-Griffin Act (1959) diminished the power and put unions and management on a more equal footing. Reagan appointees to the NLRB reversed several rulings favorable to unions.

8. In recent years, union membership has declined as a percentage of the U.S. labor force, except among public employees.

9. Factors that enhance monopoly power and make the demand for labor more inelastic increase the strength of unions.

10. Factors that make the economy more competitive weaken union strength. Right-to-work laws, imports, and deregulation all fit in this category.

NEW TERMS

featherbedding	United Mine Workers	National Labor Relations	AFL-CIO
exclusive union	(UMW)	Board (NLRB)	Landrum-Griffin Act
craft unions	wildcat strikes	Congress of Industrial	American Federation of
inclusive union	Industrial Workers of the	Organizations (CIO)	State, County, and
industrial unions	World (IWW)	Taft-Hartley Act	Municipal Employees
bilateral monopoly	yellow-dog contracts	closed shop	(AFSCME)
National Labor Union	injunctions	union shop	Humphrey-Hawkins Act
Knights of Labor	Norris-La Guardia Act	right-to-work laws	Worker Adjustment and
American Federation of	Wagner Act	mediation	Retaining Notification
Labor (AFL)	secondary boycotts	arbitration	Act (WARN)
business union			

QUESTIONS FOR DISCUSSION

1. Do unions raise wages? If so, at whose expense?

2. Is there a difference in the way inclusive unions and exclusive unions organize an industry? Which is more difficult?

3. Explain how closed shops and union shops differ. What are right-to-work laws?

4. Suppose César Chavez was successful in organizing the grape pickers in California. What would have been the likely effect on the price of California wine? What would have been the likely effect in the number of grape pickers employed? Would the fact that the border with Mexico is relatively easy to cross and that the supply of undocumented workers is relatively elastic have any impact on Chavez's organizing costs?

5. Has union strength in the North had any impact on business activity in the South?

6. Public employee unions have increased in strength, yet many states and the federal government forbid these unions from going on strike. Can you think of any reasons why this should be so? Is a police officer in Los Angeles any different from a bank guard there?

7. Is the American Medical Association (AMA) a union?

8. Unions are often viewed as existing simply to bargain for higher wages for their members. What other things do unions do?

9. In the fall of 1987, the Players Association of the National Football League went on strike. The strike lasted four weeks and was unsuccessful from the players' point of view. Why?

10. How do unions affect the distribution of labor income?

11. How do unions affect the distribution of income?

12. Why has union strength (measured as the percentage of the work force that is unionized) declined in the past twenty-five years?

13. What do labor unions maximize?

14. Public employees who are union members should have (should not have) the right to strike. Which of these positions do you support? Defend it.

15. Why might labor union leaders and business leaders be in Washington lobbying for the same legislation? Can you think of any areas on which such legislation might focus?

Suggestions for Further Reading

Blair, Roger D., David L. Kaserman, and Richard E. Romano. "A Pedagogical Treatment of Bilateral Monopoly," *Southern Economic Journal* (April 1989): 831–841. An article showing that many intermediate economic texts incorrectly present the case of bilateral monopoly.

Freeman, Richard B., and James Medoff. *What Do Unions Do?* New York: Basic Books, 1984. A study that claims unions are good for America because they increase productivity.

Hirsch, Barry T., and John T. Addison. *The Economic Analysis of Unions: New Approaches and Evidence.* Boston: Allen and Unwin, 1986. An evaluation of the literature on the economics of labor unions, with over thirty pages of bibliography.

Hughes, Jonathan. *American Economic History.* Glenview, IL: Scott, Foresman, 1990. A well-written economic history of the United States with a good chapter (21) on the early years of the labor movement.

Neff, James. *Mobbed Up: Jackie Presser's High-Wire Life in the Teamsters, the Mafia, and the FBI.* New York: Atlantic Monthly Press, 1990. An interesting account of Presser's activities as president of the Teamsters Union. According to one reviewer, the book "oozes with the sleaze of Teamster activity."

Wendland, Michael F. "The Calumet Tragedy." *American Heritage* (April/May 1986): 38–48. A vivid account of union busting in northern Michigan in 1913, which resulted in deaths and ultimately the making of a ghost town.

1. Define:
   a. economic rent,
   b. single tax,
   c. capitalized value,
   d. crowding out,
   e. roundabout production,
   f. functional distribution of income.
2. Discuss the sources of profit and the role that profit plays in a market economy.
3. List the influences that help determine the distribution of income.

INTRODUCTION

In an earlier chapter, labor markets were used to illustrate the marginal productivity theory of factor pricing. As you know, there are other factors of production that generate income for their owners. Most of the theory that describes labor markets holds for these other factors. Firms demand the services of land and capital because land and capital are productive. Like the demand for labor, the demand for land and capital is derived from the demand for the products they help produce. The price that firms are willing to pay for the services of land and capital depends on their marginal productivity. Rather than repeating the discussion of the marginal productivity model, this chapter discusses the important differences between the other factor markets and labor markets. We will examine rent and interest, the payments to the owners of land and capital. We will conclude with a discussion of profits, the payment to enterprise.

CHAPTER 29

RENT, INTEREST, AND PROFIT

LAND AND RENT

The property income that has generated the most political interest in the United States is rent. To begin, we must define the concepts of land and rent. To the British economists of the eighteenth and nineteenth centuries, land was the input to the productive process that was fixed by nature. Such assets as arable acreage, water, oil, and coal all qualified as land. Recall that if something is fixed in supply, its supply curve is perfectly inelastic. If the supply of land is perfectly inelastic, as in Figure 1, its price is determined solely by changes in demand. Such a price is known as a **demand-determined price**. In Figure 1, if the demand curve is D_0, the price is zero. As the demand curve shifts to D_1, D_2, and D_3, the price rises to P_1, P_2, and P_3, respectively. These prices are not actually rent, but they are related to rent. *Rent* is the payment for the productive services of land, not the price of the land itself. The price of the land would be the present value of the expected future flow of rent payments for future years' productive services.[1]

demand-determined price
A price that is determined solely by changes in demand because supply is perfectly inelastic.

---

1. To review the concept of present value, refer to the earlier chapter on costs and profits.

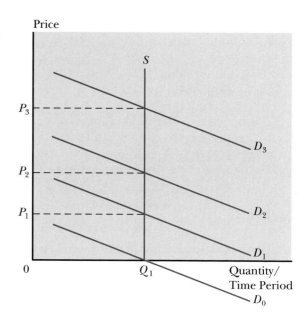

FIGURE 1
THE SUPPLY OF LAND
If the supply of land were
perfectly inelastic, the
price of land would be
determined solely by the
position of the demand
curve.

ECONOMIC RENT

The idea of rent can be generalized to apply to any factor of production. Economic rent is technically a payment greater than the amount necessary to bring a factor into productive use. In other words, in Figure 1, all the payments to land are rent because the amount Q_1 is fixed, and the payments don't bring any more land into existence. This supply curve is different from the labor supply curves described earlier. In the labor market, higher wage rates increase the quantity of labor supplied, and marginal workers enter the market only at the higher wage rate. One essential difference between labor and land is that people have alternatives to work, such as leisure, which have utility.

Economic rent is a surplus paid to the owner of the factor of production. Because it is a surplus, this rent could be taken away with no effect on economic activity. For example, suppose actor Harrison Ford's skills are such that he has only two work alternatives: being a carpenter and earning $35,000 per year or being an actor and earning $2,500,000 per year. Assume that all other aspects of the two alternatives are equal. Under such circumstances, Ford is earning economic rent as an actor. If the two occupations are equally attractive to him, he could be paid $35,001 for being an actor, and he would continue to act.[2] The government could tax away $2,464,999 of his earnings as an actor, and he would not change his behavior. An idea similar to this was suggested by Henry George as a method of raising money to conduct governmental activity.

THE SINGLE TAX

single tax
A tax proposed by Henry George to capture the economic rent on land.

In 1879, Henry George (1839–1897) wrote a book entitled *Progress and Poverty*, which suggested a single tax on land. A **single tax** is a tax on land to capture its economic rent. George argued that the return to land was

2. Competition among movie studios and producers for stars has kept Ford's earnings above $35,001.

a surplus of unearned income and should be taxed away by the government. A social reformer, George felt that this land tax should be the only tax that government collects. His followers became known as the single taxers, and some are still active today.

George's proposal rested on two basic ideas. First, the rent was unearned, and landowners were receiving the return simply because they held good land. If you think about this, it has political appeal. Why should someone get rich just because his or her grandfather happened to stake a claim on a piece of land that was located in a future population center? Second, taking this rent from landowners would not affect economic activity because the supply was perfectly inelastic. In other words, the tax wouldn't cause less land to be supplied, as an income tax causes less labor to be supplied.

ECONOMIC FUNCTIONS OF RENT

The single tax movement died because of political reasons (landowners are a strong political force) as well as some serious theoretical flaws. The first weakness is the idea that the quantity of land is fixed. Remember, when economists draw a demand or supply curve, they hold quality constant. It is possible to make improvements in the quality of land, thus increasing the quantity of land of a given quality. Anyone who has seen agriculture in the Arizona or California deserts can attest to this fact. Increasing payments for land cause more land to be irrigated, increasing the quantity of arable land supplied. If the return to land were taxed away, this incentive to improve land would be gone. Similarly, swamps can be drained, and land can be reclaimed from the sea with dikes, as in the Netherlands. For example, several years ago, there was a proposal to build a new airport near downtown Chicago. The idea was to build a dike in Lake Michigan, pump out the water, and build an airport at the bottom of the lake. Such projects would not even be considered if the single tax were in effect.

The second problem with George's idea is that rents do serve a very important function, even if they have no influence on the quantity of land in existence. George argued that the rent the landowners receive plays no part in creating incentives for them to supply land. On the other hand, the payment made by the user of the land (the firm) ensures that the land is put to its highest-valued economic use. For example, suppose there is a choice acre of vacant land near your school. What should this land be used for—a McDonald's, a massage parlor, a church, or a dump? In a market system, the use will be determined on the basis of who is willing to pay the most. In other words, the market decides between competing uses for the land. If payments to landowners were not made, some kind of planning system would be needed to determine the allocation of land among competing uses.[3]

THE CAPITALIZATION OF RENT

Rent is an income flow to the owner of land in payment for its current use. Often, however, economists speak of the price of land as the lump

---

3.   In a mixed economy, zoning commissions or boards may play the role of such a planning system. If they don't allow the most economic use of a piece of land, they are taxing the owner's right to the income from that land.

Henry George may have been the most widely read economist of all time. His book *Progress and Poverty* (1879) sold millions of copies. Measured by per capita sales at the time of publication, this book is the most popular economics book of all time.

Henry George was born in Philadelphia in a lower middle-class environment. He had almost no formal education and went to sea at age fourteen. He ended up in San Francisco and became a journalist. His interests in political economy were fueled by his experience in that job. George ran for the legislature in California but was defeated, mainly because of his strong opposition to state subsidies for railroads.

George loved to read, and he eventually turned his hand to writing about economics and social commentary. Between 1870 and 1886, he published numerous books and articles, but it was *Progress and Poverty* that brought him international fame. In it, George explained rising land values of the time by general economic growth and westward expansion. George's single tax on the site value

of land was based on the argument that there was no reason why landowners should get rich because of the simple economics of increased demand brought about by the westward expansion of the U.S. population. The increasing value of the land, George argued, was in no way determined or affected by the owners of the land. In this sense, George was arguing that the rising value of land created a "windfall" profit, much in the same way that President Carter argued that deregulation of oil creates "windfall" profits for holders of oil reserves.

George's book and his idea of a single tax made him immensely popular. In 1886, he re-entered politics. This time he ran as the Labor and Socialist Parties' candidate for mayor of New York City. George was so popular that it took a major coalition of other parties to defeat him. He ran again in 1897 but died during the campaign. The Henry George School of Social Science, which still promotes his ideas, can be found at 5 East 44th Street in New York City.

sum at which the buyer and seller exchange title to the resource. There is a simple relationship between the value of a piece of land, or any resource, expressed as a lump sum or a flow. The market price of a piece of land is the capitalized value of the rent. **Capitalized value** is the present value of a stream of future rent payments.

The capitalized value is the amount of money that would earn the annual rent if invested at the current market rate of interest. It can be calculated using the present value technique discussed in the chapter on firms and production. Changes in the stream of rent payments will thus have an impact on the capitalized value. A good example is the value of farmland. For a farmer, the rent from farmland is the income that is produced from farming the land. When farm income falls, the capitalized value of the farmland falls. In some Midwestern states, the selling price of farmland fell by over 50 percent in the mid-1980s. To compound the misery of some farmers (and their bankers), many had used their land, which was falling in value, as collateral for bank loans. They ended up owing banks more than the market value of their land.

LOCATIONAL RENTS
In the chapter on perfect competition, we discussed differential rent theory. The topic arose because firms in perfect competition may appear to be earning economic profits that are actually economic rents to resources owned by the entrepreneur. Perhaps the most basic kind of such a rent is a locational rent. If the seller of a good or service can locate so that the cost of transportation for customers is lower at that location than at the competing locations, the seller can then charge a higher price. If you could find out the location of the interchanges on a new interstate highway, you could buy the land and make a huge profit after the highway is announced. Ocean-front property has a higher market price than does land next to a sewage plant. An acre of land is more expensive in New York City than in Fair Play, South Carolina. These price differences are due to differences in locational rents along interstate highways, on the ocean, and in urban areas.

CAPITAL AND INTEREST

The capital market is the market in which the factor of production capital is exchanged. The term *capital* is, however, used in a number of ways. The economic definition of capital is the tangible equipment, the machinery and buildings, that is used to produce goods and services for consumption. In popular usage, capital consists of the funds (money) borrowed and loaned for the purchase of physical capital. Markets for such funds are close to the extreme of perfect competition.

ROUNDABOUT PRODUCTION
People produce goods so that they can consume. In a sense, therefore, the object of all production is consumption. It is clear, however, that even the most primitive societies make tools to use for production so that they can ultimately increase their output and consume more. These tools are

capitalized value
The present value of a stream of future rent payments.

roundabout production
The creation of physical capital (such as tools) that enhances productive capacity and ultimately allows increased output of consumer goods and services.

capital. The production of physical capital to enhance production instead of final goods for consumption is sometimes referred to as **roundabout production**. That is, roundabout production is the creation of capital goods (such as tools) that enhance productive capacity and ultimately allow increased output. The capital goods that are produced are purchased, or rented by firms, as factors of production. The firm borrows the money it needs to acquire this capital in the market for loanable funds (the capital market).

THE DEMAND FOR CAPITAL

Firms demand capital because it is productive. We can derive a marginal revenue product (MRP) curve for capital just as we did for labor. Such a curve is shown in Figure 2. Just as the demand for labor was a demand for units of input (hours worked), the demand in the market for capital is for physical units. In this example, it is a demand for computers. It is important to realize that the demand for capital is not a demand for money or loanable funds but rather a demand for physical capital.

We can aggregate a firm's demand for all the different types of physical capital it uses by converting this demand into a demand for dollars to purchase (or rent) that physical capital. The price of borrowing money in order to invest is the interest rate. Just as the quantity demanded of computers will increase as the price of computers falls, the quantity of dollars demanded to acquire physical capital will increase at lower rates of interest. You can see this more clearly by examining Figure 3, which shows demand and supply of loanable funds for the firm and in the market for loanable funds. The supply of loanable funds comes from business and household saving. Firms build up a supply of funds out of profits in order to invest them, and individuals save in order to consume more in the future. At higher interest rates, people will save more because present consumption given up will allow greater consumption in the future. As a result, there is an upward-sloping supply curve in the market for loanable funds.

FIGURE 2
THE FIRM'S DEMAND FOR CAPITAL
The marginal revenue product of capital (computers in this case) is the firm's demand for capital.

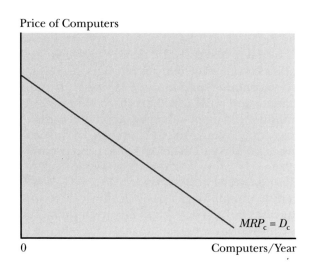

Price of Computers

$MRP_c = D_c$

0   Computers/Year

Japanese investors have been buying property and business firms in the United States, making a lot of Americans nervous and angry. When Columbia Pictures was purchased by Sony for $3.4 billion, *Newsweek* lamented that "a piece of America's soul" had been sold. When Mitsubishi purchased Rockefeller Center, *The New York Times* claimed that "a vital piece of American landscape" was sold.

To the economist, this hostility seems strange. That vital piece of American landscape isn't going to be crated up and shipped to Tokyo. It would be hard to imagine that Columbia's new Japanese owners plan to stop making movies in the United States and turn all the firm's resources to making movies of Sumo wrestlers. So why are so many Americans concerned? Does whether Mitsubishi or the Rockfeller family owns Rockfeller Center really matter?

Judging from the press, it seems to matter to a lot of people. Typical is a book called *Selling Out*, which contains chapters such as "Stealing the Crown Jewels," "Colonizing Hawaii," and "The Twenty-Fourth Ward."[a] There are twenty-three wards in Tokyo, and the authors are suggesting that Tokyo is soon to take over Los Angeles. They base their claim on the fact that twenty-eight of the thirty-five most significant buildings in downtown Los Angeles are owned by Japanese nationals. The other seven are owned by Israeli nationals (two), British nationals (three), Korean (one), and American (one). The Japanese claim that they buy high-rise buildings in large cities because people invest in what they are comfortable with, and the Japanese understand high-rise buildings—Tokyo is full of them. Critics seem to think that once the Japanese have the market cornered, they will raise rents and exploit the tenants. These critics don't seem to understand that the previous owners might go out and build some new buildings with the money they got from the Japanese. Another

INTERNATIONAL PERSPECTIVE

CALIFORNIA, THE TWENTY-FOURTH WARD

complaint against the Japanese is that they pay too much. This complaint must come from someone other than the sellers!

At present, Japanese direct investment in the United States represents about 1.5 percent of all U.S. corporate assets. These investments have grown significantly in the last four years, but they are still lower than those of many other countries. British direct investment in the United States is five times the present level of Japanese direct investment. In 1989, Japanese direct investment in the United States surpassed Dutch direct investment in the United States for the first time. When was the last time you heard someone complain about the Dutch? Furthermore, U.S. citizens still own more assets abroad than foreigners own in the United States.

So why all the fuss about the Japanese? Some Japanese leaders suggest that Americans are racists— that they don't care about a threat from the British or the Dutch but feel threatened by the Japanese. Joseph Nocera, writing in *Esquire*, suggests something different.[b] He suggests that the arrogance of the Japanese offends Americans. The Japanese earn the dollars to invest in the United States because of the trade imbalance between Japan and the United States. The Japanese claim that this trade imbalance is structural, yet they protect their industries from U.S. imports.

The furor over Japanese direct investment in the United States may be indicative of political problems on the horizon. Foreign direct investment is not bad. It is not a sign of U.S. decline. Would you invest in a declining country? The United States is not losing its real estate or its soul. Americans are, however, losing their political patience with the Japanese. American exporters want to be treated fairly and the evidence is that the Japanese do not play fair in terms of granting access to their markets.

a.   Douglas Frantz and Catherine Collins, *Selling Out* (Chicago: Contemporary Books, 1989).
b.   Joseph Nocera, "Whose Land Is This Land?" *Esquire* (March 1990): 62–63.

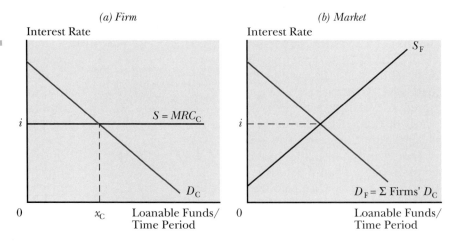

FIGURE 3
THE MARKET FOR
LOANABLE FUNDS
The supply of capital
to the firm is perfectly
elastic at the interest rate
set in the market for
loanable funds. The
firm invests in capital
until the marginal
revenue product of
capital is equal to the
market rate of interest.

In Figure 3, the market demand curve for capital is the summation of all the individual firms' demand curves for capital expressed as the demand for loanable funds. The firms' demands are based on their marginal revenue product curves for physical capital. The market rate of interest, i, determines the supply of capital available to firms in the competitive capital market. The firm can borrow all it wants to at the market rate of interest, which means that its marginal resource cost curve (and its supply curve) is perfectly elastic. We can thus determine the amount of borrowing by the firm, which in this case is x_C.

INTEREST RATES, INFLATION, AND RISK

The preceding analysis mentioned only one rate of interest. You know that there are in fact many interest rates, so which one is used for analyzing the capital market? This question is important in both microeconomics and macroeconomics because the interest rate is both a price (a micro variable) and an important aggregate that affects output and employment. In order to answer this question, we have to distinguish between the real rate of interest and the nominal rate of interest. The rate that is observed, or the market rate, is the nominal rate. Of course, we don't observe just one interest rate. We observe a whole family of interest rates. The various rates depend on who the borrower is, how much risk the lender perceives, and how long the repayment period is. Short-term loans ordinarily carry lower rates than long-term loans. Risky borrowers pay more than safe, dependable borrowers. Because there is a variety of interest rates, economists generally use the rate on U.S. Treasury bills (T-bills) as an indicator of how the market is doing. The T-bill rate is the interest rate the government, the least risky borrower possible, pays on its short-term borrowing.

Interest rates generally rise and fall together, so it's reasonable to pick out one important rate and use it to represent the overall level of interest rates. The spreads between rates, however, will vary over the course of the business cycle. As private borrowers begin to look riskier relative to the government, lenders will be more reluctant to lend to them and more in-

WHAT CAUSES HIGH INTEREST RATES?

Interest rates are higher:
- when expected inflation increases,
- with riskier loans,
- for longer time periods,
- when the demand for loanable funds increases,
- when the supply of loanable funds decreases.

clined to buy T-bills. The rate to private borrowers rises relative to the T-bill rate. The difference between the T-bill rate and the rate to private borrowers for the same length of time is called the risk premium. Risk premiums generally rise during recessions and fall during expansions.

The real rate of interest isn't observed. The real rate of interest is the nominal rate of interest minus the expected rate of inflation. When lenders set an interest rate, they consider inflation as well as risk. If prices are rising, the dollars they are being repaid will be worth less and less with each successive payment. Lenders want to get back, not the number of dollars they lent plus some interest, but the purchasing power they lent plus some interest. On the other side of the market, borrowers are also making calculations of what a loan really costs them, considering that they can repay with dollars that are declining in value. Thus, an inflation premium is included in the nominal interest rate.

COMPETITION FOR CAPITAL

The market interest rate allocates loanable funds among competing firms and among competing uses exactly like the wage rate allocates labor services. Expanding on this idea a little will allow you to see why some economists are so concerned about federal budget deficits. Consider the fact that there are more than just business firms demanding loanable funds. There are two other important groups on the demand side of the market for loanable funds. Consumers demand loanable funds to finance the part of their consumption that is obtained on credit. They borrow to buy homes, furniture, automobiles, and college educations. The other demander of loanable funds is the government. At all levels, federal, state, and local, governments borrow loanable funds. The market for loanable funds is, therefore, composed of three important segments. Demand from all of these is added to give D_F in Figure 4. The market for loanable funds has a supply of S_F and a demand of D_F. The demand curve is the summation of the household demand for loanable funds, the business demand for loanable funds, and the governmental demand for loanable funds. At the resulting interest rate, i, a representative firm adds x units of capital to its capital stock.

What happens, *ceteris paribus,* when the government increases its borrowing? Government demand for loanable funds increases, causing total demand to increase to D_F'. The interest rate rises to i_1. This higher interest rate means that the supply curve for the firm has shifted to the left.

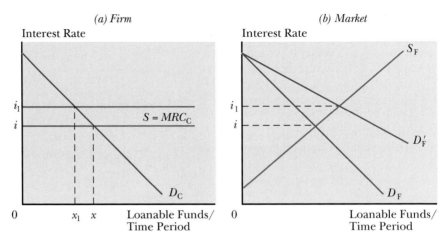

FIGURE 4
CROWDING OUT
The market demand for loanable funds is composed of household, business, and governmental demand. An increase in governmental borrowing will cause the market rate of interest to rise. Firms' response to this increased price of capital is to decrease the quantity demanded. Economists say that firms have been crowded out of the market for loanable funds.

The firm will decrease its investment from x to x_1. The government has crowded some businesses (and households) out of the capital market. Interest rates allocate loanable funds among the three demanders. When the government bids interest rates up, households and businesses will get fewer of these funds.

Many political and business leaders are worried about this crowding out. They believe that this effect is a very real burden of the federal deficit. They argue that the large amounts of borrowing by the government bids up the interest rate and attracts investment funds away from business. When this happens, business investment does not grow as much as it would have and the productivity of the economy suffers. Recall that increases in the capital stock raise the overall demand for labor. Crowding out may also hold down the wages of workers by keeping the demand for labor from growing as fast as it otherwise would have.

ENTERPRISE AND PROFITS

Profits are a residual. They are what's left for the entrepreneur after land, labor, and capital have been paid. This is not to say that profits are not important. As you saw earlier, the quest for profits makes them the prime mover of a market economy. If profits are above normal levels, they will be a signal for firms to enter an industry. If below normal profit is earned, firms will leave the industry. In addition, potential profit is the incentive for innovative activity and risk taking. The entrepreneur takes chances and bets on the future because of the perceived chance to earn profit. Henry Ford installed the assembly line because he thought it would increase efficiency and lead to higher profits. The profit motive drove him to be innovative.

THE SOURCE OF PROFITS
As you have learned, monopoly and other restrictions on markets are a source of profit. Entrepreneurs are therefore very likely to spend a great deal of time trying to monopolize their market. In fact, much of the teach-

A multinational corporation can be loosely defined as a corporation with headquarters in one country and plants in one or more other countries. The essential condition is usually considered to be direct ownership rather than simply financial interest in foreign firms.

Why would a firm go build a production facility abroad rather than export to that country or invest in a local firm there? After all, it can be a hassle to deal with foreign governments and markets that are unfamiliar. It is difficult and costly to get managers to move to foreign countries for long periods of time. Economic theory suggests that the rate of return on investment abroad must be greater by enough to compensate for the additional risks and uncertainty. In fact, if capital markets functioned worldwide as efficiently as in the United States and if worldwide product markets were competitive, there would be no economic rationale for multinational corporations. Exporting would be one alternative. Portfolio investment, or the transfer of capital to foreign entrepreneurs whose knowledge of the local conditions gives them an advantage, would be the second option. The existence of multinationals must therefore be explained by imperfections in product and/or capital markets.

The most obvious explanation is that there isn't free trade and multinationals exist in part to overcome barriers to international trade. Several other imperfections in product markets can be used to explain the existence of multinationals:

INTERNATIONAL PERSPECTIVE

MULTINATIONAL CORPORATIONS

• The investing firm may have patents and technology that it is unwilling to transfer without a great deal of control.

• The investing firm may have a highly differentiated product, such as Pepsi Cola, which gives it some degree of monopoly power. The investing firm can only exploit its brand name capital through direct ownership.

• The investing firm may have control over a raw material or other input that gives it a limited degree of monopoly power.

In all three of these cases, direct ownership would provide the control necessary to exploit any monopoly power that might be present.

There has been a great deal of direct foreign investment by Japanese automakers in the United States. This investment can be explained by some of the above imperfections. First, free trade does not exist. There has been a great deal of "voluntary restraint" of auto exports to the United States by the Japanese. They limit their exports because they are afraid the United States will impose even stricter quotas. It is a good move politically to build plants in the United States because this move dilutes the argument that jobs are lost to Japanese producers. In addition, the Japanese have production and management techniques that are unique. They also produce a differentiated product in that U.S. consumers view Japanese autos to be of very high quality.

ing that goes on in business schools is training in how to differentiate products, develop innovative products, and finance acquisitions. All of these actions are aimed at creating market power and generating profits. Any entrepreneur would choose to be a monopolist, rather than to be in competition. There is, of course, nothing wrong with the search for profit. It is Adam Smith's invisible hand at work. Most monopolies will be temporary, because new entry into the market will erode their success.

The entrepreneur engages in risky activities in search of profits. There is a great deal of uncertainty in the economy. The entrepreneur assumes risk and is rewarded for his or her talent, wisdom, or luck with profit. It is important to note the difference between uncertainty and risk. Many risks are insurable. You can buy auto insurance or fire insurance to protect yourself against risk because insurance companies are able to predict very accurately the average rate of occurrence of auto accidents or fires. The entrepreneur is instead assuming uninsurable risks. These uninsurable risks are the uncertainties surrounding demand and supply. Will a product sell, and can it be sold for a price that is higher than the costs of production? If the answer is yes, the entrepreneur will make a profit for assuming the risk of this uncertain outcome. If the answer is yes *and* other firms can be kept from entering the market, the entrepreneur will have two sources of profit.

The entrepreneur is also involved in innovation. If the entrepreneur can produce a new or better product or find a way to produce an existing product faster or more efficiently, profit will result. Innovations can even include managerial techniques that give a firm a cost advantage. If such innovations can't be patented, and they usually can't, they will quickly be copied by competing firms. Competition will force entrepreneurs to make further innovations, if profits are to be maintained. This race after profits gives the market system its vitality.

Are Profits Too High?

To much of the American public, profit is a four-letter word. It is often combined with an adjective to form phrases with a distinctly negative connotation, such as "windfall profit" or "obscene profit." This attitude toward profit arises from a very common misperception about how high profits are for U.S. corporations. A public opinion poll asked consumers how high they thought profits were in U.S. manufacturing.[4] The average consumer thought that after-tax profits in manufacturing were 37 percent of sales and that a 27 percent profit on sales was "reasonable." The profit level in manufacturing at the time of the poll was only 3.8 percent of sales.

Profits play a very important role. First and foremost, they are the signal of the market system. Second, they reward entrepreneurs for organizing production, monitoring shirking, and coordinating team production. Finally, profits generate the incentive to innovate and strive for greater efficiency.

---

4.   Opinion Research Corporation, "Public Attitudes toward Corporate Profits," *Public Opinion Index* (August 1983).

THE DISTRIBUTION OF INCOME

This chapter, in combination with the chapter on labor markets, provides a theory that explains why the distribution of income is what it is. Basically, the theory says that, given private property and competitive market conditions, market forces will produce a certain distribution of income. Labor will be paid according to its productivity, and the owners of capital and land will receive payments according to the productivity of the factors they own. Any event that causes the marginal productivity of a factor to increase will increase the payment that factor receives.

The theory that productivity determines factor income has received much criticism since it was first developed by John Bates Clark. Clark was looking for a natural law to explain how the distribution of income was determined. The criticisms of his marginal productivity theory have almost all been on the grounds of **distributive justice**, a normative argument for a particular distribution of income. Critics argue that the market-determined income distribution is unfair because the old, the sick, the young, and the handicapped, among others, do not receive a fair share since they are not as productive as others. Another normative criticism of marginal productivity theory rests on the premise that social productivity rather than economic productivity should determine income. In a market system, a writer of pornographic novels often earns more than a writer of poetry. Some critics say this is undesirable.

distributive justice
A normative argument for a particular distribution of income.

You should recognize such criticisms for what they are—normative, ethical considerations and not positive criticisms of the theory. Think back to our early discussion of the role of theory. A theory is valuable if it provides a good explanation of some aspect of the real world. According to this test, marginal productivity theory stands up quite well.[5]

INCOME DISTRIBUTION AND THE MARKET

As you have seen, the distribution of income in a market economy is determined by the payments to factors of production, especially to labor. Wages are the largest component of income. However, other sources of income—rent from land, interest on capital, and profit for enterprise—often make the difference between an average income and a high one.

Assume that the market for the factors of production (land, labor, capital, and enterprise) is perfectly competitive. What then determines the distribution of income, and is this outcome just or equitable? The economic theory developed in this chapter offers a clear and positive answer to the first part of this question. Marginal productivity theory allows economists to analyze how factor incomes change in response to changing market conditions. The second part of the question is normative. The distribution of income arising from the market may not be judged satisfactory. Decisions about changing the distribution of income involve value judgments about the "needs" of certain groups, as well as some positive statements about the effects of redistribution on incentives.

5.   For a review of empirical studies of marginal productivity theory, see David Kamerschen, "A Reaffirmation of the Marginal Productivity Theory," *Rivista Internazionàle di Sciènze Econòmici e Commerciàli* (March 1973).

TABLE 1
THE FUNCTIONAL
DISTRIBUTION OF INCOME
IN THE UNITED STATES

DECADE ENDING	SHARE OF TOTAL INCOME				
	WAGES AND SALARIES	PROPRIETORS' INCOME	CORPORATE PROFITS	INTEREST	RENT
1920	60.0%	17.5%	7.8%	6.2%	7.7%
1940	64.6	17.2	11.9	3.1	3.3
1960	69.9	11.9	11.2	4.0	3.0
1980	75.9	7.1	8.4	6.4	2.2
1990	73.6	8.9	6.8	10.4	0.3

Source: 1920 to 1980 data adapted from Irving Kravis, "Income Distribution: Functional Share," *International Encyclopedia of Social Sciences*, vol. 7; 1990 data from *Economic Indicators* (Washington, DC: U.S. Government Printing Office, February 1991).

THE FUNCTIONAL DISTRIBUTION OF INCOME

The pattern of payments to the factors of production (rent, wages, interest, and profit) is called the **functional distribution of income**. This distribution (shown for the United States in Table 1) is determined by the supply of and demand for factors of different kinds and qualities. Wages and salaries are the largest single component of income and have increased in relative importance compared to earlier periods.

functional distribution of income
The pattern of payments to the factors of production (rent, wages, interest, and profits).

THE RETURN TO SPECIFIC FACTORS

The demand for any factor of production is derived from the demand for the goods and services that the factor is used to produce. The value of any productive resource depends on the value of what it produces. Differences in factor incomes result from differences in factors' productivity and in the demand for the final products.

Given factor inputs of equal physical productivity, the highest reward will go to those factors employed in the industry whose products are most highly valued in the market. The return to a factor will also be affected by the physical productivity of the other factors with which it is combined in a production process. Thus, it is possible that labor (or another factor) of equal quality will receive different earnings when combined with different amounts and qualities of other factors of production.

Examples of productivity-related differences in factor earnings are easy to find. A piece of land near a new interstate highway will be more valuable than a comparable piece of land elsewhere because of the highway. An engineer employed in a firm with a highly successful new product might receive a higher salary than an equally skilled engineer at another firm. A quarterback on a winning NFL team might receive a higher salary because he was at the right place at the right time with the right set of teammates.

MARGINAL PRODUCTIVITY AND EFFICIENCY

An important advantage of letting the market determine income distribution is that rewards will then be linked to efficiency of resource allocation. *Ceteris paribus*, factors flow to those uses with the highest rewards, that is, those in which their productivity is most highly valued. Such a system rewards and thus encourages higher productivity. In freely operating markets, the returns to factors of equal productivity will tend to be equal (or nearly so). Over time, factors will tend to transfer to their highest-valued use.

The market-determined distribution of income may be unsatisfactory in other ways, however. Not only is this distribution very unequal, but it also involves a great deal of chance. Most individuals will avoid risk unless they can be compensated for assuming it. An individual's future income is subject to a high degree of uncertainty. Most of this uncertainty cannot be shifted or avoided through private effort. Risk aversion reduces the efficiency of allocation of productive inputs, especially labor. The situation creates a demand for government programs to reduce income uncertainty. Government may respond either by reducing the risk itself or by implementing various types of insurance plans. Reducing the risk can take the form of education programs, various types of job security, or mandating of private pension and disability programs. Insurance plans include Social Security, unemployment insurance, deposit insurance on bank deposits, and welfare, all of which were instituted in the 1930s and are collectively known as the "social safety net."

In the next chapter we will consider the normative aspect of income redistribution. There is perhaps no other topic in economics or politics that generates more controversy. How and to what degree should government redistribute income?

SUMMARY

1. Land is the factor of production that is in fixed supply. Rent is the return to this fixed factor. Economic rent is a payment above the amount necessary to bring a factor into a given use.

2. Henry George proposed a single tax on land. One important problem with this proposal is that if rents weren't paid, a planning authority would have to decide among competing uses of land.

3. Roundabout production is used to describe the production of physical capital to enhance productivity.

4. Capital, like the other factors of production, is demanded by firms because it is productive. The payment to capital is interest. As interest rates rise, the quantity of capital that firms demand will decrease.

5. When an increase in the interest rate as a result of government borrowing reduces private borrowing, econ-

omists say that crowding out is taking place in the capital market.

6. Profits are the residual amount that entrepreneurs receive. They can exist because of monopoly power, risk taking, or innovation. In a market economy, profits serve as the signal for firms to either enter or leave a particular industry.

7. Marginal productivity theory explains how the distribution of income is determined in a market economy. It says nothing normative about this distribution.

8. Income distribution is determined largely by forces in factor markets. Wages and salaries are by far the largest component of income.

9. Different types of labor, land, or capital earn different rewards depending on their productivities and the industries in which they are employed.

NEW TERMS

demand-determined   capitalized value   functional distribution
  price   roundabout production   of income
single tax   distributive justice

QUESTIONS FOR DISCUSSION

1. What is economic rent? Have you ever earned economic rent? Would taxation of this rent have caused you to behave differently?

2. What does it mean to say profits are a residual?

3. In what ways are economic rent and economic profit similar?

4. Why is the interest rate called the price of borrowing money?

5. Third World countries often complain that they are "ripped off" by multinational corporations because these corporations earn excessively high profits in host countries compared to their profits in their home countries. Can you think of any economic explanation for these higher profits?

6. When major airports are built in rural areas, commercial and residential buildings often spring up around them. The housing prices are often lower than for comparable houses in other areas. Why? If the residents band together and force planes to use noise abatement methods or follow different landing patterns, what is likely to happen? What does this represent to the homeowners?

7. Why do the activities of city and county zoning boards elicit such strong feelings?

8. The role of entrepreneurs in the production process is often misunderstood. What do entrepreneurs do that makes them so important in a market economy?

9. If your college raised your tuition by $1, would you drop out of school? If it raised tuition by $1,000, would you drop out? How about $10,000?

10. What is meant by distributive justice?

11. What conditions determine wages? What causes some people with equal skills to receive different wages? Would more competitiveness in the economy reduce or increase these differences?

12. What purpose do profits serve? Why do some people think that they are too high?

13. If part of Harrison Ford's earnings as an actor is viewed as a rent, then this part of his pay could be taken away and he would still keep acting. Some people argue that it is necessary to pay such rents in order to ensure a future supply of actors (the same argument could hold for NFL running backs). Explain this argument.

14. What does roundabout production mean?

15. What is meant by the functional distribution of income?

SUGGESTIONS FOR FURTHER READING

Aaker, David A., and Robert Jacobson. "The Role of Risk in Explaining Differences in Profitability," *Academy of Management Journal* (June 1987). A recent study that shows that risk, systematic and unsystematic, has significant impacts on the return on investment.

Herbert, Robert F., and Albert N. Link. *The Entrepreneur.* New York: Praeger, 1982. A good source of ideas about what it takes to be a successful entrepreneur.

Lindholm, Richard W., and Arthur D. Lynn. *Land Value Taxation: The Progress and Poverty Centenary.* Madison, WI: University of Wisconsin Press, 1982. This volume includes papers presented at a symposium commemorating the 100th anniversary of Henry George's *Progress and Poverty*. Many, but not all, of the papers are by present-day economists who support George's view.

1. Use a Lorenz curve to describe the distribution of income.
2. Describe how poverty is measured in the United States.
3. Identify the groups most likely to be poor.
4. Analyze the effects of discrimination on wage differences.
5. Summarize the arguments for and against the redistribution of income through government.
6. Discuss the advantages and disadvantages of:
    a. promoting equality of opportunity versus promoting equality of results.
    b. redistributing in kind versus redistributing in cash.
    c. redistributing on a centralized basis versus redistributing on a local or state basis.
7. Describe current government transfer programs.

CHAPTER 30

Income Distribution: Poverty, Discrimination, and Welfare

INTRODUCTION

No single topic in economics generates more controversy than income distribution and government policies for income redistribution. The market generates an unequal distribution of income. The government is a powerful tool for redistribution, although it does not always redistribute from the rich to the poor. This chapter examines the actual distribution of income, the measures of income distribution and poverty, the effects of labor market discrimination, and the role of government in redistributing income.

As scientists, economists have been reluctant to propose schemes for the redistribution of income. This is because value judgments are necessary to choose among alternative income distributions. However, many economists, philosophers, and politicians have developed normative standards for the distribution of income. Plato was explicit about such a rule. He argued that no one in a society should be more than four times richer than the society's poorest member. In general, there are three major normative standards for redistribution: need, equality, and productivity. The principle of pure communism as put forward by Karl Marx was "to each according to his needs, from each according to his abilities." The principle of pure equality would provide the same income for everyone. The productivity standard is also often referred to as the contributive standard. In a pure market system, this standard is the marginal productivity theory of John Bates Clark, discussed in an earlier chapter.

In the United States, the three standards for income distribution are combined. Productivity is the primary standard. However, there is redistribution to the poorer members of society. Part of this redistribution is done privately through charitable giving and part is done publicly through governmental programs at all levels of government. Income redistribution through government pits one group (taxpayers) against another group (recipients). There is less resistance by taxpayers to income redistribution in a high-growth economy. Society can provide for the poor, the elderly, and other groups out of growing income and output. When economic growth is slow, however, redistribution to some means a reduced share for others. Slow economic growth makes the debate over how and how much to redistribute income much more intense.

THE PERSONAL DISTRIBUTION OF INCOME AND POVERTY

In the last chapter, you learned about the functional distribution of income. The distribution of income in a market economy is determined primarily by the ownership of the factors of production and by the prices paid to the factors of production.

The functional distribution of income is one way of looking at income distribution. Another way of describing income distribution is according to how income is divided, equally or unequally, among individuals or households. This measure is called the **personal distribution of income**.

LORENZ CURVES

A **Lorenz curve** is a graph showing the cumulative percentage of income received by a given percentage of households, whose incomes are arranged from lowest to highest. It is constructed by cumulating the percentage of households on the horizontal axis and the percentage of income on the vertical axis. Figure 1 shows Lorenz curves for three societies. A perfectly egalitarian society would have the Lorenz curve labeled distribution A. If incomes were equally distributed, the lowest 10 percent of all households would receive 10 percent of total income, the highest 20 percent would receive 20 percent of total income, and so on. When household incomes are not uniform, the Lorenz curve diverges from the 45-degree line of perfect equality. Distribution B in Figure 1 would be found in a less egalitarian society. The greater the difference between the 45-degree line and the Lorenz curve, the greater the inequality in the income distribution. In Figure 1, distribution C represents more inequality than distribution B.

Lorenz curves for different countries can be used to compare levels of

personal distribution of income
A measure of how total income is divided among individuals or households.

Lorenz curve
A graph showing the cumulative percentages of income received by various percentages of households.

FIGURE 1
LORENZ CURVES
A Lorenz curve shows the percentage of income received by all percentages of households. A perfectly egalitarian society would have a Lorenz curve represented by distribution A. Distributions B and C represent more unequal distributions of income.

income inequality. Sweden's Lorenz curve comes fairly close to the 45-degree line. Less developed countries tend to have curves that are farthest from the 45-degree line. Lorenz curves can also be used to show how the distribution of income changes over time. The data in Table 1 for 1929 and 1988 are graphed as Lorenz curves in Figure 2. Both Table 1 and Figure 2 indicate that the income distribution in the United States has become more equal since 1929.

A Lorenz curve must be interpreted with caution for two reasons. First, Lorenz curves describe the *relative* distribution of income among households. A Lorenz curve might indicate that the lowest 20 percent of the households have only 5 percent of the income, but it doesn't say if this amount of income is high or low in an *absolute* sense. This 5 percent could be enough income to make everyone in the lowest 20 percent well fed, well housed, and well clothed. A Lorenz curve only shows the degree of inequality. By itself, it does not measure either wealth or poverty.

Second, Lorenz curves show how income is distributed among households at a given time. If the households in the lowest 10 percent change over time, the Lorenz curve will give an incorrect picture of relative poverty. The typical household's income changes in a predictable way over time. Income tends to be low when wage earners are young, increases as they reach middle age, and declines in their retirement years. This life-cycle pattern means that households will move around in the income distribution over time.[1] Since the Lorenz curve shows an income distribution at a specific time, it may make income inequality appear greater than it is over time.

One useful source of information on the behavior of income distribution over time is the Panel Study on Income Dynamics (PSID) from the Institute for Social Research at the University of Michigan.[2] The PSID has followed the income and employment history of 5,000 U.S. families since 1968. These data show considerable mobility among income levels. For example, of those who were at the top or the bottom of the income scale in 1971, only about half had been in the same relative position in 1968.

SHARE RECEIVED BY	1929	1947	1960	1972	1979	1983	1988
Lowest Fifth	3.5%	5.1%	4.8%	5.4%	5.3%	4.7%	4.6%
Second Fifth	9.0	11.8	12.2	11.9	11.6	11.1	10.8
Middle Fifth	13.8	16.7	17.8	17.5	17.5	17.1	16.9
Fourth Fifth	19.3	23.2	24.0	23.9	24.1	24.4	24.1
Highest Fifth	54.4	43.3	41.3	41.4	41.6	42.7	43.7
Highest 5 Percent	30.0	17.5	15.9	15.9	15.7	15.8	16.9

TABLE 1
INCOME DISTRIBUTION
IN THE UNITED STATES,
1929–1988

Source: U.S. Department of Commerce, Bureau of the Census, *Statistical Abstract of the United States* (Washington, DC: U.S. Government Printing Office, 1990).

1.   Morton Paglin found that when life-cycle changes were taken into account, there was about 50 percent less inequality than would be inferred from simple Lorenz curves. Further, Paglin found that adjusting for life-cycle changes revealed a significant trend toward a more equal distribution of income in the United States. See Morton Paglin, "The Measurement and Trend of Inequality: A Basic Revision," *American Economic Review* (September 1975): 598–609.
2.   Greg Duncan et al., *Years of Poverty, Years of Plenty: The Changing Economic Fortunes of American Workers and Families* (Ann Arbor, MI: Institute for Social Research, 1984).

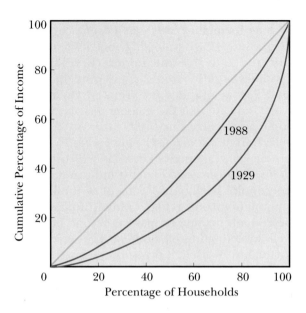

FIGURE 2
INCOME DISTRIBUTION IN THE UNITED STATES, 1929 AND 1988
Plotting Lorenz curves for the United States for 1929 and 1988 shows that the distribution of income has become more equal.

Changes in family composition—births, deaths, divorces, marriages, and children leaving home—had the largest influence on relative economic well-being. This finding supports the life-cycle view of income distribution. The PSID data also suggest that the poor may not all be caught in a poverty trap. Many are temporarily rather than permanently poor.

MEASURING POVERTY

Income distribution is not just a relative concept. Statistics on starvation, malnutrition, and disease show that poverty has an absolute meaning as well. Determining the level of income that marks the border between poverty and nonpoverty is difficult, because poverty is both absolute and relative. People who are relatively poor in one country may be well off by the standards of another country or by the standards of the same country at an earlier time.

The U.S. government first established an official definition of poverty in 1964. The definition was based on the cost of a minimally adequate diet. This figure was then multiplied by three, since the typical household spent one-third of family income on food. In 1964, the poverty income level for a family of four was $3,000 ($1,000 for food times 3) or below. In 1988, the official poverty income level was defined as $6,024 or below for a single individual and $12,092 or below for a family of four. The poverty threshold has been adjusted each year for inflation. However, no adjustment has been made for real income growth or for relative poverty. As a consequence, the poverty threshold has fallen from 44 percent of the median family income in 1964 to 31 percent of the median family income in 1988.

Table 2 shows that from 1959 to 1979, the fraction of the U.S. population below the poverty level decreased. Cuts in social programs and high unemployment rates reversed that trend in the early 1980s. By 1988, however, the percentage was back at the 1980 level.

The poverty rate is a rather crude measure of poverty or changes in

Year	Percentage
1959	22.4
1970	12.6
1975	12.3
1980	13.0
1983	15.2
1984	14.4
1985	14.0
1986	13.6
1987	13.4
1988	13.1

Table 2
Percentage of U.S. Population with Income below the Poverty Threshold, 1959–1988

Source: U.S. Department of Health, Education, and Welfare, *Social Security Bulletin, Annual Statistical Supplement* (Washington, DC: U.S. Government Printing Office, 1987).

poverty because this number gives no indication of how poor the people are. A person whose income is $1 below the threshold is counted as poor, and so is a person whose income is $3,000 below the threshold. If cash transfers bring the first person's income up by $2, the poverty rate falls. If transfer payments raise the second person's income by $2,000, the poverty rate is unchanged. However, these data do provide some indication of how much poverty exists and how it changes over time.

The poverty rate shown in Table 2 has been criticized by some economists because it only counts transfer payments such as Social Security, unemployment compensation, and Aid to Families with Dependent Children. Since 1965, an increasing fraction of programs for the poor have taken the form of in-kind transfers. In 1989, the Bureau of the Census refigured the poverty rate by also counting as income the cash equivalent value of three major in-kind programs: food stamps, housing assistance, and Medicare. These adjustments produced a poverty rate of 10.5 percent in 1988 compared to the 13.1 percent official rate.[3]

Who Are the Poor?

In the United States, the poor come from all parts of the country and every age group. However, it is possible to find certain social, geographic, and racial characteristics of the poor. Geographically, for example, the poor tend to live in the rural South and in Northern cities. Poverty is more common in rural areas than in cities. Table 3 points out some other important characteristics of people living below the poverty line in the United States. Almost 12 percent of the population fell below the poverty threshold in 1985. However, the poverty rate was above 15 percent for certain segments of the population. Nonwhites are much more likely to be poor. Age is also an important factor. Children represent a large fraction of those below the poverty level. In fact, poverty has shifted from being a problem of the elderly to being a problem of female-headed households

3.   Spencer Rich, "Defining Poverty: A Science or an Art," *The Washington Post National Weekly Edition* (12 November 1989): 31. This article also contains a good summary of how the poverty number was first developed and Congressional criticisms of it.

TABLE 3
POVERTY INCIDENCE IN THE
UNITED STATES, 1988

CHARACTERISTICS	PERCENTAGE BELOW THE POVERTY LINE
All Persons	13.1
Adult male in household	10.8
No adult male (female-headed household)	33.6
Household head under twenty-four years old	29.7
Household head under twenty-four years old and black	59.6
Household head sixty-five or older	6.6
Household head sixty-five or older and black	17.1
Households with children under eighteen	
One child	10.4
Two children	9.9
Three children	14.0
Four children	20.8
Less than eight years of schooling	25.0
High school graduate	8.9
Some college (one year or more)	3.5
Employed (50–52 weeks)	3.5
Unemployed (1–49 weeks)	19.4
Did not work	23.9

Source: U.S. Department of Commerce, Bureau of the Census, *Statistical Abstract of the United States 1990* (Washington, DC: U.S. Government Printing Office, 1990).

with small children.

Nonwhites are more likely to be poor than whites partly because of racial discrimination. In addition, nonwhites are also more likely to be poor because a higher percentage are under seventeen, have less education, or live in female-headed households. Whatever the cause of race-related poverty, Figure 3 shows that the nonwhite-white income difference has improved very little for males but a lot for females (white females, however, only earn about 60 to 65 percent of the annual earnings of white males). After some interim improvement, the black-white income ratio was about the same for males in 1988 as it was in the late 1950s.

The figures show that poverty in the United States is greatly influenced by behavior regarding work, education, and marriage. One encouraging sign is that the educational achievement of nonwhites has been increasing. This increase should eventually be reflected in higher income levels. Professor Thomas Sowell argues that monetary returns to education are much higher for minority individuals than for nonminority individuals.[4]

THE REGIONAL DISTRIBUTION OF THE POOR

The share of the population living in poverty varies widely among regions in the United States. For example, in Albany, Georgia, 8.47 percent of all families were headed by females and below the poverty line. The same figure for Sheboygan, Wisconsin was 1.1 percent. In Detroit, Michigan, the figure was 4.9 percent. In Toledo, Ohio, the out-of-state metropolitan

4.   See Thomas Sowell, *Race and Economics* (New York: David McKay Co., 1975). Sowell's points were discussed in the chapter on marginal productivity theory and labor markets.

Thomas Sowell, an economist at the Hoover Institution at Stanford University, has a B.A. from Harvard, an M.A. from Columbia, and a Ph.D. in economics from the University of Chicago. He uses microeconomic theory to analyze race-related problems of income distribution in the United States.

In one study, Sowell examined the impact of affirmative action programs on employment by institutions of higher education. He concluded that such affirmative action programs did not fulfill the intent of the Civil Rights Act of 1964. That law rejected quotas and placed the burden of proving discrimination on the government. In practice, the burden of proof has fallen on the employer, increasing costs for higher education. In addition, Sowell questioned whether such programs were necessary. His data indicate that salaries of black academics equaled or surpassed salaries of white academics with comparable training and credentials before the law was applied in 1971. Sowell's findings also suggest that male-female salary differences at colleges and universities are not primarily the result of employer discrimination but are better explained by social patterns that place heavier family responsibilities on females.

In the book *Ethnic America: A History* (1981), Sowell examined the experience of successive waves of immigrants. He concluded that disciplined hard work and entrepreneurial ability can surmount poverty and bigotry. The impressive record of West Indian blacks suggests that being black is not an overwhelming obstacle to success in the United States.

In all of his work, Sowell uses economic theory to examine social policy questions of considerable interest. He does not shy away from very sensitive questions of race and discrimination. Sowell's ideas and arguments are set forth in *Affirmative Action Reconsidered* (1975), *Black Education: Myths and Tragedies* (1970), *Race and Economics* (1975), *Knowledge and Decisions* (1980), *Ethnic America: A History* (1981), and *Markets and Minorities* (1981).

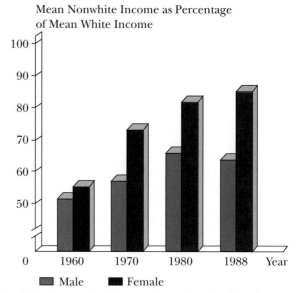

FIGURE 3
NONWHITE-WHITE INCOME RATIOS
Despite some increases in the 1970s, the nonwhite-white income ratio for males improved only moderately between 1960 and 1988. The improvement for nonwhite females, however, was dramatic.

Source: Reynold Farley, "Assessing Black Progress: Employment, Occupation, Earnings, Income, Poverty," *Economic Outlook U.S.A.* (1986)13: 14–19.

area closest to Detroit, it was 3.8 percent.

Research into these regional differences in poverty rates has led to an interesting economic finding. Low-income, female-headed families respond to economic incentives and move to capture higher welfare benefits. Norman Cloutier and Anthony Loviscek have examined the effects of differences among states in payments for Aid to Families with Dependent Children (AFDC), a transfer program aimed at helping poor children.[5] Their research shows that local economic conditions, especially the unemployment rate, are the most important factors affecting the number of families receiving AFDC assistance. However, metropolitan areas in states with high AFDC benefits located near states with low benefits will experience an increase in the number of their AFDC families. The most recent pair of cities to experience this kind of movement has been Chicago and Milwaukee. Wisconsin raised its AFDC benefits relative to those in Chicago, and AFDC families moved to Milwaukee to capture the increase. This result comes as no surprise to economists. Rational individuals respond to incentives. Welfare mothers are no different from other self-interested individuals.

DISCRIMINATION AND THE DISTRIBUTION OF INCOME

How big a role does race and sex discrimination play in income distribution? Since the Civil Rights Act of 1964, discrimination in employment has been illegal. Many companies, in part to show their compliance with fed-

5.   Norman Cloutier and Anthony Loviscek, "AFDC Benefits and the Inter-Urban Variation in Poverty among Female-Headed Households," *Southern Economic Journal* (October 1989): 315–322.

eral law, embarked on affirmative action programs in the 1970s. Yet black-white and male-female wage (and income) differences remain high. These differences, however, do not mean that discrimination accounts for the income distribution pattern. Earning differences can be shown to depend at least partly on other influences.

THE DEMAND AND SUPPLY OF DISCRIMINATION

Labor market discrimination today rarely takes the form of setting wages or hiring on the basis of sex or race, which would violate federal laws. Discrimination is usually more subtle, consisting of channeling workers by sex or race into occupations that are "more suitable" for females or non-whites. As a result of such channeling, certain work categories have a greater supply of workers and lower wage rates than they otherwise would. Traditionally, females were directed into teaching and secretarial work. Many personal service occupations show a high proportion of minority workers. Table 4 shows the concentrations of blacks and females in certain occupations. Females account for 45 percent of the labor force, and blacks account for 10 percent. Females are heavily concentrated in sales, clerical, and private household work. However, they have made progress in recent years in some higher-paying occupations, doubling their representation in medicine and showing impressive gains in law and management. Blacks have also broadened their representation in higher-paying occupations but are still overrepresented in low-paying service and blue-collar occupations.

Figure 4 illustrates the effects of channeling on wage differences. If a majority of workers in some occupations are able to exclude other workers by sex or race, the supply curve of workers for the exclusive occupations will be S_e' rather than S_e. Wage rates for workers in these jobs will be higher than they would otherwise be (W_e rather than W_0). At the same time, the supply curve of workers in minority or female occupations shifts to the right (from S_m to S_m'). The result of channeling is a lower wage rate (W_m rather than W_0) in the minority or female occupations than it would

	1972		1988	
	PERCENT FEMALE	PERCENT BLACK	PERCENT FEMALE	PERCENT BLACK
Total employed	38.0	9.5	44.7	10.1
Physicians	9.3	2.2	20.0	3.3
Lawyers and judges	3.8	1.6	19.5	3.3
Managers and administrators	19.0	1.6	44.7	6.1
Sales workers	41.6	3.0	48.9	6.1
Secretaries	99.4	6.4	99.1	7.1
Carpenters	0.5	5.0	1.4	5.2
Textile operatives	55.2	15.3	90.1	18.0
Cleaning service workers	32.8	28.6	42.6	23.0

TABLE 4
EMPLOYED PERSONS BY SEX, RACE, AND OCCUPATION, 1972 AND 1988

Source: U.S. Department of Commerce, Bureau of the Census, *Statistical Abstract of the United States 1990* (Washington, DC: U.S. Government Printing Office, 1990).

FIGURE 4
LABOR MARKET
DISCRIMINATION
(*a*) If workers are
excluded from certain
occupations, the supply
curve will shift from S_e
to S'_e. The wage rate will
rise to W_e in the excluded
occupations. The exclu-
ded workers will be chan-
neled into minority
occupations. (*b*) The
supply curve in the
minority occupations
shifts from S_m to S'_m, and
the wage rate falls to W_m.

(a) Exclusive Occupations

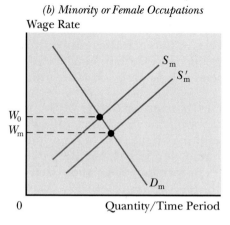

(b) Minority or Female Occupations

otherwise have been. Such wage differences constitute discrimination
only to the extent that they result from workers being excluded from one
group of occupations and channeled into another. If there are real productivity differences between the two kinds of occupations in Figure 4
(reflected in different demand curves), market forces would produce different wage rates even in the absence of racial or sexual discrimination.
In the real world, productivity differences and channeling effects may coexist in the same markets.

DOES LABOR MARKET DISCRIMINATION EXIST?

In the United States, discrimination in employment is illegal by the 1964
Civil Rights Act and the 1965 Equal Employment Opportunity Act, but
wage differences persist. There is some evidence that labor market discrimination exists. For example, in 1989, *Money* magazine reported that
blacks earn 10 to 26 percent less than whites with similar educational back-
grounds.[6] In addition, a study by Michael Robinson and Phanindra Wunnava showed that female hourly earnings in full-time non-union jobs
would be 25 percent higher in the absence of "direct discrimination."[7]

In order to measure labor market discrimination, it is necessary to separate the effects of productivity differences from other reasons for male-
female or black-white earnings differences. The first group of differences
is called the productivity gap, and the second, the wage gap. Historically,
females and minorities have made less investment in human capital (education, training, and job experience) than white males and thus have lower
productivity on the average. Studies suggest that about three-quarters of
the earnings differences can be explained by differences in human capital, by occupational choice, or by other objective characteristics such as
age, health, and geographic location. Do these studies mean that discrimination is not an important explanation for wage differences? No! Consider the effect of discrimination on the incentive to invest in human cap-

6.   Walter L. Updegrave, "Race and Money," *Money* (December 1989): 152–172.
7.   Michael D. Robinson and Phanindra V. Wunnava, "Measuring Direct Discrimination in Labor Markets Using a Frontier Approach: Evidence from CPS Female Earnings Data," *Southern
Economic Journal* (July 1989): 212–218.

ital and the effect of channeling on occupational choice. The productivity gap is not independent of the wage gap.[8] Thus, it is difficult to determine precisely how much of current wage differences reflect past and present discrimination and how much would persist even in a discrimination-free world.

OTHER EXPLANATIONS OF MALE-FEMALE EARNINGS DIFFERENCES

A number of recent studies have identified other explanations for male-female earnings differences, besides discrimination. These explanations include career interruptions, role differentiation, relative number of hours worked, and geographic mobility.

CAREER INTERRUPTIONS. Many working females leave the labor force at least once during their lives. Donald Cox examined the effects of such career interruptions, using data from Social Security records.[9] Cox found that lifetime earnings of females are reduced by these interruptions. Income growth is closely linked to job experience, which increases human capital. Interruptions disrupt the acquisition of experience. Cox also suggested that channeling is not entirely based on discrimination, at least for females. Some jobs more readily allow for career interruptions without loss of skills or continuity. These jobs may be more attractive to females because they blend better with bearing and caring for children.

ROLE DIFFERENTIATION. Economist Victor Fuchs argues that much of the observed pay inequality between males and females is the result of "role differentiation."[10] Fuchs uses this term to indicate that society has different expectations for males and females. Fuchs contends that role differentiation begins in childhood and influences the decisions females make about schooling, location, occupational choice, and time spent in the labor market. Role differentiation often encourages a female to choose a job location and job responsibilities that are compatible with her husband's job choice or that lend themselves to career interruptions. Role differentiation is also reflected in hours worked and geographic mobility. Fuchs argues that lower salaries due to role differentiation do not really constitute discrimination in a narrow sense. Instead, they are the result of choices made by females based on widely held social values. In the last twenty years more females have chosen to enter previously male-dominated occupations, and U.S. wage differences between the sexes have begun to fall.

RELATIVE NUMBER OF HOURS WORKED. Females average fewer hours in paid employment than males. Some comparisons of average earnings—such as the popular statement that females earn 60 percent as much as males—do not correct for that fact. And even that 60 percent ratio has begun to change. It is approaching 67 percent. After correcting for differences in hours

---

8. For a discussion of the interaction between the wage gap and the productivity gap, see Thomas D'Amico, "The Conceit of Labor Market Discrimination," *American Economic Review Papers and Proceedings* (May 1987): 310–315.

9. Donald Cox, "Panel Estimates of the Effects of Career Interruptions on the Earnings of Women," *Economic Inquiry* (July 1984): 386–403.

10. Victor Fuchs, "Recent Trends and Long-Run Prospects for Female Earnings," *American Economic Review Papers and Proceedings* (May 1984): 235–242.

worked, the remaining sex-related difference in earnings is even less.[11]

GEOGRAPHIC MOBILITY. Immobility of labor increases any monopsony power in local labor markets. Married females often refuse attractive job offers because of the geographic location of their husband's job. They may limit their job searches to areas close to home. Robert H. Frank has found that such locational restrictions may explain as much as 23 percent of the wage difference between males and females.[12]

One approach to evaluating sex differences in earnings is to compare the earnings of single males and single females. Some studies show that single females, who have the same incentives as males to invest in human capital, to minimize career interruptions, to work longer hours, and to be geographically mobile, earn almost the same wages as males.[13] In fact, Janet Norwood, commissioner of the U.S. Bureau of Labor Statistics, revealed in a speech at Vanderbilt University that "teenage and young adult women have median earnings that are more than 90 percent of the earnings of men of comparable age." She called the narrowing of this gap "quite significant."[14]

DISCRIMINATION AND MARKET FORCES

Some economists argue that racial or sexual discrimination will not persist over time in a market system because it is costly to entrepreneurs. There would be large numbers of minority and female workers who would be earning low salaries but who would have basically the same education and work skills as white male workers. A profit-motivated entrepreneur could hire these minority and female workers and produce goods and services more cheaply than other firms using the more expensive labor. Thus, the profit motive would work to undermine discrimination.

Some economic historians argue that the Jim Crow laws enacted in the South in the late nineteenth and early twentieth centuries were a response to the threat that market forces would undermine racial discrimination. Jim Crow laws were intended to put the force of law behind segregation and discrimination. These laws were eventually overridden by federal legislation. In South Africa, apartheid was needed to maintain a racially segregated system that economic forces would otherwise have undermined.

If market forces work to undermine discrimination and laws penalize discrimination, why do the data show persistent white-black, female-male income differences? One reason is that different sectors of the economy and different occupations adjust to change with different speeds. It is clear that professional athletics has adjusted very quickly to changing laws and customs, and the medical profession has adjusted quite slowly. The presence of monopoly power and licensing as well as the length of time it takes to train for an occupation may influence the speed of adjustment.

Persistent discrimination also reflects an interaction between discrimi-

11. Robert Pear, "Earnings Gap Is Narrowing Slightly for Women," *New York Times* (3 October 1983).

12. Robert H. Frank, "Why Women Earn Less: The Theory and Estimate of Differential Overqualification," *American Economic Review* (June 1978): 360–373.

13. See Thomas Sowell, "Affirmative Action Reconsidered," *The Public Interest* (Winter 1976): 47–65; and James Gwartney and Richard Stroup, "Measurement of Employment Discrimination According to Sex," *Southern Economic Journal* (April 1973): 575–587.

14. Frank Swoboda, "Closing the Economic Gender Gap," *Washington Post* (4 December 1989): 22.

nation and characteristics that affect productivity (education, training, experience, and occupational choice). Females or minorities, who expect to be offered lower salaries or to be excluded from desirable occupations, may invest less in human capital. As it became clear in the 1970s that jobs formerly closed to most females and minorities were now accessible, the numbers of females and minorities in those jobs began to rise. The information that provides the basis for such changes is disseminated and absorbed slowly.

Discrimination begets poverty, and poverty begets little investment in human capital. Although discrimination is not the sole source of poverty, it does have a contributing effect. Government can help combat discrimination with laws forbidding employment discrimination and with equal treatment for government employees regardless of race or sex. These policies by themselves, however, are not enough to eliminate poverty. The government may also be called upon to take action that changes the income distribution determined by the market.

INCOME REDISTRIBUTION

Citizens may support income redistribution for a variety of reasons. First, some people have **interdependent utility functions**, which means that their well-being is dependent on the well-being of others. These people would support programs to redistribute income because such redistribution increases their utility. Second, some people might view poverty as a negative external effect, like air pollution—something that makes the environment less appealing. This group would support redistribution to improve their surroundings. They might, for example, support food stamp legislation to help hungry people. Finally, redistribution can be viewed as an insurance policy. People might support redistribution as a safety net, realizing that they might become poor at some time.

interdependent utility functions
Preference patterns in which some people's well-being is dependent on the well-being of others.

PRIVATE INCOME REDISTRIBUTION AND THE ROLE OF GOVERNMENT

Income redistribution in the United States, and many other countries, has been carried out by both the private sector and the public sector. Many public goods or goods with some public benefits are produced at least partly in the private sector. There are private roads, private schools, private outdoor concerts, and other goods and services that generate collective benefits but are privately produced. Income redistribution is another activity with public benefits that is produced at least in part by the private sector. The motives for voluntary redistribution through private charities are the same as those that lead individuals to support public redistribution.

It is not likely that private redistribution alone will achieve the desired level of income transfers. Individuals in a large group will recognize that their contribution is too small to significantly affect total redistribution. Each person has an incentive to free-ride on the contributions of others. If all followed this strategy, there would be no private redistribution. There is not enough private redistribution.

The person who gives to others because of personal satisfaction gained from the act of charity does not experience an incentive to free ride. However, for some people, the nature of the benefit is seeing less poverty in the world. In this case, giving by others diminishes the need for an individual to give, and the free-rider problem can arise.

An important influence on the amount of private redistribution is the size of the group in which redistribution takes place. In a relatively small, homogeneous group, there is likely to be relatively more private redistribution. Think about the Mormon church and the Amish sects, for example, or small towns versus large cities. Greater charity in small groups is consistent with the view that the effects associated with poverty are more significant (observable) when the group size is smaller. Thus, at the national level, a small country with a relatively homogeneous population, such as Sweden, would seem likely to practice more redistribution than a large "melting-pot" country, such as the United States.

Although private redistribution has an important role to play, since the 1930s Americans have expected the government to play a major role in redistributing income and alleviating poverty. For both private and public redistribution, several important questions about the best way to redistribute must be resolved.

EQUALITY OF OPPORTUNITY OR EQUALITY OF RESULTS?
One important question concerns the goal of redistribution. Should this goal be equality of opportunity or equality of results? To the extent that labor market discrimination leads to an unequal income distribution and poverty, there may be a need for policies that create greater equality of opportunity. Such policies would mandate government investment in human capital through technical schools, student loans and grants, or training programs. They might also impose penalties on employers who engage in discrimination that is not based on productivity differences. Such policies should offer the working poor a chance to improve their earnings and escape from poverty.

Government or private programs that reduce unemployment and improve the match between workers and jobs are also indirect forms of poverty relief. Not only do these programs increase total output, they generally improve job opportunities and earnings for workers at the lower end of the wage scale. Anything that the government does to promote economic growth and reduce cyclical fluctuations will also reduce unemployment for all groups. Since the poor are so often the last hired and first fired, they would benefit more than most from such programs. Even programs that reduce the obstacles to working, such as those that improve public transportation or subsidize day care, help the poor who can work.

Programs to alleviate poverty by creating work opportunities and improving the potential to earn result in equality of opportunity. Giving everyone an equal chance at success in the labor market is consistent with the values of freedom, incentives, and individual choice implicit in a market economic system. However, equality of opportunity does nothing to help those who are too old, too young, too sick, too disabled, or too unskilled to participate in the market as workers or those who have to care for very small children. The only programs that will reach these poor are programs that are aimed directly at equality of results.

The fraction of the poor outside the labor force, or not expected to work, has risen dramatically in the last fifty years. In 1939, less than one-third of poor households were classified as composed of persons not able to work for one of the reasons listed above. Today, closer to two-thirds of poor households are headed by a person who is elderly, a student, disabled, or a female with one or more preschool children. These people do not benefit from the rising tide of economic growth and increased job opportunities unless there is a deliberate effort to share those gains through a redistribution program.[15]

IN CASH OR IN KIND?

Once the decision is made to alter the market-determined distribution of income, the next question concerns the form in which payments should be made. Should cash transfers, such as a guaranteed income, be used? Or should income be redistributed through in-kind transfers of goods and services, such as housing, food, or health care?

Many forms of income redistribution, both private and public, are in-kind transfers of specific goods or services. In-kind transfers are popular among private charities. Examples include soup kitchens, shelters for the homeless, and Meals on Wheels for shut-ins. In-kind transfers are based not on a desire to reduce income inequality but rather on a desire to ensure the provision of basics, such as food and shelter. James Tobin calls this motivation specific egalitarianism.[16] Economists tend to be general egalitarians, on the other hand. Most would argue for giving cash instead of specific goods and services because a transfer of cash allows more options and maximizes the freedom of the recipient. This argument is based on the assumption that the goal is to maximize the utility of the recipients. Tobin argues, however, that the majority of people are specific egalitarians. They are concerned with ill-clothed and ill-fed people, not with general inequality. If this observation is correct, there should be more transfers made in kind rather than in cash. For the last twenty-five years most of the growth in government transfers to the poor has been in-kind.

Nobel laureate James Buchanan argues that the preference of voters for in-kind rather than cash transfers simply means that they are maximizing their own utility as donors rather than maximizing the utility of welfare recipients by allowing them freedom of choice.[17] The donor/voter's motive for income redistribution may not be concern for the welfare of the recipients but rather a desire to eliminate some perceived problem—homeless people on the streets, slum housing, or students who disrupt the learning process in public schools because of illness or hunger. Providing specific goods or services is a more direct way of accomplishing that goal.

WHICH LEVEL OF GOVERNMENT?

A final issue in designing an income redistribution program is deciding which level of government should be responsible. Until the 1930s, alleviating poverty was a responsibility of state and local governments. The

15. Economic growth as a solution to poverty was criticized on this basis by Sheldon Danziger and Peter Gottschalk, "Do Rising Tides Lift All Boats? The Impact of Secular and Cyclical Change on the Poor," *American Economic Review Papers and Proceedings* (May 1986): 405–410.
16. James Tobin, "On Limiting the Domain of Inequality," *Journal of Law and Economics* (October 1970): 263–277.
17. James M. Buchanan, "What Kind of Redistribution Do We Want," *Economica* (May 1968): 62–87.

Great Depression led to greater involvement by the federal government. In the late 1960s and through the 1970s, strong arguments were made for centralized provision of such programs. Social Security is a federal program, but other programs are shared by levels of government. States that offered high welfare benefits attracted low-income migrants from states where benefits were lower. Thus, some economists argue, states that wanted to offer higher benefit levels were deterred from doing so by fear of attracting more recipients than they could afford. Furthermore, advocates of centralizing welfare argue that the level of income support a household receives should depend on its "needs" (ages, family size, and health) rather than the fiscal wealth of the state in which it is located. Redistribution from richer to poorer individuals would also lead to equalization among states, so even those who lived in poor states but weren't poor would benefit from lower state taxes.

After two failed efforts to centralize welfare in the 1970s (Nixon's Family Assistance Plan and Carter's Program for Better Jobs and Income), it became clear that such plans were not politically feasible. Several reasons have been suggested for this failure. If support for income transfers depends heavily on a desire to eliminate negative external effects (such as crime or blight), then support for redistribution in one's own area will be stronger because the benefits will be concentrated there. Even if taxpayers are interested in increasing the utility of the recipient rather than their own utility, they will still receive more satisfaction from seeing the poverty relief that results from spending in their own area. Thus, if a large part of the benefits of poverty relief are captured at the state or local level, there is reason for a large part of the benefits to be financed at that level as well. In addition, the appropriate level and combination of benefits may vary from state to state. If most of the poor live in rural areas in state *A,* there may be less need for food programs than in state *B*. A state with a high proportion of elderly residents or a cold climate will opt to offer more medical care or heat assistance benefits than another state. A state with more children might put more resources into day care or remedial education. Tailoring the benefits to local needs and the preferences of the local electorate is another reason for giving states a major role.

In 1982, such reasoning led the Reagan administration to propose sorting out welfare programs and returning more of the responsibilities to the states. Like Nixon's centralizing proposal, Reagan's proposal was decisively rejected. The proposal was politically unpopular because the funds to pay for the programs would not come from the federal government. After two decades of failed attempts to sort out responsibility for the poor, income redistribution programs in the United States continue to be funded by the federal government, state governments, local governments (in large cities), and private philanthropic organizations.

REDISTRIBUTION TO THE MIDDLE-INCOME CLASS

Not all redistribution is to the poor or for the poor. Nobel laureate George Stigler and Gordon Tullock point out that people try to use government programs as a way to redistribute income to themselves rather than to others.[18] Stigler theorizes that the government will use its power to extract resources that would not be provided by voluntary agreement in the society. Any group that can gain control of the government can then use this power to its own benefit. Stigler argues that the group that controls government is the middle class. Thus, most public expenditures are made for the benefit of the middle class.

Tullock argues that only a small portion of government transfers go to the poor.[19] He argues that, due to the nature of the voting process, relatively more resources will be taken from the rich in taxes. However, it is not entirely clear how they will be distributed. Since the support of middle-income voters is necessary to obtain the authority needed to take resources from other members of society, he expects that money flows from both ends of the income ladder toward the middle.

Both Tullock and Stigler believe that income redistribution tends to be captured by the dominant political group, the middle class. Both of them present examples of redistribution, such as farm subsidies and support for higher education, that mainly benefit individuals in the middle class. Much redistribution is directed to special interests or is absorbed by bureaucracy, and little of that flow benefits the poor.

GOVERNMENT TRANSFER PROGRAMS IN PRACTICE

Until the 1930s, programs to relieve poverty were small scale, provided mainly by local government and private charity. In the Depression, state and local governments were swamped with demands, and the present system of federal and federally assisted income transfer programs was born. These programs include Social Security for workers who are retired or disabled and survivors of deceased workers, unemployment compensation for the temporarily unemployed, and welfare programs for those unable to work.

SOCIAL SECURITY

Social Security, established in 1935, was initially an old-age pension program. It was later expanded to include survivors' benefits (1939) and disability insurance (1950). Social Security was designed to relieve poverty for several major groups of poor persons: the old, the dependent survivors of deceased workers, and the disabled. In 1965, a program of health care for the elderly (Medicare) was incorporated into Social Security. Except for Medicare, Social Security is a cash transfer program with no in-kind benefits.

Social Security payments are financed by a tax on workers and employers, each paying an equal amount. Many workers believe that their employers actually pay the other half of their Social Security payment. Microeconomic theory reveals that at least part of the other half is in fact paid by workers who earn lower wages than they would receive if there

---

18. George J. Stigler, "Director's Law of Public Income Redistribution," *Journal of Law and Economics* (April 1970): 1–10.
19. Gordon Tullock, *Economics of Income Redistribution* (Boston: Kluver-Nijhoff, 1983), Chapter 5.

The social welfare system is a broad term encompassing all of the transfer payments and social services that governments provide to individual citizens. Some of these programs are based on a means (level of income) test and others go to all citizens. Children's allowances in Canada, for example, are provided to all families. Since these grants are taxable income, some of the funds are recovered in tax payments from higher-income families. Education up to a certain level is traditionally provided to all citizens in industrial countries regardless of income. Food stamps and subsidized public housing, however, are subject to an income test.

Despite the hue and cry for welfare reform, social welfare expenditures in the United States are actually low relative to those of most other industrial countries. Only Japan spends a lower percent of its total income on welfare programs. Japanese society places much greater responsibility for welfare on the family. The elderly, for example, are much more likely to live with their grown children than they would be in the United States.

All major industrial countries have some type of publicly funded old age pension system and some provision for unemployment and dis-

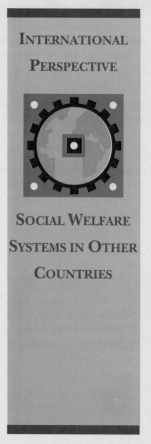

INTERNATIONAL
PERSPECTIVE

SOCIAL WELFARE
SYSTEMS IN OTHER
COUNTRIES

ability insurance. The nature of welfare benefits varies widely, however. Health care is more likely to be provided at public expense in European nations. Public housing has been an important component of social welfare in the United Kingdom, where until recently 28 percent of the population lived in "council houses" (public housing rented at subsidized rates). In Scandinavian countries, the political consensus is that a basic standard of living is a right. Therefore, certain basic social services and social insurance programs (unemployment, disability, and so on) are provided to everyone without an income test.

The emphasis on individualism and the concern over work incentives that pervade the welfare debate in the United States receive less attention elsewhere, except from the Conservative government in the United Kingdom. Support for the welfare state was at its peak in European countries and in the United States in the 1960s and 1970s. In the 1980s, Japan continued to expand its social insurance programs, but the nations of Western Europe as well as the United States were carefully reconsidering the level of public expenditure on social welfare.

SOCIAL WELFARE EXPENDITURES
(INCLUDING EDUCATION)

COUNTRY	PERCENTAGE OF GDP	PERCENTAGE OF GOVERNMENT SPENDING
Japan	17.5	46.7
United States	20.8	58.3
Canada	21.5	53.4
United Kingdom	23.7	51.0
France	29.5	61.0
Sweden	33.4	52.2

Source: Richard Rose and Rei Shiratori, *The Welfare State East and West* (Oxford, UK: Oxford University Press, 1986).

were no Social Security tax. Figure 5 shows why this is the case. Before the Social Security tax, the supply of labor facing the firm is S_0, and the firm's demand is D. The equilibrium wage is W_0. Adding a Social Security tax equal to $B - A$ (or the length of line AB) shifts the supply curve facing this firm to S_1. If supply is fairly elastic but demand is relatively inelastic, most of the tax falls on the worker. The gross wage (including the tax) rises to W_g, but the net wage taken home by the worker falls to W_n. The actual division of the burden of the tax between worker and employer depends, not on the legislation that says half on each, but on the relative elasticities of supply and demand for labor. Economists believe that most of the tax falls on the worker because the market supply of labor is very inelastic.

Social Security is the largest income redistribution program in the United States. It incorporates some aspects of insurance. Workers must contribute to the program for a specified minimum period of time in order to be eligible for benefits. Workers do not have a choice about participating. With very few exceptions, everyone who holds a paying job earning more than \$50 a quarter must pay the Social Security tax, including self-employed individuals. Once workers become eligible to receive benefits, they receive them regardless of how much non-wage income they have in the form of interest, dividends, and/or private pensions. Retired individuals in some age categories face a reduction of benefits if they earn wage income, but not non-wage income. This rule discriminates against poorer retirees, because the only way most of them can supplement their retirement income is with wage income. Higher-income retirees collect interest, dividends, and/or private pensions without loss of Social Security benefits.

Until recently, Social Security benefits were not subject to federal income tax, and even now, most of these benefits are not taxable. Since 1985, Social Security recipients with adjusted gross incomes above \$25,000 (\$32,000 for married couples) have to pay income taxes on one-half of their Social Security benefits. This rule affected 15 percent of the recipients. Even with this change in the law, a large share of Social Security benefits still

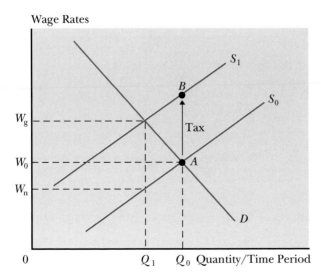

Wage Rates

0 Q_1 Q_0 Quantity/Time Period

FIGURE 5
WHO PAYS
SOCIAL SECURITY TAXES?
The higher price of labor, including the Social Security tax, reduces the number of workers employed from Q_0 to Q_1. The gross wage, including Social Security taxes, rises from W_0 to W_g, but the worker's net wage falls to W_n. The shaded area is the tax burden on workers in the form of lower wages.

goes to people who are not poor. In fact, some of the taxes paid by the working poor are being transferred to the rich through Social Security.

When Social Security was established as a compulsory retirement system, many people believed that their payments went into a trust fund. In fact, the account into which workers and employers pay their taxes is called the Social Security Trust Fund. However, it is simply a fund into which current workers pay and from which current beneficiaries receive payments. No money is held and invested for workers as a pool from which they will later receive income, as true of private pensions and annuities. It is amusing that on a regular basis some enterprising journalist "discovers" that the Social Security Trust Fund is a sham.[20]

The Social Security system is a tax-and-transfer mechanism. Individuals are taxed during their working years to pay benefits to those who are retired, disabled, or surviving dependents of covered workers. In the early years of the Social Security system, the funds coming in were more than adequate because there were many workers and few retired people. However, the age distribution of the U.S. population has changed greatly since that time. Table 5 shows this dramatic shift in the working versus the retired population. In 1950, an individual worker's payments had to support only 6 percent of one recipient's benefits. In 1991, each worker had to be taxed enough to support 35 percent of one recipient's benefits. Coupled with the increasing level of benefits, the changing ratio of workers to beneficiaries has created a heavy burden on workers. In 1980, Social Security taxes represented 30.5 percent of federal tax collections. By 1990, the Social Security share of federal tax revenues had grown to 37.0 percent. That's an increase of 21 percent in ten years. In 1990, Social Security benefits represented 20 percent of federal expenditures.[21]

Can today's workers rely on promised future Social Security payments? Many of today's workers are concerned about whether they will receive the benefits they are being promised. Reforms made in 1985 strengthened the stability of the system. These changes were (1) reducing the growth in benefit levels (including eliminating survivor benefits to college students and delaying retirement ages in the future), (2) broadening the categories of workers required to participate, so there will be more con-

TABLE 5
SUPPORT FOR
SOCIAL SECURITY
RECIPIENTS

YEAR	WORKERS PER SOCIAL SECURITY BENEFICIARY
1950	16.0
1960	5.0
1984	3.3
2010	3.0
2034	2.0

Source: The *1984 Annual Report of Board of Trustees of the Federal Old Age and Survivor's Insurance and Disability Trust Funds* (Washington, DC: Social Security Administration, 1984).

20. See, for example, Howard Gleckman, "Social Security's Dirty Little Secret," *Business Week* (29 January 1990): 66–67.
21. See "Bush Faces a Tax Steamroller," *Fortune* (12 February 1990): 8; and "Social Security's Big Fix," *U.S. News & World Report* (2 January 1990) 27–28.

tributors, (3) raising the Social Security payroll tax rate, and (4) raising the income base (the amount of income subject to the payroll tax). These last two changes increased Social Security revenues so much that the deficit turned into a surplus. In 1990, Social Security collected $380 billion in payroll taxes and paid out $249 billion in benefits. By 1993, the annual surplus is expected to grow to over $150 billion. In response to this surplus, Senator Daniel Moynihan has led a movement to reduce the payroll tax and relieve this tax burden on workers.[22]

TRANSFERS TO THE ELDERLY

Earlier in this chapter, we presented the arguments of George Stigler and Gordon Tullock that government is used by organized groups in society to capture income transfers. Since one of the fastest-growing and most politically organized groups is the elderly, that group might be expected to capture an increasing share of government transfers.

Recent experience supports this prediction. In the last several decades, the economic well-being of the elderly has increased greatly in the United States. In 1959, 35 percent of those over sixty-five had incomes below the poverty line, compared to 22 percent for the population as a whole and 27 percent for children under eighteen. The largest segment of the poor in 1959 were those over sixty-five. By 1990, only 12 percent of those over sixty-five were below the poverty line. If in-kind transfers are counted, the number falls to 5 percent. Professor James Schulz observed, "Poverty among the elderly, as measured by the poverty index and adjusted for nonmoney income, has virtually disappeared."[23] Much of this decline is due to the vast amounts of federal resources that are going to the elderly. People over sixty-five make up 12 percent of the population and receive 27 percent of federal spending. If you exclude defense spending, interest on the national debt, and foreign aid, people over sixty-five receive 48 percent of federal spending.

A second factor has also helped reduce poverty among the elderly. The wealth of those over sixty-five has increased dramatically in the last few decades. Professors Daphne Greenwood and Edward Wolff have examined household wealth by demographic group.[24] They report that in earlier decades older Americans consumed the wealth they had built up in their working years, while younger Americans built up their wealth in anticipation of retirement. This pattern changed in the late 1970s and early 1980s. Between 1973 and 1983, the average wealth of those sixty-five to sixty-nine years old increased from $169,366 to $321,562 in constant (1985) dollars. In contrast, in the same time period, the average wealth of those twenty-five to thirty-four years old decreased from $59,624 to $49,046 in constant (1985) dollars. This increase in wealth for the elderly is mainly related to rapidly rising real estate values during the period.

What has been occurring is that income transfers going to the elderly have been increasing at the same time that their wealth is increasing rela-

---

22. See, for example, Paul Craig Roberts, "It's High Time We Retired the Social Security Tax Surplus," *Business Week* (15 January 1990): 13.

23. Subratra N. Chakravarty and Katherine Weisman, "Consuming our Children," *Forbes* (14 November 1988), 223.

24. "Consuming our Children," 223.

tive to those who are paying for the transfers. The transfers to the elderly have become entitlements. Social Security is the biggest entitlement program. As you have seen, Social Security benefits represent 20 percent of federal spending. Benefits are given to all qualified individuals above a certain age, regardless of their financial situation. Medicare is another entitlement of the elderly. When it was established in 1965, this program was projected to cost $8.8 billion in 1990. Even after adjusting for inflation that estimate was far off the mark. In 1990, Medicare cost $111 billion in 1965 dollars.

The trend toward transferring more resources to those who are relatively well off has begun to cause some concern. As demographer Samuel Preston observes, "The United States has become the first society in history in which the poorest group in the population is the children, not the aged."[25] The concern among economists arises from the fact that money spent on children is at least partly an investment in the future productivity of the economy. In contrast, money spent on the elderly generally goes into consumption to make their lives more comfortable.

The solution to this dilemma is simple enough in principle, but borders on the politically impossible. Entitlement to these transfers would have to be abandoned. The original purpose of the Social Security system and related programs was to provide a safety net. Professor Gary Becker has argued that Social Security benefits should go only to the elderly poor. "When all pretense is dropped that Social Security is an annuity system, separate taxes to finance benefits make as little sense as separate taxes to finance the food stamp program."[26] Becker realizes his proposal is politically difficult, but he argues that it will eventually have to be implemented because the present system cannot sustain itself. The political difficulty is easy to pinpoint. The very young can't vote, the relatively young don't vote, and the elderly have the highest voter participation rate. In addition, the American Association of Retired Persons keeps them fully informed about their entitlements.

UNEMPLOYMENT COMPENSATION

Unemployment compensation is a transfer program financed by a tax on employers and administered by the states, which set benefit levels and eligibility requirements. Unemployment compensation is intended to be a temporary replacement of lost income while a worker is between jobs or temporarily laid off. The program has been criticized as providing "paid vacations" while workers go through the motions of searching for jobs. It has also been praised as providing a safety net for unemployed workers while they match their skills to the best available jobs, making labor markets more efficient. Of all income transfer programs, this one is the least criticized because benefits are of a temporary nature.

WELFARE

The group of programs lumped together as "welfare" began in the 1930s with Aid to the Aged, Aid to the Disabled, and Aid to Dependent Children (later Aid to Families with Dependent Children, or AFDC). These pro-

25. "Consuming our Children," 231.
26. Gary S. Becker, "Social Security Should Benefit Only the Elderly Poor," *Business Week* (16 January 1989): 20.

grams identify groups of people not expected to work. Costs are shared between the federal and state governments. There are different eligibility requirements and benefit levels in different states. In the 1960s, these programs were expanded and new ones were added as part of President Johnson's War on Poverty. Aid to the Aged, Aid to the Disabled, and several smaller programs were merged into Supplemental Security Income, a federally funded program, in 1972.

In the 1960s, there was an increase in in-kind programs, including food stamps, public housing, Medicaid, legal aid, Head Start for preschool children, and job training programs. These efforts to improve the welfare of the poor were designed to ensure that they consumed the "right mix" of goods and services, especially in the areas of health, nutrition, education, and training.

THE WELFARE REFORM DEBATE

Welfare reform is, of course, high on the political agenda. The ongoing debate was started by the 1982 proposal to return the largest welfare program, Aid to Families with Dependent Children, to the states and also by a controversial 1983 book by Charles Murray, *Losing Ground*. In this book, Murray argued that the current welfare system encourages people to do the wrong things—to avoid working, to have more children, and to become welfare-dependent. Also, the pressures of the budget deficits during the 1980s led to a re-examination of all areas of federal spending, and some of the most vulnerable programs were social welfare programs. Thus, the 1980s debate on welfare reform centered on three issues: the relative roles of the state and federal governments, work incentives, and cost containment.

The issue of how responsibilities should be shared between state and federal governments was at least temporarily put to rest in 1981 and 1982. Although the federal government reduced grants to state and local governments for social welfare programs, states rejected a proposal that they assume full responsibility for Aid to Families with Dependent Children in 1982.

Critics of welfare programs argue that they discourage work. With multiple benefits, it is very likely that a welfare client who takes a job will be worse off. For such welfare recipients, taking a job means losing not only cash benefits but also medical help, subsidized housing, and other benefits from overlapping programs. In order to determine the effects of welfare programs on work incentives, the federal government sponsored four large-scale experiments to measure how various levels of benefits would affect individuals' work efforts. Households in New Jersey, Pennsylvania, rural areas of North Carolina and Iowa, Gary (Indiana), Seattle, and Detroit were studied at various times from 1969 to 1982. The researchers concluded that higher benefit levels did lead to some modest reductions in work effort, especially among females.[27]

27. For a detailed appraisal of the results of the income maintenance program, see *Lessons from the Income Maintenance Experiments*, Alicia H. Munnell (ed.), proceedings of a conference sponsored by the Federal Reserve Bank of Boston and the Brookings Institution, 1986.

THE NEGATIVE INCOME TAX

The high cost of maintaining the bureaucracy to administer in-kind programs has led policy makers to search for another solution to the welfare
problem. One popular proposal is the negative income tax. A **negative income tax** is a transfer of income from the government to the poor based
on a formula similar to the present income tax system. A positive income
tax is a transfer to the government from citizens. Milton Friedman first
suggested replacing the existing welfare system with a negative income tax
in the 1960s.[28] The negative income tax is popular among economists because of its simplicity and positive work incentive.

Under a negative income tax, everyone would be guaranteed some
minimum income. Thus, the first problem is to decide what the minimum
income should be. This decision is strictly normative. Economic theory
offers no clue as to what this level should be. One approach would be to
calculate a typical poverty-level budget at current prices as the standard.

In addition to the minimum income guarantee, a negative income tax
also must designate a negative tax rate, which is the rate at which transfer
payments are reduced per additional dollar of earned income. These two
elements determine a third element, the break-even income, which is the
level of income at which a household neither pays income taxes nor receives benefits. In Friedman's plan, the minimum income guarantee
varies with family size. For example, a family of four might have a guaranteed income of $6,000. Suppose the negative tax rate is 50 percent. That
is, for each dollar the family earns, it loses 50¢ of welfare payments. When
the household earns $12,000, it will lose its last dollar of benefits and live
on earned income only. Since the household keeps part of its welfare
benefits when it earns a modest income, work incentives should be
stronger than under the present welfare system.

Table 6 gives benefits for four households, assuming a $6,000 income
guarantee and a 50 percent negative tax rate. The transfer payment received by a household is $6,000 minus 50 percent of any income earned
that is less than $12,000. The amount that a household receives can be de-
termined by the formula

$$W = IG - (t_n \times EI),$$

where W is the welfare payment, IG is the income guarantee, t_n is the
negative tax rate, and EI is the earned income. After the household passes
the break-even income level, at which it receives no more transfer payments, it starts paying income taxes. With an income guarantee of $6,000
and a negative tax rate of 50 percent, the break-even point would occur
at $12,000. Table 6 also shows how another $100 of income would benefit
each household.

The relationship between the three elements—the minimum income
guarantee, the negative tax rate, and the break-even income—creates
some difficult trade-offs. In order to provide a guaranteed income high
enough to ensure a minimum standard of living and a negative tax rate low
enough to encourage work, the break-even income would be very high.
This combination of choices would raise the cost of the system (requiring

28. See Milton Friedman, "The Case for the Negative Income Tax," in *Republican Papers*, M. R.
Laird (ed.) (New York: Praeger, 1968).

negative income tax
A transfer of income
from the government
to the poor based on a
formula similar to the
present income tax sys-
tem and implemented
with a minimum income
guarantee and a negative
tax rate.

	HOUSEHOLD			
	A	*B*	*C*	*D*
Earned income	0	$2,000	$4,000	$12,000
Welfare payment	$6,000	$5,000	$4,000	0
Disposable income	$6,000	$7,000	$8,000	$12,000
Increase in income	$100	$100	$100	$100
Earned income becomes	$100	$2,100	$4,100	$12,100
Tax rate	–50%	–50%	–50%	+15%
Welfare payment	$5,950	$4,950	$3,950	0
Disposable income	$6,050	$7,050	$8,050	$12,085

TABLE 6
INCOMES OF FOUR
HOUSEHOLDS WITH A
NEGATIVE INCOME TAX

higher positive tax rates above the break-even income) and extend welfare benefits much higher up the income scale. The break-even income could be reduced by lowering the guaranteed income, but a low minimum income would penalize those who are unable to work and totally dependent on transfers—the aged and the handicapped, for example. Alternatively, the break-even income could be lowered by using a higher negative tax rate, but that higher tax on earnings would discourage work.

A major attraction of the negative income tax is that it would provide public funds directly to the poor rather than funneling them through a large welfare bureaucracy. It would, therefore, cost less for the same amount of redistribution because funds would go directly to reducing poverty. Such a system would reduce the cost of administering welfare programs, which have grown to include a vast array of in-kind transfers.

The negative income tax is also attractive to recipients. It is objective and impersonal, allowing recipients to maintain a sense of dignity and entitlement. Instead of cutting off funds to those whose income is just above the poverty level, the negative income tax would provide aid to the nearly poor as well. Perhaps the most important advantage, however, is that the negative income tax does not destroy work incentives as much as the current system, which reduces transfers by 100 percent of any earned income. If a person on welfare earns $1,000, benefits fall by $1,000. A system that allows individuals to keep a portion of what they earn would strengthen work incentives.

Proponents of a negative income tax do not want to see it superimposed on the current system. Instead, they argue it should replace all direct public-assistance programs. This plan is considered by many economists to have decided advantages over other welfare reform proposals. One major obstacle to its adoption is the self-interest of those presently employed in the welfare bureaucracy. Other obstacles include preferences for in-kind programs, concerns about cost, and resistance to centralizing welfare at the federal level.

President Nixon tried to institute a negative income tax (the Family Assistance Plan) in 1971 but succeeded in only two small areas: SSI (Supplemental Security Income) for the aged and the extension of food stamp benefits. President Carter proposed a similar plan in 1978, the Program for Better Jobs and Income, but again it was not enacted. Both plans failed for three reasons: (1) the high cost of a program with an adequate income guarantee and a low enough negative tax rate, (2) opposition to federalizing of welfare, which had always been at least partly a state and local responsibility, and (3) the opposition of the "iron triangle" of congressional committees that oversee programs, beneficiaries, and government bureaucracies that administer existing programs.

WORKFARE PROGRAMS

How to provide work incentives while containing costs was answered in 1986 with the development of a variety of experimental programs at the state level. These **workfare programs** encourage or require welfare recipients who are able to work to take jobs, sometimes in the public sector, or to enter training programs that should lead to jobs, as a condition for continuing to receive benefits. Another aspect of workfare programs is a specification of the point at which mothers of small children are expected to go to work. As more and more women have chosen to work outside the home while their children are still small, the age at which children are expected to be placed in day care so that their mothers can work has been reduced from six years to three. These workfare programs have appeal for both liberal and conservative politicians. They combine the liberal approach of giving where there is need with the conservative approach of giving to those who contribute. In addition, some states have privately contracted the training of workfare recipients for long-term employment. This approach also won support from conservative politicians.

The most celebrated workfare program was established in Massachusetts, where a voluntary program involving training, day care, and help with job searches has produced promising results. The initial cost was high, especially when day care and training programs were involved, but the eventual cost savings from reduced welfare payments were expected to be substantial. The **Family Support Act of 1988** incorporated some aspects of these experimental state workfare programs. This legislation attempted to transform an entitlement into a reciprocal obligation. Getting a welfare check carried the obligation to accept a job or participate in activities to prepare for accepting a job. The results of this reform are only starting to be apparent. Some preliminary analysis of the results is encouraging. With resources and time, it appears that workfare programs can be moderately successful.[29]

THE WELFARE DEBATE IN THE 1990s

President Bush ran his 1988 campaign talking about a kinder and gentler society. To many this vision meant a call for more income redistribution to make society "more fair." Bush seemed to have something other than such redistribution in mind, however. In his speeches, he often refers to his concept as "a thousand points of light." These points of light are private redistributive efforts and voluntarism, such as students giving their time to help the illiterate learn to read or churches sponsoring shelters for the homeless.

workfare programs
State welfare programs that require those receiving welfare who are able to work to take jobs or to participate in training programs in order to be eligible for benefits.

Family Support Act of 1988
A federal law that incorporates some aspects of state workfare programs, turning entitlements into obligations to take jobs or enter job training programs.

29. For a review of the studies of transfer programs that require work or training, see Judith M. Gueron, "Work and Welfare: Lessons on Employment Programs," *Journal of Economic Perspectives* (Winter 1990): 79–98.

As you can see, there are conflicting policies and programs in the area of income redistribution. Many of the studies by economists disagree on the extent of the problem with the welfare system and what should be done about it. Thus, we end this chapter with the sentence that started it: No single topic in economics generates more disputes than income distribution and government policies for income redistribution.

SUMMARY

1. The Lorenz curve measures the relative distribution of income in an economy. The Lorenz curve, however, does not reflect the life-cycle pattern of income earning and may therefore give a false impression of how much income inequality exists over time.

2. Discrimination in labor markets channels certain groups into certain occupations. Some of the inequality that might appear to be the result of discrimination is actually due to differences in productivity or other objective characteristics.

3. To the extent that discrimination exists in the labor market, total output is lower than it could be if all resources were used in the most efficient manner.

4. Market forces will work against discrimination, because discrimination is costly and entrepreneurs can reduce the costs of production by not discriminating.

5. There is some evidence that welfare recipients, like other economic actors, will migrate to areas where benefits are higher.

6. Income redistribution can be viewed as a public good that is underprovided because of free-riding behavior.

7. In-kind transfers have expanded in the last twenty-five years and reduced the incidence of poverty in the United States.

8. Individuals may support income redistribution programs because they have interdependent utility functions, because of an insurance motive, because they view poverty as a negative external effect, or because they are seeking to use the political process to transfer income to themselves.

9. The Social Security system is a tax-and-transfer mechanism. The changing age distribution of the population is putting pressure on the financial viability of the system.

10. The elderly in America are receiving an increasing share of transfers at a time when their wealth is increasing.

11. The United States response to poverty has taken three distinct forms: to provide training and job opportunities, to provide social insurance, and to provide direct assistance to those who are unable to work because of age and health problems.

12. Current welfare reform proposals center on cost control, the federal-state mix in financing and administration, workfare programs, and greater reliance on private voluntary efforts.

13. The negative income tax has been suggested as a mechanism to ensure a minimum level of income while providing work incentives. The trade-offs between the minimum income guarantee, the break-even income, and the negative tax rate make it difficult to design a negative income tax system that is adequate, not too costly, and preserves work incentives.

NEW TERMS

personal distribution of
    income
Lorenz curve

interdependent utility
    functions
negative income tax

workfare programs
Family Support Act of
    1988

QUESTIONS FOR DISCUSSION

1. How is the official poverty level of income determined? Is it a meaningful measure?

2. Why are some people poor? What would you do if you were in a position to take some action?

3. Do you think a negative income tax would solve the problem of poverty in the United States? Why or why not?

4. Should society be concerned with relative poverty or absolute poverty? How would dealing with absolute poverty differ from dealing with relative poverty?

5. Why do many economists feel that markets will work to undermine discrimination in labor markets?

6. "The social safety net is intended to catch those who fall in, not those who jump in." Discuss the implications of this statement for designing an income support system.

7. Why are there long-term problems with the financial health of the Social Security system? Identify some possible solutions.

8. Find the missing value in each of the three elements of the negative income tax.

a. Minimum income guarantee, $4,000; break-even income, $12,000; negative tax rate, _____.

b. Minimum income guarantee, $5,000; negative tax rate, 50 percent; break-even income, _____.

c. Negative tax rate, 30 percent; break-even income, $9,000; minimum income guarantee, _____.

9. What problems with the welfare system are workfare programs designed to solve?

10. Why does society redistribute income to the poor? Why is private charity likely to be inadequate?

11. Public education is an in-kind transfer to all people in certain age groups. Who benefits more, the poor or the well-to-do?

12. How would George Stigler explain the fact that transfers to the elderly have increased so significantly in the last two decades? Would Gordon Tullock find this surprising? Why or why not?

13. Why do AFDC recipients move? Does it surprise you that they do?

14. Do you favor equality of opportunity or equality of results?

15. How do you think Congress should address the question of entitlement programs for the elderly?

SUGGESTIONS FOR FURTHER READING

Gabriel, Paul E., Donald R. Williams, and Susanne Schmitz. "The Relative Occupational Attainment of Young Blacks, Whites, and Hispanics," *Southern Economic Journal* (July 1990): 35–46. A recent empirical study that shows that labor market discrimination plays a role in the occupational attainment of black males.

Hurd, Michael D. "Research on the Elderly: Economic Status, Retirement, and Consumption and Saving," *Journal of Economic Literature* (June 1990): 565–637. A survey of recent economic research on the elderly.

Levy, Frank, and Richard C. Michel. *The Economic Future of American Families: Income and Wealth Trends.* Washington, DC: Urban Institute Press, 1991. A look at patterns of income inequality over the last two decades.

Murray, Charles. *Losing Ground: American Social Policy, 1950–1980.* New York: Basic Books, 1984. A controversial book that argues that three decades of well-meaning social programs were a failure. Murray followed it with *In Pursuit: Of Happiness and Good Government* (New York: Simon & Schuster, 1988), which argues that the poor can only be helped by local religious, social, and community organizations.

O'Rourke, P. J. "Octogenarians at the Gate," *Rolling Stone* (19 April 1990): 41–43. A satire about transfers to the elderly.

Penner, Karen. "The Free Market Has Triumphed, But What About the Losers?" *Business Week* (25 September 1989): 178–179. An editorial in a conservative business publication that calls for a more equitable society.

Tullock, Gordon. *Economics of Income Redistribution.* Boston: Kluwer-Nijhoff, 1983. This very readable analysis of governmental transfer policy criticizes a variety of programs.

MARKET FAILURE, GOVERNMENT FAILURE, AND PUBLIC CHOICE

9

1. Discuss the economic impact of property law, tort law, and contract law.
2. Define:
   a. externalities,
   b. public goods,
   c. free riding.
3. Diagram cases of both negative and positive externalities.
4. State the Coase theorem, and list the conditions under which it holds.
5. Explain how free-riding behavior results in the underproduction of public goods.
6. Explain how income redistribution and education have some characteristics of public goods.

CHAPTER 31

MARKET FAILURE AND GOVERNMENT INTERVENTION

INTRODUCTION

We have spent a great deal of time examining economic outcomes of market forces. Two of these market outcomes that are often viewed as unsatisfactory are the failure of markets to produce the optimal quantity (and price) of a good when there is monopoly power and the poverty that is often the result of the market distribution of income. Additional instances of market failure exist because of externalities and public goods. In this chapter, we examine the economic arguments for government intervention to correct for market failure.

Even an almost pure market system needs some minimal government to provide a legal system in order to define and protect property rights. We will therefore begin with a discussion of the legal system as the most basic function of government. Then we will examine the existence of externalities and public goods as arguments for governmental intervention into the market.[1]

LAW, ECONOMICS, AND GOVERNMENT

As Adam Smith noted, one of the basic roles of government is to define and enforce property rights. Thus, to an economist, law is the basic framework of any economy. In the United States, government's effect on the allocation of resources is defined by law and the interpretation of law. In recent years, economists have spent a great deal of time extending economic analysis to explain the purposes and effects of legislation (statute law) and judicial decisions (common law).[2] Both types of laws can be analyzed from an economic perspective, although in different ways.

---

1. Recall from Chapter 2 that the functions of government are allocation, stabilization, and redistribution. Stabilization is a topic discussed in macroeconomics. Redistribution was covered in the last chapter. Here we give a closer look at certain aspects of the allocation question.
2. See Richard A. Posner, *Economic Analysis of Law* (Boston: Little, Brown, 1972); and Werner Z. Hirsch, *Introduction to Law and Economics* (New York: McGraw-Hill, 1980).

Statute law is of interest because of the incentives statutes create and the way they alter existing property rights. *Common law* changes through judicial decisions, and these precedents alter incentives for decision making. Lawyers are interested in the applications of specific decisions to other cases. Economists are more concerned with how these decisions affect the economy by altering incentives.

In analyzing law, economists search for the economic reasoning implicit in legislation and judges' decisions. It is most common to divide laws into three major areas. **Property law** relates to the enforcement of property rights. Enforcement of property rights is one of the basic requirements of any economic system. **Tort law** deals with intentional and unintentional wrongs imposed by one party on another. **Contract law** deals with the enforcement of voluntary exchanges.

The important relationships between economics and law have been studied intensively in recent years by both economists and lawyers. Economics deals with property rights and exchange, which are the most basic elements of a market system. Precedents in common law or changes in statute law will have profound effects on economic activity. Laws (more correctly, the courts' interpretation of laws) determine the private-public mix in our economy.

property law
Law that concerns the enforcement of property rights.

tort law
Law that deals with intentional and unintentional wrongs inflicted by one party on another.

contract law
Law that deals with the enforcement of voluntary exchanges.

PROPERTY LAW

The law in the United States is generally compatible with the economic principle that the economy operates more efficiently under a system of exclusive, transferable property rights. The most important exceptions occur in two areas in which high transactions costs create market failure or interfere with the efficiency of market outcomes.

The first exception concerns incompatible uses of property. Incompatibility exists when the rights of the parties are in conflict. Noise, air, and water pollution are but a few examples. An attractive hazard such as a swimming pool or a construction site is another example. Cases involving incompatible uses are often treated as matters of nuisance. In many of these cases, the court will simply issue an injunction requiring that the party responsible for the nuisance cease and desist. This may appear to be the most fair or equitable solution, but it is not necessarily an efficient solution from an economic viewpoint.

The second exception to property law's compatibility with the principles of a free market is the doctrine of **eminent domain**. The principle here is that government has the legal right to purchase property at "fair market value" if it is deemed to be in the public interest. In these cases, the owner's property right is reduced in value because the owner cannot refuse to sell. Condemnation proceedings are court cases in which the government tries to take property away from an owner by arguing that the government's rights are more important. Governments often invoke eminent domain for construction of public facilities, such as parks, roads, or dams.

eminent domain
A doctrine that gives government the right to buy property at "fair market value" if the purchase is in the public interest.

TORT LAW

A **tort** is a wrongful action (or failure to act) by an individual that causes damage to the person or property of another individual. For example, if reckless behavior on your part injures another person, that person may

tort
A wrongful action (or failure to act) that causes damage to the person or property of another individual.

sue you for damages. Payment of these damages can be justified on the basis of equity. The payment restores the original distribution of income or assets. Payment of damages can also be justified on the basis of efficiency. It makes you bear the costs of your reckless action and thus increases the incentive to be more careful. For example, if you are responsible for any damage your dog may do by biting people or damaging property, you will be more likely to take precautions to keep your dog from inflicting such damage.

The equity principle requires a transfer payment from the wrongdoer to the individual who has been damaged. The impact of the efficiency principle is quite different. The law establishes a precedent for the ownership of property rights. Tort law is used to determine who has the property right when it is in dispute.[3]

CONTRACT LAW

The economics of exchange and contract law are similar in the sense that individuals are presumed to enter into contracts only if they stand to gain. Parties to contracts may end up in court not because the contracts were bad (for either of the parties), but rather because one party failed to satisfy a provision. This most often happens when the contractual exchange fails to take place on time or when the cost/benefit calculation of one party changes.

Contracts usually are not set aside by the courts if the intent is reasonably clear. On the other hand, the courts have set contracts aside if (honest) mistakes have been committed. If one party has been induced to accept a contract through fraud, duress, or incapacity, the court will refuse to enforce the contract.

Contracts, and court decisions under the common law of contracts, are important in economics because contracts, whether they are expressed or implied, form the basis of exchange. Exchange is influenced by contract law, and contract law alters the incentives that affect exchanges. For example, the courts have ruled that a college catalog or a course syllabus represents a contract with a student. This ruling has altered the terms of the production and sale of higher-education services.

EXTERNALITIES

externalities
Costs or benefits associated with consumption or production that are not reflected in market prices and fall on parties other than the buyer or seller.

Externalities are costs or benefits associated with consumption or production that are not reflected in market prices. The cost or benefit is external because it falls on parties other than the buyer or seller. Externalities represent a form of market failure.

The most frequently cited example of an externality is pollution. For example, a firm producing steel must purchase iron ore, electricity, labor, and other inputs. The costs of these factors are embodied in the price of the steel. However, in producing steel, the firm also uses clean air and produces air pollution. Yet the firm doesn't compensate those individuals

---

3.   See Chapter 19 of Allan C. DeSerpa, *Microeconomic Theory: Issues and Applications* (Boston: Allyn and Bacon, 1985) for a very thorough and readable discussion of the economics of tort law.

The Japanese legal system is quite different from the U.S. legal system in that it puts a great deal of emphasis on arbitration and compromise in resolving conflicts. Since most relationships, including economic ones, are considered social relationships in Japan, there is great reliance on informal means of settling disputes. The traditional Japanese citizen views being brought to court as a source of personal shame.

The difference in the two systems is most apparent in the area of tort law. The most common way of resolving a damage case in Japan is for the injured party to renounce its right to indemnity. The wrongdoer comes to offer apologies and offer a sum of money in compensation. The sum offered is often a token amount and is frequently much less than the value of the damages suffered by the victim. The victim is moved by the sympathy and sincerity of the responsible party. It is not the amount of the compensation but the sincerity of the responsible party that is socially important. Sometimes the victim is so moved by the sincerity of the responsible party that all compensation is refused. Even when the victim is not satisfied with the offer of compensation, the courts are avoided. Instead, the victim appeals to someone who has authority to achieve an amicable solution. In this way, both parties are able to save face.

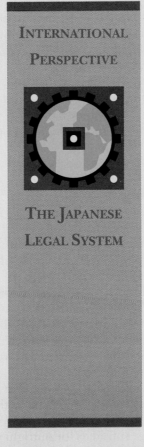

INTERNATIONAL PERSPECTIVE

THE JAPANESE LEGAL SYSTEM

This Japanese attitude about the law extends to contracts. This difference can cause problems in international transactions. The Japanese, with their dislike of the courts' emphasis on conflict, prefer to negotiate a relationship rather than a contract. They can't predict the disputes that may arise but prefer to settle disputes in an informal manner. They dislike the use of the courts because the courts assign fault, resulting in a loss of "face" for the guilty party.

The differences between the United States and Japanese legal systems are striking and are based on differences in the cultures of the two countries. The Japanese legal system is very centralized. There are no local or state laws in Japan. This reflects the strong group orientation and concentration of authority in Japan. In the United States, there is much more individualism and disdain for authority. Americans view the legal system as a way of asserting their individual rights and are much more likely to resort to the courts to resolve disputes. These cultural differences will affect economic transactions and must be addressed when doing business with the Japanese. The Japanese have been quick to understand the U.S. system and have adapted to it when doing business in the United States. Americans have been slower to adapt to the Japanese system of doing business in Japan.

who give up the clean air. As a result, the cost of using the air is not embodied in the price of the steel. This cost is external to the production of the steel.

Many problems due to externalities result from the fact that property rights to certain resources are not clearly defined. Clean air is a resource that is not owned by anyone. Therefore, the steel mill can use clean air and not compensate those who give it up, because there is no clearly defined owner to demand payment.

Externalities can be positive or negative. Air pollution is a negative externality and so is the noise resulting from the use of a snowmobile. The cost that this noise imposes on other individuals may not be taken into account in the price of snowmobiles or snowmobiling. It is external to any economic calculation.

Positive externalities are not so obvious. Inoculations against contagious diseases or spraying to control mosquitoes are examples of activities that generate positive externalities. Benefits accrue to others if enough people are inoculated or enough mosquito breeding areas are sprayed, but these benefits are not considered by those deciding on whether or not to incur the cost. Education is another good example of a positive externality. Society benefits from an individual's education. An individual who is educated is likely to be a better citizen and to be less dependent on others. In addition, that individual is likely to be a more productive person, increasing national income. Yet individuals, in deciding how much education to pursue, do not consider these benefits because they are external to them. The individual is not able to charge those who enjoy the external benefit of his or her education.

To the extent that externalities exist, the market has failed. Private market decisions will result in too little or too much of certain items being produced. Corrective action on a collective basis may be needed. The government can influence production or consumption that creates externalities through taxes, subsidies, or outright prohibitions or by requiring citizens to consume certain goods, such as inoculations and education.

EXTERNAL BENEFITS

In order to analyze the economic implications of a positive externality, suppose Figure 1 represents the market for automobile tires. D_p represents the private demand for automobile tires, and MC represents the marginal cost. Consumers will purchase Q_1 tires at price P_1. Assume that EB represents the marginal external benefits arising from the consumption of new tires. External benefits exist when people consume more new tires, because their cars are safer and the chance of an accident involving others decreases. This greater safety is a social benefit. EB can be viewed as the summation of the demand curves of people other than the immediate consumers of the product. It has a negative slope, like all demand curves.

Adding EB and D_p vertically gives the true demand curve, labeled $D_p + EB$. The two demand curves are summed vertically instead of horizontally because we are interested in marginal benefits of all who gain at various quantities consumed. We are not summing the additional amounts consumers want to purchase but rather how they value these

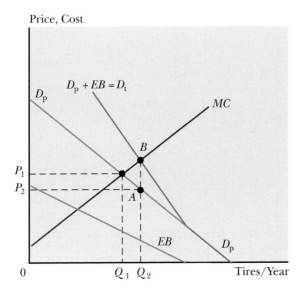

Price, Cost

$D_p + EB = D_t$

D_p

MC

B

P_1

P_2

A

EB

D_p

0   Q_1 Q_2 Tires/Year

FIGURE 1
THE CASE OF EXTERNAL BENEFITS
External benefits cause the true demand curve, $D_p + EB$, to lie above the private demand curve, D_p. The market outcome, Q_1, is smaller than the socially efficient level of consumption, Q_2.

units. If the external benefits are considered, the combined valuation ($D_p + EB$) indicates that Q_2 rather than Q_1 tires should be consumed. In other words, the existence of the positive externality resulted in this good being underproduced and underconsumed.

It is easy to see how government could correct this market failure. A subsidy to consumers equal to the length of line AB on the graph would reduce the price consumers pay to P_2 and bring about the socially optimal level of consumption, Q_2. This level is the social optimum because it includes the tire production demanded by those who are not counted by the market mechanism. Alternatively, government could require the purchase of Q_2 tires per year. Vehicle inspections, which some states require, are also attempts (rather crude ones) to reach this social optimum.

EXTERNAL COSTS

Earlier, we used air pollution as an example of an external cost. If you live near a steel mill, you are forced to breathe polluted air without being compensated for the fact that the mill is using the air as a place in which to dump some of its debris. The economic importance of this behavior is that the polluting firm avoids paying part of the costs of production. It is quite simple to determine the theoretical effects of such externalities. It is more difficult to determine how to correct them.

Pollution causes damage, or social costs, to those in the general area. **Social costs** are costs that are borne by society or some group without compensation. Negative externalities impose damages, or social costs, on groups in the population. This situation is represented in Figure 2. Assume that the polluter is in a competitive industry that is generating a negative externality. The demand curve is the usual market demand curve for the good or service. The supply curve is the summation of all the individual firms' marginal cost curves (above their average variable cost curves). This supply curve includes all private costs but not marginal social costs. Equilibrium is reached at price P_1 and output Q_1.

social costs
Costs that are borne by society or some group in society without compensation.

FIGURE 2
EXTERNALITIES AND
MARKET EQUILIBRIUM
When the social cost of
the negative externality
(*SC*) is added to the
marginal cost curves of
the competitive firms (*S*),
the true supply curve (*S*$_t$)
is found. This true supply
curve indicates that too
much of the good is
produced at too low a
price, unless the externality is taken into account.

Now suppose we know the value of the marginal social costs generated by the externality, represented by the curve *SC*. The social costs are zero when no output is produced and are assumed to increase at a constant rate. If we add these marginal social costs to the supply curve, we get the true supply curve, *S*$_t$. This curve is the summation of the social costs and the private costs embodied in the firms' marginal cost curves. The socially optimal level of production is not Q_1 but the smaller Q_2. The price associated with efficient production is P_2, which is higher than P_1.

It is clear that when the social costs of production are included, the good becomes more expensive. It isn't that these costs weren't being borne before. They weren't being borne by the producers or the consumers of the good. Instead, they were being paid by those who live near where production is taking place. In failing to take into account the social costs, the firm was producing too much of the good and charging the consumer too low a price because it was not paying some of the costs of production.

In the real world, when production or consumption of a good causes negative externalities, the people who bear those costs subsidize consumers of the product. For example, the people who live in Gary, Indiana, where steel is produced, bear costs that allow consumers of steel to pay lower prices. A person who buys a steel and chrome kitchen set in Orlando, Florida, is subsidized by someone who lives in Gary. If steel producers had to pay for the negative externalities they create, less steel would be produced, and it would be sold for a higher price. The general theoretical conclusion is that when negative externalities exist, the amount of production will not be optimal. Too much output will be produced at too low a price.

It is very important to understand that even if the cost of an externality such as pollution is placed on the buyer and seller of the good or service, this action does not cause the amount of pollution to fall to zero. Only if production of the good or service falls to zero will the resulting pollution fall to zero. In the example in Figure 2, the price paid by buyers rose from P_1 to P_2 when social costs were included, but some pollution and the costs associated with it continued. In other words, there is an "optimum" amount of pollution determined by the market process.

INTERNALIZING NEGATIVE EXTERNALITIES

According to economists, the trick to controlling the social costs of negative externalities is **internalization** of those externalities. This means that producers are forced to take account of the costs they impose on other members of society in their production decisions. When internalized, the externality is incorporated into the market price. In terms of Figure 2, the firm should have to bear the social costs SC so that S_t becomes the supply curve. How can this be done? It would be a simple matter if the social costs could easily be determined. It is easy to analyze the theoretical case, as in Figure 2, but in the real world it is very difficult to come up with a dollar value. You can determine the dollar value of having to paint your house more often because of air pollution, but what is the cost of a certain number of people dying because of respiratory problems? How much is not being able to have a cookout in the back yard worth? If government officials could determine these costs, they could place a tax on the industry that would shift the supply curve up just the right distance (to S_t in Figure 2). The market solution would then be an optimal price of P_2 and an optimal output level of Q_2.

Governmental policy makers could also charge firms for the amount of negative externalities they create. Each firm could be monitored and charged for air pollution on a monthly basis. It would be possible to put a meter on each smokestack and measure the pollutants. Then firms could be charged for the air they pollute just as they are charged for the electricity or labor they use. This pollution charge would cause costs to rise and move production toward the socially optimal level. This solution, however, has the same problem as taxation—determining the correct charge per unit of pollutant.

Although there are problems, it can be argued that there is a need for government to intervene in the market process under circumstances when there are negative externalities. When markets don't produce socially optimal results, it may be appropriate for government to step in to attempt to correct for the market imperfection. It is not always necessary for government to correct for social costs, however. Private groups may form in an effort to prevent or limit negative externalities. A good example of such a group is a condo association. Condo associations set up rules of behavior and rules for upkeep of facilities that are designed to limit or prevent residents from creating certain types of negative externalities. By buying a condo, an individual voluntarily limits his or her own behavior.

internalization
The incorporation of the social costs of negative external effects into the market price.

THE COASE THEOREM AND SMALL-NUMBER EXTERNALITIES. In an article that has had wide influence on how economists think about externalities, Ronald Coase considered cases in which the number of affected parties is small. He concluded that, in such cases, individual maximizing behavior will correct for a negative externality without the need for govern-

For years, apples and bees were used as a classic illustration of the externality problem. It was alleged that markets broke down because apple growers' orchards provided a positive externality (nectar) for bee farmers, but the orchard owners received no payment for this nectar. On the other hand, the bees provided pollinating services to orchard owners, but beekeepers were not compensated for this necessary service. As a result, intervention would be needed to make orchard owners grow more nectar-yielding apple trees and beekeepers provide more pollinating bees.

Steven Cheung refused to take this classic illustration of market failure at its face value.[a] He went into apple orchards to determine if these two externalities did indeed produce market value. To everyone's surprise, except perhaps Cheung's, he found that the market worked quite well without government intervention. An active market for beehive placement was in operation. Where the honey yield was great, beekeepers paid the orchard owner an "apiary rent" in order to place hives in these high production spots. When the honey yield was low, the orchard owner paid a "pollination fee" to induce beekeepers to place hives in these places. Cheung even found that beekeepers move hives to different states to pollinate crops in different seasons.

Cheung's study is important because it shows that markets can adapt well and that market failure may be less widespread than might appear. The lesson for policy makers is that they should be very careful in determining whether market failure exists before proposing political or governmental solutions.

ECONOMIC
INSIGHT

THE FABLE
OF THE BEES

a.   See Steven N. S. Cheung, "The Fable of the Bees: An Economic Investigation," *The Journal of Law and Economics* (April 1973).

ment intervention.[4] The **Coase theorem** states that when there are small numbers of affected parties, a property right assignment is sufficient to internalize any externality that is present. Coase demonstrated that if property rights are clearly defined, the affected individuals will take action to internalize the externality. The only government intervention required to solve the problem is enforcement of property rights.

Consider, as Coase did in his paper, a case where there are only two parties involved in a dispute, a wheat farmer and a cattle rancher. The negative externality is the damage done by cattle roaming on unfenced land. As the rancher increases the size of the herd, the damage done by straying cattle will increase. To approach an optimal result, it is necessary to compel the rancher to take these costs into account, as illustrated by Figure 2. If government intervenes, it is likely to solve the problem by requiring the rancher to pay the farmer for the damage to the farmer's wheat. In this case, the rancher would restrict the number of cattle in the herd until marginal cost equaled marginal revenue (the marginal cost includes the damage to wheat). In Figure 3, $D = MR$ represents the demand and marginal revenue curve of raising cattle, MC represents the marginal cost of raising cattle, and SC represents the marginal social cost, or the cost of the negative externality (the damage to the wheat). Without any internalizing of the social cost, the rancher would raise Q_1 cattle per year, and the farmer would incur a dollar loss to the wheat crop of W_1 for the last (marginal) cow raised. Government intervention would force the rancher to act on the basis of the joint $MC + SC$ curve through some tax scheme or direct regulation. As a result, the rancher would raise only Q_2 cattle.

Coase shows that even if government did not intervene, the same solution would result. According to Coase, all that is necessary is that property rights be defined and enforced. First, assume that the farmer's prop-

Coase theorem
The idea that well-defined property rights are sufficient to internalize any external effect that is present, when there are small numbers of affected parties.

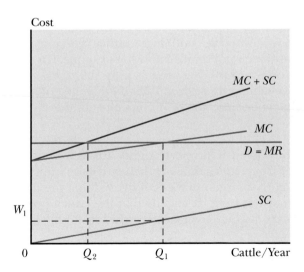

FIGURE 3
THE COASE THEOREM
The Coase theorem shows how externalities are internalized by the assignment of property rights. The social cost (SC) is automatically added to the marginal cost curve (MC) to form $MC + SC$, the true cost of raising cattle. The optimal output, Q_2, will result because a bribe or payment equal to the social cost will automatically come about.

4.   Ronald Coase, "The Problem of Social Cost," *Journal of Law and Economics* 3, (October 1960): 1–44.

erty rights include the right not to have the wheat harmed. The rancher will then be forced to pay damages, shown by the SC curve, and will add these to production costs. The rancher will then raise Q_2 cattle. On the other hand, suppose the rancher has the right to let the cattle roam. The important question then is how much the farmer will be willing to "bribe" the rancher to keep the cattle away. The farmer will be willing to pay the rancher an amount just slightly less than the cost of the damage done by the cattle because this makes them *both* better off than allowing the cattle to damage the wheat. The farmer would pay W_1 for the last cow not raised. The rancher then must include these bribes as opportunity costs because if the cattle are raised, the bribes will not be paid. When these opportunity costs are added to the marginal cost curve, the rancher will raise Q_2 cattle. The result is that Q_2 cattle will be raised regardless of who has the property rights, as long as those rights are defined and the number of people involved is small. Small numbers are necessary because the farmer and rancher must get together and work out a solution.

Note that the Coase solution says only that the allocative results, or the number of cattle produced, will be the same whoever has the property rights. It says nothing about the distribution of income. Assigning property rights does affect who is better off. In the first case, the farmer's income is higher. In the second, the rancher's income is higher. The assignment of rights might have to be resolved by the law or through the political process since it involves an issue of equity, not economic efficiency. It's not really clear whether the rancher is imposing costs on the farmer (by damaging the wheat crop) or the farmer is imposing costs on the rancher (by restricting the grazing range of the herd). That is why there are legislatures to define property rights and courts to interpret and enforce them.

The importance of the Coase theorem is that it draws attention to the role of property rights. Many social problems result from ill-defined or nonexistent property rights. Consider, for example, the case of buffalo and cattle in the Old West. Why were buffalo almost wiped out while cattle thrived? The animals are very similar and roamed the same country. The answer is simple. Nobody owned the buffalo, or rather everyone had a right to shoot them.[5] Consider air pollution as another example. If a copper mine dumped tailings on your yard, you would sue for damages or expect payment for the use of your land as a dump. Yet if the mine polluted the air, you would be helpless because you don't own the air above your land.

LARGE-NUMBER EXTERNALITIES. Even if property rights are well defined, there may still be problems from externalities. If there are large numbers of people sustaining damages or large numbers of firms doing the damage, the Coase theorem may not hold. It may be that the costs of organizing the involved parties are too high to make it worthwhile for the dam-

---

5. For a discussion of how to protect eagles by assigning property rights to them, see Ryan C. Amacher, Robert D. Tollison, and Thomas D. Willett, "The Economics of Fatal Mistakes: Fiscal Mechanisms for Preserving Endangered Predators," *Public Policy* 20, no. 1 (Summer 1972): 411–441.

aged individuals to sue for damages or organize a bribe. The individuals damaged would have to mount a door-to-door campaign, advertise in newspapers, and form a group for joint action. If the damaging firms are hard to identify, the problem is even greater. In an area with severe air pollution, it would be necessary to determine how much each of many firms contributes to this problem and who should be sued (or bribed). Because the information and transactions costs increase rapidly as the number of parties increases, it is often argued that the Coase theorem cannot fix the market failure that externalities create.

GOVERNMENT INTERVENTION AND EXTERNALITIES. Since the Coase theorem may not work, government intervention may be required to correct a negative externality. Government intervention usually takes the form of direct controls, and such controls often lead to unfairness. Suppose the government requires all cars to have a pollution control device that costs $300. The salesperson who drives a great deal and, as a result, pollutes a great deal pays very little on a per-unit-of-pollution basis. In contrast, the retired couple who drive very little must pay the same $300, although they pollute very little. In addition, government intervention affects the distribution of income. For example, as auto prices rise because of required pollution equipment, the poor are affected more than the rich because the poor spend a higher proportion of their income on cars.

Since government intervention almost always raises costs, it is important that policy makers be sure that the social costs are indeed worth correcting. Sometimes the government makes mistakes when it intervenes in markets, and these mistakes raise costs of production. Mistakes are to be expected because governmental decision making, like private decision making, is carried out by individuals with certain expectations, facing certain incentives. Governmental decision makers aren't incentive-free, they simply face different incentives than private decision makers.

Externalities have received much attention in recent years. This attention may cause some to overestimate their real costs. We have all seen gruesome pictures of oil spills and fish kills. However, this kind of damage seems to be of short duration. This is not to say that such damage is insignificant. However, the cost of correcting for a negative externality may in some cases exceed the damage it causes. Policy makers need to consider these costs before racing headlong into wholesale government regulation of externalities. They also need to consider what form that intervention should take.

The federal government has usually responded to calls to control negative externalities by creating regulations. These regulations impose costs on firms. The regulatory bodies themselves spend large amounts of money on enforcement. The costs imposed on firms are hard to estimate until the required action is actually taken. For example, a regulation to keep copper mines from polluting the air may cause them to close because of increased costs of production. In considering the costs of the regulation, an economist would examine its impact on the affected industry and region. Production may move to a state (or country) that has less stringent regulation. Some geographic regions may compete for industrial growth by offering fewer environmental or economic regulations.

Thus, in attempting to correct for the market distortions caused by negative externalities, government regulation can lead to other distortions.

Each call for regulation should be considered carefully. Some externalities may have already been corrected by market mechanisms. For example, houses near airports sell for lower prices because of airport noise. The people who buy these houses are freely choosing to do so because the lower price compensates for the noise. To change the law because these people don't like the noise would generate a windfall gain for them. It is not surprising that these residents should lobby for such a change, but it cannot be justified economically. The problem is complicated, however, by the fact that some residents may have purchased their homes before the noise became bad. These individuals lose twice. They suffer the cost of the noise and also a reduction in the value of their homes. It might make sense to compensate this group of individuals.

A recent battle concerning negative externalities and the need for government intervention has taken place over cigarette smoking and the rights of nonsmokers. The issues involved in this political battle point once again to the property rights that are at the heart of most such questions. Some states and localities have passed laws prohibiting smoking in some areas (public buildings) and requiring nonsmoking areas in restaurants and other such businesses. Are such laws necessary? If private demand for either smoke-free or smoking areas were high enough, some restaurants and other firms would fill the demand without the need for government action. In fact, some restaurants have done this without the pressure of laws. The recent opening of a motel chain for nonsmokers gives support to the feasibility of a private solution to some problems of negative externalities.

MARKETS FOR POLLUTION RIGHTS

More than a century ago, the famous economist John Stuart Mill wrote in his *Principles of Political Economy* (1862): "If from any revolution in nature the atmosphere became too scanty for the consumption, . . . air might acquire a very high marketable value." In the 1980s, he was proven correct as the market began to be used to allocate pollution rights. Economists have long argued for such a system rather than a regulatory approach. In 1970, Congress passed the **Clean Air Act**, which empowered the Environmental Protection Agency (EPA) to set standards for six pollutants and required each state to impose standards that would be met at each emission source. In other words, if emissions were to be reduced by 10 percent, all sources of the pollutant would have to be reduced by 10 percent. This act has since been renewed and extended to more pollutants and greater reductions.

Clean Air Act
A federal law passed in 1970 that empowered the EPA to set emission standards and impose standards on polluters.

Some economists argued that it would be more efficient to allow the market to solve this problem. Marketing the right to pollute would make it possible to hold pollutants at the desired level and at the same time allocate them to the producers who are willing to pay the highest price. Firms that wished to expand production could do so only if the market value of their product enabled them to purchase the right to use the scarce commodity, air quality. In addition, if pollution rights had a value, firms would have the incentive to search for other ways to produce their

The idea of charging for the privilege of polluting is not unique to the United States. Among the nations that use this approach to controlling water pollution are France, Germany, and the Netherlands. France uses a sewage tax on households and commercial enterprises to fund pollution abatement programs. Because the tax is based on the amount of water used, there is some link between the amount of tax paid and the amount of demand that a customer places on the waste treatment system. Charges to firms, which are also used to raise revenue for pollution abatement, are not linked as closely to the amount of waste discharged. France also uses fees for pollution abatement. By introducing the system through low charges on a few pollutants and gradually expanding coverage and increasing the rates, the French government has encountered very little political opposition to this program.

The German system is similar, except that it is administered by local governments. Charges

INTERNATIONAL PERSPECTIVE

PAYING TO POLLUTE IN EUROPE

depend on the type and size of the industry. Like France, Germany earmarks the revenues to pay for water quality improvement. However, economic efficiency only requires that the tax or charge be set so as to reduce the level of emissions to the socially optimal level. It says nothing about how the revenue should be used.

The Netherlands has a system of effluent charges that has been in use for more than three decades. Like France and Germany, the Netherlands earmarks the revenue for pollution abatement. Because effluent charges in this country are much higher than in the other two, however, it appears that the charges have had a significant effect on improving water quality. It is interesting to note that in the Netherlands, environmental groups have supported charges as a method of reducing pollution and industry has lobbied for a regulatory approach. These preferences seem to suggest that the market is the more effective method of pollution control!

Source: Robert W. Hahn, "Economic Prescriptions for Environmental Problems: How the Patient Followed the Doctor's Orders," *Journal of Economic Perspectives* (Spring 1989): 95–114.

products and for ways to control their emissions. If they discovered new methods of emission control, they could sell both the new technology and their pollution rights.

This idea came into use in the 1980s. In 1979, the EPA endorsed a "bubble" concept. The bubble concept allows a group of plants in the same region to adjust their emissions to achieve regional clear-air standards. The economics of the idea is simple. If the plants in the bubble are all owned by the same company, the company achieves the desired level of pollution by shifting emission control from higher-cost to lower-cost sources until the marginal cost of control is the same at each source. This approach minimizes the total cost of pollution abatement. If the plants in the bubble belong to different firms, it is a bit more complicated, but the principle is the same. The plant manager with high costs of pollution control will look for savings by paying neighboring firms in the bubble whose costs are lower to cut their emissions more and sell some of their pollution rights. This approach achieves abatement in the bubble at the lowest cost.[6]

Such bargaining may seem difficult to achieve, but by 1987 there was evidence that a market was working in pollution rights. In California, several plants financed the installation of new technology that saved on emissions by selling their rights to pollute to other companies. These other companies found it less expensive to buy pollution rights than to purchase a more costly technology. In 1984, a private firm, AER*X, was formed to serve as a broker in pollution rights. In 1990, this firm had revenue of more than $1 million a year and was experiencing a rate of growth of more than 30 percent per year.[7]

President Bush's proposals for the 1990s make use of this concept. Acid rain is perhaps the biggest pollution problem the United States presently faces. Bush proposed to solve this problem by setting annual limits on the emission of acid-producing pollutants. Under his proposal, 107 utilities, chiefly in the Midwest, would be allowed to generate a certain level of sulfur dioxide every year based on the level of electricity generation. The utilities would be free to choose how to meet these standards. Those close to Western sources of low-sulfur coal might switch fuels, and others might install anti-pollution technology. Still others might shut down. Beginning in 1995, the utilities would be free to sell their "allowances," regardless of how they had met them. By the year 2000, utilities in areas where more electricity was needed could purchase "allowances" from utilities in slow-growth areas.

PUBLIC GOODS

Public goods have two important characteristics. First, once they are produced, no one can be excluded from consuming them. Second, they are

---

6.   For a more detailed discussion on the market for pollution rights and the bubble concept, see Bruce Yandle, "The Emerging Market in Air Pollution Rights," *Regulation* (July/August 1978): 21–28; and M. T. Maloney and Bruce Yandle, "Bubbles and Efficiency," *Regulation* (May/June 1980): 49–52.

7.   For a discussion of AER*X, see Michael Weisskopf, "The Pollution Peddlers," *The Washington Post National Weekly Edition* (26 November 1989): 9.

not depleted by consumption. If an individual consumes a public good, this action does not reduce the amount of the good available for other individuals to consume. Economists refer to these two characteristics of public goods as nonexcludability and nonrivalry. Public goods were introduced in Chapter 2. We expand on that discussion here because of the close relationship between public goods and externalities. These concepts are not really two separate and distinct arguments for government intervention. The arguments are actually the same. A public good is simply a good that has very strong external benefits that are nonexcludable and nonrival.

PURE PUBLIC GOODS VERSUS PURE PRIVATE GOODS

A pure public good is one that is consumed (automatically) by all members of a community as soon as it is produced. It is impossible to exclude individuals from consumption, and the good is perfectly nonrival. In contrast, a pure private good has a price equal to the full opportunity cost of production, and its consumption provides benefits only to the individual (or group) that purchases the good.

It is, of course, difficult to come up with examples of pure public or pure private goods. No good is purely public because no good can be perfectly nonrival in consumption. Almost any public good, such as a road, a park, or a library, gets congested at some point and loses the characteristic of nonrivalry. At the other extreme, the more private a good is, the easier it is to exclude consumption. The more any individual consumes, the less there is for others to consume. A bottle of orange soda is a good example of a private good. A wilderness park might be an example of a public good if citizens consume the idea of wilderness it embodies even though most of them don't ever visit it. Many of the appeals for the preservation of certain species or habitats are based on this idea. The spotted owl or the rain forest has an appeal for people, even those who do not go out and see the owl or walk in the forest. However, a theme park, such as Disneyland, can clearly be private, and an empty soda bottle on the side of the road is a public good in a negative sense—a public bad.

THE FREE-RIDER PROBLEM

Since nonexcludability is an essential feature of a public good, it is possible for individuals to consume such a good without paying for it. Economists call this behavior free riding. Since it is impossible (or at least costly) to exclude you from consumption of a public good whether you pay or not, you may choose to hide your demand for the good, let others pay for it, and still consume it. Thus, free riding makes it difficult for the market to measure actual demand. An example of a free rider would be a weekend sailor using Coast Guard markers to locate a safe channel into a busy harbor.

Because a public good is nonrivalrous and nonexcludable over a large group, it is likely that the market will not provide enough of the good. It is difficult to free ride in a small group, where everyone knows how much each person contributes and social pressure makes it costly for individuals not to contribute. In many rural communities, this type of social pressure is a way of overcoming the free-rider problem. If you don't help rebuild a barn that has been burned, you can't expect help from your neighbors if you run into problems. The free-rider problem, however, increases as the size of the group increases.

The free-rider problem can be better understood by examining Figure 4. For simplicity, assume that there are only two demanders of national defense. (If this simplifying assumption bothers you, assume that there are two groups that have different demands for defense.) The demand curve of each individual is derived in the same way as demand curves for private goods are derived. The two demand curves reflect the amount each is willing to pay for a given "quantity" of defense. If MC represents the marginal cost of national defense, the private market will produce Q_1 units of defense, which will be purchased by consumer b and consumed by both consumers a and b. However, the marginal benefits of additional units of national defense are determined by a vertical summation of the two individual demand curves. The result is a demand curve, $D_a + D_b$, for the public good national defense. We can now determine the optimal level of production of national defense. At price P_1, Q_2 units of national defense represent the efficient level of production. In this case, individuals have every incentive to hide their demand for national defense and consume amount Q_1.

Government financing of a public good overcomes the strategic hold-out part of the free-rider problem. Forced tax collection compels the free rider to pay. It does, however, lead to another problem. In Figure 4, individual demand curves are summed to determine the "correct" demand for a public good such as defense. In reality, this demand is the demand of millions of people for the good. How could all their demand curves be measured? The answer to this difficult problem is that the political process reveals the demand for public goods. Voting for candidate x over candidate y is, at best, a very imperfect mechanism for determining the "correct" level of public good provision.

FIGURE 4
THE MARKET FOR NATIONAL DEFENSE
Since national defense is a public good and thus nonrival, the demand curve for it is found by vertically summing the individual demand curves (D_a and D_b).

MARKET FAILURE AND GOVERNMENTAL REMEDIES		
MARKET FAILURE	**EXAMPLE**	**GOVERNMENTAL REMEDY**
• Positive externality	Well-maintained houses	Zoning Fines Subsidies Deed restrictions
• Negative externality	Pollution	Prohibitions Fines Selling pollution rights User fees
• Public goods	National defense	Provision
• Natural monopoly	Electric company	Regulation Taxation

Volunteer groups can be more successful than governments in over-coming the free-rider problem and providing public goods under certain conditions. The group must be small—such as a small town, where peer pressure and visibility make free riding difficult. Volunteer fire departments and volunteer recreation programs flourish in small towns. In addition, clubs and associations can be formed to provide public goods. The condo association mentioned earlier does this. For example, some home-owners associations in Arizona require members to have grass in their yards rather than unimproved desert. A second condition that allows volunteer groups to overcome the free-rider problem is the existence of private benefits blended with the social benefits. For example, members of a garden club working for city beautification may derive private benefits from both the companionship of other members and the personal enjoyment of a more beautiful town.

PUBLIC GOODS IN PRACTICE

Economists use the distinction between private and public goods to attempt to determine what projects and activities should be undertaken by the government. The idea is to try to determine which markets might show a more nearly optimal level of output if government intervened in the process. This type of analysis is distinctly different from asking what projects and activities *will* be undertaken by government. In truth, the economic distinction between public goods and private goods has little to do with what goods and services government actually provides. Governments supply many goods that have the characteristics of private goods. At the same time, many goods that at least partly fit the economic definition of public goods are privately supplied, often by volunteer groups, nonprofit organizations, clubs, and, in some instances, the market.

Politicians often incorrectly classify goods as public or private based on who supplies them. For example, garbage removal may be considered a local public good even though it might be better classified in theory as a private good with some positive external effects. In fact, many goods (food, recreation, education, garbage removal, police protection, and so on) could be classed as both private goods and public goods depending on whether they are supplied privately or by government. The supplier may vary from one jurisdiction to another. The economist can ask what determines the goods a political unit will choose to supply. An analysis of the political process as interest-group activity is developed in the next chapter to address this question.

INCOME REDISTRIBUTION AS A PUBLIC GOOD

The argument for government redistribution of income is often based on viewing such activity as a public good. If a society decides that the income distribution resulting from the market is unsatisfactory, it can pursue deliberate redistribution. You know that if income redistribution is a public good, less than the optimal amount of redistribution will take place in the absence of government intervention. Free riders will think that there is no need to help the poor because others will give. Voters, as a result, may decide to redistribute income through government and tax all citizens to achieve a more acceptable outcome than the market-produced outcome. The fact that government does some redistribution of income in most market economies suggests that such redistribution is widely viewed as having at least some characteristics of a public good.

EDUCATION AS A PUBLIC GOOD

It is easy to see how getting a college degree is an investment in human capital. Your income will be higher because you have developed marketable skills that make you more productive. Economists argue that all schooling is investment in human capital. According to this argument, even primary and secondary schooling increases the productivity of the work force. This claim has been supported with a great deal of research that showed the positive effects of education on economic growth. If this is true, some of the return to education does not go to the individual being educated. Therefore, individuals will not invest heavily enough in education.

Much of this theory and empirical work was used to support an argument that education is a public good and should receive increased public financing. This argument was based on the fact that trained and educated workers cannot directly capture all the gain from their education. Some of the benefits spill over to society in general. These positive externalities consist of increased economic growth for the nation, a more informed electorate, greater political participation, improved and extended research, and reduction in crime and other antisocial activity. Since these gains cannot be captured by individuals, they will choose to invest too little in education. Government can correct for this market failure by subsidizing the investment in private education or by direct public production of education (along with compulsory attendance).

WELFARE ECONOMICS

The body of economic theory that concentrated on market failures and sought remedies for them was developed in the 1930s, 1940s, and 1950s in the United States. This body of theory is part of a larger and older branch of economic theory that deals with normative policy prescriptions and is called welfare economics. The market failures were negative externalities, the underprovision of public goods, inequitable distribution of income (which was the topic of the last chapter), and economic instability (which is covered in macroeconomics).

The theoretical conclusions led to the policy approach that government could and should intervene to correct for market failures. Collective choice through the political process would ensure that the society would (1) correct the externality, (2) produce the "correct" amount of the public good, (3) create an "equitable" distribution of income, and even (4) "fine-tune" the economy to a desired level of employment and price stability. This very optimistic theory envisioned collective choice and government operating to make the world a much better place through the use of enlightened economic policies. The next chapter will examine some of the problems associated with government intervention to correct market failure.

SUMMARY

1. Laws, and changes in laws due to court decisions, have important impacts on incentives. Laws and their interpretation affect the allocation of resources in a mixed economy.

2. Externalities distort market outcomes because a cost or a benefit of the production process is not included in the economic decision-making process. This cost (or benefit) results in underproduction (or overproduction) of the good.

3. The Coase theorem shows that natural market forces can solve problems of externalities if few people are involved and property rights are well defined.

4. Public goods are underproduced because some individuals will free ride.

5. Market failure exists because of monopoly power, externalities, and public goods. Market failure often results in a call for political action to correct the problem.

New Terms

property law   eminent domain   social costs   Coase theorem
tort law   tort   internalization   Clean Air Act
contract law   externality

Questions for Discussion

1. Does air or water pollution exist where you live? What should be done about it? Should the pollution be done away with entirely? How much more in taxes or higher prices for goods would you be willing to pay in order to have less pollution?

2. Is education a public good? If not, why should taxes help to pay for the college education of some individuals?

3. Why are tennis courts sometimes provided as public goods even though it would be relatively easy to exclude free-riding behavior?

4. Does football at Big Ten schools generate any externalities for students who attend these universities?

5. If you happen to live in a dorm or in an apartment populated by students, there is most likely a great deal of noise. Is there a Coase solution to deal with this externality?

6. Distinguish between public goods as defined by economists and goods that governments provide for the public.

7. What is welfare economics?

8. Why are the individual demand curves for public goods summed vertically rather than horizontally like those for a private good?

9. What is free-riding behavior? Have you ever practiced free riding? Did it work? How could it have been prevented?

10. Discuss whether each of the following is a public good or a private good.
   a. National defense
   b. A lighthouse
   c. Income redistribution
   d. Education
   e. An Apple computer
   f. A Buick
   g. Medical care

11. A main idea of the Coase theorem is that parties to a dispute have incentives to settle the dispute through negotiation. This idea has become standard fare in law school discussions of torts, property, and contracts. Professor Coase, in fact, wound up teaching in the law school at the University of Chicago. Can you think of reasons why some lawsuits would end up in court rather than being settled through negotiation?

12. Suppose you were in charge of a government program to charge firms for the right to pollute. How *should* you set the price?

13. Which business firms will take action to reduce the amount they are polluting and which business firms will pay the fee you set in Question 12?

14. Will any of the firms on which you placed fees in Questions 12 and 13 be forced out of business? Which ones?

15. Why do indefinite or poorly defined property rights generate externalities?

SUGGESTIONS FOR FURTHER READING

Browning, Edgar K., and Jacqueline M. Browning. *Microeconomic Theory and Applications*, 3rd ed. Boston: Little, Brown, 1989. An intermediate text that contains discussion of external effects and public goods.

Posner, Richard A. *Economic Analysis of Law*. Boston: Little, Brown, 1972. The standard reference for the application of economics to legal issues.

Stigler, George J. *Memoirs of an Unregulated Economist*. New York: Basic Books, 1988. The memoirs of the Nobel Prize–winning economist provide a witty overview of the impact of theory on policy. Chapter 5 contains a delightful account of the development of the Coase theorem.

Tietenberg, Thomas H. *Environmental and Natural Resource Economics*, 2nd ed. Glenview, IL: Scott, Foresman, 1988. A well-written textbook that deals with solutions to environmental pollution.

1. Define:
   a. public choice,
   b. rent seeking,
   c. rent defending,
   d. median voter theorem,
   e. logrolling.
2. Explain the biases public choice economists have identified in the political process.
3. Describe how the self-interested behavior of politicians results in rent extraction.
4. Identify the costs of rent seeking and rent defending.
5. Explain why government grows in terms of logrolling and bureaucratic incentives.
6. Explain the bias against new products and new technology that is created by regulation.
7. List some of the methods of privatization.
8. Identify the basic ideas of the Austrian school of economics.
9. Discuss the main themes of radical economic thought.

CHAPTER 32

GOVERNMENT FAILURE AND PUBLIC CHOICE

INTRODUCTION

The last chapter examined economic arguments for government intervention in markets to correct for negative externalities and provide public goods. This chapter analyzes some of the costs of such intervention. Public choice economists have identified ways in which government intervention introduces new problems and biases into the economic system. We will examine these effects and how they might affect the growth of government. Finally, we will examine some other theories about the microeconomic role of government.

PUBLIC CHOICE THEORY

Public choice theory is relatively new. It is perhaps easiest to use the definition provided in the 1988 annual report of the Center for the Study of Public Choice at George Mason University:

"Choice" is the act of selecting from alternatives. "Public" refers to people. But "people" do not choose. Choices are made by individuals, and these may be "private" or "public." A person makes private choices as he goes about his ordinary business of living. He makes "public choices" when he selects among the alternatives for others as well as for himself. . . . While traditional economic theory has been narrowly interpreted to include only the private choices of individuals in the market process, traditional political science has rarely analyzed individual choice behavior. [Public choice theory] is the intersection of these two disciplines; the institutions are those of political science and the method is that of economic theory.

Public choice theory is not as optimistic as welfare economics (discussed in the last chapter) about the potential for government intervention to improve market outcomes. Public choice economists apply the same tools of analysis and simplifying assumptions to the collective choice process and to the private market. These economists recognize that there are market failures. They do not ignore externalities, public goods, unequal income distribution, and macroeconomic cycles. They do, however, argue that collective choice and the intervention of government in the market do not work perfectly either. The weaknesses of the political process mean that government intervention does not work in the ideal way suggested by welfare economists. Public choice analysis begins with the assumption that people who act in a self-interested way when making personal economic decisions are the same people who vote, run for office, or are employed in the bureaucracy. Individuals bring their self-interest to the political process.

Public choice theory is as much political science as it is economics. Public choice analysis seeks to understand how economic incentives and individual self-interest affect political outcomes. For example, public choice economists expect the voter to be ill-informed because the cost of informed voting is extremely high. They view the politician as a vote maximizer, putting coalitions together to attract a majority of voters. Bureaucrats are not profit maximizers but seek instead to maximize budgets and/or to ensure the stability of their jobs. According to the public choice economist, the result of such self-interested behavior in the public sector is that government is an imperfect intervener in its attempt to correct for market failures. One of the most important insights that emerges from public choice theory is that small groups with strong interests will often get their way politically because it is irrational (unprofitable) for the majority to oppose them.

William C. Mitchell has succinctly summarized ten public sector biases that produce this less-than-optimal intervention into the market.[1] This list provides a good foundation for understanding the thinking of public choice economists:

1. Proposals with long-delayed benefits are likely to be adopted only if their costs are unknown or can be deferred or concealed.
2. Proposals offering readily apparent short-term benefits and deferred costs stand a good chance of adoption.
3. Proposals that concentrate benefits and diffuse costs stand an excellent chance of adoption. (A direct majority voting system might induce the opposite, depending on the relative sizes of the individual tax share and benefit.)
4. Proposals to abolish programs or reduce public spending have a low probability of adoption. Electoral rewards go to politicians who propose new programs or expansions and extensions of existing programs.
5. Packages of reform proposals stand a better chance of adoption than individual reform proposals, even if none of the packages' components would be accepted by a majority of voters if considered separately.
6. Direct transfer programs, which clearly designate specific and limited

---

1.   William C. Mitchell, *The Anatomy of Public Failure: A Public Choice Perspective*, Original Paper No. 13 (Washington, DC: International Institute for Economic Research, 1978).

When election time rolls around, voters are bombarded with messages concerning their civic responsibility to vote. These statements are often accompanied by complaints about low voter turnouts for U.S. elections.

But think about it rationally for a minute. What are the costs of voting? You must register to vote. You must spend time getting to the polls. You must wait in line at the polls. Most important, you must spend time becoming informed on the issues and the candidates. What are the benefits of voting? It is possible that you might be able to affect the outcome, but the probability of your vote being important is tiny, especially in national elections. Perhaps you vote because you get a feeling that you have done your duty, or you receive satisfaction from participating in civic affairs. These feelings must

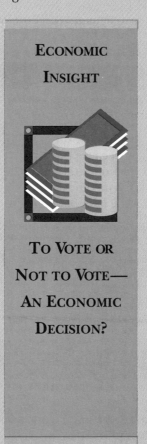

be important, or even fewer people would vote. If society as a whole really wanted more people to vote, however, there are ways to make it less costly to vote. (One reason that many states make election day a legal holiday is to encourage voting.) If you don't think costs affect turnout, answer this question: Do more people vote when the weather is nice or when it is bad?

How could the cost of voting be lowered or the benefits increased? Some methods are postcard registration, transportation to the polls, and more voting places so that lines are shorter. Coffee and doughnuts at the polls might lure a few hungry voters, or rock bands might bring in younger voters (but perhaps keep older ones away). If you think about it, perhaps you can suggest even more voter-luring techniques to your local election board.

benefits to certain persons or groups, stand little chance of adoption.

7. Proposals that rely on inefficient, complex, multiple revenue sources are preferred over those financed by simple, direct taxation.

8. Proposals that tax market efficiency stand a better chance of adoption than proposals that reward efficiency.

9. Proposals that limit consumption (such as price ceilings and rationing) as a response to product shortages are preferred over proposals that encourage increased production.

10. Policies that protect consumers by restraining producers are preferred over policies that simply improve the information level of consumers.

The implications of such biases for policy analysis are striking. Policy problems exist because two imperfect mechanisms are at work. The market fails because of externalities, underproduction of public goods (including unequal income distribution), and business cycles. The collective political process fails because the participants in that process are responding to incentives other than those assumed by the welfare economists. Policy makers must, therefore, choose between two imperfect mechanisms in attempting to solve any policy problem. The policy maker must examine the biases inherent in both the market solution and the collective political solution. It will not always be clear that the cost of intervention is less than the cost of inactivity. Therefore, the public choice approach may lead to a prescription of no intervention in many cases, on the grounds that the cure could be worse than the disease.

RENT SEEKING

In previous chapters, we discussed the concept of rent. Economic rent is the economic return over opportunity cost. It was defined in the chapter on perfect competition as the payment to any factor of production greater than the amount necessary to bring that factor into productive use. In the chapter on monopoly, we raised the issue of monopoly rent seeking, an additional economic cost incurred by individuals seeking to establish monopolies. Thus, from a societal viewpoint, monopolists "waste" resources (in addition to the deadweight loss of monopoly) by incurring the costs of certain economic activities aimed at establishing a monopoly. If you are uncertain about these two uses of the term *rent*, you should review the relevant sections of the earlier chapters.

rent seeking
The commitment of scarce resources to capture returns created artificially.

We now want to look at the concept of rent seeking in a broader sense. **Rent seeking** is defined as the commitment of scarce resources to capture returns created artificially (by government or quasi-government units). Rent-seeking analysis is used by economists to describe how people or firms compete for artificially contrived transfers. Consider the case in which a government decides to confer a monopoly privilege, for example, the contract to be the sole supplier of food services at a state university. A great deal of effort will be spent to obtain that contract. Lobbyists will work in the legislature, firms will give campaign contributions to legislators, and lawyers will draw up contracts. All these efforts are directed toward seeking a rent that has been artificially created by the state. None of this activity will cause the price of the commodity to fall, as in the case in which rents are eroded by normal competitive forces. This rent seeking is a real cost to society because competition for governmentally created rents, unlike the "real" rents discussed earlier, does not generate increased supply.

THE COST OF RENT SEEKING

Gordon Tullock, in attempting to measure the costs of rent seeking, was the first to develop the concept.[2] Figure 1 shows a market demand curve D yielding a competitive equilibrium (price P_c and quantity Q_c) and a monopolistic equilibrium (price P_m and quantity Q_m).

As you learned in the chapter on monopoly, the deadweight loss of monopoly is traditionally taken to be the area of triangle ABC in Figure 1. The area of the rectangle P_cP_mAB is supposed to be the transfer from consumers to monopolists in the form of monopoly profits. But Tullock argues that many of the resources represented by that area do not represent a transfer from consumers to producers. The expenditures to capture these profits turn them into a social cost of monopoly. In fact, if competition for the monopoly were vigorous, the area of rectangle P_cP_mAB would be exactly equal to the resources wasted in competition for the monopoly privilege. The using up of economic rent in the "cost of capture" is unproductive in the sense that it uses scarce resources but does not generate any economic activity that lowers price or increases output.

LEGISLATION AND RENT SEEKING

We can use Tullock's concept of rent seeking to explain governmental action as a form of self-interested behavior by politicians and voters. Many actions of government can be explained by this analysis. In fact, it might

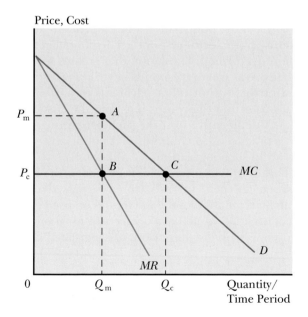

FIGURE 1
THE COSTS OF RENT SEEKING
The deadweight loss of monopoly is the area of triangle ABC, but rent seeking could use up an amount equal to rectangle P_cP_mAB, as rent seekers compete for the monopoly right.

2.   Gordon Tullock, "The Welfare Costs of Tariffs, Monopolies, and Theft," *Western Economic Journal* (now *Economic Inquiry*) (June 1967).

be argued that an industry of rent seekers exists in most state capitals and most certainly in Washington, D.C.

There are at least two broad applications of this interest-group theory of legislation. The first explains the types of government regulation. George Stigler described the benefits and costs to various interest groups of using the state as a vehicle to increase their own wealth.[3] Some groups, such as agricultural interests, seek income transfers from the state. Other groups, such as automobile producers, use the state to fend off regulation that would have a negative impact on costs and profit. In some cases, management and labor join together to use the state for their mutual benefit at a cost to consumers, such as in attempts to restrict imports.

The second application focuses on the economic behavior of legislatures. In this analysis, the politician is responsible for brokering transfers from one group to another. One can view the politician as an entrepreneur putting together coalitions of rent-seeking groups. Consider the public provision of education as an example. In the United States, education through the twelfth grade is mainly produced in the public sector. A public choice economist would argue that even if education is a public good, there is no reason to believe that representative democracy can create the incentives necessary to internalize the external benefits of education. Instead, such economists expect office holders to broker benefits to certain subsets of the population, including (but not limited to) members of the educational bureaucracy and organized student or parent groups. So, what started as a correction of market failure ends in a solution that is quite far removed from the optimal correction. It might reasonably be called government failure.

POLITICIANS AS RENT EXTRACTORS

In most of the literature on rent seeking, the politician is viewed as a broker for private rent seekers. Fred S. McChesney has focused on the politician as the rent extractor.[4] He sees the politician as an independent actor making demands to which the private sector responds. The politician first threatens to extract private rents through legislation that creates special taxes or new regulations. The private sector responds by striking bargains in the form of campaign contributions or other payments to protect its rent. As long as the cost of protecting the rent is less than the costs imposed by the threatened law, the incentive to strike such bargains exists. McChesney reports that this practice is so common that politicians even have a name for it. They refer to such legislation as "milker bills."

The example that McChesney uses to support his argument is the Federal Trade Commission's "used car rule." In 1975, Congress passed a law that ordered the FTC to initiate regulation of the warranties on used cars. The FTC developed a procedure that would have been costly for used car dealers. While the procedure was being written, Congress legislated itself

---

3.   George Stigler, "The Theory of Economic Regulation," *Bell Journal of Economics and Management Science* (Spring 1971).
4.   Fred S. McChesney, "Rent Extraction and Rent Creation in the Economic Theory of Regulation," *Journal of Legal Studies* (January 1987): 101-118. For an interesting discussion of the rent extraction and rent defending that took place during the formulating of tax reform legislation, see Laura Saunders, "One Man's Problem Is Another's Opportunity," *Forbes* (March 7, 1988): 105–112.

a veto over FTC action. After the FTC formulated its rule, Congress held hearings. Used car dealers and their trade associations descended on Congress. Congress in turn vetoed the FTC rule. What rent was extracted? McChesney reports that 89 percent of those in Congress who supported the veto and ran again in 1982 received contributions from the National Auto Dealers Association (NADA). The average contribution was over $2,300, and contributions were received by sixty-six members of Congress who had not previously been supported by NADA.

RENT DEFENDING

John T. Wenders has extended the analysis of rent seeking by drawing attention to the fact that consumers also spend resources defending their consumer surplus from rent seekers.[5] Wenders recognizes that this activity might more correctly be called consumer surplus defending, but he prefers to label it **rent defending**. Consumers would be willing to pay an amount represented by the area of rectangle P_cP_mAC in Figure 1 to prevent the market from being monopolized. As you saw in an earlier chapter, that area represents consumer surplus. Consumer surplus is the extra utility that consumers gain due to the fact that they pay less than they would be willing to pay for the item because all units are sold for the price of the last, or marginal unit.

> **rent defending**
> Actions by consumers to keep their consumer surplus from being captured by rent seekers.

Rent seekers and rent defenders are bidding for the same resources. Rent seekers are bidding for the monopoly privilege. Consumers are willing to spend a similar amount to prevent the rent seekers from acquiring a monopoly. Wenders shows that this situation is analogous to that of Prisoner's Dilemma. If either party spends less, it will lose to the party spending more. This situation ensures that exactly *double* the amount represented by P_cP_mAC in Figure 1 will be spent seeking the monopoly and defending the consumer surplus.

The concept of rent defending expands the analysis of rent seeking. The implication is that in some situations the cost of regulation is much higher than it is traditionally thought to be.

ANALYSIS OF THE POLITICAL MARKET

According to the self-interest theory of government, the size of government increases as a result of rent-seeking activity by firms and individuals and brokering activity by politicians. There are other forces at work to influence the type of governmental programs that are created by politicians. Still other forces tend to increase the size of government, and at least one tends to reduce it.

THE MEDIAN VOTER THEOREM

The **median voter theorem** predicts that under majority rule, politicians will adopt the positions of voters near the center of the political spectrum. To see why politicians move to the center, refer to Figure 2. Assume that

> **median voter theorem**
> A theory that predicts that under majority rule, politicians will reflect the positions of voters near the center of the political spectrum.

5.   John T. Wenders, "On Perfect Rent Dissipation," *American Economic Review* (June 1987): 456–459.

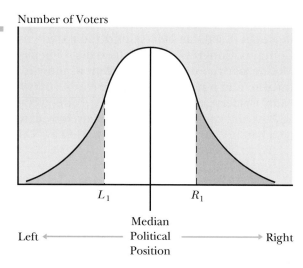

FIGURE 2
THE MEDIAN VOTER MODEL
If two politicians are running against one another, they will both move toward the median position to capture votes.

political preferences in society are continuous from left to right and distributed under the normal curve in the figure. If there are two candidates R_1 and L_1 who are at equal distances from the center, they will get the number of votes represented by the area under the curve on their side of the median line. They tie at the polls. Candidate R_1 will realize that he can steal some votes by moving toward the median, because he can count on all the voters to his right. Candidate L_1 will realize what is happening, and she will also move toward the center in an attempt to get a majority of the votes cast. As a result, both politicians will end up near the median political position, where there are the same number of voters to the left and the right.

The median voter theorem can be used to explain why public spending is aimed at groups in the middle of the political stream, especially in a two-party system. Why, for example, do politicians worry more about catastrophic medical treatment for Alzheimer's than they do for AIDS? The median voter theorem is the basis of Stigler's and Tullock's argument presented in the chapter on income distribution—that most of the redistribution of income will be from the rich and the poor to the middle class.

LOGROLLING

logrolling
Vote trading in the legislative process.

When many issues are before a legislative body at the same time, the outcome most preferred by voters on some issues may not result. This failure is due to **logrolling**, which is a form of exchange in which a politician trades support on one issue for support on another issue. Logrolling is the direct exchange of support. The senator from Oklahoma votes for the military base in South Carolina in exchange for a vote by the senator from South Carolina for the water project that will make Tulsa a seaport.

Economists don't know much about the properties of logrolling except that it does not necessarily produce optimal levels of public output. The size of the budget may be too large and its breakdown may be altered as a result of logrolling. The overall outcome depends on the coalitions that surface. It is probably safe to infer that logrolling does not enhance the efficient use of resources.

It often is argued by economists that geographically based representative democracy and logrolling produce too much government spending of the "pork barrel" type. This excess spending results from the fact that citizens see the cost of their local projects being shifted to citizens of other states or districts and reward their elected officials for delivering such projects. With most representatives attempting to be successful at this political "game," logrolling creates larger than desired levels of government spending.

BUREAUCRATS AND BUREAUS

Once a governmental unit has decided how much of a public good to produce and how to pay for it, the legislature and the executive branch (president, governor, mayor) usually turn the job of supplying the good over to a bureau (a government agency or department). In a few cases, governmental units simply purchase privately supplied goods with tax revenue. A classic case of using private suppliers exists in Scottsdale, Arizona, where fire protection is privately supplied and some part of it is purchased by the local government. Garbage removal is also often privately supplied. More often, however, a bureau is responsible for production of a public good.

Bureaus and bureaucrats further cloud the analysis of government intervention because they are charged with the delivery of public goods. The role of bureaus and bureaucracy creates many problems in supplying public goods. The first problem is that it is extremely difficult, if not impossible, to monitor the efficiency of a bureau. Bureaus do not usually produce measurable outputs. Instead, they produce activities. For example, a bureau might produce fire protection, education, or defense. These activities are usually monitored by examining spending rather than by measuring outputs. Citizens may be more interested in output levels. Sometimes there is a partial measure of output, such as the number of students educated or length of response time for fire-fighting units. But how can the value of the outputs of the Department of Defense be measured? The value of such outputs must usually be inferred from the activity of the bureau, and that activity is most often measured by the size of the expenditure on it. Thus, worries over the quality and quantity of education or defense are generally reduced to calls for increased spending on the activity itself.

MONOPOLY PROBLEMS

The problem of monitoring bureaus is further complicated by the fact that bureaus are almost always monopoly suppliers dealing with a single purchaser, the government. This relationship makes the monitoring function of the governmental committee charged with oversight of the bureau difficult at best. The rationale for a monopoly supplier is that it avoids inefficient duplication. This reasoning may or may not be valid. However, the legislative committee charged with supervising the monopoly supplier has no competing information by which to judge its efficiency.

This point has surfaced in recent years in debates concerning the public funding of education. Conservative and Libertarian social critics have suggested a voucher system as a way to introduce competition into public education. Under a voucher system, each student receives a "chit" that can be used for tuition at any school. These social critics argue that the resulting competition would improve the quality and quantity of publicly financed education.

BUDGET MAXIMIZING

Still another problem is created by the way in which bureaucrats are rewarded. As we discussed in a previous chapter, entrepreneurs or hired managers in the private sector generally lay claim to any profit and, therefore, have ample incentive to increase efficiency. In a public bureau, the manager has no such stake. In fact, it may even be that the bureau manager's salary is inversely related to efficiency. This perverse situation can result when salary increases are tied to the size of the budget and the budget grows (in part) because of inefficiency.

There are many possible goals that bureaucrats could substitute for the private manager's goal of profit maximization. Among these other motivations are salary, perquisites of the office, power, public reputation, patronage, bureau output, ease of management, or investment in future private-sector employment. Government officials should keep these competing motivations in mind when they establish bureaus and when they evaluate bureau managers' behavior. All of these motives will give different results from what welfare economists expect to occur with government intervention. Keep in mind that there is an internal contradiction in expecting a government official to try to control the size of a bureau.

THE INHERENT BIAS AGAINST INNOVATION

Government regulation has a built-in bias against new products and new technology. This bias clearly exists in the area of food and drugs and holds generally for any product that faces regulatory approval. The reason is that old products are on the market until they are proven too harmful, but new products cannot be introduced until they are proven safe. This requirement greatly retards innovation in some areas of the U.S. economy. For example, many U.S. citizens routinely travel to Europe or Mexico to receive innovative medical treatment. The list of innovative drugs not available in the United States is very long. Somatotropin for pituitary deficiency, disopyramide for heart patients, propranolol for blood pressure, and sodium valprote for epilepsy were all available in Europe five to ten years before they could be used in the United States.

Similar situations have existed for other products and techniques. For six years, Chemical Waste Management has been seeking permission to burn waste 140 miles at sea. The technique has been used in Europe for more than fifteen years. Also, *60 Minutes* reported on a similar incident in Texas. A firm used a harmless predatory insect to keep harmful bugs out of stored grain. The insect replaced previously approved pesticides that some consumers found unacceptable. The FDA shut the firm down, ruling that the insect was an unapproved additive to the grain, even though its use was recommended by the Department of Agriculture.

Perhaps the most illuminating story about old versus new products relates to sugar substitutes. In 1977, the FDA proposed a ban on saccharin because it had been linked to cancer. Saccharin had been sold in the United States for almost a hundred years. The makers of saccharin fought

Mikhail Gorbachev quickly became a world politician of the first rank. *Time* magazine named him man of the decade in 1989. His agenda of *perestroika* (economic restructuring) and *glasnost* (openness) has created profound change in the Soviet Union and Eastern Europe. So far, glasnost has been much more successful than perestroika.

Property rights and the ability to exchange such rights are essential for markets to function. It is disagreement over such rights that stands in the way of the success of perestroika. This problem is fundamental because the very definition of communism requires collective ownership of the means of production, distribution, and exchange. Marxist-Leninism was built on the contention that private property is theft.

The struggle to reform in the Soviet Union has produced some interesting definitions. In 1988, a "law on cooperatives" was passed. In effect, this law permitted private business. The term "co-op" was used to make private business sound as though it is compatible with socialism.

INTERNATIONAL PERSPECTIVE

A PROBLEM WITH PERESTROIKA

Perestroika has also led to some increase in private farming. Private leases on farming land are now available for up to fifty years. There is a great deal of resistance to these private property rights. Again, an imaginative word has been developed to describe this new private property. It is called "citizens' property" to make it compatible with socialism.

The success of perestroika will depend on the development of private businesses and the expansion of private property, not only in agriculture but all segments of the Soviet economy. The development of citizens' property in the agriculture sector has proceeded very slowly. Perhaps the memory of Stalin is still vivid in the Soviet minds. In the 1930s, Stalin "liquidated" some 20 million farmers to destroy private farming and collective agriculture. That collective agriculture has been a failure is not subject to debate, but private farmers have faced continuous obstacles from the Communist bureaucracy. There is now cautious optimism that the failure of the August 1991 coup will allow agrarian reform to move forward more rapidly.

the ban in Congress, and it was overruled. At the same time, it took G. D. Searle eight years and large sums of money to win FDA approval of an alternative sweetener, aspartame. Aspartame might have saved countless lives if it had been approved more quickly.

The moral of such stories is a simple one. Regulation has slowed the introduction of new products. This type of regulation may be having a significant impact on U.S. competitiveness in world markets. Peter Huber commented:

I strongly suspect that if Henry Ford had to bring out his Model T in today's environment, the courts and the regulators would have stopped him. Darn thing was dangerous; why you could break your arm cranking it. Of course, horses were dangerous, too, but as an established technology, horse transportation would have fared better in the courts and regulatory halls than transportation by new fangled flivver.[6]

WHAT IS THE ANSWER?

These problems of government intervention lead to disturbing conclusions. You saw in previous chapters, especially the one on monopoly, that markets do not always produce beneficial results. The chapter on market failure and government intervention added externalities and public goods to the list of market failures. But this chapter showed that political action designed to correct market failure introduces a whole set of new problems. The net result is a messy one. Markets may fail, but governments also can fail. Government and government representatives do not always work in the public interest.

This view of government failure as a parallel to market failure has been widely accepted among policy makers and voters. The important point is that economists can identify market failure and government failure and allow policy makers to sort out the least harmful solution to policy problems that affect everyone.

PRIVATIZATION

privatization
The transfer of governmental activities and/or assets to the private sector.

One political movement has worked against the tendency of governments to grow. This trend is most often referred to as privatization. **Privatization** is the transfer of governmental activities and/or assets to the private sector. In response to what some observers consider to be excessive growth of government, privatization has been increasing not only in the United States but worldwide. In England, the Thatcher government was very active in a major program of privatizing numerous state-owned industries. In the People's Republic of China, "the reform of the basic tenets of the system" involves elements of privatization. In the United States, privatization has been done mostly by local governments, but the concept may spread to state and federal governments.

The advantages of privatization are that it reduces government spending and is politically feasible because it does not eliminate the service. The spending reductions come from several sources:

1. Privatization introduces competition and the resulting efficiencies.

---

6. Peter Huber, "Who Will Protect Us from Our Protectors?" *Forbes* (13 July 1987): 23.

2. It permits smaller localities to join together into more efficiently sized units for purchasing services.
3. It removes government from labor negotiations and retirement commitments.
4. It transfers revenue-consuming activities to private firms that pay taxes and produce revenues.

U.S. cities and localities have used seven methods to privatize services. These methods are summarized in Table 1. Privatization can also result inadvertently from failure of governments to deliver a quality service. United Parcel Service's (UPS) success in competing with the U.S. Postal Service is perhaps the best example of such a governmental default. Privatization was a hot topic in the 1980s and can be expected to be an even hotter item for state and local governments in the 1990s.

OTHER SCHOOLS OF THOUGHT

Public choice theory, outlined earlier in this chapter, applies microeconomic analysis to the political process. We now draw your attention to two other schools of economic thought that are usually ignored in a beginning economics course. Both offer some useful insights on the appropriate role of government and the nature of government failure.

TABLE 1
METHODS OF
PRIVATIZATION

METHOD	DESCRIPTION	ADVANTAGES	EXAMPLES
Contracting	Competitive letting of bids	Competitive and can be seasonal	Public works Transportation
Franchises	Grant franchise to operate and charge fee	Can get some revenue without having to provide service	Garbage pickup Airports
Subsidies	Help defray costs of private provider	Cheaper than public provision	Cultural arts Youth activities
Vouchers	Coupon to purchase good or service	Can shop in marketplace— competition	Food stamps School lunches
Volunteers	Ask people to work for free	No-cost services— large pool of people	Tutoring School guards Consulting
Self-help	Variation on volunteerism	No-cost services	Neighborhood watch
Tax incentives	Grant tax concessions	Reduces public need to supply and can be used at federal, state or local level	Income tax credit for child care expenses

Source: Adapted from John C. Goodman, ed., *Privatization* (Dallas: The National Center for Policy Analysis, 1985), 37.

THE AUSTRIAN SCHOOL

The Austrian school has its roots in the work of Ludwig von Mises and Nobel laureate F. A. Hayek.[7] Economists of this school start their analysis from the assumption that policy makers make economic decisions in a state of partial ignorance. Individual consumers and producers plan with incomplete and/or incorrect knowledge of the future. Markets play the role of providing feedback, which coordinates actions as individuals adjust their incorrect plans to changing relative prices. Individuals are frustrated, but by adjusting to changes in relative prices they are better off than they would have been before the adjustment.

The Austrian school is in many ways very close to public choice theory. Economists of the Austrian school argue that political manipulation of the economy is microeconomic in nature, rather than macroeconomic. In their view, politicians do not seek to influence the unemployment rate or the inflation rate, but rather try to influence certain markets for their own gain. For example, one politician may work to create subsidies for farmers. Another may work for aid to urban slum dwellers. The result of these actions is that the size of government increases, with many programs that are difficult to control, much less to reduce.

Economists of this school take a strong stand against governmental planning. This stand is based on four points made by one of the best-known members of the school, F. A. Hayek. The first is that planning always results in more planning because people will circumvent the rules of the planner. As a result, the planner will devise more rules, which lead to more circumvention, which produces still more rules. Hayek referred to this process as "the road to serfdom." Hayek's second point about governmental planning is that no matter how detailed the plan, it can't cover all the specific cases. A bureaucracy will be needed to implement the plan. This bureaucracy will grow powerful and corrupt. Hayek's third point is that high morale is so important to the success of governmental planning that any critics of the plan must be silenced. Hayek's last point is that "the worst get to the top." His point is that governmental planning leads to a dictator. One of the great appeals of Hayek's work is that it so accurately describes the path followed by most countries that have tried central planning. As you will see in a later chapter, the Soviet Union and the People's Republic of China are trying to address some of their internal problems. The Austrian school would argue that these countries' problems are caused by planning, and reforms in the context of planning are doomed to failure.

Perhaps the leading spokesman of the Austrian school in the United States is Murray Rothbard. Professor Rothbard views conservative economists who are suspicious of government intervention as "wimpy moderates" because they do not view *all* government intervention as "not only ineffectual, but also pernicious, and counterproductive."[8] Rothbard and the Austrian school are opposed to any intervention in the macro economy. Although they believe that money matters in the economy, they

---

7.   A very good survey of the Austrian school can be found in Thomas Sowell's *Knowledge and Decision* (New York: Basic Books, 1981). In the United States, this school of thought is embodied in the Ludwig von Mises Institute, which has its offices at Auburn University.

8.   Peter Brimelow, "No Water Economics," *Forbes* (6 March 1989): 86.

don't think that monetary policy can be carried out because it requires impossibly precise assumptions about the economy.

RADICAL ECONOMIC THOUGHT

Unlike the Austrian school, radical economists are critical of both the market and government in a capitalistic system. Radical economists in the United States draw on the tradition of Karl Marx and Marxist thought, which we will discuss in a later chapter. These economists do add several new lines of attack on capitalism.[9] The basic difference between radical economics and other schools of economic thought is that all other economists (including public choice and Austrian) see a basic harmony in the economic system and believe that most problems can be solved by relying on market forces. Radicals contend that solutions to the problems of modern capitalism can only be found by restructuring industrial capitalism. In addition, radical economists regard orthodox economists as being much too narrow in their analyses.

The main themes of radical economics are monopoly power, state power, exploitation, imperialism, and waste and alienation. Radicals believe that the U.S. economy is dominated by large corporations and that small firms play an insignificant role. These large corporations set arbitrary prices and manipulate consumer wants. The state is viewed as the protector and fostering agent of the powerful monopolies. The radicals see the federal government as controlled by big companies. They believe that the state sets economic policy, including defense spending, in the interest of big business.

Radicals challenge the marginal productivity theory of income determination (discussed in an earlier chapter). They argue that monopolistic firms, unequal opportunity, and the unjustifiable private ownership of capital make this theory defective. They base their description of factor incomes on dual, or segmented, labor markets. **Dual labor markets** result from artificial barriers in labor markets that keep some workers in jobs with low wages. Radicals argue that these two labor markets consist of one in which pay is good and advancements are possible and a second in which pay is low and opportunities for advancement are nonexistent. These dual labor markets are a result of a conscious effort on the part of capitalists to restrict advancement to certain groups in the labor force. As a result, a large fraction of the labor force is doomed to dead-end jobs for life, with low pay, little job security, and no opportunities for advancement.

dual labor markets
The radical economists' idea that there are two labor markets because of artificial barriers that keep some workers earning low wages.

Radicals argue that the main obstacle to third-world development is the imperialism of industrial capitalism. Radicals claim (and here they differ from Marx) that industrial capitalists receive capital from the underdeveloped world and that the terms of trade are exploitive of poorer countries. Radicals would support the New International Economic Order, which was discussed in an earlier chapter, as a way to change these conditions.

Finally, radicals argue that resources are wasted in a capitalistic system. This waste is the amount of money spent on such items as expensive au-

9.   Most radical economists in the United States are members of the Union of Radical Political Economy (URPE). URPE publishes a journal, *The Review of Radical Political Economics*, which you can check if you are interested in learning more about radical economics.

tos, furs, alcohol, and drugs, as well as the billions of dollars spent on advertising, which radicals claim is used to manipulate consumer wants. Radicals argue that this waste and the power of monopolies contribute to alienation. Since individuals have little control over their destiny, they consume high levels of unnecessary consumer goods and feel alienated from society.

Radical economists have challenged the mainstream to examine more closely some of the weaknesses of capitalism. The response of most economists has been not to take the radicals too seriously (or to ignore them completely). Radical ideas have, however, led to suggestions for "tinkering" with capitalism in some areas, especially in control of monopoly power. The radicals have also provided useful insights into how special-interest groups use government to serve their own self-interests. These insights are not unlike those of public choice economists. The most serious weakness of the radical economic critique of capitalism is that it is negative. The radical analysis identifies problems but does not present feasible solutions.

Summary

1. Government often supplies goods that aren't public goods because there is political demand for them.

2. Public choice theory identifies biases in the political process and applies economic analysis to political processes and outcomes.

3. Rent seeking is the economic description of individuals' use of the political process to generate income transfers to themselves or to groups they support.

4. Politicians can threaten to pass taxes or regulations in order to extract rents from private parties.

5. Rent defending is the process by which consumers attempt to defend their consumer surplus from rent seekers.

6. The median voter theorem suggests that under majority rule politicians will adopt positions near the middle of the political spectrum.

7. Logrolling in a legislature increases the size of budgets. Legislators agree to vote for a colleague's project in return for a vote on their project.

8. Bureaucratic decision making is different from firm decision making because bureau managers face a different set of incentives than private sector managers do.

9. Government regulation introduces a bias against new products and new technology.

10. Privatization of government assets or activities permits provision of goods and services to be done more efficiently by relying on market (and other) forces.

11. The Austrian school of economic thought assumes that decision makers proceed on the basis of incorrect and/or incomplete information. The school makes a strong case against economic planning by governments.

12. Radical economics, which is related to Marxism, is based on the belief that monopoly capitalism, protected by government, is manipulative and exploitive.

New Terms

rent seeking	median voter theorem	privatization
rent defending	logrolling	dual labor markets

QUESTIONS FOR DISCUSSION

1. Should the government intervene in every case in which an externality exists?

2. What is public choice theory?

3. Why do public choice economists argue that direct transfer programs that clearly target a limited group stand little chance of adoption?

4. Why is it so hard to cut public programs once they are started?

5. Why do government programs that concentrate benefits and diffuse costs have a better chance of being enacted than those that benefit many and impose costs on a few?

6. How can politicians be rent extractors?

7. How can logrolling increase the size of government?

8. Is public choice theory pessimistic? What is its criticism of welfare economics (discussed in the preceding chapter)?

9. When Governor George Wallace of Alabama was campaigning for the U.S. presidency, he was fond of saying that there wasn't a "dime's worth of difference between the other candidates." Does his claim make any economic sense?

10. Is it possible for interest groups in Washington to engage in logrolling? How would they do it?

11. Why do bureaucracies not always serve the public interest?

12. Why, according to public choice theory, is it not rational to vote?

13. Why do members of the Austrian school take such a strong stand against central planning?

14. What is the Austrian school's argument against governmental planning?

15. How do radical economists challenge the marginal productivity theory of income distribution?

SUGGESTIONS FOR FURTHER READING

Buchanan, James M., and Robert D. Tollison. *The Theory of Public Choice-II.* Ann Arbor: University of Michigan Press, 1984. This book contains a series of articles related to applications of public choice theory.

Frey, Bruno S. *International Political Economics.* New York: Basil Blackwell, 1984. This book applies public choice theory in an international setting.

Heilbroner, Robert L. *The Nature and Logic of Capitalism.* New York: Norton, 1985. A critical look at capitalism from a (traditional) liberal perspective.

Lee, Dwight R., and Richard B. McKenzie. *Regulating Government.* New York: Lexington Books, 1986. This book uses public choice theory to explain government intervention into the market and why a constitution is needed to restrain government.

Lindbeck, Assar. *The Political Economy of the New Left: An Outsider's View,* 2nd ed. New York: Harper & Row, 1977. Presents a critical review of the radical economics movement.

Vickers, John, and George Yarrow. *Privatization: An Economic Analysis.* Cambridge, MA: MIT Press, 1988. An account of the privatization experience in Great Britain.

1. Evaluate the following U.S. farm policies:
   a. support prices,
   b. acreage allotment,
   c. marketing orders,
   d. target prices,
   e. Food Security Act.
2. Use a graph to illustrate the farm problems of the United States.
3. Explain optimal city size in terms of economies and diseconomies of agglomeration.
4. Discuss how the provision of local public goods is complicated by spillovers.
5. Explain and evaluate the Tiebout hypothesis.
6. Define and give examples of the tragedy of the commons, and explain why government must either regulate or assign property rights to solve the problem.
7. Identify the problems that can arise when resources are used by several nations.

CHAPTER 33

AGRICULTURE, CITIES, AND THE ENVIRONMENT: CASE STUDIES IN MARKET FAILURE AND GOVERNMENT FAILURE

INTRODUCTION

This chapter applies the theories discussed in the last two chapters to three real-world concerns: agricultural policy, urban problems, and the global environment. You often hear or read about the demise of the family farm and the crisis in agricultural markets. In some areas of the country, traditionally conservative farmers have even used the tactics of protest movements in efforts to draw political attention to their economic problems. The basic tools of economic analysis can provide many insights into the role of market failure and government failure in creating the problems in the agricultural sector.

The issues facing urban America are in many instances not unique to cities but are simply more severe there. For example, pollution and crime are found in all parts of the world, but they are more serious problems in urban areas. Pollution, crime, and other negative externalities associated with living in cities are examples of market failures that government intervention has failed to solve.

Finally, the 1990s have already been labeled the decade of the environment. Reports in the news cause concern about massive oil spills, depletion of the ozone layer, exhaustion of nonrenewable resources, acid rain, the greenhouse effect, the destruction of tropical rain forests, and the pressure of world population on a fragile ecological system. The market system tends not to take a very long view. Critics argue that environmental problems result from failure to plan far enough ahead or to consider the needs of future generations. Governments have attempted to intervene to protect the environment for future generations, but these attempts at correcting market failure bring their own problems.

THE FARM PROBLEM

Government involvement in agriculture has a long history in the United States, beginning with the Homestead Act of 1862. During the Great Depression, direct income and price support programs began. Those who favored such government intervention believed that the market failed in agriculture in several ways. The structure of agriculture is very competitive, with a large number of firms (farms). Farmers face unstable prices for their products, so their incomes vary greatly from year to year. Unpredictable weather, international trading patterns that are subject to government influence, and technological changes aggravate the market instability.

U.S. agriculture presents a case study of what happens to well-intentioned government policy as the government becomes part of the problem. Even when it is recognized that policies are unsuccessful, it is politically very difficult to reduce or eliminate the government's role. Professor George Stigler has put it this way:

One finding has been that small groups do better in politics than large groups, certainly per capita and at times in the aggregate. Today American farmers and their families comprise a little over 2 percent of the population but they get about $40 billion in governmental outlays for income stabilization and all kinds of regulations and special programs (restrictions of crops, preferential interest rates, subsidized electrical utilities, etc.). As late as 1950 farmers and their families were about 15 percent of the population and received about $3 billion from total federal government outlays, as compared with $40 billion (about $9.5 billion in 1950 dollars) in the 1980s. That is about a sevenfold increase in payments per farm operator in dollars of stable purchasing power.[1]

In the short run, the farm problem is simple enough to understand. First, agricultural production takes place in a very competitive market that closely resembles the basic supply and demand model developed in Chapter 3. Second, the demand for farm products is price-inelastic. Third, weather plays a significant role in determining the yield of any crop. These conditions together mean that the revenue a farmer receives from year to year can be highly variable.

The irony is that in years of good harvests many farmers may be in worse shape than in years of poor harvests. This situation is depicted in Figure 1. Assume that in the first year farm output sold at a price of P_1, so Q_1 units were sold, and farmers received a total revenue of $P_1 \times Q_1$. The next year, the weather was very good and the crop was large, so the supply curve shifted to S_2. Price fell to P_2, and consumers purchased Q_2 units. Since demand is inelastic, farmers received less revenue than they did the year before ($P_2 \times Q_2$ is less than $P_1 \times Q_1$). The large fall in price brought only a small increase in sales.

The long-run problem for U.S. farmers is largely the result of huge increases in their productivity in the last century. It takes fewer and fewer farmers to produce the same amount of food. In the early nineteenth cen-

1. George J. Stigler, *Memoirs of an Unregulated Economist*, New York: Basic Books, Inc., 1988, 118–119.

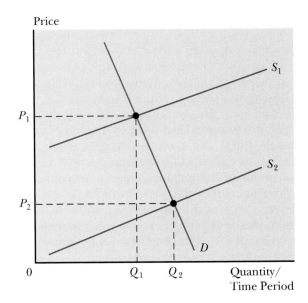

FIGURE 1
THE MARKET FOR FARM OUTPUT
The market for farm output has erratic supply (due to changes in the weather) and inelastic demand. Thus, the total revenue a farmer receives in any one year can be highly variable, and an increase in quantity supplied can reduce total farm income.

tury, more than half of the U.S. labor force was engaged in farming. Now less than 2 percent of the work force is employed in agriculture.

Some observers regard the instability of farm income and the decline of opportunities in agriculture as forms of market failure, although they do not fit into any of the categories of market failure identified in earlier chapters. In addition, as you saw in the last chapter, government intervention often does not succeed. One of these failures occurs when government follows policies that benefit special interests even though the costs to society exceed the benefits.

Many of the arguments to save the family farm are intended to stop the trend toward fewer and fewer agricultural workers. Even some non-farmers support maintaining the current number of farms. They argue that smaller farms are more environmentally benign than huge agri-industry. Farmers have political power, so there has been governmental response to their calls for action. Among the forms of this response have been agricultural price supports and managing production.

SUPPORTING PRICES

Before 1973, the **agricultural support program** consisted of attempts to achieve parity for farmers through the use of price supports. **Parity** is a one-to-one ratio between the average price of farm products and the prices of what farmers buy. In practice, achieving parity means creating **support prices**, or price floors, which are prices maintained above equilibrium levels by the government. The idea behind support prices is to link farm prices to a parity index that maintains the purchasing power of farmers at the level of some base period. For example, if a bushel of wheat bought five gallons of gasoline or two pairs of shoes in the base period, the price of a bushel of wheat should be kept high enough to permit the same purchases today. Highly respected agricultural economist and Nobel laureate T. W. Schultz described parity as "a vulgar economic con-

agricultural support program
Attempts by the federal government to achieve parity for farmers through the use of price supports.

parity
A one-to-one ratio between the average prices of farm products and the prices of what farmers buy.

support prices
Price floors for agricultural products maintained by the government, which purchases any surplus to keep the price from falling.

cept."[2] It is vulgar to Schultz because it does not allow changes in the relative prices of agricultural and nonagricultural products over time.

You saw the effect of price floors in an earlier chapter, so Figure 2 should be familiar. When there is a price floor above the equilibrium price, the quantity supplied exceeds the quantity demanded at the imposed price, and a surplus develops. If the price floor is to be maintained, demand must be increased. However, the government can't sell the surplus on domestic markets, or the price will fall back to the equilibrium price. In the 1950s and early 1960s, the government reacted to this dilemma by building storage bins and storing farm products. The Department of Agriculture sold some of the surplus food to poor countries under the Food for Peace program and distributed some to school lunch programs and welfare recipients. Most of the surplus was just stored, however. At the high point of this storage activity in 1961, the U.S. government had 1.3 billion bushels of wheat and 1.7 billion bushels of corn in storage.

There are some steps that could be taken to dispose of such a surplus. The government could destroy the surplus, but this action would upset those who consider it wasteful.[3] The government could give the surplus away to poor countries, but this might anger other countries who are trying to sell their farm products. The government might distribute the surplus in its own country. In the 1980s, the Reagan administration distributed large amounts of surplus cheese to people over age 65. Some of this cheese went to people who were quite prosperous, including retirees

FIGURE 2
PRICE FLOORS IN AGRICULTURE
If the government imposes a price floor (price support) above the market-clearing price, a surplus will result.

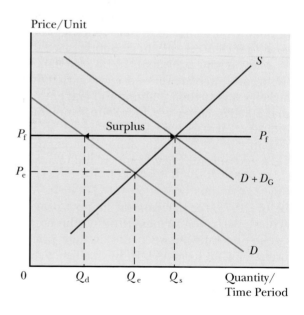

2.   T. W. Schultz, "Tensions between Economics and Politics in Dealing with Agriculture," Agriculture Economics Paper No. 84:24, Department of Economics, University of Chicago (10 August 1985): 5.
3.   The Canadian government once destroyed 28 million eggs. See Patrick Howe, "Unscrambling the Egg Market: A Lesson in Economics," *Common Sense Economics* 2 (Spring 1977): 42–47. For some ludicrous stories of price supports gone amok, see *Fortune* (25 November 1985): 149; (9 December 1985): 150.

with a great deal of accumulated wealth. The government could sell the surplus to other countries if customers could be found. Another alternative would be to retain the surplus for future emergency needs. Regardless of the disposal problems, it is absolutely necessary for the government to buy the surplus it has created.

MANAGING PRODUCTION

In the mid-1950s, the U.S. government decided that the purchase and storage of farm surpluses was too costly and that managing production was a better alternative. The new policy called for the government to maintain the price floor by keeping the quantity supplied at lower levels than would exist without government intervention. With this policy, the government was trying to shift the supply curve to the left in order to maintain the higher price without creating a surplus.

The first government attempt to manage production was known as the soil bank program. In the **soil bank program**, which was started under President Eisenhower in the 1950s, farmers were paid to let their land lie idle. A second attempt to reduce production was the acreage allotment. An **acreage allotment** sets a limit on the number of acres that can be used to produce a specific crop. The government must determine who gets what acreage allotment. For tobacco, for example, the decision is based on past levels of production. If your parents had a tobacco acreage allotment and you bought or inherited their farm, you would be entitled to an allotment based on their share of past production.

A long-term government program aimed at reducing supply is the **Conservation Reserve Program (CRP)**. This program pays farmers to remove land from production for ten years or more. In 1990, the total amount of farm land in this program was about 25 million acres. Payments to farmers in the program in that year were over $1.5 billion.[4]

The supplies of many crops that are not directly subsidized by the federal government are controlled by marketing orders. The system of marketing orders started in 1937 with the goal of maintaining farm income and stable marketing conditions. **Marketing orders** establish producer cartels that control the supply of certain agricultural commodities not subject to price supports. The federal government enforces these cartel agreements through a system of fines for growers. Marketing orders are very common in the fruit-growing industry. The influence of these cartels on supply can be enormous. For example, in 1983, 20 million cases of lemons were destroyed to keep them off the market. The amount of lemons destroyed in 1983 exceeded the amount sold to consumers.[5]

The transfer to farmers through marketing orders is a bit different from the transfer through support payments. In support programs, the payment from the government to the farmer represents a transfer from all taxpayers. Under marketing orders, the subsidy takes the form of a federally enforced artificially high price. This subsidy is a transfer from the consumers of specific products to the growers of those products.

soil bank program
Federal agricultural program beginning in the 1950s under which farmers were paid to let their land lie idle in order to reduce the supply of farm products.

acreage allotment
A limit set by the government on the number of acres that can be used to produce a specific crop, based on past production levels.

Conservation Reserve Program (CRP)
A federal program that pays farmers to remove land from production for ten years or more.

marketing orders
A federal program that establishes producer cartels that control the supply of certain agricultural products not subject to price supports.

---

4.   Jeffrey D. Karrenbrock, "The 1988 Drought: Its Impact on District Agriculture," *Review*, Federal Reserve Bank of St. Louis (May/June 1989): 8.

5.   Doug Bandow, "Federal Marketing Orders: Good Food Rots While People Starve," *Business and Society Review* (Spring 1985): 41.

Attempts to manage farm production directly by reducing inputs have not been very effective because most farmers are good entrepreneurs. Under the soil bank program, almost all farmers took their least productive land out of production with little decline in output. In the acreage allotment program, farmers had an incentive to cultivate the allowed acres very intensively in an effort to produce nearly the same output on fewer acres. Marketing orders have been more effective in reducing quantity supplied. Farmers cannot benefit by increasing productivity and output when the government specifies the maximum allowed output.

INCREASING DEMAND

In addition to trying to restrict supply, another way to raise prices for agricultural products is to increase demand. There have been some governmental attempts to do this. The Department of Agriculture (USDA) has engaged in export promotion. Programs have been created by the USDA and some land grant universities to assist companies in penetrating foreign markets. In other cases, the government has sold agricultural products directly to foreign countries, most often the Soviet Union.

Another demand-increasing program is the food stamp program. In this program, the USDA gives food stamps to the poor to enable them to buy more agricultural products. This program redistributes income at the same time that it increases the demand for agricultural products.

RECENT FARM POLICY

target prices
Prices the government considers to be fair for farmers, used to determine subsidy payments.

Since 1973, there have been some changes in the system of agricultural price supports. For some products, there are no longer price floors. Instead, the government sets target prices. **Target prices** are prices the government considers to be fair for farmers. The market is allowed to clear, and the USDA then compares the equilibrium price to the target price. The government then pays each farmer the difference between the target price and the market-clearing price. Target prices have less of a distorting effect than support prices because the relative prices of agricultural products are allowed to change. Also, the government does not have to purchase and store the surplus product. Finally, the subsidy aspect is more apparent with target prices than with support prices.

During the 1980s, the Reagan administration made some attempts to reduce the price support programs. The first attempt in early 1981 kept a scheduled rise in target prices for milk from going into effect. This move did not do away with supports, but did prevent an increase at that time.

payment in kind (PIK) program
A federal agricultural program similar to the soil bank program, but with payments made in surplus commodities rather than in money.

In 1982, President Reagan initiated a **payment in kind (PIK) program**. The idea was to eliminate the overproduction (caused by the existing support prices) and deal with the huge stocks of farm surpluses. For example, the program gave a farmer 8,000 bushels of stored corn, which the farmer would sell, in exchange for not producing 10,000 bushels. The PIK program was similar to the soil bank program, but payment was made in surplus commodities rather than in money. The result was the same as for the soil bank program. Farmers idled 47 million acres of land in 1983, but they put aside their least productive land and worked the best land more efficiently. The percent drop in production was much less than the percentage of land set aside.

The European Community (EC) maintains a common agricultural policy (CAP) for its member nations. Unlike agricultural policy in the United States, which is based on paying not to produce, CAP says "pay for everything produced." This system of guaranteed payment has produced huge surpluses that are either stored and are rotting or are sold to the Soviet Union at bargain basement prices.

CAP has resulted in what are jokingly referred to as the French wine lake, the European grain mountain, and the great olive oil sea. Great Britain has 150 storage depots that are stuffed full of grain and butter. A junior minister in Margaret Thatcher's government testified in the House of Commons that the cost of storing and disposing of stocks of cereals, sugar, wine, milk, and beef was about $25 million per day. A "rancher" with three or more cows is entitled to a subsidy from the EC! In Germany, many people have become cow ranchers. Bavaria is full of cottages on small plots of land with three cows. Former Prime Minister Thatcher complained, "In Europe, believe it or not, the subsidy for every cow is greater than the personal income of half the people in the world."[a]

INTERNATIONAL PERSPECTIVE

AGRICULTURAL POLICY, EUROPEAN COMMUNITY STYLE

One of the major beneficiaries (besides the farmers) of this transfer from taxpayers in the EC is the Soviet Union. The Soviet Union has learned to use EC-subsidized surpluses as a way of supplementing its poor agricultural output. Great Britain has sold increasingly large amounts of its surplus output to the Soviet Union. In 1984, sales from Great Britain to the USSR equaled 125,000 tons of products per week, and 35,000 tons per week were sold to Communist countries of Eastern Europe. The prices were deeply discounted from those paid to farmers. Flour was sold at an 80 percent discount; sugar, 72 percent; butter, 60 percent; beef, 88 percent; and wine, 97.5 percent.[b] The Soviets may be taking some lessons from capitalists. At least they know how to profit from the central planning of other governments!

As the EC prepares for complete economic integration in 1992, changes in CAP are high on the agenda. The protection given to agriculture may become a victim of full integration. As economies become more internationalized, the costs of such agricultural subsidies become more visible. The more apparent they become, the more politically vulnerable they will be. CAP will be a political "hot potato" in the 1990s.

a. U.S. News & World Report (30 November 1987): 9.
b. Edward Pearce, "Buying the Farm with the EEC," National Review (18 October 1985): 42–44.

Food Security Act
A 1985 federal law that sets target prices and requires farmers to agree to keep part of their land idle.

The Food Security Act of 1985. In 1985, Congress passed the **Food Security Act.** The intent of the law was to make U.S. agricultural products more competitive on world markets. The law eliminated the price support programs that caused their prices to be above world market prices. The Food Security Act sets target prices and requires farmers to agree to keep part of their land idle. Thus, it combines elements of both the target price and soil bank programs. Farmers sell their products at world market prices, and the government pays them a deficiency payment equal to the difference between the target price and the world price. The target price is supposed to be related to the costs of production.

In 1986, the target price of wheat was $4.38 per bushel, and the world market price was around $2.75 per bushel. As a result, U.S. taxpayers had to make a payment of $1.63 for every bushel of wheat sold. As you might imagine, the cost of the Food Security Act is enormous. When Congress debated the bill in early 1985, the cost over its five-year life was estimated at $35 billion. When President Reagan signed the bill in November 1985, his advisers estimated that cost to be $52 billion. In November 1989, the Congressional Budget Office reported that the actual cost for only the first *three* years of the program was $70 billion.

Save the Family Farm Act. In 1987, Senator Tom Harkin of Iowa and Congressman Richard Gephardt of Missouri introduced the Save the Family Farm Act. The goal of this act was to raise farm prices by drastically decreasing farm output (by more than half). Farmers would be given the opportunity to control production by voting mandatory limits on the amount of farm land that could be put into production. Farmers would face penalties if they did not limit production. However, the bill did not specify what the penalties would be. *Business Week* commented that the Harkin-Gephardt bill sounded "borrowed from a Soviet economic plan."[6]

Supporters of the bill argued that, although prices to consumers would increase, taxpayers would save billions in subsidy payments. One difficulty with this proposal was that, if it were successful in raising U.S. prices, imports would be cheaper and import competition would drive the artificially high U.S. prices down to world market levels. Thus, the program could only achieve its goal with more restrictive tariffs and quotas on agricultural imports than existed at the time. The Save the Family Farm Act did not pass in 1987, but it will be introduced again.

Conflicting Effects of Farm Policies

Many of the federal government's farm policies work at cross purposes. Consider, for example, the price support program, which guarantees farmers an unlimited market for grains and dairy products. Farmers expand production because they know they have a buyer to generate the cash flow to meet their payments on expensive machinery and heavily mortgaged land. Thus, this policy works to stimulate production. Other programs, such as the soil bank and marketing orders, are intended to decrease production.

---

6.   Michael A. Pollock, "Farmers Will Reap a Bumper Crop of Supports," *Business Week* (12 January 1987): 83.

In 1986, the federal government set out to mop up the milk glut created by price supports and in the process created a new problem. In a sweeping offensive called the Dairy Termination Program, the government sought to eliminate 12.3 billion pounds of milk from the market by buying up dairy herds and selling the animals for beef. In order to participate in the program, farmers had to agree to stay out of the dairy business for five years. Almost $2 billion was spent to get 14,000 farmers out of the milk business. Groups representing beef producers were quick to respond. The program designed to increase milk prices by cutting supply had the opposite effect on beef prices. Prices fell as the supply of beef increased. The California Cattlemen's Association demanded compensation for their losses of from $25 to $60 per head of beef.

Under still another program, the **Soil Conservation Service**, grants were given to encourage farmers to conserve land (rather than produce full tilt) by fallowing fields, contour plowing, and other conservation techniques. (All of these techniques temporarily reduce crop yields.) The price support and the soil conservation programs, both costing taxpayers, work in opposite directions. One creates incentives to expand production. The other offers incentives to contract production.

Soil Conservation Service
A federal program under which grants were given to encourage farmers to contract production by fallowing fields, contour plowing, and other conservation techniques.

STATE REGULATION OF AGRICULTURE

The latest development in government intervention in the agricultural market has been at the state level. In the late 1980s, several states passed legislation that made it more difficult for large corporate farms to operate. Laws passed in Kansas, Iowa, Nebraska, South Dakota, and Minnesota prevent corporations with more than a certain number of stockholders (usually fifteen) from owning land. The intent of such legislation is to preserve the family farm. As Kansas state representative Bruce Larkin said, "The intent of these laws is to keep the family farm in place. Without a family farm structure, rural communities will dry up and wither away."[7] The legislation ignores the economic fact of life that family farms are disappearing. They are being replaced by large-scale corporate farming. Legislation is not going to change this trend.

One outcome of such state legislation has been an economic boon to adjacent states. National Farms, Inc. is building a 1,200-acre hog farm near Brush, Colorado. The company had originally planned to build this farm in South Dakota, but South Dakota passed anti-corporate farm legislation in 1988. The farm produces 300,000 hogs a year and employs 200 farm workers. Maybe some of the unemployed family farmers in South Dakota will move to Colorado to find work!

In early 1990, the state of Wisconsin passed a law prohibiting the sale of milk from cows that had been given a newly developed hormone that dramatically increased milk production. Supporters of the bill argued that health officials were concerned about possible effects of this hormone on humans. Wisconsin lawmakers maintained that they were worried about potential health risks from the hormone. Cynics argued that the lawmakers saw the bill as a way to reduce the potential supply of milk.

---

7.   This quote and the facts in the next paragraph from Charles Siler, "Where Did All the Pigs Go?" *Forbes* (19 March 1990): 152–156.

THE FUTURE OF FARM POLICY

U.S. agriculture policy is at a crossroads. The average annual direct subsidy to the average American farmer is more than twice the mean family income in the United States. Two options are open to policy makers. The first is to follow a protectionist, supply management policy. The second option is to confront the challenge presented by other countries in recent tariff negotiations. These negotiations have developed an agreement to negotiate all barriers affecting trade in agricultural products. In 1991, the United States proposed an initiative that would eliminate all agricultural price supports in all member countries by the year 2000. Under this proposal, all government payments to farmers would be "decoupled" from farm production. This change would be drastic in that it would make the payments to farmers into direct welfare benefits rather than transfers through other mechanisms.[8]

Like many social problems, the farm problem cannot be resolved with the tools of economics. These tools can, however, point out some basic options. There are too many resources in the agricultural industry relative to the demand for its output. The resources are encouraged to stay there by transfer payments made to farmers out of general tax revenues. Taxpayers' income is being redistributed to farmers, keeping resources in the farm industry that would otherwise be attracted to other industries. In 1990, the direct budget costs of federal agriculture programs were more than $1,000 for every nonfarm family in the United States. These payments represent a significant share of federal tax revenues and do not include the off-budget transfers to farmers.

The basic tools of economics do not reveal whether this situation is good or bad or predict whether anything will be done to change it. The answer to the first question is a value judgment concerning whether society thinks it is good or bad to maintain the present level of resources in agriculture. The answer to the second question will, in part, depend on the political strength of farmers and the farm constituency relative to other groups.

URBAN ECONOMICS

The study of urban economics also illustrates the problems of market failure and government failure. Government failure occurs when government responds to market failures in a less than optimal way. In this case, market failure consists of the negative externalities associated with population density. These externalities include crime, traffic congestion, environmental pollution, and noise pollution, to name a few. In addition, provision of public goods in many urban areas is complicated by the number of political divisions. In the 1970s, the growth of population in cities was slower than the population growth in rural areas and in suburbs. This trend was seen at the time as due in part to the energy crisis and high gasoline prices. The 1980s saw a reversal of this trend, with population growth

---

8.   See E. C. Pasour, "Farm Programs Hurt Everyone—Even Farmers," *The Independent* (Vol. II, No. 1, 1989): 3.

in cities exceeding growth in areas outside of cities. Also during the 1980s, the Reagan administration sharply reduced the amount of federal government transfers that had been going to U.S. cities.

HOW LARGE SHOULD A CITY BE?

Cities come in all sizes, both in population and in land area. There are very small cities that seem to offer their residents a satisfactory collection of public and private goods and services. Very large cities offer a greater variety of services and attractions to residents and visitors. The most desirable size for a city depends on the balance between the advantages and disadvantages of a large population.

ECONOMIES OF AGGLOMERATION. Urban areas spring up because of economies of scale. Urban economists use the more specific term **economies of agglomeration** to describe the cost savings that individuals enjoy when enough of them locate in one relatively small area. The reasons for these lower average costs are similar to the reasons for cost savings to a firm when economies of scale exist. The savings result because the size of the city yields enough local demand for highly specialized suppliers. In addition, large pools of specialized labor exist in urban areas, again because the demand is large enough to attract enough workers.

> **economies of agglomeration**
> The cost savings that individuals enjoy when enough of them locate close together in or near a large city.

The broadcasting industry is a good example of this principle at work. Broadcasting is concentrated in New York City and Los Angeles. This concentration represents demand for writers, actors, musicians, dancers, technicians, directors, and designers and for firms that specialize in the equipment these individuals use. Start-up costs for new firms are lower because suppliers are close at hand. New firms and new artists locate in these areas in order to take advantage of these cost savings.

Economies of agglomeration usually take the form of efficiencies in production and information gathering. However, agglomeration can also result in a wider variety of consumption alternatives. This wider range of consumption choices can attract residents and lead to further agglomeration. Economists in recent years have gathered data on urban areas to make separate forecasts of economic activity for them. The motivation behind this separation is that macro modeling and forecasting for the whole economy overlooks pockets of economic activity in some areas. In other words, a recession in the United States as a whole doesn't necessarily mean a recession in all parts of the country. A smart entrepreneur needs to know what is going on in the economy at a micro level.[9]

Although some costs are lower as agglomeration takes place, others increase because of **diseconomies of agglomeration**. There are both negative and positive externalities associated with urban growth. The two most obvious negative externalities are crime and pollution.

> **diseconomies of agglomeration**
> The additional costs that individuals must pay when too many of them locate in one city (thus creating negative external effects for one another).

OPTIMAL CITY SIZE. Since there are economies and diseconomies associated with agglomeration, there should be some optimal city size. This optimum is the size at which the value of the benefits exceeds the total cost

9. John Case, "The Economic Microscope," *INC.* (November 1989): 27.

of the negative externalities by the greatest amount. In terms of micro-economic theory, the optimal size is that for which the marginal agglomeration benefits are equal to the marginal agglomeration (congestion) costs. The optimal size of a city changes as these costs and benefits change. For example, if a technological change made crime prevention cheaper, the model predicts an increase in optimal city size. If technology reduced the diseconomies of agglomeration, optimal city size would increase. In addition, to the extent that demand for the consumption activities supplied by cities is income-elastic, the incomes of residents and potential residents will affect the optimal size of that city. An increase in income will increase the optimal size of urban areas, *ceteris paribus*.

The decision about optimal size will be made by thousands of individuals. Migration out of and into cities will be driven by individual decisions about the value of the positive and negative externalities associated with city size. Differences in tastes and preferences will ensure a variety of sizes of cities. Most economists would argue that such a decentralized process is superior to some governmental decision about how large a city should be. Policy makers can, however, have some influence on city size through zoning, taxes, and transportation systems. They may move a city's size toward or away from the optimum by changing the costs and benefits individuals face in locating there. Both market forces and policy decisions determine the optimal size for each city, and the optimum is always in a state of flux.

SMALL TOWNS AND LARGE CITIES. Large cities in the United States continue to grow, but a large part of the U.S. population still lives in smaller towns and cities that lack both the attractions and the problems of New York, Detroit, or Houston. Many of these smaller towns have lost population. Even those that have grown now enjoy fewer retail services than several decades ago. The booming main streets of the first half of the twentieth century have given way to many empty storefronts since retail outlets have moved to malls that serve a cluster of small towns in a single central location. Economies of agglomeration in retailing have led to the centralization of shopping at the expense of small-town main streets.

NEW SUBURBS. The traditional role of the central city is changing. Historically, suburbs grew away from the central city, but most suburban residents commuted there for work, entertainment, and shopping. This pattern has changed as the information age is decentralizing cities, and it is no longer necessary to commute. All kinds of businesses have moved out of the city and into the suburbs, where, among other things, the rents are cheaper. Barbara Boggs Sigmund, the mayor of Princeton, New Jersey, refers to these new suburbs as "urbanoid villages." Sigmund is critical of urbanoid villages, arguing that they breed traffic, fail to deliver services, and hinder rather than promote community.[10]

---

10. Betsy Morris, "New Suburbs Tackle City Ills While Lacking a Sense of Community," *The Wall Street Journal* (26 March 1987): 1.

URBAN PUBLIC GOODS AND THE SPILLOVER PROBLEM

Public policy to solve urban problems is complicated by the number of political entities involved in these areas. For example, metropolitan Atlanta has fifty-three separate local governments. These governments do not always cooperate and are often in direct competition for projects and development funds. This competition adds a new dimension to the concept of government failure. It can lessen the potential for government failure by making governments more sensitive to voter demand, but it can also contribute to government failure by making it harder to overcome the free-rider problem.

The problem of supplying public goods is especially complicated when there are many local governments in an urban area. With many political subdivisions, the external benefits of the provision of a public good may spill over into different jurisdictions, making the provision of that public good much more difficult. For example, Figure 3 represents the demand for crime prevention by two groups of citizens in a political subdivision of an urban area. D_a represents the demands of group a, and D_b the demand of group b. Since crime prevention is a public good, it is subject to the free-rider problem discussed earlier. The true demand curve is found by vertically summing the two demand curves. The socially optimal provision of the public good is amount Q_1 at price P_1. Assume for a moment that it is possible to overcome the free-rider problem and that the citizens of the subdivision vote to tax themselves an amount equal to rectangle $0P_1AQ_1$ and supply the optimal amount of crime prevention.

The optimal amount of crime prevention will still not occur if some of its benefits spill into other jurisdictions. In Figure 3, D_c represents the demand of people who live outside the political subdivision for crime prevention inside the subdivision. They have a demand because they come to work and/or shop in the subdivision. In addition, they live close enough to fear that criminal activity might easily spread to where they live. Since they do not vote and pay taxes in the jurisdiction, their demand is not in-

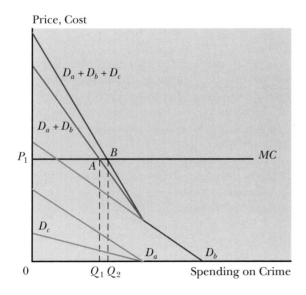

FIGURE 3
THE MARKET FOR CRIME PREVENTION
Crime prevention is a local public good. If D_a and D_b represent the demand of two groups within a jurisdiction, the optimal amount of crime prevention is Q_1. However, if some of the benefits spill into other jurisdictions and the demand of residents there is represented by D_c, the optimal amount of the public good is Q_2.

corporated into the political decision to supply amount Q_1. If it were, the demand curve (again a vertical summation) would be $D_a + D_b + D_c$ and the optimal amount of spending on crime prevention would be equal to rectangle $0P_1BQ_2$. The conclusion of this analysis is that internalizing externalities within a political subdivision becomes much more difficult when the externalities spill across political boundaries.

SOLVING THE SPILLOVER PROBLEM. Revenue sharing, or grants from higher to lower levels of government, is one way to overcome the spillover problem and increase the provision of goods with positive externalities. The state or federal government can help overcome such local urban problems through the use of grants. In the 1970s, this type of grant was very popular. In 1979, 38 percent of the revenue of U.S. cities came from higher levels of government, mostly the federal government. The Reagan administration reduced such grants, forcing urban governments to rely increasingly on their own sources of revenue.[11] By 1985, this type of grant accounted for only 29 percent of local revenues.

Fiscal conservatives are critical of grants from higher to lower levels of government for two reasons. First, they argue that the federal government should not transfer such funds when the federal budget has huge deficits. Second, they argue that these grants make local officials less fiscally accountable than they would be if they had to raise taxes in order to spend. Proponents argue that such grants can redistribute income from richer to poorer areas and compensate cities for some of the positive externalities that are enjoyed by nonresidents.

user charges
Fees that cover part or all of the cost of a public service.

One possible way to solve the spillover problem without resorting to revenue sharing is through **user charges**, or fees that cover part or all of the cost of a public service. User charges can finance some public goods, at least partially. Local governments can charge different fees to residents and nonresidents. This type of payment schedule works very well for recreational and cultural programs. For example, Greenbelt, Maryland requires proof of residence in order to pay a lower resident fee for swimming lessons and tennis classes at community recreation areas. Most state universities have a tuition schedule that charges less to state residents than to out-of-state students.

THE TIEBOUT SOLUTION. In a famous article, Charles Tiebout argued that the provision of local public goods is best done by small homogeneous jurisdictions.[12] The smaller the jurisdiction, the more responsive the government will be to its citizens. Citizens in an urban area will choose to live in a certain jurisdiction by buying into its package of local public goods and tax prices. For example, in the Washington, D.C. area, individuals can choose to live in the District or five adjacent counties, two in Maryland and three in Virginia. Each offers different tax levels, transportation services, housing quality, and local public goods.

Tiebout argues that a market exists for local public goods in which con-

---

11. See Richard P. Nathan and Fred C. Doolittle, "Federal Grants: Giving and Taking Away," *Political Science Quarterly* (Spring 1985): 53–74.
12. Charles M. Tiebout, "A Pure Theory of Public Expenditures," *Journal of Political Economy* (October 1956): 416–424.

sumers "vote with their feet" by moving to areas that provide satisfactory combinations of taxes and services. Further, he argues, the price of housing in an area will reflect the relative desirability of what is offered to the voter-consumers. The **Tiebout hypothesis** is that voters will influence local public goods through their choice of locations. This idea is closely related to the concept of privately supplied public goods discussed in the chapter on market failure. Competition among suppliers of local public services (local governments) forces them to offer more desirable combinations of spending and taxing, since individuals will migrate to those jurisdictions that have the most attractive mix.

Tiebout hypothesis
The idea that competition among local governments as suppliers of local public services will force them to offer the desired combination of spending and taxing to voters, who will migrate to those jurisdictions that produce that combination.

PRIVATIZING: THE CASE OF LOW-INCOME HOUSING

One strategy used by some cities to hold down their tax burdens is privatization, or shifting production of some services to the private sector. Low-income housing is an example. Federally funded programs to provide public housing in the 1960s and 1970s produced very unsatisfactory results in most cities. It was usually easy to identify "the project" by its many boarded-up windows and slumlike appearance. Indeed, in many cities the housing projects built in the late 1960s have been abandoned. Some have even been torn down.

The Local Initiative Support Corporation (LISC), with financing from the Ford Foundation, has tried a different approach—privatizing the process of supplying low-cost housing. The result is low-income housing that has a blend of public and private financing. LISC works with local community groups to determine what is needed in housing. These local groups use public money, foundation grants, and loans from private mortgage lenders to rebuild an area. The group then takes ownership of and manages the housing units. The results have been impressive. Pride of ownership (transferable property rights) has meant better maintenance, and these rebuilt areas have become models that other cities can emulate. The key element has been incentives at the tenant level, resulting in tenant associations that maintain and police the areas.[13]

IS MASS TRANSPORTATION A PUBLIC GOOD?

Many cities are expanding or building new mass transportation systems. These systems can cover an entire metropolitan area, in some cases crossing city or even county lines. For example, the Metropolitan Atlanta Rapid Transit Authority (MARTA) runs bus and train service from distant suburbs into downtown Atlanta. Perhaps the "snazziest" urban mass transportation system is the Metro in Washington, D.C. The system features clean facilities (in contrast to the subway in New York City) with a space-age look. In 1990, the Washington Metro was a 47-mile system. It will cost more than $6 billion when it is complete. Some critics have joked that it would have been cheaper to buy every citizen of the District of Columbia a new Mercedes automobile.[14]

13. See James Cook, "Priming the Urban Pump," *Forbes* (23 March 1987): 63–64. On the other hand, privatization has taken some of these properties out of the supply of low-income housing, creating what some view as a "time bomb." See Michel McQueen, "Inadequate Supply of Housing for Poor Could Become Worse, Panel Warns," *Wall Street Journal* (28 April 1988): 10.
14. See David M. Stewart, "Rolling Nowhere," *Inquiry* (July 1984): 18–23.

Are such systems worth the cost? Proponents argue that mass transportation is a public good. Positive externalities are produced by urban bus and subway systems. Low-cost transportation increases population density, which increases the urban tax base. Economic development increases because the dense population attracts businesses. The transportation network also allows the labor force easier access to work sites. Finally, mass transportation reduces air pollution, congestion on the roads, and parking problems. During the energy crisis, an important argument for building mass transportation networks was that they use less of scarce energy resources. Proponents claim that all these positive externalities are of sufficient value to make the benefits of mass transportation exceed the costs of construction.

Critics disagree. They argue that subsidized public transportation transfers income from taxpayers to users of the system. The systems represent a huge subsidy to riders. Critics say that proponents have exaggerated the benefits of such systems and that the costs actually exceed the benefits. For example, the benefits of low-cost transportation in allowing the density of the population to increase are often offset by higher land prices as the demand for urban housing increases. As a result, those who benefit most from public transportation are landowners in the urban area. There is also little evidence that road congestion and air pollution are much improved by such systems. In fact, after the Metro opened, some studies showed that rush-hour traffic into the District of Columbia actually increased.

Transportation, parking, and road congestion are problems facing all urban policy makers. The debate over mass transportation hinges on determining a value for its positive externalities. These benefits must then be weighed against the costs of the project. Conflicting views arise even among economists because it is very difficult to put an accurate monetary value on a positive externality.

The majority of Americans now live in an urban environment. Many are concerned about the spillovers that occur among individuals living close together: noise, pollution, crime, congestion, and other urban problems. As urban populations have grown in the United States and throughout the world, total world population and economic activity have also grown. This growth has created more pressures on scarce resources and more external effects that spread over greater distances of time and space. Concern about these issues has led economists and others to expand their focus beyond rural and urban environments to the global environment.

THE FUTURE OF THE ENVIRONMENT

Many forms of pollution are problems that have market-based solutions based on assignment of property rights. When the negative externalities and the number of people affected are small, it is easier to apply the Coase theorem and resolve those problems through assignment of property rights and negotiation. However, for larger problems, such as acid rain, depletion of the ozone layer, and global climate change, it becomes more difficult to find simple market-based solutions. These problems often extend across national boundaries and over several generations.

In Chapter 2, we presented a spectrum of categories of goods and services that ranged from public goods to positive external effects to private goods to negative externalities to public bads. Most environmental problems lie at or near the public bad end of that spectrum.

THE TRAGEDY OF THE COMMONS

One of the most famous articles of the twentieth century in the field of environmental economics was published in 1948 in *Science* magazine. The author was Garrett Hardin, and the title was "The Tragedy of the Commons."[15] In this article, Hardin addressed the overuse of a **common access resource**, the common grazing land that was found in English villages before enclosure laws assigned such land to specific owners. He pointed out that private owners use their resources at an optimal rate so as to maximize their benefits over time. The same is not true of resources held in common. For such resources, each user has an incentive to overuse the common property to the point where the marginal benefits are zero, because the marginal cost is zero. This overuse is the **tragedy of the commons**.

If a farmer does not put an extra cow to graze on the commons, that farmer does not benefit by having more forage for his other cows or less exhaustion of the common grazing land. The space that farmer doesn't use will be occupied by some other farmer's cow. Since everyone faces the same incentives, the commons will be overgrazed and eventually become useless for all the owners. The benefits from overuse go to the individual, but the costs are spread among the entire group.

The only solution to this problem of overuse of common property resources is to either assign property rights to individuals or have the government or other authority regulate the use in the common interest. If one farmer owns the commons, that farmer will use it at the optimal rate, because all of the costs and benefits will be internalized. If the farmer puts an extra cow to graze, it is that farmer's private property that is being depleted. The future costs will all fall on the farmer and the farmer's heirs rather than on the entire community. Assigning property will thus result in an efficient solution.

As you learned in an earlier chapter, opportunities to assign property rights are more widespread than might be expected. Air pollution rights have been assigned, bought, sold, and traded in the United States. The charging of fines or fees for polluting is quite similar to the purchase and sale of property rights to use the air or water for disposal of wastes. In this case, the property rights have been assigned to the government, which charges for the use of the property. Some common access resources do not lend themselves to assignment of property rights, however. Sometimes it is difficult to identify the individuals who create the problem, the individuals who are hurt by the activities of others, or the possible long-term effects of certain uses of common resources. In other cases, the commons extends across national boundaries, making it difficult for governments to intervene because several governments with different constituencies and agendas are involved.

common access resource
A resource that is not owned by any individual but is available for all to use.

tragedy of the commons
The overuse of common access resources.

15. Garrett Hardin, "The Tragedy of the Commons," *Science* (August 1948): 16–48.

The air, the water, the earth's crust, the ozone layer—all of these are common access resources for everyone on earth. The concern about these global commons is expressed in a variety of ways. Is there a greenhouse effect resulting from too much carbon dioxide emission? If so, the result might be global warming with catastrophic results, such as flooding of coastal cities and creation of deserts where there had been forests and fields. Are human actions destroying the ozone layer that provides protection from the most harmful effects of the sun's rays? Are nonrenewable resources being exploited at a rate that will inflict suffering on future generations? Are renewable resources—trees, fish, whales—being used up at rates faster than they can be replaced? Are humans going to suffocate in their wastes as they pollute the air and water and pile up trash faster than places can be found to put it? These are the major questions posed by those concerned with the use and misuse of the global commons.

THE INFORMATION PROBLEM

Managing the global commons is complicated by two important problems. One is the problem of getting adequate information. In the case of global warming, scientists can determine changes in the gases in the atmosphere, but it is harder to predict precisely how much warming will result and what its impact will be on specific regions. For nonrenewable resources, it is difficult to anticipate improvements in extraction technology and development of substitutes. The same is true to some extent for renewable resources. In the case of hazardous wastes, long delays are common between the disposal of wastes and the recognition of their hazardous effects. At Love Canal in New York, residents ultimately had to abandon their homes because of hazardous wastes beneath their sites. Love Canal is one of the most famous cases of delayed impact in U.S. history.[16]

In statistics, there are two types of error that can be made: accepting a hypothesis as true when it is false and rejecting a hypothesis as false when it is in fact true. Statisticians and scientists tend to pay more attention to avoiding the first type of error, because in their work that type is generally more damaging or costly. In the case of the global environment, however, both types of error are significant. If the dangers of global warming are real and imminent, and this true hypothesis is rejected because it cannot be verified, then the costs will be large and irreparable. Suppose, however, that the hypothesis is accepted, and governments act to restrain economic activity, save the rain forest, and reduce carbon dioxide emissions. Then the forecasts turn out to be wrong, or the forecasts are right but scientists develop a technological solution, or the forecasts are right but the damage is very minimal. In this case, we will have unnecessarily given up output, economic growth, and present consumption.

Many economists point to past experiences to show that the first kind of error, acting on a prediction that turns out to be false or at least overstated, is very common. Nineteenth-century economist Thomas Robert

---

16. Often the discovery of hazardous waste disposal in the land or water resembles a mystery story. For an account of one such story, involving pesticides in the water supply, see "A Tale of Two Towns," *Yankee* (May 1990): 66.

Externalities often spill over national borders. For example, acid rain produced by electric power plants in the United States has destroyed trees in Canada, resulting in political tension between the two countries. However, no environmental event of recent years has produced as many international problems as the Soviet nuclear accident at Chernobyl in 1986.

The accident itself was staggering: 31 people were confirmed as dead, 200 were seriously injured, and 135,000 Ukrainians were evacuated from their homes, perhaps never to return. As serious as these costs are, they were far from the only costs of the accident. Some 1,300 miles from Chernobyl, the Lapps of Norway, Sweden, and Finland were faced with a complete change in their economy and culture.

The reindeer is the core of the Lapp economy and culture. It provides meat, knife handles, glue, and skin for tents, coats, and shoes. Lichens are the reindeer's primary food source. These lichens soaked up so much radiation after Chernobyl that they may not be safe for more than three decades.

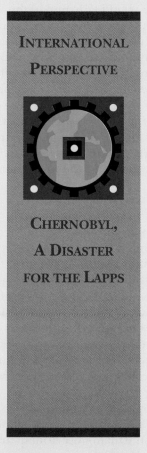

INTERNATIONAL PERSPECTIVE

CHERNOBYL, A DISASTER FOR THE LAPPS

Sweden and Norway averted immediate catastrophe for the Lapps by purchasing all the reindeer meat produced in 1986. Government officials then destroyed the meat or sold it to mink ranchers. This program cost Sweden more than $20 million in 1986. Swedish government officials believe that the Soviets are responsible for the radiation damage, and they are angered at Soviet refusal to compensate the Lapps for their economic loss.

This incident illustrates a growing political problem. Environmental externalities will become increasingly important in the years ahead. Environmental problems within national boundaries can be solved through the political process. Such solutions are difficult enough. Think of the political fighting over site selection for low-level nuclear dumps! What is difficult within a nation, however, becomes nearly impossible when two or more nations are involved. Therefore, increasing levels of international tension over externalities that spill over national boundaries are inevitable.

Source: *U.S. News and World Report* (23 March 1987): 36; (20 July 1987): 14.

Malthus forecasted an imminent crisis of starvation because population was growing faster than the food supply. Advances in agricultural technology proved him wrong. In the middle of the nineteenth century, there were great fears of extinction of the whales, who were valued for whale oil for lighting purposes. Kerosene lamps and then electricity replaced whale oil, and the whales did not disappear. In the 1930s, the fertile farmlands of the Midwest turned into a dust bowl, and some observers thought that farm practices were creating a new desert. Today this land is again highly productive. Even the energy crisis of the 1970s disappeared as higher oil prices led to discovery of new reserves and more conservation. However, the fact that disasters have been averted in the past through technological change or discoveries does not necessarily mean that such solutions will arise in the future. People's positions on environmental issues depend on their faith in technological innovation.

THE SOVEREIGNTY PROBLEM

The second problem that complicates managing the global commons is the fact that the air and water span many nations. Thus, sovereignty over the global commons is divided. The tragedy of the commons does not necessarily represent a market failure. It may be a failure to use the market by assigning property rights or a failure by government to adequately regulate the use of common access resources. The assignment of property rights and the regulation of the commons are responsibilities of governments. However, some of the most important conflicts over the use of common access resources cross national boundaries. England exports sulfur dioxide to Scandinavia, where acid rain damages the forests. Japan continues to kill large numbers of whales, while other nations try to restrain the harvest of whales in hopes of saving them from extinction. Brazil is chopping down its tropical rain forests, which absorb a great deal of carbon dioxide and help to slow the greenhouse effect around the world. The Brazilian government argues that if it were not for the emissions from industrial nations that consume most of the fossil fuels, the rain forest would not be an issue. The United States consumes fossil fuels at a higher rate than any other nation and has been criticized for failing to restrain such consumption with high taxes, as most other industrialized nations do. Even the huge oceans that girdle the globe have shown some serious damage from the disposal of wastes by many nations. Some cooperation between governments in either assigning property rights or regulating use of common access resources is essential in order to find solutions for these problems.

THE RAIN FOREST, CARBON DIOXIDE, AND GLOBAL WARMING

It is difficult to determine whether global warming is occurring. The data on weather and climate that have been assembled over decades, as well as centuries of experience, indicate that weather is highly variable. Some climatologists have argued that the earth is headed for ecological disaster because of clear cutting of the forests—especially tropical rain forests—that absorb carbon dioxide. Figure 4 shows the recent increase in the concentration of carbon dioxide in the atmosphere, mainly due to the heavy use of fossil fuels in the twentieth century. The increased carbon dioxide

Concentration of Carbon Dioxide (ppm)

FIGURE 4
CARBON DIOXIDE IN THE
ATMOSPHERE, 1958–1984
This diagram, based on
samples taken at Hawaii's
isolated Mauna Loa
observatory, shows that
there has been a steady
increase of about 0.5
percent per year in the
concentration of carbon
dioxide in the earth's
atmosphere.

traps the earth's radiated heat in the atmosphere rather than allowing it to escape. Higher levels of carbon dioxide should result in global warming. However, the amount of increase in global temperature and the resulting effects on weather and climate patterns are uncertain. Effects will be stronger in temperate zones than in tropical zones. The danger of melting of the polar ice caps and flooding of coastal cities is an extreme possibility. The impact of global warming on world food production could also be serious. Changing weather patterns would dry up some areas and provide other, previously dry areas with more water than they could effectively use.

In the United States, there has been no great reduction in forest lands that absorb carbon dioxide, but there has been increased production of carbon dioxide from burning fossil fuels (especially gasoline). Throughout the world, however, population pressures have led to loss of forests. Tropical rain forests are especially effective in absorbing carbon dioxide from the atmosphere, so concerns have focused on those forests rather than on other facets of the problem.

Market mechanisms play a part in both the problem and potential solutions. The demand for tropical hardwoods as building materials in developed countries and the need for more agricultural and grazing land have been powerful incentives for cutting down rain forests. One possible market force in the opposite direction results from the discovery of valuable natural substances in the rain forests that can be used for producing medicines, food additives, and cosmetics.[17] Yet another market force has been the purchase of tracts of rain forest by citizen groups in developed countries. The new owners preserve the trees rather than cut them down. The overall impact of such efforts has been very modest, however.

17. "Saving Brazil's Forests," *Newsweek* (1 May 1989): 50.

Individual governments can certainly act to reduce carbon dioxide emissions or to preserve forests. However, just as no individual has enough incentive to preserve the commons, no individual government has an incentive to act to prevent global warming unless other governments also act. In the absence of a single sovereign government to regulate the use of the rain forest as a global commons, the role of governments has been limited to efforts to negotiate preservation. The United States and other developed nations that have made loans to tropical nations such as Brazil have offered to forgive part of that debt in exchange for a commitment to preserve the rain forest. Such efforts have met with little response. Since the problem of carbon dioxide in the atmosphere is linked to both destruction of forests and use of fossil fuels, it is difficult to identify a single cause or a single nation that is responsible.

ACID RAIN

Closely related to global warming is the problem of acid rain. Sulfur dioxide and nitrous oxide combine with water in the atmosphere to create sulphuric acid and nitric acid. When it rains, the rain has a strong acid component that is damaging to plant and animal life. Scientists have documented the negative impact of acid rain on fish and plant life in lakes. The effect of acid rain on forests is not as clearly established.

The problem of acid rain is part of a broader problem of air quality that has been addressed by governments in many nations. Within nations, there is an incentive to clean up air in order to improve the immediate environment and reduce health risks. The battle lines within a country are drawn between those who wish to use the air for the disposal of wastes and those who wish to preserve its quality. What makes acid rain different from other kinds of air pollution is that spillovers between nations are more evident with acid rain than with other types of air pollution.

Certain countries are net exporters of sulfur emissions. The United Kingdom, for example, imports one-fifth of its sulfur and exports two-thirds of its sulfur-based emissions to Western Europe. Net importers of pollutants include West Germany, Austria, and the Scandinavian countries.[18] Within the United States, emissions in the Midwest have their greatest impact in the Northeastern states. Efforts to control acid rain within the country have pitted the producers and users (mainly electric utilities) of high-sulfur coal against environmentalists and residents and firms in the affected areas. Within the United States, the battle over amendments to the Clean Air Act is waged in Congress almost annually. These amendments represent the current trade-offs between the interests of these two conflicting groups.[19] In Europe, the European Community has provided a broader base for discussion and resolution of acid rain spillovers between countries.

18. Sandra Postel, *Air Pollution, Acid Rain, and the Future of Forests,* Worldwatch Paper No. 58 (Washington, DC: World Watch Institute, March 1984). This publication provides a good review of the scientific evidence on acid rain.
19. For a discussion of the political battles over acid rain in the United States, see Richard Meyer and T. Bruce Yandle, "The Political Economy of Acid Rain," *Cato Journal* (Fall 1987): 527–545.

MOUNT TRASHMORE IN YOUR BACKYARD: WASTE DISPOSAL

The disposal of household and industrial wastes has become a major problem for local governments in the United States. Wastes can be grouped into three classes: hazardous, recyclable, and other. Each type presents different disposal problems and potential solutions.

RECYCLABLE AND OTHER NONHAZARDOUS WASTES. Americans—and others—discard an enormous amount of waste each year. Some of this waste has no recoverable value and must be burned or buried in a commons, the local landfill or city dump. New Jersey has an above-ground landfill with the picturesque name of Mount Trashmore! Some household waste is disposed of through the sewer system, especially for households with garbage disposals. A large part of household waste can in fact be reused. Recycling recovers valuable nonrenewable resources (aluminum cans and petroleum-based plastics, for example), reduces the pressure on renewable resources (newspapers and glass), and lowers the amount of space and effort that must be devoted to disposal.

Until recently, most households had little incentive to recycle. It took time and effort to separate the trash and take recyclable items to an appropriate place. There was no penalty for failure to recycle and no rewards for cooperation. In recent years, this situation has changed. Trash disposal is largely the responsibility of local governments, and these and state governments have been innovative and effective in changing the costs and benefits people face in recycling. Local governments took this initiative because of the incentives they faced. Rising land prices, increasing federal regulations on site preparation, and hauling of trash over greater distances created an immediate and powerful incentive to act.

Figure 5 shows the shift in costs and benefits facing the individual household. MB_1 is the marginal benefit curve for recycling in the first year. Perhaps there were a few deposit bottles that could be returned, a small payment for aluminum cans, and some sense of contributing to community well-being. However, the marginal cost of recycling was high, because of the distance the recycler had to travel. Under these circumstances, the representative household only engaged in amount Q_0 of recycling. Then the local government established a recycling center. This act reduces the cost of recycling and shifts the marginal cost curve downward. The local government also started a campaign of education and persuasion that changes preferences, increasing the perceived benefits (MB_1 shifts to MB_2). These actions were typical for local governments in the 1970s and early 1980s. They had an effect on some households, but did not greatly reduce the amount of waste disposal (in the diagram, wastes fell only from Q_1 to Q_2). Effective waste reduction and recycling required more powerful incentives for both governments and citizens.

Further increases in land costs, higher payments for recycled materials, and other pressures caused some local governments to step up their efforts. These efforts shifted both the marginal benefit curve and the marginal cost curve to the right. One city in Oregon used a combination of carrot and stick to promote recycling. Households were given two kinds of containers for waste pickup. The first, general and unsorted waste, carried a fee that increased sharply with added pickups each month. The sec-

Marginal Cost, Marginal Benefit

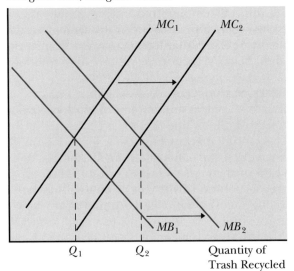

FIGURE 5
MARGINAL COSTS AND BENEFITS OF RECYCLING
With the original marginal cost curve, MC_1, and the original marginal benefit curve, MB_1, the costs of recycling were too high and the perceived benefits too low to result in a very large volume of recycling. The combination of lower costs (a recycling center) and higher perceived benefits (result of an education campaign) shifts the curves. The result is some increase in recycling, from Q_1 to Q_2. Further increases in recycling (to Q_3) can be brought about by making it more convenient to recycle (separation containers, curbside pickup) and more expensive not to (higher pickup fees for unsorted trash).

ond kind of container was separated into color-coded sections for plastics, glass, aluminum, and paper. Pickups from the color-coded containers were free. This plan combined a substantial cash benefit for not using the unsorted pickup with much lower costs of recycling because of the sorting bins and curbside pickup. Other cities have used similar combinations of positive and negative incentives. Recycling is an excellent illustration of how local governments can use market incentives to reduce overuse of a local commons, the city dump.

HAZARDOUS WASTES. Hazardous wastes represent a more serious problem. There is no good way of disposing of such wastes without endangering the air, water, or soil in the area. No one wants to live near the refuse of a nuclear power plant or a chemical plant. In fact, this reluctance to accommodate hazardous waste disposal sites produced a new acronym, NIMBY, which stands for "not in my back yard." Some states have resisted disposal of hazardous wastes, sometimes not even allowing such wastes to pass through en route to another destination. Many states have raised their fees for disposal of such wastes as both a deterrent and a revenue source. As firms find it increasingly difficult and costly to dispose of hazardous wastes, they are forced to seek other solutions. Reuse of waste materials or changes in technology that reduce the amount of hazardous wastes produced are alternatives.

Most of the horror stories about hazardous wastes result from past dumping, when there was less knowledge of the dangers and less government regulation. Hazardous waste problems, chiefly due to industrial wastes, are present in every state and will be costly to clean up. The Environmental Protection Agency's Superfund is earmarked for correcting such past mistakes.[20] Unlike global warming and acid rain, hazardous wastes represent a problem that can be addressed through a combination of market incentives and government regulation.

CHALLENGES FOR THE FUTURE

The environmental issues covered here are not the only ones. For example, the ocean is the ultimate common access resource, and little progress has been made in conserving its bounty or controlling its use as a waste dump. The optimal rate for exploiting renewable and nonrenewable resources will be found only through a combination of market incentives, technological innovation, government regulation, and intergovernmental cooperation. Problems of conserving common access resources, whether local or global, represent a serious and substantial challenge to policy makers. Imperfect information, lack of coordination between nations, and a natural tendency to overuse and exhaust common access resources complicate the problem. It will require innovative strategies, use of market mechanisms, and intergovernmental cooperation to protect the environment for generations to come.

SUMMARY

1. The long-run problem for American farmers is the result of huge increases in productivity in the last century. In the short-run, farmers' problems result from the fact that the farm sector is very competitive, has very inelastic demand, and is affected heavily by the weather.

2. Most federal governmental farm policies are aimed at slowing the trend toward fewer agricultural workers.

3. The various price support programs work primarily on the supply side of the agricultural market. The major programs have attempted to support prices or to manage production, often with conflicting results.

4. Cities are formed and grow because of economies of agglomeration. The optimal city size is where the total benefits of agglomeration exceed the diseconomies of agglomeration by the greatest amount.

5. Supplying local public goods in urban areas is complicated by the division of the area into many political

subdivisions. The Tiebout hypothesis is that voters will solve the spillover problem by choosing to live in the jurisdiction that provides the desired combination of services and taxes.

6. The tragedy of the commons is the overuse of common access resources. Each user of such a resource has the incentive to use that resource to the point where marginal benefits are zero. Common access resources must be regulated or assigned to individuals in order to attain efficient use of these resources.

7. Managing the global commons is even more complicated because of jurisdictional and informational problems. Acid rain is a good example of the problems of the global commons.

8. A blend of market incentives and regulation can be effective in addressing many environmental problems.

---

20. The Superfund is financed out of a fee on chemical feedstocks and is used to finance chemical waste cleanups. For a critical review of the performance of Superfund, see T. Bruce Yandle, "Taxation, Political Action, and Superfund," *Cato Journal* (Winter 1989): 751–764.

NEW TERMS

agricultural support
    program
parity
support prices
soil bank program
acreage allotment

Conservation Reserve
    Program (CRP)
marketing orders
target prices
payment in kind (PIK)
    program

Food Security Act
Soil Conservation Service
economies of
    agglomeration
diseconomies of
    agglomeration

user charges
Tiebout hypothesis
common access resource
tragedy of the commons

QUESTIONS FOR DISCUSSION

1. What are the short-term and long-term problems facing farmers? Why might these problems be considered market failures?

2. Suppose you are a producer in the shoe industry, and you have found that you have to sell 10 percent more shoes this year to buy the same amount of groceries and other items as in the past. How would you go about making a parity argument for supporting the price of shoes? Why would tariffs or other protective measures be needed along with price supports?

3. If the government creates support prices for shoes, will there be a surplus of shoes? If there is, what can the government do about that surplus that is similar to some of the farm programs?

4. Suppose you were sent to a city you had never visited before to determine whether that city needed more residents or already had too many. What criteria would you use to answer that question?

5. Another global environmental problem is the depletion of the ozone layer of the atmosphere, which screens out cancer-causing ultraviolet radiation. The ozone layer is being depleted by the use of chlorofluorocarbons (CFCs) in air conditioners, refrigerators, and spray cans. How is this an example of the tragedy of the commons? How can markets and governments contribute to a solution?

6. How is a common access resource different from a private resource?

7. Suppose you belong to a sailing club, which owns a dock and a boat. Will these be kept in better or worse shape than an individually owned boat and dock? Why or why not?

8. What is the distributional difference between support payments to farmers and marketing orders?

9. Why do programs such as the soil bank and acreage allotment programs have a smaller than expected influence on the supply of agricultural products?

10. In what way is the Tiebout solution for the provision of local public goods similar to the Coase theorem (discussed in the preceding chapter) for dealing with negative externalities?

11. Is a city park a common access resource? How can crowding be controlled?

12. Cattle and buffaloes are very similar animals, yet buffaloes were shot almost to extinction, while cattle were left alone in the same habitat. Why?

13. Today farmers represent about 2 percent of the U.S. population, but they get more than $40 billion in governmental outlays. This is much more than farmers received in 1950, when they were a much larger segment of the population. Does it make sense for farmers to be getting more powerful politically as their share of the voting population decreases?

14. Nobel prize–winning economist T. W. Schultz has referred to parity as "a vulgar economic concept." What did he mean?

15. Should mass transportation be viewed as a public good?

SUGGESTIONS FOR FURTHER READING

Galston, William A. *A Tough Row to Hoe: The 1985 Farm Bill and Beyond.* New York: Hamilton Press, 1985. This book covers the issues underlying the debate over the 1985 farm bill.

Harden, Garrett, and John Baden (eds.). *Managing the Commons.* San Francisco: W. H. Freeman, 1977. This collection of readings contains classic articles and a variety of perspectives on the issue of managing common access resources.

Heilbrun, James. *Urban Economics and Public Policy,* 3rd ed. New York: St. Martin's, 1987. A textbook that covers urban economic issues in detail.

O'Rourke, P. J. "Manuregate." *Rolling Stone* (12 July 1990): 45–48. A satirical view of the farm problem.

Postel, Sandra. *Air Pollution, Acid Rain, and the Future of Forests,* Worldwatch Paper No. 58. Washington, DC: World Watch Institute, March 1984. This paper and others in the series address a variety of environmental policy issues. A later one is Hilary French, *Clearing the Air: A Global Agenda,* Worldwatch Paper No. 94 (January 1990).

Regulation (Winter 1990). An entire issue is devoted to environmental issues.

Samuelson, Robert J. "The Absurd Farm Bill." *Newsweek* (6 August 1990): 51. An editorial that suggests that the farm lobby is successful because the public considers farmers deserving of the billions of dollars spent to subsidize them.

Smith, Lee. "How to Cut Farm Spending." *Fortune* (10 November 1986): 97–103. An essay that argues that the government should stop paying farm subsidies and adopt a straightforward welfare program for farmers.

Stavins, Robert N., and Adam B. Jaffe. "Unintended Impacts of Public Investments on Private Decisions: The Depletion of Forested Wetlands." *American Economic Review* (June 1990): 337–352. An article that shows how public infrastructure investment in flood control results in private decisions that reduce forested wetlands.

Tietenburg, Tom. *Environmental and Natural Resource Economics,* 2nd ed. Glenview, IL: Scott, Foresman, 1987. A standard textbook that addresses environmental issues.

THE WORLD ECONOMY 10

AFTER STUDYING THIS CHAPTER, YOU SHOULD BE ABLE TO:

1. Describe the benefits of free trade.
2. Distinguish between absolute and comparative advantage, and discuss the gains from trade based on comparative advantage.
3. Identify the effects of a tariff and a quota.
4. Discuss the arguments for trade protection.
5. Explain why firms build foreign plants and what the economic effects are.

INTRODUCTION

CHAPTER 34

INTERNATIONAL TRADE

Except for the international perspectives, this book has generally ignored the rest of the world in order to concentrate on how the U.S. economic system operates. Yet the world is increasingly an important part of the American economy. You may drive a Japanese car, drink coffee from Brazil, eat Mexican tomatoes and Honduran bananas, or take pictures with a German camera. Chances are there is a plant of a foreign-owned multinational corporation close to where you live.

Even for a country as large as the United States, where trade with other countries is a relatively small fraction (about 10 to 12 percent) of GNP, international trade has become increasingly important. The percentage of output and sales entering into international trade has doubled in the last 15 years. Foreign competition is important to major industries such as textiles, steel, and autos. Immigration (both legal and illegal), foreign investment in the United States and American investment abroad, and the ups and downs in the value of the dollar are all issues in the news.

International economics is usually separated into two parts: international trade and international finance. International trade deals with the microeconomic questions of who produces what and who trades with whom and why, as well as with multinational firms, tariffs, and quotas. International finance examines the determinants of exchange rates between national currencies, the balance of payments, and the relationship between domestic macroeconomic concerns and the foreign sector.

This chapter covers international trade and the next chapter looks at international finance. You need to recognize, however, that trade and finance are closely related. For example, changes in the price of the dollar affect U.S. imports and foreign demand for U.S. exports. An inflow of investment from abroad can affect output, employment, and interest rates in the United States.

WHY NATIONS TRADE

The reasons for international trade are really no different from the reasons for trade between individuals who live in the same country. It is important to realize that in most cases international trade takes place between individuals and firms. When we speak of trade between the United States and Japan, we are really talking about trade between individuals

890

and firms in these countries. These individuals and firms trade for the same reasons that individuals and firms within a country trade. Trade takes place because of the availability of a better product or a better price or because of an opportunity for profit. Exactly what determines the patterns of trade between nations and how much each nation benefits have been important concerns to economists as long as there have been nation states and economists.

Before Adam Smith, the dominant view was that government should direct many spheres of economic activity, especially international trade. This view, called mercantilism, put heavy emphasis on control of shipping, maintaining colonies, discouraging imports, and promoting exports. Two famous economists are responsible for developing the arguments for a policy of free trade. One was Adam Smith, whose *Wealth of Nations* in 1776 made a strong case for freedom in every sphere of economic activity. The other was David Ricardo, a distinguished nineteenth-century British economist and member of Parliament who was very interested in the practical question of what trade policy England should pursue. He developed the principle of comparative advantage in his classic 1814 book, *Principles of Political Economy and Taxation.*

THE BENEFITS OF EXCHANGE

It is easier to envision the processes at work in international trade by focusing first on exchange rather than production. Consider Heather and Peter, who are both stamp collectors. Like most stamp collectors, they expand their collections by trading duplicates of stamps they have. Let's say that Heather has the complete 1938 Presidential series and several extras. Peter has some gaps in that series, but has some extra Canadian stamps that he would like to trade and that Heather would like to have. They work a deal. She trades three Presidential stamps for five Canadian stamps. As an outside observer, you might say that the trade was one of "equal values." That may be true in a market sense, but the stamps weren't of equal value to Peter and Heather. Heather wanted the Canadian stamps more than she wanted the extra Presidential stamps, and Peter felt just the opposite. They both were better off as a result of the trade.

Economists who look at international trade emphasize the **gains from trade**, or the increase in economic well-being that comes from specialization and exchange. The emphasis on exchange is one aspect of the theory of international trade that makes it different from the rest of microeconomics. However, we have to back up one step from exchange to production. Rarely do people trade solely out of existing stocks of goods. People produce in order to trade. The explanation of how people and nations decide what to produce for trade is based on the concepts of absolute advantage and comparative advantage.

gains from trade
The increase in economic well-being resulting from specialization and exchange.

ABSOLUTE ADVANTAGE

Suppose Heather and Peter are sister and brother, and their parents want the 12 windows in the house washed and the 24 square yards of leaves raked. Heather and Peter estimate their output as shown in Table 1. If this brother and sister divided the tasks equally, they would each have to wash half the windows (6 for Heather, which would take her $1\frac{1}{2}$ hours, and 6

TABLE 1
AN EXAMPLE OF
ABSOLUTE ADVANTAGE

	WINDOWS PER HOUR	SQUARE YARDS OF LEAVES PER HOUR
Heather	4	6
Peter	2	8

for Peter, which would take him 3 hours) and rake 12 square yards of leaves (which would take Heather 2 hours and Peter $1\frac{1}{2}$ hours to complete). At the end of a long afternoon, Heather would have worked $3\frac{1}{2}$ hours, and Peter would have worked $4\frac{1}{2}$ hours. On the other hand, if they each specialized in what they do better, Heather could have all of the windows washed in just 3 hours and Peter could have all of the leaves raked in 3 hours. There would be a clear gain of a valuable $\frac{1}{2}$ hour for Heather and $1\frac{1}{2}$ hours for Peter.

Both Heather and Peter are better off if they specialize, because each has an **absolute advantage**. Heather is more efficient than Peter at washing windows, and Peter is more efficient than Heather at raking leaves. It's not difficult to convince anyone of the benefits of specialization and trade when there is a clear absolute advantage for each partner.

absolute advantage
The ability to produce something using fewer resources than other producers use.

COMPARATIVE ADVANTAGE

Suppose, however, that one partner is better at both. Assume that Heather is better at *both* window washing and leaf raking. The production rates for Heather and Peter in this case are shown in Table 2. Is there still an opportunity for specialization and trade? If they continue to divide the tasks equally, Heather will spend $1\frac{1}{2}$ hours on her 6 windows and 2 hours on 12 square yards of raking. She's through in just $3\frac{1}{2}$ hours. Poor Peter, however, has to spend 6 hours on windows and 3 hours on leaves, for a total of 9 hours of work. Can Heather do something to make Peter better off without spending any more of her own time working?

Suppose they specialize. This time it's not as obvious who should specialize in what. The concept of opportunity cost provides an answer. When Heather rakes 6 square yards of leaves, she's giving up 4 clean windows she could have "produced" in that time. A clean window costs her $1\frac{1}{2}$ square yards of raking. For Peter, a clean window costs 4 square yards of raking. Clearly, Heather's window washing is cheaper than Peter's in terms of alternatives. Heather has a **comparative advantage** in window washing because her opportunity cost is lower in that activity than in the other one. Peter also has a comparative advantage in raking, even though he has an absolute disadvantage in both activities. His opportunity cost of raking leaves is only $\frac{1}{4}$ of a clean window per square yard, and Heather's

comparative advantage
The ability to produce something at a lower opportunity cost than other producers face.

TABLE 2
AN EXAMPLE OF
COMPARATIVE ADVANTAGE

	WINDOWS PER HOUR	SQUARE YARDS OF LEAVES PER HOUR
Heather	4	6
Peter	1	4

is ⁴⁄₆, or ²⁄₃. So Peter should specialize in that activity in which he has a comparative advantage, that is, in which his opportunity cost is lower.

Heather and Peter implement a policy of specializing on the basis of comparative advantage. Heather washes all the windows, which takes her 3 hours. Peter rakes all the leaves, which takes him 6 hours. By specializing on the basis of comparative advantage, both of them are better off! They have produced the same "output" (clean windows and a leaf-free yard) with considerably less input. Heather saved ½ hour, and Peter saved 3 hours. Both parties gained from specialization.

FROM INDIVIDUALS TO NATIONS. The same principles that determine specialization for two individuals in simple situations apply to more complex situations involving individuals and firms in groups, regions, or nations. Trade between nations is also based on comparative advantage. By specializing, both parties can gain from trade. For simplicity, economists usually use a two-country, two-commodity example. The same analysis applies to situations involving more countries or more commodities.

Suppose there are two countries called Inland and Outland. Before they discover one another, they are producing the products shown in Table 3. Outland, like Peter, is able to produce less of both commodities. This lack of absolute advantage may be due to Outland's resources being less efficient, or Outland may just be a smaller or poorer country with fewer resources. The reason for absolute advantage or absolute disadvantage makes no difference for comparative advantage and the gains from trade.

The output numbers for Inland and Outland in Table 3 represent points on their production possibilities curves. (To keep things simple, both production possibilities curves are assumed to be straight lines as in Chapter 3.) One more piece of information is needed in order to draw the straight-line production possibilities curve for each country. Assume that each country is devoting two-thirds of its resources to steel and one-third of its resources to cloth. This assumption makes it possible to calculate the end points of their production possibilities curves.

If Inland specializes in cloth, the country can produce 225 bolts. If it specializes in steel, it can produce 75 tons. If Outland specializes in cloth, the country can produce 180 bolts. If it specializes in steel, it can produce 30 tons. These points give the production possibilities curves in Figure 1.

Which country should specialize in what product or mix of products? The answer lies in the two countries' opportunity costs. For Inland, the opportunity cost of producing 75 tons of steel is 225 bolts of cloth not produced, or 3 bolts of cloth per ton of steel. For Outland, the same calculation says that 1 ton of steel costs 6 bolts of cloth. Inland's steel is cheaper

COUNTRY	STEEL (TONS)	CLOTH (BOLTS)
Inland	50	75
Outland	20	60
World Total	70	135

TABLE 3
PRODUCTION
POSSIBILITIES
WITHOUT TRADE

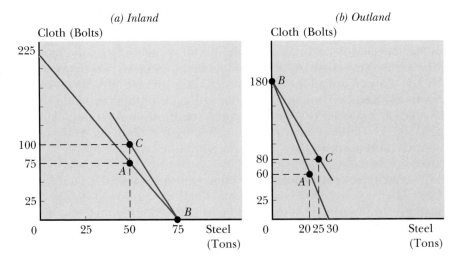

FIGURE 1
PRODUCTION POSSIBILITIES
CURVES FOR INLAND AND
OUTLAND
The production possibilities curve illustrates the gains from specializing on the basis of comparative advantage. Each country moves from pretrade production and consumption (point A), to output with specialization (point B) and then to consumption after trade (point C).

in terms of cloth forgone. Measuring the cost of cloth in terms of steel, on the other hand, gives these results: One bolt of Inland cloth costs $\frac{1}{3}$ of a ton of steel, and one bolt of Outland cloth costs only $\frac{1}{6}$ of a ton of steel. Measured in terms of opportunity costs, Outland's cloth is cheaper. The result of specialization is shown in Table 4.

Total world output has increased, without using additional resources, by 5 tons of steel and 45 bolts of cloth. Are the two countries better off?[1] Not yet. After all, they could have been producing those combinations anyway. It is only after trade that they can be better off.

THE TERMS OF TRADE. At what rate will Inland and Outland trade steel for cloth? Inland will not accept less than 3 bolts of cloth for a ton of steel, because this country can do that well producing its own cloth. Outland will not offer more than 6 bolts of cloth per ton of steel, because more than that would make it cheaper not to specialize. Anywhere between 3 and 6 bolts of cloth per ton of steel should be a mutually acceptable trading ratio. Let's make it 4 bolts of cloth for 1 ton of steel. This ratio is called the **terms of trade**. The exact terms of trade will lie somewhere between the parties' opportunity costs. Exactly where the terms of trade falls between those limits depends on the relative strength of demand for both products in both countries.

terms of trade
The ratio at which one product is exchanged for another.

TABLE 4
PRODUCTION
BEFORE AND AFTER
SPECIALIZATION

	BEFORE SPECIALIZATION		AFTER SPECIALIZATION	
	STEEL	CLOTH	STEEL	CLOTH
Inland	50	75	75	0
Outland	20	60	0	180
Total	70	135	75	180

1.   To be sure that they are better off without knowing anything about their tastes and preferences, we need to be sure that each country has at least as much of one good as before and more of the other.

There are numerous after-trade combinations of steel and cloth that could make both countries better off. One possibility is to let Inland take all of its gains from trade in extra cloth, keeping its steel consumption at the original level of 50 tons and trading away the other 25 tons to Outland for 100 bolts of cloth. That exchange leaves Outland with 25 tons of imported steel and 80 bolts of domestic cloth, a consumption combination that represents more of both goods. The results of trade are summarized in Table 5.

These new consumption points are shown in Figure 1. Point *C* in part (*a*) shows Inland consuming 50 tons of steel and 100 bolts of cloth. Point *C* in part (*b*) represents a consumption combination of 25 tons of steel and 80 bolts of cloth for Outland. In each graph, this point lies along a "terms of trade" line, or a **consumption possibilities curve**, beginning at point *B* (total production with specialization) and having a slope of ¼ (1 steel to 4 cloth). Each country is able to get beyond its production possibilities curve by separating production (at point *B*) from consumption (at point *C*). The gains from trade are the same kinds of improvements in well-being that a country gets from having additional economic resources. Point *C* in each case represents one of many trade and consumption combinations that makes that partner better off.

consumption possibilities curve
A line showing the consumption combinations attainable through trade.

THE BASIS OF COMPARATIVE ADVANTAGE. What makes Inland better at producing steel and Outland better at producing cloth? For some products, the reasons are obvious. Climate determines the cheapest place to produce bananas, potatoes, and other agricultural products. Mineral resources determine other production patterns. Some products use a high proportion of unskilled labor relative to capital and other inputs. These products will be produced in countries with relatively large amounts of low-cost, unskilled labor. Other products require relatively more skilled labor, capital, or fertile land. These products will be produced in countries where those resources are abundant.

Still other products follow what economist Raymond Vernon called the **product cycle**. When the product is introduced, it will be exported by the country in which it was developed. But as the product and the production process become standardized, production will eventually migrate to other countries with a suitable resource mix. Automobiles, whose production technology was developed in the United States, are now produced almost everywhere. Textile was originally developed in England, but the production of simple cotton textiles (the most standardized part of the industry) has migrated around the globe in search of the inexpensive, low-skill labor that is used heavily in their manufacture.

product cycle
A series of stages, from development to standardization, through which a new product passes.

	BEFORE SPECIALIZATION		AFTER SPECIALIZATION		AFTER TRADE	
	STEEL	CLOTH	STEEL	CLOTH	STEEL	CLOTH
Inland	50	75	75	0	50	100
Outland	20	60	0	180	25	80
Total	70	135	75	180	75	180

TABLE 5
GAINS FROM TRADE

Sometimes the explanation for comparative advantage lies in historical accident. A product starts being produced in country *A* because that is where it was invented, or because its citizens want such a product. Country *A* develops the skills and resources needed to produce that product, including related industries that supply inputs or use the product in making other goods. If *A*'s resources are suited to the production of the good, *A* is likely to have a comparative advantage that it can retain for some time. If the world market is not large, there may be room only for a few suppliers who take advantage of cost savings in large-scale production. The first producer may enjoy a lasting advantage for that reason.

All these factors may explain the existence of comparative advantage. The important point is that it is possible for both partners to increase output and economic well-being by specializing on the basis of comparative advantage, no matter how that advantage originated.

OTHER BENEFITS FROM TRADE

There are at least two other important benefits from trade besides the increased output from comparative advantage. One is competition. The other is economies of scale.

Trade increases the number of competing firms from whom consumers can buy, widening their range of choices of goods and suppliers. This benefit of trade can be very important if the domestic industry has only a few firms. For example, car buyers in the United States have a wide range of choices because of international trade, although there are only a few domestic producers. As a result of foreign competition, domestic producers have responded to demands of some car buyers for smaller, more fuel-efficient cars.

Access to a large world market instead of a smaller domestic one may enable firms to operate at a more efficient scale. Producers of mainframe computers, aircraft, and heavy machinery need a very large market in order to produce at a scale that results in the lowest possible costs per unit.

THE WHY AND HOW OF PROTECTION

With all of these good reasons for free trade, why are some U.S. firms and industries protected from foreign competition? Many arguments are offered by firms that have to compete with imports, but most of these arguments come down to one reason—income distribution. A country as a whole benefits from free trade, but not everyone benefits equally.

Protection of domestic industries is accomplished with two main tools: tariffs and quotas. A **tariff** is a tax on imported goods or services. The tariff can be specific (based on weight, volume, or number of units) or *ad valorem* (figured as a percentage of the price). The average U.S. tariff is less than 5 percent. Many items bear no tariff at all, and a few items have large tariffs.

A **quota** is a quantity limit. It specifies the maximum amount of a good or service that can be imported during a given time period (usually a year). Quotas can be global (limiting total imports of widgets from all foreign suppliers to 1,000 widgets per year) or geographic (assigning quotas

tariff
A tax on imported goods or services.

quota
A limit on the amount of a good or service that can be imported during a given time period.

to specific countries). Quotas also can be combined with tariffs in a **tariff quota**. In this case, a certain amount of a good from one country is allowed to enter another country without a tariff. For amounts in excess of that limit, a tariff is applied.

EFFECTS OF A TARIFF

Figure 2 illustrates the effects of a tariff. In this figure, Inland produces, consumes, and imports cheese. The domestic supply curve is S_d. The domestic demand curve is D_d. Because Inland is a small country, its purchases of imported goods do not affect the world price of those goods. Inland can buy all the cheese it wants at the world price, P_w. At P_w, domestic producers are producing A pounds and consumers are buying B pounds. The difference between production and consumption is imports of $B - A$ pounds of cheese.

P_t is the price of imported cheese after Inland imposed a tariff equal to T. Since the tariff drives up the price, consumers buy less. Cheese consumption falls to C. Domestic producers move up along their supply curve to E. They get a bigger share of the smaller market. Imports decrease from $B - A$ to $C - E$.

Who gains? Domestic producers, including their owners, workers, and suppliers. These firms can charge a higher price and have a larger market share, which benefits everyone connected with them. Government also gains some tariff revenue. Who loses? Domestic consumers are paying more and getting less, so they lose. Foreign producers have lost sales. Also, the country imposing the tariff has given up some of the benefits of free trade noted earlier—more output, competition, and economies of scale. Since foreign cheese producers are more efficient than most of Inland's domestic cheese producers, this country is switching from more efficient to less efficient producers.

EFFECTS OF A QUOTA

Quotas are similar to tariffs. In fact, they can be represented by the same diagram. The main difference is that quotas restrict quantity, and tariffs

tariff quota
A combination of a quota and a tariff that allows a certain amount of a good or service to be imported without paying a tariff and imposes the tariff on further imports.

FIGURE 2
EFFECTS OF A TARIFF OR QUOTA
A tariff $T = P_t - P_w$ or an equivalent quota $C - E$ raises prices for domestic consumers (from P_w to P_t), reduces imports (from $B - A$ to $C - E$), lowers consumption (from B to C), and increases domestic output and sales from (A to E).

TARIFFS VERSUS QUOTAS

A Tariff	A Quota
• Raises prices	• Raises prices
• Reduces imports and consumption	• Reduces imports and consumption
• Increases domestic output	• Increases domestic output
• Produces government revenue	• Creates monopoly profits for those with import licenses
• Lets imports rise when demand increases	• Makes prices rise when demand increases

work through prices. If, in Figure 2, the government imposed a quota in the amount of $C - E$ on cheese, the effects on price, domestic production, consumption, and imports would be the same as those of the tariff $T = P_t - P_w$. There are a couple of important differences, however.

First, a tariff raises revenue for the government, in the amount of the shaded area in Figure 2. A quota generates no government revenue.[2] All the benefits of a quota go to protected domestic producers and to those importers who manage to get the scarce and valuable import permits used to implement quotas. Permit holders can buy the good at the low foreign price and resell it at the higher domestic price. The difference between the price the importer pays the foreign supplier and the price the importer can charge the domestic consumer $(P_t - P_w)$ times the number of units imported is a monopoly profit that comes from having a license to import. Note that this monopoly profit is equal to the revenue the government would have received under a tariff.

Second, suppose demand increased in the country. With a tariff, the quantity of imports would increase. With a quota, only the price would increase. Originally, the tariff T and the quota $C - E$ had the same effect on prices and quantities. As Figure 3 shows, however, when demand shifts from D_d to D'_d under a tariff, imports rise to $H - E$ and consumption rises to H. With a quota, price rises to P_f. Imports remain the same ($C - E = G - F$). Domestic production rises to F, and consumption rises slightly to G.

Several U.S. economists examined the redistributional effects of protectionism in the steel industry, using techniques borrowed from finance and accounting.[3] They examined changes in the value of the stock of steel companies to determine if these firms capture the monopoly profits generated by tariffs and quotas. The owners of steel firms captured a substantial portion of the economic rent created by trade restrictions on steel. Not all firms gained equally. The smaller, more integrated producers gained the most. Those firms that were less profitable before the protection gained the most from it. These findings are consistent with the analysis presented here.

2. In the 1980s proposals were made that would require the government to auction the right to import under a quota to the highest bidder. If this kind of policy was adopted, then quotas could also be used to raise revenue for the government.

3. Stefanie Lenway, Kathleen Rehbein, and Laura Sparks, "The Impact of Protectionism on Firm Wealth: The Experience of the Steel Industry," *Southern Economic Journal* (April 1990): 1079–1093.

FIGURE 3
EFFECTS OF A TARIFF OR QUOTA WHEN DEMAND INCREASES
Under a tariff, an increase in demand increases the quantity of imports (from $C - E$ to $H - E$) and consumption (from C to H) but leaves the price unchanged (at P_t). With a quota, increased demand leads to a rise in price (from P_t to P_f) and in domestic production (from E to F). Consumption rises slightly (from B to G). Imports are unchanged ($G - F = C - E$).

Most economists prefer free trade to either tariffs or quotas. If they have to choose, they usually consider a tariff less harmful than an equivalent quota. A tariff does allow imports to increase in response to increases in demand. Also, at least some of the tariff revenue goes to the government, which uses it to further the general welfare. Also, a tariff is more visible and therefore easier to eliminate. A quota is less obvious and more likely to remain in place indefinitely.

NONTARIFF BARRIERS TO TRADE

In addition to tariffs and quotas, there are other kinds of government barriers to trade. Domestic laws or policies other than tariffs and quotas that interfere with the free exchange of goods and services across national borders are called **nontariff barriers**. Some of these barriers are intentional. One example is *domestic preference laws* requiring the government to favor domestic suppliers when making purchases for government agencies and programs. Other nontariff barriers are laws or regulations enacted for domestic reasons that make it more difficult for foreign suppliers to compete. For example, it may be difficult for a foreign supplier to comply with U.S. safety standards and labeling requirements. A common form of nontariff barrier is requiring excessive paperwork that adds to costs and reduces profits for foreign suppliers and domestic importing firms. In France, a shortage of customs inspectors constitutes a nontariff barrier because it creates long delays and thus discourages imports.

Sometimes nontariff barriers work the other way. Some U.S. laws and regulations make it more difficult for domestic firms to sell abroad. If American products must meet higher safety standards, for example, the American firm may not be able to compete with foreign producers who do not have to incur those costs.

Another type of nontariff barrier is antidumping codes. Dumping con-

nontariff barriers
Trade restrictions other than tariffs and quotas.

In May 1989, the United States took action against Japan, Brazil, and India for unfair trade practices. The U.S. government demanded that these countries end unfair practices and threatened retaliatory tariffs on selected goods from their countries if action was not forthcoming. Reporting on this development, *U.S. News & World Report* noted that President Bush suggested to one of his economic advisers, "Maybe we ought to take action against a whole bunch of countries—including ourselves."

The United States is a very open market, but there are numerous barriers to trade that its trading partners regard as unfair. These barriers include "voluntary restraints" on automobiles, customs user fees on boats, planes, and trucks, Superfund taxes on petroleum products, quotas on cheese, ice cream, and sugar, a 35¢ per gallon tariff on orange juice, steel restraints, antidumping laws, and consumer preferences for American products. Professor Gary Hufbauer estimates that tariffs, quotas, and nontariff barriers cost American consumers more than $80 billion annually.

Antidumping laws can be a bureaucratic and legal nightmare. A 1989 hearing before the International Trade Commission (ITC) offers a case study. In 1989, Torrington Company, a Connecticut-based maker of ball bearings, claimed firms in eight European countries

ECONOMIC

INSIGHT

U.S. BARRIERS TO

IMPORTS

were engaging in unfair trade practices (dumping). Torrington reportedly budgeted $1 million for the legal battle. The ITC ruled in Torrington's favor that bearings were being dumped in the U.S. market at 60 percent below their home market value. U.S. producers of power tools and machinery were not happy with this ruling. They pointed out that there was a shortage of such bearings in the United States and that Torrington was producing at capacity. They thought the ruling disadvantaged them in export markets because the price of ball bearings they use went up significantly.

Buy American mandates create another barrier that foreign countries claim is unfair. These legal requirements are most commonly found in the defense industry, road construction, and mass transit. Such preferential treatment generally gives American suppliers a price advantage over foreign suppliers. A recent European Community publication refers to these preferences as "permanent discrimination in favor of U.S. products."

Criticism of U.S. barriers to imports by U.S. trading partners conveniently ignores the fact that their barriers are just as irksome to U.S. firms trying to export. As you can see, however, and as Professor Hufbauer reports, the costs of U.S. barriers are significant to American consumers.

Source: Clemens P. Work with Robert F. Black, "Uncle Sam as Unfair Trader," *U.S. News & World Report* (12 June 1989): 42–44.

sists of selling a good at a lower price in a foreign country than in the firm's home country. Firms may dump abroad to get rid of surpluses, to take advantage of differences in elasticity of demand (price discrimination), or to establish a foothold in a competitive market. Most countries, including the United States, have antidumping regulations that forbid this practice as unfair competition. If a foreign firm is accused of dumping (usually by a competing firm in the importing country), the International Trade Commission will hear the case and may impose a duty on the dumped good to counteract the price difference. American firms often claim dumping is being done in order to make selling in the United States more difficult for foreign competitors.[4]

U.S. COMMERCIAL POLICY

The set of actions that a country undertakes to deliberately influence trade in goods and services is its **commercial policy**. For most of its history, the United States has had high tariffs and other trade restrictions. The highest U.S. tariff ever was imposed by the Smoot-Hawley Act of 1930, an average charge of 53 percent.

commercial policy
The set of actions that a country undertakes to deliberately influence trade in goods and services.

Since 1934, the United States has greatly reduced tariffs and other trade barriers by negotiating treaties with other countries. Trade barriers were reduced under a series of Congressional acts, beginning with the Reciprocal Trade Agreements Act of 1934. Regular trade negotiations led to reductions in tariffs by the United States and its major trading partners. The latest complete series of trade negotiations, which took place from 1974 to 1979, was called the Tokyo Round. After the tariff cuts agreed to in that round were finally implemented, the average U.S. tariff was only about 4.2 percent. The Tokyo Round also involved some agreements on reducing nontariff barriers. In 1986, a round of negotiations called the Uruguay Round began. In December 1990, the talks broke down over trade in agricultural products. The European countries were unwilling to lower their agricultural supports and the protection necessary to maintain them.

THE POLITICS OF PROTECTION

Reducing tariffs does not result in free trade. Quotas still protect autos, steel, textiles, and other industries. Nontariff barriers are still an important impediment to free trade. As the value of the dollar rose from 1981 to 1985, making imports cheap and exports expensive for the United States, pressures for protection rose. These pressures fell, however, as the dollar declined in 1986 and 1987. Critics of free trade point to the success of Japan and Korea, which experienced economic growth with very restrictive trade barriers. The battle between free trade and protectionism is an ongoing one.

Most demands for protection come from industries that once had a

---

4. For a clear, nontechnical review of the different types of nontariff barriers, see Cletus C. Coughlin and Geoffrey E. Wood, "An Introduction to Non-Tariff Barriers to Trade," *Review*, Federal Reserve Bank of St. Louis (January/February, 1989): 32–46.

comparative advantage but lost it when other industries developed even greater relative efficiency. Such demands also come from industries where monopoly or oligopoly conditions allowed them to ignore the need to improve technology and productivity. Shoes, clothing, steel, and, most recently, automobiles are U.S. industries that have asked for protection because they have lost a comparative advantage. Part of the problem with steel and automobiles is that they have been slow to modernize and to respond to changes in consumer preferences.

It is easy to identify gainers and losers from tariffs and quotas. Consumers lose. Foreign producers lose sales. Domestic competitors gain. One loser who does not show up in Figures 2 and 3 is the U.S. exporter. When one country raises tariffs, other countries are likely to do so in response, and the first country's exports fall. Thus, political support for free trade should come from a coalition between exporting firms and consumers, with help from wholesalers and retailers of imported goods. However, such a diverse group is not easy to organize and hold together.

Firms that gain from protection spend large sums of money in lobbying to get or keep a tariff or quota. Consider a tariff on shoes. As a consumer, you may find that the tariff only costs you a few more dollars a year, so it's hardly worthwhile to lobby against the tariff. But if you are a worker whose job in a shoe factory depends on protection or a shoe manufacturer losing sales to imports, you will work much harder to get and keep protection. Even though the total benefits of free trade would exceed the costs, complaints from a few big losers tend to generate far more noise and attention than the lobbying for free trade. If the losers are concentrated in certain regions, the American system of representation by states and districts makes it easier for them to develop "client" relationships with their members of Congress.

COMMON ARGUMENTS FOR PROTECTION

When workers and owners from import-competing firms go to Washington to lobby for protection, they use some tried and true arguments for protection. Some of these arguments have some economic validity. Others have strong political or emotional appeal, but weak economic foundations. We will discuss the most common arguments for protection in this section and then turn to two very sophisticated ones.

INFANT INDUSTRY ARGUMENT
One theoretically valid argument for protection is the infant industry argument. An infant industry is a new industry that is not yet ready to compete with established foreign producers. Given some time (and sheltered conditions) to master the technology, establish a reputation, train workers, and reach economies of scale, the infant industry may eventually be competitive. Comparative advantage can change over time. Temporary protection could give an infant industry the chance to acquire a comparative advantage and "catch up" with established foreign firms.

This argument is only valid if the protected industry will be competitive in time. There is no reason to protect industries that will never be competitive, wasting scarce resources that could be better used elsewhere. There should be no need to protect industries that will quickly become competitive, because entrepreneurs (and lenders) should be able to see past the early losses to profits. The only industries that really qualify are those that generate some kinds of external benefits to society that they are unable to recoup in the early years. Thus, the few deserving infant industries are those that are not profitable by simple cost and revenue calculations, but are worth protecting because they meet two tests:

1. They will eventually be able to compete in the market without protection.
2. They generate benefits to society that are worth the cost of a tariff.

What kinds of external benefits might an infant industry create? Examples include developing roads and power sources that are then available to other industries, training a labor force that may migrate to other firms, or producing a low-cost input that other industries can use. Benefits such as these are likely to be created in less developed countries. It's difficult to make a convincing case for protecting an infant industry in a developed country such as the United States. Even in less developed countries, this argument is easily abused by overstating external benefits and underestimating how long it will take for the industry to be competitive.

NATIONAL DEFENSE ARGUMENT

Another common and economically valid argument for protection is national defense. The product of this industry may be needed in wartime, the argument goes, but the domestic producer can't compete with cheaper foreign producers. Without protection during peacetime, the firm may not be here when war comes and foreign supplies are cut off. This argument gained merit after the War of 1812. England had been the United States's main trading partner and then became an enemy who successfully blockaded the U.S. coast. Again, during World War II, German interference with shipping created problems in obtaining some needed supplies.

However, this argument make less sense for the United States today. The government stockpiles strategic raw materials, and most products needed in wartime are those in which the United States has a comparative advantage, such as heavy machinery, sophisticated electronics, and aircraft. Economists Leland Yeager and David Tuerck argue that the national defense argument only applies in the case of another World War II, what they describe as a "prolonged non-nuclear war of attrition."[5] But, they argue, the more likely kinds of wars—the kind the Pentagon seems to be preparing for—are either "brush fire" wars, such as Panamanian invasion of 1990 and other localized battles, which do not affect U.S. access to supplies, or else all-out nuclear war, in which case there would be no time to resupply. Even the 1991 Gulf War, which was too large to be called a "brush fire," did not affect U.S. access to shipping and supplies.

---

5.   Leland B. Yeager and David G. Tuerck, *Foreign Trade and U.S. Policy* (New York: Praeger, 1976).

Balance of Payments Argument

Most other arguments for protection have more emotional or political appeal than economic logic. Proponents of protection argue that a balance of payments deficit (or at least that part of the deficit that is accounted for by exports and imports) could be reduced by imposing tariffs and importing less. Up to a point, this argument is correct, but only in the short run. Over time, tariffs encourage the development of domestic industries producing import substitutes, usually products in which the nation has a comparative disadvantage. This policy encourages inefficient use of scarce resources. Furthermore, tariffs usually lead to retaliatory tariffs on the exports of the country imposing the tariff.

Employment Argument

The employment argument suggests that reducing imports can create jobs producing import substitutes. However, the cost of doing so is high. Protectionism encourages misallocation of resources and tends to lead to retaliation. The tariff-imposing country may gain jobs in import-competing industries and lose them in more efficient exporting industries. Employment may also be lost if domestically produced items cost more or are of inferior quality. Thus, less is demanded and jobs are lost.

Cheap Foreign Labor Argument

The cheap foreign labor argument popular among protectionists goes something like this: "We're just as efficient as the foreign competition—we use the same machinery and technology and produce at least as high a quality product. However, U.S. labor costs are at least $7.00 an hour, and firms in some foreign countries have to pay only $1.00 an hour. How can we possibly compete?"

There are several possible answers. One is that cheap labor often means lower productivity. Another is that labor, especially unskilled labor, may be cheap in some countries, but other inputs such as capital and skilled labor are relatively expensive. A country such as the United States should concentrate on producing those products that use relatively more of its abundant (and, therefore, relatively less expensive) resources, capital, and skilled labor.

SOPHISTICATED ARGUMENTS FOR PROTECTION

Two sophisticated arguments from the highly mathematical literature of trade theory are valid arguments for trade restriction. These arguments are so advanced that they rarely appear in beginning economic textbooks. We include them here because we don't want to leave you with the impression that all economists favor free trade in all situations. This section will introduce you to the very basic ideas behind these arguments. You can learn more through the suggestions for further reading if you are interested.

Optimal Tariff Argument

If the price elasticity of demand for imported goods is greater than zero and the price elasticity of foreign supply is less than infinite, the imposition of a tariff raises the price of the foreign good by less than the amount of the tariff. The tariff causes the foreign supplier to lower prices in order to maintain sales. The country imposing the tariff then experiences a gain in its terms of trade, because the price of its imports has fallen while the price of its exports remains the same.

This effect on the terms of trade gives rise to the concept of an optimal tariff. An **optimal tariff** is a tariff that maximizes a nation's net gain from altering its terms of trade. At one extreme, if the supply of imports were perfectly inelastic, the optimal tariff would be infinite because the importing country would be a pure monopsonist. At the other extreme, where the import supply was perfectly elastic, the optimum would be zero.

optimal tariff
A tariff that maximizes a nation's net gain from altering its terms of trade.

The optimal tariff argument is valid within its restrictive assumptions. The main assumption is that the foreign countries do not retaliate. If other countries see their terms of trade deteriorate and retaliate with an optimal tariff of their own, the flow of trade diminishes. After a series of retaliations and counter-retaliations, world welfare will be diminished. All countries will be at lower consumption levels. Another problem is that application of optimal tariffs would be very difficult in practice. It would require that policy makers know the elasticities of demand for the traded goods. It is difficult to determine these elasticities, and they change over time.

The optimal tariff argument suggests using a country's monopsony power to provide a gain to it by imposing a tariff that causes the rest of the world to suffer a loss. It is likely that such a gain would be only a short-term one, as the rest of the world would soon retaliate.

THE THEORY OF THE SECOND BEST

The **theory of the second best** is an argument in favor of tariffs as distortions needed to offset other distortions. Monopoly, government policies, and externalities often cause a divergence between private and social costs and benefits, and governmental policy may not be able to eliminate this divergence in order to pursue the first-best policy of free trade. Then a second-best policy of tariffs may be useful to introduce new distortions that eliminate the existing distortions.

theory of the second best
A theory that a second-best policy of tariffs may be useful to introduce new distortions that eliminate existing distortions.

The theory of the second best can be used to justify import restrictions on a selective basis when external effects make the private costs to a domestic producer higher than the social costs to the country. Consider, for example, an excise tax on a domestically produced good, automobile tires. This tax raises the cost of producing tires because that cost will include the portion of the tax that is a transfer from tire producers to the government. As a result, domestic production of tires is lower, and imports of tires are higher than they would be without the excise tax. The country is importing tires at a higher social price than it would cost to produce them at home. An import duty equal to the excise tax would increase the domestic production of tires to the point where the marginal social cost of imported tires and the marginal cost of domestic production are equal.

If government-created cost differences or foreign trade restrictions affected all industries equally, they would not affect comparative costs and distort the efficient pattern of specialization and trade. It is only when these factors affect different industries differently that there may be a distortion of relative prices that justifies some kind of protection. For example, the minimum wage has more impact on costs for industries that use large amounts of unskilled labor than for industries that use primarily highly skilled labor and capital. Thus, the minimum wage raises the costs of the first type of industry more than the second.

The theory of the second best is not limited to trade theory. It recognizes that whenever market prices fail to reflect real opportunity costs, a second-best policy may be appropriate. You should remember, however, that the first-best policy is free trade.

FAIR TRADE AND THE MAINTENANCE OF THE U.S. MARKET

fair trade
The idea that the United States should impose trade barriers equivalent to those that its trading partners place on U.S. exports.

If there are so few valid economic arguments for protection, why does protection exist? There is a group of politically appealing arguments labeled **fair trade**. The concept of fair trade is often described as a "level playing field." If foreign countries erect tariff barriers, nontariff barriers, or quotas that limit U.S. firms' exports to those countries, protectionists argue that the United States should do the same. For example, if the Japanese make it very difficult or expensive for their citizens to buy U.S. automobiles or beef, protectionists say that Americans should treat Japanese exports the same way.

One version of the fair trade argument is called maintenance of markets. Some protectionists argue that it is more costly to operate in the U.S. market than in other markets. U.S. firms pay high corporate taxes, face strict environmental and safety standards, and have to comply with employment regulations such as affirmative action, minimum wage, and overtime pay. Many foreign producers, especially in less developed countries, do not incur similar costs. They can participate in the U.S. market without incurring the costs of maintaining it. This issue has received considerable attention recently because of the proposed free trade area between the United States and Mexico. Mexico has lax environmental standards and few employment regulations.

These fair trade arguments are usually put forward by organized lobbies for industries that are losing sales to foreign competitors. The appeal makes sense to the average voter, because it is couched in terms of fair play and equal treatment. Coupled with arguments against trading with Communist countries and other political enemies, the case for "fair trade" looks even more appealing. International trade differs from domestic trade in that the political dimension carries much more weight. Political concerns help to explain why the economically sound practice of free trade is rarely implemented.

Advocates of protection on the basis of fair trade or maintenance of the U.S. market offer two policy solutions. The more traditional one is a tariff on foreign goods. This tariff would be equivalent to the restrictions placed on U.S. exports by other countries or to the excess cost of maintaining the U.S. market. Computing the appropriate tariff in either case would be a difficult task. For some European nations, with large government sectors and restrictive laws governing employment, the appropriate tariff might actually be negative.

In November 1989, Canadian voters approved the U.S.–Canada Free Trade Agreement (FTA). The FTA called for a ten-year phase-in of complete free trade. Before the pact, about 75 percent of the markets between the two countries had free trade. Autos have been freely traded since 1965. The beneficiaries of this agreement were predicted to be primarily Canadian consumers and U.S. producers, because Canadian tariffs were about three times higher than U.S. tariffs. For example, two months after the agreement was signed, some Harley-Davidson motorcycle models sold for $2,000 less in Canada than they had before the pact.

Freer access to U.S. markets has contributed to a surge of business investment in Canada. The Royal Bank of Canada has reported an increase in plant and equipment investment of more than 28 percent since the signing of the agreement. Canada's Economic Council has estimated that when this investment boom is over, it will have produced more than 250,000 new jobs in Canada. On the American side, business is also booming. Buffalo, New York has reaped some benefits from the agreement, being viewed by those in Toronto as "the cheap side of the border." Shoppers from Toronto head south to purchase computers, clothes, televisions, gasoline, and liquor. Two-way trade between the United States and Canada increased more than 10 percent in the first year of the agreement.

Not everyone is happy with the agreement. Polls in Canada indicate that a majority of the population has turned against it. The Liberal Party has promised to repeal the deal if returned to power. This is understandable because there are winners and losers in free trade. The losers are more visible. Firms that aren't competitive don't survive. The strong Canadian labor unions were opposed to the agreement and still oppose it. Bruce Campbell, an economist with the Canadian Labor Congress, claims that "free trade is a bad deal for Canadians." He would be more correct to say that free trade is a bad deal for Canadian labor union members.

Free trade of sorts is also booming on the southern border of the United States. *Maquiladoras*, or border plants, are booming along the U.S.–Mexican border. Nearly half a million Mexicans are employed in almost 2,000 plants. These plants receive shipments of parts from U.S. manufacturers and assemble the parts into complete products. Any tariffs are due only on the value added. General Motors assembles auto parts in more than thirty *maquiladoras*. In 1986, this trade amounted to $29.7 billion. It grew to more than $65 billion in 1990.

Mexican President Carlos Salinas de Gortari wants free trade between Mexico and the United States to expand. Mexican and U.S. officials have been exploring a free trade agreement like the one negotiated with Canada. Administration officials look favorably on such proposals, but face tough opposition in Congress. Organized labor in the United States, like that in Canada, is strongly opposed to such an agreement. Labor leaders argue that Mexican firms enjoy an unfair advantage because they do not have to meet the environmental and safety standards that U.S. firms do. Owen F. Bieber, president of the United Auto Workers, argues that a free trade pact with Mexico would mean "there'll be a hell of a lot more empty factories in the United States of America." Perhaps Bieber and Campbell have the same speech writer!

ECONOMIC INSIGHT

THE UNITED STATES AND FREE TRADE PACTS

Sources: Stephen Baker, "Along the Border, Free Trade Is Becoming a Fact of Life," *Business Week* (18 June 1990): 41–42; Alan Freeman, "Free-Trade Pact Creates Winners, Losers," *Wall Street Journal* (7 February 1989): A20; Peter Dworkin, "Unhappy Birthday for a Free-Trade Pact," *U.S. News & World Report* (5 February 1989): 54–59.

An alternative solution was suggested by Senator Phil Gramm of Texas (trained as an economist) and former Representative Jack Kemp of New York. Gramm and Kemp are basically in favor of free trade, but are also responsive to political pressures for protection based on fair trade arguments. They propose trading with each country on the basis that it trades with the United States. They believe that this policy would result in freer trade because the U.S. market is so important to other countries that they will lower their barriers rather than see barriers raised in the United States. The appeal of this policy is that it responds to arguments for fair trade and maintenance of the market with economic incentives to promote free trade and specialization based on comparative advantage. This solution demands reciprocity, waving a stick of protectionism in order to get other governments to move toward freer trade.

MOVEMENT OF RESOURCES

If trading countries benefit from the flow of goods and services, what about benefits from the flow of inputs? Labor, capital, and raw materials also move between countries. When they do, objections are sometimes raised by those who are threatened by foreign competition. Foreign competition is unpopular with the owners of factors of production, whether the competition is in product markets or in factor markets. Thus, these owners seek restrictions on the movement of factors as well as on the movement of goods.

Organized labor, for example, opposes immigration of workers and construction of plants abroad. Newly arrived workers compete for jobs and depress wages. An offshore plant of a U.S. firm means more jobs for foreign workers and fewer jobs for American workers. Domestic firms oppose letting their foreign competitors locate inside the country with no tariff wall for protection. Canada is cautious about letting U.S. firms build new plants in that country, and countries such as Kuwait and Japan have even tighter restrictions. Emotional and political arguments are sometimes stronger than economic concerns. Many U.S. citizens are unhappy about the purchase of U.S. banks, farmland, and resort islands by foreign firms and individuals, even when there are no obvious adverse consequences.

The United States puts fewer restrictions than most countries on the inflow or outflow of capital. Except for strategic raw materials (those needed for national defense), there are no restrictions on the flow of natural resources. Exports of natural resources such as oil and copper are often restricted by countries with some market power as suppliers. Some of these countries use controls on exports of these resources to generate revenue for their governments or to attract industries that use the resources as raw materials in manufacturing. Cartels are sometimes formed to take advantage of such market power when that power is shared among a small number of countries.

Immigration policy has been a source of much debate in the United States. After several previous attempts, Congress finally passed a new immigration bill in 1986. The most controversial provisions of that bill centered on illegal aliens, who have come to the United States in large numbers in the last twenty years. The bill made it possible for illegal aliens who resided in the United States prior to 1982 to become citizens but also imposed stiff penalties on employers who hire illegal aliens. The large number of illegal aliens who were residing in the United States when the law was passed was due to past restrictive immigration quotas. Organized labor has generally opposed raising or eliminating immigration quotas because it wants to protect jobs for U.S. citizens.

In general, the movement of inputs between countries can substitute for free movement of goods. If a country is poor in raw materials, capital, or skilled labor, it has two possible remedies. It can import goods that incorporate large quantities of those inputs, or it can import those inputs and produce its own final products. Both kinds of trade should bring benefits. In the absence of artificial barriers, market considerations determine which choice is more efficient—to move the final product or to move the input.

MULTINATIONAL CORPORATIONS

Another important influence on patterns of trade and factor movements is the multinational firm. A **multinational corporation** is a firm with headquarters in one country and plants in one or more other countries. Many large and well-known multinationals are headquartered in the United States, including Ford, General Motors, IBM, and AT&T. (So are many smaller and less-known ones.) Other large multinationals are headquartered in other countries, especially Japan (Honda and Mitsubishi) and European countries (Shell Oil, Nestlé, Michelin, and BASF). Multinationals have been around for a long time, but most of their growth has occurred since World War II.

multinational corporation
A firm with headquarters in one country and plants in one or more other countries.

WHY FIRMS GO ABROAD
Why do firms build plants in foreign countries? Why not just export or invest in a local firm that can produce the product? Exporting may not be feasible because of trade barriers, perishability, or a need to produce a product tailored to the local market. Investing in a local firm by purchasing stock or making a loan is sometimes feasible. Often, however, the investing firm wants more control over management, product quality, or patented processes. Sometimes the only way to get access to local resources, especially raw materials, is to build a plant.

U.S. labor unions oppose building plants abroad, arguing that firms are in search of cheap foreign labor. Unions would rather see plants built in the United States and goods exported. However, trade barriers or the unique needs of foreign markets are much more common reasons for building foreign plants than the attraction of cheap labor. Furthermore, U.S. workers have found jobs in the many plants in the United States owned by foreign multinationals, especially Japanese-owned firms. The lower wages and different management style of Japanese companies have meant adjustments not only for their American employees but also for their American competitors.

EFFECTS OF MULTINATIONALS

Multinationals are accused by their critics of stifling competition in the countries in which they locate, creating balance of payments problems, and leading to unhealthy concentration of economic and political power. Advocates argue that multinationals often increase competition, speed up the transfer of capital and technology, and help counteract artificial barriers to trade.

COMPETITION. In some cases, the multinational "shakes up" domestic competitors, forcing them to try harder when they can no longer hide behind a protective tariff wall. On the other hand, multinationals often simply buy out local competitors or keep local competition from developing. Sometimes multinationals increase competition, and sometimes they reduce it. Japanese multinationals and others have generally been regarded as beneficial in the United States. They compete for resources and markets with established American firms that must adjust or decline.

TRANSFER OF TECHNOLOGY. Multinationals expedite the flow of technology between countries. They make available to their foreign subsidiaries processes and methods that they would be reluctant to share with competitors. Less developed countries sometimes argue, however, that this transfer doesn't spill over to other industries for maximum benefit. They also argue that multinationals, which are generally from developed industrial countries, don't try very hard to adapt technology to the local mix of available resources.

LARGE MULTINATIONALS AND SMALL COUNTRIES. Probably the most serious concern about multinationals is that small countries are at a disadvantage in dealing with these large firms. Such a firm may have an annual revenue much larger than the host country's GNP. The multinational may be the largest employer, landowner, and taxpayer in a small country. A multinational represents a threat to the sovereignty of a host country when the firm is larger and more powerful than the government.

Despite these problems, there are real benefits to having multinationals. They provide a way for resources and technology to flow around trade and cultural barriers, which has been very beneficial to the world economy. In most cases, they promote the free-trade goals of more output with less effort that were the concern of classical economists two centuries ago when they formulated the theory of comparative advantage.

SUMMARY

1. Trade takes place because both parties benefit. Trade is based on the principle of comparative advantage, which means that each country produces that product for which its opportunity cost is lower in terms of other production.

2. Specialization increases total output, and trade allows that increase to be shared. Trade also increases competition and allows countries to take advantage of economies of scale for some products.

3. Tariffs, quotas, and nontariff barriers interfere with free trade. A tariff or quota will raise the price, reduce imports, reduce consumption, and increase domestic production.

4. The United States has had high tariffs for most of its history but has reduced tariffs and other trade barriers since 1934.

5. Arguments for protection include protecting infant industries, national defense, balance of payments, employment, and cheap foreign labor. The first two have some validity but must be applied with caution. Most arguments for protection are really thinly disguised requests for income redistribution. The optimal tariff and the theory of the second best are two sophisticated arguments for tariffs.

6. Fair trade arguments call for consideration of the costs imposed on firms by U.S. laws.

7. Movements of resources can substitute for trade in goods and services.

8. Multinational corporations may increase competition in some cases and decrease it in others. They increase the transfer of technology between countries but may have too much power in small, less developed countries.

NEW TERMS

gains from trade	product cycle	nontariff barrier	fair trade
absolute advantage	tariff	commercial policy	multinational
comparative advantage	quota	optimal tariff	corporation
terms of trade	tariff quota	theory of the second best	
consumption possibilities curve			

QUESTIONS FOR DISCUSSION

1. Consider the following situation for Upland and Downland. Each country devotes half of its resources to producing bananas and half to producing apples, and the figures given are what they produce in the absence of trade.

COUNTRY	APPLES (TONS)	BANANAS (TONS)
Upland	40	80
Downland	60	60

Do these figures indicate an absolute advantage, a comparative advantage, or both? What is each country's opportunity cost of producing apples? By how much will to-

tal output rise when they specialize? Can you find a better consumption combination for each country through trade?

2. Represent the information in Question 1 on a graph as a pair of production possibilities curves.

3. Who gains and who loses from a tariff? How do the effects of tariffs differ from the effects of quotas?

4. If you were running a small country, why might you have mixed feelings about the building of a plant there by a big multinational?

5. Among the U.S. industries that have received tariff protection in recent years are textiles and autos. Use one or more of the arguments in this chapter to present a case for protection of one of these industries.

6. Write a criticism of the case you made in Question 5, citing the benefits of free trade.

7. A tariff is proposed on imported pineapple. Economists calculate that 1 million pineapple buyers will incur additional costs of $2 each. Five thousand pineapple workers will earn an additional $100 a year. One hundred unemployed workers will find jobs at an average salary of $10,000. One hundred owners of pineapple packing firms will experience an average income increase of $5,000. What are the total gains to the gainers and the total losses to the losers? Are there other losses not counted in these figures? Do you think the tariff is likely to be enacted?

8. Why do multinational firms go abroad?

9. Why do economists generally prefer tariffs to quotas?

10. Why is an economy's consumption possibilities curve different from the production possibilities curve? How does a consumption possibilities curve help explain the benefits of trade as similar to the benefits of economic growth?

11. Can the government completely eliminate imports of some goods even if there is general agreement that such restrictions are appropriate? How does the experience with illegal immigration and illegal drugs support your argument?

12. Assume that the United States can produce 3 mainframe computers or 3,000 pairs of shoes with one unit of resource, and Italy can produce 1 mainframe computer or 2,000 pairs of shoes with one unit of resource. Could specialization and trade increase world output and consumption?

13. Given the data in Question 12, how will firms in the United States and Italy know what to produce? Who or what will tell them what to produce and what to import?

14. Why might competing domestic producers and importing firms prefer quotas to tariffs?

15. U.S. companies are often criticized as being too focused on the domestic market and not concerned enough with exporting. Business schools in the United States have been blamed for this domestic emphasis and have responded by "internationalizing" the business curriculum. Can you suggest economic reasons why U.S. firms have historically concentrated on the domestic market?

SUGGESTIONS FOR FURTHER READING

Business Week: Special 1990 Bonus Issue (June 15, 1990). An entire special issue devoted to international trade.

Dertouzos, Michael L., Richard K. Lester, Robert M. Solow, and the MIT Commission on Industrial Productivity. *Made in America: Regaining the Productive Edge.* Cambridge: MIT Press, 1989. A report by an MIT commission on U.S. industrial importance that addresses issues of American competitiveness in world markets. Chapter 2 discusses the U.S. economy in the changing world environment.

Helpman, Elhanan, and Paul R. Krugman. *Trade Policy and Market Structure.* Cambridge: MIT Press, 1989. A highly theoretical treatment of trade policy that demonstrates that when markets are not competitive, government intervention can improve welfare. This argument calls into question the argument for a unilateral free trade policy.

King, Philip. *International Economics and International Economic Policy: A Reader.* New York: McGraw-Hill, 1990. A collection of readings on current issues in trade policy. Includes material on Japan's trade policy, strategic trade, Europe 1992, and multinational companies.

Root, Franklyn R. *International Trade and Investment.* Cincinnati, OH: South-Western, 1990. An intermediate-level textbook covering both international trade and international finance.

Vargish, George. *What's Made in the U.S.A.* Saddle River, NJ: Vargish International, 1988. A book written by a businessman that attacks free trade as a "national catastrophe" and repeats many of the arguments for protectionism discussed in this chapter.

Yeager, Leland B., and David G. Tuerck. *Foreign Trade and U.S. Policy.* New York: Praeger, 1976. This book presents the case for free trade and a criticism of protectionism in theory and practice, with many examples and illustrations from Congressional hearings.

1. Describe how the market for currencies is different from other kinds of markets.
2. Diagram and explain the operation of the foreign exchange market.
3. Explain what causes shifts in supply and demand for foreign exchange and how countries can deal with persistent disequilibrium in the foreign exchange market.
4. Explain the relationship between the foreign exchange market and the balance of payments.
5. Discuss how the forward market works.
6. Identify the components of the balance of payments accounts and measure the deficit or surplus.
7. Describe how the gold standard and the Bretton Woods system worked, and explain why neither is used today.
8. Discuss the advantages and disadvantages of floating rates.
9. Explain what exchange control is and why countries use it.

CHAPTER 35

INTERNATIONAL FINANCE

INTRODUCTION

International finance seems very unlike other topics in economics. It involves foreign exchange markets, hedgers and speculators, floating rates and gold hoarders, balance of payments deficits and surpluses, the ups and downs of the U.S. dollar, and dealing under the table by international banks to affect currency prices. In fact, the foreign exchange market is really very similar to other markets.

The preceding chapter described international trade in goods and services, but not exchange of currencies or financial assets. One important difference that distinguishes trade *within* nations from trade *between* nations is that people in different countries use different currencies. To pay for goods purchased abroad, a buyer must acquire foreign currency. It is relatively easy for U.S. citizens to purchase foreign currency, but obtaining foreign exchange is more difficult in many other countries.

This chapter looks at the market for currencies and what determines the price of one currency in terms of another (the exchange rate). It also describes the accounting statement for the foreign sector—the balance of payments—and its links to the domestic economy. Finally, we will examine different kinds of international monetary systems to see how they work and how they affect trade between countries.

THE MARKET FOR FOREIGN EXCHANGE

The network of banks and financial institutions through which buyers and sellers exchange national currencies is called the **foreign exchange market**. The foreign exchange market works much like the market for wheat, apples, or skateboards. There is a supply curve, a demand curve, and an equilibrium price and quantity. There are also conditions that are held constant (*ceteris paribus* conditions). When these conditions change, the curves shift and the equilibrium price and quantity change.

foreign exchange market
The network of banks and financial institutions through which buyers and sellers exchange national currencies.

913

SUPPLY AND DEMAND FOR FOREIGN EXCHANGE

Figure 1 represents the foreign exchange market as it appears to U.S. buyers and sellers. In this figure, foreign currencies are represented by the German mark (DM). The price of foreign exchange is measured in dollars.[1] Citizens of other countries supply foreign exchange in order to buy U.S. exports, to travel or invest in the United States, or to purchase U.S. services or assets. U.S. citizens demand foreign exchange in order to import foreign goods and services (including traveling abroad) and to invest in foreign assets.

In Figure 1, the equilibrium price of the mark is 50¢, and the equilibrium quantity is 100 million. At a price of 70¢ per mark (equivalent to 1.4 marks per dollar), there would be a surplus of foreign exchange of 60 million marks. Quantity supplied is 130 million marks, and quantity demanded is only 70 million. At 30¢ per mark (equivalent to 3.3 marks per dollar), there would be a shortage of foreign exchange of 60 million marks (130 million marks demanded less 70 million marks supplied).

SHIFTS IN SUPPLY AND DEMAND

Demand for foreign exchange will increase if something causes U.S. citizens to want to import more foreign goods and services or to invest more abroad. The supply of foreign exchange will increase if foreigners want to buy more U.S. goods and services or invest more in the United States. Recall from Chapter 3 that demand curves shift when the *ceteris paribus* conditions change. Some of those demand shifters, including changes in tastes, population, and income, apply here. Others work a little differently because the foreign exchange market is a macroeconomic market.

The price of a good is affected by changes in the prices of related goods. For example, demand for coffee is affected by the price of tea. In the foreign exchange market, it is aggregate rather than individual prices that matter. Aggregate price changes that can affect foreign exchange are

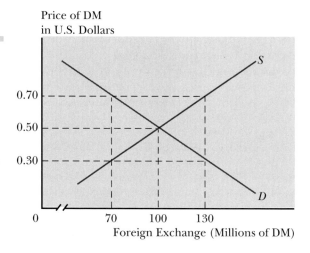

FIGURE 1
THE FOREIGN EXCHANGE MARKET
The foreign exchange market shows the supply of foreign exchange (German marks) from abroad, the demand for foreign exchange by U.S. citizens, and the equilibrium price (50¢ per mark) and quantity (100 million marks).

1.   This market can also be represented as the supply and demand for U.S. dollars, but we will focus on the U.S. market for other countries' currencies.

changes in the price level in the United States relative to the price level abroad or changes in the prices of U.S. exports in general relative to prices of foreign goods. Note that the price on the vertical axis in Figure 1 is the price of foreign exchange. Changes in other prices, including the domestic price level, can shift the supply and demand curves for foreign exchange. If the U.S. price level rises more than foreign price levels, imports become cheaper relative to domestic goods, and Americans will want to buy more imported goods. Rising domestic prices shift the U.S. demand curve for foreign exchange rightward. U.S. citizens demand more foreign exchange to buy more imported goods. At the same time, the U.S. supply curve for foreign exchange shifts to the left because foreigners want to buy fewer American exports at higher prices. In fact, economists who forecast changes in exchange rates find that changes in relative price levels are the most significant determinant.[2]

Changes in relative interest rates also shift demand for foreign exchange. If interest rates are higher abroad, Americans will demand more foreign exchange to buy foreign financial assets, such as bonds or bank deposits. From 1981 to 1985, interest rates in the United States were higher than in most other countries, attracting an inflow of foreign capital. This increased supply of foreign exchange drove the price of foreign currencies down, or the price of the dollar up. As U.S. interest rates fell after 1985, the price of the dollar also fell (that is, the prices of marks, yen, and pounds began to rise).

Another source of shifts in demand for foreign exchange is changes in government restrictions on trade, such as tariffs, quotas, and nontariff barriers. These commercial policy tools are often used intentionally to shift the demand for foreign exchange, either to change the currency price or to "cure" a shortage of foreign exchange (balance of payments

---

SOURCES OF SHIFTS IN SUPPLY AND DEMAND FOR FOREIGN EXCHANGE

Changes in:

- relative price levels,
- relative incomes,
- relative interest rates,
- tastes and preferences,
- population,
- technology,
- input cost and availability,
- tariffs, quotas, and nontariff barriers,
- export subsidies.

---

2.   The theory that changes in exchange rates result primarily from changes in countries' relative price levels is called purchasing power parity. Much attention was given to using price level changes to predict exchange rates in the 1970s and 1980s under floating exchange rates. Most studies indicate that purchasing power parity explains long-run exchange rate changes well but not short-run variations.

deficit). Export subsidies and promotions encourage foreign purchases and shift the supply of foreign exchange to the right. Finally, demand for foreign exchange shifts when there are changes in technology or input costs, which can change demand for foreign inputs or foreign products.

The same kinds of factors that shift one nation's demand for foreign exchange also operate to shift other countries' supply of foreign exchange. Changes in a country's relative price level or income, tastes, population, technology, interest rates, and tariffs and quotas all affect the supply of foreign exchange from other countries.

UNIQUE FEATURES OF THE FOREIGN EXCHANGE MARKET

The foreign exchange market has several unique features. First, the operations of this market have important macroeconomic implications. What happens in the market for foreign exchange affects (and is affected by) interest rates, output, and price levels. Second, governments are often heavily involved in setting the price, often in an attempt to limit its fluctuations. Third, a well-developed forward market exists for foreign exchange, where people make contracts for future deliveries of currency at a fixed price. Finally, the foreign exchange market sometimes suffers from persistent disequilibrium.

MACROECONOMIC IMPLICATIONS. U.S. exports and imports, which are heavily influenced by changes in exchange rates, each constitute about 10–11 percent of GNP. In addition, the foreign exchange market supports some large transactions in financial assets, such as stocks and bonds. Exports, imports, and capital transactions affect the domestic economy in many ways. A rise in exports can increase output, but expanding output puts upward pressure on the price level. Rising imports can reduce domestic output but will also reduce inflationary pressures. An inflow of foreign capital can drive up interest rates, the money supply, and prices. The opposite is true for a capital outflow. Thus, any macroeconomic model of the U.S. economy must incorporate the foreign sector if it is to predict output, employment, prices, and interest rates accurately.

Domestic events also affect exports, imports, and trade in capital assets. Changes in output, prices, and interest rates spill over into the foreign sector. Rising output means rising income, some of which will be spent on more imports. A fall in output and income will reduce imports, as it did in the 1981–1982 recession. Rising U.S. prices (relative to foreign prices) encourage U.S. citizens and foreigners to substitute cheaper goods made in other countries for more expensive American products. When the price level rises faster in the United States than abroad, exports fall and imports rise. Falling prices, or prices rising more slowly than in the rest of the world, stimulate exports and discourage imports. Higher interest rates attract capital from abroad, but lower interest rates encourage U.S. capital owners to try to earn a higher return in other countries. All these changes shift the supply and demand for foreign exchange, and thus change currency prices under the present floating exchange rate system.

GOVERNMENT INTERVENTION. Governments have always been heavily involved in the market for their own currencies. Even with floating rates, governments don't always allow the market to completely determine the prices of their currencies. A government may want to keep the price of its currency from falling because of national pride or because of the effect on the terms of trade.[3] Alternatively, a government may want to keep the price of the currency from rising too high because such an increase would make it more difficult for the country's exporters to compete and easier for imports to undersell domestic goods. In small countries where foreign trade is a large part of total economic activity, monetary authorities may be concerned about the effects of changes in the currency's price on the volume of the country's monetary reserves and the money supply. Finally, a government may want to keep the price of the currency stable in order to encourage trade and foreign investment by minimizing risk and uncertainty.

Governments set and maintain prices in other markets, including minimum wages, farm price supports, and rent controls. In these markets, the government usually sets either a floor price or a ceiling price. In the market for foreign exchange, governments historically have set both a floor and a ceiling.

THE FORWARD MARKET. Another special feature of the foreign exchange market is a well-developed **forward market**, in which contracts are made for future delivery of specific amounts of currency at a specified price. Forward (or futures) markets also exist in other goods and services. Probably the best-known forward market is the commodities market, where contracts for the future delivery of corn, wheat, pork bellies, copper, tin, gold, and other metals and agricultural goods are traded.

Traders who try to reduce their risk by buying or selling contracts for future delivery are called **hedgers**. Those who are willing to assume risk in return for the chance of a profit are called **speculators**. Let's look at a simple illustration of how hedgers and speculators interact in the foreign exchange market. Suppose a Honda dealer in the United States receives a shipment of Hondas from Japan. The dollar cost of the shipment is $100,000, but the contract calls for payment in six months in yen. The yen is trading for 150 yen per U.S. dollar, so the dealer owes 15 million yen. What the dealer needs in six months is not $100,000, but however many dollars it takes at that time to buy 15 million yen. Suppose the dealer thinks the price of a dollar in six months will be only 120 yen. Then the payment will cost the dealer more dollars—$125,000, to be precise. There goes the profit! If the dealer can find someone now who will guarantee a reasonably attractive price, say 145 yen to the dollar, that will eliminate the exchange risk. The dealer can concentrate on the business of selling cars and motorcycles.

What about the opposite situation—that of the speculator? Chances are the speculator is a large commercial bank, with many forward transactions in many directions. There is probably some Japanese firm in need of dollars that can be matched with the U.S. car dealer's need for yen.

forward market
The market in which contracts are made for future delivery of specific amounts of currency at a specified price.

hedgers
People who try to reduce their risk by buying or selling contracts in the forward market for currency.

speculators
People who assume risk in the forward market for currency in return for the chance of a profit.

---

3.   If the price of U.S. currency falls, then Americans have to pay more U.S. dollars (and therefore more U.S. goods) for foreign goods. Giving up more U.S. goods per unit of foreign good makes U.S. consumers worse off. The ratio of U.S. goods exchanged to foreign goods received is called the gross barter terms of trade.

Some speculators are gambling on changes in currency prices. Perhaps the speculator who offered the car dealer 145 yen per dollar expects the price of yen to go to 160 yen per dollar. If the dealer can buy dollars at 145 yen per dollar and sell them at 160, there will be a profit of 15 yen on each dollar bought and sold.

The forward market in foreign exchange has been around for a long time. Since 1973, when most countries adopted floating exchange rates, the forward market has played an important role in encouraging foreign exchange by reducing risk.

PERSISTENT DISEQUILIBRIUM. If the price of currency is set by the government, it may not be a market-clearing price. If it isn't, there will be a persistent disequilibrium, that is, constant surpluses or shortages of foreign exchange. This situation is shown for the United States in Figure 2. The market shows a shortage of foreign exchange because the price of 40¢ per mark is too low for equilibrium. The quantity of marks demanded exceeds the quantity supplied by 50 million marks.

One way to deal with this problem is to change the price of the currency. Another way is to try to shift supply or demand for foreign exchange in order to make the curves intersect at the official price. A third possibility is for the government to ration foreign exchange. Finally, if the government has some foreign exchange reserves, it may draw on those reserves to meet the shortage, hoping that the shortage will eventually disappear of its own accord.

balance of payments deficit
An excess of a country's foreign spending over its foreign earnings for a given year.

A shortage of foreign exchange is equivalent to a balance of payments deficit. A **balance of payments deficit** is an excess of a country's foreign spending over its foreign earnings for a given year. In Figure 2, that difference amounts to 50 million marks. (At 2 marks per dollar, 50 million marks translates into $25 million.) A nation can instead have a balance of payments surplus (foreign earnings exceed foreign spending) or an equilibrium in foreign exchange (inflows and outflows are equal). Before exploring the various ways of dealing with disequilibrium, it would be helpful to know a little more about how such surpluses and deficits are measured. The source of that information is the balance of payments.

FIGURE 2
DISEQUILIBRIUM IN THE FOREIGN EXCHANGE MARKET
At 40¢ per mark, the quantity of foreign exchange demanded exceeds the quantity of foreign exchange supplied by 50 million marks. This gap between supply and demand corresponds to a balance of payments deficit.

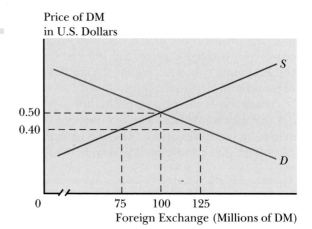

Price of DM in U.S. Dollars

Foreign Exchange (Millions of DM)

THE BALANCE OF PAYMENTS

The yearly summary of the transactions between residents of one country and residents of the rest of the world is that country's balance of payments. The **balance of payments** is an income statement—a summary of the flows of goods, services, and assets in and out of a country in a given year.

The balance of payments was a matter of great concern to the United States from 1945 to 1973. During that period, there was a fixed rate of exchange for the dollar, or a currency price set and maintained by the U.S. government. Every time the U.S. balance of payments was in deficit (which was most of the time), U.S. reserves fell, putting greater downward pressure on the price of the dollar. Since 1973, the balance of payments has been less important. However, it still provides several kinds of useful information. Table 1 presents a simplified summary of the U.S. balance of payments for 1990.

The pluses and minuses in the table have important meanings. A transaction that gives rise to a payment to the United States or a claim to future payment is entered with a plus sign. A transaction resulting in a payment by the United States or a claim for future payment is entered with a minus sign.

balance of payments
An annual summary of the transactions between residents of one country and residents of the rest of the world.

CURRENT ACCOUNT			
Merchandise exports	+389,286		
Service exports	+130,623		
Merchandise imports		−497,966	
Service imports		−107,699	
Investment income (net)	+7,533		
Unilateral transfers		−21,073	
Balance on current account			−99,296
CAPITAL ACCOUNT			
Changes in foreign private assets in the United States	+56,767		
Changes in U.S. private assets abroad		−62,063	
Changes in government assets other than reserves (net)		−33,749	
Balance on capital account			+28,453
STATISTICAL DISCREPANCY			+73,002
Overall balance			−2,159
SETTLEMENT ACCOUNT			
Changes in U.S. reserve assets	+9,151		
Changes in foreign official holdings of dollars	+47,516		
Balance in settlement account			+56,667

TABLE 1
U.S. BALANCE OF PAYMENTS, 1990 (MILLIONS OF DOLLARS)

Source: Adapted from U.S. Department of Commerce, *Survey of Current Business* (Washington, DC: U.S. Government Printing Office, March 1991).

COMPONENT ACCOUNTS

The balance of payments provides a lot of useful information. The sum of merchandise and service exports and imports (the balance of trade) indicates how competitive U.S. exports are compared to earlier years. The deficit in the balance of trade in the last decade has been a matter of great concern to policy makers. The buzzword "competitiveness" reflects concern for the big gap between U.S. exports and imports.

current account
The part of the balance of payments that summarizes transactions in currently produced goods and services.

The current account, which adds investment income and a few other items to the balance of trade, is roughly equivalent to the part of the national income accounts called net foreign investment. The **current account** is the part of the balance of payments that summarizes transactions in currently produced goods and services, including merchandise, services, investment income, and several smaller items. Note that in 1990 the United States had a large deficit for this account, reflecting an excess of imports over exports. From 1960 to 1971, the United States regularly had a surplus on this account. Prior to the 1980s, the largest deficits in the current account were $14 billion in 1977 and $15 billion in 1978. After some small surpluses in 1980 and 1981, the deficit in the current account reappeared and grew rapidly from $9 billion in 1982 to $46 billion in 1983, $117 billion in 1985, and $161 billion in 1987. These figures set off a wave of alarm about loss of U.S. competitiveness with foreign products. Part of the reason for the current account deficit, however, was the high price of the dollar. The price of the dollar was bid up in foreign exchange markets by a demand for dollars to invest in the United States. The value of the dollar began to fall, and, after a lag, there was some decline in the current account deficit beginning in 1988. The current account is linked to the capital account through changes in the market for the U.S. dollar. In 1990, the deficit fell to $99 billion, a decline of 38.5 percent from the 1987 high.

capital account
The part of the balance of payments that summarizes purchases and sales of financial assets.

The **capital account** is the part of the balance of payments that summarizes purchases and sales of financial assets, such as bonds, short-term debts, bank deposits, stocks, and foreign plants. This category showed a surplus in 1990, although the surplus was even larger a few years earlier when high U.S. interest rates attracted foreign capital. The figure of $57 billion in foreign private investment in the United States is enormous compared to past experience. The outflow of private U.S. investment of $62 billion is small compared to levels of investment abroad in previous years. This pattern of a large net inflow of foreign private capital has existed only in the last few years.

statistical discrepancy
The part of the balance of payments that reflects unrecorded transactions and inaccurate estimates of spending by tourists.

The category of statistical discrepancy is often rather large. The **statistical discrepancy** is the part of the balance of payments that reflects unrecorded transactions (such as workers' remittances, smuggling, and other illegal activities) and inaccurate estimates of spending by U.S. tourists abroad or by foreign tourists in the United States. There is a good reason for this entry. Balance of payments accountants do not have perfect information. When the discrepancy is large, as it was in the 1980s, it is believed to consist mainly of unrecorded bank deposits. Thus, a negative statistical discrepancy suggests additional (unrecorded) capital inflows.

SURPLUSES, DEFICITS, AND SETTLEMENT ACCOUNT

The sum of the current account, the capital account, and the statistical discrepancy is the surplus or deficit in the balance of payments. In 1990, there was a deficit of about $2 billion. At 1990 exchange rates, the demand for foreign exchange in the United States exceeded the supply of foreign exchange by about $2 billion. That figure is not large relative to some of the other sums in the accounts. A moderate balance in the settlement account and a corresponding moderate surplus or deficit in the other three accounts is normal even under a floating exchange rate. When the price of currency is allowed to adjust to clear the foreign exchange market, the small surplus or deficit at the end of the year reflects the fact that the market is moving toward equilibrium but hasn't arrived there. Under a fixed exchange rate, surpluses or deficits would be larger, reflecting the fact that when price is not allowed to adjust, a disequilibrium (surplus or deficit) can be large and persistent.

The **settlement account** is the part of the balance of payments that explains how a deficit or surplus was financed. In 1990, the deficit was settled by selling foreign exchange in the amount of about $2 billion. The Federal Reserve watches changes in foreign exchange reserves closely because they are a component of the monetary base and can affect the size of the U.S. money supply.

settlement account
The part of the balance of payments that explains how a deficit or surplus was financed.

Under the present system of floating exchange rates, persistent surpluses or deficits suggest that the price of a country's currency is likely to rise or fall. Under floating rates, a market-determined rise in the price is called **appreciation**, and a market-determined fall is called **depreciation**.

Although the United States and most major industrial countries allow their currency prices to float, many other countries maintain a fixed price for their currencies. However, a floating rate can be either clean or, more commonly, dirty. A clean float means that there is no government intervention to influence the currency's price. A dirty float implies some government involvement in the market to limit fluctuations. This activity has been common in recent years.

appreciation
A rise in the market price of a currency due to market forces.

depreciation
A fall in the market price of a currency due to market forces.

INTERNATIONAL MONETARY SYSTEMS

Although most industrial countries have floating rates, four different international monetary systems have been tried in the past. Two of them, exchange control and floating rates, continue to be used by most countries. Some economists and policy makers advocate a return to one of the other two systems, the gold standard or the Bretton Woods system. No discussion of international finance would be complete without considering these four alternatives.

Consider what goals an international monetary system might be designed to achieve. Many traders and bankers prefer fixed or at least stable exchange rates. Stable rates reduce much of the uncertainty and the need for hedging in international transactions, making foreign trade more like domestic trade. Another goal that has widespread support is freedom of trade and capital movement, so nations can enjoy the benefits of specialization and trade. Still another goal that many countries want is freedom in domestic monetary and fiscal policy. If the government feels a need to fight recession or contain inflation, it should be free to do so without having to worry about the effects of its policies on the balance of payments or international transactions. Finally, a satisfactory system ensures equi-

In Dyersville, Iowa, a baseball field was built for the set of the 1989 movie *Field of Dreams*. The baseball field was carved out of a cornfield owned by farmer Don Lansing. It is beautifully groomed and maintained. *Field of Dreams* was a box office smash in baseball-crazy Japan. As a result of the movie's success, a Japanese tour operator began to include Dyersville, Iowa in one of its tours. Lansing hasn't (yet) started charging tourists to see the ball park, but he took donations from the more than 8,500 Japanese who visited in the first twelve months after the tour began to include his farm. Lansing hasn't made so much that he has give up farming, but his experience is an indication that foreign tourism is becoming big business in the United States.

Until very recently, American spending on foreign tourism was greater than foreign spending on tourism in the United States. The balance of tourism trade was positive in 1989, for the first time since the U.S. Department of Commerce started keeping records on tourism. In other words, the United States became a net exporter of tourism for the first time in 1989, when 39 million foreign tourists spent $44 billion in the United States. This total was $1.2 billion more than U.S. tourists spent in foreign countries in

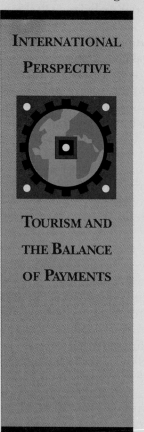

INTERNATIONAL PERSPECTIVE

TOURISM AND THE BALANCE OF PAYMENTS

that year. As recently as 1985, the United States had a $9 billion deficit in the tourism account. Foreign tourism continues to grow. The number of foreign tourists visiting the United States in 1995 is projected to be four times the number who came in 1985.

Most foreign tourists in the United States (65 percent in 1989), come from Mexico and Canada. However, Japanese tourists account for much of the spending surplus. Although Japanese tourists represent only 8 percent of the foreign tourists visiting the United States, they are big spenders, accounting for 19 percent of tourists' spending. It appears that Americans are buying Japanese autos and selling Japanese tourists greens fees on golf courses and shopping sprees in fancy boutiques in exchange.

Most foreign tourists in the United States follow the same pattern that Americans do when they go abroad for the first time. They go to major cities. As a result, New York, San Francisco, Los Angeles, and Miami are big draws for foreign tourists. Orlando, home of Disney World, is a close fifth. After foreign tourists have seen the cities, they tend to concentrate on the West. Perhaps all those Western movies are now paying off in tourist dollars!

Source: Evan McGlinn, "Good News for the Balance of Payments," *Forbes* (25 June 1990): 36–38.

librium in the balance of payments. The system should have some way of correcting deficits and surpluses. The various international monetary systems attain these goals in different degrees.

THE GOLD STANDARD

From the late nineteenth century until the 1930s, most industrial countries were on the gold standard. The **gold standard** was an international monetary system in which currencies were defined in terms of gold, money supplies were tied to gold, and balance of payment deficits were settled in gold. Gold served as money in most of the world for centuries. Thus, gold was a logical choice for settling accounts between countries with different national currencies. A country on the gold standard was supposed to observe three rules:

1. To define the value of its currency in terms of gold content. Under the gold standard, the dollar price of an ounce of gold was $20.67 from 1837 to 1934, and the price of gold in British pounds was £4.25. The price of each currency in gold automatically determined the exchange rates between the two countries. The British pound was worth $4.86 ($20.67 divided by £4.25).
2. To have its money supply consist of gold or be tied to the gold stock in some fixed ratio. For example, the ratio of gold to currency in the United States was 1:4 in the nineteenth century. The nation's supply of currency could not exceed four times its gold stock. The money supply could be less than the maximum, however.
3. To require its central bank or monetary authority to buy gold from anyone or to sell gold to anyone at the official price.

CORRECTING DEFICITS AND SURPLUSES. These rules, if followed, automatically corrected deficits and surpluses in the balance of payments. When there was a deficit (surplus of U.S. dollars offered for foreign exchange), the price of foreign exchange would tend to rise. As the dollar price of foreign exchange started to rise, U.S. citizens would find that they could get more pounds or francs per dollar by exchanging their dollars for gold at the Fed, shipping the gold abroad, and exchanging it there for pounds or francs. As gold flowed out of the country, the U.S. money supply would shrink, and prices and output would fall.

When prices fall in the United States, exports rise and imports fall. There is a shift in demand and supply for foreign exchange. Foreigners supply more of their currencies to buy more of relatively cheaper U.S. exports. At the same time, U.S. citizens demand less foreign exchange because they want to buy less of other countries' relatively more expensive products. Also, as U.S. output and national income fall, Americans buy less of everything, including imports.

Figure 3 shows these effects. Again, German marks (DM) represent all foreign currencies. The official price of the mark is 40¢, and the cost of shipping 1 mark's worth of gold is 5¢. In a free market, the equilibrium price of the mark would be 50¢. Because the United States is on the gold standard, the price of foreign exchange cannot rise above the official price plus the cost of shipping the gold to Germany. Thus, at the maxi-

gold standard
An international monetary system in which currencies were defined in terms of gold, money supplies were tied to gold, and balance of payment deficits were settled in gold.

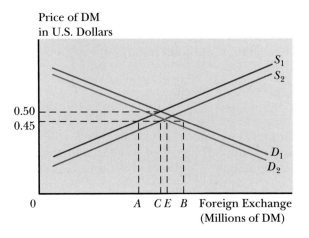

FIGURE 3
AUTOMATIC ADJUSTMENT
UNDER THE GOLD
STANDARD
At 45¢ per mark, gold
flows out of the country
to cover the deficit
$B - A$. The gold outflow
shrinks the money supply,
reducing income and
prices. Lower income and
prices reduce demand for
imports (from D_1 to D_2)
and increase the supply
of foreign currency to
buy U.S. exports (from S_1
to S_2). The deficit shrinks
from $B - A$ to $E - C$.

mum price of 45¢, amount $B - A$ of gold flows out of the United States.
That outflow shrinks the U.S. money supply, lowering national income
and the price level and shifting supply and demand for foreign exchange
to S_2 and D_2. The deficit falls to $E - C$. This process of gold flows and
shifts in supply and demand continues until the official price is restored
and the deficit is eliminated.

The effects of the gold flow are reinforced by events in the other country into which gold is flowing. The other country's money supply expands,
raising income and prices and further shifting supply and demand in the
correct direction. This automatic correction of deficits and surpluses, recognized in the early eighteenth century by David Hume, is called the
specie flow mechanism. (Specie refers to coined money with a commodity value, such as gold or silver.)

specie flow mechanism
The automatic correction
of deficits and surpluses
in the balance of pay-
ments through the effects
of gold flows on money
supplies.

HISTORICAL EXPERIENCE. The gold standard worked fairly well in the late
nineteenth and early twentieth centuries. Numerous discoveries of gold
in California, Colorado, Alaska, Canada, and South Africa provided an adequate supply of gold for stock. The gold standard meant that governments could not control their money supplies, but nineteenth-century
governments didn't pursue an active monetary policy anyway. There were
few major disturbances, such as wars and revolutions, that might have
caused shifts in supply and demand so great that they would have been
difficult and painful to correct.

World War I marked the end of the gold standard, although some
countries (including the United States) remained on it until the 1930s.
The gold standard's main attractions were fixed exchange rates and automatic correction. The slow growth in the supply of gold in the twentieth century and the gold standard's restrictions on monetary policy were
serious problems that could not be resolved.

The gold standard achieved three of the four goals of an international

The idea of returning to the gold standard has never died. It just went underground, surfacing as regularly as the groundhog every February. Although the Reagan administration never officially endorsed returning to the gold standard, some of Reagan's financial advisers were inclined in that direction. Jude Wanniski, in a popular book on supply side economics, *The Way the World Works*, argued very strongly for a return to the gold standard.[a]

Why does this idea keep returning? In part, it is because gold seems to offer a degree of certainty that paper money does not. When governments have gone down in revolutionary flames, new governments have usually restored faith in the currency by tying it to gold. When refugees leave countries in turmoil, the safest way to transport their wealth is in the form of gold. Fifty years after the gold standard was abandoned, some people still think of gold as the only universal money.

Gold buffs, however, are not sentimental. Most of them are hard-headed profit seekers. Many invested in gold as its price made its dramatic rise from $35 an ounce in 1967 (the official price, maintained by central banks) to over $1,000 an ounce in the mid-1970s in a free market. (Some also had the foresight to get out of gold before its price dropped sharply to under $400 an ounce in the early 1980s.) They didn't invest because of the demand for gold to use for jewelry and dental work. They invested because gold was, is, and probably always will be considered money by a substantial part of the world. The gold buffs would like gold to be *the* money of the world again in the same way it was in earlier centuries.

ECONOMIC
INSIGHT

THE GOLD BUFFS

Gold buffs usually want to return to the gold standard because they do not trust the government to control the money supply. They would rather have the money supply determined by the impersonal forces of the marketplace and the supply of monetary gold. Give governments the freedom to print money, they argue, and political pressures will sooner or later run up the money supply and the price level.

One argument offered against returning to the gold standard is that the chief advantage of gold is also its chief disadvantage. No one can control the supply of gold. Big discoveries can cause inflation and have done so in the past. Very slow growth of the gold supply relative to growth of output and population can lead to deflation, which can be very painful. Gold buffs argue that at $400 an ounce, the supply is much greater than it was fifty years ago, because an ounce now represents much more money and because there is more incentive to mine gold at the higher price. They admit, however, that it would be necessary to fix the price of gold. Over time, that fixed rate would fail to encourage more gold mining as the cost of finding and retrieving gold increases.

The main reason why gold buffs are unlikely to get their way is that governments don't like to tie their own hands. Returning to the gold standard would mean giving up any sort of stabilization policy. No elected government is going to be willing to give up that option. The argument will go on, but as nations adapt to floating rates, the likelihood of going back on the gold standard gets smaller and smaller each year.

a.   Jude Wanniski, *The Way the World Works* (New York: Basic Books, 1981).

monetary system: stable exchange rates, freedom of trade and capital movement, and balance of payments equilibrium. It sacrificed independent monetary and fiscal policy. If the money supply is controlled by gold flows, little discretion is left to the monetary authority to use the money supply to change the levels of output, employment, and prices. This drawback, combined with the problem of ensuring an adequate gold supply, makes a return to the gold standard very unlikely.

BRETTON WOODS SYSTEM

Bretton Woods system
The international monetary system in effect from 1945 to 1973, based on infrequent changes in currency prices, ample reserves, and the dollar as key currency.

From 1945 to 1973, international monetary arrangements were governed by the **Bretton Woods system**, named for the small New Hampshire town where delegates from major countries met to create a new international monetary system. The Bretton Woods system had some of the characteristics of the gold standard and some of the advantages of floating rates.

OPERATING RULES. Under the Bretton Woods system, a country defined a par value for its currency in terms of gold. The government was then obliged to keep its currency price within 1 percent of that par value.[4] Central banks bought and sold their countries' currencies in exchange for gold, dollars, or other foreign currencies in order to maintain the currency's price at par value.

The Bretton Woods system differed from the gold standard in that there was no connection between gold, deficits, and the money supply. Countries could pursue independent monetary policies instead of linking their money supply to their holdings of gold. Since there was no automatic correction for deficits and surpluses, a balance of payments disequilibrium might last indefinitely. Because of this problem, the designers of the Bretton Woods system created a pool of **international monetary reserves**, or funds that countries could borrow to settle deficits and repay when they ran surpluses. Reserves consisted of gold, dollars, and other currencies. These reserves were kept at a newly created institution, the International Monetary Fund (IMF). The **International Monetary Fund (IMF)** was the agency that supervised the operation of the Bretton Woods system by recording par values, consulting on devaluations and revaluations, and maintaining a pool of reserves.

international monetary reserves
The pool of gold and major currencies created under the Bretton Woods system, from which countries could borrow to settle deficits and replenish from surpluses.

International Monetary Fund (IMF)
The agency that supervised the operation of the Bretton Woods system by recording par values, consulting on devaluations and revaluations, and maintaining a pool of reserves.

What happened if a country kept running deficits and borrowing from the IMF? The pool of reserves was not intended to sustain deficits forever—just long enough for the situation to get back to normal. If a disequilibrium continued, the Bretton Woods system had a second method for coping with deficits (or surpluses). A country with a persistent deficit could change the currency's price, or the exchange rate. Thus, the Bretton Woods system did not mandate unchangeable currency prices, a central feature of the gold standard. In this respect, the Bretton Woods system was more like floating rates, except that currency prices changed infrequently by large amounts instead of frequently by small amounts.

---

4. The Bretton Woods system, like the gold standard, had both a floor and a ceiling price for each currency. Under the gold standard, the floor and ceiling prices were determined by the cost of shipping gold. Under the Bretton Woods system, the floor and ceiling prices were arbitrarily set at 1 percent above and below the official price.

WHY THE BRETTON WOODS SYSTEM FAILED. The key to the failure of Bretton Woods system lay in the difficulty of finding enough reserves. Since there was not enough gold, the next choice was the U.S. dollar, for two reasons. First, at the end of World War II, the United States had two-thirds of the world's monetary gold stock and was the only nation willing to redeem its currency in gold. Second, the United States dominated world trade as the biggest supplier and the biggest customer. Because dollars were so popular and so useful, they were even used to make payments when no U.S. citizens or firms were involved. A currency that serves as a major reserve asset and is used in transactions between third-party nations is called a **key currency**. The dollar, as the most popular key currency, joined gold as the second major form of international reserves.

> **key currency**
> A currency that serves as a major reserve asset and is used in transactions between third-party nations.

Unfortunately, since the Bretton Woods system provided for no built-in corrections, deficits became large and persistent for many countries. Demand for reserves grew rapidly. The United States obliged by creating reserves. To create reserves, the United States ran deficits. The bigger and more frequent these deficits were, the more reserves were created. But the more dollars that were outstanding, the less likely it became that the United States would be able to redeem them from its dwindling gold stock. It became more likely that a devaluation of the dollar would be necessary to correct the deficits. No one wanted to be holding dollars when they were devalued, because of the financial loss. The pending crisis came to a head in 1971, when foreigners started turning in dollars for gold. The United States was forced to suspend the redemption of dollars for gold in August 1971—an event known as the "closing of the gold window." In December 1971, the dollar was devalued by about 8 percent, raising the dollar price of gold from $35 to $38. In February 1973, the dollar was devalued again, raising the dollar price of gold to $42. After the second devaluation, the United States and its major trading partners all switched to floating rates.

The Bretton Woods system was an attempt to have the best of all possible worlds. Nations wanted stable exchange rates, independent monetary policy, and free trade. The Bretton Woods system sacrificed balance of payments equilibrium. The failure of Bretton Woods reminded policy makers that there must be some mechanism to deal with deficits. Once the nations of the world recognized that problem, Bretton Woods could not survive.

FLOATING EXCHANGE RATES

A system of floating exchange rates represents a pure market approach to foreign exchange, in which any shift in supply or demand will change the price of a currency. This system had been tried by some countries, such as Canada, but was not widely adopted until 1973. In February 1973, the United States totally abandoned its commitment to fixed exchange rates. Japan quickly followed suit and allowed the yen to float against the dollar. Within a month, the finance ministers of the European Economic Community announced that they would allow their currencies to float. Most major industrial countries have had floating exchange rates since 1973. Figure 4 shows that the price of the U.S. dollar has fluctuated a great deal under floating rates.

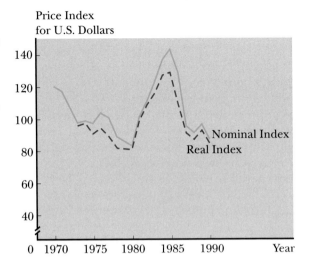

FIGURE 4
THE RISE AND FALL OF THE U.S. DOLLAR
The dollar was devalued in 1971 and again in early 1973. Beginning in 1973, the dollar has floated. Its value has fluctuated in both nominal terms (solid line) and real terms (dashed line—corrected for price level changes) against currencies of the major trading partners of the United States.

Floating exchange rates work on the basic principles of supply and demand. Floating rates support all of the suggested goals for an international monetary system except stable exchange rates. If exchange rate adjustments clear the market, then the balance of payments should always be at or near equilibrium. Thus, there will be no need to shift the curves to intersect at a fixed price or to use restrictions in order to make international payments balance.

When countries first began to use floating exchange rates, there was widespread fear that the volume of trade would shrink because exchange rates would be very unstable. Although exchange rates have been unstable, well-developed forward markets have ensured that this instability does not discourage international trade. One serious problem has been that when a currency's exchange rate falls, it often falls below its ultimate equilibrium before rising back to that equilibrium. In the interim, the exchange rate is still incorrect but it is too low instead of too high. During this time, price signals to importers, exporters, consumers, and producers are distorted. Decisions are made that would not be profit-maximizing at the correct exchange rate.

Floating rates have not resulted in balance of payments equilibrium. Why? Part of the problem is measurement, but another part reflects a basic truth about market equilibrium. Equilibrium is never where the market is, but rather the direction in which it is headed. If supply and demand shift often, the market may always be in the process of moving from one equilibrium to another. However, deficits and surpluses generally have been much smaller under floating rates than they were under fixed rates.[5] In fact, the floating rate system has worked fairly well during severe shocks (major supply and demand shifts), such as the OPEC oil price hike that created large deficits and surpluses and the 1981–1982 recession.

The floating rate system established in 1973 is not a completely free

---

5.   The United States has had large deficits in its balance of trade in recent years, but those have been largely offset by inflows of foreign capital.

market in practice. Governments continue to intervene in the market, buying and selling their own currency to limit swings in the price. Countries have not allowed the market alone to determine exchange rates, but they are closer to doing so than ever in the past. Although there is still some unhappiness with floating rates, there is little pressure to return to a fixed rate system. Many government officials are reluctant to go back on the gold standard or to return to the Bretton Woods system because both would limit their flexibility of action.

EXCHANGE CONTROL

The last international monetary system, exchange control, is used by most less developed countries and sometimes by major industrial nations. **Exchange control** means that a country's government requires all earnings of foreign exchange to be turned over to it and then sells the foreign currencies to those who want to import, travel abroad, or invest in other countries.

> **exchange control**
> A system in which the government purchases all incoming foreign exchange and is the only source from which foreign exchange can be legally purchased.

Usually, a country adopts exchange control because the currency price is too high and the country doesn't want to change it. Without exchange control, the balance of payments would be in deficit. Typically, the country that uses exchange control has limited reserves and little international credit. By insisting that everyone turn in their foreign currency to the government, which then sells it, the country can make its balance of payments accounts balance.

Exchange control accomplishes three of the goals cited earlier: stable exchange rates, independent monetary and fiscal policy, and no apparent deficit in the balance of payments. However, free trade is sacrificed. In addition, black markets almost always exist. People make side deals in foreign exchange in order to bypass the government. Bribery, smuggling, and falsified reporting of earnings from exports and the cost of imports are regular events in countries with exchange control.

However, exchange control can accomplish other objectives. Often there are multiple exchange rates—different rates for buying, selling, and different uses. Suppose the government wants to encourage factory construction and discourage luxuries. It can charge a low price for foreign exchange to people who want to import machinery and a high price to those who want to buy air conditioners and yachts. Thus, the government can promote specific consumption and production goals. Also, the government can gain revenue for public purposes by buying foreign currencies at a low price and selling them at a higher price.

In some countries, such as China, exchange control involves two kinds of currency. One is used solely by foreigners, such as tourists and approved traders, and the other is used by ordinary citizens. Some stores and service institutions, such as hotels, accept only the first kind. In this way, the government can closely control the use of foreign exchange, deciding who buys imports and who gets the currency that foreigners spend in the country. With this type of exchange control, black markets are less likely, because the country's citizens are not allowed to hold exchangeable currency.

Some degree of exchange control is practiced by all but a few industrialized countries. Total or partial exchange control can coexist with ei-

One problem of a floating rate system is the difficulty of measuring changes in the price of one currency when others are moving around at the same time. If the price of the dollar is measured in French francs instead of Japanese yen, the picture of what is happening to the dollar may look very different.

One way to obtain a consistent measure of a currency's price is to use special drawing rights (SDRs). These drawing rights are issued by the International Monetary Fund and are only exchanged among central banks. One SDR equaled one U.S. dollar before the 1971 devaluation. This international "currency" provides a constant measuring rod. In the table titled "Currency Units per U.S. Dollar," for example, are the prices of the dollar in March 1977 and February 1991, measured in francs, yen, and SDRs. The SDR price is the most accurate reflection of changes in the price of the dollar because it is the only constant measuring rod. The dollar rose relative to the franc and fell sharply with respect to the yen. The dollar also fell when measured in SDRs. (Note from Figure 4, however, that there were some sharp ups and downs in the interim.)

INTERNATIONAL

PERSPECTIVE

WATCHING

CURRENCIES

UNDER

FLOATING RATES

Measured in SDRs, the dollar and most other currencies have had a lively market since 1973. After the first devaluation (in December 1971), the dollar was worth 0.92105 SDRs. After the second devaluation (in February 1973), the dollar dropped to 0.82895 SDRs. During the ups and downs that followed, the dollar hit a low of 0.74141 SDRs—more than 25 percent below its 1971 price. It rebounded sharply to a high of 1.035 SDRs in 1985 before dropping back to 0.7039 SDRs in February 1991.

Other currencies have seen equally dramatic shifts in prices. The table titled "Currency Units per SDR" gives the high and low values since 1975 for five major currencies. Daily rates (including forward prices) are published in most major newspapers. Long-term trends can be followed in *International Financial Statistics*, a monthly publication of the International Monetary Fund (and the source of these exchange rate figures). Importers, exporters, foreign exchange dealers, lenders, and multinational corporations all follow these figures carefully to make decisions about what to trade, when to trade, and at what price.

CURRENCY UNITS PER U.S. DOLLAR

	MARCH 1977	FEBRUARY 1991	PERCENT CHANGE
French franc	4.9780	5.1770	+3.9
Japanese yen	282.7000	132.0000	−53.3
SDRs	0.8639	0.7039	−18.5

CURRENCY UNITS PER SDR

CURRENCY	1971 VALUE	LOW VALUE (DATE)	HIGH VALUE (DATE)
U.K. pound sterling	0.4250	0.8476 (1984)	0.4250 (1975)
French franc	5.6718	9.4022 (1984)	5.2510 (1985)
Canadian dollar	1.0809	1.6703 (1990)	1.1725 (1975)
German mark	3.5481	3.0857 (1984)	2.1378 (1991)
Japanese yen	341.7800	368.4700 (1974)	175.2000 (1987)

ther a fixed rate or a managed float, although fixed rates are more common. The major industrial countries have adopted floating rates, but the majority of nations do not have floating currencies. Most countries still maintain a fixed exchange rate or "peg" their currency to a major currency. For example, many former French colonies in Africa keep a fixed relationship between the price of their currency and the French franc. Since France is still their major trading partner, this link creates a fixed exchange rate for most of their transactions. If the price of the franc falls 10 percent relative to the dollar, the price of a currency pegged to the franc will also fall by 10 percent relative to the dollar. The pegged currency will still have the same relationship to the franc.

A combination of floating rates, managed floats, exchange control, fixed rates, and pegged rates make up the hodgepodge international monetary system of the 1990s. It will be interesting to see how the Soviet Union and the countries of Eastern Europe manage their currency prices as they move from planned economies to market systems.

Summary

1. Unique features of the foreign exchange market are the forward market, government price setting, and effects on important macroeconomic variables.

2. U.S. demand for foreign exchange reflects demand for foreign goods, services, and financial assets. The supply of foreign exchange reflects foreigners' desire to buy U.S. exports of goods and services and/or U.S. financial assets.

3. Surpluses and shortages in the market for foreign exchange are equivalent to surpluses and deficits in the balance of payments.

4. Shifts in supply and demand for foreign exchange result from changes in relative prices, incomes, interest rates, tastes, population, technology, and input cost and availability.

5. The forward market reduces the risk connected with changing currency prices.

6. Disequilibrium often persists in the foreign exchange market. Ways in which government can deal with this disequilibrium include changing the currency's price, shifting the supply and demand curves, rationing, and drawing on reserves.

7. The balance of payments is a summary of transactions between U.S. residents and foreigners. It is divided into four accounts: the current account, the capital account, the statistical discrepancy, and the settlement account. The sum of the first three is the deficit or surplus. The settlement account explains how the deficit or surplus was financed.

8. The gold standard relied on movements of gold to settle deficits. Gold flows changed money supplies, affecting prices and income and shifting supply and demand for currency.

9. The Bretton Woods system was established in 1945 to provide some stability in exchange rates. It relied on reserves to settle deficits. It broke down because it was too dependent on a single currency—the dollar—which could not be devalued.

10. Floating exchange rates, determined in the market, have been widely used since 1973.

11. Under exchange control, all sales and purchases of foreign exchange pass through the government. Many less developed countries use exchange control. Usually, black markets in currency develop under this system.

New Terms

foreign exchange market	balance of payments	depreciation	International Monetary
forward market	current account	gold standard	Fund (IMF)
hedgers	capital account	specie flow mechanism	key currency
speculators	statistical discrepancy	Bretton Woods system	exchange control
balance of payments	settlement account	international monetary	
deficit	appreciation	reserves	

QUESTIONS FOR DISCUSSION

1. Look up the balance of payments for the United States for the last year in the *Federal Reserve Bulletin.* See if you can put it into the simplified format of Table 1 and calculate the surplus or deficit. How has it changed in the last few years?

2. What might shift a country from equilibrium into a deficit in its balance of payments? How would the deficit be dealt with under each of the four international monetary systems—the gold standard, the Bretton Woods system, floating exchange rates, and exchange control?

3. Why is the forward market especially important with floating exchange rates?

4. How do changes in prices and incomes in one country affect the supply and demand for its currency? What about changes in prices and incomes in other countries?

5. Why do some people want to return to the gold standard? What drawbacks does the gold standard have?

6. If interest rates rise in the United States, what happens to the supply, demand, and price of the dollar? Why? How might this affect U.S. exports and imports of goods and services?

7. In what part of the U.S. balance of payments (Table 1) would each of the following transactions be incorporated?

a.   Sale of tractors to Poland

b.   Gift of tractors to Mexico

c.   U.S. citizen's purchase of a restaurant meal in Canada

d.   British resident's purchase of U.S. government bonds

8. How does a recession in one country affect economic conditions in another country?

9. The ways of dealing with a disequilibrium in the foreign exchange market are to change the currency's price, ration, shift the supply and demand curves into equilibrium at that price, or draw on or accumulate reserves. Identify the international monetary system that uses each of these as its primary way to deal with disequilibrium.

10. Why is there a statistical discrepancy in the balance of payments?

11. Do floating exchange rates do away with a country's need to maintain reserves?

12. How would you describe the current international monetary system? How did it evolve?

13. Stories in the press often draw attention to the fact that the balance of trade between the U.S. and Japan is in deficit. In itself, is this bilateral deficit a meaningful number?

14. How would each of the following be likely to affect supply or demand for the U.S. dollar? What should happen to its price?

a.   A recession in Japan, Canada, and Western Europe, the major trading partners of the United States

b.   A fall in the U.S. interest rate relative to that in the rest of the world

c.   More rapid inflation in the United States than in the rest of the world

d.   An export boom in U.S. movies and television shows

15. Graph the foreign exchange market for the zloty, the currency of Poland, to indicate an equilibrium price of 20¢ and an equilibrium quantity of 50 million. Is there a surplus or a shortage at prices of 40¢ and 10¢?

SUGGESTIONS FOR FURTHER READING

Melamed, Leo (ed.). *The Merits of Flexible Exchange Rates: An Anthology.* Fairfax, VA: George Mason University Press, 1988. A collection of articles by eminent economists in support of flexible exchange rates.

Pool, John Charles, and Steve Stamos. *The ABCs of International Finance.* Lexington, MA: Lexington Books, 1987. A simple, nontechnical discussion of current international finance issues, emphasizing the evolution of the international monetary system and the problems of debtor nations, including the United States.

Root, Franklin R. *International Trade and Investment,* 6th ed. Cincinnati: South-Western, 1990. An intermediate textbook on international trade and international finance.

Yeager, Leland B. *International Monetary Relations: Theory, History, and Policy.* New York: Harper & Row, 1976. A classic reference on international finance with a solid treatment of history and policy.

1. Define:
   a. capitalism,
   b. socialism,
   c. communism,
   d. fascism.
2. Contrast socialism and capitalism.
3. Describe the major features of and the differences in the economic systems of:
   a. the Soviet Union,
   b. the People's Republic of China,
   c. Cuba,
   d. Yugoslavia,
   e. Great Britain.
4. Define:
   a. input coefficients,
   b. shadow prices,
   c. the socialist controversy,
   d. the competitive solution.
5. Discuss prospects for economic reform in China, Eastern Europe, and the Soviet Republics.
6. Identify the unique characteristics of the Japanese economy.

CHAPTER 36

COMPARATIVE ECONOMIC SYSTEMS IN THEORY AND PRACTICE

INTRODUCTION

The past few years have seen staggering and revolutionary changes in the world. Political and economic reform has been the order of the day in much of the Communist world. Indeed, many writers now use the words "formerly Communist" when referring to some of the countries of Eastern Europe and the Soviet Union. Few would have thought that on November 17, 1989, Berliners from both sides would be dancing on the Berlin Wall as it came tumbling down, while the East German guards watched. A week earlier, getting close to the east side of the wall would have probably meant death.

This chapter will examine the events of the recent past and speculate on what might occur as these economic and political changes mature. There is much uncertainty surrounding these reforms. The introduction of markets and market mechanisms means choice and uncertainty in countries where security and sameness ruled. To some individuals, this choice and uncertainty will be very unsettling.

To begin, it is important to define some basic differences in economic systems. People often discuss other economic systems without really knowing how to define such terms as capitalism, socialism, and communism. What are the key differences among these systems, and to what degree do these differences affect economic outcomes? Chapter 2 stated that all economic systems are mixed systems and that economic theory can be used to analyze any economic system. That statement was valid because the concepts of opportunity cost, the law of demand, the principle of diminishing returns, specialization, exchange, efficiency, and self-interest do not differ from country to country. Competing ideologies may respond to these concepts differently, but no ideology can eliminate their impact on economic life.

You might ask, if the economics you have learned is good for all systems, why include a chapter on comparative systems? The answer is that politics, cultures, and ideology mix with economics to create widely differing economic-political systems. These different mixes will be important as the various countries of Eastern Europe pursue reform. It is therefore necessary to examine the way economics works in different political and historical settings.

To introduce the subject of comparative economics, we will begin with an attempt to define ideological systems. We will then examine some of the different forms of communism as well as recent changes in a number of countries. Next, we will present a decision-making approach to the analysis of differing systems and discuss advantages and disadvantages of economic planning. Finally, we will examine reform movements in China and the Soviet Union and outline the unique features of the Japanese form of capitalism.

IDEOLOGIES

Chapter 2 divided economic systems into three major groups, labeled traditional, planned, and market. The field of comparative economics subdivides the last two categories, which include all modern industrial economies, in order to classify economies more precisely. A very common approach, and perhaps the oldest, is to classify economic systems according to two criteria: the underlying political philosophy, and the ownership of the factors of production. This might be called the *isms* approach because it concentrates on four major political philosophies: capitalism, socialism, communism, and fascism.

Even this approach oversimplifies the diversity that exists in economic systems. There are numerous economic systems in the world. The term *capitalism* is often applied to the economic systems found in Western democracies, but there are significant differences among economic institutions in the United States, Great Britain, France, and Sweden. Similarly, the economic systems in Eastern Europe and the Soviet Union were labeled communist before the reforms began, but there were important differences in the institutions of the Soviet Union, Yugoslavia, and Romania. This complexity makes it difficult to separate the critical elements of the four basic economic systems. Economists must identify the differences in institutions and then determine if these differences are the reasons for differing economic behavior. The most important factor distinguishing the four *isms* is in the ownership of the factors of production.

CAPITALISM

capitalism
An economic system characterized by private ownership of the factors of production by individuals or groups of individuals.

Capitalism is an economic system characterized by private ownership of the factors of production by individuals or groups of individuals. In pure capitalism, these individuals would be free to use their property as they see fit. Any limitations on the use of the property diminish its value to the owner. Private property holders are at the center of the decision-making process in capitalism.

A system based on private ownership is one in which individuals maximize their own well-being, in terms of either profit or utility. The term *capitalism* is interpreted very broadly to allow for a great deal of government intervention, as long as the primacy of private ownership is retained. It is therefore possible for systems as divergent as the U.S. economy and the British economy to be labeled capitalist.

SOCIALISM

Under a system of **socialism**, the nonhuman means of production are owned by society or the state. Socialism has its theoretical roots in the work of Marx and its real-world roots in various twentieth-century revolutions and their leaders. Socialism shifts the decision-making authority from individual entrepreneurs to a central authority. This central authority makes the major economic decisions. Utopian socialists see this central authority as promoting the "common good," usually greater equality and/or economic development. Critics of socialism point out that this authority may develop into a centralist, personal dictatorship, such as that of Stalin in the Soviet Union or Nicolae Ceausescu in Romania. Fidel Castro of Cuba is a living example of this tendency.

Like capitalism, socialism comes in many forms. There is utopian socialism, such as the Fourier movement in the United States in the early to mid-nineteenth century. Utopian socialists established communes with shared possessions and cooperative labor. Other variations, such as the Social Democratic parties in Western Europe, have become forceful political movements. For instance, François Mitterand, a socialist, was elected president of France in 1981 and 1988. Because the term *socialism* is used to describe a great variety of people and ideas, it is almost meaningless to label someone a socialist or a set of institutions socialistic.

> **socialism**
> An economic system in which the nonhuman means of production are owned by society or the state.

COMMUNISM

To Karl Marx, **communism** was the final stage of the progression from capitalism, with socialism representing the middle stage. Under communism, Marx foresaw the end of scarcity, the end of conflict among the classes, and the creation of a new social order. An ideal member of this new order would no longer be the self-interested individual on which most economic analysis is based. The true communist would put the interest of the larger community above personal self-interest. In the final stage, individuals would receive goods and services according to their needs, and the state would wither away until all it did was administer the economy. The organizational structure that Marx foresaw under communism is not at all clear. Presumably everyone would contribute labor in exchange for goods and services needed. One major problem is how those needs would be defined and determined. A second problem is the motivation that would drive the system and create incentives. In the absence of self-interest, the motivation would have to lie in the development of this new economic order.

> **communism**
> The final stage in the theory of Karl Marx, in which the state has withered away and economic goods are equally distributed.

FASCISM

In the countries that have practiced **fascism** (which include Spain, Portugal, Germany, and Italy), monopoly capitalism and private property were combined with a strong authoritarian central government headed

> **fascism**
> An economic system that combines monopoly, capitalism, private property, and a strong authoritarian central government.

Political-legal developments in China, Hong Kong, and Taiwan and economic comparisons among them demonstrate much about capitalism and socialism. The varying levels of economic development invite comparison because the areas are similar in many ways, including culture. The essential differences are political and economic.

In 1997, the 100-year lease that the British have for Hong Kong expires, and the territory reverts to Chinese rule. This change is expected to have a profound effect on Hong Kong. There are virtually no government impediments to doing business in Hong Kong. A corporation can be started for a fee of only $250, and there are no reporting requirements. Hong Kong has no currency exchange controls, no tariffs, and no quotas. The entrepreneurs in this prosperous capitalist state are casting a wary eye on 1997 and the arrival of the Communist Chinese. In 1997, the country will go from almost pure *laissez-faire* capitalism to communist rule. Many of Hong Kong's successful entrepreneurs are looking for a haven in Taiwan,

Singapore, or other parts of Southeast Asia. Some have moved as far away as Jamaica.

Taiwan provides another interesting contrast to mainland China. Chinese nationalists who fled mainland China during the Communist revolution in 1949 went to Taiwan. There they dominated the native Taiwanese majority and established a market-directed economy. The People's Republic of China insists that Taiwan is a province of China and that reunification is inevitable. The Taiwanese insist that they must remain independent. A comparison of China and Taiwan seems to indicate that economic development is faster under capitalism than under socialism. In 1950, the socialistic People's Republic and capitalistic Taiwan had basically the same level of development. Today, the average income in Taiwan is about $3,000 per year, more than ten times the per capita income in China. Perhaps this fact is understood in China, where elements of market capitalism are being introduced in the disguise of economic reform.

by a charismatic dictator. This combination promoted monopoly and then imposed "national interests" on that monopoly structure. Fascism lacks both the large degree of personal freedom that is a characteristic of free-enterprise capitalism and the egalitarian ideals of socialism and communism.

USE OF THE *ISMS* APPROACH

The drawback of using the *isms* approach to compare economic systems is that it is too simplistic and does not include many of the keys to determining control over resources. The *isms* approach tends to equate ownership with control and control with decision-making power over the factors of production. This connection is becoming less clear over time. For example, in the Soviet Union, before the reform movement, the leaders of the government did not own much of anything, yet they clearly controlled the system. In the United States, many people own land, but they cannot use it as they please because of zoning or environmental regulations.

All economies are mixed in varying degrees. That is, they contain elements of socialism (or planning) and elements of capitalism (or markets). Therefore, the *isms* approach, though often used in political-economic classification schemes (and political rhetoric), has serious limitations. In fact, applying this classification scheme would be likely to produce just two sets of systems, capitalism and socialism. Yet no serious analyst would consider a scheme that places the United States, France, and Great Britain in one category to be very meaningful. However, capitalism and socialism, like pure competition and monopoly, offer theoretical models to aid in understanding real-world mixed systems.

The *isms* approach remains popular because it is the one almost always used by politicians and journalists. A statement made in 1990 by a member of the Leningrad Communist Party is typical. Pyotr S. Filipov is quoted as saying: "We must hurry away from Marxism-Leninism, through Socialism, to Reaganism."[1] What does this mean and how do the Soviets expect to accomplish such a reform? In this chapter we will try to address these issues so you can give an informed answer to such a question.

CONTRASTING CAPITALISM AND SOCIALISM

Recognizing that there is no such thing as a pure system, we can construct a continuum and attempt to place countries on it. Figure 1 presents such a continuum. On one end is pure, market-directed capitalism, and on the other end is pure, centrally planned socialism. (The Soviet Union and the countries of Eastern Europe have been omitted from Figure 1 because it is unclear what the outcome will be in these reforming nations.) Capitalism and socialism are the two polar extremes of economic systems. Contrasting the distinguishing features of these two types of economic systems will help in evaluating real-world systems.

Private property rights are an important feature of capitalism because they create incentives and make exchange possible. In capitalism, the property rights to resources and factors of production, including labor, are vested with the individual. Workers are free to move about, but they

1. *National Review* (29 August 1990): 11.

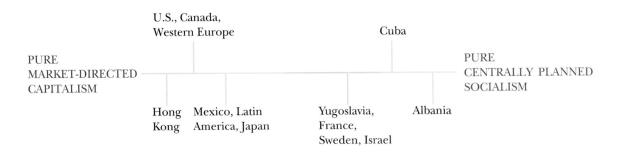

FIGURE 1
A CONTINUUM OF
ECONOMIC SYSTEMS
No country has an
economic system that
represents a pure type.
All countries mix market
and planning to some
degree. It is possible to
place countries along a
continuum, as shown
here, on the basis of their
relative reliance on the
market or on a plan.

are not guaranteed jobs. In socialism, the state is vested with property rights, including property rights to the individual's labor. As economic reforms proceed in the Soviet Union and Eastern Europe, property rights and who owns what are important issues in these reforms. Government officials in these countries are arguing over the ownership of resources, including a new division between public and private ownership.

Under socialism, especially in China, people are often assigned jobs in certain geographic locations and do not have the freedom to switch occupations or geographic location. The method of job assignment in the U.S. military is similar to that in most socialist states. Workers have greater job security but less freedom to choose jobs than in a market system. Investment decisions follow a similar pattern. Under capitalism, individuals seeking profits make these decisions. Under socialism, a central plan determines the level and composition of investment. Production decisions and decisions that affect the distribution of income are also made by the central planning authority under socialism. These decisions are the *what* and *for whom* questions of Chapter 2.

MARX, MARXISTS, AND MARXISM

Perhaps no other economist has had more effect on the political shaping of the world than Karl Marx, who with Friedrich Engels, published the *Communist Manifesto* in 1848. This book, along with Marx's *Das Kapital*, published in three volumes in 1867, 1885, and 1894, is the philosophical basis for a widely divergent group of economic-political systems. In recent years, almost all communist governments have claimed to be Marxist. Therefore, it is necessary to distinguish between Marx and Marxism (or Marxists).

The central ideas of Marx's economic theory are easy to outline. He believed that every society would evolve through the historical stages of tribal communism, slavery, feudalism, capitalism, socialism, and, finally, communism. The most important transition would come when capitalism decayed because of internal conflict and was succeeded by socialism. The regular cyclical ups and downs of a capitalist economy (the business cycle) would become more and more severe until capitalism finally collapsed. Marx saw the empire building of European countries in the nineteenth century as an attempt to postpone the inevitable failure of capitalism. He believed that when socialism was replaced by communism, scarcity would disappear, and workers would produce without material incentives.

ESSENTIAL DIFFERENCES BETWEEN CAPITALISM AND SOCIALISM		
	CAPITALISM	SOCIALISM
• Property rights	Resources are owned by individuals or groups of individuals.	Resources are owned by the state.
• Labor	Workers have a property right to their own labor. They are self-employed or work for private firms.	Workers are employed by the government and are usually not allowed to change jobs.
• Investment	Investment is determined and undertaken by entrepreneurs.	Investment is determined and undertaken by government.
• Production mix	What is produced is determined by market forces.	What is produced is determined by central plan.
• Distribution of income	Distribution of income is determined by market forces, productivity, and ownership patterns.	Distribution of income is determined by central plan.
• Incentives	Labor, management, and entrepreneurs respond to wages, prices, and profits.	Often many nonmaterial incentives are used.

The countries to which communism has spread have been those in which the level of industrialization was very low. This pattern is inconsistent with what Marx predicted. What, then, is the significance of Marx's writings?

The significance of Marx's writings lies not in the accuracy of his predictions but rather in the theoretical, philosophical, and political movements spawned by his work. Communist parties in many countries consider themselves Marxists and appeal to the writings of Marx to justify their views on various issues. In some respects, they are similar. They all condemn the "exploitation" of workers under capitalism and forbid the use of the term *profit*. Countries in which Communists are in power all claim to have full-employment economies and to have overcome the unemployment problem of capitalistic systems. There are also wide differences among Communist countries, however. Countries as diverse as China, Yugoslavia, the Soviet Union, Albania, Romania, and Cuba have all at one time or another claimed to be the true Marxists. Many of the economic reform movements in these countries still use Marxist terminology in their political statements. The significance of Marx is that he was the father of a political, as well as an economic, movement.

LEADERISMS

Socialism was Marx's intermediate stage between capitalism and communism. Under socialism, the decision-making authority shifts from individual entrepreneurs to a central authority, which Marx called the "dictatorship of the proletariat." In practice, the central authority has almost always been personified by a dominant individual. It is thus possible to view many of the offshoots of Marxism as the products of the interaction of Marxist ideas with the personalities of strong-willed leaders. Thus, for example, the Soviet economic and political reforms may have a curious result if they succeed. Gorbachev had to be a strong leader to initiate the reforms, but any success in these reforms will reduce his power. This effect became evident early in his term of office as competition for the right to lead the Soviet Union quickly developed.

LENINISM

Vladimir Lenin (1870–1924) was active in developing the Communist Party in Russia and led that country's successful Bolshevik Revolution in 1917–1918. He claimed to be a follower of Marx but developed new directions for the achievement of communism. Lenin refused to wait for the maturation of capitalism and instead developed a different model for revolution based on four essential ingredients: (1) a small, revolutionary elite, (2) economic underdevelopment (the opposite of Marx's industrialization), (3) a discontented peasantry, and (4) war against an outside force. Lenin's formula worked in Russia and in Yugoslavia, China, Vietnam, and Cuba. In fact, Lenin's formula applies to almost all cases where communism has taken root. The exceptions are those countries of Eastern Europe in which the Soviet Union imposed communism after World War II.

War Communism
An economic system of rigid administrative control imposed by Lenin in Russia during the civil war following the Bolshevik Revolution.

Lenin was the first Communist to be faced with the task of setting up an economic system after the political system was secure. **War Communism** was the economic system that Lenin imposed on Russia immediately after the Bolshevik Revolution. This system instituted rigid administrative control of the economy in an attempt to marshal the resources needed to engage in a civil war with the non-Communist White Russians. Widespread nationalization of industry took place, and all private trading was outlawed. All labor mobility was rigidly controlled, and money as an exchange mechanism almost disappeared. This period is difficult to evaluate. Some economic historians claim that Lenin instituted War Communism only because of the demands of fighting a civil war.[2]

New Economic Policy (NEP)
A program that replaced War Communism in 1921 in the Soviet Union and was an attempt at market socialism.

By 1921, the economy had seriously deteriorated. Lenin responded by abandoning War Communism and instituting a program referred to as the **New Economic Policy (NEP)**. This policy was an attempt at market socialism, with planning for only the key industries in the economy. The remainder of the economy was left to respond to basic market forces. There was very rapid economic growth during this period, and the Soviet economy quickly recovered from the protracted civil war. Lenin died in 1924. In 1926, the NEP came to an end for a variety of reasons. One reason was that the move toward a market economy during NEP greatly reduced the power of the Communist Party to channel and direct the course of economic development. Many parts of the current reform in the Soviet Union resemble the NEP.

---

2.   Others claim Lenin instituted War Communism out of a desire to see such a system evolve as the economic application of communism. For this view, see Paul Craig Roberts, *Alienation and the Soviet Economy* (Albuquerque: University of New Mexico Press, 1971).

STALINISM

After Lenin's death, there was open dispute in the Soviet Communist Party over the direction of development. The **Great Industrialization Debate** was an open debate that took place in the Soviet Union from 1924 to 1928 concerning the correct way to industrialize the economy.[3] The left wing of the party, led by economist E. A. Preobrazhensky, argued that the country should make a concerted effort toward rapid industrialization of key sectors of the economy. This policy would be carried out by the central allocation of investment expenditures. N. I. Bukharin, who was the spokesperson for the right wing, disagreed with this position and stressed balanced growth of the economy. Bukharin argued that all sectors of the economy must grow together because they all support and feed one another.

Joseph Stalin (1879–1953) was both an observer and a participant in the debate. Stalin played one side against the other while forming a power base. At the time of Lenin's death, Stalin allied himself with the right wing of the party in order to counteract the power of Leon Trotsky and the left wing. This alliance allowed Stalin to discredit and weaken the left wing, a task he accomplished by 1927. He then turned on the right wing and, by 1928, had its leaders denounced by the party. Stalin was then in complete control, since he had purged all dissidents.[4]

The planning system that Stalin adopted was centrally directed and was set up in five-year increments. Five years was chosen since it is possible to complete most investment projects in that period. Stalin's first five-year plan was an extreme version of the left-wing industrialization proposal. Its achievement required very centralized planning, investment in heavy industry, and forced collectivization in the agricultural sector, which was expected to supply food and raw materials. Industrialization was very rapid, but the costs of this policy in human terms were great. Millions of people were purged. Many others starved to death because the peasants resisted forced centralization by destroying crops and livestock.

The Soviet Union's rigid system of central planning up to 1989 was the legacy of Stalin. Today, the term *Stalinism* is associated with a ruthless dictatorship as well as with a highly centralized planning structure. However, Stalinism is not openly practiced in any Communist country today.

MAOISM

In China, the Communist Party came to full power in October 1949, after decades of struggle. Mao Zedong was the revolutionary leader who took command, just as Lenin's formula for communist revolutionaries had predicted. In the early years of Chinese Communism, the goal was industrialization, much as it had been in the Soviet Union. However, this policy was formulated without the help of Moscow. The Chinese Communist Party, from the very beginning, was fiercely independent of the Soviet Union.

In 1958, the Great Leap Forward was announced. The **Great Leap Forward** was a modernization plan to increase per capita income in China by 25 percent in five years. Many of the programs were ill-conceived, such

Great Industrialization Debate
An open debate that took place in the Soviet Union from 1924 to 1928 concerning the correct way to industrialize the economy.

Great Leap Forward
A modernization plan that was launched in 1958 to increase per capita income in China by 25 percent in five years.

3.   See Alexander Erlich, *Soviet Industrialization Debate, 1924–1928* (Cambridge, MA: Harvard University Press, 1960).
4.   For an excellent economic history of the Soviet Union, including this period, see Alec Nove, *An Economic History of the USSR* (London: Penguin, 1975).

as the production of steel on a small scale in backyard furnaces. The result was a product of poor quality that was not useful as input to further manufacturing processes. The Great Leap Forward included the collectivization of Chinese agriculture. Mao sought to mobilize the huge underemployed population of China in collectivized agriculture. The result was disastrous. In two years, agricultural production fell by 20 percent and widespread starvation occurred. Mao was ousted from control, and a pragmatic leadership took over. With the aid of revolutionary youth, Mao was able to return to power in 1966 through a political coup.

Cultural Revolution
The high point of Mao's power in China, characterized by a radical restructuring of the economy from 1966 through 1969.

The period from 1966 through 1969, called the **Cultural Revolution**, represented the high point of Mao's power. The Cultural Revolution embraced revolutionary values. Mao envisioned a completely classless society, organized as a collective operation rather than as a state enterprise, as in the Soviet Union. The motivation for the society was to be completely altruistic, embracing the concept of the "new man" who responds to social rather than to material incentives. The Cultural Revolution almost destroyed the educational system. Professors were sent to work in communes and factories. Education came to a standstill during this period. The Cultural Revolution was also an economic disaster. As a result, in 1969, Mao turned more authority over to Chou En-Lai, who tempered some of the more drastic policies.

The Chinese economy has changed often and in different directions. Not enough information is available to evaluate the success of Maoism in promoting economic development. Several economists who have traveled to China give strikingly different reports. For example, John Gurley argues that China made great strides and has eradicated poverty, but James Tobin claims that there was not much economic progress under Mao.[5] He argues that almost any system that brought peace to the country would have achieved some economic success, since China was torn by revolution and war for several decades before 1949.

After Mao's death in 1976, the new leaders pursued a development strategy that was often openly hostile to Mao's ideas. They attacked the "Gang of Four," Mao's widow and three other radicals. In attacking the Gang of Four, the leaders attacked the ideas of the Cultural Revolution and, in fact, Mao himself, although they were careful not to name Mao. *Newsweek* reported that Chinese officials argued that "Chairman Mao was deceived by the Gang of Four."[6] The Gang of Four were tried and convicted in 1981.

CASTROISM

Fidel Castro, who overthrew the Batista government in Cuba in 1958, learned the lesson of Lenin's formula for revolution very well. He led a small group of committed revolutionaries in an country with a large, discontented peasant class and an underdeveloped economy. The United States served as an outside enemy that he used to unify the diverse elements within Cuba. In many ways, the Cuban system resembles early Chi-

5.   John Gurley, "Maoist Economic Development," and James Tobin, "The Economy of China: A Tourist's View," in Edwin Mansfield, *Economics: Readings, Issues, and Cases* (New York: W. W. Norton, 1977).
6.   *Newsweek* (30 October 1978): 50.

nese communism. For example, Castro has placed heavy emphasis on creating a "new man."[7] The goal was to remove all social inequities and motivate workers with moral incentives rather than with material ones. Castro's vision is very close to Marx's view of the final stage of communism. His policy was in large part the work of Che Guevara. The Soviets, who were financially underwriting the Cuban economy, were skeptical of the plan.

Rather than attempt to industrialize the Cuban economy rapidly, Castro concentrated on agriculture and sought to exploit the export potential of the sugar cane industry. This policy required the transfer of labor from cities to rural areas, the exact opposite of what occurred under European Communist regimes. The Cuban economy remains heavily reliant on agriculture. Planning in Cuba is carried out by the System of Budgetary Finance, a centralized planning system that views the economy as a single firm to be rigidly controlled by the central authority.

Castro faces severe problems. The Cuban economy had been receiving more than $5 billion annually in subsidies from the Soviet Union. With reform in the Soviet Union, these subsidies were phased out beginning in 1991. When the Soviet aid declined, the Cuban GNP fell 30 percent. Castro responded by sending 100,000 "volunteers" into the countryside to plant and harvest crops. He called on Cubans to tighten their belts and create a new agricultural class. This move created unrest among the youth, but they appear too apathetic or frightened to protest. Many experts predict that Castro will be the next Communist leader to be deposed. In fact, a group of Cuban-Americans in Miami has drafted a constitution and is planning economic programs for a post-Castro Cuba. The group, called The Cuban American National Foundation, is headed by Jorge Mas Canosa, a successful Florida businessman.[8]

RETREAT FROM SOCIALISM: THATCHERISM

Just as strong leaders have had a significant influence on socialism, some leaders have left a mark on capitalism. Margaret Thatcher led a retreat from socialism through significant reprivatization of the British economy. She served the longest continuous term as British Prime Minister in the twentieth century. In December 1990, Thatcher stepped down as Prime Minister when she was challenged for the leadership of the Conservative Party. Thatcher was often linked with former President Reagan as a proponent of supply side economics and privatization. However, her program aimed at decreasing the size of government was far more successful than Reagan's. Thatcher reduced income taxes in order to reverse the "talent drain" of entertainers and other highly paid individuals from Britain. She convinced Parliament to pass legislation that greatly reduced the power

---

7.   For a good review of Castro's Cuba, see Carmelo Mesa-Lago (ed.), *Revolutionary Change in Cuba* (Pittsburgh: University of Pittsburgh Press, 1971).

8.   See "Gorbachev Will Soon Make Castro More of an Island," *Business Week*, (16 July 1990): 47; Anthony Daniels, "The Last Days of Fidel Castro," *National Review* (5 March 1990): 29–32; "Soon to Come: Capitalist Cuba", *National Review* (17 September 1990): 19–20. The Council for Inter-American Security sponsored a contest, a pool to predict when Castro will fall from power, and received 300 predictions. Former U.N. Ambassador Jeane Kirkpatrick predicted "by the end of 1991," and Texas oilman Nelson Bunker Hunt predicted October 5, 1993. See "Betting on Fidel's Fall," *Forbes* (1 October 1990): 17.

of labor unions by requiring that they poll their members before calling a strike.

Perhaps the most important element of Thatcherism was the privatization of the British economy. When she became Prime Minister in 1979, the economy was best described as one in which large governmental enterprises were deadlocked with large labor unions. (This situation was referred to as the "British Disease.") During her tenure, she reversed the trend by selling off more than $31 billion in state-owned industries to private investors. These sales included the government's share in British Gas, Rolls-Royce, British Airways, and British Petroleum. Her action and the effect it had on productivity (productivity increases have averaged over 3 percent) inspired similar privatization policies in Italy and France.

ORGANIZATION AND DECISION-MAKING APPROACH TO COMPARING ECONOMIC SYSTEMS

We have been comparing economic systems in terms of how the underlying ideology affects their organization. In many cases, a dominant personality's interpretation of that ideology shaped an entire system. Some of you may have found this an exciting and useful way to categorize the world. Others may have found it frustrating to examine individual systems, rather than developing general principles as to how different systems are organized and how they affect behavior. The first approach has been the way most economists have historically examined alternative economic systems. A second approach is to formulate organizational principles using economic theory as a coherent analytical framework.[9]

THE DECISION PROCESS: DECISION MAKERS, INCENTIVES, AND INFORMATION
To understand an economic system, it is necessary to examine the organizational setting for the production of goods and services *and* the institutional setting for the distribution of those goods and services. The important questions concern the structure of decision making in production and distribution. One such question is which individuals, and at which levels, make the major decisions concerning production and distribution. In the United States, production decisions are made at the entrepreneurial level. In the Soviet Union, these decisions until recently were made at the planning level.

Once the assignment of decision-making responsibility has been made, the next question concerns the motivation for the decision makers. Do the decision makers bear the costs of wrong decisions or reap the rewards of correct decisions? It is also necessary to determine how one person's participation in the decision-making process influences another's. Also, it is possible to change an individual's internal values. In other words, do institutions affect individuals' value systems?

Once these two aspects of the decision-making structure are determined, the informational structure of the economic system can be ana-

---

9.   For a comprehensive development of this approach, see Egon Neuberger and William J. Duffy, *Comparative Economic Systems: A Decision-Making Approach* (Boston: Allyn and Bacon, 1976).

lyzed. The informational structure is the way in which individuals learn about their options so they can act on them. In the U.S. economy, prices are an important source of information. In the Soviet economy, the plan plays this role. As decision making becomes centralized, more and better information is critical because the costs of wrong decisions are so much higher. System questions are largely microeconomic in nature.

THE ENVIRONMENT
A country's environment is its social structure, physical conditions, and international situation. Some of the more critical aspects of the environment in terms of possible impact on the economic system are the level of economic development, the size of the country in area and population, the availability of natural resources within the country and from safe allies, the values of the people (religious, cultural, and so on), the political system, the size of the country relative to its near neighbors, the level of development relative to the rest of the world and relative to near neighbors, and the sphere of influence in which the country lies (American, Soviet, or Chinese, for example). These are only a few of the influences on an economic system, but they are representative of the concept of environmental influence.

ECONOMIC PERFORMANCE
The way in which an economy performs is an important evaluation measure. Economists usually focus on the performance of the gross national product (GNP) and examine growth in per capita production, stability of production (business cycles can be socially destabilizing), and equity in income distribution. These measures of performance are mostly macroeconomic in nature.

POLICY CHANGES
Some policy changes can be made within a system without changing the underlying fabric of the system. These changes consist of marginal changes in the system and its environment in order to affect performance. Policy changes can influence the system in a positive or negative way. A "good" system might develop "bad" policies that produce "bad" performance and in turn result in a negative change in the "good" system. For example, a central planning policy decision to consolidate farms into larger units or to shift from corn to wheat can increase (or reduce) productivity and efficiency. Recent policy changes in the Soviet Union and some countries in Eastern Europe affect the entire system.

INTERACTION OF SYSTEMS, ENVIRONMENT, PERFORMANCE, AND POLICY
Of course, all these organizational elements interact in a complex fashion. Using this terminology, however, can help in understanding how economic systems differ and in what ways they are similar. For example, consider a small country with the Soviet Union or the United States as a close neighbor. How would this affect the development of its economic system? Having the Soviet Union nearby had a profound effect on the countries of Eastern Europe, but the Soviet Union has pulled back, even allowing the reunification of the two Germanys in 1990. Similarly, being close to

the United States has affected the trade pattern, the output mix, and the level of development in Canada, Mexico, and the Caribbean. What environmental factors caused the Industrial Revolution to spread from England to the United States but not to Russia?

How might performance influence an economic system? Performance is part of Lenin's formula: If things get bad enough, there might be a revolution. On the other hand, if economic conditions stagnate in a Communist country after a revolution, there might be a move toward capitalism or market socialism. There are many complex questions, and the organization and decision-making approach may give you a start in organizing your thoughts. This approach gives some insight into the many and varied forms of capitalism and socialism.

PLANNING

Throughout this chapter, whether we were using the *isms* approach to systems or a more structured organizational approach, we continually encountered the issue of planning. Who directs production, who makes decisions, and who bears the costs for wrong decisions or receives the rewards for correct decisions? Planning is the essence of the problem of understanding systems. The question is not whether planning should take place but rather who should do the planning. General Motors plans, homebuilders plan, wheat farmers plan—and so do you. The key question is the degree of centralization of planning and control. At the market extreme, the answer would be that only individual consumers and entrepreneurs should plan. At the command extreme, the position would be that only the central authority should plan.

THE SOCIALIST CONTROVERSY

Marx had little to say about the actual workings of the economic system under socialism. Instead, Marx criticized capitalism and left the development of the economics of socialism to his followers. In 1922, a professor at the University of Vienna, Ludwig von Mises, wrote a famous article, "Economic Calculation in the Socialist Commonwealth."[10] This article claimed that rational economic calculations were impossible under socialism. Von Mises based his argument on a number of factors, but the essence was quite simple. If the state owned the factors of production (other than labor), it would have to allocate them among competing uses. Without a market to determine prices, this task would be impossible. A simulated market with shadow prices could not supply correct information because of the absence of the profit motive. **Shadow prices** are simulated market prices used by economic planners.

shadow prices
Simulated market prices used by economic planners.

socialist controversy
A debate between Ludwig von Mises and Oskar Lange concerning the feasibility of planning without markets.

The **socialist controversy** was a debate between von Mises and Oskar Lange concerning the feasibility of planning without markets.[11] Von Mises argued that "the most serious menace to socialist economic organization"

10. Ludwig von Mises, "Economic Calculation in the Socialist Commonwealth," in F. A. Hayek (ed.), *Collectivist Economic Planning* (Clifton, NJ: Augustus M. Kelley, 1967), 103.
11. For a thorough discussion of the socialist controversy, see Paul R. Gregory and Robert C. Stuart, *Soviet Economic Structure and Performance* (New York: Harper & Row, 1974).

was the lack of rewards for correct managerial decisions and penalties for incorrect managerial decisions. Lange, a famous Polish economist who at the time was on the faculty at the University of Chicago, responded to von Mises by developing a model sometimes referred to as the **competitive solution**. In this model, Lange tried to prove that a socialist economy with a combination of central *and* local decision making can arrive at the same efficiency as attained with perfect competition. Prices are set by the central authority. Local managers are told to maximize profits, although they cannot keep these profits. They are solely accounting profits. If shortages or surpluses develop, the price is changed, and in this way an equilibrium price is finally reached. One of the most telling criticisms of Lange's solution, however, is that in a market system, profits are not merely a measure of success but the *incentive* to succeed.[12]

> **competitive solution**
> The model developed by Oskar Lange in an attempt to show that a planned economy could theoretically reach the efficiency of an economy with competition.

The debate over the feasibility of centralized planning has never been resolved. Is it possible for a central authority to make the calculations necessary to produce efficiently? In a later article that might be considered an extension of this debate, Nobel laureate F. A. Hayek said no.[13] Hayek argues that information is the friction in the system that causes economic models to diverge from the ideal system of either von Mises or Lange. Information is costly to develop and spread, using up scarce resources that must be taken away from other uses. Hayek argued that market systems are superior because they need less information than do centrally planned systems.

Recall from Chapter 2 what happens in a planned economy and a market economy when an earthquake destroys a copper mine. What happens in each economy? In the market economy, the price of copper will rise, reflecting the decrease in supply. Profit-minded entrepreneurs will substitute cheaper metals to minimize costs. In a planned economy, the planners must first be informed of the disaster. The planners must then make some estimate of the severity of the scarcity. They then inform each user of copper that in the future less copper will be available and that other metals should be substituted. The planners must also contact producers of other metals and tell them to ship to the enterprises that had been using copper. In addition, the planners will have to set priorities for use of the available copper. In the market system, this priority setting was done by the increase in price.

Hayek's position is quite simple: Central planning can never be as efficient as a market system because it requires the use of so many resources in transmitting information. The market system, on the other hand, minimizes the amount of information needed. In 1989, there were severe earthquakes in San Francisco (during the World Series) and in Soviet Armenia. The speed of adjustment in the earthquake zones was much faster in San Francisco, reflecting the positive role that the market can play in speeding the process of economic recovery. Recent developments in planned economies also lead to the conclusion that Hayek was right. The inefficiencies of central planning became too expensive, and market reforms were required to stimulate economic growth.

12. Paul Craig Roberts, "Oskar Lange's Theory of Socialist Planning," *Journal of Political Economy* (May-June 1971): 562–568.
13. F. A. Hayek, "The Use of Knowledge in Society," *American Economic Review* (September 1945): 519–528.

HOW TO PLAN

The fact that central planning may be inefficient does not change the fact that it is undertaken. Most socialist countries still rely heavily on central planning to move production in the desired direction. Therefore, we need to look at how planning takes place in a command economy.

First, priorities must be established. Someone has to decide what to produce. In the early years of Soviet planning, such decisions were made at the aggregate level. The first plan was, in fact, called the "State Plan for the Electrification of Russia." Until recently, planning was still done by the state planning commission, commonly called the **Gosplan**. Whether to produce consumer or investment goods was the first aggregate planning decision in the Soviet Union. Since the goal of the early leaders was rapid economic growth, they decided to produce investment goods at the expense of consumer goods. As a result, very few consumer goods were available, forcing consumers to save. This pattern of production permitted heavy investment and very rapid rates of economic growth. There were, and still are, shortages of consumer goods in the Soviet Union.

Once planners decided what to produce, they turned their attention to how much to produce. This is a difficult planning problem because the amount produced depends on the productive capacity of the existing industries and on the resources that will be available during the period. Production uses up resources. Therefore, the planners have to make sure that the resources to be used for the final output will be available. At this stage, the various industries are brought into the picture, and the ministries, one for each major industry, make their plans ahead of the overall plan. Once all plans are finalized, they are communicated to productive enterprises so they can take the necessary action to put the plans into operation. Planning is an ongoing process. Even though the planning period is usually expressed in five-year increments, there is continuous revision and implementation.

The planning process itself used up a great deal of time and productive resources. The individuals who engaged in the planning were highly trained engineers and economists, people taken out of other productive activities in order to plan. It is not, therefore, difficult to understand the burden that planning places on an economy. Ironically, many of the poorest countries, where most Communist revolutions have taken place, are the very ones that can least afford the luxury of planning, because of the high opportunity cost of the resources used in the planning process.

INPUT-OUTPUT ANALYSIS

The complexity of planning led to the development of methods to make it more effective. Input-output analysis, developed by Nobel prize–winning economist Wassily Leontief, shows that everything depends on everything else. These interrelationships are what make planning so difficult, because specific plans must be made as to how much of each good is to be produced, by whom, and for whom. **Input-output analysis** is an attempt to quantify the flows between different sectors of the economy.

Table 1 is an input-output table for a small economy in which there are only a few industries to control. There are only three industries: electric-

Gosplan
The state planning commission in the Soviet Union.

input-output analysis
An attempt to quantify the flows between different sectors of the economy for purposes of economic planning.

		OUTPUTS				
		Electricity	Trucks	Steel	Consumption	Total Output
INPUTS	Electricity	1,000	1,500	5,000	1,500	9,000 kilowatts
	Trucks	1,000	1,500	2,000	1,000	5,500 trucks
	Steel	4,000	3,000	8,500	3,500	19,000 tons
	Labor	2,000	500	3,000	0	5,500 worker-days

TABLE 1
INPUT-OUTPUT
TABLE FOR A SIMPLE
THREE-INDUSTRY
ECONOMY

ity, trucks, and steel. There is also a labor sector and a category of consumption. The input to labor is consumption. Reading across the rows of Table 1 gives the output of each industry and of labor and shows how that output is distributed. One of the reasons that input-output tables are especially useful in command economies is that physical units are used, and prices of outputs and inputs are not needed for the analysis. The fact that no prices are needed is important in a system where market prices are not available and the prices that exist do not necessarily reflect relative scarcity.

To interpret this input-output table, read across the rows. For example, the steel industry has a total output of 19,000 tons, which is sold or allocated by the central authority to the following sectors: 4,000 tons to the electricity industry, 3,000 tons to the truck industry, 8,500 tons to the steel industry, and 3,500 tons to the consumer goods sector. Reading down a column shows the inputs that are needed to produce the output. For example, in order to produce the 19,000 tons of steel, the steel industry uses the following inputs: 5,000 kilowatts of electricity, 2,000 trucks, 8,500 tons of steel, and 3,000 worker-days of labor. The simple arithmetic of input-output tables can be used to plan future output.

The key assumption in input-output analysis is that production takes place in all industries at *constant* costs. There are no economies or diseconomies of scale. If planners want to double the production of the steel industry, all they need to do is double the inputs. Regardless of the level of output planned, the amount of inputs required per unit of output remains the same. However, for large increases in output, this assumption is very unrealistic.

The numbers in Table 2 can be used to calculate the input needed to produce additional units of output. These numbers are referred to as input coefficients. An **input coefficient** shows the ratio of the amount of an input to the total output of an industry. Each input coefficient in Table 2 can be calculated by dividing each value in a column of Table 1 by the to-

input coefficient
In input-output analysis, the ratio of the amount of an input to the total output of an industry.

		OUTPUTS		
		Electricity	Trucks	Steel
INPUTS	Electricity	0.11	0.27	0.26
	Trucks	0.11	0.27	0.11
	Steel	0.44	0.55	0.47
	Labor	0.22	0.09	0.16

TABLE 2
INPUT COEFFICIENTS
FOR THE ECONOMY
OF TABLE 1

tal output of that industry. For example, the input coefficient of electricity in the truck industry is 0.27 kilowatts/truck (1,500/5,500). Input coefficients can be used to plan increases in output. Examine the column for trucks. The input coefficient tells what increase is needed from each supplying industry in order to get a given increase in output of trucks.

The input-output information in Tables 1 and 2 can be used to plan for the three-industry economy. Suppose planners want to expand the output of the electricity industry by 2,000 kilowatts. That expansion in output would require 220 kilowatts of electricity, 220 trucks, 880 tons of steel, and 440 worker-days. These inputs are found by multiplying the applicable input coefficients by the desired increase in output. Planners would, therefore, be able to direct these industries to deliver the required inputs to produce the planned output.

You should note that there are feedback effects in this process. In order to produce more electricity, some electricity must be consumed in producing the additional steel and trucks used to produce electricity. Feedback occurs throughout this interdependent system. The example assumes that there is no limit to the capacity of any sector of the economy. In fact, however, this may not be the case. In order to produce more electricity, it may be necessary to build new power generators. Generators require time to produce, causing a delay in fulfilling the plan.

The problems of using input-output analysis for planning stem from the fact that the coefficients are constant and are calculated on the basis of historical experience. In other words, the required inputs are calculated on the assumption that the same input mix as that used in the time period for which the table of input coefficients was compiled will continue to be used.

PROBLEMS OF CENTRAL PLANNING

The technique of planning seems simple in theory. The calculations for a realistic economy are usually overwhelming, however. Think about the size of an input-output table for an economy with 100 industries, 1,000 industries, or 5,000 industries. The interdependencies between the industries become mind-boggling, or even computer-boggling.

The significant problems of planning begin after the plan has been created. There are the problems of implementing the plan, as well as the problems of creating and maintaining incentives that induce workers and managers to support the plan. Managers have incentives to overstate their "needs" for inputs and to hoard materials, since they do not have to pay for them. It is not surprising that plans are often announced with a great deal of publicity and fanfare, but the poor results are often played down.

REFORMS: ECONOMIC FREEDOM AND POLITICAL FREEDOM

Socialist countries have found through experience that the application of planning has not necessarily improved economic performance. This failure was evident during the Great Leap Forward and the Cultural Revolution in China and is also suggested by the declining rate of economic growth in the Soviet Union. Because of poor economic performance, both the People's Republic of China and the Soviet Union have entered into a series of reforms aimed at introducing market forces into the economy. The difficulty with such reforms is that the economic freedom of markets always produces pressure for other types of freedom, which would reduce the power of the central authorities. The trade-off is easy to see. In order to stimulate economic growth, incentives are needed. Markets are allowed to develop in order to create these incentives. The markets diminish the control of the party and its large and powerful bureaucracy. The problem becomes acute when the economic reforms produce the inevitable demands for other freedoms. Bureaucrats can use the demands for political freedom as an excuse for reversing the economic reforms and, by so doing, restore their diminished power. Each socialist country has to cope with the conflicting goals of economic growth and tight administrative control. It is helpful to examine the reform movements in China and the Soviet Union in greater detail.

THE PEOPLE'S REPUBLIC OF CHINA

After Mao's death in 1976, there was rapid reform in China, affecting almost every aspect of the economy. Much of this reform was due to the efforts of Deng Xiaoping, Party General Secretary since December 1978.

POLITICAL, SOCIAL, AND INTELLECTUAL REFORMS. Many of the holdovers of Maoism disappeared from China in the 1980s. Before then, class labels from before the 1949 revolution were still used. These labels (peasant, landlord, intellectual, and so on) affected such things as how people were treated by the courts and whether they were allowed into schools. In the 1980s, the labels were eliminated. Intellectuals benefited from these changes, a great contrast to the days of the Cultural Revolution. They were encouraged to debate and exchange ideas with Western scholars. The results were sweeping demands for political freedom that culminated in large demonstrations.

A system of laws also evolved in the 1980s. Mao had removed all laws because they interfered with the "dictatorship of the proletariat." The new system of laws replaced the arbitrary power of party secretaries and brought some stability to the country.

ECONOMIC REFORM. The first stage of the economic reforms championed by Deng required the "readjustment" of some priorities. The first shift occurred in the output mix. To establish economic incentives, it is necessary to increase wages *and*, equally important, to produce consumer goods for people to buy with those higher wages. This change was accomplished by setting lower targets for heavy industries and increasing investment in light, consumer-oriented industries.

Most noticeable was the change away from the Maoist principle of self-reliance, that is, independence from other countries. Trade with the rest of the world was greatly expanded. Between 1975 and 1985, China's international trade increased from 3.5 percent of GDP to 16 percent of GDP.

The basic reforms of the economic system had profound effects. In agriculture, the "household responsibility system" assigned land that had been held in communes to individual families. In exchange, these farmers assumed contractual obligations to provide a certain amount of food to the state. Farmers were allowed to sell production in excess of the contracted amounts. The result was dramatic. Production increased sharply, and peasant farmers became some of the wealthiest people in China.

The industrial sector was also radically reformed. Once production goals were met, industrial enterprises could sell any surplus on the open market, or they could barter it for other goods. Profits and losses were used to reward or penalize managers. In some instances, factories that had been making losses were turned over to workers, just as communal farms were divided among households. In addition, the state started to charge industrial enterprises for the investment capital it supplied. In some cases, these "loans" were made with assigned payment schedules and interest charges, just as in capitalist countries.

The changes brought about by Deng Xiaoping were fundamental. They injected a great deal of market influence into the Chinese economy. With the market influence and the rise in foreign trade, there came other observable changes. Western dress, music, and ideas about democracy crept in. These Western influences created a danger. Deng was responsible for the reforms, which were not popular with all party leaders. The frustration of many leaders was understandable, since the freeing of the economy greatly reduced their power and influence. As a result, a political movement to reverse the reforms surfaced. In 1985, some party leaders began to complain about the "excesses" of the reforms and the "spiritual pollution" that had been created. In January 1987, the conservatives in the party finally acted when students demonstrated for democratic reforms, including freedom of expression. The student demonstrations united the police and military elements in the party leadership. The result was that Hu Yaobang, party leader, reform advocate, and likely heir to Deng's power, made a "self-criticism" and was forced to step down. He was replaced by Zhao Ziyang, whose first act was to fire the top security official for being too lenient with the student demonstrators. Zhao was described in the press as a cautious reformer.

The Chinese reform movement was at a crossroads in 1989. The economic reform produced economic gains, which in turn led to political demands. These demands led to the firing of Hu and a campaign against "bourgeois liberalization." Party leaders started stressing central planning, thrift, and reduced consumption. Factory managers remained quiet while party leaders were reasserting their political control. In June 1989, students gathered in Tiananmen Square demanding democracy. The demonstration, which included the construction of a statue copied from the Statue of Liberty, was covered in great detail by the Western news media. On June 4, 1989, the military opened fire on the students to put down what is officially known in China as "the turmoil." Thousands of students died. The commander of the 38th Army who did not obey orders to attack the students received a ten-year prison sentence. The official line is that the student movement was a counter-revolutionary rebellion. During the turmoil, Jian Zemin emerged as General Secretary of the Chinese Communist Party. He told *U.S. News & World Report,* "We do not regret or criticize ourselves for the way we handled the Tiananmen event because if we had not sent in the troops then, I would not be able to sit here today."[14]

The political backlash has restricted further economic reforms. Some Western firms that had been investing in China fear that the crackdown will reverse the economic gains. Others contend that the economic reforms have gone so far that it would be impossible to reverse them.

THE SOVIET UNION

Recent changes in the Soviet Union have been staggering. Before 1989, planning was the major feature of the Soviet economy. Gosplan supervised the planning and the implementation of the plan through approximately fifty ministries. Each ministry represented a segment of the Soviet economy. The changes were spawned by the Soviet Union's lackluster economic performance. In Stalin's time, growth rates were high. But a succession of general secretaries, including Brezhnev, Andropov, Chernenko, and now Mikhail Gorbachev, have acknowledged the poor economic performance in their speeches.

Concern focused on several areas. First and foremost, economic growth has been slow. Coupled with this slow growth were "imbalances" (shortages) in consumer areas. Wages increased, but the production of consumer goods was too low. As a result, workers had few production incentives. In addition, both shortages and surpluses were common because the plan did not adjust to changes in supply and demand. As Soviet consumers became relatively better off, they resisted purchasing shoddy merchandise, creating surpluses of some products.

The reasons for the poor performance are not hard to pinpoint. The centralization of economic decision making, based on detailed, explicit plans, led to mistakes. There was no good mechanism for channeling feedback from consumers into the plans. Ultimately, the managers of enterprises were only concerned with satisfying the central planners in the relevant ministry. This concentrated central planning, coupled with enterprise security (the firms faced no competition) and employment security (workers faced no job-loss threat), created few incentives to increase productivity or to be more responsive to consumer preferences.

REFORMS. In March 1985, Mikhail Gorbachev was made general secretary of the Soviet Communist Party following the death of Konstantin Chernenko. Gorbachev, in his fifties, represented a change from rule by elderly men from the Stalin era. His first steps in the direction of economic reform were taken in early 1987. The economic reforms are referred to as *perestroika*. Political reforms are known as **glasnost**, or openness.

Perestroika represents the first steps in economic reform. Reform was not easy to accomplish because every step toward markets and efficiency was a step away from central planning. *Glasnost* and *perestroika* are dramatic changes from earlier periods when the Soviet Union intervened first in

perestroika
Restructuring, economic reforms in the Soviet Union.

glasnost
Openness, political reforms in the Soviet Union.

---

14. Emily MacFarquhar, "Back to the Future in China," *U.S. News & World Report* (12 March 1990): 41. This issue of *U.S. News & World Report* contains three very good articles on China.

While the Soviets struggle with the political aftermath of the failed coup, some of the Eastern European countries are moving much faster in the area of economic reform. It must be kept in mind that these countries differ greatly from the Soviet Republics. For most of these countries, the main obstacle to reform was the Soviet Union. When they realized that the Soviet Union would not intervene militarily as it had in Hungary (1956) and Czechoslovakia (1968), the reform movements gained momentum.

The success of reforms in Eastern Europe is based on many factors. To begin, most of these countries have escaped the ethnic unrest that has been so devastating in the Soviet Republics. In addition, their economies were in better shape than the Soviet economy when the reforms began.

East Germany was the most developed of the Soviet bloc countries. Its reform movement has been greatly helped by its reunification with West Germany. The financial aid from the West German economy is so important that East Germany is a special case by itself. Even there, however, there have been problems. Unemployment has been high, and buyers for state enterprises have been hard to find.

Poland moved toward capitalism in a bold step. Poland's Finance Minister Leszek Balcerowicz is a former economics professor with an MBA degree from St. John's University in New York. He is an admirer of Milton Friedman. With the help of Professor Jeffry Sachs of Harvard University, Balcerowicz drafted a plan for Poland's economic reform. In 1990, inflation dropped to an annual rate of around 30 percent, compared to 3,000 percent in 1989. The

INTERNATIONAL PERSPECTIVE

REFORM IN EAST GERMANY, POLAND, HUNGARY, AND CZECHOSLOVAKIA

stores are well stocked with agricultural products from local farms and high-tech consumer goods from West Germany and Hong Kong. All restrictions on new enterprises were lifted in the fall of 1989, and 80,000 new companies sprang up in the first year. It was expected that 45 percent of all goods and services would be produced by firms in the private sector by the end of 1991.

Problems remain. Unemployment is high and consumers spend most of their income on food and shelter. The main obstacle to continued success in Poland is political. Lech Walesa and Prime Minister Tadeusz Mazowiecki fought for control of the ruling Solidarity movement in November and December of 1990. Walesa won the election and became Prime Minister in December 1990. Critics worry that his political ties to labor will undermine the reforms. Since his election, Walesa has been uncharacteristically silent about his plans.

Hungary is pursuing a very sophisticated reform package, loosely based on a Thatcher-like gradual selling of government-owned enterprises. The ability to attract foreign capital will determine its success. By the end of 1991, 45 percent of the Hungarian GNP was produced by privately owned firms.

The Czech reform is proceeding more slowly. Czech reformers do not want to sell government assets directly to foreigners or to Czech citizens. They favor a gradual approach. The Czech plan calls for vouchers to be given to citizens, who could use them to buy equity in state-owned enterprises. About 10 percent of the Czech economy had been privatized by the end of 1991.

Hungary, then in Czechoslovakia, and finally in Poland to make sure that economic reform did not mean a slide toward capitalism. In 1989, the Soviet Union did not intervene when radical change swept Eastern Europe. The most dramatic event occurred in East Germany where the Berlin Wall came down, but change also occurred in Romania, Hungary, Czechoslovakia, and Poland.

The reforms in the Soviet Union have not gone smoothly. The once powerful Red Army is in disarray. In the first half of 1990, when only 26 percent of the drafted young men showed up, the government chose not to crack down on the draft-dodgers. To complicate the military situation, several independent armies emerged in ethnic republics, including Georgia, Armenia, and Azerbaijan.[15] In August 1991, Gorbachev was the victim of a coup, but he was rescued when Boris Yeltsin's political support defeated the coup.

The reforms face at least eight problems:

1. There is no experience with markets, property rights, and exchange. There is widespread distrust of market processes.
2. Pollution is rampant in the Soviet Union (and the countries of Eastern Europe). An emerging environmental movement is demanding that more attention be paid to the environment. This will be expensive at a time when other matters are more pressing.
3. There is growing ethnic unrest. Independence movements have succeeded in the Baltics, the Ukraine, Moldavia, and Georgia. Fighting has erupted between Armenia and Azerbaijan.
4. There is growing labor unrest. Miners are the most organized and violent. They threaten to strike unless their demands are met.
5. The military is in turmoil. Senior military leaders are unhappy about their loss of status in the political apparatus.
6. Agriculture is in disarray. Although bumper harvests, the best in fifteen years occurred in 1990, food rotted in the fields because the distribution network is not adequate.
7. The economic reformers demand faster and more radical economic changes. At the same time, there is strong resistance from bureaucrats and consumers who fear higher prices.
8. Finally, the economy is in chaos. The widespread shortages are aggravated by panic buying from consumers afraid of higher rates of inflation. An illegal black market thrives. Economic conditions are likely to deteriorate before they get better.

To address these growing problems, Gorbachev teamed with his rival Yeltsin in August 1990 to announce a new 500-day program to replace the failed reform of the previous year. Under the 500-day program, the government's huge subsidies to industry were to end. The twenty remaining industrial ministries would be substantially cut back, further freeing the economy to market forces. Workers, the public, and even foreign investors would be permitted to buy state assets. The republics were to be given more control over their own resources. Most have already declared such

---

15. See "The Enemy Within?" *National Review* (17 September 1990): 7.

control.[16] The future is difficult to predict. The failed coup in August 1991 ended communist rule. The Communist Party and the KGB were shut down in Russia by Yeltsin. Other republics quickly followed suit. It is unclear what the political structure of the former Soviet Union will be.

CAN REFORMS SUCCEED IN THE SOVIET UNION? The next few years will determine whether reforms succeed in the Soviet Republics or are halted by a conservative backlash. The twin forces of *perestroika* and *glasnost* can cause opposing changes. In China, the democracy movement created a setback for the economic reform movement. In some Soviet Republics, the same result could occur.

A major problem that market reform faces is the attitude of consumers. Consumers want the standard of living that capitalism produces, but they like the safety of governmental regulation. If such attitudes prevail, it will be very difficult to institute market reforms in a democratic setting. The breakup of the Soviet Union into a loose federation of republics could be the cause for optimism. The various republics will go their separate ways, and markets may have a better chance with decentralization and the shock destruction of the centralized political power.

JAPAN

In Japan, great strides have been made in a modified capitalistic structure in the last forty years. The Japanese "miracle" is of great interest to developing countries and industrial managers in the United States. The interest stems in part from wanting to borrow those elements of the Japanese success that can be transplanted into other economies.

In 1950, Japan was starting to recover from the devastation of World War II. The U.S. Commerce Department reports that Japanese per capita income in 1950 was only about an eighth of that in the United States. Thirty-five years later, in 1990, the per capita level of income was four-fifths of that of the United States. In the 1950s, the phrase "Made in Japan" implied cheap, shoddy copies of U.S. products. In the 1990s, "Made in Japan" implies the finest of automotive and high-tech products. This rapid economic growth occurred in a country smaller than the state of California with few natural resources (Japan imports almost all of its oil) and a population half as large as that of the United States.

TAXES
Compared to Western Europe and the United States, Japan has very low taxes. Japan's taxes are around 25 percent of national income, compared to 30 percent in the United States, 35 percent in the United Kingdom, and almost 40 percent in West Germany.

---

16. See "This Time, Gorbachev May Really Turn the Economy Upside Down," *Business Week* (27 August 1990): 8; "Out of Stock," *The Wall Street Journal* (23 July 1990): 1; "Moscow's Bumper Crop of Troubles," *U.S. News & World Report* (3 September 1990): 27–28; "Who's in Charge Here?" *Forbes* (3 September 1990): 32–33; Anthony DeCurtis, "Anarchy in the Soviet Union," *Rolling Stone* (26 July 1990): 29–34; "Yeltsin's Shadow Just Keeps Getting Longer," *Business Week*, (17 September 1990): 28; and "500 Days," *Business Week* (1 October 1990): 29–30.

Supply siders in the United States argue that low taxes are an important reason for growth. They note that the tax structure in Japan is not used to redistribute income. Until very recently, there was no social insurance system, and even now it is very limited. The pre-tax distribution of income is about the same as the post-tax distribution. As a result, there are powerful incentives to engage in risky, entrepreneurial activity.

INVESTMENT AND SAVING

The Japanese people save about 20 percent of their annual incomes. These savings find their way into capital investment, which creates future income. The high rate of Japanese saving is the result of two powerful influences. The first has already been mentioned. Since only a very limited social insurance system exists in Japan, workers must save for their retirement. Second, the tax system is structured in such a way that tax credits are given for saving. In contrast, in the United States, dividends and interest—the returns to saving—are taxed, and Social Security reduces the incentive to save for retirement.

LABOR-MANAGEMENT RELATIONS

Perhaps the aspect of the Japanese economy that has generated the most interest in the U.S. business community is the labor-management relationship. Great loyalty to the firm exists in Japan. Many workers in the manufacturing sector enjoy lifetime employment to age fifty-five, when mandatory retirement occurs. These workers belong to company unions that cooperate with management in setting goals, work schedules, and plans for the company.

Certain aspects of this labor-management relationship are being tried by U.S. businesses. **Theory Z** is the idea that employees are not motivated by negative incentives, such as threats, or by monetary incentives, such as raises and promotions, but are motivated by being included as active participants in the management process. The use of quality circles is one of the tools of a Theory Z style of management. In **quality circles**, workers organize themselves into units to try to improve quality by discussing production problems and suggesting solutions. A quality circle is a kind of activist, organized, suggestion box.

Theory Z
A management theory that workers are motivated to perform if they are made part of the management process.

quality circles
Groups of workers organized to improve quality by discussing production problems and suggesting solutions.

HAS JAPAN PEAKED?

Many observers feel that the Japanese economy may have peaked in the mid-1980s.[17] They point to the fact that Japanese exports have dropped and industrial production has fallen. Other observers have predicted that younger workers in Japan will grow restless because of long working hours and high consumer prices. They will demand higher standards of living, rather than increased investment and production through higher levels of saving.

The Japanese Ministry of International Trade predicts that Japan will lose 560,000 manufacturing jobs by 2000. Some of this loss is due to the increasing tendency for Japanese firms to produce in foreign countries rather than producing in Japan and exporting. Approximately 20 percent

---

17. See "To Have and Have Not in Japan," *U.S. News & World Report* (13 February 1989): 41–42.

of Japanese manufacturing is expected to be "offshore" in 2000, compared to 5 percent in 1987.

The Japanese response to the changing economic position will be important. If Japan opens its market to foreign trade, it will be able to live off its investments rather than its production. This openness will be a challenge because changing the pattern of economic development has been disturbing to Japanese leaders. These leaders have tended to support protectionist policies in the past. In the face of rising production costs at home, a rise in protectionist policies may follow. These trends could represent a cloud on the Japanese horizon.

Still another cloud on the Japanese horizon is growing discontent among Americans about the trade relationship between the United States and Japan. Forty-four percent of Americans say they do not trust the Japanese, and sixty-one percent believe Japanese imports into the United States should be restricted. These negative attitudes are unlike the attitudes of U.S. voters to trade relations with other foreign countries.[18]

SUMMARY

1. The study of comparative systems allows economists to analyze different environments and institutions to determine how they can affect economic outcomes.

2. The most common approach to comparative economics is to classify systems according to dominant ideology. This approach is not very useful. Almost all systems can be labeled as either capitalist or socialist but differ widely within these general categories.

3. Marx's writings provide the basic political framework on which all socialist systems are based. The economic systems of these countries are, however, widely divergent. The variation in the systems has been, in many cases, the result of dominant political leaders. Thus, it is possible to distinguish among Leninism, Stalinism, Castroism, and Maoism as separate forms of socialism.

4. Another way to analyze different economic systems is to examine their organizational and decision-making differences. This approach looks at the level at which decisions are made, the informational requirements and the motivations of the decision-making units, and the interaction of system, environment, performance, and policy.

5. Planning is carried out in all economies. The key difference between systems is the level at which plan-

ning is carried out. The higher the level of planning, the greater the informational requirements of the system.

6. Central planning requires the determination of what to produce. In the Soviet Union, such planning resulted in rapid growth because the central authority decided not to produce many consumer goods. This decision generated high rates of investment.

7. Central planning relies on input-output analysis. Input-output analysis starts with historical data on the amounts of inputs necessary to produce a given output. Those data are used to determine what inputs are necessary to produce a desired output. Input-output analysis assumes that the historical production record will continue to hold.

8. After all the technical problems of planning are worked out, it is necessary to put the plan into operation. Implementation requires transmitting the plan to the production units and creating the proper incentives.

9. China and the Soviet Republics face reform movements. Economic growth in each case will depend on whether these reforms are continued or reversed.

10. The Japanese "miracle" is based on low tax rates, high saving rates, and labor-management harmony.

---

18. Lee Smith, "Fear and Loathing of Japan," *Fortune* (26 February 1990): 16.

NEW TERMS

capitalism
socialism
communism
fascism
War Communism
New Economic Policy
    (NEP)

Great Industrialization
    Debate
Great Leap Forward
Cultural Revolution
shadow prices

socialist controversy
competitive solution
Gosplan
input-output analysis
input coefficient

perestroika
glasnost
Theory Z
quality circles

QUESTIONS FOR DISCUSSION

1. How did the trade union Solidarity threaten the Communist Party in Poland? Why was the Soviet Union so interested in developments in Poland?

2. How did Lenin change the theories of Marx? Which of the two appears to be more important as the inspiration of communist revolutions?

3. Is planning an important function in all economies? Is it more important in market or command economies?

4. How would allowing the input coefficient to vary complicate input-output analysis? Is the assumption of fixed input coefficients a damaging one?

5. List as many problems of maintaining proper incentives under a central planning system as you can. Do these problems exist only in centrally planned economies?

6. How do you evaluate the performance of the Japanese economy? Are there lessons for the U.S. economy?

7. What are the weaknesses of fascism?

8. What was the period of the New Economic Policy in the Soviet Union?

9. Evaluate the two sides of the socialist controversy.

10. What is the connection between economic freedom and political freedom?

11. How can political freedom undermine economic reform in Eastern Europe, China, and the Soviet Union?

12. What are the primary obstacles facing the reform movement in the Soviet Republics?

13. Which reform movement in Eastern Europe has been the most successful? Why? Are there any lessons in this for the rest of the world?

14. Cuba is the last of the Communist countries to continue rigid planning. What are prospects for reform in Cuba?

15. Do the events of the past five years signal the death of communism and the victory of capitalism?

SUGGESTIONS FOR FURTHER READING

Doder, Dusko, and Louise Branson. *Gorbachev: Heretic in the Kremlin.* New York: Viking, 1990. A book billed as the story of how "Gorby got to the top." The authors final prediction: "It is entirely possible that Gorbachev ultimately will be rejected by the nation in a free election."

Galbraith, John Kenneth. *Economics in Perspective.* Boston: Houghton Mifflin, l987. A fast-paced economic history that extends from Adam and Eve to the present.

Gray, Francine du Plessix. *Soviet Women.* New York: Doubleday, 1990. Looks at the reform movement through the eyes of Soviet women and describes the problems they face.

Kahn, Joseph F. "Better Fed Than Red," *Esquire* (September 1990): 186–197; and "Inside Quin Cheng Prison," *Harper's* (August 1990): 17–19. Two accounts of what happened to different groups of students after the Tiananmen Square protest in China. The first chronicles the life of student leader Wu'erkaixi after his escape to Paris. The second describes life in prison for some of the arrested students.

Kotkin, Stephen. *Steeltown USSR: Soviet Society in the Gorbachev Era.* Berkeley: University of California Press, 1991. Shows how difficult Soviet reforms will be, based on interviews in a steel-producing city.

Winiecki, Jan. *The Distorted World of Soviet-type Economies.* Pittsburgh: Pittsburgh University Press, 1988. A book by a respected Polish economist that outlines the problems that faced Soviet-type economies on the eve of the reform movement.

Yoshino, M. T., and Thomas B. Lifson. *The Invisible Link: Japan's Sogo Shosha.* Cambridge, MA: MIT Press, 1986. Examines how the Japanese general trading houses coordinate trade and production.

GLOSSARY

absolute advantage The ability to produce something using fewer resources than other producers use.

accommodating monetary policy Monetary expansion that is undertaken to help the Treasury finance deficits without driving up interest rates very much.

Accord, The The 1951 agreement between the Fed and the Treasury that the Fed was no longer obliged to hold interest rates low to assist with the Treasury's debt financing.

accounting profit The difference between total sales and explicit costs.

acreage allotment A limit set by the government on the number of acres that can be used to produce a specific crop, based on past production levels.

adaptive expectations Expectations about the future that are formed by economic actors on the basis of current and past experience and that adjust slowly to changing conditions.

administered prices Prices that are relatively rigid, or changed only infrequently.

AFL-CIO Organization formed by the merger of the American Federation of Labor and the Congress of Industrial Organizations in 1955, which gave labor a more unified political front.

Agency for International Development (AID) An agency that is part of the U.S. State Department and is in charge of U.S. aid to foreign countries.

aggregate demand curve A graph showing the amounts of total real output that all buyers in an economy wish to purchase at various price levels.

aggregate expenditure (*AE*) Total planned spending by all sectors for an economy's total output.

aggregate production function A graph showing the relationship between total real output and the number of workers employed.

aggregate supply curve A graph showing the amounts of total real output that the producing sector will offer for sale at various price levels.

aggregates Quantities whose values are determined by adding across many markets.

agricultural support program Attempts by the federal government to achieve parity for farmers through the use of price supports.

allocation Any activities by government or its agents that affect the distribution of resources and the combination of goods and services produced.

allocative efficiency The use of resources to produce the goods most desired by society. Free markets allow allocative efficiency.

American Federation of Labor (AFL) An exclusive union for skilled workers founded by Samuel Gompers in 1886 as the first business union.

American Federation of State, County, and Municipal Employees (AFSCME) A union of public employees that was one of the few unions that grew in the 1970s.

annually balanced budget The view that government revenues should be equal to expenditures on an annual basis.

appreciation A rise in the market price of a currency due to market forces.

appropriate technology Methods of production that have been adapted to take advantage of the mix of resources available in less developed countries.

arbitration Third party intervention in a dispute consisting of hearing the arguments of both sides, studying their positions, and rendering a decision. In binding arbitration, both sides must abide by the decision.

arc elasticity The elasticity at the midpoint between two points on a demand curve.

asset demand for money Demand for money to hold in order to protect the value of one's assets against changes in interest rates. The asset demand for money is negatively related to interest rates.

association-causation fallacy The false notion that association implies causality.

auction markets Markets characterized by good information, many buyers and sellers, and rapid adjustments of price to changing conditions.

automatic stabilizers Changes in tax collections and transfer payments that are automatically triggered by changes in national income and tend to reduce changes in output and employment.

average fixed cost (*AFC*) Total fixed costs of production divided by number of units of output.

average physical product (*APP*) The total physical product (output) divided by the number of units of a factor used.

average revenue (*AR*) Total revenue divided by the quantity sold, or the revenue per unit sold (the price).

average total cost (*AC*) Total costs of producing a level of output divided by the number of units of output.

average variable cost (*AVC*) Total variable costs of production divided by the number of units of output.

backward-bending supply curve A labor supply curve that slopes back to the left at the point where the income effect dominates the substitution effect.

balance of payments An annual summary of the transactions between residents of one country and residents of the rest of the world.

balance of payments deficit An excess of a country's foreign spending over its foreign earnings for a given year.

balance on goods and services The difference between the value of exports and the value of imports for a country in a given year.

balance sheet A statement of assets owned, liabilities owed, and the difference between them at a point in time.

bank deregulation A policy enabling banks to compete more aggressively with nonbank financial institutions by reducing the regulations affecting them.

bank panics Sudden waves of fear that banks will not be able to pay off their depositors.

bar chart A graphic representation that expresses data using columns of different heights.

barriers to entry Natural or artificial obstacles that keep new firms from entering an industry.

barter Direct exchange of one good or service for another without the use of money.

big push strategy The development strategy calling for a major thrust on all fronts in the economy by government or by private enterprise with government inducement.

bilateral monopoly Market structure in which monopolies deal with each other as buyers and sellers, such as when an inclusive union sells labor to a monopsonistic firm.

bimetallism The use of both gold and silver as parts of the money stock.

black markets Markets in which people illegally buy and sell goods and services at prices above government-imposed price ceilings.

board of directors The individuals elected by the stockholders of a corporation to select the managers and oversee the management of the corporation.

Board of Governors Central governing body of the Federal Reserve System.

bond An interest-earning certificate that is issued by a government or corporation in exchange for borrowed funds and has a fixed face value, annual interest payment, and maturity date.

bond market A market in which the debt instruments of governments and corporations are traded.

Bretton Woods system The international monetary system in effect from 1945 to 1973, based on infrequent changes in currency prices, ample reserves, and the dollar as key currency.

budget constraint A given level of income that determines the maximum amount of goods that may be purchased by an individual.

business cycle An observed and repeated pattern of ups and downs in real output, employment, and prices.

business cycle theorists A group of economists in the nineteenth and early twentieth centuries who tried to develop explanations for cyclical patterns in economic activity.

business firm An organization formed by an entrepreneur to combine inputs in order to produce marketable outputs.

business inventories Stocks of goods held by firms from which they can make sales to meet demand.

business union According to Samuel Gompers, a union that works for economic goals without wanting to change or destroy the business organization or the political environment in which it functions.

capital The durable inputs into the production process created by people. Machines, tools, and buildings are examples of capital.

capital account The part of the balance of payments that summarizes purchases and sales of financial assets.

capital consumption allowance The national income accountants' estimate of the amount of the nation's capital stock used up in production during a year.

capital gain An increase in the market price of an asset.

capitalism An economic system characterized by private ownership of the factors of production by individuals or groups of individuals.

capitalized value The present value of a stream of future rent payments.

cartel A group of independent firms that agree not to compete but rather to determine prices and output jointly.

Celler-Kefauver Antimerger Act A federal law that strengthened the Clayton Act in 1950 by making it illegal in certain circumstances for a firm to merge with another by purchasing its assets.

certificate of deposit (CD) A deposit made with a financial institution at a specified interest rate for a given (fixed) period of time.

ceterus paribus **assumption** The assumption that everything else will remain constant, used for most economic models. (*Ceterus paribus* is Latin for "all else being equal.")

ceterus paribus **fallacy** The false notion that arises because an observer fails to recognize that variables other than the one in question have changed.

checkable deposit Balances in accounts at depository institutions on which checks can be drawn.

chiseling Cheating on a cartel agreement by lowering prices in an attempt to capture more of the market.

circular flow model A visual representation of the relationships between the factor market (in which income is obtained) and the product market (in which income is used to purchase goods and services).

classical school A group of economists in the eighteenth and nineteenth centuries who believed that the economy automatically tended toward the full-employment level of output.

Clayton Act Federal law, passed in 1914, prohibiting the acquisition of the stock of a competing company if such an acquisition would "substantially lessen competition."

Clean Air Act A federal law passed in 1970 that empowered the EPA to set emission standards and impose standards on polluters.

closed shops Firms where workers must be union members before being employed.

Coase theorem The idea that well-defined property rights are sufficient to internalize any external effect that is present, when there are small numbers of affected parties.

coefficient of price elasticity of demand (E_d) The numerical measure of price elasticity of demand, equal to the percent change in quantity demanded of a good divided by the percent change in its price.

coefficient of price elasticity of supply (E_s) The numerical measure of price elasticity of supply, equal to the percent change in the quantity supplied of a good divided by the percent change in its price.

collusion Agreements between firms in an industry to set a certain price or to share a market in certain ways.

command economy An economy in which the three basic questions are answered through central planning and control (also called a planned economy).

commercial paper Short-term loans by financial institutions to business firms.

commercial policy The set of actions that a country undertakes to deliberately influence trade in goods and services.

Commodity Credit Corporation (CCC) A U.S. government agency that makes loans to farmers as part of federal price support programs.

common access resource A resource that is not owned by any individual but is available for all to use.

communication Firms' ability to signal their intentions to each other.

communism The final stage in the theory of Karl Marx, in which the state has withered away and economic goods are equally distributed.

comparable worth A standard for determining wages that calls for equal pay for jobs that require similar levels of training, responsibility, and skills.

comparative advantage The ability to produce something at a lower opportunity cost than other producers face.

comparative statics A technique of comparing two equilibrium positions to determine the changing relationships between variables.

competitive fringe The smaller competitors in informally coordinated markets with one large, dominant firm.

competitive solution The model developed by Oskar Lange in an attempt to show that a planned economy could theoretically reach the efficiency of an economy with competition.

complementary goods Goods that are jointly consumed. The consumption of one enhances the consumption of the other.

concentration ratio A measure of the distribution of economic power among firms in an oligopolistic market.

conglomerates Firms that perform many unrelated operations or produce many unrelated products or services.

Congress of Industrial Organizations (CIO) An affiliation of industrial unions that was organized when the AFL decided not to move into mass-production industries.

Conservation Reserve Program (CRP) A federal program that pays farmers to remove land from production for ten years or more.

constant cost industry An industry in which expansion of output does not cause average cost to rise in the long run.

constrained sales maximization The hypothesis that managers' primary goal is to increase the sales of the firm because they will be rewarded by stockholders for increasing the firm's relative share of the market.

consumer durables Goods that last, on average, a substantial length of time.

consumer nondurables Goods that last, on average, only a short period of time.

Consumer Price Index (CPI) A well-known measure of inflation based on the cost of a selected market basket of consumer goods (also known as the cost-of-living index).

consumer services That part of household consumption composed of nontangible activities.

consumer surplus The extra utility derived from a purchase that has a value to the consumer greater than the market price.

consumption expenditures Sales to the household sector.

consumption function Any equation, table, or graph that shows the relationship between income of consumers (disposable income) and the amount they plan to spend on currently produced final output.

consumption possibilities curve A line showing the consumption combinations attainable through trade.

contestable markets Markets composed of large firms that are nevertheless efficient because easily reversible entry into the market is possible.

contract law Law that deals with the enforcement of voluntary exchanges.

contract markets Markets characterized by few buyers and sellers, imperfect information, long-term contracts, and sluggish price adjustments.

contractionary fiscal policy Raising taxes, lowering transfer payments, or reducing government purchases in an attempt to reduce the equilibrium level of output to one that is attainable with available resources.

convergence hypothesis The prediction that income differences among countries will shrink over time because of the transfer of technology and innovation.

coordinates The values of x and y that define the location of a point in a coordinate system.

coordination Firms' ability to relate their production decisions to those made by other firms in an industry.

corporation A form of enterprise in which stockholders are the owners of the firm but have limited liability.

cost-plus pricing The form of price regulation that allows firms a markup that is a percentage of average costs of production.

cost-push inflation Inflation that starts as a result of a decrease in aggregate supply due to wage or price increases.

countercyclical policy Government actions designed to offset the cyclical ups and downs of the macro economy.

countervailing power The offsetting power possessed by both sides of the market in a monopoly.

craft union A union composed of specific kinds of skilled workers, such as plumbers or carpenters.

credit crunch The 1966 shortage of loanable funds caused by the sudden slowing of monetary growth rates by the Fed.

credit market The aggregate market consisting of

financial institutions that channel household savings to business firms that want to invest.

cross elasticity of demand The measure of the responsiveness of changes in the quantity demanded of one good to changes in the price of another.

crowding out The negative effect on borrowing for private investment due to competition from the federal government in the credit market.

crude birth rate Number of births per thousand of population.

crude death rate Number of deaths per thousand of population.

Cultural Revolution The high point of Mao's power in China, characterized by a radical restructuring of the economy from 1966 through 1969.

currency Paper money with a specified value, issued by the government or central bank.

currency drain An increase in cash held by the public that causes a dollar-for-dollar decline in bank reserves.

current account The part of the balance of payments that summarizes transactions in currently produced goods and services.

cyclical deficit The part of a deficit that is due to a downturn in economic activity.

cyclical unemployment Unemployment caused by a decline in the level of total output.

cyclically balanced budget The idea that surpluses during expansionary periods should offset deficits during recessionary periods so that the budget balances over the course of the business cycle.

deadweight loss The lost consumer surplus due to monopolistic restriction of output.

debasement of money The practice of reminting coins of gold or silver with base metals added, thus increasing the number of coins, driving up the prices of goods, and reducing the value of each coin.

decrease in demand A shift in the demand curve indicating that at every price, consumers demand a smaller amount than before.

decrease in supply A shift in the supply curve indicating that at every price, a smaller quantity will be offered for sale than before.

decreasing cost industry An industry in which expansion of output causes average cost to fall in the long run.

deficit The difference between the federal government's revenues and expenditures in a given year (the fiscal year), when the government spends more than it collects in taxes.

demand The desire and ability to consume certain quantities of a good at various prices over a certain period of time.

demand curve A graph representing a demand schedule and showing the quantity demanded at various prices in a certain time period.

demand deposits Bank deposits on which checks can be written (also known as checking accounts).

demand-determined price A price that is determined solely by changes in demand because supply is perfectly inelastic.

demand for money The amount of money households and businesses wish to hold for making transactions and as a financial asset.

demand-pull inflation Inflation that starts as a result of a rise in aggregate demand, usually due to expansionary monetary or fiscal policy.

demand schedule A table that shows quantities demanded at various prices during a specific time period.

demographic transition The bridging of the developmental gap from falling death rates to falling birth rates, resulting in slower population growth.

dependency ratio The percentage of the population not of working age (under fifteen or over sixty-five).

dependent variable The variable, usually plotted on the vertical axis, that is affected or influenced by the other variable.

deposit multiplier Ratio between the maximum increase in the money supply and a given increase in excess reserves. It equals the reciprocal of the reserve ratio.

depreciation (1) The decline in the value of an asset, such as a machine or factory, over time. (2) A fall in the market price of a currency due to market forces.

depression A very severe recession.

derived demand Demand for a productive resource that results from demand for a final good or service. For example, the demand for labor is derived from the demand for the product that the labor produces.

diamond-water paradox The fact that diamonds, although less useful than water, are more expensive than water. That is, things with the greatest value in exchange (price) often have little value in use.

differentiated oligopoly An oligopoly that produces heterogeneous products that are very close substitutes.

differentiated product A good or service that has real or imagined characteristics that are different from those of other goods or services.

discount rate The interest rate the Fed charges on loans to banks.

discounting The technique of calculating present values by adjusting for interest that would be earned between now and some specified future time.

discretionary fiscal policy Deliberate changes in tax rates, transfer programs, or government purchases designed to change the equilibrium level of national income.

diseconomies of agglomeration The additional costs that individuals must pay when too many of them locate in one city (thus creating negative external effects for one another).

diseconomies of scale Increases in long-run average cost that are due to increased plant size.

disequilibrium An unstable situation in which variables are moving toward equilibrium but are not yet at equilibrium.

disposable income Income received by households and available to spend or save; equals PI less personal taxes.

dissaving Consuming by drawing on accumulated stocks (inventories) or financial assets.

distributive justice A normative argument for a particular distribution of income.

dominant firm The most influential firm in an industry, usually the largest firm.

double coincidence of wants The necessary requirement for barter that each trader has what the other wants and wants what the other has.

dual labor markets The radical economists' idea that there are two labor markets because of artificial barriers that keep some workers earning low wages.

dualism The coexistence of a modern, urban, market-oriented society and a rural, agriculture-based, traditional peasant society, characteristic of most less developed countries.

dumping The practice of selling in foreign markets at lower prices than in domestic markets (a form of price discrimination).

economic efficiency The least-cost method of production.

economic growth An increase in the level of real output per capita.

economic profit The difference between total sales and the total of explicit and implicit costs of production.

economic rent A payment to a factor of production in excess of its opportunity cost.

Economic Report of the President An annual report to Congress describing the state of the economy and recommending policy.

economics The study of how people and institutions make decisions about production and consumption and how they face the problem of scarcity.

economies of agglomeration The cost savings that individuals enjoy when enough of them locate close together in or near a large city.

economies of scale Declines in long-run average cost that are due to increased plant size.

elasticity The measure of the sensitivity or responsiveness of quantity demanded or quantity supplied to changes in price (or other factors).

eminent domain A doctrine that gives government the right to buy property at "fair market value" if the purchase is in the public interest.

Employment Act of 1946 A law requiring the federal government to actively promote full employment, steady growth, and stable prices through the use of fiscal and monetary policy.

endogenous variables Variables that are explained or determined within a model.

enterprise The input to the production process that involves organizing, innovation, and risk taking.

equation of exchange An identity based on the quantity theory of money that says that the money supply times the velocity of money equals the price level times real output.

excess capacity The unutilized part of existing production facilities by a monopolistically competitive firm.

excess reserves Reserves above the level required by law.

exchange control A system in which the government purchases all incoming foreign exchange and is the only source from which foreign exchange can be legally purchased.

excise tax A tax that on the purchase of a particular good, such as liquor, cigarettes, or electricity, or a broad class of goods, such as food.

exclusive union A union that restricts the supply of labor and maintains a higher-than-competitive wage for its members by excluding workers from a trade or occupation. Craft unions are exclusive unions.

exogenous variables Variables that are determined outside of a model and affect endogenous variables.

expansion A period of economic growth extending from a trough to the next peak in a business cycle.

expansionary fiscal policy Cutting taxes, raising transfer payments, or increasing government purchases to try to increase the level of income and employment.

expectations Feelings that individuals have about future conditions.

expected yield The rate of return on an asset that includes expected interest or dividends and the expected increase or decrease in its price.

expenditure multiplier Measures the impact of a given initial change in aggregate expenditures on equilibrium income and output. The multiplier is equal to $1/(1-MPC)$.

explicit costs Accounting costs or money outlays.

exports Goods and services sold to foreign buyers.

externalities Costs or benefits associated with consumption or production that are not reflected in market prices and fall on parties other than the buyer or seller.

factor market Set of markets in which owners of the factors of production sell these to producers.

factors of production The inputs of land, labor, capital, and enterprise that a firm uses to produce outputs.

fair rate of return The normal profit that a regulated industry must earn in order to stay in business.

fair trade The idea that the United States should impose trade barriers equivalent to those that its trading partners place on U.S. exports.

fallacy of composition The false notion that what holds for the parts holds for the whole.

Family Support Act of 1988 A federal law that incorporates some aspects of state warfare programs, turning entitlements into obligations to take jobs or enter job training programs.

fascism An economic system that combines monopoly, capitalism, private property, and a strong authoritarian central government.

featherbedding The maintenance of jobs that management claims are unnecessary or redundant.

federal funds market The market in which banks borrow reserves from each other.

federal funds rate The interest rate charged in the federal funds market.

Federal Open Market Committee (FOMC) Committee that supervises the conduct of the Fed's monetary policy.

Federal Reserve System (Fed) The central bank of the United States.

Federal Trade Commission Act A federal law passed in

1914 that set up the Federal Trade Commission (FTC) to police unfair and deceptive business practices.

fiat money   Money that is not a commodity and is not redeemable in any commodity.

final goods   Goods that will not be further processed or resold.

fiscal policy   The use of government spending and taxes to try to influence the levels of output, employment, and prices.

fixed factors   The factors of production that cannot be varied in the short run.

fixed investment   The part of business investment that does not add to inventories; consists of new plants and equipment and residential construction.

flow variable   A variable that is defined over a period of time.

Food Security Act   A 1985 federal law that sets target prices and requires farmers to agree to keep part of their land idle.

foreign exchange market   The network of banks and financial institutions through which buyers and sellers exchange national currencies.

45° line   A line in the first quadrant, passing through the origin, with a slope of +1, which divides the quadrant in half. If the scales on the axes are the same, the value of the x-variable is equal to the value of the y-variable along the 45° line.

forward market   The market in which contracts are made for future delivery of specific amounts of currency at a specified price.

fractional reserve banking   The practice of holding a fraction of money deposited as reserves and lending the rest.

free reserves   A bank's excess reserves less its loans from the Fed.

free riders   People or business firms who consume collective goods without contributing to the cost of their production.

frictional unemployment   Unemployment due to workers being temporarily between jobs or new entrants to the work force.

full-bodied money   Money that has a value in other uses equal to its monetary value. Coins made of precious metals are the best examples.

full employment   The level of employment at which approximately 94 to 95 percent of those who want to work are employed.

full-employment level of output   The level of real output associated with full use of all of the factors of production, especially labor.

functional distribution of income   The pattern of payments to the factors of production (rent, wages, interest, and profits).

functional finance   The idea that a balanced budget is less important than a stable economy.

gains from trade   The increase in economic well-being resulting from specialization and exchange.

game theory   A mathematical theory about rational decision making under conditions of uncertainty that can provide insight into oligopolistic behavior.

glasnost   Openness, political reforms in the Soviet Union.

GNP deflator   A current-weights index used to correct the GNP for price changes.

GNP targeting   A monetary policy that calls for the Fed to aim at some level of nominal GNP by influencing a number of variables that affect GNP.

gold standard   An international monetary system in which currencies were defined in terms of gold, money supplies were tied to gold, and balance of payment deficits were settled in gold.

Gosplan   The state planning commission in the Soviet Union.

Great Industrialization Debate   An open debate that took place in the Soviet Union from 1924 to 1928 concerning the correct way to industrialize the economy.

Great Leap Forward   A modernization plan that was launched in 1958 to increase per capita income in China by 25 percent in five years.

Green Revolution   An agricultural innovation consisting of the development of dwarf, high-yield varieties of wheat and rice that have enabled some less developed countries to improve food production.

greenbacks   Paper money issued by the U.S. government during the Civil War that was not redeemable in gold.

gross national product (GNP)   The total market value of all final goods and services produced by a nation's domestically owned factors of production during a given time period, usually a year.

gross private domestic investment   Purchases by the business sector of final output.

Hart-Scott-Rodino Antitrust Improvement Act   A 1970 federal law amending the FTC Act to require firms to report mergers or acquisitions to the FTC and Department of Justice before the fact.

hedgers   People who try to reduce their risk by buying or selling contracts in the forward market for currency.

Herfindahl Index   A summed index of concentration that takes into account all the firms in an industry.

high-employment balanced budget   The view that tax rates and transfer payments should be set so as to balance the budget at the full-employment level of output Y^*. (The actual budget need not be balanced.)

holding companies   Firms set up for the sole purpose of owning and thus controlling other firms.

horizontally integrated firms   Firms that perform many similar production operations in the same industry.

human capital   The investment made to improve the quality of people's labor skills through education, training, health care, and so on.

Humphrey-Hawkins Act   A 1978 amendment to the Employment Act of 1946 that set specific targets for output, employment, and prices.

impact lag   The time that elapses between implementation of a fiscal policy and its full effect on economic activity.

implementation lag   The time it takes after a problem is recognized to choose and enact a fiscal policy in response.

implicit costs Costs measured by the value of alternatives given up.

imports Goods and services purchased from foreign sellers.

inclusive union A union that attempts to organize all the workers in an industry and to maintain a strong bargaining position with respect to management.

income-consumption curve A curve that uses parallel budget lines to show changes in consumer equilibrium when income changes.

income effect An increase in demand for a good (or service) when its price falls, *ceteris paribus*, because the household's real income rises and the consumer buys more of all normal goods.

income elasticity of demand The measure of the responsiveness of quantity demanded to changes in income.

income statement Measure of the total flow of revenue to a household, individual, or firm over a period of time.

increase in demand A shift in the demand curve indicating that at every price, consumers demand a larger amount than before.

increase in supply A shift in the supply curve indicating that at every price, a larger quantity will be offered for sale than before.

increasing cost industry An industry in which expansion of output causes average cost to rise in the long run.

increasing opportunity cost The principle that as production of one good rises, larger and larger sacrifices of another are required.

independent variable The variable, usually plotted on the horizontal axis, that affects or influences the other variable.

indifference analysis An approach to analyzing consumer behavior based on ranking the utility of choices relative to one another.

indifference curve A plot of all combinations of goods that the consumer is indifferent among.

indifference map A set of indifference curves. Higher curves represent higher levels of utility.

indifference set Any number of combinations of goods among which the individual consumer is indifferent (has no preference).

industrial policy A growth strategy consisting of government programs to identify and encourage promising industries and to ease the decline of old industries.

industrial union An inclusive union that gains power by organizing all (or a large share) of the workers in an industry.

Industrial Workers of the World (IWW) An international union that organized U.S. steelworkers after World War I and was viewed as a socialistic organization, which contributed to its demise.

industry A group of firms producing similar or related products.

industry studies Investigations of specific industries to determine the degree of competitive behavior.

inferior good A good for which demand decreases as income increases.

inflation A sustained rise in the general, or average, level of prices.

infrastructure The basic facilities and equipment, usually publicly owned, that provide community services.

injections Spending added to the circular flow that is not paid for out of factor income. Business investment, government expenditures, and sales of exports are injections.

injunctions Court orders to cease some activity, such as ordering labor to stop a strike or walkout.

innovation The translation of inventions into products and processes that are commercially feasible and cost-effective.

input coefficient In input-output analysis, the ratio of the amount of an input to the total output of an industry.

input-output analysis An attempt to quantify the flows between different sectors of the economy for purposes of economic planning.

insatiable wants The needs and desires of human beings, which can never be completely satisfied.

insider-outsider model An explanation of labor market behavior that assumes that insiders (employed union members) will negotiate for higher real wages for themselves at the expense of jobs for outsiders, thus worsening the inflation-unemployment tradeoff.

institutional investors Large investors, including insurance companies, pension funds, and mutual funds, whose purchases and sales have an impact on the prices of investment assets.

interdependent demand Demand that depends on another type of demand. For example, a firm's demand for labor depends on the amount of other factors that the firm plans to use.

interdependent utility functions Preference patterns in which some people's well-being is dependent on the well-being of others.

interest The return to capital, one of the factors of production.

intermediate goods Goods that will be further processed before final sale.

internalization The incorporation of the social costs of negative external effects into the market price.

International Monetary Fund (IMF) The agency that supervised the operation of the Bretton Woods system by recording par values, consulting on devaluations and revaluations, and maintaining a pool of reserves.

international monetary reserves The pool of gold and major currencies created under the Bretton Woods system, from which countries could borrow to settle deficits and replenish from surpluses.

interpersonal utility comparisons Attempts to compare the utility of one individual with that of another (or others).

inventories The stocks of goods that have been produced by business firms but have not yet been sold.

investment Purchases of real, tangible assets, such as machines, factories, or inventories, that are used to produce goods and services.

investment demand schedule A graph that ranks possible investment projects for a firm in order of decreasing expected rate of return.

Investment Tax Credit (ITC) Provision offering tax

savings over and above depreciation for business firms investing in new plants or equipment. A percentage of the investment made can be subtracted from tax liability.

invisible hand The idea advanced by Adam Smith that individuals pursuing their own self-interest direct the market system toward socially desirable outcomes.

isocost line A line that shows the amounts of two inputs that can be purchased with a fixed sum of money (a firm's budget line).

isoquant A curve that shows all combinations of two inputs that can be used to produce a given output.

junk bonds High-yield, high-risk securities that are usually issued to finance a takeover of one corporation by another.

key currency A currency that serves as a major reserve asset and is used in transactions between third-party nations.

Keynesian economists Twentieth-century economists who adopted and extended John Maynard Keynes's idea that there could be persistent unemployment without government intervention.

Keynesian revolution The change in macroeconomic theory and policy that occurred when Keynes's ideas displaced the classical theory of how output and employment are determined.

kinked demand curve A demand curve with a bend in it at the price settled on in an oligopolistic industry because other firms' price cuts, but not price increases, are matched.

Knights of Labor Organized as a secret organization by Uriah Stevens in 1869, it won the first major strike in the United States against the railroad industry but had political reformist goals that led to its demise.

labor The physical and mental exertion that human beings put into production activities.

labor force Those who are working or actively seeking work.

labor force participation rate The percentage of the adult population that is employed or actively seeking work.

land Natural resources that can be used as inputs to production.

Landrum-Griffin Act An act passed in 1959 and aimed at curbing union power by making unions more democratic, restricting Communist Party members and convicted felons from union leadership, and making picketing illegal under certain circumstances.

law of demand The quantity demanded of a good or service is negatively related to its price, *ceteris paribus.*

leading sectors strategy The development strategy calling for concentration on a few successful sectors, which will then pull along other sectors in the development process.

leakages Flows out of the circular pattern that occur when factor income is received but not spent directly on purchases from domestic firms. Savings, taxes, and purchases of imports are leakages.

legal tender Money that, by law, must be accepted by private parties and governments in payment of debts and obligations.

lender of last resort A source of funds for rescuing sound banks by lending them as much as they need to meet temporary high demand from depositors.

Lerner Index of Monopoly Power (LMP) An index that evaluates the gap between price and marginal cost as a measure of monopoly power.

limited liability The fact that the stockholders of a corporation cannot be sued for failure of the corporation to meet its obligations.

liquidity The measure of how quickly a financial asset can be converted into the medium of exchange.

local monopoly A firm that has monopoly power in a geographic region because of the large distance from other suppliers of its product (or substitutes).

logrolling Vote trading in the legislative process.

long run The period of time in which all inputs, including plant and equipment, can be varied.

long-run average cost (*LRAC*) curve A curve tangent to all the possible short-run cost curves and representing the lowest attainable average cost of producing any given output.

long-run profit maximization The argument that even if managers seem to behave in accord with satisficing or constrained sales maximization, they only do so because it leads to higher profits in the long run.

Lorenz curve A graph showing the cumulative percentages of income received by various percentages of households.

M1 money stock The total of all financial assets in the United States that function as a medium of exchange: currency, traveler's checks, demand deposits, and other checkable deposits.

M2 money stock The total of M1 and small-denomination time and savings deposits at all financial institutions, money market accounts, and a few other items.

M3 money stock The total of M2 and large-denomination time deposits, repurchase agreements, and a few other items.

macroeconomic equilibrium The level of output at which there is no tendency to change. The amount that buyers wish to buy is exactly equal to what is being produced.

macroeconomics The study of the economy as a whole or of economic aggregates, such as the level of employment and the growth of total output.

marginal analysis A technique for analyzing problems by examining the results of small changes.

marginal cost The change in total cost from producing one more (or one less) unit of output.

marginal cost pricing A policy tool for forcing a monopoly to behave more like a competitive firm by regulating the monopoly price so that it is equal to marginal cost.

marginal efficiency of investment (*MEI*) curve A graph that sums the investment demand schedules for all firms in an economy. It ranks all investment possibilities for all firms according to their expected rates of return.

marginal physical product (*MPP*)   The change in total output that is produced by a unit change in a factor of production.

marginal productivity theory   An explanation of how the distribution of income is determined in a market system. Each factor is paid according to its contribution, or its marginal productivity.

marginal propensity to consume (*MPC*)   The fraction of any change in income that is consumed. The *MPC* is greater than 0 and less than 1.

marginal propensity to save (*MPS*)   The fraction of any change in income that is saved. The *MPS* is greater than 0 and less than 1.

marginal rate of substitution (*MRS*)   The trade-off ratio along an indifference curve.

marginal resource cost (*MRC*)   The cost of each additional unit of a productive resource.

marginal revenue (*MR*)   The change in total revenue from selling one more (or one less) unit.

marginal revenue product of labor (MRP_L)   The amount that an additional unit of labor adds to a firm's total revenue.

marginal utility (*MU*)   The amount of utility that one more or one less unit of consumption adds to or subtracts from total utility.

market   A place where buyers and sellers meet to exchange goods, services, and productive resources.

market-clearing price   The equilibrium price, which clears the market because there are no frustrated consumers or suppliers.

market concentration doctrine   The hypothesis that the degree of concentration in an industry is a reliable index of monopoly power and that a high concentration ratio is likely to be associated with undesirable monopoly behavior.

market demand curve   The sum of all of the individual demand curves. A market demand curve shows what quantities will be demanded by all consumers in a specific time frame in a certain market at various prices.

market economy   An economy in which the three basic questions are answered through the market, by relying on self-interested behavior and incentives.

market equilibrium   A point at which quantity demanded by consumers is equal to quantity supplied by producers. The price at which this occurs is the equilibrium price, or market-clearing price.

market for loanable funds   The market in which transactions between borrowers and lenders determine the interest rate and equate quantities of loanable funds offered to quantity demanded.

market power   The ability of buyers or sellers to affect price.

market supply curve   The sum of all of the individual supply curves. A market supply curve shows what quantities will be supplied by all firms at various prices during a specific time period.

marketing orders   A federal program that establishes producer cartels that control the supply of certain agricultural products not subject to price supports.

maximum   The point on a graph at which the *y*-variable, or dependent variable, reaches its highest value.

Measure of Economic Welfare (*MEW*)   An alternative to GNP that tries to provide a better indicator of economic well-being by adding leisure and nonmarket production and subtracting public bads.

median voter theorem   A theory that predicts that under majority rule, politicians will reflect the positions of voters near the center of the political spectrum.

mediation   Third-party intervention in a dispute consisting of attempts to keep the parties together and talking by offering suggestions and clarifying issues.

medium of exchange   A function of money in simplifying transactions by allowing people to exchange the goods and services they produce for money and then exchange money for other goods and services they want.

microeconomics   The study of individual market interactions, focusing on production and consumption by the individual consumer, firm, or industry.

minimum   The point on the graph at which the *y*-variable, or dependent variable, reaches its lowest value.

minimum wage   A price floor imposed by the federal government in the labor market.

mixed economy   An economy in which the three basic questions are answered partly by market forces and partly through government.

model   A set of assumptions and hypotheses that is a simplified description of reality.

monetarists   Twentieth-century economists who criticize Keynesian economics and stress the role of the money supply.

monetary base   The currency in the hands of the public plus reserves held by banks.

monetary policy   The use of changes in the money supply to try to influence the levels of output, employment, and prices.

monetary rule   A proposed regulation requiring the Fed to make the money supply grow at some predetermined, steady rate.

money   Any financial asset that serves as a medium of exchange, a unit of account, a standard of deferred payment, and a store of value.

money multiplier   The ratio of the actual money supply to the monetary base.

monopolistic competition   The market structure in which a large number of firms sell differentiated products.

monopoly   The market structure in which there is a single seller of a product that has no close substitutes.

monopoly power   The ability to exercise some of the economic effects predicted in the model of monopoly by restricting output.

monopoly rent seeking   The efforts and resources expended by those attempting to establish monopolies to earn monopoly profits.

monopsonistic exploitation   The difference in wages paid by a firm that has monopsony power, compared to what would be paid in a competitive market.

monopsony   A market structure in which there is a single purchaser of a factor of production.

moral suasion   Attempts by the Fed to convince depository institutions to do what the Fed favors.

multinational corporation   A firm with headquarters in one country and plants in one or more other countries.

municipal bond   Any bond issued by a state or local government to finance a capital project.

mutual fund   A financial institution that pools money from many individuals in order to invest in a diversified portfolio of assets.

name brand capital   The value that consumers place on a product because of experience, reputation, or image.

National Banking System   Agency that chartered and regulated national banks during the latter half of the nineteenth century, before the Federal Reserve System.

national banks   Banks chartered by the federal government and subject to its rules and regulations.

national debt   The total of all past budget deficits minus all past surpluses, or the net amount owed to lenders by the federal government.

national income (NI)   Income earned by the four factors of production; consists of wages, rent, interest, profit, and proprietors' net income.

National Labor Relations Board (NLRB)   A board established by the Wagner Act in 1935 and empowered to investigate employer unfair labor practices and to determine the legitimate bargaining agent for labor when there are competing unions.

National Labor Union   The first successful national union in the United States, founded in 1867 by William Sylvis.

National Recovery Administration (NRA)   A major New Deal program that was aimed at business recovery but was anticompetitive since it allowed and encouraged agreements between firms. It was eventually declared unconstitutional.

natural monopoly   A monopoly that emerges because economies of scale mean that there is room for only one firm in the market.

natural rate of unemployment   The rate of unemployment that is determined by frictional and structural factors and toward which the economy tends to return.

near money   Assets that are very similar to the kinds of assets included in the money stock. Near money is usually highly liquid.

negative externalities   Harmful spillovers to third parties that result from production or consumption of certain goods.

negative income tax   A transfer of income from the government to the poor based on a formula similar to the present income tax system and implemented with a minimum income guarantee and a negative tax rate.

negative relationship   A relationship between two variables in which an increase in the value of one is associated with a decrease in the value of the other.

net national product (NNP)   Equal to GNP minus the capital consumption allowance (depreciation).

net private domestic investment   Gross private domestic investment minus the capital consumption allowance (depreciation).

net worth   The difference between assets and liabilities for a person or firm at a point in time.

new classical economists   Late twentieth-century economists who regard monetary and fiscal policies as ineffective because individuals will anticipate and offset government actions.

New Economic Policy (NEP)   A program that replaced War Communism in 1921 in the Soviet Union and was an attempt at market socialism.

New International Economic Order (NIEO)   A proposal by the Group of 77 calling for changes in international economic institutions to redistribute income from richer nations to poorer nations through trade preferences, increased aid, and other measures.

nominal rate of interest   The rate of interest actually charged, without correction for inflation (also known as the market rate of interest).

nonprice competition   Competing with rival firms through advertising, style changes, color changes, and techniques other than lowering price.

nontariff barriers   Trade restrictions other than tariffs and quotas.

normal good   A good for which demand increases as income increases.

normal profit   The opportunity cost of capital and enterprise, or the rate of return that is necessary for a firm to remain in a competitive industry.

normative statements   A set of propositions about what ought to be (also called value judgments).

Norris-La Guardia Act   A law passed in 1932 that vastly strengthened the power of labor unions by limiting the court's use of injunctions in labor-management disputes.

(not quite) law of supply   The quantity supplied of a good or service is usually a positive function of price, *ceteris paribus.*

number equivalent   A measure of the theoretical number of equal-sized firms that should be found in an industry (the reciprocal of the Herfindahl Index).

oligopoly   The market structure in which a few firms compete imperfectly and recognize their interdependence.

open market operations   Purchases and sales of government bonds on the open market by the Fed in order to affect bank reserves.

opportunity cost   The value of the other alternatives given up in order to enjoy a particular good or service.

optimal-size plant   The plant represented by the short-run average cost curve with the lowest attainable per-unit costs.

optimal tariff   A tariff that maximizes a nation's net gain from altering its terms of trade.

origin   The intersection of the vertical and horizontal axes of a coordinate system, at which the values of both the x-variable and the y-variable are zero.

paradox of thrift   The fact that attempts by consumers to increase saving cause income and output to decline. Therefore actual saving may not increase at all.

parity A one-to-one ratio between the average prices of farm products and the prices of what farmers buy.

partnership A form of enterprise in which there is more than one owner, and the firm does not have a legal existence separate from the owners.

payment in kind (PIK) program A federal agricultural program similar to the soil bank program, but with payments made in surplus commodities rather than in money.

peak A high point in a business cycle, where output turns downward.

perestroika Restructuring, economic reforms in the Soviet Union.

perfect competition The market structure in which there are many sellers and buyers, firms produce a homogeneous product, and there is free entry into and exit out of the industry.

perfectly elastic demand Demand represented by a horizontal demand curve with a coefficient of price elasticity of demand that is equal to infinity. The quantity demanded responds in an infinite way to a change in price.

perfectly inelastic demand Demand represented by a vertical demand curve with a coefficient of price elasticity of demand that is equal to zero. There is no response in quantity demanded to changes in price.

permanent income hypothesis The view that consumption does not depend on current income alone but on past income and expected future income as well.

personal distribution of income A measure of how total income is divided among individuals or households.

personal income (PI) The income received by households; computed from NI by subtracting corporate profits taxes and undistributed corporate profits and adding net transfer payments.

Phillips curve A graph showing the relationship between the rates of inflation and unemployment for a country over a specified period of years.

pie chart A graphic representation in the shape of a pie that expresses actual economic data as parts of a whole. The sizes of the slices of the pie correspond to the percentage shares of the components.

planning curve The long-run average cost curve used in the planning stage.

point elasticity The elasticity at a particular point on a demand curve.

political business cycle A business cycle that results from the use of fiscal (or monetary) policy to influence the outcome of elections.

positive externalities Spillover benefits to third parties (free riders) that result from production or consumption of certain goods.

positive relationship A relationship between two variables in which an increase in one is associated with an increase in the other and a decrease in one is associated with a decrease in the other.

positive statements A set of propositions about what is, rather than what ought to be.

Post-Keynesians A group of late twentieth century economists who have refined and extended the work of Keynes. They stress market imperfections such as imperfect information, monopoly power, and inflexible wages and prices.

potential output The output an economy could produce if all of its resources were fully employed.

predatory pricing The act of selling below cost to destroy competitors.

present value (*PV*) The value of a future payment or series of future payments discounted to the present.

price ceilings Upper limits on prices imposed by a governmental unit. The ceiling is a price that cannot be exceeded.

price clusters Groupings of prices for similar, but not homogeneous, products.

price-consumption curve A curve that shows changes in consumer equilibrium when the price of one good on an indifference curve changes.

price discrimination The practice of charging different prices to different consumers or to a single consumer for different quantities purchased.

price elasticity of demand The measure of the responsiveness of the quantity demanded to changes in price.

price elasticity of supply The measure of the responsiveness of the quantity supplied to changes in the price.

price floors Minimum limits on prices established by a governmental unit. The floor is a price that cannot be undercut.

price index A measure of the price level in a given year relative to some base year.

price leadership The form of tacit collusion in an oligopolistic industry in which one firm, the price leader, sets the price or initiates price changes and the other firms follow that lead.

price searcher A firm that sets price in order to maximize profits and thus has monopoly power.

price taker A seller (or buyer) in perfect competition that has no influence on price and can sell any amount at the market-clearing price.

primary effect The dominant or immediate effect of a change in an economic variable.

principle of comparative advantage The idea that output will be maximized if people specialize in producing those goods or services for which their opportunity costs are lowest and engage in exchange to obtain other things they want.

principle of diminishing marginal rates of substitution The fact that as more of one good is consumed, more and more of the other must be given up to maintain indifference between the two.

principle of diminishing marginal utility The fact that the additional utility declines as quantity consumed increases. Less satisfaction is obtained per additional unit as more units are consumed.

principle of diminishing returns The fact that as more and more units of a variable factor are added to a set of fixed factors, the resulting additions to output eventually become smaller.

privatization The transfer of governmental activities and/or assets to the private sector.

Producer Price Index A group of three indices (for raw materials, semifinished goods, and finished goods) that shows what is happening to prices paid by producers and wholesalers.

product cycle A series of stages, from development to standardization, through which a new product passes.

product group A market for a set of goods that are differentiated but have a large number of close substitutes.

product market Set of markets in which goods and services produced by firms are sold.

production The process of transforming inputs into marketable outputs.

production function A description of the amounts of output expected from various combinations of inputs.

production possibilities curve A graph that depicts the various combinations of two goods that can be produced in an economy with the available resources.

productivity A measure of economic performance that shows changes in output per worker hour from one year to the next.

profit The return to enterprise, one of the factors of production. Profit is whatever remains after all other factors have been paid.

progressive tax A tax that takes a larger share (percentage) of income as income rises.

property law Law that concerns the enforcement of property rights.

property rights The legal rights to a specific piece of property, including the rights to own, buy, sell, or use in specific ways. Markets can exist and exchanges can occur only if individuals have property rights to goods, services, and productive resources.

proportional tax A tax that takes the same share (percentage) of income from all taxpayers.

public bads Negative external effects of production or consumption that impact a large number of individuals—for example, acid rain.

public choice economics A branch of economic theory that attempts to integrate economics and politics by examining the motives and rewards facing individuals in the public sector.

public goods Goods that are nonrival in consumption and not subject to exclusion.

pure oligopoly An oligopolistic industry that produces a homogeneous product.

quality circles Groups of workers organized to improve quality by discussing production problems and suggesting solutions.

quantity theory of money The theory that changes in the price level will be proportional to changes in the money supply.

quota A limit on the amount of a good or service that can be imported during a given time period.

real business cycle A cyclical pattern of economic activity resulting from changes in aggregate supply (rather than aggregate demand).

real deficit A measure of the federal budget deficit as the change in the real (inflation-adjusted) value of the national debt from one year to the next.

real rate of interest The nominal rate of interest minus the expected rate of inflation.

recession A state of an economy marked by a decline in real output for two or more successive quarters.

recessionary gap The difference between aggregate expenditure and the full-employment level of output.

recognition lag The length of time it takes to determine that an economic problem exists.

redistribution Actions by government that transfer income from one group to another.

regressive tax A tax that takes a smaller share (percentage) of income as income rises.

rent The return to land, one of the factors of production.

rent control A price ceiling imposed by a governmental unit on housing rents.

rent defending Actions by consumers to keep their consumer surplus from being captured by rent seekers.

rent seeking The commitment of scarce resources to capture returns created artificially.

representative firm A typical firm in perfect competition, one of the many identical firms in the market.

representative money Money that is redeemable in a commodity (or commodities), such as gold.

reserve ratio Fraction of deposits that banks are required to hold in reserves.

reserves Bank assets that can be used to pay depositors when checks are presented for payment, consisting of currency on hand and reserve deposits at the central bank.

residual claimant Individual, or group of individuals, who shares in the profits of an enterprise.

right-to-work laws State laws that allow people to hold jobs without belonging to unions.

risk A measure of how much the actual yield on an asset may vary from the expected yield.

risk premium The difference between interest rates charged to the safest borrowers and those charged to less safe borrowers for the same length of time.

Robinson-Patman Act A federal law that amended the Clayton Act in 1936, making predatory pricing illegal.

roundabout production The creation of physical capital (such as tools) that enhances productive capacity and ultimately allows increased output of consumer goods and services.

S corporation A hybrid type of corporation that passes income directly to the owners, avoiding the double taxation of corporate profits.

satisficing hypothesis The argument that managers do not seek to maximize profits but rather seek target levels of output and profits that are satisfactory to the ownership interests.

saving The part of households' income flow not spent on purchases of goods and services.

savings rate The ratio of combined business, household, and government saving to GNP.

Say's law The idea that supply creates its own demand, a cornerstone of classical economics.

scarcity The central economic problem that there are not enough resources to produce everything that individuals want.

scatter diagram   A graph that plots actual pairs of values of two variables to determine whether there appears to be any consistent relationship between them.

secondary boycotts   Union actions to stop an employer from doing business with other firms.

secondary effects   Effects indirectly related to the immediate effect, often smaller and felt after some time.

self-interested behavior   A basic assumption of economic theory that individual decision makers do what is best for themselves.

self-regulating markets   Markets that quickly resolve problems of shortage or surplus through price changes, quantity adjustments, or a combination of the two.

separation of ownership and control   The idea that large firms are run (controlled) by hired managers, not the owners, and the managers might have different goals from those of the owners.

settlement account   The part of the balance of payments that explains how a deficit or surplus was financed.

shadow prices   Simulated market prices used by economic planners.

shared monopoly   The model of oligopoly that says that oligopolists coordinate and share markets to act as a monopoly.

Sherman Antritrust Act   The first federal antitrust law in the United States, passed in 1890. Section 1 of the act declared every contract, combination, or conspiracy in restraint of trade to be illegal. Section 2 made it illegal to monopolize or attempt to monopolize.

shirk   To put forth less effort than agreed on.

short run   The period of time that is too short to vary all the factors of production.

short-run supply curve   The supply curve for the period in which the size of the plant cannot be varied (in perfect competition, the same as the short-run marginal cost curve).

shortage   The amount by which the quantity consumers wish to purchase at some price exceeds the quantity suppliers wish to supply at that price. A shortage can occur on a lasting basis only when a price ceiling is in effect.

shutdown point   The minimum point on the average variable cost (AVC) curve, or the level of output at which a firm minimizes its losses by ceasing operation.

single tax   A tax proposed by Henry George to capture the economic rent on land.

slope   The ratio of the change in the dependent variable (y) to the change in the independent variable (x).

social costs   Costs that are borne by society or some group in society without compensation.

social science   An academic field that studies the behavior of human beings, individually and in groups, and examines their interactions.

socialism   An economic system in which the nonhuman means of production are owned by society or the state.

socialist controversy   A debate between Ludwig von Mises and Oskar Lange concerning the feasibility of planning without markets.

soil bank program   Federal agricultural program beginning in the 1950s under which farmers were paid to let their land lie idle in order to reduce the supply of farm products.

Soil Conservation Service   A federal program under which grants were given to encourage farmers to contract production by fallowing fields, contour plowing, and other conservation techniques.

sole proprietorship   A form of enterprise in which no legal distinction is made between the firm and its owner.

specialization   Limiting production activities to one or a few goods and services that one produces best in order to exchange for other goods.

specie flow mechanism   The automatic correction of deficits and surpluses in the balance of payments through the effects of gold flows on money supplies.

speculators   People who assume risk in the forward market for currency in return for the chance of a profit.

spread   The difference between the average interest rate earned on loans and the average interest rate paid on deposits.

stabilization   Actions by government to reduce changes in output, employment, and prices.

stabilization policy   Government actions designed to smooth out sharp changes in output, employment, and the price level.

stagflation   An economic condition of slow growth, high unemployment, and inflation.

Standard Industrial Classification (SIC) system   A code devised by the U.S. Census Bureau for classifying industries using about 400 four-digit numbers.

standard of deferred payment   A function of money in providing borrowers and lenders a medium for the repayment of debt in the future.

state banks   Banks chartered and regulated by individual states, as opposed to the federal government.

statistical discrepancy   The part of the balance of payments that reflects unrecorded transactions and inaccurate estimates of spending by tourists.

stock   A certificate of ownership in a corporation.

stock market   A financial market in which ownership claims on corporations are bought and sold.

stock variable   A variable that is defined at a point in time.

stockholders   The owners of a corporation.

store of value   A function of money in providing purchasing power in a general form that can be held in order to buy goods and services in the future.

structural deficit   The part of a deficit that would persist even if the economy were at the full-employment level of output.

structural unemployment   Unemployment due to a mismatch between the skills or locations of unemployed workers and those of available jobs.

substitute goods   Goods that can be interchanged. The consumption of one replaces the consumption of the other.

substitution effect   An increase in the quantity demanded of a good (or service) because its price has fallen and it becomes a better substitute for all other goods.

supply   The quantity of a good offered for sale at various prices during a certain time period.

supply curve A graph representing a supply schedule and showing the quantities supplied at various prices in a certain time period.

supply schedule A table that shows quantities offered for sale at various prices over a particular time period.

supply siders Late twentieth century economists and policy makers who want to fight inflation and unemployment by trying to shift the aggregate supply curve to the right.

support prices Price floors for agricultural products maintained by the government, which purchases any surplus to keep the price from falling.

surplus (1) The amount by which the quantity suppliers wish to supply at some price exceeds the quantity consumers wish to purchase at that price. A surplus can occur on a lasting basis only when a price floor is in effect. (2) A situation in which the government collects more in taxes than it spends.

surplus value The difference between the value of the goods produced by labor and the subsistence wages the workers received.

T-accounts Partial balance sheets showing changes in assets and/or liabilities resulting from a transaction or group of transactions.

tacit collusion Unorganized and unstated attempts by informally coordinated oligopolies to practice joint actions.

Taft-Hartley Act Act passed in 1947 to reverse some of the Wagner Act's favoring of labor by shifting some legal rights back to employers.

tangent line A straight line just touching a curve (nonlinear graphic relationship) at a single point. The slope of the tangent line is equal to the slope of the curve at that point.

target prices Prices the government considers to be fair for farmers, used to determine subsidy payments.

tariff A tax on imported goods or services.

tariff quota A combination of a quota and a tariff that allows a certain amount of a good or service to be imported without paying a tariff and imposes the tariff on further imports.

tax-based inflation policy (TIP) A sophisticated approach to wage and price controls that ties allowable increases in prices and wages to tax breaks and penalties and uses market incentives to attempt to control price increases.

tax incidence The place where the burden of a tax actually falls after all shifting has occurred.

tax wedge The gap between prices paid by consumers and the prices (incomes) received by sellers (factor owners).

teams Groups of employees that work together to produce something.

technical efficiency The basis for minimizing the physical inputs to a production method according to some specific rule (an engineering concept).

technologically determined demand Demand that depends on techniques of production and technological progress. For example, the demand for labor will be af-

fected by the introduction of new technology in a firm or industry.

terms of trade The ratio at which one product is exchanged for another.

testable hypothesis An inference from a theory that can be subjected to real-world testing.

theory A set of principles that can be used to make inferences about the world.

theory of the second best A theory that a second-best policy of tariffs may be useful to introduce new distortions that eliminate existing distortions.

Theory Z A management theory that workers are motivated to perform if they are made part of the management process.

Tiebout hypothesis The idea that competition among local governments as suppliers of local public services will force them to offer the desired combination of spending and taxing to voters, who will migrate to those jurisdictions that produce that combination.

token money Money whose monetary value is greater than its commodity value. Modern coins, for example, are worth more as money than the metal they contain.

tort A wrongful action (or failure to act) that causes damage to the person or property of another individual.

tort law Law that deals with intentional and unintentional wrongs inflicted by one party on another.

total cost (*TC*) The sum of all the costs of production for a given level of output.

total fixed costs (*TFC*) The costs of the fixed factors of production, which can't be avoided in the short run.

total physical product (*TPP*) The amount of output that a firm produces in physical units.

total revenue (*TR*) The amount of money a firm takes in, equal to the quantity of the good or service sold multiplied by its price.

total variable cost (*TVC*) The total of costs that vary directly with output, increasing as more output is produced.

traditional economy An economy in which the three basic questions are answered by custom, or how things have been done in the past.

tragedy of the commons The overuse of common access resources.

transactions costs Costs associated with gathering information about markets (prices and quantities supplied) for consuming or producing.

transactions demand for money Demand for money in order to make purchases and carry out other day-to-day market transactions. The transactions demand for money is positively related to income.

transfer payments Income payments to individuals who provide no goods or services in exchange.

transmission mechanism The process of translating money supply changes into changes in demand, output, and the price level.

trough A low point in a business cycle, where output turns upward.

trusts Organizations set up to control the stock of other companies through boards of trustees.

tying contracts Agreements between producers and

retailers that call for the retailer to stock certain items in return for being allowed to stock other items.

unemployment rate The percentage of the labor force that wants to work but does not currently have a job.

unintended effects of policy Results that are unanticipated by policy makers but become evident through careful economic analysis.

union shops Firms where union membership is necessary for a worker to remain employed.

unit elastic demand Demand represented by a demand curve that is a rectangular hyperbola with a coefficient of price elasticity of demand equal to one. The quantity demanded responds at the same rate as any change in price.

unit of account A function of money in providing a measuring unit in terms of which goods can be valued and thus readily compared with each other.

United Mine Workers (UMW) The industrial union for mine workers.

unplanned inventory changes Changes that occur when the inventory level rises above or falls below that desired by a firm because the production level is too high or too low relative to current sales.

user charges Fees that cover part or all of the cost of a public service.

util An arbitrary unit used to measure individual utility.

utility The satisfaction that an individual expects to receive from consuming a good or service.

utility function A relationship expressing a consumer's desire to consume differing amounts of a good.

utility maximization The process by which a consumer adjusts consumption, given a budget constraint and a set of prices, in order to attain the highest total amount of satisfaction.

value of the marginal product of labor (VMP_L) A measure of the value of the additional output that each unit of additional labor adds to a firm's total, found by multiplying the marginal physical product by the price at which the firm can sell the product.

variable factors The factors of production that can be increased or decreased in the short run.

vertically integrated firms Firms that perform many sequential steps in a production process.

vicious circle of poverty A trap in which many low-income countries are caught—there is little investment because of a low level of income, and a low level of income because of little investment.

wage and price controls Government-imposed restrictions on increases in prices or wages in order to contain inflation.

wages The return to labor, one of the factors of production.

Wagner Act A law passed in 1935 that gave employees the right to organize and bargain collectively and outlawed certain unfair labor practices by employers.

War Communism An economic system of rigid administrative control imposed by Lenin in Russia during the civil war following the Bolshevik Revolution.

Wheeler-Lea Act A 1938 federal law amending the FTC Act to make unfair or deceptive acts or practices in commerce illegal.

wildcat strikes Local strikes that are unauthorized by the national union.

Worker Adjustment and Retraining Notification Act (WARN) An act passed in 1988 that required all firms with more than 100 employees to give sixty-days' notice before shutting down or laying off workers.

workfare State welfare programs that require those receiving welfare who are able to work to take jobs or to participate in training programs in order to be eligible for benefits.

x-axis The horizontal line in a coordinate system that shows the values of the independent variable; the horizontal axis.

x-inefficiency The inefficiency associated with the "slack" management of monopoly firms because of the lack of market discipline.

y-axis The upright line in a coordinate system that shows the values of the dependent variable; the vertical axis.

yellow-dog contracts Contracts that require employees to agree to refrain from union activity as a precondition for employment and that allow firms to discharge workers who violate that agreement.

yield The return on funds invested in an asset measured as a percentage of the price paid for the asset.

INDEX

I-5